THE LIVERPOOL

·ENCYCLOPEDIA·

THE LIVERPOOL ENCYCLOPEDIA

ARNIE BALDURSSON

&

GUDMUNDUR MAGNUSSON

Published by
deCoubertin Books Ltd in 2013

deCoubertin Books,
145-157 St John Street,
London, EC1V 4PY

www.decoubertin.co.uk

First hardback edition

Standard Edition
978-1-909245-08-2

Legends Edition
978-1-909245-14-3

Shankly The Great Edition
978-1-909245-15-0

A CIP catalogue record for
this book is available from the
British Library.

Printed and bound in the UK by
Butler Tanner and Dennis.

Design in Liverpool
by Leslie Priestley.

Photographs courtesy of Getty
Images and the private collections
of the authors and other Liverpool
supporters. Thank you to
Dr David France for the use of
his portrait of John Houlding.

Every effort has been made to
contact copyright holders for
photographs used in this book.
If we have overlooked you in any
way, please get in touch so that we
can rectify this in future editions.

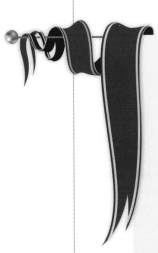

DEDICATION

MY LOVELY WIFE,

ÁSTA SÓL,

HAS SUPPORTED MY

DEDICATION TO

LIVERPOOL ENCYCLOPEDIA

AND GIVES ME

STRENGTH TO ACHIEVE

THE GOALS I SET

MYSELF IN LIFE. MY CHILDREN

ELENA AND LEON BJARTUR,

AND THE ONE WHO

WANTED TO BE A PART

OF THIS PRODUCTION PROCESS,

EXPECTED IN JANUARY 2014,

I AM THANKFUL FOR EVERY DAY.

FINALLY, TO

LIVERPOOL FOOTBALL CLUB

THAT HAS BEEN

A FAITHFUL COMPANION

OF MINE

THROUGH ALL MY LIFE.

ARNIE

....

TO MY

WONDERFUL WIFE ÓLÖF,

MY GREAT,

ADVENTUROUS DAUGHTER

ELÍSABET ÓSK

AND THE MEMORY

OF MY GRANDFATHER

GUÐMUNDUR

WHO ENCOURAGED ME

TO GET

INVOLVED IN FOOTBALL.

GUÐMUNDUR

Introduction

Arnie wrote his first draft on Liverpool's history in 1986.

I AND Gudmundur Magnusson started working together on the board of the Official Icelandic Liverpool Supporters' Club back in 1997. Iceland has a strong link with Liverpool's past as the club's first-ever European game took place in the country's capital, Reykjavík in 1964. It was an adventure for the locals to see such a strong team and their interest has been passed on from one generation to the next. We, however, do not come from such families. I fell head over heels as I read Derek Hodgson's book about Liverpool, published in Iceland in 1980 when I was nine. I wrote my first draft of Liverpool FC's history as a school essay at 15 years of age. I guess this was always meant to be. Gudmundur chose Liverpool to represent him in a computer game when he was 10 years old and that was the point of no return. In 2003 our passion for Liverpool manifested itself in the launch of *www.LFChistory.net*. The site has grown considerably in volume and importance during that period and has been officially embraced by the club as well as its huge fan base.

Following the success of our first book, *Liverpool: The Complete Record*, published in 2011, we agreed to deCoubertin Books' offer to further our documentation of Liverpool in print. Whereas *Complete Record* focused on stats and a comprehensive narrative for each season, this publication ideally complements that with profiles for every single player and key aspects of the club's illustrious history. We approached every player from as fresh a perspective as possible and wanted to infuse humanity into even the most unknown of figures. Hopefully you will appreciate our efforts, but we would never have made such progress on our own. Words cannot really do justice to the help provided by a quintumvirate of dedicated Reds. Kjell Hanssen has consistently brought forth rare newspaper articles that have been worth their weight in gold, Adrian Killen has provided us with fantastic images, Graeme and Reg Riley's research has benefited us greatly and Chris Wood's dedication to our cause almost from day one is unparalleled. Without them this book would not have reached the standard that we aimed for. Mark Anthony, Stuart Basson, Ian Beardsley, Bob Blenkinsop, Martin Brodetsky, Jim Donnelly (curator of the Unofficial Liverpool museum on Facebook), Torbjørn Flatin, Gavin Foster, David France, Jeff Gaydish, Chris Goodwin, Lee Gray, Sigfús Guttormsson, Skapti Hallgrímsson, Elizabeth Hargreaves, Vegard Heggem, Alan Hindley, Steven Horton, David Hughes, Hyder Jawad, Gerald Jensen, John Jones, Rena Liddell, Bob McCluskey, Kevin Nealon, Joe Neary, Ron Parrott, Mark Platt, Paul Plowman, Katharine Reidel, Darren Riley, Pete Sampara, George Sephton, Dave Usher and Jacqueline Wadsworth also deserve a mention for their various contributions.

WE WOULD ALSO LIKE TO THANK several former Liverpool players whom we have interviewed throughout the years. They have shed further light on their own careers and given us priceless insight into the legends who built the club and its inner workings. A collective thank you to Gerry Byrne, Ian Callaghan, Jimmy Case, Ray Clemence, David Fairclough, Joey Jones, Alan Kennedy, Jan Mølby, Phil Neal, Neil Ruddock, Ian Rush, Ian St John, Michael Thomas, Peter Thompson, Phil Thompson, John Wark and Ron Yeats.

We have overcome plenty of obstacles on the way, but establishing dates of birth and death has been notoriously difficult and we welcome any corrections that you might have, at webmaster@lfchistory.net. For those who may not be familiar to formations of old, a number of players' positions are classified according to the 2-3-5 pyramid formation which needs a brief explanation. The full-backs served as the team's prime defenders, guarding their keeper from onrushing forwards while the half-backs (left-half, centre-half and right half) were more akin to modern midfielders. The wingers were called outside-right and outside-left and the inside-forwards worked the channels on either side of the centre-forward.

Note that the statistics in the book include all seasons from 1892/93 to 2012/13. Data from the 2013/14 season onwards awaits future editions. International stats are up to 1 July 2013.

IT IS ONLY JUST to put on record my gratefulness to the Coca Cola Company and double Espressos for keeping me up on occasion beyond any rhyme or reason. Designer Leslie Priestley weaved his magic on these pages and was a true pleasure to work with as well as his son Stephen. Editor Ian Allen provided his expertise and the impressive ambition of publisher James Corbett encouraged us to greater deeds.

This book is really a culmination of our work that started 11 years ago when two Icelanders felt that a clearer vision of Liverpool FC's history was needed so we started to collect information and data. During the last 12 arduous months to make this book a reality my wife's patience was admittedly wearing thin sometimes but she has come to understand my unrelenting passion for all things Liverpool.

Arnie Baldursson

Reykjavík, Iceland,
22 JULY 2013

A'Court, Alan

RAINHILL-BORN A'Court gave Liverpool outstanding service from the day he made his debut against Middlesbrough as an 18-year-old on 7 February 1953 until his last appearance on 14 September 1964.

The *Liverpool Echo's* Leslie Edwards saw A'Court's fantastic potential when watching him in only his fourth game for Liverpool against Bolton at Anfield on 4 March 1953: 'With A'Court showing unmistakable signs of football genius – on this first look at him I rate him as outstanding of the new boys, both for courage and ability – the Liverpool attack must continue to succeed.'

FACTFILE

BORN
Rainhill,
30 September 1934
DIED
14 December 2009
POSITION
Left-winger
OTHER CLUBS
Prescot Cables,
Tranmere Rovers
(1964–66)
SIGNED FROM
Prescot Cables,
24 September 1952
INTERNATIONAL CAPS
5 England caps (1 goal),
1957–58
LFC DEBUT GAME/GOAL
7 February 1953 /
14 March 1953
CONTRACT EXPIRY
October 1964
HONOURS
Second Division
Championship 1961/62

A'Court's reputation as a schoolboy footballer had evolved steadily and he was chosen to represent Merseyside grammar schools, then Lancashire County and finally the England grammar schools' team. He played amateur football at Prescot Cables and, with scouts from the Reds, Bolton, Wolves and Everton watching with interest, he accepted Don Welsh's offer of a £10 signing-on fee to become a professional at Liverpool. A'Court got an early opportunity in the first team but unfortunately when he was establishing himself at Anfield the club was relegated in 1954. He was held in such high regard that the great Billy Liddell was moved to centre-forward to make room for him on the left flank as the club's first campaign outside the top flight for 49 years got under way. A'Court was a regular in the side for seven years and a crucial part of the Liverpool side that finally made its way out of the Second Division in the 1961/62 season, being the only player – apart from Ronnie Moran – who had been relegated eight years earlier.

A'COURT WAS STRONG and direct with awesome power in his boots, and impressed sufficiently for the England selectors to include him in their World Cup squad in Sweden 1958 while he was a second division player. This was no mean feat! He replaced the injured legend Tom Finney after England's opening game, a 2-2 draw against USSR, and featured in a goalless draw with eventual world champions Brazil and a 2-2 draw with Austria. USSR and England were equal on points in their group so a play-off was required, which A'Court and his team-mates lost 1-0.

LFCHistory.net interviewed Alan in 2004 and asked him about the incredible loyalty he showed in sticking with the club in the Second Division, despite being an England international at the peak of his powers. 'I played just under 400 games for the club and I was happy at Liverpool. Arsenal were interested and offered £12,000. I didn't want to move house, I was happy at home and I had good mates in Liverpool.' A'Court missed half of his debut season in the First Division due to niggles and strains and the papers speculated that he would soon be

replaced by Peter Thompson, who had scored Preston North End's winning goal against Liverpool in the FA Cup the previous season. As predicted, Thompson was brought in to fill the left-wing role that A'Court had made his own for so long. After not having featured in the first team for 16 months he made his farewell appearance for Liverpool in the club's first-ever European tie at Anfield, against KR Reykjavik in September 1964.

A'Court had passed his 30th birthday by a few days when he moved to Tranmere and he was perhaps unlucky to just miss out on the glory days that awaited Liverpool, having to settle for a Second Division Championship medal as his only major honour. He later became a coach, serving Norwich City, Crewe Alexandra and Stoke City. According to Bill Shankly, A'Court wasn't only important on the field but an inspiration off it as well as he noted in the *Liverpool Echo*. 'Jovial Alan A'Court is a wit and worth his weight in gold in the dressing room with his practical jokes.' Ian Callaghan said it was made easy for him to sign for Liverpool as his heroes Billy Liddell and A'Court played for the club. He paid this tribute to A'Court after Alan's passing on 14 December 2009: 'He had this ability to cross a fantastic ball and he was an inspiration to me when I was coming through the ranks as a raw 17-year-old. He was one of the nicest guys you could ever wish to meet and he took me under his wing and he took me

> HE WAS HELD IN SUCH HIGH REGARD THAT THE GREAT BILLY LIDDELL WAS MOVED TO CENTRE-FORWARD

out on social trips. He had this fantastic car, which was a Sunbeam Rapier Convertible, and it was fantastic to go in that with him.' Alan A'Court had fantastic memories of his time at Anfield as he revealed in his autobiography. 'The crowd had helped me enormously in settling into the side but then they backed every member of the team that gave everything to the cause. My best asset was my pace but Anfield is a very confined playing space and, if you were racing for

the corner, it was impossible to pull up if you really wanted to reach the ball in time. I lost count of the number of times I went flying off the pitch, ending up in the arms of the spectators, before being pushed on again. They weren't nearly so helpful to visiting wingers, who were allowed to crash in the concrete surrounds, often with painful consequences.'

> HE MADE HIS FAREWELL APPEARANCE FOR LIVERPOOL IN THE CLUB'S FIRST-EVER EUROPEAN TIE AT ANFIELD

Season	League		FA Cup		League Cup		Europe		Other		Total	
	App	Goals	App	Goals	App	Goals	App	Goals	App	Goals	App	Goals
1952/53	12	2	0	0	-	-	-	-	-	-	12	2
1953/54	16	3	0	0	-	-	-	-	-	-	16	3
1954/55	30	2	3	1	-	-	-	-	-	-	33	3
1955/56	40	6	5	0	-	-	-	-	-	-	45	6
1956/57	38	10	1	0	-	-	-	-	-	-	39	10
1957/58	39	6	5	0	-	-	-	-	-	-	44	6
1958/59	39	7	1	0	-	-	-	-	-	-	40	7
1959/60	42	8	2	0	-	-	-	-	-	-	44	8
1960/61	33	7	2	0	2	0	-	-	-	-	37	7
1961/62	42	8	5	1	-	-	-	-	-	-	47	9
1962/63	23	2	0	0	-	-	-	-	-	-	23	2
1964/65	0	0	0	0	-	-	1	0	0	0	1	0
Total	354	61	24	2	2	0	1	0	0	0	381	63

Ablett, Gary

A HARD-WORKING DEFENDER who could play either at left-back or centre-half, Gary Ablett came through the ranks at Liverpool and made his debut for the reserves on 23 November 1982.

The 21-year-old made quite an impression on his senior home debut against Nottingham Forest on 18 April 1987.

The Times reported: 'For one so young, Ablett produced a quite memorable display. He carried out his defensive duties with elegant poise and underlined his rich potential by scoring Liverpool's third goal after 68 minutes with a quite delightful volley.' This turned out to be his only goal for Liverpool.

A week later Ablett helped Ian Rush make local history as his pass led to the forward equalling Dixie Dean's record of 19 goals in Merseyside derbies. Gary Gillespie

and Barry Venison were first choice when the historic 1987/88 season started, but from the end of January onwards Ablett played every game except one due to his rivals' injuries. As the following league season kicked off Ablett found himself again in the reserves, but soon enough Venison was on the sidelines and then Gillespie was out for four months. After featuring in 49 matches in 1988/89 Ablett looked forward to the following campaign, but to his dismay he was considered second best to a number of players. Gillespie's rotten luck with injuries was again to Ablett's benefit in 1990/91 and he started 30 games for the club. Ablett was in Graeme

Souness's first XI as the following season started, but after a dismal run of results that left Liverpool in ninth place he was booted out of the team and sold to Everton for £750,000 in January 1992.

ABLETT WROTE HIS NAME in the history books by becoming the only player to win the FA Cup at both Liverpool and Everton when the Blues beat Manchester United in the 1995 final, having won the cup for the Reds in 1989. Ablett went on to make 156 appearances for Everton in four years before establishing an excellent understanding with Steve Bruce in the middle of Birmingham City's defence between 1996 and 1998. When Bruce left to become player-manager at Sheffield United, Ablett was appointed Birmingham captain. He finished his career in the unlikely venue of New York as a member of Long Island Rough Riders.

> ABLETT WROTE HIS NAME IN THE HISTORY BOOKS BY BECOMING THE ONLY PLAYER TO WIN THE FA CUP AT BOTH LIVERPOOL AND EVERTON

Subsequently Ablett spent a few years as coach at Everton's academy but in the summer of 2006 he returned to Liverpool as manager of the reserve team. It was quite seldom that a player would cross the great divide from Reds to Blues and then back again, and came as a great surprise to him. 'Crossing Stanley Park is a very strange feeling. Although I'd always been a Liverpudlian all my thoughts and

energies were suddenly focused on Everton and I wanted to prove Liverpool were wrong for letting me go. When I eventually hung up my boots and returned to England it was Everton who gave me my break on the coaching side and that's all I was concentrating on. I would never have dreamed that four years down the line I'd be crossing sides again.'

> I HAD PLAYED FOR THE BEST TWO TEAMS IN THE WORLD, COACHED FOR THE BEST TWO TEAMS IN THE WORLD

HIS RETURN TO Liverpool brought success as under Ablett's guidance the club won the Premier Reserve League North in April 2008 and a month later became national champions by convincingly defeating the southern champions Aston Villa 3-0 at Anfield. His second season in charge proved to be somewhat anti-climactic and he was sacked as part of Rafa Benítez's rebuilding of the youth system at Liverpool in the summer of 2009. But he was not out of the game for long.

On 8 July 2009 Ablett was named as the new manager of League One club Stockport County. Unfortunately they endured a miserable 2009/10 season and were relegated back to League Two. Just over two months later

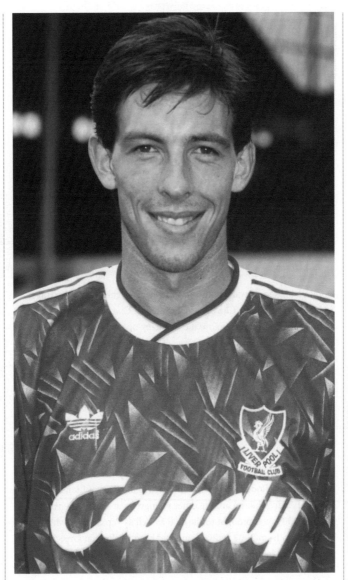

Ablett had left the club. In the summer of 2010, Ablett was offered a way back into the game by Roy Keane at Ipswich Town, who wanted to add him to his coaching staff. Unfortunately, before he was really able to make an impression, Ablett was rushed to hospital after being taken ill on the training ground. It was subsequently confirmed that the 44-year-old had non-Hodgkin's lymphoma – the same form of cancer that ex-Arsenal midfielder David Rocastle died from in 2001. Only three days passed from diagnosis to the first session of chemotherapy so it was a massive shock to Gary and his family. Gary fought the disease bravely for 16 months. 'I thought it can't be me, it just can't,' he told Everton's official website. 'I felt so strong – I had played for the best two teams in the world,

coached for the best two teams in the world. It can't be me. But unfortunately it was. In terms of what I've been through with the different regimes of the chemotherapy, the blood transfusions, the platelet transfusions, eight radiotherapy sessions, the lumbar punctures and I had a bone marrow transplant in January 2011... the list can go on and on.' Sadly the battle was one that was lost and Gary Ablett passed away on 1 January 2012, aged just 46.

FACTFILE

BORN
Aigburth, Liverpool,
19 November 1965
DIED
1 January 2012
POSITION
Left-back / Centre-half
OTHER CLUBS
Derby County (loan, 1985),
Hull City (loan, 1986),
Everton (1992–96),
Sheffield United (loan, 1996),
Birmingham City (1996–99),
Wycombe Wanderers
(loan, 1999),
Blackpool (2000),
Long Island Rough Riders
(2000–01)
JOINED
October 1981;
signed professional
19 November 1983
INTERNATIONAL CAPS
1 England U-21 cap
LFC DEBUT GAME/GOAL
20 December 1986 /
18 April 1987
CONTRACT EXPIRY
13 January 1992
HONOURS
League Championship
1987/88, 1989/90;
FA Cup 1989

Season	League		FA Cup		League Cup		Europe		Other		Total	
	App	Goals	App	Goals	App	Goals	App	Goals	App	Goals	App	Goals
1986/87	5	1	0 (1)	0	0	0	-	-	0	0	5 (1)	1
1987/88	15 (2)	0	5	0	0	0	-	-	-	-	20 (2)	0
1988/89	34 (1)	0	6	0	6	0	-	-	2	0	48 (1)	0
1989/90	13 (2)	0	0	0	1	0	-	-	0	0	14 (2)	0
1990/91	23	0	5 (1)	0	1	0	-	-	1	0	30 (1)	0
1991/92	13 (1)	0	0	0	2 (1)	0	6	0	-	-	21 (2)	0
Total	**103 (6)**	**1**	**16 (2)**	**0**	**10 (1)**	**0**	**6**	**0**	**3**	**0**	**138 (9)**	**1**

Academy

LIVERPOOL FC'S ACADEMY is located on a roughly forty five acre land in the eastern suburb of Kirkby and was opened in 1998.

The idea behind the new facility was to allow the club to have a centre for youth development and keep Melwood separate solely used for first-team matters. Then Chief Executive Peter Robinson made it a mission of his to make the Academy a reality before he retired. 'After visiting a number of academies in Europe we decided to base our own on the one at Ajax. At the time they were one of the most successful clubs in Europe when it came to producing homegrown players,' Robinson told the *Liverpool Echo*.

The first director of the Academy was Steve Heighway, who had gained considerable experience training youngsters in the US. He was originally brought to the club to oversee the youth set-up, known as the School of Excellence. 'When I started here in 1989 Peter Robinson said to me, 'We haven't produced a local player for ten years.' We had a long run with the likes of Phil Thompson and Sammy Lee, going back to Chris Lawler and Tommy Smith in the 1960s, and then a long gap.' Several players moved on from Heighway's care into the first-team picture, such as Steve McManaman, Robbie Fowler,

Dominic Matteo, David Thompson, Stephen Wright, Richie Partridge, Steven Gerrard, Jamie Carragher and Michael Owen, but they had all progressed as players before the Academy opened. Players of that calibre are hardly expected to emerge at regular intervals, but a steady flow of youngsters to form the basis of the first-team squad is the ideal. Youngsters have been produced by the Academy but they haven't been of sufficient quality and mostly ended up strengthening other teams than Liverpool, further down the League ladder. In that respect the Academy is still a work in progress, though of fantastic benefit to youngsters learning the game.

Since 2009 Liverpool have looked towards Barcelona as the blueprint for future success. Rodolfo Borrell, who coached the likes of Lionel Messi, Xavi and Andrés Iniesta among other youngsters at Barcelona from 1996 to 2009, was brought to the club as well as Pep Segura, who was at Barcelona from 2002 to 2004 and had been working in Greece since 2006. Segura left the club in 2012 but Borrell is the current head of Adacemy coaching. Four major factors are considered when assessing a youngster at the Academy: technical ability, tactical ability, mental approach to becoming a professional, and physique (speed, strength and size being crucial to English football). The 180-200 Academy members, aged from 8 to 21 years, are taught gradually to appreciate a basic understanding of the club's system of play and to work consistently within the philosophy of the club. Pass and move has been taught at Liverpool since the days of Bill Shankly; building attacks from the defensive line while displaying tactical awareness and controlling the tempo of the game is the order of the day.

The club has a widely spread network of scouts, Locally, English clubs can only recruit youngsters aged 12 to 16 within 90 miles radius of their academies and eight to 11-year-olds within 60 miles. Those rules don't apply for foreign youngsters. Liverpool search high and low for talent all over the world, but Academy director Frank McPharland emphasised the importance of the 'Scouse factor' to the *Anfield Wrap*: 'If one is English and one is Scouse, and they're at exactly the same level, we would 100 per cent always take the Scouse one, because our club's identity has always been about having local kids coming through and we're desperate to carry that on.' Once the youngest boys have reached the age at which their secondary education would normally begin, the Academy has the facilities in place to cover their academic needs as well as their sporting requirements. Every match played at the Academy is recorded for later

analysis. The recording includes the coaches' voices, an innovation introduced following research by the local university, which suggested that oral communication was very important in the boys' development. Parents are encouraged to watch their children play in such matches with the proviso that they are kept away from the pitch to avoid the sort of touchline behaviour that is sadly so prevalent at amateur level. Parents discuss their child's progress with Academy staff a few times each year. This means that they know well in advance if their child is unlikely to progress through to the first team. Of course, the dream is that they will make it, but the reality is that most won't.

Progress can be rapid for a boy who proves that he has all the necessary attributes to become a professional footballer. One such example is Andre Wisdom, the powerful defender Liverpool acquired from Bradford City at only 14 years of age. Wisdom broke into Liverpool's first team as an 18-year-old in the early stages of the 2012/13 season. Melwood coach Mike Marsh lauded Wisdom's success. 'It just shows you the input and work he's done at the Academy with all the coaches in his development.' Other former Academy boys who were allocated a first-team squad number in 2012/13 are Jon Flanagan, Adam Morgan, Jack Robinson, Suso, Dani Pacheco, Conor Coady and Raheem Sterling.

THE TWO MAIN TARGETS of the Academy are the same today as when its doors opened in 1998: 'To implement a common style of play in teams through all categories, and to provide players for the first team.' Brendan Rodgers is ready to take a real chance on youngsters, which bodes well for the future of the Academy.

> BRENDAN RODGERS IS READY TO TAKE A REAL CHANCE ON YOUNGSTERS WHICH BODES WELL FOR THE FUTURE OF THE ACADEMY

Adam,
Charlie

BORN IN DUNDEE a fortnight before Christmas in 1985, Charlie Adam didn't represent either of his local professional clubs but instead joined Glasgow Rangers shortly after his 17th birthday.

George Adams, who was head of Celtic's youth programme, later told the *Daily Mail* that Adam was quite a prospect back then. 'At 13 or 14, everyone thought he would go right to the very top,' Adams said. 'Every club in Scotland wanted him, and a few in England. Two of those clubs were Manchester United and Liverpool. But it came down to a choice between Rangers and Celtic.'

> ADAM HAD GAINED A REPUTATION AS A DEAD-BALL SPECIALIST

Adam didn't become a regular in the Rangers team until the 2006/07 season but then he was an immediate success, scoring 18 times in 74 competitive matches over two seasons. This success earned him a new five-year deal with Rangers in June 2007, but he failed to add to his goal tally in nine Scottish Premier League matches at the start of the 2008/09 season.

Stuck on the left wing and overweight, Adam was subsequently loaned out to Championship club Blackpool, for whom he was sent off on his debut! This lapse in discipline did not deter the Seasiders from signing him permanently the following summer. Adam quickly became a firm fans' favourite at Blackpool, who were promoted to the Premier League at the end of the 2009/10 season.

ADAM soon made an impression in the top flight and by mid-season Blackpool looked to be in a comfortable position in the Premier League. Liverpool tried to buy 25-year-old Adam in the January 2011 transfer window. According to manager Ian Holloway the offer was 'disgraceful' for a player key to Blackpool's survival.

Nevertheless, the club slid down the table, with relegation confirmed on the final day of the season despite Adam's efforts, endeavours that saw him nominated for the Professional Footballers' Association's Player of the Year. Blackpool activated an option to extend his contract by another year, but six weeks later he had signed for Liverpool, despite Tottenham's last-ditch effort to steal him.

At Bloomfield Road Adam had gained a reputation as a dead-ball specialist: corners, free kicks and penalty kicks, even scoring direct from a corner in February 2011. Yet Sir Alex Ferguson's claim that 'Adam's corners are worth £10million alone,' did not ring true as he struggled to impress Liverpool fans, although he did provide a few assists. He missed a penalty at Wigan in December 2011 and put another spot kick

into orbit during the shootout that followed the drawn League Cup final in February 2012.

Adam played in nearly 70 per cent of Liverpool's first-team matches in 2011/12 but his debut campaign was ended by lateral knee ligament damage suffered against QPR on 21 March 2012.

Maybe Adam was not suited to life at Liverpool, where he was just a small fish in a big pond compared to Blackpool. He left Liverpool for Stoke City on the last day of the 2012 summer transfer window.

FACTFILE

BORN
Dundee, Scotland,
10 December 1985
POSITION
Midfielder
OTHER CLUBS
Rangers (2004–09),
Ross County (loan, 2004–05),
St Mirren (loan, 2005–06),
Blackpool (2009–11),
Stoke City (2012–)
SIGNED FROM
Blackpool, £6.75million,
7 July 2011
INTERNATIONAL CAPS
23 Scotland caps
(6 at LFC), 2007–
LFC DEBUT GAME/GOAL
13 August 2011 /
27 August 2011
CONTRACT EXPIRY
31 August 2012
HONOURS
League Cup 2012

Season	League		FA Cup		League Cup		Europe		Other		Total	
	App	Goals	App	Goals	App	Goals	App	Goals	App	Goals	App	Goals
2011/12	27 (1)	2	1 (1)	0	3 (2)	0	-	-	-	-	31 (4)	2
2012/13	0	0	0	0	0	0	1 (1)	0	-	-	1 (1)	0
Total	**27 (1)**	**2**	**1 (1)**	**0**	**3 (2)**	**0**	**1 (1)**	**0**	**0**	**0**	**32 (5)**	**2**

Age

Youngest

Youngest player to make debut

Jerome Sinclair
16 years 6 days
26 September 2012

Jack Robinson
16 years 8 months 8 days
9 May 2010

John McFarlane
17 years 1 month 16 days
9 February 1929

Raheem Sterling
17 years 3 months 16 days
24 March 2012

Max Thompson
17 years 4 months 8 days
8 May 1974

Youngest goalscorer

Michael Owen
17 years 4 months 22 days
6 May 1997

Raheem Sterling
17 years 10 months 12 days
20 October 2012

JIMMY MELIA
[LIVERPOOL]

Jimmy Melia
18 years 1 month 16 days
17 December 1955

Jamie Redknapp
18 years 5 months 12 days
7 December 1991

Robbie Fowler
18 years 5 months 13 days
22 September 1993

JAMIE REDKNAPP
LIVERPOOL FC

Oldest

Oldest player to make debut

Ned Doig
37 years 10 months 3 days
1 September 1904

Paul Jones
36 years 8 months 23 days
10 January 2004

Gary McAllister
35 years 7 months 25 days
19 August 2000

Phil Bratley
33 years 9 months 7 days
3 October 1914

Mauricio Pellegrino
33 years 3 months 10 days
15 January 2005

Oldest goalscorer

Billy Liddell
38 years 1 month 24 days
5 March 1960

Gary McAllister
36 years 9 months 14 days
9 October 2001

Kenny Dalglish
36 years 1 month 14 days
18 April 1987

Ian Callaghan
35 years 11 months 5 days
15 March 1978

Donald Mackinlay
35 years 7 months 8 days
5 March 1927

Oldest player

Ned Doig 41 years 5 months 13 days		11 April 1908
Ephraim Longworth 40 years 6 months 19 days		21 April 1928
Elisha Scott 40 years 5 months 28 days		21 February 1934
Kenny Dalglish 39 years 1 month 27 days		1 May 1990
Billy Liddell 38 years 7 months 21 days		31 August 1960

Youngest line-up

22.83 years *	Wolves (away)	26 April 1965
22.97 years	Birmingham City (home)	8 May 1963
23.05 years	Everton (home)	21 November 1970
23.07 years	Arsenal (away)	28 November 1970
23.10 years	Mansfield Town (home)	22 September 1970

Bill Shankly lined up a team mostly consisting of reserves as the FA Cup final against Leeds was just a few days ahead. Of the 11 that played against Wolves only Geoff Strong featured in the cup final.

Oldest line-up

30.82 years	Newcastle United (home)	4 November 1950
30.76 years	West Ham United (home)	5 September 1925
30.74 years	Tottenham Hotspur (away)	13 December 1924
30.72 years	Bolton Wanderers (home)	30 September 1950
30.67 years	Arsenal (home)	3 January 1925

In comparison the youngest line-up ever produced by Brendan Rodgers is 23.21 years against Oldham Athletic (away) in the FA Cup on 27 January 2013. That is the seventh youngest line-up in the history of the club.

Agger,
Daniel

BETWEEN 2004 and 2006, when he joined Liverpool, Daniel Agger was voted Denmark's most promising player. He made his Brøndby debut on 25 July 2004 in a league match against OB Odense, having been on the club's books since he was 12 years old.

He got his big break earlier than expected as Brøndby's experienced centre-half, Andreas Jakobsson, was sold to Southampton. Agger was voted Brøndby's man of the match three games in a row following his emergence and was established in the first team aged just 19, never looking out of place. He earned his big move to

Liverpool after just 49 first-team games for Brøndby. Rafa Benítez was so confident about his abilities that he declared: 'He will be a Liverpool centre-back for the next ten years.'

AGGER fitted straight into the Liverpool team and it was a testament to his abilities that the great Sami Hyypia was forced to make way, for a while at least. The Danish defender scored the best goal of Liverpool's 2006/07 season with a fantastic shot from outside the penalty area against West Ham in front of the Kop in only his second league game. His stylish play earned him rave reviews and he showed his strong character against Chelsea in the Champions League semi-final at Anfield. He had difficulty in

containing Didier Drogba in the first leg at Stamford Bridge, but was man of the match in the second leg at Anfield, scoring Liverpool's goal as well. An injury to Agger's metatarsal in September 2007 wrecked the 2007/08 season as he underwent an operation that kept him out until the start of the 2008/09 season. The emergence of Martin Skrtel kept Agger on the bench until middle of October 2008 when the Slovakian injured his knee. The Dane was clearly not in his best form, but managed to get a good run in the side until Skrtel was fit again at the end of January. Agger seemed to be regaining his old form at the end of the season, but a recurrence of a back injury kept him on the sidelines for the first two months of 2009/10.

THE DANISH DEFENDER SCORED THE BEST GOAL OF LIVERPOOL'S 2006/07 SEASON WITH A FANTASTIC SHOT FROM OUTSIDE THE PENALTY AREA

Agger figured in 23 league and 13 cup matches during the 2009/10 season, sometimes at left-back, but most often in his more familiar position of centre-back. He reached his century of Liverpool matches when picked for the home leg with Unirea Urziceni on 25 February 2010.

Season	League		FA Cup		League Cup		Europe		Other		Total	
	App	Goals	App	Goals	App	Goals	App	Goals	App	Goals	App	Goals
2005/06	4	0	0	0	0	0	0	0	0	0	4	0
2006/07	23 (4)	2	1	0	2	1	12	1	1	0	39 (4)	4
2007/08	4 (1)	0	0	0	0	0	1	0	-	-	5 (1)	0
2008/09	15 (3)	1	1	0	2	1	5	0	-	-	23 (3)	2
2009/10	23	0	1	0	0	0	12	1	-	-	36	1
2010/11	12 (4)	0	1	0	1	0	3	0	-	-	17 (4)	0
2011/12	24 (3)	1	3	1	4	0	-	-	-	-	31 (3)	2
2012/13	35	3	0	0	0	0	4	0	-	-	39	3
Total	140 (15)	7	7	1	9	2	37	2	1	0	194 (15)	12

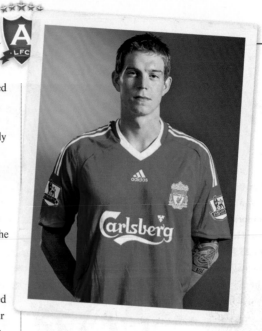

THE *LIVERPOOL ECHO'S* Dominic King celebrated the Dane's milestone. 'Agger is one of those players to whom everything about the game comes easy, a terrific, natural talent whom it is a privilege to watch in close quarters, as he has skills that many attacking players don't possess.'

Denmark's talisman in the 1980s and 90s, Michael Laudrup, was equally complimentary in an interview with Liverpool's official website in July 2011: 'Ask any player in the world, even the greats – you can't hit top form if you have niggling injuries… If he can stay fit then I think he can definitely be one of the best central defenders in the game.' Agger played in Denmark's three matches in the 2010 World Cup but unfortunately the Danes could not get past the group stage, finishing third behind the Netherlands and Japan.

'Will we ever see a fully fit Daniel Agger for the whole of a season?' has been the perennial question regarding his Reds' career. He was concussed in the first Premier League match of the 2010/11 season against Arsenal and also had other injuries that kept him out of contention in the first half of the campaign. Roy Hodgson preferred Martin Skrtel to Agger but the Dane's fortunes were revived when Kenny Dalglish took over. Unfortunately, his injury jinx struck again when he was forced to leave the field at West Bromwich Albion early in March. That was Agger's final appearance of a very disruptive season.

Not suffering from injury as much as in some previous seasons, Denmark's captain was able to play in two-thirds of Liverpool's first-team matches in 2011/12, forming a great partnership with Skrtel. Agger's silky skills and forward movement fitted nicely with the Slovakian's steely determination.

Agger should have by now played around 300-plus games for Liverpool. There is no question about his ability as he is generally considered the best defender in the squad, but the fact remains that his numerous injuries have curtailed his progress. There was much speculation about his Liverpool future at the start of the 2012/13 season, but he signed a new long-term contract with the club on 5 October 2012. In November 2012 Agger was voted the Danish Footballer of the Year for the second time in his career, an achievement he first earned in 2007. Agger lacked consistency in 2012/13 compared to the previous season, not helped by Skrtel's big loss in form. The Dane looked way more assured once Jamie Carragher slotted in by his side from end of January and Liverpool kept five clean sheets in their last eight games of the season, which was testament to the team's recovered resolve in the centre of defence. Agger enjoyed his best season since joining the Reds in terms of league appearances, having featured in a total of 35. He had only missed one league game when he was forced to sit out the last two of the campaign as he underwent proactive injections to enhance the stability of his back.

FACTFILE

BORN
Hvidovre, Denmark,
12 December 1984
POSITION
Centre-half / Left-back
OTHER CLUBS
Brøndby (1996–2006)
SIGNED FROM
Brøndby, £5.8million,
12 January 2006
INTERNATIONAL CAPS
56 Denmark caps (7 goals)
(52 (5) at LFC), 2005–
LFC DEBUT GAME/GOAL
1 February 2006 /
26 August 2006
HONOURS
League Cup 2012

Aitken,
Andrew

GOALKEEPER Andrew Aitken made his one and only Liverpool appearance in a 3-3 draw away to Blackburn Rovers on 27 December 1930.

Arthur Riley was Liverpool's number one at the time and Aitken had virtually no chance of establishing himself as the legendary Elisha Scott was Riley's understudy. Aitken's Anfield career was cut short when he broke his leg in a 6-1 loss against Stockport County's reserves on 4 April 1931.

AITKEN'S ANFIELD CAREER WAS CUT SHORT WHEN HE BROKE HIS LEG IN A 6-1 LOSS AGAINST STOCKPORT COUNTY

He returned to amateur football after he left Liverpool, but got back into the league scene with Hartlepools United of the Third Division North.

FACTFILE

BORN
Newcastle upon Tyne,
25 August 1909
DIED
October 1984
POSITION
Goalkeeper
OTHER CLUBS
Wallsend (1927–30),
Mickley, Newburn Athletic,
Hartlepools United (1936)
SIGNED FROM
Wallsend, 15 March 1930
LFC DEBUT
27 December 1930
CONTRACT EXPIRY
April 1931

	League		FA Cup		Total	
Season	App	Goals	App	Goals	App	Goals
1930/31	1	0	0	0	1	0
Total	1	0	0	0	1	0

Aldridge, John

ONCE UPON A TIME Liverpool had the luxury of dropping 30-goals -a-season strikers. John 'Aldo' Aldridge was a true goalscoring wizard and it didn't matter where he was playing, the goals kept coming. He was an exceptional header of the ball and a master of link-up play. He would receive the ball with his back to the opposition, feed it into the right channels and make his way to the box, where he was deadly.

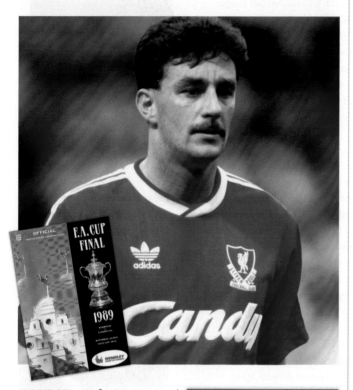

ALDRIDGE was a fervent Liverpool fan from a very early age and must have thought his chance of playing for his boyhood heroes had passed him by when he plied his trade with Oxford United. But the imminent departure of Ian Rush to Juventus meant that Kenny Dalglish needed to strengthen his attacking force and Aldridge needed no second invitation when he finally made his 'dream move' to Anfield early in 1987 at the age of 28. Aldridge had already scored 15 goals in 25 matches that season for Oxford but after joining Liverpool he only added two goals to his total for that campaign. This was perhaps not surprising as he came on as substitute in all but two of his 10 appearances for the Reds in 1986/87. Dalglish did not seem too keen on using him but told Aldridge not to worry, his time

> JOHN 'ALDO' ALDRIDGE WAS A TRUE GOALSCORING WIZARD

would come when Rush had left and other players, who complemented him better, had arrived. A few months later, John Barnes and Peter Beardsley joined Liverpool. Aldridge took over the

responsibility of leading the attack with devastating effect, scoring in each of the first nine league matches in the 1987/88 season. Having also scored in the final league game of the previous season it set a club record of scoring in 10 consecutive league matches, one that still stands. Rush was in no doubt after watching his successor in action in October 1987 that he was the right man for the job. 'I always felt that John was the main man to take over from me,' Rush told the press following Liverpool's 4-0 annihilation of QPR. 'He is scoring goals at a faster rate than I ever did, and Liverpool look a better side than they did last year. There are not many strikers around like John, and by playing with wingers they have so many more options this season.'

Normally so reliable from 12 yards, Aldridge became the first player to miss a penalty in an FA Cup final at Wembley when Liverpool were denied a League and FA Cup double by Wimbledon in 1988.

ALDRIDGE got the surprise of his life when Rush returned to Anfield after only one season at Juventus, forcing Dalglish to accommodate both of them in the same team. He rose to the challenge, scoring 31 goals during the 1988/89 season, and made amends for his penalty miss when he scored with his first touch against Everton in the 1989 FA Cup final, adding an FA Cup winners' medal to his trophy cabinet as Liverpool beat their neighbours 3-2 after extra time. He thereby completed his domestic set of honours, having

FACTFILE

BORN
Garston, Liverpool,
18 September 1958
POSITION
Centre-forward
OTHER CLUBS
South Liverpool,
Newport County (1979–84),
Oxford United (1984–87),
Real Sociedad (1989–91),
Tranmere Rovers (1991–98)
SIGNED FROM
Oxford United, £750,000,
27 January 1987
INTERNATIONAL CAPS
69 Ireland caps (19 goals)
(19 (1) at LFC), 1986–96
LFC DEBUT GAME/GOAL
21 February 1987 /
28 February 1987
CONTRACT EXPIRY
13 September 1989
HONOURS
League Championship
1987/88;
FA Cup 1989;
First Division Top-Scorer
1987/88

already won the League Cup as an Oxford player in 1986. Rush had scored the other two goals in the FA Cup final against Everton and when he had finally reached full fitness at the start of the 1989/90 season it became apparent that Kenny would prefer his old striking partner to Aldridge.

With a move to Real Sociedad looming he was allowed to come off the bench when a penalty was awarded in the 9-0 win of Crystal Palace on 12 September 1989. Peter Beardsley graciously made way for Aldridge, who tucked the spot kick away with typical efficiency and threw his shirt and boots into the Kop at the end of an emotional farewell appearance.

Season	League		FA Cup		League Cup		Europe		Other		Total	
	App	Goals	App	Goals	App	Goals	App	Goals	App	Goals	App	Goals
1986/87	2 (8)	2	0	0	0	0	-	-	0	0	2 (8)	2
1987/88	36	26	6	2	3	1	-	-	-	-	45	29
1988/89	31 (4)	21	6	6	4 (1)	2	-	-	1	2	42 (5)	31
1989/90	0 (2)	1	0	0	0	0	-	-	0	0	0 (2)	1
Total	**69 (14)**	**50**	**12**	**8**	**7 (1)**	**3**	**0**	**0**	**1**	**2**	**89 (15)**	**63**

Allan,
George

GEORGE 'DOD' ALLAN, who was described as 'a model centre; of fine physique, great speed and no fear', was Liverpool's first great goalscorer in the Football League and the club's first player to be capped for Scotland, on 3 April 1897.

Dundee native Peter D. Allan, said to be by *Scottish Sport*, 'the best known poacher of Scottish footballers for English clubs,' alerted Liverpool to George's capabilities. Allan was playing for Leith Athletic when Liverpool sent their scouts to watch him. Burnley had, in fact, already registered him as a player in the English Football League but took Liverpool's offer of £2 to tear up the contract as according to the famous scout, 'Unfortunately for Burnley, they had seen Allan at his worst.'

Allan's transfer to Liverpool was made under controversial circumstances as he had signed a contract with St Bernard's in Edinburgh as well. He was reported to the Scottish Football Association and on 14 October 1895 was suspended until 30 November, after which he was considered a bona fide Liverpool player.

Allan burst on to the scene in the 1895/96 season with a staggering 25 goals from only 20 league matches as the club won the Second Division, and would have no doubt netted more if not for his eight-game suspension. He was Liverpool's top scorer the following season with 17 goals from 34 games as Liverpool finished fifth in the First Division.

The Football League President J.J. Bentley was an admirer, writing in the *Edinburgh Evening News* in January 1897: 'In Liverpool they have one of the best centre forwards in the country. I may be mistaken, but I fancy Allan has to thank the tuition of James Ross for his advancement, for when I first saw him he was energetic, but decidedly clumsy. He is strongly built, and can stand the charge of the heaviest back with equanimity, whilst he passes most judiciously. Our Scottish friends might do worse than keep their selection optics on this young man.' Allan moved to Celtic in May 1897, where he helped the club to its fourth championship by scoring 15 goals in 17 league games. Liverpool still held his Football League registration, but quite happily paid £50 to get him back. The club wanted him to play the last match of the 1897/98 season; a friendly against league champions Sheffield United. Unfortunately his clearance did not come through in time so Allan was instead linesman in the match. In the press afterwards it was said he was the most expensive and best paid linesman ever. Liverpool finished second in the First Division in the following season with Allan scoring 11 goals in 36 games.

ALLAN had played seven games in his second spell at Liverpool when he was involved in a colourful incident with Sheffield United's goalkeeper, William 'Fatty' Foulke, that gained legendary status. Foulke was over 20 stone (125kg) and very difficult (to say the least!) to charge off the ball or into the goal – as was permitted in those days. The scene is set for 29 October 1898 when Liverpool and then League champions Sheffield United were playing at Anfield. Unlike his contemporaries, 5ft 10in and 13st 6lb (173cm and 86kg) Allan was not afraid of 'Fatty' and it was reported that 'Allan charged Foulke in the goalmouth, and the big man, losing his temper, seized him by the leg and turned him upside down'. The referee wasn't too keen on Foulke's reaction and awarded Liverpool a penalty, from which Andy McCowie scored. Liverpool won the game 2-1, with none other than Allan scoring the other goal for Liverpool. After he retired from football Foulke gave a different version of this incident when he was interviewed by the *London Evening News*.

You may have heard that there was a very great rivalry between the old Liverpool centre forward Allan and myself, that prior to one match we breathed fire and slaughter at each other, that at last he made a rush at me as I was saving a shot, and that I dropped the ball, caught him by the middle, turned him clean over in a twinkling, and stood him on his head, giving him such a shock that he never played again. Well, the story is one which might be described as a 'bit of each'. In reality, Allan and I were quite good friends off the field... What actually happened on the occasion referred to was that Allan (a big strong chap, mind you) once bore down on me with all his weight when I was saving. I bent forward to protect myself, and Allan, striking my shoulder, flew right over me and fell heavily. He had a shaking up, I admit, but quite the worst thing about the whole business was that the referee gave a penalty against us and it cost Sheffield United the match.'

Prior to the 1899/1900 season it was reported that Allan was too ill for training. In September 1899 manager Tom Watson admitted full of sorrow: 'Diseased lungs are not cured in a day. Allan's absence is now beginning to be felt, and we are able to estimate him at his worth. Poor old George!' Allan died of tuberculosis in Earlsbury, Fife, when he was only 24 years old on 17 October 1899.

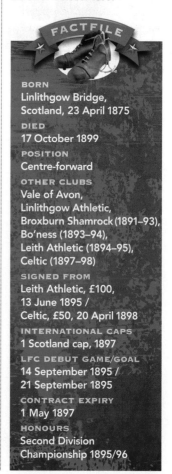

FACTFILE

BORN
Linlithgow Bridge, Scotland, 23 April 1875
DIED
17 October 1899
POSITION
Centre-forward
OTHER CLUBS
Vale of Avon, Linlithgow Athletic, Broxburn Shamrock (1891–93), Bo'ness (1893–94), Leith Athletic (1894–95), Celtic (1897–98)
SIGNED FROM
Leith Athletic, £100, 13 June 1895 / Celtic, £50, 20 April 1898
INTERNATIONAL CAPS
1 Scotland cap, 1897
LFC DEBUT GAME/GOAL
14 September 1895 / 21 September 1895
CONTRACT EXPIRY
1 May 1897
HONOURS
Second Division Championship 1895/96

Season	League		FA Cup		Other		Total	
	App	Goals	App	Goals	App	Goals	App	Goals
1895/96	20	25	2	1	4	2	26	28
1896/97	29	15	5	2	-	-	34	17
1898/99	30	8	6	3	-	-	36	11
Total	**79**	**48**	**13**	**6**	**4**	**2**	**96**	**56**

Allen,
Joe

ALTHOUGH NEW LIVERPOOL manager Brendan Rodgers had a written agreement with his previous employers, Swansea City, that he would not try to sign any players from the club for a full 12 months, there was a certain inevitability about Joe Allen leaving South Wales once it became clear that there was a clause in that agreement allowing him to leave for £15million for a big English club. Michael Laudrup, who replaced Rodgers as manager at the Liberty Stadium, accepted that it was pointless trying to keep a player who wanted to leave, adding: 'He has a great possibility to go to a big club with a manager who knows him and who will play him.'

The midfielder had been part of Swansea's set-up since he was only nine years old, progressing through the junior ranks until the day came when, aged just 17, manager Roberto Martínez gave him his Football League debut on the final day of the 2006/07 season. Progress was slow over the next couple of years and he had a spell on loan at Wrexham, but his stay there was curtailed due to an ankle injury. Once he had recovered, he became an integral part of the Swansea team that first consolidated its position in the Championship and then made a serious challenge for

promotion to the Premier League. Allen featured in the playoff final against Reading at Wembley in which his club defeated the Berkshire club 4-2. Shortly before Swansea began their inaugural season in the top division, Allen signed a contract that, without Liverpool's intervention, would have kept him in South Wales until 2015. But Allen's form, like that of his club, surpassed most people's expectations and it wasn't

just Liverpool taking an interest. Allen played in all but two of Swansea's 38 Premier League matches in 2011/12. His good form was also being recognised on the international stage. Having represented Wales at Under-17, Under-19 and Under-21 level, it was no surprise when he eventually made his debut for the senior side and at the time of his transfer to Liverpool he had eight full caps. He was also one of five Welshmen selected by manager Stuart Pearce to be in Great

Britain's squad for the London Olympics and played from the start in all four of the tournament matches. Allen is excited about playing for Liverpool and the man who signed him is confident that he will be a success. 'This boy, when you see him play, you would think he was a European player,' Brendan Rodgers told the *Liverpool Echo*. 'He is a unique player in that he is a British player who doesn't give the ball away.

He's incredible on the ball. His body work and intelligence for a 22-year-old is frightening. You will see when he comes into this team the difference he can make. His game understanding is very good, and he is in love with the football.'

RODGERS' referral to Allen as the 'New Xavi' in the documentary 'Being Liverpool' was maybe slightly excessive, but Allen started his Liverpool career superbly, delivering man-of-the-match

performances in an unfamiliar role as defensive midfielder in the absence of Lucas Leiva. The fans voted him their Standard Chartered Player of August 2012. It was expected he would relish playing further upfield as Lucas returned, but he seemed to lose confidence, still coming to terms with his move from Swansea to Liverpool. Allen missed the last two months of the season as he needed surgery on his left shoulder. 'The fans have definitely not seen the best of me yet,' Allen admitted to *Liverpoolfc.com* in April. 'It's no secret that recent months haven't gone great for me. I am confident and faithful that next season I can perform a lot better. The injury is something I'd been trying to put to the back of my mind but it was something that needed to be addressed. It had been there for a while so I'd almost grown used to it but it's got worse and worse. These things can often play on your mind.' Allen is still young and seems quite certain to find his form again and be a valuable member of the Liverpool squad.

FACTFILE

BORN
Carmarthen, Wales,
14 March 1990

POSITION
Midfielder

OTHER CLUBS
Swansea City (2007–12),
Wrexham (loan, 2008)

SIGNED FROM
Swansea City, £15million,
10 August 2012

INTERNATIONAL CAPS
13 Wales caps
(5 at LFC), 2009–

LFC DEBUT GAME/GOAL
18 August 2012 /
27 January 2013

> ALLEN STARTED HIS LIVERPOOL CAREER SUPERBLY, DELIVERING MAN-OF-THE-MATCH PERFORMANCES

Season	League		FA Cup		League Cup		Other		Total	
	App	Goals	App	Goals	App	Goals	App	Goals	App	Goals
2012/13	21 (6)	0	2	1	1	0	5 (2)	1	29 (8)	2
Total	**21 (6)**	**0**	**2**	**1**	**1**	**0**	**5 (2)**	**1**	**29 (8)**	**2**

Allman, Messina

Messina 'Dick' Allman's sole appearance in the Football League for Liverpool came at home to Bristol City on 13 March 1909, a game the visitors won 2-1.

After drifting from one club to another Allman finally found a home in the Southern League with Croydon Common, making 113 appearances and scoring 34 goals. He enlisted in the army in 1915 and served in France, but still made 32 appearances for the club during wartime. Messina was in the news in 1925 when his wife, Beatrice Ellen Allman, was charged with bigamy! Messina, who was then working as a foreman at Woolwich Arsenal, believed Beatrice was training to become a servant in Newhaven. Beatrice, instead, according to the *Western Morning News*, 'went through a form of marriage with a seaman named Stephen Winder.' Winder said he thought Beatrice was a widow. She accompanied her second 'husband' to the police station at Brighton and confessed.

FACTFILE

BORN
Burslem 1883
POSITION
Right-half
OTHER CLUBS
Burslem Highergrave (1901–03),
Burslem Port Vale (1903–05),
Reading (1905–07),
Portsmouth (1907),
Plymouth Argyle (1907–08),
Wrexham (1909–10),
Grantham (1910–11),
Ton Pentre (1911),
Leicester Fosse (1911–12),
Croydon Common (1912–16),
Crystal Palace (1919–20),
Maidstone United (1920–21)
SIGNED FROM
Plymouth Argyle, 7 July 1908
LFC DEBUT
13 March 1909
CONTRACT EXPIRY
September 1909

Season	League		FA Cup		Total	
	App	Goals	App	Goals	App	Goals
1908/09	1	0	0	0	1	0
Total	1	0	0	0	1	0

Alonso, Xabi

Xabier Alonso Olano made his debut for Real Sociedad against Logrones on 1 December 1999 in the Copa del Rey. He made 14 further appearances that season, but was then loaned out to Eibar in the Segunda Division. Sociedad were, however, struggling in the Primera Liga and new manager and former Liverpool great John Toshack recalled Alonso from his loan and in a shock move made the 19-year-old captain of the side.

The team cemented its position in La Liga the following year and blossomed in the 2002/03 season, finishing two points behind champions Real Madrid. The respected football magazine *Don Balon* elected Alonso Spanish Player of the Year.

Alonso made his international debut against Ecuador on 30 April 2003 and featured against Russia and Portugal in Euro 2004, but Spain failed to get out of the group stages. Sociedad qualified for the knockout phase of the Champions League, but were knocked out by Lyon and struggled in the league, finishing 15th.

RAFA BENÍTEZ had seen enough of Xabi to convince him of the qualities he could bring to Liverpool: strong in defence and going forward and possessing an excellent passing range. If there ever was a player moulded in the Liverpool way, it was Alonso, as he was comfortable in possession with the vision to spot passes and the ability to execute them. He was also a tough customer and maybe Benítez didn't expect that he would boast one of the best rates of successful tackles in the Premiership.

ALONSO made an instant impression at Liverpool, but suffered a broken ankle in the 2005 New Year's Day clash against Chelsea, and the difference in the team's performance was noticeable. Alonso returned to the side three months later just in time to feature in the second leg of the quarter-final clash with Juventus in the Champions League when Liverpool drew 0-0 in Turin after winning 2-1 at Anfield. The Reds were concerned when he was banned for the second leg of the semi-final against Chelsea at Anfield, but fortunately his absence didn't prevent Liverpool from reaching the final where he scored the equalising goal against Milan, pouncing on the rebound after seeing his penalty saved. Alonso was, incredibly, a European champion in his debut season at Liverpool.

His speciality became his extra-long-range strikes, scoring twice from inside his own half. His first effort was from 65 yards in the 5-3 FA Cup win over Luton in January 2006, guaranteeing a Liverpool fan £25,000. Adrian Hayward had placed his £200 bet at 125-1 after noticing that Alonso had tried several times in his debut season to score from his own half. 'I've always had a vision in my mind that it would come when the opposing keeper came out for a corner in a cup game. I couldn't believe it when Luton got a corner and the keeper started to run upfield... I thought I was going to pass out. When it went in, I went crazy,' said a delighted Adrian.

In the 2005/06 season Alonso looked forward to an FA Cup final against West Ham. Unfortunately, he picked up an ankle injury in the last league game of the season, but convinced Rafa and the medical team that he was ready for the final. Alonso managed 67 minutes before he was taken off at the Millennium Stadium, where a Gerrard-inspired Liverpool went on to secure a winners' medal for him after a penalty-shootout win.

> IF THERE EVER WAS A PLAYER MOULDED IN THE LIVERPOOL WAY, IT WAS ALONSO

ALONSO repeated his incredible feat of scoring from his own half, against Newcastle in September 2006 in a league game at Anfield. This time the distance was 70 yards and Steve Harper tried desperately to reach the shot, but to no avail. *The Independent* described it as 'one of the most audacious goals in Anfield's rich 115-year history'. Despite this wonder goal Alonso seemed to have lost his way a bit. His usually sublime passes were quite wayward and he didn't contribute as he had before. Benítez kept faith with him through the 2006/07 season that ended disappointingly in Athens, where Alonso featured in the 2-1 loss to Milan in the Champions League final.

The Basque played in fewer first-team competitive matches during his fourth season at Anfield than the previous season, just 27 out of a possible 59. He was picked from the start in the opening five league games and scored twice as promoted Derby County were thrashed 6-0 at Anfield on the first day of September. He was substituted due to a slight injury against Portsmouth in the middle of September and was out for six weeks. He was then rushed into action to face Arsenal on 28 October 2007 but limped off and missed another seven weeks. Rafa struggled to find a suitable midfield combination in his absence, rotating between Momo Sissoko, Javier Mascherano and Lucas Leiva to partner Gerrard. When Alonso returned Benítez accommodated him alongside the respective holding midfielders

by moving Gerrard further forward as a second striker behind Fernando Torres.

Alonso played 163 minutes in Spain's successful Euro 2008 tournament and came on as substitute in the 63rd minute of the final against Germany. After the tournament speculation was rife that Alonso would be moving on from Liverpool, with Gareth Barry the man expected to take his place. In the end Barry's transfer from Aston Villa never happened and Alonso went on to have perhaps his best season as a Liverpool player, making

47 first-team appearances and scoring five times, including the goal that ended Chelsea's record-breaking unbeaten home run in the league.

His tenacity returned, prompting his opponents to foul him on a constant basis, which resulted in six dismissals of opponents for fouls made on him! But Benítez's willingness the previous year to sell him seemed to have soured their relationship. Real Madrid were monitoring the situation and Alonso wanted to return home to Spain. Liverpool agreed to sell the midfielder to Madrid for a fee that

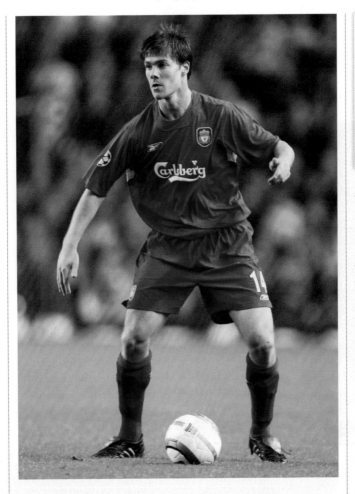

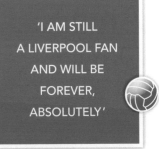

'I AM STILL A LIVERPOOL FAN AND WILL BE FOREVER, ABSOLUTELY'

was believed to be around £30million, certainly a significant profit on the £10.7million Liverpool paid Real Sociedad for Alonso's services in 2004. Alonso, who started every game of Spain's 2010 World Cup winning campaign, has always been linked with a return to Liverpool one day and is still in love with the club. 'I am still a Liverpool fan and will be forever, absolutely,' Alonso told *The Times* in 2011. 'The things that I have lived and the experiences I had during those five years are deep in my heart and the passion and respect I had for the club and its supporters are still the same. Hopefully I can transmit to my son what Liverpool Football Club means and how special it is, as he was born in the city.'

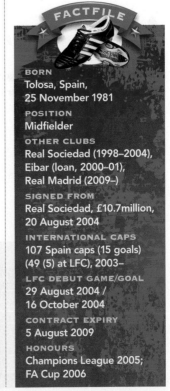

FACTFILE

BORN
Tolosa, Spain, 25 November 1981
POSITION
Midfielder
OTHER CLUBS
Real Sociedad (1998–2004), Eibar (loan, 2000–01), Real Madrid (2009–)
SIGNED FROM
Real Sociedad, £10.7million, 20 August 2004
INTERNATIONAL CAPS
107 Spain caps (15 goals) (49 (5) at LFC), 2003–
LFC DEBUT GAME/GOAL
29 August 2004 / 16 October 2004
CONTRACT EXPIRY
5 August 2009
HONOURS
Champions League 2005; FA Cup 2006

Season	League App	League Goals	FA Cup App	FA Cup Goals	League Cup App	League Cup Goals	Europe App	Europe Goals	Other App	Other Goals	Total App	Total Goals
2004/05	20 (4)	2	0	0	0	0	7 (1)	1	-	-	27 (5)	3
2005/06	29 (6)	3	5	2	0	0	11	0	2	0	47 (6)	5
2006/07	29 (3)	4	1	0	0 (2)	0	13 (2)	0	0 (1)	0	43 (8)	4
2007/08	16 (3)	2	3	0	1	0	4	0	-	-	24 (3)	2
2008/09	27 (6)	4	3	0	0 (1)	0	10	1	-	-	40 (7)	5
Total	**121 (22)**	**15**	**12**	**2**	**1 (3)**	**0**	**45 (3)**	**2**	**2 (1)**	**0**	**181 (29)**	**19**

Amoo, David

AFTER SCORING nine goals in 20 games for the Millwall Under-18 team in the 2006/07 season Amoo joined Liverpool's Academy in July 2007.

The right-winger was promoted to Melwood in 2009 and made his debut for Liverpool's first team in the Europa League third qualifying round against FK Rabotnicki on 29 July 2010. Amoo wasn't considered strong enough to challenge for a first-team place at Liverpool and was loaned out to MK Dons in League One and Hull City in the Championship for two months in the latter part of 2010/11. He spent the majority of 2011/12 on loan at League One side Bury where he played 27 league matches and scored four times. Among his goals was the winner against Preston at Gigg Lane in November 2011. He clearly impressed Preston North End, who agreed to sign him following the expiry of his Liverpool contract on 1 June 2012. After 15 substitute appearances and nine starts for Preston Amoo's one-year deal was terminated in January 2013. He subsequently

FACTFILE

BORN
Southwark, London,
13 April 1991
POSITION
Right-winger
OTHER CLUBS
MK Dons (loan, 2011),
Hull City (loan, 2011),
Bury (loan, 2011–12),
Preston North End (2012–13),
Tranmere Rovers (2013–)
SIGNED FROM
Millwall (youth), 11 July 2007
LFC DEBUT
29 July 2010
CONTRACT EXPIRY
1 June 2012

joined Tranmere Rovers. Amoo once represented London as a sprinter in the English Schools National Track and Field Championships and his personal best in the 100 metres sprint is said to be 10.5 seconds.

Season	League		FA Cup		League Cup		Europe		Total	
	App	Goals	App	Goals	App	Goals	App	Goals	App	Goals
2010/11	0	0	0	0	0	0	1	0	1	0
Total	0	0	0	0	0	0	1	0	1	0

Anderson, Eric

A skilful forward, who scored one goal in every three games at Liverpool, Eric Anderson signed in December 1951 when he was 20 years old.

He was given his debut on 28 March 1953 in a home fixture against Charlton Athletic but that was his only appearance of the season. He scored five times in 13 games the following season when Liverpool were relegated.

ANDERSON established himself in the side in the Second Division, playing in 32 league fixtures and contributing a further 10 goals. He appeared fairly regularly over the next season and a half before being replaced by a young Jimmy Melia.

FACTFILE

BORN
Manchester, 12 March 1931
DIED
July 1990
POSITION
Inside-right / Left forward
OTHER CLUBS
Barnsley (1957–59),
Bournemouth & Boscombe
Athletic (1959–60),
Macclesfield (1960–61),
Hyde United (1961),
Mossley (1961–62)
JOINED
11 December 1951
LFC DEBUT GAME/GOAL
28 March 1953 /
6 February 1954
CONTRACT EXPIRY
July 1957

ERIC ANDERSON
LIVERPOOL F.C.

Season	League		FA Cup		Total	
	App	Goals	App	Goals	App	Goals
1952/53	1	0	0	0	1	0
1953/54	13	5	0	0	13	5
1954/55	32	10	3	0	35	10
1955/56	20	6	0	0	20	6
1956/57	7	1	0	0	7	1
Total	73	22	3	0	76	22

Anelka, Nicolas

WHO COULD GUESS that one of Anelka's many destinations would be Liverpool? The former PFA Young Player of the Year has destroyed a number of golden opportunities with his attitude, including a career at Anfield. He and his brothers – who served as his agents – tested Gérard Houllier's patience and the boss refused to buy him at the end of his loan period.

One particular night, when the lights went out against Newcastle, represented Nico's golden moment at Liverpool. A superb display from the mercurial Frenchman lit up Anfield in a 3-0 win. Anelka claimed to be excited with the prospect of joining the Reds. 'Soon Liverpool will be able to sign me,' he said. 'It's a long time since I enjoyed myself so much on the pitch. Liverpool is a fantastic club. I also really like Liverpool as a city.' Many supporters were surprised when

Houllier decided not to make Anelka a permanent addition to his squad at the end of the 2001/02 season. Four goals from 20 league games had helped the club achieve second place in the Premier League, behind champions Arsenal. Instead Houllier decided to buy El Hadji Diouf, and nobody in their right mind would consider him a better signing than Anelka might have been.

PHIL THOMPSON, who was Houllier's assistant at the time, later revealed to *LFChistory.net*

> **'THE KOP APPLAUD ME AND KNOW I WANTED TO STAY'**

why Anelka wasn't purchased. 'Arséne Wenger rang up Gérard and said: "Gérard, I have to tell you. Nicolas' brothers have just rang me up and they've asked me to take Nicolas back to Arsenal." Once his brothers tried to sell Nicolas to Arsenal while he was on loan at us, that was the end.' It wasn't long before Anelka was back in English football when Kevin Keegan signed him for Manchester City, where he spent three fairly successful years, scoring 38 goals in 89 league games before he was on the move again, this time to Turkish club Fenerbahce. He helped them win the championship before signing a four-year contract at Bolton Wanderers that cost them a club record £8million. When Chelsea came calling in the January transfer window of 2008, it was hard for the player or his club to say no. The £15million fee meant that close on £90million had been spent on Anelka from the time he joined Real Madrid from Arsenal in 1999.

A CHAMPIONS LEAGUE winner with Madrid, Anelka would reach another final with Chelsea, but after a tight match that went the full distance it was his penalty kick, saved by Manchester United goalkeeper Edwin van der Sar, that meant that London clubs were still without a European Cup. In his second season at Chelsea Anelka finished top scorer of the Premier League with 19 goals. He was a member of their successful FA

Cup winning teams in both 2009 and 2010 and won his second Premier League winners' medal 12 years after winning his first with Arsenal in 1998.

In January 2012, Anelka signed for Chinese club Shanghai Shenhua. He was loaned to Juventus in January 2013 as the Turin club were short in attack due to injuries. What Anelka might have achieved had he stayed at Anfield in 2002 is only conjecture. But the significant number of goals scored for the clubs he has played for since then suggest that he could have become a really important player for the Reds. Anelka certainly believes so as he revealed ahead of Liverpool's and Bolton's New Year's Day clash in 2007: 'The Kop applaud me and know I wanted to stay. I would no doubt be at Liverpool now if Gérard Houllier had taken up the option to buy me. Everything about them fascinates me – the team, the very British stadium, the fans, the city, the red of their shirts.'

FACTFILE

BORN
Versailles, France,
14 March 1979
POSITION
Centre-forward
OTHER CLUBS
Paris St Germain (1995–97),
Arsenal (1997–99),
Real Madrid (1999–2000),
Paris St Germain (2000–02),
Manchester City (2002–05),
Fenerbahce (2005–06),
Bolton Wanderers (2006–08),
Chelsea (2008–12),
Shanghai Shenhua (2012–13),
Juventus (loan, 2013)
West Bromwich Albion (2013–)
SIGNED FROM
Paris St Germain (on loan),
£1million, 20 December 2001
INTERNATIONAL CAPS
69 France caps (14 goals)
(1 (0) at LFC), 1998–2010
LFC DEBUT GAME/GOAL
26 December 2001 /
5 January 2002
CONTRACT EXPIRY
12 May 2002

Season	League		FA Cup		League Cup		Europe		Other		Total	
	App	Goals	App	Goals	App	Goals	App	Goals	App	Goals	App	Goals
2001/02	13 (7)	4	2	1	0	0	0	0	0	0	15 (7)	5
Total	13 (7)	4	2	1	0	0	0	0	0	0	15 (7)	5

Liverpool Football Ground
The Wrench Series No. 440

ANFIELD 1923

Anfield

EVERTON PRESIDENT John Houlding was instrumental in renting a new piece of land for the club to play on between Anfield Road and Walton Breck Road on which Everton made their debut on 28 September 1884. Everton's new home simply became known as Anfield after the district it was situated in which was once a land fit only for grazing in the town of Walton on the Hill, that was made part of Liverpool Borough Council in 1836. The area was named Hanging-fields or Hangfield as the terrain had a deep slope.

Perimeter fences had to be raised around the Anfield pitch that also had a slight slope, not levelled out until in 1887. According to historian Thomas Keates, 'A hoarding of boards was fixed on the walls, and rails round the playing pitch.' Five years later Everton could receive up to 20,000 people. 'The enclosure now bears the resemblance of a huge circus, with its two immense galleries, rising tier above tier, and its covered stands stretching the length of the ground on the one side, and for the greater part of that distance on the other,' reported *Football Field*. Yet maybe comfort was sacrificed for quantity. A frustrated fan complained in the *Liverpool Echo* that 'the entrances to Anfield are a disgrace to a club with the financial position of Everton. When an important match is played the strong alone gain admission, the weak going to the wall, and very often into the mud.'

HOULDING AND EVERTON had a much-publicized split which led to the birth of Liverpool Football Club in 1892. Houlding's new club played at the Anfield ground that he had owned since 1885 while Everton moved to Goodison Park. Liverpool played their first-ever game at Anfield on 1 September 1892 when Rotherham were defeated 7-1 in a friendly before participating in the Lancashire League for which 4d was charged a game. Season tickets were available, the cheapest at 7s 6d for the uncovered stands and the most expensive at 21s for the reserved stands. As the club progressed at speed a new grand stand which represented three sides of a hexagon with a distinctive muck tudor central gable was built prior to the 1894/95 season. It was 360ft (110m) long and contained 11 rows of seats separated by 11in (28cm) for 3,000 spectators and the paddock in front was 15ft (4.5m) from the iron railings creating space for further 2,000.

The grandstand was finally covered before the start of the 1897/98 season and other alterations were made that had 'completely varied the aspects of the old Anfield ground.' The players had until now been forced to change at Houlding's establishment, the Sandon, that was just down the road, but the back end of the new stand had space for dressing rooms and offices. The first full-scale stand at the Anfield Road end was built in 1903, barrel-roofed and made from timber and corrugated iron. Few could have

envisaged the speedy progress made by Houlding's new club, conquering the League only in its ninth year of existence.

A CHANGE of ownership on 19 January 1906 brought about dramatic changes to the ground. Liverpool Football Club purchased Anfield from the owner, Sir William Houlding, whose father John had passed away in 1902, with a £10,000 loan from the Royal Liverpool Friendly Society, due to be repaid with interest in twenty years. The *Manchester Courier* reported that 'the new owners hope, by the beginning of next season, to have an enclosure

the kop
1928

worthy of the new club.' Noted architect Archibald Leitch, who had designed many of the finest grounds in England and Scotland, including Fulham's Craven Cottage, Chelsea's Stamford Bridge, Rangers' Ibrox and Newcastle United's St James' Park was hired to create the new Anfield. A new grandstand was erected by Lake Street and the old one was re-erected at Kemlyn Road on the opposite side where it remained until its demolition in 1963. The terracing now joined the Anfield Road stand and the corners were rounded so any wasted space was used fully. The pitch was raised 5ft (1.5m) with a paddock all round.

A terrace was made by Walton Breck Road which later on became

world famous as the Spion Kop *[see 'Kop' later in the book]*. Four mammoth exit gates were erected and no fewer than 47 turnstiles gained spectators entrance compared with 26 previously. The access to the pitch for the players had also been made easier as the *Cricket and Football Field* noted: 'This season the players will use the same dressing-rooms as formerly, but will have an exclusive entrance to the arena and thus escape their admirers' periodical too warm embraces.' The *Athletic News* were impressed by the club's ambition. 'Liverpool, having provided themselves with an up-to-date enclosure, now possess a home worthy of their title as League champions... when completed, the Liverpool ground will be equal to anything in the country both as regards size, convenience and equipment.' The work that had taken place was immense as explained by the reporter of the *Cricket and Football Field* who was guided through the ground in the company of Chairman John McKenna.

'Directly when the curtain fell in April the builders took possession of the enclosure and from that time onwards Anfield's interior has been one great scene of animation. When completed it is anticipated that New Anfield will accommodate 45,000 to 48,000 spectators far and away more comfortably than did Old Anfield a matter of 25,000. The banking up has necessitated hundreds of thousands of tons of ashes being deposited around the arena. Then the banking up does not merely consist of a giant slope, but rises tier after tier – constituting a mammoth four sided stand on terra firma.'

THE KOP could be quite windy and cold and finally in 1928 the Kopites were provided shelter when a new roof was built. Liverpool were on a downward spiral when Anfield's all-time record attendance was achieved on 2 February 1952 when 61,905 saw Liverpool beat Wolves 2-1 in the fourth round of the FA Cup. Liverpool were relegated in 1954 and not much was done of note to improve facilities at the ground until floodlights

were installed and switched on for the first time on 30 October 1957 when Liverpool faced Everton in the appropriately named Floodlit Challenge Cup to commemorate the 75-year anniversary of the Liverpool County FA. When Bill Shankly arrived at the club in December 1959 he wasn't very impressed by Anfield. 'The ground was an eyesore. It needed renovating and cleaning up,' Shankly said in his autobiography. 'I said to the groundsman, 'Where is your watering equipment?' There was a pipe from the visitor's dressing room and a tap. But no facilities for watering the pitch. It cost us about £3,000 to put that right. The ground was not good enough for the public of Liverpool and the team was not good enough for the public of Liverpool. The people were thirsting for success.' Four years later when the club had regained its spot in the top division the old Kemlyn Road stand was replaced by a cantilevered stand, able to hold 6,700 spectators. When Shankly had won his first league title at Liverpool and the team had entered European competition for the first time the Anfield Road end was turned into

a large covered standing area. Shankly's team had a barren spell from 1966 – 1973, but six weeks prior to the club guaranteeing its first league title for seven years the new Main stand was officially opened by the Duke of Kent. At the same time, the pylon floodlights were pulled down and new lights installed along the top of the Kemlyn Road and Main stands. The slightest of improvements were important to Shankly as Ian St John can confirm. 'He took a bemused reporter into a toilet cubicle in the new dressing room at Anfield, pulled the chain and said: 'You know it refills in 15 seconds... it's a world record.''

In 1981 the paddock in front of the Main stand was turned into seating. The Kemlyn Road stand was demolished to develop the Centenary stand with executive boxes, second tier and a cantilever roof, adding 11,000 seating spaces. The Centenary was opened on 1 September 1992, exactly 100 years after the first game was played at Anfield. The Kop was rebuilt in 1994 after the recommendations of the Taylor Report and became all seated; although it is still a single tier, the capacity was significantly reduced to 12,390. The latest development inside the ground was when an upper tier was built on the Anfield Road stand in 1998. The current capacity of Anfield, seated in the two-tiered Anfield Road end and Centenary stand and the single-tiered Kop and Main stand, is 45,276.

ANFIELD is of course more than just bricks and mortar and has become a sacred place where tears have been shed both in joy and sorrow and strong bonds been

formed beyond life and death. The fans' ashes have been scattered on the pitch, just as Bill Shankly invited his fervent followers to do. 'A family came with a man's ashes when the ground was frost-bound,' Shankly revealed in his autobiography.

> *'So the groundsman had the difficult job of digging a hole in the pitch inside the Kop net. He dug it a foot down at the right-hand side of the post facing the Kop and the casket containing the man's ashes were placed in it. So people not only support Liverpool when they're alive. They support them when they are dead. This is the true story of Liverpool. Laughingly I have said when a ball has been headed out of that particular corner of the net: 'That's the bloke in there again! He's having a blinder today.''*

Liverpool opened their doors to mourners following the Hillsborough disaster and 12 months later the memorial became an integral part of Anfield that also hosts an annual remembrance of the 96 victims on 15 April.

Shankly, who created the cauldron of noise that Anfield became so famous for, was rightfully honoured by the gates and the statue bearing his name at the ground, in 1982 and 1997 respectively. Bob Paisley, who continued Shankly's success was given a gateway of his own in 1999. Paisley was in charge when Liverpool set a club record of 85 home games unbeaten in all competitions from 7 February 1978 to 31 January 1981. Anfield has furthermore been a venue for boxing fights, concerts and internationals.

PLANS TO MOVE 300 yards away from Anfield and build a 55,000-seater stadium on Stanley Park were first announced in 2002. Rick Parry emphasised to fans through the media that 'we think we have good links to the new site without losing our history and tradition.' The AFL-designed 'First Generation Anfield' was revealed in 2007 and scrapped by new

owners George Gillett and Tom Hicks. A year later AFL brought forth 'New Generation Anfield' but lost to a rival design by American architects HKS. Liverpool's managing director, Ian Ayre, later revealed that the HKS designs and their development had come at a great cost to the club. Current owners John Henry and Tom Werner decided in 2012 that the solution was to redevelop Anfield instead of building on Stanley Park. The capacity would be in the vicinity of 60,000, by adding to the Main stand and then the Anfield Road end but the club first has to buy up 28 houses surrounding the stadium before any real work can begin. 'The idea is to increase matchday revenue to increase our spending in the transfer market, and to do that we need a much-increased capacity,' Ian Ayre explained to the press. 'We could have achieved a greater capacity in a new stadium but the cost of doing so would have been at least double what we expect to spend by staying put.' A lot of fans were relieved by this monumental decision as anyone would readily admit it would be strange to see Liverpool play anywhere else than at Anfield.

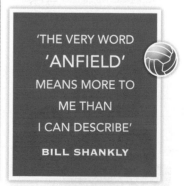

'THE VERY WORD
'ANFIELD'
MEANS MORE TO
ME THAN
I CAN DESCRIBE'
BILL SHANKLY

Appearances

All-time top appearances

1	Ian Callaghan	857
2	Jamie Carragher	737
3	Ray Clemence	665
4	Emlyn Hughes	665
5	Ian Rush	660
6	Phil Neal	650
7	Tommy Smith	638
8	Steven Gerrard	630
9	Bruce Grobbelaar	628
10	Alan Hansen	620

BILLY LIDDELL
LIVERPOOL

All-time top League appearances

1	Ian Callaghan	640
2	Jamie Carragher	508
3	Billy Liddell	492
4	Emlyn Hughes	474
5	Ray Clemence	470
6	Ian Rush	469
7	Tommy Smith	467
8	Phil Neal	455
9	Steven Gerrard	441
10	Bruce Grobbelaar	440

TOMMY SMITH
LIVERPOOL

All-time top European appearances

1	Jamie Carragher	150
2	Steven Gerrard	124
3	Sami Hyypia	94
4	Ian Callaghan	89
5	Tommy Smith	85
6	Pepe Reina	84
7	Ray Clemence	80
8	Emlyn Hughes	79
9	John Arne Riise	79
10	Phil Neal	74

IAN CALLAGHAN
LIVERPOOL

RAY CLEMENCE
LIVERPOOL

All-time top FA Cup appearances

1	Ian Callaghan	79
2	Bruce Grobbelaar	62
3	Emlyn Hughes	62
4	Ian Rush	61
5	Alan Hansen	58
6	Ray Clemence	54
7	Tommy Smith	52
8	John Barnes	51
9	Ron Yeats	50
10	Steve Nicol	50

All-time top League Cup appearances

1	Ian Rush	78
2	Bruce Grobbelaar	70
3	Alan Hansen	68
4	Phil Neal	66
5	Kenny Dalglish	59
6	Ray Clemence	55
7	Ronnie Whelan	50
8	Mark Lawrenson	50
9	Emlyn Hughes	46
10	Alan Kennedy	45
11	Graeme Souness	45

CHRIS LAWLER
LIVERPOOL

JOHN BARNES
LIVERPOOL

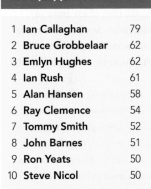

ALAN HANSEN
LIVERPOOL

All-time top consecutive appearances

		Games	First game		Last game	
1	Phil Neal	417	23 October	1976	24 September	1983
2	Ray Clemence	336	9 September	1972	4 March	1978
3	Bruce Grobbelaar	317	29 August	1981	16 August	1986
4	Chris Lawler	316	2 October	1965	24 April	1971
5	David James	213	19 February	1994	23 February	1998
6	Alan Kennedy	205	23 January	1982	31 March	1985
7	Ian Callaghan	185	17 August	1971	7 September	1974
8	Kenny Dalglish	180	13 August	1977	23 August	1980
9	Emlyn Hughes	177	31 October	1972	25 October	1975
10	Peter Thompson	153	1 September	1965	13 April	1968

PHIL NEAL
LIVERPOOL

Aquilani,
Alberto

TWENTY-FIVE-YEAR-OLD Aquilani arrived at Anfield early in August 2009 in the wake of Xabi Alonso's transfer to Real Madrid. The medical was passed despite the young Italian not having played in a competitive match since 11 March 2009 because of an ankle injury. At the time of his move to Liverpool, Aquilani had made 102 Serie A appearances for the Romans, scoring five goals.

Aquilani was born in Rome and joined his home-town club in 2002. Although he was given his debut by Fabio Capello in May 2003, later in the same year he was loaned to Serie B club Triestina. He was a regular during the 2007 Under-21 Championship held in the Netherlands, where he scored two goals and was named

in the UEFA Team of the Tournament. Aquilani was given his full international debut against Turkey in November 2006 and was in the Italian squad that competed in the finals of the European Championships during the summer of 2008.

THE ITALIAN was given the number 4 shirt vacated by Sami Hyypia, but had to wait patiently while his new colleagues made a stuttering start to the 2009/10 campaign. Eventually Liverpool supporters saw Aquilani in a first-team match when he made a 15-minute substitute appearance at Arsenal in the League Cup. He impressed enough to be given two further matches as a substitute in November before finally making his long-awaited full debut in a meaningless home game against Fiorentina in December. After that he had to be satisfied with being in the match-day squad rather than actually starting a game. Aquilani scored his first Liverpool goal when Portsmouth visited Anfield in the middle of March 2010. A second and more important goal also came at the Kop end in April as his precise finish gave the team the equaliser on aggregate against Atletico Madrid in the Europa League semi-final.

Considering he didn't play his first match until the end of October, a total of 18 Premier League and eight cup appearances was probably as much as Aquilani could have expected. He had six assists to his name

in the Premier League, ranking him 20–27th, one below Gerrard's seven assists, which is quite an accomplishment given the number of minutes he played in his sole season in England.

It soon became apparent at Anfield that Aquilani's fortunes would be better served in his homeland. He spent the whole of the 2010/11 season on loan at Juventus, playing in 32 of the 38 Serie A fixtures, and in the following campaign failed to impress AC Milan sufficiently for them to buy him outright in the summer of 2012. Finally in August 2012 Aquilani was sold for a huge financial loss to Fiorentina.

> HIS PRECISE FINISH GAVE THE TEAM THE EQUALISER ON AGGREGATE AGAINST ATLETICO MADRID IN THE EUROPA LEAGUE SEMI-FINAL

FACTFILE

BORN
Rome, Italy, 7 July 1984
POSITION
Midfielder
OTHER CLUBS
AS Roma (1999–2009),
Triestina (loan, 2003–04),
Juventus (loan, 2010–11),
AC Milan (loan, 2011–12),
Fiorentina (2012–)
SIGNED FROM
AS Roma, £17.1 million,
7 August 2009
INTERNATIONAL CAPS
30 Italy caps (4 goals)
(10 (1) at LFC), 2006–
LFC DEBUT GAME/GOAL
28 October 2009 /
15 March 2010
CONTRACT EXPIRY
3 August 2012

Season	League		FA Cup		League Cup		Europe		Total	
	App	Goals	App	Goals	App	Goals	App	Goals	App	Goals
2009/10	9 (9)	1	1 (1)	0	0 (1)	0	3 (2)	1	13 (13)	2
2010/11	0	0	0	0	0	0	1 (1)	0	1 (1)	0
Total	**9 (9)**	**1**	**1 (1)**	**0**	**0 (1)**	**0**	**4 (3)**	**1**	**14 (14)**	**2**

Arbeloa, Álvaro

ÁLVARO ARBELOA joined Deportivo in the summer of 2006 from Real Madrid, where he had mostly featured in Real's B-team, Castilla. Deportivo's financial difficulties forced them to sell Arbeloa, who had been a regular since his arrival, making a handsome profit on the deal. When Liverpool failed to bring Lucas Neill to the club, they bought Arbeloa to be Steve Finnan's understudy at right back.

Arbeloa's first two weeks at Liverpool were no picnic as he told the press in March 2008. 'My first fortnight at the club was inhumane. Rafa Benítez criticised everything I did, from the way I did some basketball practice to how I played my football. But now I am grateful to him for filling me in on how the team works.'

Arbeloa had a baptism of fire against Barcelona in the Champions League, where he showed his versatility in the left-back position and kept Lionel Messi quiet. Although he was primarily known in Spain as a right-back, in a lot of matches, especially early in the season, he was switched to the other flank; and he was also able to fill in as a central defender if required.

FACTFILE

BORN
Salamanca, Spain,
17 January 1983
POSITION
Right / Left-back
OTHER CLUBS
Real Madrid (2000–06),
Deportivo La Coruna
(2006–07),
Real Madrid (2009–)
SIGNED FROM
Deportivo La Coruna,
£2.64million,
30 January 2007
INTERNATIONAL CAPS
52 Spain caps
(9 at LFC), 2008–
LFC DEBUT GAME/GOAL
10 February 2007 /
7 April 2007
CONTRACT EXPIRY
30 July 2009

Arbeloa established himself as the team's first-choice right-back in the 2008/09 season, when Liverpool should have won the league title. The signing of Glen Johnson in the close season of 2009 led to much speculation that Arbeloa would move on, which was confirmed when he signed a five-year contract with his former club, Real Madrid.

FERNANDO TORRES was appreciative of his compatriot's contribution. 'Álvaro was a player who did a vital job for us, always played to a high level and his flexibility was a huge bonus,' he told Spanish sports magazine *Don Balon* in April 2010.

Arbeloa has played in roughly 70 per cent of Real Madrid's Primera matches in his four seasons there and in 2011/12 he added a Spanish Championship winners' medal to the Copa del Rey winners' medal won a year earlier. Arbeloa was in Spain's successful squad that won the European Championship in 2008 but only appeared in one match, against Greece, during the finals. He can also call himself a World Champion, even though he only featured for 13 minutes in the 2010 World Cup. Arbeloa was finally a regular in the team when Spain repeated their Euro success in 2012, appearing in six games.

> HE SHOWED HIS VERSATILITY IN THE LEFT-BACK POSITION AND KEPT LIONEL MESSI QUIET

Season	League		FA Cup		League Cup		Europe		Other		Total	
	App	Goals	App	Goals	App	Goals	App	Goals	App	Goals	App	Goals
2006/07	8 (1)	1	0	0	0	0	4 (1)	0	0	0	12 (2)	1
2007/08	26 (2)	0	1	0	3	0	8 (1)	0	-	-	38 (3)	0
2008/09	29	1	2	0	0	0	12	0	-	-	43	1
Total	**63 (3)**	**2**	**3**	**0**	**3**	**0**	**24 (2)**	**0**	**0**	**0**	**93 (5)**	**2**

Armstrong, Tom

GOALKEEPER TOM ARMSTRONG made his one and only league appearance for Liverpool in an away match at Sheffield Wednesday on 13 March 1920 after a couple of reserve outings. The game ended in a 2-2 draw.

Season	League App	League Goals	FA Cup App	FA Cup Goals	Total App	Total Goals
1919/20	1	0	0	0	1	0
Total	1	0	0	0	1	0

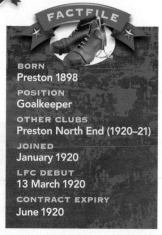

FACTFILE

BORN
Preston 1898
POSITION
Goalkeeper
OTHER CLUBS
Preston North End (1920–21)
JOINED
January 1920
LFC DEBUT
13 March 1920
CONTRACT EXPIRY
June 1920

ALAN ARNELL
LIVERPOOL

Arnell, Alan

CENTRE-FORWARD Alan Arnell moved from Sussex amateur side Worthing to Liverpool when he was 19 years old.

As Arnell was doing his national service in the Royal Sussex Regiment he couldn't sign as a professional, so it was as an amateur that he made a scoring debut on 5 December 1953, in a 5-2 home victory over Blackpool. He only played another two times that season and in just eight games the following campaign, in which he scored three more goals.

ALTHOUGH he was in and out of the side during the next few years, Arnell boasts a decent scoring record, averaging a goal every two games in the Second Division for Liverpool. Arnell's chief rival for the number 9 shirt that he most preferred was none other than Billy Liddell. 'Billy was an idol at Anfield. The local Press was biased towards him but I'm not complaining. With him around you had to be 110 per cent,' Arnell told the *Brighton Argus* in 2002. After Arnell had just featured once under Shankly since his arrival 14 months earlier he was transferred to Third Division Tranmere Rovers in February 1961. He scored 34 goals in 68 league games for Rovers but suffered relegation to the Fourth Division.

> SHANKS WAS SIMPLY OBSESSED WITH FOOTBALL. WHEN YOU TALKED WITH HIM, YOU WERE THE BEST PLAYER

> In 1961 I arranged to buy a sub-post office and newsagent's shop less than a quarter of a mile from the training ground. It was towards the end of the season and Bill Shankly, who had taken over as manager in 1959, said Swindon were interested in me and a £7,000 fee, which was quite a high fee then, was mentioned. I said I had just offered to buy a business and Shanks immediately replied – in that case, you can have a free transfer. In about one hour I was a Tranmere player. I think Shanks was a little bit naughty about that. Life under Shankly was interesting although Don Welsh was also a flamboyant manager. Shanks was simply obsessed with football. When you talked with him, you were the best player, the opposition rubbish, not worth mentioning. He was a great motivator.

FACTFILE

BORN
Chichester, 25 November 1933
DIED
5 May 2013
POSITION
Centre-forward
OTHER CLUBS
Chichester City (1949–51), Worthing (1951–53), Tranmere Rovers (1961–63), Halifax Town (1963–64), Runcorn (1964–66)
SIGNED FROM
Worthing, 24 March 1953
LFC DEBUT GAME/GOAL
5 December 1953 / 5 December 1953
CONTRACT EXPIRY
February 1961

Season	League App	League Goals	FA Cup App	FA Cup Goals	League Cup App	League Cup Goals	Total App	Total Goals
1953/54	3	1	0	0	-	-	3	1
1954/55	7	3	1	0	-	-	8	3
1955/56	23	13	4	2	-	-	27	15
1956/57	14	10	1	0	-	-	15	10
1957/58	8	1	0	0	-	-	8	1
1958/59	12	5	0	0	-	-	12	5
1959/60	1	0	0	0	-	-	1	0
1960/61	1	0	0	0	0	0	1	0
Total	69	33	6	2	0	0	75	35

Arnold, Steve

THE LONDONER turned professional for Crewe the year prior to his move to Liverpool and had only made 15 league appearances in the Third and Fourth Division before signing for the Reds.

Crewe had suffered relegation to the Fourth Division while Liverpool were going through a transitional period in the top-flight under Shankly. Steve Arnold made his second first-team appearance for the Reds in bizarre circumstances, seven months after his arrival. Liverpool incurred the wrath of the Football League, and received a large fine as a result, by making ten changes for the penultimate league match of the season at Manchester City two days after they

had won at Nottingham Forest. The reason was simple. Already in the FA Cup final, Bill Shankly wasn't prepared to allow his first-choice players to go through a punishing schedule with more important fixtures coming up. The midfielder featured mostly for Liverpool's reserves and was loaned

out to other clubs while on Reds' books. He moved to Rochdale who finished bottom of the Third Division and 12 months after leaving Anfield he was playing non-league football with Weymouth. He initially retired because of injury in 1976 but returned to non-league football two years later.

FACTFILE

BORN
Wembley, London,
5 January 1951
POSITION
Midfielder
OTHER CLUBS
Crewe Alexandra (1966–70),
Southport (loan, 1972),
Torquay United (loan, 1972),
Rochdale (1973–74),
Weymouth (1974–76),
Dorchester Town (loan, 1975),
Connah's Quay Nomads
(1978–79),
West Kirby
SIGNED FROM
Crewe Alexandra, £12,000,
9 September 1970
LFC DEBUT
16 January 1971
CONTRACT EXPIRY
12 June 1973

Season	League		FA Cup		League Cup		Europe		Total	
	App	Goals	App	Goals	App	Goals	App	Goals	App	Goals
1970/71	1 (1)	0	0	0	0	0	0	0	1 (1)	0
Total	1 (1)	0	0	0	0	0	0	0	1 (1)	0

Arphexad, Pegguy

OUTSTANDING PERFORMANCES for Leicester City at Filbert Street and at Anfield against Liverpool in the 1999/2000 season ignited Gérard Houllier's interest in the keeper.

His heroics against Arsenal in the fourth round of the FA Cup in January 2000, when he saved two penalties in the shootout, got him great recognition as well. When Arphexad was available on a free transfer the following summer Houllier brought him to Merseyside as cover for Sander Westerveld. When the Dutchman left in acrimonious circumstances it was believed that Arphexad would soon follow suit but he saw out his contract, playing the odd

reserve game. Arphexad won several medals during his spell with Liverpool but he was mostly an unused substitute. He did play his part in the club's success in the League Cup in the 2000/01 season as he was between the sticks in the third round against Chelsea and in the fourth round, when Stoke were defeated 8-0.

DURING the 2004/05 season Arphexad was on the books of Marseille but failed to play in a

single league match for the French south coast club during that brief period, which effectively saw the end of his professional career in which he only made 53 first-team appearances!

FACTFILE

BORN
Guadeloupe, 18 May 1973
POSITION
Goalkeeper
OTHER CLUBS
Brest (1989–90),
Lille (1990–91),
Lens (1991–97),
Lille (loan, 1996–97),
Leicester City (1997–2000),
Stockport County (loan, 2001),
Coventry City (2003–04),
Notts County (loan, 2004),
Olympique Marseille
(2004–05)
JOINED
Bosman free transfer,
1 July 2000
LFC DEBUT
1 November 2000
CONTRACT EXPIRY
1 July 2003
HONOURS
FA Cup 2001,
League Cup 2001, 2003;
UEFA Cup 2001

Season	League		FA Cup		League Cup		Europe		Other		Total	
	App	Goals	App	Goals	App	Goals	App	Goals	App	Goals	App	Goals
2000/01	0	0	0	0	2	0	0	0	-	-	2	0
2001/02	1 (1)	0	0	0	0	0	2	0	0	0	3 (1)	0
Total	1 (1)	0	0	0	2	0	2	0	0	0	5 (1)	0

Arrowsmith, Alf

ALF ARROWSMITH was described as a born goalscorer by Shankly but was dreadfully unlucky with injuries. He first arrived at Anfield as a fresh-faced 17-year-old in August 1960 from Ashton United, having previously scored a massive 96 goals for Derbyshire club Tintwistle Villa in the 1959/60 season, a club record that has never been broken. He had spent just four months at Ashton United and scored nine goals in seven Lancashire Combination Division Two matches when Liverpool made their move.

His name was soon on everybody's lips at Anfield because he scored no less than 81 reserve team goals between 1961 and 1963. His breakthrough into the first team arrived in the latter part of the title-winning 1963/64 season, when he scored 19 goals in 24 games. Roger Hunt, Ian St John and Arrowsmith contributed a massive 67 league goals that season as Liverpool powered to their first title for 17 years. The future looked bright for Arrowsmith but then tragedy struck. He injured his left knee badly in the 1964 Charity Shield (in the process leading to Liverpool's first recorded substitution), missed most of the season and only made a further 13 starts plus six as substitute over the next three seasons.

'I called for the ball, lost it and went to challenge the bloke,' Arrowsmith told *LFC Magazine* about the incident that destroyed his Liverpool career. 'I turned around and my studs stuck and I went straight around.

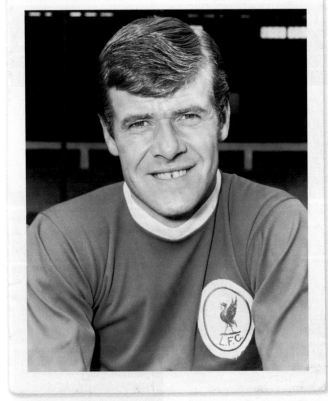

>
>
> 'APART FROM MY MUM AND US THREE THERE WAS ONLY ONE LOVE OF HIS LIFE – IT WAS LIVERPOOL FOOTBALL CLUB UNTIL THE DAY HE DIED'
>
> **JULIE ARROWSMITH**

They took me up to Walton hospital and then they hadn't got the equipment that they have now and the X-ray showed that I had broken no bones. I waited five to six weeks and the cartilage popped out in training one Friday morning. It was never the same again and it was always at the back of my mind. It was the cruciate ligament that I'd done.

Nowadays you have some surgery and are back in no time but not in them days. I was still scoring goals in the reserves but it was never the same, I didn't have the confidence. I could still hit the ball as hard, but it was the twisting and turning.'

JULIE, one of his three daughters, said after Alf's passing in 2005: 'He lived life to the full, he had lots of energy and made a lot of people smile. Apart from my mum and us three there was only one love of his life – it was Liverpool Football Club until the day he died.'

FACTFILE

BORN
Hollingworth,
11 December 1942
DIED
12 May 2005
POSITION
Centre-forward
OTHER CLUBS
Tintwistle Villa (1959–60),
Ashton United (1960),
Bury (1968–70),
Rochdale (1970–72),
Macclesfield Town
SIGNED FROM
Ashton United, £1,250,
30 August 1960
LFC DEBUT GAME/GOAL
7 October 1961 /
16 September 1963
CONTRACT EXPIRY
December 1968
HONOURS
League Championship
1963/64

Season	League		FA Cup		League Cup		Europe		Other		Total	
	App	Goals	App	Goals	App	Goals	App	Goals	App	Goals	App	Goals
1961/62	1	0	0	0	-	-	-	-	-	-	1	0
1962/63	3	0	0	0	-	-	-	-	-	-	3	0
1963/64	20	15	4	4	-	-	-	-	-	-	24	19
1964/65	7	1	1	0	-	-	0	0	1	0	9	1
1965/66	3 (2)	1	0	0	-	-	1	0	0	0	4 (2)	1
1966/67	6 (3)	2	0	0	-	-	0	0	0	0	6 (3)	2
1967/68	2 (1)	1	1	0	0	0	0	0	-	-	3 (1)	1
Total	**42 (6)**	**20**	**6**	**4**	**0**	**0**	**1**	**0**	**1**	**0**	**50 (6)**	**24**

Ashcroft,
Charlie

CHARLIE ASHCROFT finally replaced Cyril Sidlow in the Liverpool goal in the 1951/52 season, having only featured in nine first-team matches since the resumption of league football following World War Two.

Ashcroft earned the distinction of saving a penalty from Preston legend Tom Finney on the opening day of the 1952/53 season and was first choice until December 1952 when he lost his place to Russell Crossley after a disastrous spell for the club. The arrival of Dave Underwood in December 1953 further restricted his chances. Liverpool were relegated in the spring and South African Doug Rudham was signed at the start of the 1954/55 season. Ashcroft still managed 15 games in his final season, despite battling for one position with Underwood and Rudham.

ASHCROFT was signed by future England World Cup winning coach, Alf Ramsey, for Ipswich Town, who then played in the Third Division South. After only seven games he broke his arm in a reserve game and left for Coventry the following summer. He only stayed at the Sky Blues for one season, as his break hadn't healed properly so City had effectively signed a keeper who couldn't straighten his arm!

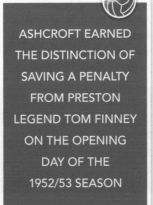

ASHCROFT EARNED THE DISTINCTION OF SAVING A PENALTY FROM PRESTON LEGEND TOM FINNEY ON THE OPENING DAY OF THE 1952/53 SEASON

FACTFILE

BORN
Chorley, Lancashire,
3 July 1926
DIED
13 March 2010
POSITION
Goalkeeper
OTHER CLUBS
Eccleston,
Chorley (loan) [prior to LFC],
Ipswich Town (1955–57),
Coventry City (1957–58),
Chorley (1958–61)
JOINED
24 December 1945
LFC DEBUT
7 September 1946
CONTRACT EXPIRY
6 June 1955

Season	League		FA Cup		Total	
	App	Goals	App	Goals	App	Goals
1946/47	2	0	0	0	2	0
1950/51	7	0	0	0	7	0
1951/52	34	0	1	0	35	0
1952/53	24	0	0	0	24	0
1953/54	6	0	0	0	6	0
1954/55	14	0	1	0	15	0
Total	**87**	**0**	**2**	**0**	**89**	**0**

Ashworth, David

LEAGUE CHAMPIONS 1921/22

LIVERPOOL

DAVID ASHWORTH was a well-known Football League referee before going into management. He was assistant manager at his local club, Rossendale, before his first managerial appointment with Oldham Athletic in 1906, shortly after the club had moved to Boundary Park. At that time the Latics were playing in the Lancashire Combination but they soon gained Football League status replacing Burslem Port Vale who resigned at the end of the 1906/07 season.

Ashworth led Oldham to a creditable third-place finish in their inaugural season as a league club and it took only a further two years before they achieved promotion to the top division as runners-up to Manchester City. Although narrowly escaping relegation in 1912, they finished as high as fourth in the 1913/14 season, towards the end of which Ashworth left to join Stockport County.

ASHWORTH agreed to become Liverpool's manager in December 1919 in the first league season in four years after the atrocities of World War One. The *Liverpool Echo* was impressed by the new Liverpool.

'What Mr Ashworth does not know about the clubs and the players is scarcely worth knowing. There is no better judge of a good footballer. Owing to his tact and good humour he has always had the players on excellent terms with one another - one secret of his success - he knows how to manage men. Without any show of authority he gets on their right side and makes them feel that he is a friend as well as a manager. When he goes into the dressing room before a match he says: 'Now then, boys, do your best!' and they do.'

The scribe at the *Echo* interviewed Ashworth ahead of his greatest challenge. 'I know all the Liverpool directors and most of the players personally and I feel certain when I get there we shall be a happy family. I consider it an honour to have a man like Mr McKenna on the board of directors, and what I have done for Oldham and Stockport I shall try and do for Liverpool. I shall do my best.' Results had been poor under manager George Patterson in the period before he was appointed. A run of 11 matches between the end of September and early December had brought just two victories. Liverpool won

eight games in a row from mid-January until mid-February, scoring 18 goals without conceding a single one. George Patterson, who had resumed his duties as secretary was pleased by his successor's progress: 'The interest in the club is enormous, and their run of League and cup successes is quite natural under the circumstances. The boys are playing fine football and for long enough the people of Liverpool have recognised this and have stood by the side although we started rather badly. It was one goal against us week by week. We turned the corner in December and confidence and good football have done the rest. The boys fear no team.' The club eventually finished in fourth spot.

Pipe-smoking Ashworth had inherited a classy group of players that he welded into the most ferocious team Liverpool fans had ever seen. Another fourth-place finish followed in 1921 before Liverpool won their third League Championship with a convincing six-point margin separating them from runners-up Tottenham. Ashworth had truly captured the hearts of the Liverpool fans and was very optimistic about the campaign ahead. 'We ought to

have a very good season. There is perfect harmony from the boardroom to the dressing room and that goes a long way.' As Christmas approached Liverpool had a one-point lead over Sunderland at the top, compared to being fifth and five points behind Burnley at the same time a year before, so the champions were in quite a strong position. A rumour was spreading that Ashworth would be in charge of his old club, Oldham, rather than Liverpool when the teams would face each other on 25 and 26 December. Ernest 'Bee' Edwards of the *Liverpool Echo* went directly to Ashworth to see if he could shed some light on the matter and reported to Liverpool fans' relief that: 'Mr Ashworth, manager of the Liverpool Football Club asks me to deny the story that is all over Oldham that he is about to become their manager.' The following day, it was evident that Ashworth had lied to Bee. 'Mr Ashworth's earliest managerial work was with Stockport County and he joined Liverpool three years ago. These have been Liverpool's most successful years, financially and in a playing sense, therefore it will come as a severe shock to all football supporters that Mr Ashworth has seen fit to leave Liverpool at their zenith and join Oldham in the depths. At any rate all Liverpool will be surprised that a change has been made, for there had been no suggestion of any movement in connection with the Liverpool Football Club for some time.' Why would Ashworth leave a team at the top

Season	Division	P	W	D	L	GF	GA	Pts	Position	Win %	FA Cup
1919/20*	1st Division	24	12	4	8	36	18	32	4	50.00	4th Round
1920/21	1st Division	42	18	9	15	63	35	51	4	42.86	2nd Round
1921/22	1st Division	42	22	7	13	63	36	57	1	52.38	2nd Round
1922/23**	1st Division	19	13	5	1	41	20	27	1	68.42	
Total		**127**	**65**	**25**	**37**	**203**	**109**	**167**	**-**	**51.18**	**-**

* Ashworth appointed on 17 December 1919 with Liverpool in 18th position
** Ashworth resigned on 20 December 1922 with Liverpool in 1st position

of the division for Oldham in twenty-first position out of a league of 22 teams? It wasn't public knowledge at the time, but Ashworth had evidently moved for family reasons as he wanted to live with his wife and daughter, who were both invalids, in Stockport that was only 11 miles away from Oldham compared to 43 miles from Liverpool. For the record Liverpool won the Championship while Oldham got relegated. However, the Reds never reached the heights or stability, achieved by Ashworth, for the rest of the 20s or indeed the 30s. Ashworth left Oldham after only 18 months in charge in his second spell at the club. In July 1924 he took the reins of first division Manchester City, but lasted less than a year and a half before being dismissed and suffered the same fate after a similarly brief spell with Walsall. He then managed two Welsh clubs; Caernarfon and Llanelli, before returning to the English game as a scout for Blackpool, the town in which he died on 23 March 1947, aged 79. One can only wonder what more Ashworth might have achieved at Anfield if it hadn't been for his sudden return to Oldham.

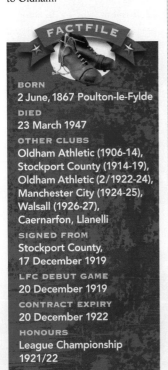

FACTFILE

BORN
2 June, 1867 Poulton-le-Fylde
DIED
23 March 1947
OTHER CLUBS
Oldham Athletic (1906-14), Stockport County (1914-19), Oldham Athletic (2/1922-24), Manchester City (1924-25), Walsall (1926-27), Caernarfon, Llanelli
SIGNED FROM
Stockport County, 17 December 1919
LFC DEBUT GAME
20 December 1919
CONTRACT EXPIRY
20 December 1922
HONOURS
League Championship 1921/22

Assaidi, Oussama

NOBODY saw this coming. In contrast to the incessant rumours and counter-rumours that are attached to English Premier League clubs during any transfer window, confirmation of Oussama Assaidi's arrival was conducted in the old 'Liverpool Way' with an announcement about the transfer only taking place after it had been completed.

Although born in Morocco, Assaidi moved with his family to the Netherlands when he was only three years old. Assaidi made his professional debut for Omniworld in February 2007, and 18 months later he moved to Eredivisie club De Graafschap and had a season and a bit there before signing for Heerenveen. Assaidi had two full seasons with Heerenveen in which he scored nine and ten goals as his club finished twelfth and fifth in one of Europe's most competitive leagues.

ALTHOUGH predominantly right-footed, Oussama can play on either flank. An effective wide player was something that was often missing from Kenny Dalglish's final season in charge. A former team-mate of Assaidi's at Heerenveen felt that he would be a good acquisition. 'A great player. Quicker running with the ball than without. He is right-footed but has been playing on the left wing. He creates chances out of nothing and has incredible ball control. Assaidi is ridiculously creative

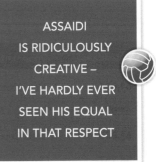

ASSAIDI IS RIDICULOUSLY CREATIVE – I'VE HARDLY EVER SEEN HIS EQUAL IN THAT RESPECT

– I've hardly ever seen his equal in that respect. A good fit for Rodgers – he could really prosper under his guidance.' Obviously time will be the test of that praise being justified, but at least Liverpool Football Club don't appear to have made a risky purchase. Assaidi has been on the fringes of the first team since his arrival and started only six games in the 2012/13 season. He has vowed to knuckle down to be given more chances to impress, but there is tough competition for places on the wings and he might have to settle for remaining a squad player.

FACTFILE

BORN
Beni-Boughafar, Morocco, 15 August 1988
POSITION
Right / Left-winger
OTHER CLUBS
Omniworld (2007–08), De Graafschap (2008–09), Heerenveen (2009–12)
SIGNED FROM
Heerenveen, £2.4million, 17 August 2012
INTERNATIONAL CAPS
13 Morocco caps (1 goal) (4 (0) at LFC), 2011–
LFC DEBUT
20 September 2012

Season	League		FA Cup		League Cup		Europe		Total	
	App	Goals	App	Goals	App	Goals	App	Goals	App	Goals
2012/13	0 (4)	0	0	0	2	0	4 (2)	0	6 (6)	0
Total	**0 (4)**	**0**	**0**	**0**	**2**	**0**	**4 (2)**	**0**	**6 (6)**	**0**

Attendances

Biggest attendance at Anfield

Attendance	Opponent	Date	Competition	Score
61,905	Wolverhampton Wanderers	2 February 1952	FA Cup 4th round	2-1
61,036	Tranmere Rovers	27 January 1934	FA Cup 4th round	3-1
61,003	Notts County	29 January 1949	FA Cup 4th round	1-0
58,757	Chelsea	27 December 1949	1st Division	2-2
57,906	Burnley	20 February 1963	FA Cup 4th round replay	2-1

Biggest attendance Away

Attendance	Opponent	Date	Competition	Score
90,832	Barcelona	5 April 2001	UEFA Cup Semi-final 1st leg	0-0
90,000	Dinamo Tbilisi	3 October 1979	European Cup 1st round 2nd leg	0-3
88,000	Barcelona	21 February 2007	Champions League 1st knockout round 1st leg	2-1
80,000	Benfica	1 March 1978	European Cup 3rd round 1st leg	2-1
78,599	Everton	18 September 1948	1st Division	1-1

Aurélio,
Fábio

FÁBIO Aurélio started his career with São Paolo in Brazil in 1997. He joined Valencia in the summer of 2000 after featuring for Brazil's Under-23 team at the Sydney Olympics. Rafa Benítez took over as coach of Valencia in 2001 and Aurélio twice celebrated winning the Spanish Championship, in 2002 and 2004, as well as winning the UEFA Cup.

However, he didn't make as many appearances as he would have liked because of injuries, only making two appearances in the successful 2003/04 season after starring for Valencia on the left flank in the previous season, playing 35 games and scoring 10 goals.

AURÉLIO'S injuries unfortunately did not desert him when he arrived at Liverpool. Just when he had started to hit peak form he ruptured his Achilles against PSV Eindhoven in the first leg of the Champions League quarter-final in the 2006/07 season. Thirteen of his 29 appearances in 2007/08 came in cup matches and Benítez seemed particularly keen to use him in the Champions League. Aurélio had his best season at Liverpool in the 2008/09 season, making 27 starts and five substitute appearances despite spending six weeks on the sidelines with injury from November through to January. He showed quick thinking when

he scored from a wonderful free kick at Chelsea in the second leg of the Champions League quarter-final. His goal even earned a celebration from Rafa on the touchline! Aurélio also scored from a free kick that was the highlight of Liverpool's tremendous 4-1 win over Manchester United at Old Trafford. He seemed to have finally nailed a regular spot in the Liverpool line-up, but then injured his knee in a freak accident playing with his son in the garden in summer 2009.

The 2009/10 season was on the whole a disappointment for the Brazilian as Emiliano Insúa established himself as first-choice left-back. Even the sale of Andrea Dossena to Napoli in January 2010 didn't significantly improve Aurélio's chances because the manager, who had a surfeit of central defenders to try and keep happy, used Daniel Agger as his left-back on occasion. Aurélio injured his thigh against Blackburn Rovers on 28 February, which ended his season.

Aurélio's contract was due to run out in the summer of 2010 and Liverpool were only ready to offer him a pay-as-you-play deal. He wanted more security and left Liverpool when his contract expired. Before the 2010/11

league season began, Aurélio re-signed for Liverpool on a two-year deal. The chances of poor Aurélio getting through an entire season without being injured were pretty slim; and so it proved. He picked up an Achilles injury and after he had recovered Roy Hodgson used him only sparingly, although he was more of a regular after Dalglish succeeded the Englishman. But when picked to start at the Emirates in the middle of April, Aurélio picked up a hamstring injury and had to be substituted for Jack Robinson with less than a third of the match played. Dalglish picked him to start in the final league match of the season away to Aston Villa and amazingly the Brazilian got through the whole match unscathed!

AURÉLIO only played in three first-team matches in 2011/12, partly due to the good form of Jose Enrique and partly because of injuries. Only 134 appearances in six seasons shows how often he was unavailable for selection. Leaving Liverpool at the age of 32, Aurélio hoped Fortune would smile on him more favourably at Gremio in his native Brazil. However, he missed his first season for them after suffering a knee ligament rupture in summer 2012.

FACTFILE

BORN
São Carlos, Brazil,
24 September 1979
POSITION
Left-back / Left-winger
OTHER CLUBS
São Paolo (1997–2000),
Valencia (2000–06),
Gremio (2012–)
JOINED
Bosman free transfer,
5 July 2006;
free transfer, 31 July 2010
LFC DEBUT GAME/GOAL
13 August 2006 /
2 March 2008
CONTRACT EXPIRY
1 June 2010 / 1 June 2012

Season	League		FA Cup		League Cup		Europe		Other		Total	
	App	Goals	App	Goals	App	Goals	App	Goals	App	Goals	App	Goals
2006/07	10 (7)	0	0 (1)	0	1	0	3 (2)	0	0 (1)	0	14 (11)	0
2007/08	13 (3)	1	0 (1)	0	3	0	7 (2)	0	-	-	23 (6)	1
2008/09	19 (5)	2	0 (1)	0	0	0	8	1	-	-	27 (6)	3
2009/10	8 (6)	0	1	0	1	0	3 (4)	0	-	-	13 (10)	0
2010/11	7 (7)	0	1	0	0	0	5 (1)	0	-	-	13 (8)	0
2011/12	1 (1)	0	1	0	0	0	-	-	-	-	2 (1)	0
Total	**58 (29)**	**3**	**3 (3)**	**0**	**5**	**0**	**26 (9)**	**1**	**0 (1)**	**0**	**92 (42)**	**4**

Ayala, Daniel

CENTRE-HALF Daniel Ayala took the same path as Antonio Barragan two years earlier when Liverpool snapped him up from Sevilla before he had signed a professional contract.

Ayala impressed on Liverpool's pre-season tours of Switzerland and Thailand and made his debut as a substitute in the first game of the 2009/10 season at Spurs. Ayala played from the start and with composure in Liverpool's first home league match against Stoke City and made another appearance as a late substitute for Dirk Kuyt shortly after Jamie Carragher had been sent off at Fulham.

TO START two matches and make three substitute appearances was probably about as much as Ayala

> AYALA IMPRESSED ON LIVERPOOL'S PRE-SEASON TOURS OF SWITZERLAND AND THAILAND

FACTFILE

BORN
Sevilla, Spain,
7 November 1990

POSITION
Centre-half

OTHER CLUBS
Hull City (loan, 2010),
Derby County (loan, 2011),
Norwich City (2011–),
Nottingham Forest
(loan, 2012–13)

SIGNED FROM
Sevilla (youth), £160,000,
17 September 2007

INTERNATIONAL CAPS
1 Spain U-21 cap

LFC DEBUT
16 August 2009

CONTRACT EXPIRY
16 August 2011

could have hoped for in the 2009/10 season. Ayala was on loan at Hull the following season until New Year's Day 2011 and spent the remainder of the campaign at Derby. Hull and Swansea both bid £850,000 when he was allowed to leave Liverpool in August 2011. Norwich City also expressed an interest and it was the East Anglian club that was ultimately successful, with Ayala's signature being secured on a four-year deal. An injury-hit season restricted Ayala to just 10 first-team appearances for Norwich in 2011/12 and in August 2012 he secured a season-long loan deal with Nottingham Forest in the Championship.

Season	League		FA Cup		League Cup		Europe		Total	
	App	Goals	App	Goals	App	Goals	App	Goals	App	Goals
2009/10	2 (3)	0	0	0	0	0	0	0	2 (3)	0
Total	2 (3)	0	0	0	0	0	0	0	2 (3)	0

Ayre, Ian

THE CURRENT Managing Director of Liverpool, whose ability to guarantee the club some very lucrative contracts has earned him a good reputation.

Ian Ayre was born in Liverpool in 1963. After moving up in the business world he turned to the tumultuous world of football and was Chief Executive and Chairman of Huddersfield Town for three years before spending three years at Premium TV, a subsidiary of NTL Incorporated, that is the dominant cable operator in Britain. He later moved to Malaysia, where he was CEO of Total Sports Asia; a brand solutions business for international sports and entertainment partners aiming to develop an Asian strategy for their brands. Tom Hicks and George Gillett Jr. wanted to utilise his knowledge of the Asian market and appointed Ayre as Liverpool's Commercial Director in 2007.

AYRE SOON proved his business acumen by securing the impressive shirt sponsorship deal with Standard Chartered Bank. Ayre survived the change of ownership and was appointed by John W. Henry and Tom Werner as the club's Managing Director on 22 March 2011, taking over from Christian Purslow, who stood down after the club's October sale to New England Sports Ventures. Liverpool's principal owner Henry told the press: "We conducted an extensive recruitment search but in the end we realised that Ian had all of the attributes necessary to lead the club forward. Ian is also from Liverpool and understands the relationships between the club, the supporters and the city."

Babb,
Phil

AFTER GOING through the youth system at Millwall without making a senior appearance Phil Babb established himself in midfield at third division Bradford City from 1990, scoring 14 goals in 80 league appearances. In July 1992 he got his big break when he moved to Premiership Coventry City. He took over the captaincy at the club and was voted Player of the Year at the Sky Blues for the 1993/94 season.

Babb became Britain's most expensive defender when he was bought for £3.6million after shining brightly for Ireland in the 1994 World Cup. His strengths were his speed, man-marking skills and tackling but his distribution of the ball, positional sense and sometimes alarming carelessness let him down. With fellow new signing John Scales he was charged with the task of solving Liverpool's defensive problems and became an integral part of Evans' 5-3-2 formation.

BABB SCORED a single goal for Liverpool that came against his former club, Coventry, on 4 September 1996. Dominic Matteo was as taken aback as everyone else at the end of the game. 'The joke was definitely on the rest of the players. Everyone said that he wouldn't score, but he kept them quiet with that goal.' Babb was delighted by his goal scored at the far post from a centre by Jason McAteer as he told the press post-match: 'The lads are still in shock, in even more shock than me. I still haven't come down yet. It's such a nice feeling to score against your old club.'

Babb was a regular in his first two-and-a-half seasons at the club but lost his way somewhat in the

otherwise impressive 1996/97 season. Mick McCarthy, then Republic of Ireland's coach, tried to analyse what had happened to the previously composed defender: 'I don't think that formation suited Babb, who has always looked more comfortable in the middle of a flat back four. It didn't help that other senior players at Liverpool were struggling at the time, and the end product was that Phil began to lose confidence.'

Injury disrupted Babb's progress in the following season, but he was back in the first XI from January 1998 onwards. Gérard Houllier gave him a chance after he took sole control of the club in the 1998/99 season, but he struggled to recapture the form that prompted Roy Evans to sign him. Babb was at the centre of the most painful and yet hilarious incident in Anfield's history on 4 October 1998. He attacked the post in front of the Anfield Road end with brute force, unsuccessfully trying to prevent Pierluigi Casiraghi's first goal for Chelsea in a 1-1 draw. Babb's privates came off the worst, prompting one fan to shout while he lay prostrate holding his manhood, 'Don't rub them Phil, count them!'

The writing was on the wall for Babb when he was left out of a weekend tournament in Belfast in July 1999 and the arrival of Sami Hyypia and Stephane Henchoz in the summer of 1999 effectively made him a spectator in his last year at the club. He was loaned for one month to John Aldridge's Tranmere in late January and helped Rovers to the League Cup final.

'DON'T RUB THEM PHIL, COUNT THEM!'

He made a surprise move to Sporting Lisbon where he enjoyed a revival of some sorts and enjoyed his football again for two years, winning the league and cup double in his second season and being voted the league's top overseas defender. Sporting offered him a new contract but he and his family wanted a return to England. He opted for Peter Reid's Sunderland in the summer of 2002 but was relegated from the Premiership in his first season and spent one year in the First Division before retiring from the game that had given him so many highs and lows.

FACTFILE

BORN
Lambeth, London,
30 November 1970

POSITION
Centre-half

OTHER CLUBS
Bradford City (1990–92),
Coventry City (1992–94),
Tranmere Rovers (loan, 2000),
Sporting Lisbon (2000–02),
Sunderland (2002–04)

SIGNED FROM
Coventry City, £3.6million,
1 September 1994

INTERNATIONAL CAPS
35 Ireland caps (25 at LFC),
1994–2002

LFC DEBUT GAME/GOAL
17 September 1994 /
4 September 1996

CONTRACT EXPIRY
1 July 2000

HONOURS
League Cup 1995

Season	League		FA Cup		League Cup		Europe		Total	
	App	Goals	App	Goals	App	Goals	App	Goals	App	Goals
1994/95	33 (1)	0	6	0	7	0	-	-	46 (1)	0
1995/96	28	0	4	0	4	0	4	0	40	0
1996/97	21 (1)	1	1	0	3	0	4 (1)	0	29 (2)	1
1997/98	18 (1)	0	0	0	2	0	1	0	21 (1)	0
1998/99	24 (1)	0	1	0	0	0	3 (1)	0	28 (2)	0
Total	**124 (4)**	**1**	**12**	**0**	**16**	**0**	**12 (2)**	**0**	**164 (6)**	**1**

Babbel, Markus

MARKUS BABBEL arrived at Anfield in June 2000 as one of the most decorated players in German football history. Two spells with Bayern Munich had seen him win the German Championship four times as well as two German Cups, three German League Cups as well as the 1996 UEFA Cup. He was also a member of his country's European Championship winning team when the tournament was held in England in 1996.

Bayern had accepted a bid from Real Madrid for Babbel's services, but he had already given Liverpool his word that he would join the Reds. Babbel became an important part of a solid defence in the club's treble cup success of 2001 as well as being an attacking threat. His energetic runs down the right and his massive experience shone through and he played in 60 out of 63 matches. Never a regular scorer nor expected to be, his most important goal in Liverpool colours was the opener in Dortmund when the Reds beat Alaves to win the 2001 UEFA Cup, presenting Babbel with his second winners' medal in the competition.

LIVERPOOL didn't have to worry about the right-back position for the next couple of years, but then life changed drastically for the German. He was taken off at half-time in Liverpool's matches against West Ham on 18 August 2001 and at Bolton nine days later, completely out of breath. Babbel was diagnosed with the

debilitating and paralysing Guillain-Barré syndrome that has destroyed many a top sportsman's career. The German refused to give up and showed extraordinary courage and determination to return only 15 months after being diagnosed with the terrible illness that had left him in a wheelchair.

'I first felt numbness in my feet four weeks ago,' Babbel said in December 2001. 'Later they felt like I had been running through snow and I was thawing them out in the warm. All of a sudden I felt much worse and I was unable to lift my legs. When I came to the hospital for tests doctors decided straight away to keep me in. I was given injections for five days and the symptoms of paralysis in my legs finally stopped. Right now I can only take a couple of steps – and that is with someone else helping me. My hands were affected too. I barely had any feeling in them.'

Babbel started four games out of five for the first team from the middle of November to early December 2002, trying to regain his former strength and fitness. A debacle of a performance in the League Cup against Aston Villa on 18 December, when he removed his shirt in disgust after being substituted in the 39th minute for Jamie Carragher, proved to be Babbel's last performance for the first team.

Surprisingly Babbel, who had been a model professional his whole career, ignited Houllier's anger by showing a lack of discipline in reserve matches, twice being sent off, against Sheffield Wednesday in February and Everton in May 2003 after headbutting young Blues' player, Michael Symes. It must have been a frustrating time for Babbel, who had clearly not regained his stamina levels by any means. Houllier voiced his displeasure with him at the end of the 2002/03 season. 'I doubt he will play for us again because I gave him many chances and it hasn't worked out. The staff has been disappointed with Markus' attitude towards the

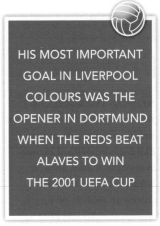

club and the fans. He is no longer in my plans. We stood by him and handed him a new contract.'

Babbel played 25 games on loan for Graeme Souness's Blackburn in the 2003/04 season and then left permanently for Stuttgart in his native Germany in the summer of 2004. Even though by now in his early thirties, Babbel showed that he was still capable of playing at a high level and in 2007 he helped Stuttgart to their first German Championship for 15 years.

Accepting that his playing days were over, Babbel became assistant coach at Stuttgart and in November 2008 he was promoted to the mid-table club's coach. Stuttgart finished the season third and qualified for the Champions League. Despite progressing to the last 16 in Europe's premier competition Stuttgart were doing abysmally in the league and only 13 months after being appointed he was sacked.

Just over five months after leaving Stuttgart Babbel was appointed as coach of Hertha Berlin and given the immediate task of returning his new club to Germany's top division, having finished bottom of the Bundesliga at the end of the 2009/10 season. Hertha returned to the Bundesliga as champions, but again Babbel did not survive a second season and was sacked with immediate effect in December 2011. On 10 February 2012 Babbel signed a 30-month contract to

Season	League		FA Cup		League Cup		Europe		Other		Total	
	App	Goals	App	Goals	App	Goals	App	Goals	App	Goals	App	Goals
2000/01	38	3	5	1	4	1	13	1	-	-	60	6
2001/02	2	0	0	0	0	0	2 (1)	0	1	0	5 (1)	0
2002/03	2	0	0	0	3	0	1	0	0 (1)	0	6 (1)	0
Total	**42**	**3**	**5**	**1**	**7**	**1**	**16 (1)**	**1**	**1 (1)**	**0**	**71 (2)**	**6**

become Hoffenheim's coach in the Bundesliga. His new club finished the season in a respectable 11th place out of 18. When Hoffenheim were third from bottom in the Bundesliga in December 2012 Babbel was sacked.

BABBEL WAS thrilled to join Liverpool at the time, even though it meant rejecting the Spanish giants, Real Madrid, as he revealed to the local press. 'As a kid, I was always watching Liverpool on television in the great times of the Eighties. So I was very honoured when I got an offer from them and I didn't have to think much about it, I just signed. It was always a dream for me to play in England. I never thought about Spain or Italy. It was mainly the tremendous atmosphere I wanted to experience. I had a taste of it in Euro 96 when I was over here with Germany, and the German players who have played in England always came back and told us amazing stories about the crowds and the buzz you get in the stadiums.'

Babel, Ryan

RYAN BABEL signed his first professional contract with Ajax in January 2004, after progressing through the youth ranks since his first affiliation as an 11-year-old.

He made his Ajax debut in a 4-0 win over ADO Den Haag in the Eredivisie on 1 February 2004 and Ajax later won the championship that season, the only time in his first spell at the club. Babel featured considerably more the following season, scoring seven goals in 13 league starts, and made the breakthrough into the international side against Romania in a World Cup qualifying match. He scored in Netherlands' 2-0 victory and became the youngest goalscorer in 68 years for the Netherlands and the fourth-youngest of all time. Babel was a key player for the Dutch team that won the UEFA Under-21 Championship, held in the Netherlands in the summer of 2007. His second goal of the tournament came during his man-of-the-match performance in the final as Serbia were defeated 4-1.

In July 2007 Babel became the third most expensive player in Liverpool's history. Much was expected of him after he was unveiled along with Yossi Benayoun. Babel made 30 appearances in the league, to which he added a further 19 appearances in cup matches. He mostly played wide on the left, seemed to be very one-footed and liked to cut inside on his right foot to produce a pass or a shot. He also showed that he was capable of taking on and beating a defender by going outside his opponent on his

left foot. Nobody could complain at his goal contribution during the season. In addition to those he created, Babel scored ten times, four in the league and six in the cups, including a brace on the night Besiktas were put to the sword at Anfield in the Champions League group stage. His final two goals of the season were also in that competition, the one that made sure there was no way back for Arsenal in the quarter-final at Anfield and the long-range extra-time shot that briefly raised hopes of a sensational climax to the semi-final at Chelsea.

BABEL SCORED TEN TIMES, FOUR IN THE LEAGUE AND SIX IN THE CUPS

BABEL failed to live up to expectations in his second season at Liverpool. He made only 13 starts, no less than 29 substitute appearances and scored four goals. He drifted in and out of games and despite having obvious skill and pace he consistently took the wrong decision on the field of play. Babel started his third season yet to properly fulfil the potential he had shown as a youngster with Ajax. One thrilling goal at Lyon apart, it didn't really happen this time either. In the mid-season transfer window, Liverpool apparently rejected a huge offer for Babel from Birmingham City and the boss kept faith with him until the end of the campaign. He tested Rafa Benítez' patience when

Season	League		FA Cup		League Cup		Europe		Total	
	App	Goals	App	Goals	App	Goals	App	Goals	App	Goals
2007/08	15 (15)	4	4	1	2	0	8 (5)	5	29 (20)	10
2008/09	6 (21)	3	2 (1)	0	2	0	3 (7)	1	13 (29)	4
2009/10	9 (16)	4	0 (1)	0	2	0	5 (5)	2	16 (22)	6
2010/11	1 (8)	1	0 (1)	0	1	0	5 (1)	1	7 (10)	2
Total	**31 (60)**	**12**	**6 (3)**	**1**	**7**	**0**	**21 (18)**	**9**	**65 (81)**	**22**

his petulance in Portugal saw him sent off at a critical stage of the Europa League tie with Benfica. The exciting young prodigy Liverpool had signed just three years earlier had started to fade and at times Babel made it easy for defenders to predict his next move. Sometimes he seemed a one-trick pony, and even that trick was nothing to write home about.

On 18 January 2011 Liverpool accepted a bid for their Dutch forward from Hoffenheim. Although both buying and selling clubs were in agreement, it initially seemed that the player could not agree personal terms with the German club. Kenny Dalglish announced that Babel would be staying at Anfield after all. However, only 24 hours later, Babel signed a two-and-a-half-year deal with the Bundesliga club. The fee was reported to be £5.8m, so considerably less than Liverpool paid Ajax for the 20-year-old in July 2007. Babel featured in almost half a century of Bundesliga games before being released in the summer of 2012. He made a short stop at his first club, Ajax, before moving to Turkish side Kasimpasa in June 2013.

BORN
Amsterdam, Netherlands,
19 December 1986
POSITION
Left-winger
OTHER CLUBS
Ajax (1997–2007),
Hoffenheim (2011–12),
Ajax (2012–13),
Kasimpasa (2013–)
SIGNED FROM
Ajax, £11.5million,
13 July 2007
INTERNATIONAL CAPS
42 Netherlands caps
(5 goals) (26 (1) at LFC),
2005–11
LFC DEBUT GAME/GOAL
11 August 2007 /
1 September 2007
CONTRACT EXPIRY
25 January 2011

Balmer, Jack

JACK BALMER was spotted by Everton when playing for Collegiate Old Boys, an amateur club that was founded to provide a football facility for old boys of the Liverpool Collegiate School.

The Blues gave Balmer a trial and he played for them as an amateur for two seasons. The Balmer name was already well known at the club as Jack's uncles, William and Robert, had both been popular players at Everton in the early part of the century. Everton decided not to keep him for a third season and Liverpool snapped Jack up, still aged only 19, in May 1935. Balmer signed professional forms for Liverpool three months later. He came back to haunt Everton in the Merseyside derby on 16 February 1938 at Goodison Park when he scored inside 30 seconds in a 3-1 win!

Jack Balmer in training with Freddie Howe

After losing potentially the best years of his career to World War Two Balmer resumed league football after the war and was the club's top scorer, equal with Albert Stubbins, as Liverpool won the League Championship for the first time for nearly a quarter of a century. It was during that season that he scored hat-tricks in three successive First Division matches in November 1946; Portsmouth, Derby and Arsenal being his victims. Naturally when Balmer had netted twice against the Gunners at Anfield the crowd wanted one more. Balmer completed his hat-trick in the 68th minute when the score was 2-2. 'All that was needed now was a Balmer goal to make three hat-tricks in succession,' reported the *Echo*. 'No sooner had the words been spoken than Eastham started the run which produced an angled chance for Balmer, who veered to the right, and put the ball into the net to the biggest cheer Anfield has ever known in its long history. Having scored a hat-trick of hat-tricks, and 10 goals in three matches, Balmer must have established a record which will stand for many a year. He was mobbed by his delighted teammates.' Balmer became the third player to achieve that feat in the top division, after Tottenham's South African Frank Osborne in 1925, with Tom Jennings at Leeds following in his footsteps in 1926. (Liverpool, incidentally, were in both instances involved in their scoring run: Osborne scored three against the Reds on 24 October 1925 at White

FACTFILE

BORN
West Derby, Liverpool,
6 February 1916
DIED
25 December 1984
POSITION
Inside-right/left forward
OTHER CLUBS
Collegiate Old Boys,
Everton (1934–35);
Brighton & Hove Albion,
Newcastle (wartime guest)
JOINED
Free transfer, 15 May 1935
LFC DEBUT GAME/GOAL
21 September 1935 /
7 December 1935
CONTRACT EXPIRY
May 1952
HONOURS
League Championship
1946/47

Hart Lane and Jennings four at Anfield on 2 October 1926). Since Balmer joined this select group of men no one has managed a hat-trick of hat-tricks in the top division.

Balmer was a prolific scorer for Liverpool throughout his career and is one of the few men to have scored over 100 times for the club in all competitions. Former Liverpool captain Don Mackinlay was a good judge of character and recalled in the *Evening Express* in 1955: 'I thought a lot of him. If Jack had had a little more "devilment" in him, he would have been one of the best inside forwards in the game.'

Balmer was a tremendously skilful and clever player, but his refusal to get stuck in with well-placed tackles made him unpopular with a certain section of the Liverpool crowd, as his former team-mate Bob Paisley noted in his book about his 50 Golden Reds: 'I don't honestly think I've ever known a player so harshly treated by Liverpool supporters as he was, but he managed to smile his way through although it hurt him deeply. He was a local lad, born and bred in Liverpool, and he gave

JACK BALMER
LIVERPOOL

BALMER, nevertheless, refused to alter his style. 'They were entitled to their opinion. Maybe I didn't go in for the crunch tackle but that kind of thing wasn't my idea of football. I was never a coward at the game but I got a shudder when I saw the boot going in.' Balmer was captain of Liverpool from 1947–49 and a coach at the club from 1952–55.

Season	League		FA Cup		Total	
	App	Goals	App	Goals	App	Goals
1935/36	17	3	0	0	17	3
1936/37	33	8	1	0	34	8
1937/38	30	13	1	0	31	13
1938/39	42	10	3	4	45	14
1945/46	-	-	2	1	2	1
1946/47	39	24	6	4	45	28
1947/48	40	15	1	0	41	15
1948/49	42	14	4	2	46	16
1949/50	9	1	0	0	9	1
1950/51	34	10	1	1	35	11
1951/52	2	0	2	0	4	0
Total	**288**	**98**	**21**	**12**	**309**	**110**

everything to his only professional club but there was a group of supporters who could never forgive him because he didn't get stuck into the tackle.'

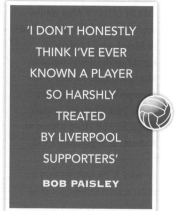

'I DON'T HONESTLY THINK I'VE EVER KNOWN A PLAYER SO HARSHLY TREATED BY LIVERPOOL SUPPORTERS'

BOB PAISLEY

Bamber, John

JOHN BAMBER started his career as a right-winger but developed into a right-half of good repute. He joined Liverpool during World War One and did not cost the club a penny. He made 24 appearances in 1919/20 as competitive league football in England resumed after a four-year absence.

Bamber was described in March 1920 in the club programme as follows: 'Since coming to Anfield his consistency has been remarkable. Never really brilliant, but always very effective, Bamber is the type of player who is bound to make a name for himself; he discards all idea of ornamentality for efficiency, and seldom is it that the keenest critic can find fault with his work in the field.' In April 1921 the *Derby Daily Telegraph* praised Bamber for being 'a powerful defender, a sixth forward, a breaker-up and forager rolled into one. Has a wonderful stock of energy, delights in loading upon his forwards the choicest of delicate ground passes, and is an artist.'

Thirty league matches followed the next season as he established himself in the side and was even chosen to represent England against Wales in March 1921. After playing the first four league matches of the 1921/22 season Bamber was stricken with appendicitis. His illness paved the way for Jock McNab and once Bamber recovered he was only in the side if McNab was unavailable. As a consequence Bamber missed out on medals as Liverpool won the League Championship twice in 1922 and 1923.

IN FEBRUARY 1924 Bamber joined Leicester City, who won the Second Division. He played for the Foxes in two seasons in the First Division before returning to Merseyside in 1927 to play for Tranmere Rovers.

BAMBER MISSED OUT ON MEDALS DESPITE LIVERPOOL WINNING THE LEAGUE CHAMPIONSHIP IN 1922 AND 1923

FACTFILE

BORN
Peasley Cross, St Helens, 11 April 1895
DIED
August 1971
POSITION
Right-half
OTHER CLUBS
St Helens Recreation, Heywood, St Helens Town, Alexandra Victoria, Leicester City (1924–27), Tranmere Rovers (1927–30), Prescot Cables (1930–32)
SIGNED FROM
Alexandra Victoria, 4 December 1915
INTERNATIONAL CAPS
1 England cap, 1921
LFC DEBUT GAME/GOAL
13 September 1919 / 14 February 1920
CONTRACT EXPIRY
February 1924

Season	League		FA Cup		Other		Total	
	App	Goals	App	Goals	App	Goals	App	Goals
1919/20	24	1	5	0	-	-	29	1
1920/21	30	1	3	0	-	-	33	1
1921/22	8	0	0	0	0	0	8	0
1922/23	4	0	0	0	-	-	4	0
1923/24	6	0	0	0	-	-	6	0
Total	**72**	**2**	**8**	**0**	**0**	**0**	**80**	**2**

Banks, Alan

LIVERPUDLIAN Alan Banks scored 10 goals for the reserves in March and April 1958, signed professional forms in May and made his debut for Liverpool a few days short of his 20th birthday against Brighton and Hove Albion at Anfield, in September 1958.

IT WAS A DREAM DEBUT too as he scored Liverpool's third goal in a convincing 5-0 victory. Despite scoring four times in five matches for the first team and 21 for the reserves in the 1960/61 season, Banks left in the summer of 1961. He was subsequently a talisman for Exeter City, scoring 109 goals in 285 games in two spells, having signed from Cambridge City in October 1963.

In a PFA survey published in December 2007, he was voted as Exeter's all-time favourite player.

Season	League		FA Cup		Other		Total	
	App	Goals	App	Goals	App	Goals	App	Goals
1958/59	3	2	0	0	-	-	3	2
1960/61	5	4	0	0	0	0	5	4
Total	8	6	0	0	0	0	8	6

Banks, Billy

AGED 21 when he made his Liverpool debut in the 1913/14 season, Billy Banks played in nine of the final 11 league fixtures, scoring four goals including a brace against Chelsea. He made a further 17 appearances the following season, adding another two goals to his total.

William Banks

Banks' career as a Liverpool player was cut short by the advent of World War One, but he played on 20 occasions for Liverpool during the war. He signed for neighbours Tranmere Rovers in April 1919 and after only a seven-month stay moved to Second Division Fulham, where he played 43 games and scored 12 goals between 1919 and 1921. Banks was described as a man of squat build (being 5ft 6½in, or 169cm) who was more of a linkman than an individual performer.

Season	League		FA Cup		Total	
	App	Goals	App	Goals	App	Goals
1913/14	9	4	0	0	9	4
1914/15	17	2	0	0	17	2
Total	26	6	0	0	26	6

Barclay, William Edward Morton

WILLIAM EDWARD Morton Barclay was Everton's vice-president when John Houlding left the presidency of the club. He stayed loyal to his boss and took part in the founding of Liverpool Football Club in 1892.

BARCLAY was so described at the time: "A great enthusiast in football management. Is a most successful organiser, a fine judge of the great game, and knows everybody in the football world. Few men have travelled so much to football matches as he. One of Mr John Houlding's staunchest supporters. He is the successful Head Master of the Industrial Schools, Everton Crescent, and is, further, widely known and everywhere esteemed. An able man all-round." Barclay was appointed the first Secretary of Liverpool, responsible for all kinds of paperwork relating to the running of the team; signing contracts and keeping deadlines. When John Houlding gave his board £500 to bring in new players Barclay went on a number of scouting missions to Scotland. However, as would be the case until the late 50s, the board of the club chose the starting line-up and signed new players, so Barclay had very little say in those matters though the role of Secretary was a rough precursor to that of the team manager's role. At that time Barclay was more of a regular administrator. It wasn't until the arrival of Tom Watson in 1896 that a sole man was considered responsible for the success or the failure of the team. John McKenna was pulling the strings, even

though he was just a regular board member; he was a man of great influence and was the club's outward face. Barclay apparently knew nothing of the club's successful application for membership of the Second Division in 1893 until he received a telegram instructing him to travel to London to help arrange the fixtures for Liverpool's inaugural season as a member of the league. That single incident indicates how much more involved McKenna was really with policy and key decisions. Neither Barclay or McKenna were hands-on with

the team during training as trainers Alec Dick and Wally Richardson were responsible for keeping the players in shape and as no one was allowed along the touchline during games change of tactics were very much in the hands of the captain, who was Andrew Hannah at the time.

Barclay left the club in August 1895 and seemed to have fallen on hard times as the Lancashire Association agreed in January 1901 to contribute five guineas to a fund being raised on his behalf. When Liverpool lost the FA Cup final to Burnley in 1914 Barclay sent the following letter to the *Liverpool Echo*, clearly keeping an eye out on the progress of his old club. 'Let me sympathise with Liverpool in just missing winning the Cup, and also sincerely and heartily congratulate the Liverpool club on the silver, nay the golden lining, to the cloud. May they have better luck from a playing point of view next season is my wish.'

SADLY IN LATE January 1917 the following was reported in the *Echo*:

> '*A Liverpool jury to-day returned a verdict of "Suicide during temporary insanity" in the case of William Edward Morton Barclay (60), a munitions storekeeper, who lodged at 45, Upper Beau-street. Barclay, who was a B.A. and B.Sc., and who had previously been in a better position, was in the habit of taking a drug for pains in the head. On Monday he was found dead, from loss of blood, in his bedroom. There were gashes on his forearm from a razor found beside him, and a letter to a friend indicated that he intended to commit suicide.*'

MR. W. E. BARCLAY,
The First Secretary.

A sad end to the life of a man who was committed to making Liverpool a force to be reckoned with.

A SAD END TO THE LIFE OF A MAN WHO WAS COMMITTED TO MAKING LIVERPOOL A FORCE TO BE RECKONED WITH

FACTFILE

BORN
Liverpool, 1856
DIED
29 January 1917
SIGNED
15 March 1892
LFC DEBUT GAME
3 September 1892
CONTRACT EXPIRY AS MANAGER
August 1895
HONOURS
Lancashire League 1892/93;
Second Division 1893/94

Season	Division	P	W	D	L	GF	GA	Pts	Position	Win %	FA Cup
1892/93	Lanc League*	22	17	3	2	66	19	36	1	77.27	3rd Qualifier
1893/94	2nd Division	28	22	0	6	77	18	50	1	78.57	3rd Round
1894/95	1st Division	30	7	15	8	51	70	22	16	23.33	2nd Round
Total**		**58**	**29**	**15**	**14**	**128**	**88**	**72**	**-**	**50**	**-**

*Lancashire League   **Lancashire League is excluded from the total*

Barkas, Harry

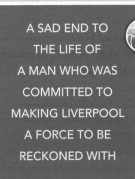

HARRY BARKAS SCORED 15 goals in 21 games for South Shields in the Third Division North in the 1929/30 season. Financial struggles forced the club to move to the neighbouring town of Gateshead, where the council was eager to acquire a football team, and adopt their name.

Barkas had netted seven in 19 matches for Gateshead in 1930/31 when Liverpool made their move. He played five matches over a period of nine months before rejoining Gateshead in 1932.

Henry, or 'Harry' as he was better known, came from a footballing family and his brothers Jimmy, Tommy, Ned and Sam were all professional footballers. Sam captained England three times.

Season	League		FA Cup		Total	
	App	Goals	App	Goals	App	Goals
1930/31	4	0	0	0	4	0
1931/32	1	0	0	0	1	0
Total	**5**	**0**	**0**	**0**	**5**	**0**

FACTFILE

BORN
Wardley Colliery, Northumberland, 21 January 1906
DIED
1974
POSITION
Centre-forward
OTHER CLUBS
Spennymoor United (1927–29),
South Shields/Gateshead (1929–30),
Gateshead (1932–33),
Jarrow (1933–34)
SIGNED FROM
Gateshead, £1,500, 30 December 1930
LFC DEBUT GAME
3 January 1931
CONTRACT EXPIRY
1932

Barmby, Nick

NICK BARMBY started his career with Tottenham, playing three seasons at White Hart Lane and winning England recognition. He joined Middlesbrough at the start of the 1995/96 season for £6.25 million.

Only 14 months later he was on the move again, this time to Everton. After a slow start at Goodison, Barmby's career was on the rise under the management of Walter Smith and he returned to the England team. With a new contract on the table at Goodison but interest from Liverpool, the biggest decision of his football life beckoned. Barmby made a courageous decision to move across Stanley Park, the first player since Dave Hickson in 1959 to be transferred from Everton to Liverpool.

> HIS MAGNIFICENT GOAL AFTER 12 MINUTES AGAINST EVERTON AT ANFIELD MADE HIM AN INSTANT HERO, SILENCING EVERTONIANS 'JUDAS' CHANTS

He made a powerful start to his Reds' career and seemed quite a useful addition on the left side of midfield. His magnificent goal after 12 minutes against Everton at Anfield made him an instant hero, silencing Everton's 'Judas' chants. In his debut season Liverpool were victorious in three cup competitions, but Barmby only featured in the League Cup final as he struggled with injuries as the campaign drew to a close. He had to settle for a place on the bench in the UEFA Cup final, having scored in three consecutive European away games en route to Dortmund, and missed the FA Cup final after participating in five earlier rounds.

The Nick Barmby who turned out for Liverpool in his second season struggled to make an impression, to say the least. Liverpool accepted Sunderland's bid for him in October 2001, but Barmby persevered and refused to leave. The writing was, however, on the wall and Leeds United was his next destination in his much-travelled career.

BARMBY only stayed two years at Elland Road before leaving on a free to his home-town club, Hull, in July 2004. That proved to be a wise move as he was a key player in Hull's rise from League One to the Premiership in four years. Hull dropped back into the Championship after just two years in the top division, but Barmby continued to roll back the years in 2010/11, playing on past his 37th birthday.

Barmby combined his playing duties with a coaching role under Nigel Pearson at the KC Stadium. When Pearson left to become Leicester City's manager in November 2011, Barmby was appointed to the post of caretaker-manager. In January 2012 Barmby signed as manager on a permanent basis. He led the team into the playoff positions, but shortly after the end of the regular season Barmby was sacked for criticising the club's owners in an interview he had given to a local newspaper.

FACTFILE

BORN
Hull,
11 February 1974

POSITION
Midfielder

OTHER CLUBS
Tottenham Hotspur
(1991–95),
Middlesbrough (1995–96),
Everton (1996–2000),
Leeds United (2002–04),
Nottingham Forest
(loan, 2004),
Hull City (2004–11)

SIGNED FROM
Everton, £6million,
18 July 2000

INTERNATIONAL CAPS
23 England caps (4 goals)
(8 (1) at LFC), 1995–2001

LFC DEBUT GAME/GOAL
19 August 2000 /
14 September 2000

CONTRACT EXPIRY
8 August 2002

HONOURS
League Cup 2001;
UEFA Cup 2001

Season	League		FA Cup		League Cup		Europe		Other		Total	
	App	Goals	App	Goals	App	Goals	App	Goals	App	Goals	App	Goals
2000/01	21 (5)	2	2 (3)	1	2 (4)	1	6 (3)	4	-	-	31 (15)	8
2001/02	2 (4)	0	0	0	1	0	3 (1)	0	1	0	7 (5)	0
Total	23 (9)	2	2 (3)	1	3 (4)	1	9 (4)	4	1	0	38 (20)	8

Barnes,
John

HIS HOME IN THE SUNNY Caribbean island of Jamaica seemed far away when 12-year-old John Charles Bryan Barnes (so christened because of his father's admiration for Welsh legend John Charles) came to England for the first time. His father had been appointed Jamaica's military attaché in London. 'I had never seen snow before,' John revealed in his autobiography. 'As our plane came in to land at Heathrow, I stared out of the window and saw all the white roofs. My heart sank. I could not imagine living in such a cold climate. But beyond the white roofs, I caught sight of what seemed like countless football pitches and my spirits lifted.'

Within a week he had found a football club, Stowe Boys Club. The team was strong and went easily into double figures against its opponents. At home in Kingston Barnes was used to playing in the middle or up front, but everybody in the Stowe team wanted to attack and couldn't care less about defensive duties. Barnes spent the next three-and-a-half years with Stowe at centre half as well as captaining the side. 'Occasionally, I dribbled out of defence. If I had wanted to I could have gone around all the opposing players and scored. Even at thirteen, I was very team-orientated. This sense of self-restraint, of sacrificing personal desire for the good of the collective, meant I was well prepared for the life of a professional.' Stowe did not have an Under-17 team so he moved to non-league Sudbury Court. Watford scouts spotted him and he was signed by the then Second Division club in the summer of 1981, aged 17. His father's duties

at the Jamaican embassy had come to an end and the family was on its way back to Jamaica. It was a big decision for John to stay behind and try to become a professional footballer, but his progress in Graham Taylor's team was swift. Luther Blissett's strike partner, Ross Jenkins, had left the team in the middle of the season and Barnes took his place up front. The Vicarage Road club were promoted to the top division at the end of the 1981/82 season.

The 1982/83 season, Watford's first ever in the top flight, was incredible. On the last day Watford beat Liverpool and Manchester United lost, meaning the Hornets captured the runners-up spot, with Barnes the key player. 'I remain proud of my scoring record and particularly the goals I managed in the 1982/83 season, the best year of my career,' he recalled. 'Even the vintage 1987/88 season at Liverpool could not match this year at Watford. Midway through the season, Zico described me as "the future of English football".' Barnes subsequently reverted to the left wing and played a part in their run to the 1984 FA Cup final. As Watford established themselves in the First Division, Barnes was regularly linked with a move to a higher-profile club. Watford finished 1986/87 in ninth place and at the end of the season Graham Taylor left for Aston Villa. Barnes was also on his way out after featuring in 233 league games, scoring 65 goals.

Barnes had plenty of options. He recalled:

Liverpool, the leading team of the era, first made overtures in February 1987 but I knew I was going to stay at Watford until the end of the season when my contract expired. If I committed myself to Liverpool in February, Juventus or Real Madrid might have come along and that would have been desperately frustrating. Holding on represented a gamble because of the threat of injury or Liverpool's interest cooling. Given my technical skills, I would be more appreciated in Italy than in England. But as the season wore on, it looked increasingly like my destination was to be Manchester United or Liverpool. Alex Ferguson was very eager to sign me but he had just bought Jesper Olsen, a left-winger. I'm not sure I would have gone to Old Trafford anyway. Liverpool seemed the best bet.

In the summer of 1987 Kenny Dalglish agreed a fee of £900,000 to bring Barnes to Anfield, where he would join forces with the recently signed Peter Beardsley and John Aldridge to form one of the club's most exciting forward lines ever.

It only took Barnes nine minutes to create a goal for Aldridge on his Liverpool debut at Highbury on 15 August 1987. His first real test was his Anfield debut on 12 September against Oxford. Liverpool boss Dalglish was delighted by his performance: 'Barnes did what we expected him to do. He made a goal, scored one, and entertained. You remember that.' The season was like a fairytale for Liverpool, with Barnes their talisman. 'Everything I tried worked: every trick or dribble, feint or pass produced something.' Barnes' greatest performance came on 17 October 1987 against league leaders Queens Park Rangers. He scored what he considers the best goal of his career. 'The memory of that match burns more vividly in my mind than any other I played for Liverpool,' Barnes remembered:

Kevin Brock tried to dribble past me and I just stuck a foot out and nicked the ball. Terry Fenwick rushed in to repair the damage so I pushed the ball to the left of him. Whenever would-be tacklers came sliding in, I tried to toe the ball past them, ride the challenge and regain balance and the ball on the other side. After I pushed the ball past Fenwick, I landed and brought the ball back with my left foot in one movement.

LIVERPOOL WON the League Championship this season with 90 points, scoring 87 goals of which Barnes claimed 15. He received rave reviews from legends in the game and got the

recognition he deserved for his part in Liverpool's dominance, when he was voted both the PFA's and Football Writers' Player of the Year.

Barnes summed the 1987/88 season up perfectly: 'We were irresistible, playing with fluency and imagination, creating chances at will. Every time Bruce Grobbelaar gathered the ball, he threw it out and we were off, weaving our way into the final third. The accuracy of our passing and each player's confident touch ensured we rarely gave away possession. So each time we got the ball, we expected to make a chance for John Aldridge or whoever was in the box. The opposition must have been terrified.' The double was on the horizon but Wimbledon shocked Liverpool in the FA Cup final.

> 'PLAYERS LIKE JOHN BARNES COME ALONG JUST ONCE IN A LIFETIME'
>
> **SIR TOM FINNEY**

The following season, Liverpool struggled to recapture their form but the Hillsborough disaster put everything in perspective. Liverpool still had to finish the season and two exciting finals were on the horizon. The Reds had a three-point lead on Arsenal before the teams met in the last league match of the season on 26 May 1989 at Anfield. Barnes received the ball in the final moments of the game. 'I decided to show some ambition for possibly the first time in the evening. What I did next cost Liverpool the Championship.' Barnes had wandered over to the right flank and if he had kept the ball and seen out the closing moments Liverpool would have

been crowned champions. Instead of bringing the ball into the corner Barnes tried to go past Kevin Richardson, who nicked the ball off him. Arsenal broke and, needing to add to their 1-0 lead to win the title on goal difference, with 91 minutes and 22 seconds of the game played Michael Thomas scored in the most dramatic fashion possible. Some 40 seconds later the game was finished; Arsenal were champions. Barnes recalled: 'In the dressing room, Ronnie Moran said to me, "What were you doing? You should have taken the ball down to the corner flag." But no one else criticised me. Everyone was too shell-shocked.'

Liverpool didn't finish this tragic season empty-handed. The big two Merseyside teams played each other in the FA Cup final and Barnes finally won his elusive cup winners' medal at the third time of asking.

BARNES joined Ian Rush in the forward line in the 1989/90 season, as Aldridge had been dropped to the bench and was soon on his way out. Barnes also took over from Aldridge as the club's penalty taker. Liverpool were inconsistent throughout the first part of the season but Barnes was very consistent in his goalscoring with 12 goals in just 20 matches. In the second half of the season he scored 16 goals in 25 matches to take his tally to 28. He was top scorer at Liverpool, two ahead of Rush and second-highest goalscorer in the league, two goals behind Gary Lineker. Barnes was voted Player of the Year again by the Football Writers' Association and joined legends such as Danny Blanchflower, Kenny Dalglish, Stanley Matthews and Tom Finney, who also won this award twice in their careers. Liverpool won the Championship in comprehensive fashion, nine points in front of Aston Villa and 17 points ahead of defending champions Arsenal. The Reds finished the season in style as Barnes scored a hat-trick in a 6-1 win over Coventry at Highfield Road.

In February 1991 Liverpool were in the familiar top position. Barnes was on his way to training when he received the astounding news that Dalglish had resigned. Liverpool's title charge petered out and Arsenal won the League Championship again. Barnes still had a good season and scored 18 goals in 45 matches.

Graeme Souness was at the helm when the 1991/92 season started. Barnes was injured in the second league match and didn't feature again until January. He played a big part in the team's march to the FA Cup final by scoring a hat-trick against Crewe Alexandra in the third round and in the sixth round his great pass enabled Michael Thomas to score the winning goal against Aston Villa. Barnes also scored one of Liverpool's penalties when they beat Portsmouth in a penalty shootout in the semi-final replay. Wembley beckoned for Barnes, but a few days before the big game he strained his calf while playing volleyball with his team-mates in a hotel pool and could only watch from the sidelines as Liverpool conquered Sunderland in the final.

In 1992 the 28-year-old was at a crossroads in his Liverpool career. The manager who had brought him to the club had left and Barnes realised this could be his last chance to sample life on the continent. He still harboured dreams about playing for Juventus, Barcelona or Real Madrid. These dreams perished in a warm-up game for the European Championships, against Finland in Helsinki on 3 June 1992. He effectively tore his right-leg hamstring to shreds and was out until November. This had a detrimental effect on his ability to take players on, as he always used his right leg when taking off on a solo run, using his left to take the ball past players. A similar injury finished Mark Lawrenson's career and Barnes was forced to change his style of play, eventually moving into central midfield. When Barnes was offered a new contract in February 1993 he decided to stay put as he could see it would be a while until he was back to his best. Yet robbed of his electrifying pace, in the 1992/93 and 1993/94 seasons he was far from the player he used to be. Souness nevertheless kept faith in Barnes, despite

criticising him in front of the other players. Barnes tried his best but his physical condition curtailed his natural instincts.

SOUNESS resigned at the end of January 1994 to be replaced by Roy Evans, who created a new role in the team for Barnes. It was plain to see that Barnes' pace had vanished and Evans wanted him to dictate play from midfield and be his coach on the field. Barnes was inspired by this new role as he understood the game better than most. He was left to hold the fort while other players attacked the opposition. Steve McManaman had taken over his role on the wing and flourished with Barnes' assistance. Evans handed Barnes the captain's armband in 1996, encouraged by his excellent improvement in form. Liverpool had the makings of a title-winning side but the captain felt their discipline let them down when it mattered. Barnes played in his first final in six years when he faced Bolton in the League Cup in 1995, and created McManaman's first goal in a 2-1 victory. Next season he envisaged lifting the famous FA Cup, but the Reds lost 1-0 to Manchester United in the 1996 final.

Barnes had an impressive start to the 1996/97 season and scored one goal in a 3-3 draw with Middlesbrough on the opening day. He clearly meant business and was in a much more attacking mood than in previous seasons. Yet his form wasn't enough to inspire the team to capture the title. On 24 April Liverpool played their European Cup Winners Cup semi-final second leg against Paris St Germain at Anfield, having lost the first leg 3-0. In the previous game Liverpool had lost 3-1 at home against Manchester United, which ended their title challenge. Barnes scored Liverpool's goal with a header, which proved to be his last for the club. A few changes were made before the second leg

against PSG and Barnes was dropped for the first time in his ten-year career at Liverpool. The Reds did their best with the fans' great support, but just fell short of the final, winning 2-0. Barnes started on the bench for the three remaining games as Liverpool fell from second to fourth. Paul Ince was bought from Inter Milan in the summer and took over from Barnes as Liverpool's captain.

A decade after Barnes arrived at Anfield from Watford in 1987, he was given a free transfer and was signed for a second time by Kenny Dalglish, now manager of Newcastle United. He stayed on Tyneside for two seasons and when he appeared for the Magpies in the 1998 FA Cup final against Arsenal, it was the fifth time he had graced Wembley's showpiece end-of-season finale. Unfortunately, as with Watford in 1984 and Liverpool in 1988 and 1996, he took a runners-up medal home with him. Following Dalglish's departure and Ruud Gullit's arrival Barnes had to seek pastures new at Charlton, who had just been promoted to the top division, to get regular football. He only appeared in 12 league matches and was unable to prevent the southeast London club from being relegated. As Charlton prepared for life back in the First Division, Barnes announced his retirement as a player at the age of 35, nearly 20 years after he had made his debut for Watford.

The eloquent and erudite Barnes was always likely to stay in the game in some capacity. However, it was still a bit of a surprise when he was appointed manager of Celtic in 1999 under Dalglish, who was Director of Football at Parkhead. It was not a happy time for either man. Celtic suffered a humiliating home cup defeat to the then minnows of Inverness Caledonian Thistle and Barnes was sacked soon after. Barnes then became the latest in a long

line of ex-Liverpool players to work in the media covering football, in his case with Channel Five.

IN SEPTEMBER 2008 he was appointed as the manager of the Jamaican national team that failed to qualify for the 2010 World Cup finals in South Africa. A couple of weeks before his contract with the Jamaican Football Federation was due to expire, Barnes confirmed that he would be returning to club management as successor to Ronnie Moore at League One club Tranmere Rovers. After a dreadful start to the 2009/10 season, with just two victories from the opening 11 matches, he was dismissed only a few days after a 5-0 thrashing at Millwall. Jason McAteer, who had been appointed as Barnes' assistant at Prenton Park, left the club at the same time.

BARNES was an experienced international when he joined Liverpool with 29 caps to his name. He had played in the 1986 World Cup, where he was only in a supporting role, but his performance against Argentina in the quarter-finals could have destroyed Diego Maradona's World Cup dream. Six minutes into the second half Maradona scored the infamous 'Hand of God' goal past Peter Shilton. Four minutes later the Argentina captain scored a brilliant individual goal as Barnes watched in awe from the bench. England were losing 2-0 when Barnes came on with 16 minutes to go. His superb pass from the left flank provided Gary Lineker with a goal. Three minutes from time Barnes made his way down the flank again and passed into the penalty area only for an Argentinian

defender somehow to get the ball away from the goal-line. Argentina went on to win the World Cup.

Barnes made his international debut against Northern Ireland on 28 May 1983. He had played nine internationals when England faced Brazil at the Maracana stadium on 10 June 1984. Barnes took centre stage a minute before half-time.

I picked up possession and began running at Brazil's defence. For all the superlatives heaped upon that run, I can honestly say that if I had seen someone to pass to I would have done. Having slipped around the first Brazilian, I looked up to see if an England team-mate was nearby. There wasn't, so I kept going. A pattern developed – look around, no support, keep going, beat another Brazilian, look around, no support, keep going, beat another Brazilian. I was not sure where I was until I found myself in front of goal facing the 'keeper. That was how the goal unfolded. I didn't appreciate what an impact my slalom dribble was having. Apparently, one Rio paper described it as "the greatest goal ever seen at the Maracana".

THIS GOAL – which many consider the finest ever scored by an England international – proved to be a burden during his England career, as many expected him to repeat this individual brilliance on a regular basis. Barnes had been in sensational form for Liverpool leading to the European Championships in Germany in 1988. However, contrary to his club position where he was allowed to roam free, he was told to stay out on the wing by England coach Bobby Robson, where he was starved of the ball. England finished bottom of their group and Barnes was given unbelievable abuse in the final match against USSR.

'THE GREATEST GOAL EVER SEEN AT THE MARACANA'

Player of the year 1988

'EVEN IF MY SCORING RECORD PROVES I COULD SCORE, I ADMIT I WAS NEVER AN OUT-AND-OUT GOALSCORER. THE ACTUAL ACT OF SCORING DID NOT MEAN THAT MUCH TO ME. I WOULD RATHER CREATE SOMETHING BEAUTIFUL THAN HAVE THE BALL BOUNCE OFF MY KNEE AND BOBBLE OVER THE LINE. I PREFERRED TO BE THE PLAYER WHO BEAT THREE MEN AND CROSSED THE BALL FOR IT TO GO IN OFF SOMEONE ELSE'S KNEE'

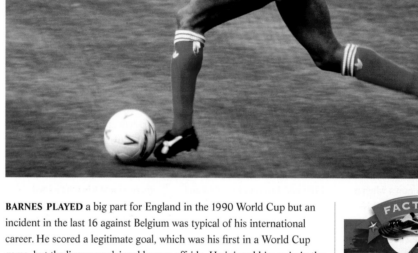

BARNES PLAYED a big part for England in the 1990 World Cup but an incident in the last 16 against Belgium was typical of his international career. He scored a legitimate goal, which was his first in a World Cup game, but the linesman claimed he was offside. He injured his groin in the second half and was on the bench when David Platt's heroics saved England in the 120th minute. Barnes started against Cameroon in the quarter-finals but had to be substituted as he couldn't shake off his groin injury. He didn't feature at all when England lost to West Germany in the semi-finals. One more international tournament finished in disappointing fashion.

When Graham Taylor resigned as England's coach it was expected that his international career was over, but in September 1994 Terry Venables put his faith in Barnes. The media wondered if Euro 96 was a realistic option for the experienced campaigner but that didn't come to fruition. His 79th international against Colombia on 6 September 1995 proved to be his last.

FACTFILE

BORN
Kingston, Jamaica,
7 November 1963

POSITION
Left-winger /
Centre-forward / Midfielder

OTHER CLUBS
Sudbury Court,
Watford (1981–87),
Newcastle United (1997–99),
Charlton Athletic (1999)

SIGNED FROM
Watford, £900,000,
9 June 1987

INTERNATIONAL CAPS
79 England caps (11)
(48 (8) at LFC), 1983–95

LFC DEBUT GAME/GOAL
15 August 1987 /
12 September 1987

CONTRACT EXPIRY
11 August 1997

HONOURS
League Championship
1987/88, 1989/90;
FA Cup 1989;
League Cup 1995;
FWA Footballer of the Year
1988, 1990;
PFA Player of the Year 1988

Season	League		FA Cup		League Cup		Europe		Other		Total	
	App	Goals	App	Goals	App	Goals	App	Goals	App	Goals	App	Goals
1987/88	38	15	7	2	3	0	-	-	-	-	48	17
1988/89	33	8	6	3	3	2	-	-	2	1	44	14
1989/90	34	22	8	5	2	1	-	-	1	0	45	28
1990/91	35	16	7	1	2	0	-	-	1	1	45	18
1991/92	12	1	4	3	0	0	1	0	-	-	17	4
1992/93	26 (1)	5	2	0	2	0	0	0	0	0	30 (1)	5
1993/94	24 (2)	3	2	0	2	0	-	-	-	-	28 (2)	3
1994/95	38	7	6	2	6	0	-	-	-	-	50	9
1995/96	36	3	7	0	3	0	4	0	-	-	50	3
1996/97	34 (1)	4	2	0	3	0	7	3	-	-	46 (1)	7
Total	**310 (4)**	**84**	**51**	**16**	**26**	**3**	**12**	**3**	**4**	**2**	**403 (4)**	**108**

Baron, Fred

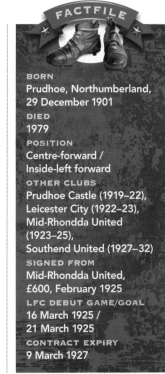

FRED BARON came into the Liverpool side for the first time in March 1925 and scored five times in the nine games he played by the end of that season as Liverpool finished fourth. According to the *Derby Telegraph* he was a 'big, stoutly built lad,' who could 'shoot with deadly force on the run.'

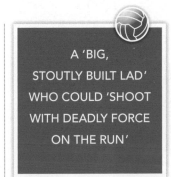

A 'BIG, STOUTLY BUILT LAD' WHO COULD 'SHOOT WITH DEADLY FORCE ON THE RUN'

He was only called on ten times the following season and added just a couple more goals to his total. His 20th and final league match for Liverpool was at Burnden Park, Bolton, on New Year's Day 1927. Baron joined Southend United in the Third Division South in March 1927 and played 64 games and scored 42 goals in his five-year stay at the club.

FACTFILE

BORN
Prudhoe, Northumberland, 29 December 1901
DIED
1979
POSITION
Centre-forward / Inside-left forward
OTHER CLUBS
Prudhoe Castle (1919–22), Leicester City (1922–23), Mid-Rhondda United (1923–25), Southend United (1927–32)
SIGNED FROM
Mid-Rhondda United, £600, February 1925
LFC DEBUT GAME/GOAL
16 March 1925 / 21 March 1925
CONTRACT EXPIRY
9 March 1927

Season	League		FA Cup		Total	
	App	Goals	App	Goals	App	Goals
1924/25	9	5	0	0	9	5
1925/26	10	2	0	0	10	2
1926/27	1	0	0	0	1	0
Total	**20**	**7**	**0**	**0**	**20**	**7**

Baron, Kevin

INSIDE-RIGHT forward Kevin Baron had played as an amateur for his home-town club of Preston North End before arriving at Anfield.

Due to his young age and diminutive stature he was once refused entry to an away ground with the doorman claiming:

'DON'T TELL ME YOU'RE A PLAYER YOU'RE ONLY A BOY'

'Don't tell me you're a player. You're only a boy.' He made six league appearances in the 1947/48 season but the side that had won the League Championship the previous year was fairly settled and Baron's youth and lack of experience kept him on the sidelines for a while.

HIS BIG breakthrough came in the 1949/50 season when he only

missed four league matches and played in Liverpool's FA Cup final team against Arsenal at Wembley. In 1951/52 Baron missed just two of the club's 42 league fixtures and scored six goals. A goal every third game in 27 league matches wasn't a bad return in the 1952/53 season. As Liverpool were relegated in 1954, Baron left for Southend United in the Third Division South. He spent four years there, scoring 45 goals in 138 league matches.

Kevin Baron died on 5 June 1971, only 44 years old. His brother, Gerard Bernard Patrick Baron, who was four years his senior, was the oldest victim, aged 67, of the Hillsborough disaster in 1989.

FACTFILE

BORN
Preston, 19 July 1926
DIED
5 June 1971
POSITION
Inside-right forward
OTHER CLUBS
Preston North End (1942–44), Southend United (1954–58), Northampton (1958–59), Gravesend & Northfleet (1959), Wisbech Town (1959–60), Aldershot (1960–61), Cambridge City (1961), Bedford Town (1961–62), Maldon Town (1962–63)
SIGNED FROM
Preston North End, September 1944
LFC DEBUT GAME/GOAL
5 January 1946 / 8 November 1947
CONTRACT EXPIRY
May 1954

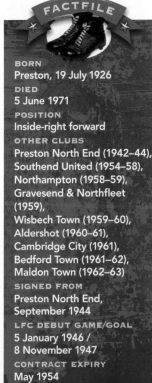

Season	League		FA Cup		Total	
	App	Goals	App	Goals	App	Goals
1945/46	-	-	3	0	3	0
1947/48	6	2	0	0	6	2
1948/49	6	2	0	0	6	2
1949/50	38	7	7	1	45	8
1950/51	7	1	0	0	7	1
1951/52	40	6	1	0	41	6
1952/53	27	9	1	0	28	9
1953/54	17	4	0	0	17	4
Total	**141**	**31**	**12**	**1**	**153**	**32**

KEVIN BARON
INSIDE FORWARD
LIVERPOOL F.C.

Baros,
Milan

MILAN BAROS was well known amongst youth scouts, but still a relative unknown on the big stage when Gérard Houllier snapped him up in July 2001. Then caretaker manager Phil Thompson was excited by his potential as he was unveiled along with loan signing Nicolas Anelka in December 2001.

'Gérard and our European scout, Alex Miller, first saw him three years ago in a youth tournament when the Czech side was outstanding. We've wanted him since then, and in the same way as Gregory Vignal and the two French boys from Le Havre, Milan is a signing who makes the future of the club very bright. I would describe him as a strong, fast player. He is a goal poacher with a lot of pace.'

Baros looked out of shape when arriving at Anfield and even Houllier admitted: 'When he first arrived I think some of my staff had thought I was already ill when I signed him! But I knew what I was signing. For the first three or four months none of my staff dared come up to me and tell me I had made a mistake in buying him, but I think in the back of their minds that is what they thought.'

BAROS was leaner and meaner at the start of the 2002/03 season and scored twice on his Premiership debut in a 3-2 win at Bolton. He won admiration for his determination to stamp his

authority on the game, and his energetic runs up field with the ball at his feet were a joy to behold. Houllier was pleased with his progress: 'The big difference has been in his weight and in learning English. He lost maybe three or four kilos over the summer and has looked sharp since then. Paolo Maldini said after the pre-season tournament in Madrid that he couldn't cope with him, and you can see why. We allowed Jari Litmanen to leave because of Milan's improvement. Jari is in his thirties while Milan is still only 20, and maybe the best of Milan will not come while I am in charge.'

The goal-hungry striker scored 12 goals in 42 matches in his first full season but his progress stuttered early in the 2003/04 season when Baros broke his ankle at Blackburn and was out for five months. He returned in fine form but was then dropped by Houllier, who left in the summer.

Baros was on the verge of quitting the club as he said Houllier had knocked the confidence out of him.

In a curious way Baros' lengthy lay-off worked in his favour, as he was hungry for action with the Czech Republic in the European Championships in the summer of 2004. Baros was the top scorer of the Euros with five goals in five games as the Czech Republic reached the semi-finals. He was expected to be firing on all cylinders when he returned to Anfield with a new manager at the helm, Rafa Benítez. He scored 11 goals in the first four months of the season but then added only two goals in the remaining 24 games as Liverpool won the Champions League for the first time. His greatest fault was being too focused on scoring himself instead of passing to a team-mate in a better position.

Benítez decided to cash in on Baros towards the end of August 2005. Aston Villa paid £6.5million for the Czech star and he repaid them with a disappointing 14 goals from 51 matches in a 17-month spell in the Midlands.

Baros, rather curiously considering their uneasy relationship at Liverpool, rejoined Houllier at French champions Lyon on 22 January 2007. Although his new club won their sixth league championship in a row Houllier was replaced by Alain Perrin and

Season	League		FA Cup		League Cup		Europe		Other		Total	
	App	Goals	App	Goals	App	Goals	App	Goals	App	Goals	App	Goals
2001/02	0	0	0	0	0	0	0 (1)	0	0	0	0 (1)	0
2002/03	17 (10)	9	0 (1)	0	2 (2)	2	3 (6)	1	0 (1)	0	22 (20)	12
2003/04	6 (7)	1	0 (1)	0	0	0	2 (2)	1	-	-	8 (10)	2
2004/05	22 (4)	9	0 (1)	0	1 (3)	2	13 (1)	2	-	-	36 (9)	13
2005/06	0 (2)	0	0	0	0	0	0	0	0	0	0 (2)	0
Total	**45 (23)**	**19**	**0 (3)**	**0**	**3 (5)**	**4**	**18 (10)**	**4**	**0 (1)**	**0**	**66 (42)**	**27**

the Czech forward played significantly less under the new manager. Towards the end of January 2008 he was unveiled as a Portsmouth player, initially on loan until the end of the season. Baros helped Portsmouth reach the FA Cup final and he received a winners' medal after coming on as a substitute for Kanu with three minutes remaining against Cardiff

City. However, he hadn't impressed Harry Redknapp enough to sign him permanently and he returned to Lyon after failing to score in 16 appearances for Pompey.

BAROS joined Harry Kewell at Turkish giants Galatasaray in the summer of 2008. He enjoyed a very successful first season in Turkey, scoring 20 goals from

31 league games. This was the highest total of league goals he had scored in a single season since becoming a professional footballer. He scored a total of

61 goals in 116 matches in Turkey. In February 2013 the 31-year-old returned to Banik Ostrava, where he started his career.

FACTFILE

BORN
Valasske Mezirici,
Czech Republic,
28 October 1981
POSITION
Centre-forward
OTHER CLUBS
Banik Ostrava (1998–2001),
Aston Villa (2005–07),
Lyon (2007–08),
Portsmouth (loan, 2008),
Galatasaray (2008–13),
Banik Ostrava (2013),
Antalyaspor (2013–)
SIGNED FROM
Banik Ostrava, £3.2million,
26 July 2001
INTERNATIONAL CAPS
93 Czech Republic caps
(41 goals) (38 (23) at LFC),
2001–12
LFC DEBUT GAME/GOAL
13 March 2002 /
14 September 2002
CONTRACT EXPIRY
23 August 2005
HONOURS
League Cup 2003;
Champions League 2005

Barragan, Antonio

SPANISH RIGHT-BACK Antonio Barragan was raised by Sevilla, but before he had even come close to making his first-team debut he refused a contract offer from the club, as Liverpool had been preparing his transfer for the previous six months. Liverpool made use of FIFA rules regarding young players who did not have professional contracts and paid a compensation fee of £240,000.

LIVERPOOL had high hopes for Barragan but he was rather surprisingly sold after just one year and one appearance back to his homeland. Barragan played 26 league games in two seasons for Deportivo La Coruna before joining Real Valladolid in the summer of 2009 after being out with a serious knee injury throughout 2008/09. He played 39 league games in two years for Valladolid but the club was relegated in his first season to Spain's second division. His career was on the rise again when he joined Valencia in August 2011.

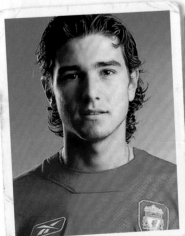

LIVERPOOL HAD
HIGH HOPES
FOR BARRAGAN

FACTFILE

BORN
Sevilla, Spain 12 June 1987
POSITION
Right-back
OTHER CLUBS
Deportivo La Coruna (2006–09),
Real Valladolid (2009–12),
Valencia (2012–)
SIGNED FROM
Sevilla (youth), £240,000,
4 July 2005
INTERNATIONAL CAPS
1 Spain U-21 cap
LFC DEBUT GAME
10 August 2005
CONTRACT EXPIRY
3 August 2006

Season	League		FA Cup		League Cup		Europe		Other		Total	
	App	Goals	App	Goals	App	Goals	App	Goals	App	Goals	App	Goals
2005/06	0	0	0	0	0	0	0 (1)	0	0	0	0 (1)	0
Total	0	0	0	0	0	0	0 (1)	0	0	0	0 (1)	0

Barton, Harold

HAROLD BARTON made 12 appearances by the end of his debut season, in 1929/30, when Liverpool finished a disappointing 12th. Although he was overlooked for the first dozen or so fixtures the following season, he was a regular in the side from November 1930 onwards.

The 1932/33 season was his most productive as he scored 13 from 36 matches, including a hat-trick when Liverpool crushed league champions Everton 7-4 at Anfield on 11 February 1933. The 11 goals scored in that game is easily the highest aggregate ever in a Merseyside derby.

IN 1934 Barton left for Sheffield United, who had just been relegated to the Second Division, and played at Bramall Lane until World War Two. Barton scored 47 goals in 203 matches for the Blades and was in the United side that lost 1-0 to Arsenal in the 1936 FA Cup final.

> THE 1932/33 SEASON WAS HIS MOST PRODUCTIVE AS HE SCORED 13 FROM 36 MATCHES

FACTFILE

BORN
Leigh, Lancashire,
30 September 1911
DIED
1969
POSITION
Right/left-winger
OTHER CLUBS
Sheffield United (1934–39);
Bradford City, Chesterfield,
Lincoln, Rotherham United,
Sheffield Wednesday
(wartime guest)
SIGNED FROM
Whitegate Juniors (youth),
November 1928
LFC DEBUT GAME/GOAL
9 October 1929
/ 7 February 1931
CONTRACT EXPIRY
June 1934

Season	League		FA Cup		Total	
	App	Goals	App	Goals	App	Goals
1929/30	12	0	0	0	12	0
1930/31	26	4	0	0	26	4
1931/32	24	8	4	4	28	12
1932/33	35	13	1	0	36	13
1933/34	6	0	1	0	7	0
Total	**103**	**25**	**6**	**4**	**109**	**29**

Bartrop, Wilf

FACTFILE

BORN
Worksop, 22 November
1887
DIED
7 November 1918
POSITION
Right-winger
OTHER CLUBS
Worksop Town (1907–09),
Barnsley (1909–14);
Nottingham Forest
(wartime guest)
SIGNED FROM
Barnsley, 13 May 1914
LFC DEBUT GAME
19 December 1914
CONTRACT EXPIRY
1915

WILF BARTROP started his career at Worksop Town in the Midland League and joined Second Division Barnsley on 21 June 1909. His stay at Barnsley was an interesting one. In his first season Barnsley reached the FA Cup final, losing 2-0 in a replay against Newcastle United.

He was almost relegated in the 1910/11 season and then reached Wembley again in 1912. This time Barnsley were victorious against West Bromwich Albion in another replayed final, scoring the game's only goal in extra time.

BARTROP played 186 matches and scored 17 goals for the Yorkshire club before he joined Liverpool

> BARTROP MADE JUST THREE LEAGUE APPEARANCES FOR LIVERPOOL DURING THE SEASON IN WHICH WORLD WAR ONE BROKE OUT

with team-mate Phil Bratley in May 1914. The pair had impressed when Barnsley faced the Reds in the first round of the FA Cup the previous January. Bartrop made just three league appearances for Liverpool during the season in which World War One broke out.

He joined the Royal Field Artillery as a gunner in a trench mortar battery and was killed in action in Belgium on 7 November 1918, four days before the Armistice.

Season	League		FA Cup		Total	
	App	Goals	App	Goals	App	Goals
1914/15	3	0	0	0	3	0
Total	**3**	**0**	**0**	**0**	**3**	**0**

Battles,
Bernard
'Barney'

BERNARD 'Barney' Battles had gained quite a reputation for himself in Scotland after winning the Scottish championship for two seasons running with Hearts and Celtic.

He was loaned to Liverpool at the end of the 1895/96 season, where he featured in two Second Division games and played in three of the four 'Test' matches which decided the promotion and relegation issues of the day. Liverpool were promoted and for his six weeks' loan he received a special gold medal and a cheque for a 'handsome sum'.

Liverpool had previously tried to get him on loan from Hearts for a Test match against Bury in the 1894/95 season. Hearts didn't release him or his team-mate Bill Michael, who Liverpool tried to get on loan as well, and the Reds were relegated.

> LIVERPOOL WERE PROMOTED AND FOR HIS SIX WEEKS' LOAN HE RECEIVED A SPECIAL GOLD MEDAL AND A CHEQUE FOR A 'HANDSOME SUM'

BATTLES WAS A PLAYER of heavyweight proportions, but made up for his girth by his enthusiasm and fearless nature. He read the game well and was a popular player. He rejoined Tom Watson's Liverpool in March 1898, prompting this verse:

> *Ben Battle was a soldier bold*
> *And used to war alarms;*
> *Barney Battles, Dundee's half-back,*
> *Not proof against Watson's charms*

Barney only made one appearance in a 2-2 draw at Anfield against Bury on 31 March 1898 before moving back to Celtic for his second spell at the Glasgow club in October 1898, again inspiring a poetic verse:

> *Back to the Celtic again*
> *Let us join in the happy refrain*
> *Out with your rattles*
> *For Big Barney Battles*
> *Is back with the Celtic again!*

Battles impressed the Scotland selectors with his performances for Celtic and he was picked for three Home Internationals in 1901 as well as featuring for the Scottish League.

ALAS, HIS LIFE was to end in tragedy and Battles was diagnosed with influenza after playing for Kilmarnock at Ibrox on 21 January 1905. The flu developed into pneumonia and he died at his home in Glasgow's Gallowgate on 9 February 1905, at the age of only 29. No fewer than 40,000 people lined the route to Dalbeth cemetery at his funeral. The income from the stands at the Scotland–Ireland match at Celtic Park on 18 March 1905, a total of £150, was donated by host club Celtic to the grieving Battles family in tribute to their former player. His wife was pregnant at the time and the boy she gave birth to, Barney Jr, went on to

play for Scotland and while at Hearts was top scorer of the 1930/31 Scottish league season with 44 goals.

FACTFILE

BORN
Springburn, Glasgow, Scotland, 13 January 1876
DIED
9 February 1905
POSITION
Left-back / Right-half
OTHER CLUBS
Broxburn (1891–92),
Bathgate (1892–94),
Hearts (1894–95),
Celtic (1895–97),
Dundee (1897–98),
Celtic (1898–1903),
Kilmarnock (1904–05)
SIGNED FROM
Celtic (on loan), March 1896
/ Dundee, £20, 28 March 1898
INTERNATIONAL CAPS
3 Scotland caps, 1901
LFC DEBUT
21 March 1896
CONTRACT EXPIRY
April 1896 / October 1898

Season	League		FA Cup		Other		Total	
	App	Goals	App	Goals	App	Goals	App	Goals
1895/96	2	0	0	0	3	0	5	0
1897/98	1	0	0	0	-	-	1	0
Total	**3**	**0**	**0**	**0**	**3**	**0**	**6**	**0**

Beadles, Harry

HARRY BEADLES' background is an interesting one. Due to economic circumstances he was forced to leave school aged 12 to work at Pryce Jones Welsh Warehouse, Newtown, as a furrier and hosier.

When war broke out he enlisted in August 1914 and a year later, while serving as rifleman in Gallipoli, Turkey, he was awarded the Serbian Gold Medal for 'Gallantry'. A Serbian observer officer had been wounded in no-man's land and, despite heavy artillery fire, Beadles saved his life. After the war Beadles' regiment was left in Palestine until mid-1919, where he displayed his football skills, being a part of the 7th Royal Welsh Fusiliers who won the British Forces (Egypt) Football League Cup Final in 1919.

Beadles returned to Newtown after the war and played for his local club from 1919 to 1920 until he moved to Merseyside, where he played for an amateur side in Liverpool, Grayson's of Garston, that represented a local shipping company. Beadles was officially employed by the firm, clocking on and off each day and being paid despite only making the tea! It appeared they were more interested in his footballing skills.

In May 1921 he and team-mate Danny Shone were signed by Liverpool. Forward Beadles started well at Liverpool, scoring six goals in 11 games as Liverpool won the League Championship for the first time in 16 years. Liverpool's side was immensely strong at this time and Beadles never fully established himself.

In August 1924, Beadles joined his old army buddy and mentor from the Fusiliers, George Latham, who was coach at Cardiff City and incidentally a former Liverpool player. Beadles was part of the Cardiff team that lost 1-0 to Sheffield United in the 1925 FA Cup final. Cardiff succeeded in winning the FA Cup by beating Arsenal 1-0 in April 1927, but Beadles was not part of that victorious side, as due to lack of funds he had been sold to Sheffield Wednesday in late November 1925. Beadles only made Wednesday's reserves and joined Southport in the Third Division

HARRY BEADLES
RIFLEMAN

North nine months later. He was captain and top scorer in each of his three seasons there, scoring 66 goals in 102 appearances.

A knee injury curtailed his career and in July 1929 he moved to Ireland to play for and coach Dundalk, which proved to be his final club.

FROM 1939 BEADLES was a hotelier at the Hillside in Huyton, Liverpool. In the late 1940s he ran a pub, the Cannon, near Anfield where he enjoyed the banter with the Liverpool and Everton fans. He also attended matches at Anfield, queuing up and paying to stand on the Kop alongside other supporters.

A SERBIAN OBSERVER OFFICER HAD BEEN WOUNDED IN NO-MAN'S LAND AND, DESPITE HEAVY ARTILLERY FIRE, BEADLES SAVED HIS LIFE

Season	League		FA Cup		Other		Total	
	App	Goals	App	Goals	App	Goals	App	Goals
1921/22	11	6	0	0	1	0	12	6
1922/23	4	0	0	0	-	-	4	0
1923/24	2	0	0	0	-	-	2	0
Total	**17**	**6**	**0**	**0**	**1**	**0**	**18**	**6**

Beardsley, Peter

PETER BEARDSLEY established himself at Third Division Carlisle United in the 1979/80 season having been rejected by Newcastle as well as a host of other clubs that didn't believe in the talents of this quiet and unassuming lad. Beardsley made an audacious move to Canadian team Vancouver Whitecaps, where he impressed Manchester United manager Ron Atkinson in a friendly in Canada and joined United in September 1982. He only featured in a single League Cup game before moving back to the Whitecaps after six months.

In September 1983 22-year-old Beardsley was on the move again, this time to his home-town club, Newcastle United, for only £150,000, arguably the best business the Northeast club has ever done. Kevin Keegan's leadership in his final season as a player inspired Chris Waddle and Beardsley to greater heights and the diminutive forward scored 20 goals as Newcastle were promoted to the First Division after a six-year absence. The Magpies remained in the lower half of the top flight during the rest of Beardsley's first spell at the club.

Beardsley's international career blossomed in the World Cup in Mexico in 1986 when he eventually started in England's third game of the finals against Poland after the team had struggled for goals in its first two games. He had only made his international debut five months earlier. Beardsley was a perfect partner for goalscorer supreme Gary Lineker, who scored a hat-trick against the Poles. Paraguay were beaten 3-0 in the following game with a Lineker brace and a Beardsley goal.

England finally succumbed in the quarter-finals to a Maradona-inspired Argentina. Beardsley also featured in the disastrous 1988 European Championships and the 1990 World Cup finals, in which England lost to West-Germany in the semi-finals.

IN 1987 BEARDSLEY had 12 months of his contract to run and Newcastle manager Willie McFaul said unless he signed a new three-year deal the club was ready to let him go. Liverpool had sold Ian Rush to Juventus for £3.2million and were willing to spend more than half of that on the Geordie. Beardsley agreed terms with Liverpool inside an hour and the club paid a British record fee of £1.9million for his services.

During the triumphant 1987/88 season the Reds destroyed the opposition with the attacking trio of Barnes, Beardsley and Aldridge, going 29 games unbeaten on their way to the title, which Liverpool clinched with Beardsley's goal at Anfield against Spurs with four matches to go. Beardsley, who had by his own admittance struggled and felt like an 'expensive passenger' for the first half of the season, scored 18 goals in 48 appearances by his debut campaign's end and earned rave reviews. He was a true wizard with the ball and his dip of the shoulder to fool the opposition became a favourite among the fans.

In the 1988/89 season Beardsley contributed 12 goals but a final-day 2-0 defeat to Arsenal robbed the Reds of the title a few weeks after the Hillsborough disaster. The League Championship was reclaimed in 1989/90 with Beardsley playing an important role, but he missed the last seven matches of the season due to a stress fracture of the knee diagnosed following the astounding 4-3 defeat to Crystal Palace in the FA Cup semi-final. The genial Geordie was taken

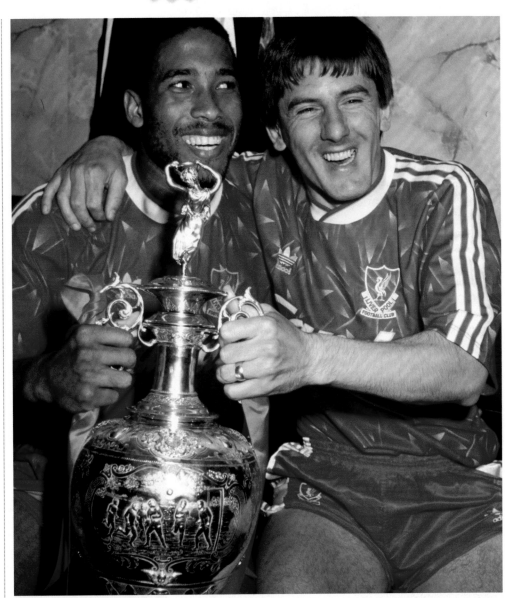

by surprise in the summer when Dalglish told him that Marseille had made a £3.6million offer for his services. Beardsley was concerned because he felt Liverpool were ready to do business, but he didn't want to uproot his young family.

BEARDSLEY was dropped on occasion and substituted once too often for his own liking in the 1990/91 season, but he didn't let his standards drop and kept his disappointment to himself. He made the ideal start to the season by scoring the winner against Arsenal in the Charity Shield. He scored a memorable hat-trick against Manchester United at Anfield on 16 September

and a brace at Goodison Park six days later. Beardsley was out for six weeks after he tore ligaments in his ankle in Steve McManaman's senior debut against Sheffield United on 15 December 1990. He had been a substitute four games running when he was finally back into the starting line-up following his injury and scored two goals in a thrilling 4-4 FA Cup draw at Goodison Park, which turned out to be Dalglish's final game as manager in his first spell at the club. Rumours of a great rift between Dalglish and Beardsley in the 1990/91 season were later put to rest: 'I never fell out with Kenny other than being devastated at being left out of the team,'

Beardsley said in 1999. 'Kenny is a good friend. I got involved in his wife Marina's charity last year, we played in a charity game together against Celtic and Kenny played in my testimonial. If I had any problem with him I wouldn't have invited him. It is wrong for people to say we fell out.'

GRAEME SOUNESS took over and it soon became apparent Beardsley wasn't to his liking, as he regretfully remembers: 'There was no way I would have asked to leave Liverpool, I was really enjoying my time there but Souness wanted me out.' Souness spent a then-record £2.9million fee on Dean Saunders from Derby County in July 1991, which

'THE CROWD STARTED TO CHANT, "WHAT A WASTE OF TALENT!"

Becton, Frank

IN 1891 Frank Becton joined the famous Preston North End 'Invincibles' team that had won the title in the first two seasons of the Football League. Becton never won the league with the Deepdale club, instead finishing runners-up three seasons running from 1891–93 before sliding down the league ladder. His best season was 1892/93 when he was top scorer at the club with 25 goals in the league and FA Cup.

Becton netted twice on his international debut for England in a 9-0 win over Ireland on 9 March 1895 but then shocked his employers by demanding a hefty pay rise. He claimed Aston Villa, Manchester City and Bolton Wanderers were interested in his services. Preston sold him for the quite substantial sum of £100 to Liverpool. He scored four goals from only five appearances by the end of that season but could not prevent Liverpool's relegation. However, Becton, George Allan and Jimmy Ross scored a total of 66 goals as Liverpool bounced straight back into the top flight.

On Liverpool's return to the First Division Becton got into serious trouble with Liverpool's management when he failed to turn up for training in October 1896. He was instantly relegated to the reserves, having played regularly up to that point, and matters went as far as Liverpool wanting to sell him for his insubordination. The *Cricket and Football Field* complimented Liverpool on their actions: 'Rules must be observed, Frank, and your friends feel sure that your place in the League team is yours by right if you only act ditto,' the paper said. 'A firm hand

prompted Everton, who intended to sign Saunders, to go for their second choice, Beardsley, for one-third of Saunders' fee.

'Howard Kendall revealed that even in his wildest dreams he didn't think that Liverpool would make me available to Everton, but he tried his luck and the gamble paid off,' Beardsley recalled. 'He was shocked when Liverpool said yes to his offer and I was surprised too, but that's life.'

Evertonians cherished Beardsley for two years, where he played 95 games and scored 32 goals and proved that Liverpool sure could have used his talents during the Souness regime. A personal highlight for Beardsley was when he returned to Anfield for his first game in a Blues' shirt on 31 August 1991. 'Just before the game the Kop chanted my name and I don't suppose that's happened too many times, an Everton player getting his name chanted by the Kop. But during the game, with Liverpool winning, the crowd started to chant, "What a waste of talent!" The Kop were a bit special to me on that day and I won't ever forget it.'

In July 1993 Beardsley rejoined his beloved Newcastle, where Kevin Keegan was now manager. Newcastle had just been promoted

to the Premier League after winning the First Division and Beardsley played brilliantly, scoring 25 goals in all competitions to go along with Andy Cole's 41 as the Magpies finished third. Newcastle finished sixth the following year and lost the title to Manchester United after dropping a 12-point lead in the 1995/96 season. Beardsley's disappointment was made even greater when he was axed from England's European Championship squad. Dalglish took over at Newcastle mid-season and the club had to settle again for second-best in the League. Beardsley brought his second spell at St James' Park to an end in August 1997, at 36 years of age, having added 157 games and 56 goals to bring his total for Newcastle to 321 games and 117 goals.

BEARDSLEY went from one club to another, desperate to lengthen his career, even rejoining Keegan at Fulham, but after a single season at Hartlepool United during which he just escaped the drop to the Conference, he ended his sensational league career.

Beardsley was awarded a testimonial by Newcastle in January 1999 and has since been part of the club's coaching staff in two spells, and was promoted to reserve team coach in July 2010.

In October 2011 Beardsley was appointed as football development manager at Newcastle, a role that will see him help drive recruitment on a local, national and global scale, and fly the flag for the Magpies around the world.

FACTFILE

BORN
Newcastle upon Tyne, 18 January 1961
POSITION
Forward
OTHER CLUBS
Carlisle United (1977–81), Vancouver Whitecaps (1981–82), Carlisle United (loan, 1981–82), Manchester United (1982–83), Vancouver Whitecaps (1983), Newcastle United (1983–87), Everton (1991–93), Newcastle United (1993–97), Bolton Wanderers (1997–98), Manchester City (loan, 1998), Fulham (1998), Hartlepool United (1998–99), Melbourne Knights (1999)
SIGNED FROM
Newcastle United, £1.9million, 14 July 1987
INTERNATIONAL CAPS
59 England caps (9 goals) (34 (6) at LFC), 1986–96
LFC DEBUT GAME/GOAL
15 August 1987 / 29 August 1987
CONTRACT EXPIRY
5 August 1991
HONOURS
League Championship 1987/88, 1989/90; FA Cup 1989

Season	League		FA Cup		League Cup		Other		Total	
	App	Goals	App	Goals	App	Goals	App	Goals	App	Goals
1987/88	36 (2)	15	7	3	3	0	-	-	46 (2)	18
1988/89	33 (4)	10	5	2	6	0	3	0	47 (4)	12
1989/90	27 (2)	10	8	4	2 (1)	1	1	1	38 (3)	16
1990/91	24 (3)	11	2 (3)	2	2	0	1	0	29 (6)	13
Total	**120 (11)**	**46**	**22 (3)**	**11**	**13 (1)**	**1**	**5**	**1**	**160 (15)**	**59**

> LIVERPOOL WANTED TO SELL HIM FOR HIS INSUBORDINATION

is naturally expected to rule well nowadays, and the example meted out to one of their best forwards may act as a deterrent to others who would do likewise.'

Becton was a popular player, with many clubs interested, so an auction took place that started with Manchester City's bid of £150 being rejected out of hand. Wolves offered £250, which Liverpool accepted, but Becton refused to join them, preferring Aston Villa who were ready to offer £250 as well. However, Liverpool were not keen on doing business with Villa because of an earlier dispute between the clubs that hadn't been resolved. An impasse had been reached but in the end the player and club settled their differences and Becton returned to the Liverpool first team in December and featured regularly for the rest of the season.

BECTON played two years with Liverpool in the First Division before finally moving to league champions Sheffield United in 1898. The Blades won the FA Cup before finishing second in the league the following season. Becton moved back to Preston in the 1900/01 season but the glory days were all gone at Deepdale and as his local club was relegated he joined Swindon Town in the Southern League. He was instrumental in keeping Swindon in the top flight of their league as he scored two goals in the Test match at the end of his first season. He stayed another year and scored

a total of 15 goals in 60 games. Frank's brothers, Martin and Tom, were both professional footballers and played for Preston North End as well. Frank died of tuberculosis aged only 36 on 6 November 1909.

Season	League		FA Cup		Other		Total	
	App	Goals	App	Goals	App	Goals	App	Goals
1894/95	5	4	0	0	0	0	5	4
1895/96	24	18	2	1	4	0	30	19
1896/97	20	5	5	1	-	-	25	6
1897/98	21	11	5	2	-	-	26	13
Total	**70**	**38**	**12**	**4**	**4**	**0**	**86**	**42**

FACTFILE

BORN
Preston, 28 October 1873
DIED
6 November 1909
POSITION
Inside left-forward
OTHER CLUBS
Fishwick Ramblers (1889–91),
Preston North End (1891–95),
Sheffield United (1898–99),
Bedminster (1899–1900),
Preston North End (1900–01),
Swindon Town (1901–03),
Nelson (1903),
Ashton Town (1903–04),
Oldham Athletic (1904)
SIGNED FROM
Preston North End, £100,
18 March 1895
INTERNATIONAL CAPS
2 England caps (2 goals)
(1 at LFC), 1895–97
LFC DEBUT GAME/GOAL
25 March 1895 /
25 March 1895
CONTRACT EXPIRY
October 1898
HONOURS
Second Division
Championship 1895/96

Beeby, Augustus

The 5ft 10in (178cm) goalkeeper with the strange-sounding name made 16 appearances for Liverpool during the 1909/10 and 1910/11 seasons, making his debut away to Woolwich Arsenal two days after Christmas in 1909. Beeby got a chance due to Sam Hardy's damaged wrist at the start of the following season, as well as for a second spell during November and December when Hardy was out again. Unfortunately for him Liverpool were going through a rather lean spell and he kept just one clean sheet as they lost seven out of the 11 games in which he featured in 1910/11.

Season	League		FA Cup		Total	
	App	Goals	App	Goals	App	Goals
1909/10	5	0	0	0	5	0
1910/11	11	0	0	0	11	0
Total	**16**	**0**	**0**	**0**	**16**	**0**

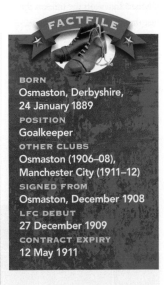

FACTFILE

BORN
Osmaston, Derbyshire,
24 January 1889
POSITION
Goalkeeper
OTHER CLUBS
Osmaston (1906–08),
Manchester City (1911–12)
SIGNED FROM
Osmaston, December 1908
LFC DEBUT
27 December 1909
CONTRACT EXPIRY
12 May 1911

Beglin,
Jim

YOUNG JIM BEGLIN was destined to join Arsenal in spring 1983 when the deal mysteriously fell through, but only a few days later he joined Liverpool on a month's loan. Only 10 days into his stay he became Bob Paisley's last signing in May 1983.

The 21-year-old got his big break in April 1985 due to Alan Kennedy's injury and even scored on his European debut with a bullet header in the semi-finals of the European Cup against Panathinaikos. The final at the Heysel Stadium in Brussels against Juventus, in which Beglin played, proved to be one of the blackest days in the club's history.

Kenny Dalglish took over from Joe Fagan and initially Kennedy reclaimed his place, with Beglin moved to the left side of midfield. Kennedy was allowed to move to Sunderland in September 1985, which showed how much faith was put in the promising Irishman. Beglin became Dalglish's first-choice left-back for the rest of the season and played a major part in the boss's winning goal against Chelsea that won the title on the last day of the 1985/86 season.

The double was sealed against rivals Everton at Wembley a week later, where for one heated moment Beglin became the centre of attention. 'The ball was running along the line and Bruce [Grobbelaar] was shouting for me to let it run, but I was thinking, if I let it run, Trevor Steven's

going to get on it,' Beglin recalled in the *LFC Magazine*. 'Bruce timed his jump thinking I was going to do as he said, but in the meantime I'd put my foot on it and I had to shield it before he got back. He got a bit panicked about it all and once he'd got the ball, he called me something unrepeatable. I told him where to go and he hit me. I thought I've got to hit him back, then you realise the occasion, and of course, Bruce was a jungle fighter, so it was probably best to leave it.'

Bob Paisley was impressed by his progress: 'He has the ideal build for a full-back. He's a strong kicker of the ball. He's naturally left-footed. He has bags of guts and determination but above all, he wants to improve. And if they're prepared to listen, then we're prepared to tell them.'

Beglin's Liverpool career came to an abrupt end when he suffered a horrific leg-break after a tackle by Everton's Gary Stevens at Goodison Park on 21 January 1987. 'I knew it was bad,' he recalled. 'The play seemed to carry on for eternity for me, but it was probably just a few seconds. I looked down and I couldn't believe where my foot was, but I knew it was where it shouldn't be, adjacent to my shin. The pain was a nightmare.' Paisley was horrified by Beglin's break: 'I've seen one or two broken legs in going on fifty years in the game, but not one made me really wince; Jim's did.'

> 'HE HAS BAGS OF GUTS AND DETERMINATION BUT ABOVE ALL, HE WANTS TO IMPROVE'
> **BOB PAISLEY**

BEGLIN LEFT LIVERPOOL in the summer of 1989 to rebuild his career at Leeds United. Only a few days into the pre-season his right knee gave way. Another operation followed and then he was loaned out to Plymouth Argyle. He returned to Leeds and featured in a few games as the club conquered the Second Division. Beglin wasn't confident his knee would stand the strain but was desperate to get his career back on track. He was loaned out to Blackburn in October 1990, but after playing for Leeds on 19 December 1990 Beglin had to accept defeat. 'My right knee was like a time bomb waiting to explode and eventually it did.' He retired from the game in 1991 and has since become known as a TV pundit.

FACTFILE

BORN
Waterford, Ireland,
29 July 1963

POSITION
Left-back / Left-winger

OTHER CLUBS
Shamrock Rovers (1980–83),
Leeds United (1989–91),
Plymouth Argyle (loan, 1989),
Blackburn Rovers (loan, 1990)

SIGNED FROM
Shamrock Rovers, £20,000,
May 1983

INTERNATIONAL CAPS
15 Ireland caps, 1984–86

LFC DEBUT GAME/GOAL
10 November 1984 /
10 April 1985

CONTRACT EXPIRY
28 July 1989

HONOURS
League Championship
1985/86;
FA Cup 1986

Season	League		FA Cup		League Cup		Europe		Other		Total	
	App	Goals	App	Goals	App	Goals	App	Goals	App	Goals	App	Goals
1984/85	10	1	2	0	0	0	3	1	0	0	15	2
1985/86	34	1	7	0	7	0	-	-	5	0	53	1
1986/87	20	0	1	0	6	0	-	-	3	0	30	0
Total	**64**	**2**	**10**	**0**	**13**	**0**	**3**	**1**	**8**	**0**	**98**	**3**

Bellamy,
Craig

CRAIG BELLAMY started his career at Norwich, making his first-team debut in the 1996/97 season. He alerted bigger clubs to his ability by scoring 13 goals in 38 games in his first full season and making his Wales debut. He scored 19 goals in 43 games the following season and after an injury-hit 1999/2000 was sold for a club record fee of £6.5million to replace Robbie Keane at Coventry.

His former manager in the Welsh international side, Bobby Gould, had great faith in the youngster. 'Bellamy is a terrific talent with tremendous flair and ability,' he said. 'He's a philosopher and disciple of the game, and travels all over Europe at his own expense, watching the top clubs and learning from the best players. I was telling Premiership managers three years ago to go out and buy him, so I think it's a great signing.' The Sky Blues were relegated from the Premier League in his only season but luckily for Bellamy Newcastle were fully aware of his talent.

Bellamy spent the next four years at Newcastle and was voted PFA Young Player of the Year in his debut 2001/02 season. His boss Bobby Robson described him as 'a great player wrapped round an unusual and volatile character.' Knee problems curtailed his career at the Magpies and Bellamy was even worried that he might never overcome them. He still managed to play 128 games and score 43 goals. After Sir Bobby left Newcastle in 2004 Bellamy had a very public falling-out with his successor, Graeme Souness, who voiced his displeasure in his notes in Newcastle's match programme: 'Craig Bellamy has been a disruptive influence from the

minute I walked into this football club with his attitude to the coaching staff, to me and to his team-mates.' Former assistant manager of Newcastle, Terry McDermott, wasn't a big fan either. 'I've never come across so much hatred and unrest over one person.'

Bellamy was sent on loan to Celtic at the end of January 2005. He scored nine goals in 15 matches in Scotland but Bellamy wasn't interested in a long-term deal. The fiery Welshman joined another fiery Welshman at Blackburn prior to the 2005/06 season. Bellamy flourished under Mark Hughes' guidance, scored 17 goals in 32 games and was considered by many the buy of the season. He had a £6million get-out clause in his contract, which Liverpool took full advantage of, and this lifelong Red joined his idols.

Bellamy was, nevertheless, very inconsistent in his only season in his first spell at Liverpool. He made 33 starts and nine substitute appearances and showed his obvious talents on occasions, but unfortunately the 'highlight' was his Tiger Woods imitation on Liverpool's club trip to Portugal when John Arne Riise faced the angry Welshman and his golf club. Bellamy made light of the incident when celebrating his goal against Barcelona in February 2007 with a mock golf swing.

His international manager, John Toshack, was impressed by Bellamy when commenting on him in November 2006: 'Craig is the nearest thing to Kevin Keegan I have seen in 20 years. For us, he led by example and is a constant threat with his pace and running. He is so like Kevin, my old strike partner at Liverpool. Kevin could turn bad passes into good ones with his determination and running, and Craig does the same.

Their work rates are very similar – Craig just runs and runs, and so did Kevin.'

Bellamy was sold to West Ham United in July 2007, but played with the Hammers for only one and a half seasons where injuries took their toll on him. But despite only managing nine goals in 26 games for 18 months he was sold for a whopping £14million to Manchester City in January 2009.

> HE HAD A £6MILLION GET-OUT CLAUSE IN HIS CONTRACT, WHICH LIVERPOOL TOOK FULL ADVANTAGE OF, AND THIS LIFELONG RED JOINED HIS IDOLS

BELLAMY SCORED four goals in 11 matches in his debut season at Eastlands. He seemed be fairly settled at City, missing only six of the 38 Premier League matches in 2009/10. He endeared himself to the City fans by scoring twice in a league match at Old Trafford, the second making the score 3-3 with time running out (however, there was still enough time for Michael Owen to grab a United winner in added time). In what turned out to be his only full season at City, Bellamy scored 10 goals from 32 Premier League matches as well as boasting eight assists. The Welshman was on the move again, but this time on a season-long loan deal to his home-town club, Cardiff City. He was immediately named club captain, scored 11 goals from 36 matches and proved instrumental with 13 assists in 2010/11. Cardiff's quest to become a Premier League club again ended in disappointment after Reading defeated them in the playoff semi-final.

> BELLAMY WAS ONE OF THE BIG SUCCESS STORIES OF THE SEASON

ON THE LAST DAY of the 2011 summer transfer window, 32-year-old Bellamy made a surprise return to Liverpool five years after he first arrived at Anfield. Bellamy had been granted a free transfer by Manchester City after the club agreed to settle the final year of the player's £90,000-a-week contract, though the compensation did not total the full £4.6million.

Liverpool's Director of Football, Damien Comolli, was pleased with adding Bellamy to Dalglish's squad:

'Both for Kenny and I it was a no-brainer. He has pace, he's a good finisher, he works hard and the timing of his runs is second to none. His work rate is really good and what we really liked is the fact he is so versatile.'

Bellamy was one of the big success stories of the season. He appeared in almost three-quarters of the 51 first-team matches, even though he was rarely asked to play twice in the same week due to his physical condition, having undergone seven knee operations. His strike took the club through to the final of the League Cup, ironically where Liverpool met Cardiff City. In the final he came on as a substitute for Jordan Henderson midway through the second half, applauded by both sets of fans. As Liverpool celebrated the win Bellamy made a point of

going to the Cardiff fans, thanking them for their reception.

He was also a substitute in the FA Cup semi-final against Everton at Wembley and created the winning goal for Andy Carroll, guaranteeing himself a starting place in the final against Chelsea. Bellamy contributed nine goals to the campaign, but failed to score in his last 13 games of which six were 'starts'.

Bellamy left for Cardiff in August 2012 as he wanted to live closer to his children. 'Even after good games I just went home and looked at the bad points. It was just nuts,' Bellamy revealed to the *Daily Mail* in March 2013. 'It must have been hard to be my team-mate but I always managed it by moving on to another club before I ended up driving everybody absolutely nuts. My method was: leave while you

are still being tolerated. This season has been the most enjoyable I have ever had in my career.'

Season	League		FA Cup		League Cup		Europe		Other		Total	
	App	Goals	App	Goals	App	Goals	App	Goals	App	Goals	App	Goals
2006/07	23 (4)	7	0	0	2	0	8 (4)	2	0 (1)	0	33 (9)	9
2011/12	12 (15)	6	2 (2)	1	4 (2)	2	-	-	-	-	18 (19)	9
Total	**35 (19)**	**13**	**2 (2)**	**1**	**6 (2)**	**2**	**8 (4)**	**2**	**0 (1)**	**0**	**51 (28)**	**18**

Benayoun, Yossi

YOSSI BENAYOUN was Israel's most promising player when he joined the famed Ajax academy at the age of 15. He had taken his whole family with him, but some of them pined for their home in Israel. Benayoun had impressed everyone at Ajax and was offered a four-year contract, which he declined for his family's sake, returning to Israel after only one year. He was criticised for returning home so early and local press claimed he would never realise his potential.

> BENAYOUN'S FIRST SEASON AT ANFIELD CAN CERTAINLY BE DESCRIBED AS SUCCESSFUL

Benayoun joined his home-town club, Hapoel Be'er Sheva, and while they were relegated, he starred for the team and scored 15 goals. Benayoun thought he had saved his team from relegation when he scored in the last minute of their final league match, but the other relegation candidates also scored and Benayoun's team went down. A photograph of Benayoun taken right after the game showed his

tearful disappointment. The photo struck the heart of Israel and 'The Kid' was beloved again.

BENAYOUN was transferred to Maccabi Haifa, where he was voted Player of the Year as the club won its first title in seven years in the 2000/01 season, and a year later triumphed in the league again. In 2003, the midfielder was on his way to Racing Santander. Benayoun starred in a struggling Santander side and established a good reputation that Rafa Benítez was very aware of. After 101 league appearances and 21 goals Santander were forced to cash in because of their financial predicament.

West Ham parted with £2.5million for the Israeli playmaker in the summer of 2005. Alan Pardew was fascinated by Benayoun after

he made his Hammers' debut and maybe did him no favours by comparing him to the world's best player at the time. 'He makes you get out of your seat. He is easy on the eye, he lets the ball drift across him like Zidane,' he said. He scored five goals and made seven assists as the Hammers finished a respectable ninth in the 2005/06 season and reached the FA Cup final. Benayoun proved very tricky for Liverpool's defence and his performance certainly played its part in Benítez signing him a year later.

BENAYOUN'S first season at Anfield can certainly be described as successful, as he featured in 47 of Liverpool's 59 competitive matches, but he was introduced as a substitute 21 times, which must have been frustrating. Benítez felt

he was a match winner but more often than to Benayoun's liking he didn't have a place for him in the starting line-up, which he tried to explain: 'I have a lot of confidence in Kuyt, Voronin, Torres and also Crouch. You can't go away with all four strikers. You must leave one behind. To go away with three strikers when we have Benayoun who can play as a second striker, is hard.' Still, 11 goals was a more than satisfactory figure for a man playing as a second striker and included hat-tricks against Besiktas in the Champions League and Havant & Waterlooville in the FA Cup. He had a knack of being 'in the right place at the right time' because no fewer than three of those six goals came when he reacted quickly to shots by his colleagues that had been saved or blocked.

> THE ONLY ENGLISH-BASED PLAYER TO HAVE SCORED HAT-TRICKS IN THE PREMIER LEAGUE, THE CHAMPIONS LEAGUE AND THE FA CUP

Benayoun made further progress in his second season as Liverpool made a championship challenge. His skill on the ball was a joy to behold and his vision second to none but he was still considered mainly an impact player, although he wasn't one to complain. 'With the number of top players we've got, you accept you are not always going to be playing and that you have to give it everything, when your chance comes along,' said Benayoun in March 2009. 'If I found myself going three or four months without setting foot on the pitch, it might be different.'

In total he scored nine times in 42 first-team appearances in the 2008/09 season and had another steady season in 2009/10, starting 29 competitive matches but significantly being replaced in 22 of them. His hat-trick in the early-season Anfield encounter with Burnley created a unique treble, making him the only English-based player to have scored hat-tricks in the Premier League, the Champions League and the FA Cup.

Ironically Benayoun's best ever form in a Liverpool shirt, in the second half of the 2009/10 season, was rewarded with a transfer to Chelsea in the summer of 2010. His move came as a surprise to fans, but Benayoun was clear about his reasons for leaving. 'There is only one reason,' he told the press in July 2011. 'Rafa Benítez. I want Liverpool fans to know the truth and for them to know I made up my mind to leave a long time ago because of Benítez. He never treated me with the respect I deserved. If I played well, I never felt he gave me credit. When I scored, I still expected to be out of the team the next game. And when the fans wanted me to play, Benítez told me he couldn't understand why. On the day before the final game of last season at Hull, Benítez pulled me to one side after training and said: "You will not be in the squad for this game. Thank you for your three years of service, now you can call your agent to do a deal with another club."'

Benayoun's first season back at a London club since 2006/07 was definitely one to forget. A serious Achilles injury kept him out of action for over half the season and although he eventually made a good recovery he only played in seven Premier League matches for Chelsea. Benayoun was loaned to Arsenal in the 2011/12 season, where he played 25 times, scoring six goals. He made six appearances on loan at one of his former clubs, West Ham, during the first half of the 2012/13 season before returning to Chelsea where his old boss, Benítez, was in charge. The club released Benayoun in the summer of 2013.

FACTFILE

BORN
Dimona, Israel, 5 May 1980
POSITION
Attacking midfielder
OTHER CLUBS
Hapoel Be'er Sheva (1995–98), Maccabi Haifa (1998–2002), Racing Santander (2002–05), West Ham United (2005–07), Chelsea (2010–13), Arsenal (loan, 2011–12), West Ham United (loan, 2012)
SIGNED FROM
West Ham United, £5million, 13 July 2007
INTERNATIONAL CAPS
90 Israel caps (24 goals) (14 (4) at LFC), 1998–
LFC DEBUT GAME/GOAL
15 August 2007 / 25 September 2007
CONTRACT EXPIRY
2 July 2010

Season	League		FA Cup		League Cup		Europe		Total	
	App	Goals	App	Goals	App	Goals	App	Goals	App	Goals
2007/08	15 (15)	4	3	3	1 (2)	1	7 (4)	3	26 (21)	11
2008/09	21 (11)	8	0 (1)	0	0	0	5 (4)	1	26 (16)	9
2009/10	19 (11)	6	1 (1)	0	0 (1)	0	9 (3)	3	29 (16)	9
Total	**55 (37)**	**18**	**4 (2)**	**3**	**1 (3)**	**1**	**21 (11)**	**7**	**81 (53)**	**29**

Benítez, Rafael

RAFA BENÍTEZ was not, and nor did he ever claim to be, a great footballer. He was, however, good enough to be part of Real Madrid's youth academy in the early 1970s before playing lower-league Spanish football for clubs Castilla (effectively Real's reserve team), Parla and Linares.

Benítez continued his academic studies whilst playing at this level. At the age of 26, by which time it was clear that he was not going on to have a great professional career as a player, Benítez was invited to join Real Madrid's coaching staff and he managed the club's under 19 and reserve teams as well as becoming assistant manager for the senior team. In 1995 he left Real for unsuccessful spells in La Liga at Valladolid, sacked after two victories in 23 games and Osasuna, sacked after just one victory in the first nine games. He finally had some degree of success when he led unfancied Extremadura into La Liga at the end of the 1997/98 season. Unfortunately, their chances of

FACTFILE

BORN
16 April 1960, Madrid, Spain
OTHER CLUBS
Valladolid (1995-96),
Osasuna (1996),
Extremadura (1997-99),
Tenerife (2000-01),
Valencia (2001-04),
Inter Milan (2010),
Chelsea (2012-13)
Napoli (2013-)
SIGNED FROM
Valencia, 16 June 2004
LFC DEBUT GAME
10 August 2004
CONTRACT EXPIRY
3 June 2010
HONOURS
FA Cup 2006;
Champions League 2005

surviving there were always slim as they had a small squad and a small budget. Defeat in the relegation play-offs saw them return to the Segunda Division and Benítez took one year off in 1999-2000 to study training methods at Manchester United, Arsenal and in Italy. Benítez returned with Tenerife in the Segunda and the Canary Island club were promoted to La Liga in 2000/01 in his first season. The reputation of this relatively unknown manager was rising and it was almost inevitable that bigger clubs who had been following his progress would show an interest.

Valencia had not won the Spanish title since 1971 when 41-year old Rafa Benítez took over from Hector Cuper in June 2001. Valencia had, however, done well in Europe reaching two successive Champions League finals, but failed to win either of them. Valencia only managed fifth place in Cuper's last season, 17 points behind champions Real Madrid. Valencia's fans expected a big-name appointment following Cuper's move to Inter. Benítez wasn't Valencia's first-choice, but probably the board was later relieved that it was turned down by more illustrious names. Valencia fans, who had felt Cuper's approach to the game was too cautious, were soon won over by Benítez when he introduced a more attacking style. Ruben Baraja, Pablo Aimar, Fabian Ayala and captain David Albelda who became the basis of his team had been bought the previous season. However the club's stars; Gaizka Mendieta and Claudio Lopez had left for Lazio. Benítez brought with him two players from Tenerife, Migel Angel Mista, who finished as Valencia's top scorer in 2003/04 with 19 goals and right-back Cristobal Curro Torres. Benítez kicked off his Valencia career in style by beating Real Madrid 1-0 on 25 August 2001. His rotation policy caused a few upsets, sometimes resting his best players, but he was confident his system would get the results. Benítez's tactics earned Valencia their first title in 31 years, winning it by a good margin of seven points over Deportivo La Coruna. Even Real Madrid's famous Galacticos were not on par with Rafa's troops.

Valencia failed to follow up to their title success and finished only fifth in the 2002/03 season, 18 points behind Real Madrid and with 15 points less than the season before. Benítez's first season in the Champions League proved to be a valiant effort, but fell short of his own ambitions. Valencia were paired with Liverpool in the Champions League first group phase. Valencia outplayed Liverpool 2-0 and 1-0, comprehensive wins that caught the attention of the Liverpool hierarchy. Valencia were knocked out in the quarter-finals by Inter on the away goals rule. Benítez began preparations for the 2003/04 season under a cloud. Valencia's Director of Sport, Jesus Pitarch, refused his plea to finance a proven goalscorer and signed instead

against his wishes winger Néstor Canobbio. Benítez was outraged: 'I asked for a sofa and they bought me a standard lamp.' Despite difficulties, Benítez's side was crowned champions with three games to go and he was obviously delighted: 'A month ago it looked pretty hopeless. We were eight points behind Real Madrid. But we never lost focus and knew this was a marathon. The team is a great long-distance runner and maintained a very high rate of form for a long period of time. Two championships in three years isn't easy - especially for a club of Valencia's size.' Valencia also beat Marseille 2-0 in the UEFA Cup final to conclude a very successful season, but Benítez's rift with the club's board hadn't healed. When Liverpool's interest was evident Valencia offered Benítez a better deal, but it was too late. His philosophy seemed to suit Liverpool perfectly: 'My ideas are near to the Milan of Arrigo Sacchi, I like technical and aggressive teams that don't allow the opponents to play. I like teams that play the ball with speed and look to score with as few passes as possible.' Guillem Balague, *Sky Sports*' analyst in Spain and self-confessed Liverpool fan was delighted with Benítez's capture: 'He was at one point obsessed with detail but he has corrected that and improved his relationship with the players. He got rid of the players that he thought weren't with him and has stuck by those who were committed to his style of management. Since then they have reaped the benefits with success both at home and in European competition. His teams might be solid at the back but they are certainly given a licence to attack. He is a studious person and a very scientific coach. I am confident he would be a massive success at Anfield.'

BEFORE BENÍTEZ'S first season in English football had even started in earnest, the new

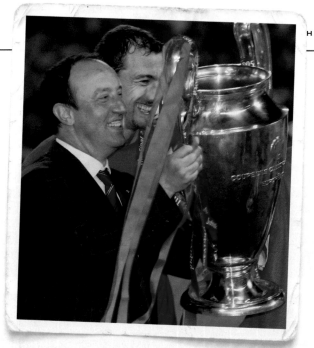

manager had to persuade his captain Steven Gerrard not to move to Chelsea, although a similar attempt to convince Michael Owen to extend his contract proved fruitless, the striker deciding to move to Spain instead. Benítez inherited from Houllier a good squad but it's probably fair to say not a great one. He immediately brought in Luis Garcia and Xabi Alonso from Spain and would in time recruit other players from his homeland. His first league season at Liverpool was a huge disappointment. Eleven of the nineteen away matches were lost and the team eventually finished in fifth place immediately behind their city neighbours Everton. It was the cup competitions that would build momentum as Rafa Benítez's debut season reached a thrilling if unlikely climax. Although humbled by Burnley in the third round of the FA Cup, Liverpool reached the final of the other domestic cup competition before losing to Chelsea after extra-time. In Europe, though, a remarkable journey began in Austria in August. As Liverpool were in Germany to face Bayer Leverkusen in the last 16 in March Benítez ventured out on the town to watch Chelsea – Barcelona live on TV. He went into an Irish bar called Jameson's that was full with Liverpool supporters and his popularity with the fans shot through the roof after that remarkable night. 'We tried to sneak in without anyone noticing and I said to the first fan 'ssshhhh be quiet', but next thing the whole place erupted and everyone was singing 'Rafa-Rafa-Benítez,' he told Liverpool's official website. 'I stayed for about 50 minutes but it was impossible to watch the game after that. All the fans gathered around me, singing, shaking my hand and taking photographs with their mobile telephones. The fans of this club are totally different to those in Spain. They are always singing. And to experience it at

close hand in the pub was just fantastic.' Some of the home legs during that epic run were reminiscent of the great evenings of the past in previous decades. The Anfield crowd immersed itself happily into the euphoric atmosphere of the evenings in particular that saw Olympiacos, Juventus and Chelsea beaten on Merseyside. Benítez proudly held the Champions League trophy aloft in Turkey in May after a truly astonishing final with AC Milan.

It was a hard act to follow but Benítez had quickly cemented himself into the hearts and minds of Liverpool's huge worldwide fan-base. Domestic success followed a year later after an FA Cup final versus West Ham every bit as tense and dramatic as the European final in Istanbul. The team's league form remained inconsistent, not good enough for any sort of serious challenge for the Championship. But on the European stage, Liverpool became the opponent most other clubs both respected and feared. Benítez's tactical awareness was a match for any of his managerial colleagues on the continent. He led Liverpool to the Champions League final for the second time in three years against AC Milan. Liverpool's comeback, however, came too late in Athens. 2007 was also the year in which the American partnership of Tom Hicks and George Gillett arrived on the scene. Money was found to bring in some of the players the manager wanted like Fernando Torres, Yossi Benayoun and Javier Mascherano.

For the first time under his tenure, Benítez led Liverpool to the summit of the Premier League after thrashing Derby County 6-0 on the first day of September 2007. However, European results were not as positive and this led to a public falling-out with the club's owners. The fans showed their public support for a manager whose position was undermined still further by an apparent attempt by the Americans to bring in Jürgen Klinsmann to replace him. A serious power-struggle developed between the club's manager and its Chief Executive as it was no secret that Benítez did not like the influence Rick Parry had over transfer negotiations and contracts. Parry announced in March 2009 that he would be leaving at the end of the season. In the same month Benítez signed a new five-year contract that would take him up to the year 2014. Liverpool ran Manchester United very close for the 2009 Premier League title and hopes were high that Liverpool would go one better in 2010. Alvaro Arbeloa and Xabi Alonso left for Real Madrid in the summer and Sami Hyypia was off to Bayer Leverkusen. 'We had the confidence we could win the league but you have to wheel and deal. You cannot bring in two or three top-class players if you don't have the money,' Benítez told the *Daily Mail* in March 2011 as he reflected on his last season at Liverpool.

'You have to sell. We sold Xabi Alonso and bought Glen Johnson, Alberto Aquilani and Sotirios Kyrgiakos. We had money but I couldn't use it because we had to meet the interest payments. We had one top-class player who was our target, Fiorentina's Stevan Jovetic. As far as I was concerned, we had the money for him in our budget. But then the owners said: 'No, no, we don't have the money.' Then he scored against us in the Champions League to help knock us out! If you have your budget and you know that is happening, fine. But my budget was always given to me as a net figure [after taxes] for wage negotiation. But in the last year it was gross - a massive difference - but I didn't know. No one told me it had changed.'

NINETEEN defeats in all competitions in 2009/10 placed even more strain on an already fractious relationship between manager and owners. Liverpool Football Club was no longer a member of the so-called "Big Four" of English football, the clubs that would regularly compete in the Champions League. The seemingly inevitable parting of the ways finally came to pass on 3 June 2010. Rafa blamed Gillett and Hicks' decision to hire Christian Purslow as managing director for his downfall. 'After 86 points and finishing second in the league, what changed? The Americans, they chose a new managing director and everything changed. The managing director is involved in all the decisions: new lawyer, new chief of press, new manager, nine new players, new medical staff, new fitness coaches – they changed everything.' Benítez has of course to shoulder some of the blame himself as he replaced his playmaker Alonso with a lesser talent in Aquilani who was injured when he arrived at Liverpool and had missed several games in two injury spells the previous season and not featured in a competitive match since March.

BENÍTEZ'S reign ended after six seasons, an era that had begun with the hope and belief that the glory days really were returning to Anfield. Less than a week after being dismissed by Liverpool, Benítez was appointed as head coach of European champions Inter Milan. Benítez's spell in Milan was an unhappy one. Although his team won the Italian Super Cup and the FIFA Club World Cup, poor league form left them at one point thirteen points adrift of the top club. He demanded that his squad would be strengthened with new signings but failed to receive the backing he wanted and was dismissed by Inter two days before Christmas in 2010.

Season	Champions League	Europa League
2004/05	Winners	-
2005/06	3rd Qualifying Rd	-
2006/07	Runners-Up	-
2007/08	Semi-Final	-
2008/09	Quarter-Final	-
2009/10	First Group Phase	Semi-Final

Season	Division	P	W	D	L	GF	GA	Pts	Pos	Win %	FA Cup	League Cup
2004/05	Premier League	38	17	7	14	52	41	58	5	44.74	3rd Round	Runners-Up
2005/06	Premier League	38	25	7	6	57	25	82	3	65.79	Winners	3rd Round
2006/07	Premier League	38	20	8	10	57	27	68	3	52.63	3rd Round	5th Round
2007/08	Premier League	38	21	13	4	67	28	76	4	55.26	5th Round	5th Round
2008/09	Premier League	38	25	11	2	77	27	86	2	65.79	4th Round	4th Round
2009/10	Premier League	38	18	9	11	61	35	63	7	47.37	3rd Round	4th Round
Total		228	126	55	47	371	183	433	-	55.26	-	-

Benítez and his wife, Montse, remained close to several charities on Merseyside and helped the Hillsborough families in their cause for justice. Benítez, who still lived in West Kirby on the Wirral, was clearly hoping to be appointed as Liverpool boss again after Roy Hodgson's dismissal and once again after Dalglish was let go. But, the call never came. After nearly two years without a coaching role, Benítez took over as interim manager at Chelsea. He was not a popular appointment, but he delivered a Champions League spot and the Europa League trophy during his successful spell. Benítez was appointed as manager of Napoli in May 2013.

Bennett,
Reuben

TRAINER REUBEN BENNETT was as hard as they come. The dour Scotsman was Shankly's henchman, a man to his liking who kept the players fit and on their toes. Shankly described him once as the hardest man in the world.

Bennett was born in Aberdeen in December 1913 and was a goalkeeper at Hull City and Queen of the South before he joined Dundee following World War Two. He started his coaching career at Dundee and then served as manager at Ayr United from 1953-55. Following his dismissal from Ayr he trained Motherwell and Third Lanark, working at the latter under Bill Shankly's brother, Bob. Bennett was appointed head coach at Liverpool in December 1958, when Phil Taylor was manager. When Bill Shankly arrived a year later, he chose to keep the club's training staff and thus Bennett became one of the original Bootroom boys along with Bob Paisley and Joe Fagan. Shankly believed if the team was fitter than their opponents it could conquer any obstacle and Bennett made sure his players got away with nothing during training. 'Reuben was hard as nails. He didn't tolerate wimps too much,' former player Willie Stevenson said in Stephen F Kelly's book, *The Boot Room Boys*.

'He considered any feeling of pain or hurt was soft. One time we were in Blackpool. It was really, really cold. We were on the beach playing in snow and the water was iced out to about 30 or 40 feet Anyhow, one of us kicked the ball into the water and Reuben says, 'Go and get it.' We told him to bugger off. So he called us a load of wimps and promptly proceeded to run into the sea, swim out, get the ball and come back and carry on playing. He only had shorts and a T-shirt on. We all had balaclavas, hats, gloves and pullovers.'

Bennett's no-nonsense approach made him a favourite with Shankly and even though he was sometimes ruthless with the players the chain-smoking Scot was pleasing company. 'He was very popular with the players. He used to tell us all these stories from when he was in Scotland, all grossly exaggerated! In the afternoons you'd see him standing outside Anfield in short sleeves when it was ten degrees below,' Roger Hunt said in *The Boot Room Boys*.

WHEN JOE FAGAN was promoted to first-team coach in 1971 the Scot's role changed from head of training to 'special duties'. Amongst other projects he was sent on scouting trips in Europe to spy on Liverpool's opponents, delivering valuable info that allowed Paisley to dominate Europe in his time in charge. Bennett was still part of the Liverpool groundstaff when he died in 1989.

Reuben Bennett was a vital part of the synergy that created the enormous success Liverpool enjoyed since Shankly revived the club. 'There was no animosity between Bob, Bill, Joe Fagan and Reuben Bennett,' said Willie Stevenson. 'That's unusual with four people who were all personalities in their own right to get on so well. That was the most remarkable thing as far as I was concerned.'

> 'HE AND SHANKS WERE BORN OUT OF THE SAME POD, EXACTLY THE SAME MENTALITY'
> **DAVID FAIRCLOUGH**

Bennett,
Tom

TOM BENNETT scored no less than 77 wartime goals in 70 matches for Liverpool.

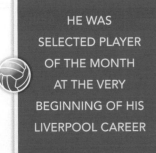
BENNETT SCORED
NO LESS THAN
77 WARTIME GOALS
IN 70 MATCHES

HOWEVER, Bennett's solitary 'official' game for Liverpool came in the ninth match of the 1919/20 season, away to Chelsea, when he replaced Fred Pagnam, who had played in all eight previous matches. Bennett never played for Liverpool again and neither, incidentally, did Pagnam. Bennett was suffering from pleurisy and was awarded a benefit match at Anfield on 27 September 1920 featuring Liverpool against an International XI. At the end of 1920 it was reported that Bennett was thoroughly fit again so he went for a month's trial at Liverpool, but wasn't signed as he had clearly not recovered sufficiently. He made four appearances for Rochdale in 1921, scoring one goal. Bennett died on 11 January 1923 at the early age of 31.

	League		FA Cup		Total	
Season	**App**	**Goals**	**App**	**Goals**	**App**	**Goals**
1919/20	1	0	0	0	1	0
Total	**1**	**0**	**0**	**0**	**1**	**0**

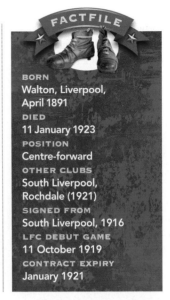

FACTFILE

BORN
Walton, Liverpool,
April 1891
DIED
11 January 1923
POSITION
Centre-forward
OTHER CLUBS
South Liverpool,
Rochdale (1921)
SIGNED FROM
South Liverpool, 1916
LFC DEBUT GAME
11 October 1919
CONTRACT EXPIRY
January 1921

Berger,
Patrik

PATRIK BERGER tasted success at an early age. He was in the Czech Under-16 squad that became European champions in 1990. Berger started on the books of Sparta Prague but their rivals Slavia were quicker to react when Berger was eligible to sign a professional contract at 18. Berger spent four years with Slavia but Sparta dominated the league. He joined Borussia Dortmund in 1995 but although the club won the championship in his only season he was mostly on the bench. Berger didn't like the fact that the coach saw him as a defensive midfielder.

HE WAS
SELECTED PLAYER
OF THE MONTH
AT THE VERY
BEGINNING OF HIS
LIVERPOOL CAREER

Four weeks after the conclusion of the 1996 European Championships in England, where the Czech Republic were runners-up to Germany, Roy Evans signed Berger, who had featured in a more attacking role for his national team. By the beginning of September Berger had shaken off a minor calf problem and his Liverpool career got off to a glorious start. Two shots with his deadly left foot beat Leicester in only his second substitute appearance. 'I've never seen a ball move so fast in my life. It's a good job I didn't get in the way of either shot or I'd have been back in the net with them,' said Leicester goalkeeper, Kasey Keller, still petrified.

BERGER'S FIRST GAME in the starting line-up against Chelsea resulted in two more goals and he was selected Player of the Month at the very beginning of his Liverpool career. He was clearly seen as an out-and-out

striker by Evans, threatening Stan Collymore's place in the team as the ex-Forest striker struggled to recapture the form that had seen him and Fowler score 55 goals the previous season. Berger couldn't keep up his scoring ratio as he had never been a real striker, and finished with nine goals in his first season. On 5 October 1997 he scored a hat-trick in a 4-2 win over Chelsea at Anfield that turned out to be his only goals in the

league that season. Evans was furious when Berger refused to be on the bench for a Premier League game against Bolton on 7 March 1998. 'I only want people who want to play for Liverpool,' Evans raged. 'To involve him would not only be an insult to the other players but to everyone at the club. There's no point of having people on the bench if they are not in the right frame of mind. We're looking for offers for Patrik but he won't be going out on the cheap or on loan. He wants to play all the time but to do that you've got to be consistent.' In the summer of 1998 Berger said he was going to Prague to contemplate his future with Liverpool.

Berger's saviour came in the form of Gérard Houllier that summer. He put him in the first XI behind the strikers and although his first two games in the 1998/99 season were quiet, Berger repaid Houllier's faith in him by scoring four goals in the next five.

FANTASTIC GOALS AGAINST WIMBLEDON, LEEDS UNITED, MANCHESTER UNITED AND TOTTENHAM ARE FOREVER KEPT IN THE MINDS OF LIVERPOOL SUPPORTERS

HIS OVERALL GAME improved and Berger seemed finally settled on Merseyside after making 39 starts that season. Berger's game blossomed at the turn of 2000 and fantastic goals against Wimbledon, Leeds United, Manchester United and Tottenham are forever kept in the minds of Liverpool supporters. Houllier was pleased by his progress as he told the press in April 2000. 'Patrik has scored nine goals for us this season, and he is improving all the time. I would say he has been directly involved in a third of the goals we have scored this season. He has either scored them, created them, been fouled for free kicks, or delivered the free kicks to score. He is a very good midfield player. He likes to run, he likes to do his defensive duties well, and his understanding of the game and his realisation of the needs of his team is getting better. He has a very good partnership with Dominic Matteo. He is willing to work with him and doing his share of the defensive work.'

The 2000 European Championships turned out to be a disappointment for Berger and the Czech Republic. As he had been sent off in a qualifier against the Faroe Islands he had to sit out the first two games of the Euros that ended in defeat against the Netherlands and France, and when he finally made his debut against Denmark it was too late to save the Czechs. Berger was out for five months with a knee ligament injury in the successful 2000/01 season but he made a late cameo in the FA Cup final against Arsenal and set up Michael Owen's winner four minutes from time. Again he played a bit part in the 2001/02 season and at the start of the following season it was clear that his future would lie elsewhere in the summer.

BERGER moved to Portsmouth in 2003 and his impact on the south coast was immediate, as he scored against Aston Villa on the opening day of the season. A few weeks later he scored the winning goal against Liverpool. Early in 2004 he had to undergo knee surgery and his appearances for Portsmouth from then on were limited. He was released by Pompey in June 2005 and joined Aston Villa on a two-year contract. The Czech continued to suffer from injuries in the Midlands and was loaned to Stoke City. After he returned to Villa Park, his general fitness seemed improved. Shortly after the end of the 2006/07 season, Berger signed a one-year extension to his contract but played little football in the subsequent 12 months and alienated his manager Martin O'Neill by advising his club captain, Gareth Barry, to make a move to Liverpool once interest from his former club became known. Berger was fined two weeks' wages and suspended from the training ground.

Once a free agent in 2008 Berger returned to his homeland and at the age of 34 signed a two-year contract with Sparta Prague. Berger retired from football in January 2010 due to persistent knee problems but still features on occasion for Dolni Chabry, a sixth-division side situated in the suburbs of Prague.

'I can't say my Liverpool career has been great. Nor can I say it has been bad,' he said during the 2002/03 season. 'I've had good times, I've had bad times. Actually I have been through everything since I have been at Liverpool. Whatever you can experience, I have experienced.'

FACTFILE

BORN
Prague, Czech Republic,
10 November 1973
POSITION
Forward / Attacking
midfielder / Left-winger
OTHER CLUBS
Slavia Prague (1991–95),
Borussia Dortmund (1995–96),
Portsmouth (2003–05),
Aston Villa (2005–08),
Stoke City (loan, 2006–07),
Sparta Prague (2008–10),
Dolni Chabry
SIGNED FROM
Borussia Dortmund,
£3.25million, 1 August 1996
INTERNATIONAL CAPS
44 Czech Republic caps
(18 goals) (23 (9) at LFC),
1993–2001
LFC DEBUT/GOAL
7 September 1996 /
15 September 1996
CONTRACT EXPIRY
1 July 2003
HONOURS
FA Cup 2001;
UEFA Cup 2001

Season	League		FA Cup		League Cup		Europe		Other		Total	
	App	Goals	App	Goals	App	Goals	App	Goals	App	Goals	App	Goals
1996/97	13 (10)	6	1 (1)	0	3	1	6	2	-	-	23 (11)	9
1997/98	6 (16)	3	0 (1)	0	2 (1)	1	1 (1)	0	-	-	9 (19)	4
1998/99	30 (2)	7	2	0	1	0	6	2	-	-	39 (2)	9
1999/2000	34	9	1	0	1 (1)	0	-	-	-	-	36 (1)	9
2000/01	11 (3)	2	0 (1)	0	1	0	3 (2)	0	-	-	15 (6)	2
2001/02	12 (9)	1	0 (1)	0	1	0	1 (7)	0	0 (1)	0	13 (18)	1
2002/03	0 (2)	0	0	0	1	1	0 (1)	0	0	0	1 (3)	1
Total	**106 (42)**	**28**	**4 (4)**	**0**	**9 (2)**	**3**	**17 (11)**	**4**	**0 (1)**	**0**	**136 (60)**	**35**

Berry, Arthur

ARTHUR BERRY won two gold medals with England in the 1908 and 1912 Olympics. He and Vivian Woodward are the only players to be on both winning teams. He was educated at Denstone, a college famous for its sporting success.

He was the school's cricket captain and tremendously athletic. The school magazine reported: 'Arthur Berry incited the rest of the team to greater keenness by his splendid fielding; as a batsman he seemed able to hit anything and rarely failed to make runs. As a bowler he met with great success, being fast with a deadly swerve. A magnificent fielder, and won the bat offered for this department.' Berry studied law at Oxford and was prominent in the University's team.

His father was Edwin Berry, who was Liverpool's chairman from 1904 to 1909, which led to Arthur's first spell at the club. Arthur played his first reserve game in April 1906 and made his first-team debut in April 1908 when the Reds lost 3-1 to Newcastle. The match programme commented that if amateur Berry 'cares to take to the game seriously he will be an excellent forward,' suggesting he should become a professional. However, Arthur left in September 1909 for Fulham, but he was still living up north and found it difficult to travel to London, so he joined Everton in February 1910. He rejoined Liverpool in June 1912, but only added one appearance to bring his total to four.

As an amateur he featured for a number of teams, utilising his freedom of movement between clubs. Arthur was an FA Amateur Cup winner in 1913 with Oxford City, which was his only club honour. Arthur, still an amateur, retired from football in 1914, served as adjutant of the Lancashire Fusiliers during World War One, then eventually joining the family law firm, which his father headed.

FACTFILE
BORN
Liverpool, 3 January 1888
DIED
15 March 1953
POSITION
Inside-right forward
OTHER CLUBS
Oxford University, Wrexham (six spells from 1907–14), Fulham (1909), Everton (1910–11), Oxford City (1912, 1913–14), Northern Nomads (1914)
JOINED
Oxford University, 1906; Unaffiliated, June 1912
INTERNATIONAL CAPS
1 England cap, 1919; 32 amateur caps (13 goals)
LFC DEBUT
11 April 1908
CONTRACT EXPIRY
September 1909 / 14 November 1912

Season	League		FA Cup		Total	
	App	Goals	App	Goals	App	Goals
1907/08	1	0	0	0	1	0
1908/09	2	0	0	0	2	0
1912/13	1	0	0	0	1	0
Total	4	0	0	0	4	0

Bimpson, Louis

LOUIS BIMPSON
LIVERPOOL

BIG AND STRONG, Louis Bimpson was a handful for defences in the Second Division, rotating between the inside-right position and centre forward. Scoring runs of four goals in five appearances and 11 goals in 16 in seasons 1957/58 and 1958/59 respectively showed he had a knack for delivering the goods.

He was given his debut at Aston Villa on 7 March 1953 and played in seven more league games before the end of the season, scoring three goals. His most productive season for Liverpool was in 1953/54, when he hit the net 12 times in 24 league matches. On his day he could be brilliant: a brace against Manchester United in August 1953 and a four-goal show in the first half against Burnley at Anfield a month later prove that. But he was never considered to be a regular in the side and when Dave Hickson arrived from Goodison in November 1959, Bimpson faded out of the first-team picture altogether and was transferred to Blackburn Rovers two weeks later.

In joining First Division Blackburn, Bimpson took a step up the league ladder, scoring eight goals in 29 matches from 1959 to 1961. He starred in Rovers' cup run in 1960 when he scored in the 4-1 victory over Sunderland in the third round and netted a brace in a 3-1 win at Tottenham in the fifth round. Rovers went all the way to Wembley where Bimpson wore the No. 7 shirt. Rovers struggled on the day, losing 3-0 to Wolverhampton Wanderers in the so-called 'Dustbin final' as Wolves' players were pelted with all kinds of garbage by the Rovers' fans when they were on their victory lap.

FACTFILE
BORN
Rainford, 14 May 1929
POSITION
Centre-forward / Inside-right forward
OTHER CLUBS
Burscough (1951–53), Blackburn Rovers (1959–61), Bournemouth & Boscombe Athletic (1961), Rochdale (1961–63), Wigan Athletic (1963–65), Burscough
SIGNED FROM
Burscough, 28 January 1953
LFC DEBUT GAME/GOAL
7 March 1953 / 3 April 1953
CONTRACT EXPIRY
19 November 1959

Season	League		FA Cup		Total	
	App	Goals	App	Goals	App	Goals
1952/53	8	3	0	0	8	3
1953/54	24	12	0	0	24	12
1954/55	8	2	1	0	9	2
1955/56	8	0	1	0	9	0
1956/57	21	6	0	0	21	6
1957/58	7	4	3	1	10	5
1958/59	15	11	1	0	16	11
1959/60	5	0	0	0	5	0
Total	96	38	6	1	102	39

Biscan,
Igor

WHEN GÉRARD HOULLIER saw the opportunity to snap up Igor Biscan from Dinamo Zagreb in December 2000 to challenge Didi Hamann for the defensive midfielder position he grabbed it with both hands. Biscan arrived in the winter break of the Croatian season but initially struggled to make an impression in a red shirt as Liverpool charged on to a dramatic treble in the 2000/01 season. He did score his first goal in the League Cup semi-final against Crystal Palace at Anfield and featured from the start in the final win over Birmingham.

The 2001/02 and the 2002/03 seasons were a nonstarter for Biscan, but he started 35 games in 2003/04 as Houllier used his versatility, fulfilling a pre-season promise. 'I think he will be playing more this season. He can play at

FACTFILE

BORN
Zagreb, Croatia, 4 May 1978
POSITION
Midfielder / Centre-half
OTHER CLUBS
Dinamo Zagreb (1995–2000),
Samobor (loan, 1997–98),
Panathinaikos (2005–07),
Dinamo Zagreb (2007–12)
SIGNED FROM
Dinamo Zagreb, £5.5million,
7 December 2000
INTERNATIONAL CAPS
17 Croatia caps (1 goal)
(5 (0) at LFC), 1999–2001
LFC DEBUT/GOAL
10 December 2000 /
24 January 2001
CONTRACT EXPIRY
1 July 2005
HONOURS
Champions League 2005;
League Cup 2001, 2003

centre midfield and centre-back. He is strong and powerful and quick. Sometimes he loses the ball when he passes, but then who doesn't? I prefer players who try things,' Houllier said. Biscan had the odd slip-up in the centre of defence as he was paired with Sami Hyypia in the absence of Stephane Henchoz, who was getting rather injury-prone.

RAFA BENÍTEZ took over from Houllier in the summer and he told Biscan to focus on being a midfielder, seemingly to the player's relief. 'My confidence suffered playing at the back but that's not an excuse. I'm aware I took some of the brunt of the fans' frustration but that's not a problem. I suppose the fact I'm playing in central midfield is one of the reasons why I'm playing better,' Biscan explained.

Undoubtedly Biscan's best moments came under Benítez when he solidified his cult hero status on the Kop. He had been told he had no future at Anfield by Rafa in December and would be allowed to leave in the summer when his contract expired, but played his part in the Champions League run that ended in success in Istanbul, most notably away to Deportivo La Coruna in the group phase when he went on a few galloping runs which were reminiscent of absent captain Steven Gerrard. Biscan played from the start against Leverkusen in the last 16, Juventus in the quarter-finals and in the semi-finals against Chelsea but remained on the bench in the final.

LFChistory.net asked Biscan in 2002 what his routine as a professional footballer was like.

'It's quite boring to be honest. Every day is almost the same. Wake up in the morning, go to training, have lunch here at Melwood, rest. I watch television or maybe sleep for an hour and a half or two. Maybe you do something together with your friends, then you go to sleep and wake up to train again the next morning.'

After the Champions League win, Biscan went to Greece to ply his trade with Panathinaikos and after two-and-a-half years the 29-year-old returned to Croatia to take over the captaincy of Dinamo Zagreb. Dinamo were Croatian champions in both 2008 and 2009 as well as lifting the Croatian cup in the same years. Injuries restricted Biscan to only 61 league games in five seasons in Zagreb and he retired in 2012.

EVEN TODAY the chants of 'Igor, Igor, Igor!' and 'Igor Biscan, He is a giant of man, He should be playing for Milan,' can be heard echoing in the pubs surrounding Anfield. Biscan values his time at Liverpool: 'When you play for big clubs you know you'll have good periods and bad periods. If you come through the bad times then that's what makes you a better person and a better player. The Liverpool fans have been great with me. It gives me a really nice feeling and makes me feel special when they chant my name.'

> 'THE LIVERPOOL FANS HAVE BEEN GREAT WITH ME'

Season	League App	League Goals	FA Cup App	FA Cup Goals	League Cup App	League Cup Goals	Europe App	Europe Goals	Other App	Other Goals	Total App	Total Goals
2000/01	8 (5)	0	3 (1)	0	4	1	0	0	-	-	15 (6)	1
2001/02	4 (1)	0	0	0	0	0	1 (3)	0	0 (1)	0	5 (5)	0
2002/03	3 (3)	0	0 (1)	0	2 (1)	0	0 (3)	0	0	0	5 (8)	0
2003/04	27 (2)	0	1	0	2	0	5 (2)	0	-	-	35 (4)	0
2004/05	8 (11)	2	1	0	4 (2)	0	8 (1)	0	-	-	21 (14)	2
Total	**50 (22)**	**2**	**5 (2)**	**0**	**12 (3)**	**1**	**14 (9)**	**0**	**0 (1)**	**0**	**81 (37)**	**3**

Bjørnebye, Stig Inge

**SO BEGINS the fairytale...
Stig Inge Bjørnebye scored the
winning goal in the Norwegian
cup final for Rosenborg. The
following day Liverpool boss,
Graeme Souness, was on the
phone offering him a contract. A
couple of days at the end of 1992
changed his life in an instant.**

Bjørnebye nevertheless had a
baptism of fire when he made his
debut against Coventry City on
19 December 1992. Liverpool lost
5-1 at Highfield Road, which was
the club's biggest defeat in 16
years. The Norwegian struggled
with life in the Premiership in
the first two seasons but his
breakthrough came in the 1994/95
season. Unfortunately he then
suffered a broken leg reaching for
a cross while his studs got caught
in the grass when playing against
Southampton in April 1995.

Due to the injury he only played
two games in the 1995/96 season
but his career hit peak form in
1996/97 when the Reds finally
mounted a serious assault on the
title, although it failed in the last
stages. He delivered pin-point
passes into the penalty area
providing plenty of goals for
Fowler and Collymore and was
voted in the Premier League
Team of the Year.

BJØRNEBYE became one of
Houllier's first casualties when he
overhauled the squad in the
summer of 2000 after he hadn't
featured at all in the previous
season and had been loaned out
to Brøndby for the last couple of
months. He rejoined Souness at
Blackburn and after regaining
his fitness he featured in Rovers'
successful promotion season and
returned to the Premier League,
where he played 23 games in the
2001/02 season before fracturing
his eye-socket in training in April

and had to undergo corrective surgery after complaining about blurred
vision. Although Bjørnebye finally returned seven months later his
comeback against Wigan saw another injury, this time to his foot. When
he was recuperating in Norway he was rushed to hospital and surgeons
were forced to bypass two failing arteries in a five-hour operation to save
his foot from being amputated.

Sadly Bjørnebye was forced to retire from football in March 2003.
Souness was sorry on behalf of the dependable Norwegian: 'It's a very
sad day. As far as I am concerned it could hardly be worse, for Stig is the
consummate dedicated professional. He is as good a professional as any

I have worked with, I couldn't
name anybody better and he is
a fine role model and a proper,
proper human being. Stig has
had a wonderful career, it's a
great shame that it has to end with
a freak training-ground accident
as he felt, quite rightly, that he
could have played longer.'

STIG INGE'S father, Jo Inge,
was a ski jumper, who competed
in the 1968 Winter Olympics
in Grenoble and the 1972 Winter
Olympics in Sapporo.

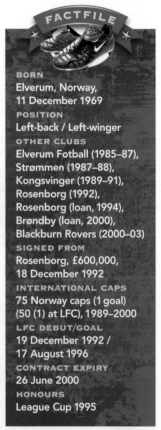

FACTFILE

BORN
Elverum, Norway,
11 December 1969
POSITION
Left-back / Left-winger
OTHER CLUBS
Elverum Fotball (1985–87),
Strømmen (1987–88),
Kongsvinger (1989–91),
Rosenborg (1992),
Rosenborg (loan, 1994),
Brøndby (loan, 2000),
Blackburn Rovers (2000–03)
SIGNED FROM
Rosenborg, £600,000,
18 December 1992
INTERNATIONAL CAPS
75 Norway caps (1 goal)
(50 (1) at LFC), 1989–2000
LFC DEBUT/GOAL
19 December 1992 /
17 August 1996
CONTRACT EXPIRY
26 June 2000
HONOURS
League Cup 1995

Season	League App	League Goals	FA Cup App	FA Cup Goals	League Cup App	League Cup Goals	Europe App	Europe Goals	Other App	Other Goals	Total App	Total Goals
1992/93	11	0	2	0	0	0	0	0	0	0	13	0
1993/94	6 (3)	0	0 (1)	0	0	0	-	-	-	-	6 (4)	0
1994/95	31	0	5 (1)	0	7	0	-	-	-	-	43 (1)	0
1995/96	2	0	0	0	0	0	0	0	-	-	2	0
1996/97	38	2	2	0	4	0	8	2	-	-	52	4
1997/98	24 (1)	0	0	0	3	0	4	0	-	-	31 (1)	0
1998/99	20 (3)	0	2	0	2	0	4	0	-	-	28 (3)	0
Total	**132 (7)**	**2**	**11 (2)**	**0**	**16**	**0**	**16**	**2**	**0**	**0**	**175 (9)**	**4**

Blanthorne, Bob

BOB BLANTHORNE was secured from neighbours Birkenhead in November 1905 and finished as top scorer of Liverpool's reserves with 22 goals in the 1905/06 season.

> TOP SCORER OF LIVERPOOL'S RESERVES WITH 22 GOALS
> **1905/06**

After netting another 17 goals in the following season Blanthorne finally got his chance with the first team, but his two league appearances at the end of 1906/07 against Bristol City and Middlesbrough proved to be his only appearances for the seniors.

THE CHIEF complaint about him at Liverpool was that he lacked 'speed and dash'. Blanthorne looked forward to his challenge at Newcastle, but sadly broke his leg in the opening game of the

1908/09 season, which proved detrimental to the rest of his career. He was out for a season and a half and, having recovered his fitness with Newcastle's reserves, joined Hartlepools United in January 1911.

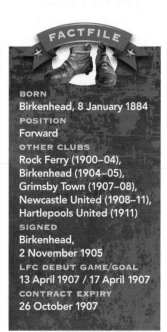

FACTFILE

BORN
Birkenhead, 8 January 1884
POSITION
Forward
OTHER CLUBS
Rock Ferry (1900–04),
Birkenhead (1904–05),
Grimsby Town (1907–08),
Newcastle United (1908–11),
Hartlepools United (1911)
SIGNED
Birkenhead,
2 November 1905
LFC DEBUT GAME/GOAL
13 April 1907 / 17 April 1907
CONTRACT EXPIRY
26 October 1907

Season	League		FA Cup		Total	
	App	Goals	App	Goals	App	Goals
1906/07	2	1	0	0	2	1
Total	2	1	0	0	2	1

Blenkinsop, Ernie

ERNIE BLENKINSOP began his professional career at Hull City, who paid his local club in the mining village of Cudworth £100 and a barrel of beer (80 pints) for his services. Blenkinsop worked in the Grimethorpe and Brierley pits from the early age of 13 until he was 18 and once cheated death when the roof collapsed in the gallery in which he was working. He threw himself to the ground, where he was buried by the debris, and was certain that if he had stayed upright he would have been killed.

Blenkinsop, who had been scouted by Doncaster Rovers before Hull made their move, wanted to serve out his notice in the mines but his manager insisted that he joined Hull straight away, as a week was a long time in that hazardous profession. He started out as an inside-left, but was early on converted to left-back. He was very skilful, his positional play impeccable and his delivery accurate. Blenkinsop preferred to play the ball out of defence instead of just hoofing it upfield. The former England captain was almost 32 years of age when he joined Liverpool from Sheffield Wednesday, where he had played

> HE THREW HIMSELF TO THE GROUND, WHERE HE WAS BURIED BY THE DEBRIS, AND WAS CERTAIN THAT IF HE HAD STAYED UPRIGHT HE WOULD HAVE BEEN KILLED

424 games from 1923 to 1934 and won the League Championship two years in succession in 1929 and 1930. Blenkinsop is a proper Wednesday legend and said to have been one of the best left-backs England has ever produced.

SIR STANLEY MATTHEWS had memorable battles with Blenkinsop, as he recalled in his autobiography. 'I found the first tackle a full-back ever made on me in a game was usually the hardest as he tried to unnerve me for the remainder of the match. Ernie Blenkinsop, who played for Sheffield Wednesday and later captained Liverpool, would do this. His first tackle could be a bone crusher if you weren't careful and as we both came out of it he'd say, "That's just to let you know I'm here." As if I needed reminding, and this from a player who had been spotted playing for his local church team in Yorkshire.'

Blenkinsop was at Anfield for three-and-a-half years, during which he shared the captaincy with his former England colleague Tom Cooper. 'Cartilage trouble', as he referred to his injuries himself, suffered against Derby on 24 November 1934 ruined his first full season. He was operated on successfully and only missed five league matches in the 1935/36 season. His bad luck continued in the following season when more cartilage damage in the knee, picked up against Everton on 19 September 1936, sidelined him for the rest of the campaign. Prior to signing for the club in the 1937/38 season a clause was included that stated if Blenkinsop was not a regular member of the first team at the end of September his engagement would be reconsidered. Only having featured in two games in the season, he joined Cardiff City in the Third Division South on 26 November 1937.

FACTFILE

BORN
Cudworth, Yorkshire,
20 April 1902
DIED
24 April 1969
POSITION
Left-back
OTHER CLUBS
Cudworth Village (1917–21),
Hull City (1921–23),
Sheffield Wednesday
(1923–34),
Cardiff City (1937–39);
Buxton,
Bradford Park Avenue,
Halifax Town, Bradford City,
Hurst (wartime guest)
SIGNED FROM
Sheffield Wednesday, £6,500,
15 March 1934
INTERNATIONAL CAPS
26 England caps, 1928–33
LFC DEBUT
17 March 1934
CONTRACT EXPIRY
26 November 1937

The Yorkshireman kept a detailed autograph book, which he would leave outside the dressing room for players to sign over a three-to-four-year period in the 1930s. This great collection contains signatures from his time at Sheffield Wednesday, England and Liverpool. He even collected the signatures of the medical staff that operated on his knee in the Liverpool Nursing Home! Blenkinsop set a record for consecutive international appearances, playing in every England game from 17 May 1928 to 1 April 1933, 26 in total, and he captained the national team on four occasions.

Blore, Reginald

WREXHAM-BORN forward **Reginald Blore came through the junior ranks at Anfield and made his only league appearance for Liverpool as a 17-year-old at Stoke City on 17 October 1959.**

He was transferred to Southport in July 1960, where he scored 55 goals in 139 Fourth Division games. He spent two years as a reserve at First Division Blackburn from 1963 to 1965, but got his career back on track with Oldham Athletic, for whom he made 182 league appearances as a midfielder between 1965 and 1970. Blore was an accomplished golfer and won the Professional Footballers' Golf Championship in 1968.

FACTFILE

BORN
Wrexham, Wales,
18 March 1942
POSITION
Right-winger
OTHER CLUBS
Southport (1960–63),
Blackburn Rovers
(1963–65),
Oldham Athletic (1965–70),
Bangor City (1970–71),
Ellesmere Port Town
(1971–72)
JOINED
22 May 1957; signed
professional 13 May 1959
LFC DEBUT
17 October 1959
CONTRACT EXPIRY
4 July 1960

Season	League		FA Cup		Total	
	App	Goals	App	Goals	App	Goals
1933/34	9	0	0	0	9	0
1934/35	16	0	0	0	16	0
1935/36	37	0	0	0	37	0
1936/37	7	0	0	0	7	0
1937/38	2	0	0	0	2	0
Total	**71**	**0**	**0**	**0**	**71**	**0**

Season	League		FA Cup		Total	
	App	Goals	App	Goals	App	Goals
1959/60	1	0	0	0	1	0
Total	**1**	**0**	**0**	**0**	**1**	**0**

Boersma, Phil

PHIL BOERSMA made his first-team debut almost two years after featuring for the reserves for the first time as an 18-year-old in November 1967. He got a proper run in the side from November 1970 to March 1971 when Alun Evans was absent with injury. Kevin Keegan arrived in 1971 and struck up a terrific understanding with John Toshack in the forward line. An injury to Toshack in September 1972 gave Boersma a chance to establish himself in the side, but he lost his place on the Welshman's return two months later. He did manage to make 26 starts and scored four goals during the club's successful UEFA Cup run. He also scored seven times in the league that season as the Reds won the title.

BOERSMA continued to be a good 'squad' player the following season but walked out on Liverpool when he found that he would not be named as substitute in the 1974 FA Cup final against Newcastle. He threatened that he would never play for the club again, but Boersma and Liverpool resolved their issues.

New boss Bob Paisley was thankful for Boersma's most productive spell at the club, which came at the start of the 1974/75 season when he scored 10 goals in 11 games while Keegan was serving his ban for being sent off in the Charity Shield against Leeds. Paisley found room for Boersma in midfield on Keegan's return but by November the local boy had lost his spot. Boersma was mostly on the bench in the first months of the 1975/76 season and moved to Middlesbrough in December 1975, where he met Graeme Souness. In 1991 he returned to Anfield as manager Souness's right-hand man, a partnership they had developed at Rangers. He then followed Souness to Galatasaray, Southampton, Torino, Benfica, Blackburn Rovers and Newcastle United.

'I was a totally different type to Kevin Keegan,' Boersma told *LFC magazine*. 'Shanks would always stick by what he thought was his strongest team. He went with Toshack, Keegan and Heighway. I just came in and did my bit and even in that period in '74 when Kevin came back, it was me, Ray Kennedy and Stevie up front.

HE SCORED 10 GOALS IN 11 GAMES WHILE KEEGAN WAS SERVING HIS BAN FOR BEING SENT OFF IN THE CHARITY SHIELD

I THINK he dropped Kevin into midfield for a couple of games. He didn't do too well and we swapped over again. I went into midfield and Kevin went up front. I would have played left wing, right wing, up front, anywhere. I still enjoyed my time at Liverpool. It was just so difficult to get a chance.'

FACTFILE

BORN
Kirkby, Liverpool,
24 September 1949
POSITION
Forward / Midfielder
OTHER CLUBS
Wrexham (loan, 1970),
Middlesbrough (1975–77),
Luton Town (1977–78),
Swansea City (1978–81)
JOINED
1965; signed professional
September 1968
LFC DEBUT/GOAL
24 September 1969 /
4 November 1970
CONTRACT EXPIRY
1975
HONOURS
League Championship
1972/73;
UEFA Cup 1973

Season	League		FA Cup		League Cup		Europe		Other		Total	
	App	Goals	App	Goals	App	Goals	App	Goals	App	Goals	App	Goals
1969/70	4	0	0	0	0 (1)	0	1	0	-	-	5 (1)	0
1970/71	13 (2)	1	3	0	0	0	2 (1)	2	-	-	18 (3)	3
1971/72	3 (2)	0	0 (1)	0	0	0	0	0	0	0	3 (3)	0
1972/73	19	7	0 (1)	0	2 (1)	2	5 (3)	4	-	-	26 (5)	13
1973/74	13 (2)	3	4 (1)	1	0	0	1 (1)	0	-	-	18 (4)	4
1974/75	20 (1)	6	0	0	3	1	4	2	1	1	28 (1)	10
1975/76	1 (2)	0	0	0	0 (1)	0	0 (1)	0	-	-	1 (4)	0
Total	73 (9)	17	7 (3)	1	5 (3)	3	13 (6)	8	1	1	99 (21)	30

Books

THERE HAVE BEEN many fantastic books written about the subject of Liverpool FC throughout the decades. Autobiographies of players past and present are popular and books on the rich history of the club arouse curiosity. This is not by any means a complete list of books published relating to Liverpool FC, as that would be an almost impossible task, but simply an overview of the ones that might pique your interest and be worthwhile to the reader.

Autobiographies:

Gary Ablett,
The Game of My Life 2012;
Alan A'Court,
My Life in Football 2003;
Rafa Benítez,
Champions League Dreams
with Rory Smith 2012;
Ian Callaghan,
The Ian Callaghan Story
with John Keith 1975;
Jamie Carragher,
Carra 2009;
Kenny Dalglish,
My Liverpool Home 2010;
Robbie Fowler,
Fowler 2006;
Steven Gerrard,
My Autobiography 2007;
Bruce Grobbelaar,
More Than Somewhat 1986;
Didi Hamann,
The Didi Man: My Love Affair
with Liverpool 2012;
Sami Hyypia,
From Voikkaa to the Premiership
2002;
Craig Johnston,
Walk Alone with Neil Jameson
1990;
Rob Jones,
Robbed: My Liverpool Life 2012;
Kevin Keegan,
with John Roberts 1977;
Alan Kennedy,
Kennedy's Way 2005;
Ray Kennedy,
Ray of Hope with Dr. Andrew Lees
1993;
Billy Liddell,
My Soccer Story 1960;
Jan Mølby,
Jan The Man: From Anfield to
Vetch Field 2007;

Bob Paisley,
My Autobiography 1983;
Bill Shankly,
with John Roberts 1976;
Tommy Smith;
I Did It the Hard Way 1980;
Ian St John,
Boom at the Kop 1966;
Graeme Souness,
No Half Measures with Bob Harris
1985;
Phil Thompson,
Stand Up Pinocchio 2008;
John Wark,
Wark On 2009.

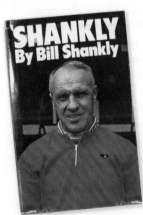

Fans' Autobiographies:

Nicholas Allt,
The Boys From the Mersey 2005;
Neil Dunkin,
Anfield of Dreams:
A Kopite's Odyssey 2008;
Alan Edge,
Faith of Our Fathers 1997;
Brian Reade,
40 Years With the Same Bird
2008.

Biographies:

Ian Callaghan,
Cally on the Ball by John Keith
2010,
Kenny Dalglish,
by Stephen F. Kelly 1997;
Roy Evans,
Ghost on the Wall by Derek Dohren
2004;
Joe Fagan,
Reluctant Champion by Mark Platt
with Andrew Fagan 2011;
Liverpool Heroes,
by Ragnhild Lund Ansnes 2012;
Geoff Twentyman,
Secret Diary of a Liverpool Scout
by Simon Hughes 2011.

Historical:

Arnie Baldursson
and Gudmundur Magnusson,
Liverpool: A Complete Record
2011;
Dave Ball and Ged Rea,
The Ultimate Book of Stats
and Facts 2001;
Eric Doig and Alex Murphy,
The Essential History of Liverpool
2003;
Stephen Done and
Jeff Anderson,
The Official Illustrated History
2002;
Stephen Done and
David Walmsley,
The Treasures of Liverpool FC
2004;
Kjell Hanssen,
Dicky Sams: Liverpool FC in Blue
and White 2009;
Derek Hodgson,
The Liverpool Story 1978;
Steven Horton,
Ending The Seven-Year Itch
1972-73 2012;
John Hynes,
The Irish Kop 2009;
Stephen F. Kelly,
Boot Room Boys 1999;
Stephen F. Kelly,
The Kop: Liverpool's Twelfth Man
1993;
Doug Lamming,
Who's Who of Liverpool 1989;
Peter Lupson,
Across the Park 2009;

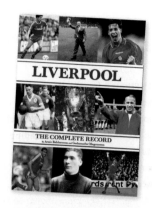

Bob Paisley and Peter Oakes,
Bob Paisley - My 50 Golden Reds
1990;
Brian Pead,
Liverpool: Champion of
Champions 1990;
Mark Platt and Gary Shaw,
At The End of the Storm 2009;
Mark Platt,
Cup Kings 1965 2000;
Mark Platt,
Cup Kings 1977 2003;
Ivan Ponting,
Player by Player
published 1990-2009;
Ivan Ponting and Steve Hale,
Liverpool in Europe 2001;
Brian Reade,
An Epic Swindle 2011;
The Real Bob Paisley,
Trinity Mirror 2007;
The Real Shankly,
Trinity Mirror 2007;
Graeme and Reg Riley,
Liverpool: Match by Match
Volume One 1892-1900 2012;
Graeme and Reg Riley,
Liverpool: Match by Match
Volume Two 1900-1908 2013;
Gary Shaw and Mike Nevin,
On the March with Kenny's Army
2011;
Paul Tomkins,
Dynasty: Fifty Years of Shankly's
Liverpool 2008;
Paul Tomkins,
Pay As You Play: The True Price
of Success in the Premier League
Era with Graeme Riley and
Gary Fulcher 2010;
Paul Tomkins and
Jonathan Swain,
Golden Past, Red Future:
Liverpool FC - Champions of Europe
2005;
John Williams,
Red Men 2010.

Bootroom

ANFIELD'S famous Bootroom was a small area off a long corridor that ran at ground level in the Main stand at the stadium. As its name indicates, it was a room where the squad's boots were kept.

It was introduced during Bill Shankly's reign as manager where his coaching staff would have an informal place to meet to discuss matches past and present, players, tactics, anything to do with the club really. It was also the location where visiting managers were often invited to join the home team staff in the immediate aftermath of a first-team match at Anfield.

The members of the Bootroom were part of quite an exclusive club as youth team coach John Bennison recollected in Stephen F. Kelly's book *The Boot Room Boys*. 'Reuben [Bennett] had his own room but he'd come in. Shanks, Tom Saunders and Geoff Twentyman, all had their own offices. But in the Bootroom was Joe Fagan, Ronnie Moran, Roy Evans and myself. Now Bob would come in but he had his own office and he wouldn't hang up his coat up in the Bootroom.' Chris Lawler, Tommy Smith and Phil Thompson also became members in due course, reflecting their value to the coaching set-up as a whole and the high regard with which they were held by more senior employees of the club. The Bootroom was a place where all men were equal and everyone's input was appreciated, whether the discussion revolved around the senior team, the reserves or the youth team. Paisley, Fagan and Evans would all eventually become managers of the club, which reflected the club's policy at the time of 'promoting from within'. In addition to that trio, Ronnie Moran's grounding in the Bootroom philosophy was

invaluable when he was asked to step in as caretaker in both 1991 and 1992.

A CERTAIN mystique enveloped the Bootroom as the trophies continued to pile up. But the reality was that there was no magic formula concocted by the men who met there. It was a pooling of resources and a mixture of ideas from experienced football men who only ever wanted the best for the club they worked for. Visiting managers and inquisitive journalists might have hoped that some of the 'magic' would rub off on them. But the reality is that there was no magic. 'There was a chart on the wall and it had 13 League Championships and it just went on and every year, they would scratch out the number and add a new one,' Phil Thompson noted in *The Boot Room Boys*. 'There were notes all over it and it was ripped but that stayed year upon year. And someone had written 'just like Real Madrid' on it. It stayed there for years from 1978/79. It was looking at

the things that happened before, that drove them on to succeed all the more.' This approach certainly worked because the success different Liverpool teams had for twenty years was staggering. Meticulous diaries were kept by the coaching staff recording everything that happened at both Anfield and Melwood and they were often referred to because if something had worked before, the belief was that it would work again.

'There was little evidence to suggest this room was even part of a football club,' Joe Fagan reflected. 'In time it would become furnished with luxuries like a rickety old table and a couple of plastic chairs, a tatty piece of carpet on the floor and a calendar on a wall that would later be adorned with photographs, ripped from newspapers, of topless models.' The simplistic surroundings did not give away the cunning behaviour of its regular occupants. 'When visiting managers and coaches were invited in for a drink, they usually

the Boot Room Boys

accepted gratefully, aware of the honour,' Kenny Dalglish said in *My Liverpool Home*. 'They'd perch on a skip, sipping whisky from an old glass, totally unaware they had walked into an ambush. Joe, Ronnie and Tom should have worn masks they staged so many hold-ups in the Bootroom. "You're building a good team there. Got any kids coming through?" Joe asked. Responding to such flattery, the visiting manager would talk about some promising teenager on the books of his club. Within days, Liverpool scouts would be checking him out. They were weighing people up, finding out tiny details about what made their team tick, building up a mental dossier on opponents' strengths and weaknesses.'

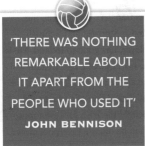

Borini,
Fabio

The demolition of the Bootroom took place when Graeme Souness was manager. Was he solely to blame? It is very doubtful if his predecessor Kenny Dalglish would have allowed anybody to ruin this sacred place. Peter Robinson was the club's chief executive at the time and he doesn't blame Souness as it was a general decision taken by the hierarchy of the club. 'Initially a lot of players didn't have cars and we felt that it would be better for the players to report directly to Melwood each day and to train and be fed there rather than to ride up and down in an old coach as they used to. Football was moving on. We also needed to have an after-match press-room and that was the ideal area for it.' Just imagine if the Bootroom would have been allowed to stay. It would be quite an attraction for fans all over the world.

ALTHOUGH sadly the fabled Bootroom will never return to its former glory, its place in the club's history can never be underestimated and its name lives on in the Sports Café that is situated close to the club's museum and stadium shop at Anfield as well at the Cheshire Oaks Designer Outlet, near Ellesmere Port. Ten years after leaving Liverpool Football Club, John Bennison reflected on his time as a Bootroom boy. 'It's amazing how so much intrigue and mystique surrounds what was basically an old broom cupboard. To look at, it was nothing special. It measured about eight feet square and there was nothing remarkable about it apart from the people who used it.'

WHEN ITALIAN international striker Fabio Borini signed a contract to join Liverpool in the middle of July 2012, the Reds became the third English club he had been on the books of even at the early age of 21. He was, however, a footballer already well known by the manager who signed him, because Brendan Rogers had been Swansea's manager when the Italian was loaned to the Welsh club by Chelsea for the closing weeks of the 2010/11 season.

Liverpool's new boss explained why he was so keen to complete this signing: 'I think the supporters will love him. He's a multi-functional player who can play in a number of positions and someone I believe has got great growth. He is arguably the best physical player I've worked with in terms of his pace, power and fitness. Mentally, he's very strong.'

After scoring 10 goals in 11 matches for Chelsea reserves in the 2008/09 season, Borini played in eight first-team games for the Londoners. Borini performed well under Rogers at Swansea with six goals in nine Championship matches, but once his loan expired he had reached an agreement to sign for Parma.

Less than two months after signing for Parma in 2011, he moved on to Roma, initially on loan but with Roma having an option to make the deal permanent later. Borini was not given much of a chance in the first half of the season at the club but once he got going there was no stopping him, his best run being 10 goals in 14 matches from 26 October 2011 to 10 March 2012. The loan was upgraded to a co-ownership deal and in the summer of 2012 Roma outbid Parma in a blind auction, parting with £4.3million to secure the other 50 per cent of his registration.

BORINI was in Italy's 23-man Euro 2012 squad but was one of only two outfield players not to see any action. He can play on either the left or right flank as well as up front and hopefully he will deliver steely determination to Liverpool's cause, serving as a direct replacement for Dirk Kuyt, who departed to Turkey in summer 2012.

Liverpool supporters saw his trademark 'dagger celebration' as early as his home debut, against Gomel in the Europa League, but Borini's hopes were dashed when he broke a bone in his foot and was sidelined until January 2013.

'It was extremely frustrating because in the last three years I have got injured for three months every year in October,' he told *liverpoolfc.com* in January. 'I haven't played a full season yet because of those injuries, but I hope they'll stop.' Soon after making this comment Borini dislocated his shoulder against Swansea and was out for two and a half months. He returned at St James' Park on 27 April and netted his first league goal coming on as a substitute in the 6-0 win. Borini performed excellently in the European U-21 Championship finals during the summer, scoring two tremendous goals in the semi-final and the final, which Italy lost 4-2 to Spain.

FACTFILE

BORN
Bentivoglio, Italy,
29 March 1991
POSITION
Forward
OTHER CLUBS
Chelsea (2007–11),
Swansea City (loan, 2011),
Parma (2011–12),
AS Roma (2011–12)
SIGNED FROM
AS Roma, £10.4million,
13 July 2012
INTERNATIONAL CAPS
1 Italy cap, 2012
LFC DEBUT/GOAL
2 August 2012 /
9 August 2012

Season	League		FA Cup		League Cup		Europe		Total	
	App	Goals	App	Goals	App	Goals	App	Goals	App	Goals
2012/13	5 (8)	1	1	0	0	0	4 (2)	1	10 (10)	2
Total	**5 (8)**	**1**	**1**	**0**	**0**	**0**	**4 (2)**	**1**	**10 (10)**	**2**

Bovill, John

WHEN CHESTERFIELD Town lost its league status in 1909, fiery-tempered John Bovill stayed with the club, scoring 31 goals in 77 Midland League games.

TWO YEARS LATER he moved to Anfield and made 29 appearances for Liverpool in the period leading up to World War One. The bulk of those games were in the 1911/12 season, when he scored seven times from 25 matches. He was to make only a further four appearances for the club in the next two seasons, the club programme complaining that his main fault was 'lack of deadliness in front of goal,' but his main strength that he was a 'hard worker' who delivered 'neat, low forward passes of value to his partners.' The *Liverpool Echo* reported on his transfer: 'John Bovill, the ex-Chesterfield and Scottish player, has gone to Ireland. He is to help Linfield, and Ireland will be all the richer in good fun, for this comedian of a player will delight the Irish folk even more than he did the Liverpool crowd.'

> IRELAND WILL BE ALL THE RICHER IN GOOD FUN, FOR THIS COMEDIAN OF A PLAYER WILL DELIGHT THE IRISH FOLK

FACTFILE

BORN
Rutherglen, Lanarkshire, Scotland 21 March 1886
POSITION
Inside-right forward
OTHER CLUBS
Strathclyde Juniors, Rangers (1907–08), Blackburn Rovers (1908–09), Chesterfield Town (1909–11), Linfield (1914–19)
SIGNED FROM
Chesterfield Town, April 1911
LFC DEBUT/GOAL
4 September 1911 / 4 November 1911
CONTRACT EXPIRY
May 1914

Season	League		FA Cup		Total	
	App	Goals	App	Goals	App	Goals
1911/12	23	7	2	0	25	7
1912/13	1	0	0	0	1	0
1913/14	3	0	0	0	3	0
Total	**27**	**7**	**2**	**0**	**29**	**7**

Bowen, George

GEORGE BOWEN
LIVERPOOL

GEORGE BOWEN had no doubt impressed Liverpool when he scored both Wolves' goals in a 2-1 win at Molineux six months prior to his September 1902 move to the Reds.

Right-winger Bowen had a very unlucky career at Liverpool. He only made two first-team appearances, both in league matches at the start of the 1901/02 season. His debut came in the Anfield derby against Everton on 14 September 1901 in which his beautiful centre was finished by Bill White for Liverpool's first goal in a 2-2 draw.

BOWEN kept his place but never featured for the first team again after breaking his leg in the away game at Sunderland. He made a return with the reserves a year later before moving back, still injured, to Wolves, where he had made 48 appearances and scored 13 goals in the First Division in his first spell at the club from 1899 to 1901. In his second spell he only made three appearances and scored one goal before joining Second Division Burslem Port Vale in the 1904/05 season.

FACTFILE

BORN
Walsall, July 1875
POSITION
Right/Left winger
OTHER CLUBS
Bridgtown Amateurs (1895–99), Wolverhampton Wanderers (1899–1901), Wolverhampton Wanderers (1902–04), Burslem Port Vale (1904–05), Bloxwich Strollers (1905–06)
SIGNED FROM
Wolverhampton Wanderers, May 1901
LFC DEBUT
14 September 1901
CONTRACT EXPIRY
17 September 1902

Season	League		FA Cup		Total	
	App	Goals	App	Goals	App	Goals
1901/02	2	0	0	0	2	0
Total	**2**	**0**	**0**	**0**	**2**	**0**

Bowyer, Sam

SAM BOWYER
LIVERPOOL

FORWARD Sam Bowyer made 45 league and three FA Cup appearances for Liverpool during the years which led up to World War One.

Bowyer's most telling contribution for Liverpool in a cup tie was the two goals he scored in three minutes against Gainsborough Trinity in the middle of January 1911, having been scolded for lack of accuracy in his shooting in the match programme a month earlier. After scoring in every third game for the Reds he moved to Second Division Bristol City where he scored 14 goals in 40 matches between 1912 and 1913.

FACTFILE

BORN
Northwich, 12 October 1887
DIED
11 April 1961
POSITION
Forward
OTHER CLUBS
Earlestown (1905–07),
Bristol City (1912–13),
Bedminster (1913–15),
South Liverpool (1915)
SIGNED FROM
Earlestown, £95,
2 March 1907
LFC DEBUT/GOAL
7 September 1907 /
1 October 1908
CONTRACT EXPIRY
15 February 1912

Season	League		FA Cup		Total	
	App	Goals	App	Goals	App	Goals
1907/08	4	0	1	0	5	0
1908/09	14	4	0	0	14	4
1909/10	12	6	1	0	13	6
1910/11	13	4	1	2	14	6
1911/12	2	0	0	0	2	0
Total	**45**	**14**	**3**	**2**	**48**	**16**

Boys' Pen

IT IS NOT known exactly when a boys' enclosure was first opened at Liverpool's Anfield stadium, although it probably wasn't until after World War One. It was definitely in place throughout most of the 1920s and 1930s, when it was located in the Paddock of the old Kemlyn Road stand and ran from around the halfway line on that side of the stadium up to the Anfield Road enclosure.

It was a popular area for youngsters to congregate and watch the team and there doesn't seem to be any record of bad behaviour until Leeds United came to Anfield for a First Division fixture on Saturday 5 February 1938. Apparently on this day kids inside the boys' enclosure threw orange peel onto the pitch, which might or might not have been directed at visiting players. But the club was warned and was ordered to have a policeman patrol this area of the stadium at future home matches.

By the time The Football League was able to resume its programme in the 1946/47 season, the kids' enclosure in the front of the Kemlyn Road stand had been moved to a raised area of the Kop with its own entrance in Lake Street on the Main stand side of the stadium. It was a wise decision, perhaps made in the aftermath of the death of 33 spectators at a horribly overcrowded Burnden Park, Bolton earlier in the year with the move endorsed by another bad incident of overcrowding in Liverpool's second home First Division match of the season against Chelsea on 7 September 1946 which forced hundreds of dehydrated spectators to seek refuge on the track around the pitch on an almost unbearably hot day for both playing and watching.

SO THE BOYS who attended Liverpool's home matches finally had a place they could call home. But it was far from a welcoming home and the kids who supported visiting teams knew better than to go in there. Robbie "Mottman" Ashcroft, who spent many a match watching his team from this vantage point recalls: 'The kids who went on the Boys' Pen were hard. You had to be a survivor

> **'THE KOP WAS WARM AND FRIENDLY - THE BOYS' PEN WAS ANGRY, AGGRESSIVE AND MEAN'**
> **ROBBIE ASHCROFT**

even to queue up. You could not show fear. Fear would be pounced on. There were no away fans but the number of scraps before, during and after the match was scary. The Kop was warm and friendly - the Boys' Pen was angry, aggressive and mean.'

THE PEN was once described as a valid inspiration for William Golding's *Lord of the Flies*. The boys in the Pen would try to break out of it into the freedom of the Kop, not easy because of the railings surrounding it, risking broken limbs or being impaled on rusty metal. The Kopites would follow this sideshow with great interest, cheering the brave souls on, catching the successful ones, who disappeared quickly into the crowd before they could be caught by the stewards.

So these were the little Kopites of the future, the kids who dreamed of the day when they would be old enough to join the adults on the other side of the barbed wire that kept them in their own little corner.

A supporter with many years' experience of watching Liverpool at Anfield, Christopher Wood, recalls a momentous occasion when that screeching was not just tolerable but effective. It happened at the home derby with defending champions Everton on 21 November 1970, shortly after the visitors had taken a two-goal lead.

Wood was standing in the Paddock in front of the Main stand. 'I was alerted by a sound coming from somewhere to my right. Treble voices from the Boys' Pen started to chant 'No Surrender', faintly at first and then louder with each repetition as others joined in. Within seconds adult voices from the main terrace were chanting too, drowning out the rallying cry that those lads in the Pen had started. It boomed out in defiance from twenty thousand plus throats young and old. People remember the comeback of November 1970; they remember the goals. But how many remember, as I do, how a bunch of kids refused to allow their blind faith to waver in the face of adversity and began a call to arms that resulted in a famous and emotional victory?'

The Boys' Pen died a natural death as the 1970s became the 1980s. In a way, considering all the mayhem that went on in there, it was perhaps fortunate to survive for as long as it did. But it would have had to disappear post-Hillsborough anyway. Perhaps older supporters recalling the time they spent in there have more bad memories than good. But it was still an important part of their upbringing. Terry McDermott and

John Aldridge graduated from the Boys' Pen to the Kop and then, like Phil Thompson, on to the famous turf as well. 'When I looked up at the Pen during matches, it always felt strange. That was where it really started for me,' Thompson remembered after he got into the first team.

THE BOYS' PEN in the Kop was a strange place. It was often a dangerous place. It was a place where you had to grow up fast, where you entered as a boy and then, when your apprenticeship had been served, you left it as a man.

Bradley,
James

'BRADLEY possesses a splendid idea of the requirements of a successful half back, and the forwards in front of him cannot complain of the accurate attention. He believes in keeping the ball on the turf, and his clever tackling is only equalled by the skilful manner in which he places to his front rank,' said the club programme of 2 February 1908.

James Bradley started out with a local team, Goldenhill Wanderers, in the coalmining village of Goldenhill where he was born and raised. After only one season he signed for Stoke, where he made 199 appearances in the First Division from 1898 to 1905. At the end of the 1904/05 season he was supposed to join Plymouth Argyle but the Football Association would not sanction the deal.

HE JOINED LIVERPOOL a few months later despite having had a run-in with one of their players in a First Division match on 17 October 1903. Bradley got into a fight with Fred Buck and they were both sent off. Buck was banned for six weeks but Bradley only 14 days.

Bradley made his first appearance for Liverpool in a home league fixture with Birmingham City on 23 September 1905 and played in 32 league matches in his debut season, collecting a League Championship medal in the process. He would miss only 18 league matches over the next four seasons and it wasn't until the 1910/11 season that his position at left-half was threatened. On one unusual occasion Bradley played in Liverpool's goal on 25 December 1909, donning the goalkeeper's jersey in Sam Hardy's absence. Hardy had dislocated a finger whilst diving for a shot against Villa the week before. The directors assumed he would be playing so they allowed reserve keeper Augustus Beeby to travel with the reserves and Malone, the third choice, to play in another game. Shortly before kick off, with no Hardy in sight, one of the staff appeared holding a telegram dated 22 December saying that he would definitely not be fit and so would not travel. The directors asked for a volunteer and Bradley

stepped forward, and McConnell, who was only by chance at the ground, stepped in at half-back. The big England international must have been proud to see his unlikely understudy keep a clean sheet in a 3-0 win over Bolton Wanderers. In 1913 Bradley rejoined Stoke after the club had resigned from the Football League.

Season	League		FA Cup		Other		Total	
	App	Goals	App	Goals	App	Goals	App	Goals
1905/06	32	0	5	0	1	0	38	0
1906/07	36	1	4	0	-	-	40	1
1907/08	34	3	4	3	-	-	38	6
1908/09	34	1	2	0	-	-	36	1
1909/10	30	0	0	0	-	-	30	0
1910/11	4	0	0	0	-	-	4	0
Total	**170**	**5**	**15**	**3**	**1**	**0**	**186**	**8**

Bradshaw, Thomas Henry 'Harry'

HARRY BRADSHAW became the first Liverpool player to achieve international honours, when he played on the left flank as England beat Ireland 6-0 on 20 February 1897. In these nascent days at Anfield, Bradshaw was Liverpool's centre-forward and the biggest star that the club had possessed.

He started out with Liverpool Nomads in 1889, before featuring in Everton's reserves in the Lancashire Combination for one season. He stayed one year at Northwich Victoria, where he played 22 games and scored eight goals in the Second Division. Bradshaw scored seven goals from 14 appearances to help Liverpool to the Second Division Championship in their debut season in the Football League in 1893/94. In the difficult season which followed, with the club being immediately relegated, he was the club's only 'ever-present' in the league and found the net 17 times. Although he would immediately pick up another Second Division winners' medal in 1895/96, Bradshaw scored just 11 times. But as he had switched to the wing by then, this was understandable.

His versatility in being able to play on the left and in the centre was a useful asset but he was criticised for dallying on the ball with the 'usual results'. The pros, though, far outweighed the cons and soon after his England debut *Lloyds Weekly Newspaper* claimed that Bradshaw 'undoubtedly ranks as one of the finest rising forwards in the country at the present time.'

Bradshaw joined Tottenham before the 1898/99 season and featured mainly as a left-winger playing an exhausting total of 52 matches and scoring 13 goals in his only season at Spurs.

He then moved to Thames Ironworks (later West Ham) in the summer of 1899 and was made club captain. He played his last game of football on 9 December 1899, in which he scored in a 2-1 loss against Millwall. He got kicked in the leg and was ordered to rest for three weeks.

On Christmas Day 1899 Harry watched Spurs play Portsmouth in the morning. After the match he went with some of the players to the Bell and Hare close by, where he had one glass of whisky. At 2:15pm he went home to his residence at 5 Shelbourne Road, Tottenham. No sooner had he entered the house when he

vomited excessively. He threw himself on his bed and complained of violent pains in the head and chest. Before a doctor could attend to him, 26-year-old Harry had a fit and died.

Elizabeth Bradshaw, Harry's widow, stated that during a football match four years previously he was kicked on the head, and on the following Saturday was again kicked in the same place. The doctor who attended him said that Harry had ruptured an eardrum. From that time forward he suffered from pains in the head and discharges from the ears. Tottenham player John Jones, who had been Harry's friend from childhood, said that since the incidents Harry had to put his hands to his ears to ease the suffering from heading the ball. He had been with Harry at the day of his passing and said he had looked in the best of health when he left him.

THE POSTMORTEM showed Harry's death attributable to a ruptured blood vessel in the brain, which was possibly because of the head injury he received four years earlier, but might also have been due to the strain put on the blood vessel while vomiting. It was impossible to say for certain what the cause of his death was, according to the coroner's report. On 2 April 1900 Tottenham and Thames Ironworks played a charity match to raise money for Harry's widow and two young children.

HARRY BRADSHAW
LIVERPOOL

> BRADSHAW SCORED SEVEN GOALS FROM 14 APPEARANCES TO HELP LIVERPOOL TO THE SECOND DIVISION CHAMPIONSHIP IN THEIR DEBUT SEASON

FACTFILE

BORN
Liverpool, 24 August 1873
DIED
25 December 1899
POSITION
Centre-forward / Left-winger
OTHER CLUBS
Liverpool Nomads (1889–91),
Everton (1891–92),
Northwich Victoria (1892–93),
Tottenham Hotspur (1898–99),
Thames Ironworks (1899)
SIGNED FROM
Northwich Victoria,
14 October 1893
LFC DEBUT/GOAL
28 October 1893 /
4 November 1893
CONTRACT EXPIRY
May 1898
HONOURS
Second Division
Championship
1893/94, 1895/96

Season	League		FA Cup		Other		Total	
	App	Goals	App	Goals	App	Goals	App	Goals
1893/94	14	7	3	2	1	1	18	10
1894/95	30	17	3	1	1	0	34	18
1895/96	26	11	2	1	4	2	32	14
1896/97	25	4	3	0	-	-	28	4
1897/98	23	4	3	1	-	-	26	5
Total	**118**	**43**	**14**	**5**	**6**	**3**	**138**	**51**

Bradshaw, Tom 'Tiny'

> 'TINY
> WENT OUT TO PLAY
> FOOTBALL
> AND LET THE BEST
> MAN WIN'
>
> **DIXIE DEAN**

NICKNAMED 'TINY', Bradshaw was a giant of a man in the Liverpool team through the 1930s. Already a veteran of 208 league games with Bury in the Second and First Division when he arrived at Liverpool, he had also played once for the Scottish international side two years prior, an occasion marked by Scotland's greatest performance: a 5-1 drubbing of England in front of 80,000 at Wembley that saw the team dubbed 'The Wembley Wizards'.

Used as a right-half in his Liverpool debut season, 1929/30, Tiny played in the last 17 league matches. He was just as comfortable at centre-half, a position he made his own over the next seven seasons, captaining the side from 1931–34. Tiny was literally a tower of strength in defence for the club, which unfortunately had a below average decade in the 1930s.

Leslie Edwards at the *Echo* was a big fan: 'A giant at 6ft 3in [190 cm], but amazingly agile. He had the build of Ron Yeats and the touch of Alan Hansen, who were also Scottish. Tiny was a marvellous defender and the only man I have ever seen come anywhere near him was John Charles.'

Liverpool's main foe was Everton's goal machine, Dixie Dean, who had great respect for Tiny. 'In all the times I played against him he never used any of those sly little tricks that others did, like pulling you back by your shirt or shorts. Tiny went out to play football and let the best man win.'

Season	League App	League Goals	FA Cup App	FA Cup Goals	Total App	Total Goals
1929/30	17	0	0	0	17	0
1930/31	35	0	1	0	36	0
1931/32	42	0	4	0	46	0
1932/33	39	3	1	0	40	3
1933/34	39	0	4	1	43	1
1934/35	31	0	2	0	33	0
1935/36	41	0	2	0	43	0
1936/37	31	0	0	0	31	0
1937/38	2	0	0	0	2	0
Total	**277**	**3**	**14**	**1**	**291**	**4**

FACTFILE

BORN
Coatbridge,
North Lanarkshire, Scotland,
7 February 1904
DIED
22 February 1986
POSITION
Centre-half / Right-half
OTHER CLUBS
Woodside Juniors (1920–22),
Bury (1922–30),
Colchester United (1938),
Third Lanark (1938–39),
South Liverpool (1939–40)
SIGNED FROM
Bury, £8,000, January 1930
INTERNATIONAL CAPS
1 Scotland cap, 1928
LFC DEBUT/GOAL
25 January 1930 /
3 September 1932
CONTRACT EXPIRY
September 1938

Bratley, Phil

PHIL BRATLEY was part of the Barnsley side that won the FA Cup in 1912 after a replay against West Bromwich Albion. He was Barnsley's hero in the replayed semi-final against Swindon Town when he scored the only goal of the game.

When Harry Lowe was out with injury Bratley made his Liverpool debut in a disastrous 5-0 defeat to Everton at Anfield in October 1914.

HE HAD A RUN of nine matches in the side while Lowe was out of action for three months. Bratley made a further four appearances before the end of the season, bringing his total number of games for the club up to 13. 'Old man' Bratley featured in nine matches for Rotherham County following World War One, then into his forties, before concluding his career in the Midland League with Worksop Town.

Season	League App	League Goals	FA Cup App	FA Cup Goals	Total App	Total Goals
1914/15	13	0	0	0	13	0
Total	**13**	**0**	**0**	**0**	**13**	**0**

FACTFILE

BORN
Rawmarsh, Yorkshire,
26 December 1880
POSITION
Centre-half
OTHER CLUBS
Rawmarsh (1896–1902),
Doncaster Rovers (1902–04),
Rotherham County (1904),
Rotherham Town,
Barnsley (1910–14),
Barnsley (wartime guest),
Rotherham County (1919–21),
Worksop Town
SIGNED FROM
Barnsley, May 1914
LFC DEBUT
3 October 1914
CONTRACT EXPIRY
1915

Brierley,
Ken

SKILFUL left-winger Brierley had played over 50 league matches for Oldham Athletic in the Third Division North before signing for league champions Liverpool in February 1948. He appeared in 10 of the last 11 matches of the 1947/48 season and notched his first goal for the club as Everton were beaten 4-0 at Anfield on 21 April 1948.

Brierley never really established himself in the Liverpool team and the highest number of league appearances he made in a season was just 13, in 1948/49. He returned to his former club Oldham in March 1953.

ALBERT STUBBINS recalled an amusing story from when Brierley signed for Liverpool. 'George Kay was meticulous about drinking before a game,' Stubbins said in an interview with *LFC Magazine* in 2001 'On the Friday night before a home game we'd stay at a hotel in Southport. I remember one occasion; we'd just signed an

> 'WHEN YOU ARE A LIVERPOOL PLAYER, YOU DO NOT DRINK BEFORE A GAME!'

inside left from Oldham called Ken Brierley. We sat down for lunch and Ken was there with a glass of beer. That was unheard of and we couldn't believe it. Anyway, as we took our seat, Ken asked Jack Balmer, who was our captain, if it was okay. Jack replied, "Oh yes, we always have a pint before a game." When George Kay came in, he walked straight over to Ken and pulled the glass away. Ken was astonished and George told him straight, "When you are a Liverpool player, you do not drink before a game!"'

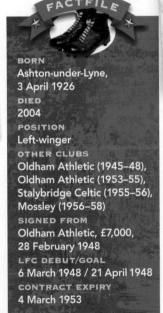

FACTFILE

BORN
Ashton-under-Lyne,
3 April 1926
DIED
2004
POSITION
Left-winger
OTHER CLUBS
Oldham Athletic (1945–48),
Oldham Athletic (1953–55),
Stalybridge Celtic (1955–56),
Mossley (1956–58)
SIGNED FROM
Oldham Athletic, £7,000,
28 February 1948
LFC DEBUT/GOAL
6 March 1948 / 21 April 1948
CONTRACT EXPIRY
4 March 1953

Season	League		FA Cup		Total	
	App	Goals	App	Goals	App	Goals
1947/48	10	1	0	0	10	1
1948/49	13	0	1	0	14	0
1949/50	11	5	0	0	11	5
1950/51	5	0	0	0	5	0
1951/52	11	1	0	0	11	1
1952/53	10	1	0	0	10	1
Total	**60**	**8**	**1**	**0**	**61**	**8**

Bromilow,
Tom

TOM BROMILOW had just left the British Army when he joined Liverpool. The club's secretary George Patterson recalled: 'His signature was obtained in the strangest manner. He came to the ground in uniform during the war and asked for a game. I asked George Fleming, who was in charge of the second team then, how he was fixed and he said he could do with another player; Bromilow played at outside-right and was an instant success. When the war ended he signed as a professional. Eventually he took his place in the first team when Lacey was playing an international match for Ireland. I should think that it is one of the luckiest signings I have made.'

McNab, Wadsworth and Bromilow in training

BROMILOW made his full Liverpool debut on 25 October 1919 at Burnley's Turf Moor. Liverpool won 2-1 and the club programme later reported that 'quite a good impression was created by the local lad Bromilow at right half-back; it was asking a great deal of him to place him against such a clever pair as Lindsay and Mosscrop, but he came out of the ordeal with

> 'I SHOULD THINK THAT IT IS ONE OF THE LUCKIEST SIGNINGS I HAVE MADE'
> **GEORGE PATTERSON**

distinct credit.' The club programme of 18 February 1920 noted that Bromilow had 'not yet figured on the losing side with the Reds. In all he has taken part in fourteen engagements, including two cup ties which have resulted in ten victories and four drawn games, with a goal record in his side's favour of 23 and only five against. Bromilow's advent and McKinlay's retirement to full-back has proved a most judicious move in the re-arrangement of the club's resources.'

LIVERPOOL lost eventually with Bromilow two games later but had greatly improved, finishing 4th having been as low as 18th in December. He played in a total of 28 games during his debut season and would miss only five matches

over the next three seasons, which included the club's third and fourth League Championships.

Bromilow usually played at left-half and formed a powerful half-back trio with Jock McNab and Walter Wadsworth. Bromilow was said to be 'more dainty and artistic than either of his two colleagues, but is eminently efficient none the less.'

BROMILOW made his final appearance for the club at Blackburn on the last day of the 1929/30 season after an immensely successful career at the Reds. He was fondly remembered by Liverpool fans and came fifth in a poll among them in 1939 when they were asked to name the best ever Liverpool player.

Bromilow started his coaching career in the summer of 1930 in Amsterdam, Holland. In October 1932 he was appointed manager of Burnley, who had been relegated to the Second Division two years earlier. The highlight of his time at Turf Moor was when the Clarets reached the semi-finals of the FA Cup in the 1933/34 season. Bromilow left in July 1936 for Crystal Palace in the Third Division South.

Liverpool, however, was never far from his thoughts and when the role of manager at Anfield became vacant he applied with 51 others,

but George Kay was appointed in August 1936. Bromilow left the Eagles after only one season, taking charge of Newport County in 1936/37, then returning to Palace, finishing runners-up in the Third Division South before the outbreak of World War Two. He managed Leicester City during the war, winning the League South title and Midland Cup. He returned to Newport for a couple of years, before joining Leicester again, this time as scout. Bromilow died suddenly on a train in Nuneaton on 4 March 1959 while scouting a cup game between Wrexham and Merthyr Tydfil for Leicester.

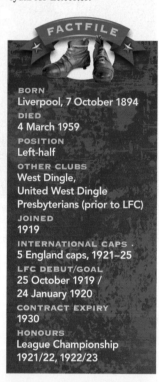

FACTFILE

BORN
Liverpool, 7 October 1894
DIED
4 March 1959
POSITION
Left-half
OTHER CLUBS
West Dingle,
United West Dingle
Presbyterians (prior to LFC)
JOINED
1919
INTERNATIONAL CAPS
5 England caps, 1921–25
LFC DEBUT/GOAL
25 October 1919 /
24 January 1920
CONTRACT EXPIRY
1930
HONOURS
League Championship
1921/22, 1922/23

JOSEPH BROUGH
LIVERPOOL

Brough,
Joseph

AMATEUR JOSEPH BROUGH left Burslem Port Vale in 1906 for Stoke, after financial difficulties saw their resignation from the Football League.

He subsequently rejoined the new Vale, who had dropped Burslem from its name in 1907, and netted a club record 43 goals in the 1909/10 season. Brough moved to Liverpool and made 11 appearances as a forward during 1910/11, scoring three goals. He moved to Bristol City in January 1912 after featuring only for Liverpool's reserves in the previous 12 months.

FACTFILE

BORN
Burslem, 9 November 1886
DIED
5 October 1968
POSITION
Inside-right forward
OTHER CLUBS
Smallthorne (1903–06),
Burslem Port Vale (1906–07),
Stoke City (1907–08),
Tottenham Hotspur (1908–09),
Port Vale (1909–10),
Bristol City (1912–13),
Port Vale (1913–22)
SIGNED FROM
Port Vale, August 1910
LFC DEBUT/GOAL
10 September 1910 /
17 September 1910
CONTRACT EXPIRY
January 1912

Season	League		FA Cup		Other		Total	
	App	Goals	App	Goals	App	Goals	App	Goals
1919/20	23	1	5	0	-	-	28	1
1920/21	40	0	3	0	-	-	43	0
1921/22	40	2	3	0	1	0	44	2
1922/23	41	3	4	0	-	-	45	3
1923/24	27	0	5	0	-	-	32	0
1924/25	21	0	2	0	-	-	23	0
1925/26	30	1	3	0	-	-	33	1
1926/27	40	0	4	0	-	-	44	0
1927/28	42	3	2	0	-	-	44	3
1928/29	28	1	2	0	-	-	30	1
1929/30	9	0	0	0	-	-	9	0
Total	**341**	**11**	**33**	**0**	**1**	**0**	**375**	**11**

Season	League		FA Cup		Total	
	App	Goals	App	Goals	App	Goals
1910/11	11	3	0	0	11	3
Total	**11**	**3**	**0**	**0**	**11**	**3**

Brownbill, Derek

DEREK BROWNBILL came through the junior ranks at Anfield before signing professional forms after he turned 18.

He only played once for the first team, in a league match away to Birmingham City on 15 September 1973. He was substituted for Brian Hall when Liverpool were losing 1-0 and Hall promptly scored the equaliser with just five minutes left. After leaving Anfield in February 1975, Brownbill went on to play 140 games in the lower divisions for Port Vale and Wigan Athletic. He immigrated to the USA to play for Cleveland Cobras and then went home again to play amateur football. He became player-manager at Warrington Town and then managed Curzon Ashton before returning to Warrington. He stepped down in 2009 as the club's director of football after more than two decades of service.

FACTFILE

BORN
Liverpool, 4 February 1954
POSITION
Midfielder
OTHER CLUBS
Port Vale (1975–78), Cleveland Cobras (1978), Wigan Athletic (1978–80), Stafford Rangers (1980), Oswestry Town, Morecambe, Witton Albion, Warrington Town
JOINED
March 1970; signed professional February 1972
LFC DEBUT
15 September 1973
CONTRACT EXPIRY
February 1975

Season	League		FA Cup		League Cup		Europe		Other		Total	
	App	Goals	App	Goals	App	Goals	App	Goals	App	Goals	App	Goals
1973/74	1	0	0	0	0	0	0	0	-	-	1	0
Total	1	0	0	0	0	0	0	0	0	0	1	0

Browning, John

JOHN BROWNING made his Reds' debut towards the end of the 1934/35 season, playing in three of the last four league fixtures.

But due to the consistency of Jimmy McDougall, the Scotsman was only picked six times in 1935/36 and that was the highest number of appearances he made for the club during any one season. His father, John senior, was a Scottish international who scored 63 goals in 217 games for Celtic between 1911 and 1919. His reputation suffered a bitter blow when in 1924 he and ex-Rangers player, Archie Kyle, were found guilty of attempting to bribe Bo'Ness player Peter Brown. John received 60 days hard labour for this misdemeanour. John Jr. moved to Southern League's Gillingham in August 1939. He moved to Dumbarton only three months later at a time when World War Two had derailed the British game. As well as featuring for Dumbarton he worked for the government. Liverpool held Browning's Football League registration until 1946.

FACTFILE

BORN
Alexandria, Scotland, 27 January 1915
DIED
14 August 1971
POSITION
Left-half
OTHER CLUBS
Bridgton Waverley (1931–32), Dunoon Athletic (1932–34), Gillingham (1939); Dumbarton, Albion Rovers (wartime guest) Cowdenbeath (1946–47)
SIGNED FROM
Dunoon Athletic, March 1934
LFC DEBUT
20 April 1935
CONTRACT EXPIRY
1946

Season	League		FA Cup		Total	
	App	Goals	App	Goals	App	Goals
1934/35	3	0	0	0	3	0
1935/36	6	0	0	0	6	0
1936/37	3	0	0	0	3	0
1937/38	5	0	0	0	5	0
1938/39	2	0	0	0	2	0
Total	19	0	0	0	19	0

Bruton, Les

ONCE DESCRIBED as a "human tank" Les Bruton came into his own at Blackburn after a slow start to his career.

HE SCORED 23 goals in 38 First Division appearances at Rovers from 1929 to 1931. He lost his place in Rovers' starting line-up in the 1931/32 season and was transferred to Liverpool, where he made a couple of appearances in February 1932. His debut came away to West Ham in a 1-0 defeat in the league and he also played in the FA Cup defeat by Chelsea a week later at Anfield. Bruton made seven more appearances the following season with his only goal coming at Chelsea on 27 December 1932.

ONCE DESCRIBED AS A "HUMAN TANK"

Season	League		FA Cup		Total	
	App	Goals	App	Goals	App	Goals
1931/32	1	0	1	0	2	0
1932/33	5	1	1	0	6	1
Total	**6**	**1**	**2**	**0**	**8**	**1**

FACTFILE

BORN
Foleshill, Coventry,
1 April 1903
DIED
2 April 1989
POSITION
Inside-left forward
OTHER CLUBS
Bell Green Wesleyans,
Foleshill (1919–22),
Southampton (1922–26),
Peterborough & Fletton
United (1926–27),
Raith Rovers (1927–29),
Blackburn Rovers (1929–32),
Leamington Town (1933–35)
SIGNED FROM
Blackburn Rovers,
February 1932
LFC DEBUT/GOAL
20 February 1932 /
27 December 1932
CONTRACT EXPIRY
19 July 1933

Buck, Fred

DIMINUTIVE forward Fred Buck was selected for the first eight league games of the 1903/04 season but on 17 October 1903 was sent off for kicking and punching a Stoke player by the name of James Bradley, who signed for Liverpool two years later. The Football League suspended Buck for six weeks, from 27 October onwards.

Buck returned for the home match with Wolverhampton a couple of weeks before Christmas but was immediately left out again and made only a further four appearances in the first team. Buck's only goal for Liverpool came in the Boxing Day defeat by Blackburn Rovers at Anfield.

IN HIS second spell at West Bromwich Albion from 1906 to 1914 he won the Second Division in 1911 and was a runner-up in the 1912 FA Cup, where he featured at centre half. He made over 300 league appearances for Albion in the First and Second Division and scored more than 70 goals.

BUCK'S ONLY GOAL FOR LIVERPOOL CAME IN THE BOXING DAY DEFEAT BY BLACKBURN ROVERS AT ANFIELD

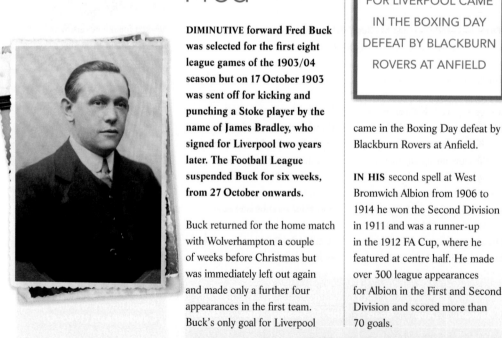

Season	League		FA Cup		Total	
	App	Goals	App	Goals	App	Goals
1903/04	13	1	0	0	13	1
Total	**13**	**1**	**0**	**0**	**13**	**1**

FACTFILE

BORN
Audley, Staffordshire,
2 November 1879
DIED
5 June 1952
POSITION
Inside-right forward
OTHER CLUBS
Stafford Wesleyans
(1895–97),
Stafford Rangers
(1897–1900),
West Bromwich Albion
(1900–03),
Plymouth Argyle
(1904–06),
West Bromwich Albion
(1906–14),
Swansea Town (1914–17)
SIGNED FROM
West Bromwich Albion,
May 1903
LFC DEBUT/GOAL
5 September 1903 /
26 December 1903
CONTRACT EXPIRY
March 1904

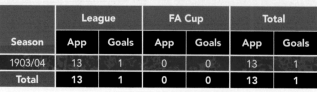

LIVERPOOL
IN 'ACTION'
1895

KEITH BURKINSHAW
LIVERPOOL

Bull,
Ben

JUST A SINGLE first-team appearance is recorded for Ben Bull.

HE TOOK OVER from regular right-winger Malcolm McVean when Liverpool played host to Lincoln City on 25 January 1896. Lincoln were thrashed 6-1 and he scored Liverpool's second goal, which was described as follows by the *Liverpool Mercury*: 'Geary a little later on dashed down the wing with a swift run and centred, and, after Bull had shot against the post, the same player very neatly sent into the net.' Despite his goal Bull didn't keep his place

in the side and McVean came back for the remainder of the season, at the end of which Liverpool won the Second Division.

FACTFILE

BORN
Leicester, 1872
POSITION
Right-winger
OTHER CLUBS
Loughborough Town
(1893–95)
SIGNED FROM
Loughborough Town,
December 1895
LFC DEBUT GAME/GOAL
25 January 1896 /
25 January 1896
CONTRACT EXPIRY
1896

Burkinshaw, Keith

KEITH BURKINSHAW'S only appearance for Liverpool came in a home fixture with Port Vale on 11 April 1955.

THE centre-half was transferred to Workington in December 1957, for whom he played nearly 300 league matches, first in the Third Division North and then the Fourth Division when the league system was reorganised in 1958. He also made over 100 league appearances for Scunthorpe.

Burkinshaw is best known for his spell as manager of Tottenham Hotspur from July 1976 until May 1984. He won the FA Cup two years in succession in 1981 and 1982 and the UEFA Cup in his last season as manager of Spurs.

FACTFILE

BORN
Higham, Barnsley,
23 June 1935
POSITION
Centre-half
OTHER CLUBS
Denaby United (1950–52),
Wolverhampton Wanderers
(1952–53),
Workington (1957–65),
Scunthorpe United
(1965–68)
SIGNED FROM
Wolverhampton Wanderers,
November 1953
LFC DEBUT
11 April 1955
CONTRACT EXPIRY
December 1957

Season	League		FA Cup		Other		Total	
	App	Goals	App	Goals	App	Goals	App	Goals
1895/96	1	1	0	0	0	0	1	1
Total	1	1	0	0	0	0	1	1

Season	League		FA Cup		Total	
	App	Goals	App	Goals	App	Goals
1954/55	1	0	0	0	1	0
Total	1	0	0	0	1	0

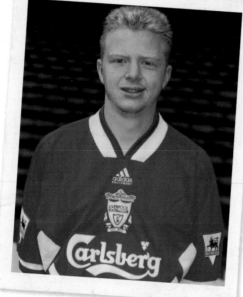

Burrows, David

DAVID 'BUGSY' BURROWS was a few days short of his 20th birthday when Kenny Dalglish signed the no-nonsense left-back from West Bromwich Albion. He went straight into the team for a home match against Coventry just two days later and would go on to make a further 20 league appearances before the end of a season that was overshadowed by the Hillsborough disaster.

A year later Burrows picked up a League Championship winners' medal after Liverpool again reached the summit of English football with their 18th league title. Another highlight was when he featured in Souness's side that won the FA Cup at Wembley in 1992.

In September 1993 Burrows was transferred to West Ham with Mike Marsh, in a swap deal for Julian Dicks. Burrows didn't get

on too well with Souness, as he revealed a few years later.

'I was desperately unhappy during my time with him [Souness] at Anfield,' Burrows remembered. 'It soon became clear that he didn't fancy me, and when a manager gets that into his head you haven't a chance. I was happy when the deal was done for me to join West Ham.'

> BURROWS PICKED UP A LEAGUE CHAMPIONSHIP WINNERS' MEDAL AFTER LIVERPOOL AGAIN REACHED THE SUMMIT OF ENGLISH FOOTBALL

FACTFILE

BORN
Dudley, 25 October 1968
POSITION
Left-back
OTHER CLUBS
West Bromwich Albion (1983–88), West Ham United (1993–94), Everton (1994–95), Coventry City (1995–2000), Birmingham City (2000–02), Sheffield Wednesday (2002–03)
SIGNED FROM
West Bromwich Albion, £550,000, 20 October 1988
INTERNATIONAL CAPS
7 England U-21 caps
LFC DEBUT GAME/GOAL
22 October 1988 / 31 August 1991
CONTRACT EXPIRY
17 September 1993
HONOURS
League Championship 1989/90; FA Cup 1992

Burrows had a tempestuous time at Birmingham where he clashed with two managers. He was quite understandably very upset with Trevor Francis when he left him out of the side that lost the League Cup final against Liverpool in March 2001, and was thrown out of the club after a training ground bust-up with Steve Bruce in February 2002. A month later he moved to Sheffield Wednesday but serious injuries to his collar-bone and hamstring forced him to end of his playing career at the age of 34.

Busby, Matt

MATT BUSBY, along with Tiny Bradshaw and Jimmy McDougall, formed an all-Scottish half-back line that certainly ranks with the best the club has possessed in its history. Busby started out as a youth-team player at Alpine Villa where he won the Under-18 Scottish Cup before moving to Denny Hibernian. He had been watched by scouts from Rangers and Celtic, but when Busby went on a trial to Rangers they found out he was a Catholic, and then Celtic weren't impressed that he had been at Rangers.

INSTEAD HE MOVED south to Manchester City as an inside-forward in February 1928, but they moulded him into a classy half-back. Busby was relieved to make the grade: 'There were only two ways for boys to go in those days: down, working in the pits, or up, if you happened to be good at football.' In seven years Busby played 226 Football League games for City. His biggest disappointment was losing the FA Cup final 3-0 to Everton in 1933 but the highlight was winning it a year later, when Portsmouth were beaten 2-1.

> HE IS THE RICHEST AND MOST PRACTISED PASSER THE GAME HAS EVER KNOWN
> **LIVERPOOL ECHO**

At 26 Matt Busby was an experienced professional when he was signed by Liverpool in March 1936 for £8,000. He almost immediately took over the right-half position from Bob Savage. Busby didn't miss many matches over the next three

Season	League		FA Cup		League Cup		Europe		Other		Total	
	App	Goals	App	Goals	App	Goals	App	Goals	App	Goals	App	Goals
1988/89	16 (5)	0	3	0	0	0	-	-	0	0	19 (5)	0
1989/90	23 (3)	0	2 (1)	0	3	0	-	-	1	0	29 (4)	0
1990/91	34 (1)	0	5	0	3	0	-	-	1	0	43 (1)	0
1991/92	30	1	6	0	5	0	7	0	-	-	48	1
1992/93	29 (1)	2	0	0	5	0	4	0	1	0	39 (1)	2
1993/94	3 (1)	0	0	0	0	0	-	-	-	-	3 (1)	0
Total	**135 (11)**	**3**	**16 (1)**	**0**	**16**	**0**	**11**	**0**	**3**	**0**	**181 (12)**	**3**

FACTFILE

BORN
Orbiston, Lanarkshire,
Scotland, 26 May 1909
DIED
20 January 1994
POSITION
Right-half
OTHER CLUBS
Denny Hibernian (1927–28),
Manchester City (1928–1936);
Chelsea, Middlesbrough,
Reading, Brentford,
Bournemouth & Boscombe
Athletic,
Hibernian (wartime guest)
SIGNED FROM
Manchester City, £8,000,
11 March 1936
INTERNATIONAL CAPS
1 Scotland cap, 1933
LFC DEBUT GAME/GOAL
14 March 1936 /
10 April 1936
CONTRACT EXPIRY
1939

> 'PEOPLE LIKE
> HIM WEREN'T SOLELY
> TIED DOWN WITH
> TACTICS, WHICH WAS
> A VALUABLE LESSON
> FOR ME'
> **BOB PAISLEY**

game with one shrewd pass, which always went speedily and accurately to the right man. There was never anything slipshod about Matt. Only the best would do and no matter where the ball was he was always working, always taking up position, always thinking a couple of moves ahead of anyone else.' Lawton said in his book *My Twenty Years of Soccer*.

MATT BUSBY was appointed as coach and assistant manager to George Kay at Anfield for £10 per week in May 1944. However, his views on how football should be played and governed were not shared by Liverpool's board. In February 1945, Busby, who was at this time an instructor at the Royal Military College, was released from his coaching position at Anfield. A few days later he accepted the manager's position at Manchester United.

seasons when Liverpool were a mediocre First Division team, but like so many of his contemporaries, Busby's playing career was cut short by World War Two.

Busby's greatest strength on the field was his passing. The *Liverpool Echo* waxed lyrical about him in September 1936: 'Busby goes far up, if so inclined and when he starts his upward trend one knows his command of the ball will be such he will not be dispossessed. He is the richest and most practised passer the game has ever known. Hence he appears in a blinding light when compared with some other half-backs.'

Tommy Lawton, the English striker extraordinaire, praised Busby's strengths as a player. 'Probably the classiest wing half-back I have ever met was Matt Busby. It was uncanny to see him change the direction of a

Matt Busby, Jack Balmer, Jim Harley, Willie Fagan and Don Welsh

It was a bold step but his achievements at Old Trafford were nothing short of astonishing, with the birth of the 'Busby Babes', five First Division Championships and two FA Cups. He survived the Munich air crash and then a decade later masterminded the European Cup winning team of 1968. Sir Matt Busby is rightly considered one of the best managers of all time. Liverpool supporters may be unhappy that he made United the force it is but they can be grateful to Busby for being the man who contacted Liverpool manager George Kay, suggesting he take a look at a lad called Billy Liddell. Busby was quite correct when he later said that the day Liddell arrived on Merseyside was 'a very fortunate day for Liverpool.'

WHEN BOB PAISLEY joined Liverpool Busby was club captain and they remained the best of friends. Paisley said: 'Matt Busby was a man you could look up to and respect. He'd played the game and people like him weren't solely tied down with tactics, which was a valuable lesson for me.'

	League		FA Cup		Total	
Season	**App**	**Goals**	**App**	**Goals**	**App**	**Goals**
1935/36	11	1	0	0	11	1
1936/37	29	1	1	0	30	1
1937/38	33	0	3	0	36	0
1938/39	42	1	3	0	45	1
Total	**115**	**3**	**7**	**0**	**122**	**3**

Bush, Tom

TOM BUSH was one of so many players whose careers were disrupted by World War Two. He was a centre-forward at Shrewsbury Amateurs where he scored 50 goals in the season previous to joining Liverpool, but was used as a defender at the Reds. He first played for the first team at the end of December 1933 and made a further 57 league and seven FA Cup appearances by the time hostilities broke out in September 1939, and although he returned to Anfield when the war was over he was by then a peripheral figure.

BUSH HAD to fly across the Atlantic from Liverpool's 1946/47 pre-season tour in America to be by his daughter's bedside. Tragically, nine-month-old Christine Ann Bush died on 29 May 1946.

Tom made three appearances as Liverpool won the League in the ensuing season. The last of his 61 league appearances came against Preston North End on 7 April 1947, over 13 years after he had made his debut. His solitary goal for the club came at Sunderland on 17 December 1938.

After Bush retired as a player he was for many years in charge of bringing players through the youth

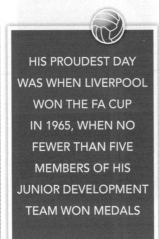

HIS PROUDEST DAY WAS WHEN LIVERPOOL WON THE FA CUP IN 1965, WHEN NO FEWER THAN FIVE MEMBERS OF HIS JUNIOR DEVELOPMENT TEAM WON MEDALS

system at Liverpool, preparing them for the reserves and then hopefully the first team. He also dealt with the administrative side of the A team, working out travel arrangements, booking meals and doing similar tasks in the daily running of a football club. Much of his work was done away from Anfield in close co-operation with chief scout Geoff Twentyman by interviewing parents of youngsters who Liverpool had interest in bringing to the club.

HIS PROUDEST day was when Liverpool won the FA Cup in 1965, when no fewer than five members of his junior development team won medals: Roger Hunt, Ian Callaghan, Tommy Smith, Tommy Lawrence and Gerry Byrne. He spent 37 years at the club apart from his war service.

TOM BUSH
LIVERPOOL

FACTFILE

BORN
Hodnet, 22 February 1914
DIED
20 December 1969
POSITION
Half-back
OTHER CLUBS
Shrewsbury Amateurs
(1929–33);
Brighton & Hove Albion,
Leeds United, Fulham
(wartime guest)
SIGNED FROM
Shrewsbury Amateurs,
March 1933
LFC DEBUT GAME/GOAL
30 December 1933 /
17 December 1938
CONTRACT EXPIRY
1947

Season	League		FA Cup		Total	
	App	Goals	App	Goals	App	Goals
1933/34	2	0	0	0	2	0
1936/37	9	0	0	0	9	0
1937/38	24	0	5	0	29	0
1938/39	23	1	2	0	25	1
1945/46	-	-	1	0	1	0
1946/47	3	0	0	0	3	0
Total	61	1	8	0	69	1

Byrne, Gerry

LIVERPOOL-BORN Byrne signed professional forms aged 17 after coming through the junior ranks at Anfield. He was spotted by chain-smoking Liverpool scout Tosh Moore at 15 when featuring for Liverpool Catholic Schoolboys.

Byrne made his league debut at Charlton Athletic on 28 September 1957, but that was his only outing that season. Perhaps it was because Liverpool lost 5-1, or maybe because he scored an own goal! It was, he recalled, a humiliating experience. 'I wish the ground would swallow me up when you score a goal like that. I just passed it back to Tommy Lawrence and he wasn't there. I got terrible abuse from the crowd,' Byrne said. The experienced full-back pairing of John Molyneux and Ronnie Moran prevented Byrne from making more than a handful of appearances during the next two years, but Bill Shankly's arrival in late 1959 changed his prospects completely as the new manager seemed to take a liking to the tough-tackling full-back, who got a break when Moran was seriously injured in the autumn of 1960.

Newcomer Tommy Smith could vouch for Byrne's toughness. 'I was only fifteen and playing in a five-a-side game at Melwood,' Smith said. 'I nutmegged Byrne and scored and I was on top of the world. A couple of minutes later a ball dropped between us, I went to head it and Gerry headed me and I went down with a gashed eye. As I lay on the ground covered in blood, Shankly strolled across, looked down at me and said, "Lesson number one, never nutmeg Gerry Byrne, son, and think you can get away with it."'

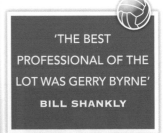

Byrne played in the remaining 33 league games of the 1959/60 season and was a regular from then on. He was an uncompromising character on the field. 'I was nicknamed the "Crunch". I was a clean player. I was hard, but fair,' he told *LFChistory.net*. 'I used to wait for the ball to come and then I was on my way. You hit someone when the ball was there and that was it. That's how I got the crunch. I didn't go after players intentionally. I was never sent off in my life.'

Byrne might not have been as well known as some of his colleagues but his courage was never in question; and that was never shown more clearly than on the day Liverpool finally won the FA Cup for the first time. He was injured very early on in the 1965 final against Leeds United at a time before substitutes were allowed. Bob Paisley was Liverpool's physio at the time and ran on to the field. 'Gerry had clattered into the chunky Bobby Collins. As soon as I reached him I knew that my initial touchline diagnosis had been painfully accurate. He had broken his collar-bone,' Paisley said in his book "50 Golden Reds". 'My first reaction should have been to wave to the bench to call for a stretcher. But Gerry got in first. Looking up at me he pleaded: "Don't tell anyone!" I asked: "Do you know it's broken?" Gerry knew – but still insisted on playing on through the remaining 87 minutes and, as it happened, another half hour of extra time. He told me defiantly: "I can get by." And he did, in one of the bravest Wembley displays I have ever witnessed.'

The extent of his injury was not revealed until the final was over, by which time Byrne had a winners' medal in his pocket and an important involvement in the first, vital breakthrough goal scored by Roger Hunt early in extra time. Shankly was in awe of Byrne's performance. 'Gerry's collar-bone

was split and grinding together yet he played on in agony. It was a performance of raw courage from the boy.'

Byrne was in England's World Cup winning squad in 1966 alongside team-mates Roger Hunt and Ian Callaghan, although he failed to make an appearance in the finals. In 2009 he was finally presented with a winners' medal at a special ceremony in London. Byrne had celebrated his 30th birthday a few days into the 1968/69 season, but the injury problems which had wrecked most of the 1966/67 season for him ended his career prematurely.

'I got injured after the World Cup. There was nobody near me.

I twisted and my studs stayed in the ground,' Byrne revealed to *LFChistory.net* in 2008.

Byrne's reward for a career which had seen him play 333 times for the first team was a testimonial match attended by nearly 40,000 people, who braved appalling conditions to pay tribute to a man who had been an integral part of Shankly's success.

Bill Shankly had nothing but the utmost respect for Gerry Byrne, as he revealed in 1975. 'I've had many skilful men and the likes of Peter Thompson, Ian St John, Kevin Keegan and Steve Heighway were the ones who caught the eye. But the best professional of the lot was Gerry

Byrne. He wasn't flashy and he wouldn't score you goals. But he was hard and skilful and gave you everything he had. More than that he was totally honest, which is the greatest quality of all. He was a true Liverpudlian who couldn't look his fellow Scousers in the face after a game unless he'd given everything he had for 90 minutes.'

FACTFILE

BORN
Liverpool, 29 August 1938
POSITION
Right/Left-back
JOINED
August 1953;
signed professional
30 August 1955
INTERNATIONAL CAPS
2 England caps, 1963–66
LFC DEBUT GAME/GOAL
28 September 1957 /
3 February 1962
CONTRACT EXPIRY
December 1969
HONOURS
League Championship
1963/64, 1965/66;
Second Division
Championship 1961/62;
FA Cup 1965

Season	League App	League Goals	FA Cup App	FA Cup Goals	League Cup App	League Cup Goals	Europe App	Europe Goals	Other App	Other Goals	Total App	Total Goals
1957/58	1	0	0	0	-	-	-	-	-	-	1	0
1958/59	1	0	0	0	-	-	-	-	-	-	1	0
1959/60	5	0	0	0	-	-	-	-	-	-	5	0
1960/61	33	0	2	0	3	0	-	-	-	-	38	0
1961/62	42	1	5	0	-	-	-	-	-	-	47	1
1962/63	38	0	6	0	-	-	-	-	-	-	44	0
1963/64	33	0	4	0	-	-	-	-	-	-	37	0
1964/65	40	0	8	0	-	-	7	1	1	1	56	2
1965/66	42	1	1	0	-	-	9	0	1	0	53	1
1966/67	9	0	2	0	-	-	0	0	1	0	12	0
1967/68	27	0	1	0	2	0	6	0	-	-	36	0
1968/69	2 (1)	0	0	0	0	0	0	0	-	-	2 (1)	0
Total	**273 (1)**	**2**	**29**	**0**	**5**	**0**	**22**	**1**	**3**	**1**	**332 (1)**	**4**

Cadden, Joe

GLASGOW-BORN centre-half Cadden signed for Liverpool in June 1948 after impressing the club's management on their USA tour.

He moved to the States after being discharged from the army at the end of World War Two. He didn't make his debut until 23 September 1950, by which time he had already passed his 30th birthday. Only four more first-team appearances followed before he was transferred to Grimsby Town in July 1952, where he only made one appearance in the Third Division North before moving to Accrington Stanley in the same division where he played 17 league games.

Season	League		FA Cup		Total	
	App	Goals	App	Goals	App	Goals
1950/51	4	0	0	0	4	0
1951/52	0	0	1	0	1	0
Total	**4**	**0**	**1**	**0**	**5**	**0**

Callaghan, Ian

IAN CALLAGHAN was a 15-year-old when he first registered on Liverpool's books for £10. When Billy Liddell was asked in 1961 if Liverpool had in their ranks a worthy successor to his crown, he didn't harbour any doubts: 'There is always someone to follow on. They have one at Anfield already, a youngster named Ian Callaghan. I played with him twice, watched his progress and I believe he'll be a credit to his club, the game and to his country,' he stated at the time. These were prophetic words indeed.

Callaghan played his first game only six days after his 18th birthday, replacing his boyhood hero Liddell. Liverpool beat Bristol Rovers 4-0 but Callaghan's performance captured the imagination.

Callaghan with Jimmy Melia and Gerry Byrne in 2008. A total of almost 1,500 games for the Reds between them!

When the final whistle went 27,000 spectators applauded him off, along with both set of players as well as the referee! The headline in the *Daily Post* read: 'A Callaghan debut to remember'. In the *Daily Express* Graham Fisher wrote: 'For Liverpool right-winger Ian Callaghan, veteran of four Central League games, he just ended the most accomplished League debut I've had the pleasure to witness.' Callaghan remembers well the prelude to his debut, as he told *LFChistory.net*. 'I went on the bus when I made my debut. People didn't have cars. I thought I was giving me plenty of time but they were queuing at the bus-stop to go to the match. They all knew who I was as it was in my neighbourhood. Several of them said: "Let Cally get on the bus, he's playing." I went at the front of the bus. I got off at the ground, played and got the bus home.'

BILL SHANKLY did not, however, want to rely on such a young man so soon and bought Kevin Lewis before the start of the 1960/61 season. Lewis scored 22 goals in 36 games and Callaghan had to bide his time. Liverpool were promoted in 1961/62 and from November that season he was finally a regular and stayed that way for the next 15 years!

During the first part of his career Callaghan played on the right wing with Peter Thompson on the left. They were a dangerous duo and created a number of goals for Roger Hunt and Ian St John. Callaghan only stood 5ft 7in (170cm), but he was blessed with great speed. 'I used to take the full-back on and get to the by-line. That was my strength.' Peter Thompson certainly enjoyed playing with Callaghan: 'The boss was a great influence. He made me believe I was the greatest winger in Europe, and he made Ian Callaghan believe he was better than I was! Cally and myself complemented each other perfectly. He was direct whereas I would tend to dwell on the ball a lot more and try to beat people. Some games one of us would be struggling, the defender facing Cally may have been faster than him or the right-back could handle a dribbler like myself, so we'd simply switch flanks and it'd work."' When Dixie Dean was asked if he could have repeated his record of scoring 60 league goals in one season in modern football he answered: 'If I could play between Ian Callaghan and Peter Thompson I'd still get my 60 goals a season.'

Callaghan's favourite memory from his career is the 1965 FA Cup final.

'IAN CALLAGHAN
WILL GO DOWN AS
ONE OF THE GAME'S
TRULY GREAT PLAYERS'
BILL SHANKLY

The game stood at 1-1 in extra time after goals from Roger Hunt and Billy Bremner. Callaghan crossed from the right and St John headed the winner into the net. This historic FA Cup win came between two Championships in 1964 and 1966.

This was the golden age of Bill Shankly's 60's side. 'Ian Callaghan is everything good that a man can be. No praise is too high for him,' Shankly said. 'He is a model professional, and a model human being. If there were eleven Callaghans at Anfield there would never be any need to put up a team sheet. You could stake your life on Ian. Words cannot do justice to the amount he has contributed to the game. Ian Callaghan will go down as one of the game's truly great players.'

In the 1970/71 season Callaghan underwent a knee operation and Brian Hall took his place on the right wing. When Callaghan returned Shankly moved him to the centre of midfield, prolonging his Liverpool career by seven years. Callaghan's great reading of the game and incredible work rate made him ideal for this position. Callaghan set a new record of appearances for Liverpool on 15 August 1972, breaking Billy Liddell's long-standing club record of 534. Three championship medals – in 1973, 1976 and 1977 – followed. Callaghan played in four FA Cup finals, winning in 1965 and 1974, but finishing on the losing side in 1971 and 1977. He won the UEFA Cup twice, in 1973 and 1976. In 1977 Liverpool

won the European Cup for the first time after beating Borussia Mönchengladbach 3-1 in Rome, and they celebrated their second European Cup win in 1978. Callaghan had lost his place to Graeme Souness by then but he was on the bench in the Wembley final.

That was to be the last time his name appeared on Liverpool's team sheet. He had gone through the whole of his Liverpool career without being sent off or even booked when the referee took his name down in Callaghan's penultimate game for Liverpool in March 1978. 'It was against Nottingham Forest in the League Cup. We played at Wembley on the Saturday and we drew and the replay was at Old Trafford,' Callaghan remembered. 'The referee was Pat Partridge. He had given a penalty. Phil Thompson tackled a guy and it was a yard outside the box. It went a bit mad after that and people were tackling. The ball bounced between this Scouser, called Peter Withe, and myself and I went in and he went in. I caught him in the chest and [the ref] took my name. The club tried to get it taken away, but they didn't. Tommy Smith said that I should have been booked more than him!'

In September 1978, after 19 seasons with Liverpool, Callaghan called it a day at the club having enjoyed the summer in the States. 'I went to America straight after the European Cup final at Wembley. I flew out the next day to sign for Fort Lauderdale on loan from Liverpool,' Callaghan said. 'Gordon Banks was in goal for us. I roomed with George Best for five months. That was an experience! Bob had signed Graeme Souness earlier, who was a great player. Bob said: "I'll give you a rise, but I want you to play in the reserve team to help the young players come along." I wanted to play more and wasn't ready for reserve team football so I signed for Swansea.'

CALLAGHAN played with Tommy Smith at John Toshack's Swansea on weekends, but still trained with Liverpool during the week. In 1981 Callaghan was going to retire following a short spell in Ireland but was persuaded by his old mate Alan A'Court, who was assistant manager at Crewe, to share his experience in the game.

'Alan turned up and asked me if I would come to Crewe just for a month to play in midfield, settle the youngsters down. I said: "No, no, I've finished." He was very persistent. I ended up going for a month and was five months there. Then I did my Achilles tendon and I called it a day.' Callaghan was two months short of his 40th birthday.

Liverpool FC's Membership manager Suzanne Cohen told a great story about Callaghan to the Official Liverpool FC website in January 2009 that offers valuable insight into this great man. 'My all-time favourite memory so far was when we had a new door fitted in the office. Ian Callaghan came in quite a lot and one day he noticed this door. I remember Val Rice saying to him: "Yes Ian, we decided that as we've got the Paisley Gates and the Shankly statue, it was about time we unveiled something like the Callaghan door." We then made a little sign and put a ribbon across it. He even cut it himself to officially declare it open! Moments like that are priceless.'

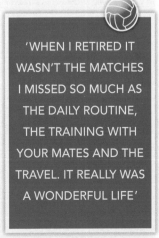

'WHEN I RETIRED IT
WASN'T THE MATCHES
I MISSED SO MUCH AS
THE DAILY ROUTINE,
THE TRAINING WITH
YOUR MATES AND THE
TRAVEL. IT REALLY WAS
A WONDERFUL LIFE'

LIVERPOOL 1977
Champions of Europe

FACTFILE

BORN
Toxteth, Liverpool,
10 April 1942
POSITION
Right-winger / Midfielder
OTHER CLUBS
Fort Lauderdale Strikers
(loan, 1978),
Swansea City (1978–81),
Canberra City (loan, 1979),
Cork United (1981),
Crewe Alexandra (1981–82)
JOINED
1957; signed professional
28 March 1960
INTERNATIONAL CAPS
4 England caps, 1966–77
LFC DEBUT GAME/GOAL
16 April 1960 /
4 November 1961
CONTRACT EXPIRY
15 September 1978
HONOURS
League Championship
1963/64, 1965/66, 1972/73,
1975/76, 1976/77;
Second Division
Championship 1961/62;
FA Cup 1965, 1974;
European Cup 1977, 1978;
UEFA Cup 1973, 1976;
FWA Footballer of the Year
1974

Ian Callaghan boasts one of the most remarkable careers of any player in Europe past or present. He was the epitome of the professional footballer and is a gentleman off the field. He is the club's record appearance holder with 857 games and was the first Liverpool player to be voted FWA Footballer of the Year, in 1974. Strangely enough he only played four times for his country. He was part of the World Cup winning squad in 1966, playing one game, but incredibly 11 years and 79 days passed from his second to his third cap. On 10 June 2009 Ian Callaghan was finally presented with a World Cup winners' medal at a special ceremony in London, nearly 43 years after the event.

When Liverpool won the European Cup for the first time in 1977 Callaghan was the only player who had also played in Liverpool's first European game in 1964 or indeed featured in the Second Division for the club. Charles Lambert, a *Liverpool Echo* reporter, gave Callaghan this praise: 'As great a Liverpool institution as the Mersey Ferries.' All things considered it is highly unlikely that Ian Callaghan's record of games played for Liverpool will ever be broken. Cally himself has the final word: 'I can honestly say I enjoyed every minute of my career. Yet when I retired it wasn't the matches I missed so much as the daily routine, the training with your mates and the travel. It really was a wonderful life.'

Season	League		FA Cup		League Cup		Europe		Other		Total	
	App	Goals	App	Goals	App	Goals	App	Goals	App	Goals	App	Goals
1959/60	4	0	0	0	-	-	-	-	-	-	4	0
1960/61	3	0	0	0	2	0	-	-	-	-	5	0
1961/62	23	1	5	0	-	-	-	-	-	-	28	1
1962/63	37	2	6	0	-	-	-	-	-	-	43	2
1963/64	42	8	5	0	-	-	-	-	-	-	47	8
1964/65	37	6	8	1	-	-	9	1	1	0	55	8
1965/66	42	5	1	0	-	-	9	0	1	0	53	5
1966/67	40	3	4	0	-	-	5	1	1	0	50	4
1967/68	41	3	9	0	2	1	6	3	-	-	58	7
1968/69	42	8	4	1	3	1	2	0	-	-	51	10
1969/70	41	3	6	0	2	0	3 (1)	2	-	-	52 (1)	5
1970/71	21 (2)	0	4 (1)	0	1	0	5	0	-	-	31 (3)	0
1971/72	41	2	3	0	3	0	4	0	1	0	52	2
1972/73	42	3	4	0	8	1	12	0	-	-	66	4
1973/74	42	0	9	0	6	3	4	0	-	-	61	3
1974/75	41	1	2	0	3	0	4	1	1	0	51	2
1975/76	40	3	2	0	3	0	12	1	-	-	57	4
1976/77	32 (1)	1	4 (1)	0	2	1	7	0	1	0	46 (2)	2
1977/78	25 (1)	0	1	0	7	0	6	1	1	0	40 (1)	1
Total	**636 (4)**	**49**	**77 (2)**	**2**	**42**	**7**	**88 (1)**	**10**	**7**	**0**	**850 (7)**	**68**

Camara,
Titi

TITI CAMARA can hardly be considered a failure at Anfield. Although he was only at Liverpool for 18 months he was a popular player with the supporters and lit up Anfield on occasion with his sublime skills.

His scoring debut for Liverpool against Sheffield Wednesday was a sign of extraordinary things to come, as the *Liverpool Echo* noted: 'And then there is Titi Camara. Or "Allez Titi" as the red, green and yellow banner read. His debut Premiership goal – a left-foot shot from just inside the area six minutes from time after Srnicek had pushed a 25-yard piledriver from Fowler straight into his path – was reward for [an] eye-catching display. The theory remains that Camara, for all his instant love affair with the supporters, will prove a better substitute in the long run; able to change the course of games in that role rather than from the start.'

CAMARA started 24 and made 13 substitute appearances during the 1999/2000 season and scored 10 goals, all but one of which came when he was in the starting line-up. His best goal was possibly his second, a brilliant curling shot at Elland Road, or maybe the 'screamer' against Coventry at the Kop end on the day the club celebrated the 40th anniversary of Bill Shankly's arrival at Anfield.

His most emotional moment in a Liverpool shirt came one evening late in October 1999 when he slumped to his knees in front of the Anny Road end after scoring

what turned out to be the winning goal against West Ham, having been told only hours earlier that his father had died. To play at all under such circumstances, never mind score the winning goal, was testament to his courage. 'I would like to pay Titi a special tribute because today was special for him,' Houllier told the press following the match. 'He lost his dad during the day but he told me, "I want to play for my father." He was crying after he scored because it was such an emotional day.'

Camara's time at Liverpool was effectively over after only one season, when he fell dramatically out of favour with Houllier. The Frenchman said in October 2001: 'Titi got injured at half-time in the pre-season friendly with Parma on August 12th. He is the only player I know who has got injured without playing. The injury was so bad that he could only come back seven weeks later. I don't know what kind of injury he had.'

Camara finally made the bench for the game with Slovan Liberec on 26 October, after being excluded from the squad for the two

previous games. Houllier and Titi had both had enough of the impossible situation. 'The following day Titi came to see me and said he did not want to play for Liverpool and that he wanted to leave,' Houllier said. 'If he doesn't want to play for Liverpool and wear the red shirt, then that's it.'

TWO MONTHS later the Guinean moved to West Ham. For many Liverpool supporters, though, despite his short stay at club Titi retains something of a 'cult hero' status – a status reflected in him being voted in 91st position in the 2006 poll '100 Players Who Shook The Kop', which was conducted by the Official Liverpool FC website.

Unfortunately Titi's move to Harry Redknapp's Hammers did not revive his career despite his best intentions. 'I've come to West Ham to play, play, play – and score, score, score!' Titi declared. 'If it was a question of money, I could have stayed at Liverpool and picked it up. I need to play, and if I don't it is totally pointless.' He remained at Upton Park for two-and-a-half years but only played in 14 matches and failed to score in any of them.

By now past his 31st birthday, he went on a four-month loan to Saudi Arabia in January 2003, where he enjoyed life's riches, living in the presidential suite at the Jeddah Meridien Hotel with servants, drivers and security staff on call 24 hours a day. When he scored a hat-trick in his second game he was rewarded with three luxury cars. Next stop was Qatar, then Titi finally went back to France where he had started his professional career. In June 2009 Titi took over as manager of Guinea's national team, a post he held for four months. At the end of 2010 Titi was appointed Guinea's Sports Minister and remained in office until October 2012 when he was forced out in a government reshuffle.

'At Liverpool, I was lucky enough to be playing for a great club, but unfortunately things didn't go well,' he would recall. 'I would have liked to have continued my career there, but that's football, that's destiny. The memories I have from Anfield will stay with me right until my final days.'

FACTFILE

BORN
Conakry, Guinea,
17 November 1972
POSITION
Centre-forward
OTHER CLUBS
Saint-Etienne (1990–95),
Lens (1995–97),
Olympique Marseille
(1997–99),
West Ham United (2000–03),
Al Ittihad (loan, 2003),
Al Siliya (2003–04),
Amiens (2004–06)
SIGNED FROM
Olympique Marseille,
£2.6million, 1 June 1999
INTERNATIONAL CAPS
38 Guinea caps (23 goals)
(4 (4) at LFC), 1992–2004
LFC DEBUT GAME/GOAL
7 August 1999 /
7 August 1999
CONTRACT EXPIRY
21 December 2000

Season	League		FA Cup		League Cup		Total	
	App	Goals	App	Goals	App	Goals	App	Goals
1999/2000	22 (11)	9	2	1	0 (2)	0	24 (13)	10
Total	22 (11)	9	2	1	0 (2)	0	24 (13)	10

Cameron,
James

JAMES CAMERON made four appearances for Liverpool's first team, during the disastrous 1894/95 First Division campaign.

Liverpool picked up only one point from the four games the defender played in, scored twice and conceded 11 goals.

FACTFILE

BORN
Glasgow, Scotland, 1868
POSITION
Defender
OTHER CLUBS
Rangers (1883–87), Glasgow Perthshire (1888–92), Linthouse (1893), Glasgow (1893–94), Pollokshields (1895–97)
SIGNED FROM
Glasgow, 8 May 1894
LFC DEBUT
6 October 1894
CONTRACT EXPIRY
1895

Season	League		FA Cup		Other		Total	
	App	Goals	App	Goals	App	Goals	App	Goals
1894/95	4	0	0	0	0	0	4	0
Total	4	0	0	0	0	0	4	0

Cameron,
Jonathan

SCOTTISH FORWARD Cameron scored twice on his debut in an 8-0 win over Higher Walton in September 1892.

In total he played nine games in Liverpool's inaugural season and scored five goals, certainly an impressive record. His final outing for the club was memorable: a 2-1 win at Heywood Central, which was played in six inches of snow!

FACTFILE

BORN
Unknown
POSITION
Inside-left forward
OTHER CLUBS
Renton (1890–92)
SIGNED FROM
Renton, 1892
LFC DEBUT GAME/GOAL
3 September 1892 /
3 September 1892
CONTRACT EXPIRY
1893
HONOURS
Lancashire League Championship 1892/93

Season	League		FA Cup		Other		Total	
	App	Goals	App	Goals	App	Goals	App	Goals
1892/93	-	-	2	1	7	4	9	5
Total	0	0	2	1	7	4	9	5

Campbell,
Bobby

BOBBY CAMPBELL featured in 13 matches in Bill Shankly's inaugural season as manager that was the midfielder's second campaign as a first-team player.

His playing career was cut short by injury soon after his 30th birthday. Campbell subsequently embarked on a colourful managerial career in 1976, when he was George Best's manager at Fulham. He was sacked in 1980 but made Portsmouth Third Division champions three years later. Following a spell in Kuwait from 1985–86 he was appointed as John Hollins' assistant at Chelsea in the 1987/88 season. When Hollins was dismissed Campbell took over as caretaker manager but was unable to save the London club from relegation. Campbell was hired full-time and Chelsea won the Second Division, then finished fifth the following season. Campbell was sacked when the team failed to live up to expectations in the 1990/91 season. He moved again to Kuwait in 1993, where he stayed one year. Campbell is one of Roman Abramovich's closest friends and is often seen by his side at games at Stamford Bridge.

FACTFILE

BORN
Liverpool, 23 April 1937
POSITION
Midfielder
OTHER CLUBS
Wigan Athletic (1961), Portsmouth (1961–66), Aldershot (1966–67)
JOINED
1952; signed professional 11 May 1954
LFC DEBUT GAME/GOAL
15 September 1958 /
20 September 1958
CONTRACT EXPIRY
1961

BOBBY CAMPBELL
LIVERPOOL

Season	League		FA Cup		League Cup		Total	
	App	Goals	App	Goals	App	Goals	App	Goals
1958/59	10	1	0	0	-	-	10	1
1959/60	13	1	0	0	-	-	13	1
1960/61	1	0	0	0	1	0	2	0
Total	24	2	0	0	1	0	25	2

Campbell, Don

THE ENGLAND YOUTH international defender didn't get any first-team opportunities until the 1953/54 relegation season, one of 31 players called on by manager Don Welsh during that traumatic year.

Campbell finally got a decent run in the first team under the leadership of Phil Taylor in the 1957/58 season, seven years after signing for the club.

He was transferred to Fourth Division Crewe Alexandra in the summer. He ended up in non-league football, working as a painter and decorator.

Season	League		FA Cup		Total	
	App	Goals	App	Goals	App	Goals
1953/54	2	0	0	0	2	0
1954/55	12	0	0	0	12	0
1956/57	6	1	0	0	6	1
1957/58	27	1	1	0	28	1
Total	47	2	1	0	48	2

FACTFILE

BORN
Bootle, Liverpool,
19 October 1932
POSITION
Left-half
OTHER CLUBS
Crewe Alexandra (1958–62),
Gillingham (1962–64),
Folkestone Town (1964–67),
Margate (1967–69),
Canterbury City (1969)
JOINED
November 1950
LFC DEBUT GAME/GOAL
14 November 1953 /
19 April 1957
CONTRACT EXPIRY
July 1958

Campbell, Ken

KEN CAMPBELL became Liverpool's last line of defence before the final seven league games of the 1911/12 season, when the club was in serious relegation trouble.

Tom Watson showed immense faith in such an inexperienced 20-year-old. Liverpool survived by winning three out of their last four games, with Campbell keeping three clean sheets. Watson was quite content with his new goalkeeper, who was recognised as one of the very best captures of the 1911/12 season. Watson told the club's board at its annual meeting; 'And he only cost us £10 – and the travelling expenses.'

LIVERPOOL'S first-choice keeper for the previous seven years, Sam Hardy, moved to Villa Park at the end of the season and Campbell missed only one First Division match during the 1912/13 season. The man who replaced him on that occasion, the young Elisha Scott, would subsequently ensure that Campbell's spell as Liverpool's first-choice keeper wasn't as dominant as his talent warranted.

Campbell only missed four league games in the 1913/14 season but before the halfway point of the following season Scott had taken over between the posts. According to a contemporary profile of Campbell he was said to be 'the idol of the Anfield crowd, especially the ladies'.

When World War One ended and league football resumed, Campbell did find himself first choice again, but only because of Scott's unavailability. When Scott returned in goal Campbell almost immediately joined Partick Thistle, but was still living on Merseyside and travelling north for games.

Finally, in the summer of 1922 the Scottish international surprised everybody, except his family, by moving to New Brighton,

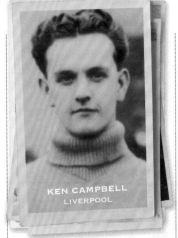

KEN CAMPBELL
LIVERPOOL

a Lancashire Combination club. He wanted to move closer to home and opened a sports outfitter in nearby Wallasey later that year, which was to become his base for the rest of his life. On the playing front, he moved to Stoke in March 1923, but featured mainly in the Second Division as the Potters were relegated a couple of months after he joined them.

CAMPBELL tasted life in the top flight once more with newly promoted Leicester City, who finished seventh in the First Division in his second season. Leicester finished third and second in the next two seasons, but Campbell was no longer first choice by then. He spent the final couple of years of his career at New Brighton, returning there in 1929.

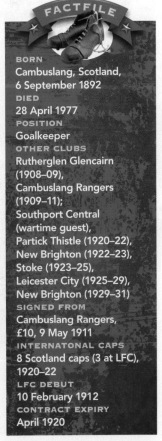

FACTFILE

BORN
Cambuslang, Scotland,
6 September 1892
DIED
28 April 1977
POSITION
Goalkeeper
OTHER CLUBS
Rutherglen Glencairn (1908–09),
Cambuslang Rangers (1909–11);
Southport Central (wartime guest),
Partick Thistle (1920–22),
New Brighton (1922–23),
Stoke (1923–25),
Leicester City (1925–29),
New Brighton (1929–31)
SIGNED FROM
Cambuslang Rangers,
£10, 9 May 1911
INTERNATONAL CAPS
8 Scotland caps (3 at LFC),
1920–22
LFC DEBUT
10 February 1912
CONTRACT EXPIRY
April 1920

Season	League		FA Cup		Total	
	App	Goals	App	Goals	App	Goals
1911/12	7	0	0	0	7	0
1912/13	37	0	4	0	41	0
1913/14	34	0	8	0	42	0
1914/15	15	0	0	0	15	0
1919/20	32	0	5	0	37	0
Total	125	0	17	0	142	0

Captains

Andrew Hannah	1892-1895	Laurie Hughes	1954-1955
Jimmy Ross	1895-1897	Billy Liddell	1955-1958
John McCartney	1897-1898	Johnny Wheeler	1958-1959
Harry Storer	1898-1899	Ronnie Moran	1959-1960
Alex Raisbeck	1899-1909	Dick White	1960-1961
Arthur Goddard	1909-1912	Ron Yeats	1961-1970
Ephraim Longworth	1912-1913	Tommy Smith	1970-1973
Harry Lowe	1913-1915	Emlyn Hughes	1973-1979
Ephraim Longworth / Don Mackinlay	1919-1920	Kenny Dalglish	1979
		Phil Thompson	1979-1982
Ephraim Longworth	1920-1922	Graeme Souness	1982-1984
Don Mackinlay	1922-1928	Phil Neal	1984-1985
Tom Bromilow	1928-1929	Alan Hansen	1985-1988
James Jackson	1929-1931	Ronnie Whelan	1988-1989
Tom Bradshaw	1931-1934	Alan Hansen	1989-1990
Ernie Blenkinsop / Tom Cooper	1934-1935	Ronnie Whelan / Steve Nicol	1990-1991
Ernie Blenkinsop	1935-1936	Mark Wright	1991-1993
Ernie Blenkinsop / Tom Cooper	1936-1937	Ian Rush	1993-1996
		John Barnes	1996-1997
Tom Cooper	1937-1939	Paul Ince	1997-1999
Matt Busby	1939-1940	Jamie Redknapp	1999-2002
Willie Fagan	1945-1947	Sami Hyypia	
Jack Balmer	1947-1950	/ Robbie Fowler	2000-2001
Phil Taylor	1950-1953	Sami Hyypia	2002-2003
Bill Jones	1953-1954	Steven Gerrard	2003-

Liverpool Captain Jack Balmer leading the team out alongside Everton Captain T.G.Jones

TOM BRADSHAW
[LIVERPOOL CAPTAIN]

Carlin, John

JOHN CARLIN first appeared in Liverpool's forward line at Stoke on 17 January 1903.

THIS WAS his only game of the season and the only match missed by Liverpool's star striker Sam Raybould, who scored 32 times in 34 games that campaign. In view of the club's reliance on Raybould to score, perhaps it was not surprising that Carlin's debut for the club was one of only six matches in which it failed to score during the league campaign.

The club programme commented on him in a preview to the 1904/05 season: '[Carlin] is so clever and has such knowledge of the game that one is forced to explain "What a pity it is that he is only a little 'un." He is apt to be lost in a melee in front of goal.'

Carlin never settled in Liverpool's first XI and the highest number of appearances he made in a single season was the 16 he managed during 1905/06 when he scored six goals, a vital contribution to the club's second league title.

FACTFILE

BORN
Liverpool, 1876

POSITION
Inside-right/left forward

OTHER CLUBS
Barnsley, Preston North End (1907–09)

SIGNED FROM
Barnsley, 5 December 1902

LFC DEBUT/GOAL
17 January 1903 / 23 January 1904

CONTRACT EXPIRY
18 May 1907

HONOURS
League Championship 1905/06

Season	League App	League Goals	FA Cup App	FA Cup Goals	Other App	Other Goals	Total App	Total Goals
1902/03	1	0	0	0	-	-	1	0
1903/04	5	1	0	0	-	-	5	1
1904/05	4	1	1	0	-	-	5	1
1905/06	14	6	2	0	0	0	16	6
1906/07	8	0	0	0	-	-	8	0
Total	**32**	**8**	**3**	**0**	**0**	**0**	**35**	**8**

LIVERPOOL

LEAGUE CHAMPIONS 1905-1906

Carlin,
Willie

WILLIE CARLIN came through the junior ranks at Anfield but only made one first-team appearance for the club, in a 2-2 draw against Brighton at Anfield on 10 October 1959.

A promising youngster who had represented his country at schoolboy and youth levels, the pint-sized dynamo played 445 matches and scored 74 goals in all four divisions of the Football League. He was transferred to Third Division Halifax Town in August 1962, who were relegated at the end of the season. Carlin's career took an upward turn when he helped Brian Clough's Derby to win the Second Division. He was a regular for one season in the top flight before being sold to Leicester, who subsequently won

the Second Division title. Again, Carlin didn't stay for long in the upper echelons as he was sold to Third Division Notts County in September 1971. He finished his playing career with Second Division Cardiff City.

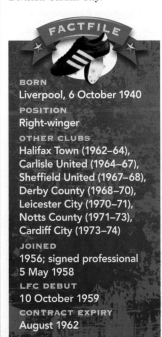

BORN
Liverpool, 6 October 1940
POSITION
Right-winger
OTHER CLUBS
Halifax Town (1962–64),
Carlisle United (1964–67),
Sheffield United (1967–68),
Derby County (1968–70),
Leicester City (1970–71),
Notts County (1971–73),
Cardiff City (1973–74)
JOINED
1956; signed professional
5 May 1958
LFC DEBUT
10 October 1959
CONTRACT EXPIRY
August 1962

Season	League		FA Cup		Total	
	App	Goals	App	Goals	App	Goals
1959/60	1	0	0	0	1	0
Total	**1**	**0**	**0**	**0**	**1**	**0**

Carney,
Len

LIVERPUDLIAN Len Carney was a university graduate and history teacher who went on to be headmaster of Chadderton Grammar School in Oldham.

HIS HEROICS SAVED
THE DAY FOR
LIVERPOOL, WHO
WENT ON TO
WIN THEIR
FIFTH LEAGUE TITLE

Carney, who featured in 33 games and scored 15 goals for Liverpool during wartime, during which he won the Distinguished Service Order for bravery, was 31 years old when he made his proper debut at Sheffield United on the opening day of the first full season following World War Two. 'Len Carney, fair-haired schoolmaster, crashes into big-time football,' the press reported. Carney scored

the game's only goal in the very last minute with a 'gliding header'.

HIS HEROICS saved the day for Liverpool, who went on to win their fifth league title. He kept his place in the starting line-up in the game following his scoring debut but that turned out to be his last appearance during this historic season.

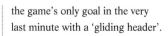

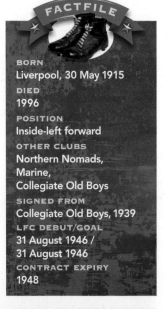

BORN
Liverpool, 30 May 1915
DIED
1996
POSITION
Inside-left forward
OTHER CLUBS
Northern Nomads,
Marine,
Collegiate Old Boys
SIGNED FROM
Collegiate Old Boys, 1939
LFC DEBUT/GOAL
31 August 1946 /
31 August 1946
CONTRACT EXPIRY
1948

Season	League		FA Cup		Total	
	App	Goals	App	Goals	App	Goals
1946/47	2	1	0	0	2	1
1947/48	4	0	0	0	4	0
Total	**6**	**1**	**0**	**0**	**6**	**1**

Carr, Lance

AN ACCOMPLISHED cricketer and boxer, and son of a professional runner, Lance Carr utilised his physical strength and electrifying pace on the left wing.

The South African had just one extended run in the first team, when he featured in 23 of 28 games in the 1935/36 season. He replaced Alf Hanson on 7 September 1935 when Everton visited Anfield and created the first two goals for Liverpool who went on to beat Everton 6-0, which is still the Reds' biggest win over their blue rivals. Imagine Carr's shock when four days later Manchester City beat Liverpool by the same scoreline! He scored in the following game when Liverpool beat Grimsby 7-2. Clearly, no regular results in those days!

Carr enjoyed being a firm fixture in the side for the first time in his Liverpool career with his compatriot Berry Nieuwenhuys on the opposite wing. They had arrived together from South Africa in September 1933 after being spotted by the father of their compatriot Arthur Riley, who was still keeping goal for Liverpool.

THE HIGHLIGHT of Carr's post-Liverpool career was winning

the Third Division South with Newport County in the 1938/39 season. He played 42 games and scored eight goals in his only season at Bristol Rovers after the resumption of league football before going on a free transfer to Merthyr Tydfil in July 1947. Carr later became a businessman in London and died in Greenwich on 28 April 1983, aged 73.

FACTFILE

BORN
Johannesburg, South Africa, 18 February 1910
DIED
28 April 1983
POSITION
Left-winger
OTHER CLUBS
Johannesburg Calies (1927–29), Boksburg (1929–33), Newport County (1936–37), South Liverpool (1937–38), Newport County (1938–46); Bristol City, Swindon Town, Aldershot (wartime guest), Bristol Rovers (1946–47), Merthyr Tydfil
SIGNED FROM
Boksburg, 11 September 1933
LFC DEBUT/GOAL
16 December 1933 / 19 April 1935
CONTRACT EXPIRY
22 October 1936

Season	League		FA Cup		Total	
	App	Goals	App	Goals	App	Goals
1933/34	2	0	0	0	2	0
1934/35	8	2	0	0	8	2
1935/36	21	6	2	0	23	6
Total	**31**	**8**	**2**	**0**	**33**	**8**

Carragher, Jamie

A LOCAL LAD whose fighting abilities and sense of humour endeared him to supporters and team-mates alike, Carragher became the Scouse rock at the heart of the Liverpool defence.

He excelled at both domestic and European level, leading the charge to Jerzy Dudek's goal following his penalty save from Andriy Shevchenko in Istanbul even though Carragher had suffered from agonising leg cramp in extra time. Carra wore his Liverpool heart on his sleeve and his frustration could boil over when things were not going according to plan.

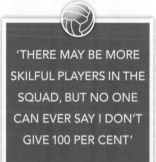

'THERE MAY BE MORE SKILFUL PLAYERS IN THE SQUAD, BUT NO ONE CAN EVER SAY I DON'T GIVE 100 PER CENT'

'Jamie Carragher is the true boss in the dressing room. He is very bad-tempered, he orders everybody around and yells a lot,' said Álvaro Arbeloa, who was on the receiving end of Carra's very public outburst at the Hawthorns in May 2009. Carragher had, though, the best interests of Liverpool at heart and

he transmitted more positive vibes than negative to his colleagues, as Chris Kirkland noted: 'He's the joker of the squad all right. Carra is always the life and soul of the party. If we win a game and go out to celebrate, he's the first one on the microphone. Every club needs someone like Carra. You can't buy team spirit and with him around the atmosphere in the dressing room is always brilliant.'

It was Roy Evans, in his penultimate full season as sole manager, who gave the soon-to-be 19-year-old his first-team debut in January 1997, as a substitute for Rob Jones in a League Cup tie at Middlesbrough. It was a debut that had been expected for a while because Carragher's presence had been carefully monitored through his days at the Football Association's School of Excellence at Lilleshall and as a member of Liverpool's successful Youth Cup winning team of 1996. His first start was marked in fine style by heading in a left-wing corner in front of the Kop to set his team on the way to a comfortable 3-0 victory over Aston Villa.

Carragher was supposed to feature at centre-half, but Bjørn Tore Kvarme had been cleared to play following his move from Rosenborg at 5pm the night before the game. Fortunately for Carragher Patrik Berger was sick so he did feature after all but as a midfielder. The Villa goal was one of the highlights of his career. 'I was a bit nervous, but it was more excitement really. I got booked after 20 seconds, that calmed me down.'

'CARRA IS THE BEST DEFENDER I'VE PLAYED WITH AT LIVERPOOL AND THE WORST FINISHER I'VE EVER PLAYED WITH!'

STEVEN GERRARD

Carragher became a more regular member of the team with 20 starts and three more as substitute in the disappointing 1997/98 season. Once Gérard Houllier had taken over following the departure of Roy Evans, the Bootle boy became a key player for the Frenchman for the rest of his reign at Anfield.

Carragher was not to everyone's taste, as he himself recognised. 'I don't go on the websites or anything but I believe there's murder there after a game if we have got beaten. But I'm not kidding people, if the team were to get beaten then I know I'd be one of the first to get criticised!' His number of appearances only dipped once below 50-a-season for Houllier, but his absence was excusable as he broke his leg at Blackburn's Ewood Park on 13 September 2003, which kept him out for four months.

CARRAGHER'S versatility as a defender proved to be absolutely vital for him as he held his ground

despite many attempts by newcomers to push him out of the first XI. He could adapt to any given situation, which ultimately proved the foundation for his long and successful career. He established himself as the team's regular right-back before moving to the left when Markus Babbel arrived at the club. Rafa Benítez saw Carragher as an ideal centre-half and in the Spaniard's first two seasons in charge, which ended with victories in the Champions League and the FA Cup, he made 56 and 57 first-team appearances respectively. His performances defied belief, as Alan Hansen noted following Liverpool's monumental win over Chelsea in the Champions League semi-final at Anfield in May 2005. 'The way he held Chelsea at bay was unbelievable. I'm sitting there in awe of how many times he intercepted, blocked and covered.'

Carragher scored an own goal in the 2006 FA Cup final and they came more readily for him than actually scoring for his own team, as Steven Gerrard pointed out light-heartedly. 'Carra is the best defender I've played with at Liverpool and the worst finisher I've ever played with!' Carragher managed to put the ball eight times into his own net, including

twice in the same game against Manchester United in September 1999. It's probably an inevitable part of a defender's life that he will sometimes unwittingly make the crucial contact or deflection that can prove costly. The number of goals Carragher prevented by his last-ditch tackling and self-sacrifice for the team far outweighs any 'damage' he may have done. 'For me Jamie is one of the best defenders in Europe,' Rafa Benítez said in March 2007. 'He is always focused on the game, always trying to learn. That is the key for me because each season he improves a little bit. He reminds me of a hunting dog, when I want something specific done in defence he is very willing to learn. He is always shouting and talking to the others. He is good for the young players, showing them what to do and how to play.'

'FOR ME JAMIE IS ONE OF THE BEST DEFENDERS IN EUROPE'

RAFA BENÍTEZ

A couple of nasty injuries restricted Carragher to only 38 of the team's 54 first-team matches during the 2010/11 season. He enjoyed a well-deserved testimonial at Anfield in September 2010, when a mixture of Liverpool players past and present played an Everton team, with all proceeds from the game going to local charities through the Carragher 23 Foundation. Carragher appeared in 60 per cent of the club's first-team matches in 2011/12 but 21 Premier League appearances was his lowest total since the 2003/04 season. He turned 34 years old during the campaign and was no longer an automatic choice. But Brendan

Rodgers knew that Carra's mere presence was of the utmost importance to the squad. 'Jamie has been an absolute model professional. I feel we are a quiet team, and maybe we've needed players who can organise and manage inside the game. You need a voice in your team, and you don't get a louder voice than Carra's!' Carragher was put back into the starting line-up and was fully expected to play one more campaign, but he announced in February 2013 that he would retire at the end of the season.

Carragher had a historic career at Liverpool. He made his 137th European appearance for the club in March 2011, a British record at the time although he was subsequently overtaken by Ryan Giggs. On 9 May 2011 he overtook Emlyn Hughes and Ray Clemence in making his 666th competitive appearance for the club, leaving just Ian Callaghan ahead of him in the club's all-time appearance list. A remarkable feat!

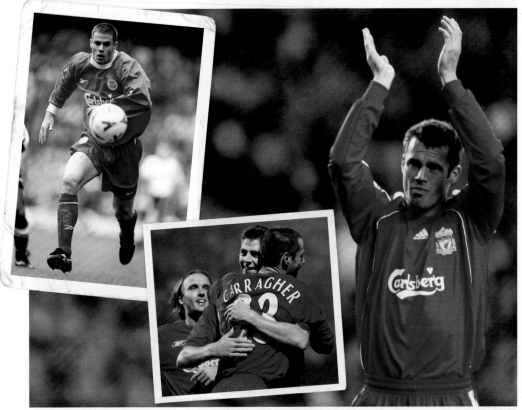

FACTFILE

BORN
Bootle, Liverpool, 28 January 1978
POSITION
Defender / Midfielder
JOINED
1987; signed professional 9 October 1996
INTERNATIONAL CAPS
38 England caps, 1999–2010
LFC DEBUT/GOAL
8 January 1997 / 18 January 1997
CONTRACT EXPIRY
19 May 2013
HONOURS
FA Cup 2001, 2006; League Cup 2001, 2003, 2012; Champions League 2005; UEFA Cup 2001

Season	League		FA Cup		League Cup		Europe		Other		Total	
	App	Goals	App	Goals	App	Goals	App	Goals	App	Goals	App	Goals
1996/97	1 (1)	1	0	0	0 (1)	0	0	0	-	-	1 (2)	1
1997/98	17 (3)	0	0	0	2		1	0	-	-	20 (3)	0
1998/99	34	1	2	0	2	0	6	0	-	-	44	1
1999/2000	33 (3)	0	2	0	2	0	-	-	-	-	37 (3)	0
2000/01	30 (4)	0	6	0	6	0	12	0	-	-	54 (4)	0
2001/02	33	0	2	0	1	0	16	0	0 (1)	0	52 (1)	0
2002/03	34 (1)	0	3	0	3 (2)	0	11	0	0	0	51 (3)	0
2003/04	22	0	3	0	0	0	4	0	-	-	29	
2004/05	38	0	0	0	3	0	15	0	-	-	56	0
2005/06	36	0	6	0	0	0	13	1	2	0	57	1
2006/07	34 (1)	1	1	0	0 (1)	0	13	0	1	0	49 (2)	1
2007/08	34 (1)	0	3 (1)	0	3	0	13	0	-	-	53 (2)	0
2008/09	38	1	3	0	0 (1)	0	12	0	-	-	53 (1)	1
2009/10	37	0	2	0	1	0	13	0	-	-	53	0
2010/11	28	0	0	0	0	0	9 (1)	0	-	-	37 (1)	0
2011/12	19 (2)	0	5	0	3 (2)	0	-	-	-	-	27 (4)	0
2012/13	16 (8)	0	1	0	2	0	10 (1)	0	-	-	29 (9)	0
Total	**484 (24)**	**4**	**39 (1)**	**0**	**28 (7)**	**0**	**148 (2)**	**1**	**3 (1)**	**0**	**702 (35)**	**5**

Carroll,
Andy

A GEORDIE through and through, Andrew Thomas Carroll was born in Gateshead and signed a professional contract with Newcastle United when he was only 17 years old. He made four Premier League appearances for the Magpies in 2006/07, in addition to becoming the club's youngest ever player to feature in a European fixture, when he played against Palermo on 2 November 2006.

His FA Cup debut came two months later against Birmingham City. Carroll first played for England's Under-19 side in 2007 after Scotland had named him in their U-19 side, as he was eligible to play for both countries. In 2007 he was the recipient of a 'rising star' award bearing the name of Newcastle legend Jackie Milburn. Carroll scored his debut goal in a 2-2 draw against West Ham on 10 January 2009 and added two more in a total of 16 matches as Newcastle were relegated from the Premier League.

THE SIZE OF THE FEE ASTOUNDED THE FOOTBALL WORLD, £35MILLION, MAKING CARROLL THE MOST EXPENSIVE BRITISH PLAYER IN HISTORY

HIS CAREER BLOSSOMED in 2009/10 when he scored 17 goals as Newcastle returned to the top division as winners of the Football League Championship. In the summer of 2010 Carroll was handed the legendary No. 9 shirt at Newcastle that Jackie Milburn, Malcolm Macdonald and Alan Shearer had worn with such distinction. 'Alan Shearer was my idol as a young lad and who would have thought I'd be following in his footsteps?' Carroll enthused. 'It's every young Geordie lad's dream to be the Newcastle United number nine.'

The famous shirt certainly did Carroll no harm as the goals continued to flow when Newcastle resumed their place at English football's top table. He had delivered 11 goals from 19 league games halfway through the season. Liverpool had already seen first-hand his all-round strength and shooting capabilities at Newcastle in December. He beat Pepe Reina from distance and had a hand in the other two goals in a 3-1 victory. Incoming Newcastle manager Alan Pardew attempted to dissuade potential suitors for his in-form striker by declaring that he was not for sale. A week later Carroll was injured during a defeat at Tottenham. The striker was unavailable for selection, but Liverpool still made their move towards the end of the January transfer window.

Kenny Dalglish already knew that Fernando Torres was leaving for Chelsea and he had to act swiftly to secure an adequate replacement. The size of the fee astounded the football world, £35million, making Carroll the most expensive British player in history. Liverpool's Director of Football at the time, Damien Comolli, said the deal was worth making as it was a part of a bigger picture, as he told *The Times* in December 2012. 'The way we looked at it, we were selling two players, Fernando Torres and Ryan Babel, and we were bringing two in, Luis Suarez and Carroll, and we were making a profit and the wage bill was coming down as well. It was a four-player deal.'

Carroll needed a month to recover from his injury and had to wait until his sixth match for his first goal against Manchester City at Anfield, a ferocious left-foot strike from the edge of the penalty area. He added a second ten minutes before half-time with a towering header from a Meireles cross.

For much of the 2011/12 season the enormous transfer fee seemed to hang like a millstone around the young striker's neck. Only nine goals from 47 first-team matches did not seem to represent good value for money. But big Andy persevered and got his reward in the middle of April when he headed late winners against Blackburn in the Premier League and against Everton in the FA Cup semi-final. He scored in the FA Cup final against Chelsea and was denied a second goal by a miraculous save. His improved form towards the end of the season earned him a place in Roy Hodgson's 23-man squad for the Euros, where he made two substitute appearances and started

Season	League		FA Cup		League Cup		Europe		Total	
	App	Goals	App	Goals	App	Goals	App	Goals	App	Goals
2010/11	5 (2)	2	0	0	0	0	1 (1)	0	6 (3)	2
2011/12	21 (14)	4	4 (2)	4	4 (2)	1	-	-	29 (18)	9
2012/13	0 (2)	0	0	0	0	0	0	0	0 (2)	0
Total	**26 (18)**	**6**	**4 (2)**	**4**	**4 (2)**	**1**	**1 (1)**	**0**	**35 (23)**	**11**

once, scoring one goal in the 3-2 win over Sweden as England tried to cope up front without suspended Wayne Rooney.

YET AS SOON as Brendan Rodgers took over at Liverpool it was abundantly clear that Carroll didn't suit his requirements. After appearing twice for Liverpool as substitute for a total of 17 minutes in the 2012/13 season Carroll was loaned on 30 August 2012 for the remainder of the campaign to Sam Allardyce's West Ham, leaving the Reds a striker short until January following the collapse of the deal to bring Clint Dempsey in from Fulham. Carroll was out for four weeks with a hamstring injury suffered in his first game for the Hammers, against Fulham. He did not get on the scoresheet in his first eight games, but he finally hit form for West Ham in November, scoring seven goals in 16 appearances as well as delivering a few assists until the end of the season. Carroll completed a £15million permanent move to West Ham in June 2013, signing a six year contract.

Carson,
Scott

SCOTT CARSON made his Leeds debut when coming on as a substitute in a 3-0 defeat against Middlesbrough on 31 January 2004. Paul Robinson was sent off in the 88th minute and Carson's first task was to try to save a penalty, but he didn't succeed.

He was kept out of Leeds' starting line-up in the 2004/05 season by Neil Sullivan and wanted a new challenge. Liverpool won the race with Chelsea to sign the England Under-21 keeper in January 2005.

Carson was Jerzy Dudek's understudy, but his quest to become Liverpool's number one keeper became considerably more complicated with the arrival of Pepe Reina in July 2005. After only nine games in two years, including a great performance in the quarter-finals of the Champions League against Juventus at Anfield, he went on loan to Charlton Athletic, who were then relegated from the Premier League. Luke Young, skipper of Charlton, was still very impressed. 'Since Scott came to Charlton he's been an absolute revelation and made save after save. Give him time to settle and he will become a top, top goalkeeper.'

RAFA BENÍTEZ wanted to keep Carson at Anfield but he was still in England's plans and could not afford to be an unused understudy. When Carson did leave Liverpool he preferred Premier League newcomers West Bromwich Albion to Stoke, which didn't

seem such a wise choice when Stoke finished 12th in the Premier League and Albion were relegated. Baggies manager Roberto Di Matteo made Carson club captain at the start of the 2009/10 season and he featured in 40 of 46 matches in the Championship as the West Midlands club made an immediate return to the Premier League. Carson's form dipped halfway through the 2010/11 season and he was replaced for a few matches for Boaz Myhill, but Carson was back in favour with the arrival of Roy Hodgson in February 2011. In July 2011 Carson completed a surprising transfer to Turkish club Bursaspor. 'Going abroad never crossed

my mind,' the keeper said in November 2011. 'Once Bursaspor made contact and West Brom were willing to speak to them I thought that was the writing on the wall. The football is great and the atmospheres are unbelievable so I'd recommend it to other English players.'

CARSON has made four appearances for the England international team as well as taking part in 29 Under-21 internationals. His international career suffered after he made a terrible error against Croatia at Wembley in a 3-2 European Championship qualifier defeat on 21 November 2007. England failed to reach Euro 2008 and manager Steve McLaren was sacked the following day.

Season	League		FA Cup		League Cup		Europe		Other		Total	
	App	Goals	App	Goals	App	Goals	App	Goals	App	Goals	App	Goals
2004/05	4	0	0	0	0	0	1	0	-	-	5	0
2005/06	0	0	1	0	1	0	2	0	0	0	4	0
Total	4	0	1	0	1	0	3	0	0	0	9	0

Carter,
Jimmy

WINGER JIMMY CARTER earned himself a good reputation at Millwall after earlier spells with Crystal Palace and Queens Park Rangers. He was part of the Lions squad that gained promotion to the top flight for the first time in the southeast London club's history in 1988.

After signing for Kenny Dalglish on 10 January 1991 he went straight into the team for a league match at Aston Villa two days later. *The Guardian* commented on his performance in his second match against Wimbledon that he was 'like a Millwall player masquerading in a Liverpool shirt', but he still got the bubbly for being voted man of the match. When Dalglish left Anfield only six weeks after Carter's arrival, the Londoner had lost his place in the starting line-up. In June 2011 he told the *Daily Post* in North Wales that Dalglish's departure completely took the wind out of his sails. 'I get a bit of stick now and again from Liverpool fans and outsiders who say "what the hell was Kenny doing?" In a way I feel like I've let Kenny down because I wasn't successful there. That's the bottom line.' Carter only made eight appearances at the club; five under Dalglish and three under his successor, Graeme Souness. It was clear that Souness didn't rate the 25-year-old as he

substituted Carter at Stamford Bridge after he had come off the bench earlier in the game.

SOUNESS recouped over half of the club's purchase price when Arsenal paid £500,000 to take Carter back to London in October 1991. Carter spent over three years at Highbury but only played 30 matches and was twice loaned out to Oxford United before making a permanent move to Portsmouth in Football League One in 1995. Three years, 80 games and six goals later he was back at Millwall, but his second spell with the club was nowhere near as successful as his first. At the end of the 1998/99 season he had to retire as a player at the age of 33 due to a serious back injury.

FACTFILE

BORN
Hammersmith,
9 November 1965
POSITION
Right-winger
OTHER CLUBS
Crystal Palace (1980–85),
Queens Park Rangers
(1985–87),
Millwall (1987–91),
Arsenal (1991–95),
Oxford United
(loan, 1994 and 1994–95),
Portsmouth (1995–98),
Millwall (1998–99)
SIGNED FROM
Millwall, £800,000,
10 January 1991
LFC DEBUT
12 January 1991
CONTRACT EXPIRY
8 October 1991

Case,
Jimmy

A TOUGH-TACKLING midfielder who took no prisoners, Jimmy Case was also renowned for his ferocious shooting ability, scoring more than a fair amount of goals for Liverpool. His credentials, however, were established locally when during a football game with coats as goalposts between the Garston Church Choir and the Allerton Scouts he gave the goalkeeper of the Choir a hefty kick when the score was 23-22. Case had proved his reputation as a winner, if not a bad loser. Even though his team lost, Case's legend was born.

He already possessed a tremendous shooting power and when he was an eight-year-old he took the goal kicks because no one in his team could kick as hard. Case learned to survive on the football field while playing for dockers' club Blue Union in Garston aged only 16, regularly facing 30-somethings that showed the teenager no mercy. A year later he started playing for non-league South Liverpool where he was noticed by Liverpool scouts Tom Saunders and John Bennison.

Case told *LFChistory.net* about the beginnings of his glittering career at Liverpool: 'They asked me to go for a two-week trial at Liverpool. I took two weeks off work because I was an apprentice electrician as well. At the end of the two weeks they asked me to sign full-time, but I actually turned them down because I had done two years of my electrician's apprenticeship, which is a four-year term, and I wanted to continue that, which in the end I did. Liverpool took over my semi-professional contract at

Season	League		FA Cup		League Cup		Europe		Other		Total	
	App	Goals	App	Goals	App	Goals	App	Goals	App	Goals	App	Goals
1990/91	2 (3)	0	2	0	0	0	-	-	0	0	4 (3)	0
1991/92	0	0	0	0	0	0	0 (1)	0	-	-	0 (1)	0
Total	**2 (3)**	**0**	**2**	**0**	**0**	**0**	**0 (1)**	**0**	**0**	**0**	**4 (4)**	**0**

South Liverpool and I did that for two years until I was 20, signed full-time pro and by the time I was just short of 21 years of age that's when I made my debut.'

Case was an instant success when he made his league debut at Anfield on the final day of the 1974/75 season against Queens Park Rangers. He established himself the following season, making 39 appearances for the first team in all competitions and scoring 12 times, three of which came on a foggy December night on Merseyside as the Poles from Wroclaw were defeated in the UEFA Cup. Case also scored important goals in the quarter-final and the final of that competition and added a European winners' medal to the League Championship medal in his first full season.

CASE'S long-range shooting became a feature of his game and many of the 46 goals he scored for the club came from distance, like the majestic turn and volley in the 1977 FA Cup final against Manchester United. He added another Championship medal in his second full season and was also a member of the team that finally won the greatest prize of all, the European Cup, on that famous night in Rome. He would go on to win two more winners' medals in that tournament plus another two in the domestic championship.

Case was a fierce competitor whose reputation preceded him, and Manchester United and

England captain Bryan Robson once remarked: 'I won't say he was dirty but certainly the hardest opponent was Jimmy Case. He could certainly look after himself. He was very clever about it as well.' Case certainly made an impression on his opponents. 'The ball is there to be won,' Case reflected. 'It stems back to where you go to school. An eight-year-old is told by his sportmaster: "If you hold back, you're the one who will get hurt." I took them words on board, and let's put it this way, I never held back. Later on in life you get a reputation that you go into for 50-50, full blooded every day. After that you don't really need to get in, you just go towards it and if it's 50-50, he'll back off.'

Although an integral part of the team, only missing the last five games of the 1979/80 league campaign, many of Case's appearances the following season were as substitute after losing his place to Sammy Lee. Case admitted contributing to his own downfall. 'I left Liverpool when I was 28. I think it was just that – without being controversial – you get in a few scrapes, you're breathalysed and you're caught fighting in a hotel in Wales like me and Ray Kennedy were, and the club didn't look upon that too kindly.'

IN SUMMER 1981 he was transferred to Brighton and Hove Albion, with whom he returned to Anfield two years later and scored the goal which knocked his former club out of the FA Cup. He joined Southampton and continued playing league football to a high standard for several more seasons.

'We played with supreme confidence because we knew how good the fella was next to us,' he would say of his time at Liverpool. 'I always considered myself – I know I get told different from time to time – as a bread-and-butter player. A fetcher and carrier to fill in the spaces on the right-hand side and work hard. Then you had the flair players like Kenny Dalglish and Terry McDermott, but they couldn't play without us anyway.'

FACTFILE

BORN
Allerton, Liverpool,
18 May 1954
POSITION
Midfielder
OTHER CLUBS
Blue Union (1969–70),
South Liverpool (1970–72),
Brighton & Hove Albion
(1981–85),
Southampton (1985–91),
Bournemouth (1991–92),
Halifax Town (1992–93),
Wrexham (1993),
Wanneroo British (1993),
Darlington (1993),
Sittingbourne (1993),
Brighton & Hove Albion
(1993–95),
Bashley (1997–98)
SIGNED FROM
South Liverpool, £500,
1 May 1973
LFC DEBUT/GOAL
26 April 1975 /
23 August 1975
CONTRACT EXPIRY
19 August 1981
HONOURS
League Championship
1975/76, 1976/77,
1978/79, 1979/80;
League Cup 1981;
European Cup
1977, 1978, 1981;
UEFA Cup 1976

Season	League App	League Goals	FA Cup App	FA Cup Goals	League Cup App	League Cup Goals	Europe App	Europe Goals	Other App	Other Goals	Total App	Total Goals
1974/75	1	0	0	0	0	0	0	0	0	0	1	0
1975/76	27	6	2	0	1	1	7 (2)	5	-	-	37 (2)	12
1976/77	24 (3)	1	7	4	1	0	6	2	1	0	39 (3)	7
1977/78	30 (3)	5	0	0	8	2	9	4	1	0	48 (3)	11
1978/79	37	7	5 (1)	1	1	0	4	1	-	-	47 (1)	9
1979/80	37	3	5	1	7	0	2	1	1	0	52	5
1980/81	14 (10)	1	1 (1)	1	3 (1)	0	2 (3)	0	1	0	21 (15)	2
Total	170 (16)	23	20 (2)	7	21 (1)	3	30 (5)	13	4	0	245 (24)	46

Cavalieri,
Diego

DIEGO CAVALIERI had a difficult task to displace Pepe Reina as Liverpool's number one. He was the third Brazilian who put pen to paper at Liverpool, following in the footsteps of Fábio Aurélio and Lucas Leiva.

The shot-stopper played over 100 games for Palmeiras after making his debut in 2002, but when he joined Liverpool he had been second choice to World Cup winner Marcos. As expected Cavalieri mainly got his chance in his debut season in cup competitions. He conceded one goal against Crewe in the third round of the League Cup and was hardly impressive in Liverpool's 4-2 loss at Tottenham in the fourth round. He was between the sticks against PSV Eindhoven in December 2008 when Liverpool had already progressed from the group phase of the Champions

League, and kept a clean sheet in the third round of the FA Cup against Preston North End.

REINA'S FORM and stature were enough to ensure that Cavalieri remained on the bench most of the time the following season, with his only appearances being against Leeds and Arsenal in the League Cup, a Reading replay in the FA Cup and the final Champions

League group match with Fiorentina, by which time Liverpool had already been eliminated from the competition. On 23 August 2010 he moved to newly promoted Serie A side, Cesena, to play on a regular basis. Cavalieri spent six months at Cesena where the coach elected to play a 41-year-old veteran ahead of him. Shortly after his 28th birthday, Cavalieri returned to his

homeland to sign for Fluminense. He played a key role in the club's Brazilian Championship title win in 2012.

FACTFILE
BORN São Paulo, Brazil, 1 December 1982
POSITION Goalkeeper
OTHER CLUBS Palmeiras (2001–08), Cesena (2010), Fluminense (2010–)
SIGNED FROM Palmeiras, £3.5million, 11 July 2008
INTERNATIONAL CAPS 2 Brazil caps, 2012–
LFC DEBUT 23 September 2008
CONTRACT EXPIRY 23 August 2010

Season	League App	League Goals	FA Cup App	FA Cup Goals	League Cup App	League Cup Goals	Europe App	Europe Goals	Total App	Total Goals
2008/09	0	0	1	0	2	0	1	0	4	0
2009/10	0	0	1	0	2	0	1	0	4	0
2010/11	0	0	0	0	0	0	2	0	2	0
Total	**0**	**0**	**2**	**0**	**4**	**0**	**4**	**0**	**10**	**0**

Chadburn,
John

DESCRIBED as a humorous character in the dressing room and on the training ground, but with a volatile temper on the pitch, John Chadburn made his name with West Bromwich Albion, who were relegated from the First Division in the 1900/01 season but won the Second Division straight away and finished seventh in the top flight in his last season there.

CHADBURN featured for Albion as right-back and right-winger and moved to Liverpool after 48 games and four goals. He was one of four different players to feature at right-back in the opening ten

league fixtures of the 1903/04 season before a fifth, Alfred West, came into the side on 7 November 1903 and held on to his place for the rest of a campaign that ended in relegation.

FACTFILE
BORN Mansfield, 12 February 1873
DIED 10 December 1923
POSITION Right-back
OTHER CLUBS Leicester Fosse, Mansfield Unitarians (1891–92), Mansfield Greenhalgh (1892–93), Lincoln City (1893–94), Notts County (1894–97), Wolverhampton Wanderers (1897–1900), West Bromwich Albion (1900–03), Plymouth Argyle (1904–05), Mansfield Mechanics (1905–06), Mansfield Town, Mansfield Woodhouse Rangers
SIGNED FROM West Bromwich Albion, 11 May 1903
LFC DEBUT 5 September 1903
CONTRACT EXPIRY March 1904

Season	League App	League Goals	FA Cup App	FA Cup Goals	Total App	Total Goals
1903/04	2	0	0	0	2	0
Total	**2**	**0**	**0**	**0**	**2**	**0**

Chadwick,
Edgar

EDGAR CHADWICK spent the autumn of his career at Liverpool, after a sensational period at Everton from 1888–99. He signed for the Blues before the inaugural Football League season of 1888/89 and played 300 games scoring 110 goals. His highlight was winning the League Championship in 1891.

The 5ft 6in (167cm) left-winger was called 'King of the dribblers and master of the ball', as Victor Hall recalled in the *Liverpool Echo* in the 1920s. 'To see Edgar Chadwick in play was to realise for the first time what the art of "dribbling" really meant. As a player he never appeared to be speedy, he had not the build or the symmetry of wind and limb that indicates pace. Coming of Lancashire stock, he had rather the loose awkward build that even when stripped for play is so deceptive in other fields of athletics. In manner Edgar was shy and diffident. He had that modest, unassuming manner both on and off the field of play, that one finds so frequently in really great players.'

EDGAR CHADWICK
LIVERPOOL & ENGLAND

Chadwick joined Burnley aged 30, but despite being the top scorer of the team with ten goals he couldn't prevent their relegation to the Second Division. He moved to Southampton where he was victorious in the Southern League before featuring in the 1902 FA Cup final, where the Saints lost 2-1 to Sheffield United in a replay. That defeat completed an unwanted hat-trick for Chadwick,

who had twice before been on the losing side with Everton in a Cup final, in 1893 and 1897. After two years at Southampton Chadwick wished to move on so he purchased his transfer from Burnley, who still held his Football League registration, for £25.

CHADWICK played in the Reds' forward line for two seasons between the League Championship wins of 1901 and 1906. His team-mates undoubtedly learned a lot from playing with him as according to the club programme 'he had a kindly disposition to new players and especially to young ones coming along'. Chadwick missed only five of the 34 First Division matches in the 1902/03 season and scored seven times, including two in the 9-2 demolition of Grimsby Town at Anfield on 6 December. He added a further 15 matches to his total,

Chadwick, seated front row on the right with the England team in 1893

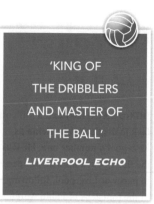

of which 11 were defeats, in the disastrous 1903/04 campaign.

A PIONEER for Englishmen coaching abroad, he became a respected coach in the Netherlands and took charge of the Dutch national team in 1908, a post he held until November 1913. He guided the team to bronze medals in the 1908 and 1912 Olympics. Chadwick returned to Blackburn to work as a baker and made one final appearance as a wartime guest for Blackburn Rovers against Manchester United on 11 November 1916, at the age of 47!

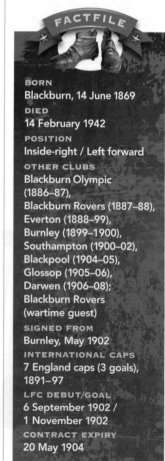

FACTFILE

BORN
Blackburn, 14 June 1869
DIED
14 February 1942
POSITION
Inside-right / Left forward
OTHER CLUBS
Blackburn Olympic (1886–87),
Blackburn Rovers (1887–88),
Everton (1888–99),
Burnley (1899–1900),
Southampton (1900–02),
Blackpool (1904–05),
Glossop (1905–06),
Darwen (1906–08);
Blackburn Rovers (wartime guest)
SIGNED FROM
Burnley, May 1902
INTERNATIONAL CAPS
7 England caps (3 goals), 1891–97
LFC DEBUT/GOAL
6 September 1902 /
1 November 1902
CONTRACT EXPIRY
20 May 1904

Season	League		FA Cup		Total	
	App	Goals	App	Goals	App	Goals
1902/03	29	7	1	0	30	7
1903/04	14	0	1	0	15	0
Total	**43**	**7**	**2**	**0**	**45**	**7**

ENGLAND

Chairmen

Edwin Berry was appointed the first chairman of Liverpool when the club was founded but he had to resign shortly into his tenure to attend to his other business interests.

John Houlding

JOHN ASBURY
{ CHAIRMAN }

Chairmen of Liverpool Football Club

1892	Edwin Berry
1892-1896	John Houlding
1896-1904	William Houlding
1904-1909	Edwin Berry
1909-1913	John McKenna
1913-1917	John Asbury
1917-1919	John McKenna
1919-1924	Walter Robert Williams
1924-1926	Robert L. Martindale
1926-1932	Thomas Crompton
1932-1935	William Henry Cartwright
1935-1941	W.J. Harrop
1941-1944	Robert Lawson Martindale, Jnr.
1944-1947	William H. McConnell
1947-1950	Samuel R. Williams
1950-1953	George A. Richards
1953-1956	W. J. Harrop
1956-1964	Thomas Valentine Williams
1964-1967	Sidney C. Reakes
1967-1969	Harold Cartwright
1969-1973	H.E. Roberts
1973-1990	John Winston Smith
1990-1991	Noel White
1991-2007	David Moores
2007-2010	Tom Hicks and George N. Gillett
2010	Martin Broughton
2010-	Tom Werner

WALTER ROBERT WILLIAMS

Three father and sons were chairmen;
John and William Houlding, Robert L. Martindale Snr. and Jnr. and Walter and Samuel Williams.

Three chairmen died while in office:
Robert L. Martindale on 9 March 1926,
William H. McConnell on 7 August 1947
and W.J. Harrop in February 1956.

John McKenna

Chalmers, Billy

BILLY CHALMERS made just two league appearances for Liverpool, both coming during the 1924/25 First Division season when he deputised for left-winger Fred Hopkin for the unsuccessful visit to Birmingham City on 29 November 1924 and the 4-0 home victory over Bury on 24 January 1925.

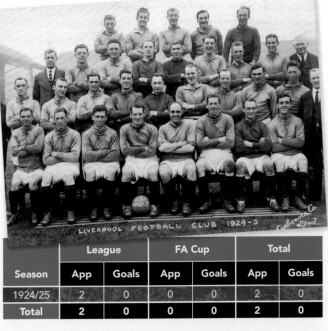

LIVERPOOL FOOTBALL CLUB 1924-5

Season	League		FA Cup		Total	
	App	Goals	App	Goals	App	Goals
1924/25	2	0	0	0	2	0
Total	**2**	**0**	**0**	**0**	**2**	**0**

FACTFILE

BORN
Aberdeen, Scotland,
3 April 1901
DIED
1997
POSITION
Left-winger
OTHER CLUBS
Old Aberdeen (1919–23),
Tranmere Rovers (1925–26)
SIGNED FROM
Old Aberdeen, August 1923
LFC DEBUT
29 November 1924
CONTRACT EXPIRY
June 1925

Chambers, Harry

TOM WATSON liked the look of the bowlegged, pigeon-toed and ever-smiling Northern boy who knocked on his door in 1915. Henry 'Harry' Chambers turned out to be the last player Watson ever signed for Liverpool before he passed away on 6 May 1915. Chambers only played a couple of reserve games for Liverpool before league football was suspended due to World War One. He became a soldier but was soon invalided out of the Army and while convalescing in Ulster he guested for Belfast Distillery and Glentoran.

Chambers had a lethal left foot and a brilliant football brain and was a key member of the Liverpool team that won the First Division in successive seasons in 1921/22 and 1922/23, scoring 41 goals in 71 matches. He was the club's top scorer for four successive seasons from 1919/20 to 1922/23, but only scored seven goals in the 1924/25 season after being out with injury for the first two months of the campaign. His injury concerned a scribe who wrote in the match programme: 'There has been a lack of that intelligent footwork which carried the side through so successfully during the championship campaigns, and the return of the International, whose presence inspires his colleagues, will be eagerly awaited.'

'Smiler' played eight internationals for England, scoring five goals from his debut on 14 March 1921 in a British Home Championship game against Wales in Cardiff until his last selection on 20 October 1923 against Ireland at Windsor Park. His debut goal came in a friendly against Belgium on 21 May 1921 in Brussels. He scored both England's goals in a 2-0 win over Ireland on 21 October 1922, his second being England's 400th goal. He scored his fourth and fifth goal against Wales and Belgium in March 1923.

Liverpool fans were shocked to hear in March 1926 that Chambers wanted to leave the club and had been placed on the transfer list. This was described as no less than the 'biggest noise in the football world'. Chambers was the darling of the supporters due to his cheerfulness, which rubbed off on everybody around him. He had scored nine goals in the 1925/26 season but since netting a hat-trick against Newcastle on Christmas Day had only scored once in two-and-a-half months. His frustration had clearly boiled over.

Ernest 'Bee' Edwards at the *Liverpool Echo* got an exclusive from 'Smiler' on the reasons why he wanted to depart Anfield. 'Sometimes you get fed up,' Chambers lamented:

Well, I'm more than fed up. Not with the team, spectators, the boys or the directors, you know, but just fed up. I think if I got away I should do better than I am doing. A change is good for anyone when they have got into a rut. I don't imply that I have been playing a blinder or that I have been playing badly, but it seems that a move at this critical juncture will do me good and bring me back to the best possible form. I am longing for a change of surroundings, and I hope it shall not be long before I move.

Thankfully Chambers found his scoring instincts again, netting seven goals in the remaining 11 games of the season, and was the top scorer of the team the following season by scoring 21 goals in 46 games.

> CHAMBERS WAS THE DARLING OF THE SUPPORTERS DUE TO HIS CHEERFULNESS, WHICH RUBBED OFF ON EVERYBODY AROUND HIM

After playing nine games without getting on the scoresheet in his final season, 1927/28, Chambers was knocked down by a car while riding a bicycle. He later failed to recover damages for the incident in court. Chambers said because of the accident he had lost his form and failed to win back his place in the Liverpool team. A doctor said he could not discover anything physically wrong with Chambers and that his loss of form might be due to anxiety over the result of the court case. After an absence of two months from the first team Chambers returned, adding four goals and taking his total for the club past the 150 mark before he was transferred in March 1928 to West Bromwich Albion, who had just been relegated from the First Division.

HARRY CHAMBERS

Chambers was by that time aged 32 and maybe had slowed down a bit, but he was still very adept at reading the game and was converted to centre-half with resounding success. Chambers joined Hereford United from Oakengates Town in the Birmingham League in January 1933. He played a total of 18 times for Hereford during 1932/33 before returning to Oakengates the following season, playing for the club until he was 51! He passed away all too soon on 29 June 1949, aged 52.

Season	League App	League Goals	FA Cup App	FA Cup Goals	Other App	Other Goals	Total App	Total Goals
1919/20	34	15	0	0	-	-	34	15
1920/21	40	22	3	2	-	-	43	24
1921/22	32	19	3	2	1	0	36	21
1922/23	39	22	4	3	-	-	43	25
1923/24	30	13	5	4	-	-	35	17
1924/25	27	7	4	0	-	-	31	7
1925/26	42	17	3	0	-	-	45	17
1926/27	42	17	4	4	-	-	46	21
1927/28	24	3	2	1	-	-	26	4
Total	**310**	**135**	**28**	**16**	**1**	**0**	**339**	**151**

Charity/Community Shield

THE FOOTBALL ASSOCIATION Charity Shield, renamed the **Football Association Community Shield** from 2002, is known as the traditional curtain-raiser to a new English season between the reigning League champions and the FA Cup-holders. However, the shield's early years saw a rather different format and it wasn't until 1921 that a match actually took place between the champions, (Burnley, and the cup-winners, Tottenham Hotspur.

In 1908, when the oddly-shaped trophy was presented for the first time, the match-up was between the First Division champions, Manchester United, and the Southern League champions, Queens Park Rangers. The forerunner of the Charity Shield had been the Sheriff of London Charity Shield, a contest devised by Sir Thomas Dewar when he was Sheriff, which was competed for between 1898 and 1907.

Liverpool's first involvement with either came in 1906 when the newly-crowned First Division champions were invited to compete for the Sheriff of London Shield against the amateurs of Corinthian Football Club, whose strictly amateur ethos had quaintly prevented them from joining the Football League or participating in the FA Cup as they would be competing for prizes. Twenty-four years after the club was founded, the rules had been relaxed enough to allow them to face Liverpool at Fulham's Craven Cottage. The Merseysiders were comfortable winners by five goals to one with forward Joe Hewitt scoring a hat-trick. The shield itself, commissioned by Dewar, was over 6ft high.

LIVERPOOL'S next involvement came in 1922 when they faced Huddersfield Town at Old Trafford eleven days after the Yorkshire club had won the FA Cup by beating Preston North End 1-0 at Stamford Bridge in London. This would be the last time the shield would be played for at the end of the season in which the participants had won their honours. It was also the first time that both competing teams were from the north of England, which is why a northern venue was selected to host the match. Huddersfield repeated their FA Cup-winning score in defeating Liverpool by a single goal.

LIVERPOOL RETAINED the Championship in 1923 and their opponents at the start of the 1923/24 season ought to have been the first club to win the FA Cup at the recently-opened Wembley Stadium, Bolton Wanderers. But instead 1923 was the first of five years in the 1920s in which an English professional team met an English amateur team. The League winner v FA Cup winner format would not return until 1930.

If the team that won the league also won the cup, the FA's decree was that the League runners-up or the beaten FA Cup finalists would provide the opposition for the champions. In 1971 Arsenal won both trophies and Liverpool were invited to play for the shield as the beaten FA Cup finalists but Arsenal decided not to participate and their place went instead to the 1971 Second Division champions, Leicester City. At Filbert Street, Leicester's first-half goal from full-back Steve Whitworth condemned Liverpool to their second 1-0 defeat in the annual match that many had begun to see as just a glorified pre-season friendly.

The prestige finally arrived in 1974 when on the FA Secretary Ted Croker's initiative moved the Charity Shield match to Wembley, offering the national stadium as an incentive to the English champions and FA Cup-winners, both of whom had refused to contest the shield in the previous two years; Derby County and Leeds United in 1972 and Liverpool and Sunderland in 1973. Liverpool's three consecutive appearances in the Charity Shield in the middle of the 1960s had seen two draws against West Ham United and Manchester United and one win over Everton. The opportunity of playing at Wembley in the 1970s was too good to turn down. The FA's decision backfired in dramatic fashion. A brutal match between Liverpool and Leeds United saw both Kevin Keegan and Billy Bremner dismissed by referee Bob Matthewson who, frankly, could have sent other players to join them in the dressing-room. The offending players were heavily fined and each banned for 11 matches. In the same match, Liverpool became the first winners of the shield to do so by winning a penalty shootout.

The 1970s and 1980s were golden decades for Liverpool FC and qualifying to play for the shield

was almost an annual occurrence. Between 1974 and 1989 the club played at Wembley 11 times out of a maximum of 16, competing eight times as League champions, twice as Cup-winners and once as both, in 1986. On only two of those occasions did a Liverpool team lose, although the shield was shared with Manchester United in 1977 and with Everton in 1986, something that would happen again with United in 1990.

After losing as Cup-winners to Leeds United in 1992, it would be another nine years before Liverpool qualified again, during a six-year period in which the venue was switched to the Millennium Stadium in Cardiff while Wembley was being rebuilt. On the back of three cup successes in the spring months of 2001, Liverpool finally overcame Manchester United in the Charity Shield at the fifth attempt after three drawn matches and one defeat against their rivals. Early goals by Gary McAllister and Michael Owen saw United off.

A YEAR LATER the Charity Shield became the Community Shield and Liverpool lost to Arsenal, their only defeat in the seven matches they played at the Millennium Stadium in various competitions between 2001 and 2006.

Only Manchester United with 15 victories and four drawn matches have a better record than Liverpool in this fixture. Liverpool have 10 wins and five draws. It still isn't seen as a particularly prestigious match but it is a good day out for the supporters. The manager of one of Liverpool's rivals described the Community Shield as being 'a barometer for fitness.' That's probably how Liverpool have seen it as well, as just another match to play in a hectic pre-season schedule. Winning the shield isn't particularly important on its own, but what has to be achieved to qualify is of utmost importance.

Charlton, John

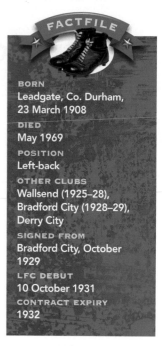

JOHN CHARLTON
LIVERPOOL

THE LEFT-BACK represented Liverpool on just three occasions during the 1931/32 First Division campaign.

Given his debut on 10 October 1931 in a home game with West Ham, John Charlton was not selected for the next five league matches before making consecutive appearances against Manchester City and Arsenal towards the end of November 1931.

	League		FA Cup		Total	
Season	App	Goals	App	Goals	App	Goals
1931/32	3	0	0	0	3	0
Total	3	0	0	0	3	0

FACTFILE

BORN
Leadgate, Co. Durham,
23 March 1908
DIED
May 1969
POSITION
Left-back
OTHER CLUBS
Wallsend (1925–28),
Bradford City (1928–29),
Derry City
SIGNED FROM
Bradford City, October
1929
LFC DEBUT
10 October 1931
CONTRACT EXPIRY
1932

Charnock, Phil

PHIL CHARNOCK became a record holder when he made his debut for Liverpool against Apollon Limassol on 16 September 1992, coming on as a substitute when the Reds were 5-0 up at Anfield. He was the club's youngest player to ever appear in a European match, aged 17 years and seven months. He added only one appearance to his Liverpool total when he was replaced at half-time in a disastrous 4-4 draw against lower-league Chesterfield in the League Cup.

> HE WAS THE CLUB'S YOUNGEST PLAYER TO EVER APPEAR IN A EUROPEAN MATCH

CHARNOCK had a brief loan spell at Blackpool in 1996 and shortly afterwards joined Crewe Alexandra. Although often injured during his six years at Gresty Road, Charnock made over 150 league appearances for the Cheshire club, scoring eight times, before he joined Port Vale in 2002. Charnock subsequently tried his luck in Northern Ireland, firstly with Linfield and then later with

FACTFILE

BORN
Southport, 14 February 1975
POSITION
Midfielder
OTHER CLUBS
Blackpool (loan, 1996),
Crewe Alexandra (1996–2002),
Port Vale (2002–03),
Bury (2003),
Linfield (2003–06),
Ballymena United (2006),
Fleetwood Town (2006–07),
Leigh RMI (2007–08),
Mossley (2008)
JOINED
1987; signed professional
16 March 1992
LFC DEBUT
16 September 1992
CONTRACT EXPIRY
1996

Ballymena United. Unfortunately, the player's injury problems returned, particularly to his knee, and he missed a complete season while on Linfield's books. He retired from football in 2008 because of injury.

	League		FA Cup		League Cup		Europe		Other		Total	
Season	App	Goals	App	Goals	App	Goals	App	Goals	App	Goals	App	Goals
1992/93	0	0	0	0	1	0	0 (1)	0	0	0	1 (1)	0
Total	0	0	0	0	1	0	0 (1)	0	0	0	1 (1)	0

Checkland, Francis

FRANCIS CHECKLAND made five consecutive league appearances for Liverpool early in the 1921/22 season when he replaced right-half John Bamber, who had contracted appendicitis.

However, Jock McNab soon made the position his and Checkland never played for Liverpool's first team again. In 1923/24 Checkland moved to Tranmere Rovers where he featured in 17 games in the Third Division North over the next couple of seasons.

Season	League		FA Cup		Other		Total	
	App	Goals	App	Goals	App	Goals	App	Goals
1921/22	5	0	0	0	0	0	5	0
Total	5	0	0	0	0	0	5	0

Cheyrou, Bruno

BRUNO CHEYROU came to Anfield with good credentials, but seemed a bit lost in English Premiership football. Being hailed as 'the new Zidane' by Gérard Houllier, who had brought him to England, became a burden rather than an inspiration.

Even after struggling to impress in his first season his compatriot was still banging the Cheyrou drum. 'For me, Bruno has all the assets to reach the level that separates a good player from a great player. He has a great individual technique, he passes the ball well, he has an excellent touch of the ball and the essential tactical sense,' said Houllier. 'Like other French players before him, he probably needs a little more time. Remember the first season at Arsenal? Everyone laughed at Robert Pires.' Cheyrou did have a couple of highlights along the way. His excellent goal secured Liverpool's first win in

the Premier League at Stamford Bridge on 7 January 2004 and two goals against Newcastle in the FA Cup later that month saw him voted the best player of the fourth round. Cheyrou was happy to be finally part of the Liverpool team. 'It meant a lot to me when Steven Gerrard came up to me after the game and hugged me,' Cheyrou said. 'This season, I felt I still had to earn the respect of my team-mates

here. I was not the worst player in the world a week ago, and I'm not the best player in the world now.' Unfortunately a month later Cheyrou was back on the bench again.

HE WAS loaned out to Marseille in the 2004/05 season and then Bordeaux in 2005/06 with the prospect of making it a permanent transfer. Neither team was sufficiently impressed, but Stade

Rennais took the plunge and he became a firm fixture in their starting XI as a holding midfielder. By the end of the 2007/08 season, he had made nearly as many league appearances for Stade Rennais as he had for Liverpool, Marseille and Bordeaux combined.

In January 2010 the 31-year-old moved to Cypriot club Anorthosis Famagusta. After six months in Cyprus, Cheyrou returned to France, signing a two-year deal with Nantes, where he made 41 appearances in two seasons in Ligue 2.

Season	League		FA Cup		League Cup		Europe		Other		Total	
	App	Goals	App	Goals	App	Goals	App	Goals	App	Goals	App	Goals
2002/03	8 (11)	0	2	0	1 (1)	0	3 (2)	1	0 (1)	0	14 (15)	1
2003/04	9 (3)	2	3 (1)	2	0	0	1 (2)	0	-	-	13 (6)	4
Total	17 (14)	2	5 (1)	2	1 (1)	0	4 (4)	1	0 (1)	0	27 (21)	5

Childs, Albert

LIVERPOOL 1954

LIVERPOOL-BORN England amateur international 'Bert' Childs replaced regular right-back Ray Lambert for two consecutive matches in the First Division in the autumn of 1953. Childs experienced the best and worst of Liverpool's season as his first game resulted in a 4-0 home win over Derby County when Louis

Bimpson scored all four in the first-half whereas seven days later the Reds were humiliated 6-0 by Charlton Athletic at the Valley.

Season	League		FA Cup		Total	
	App	Goals	App	Goals	App	Goals
1953/54	2	0	0	0	2	0
Total	**2**	**0**	**0**	**0**	**2**	**0**

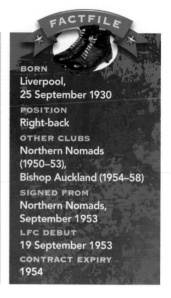
Chisnall, Phil

PHIL CHISNALL was a schoolboy star forward, who in 1958 was snapped up by Manchester United where he played 47 games and scored 10 goals from 1961–64. Shortly after Chisnall featured for the England Under-23 team against West Germany in a 4-2 win at Anfield, Bill Shankly contacted his good friend Matt Busby and made a bid for his services.

Chisnall, who had already tasted European action with United, made his second Reds' appearance in the club's first ever European game against KR Reykjavik in Iceland and scored in a 5-0 victory.

His league debut followed five days later in a 3-2 win over Arsenal at Anfield on the opening day of the season. He didn't play again in the league until the final four games of the same season, which also saw his only league goal for the club, in a 2-0 home victory over Chelsea. Chisnall recalled: 'In the space of a year I played under Matt Busby, Bill Shankly and Alf Ramsey, who was manager of England Under-23s at the time. At United we had Busby, who was the quiet type, and Jimmy Murphy who was the passionate Welshman. At Liverpool it was the other way around, with Shankly the passionate one and Bob Paisley the calming influence. Ramsey was different again, quite prim and proper.' The following 1965/66 season Chisnall was stuck in the reserves where he scored 16 goals; he made his final appearance for the first team as a replacement for Geoff Strong in the first leg of the European Cup Winners' Cup semi-final against Celtic in Scotland on 14 April 1966. Liverpool lost 1-0 but progressed to the final where they lost 2-1 to Dortmund.

CHISNALL MADE HIS SECOND REDS' APPEARANCE IN THE CLUB'S FIRST EVER EUROPEAN GAME AGAINST KR REYKJAVIK IN ICELAND

Chisnall did not make the grade at Anfield due to the sheer strength of the first XI, as he later told the *Liverpool Echo*: 'It was a great side with players like Ian St John, Ian Callaghan, Peter Thompson, Roger Hunt, Willie Stevenson, Gordon Milne and Tommy Smith, so it was always going to be tough to get into the side.'

He went on to play 160 games and score 31 goals for Southend United in the Fourth Division from 1967–71, before having one last season with Stockport County, retiring at 29 due to knee trouble.

CHISNALL is the last player to have been transferred directly from

Manchester United to Liverpool. 'Back then it was just a footballer moving from one club to another,' Chisnall told the *Echo*. 'I was able to go to Old Trafford and play for Liverpool and get a good reception from the crowd. The only person who was bothered was the missus. I told her I was going to play for Liverpool and it meant she had to take all the curtains down, pack up and move down the East Lancs Road. She wasn't too pleased.'

Season	League		FA Cup		League Cup		Europe		Other		Total	
	App	Goals	App	Goals	App	Goals	App	Goals	App	Goals	App	Goals
1964/65	6	1	0	0	-	-	1	1	0 (1)	0	7 (1)	2
1965/66	0	0	0	0	-	-	1	0	0	0	1	0
Total	**6**	**1**	**0**	**0**	**0**	**0**	**2**	**1**	**0 (1)**	**0**	**8 (1)**	**2**

Chorlton, Tom

TOM CHORLTON missed the majority of the 1907/08 season as he was suffering from typhoid fever. This versatile, skilful defender had been on the fringes of the team, making 11 games on average in his first three campaigns. He made the breakthrough in 1908/09 and was the only ever-present in the 1909/10 season.

Chorlton lost his place following a miserable run of five defeats in the first seven league games in the following season. He was the club's penalty-taker for a while, as he had been at Accrington Stanley, and scored four of his eight goals for Liverpool from the penalty spot. After finishing as a player after World War One Chorlton spent a period as a trainer at Manchester City.

LIVERPOOL 1949/50

FACTFILE

BORN
Ashton, Cheshire, 1881
POSITION
Defender
OTHER CLUBS
Heaton Mersey Juniors (1897–99),
Northenden (1899–1900),
Stockport County (1900–02),
Accrington Stanley (1902–04),
Manchester United (1912–14),
Stalybridge Celtic (1914)
SIGNED FROM
Accrington Stanley, May 1904
LFC DEBUT/GOAL
24 September 1904 /
29 October 1904
CONTRACT EXPIRY
31 August 1912
HONOURS
Second Division
Championship 1904/05

Chorlton was described by a *Liverpool Echo* scribe in 1910 as follows:

As a player and a man Liverpool likes Chorlton. There is no 'side' about him. Once a half-back, once a big forward with exceedingly strong centres, Chorlton is now settled at full-back, and in that time he has shown his versatility by occupying both positions for the benefit of others who have been introduced. His build catches the eye, his muscles are large, and his leg a pattern to many who do not exercise. His play has been of a good, level order and his service to Liverpool of great value. At times he does not manage to catch the ball full, but where is there a defender who does not blunder?

Season	League		FA Cup		Other		Total	
	App	Goals	App	Goals	App	Goals	App	Goals
1904/05	12	3	0	0	-	-	12	3
1905/06	6	1	0	0	0	0	6	1
1906/07	14	0	1	0	-	-	15	0
1907/08	7	1	0	0	-	-	7	1
1908/09	33	3	2	0	-	-	35	3
1909/10	38	0	1	0	-	-	39	0
1910/11	7	0	0	0	-	-	7	0
Total	**117**	**8**	**4**	**0**	**0**	**0**	**121**	**8**

Christie, Frank

FRANK CHRISTIE was obtained from St Johnstone Young Men's Club during World War Two but he only made it as far as the reserve team at Liverpool. He was loaned out to Forfar in 1945/46 and bought by the club at the end of the season.

FRANK CHRISTIE

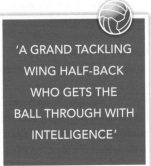

'A GRAND TACKLING WING HALF-BACK WHO GETS THE BALL THROUGH WITH INTELLIGENCE'

1950/51 season and left the club in January 1951. He became a resounding success with East Fife in Scotland, described as 'a grand tackling wing half-back who gets the ball through with intelligence'. Christie was East Fife's manager from 1973–76.

FACTFILE

BORN
Scone, Perthshire, Scotland, 17 February 1927
DIED
1996
POSITION
Left-half
OTHER CLUBS
St Johnstone Young Men's Club (1944–45),
Forfar Athletic (1946–49),
East Fife (1951–58)
SIGNED FROM
St Johnstone Young Men's Club, 19 July 1945 /
Forfar Athletic March 1949
LFC DEBUT
15 March 1950
CONTRACT EXPIRY
22 May 1946 / January 1951

Three years later left-half Christie returned to Liverpool to make another attempt to succeed south of the border. He spent a year in the reserves before making his long-awaited first-team debut in the unusual position of outside-left in a goalless draw with Manchester United on 15 March 1950 at Old Trafford. Christie played as a left-half in a 1-0 win over Charlton Athletic, a 5-1 defeat against Newcastle United and a 1-0 loss to Burnley. He went back to the reserves in the

Season	League		FA Cup		Total	
	App	Goals	App	Goals	App	Goals
1949/50	4	0	0	0	4	0
Total	**4**	**0**	**0**	**0**	**4**	**0**

Cissé,
Djibril

DJIBRIL CISSÉ joined Auxerre as a youngster and his star shone brightly in the 2001/02 season, scoring all kinds of goals, some of them truly spectacular, and finishing as top scorer in France with 22 goals from 29 league games.

Gérard Houllier was a firm admirer and signalled his intentions to his old friend Guy Roux, Auxerre's manager. 'Gérard and I speak all the time and it does not usually take him long to get round to the subject of Djibril,' revealed Roux. 'With his pace he would be one of the most destructive strikers in the English game.' Cissé realised he was going nowhere yet and had a somewhat disappointing 2002/03 season, scoring 14 goals in 33 league games.

FACTFILE

BORN
Arles, France,
12 August 1981
POSITION
Centre-forward
OTHER CLUBS
Auxerre (1999–2004),
Olympique Marseille
(loan, 2006–07 + transfer
2007–09),
Sunderland (loan, 2008–09),
Panathinaikos (2009–11),
Lazio (2011–12),
Queens Park Rangers
(2012–13),
Al Gharafa (loan, 2013)
Kuban Krasnodar (2013-)
SIGNED FROM
Auxerre, £14.5million,
1 July 2004
INTERNATIONAL CAPS
41 France caps (9 goals)
(14 (6) at LFC), 2002–11
LFC DEBUT/GOAL
10 August 2004 /
14 August 2004
CONTRACT EXPIRY
9 July 2007
HONOURS
Champions League 2005;
FA Cup 2006

In the summer of 2003 Roux persuaded him to stay for one more season. Liverpool-bound Cissé played superbly in his final year, scored 26 goals in 38 league games and was again king of the scoring charts in the French league, by a good margin of six from Alexander Frei at Stade Rennais and seven from Marseille's Didier Drogba. In total Cissé scored 70 goals in 128 league games during his six seasons at Auxerre.

IRONICALLY, two weeks before Cissé's arrival at Anfield on 1 July 2004, Houllier left the club. He now had to impress Rafa Benítez, which was no easy undertaking. By October Cissé admitted to *LFC Magazine* he was struggling in his new surroundings. 'The game is much faster and more physical than I am used to and I am being singled out for close marking. Milan [Baros] likes to have the ball at his feet and the goal in front of him so he can run at players and commit them, getting in behind them and shooting. I like the ball in space so I have time to assess my options. I think we can blend together well,' Cissé said convincingly.

In only his 15th game for Liverpool, having scored three goals, Cissé suffered a fracture of the tibia and fibula of his left leg against Blackburn on 30 October 2004. He was out of action for six months, returning in the second leg of the quarter-finals of the Champions League against Juventus. If he hadn't been given the right treatment Cissé's career might have ended there and then. 'My bones were overlapping and I had no circulation in my foot,' Cissé said. 'They had to pull my bones back into place with their hands. If they had waited until I got to the hospital I might have lost my leg.' Cissé was a substitute in nine of the ten games

he featured in the rest of the season including the Istanbul final, where he played 35 minutes and scored Liverpool's second penalty in the shootout.

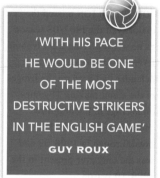

Cissé scored six goals in his first nine matches of the 2005/06 season but the majority of them came against weak opponents in the qualifying rounds of the Champions League. He was happy with his progress: 'I was worried about getting back my acceleration. But in the tests, I was the one who jumped the highest and ran the fastest. No one at Liverpool can beat me. Djibril is back!' Two of his goals, though, came in the European Super Cup final against CSKA Moscow, when he guaranteed a 3-1 victory in extra time.

CISSÉ didn't command a regular place in the team but two consecutive starts inspired winning goals against Blackburn and Anderlecht in the middle of October. However, he struggled to find any consistency as the season progressed and Rafa was not too happy. 'At Auxerre he didn't have any responsibility for defending or the tactics of the team. Now at a big club like Liverpool he needs to learn that he has to work for his team-mates, who are also very good players. He has to understand the difference between a club that plays to win games and a club that plays to win trophies.'

In January 2006 Cissé had to deny claims made by his brother and

one-time agent Hamed that a deal with Marseille was '90 per cent done' and insisted: 'I'm in Liverpool for three more seasons and I'm not going to leave. It hurt me because it's my own family who talk rubbish.' However, Marseille sporting director Jose Anigo insisted his club would continue their pursuit. 'In football what you say one day might not be true any more the next.'

CISSÉ scored one goal from the middle of November to the middle of March but finished the season with a flourish. He scored seven goals in his last ten games

including the opening goal in the FA Cup final win over West Ham. As Liverpool were in contract discussions with Marseille and Lyon over Cissé's transfer he suffered another double fracture of the tibia and fibula, this time of his right leg, in a friendly for France against China. He missed the World Cup in Germany but a loan deal was agreed that took him to Marseille in July 2006.

Cissé scored 15 goals in 25 games, including two in the Cup final against Sochaux which Marseille lost in a penalty shootout. After lengthy negotiations the player

was sold to Marseille early in July 2007 for £6million. Cissé scored 22 goals in 50 matches for Marseille in 2007/08 but he wanted a return to England where his wife was still living.

In August 2008 he signed a one-year loan deal with Sunderland where he played 38 games and scored 11 goals. Cissé returned to Marseille but within a few weeks the French club had negotiated a £6.8million transfer that took him to Panathinaikos.

His efficiency with Panathinaikos secured him a four-year contract

> HE SCORED SEVEN GOALS IN HIS LAST TEN GAMES INCLUDING THE OPENING GOAL IN THE FA CUP FINAL WIN OVER WEST HAM

with Italian Serie A club Lazio in July 2011. He had only scored five goals in 27 matches when he signed for Queens Park Rangers a few months later and helped keep the club in the Premier League.

DURING the 2012/13 season Cissé struggled for form and was loaned to Al Gharafa in Qatar before being released from Rangers in the summer.

Season	League		FA Cup		League Cup		Europe		Other		Total	
	App	Goals	App	Goals	App	Goals	App	Goals	App	Goals	App	Goals
2004/05	10 (6)	4	0	0	0	0	4 (5)	1	-	-	14 (11)	5
2005/06	19 (14)	9	3 (3)	2	0	0	6 (8)	8	1	0	29 (25)	19
Total	29 (20)	13	3 (3)	2	0	0	10 (13)	9	1	0	43 (36)	24

Clark, Bob

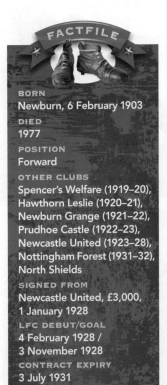

FACTFILE

BORN
Newburn, 6 February 1903
DIED
1977
POSITION
Forward
OTHER CLUBS
Spencer's Welfare (1919–20), Hawthorn Leslie (1920–21), Newburn Grange (1921–22), Prudhoe Castle (1922–23), Newcastle United (1923–28), Nottingham Forest (1931–32), North Shields
SIGNED FROM
Newcastle United, £3,000, 1 January 1928
LFC DEBUT/GOAL
4 February 1928 / 3 November 1928
CONTRACT EXPIRY
3 July 1931

BOB CLARK, who could feature anywhere up front and was 'built like an elephant', won the League Championship with Newcastle in 1927, and was a perfect partner for Hughie Gallacher. He played 77 league games and scored 16 goals in five years until he moved to Liverpool in the middle of the 1927/28 season.

He was introduced into the Liverpool side when he played in two defeats against West Ham and Portsmouth in early February 1928. He played in 32 consecutive league matches the next season, scoring nine goals. Clark featured in the opening three league fixtures of 1929/30 before losing

his place, and was only called on once more in his last season at the club, on 28 March 1931, signing off with a goal when Liverpool defeated Portsmouth 3-1.

Clark did have his moments in a Liverpool shirt, as is evident from this *Liverpool Echo* report of the club's 8-0 victory over Burnley on Boxing Day 1928:

Clark is one of the few footballers who really enjoys his football. He loves to make a tackle with one foot and, having missed the ball, he completes the boyish trick of putting his other foot out behind foot number one [basically an early description of a two-footed tackle!]. But he is seen at his best, when he is bringing a ball down by a trapping movement. Yesterday against Burnley he got his first goal, through charging Lindsay out of the way and dribbling round one of his own players. That's Clarky, he would dribble round his own side, the referee and anyone else between him and goal. Dribbling is a joy to watch when Clark is in this mood. Although the crowd at times do not echo my enthusiasm when he goes backward to go around the same player twice or even thrice.

Season	League		FA Cup		Total	
	App	Goals	App	Goals	App	Goals
1927/28	2	0	0	0	2	0
1928/29	32	9	3	0	35	9
1929/30	4	1	0	0	4	1
1930/31	1	1	0	0	1	1
Total	39	11	3	0	42	11

Cleghorn, Tom

TOM CLEGHORN

TOM CLEGHORN was a popular player at Blackburn Rovers, where his energetic performances at half-back were reputedly worth the admission price alone.

He was described by a Blackburn historian as 'A great little player who never knew when he was beaten. He worked like a demon, tackled effectively and headed the ball with wonderful skill. His value was enhanced by the judgement he displayed in feeding the forwards. On many occasions Cleghorn roused crowds to a frenzy of enthusiasm.' Standing just 5ft 5in (166cm), Cleghorn played 48 games for Rovers from 1894–96 in the First Division.

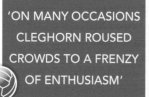

'ON MANY OCCASIONS CLEGHORN ROUSED CROWDS TO A FRENZY OF ENTHUSIASM'

CLEGHORN made his debut for Liverpool on 21 March 1896 in a home fixture in the Second Division with Burton Swifts, which Liverpool won 6-1. He played in the last six games of that successful season which saw Liverpool go up again. Cleghorn made a further 17 league appearances in 1896/97 before being one of the club's two

'ever-present' players (the other was keeper Harry Storer) in 1897/98. The next season was his final one at the club during which he took his total games tally up to 56. Cleghorn also played in ten FA Cup ties for Liverpool and his only senior goal for the club came in that competition, a 4-3 first round victory over Burton Swifts on 30 January 1897.

FACTFILE

BORN
Leith, Edinburgh, Scotland, 13 February 1870
POSITION
Left-half
OTHER CLUBS
Leith Athletic (1892–94), Blackburn Rovers (1894–96), Portsmouth (1899–1903), Plymouth Argyle (1903–05)
SIGNED FROM
Blackburn Rovers, March 1896
LFC DEBUT/GOAL
21 March 1896 / 30 January 1897
CONTRACT EXPIRY
August 1899

Season	League		FA Cup		Other		Total	
	App	Goals	App	Goals	App	Goals	App	Goals
1895/96	3	0	0	0	4	0	7	0
1896/97	17	0	5	1	-	-	22	1
1897/98	30	0	5	0	-	-	35	0
1898/99	6	0	0	0	-	-	6	0
Total	**56**	**0**	**10**	**1**	**4**	**0**	**70**	**1**

Cleland, James

LIVERPOOL were seriously depleted through injuries to key men and got inside-left James Cleland on loan for the Test match at the end of the 1894/95 season.

Liverpool had finished bottom of the First Division that season and were relegated after losing 1-0 to Bury despite Cleland's help. He was a Scottish international by then, having earned his only cap on 28 March 1891 against Ireland.

FACTFILE

BORN
Lanarkshire, Scotland, 1870
POSITION
Inside-left forward
OTHER CLUBS
Minerva (1889–92), Royal Albert (1892–94), Third Lanark (1894–95), St Bernard's (1895–96), Abercorn (1896–97), Partick Thistle (1897–98)
SIGNED FROM
St Bernard's (on loan), April 1895
INTERNATIONAL CAPS
1 Scotland cap, 1891
LFC DEBUT
27 April 1895
CONTRACT EXPIRY
April 1895

Season	League		FA Cup		Other		Total	
	App	Goals	App	Goals	App	Goals	App	Goals
1894/95	0	0	0	0	1	0	1	0
Total	**0**	**0**	**0**	**0**	**1**	**0**	**1**	**0**

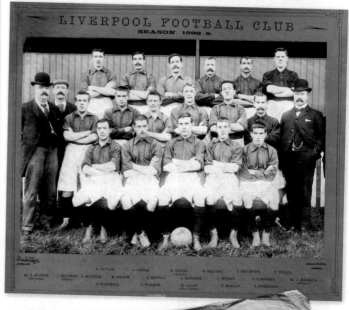

LIVERPOOL 1898/99

*Back row - **Dunlop, A. Goldie, Storer (Captain), McQueen, Stevenson, Wilkie***
*Middle - **Watson (Secretary), Chapman (Trainer), McCowie, W. Goldie, Howell, Raisbeck, Wilson, Cleghorn, McKenna (Director)***
*Front - **Marshall, Walker, Allan, Morgan, Robertson***

Clemence, Ray

RAY CLEMENCE was a fresh-faced 18-year-old at Scunthorpe United when Bill Shankly brought him to Anfield in June 1967. Despite his young age he had made 46 appearances for the Third Division club. Shankly even told him Tommy Lawrence was over the hill and he would be in the team inside six months to convince him to join. Shankly liked the look of him: 'He's a nicely built lad, with one or two mannerisms, and maybe a wee bit cocky. But we're getting him in plenty of time to work on him.'

Clemence had to serve a frustrating two-and-a-half year apprenticeship in the reserves before becoming a regular. A rare exception was a League

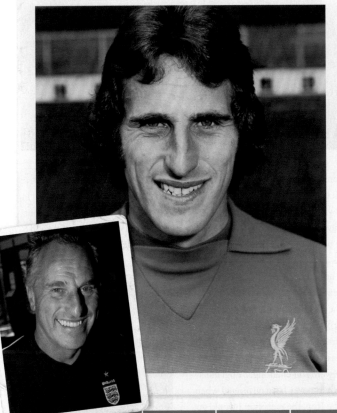

Cup tie against Swansea in September 1968, which was an interesting experience, as Clemence told *LFChistory.net*: 'It was a horrible night, lashing down with rain and a gale-force wind. I had a particularly poor night when kicking the ball was concerned. I remember one soul shouting out from the Anfield Road end, knowing my kicking would put Swansea on the attack every time I had the ball: "Clemence, take an early shower." Obviously he didn't realise what was to come in the next 14 years.'

Clemence's second and third game came one year after his debut but he could hardly showcase his talent as Liverpool conquered Dundalk 10-0 and 4-0 in the European Fairs Cup.

As the 1960s ended, Shankly was starting to break up the team which had brought him so much success. Tommy Lawrence lost his spot following an awful FA Cup quarter-final defeat at Watford on 21 February 1970 and seven days later Clemence was one of a number of changes made for the visit of Derby County; he had established himself firmly as first-choice keeper by the end of that season. In the next 11 years Clemence only missed six league matches!

In the 1970/71 season Clemence only conceded 22 goals in 41 First Division matches, a record which was surpassed in 1978/79 when just 16 goals were conceded, with Clemence an ever-present for the sixth time. It was no coincidence Liverpool were the best team as they had the best defence: Clemence, Phil Neal, Alan Kennedy, Phil Thompson and Alan Hansen. Clemence kept 28 clean sheets and only conceded four goals at Anfield in 21 games in this fantastic season! His positional sense and quick reactions led to England caps galore and his tally would have been even higher had Peter Shilton not been around at the same time.

CLEMENCE was crucial to Liverpool's immense success and had a number of memorable moments when the Reds conquered Europe. His crucial save from Uli Stielike when the 1977 European Cup Final was tensely balanced at 1-1 helped Liverpool achieve perhaps the most memorable result in the club's illustrious history. His penalty save from Jupp Heynckes prevented Liverpool from losing the 1973 UEFA Cup final on the away-goals rule. Another brilliant save from a spot kick at Dresden in the UEFA Cup three years later also prevented a quarter-final exit and the Reds went on to win the cup that year as well. Clemence's remarkable consistency and athleticism turned many a draw into a victory and many potential defeats into draws and wins.

Clemence's final game for Liverpool was appropriately on the sort of grand stage to which he had become accustomed. He kept a clean sheet as Real Madrid were beaten in Paris as Liverpool lifted their third European Cup. It was a shock for Liverpool's management as well as fans when Clemence, who was approaching his 33rd birthday, declared he wanted to leave the club just as

Season	League		FA Cup		League Cup		Europe		Other		Total	
	App	Goals	App	Goals	App	Goals	App	Goals	App	Goals	App	Goals
1968/69	0	0	0	0	1	0	0	0	-	-	1	0
1969/70	14	0	1	0	0	0	2	0	-	-	17	0
1970/71	41	0	7	0	3	0	10	0	-	-	61	0
1971/72	42	0	3	0	3	0	4	0	1	0	53	0
1972/73	41	0	4	0	7	0	12	0	-	-	64	0
1973/74	42	0	9	0	6	0	4	0	-	-	61	0
1974/75	42	0	2	0	4	0	4	0	1	0	53	0
1975/76	42	0	2	0	3	0	12	0	-	-	59	0
1976/77	42	0	8	0	2	0	9	0	1	0	62	0
1977/78	40	0	1	0	9	0	9	0	1	0	60	0
1978/79	42	0	7	0	1	0	3	0	-	-	53	0
1979/80	41	0	8	0	7	0	2	0	1	0	59	0
1980/81	41	0	2	0	9	0	9	0	1	0	62	0
Total	**470**	**0**	**54**	**0**	**55**	**0**	**80**	**0**	**6**	**0**	**665**	**0**

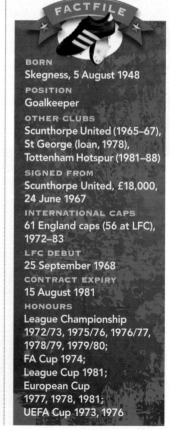

newcomer Bruce Grobbelaar was staking a claim to the number one jersey.

'I came off the field afterwards and went into the dressing room,' Clemence explained to *LFChistory.net*. 'There was champagne everywhere and TV cameras. It was just another day at the office for me. It was there and then that I made the decision that to perform at the level I had always pushed myself to, I just needed a new challenge. I had won everything there was to win at Liverpool.'

Clemence, who had another two years left of his contract, told Bob Paisley and Peter Robinson about his decision two weeks after the final:

Peter Robinson said: 'Well, are you sure it's nothing else. Can we do anything?' I'm sure they would have given me probably a bigger contract if I had pushed for it. But I said, 'It's not that, it's just literally I need to change. I've loved every minute of this here and I don't want it to turn sour.' I had seen other great players stay a little bit too long at Liverpool and then moving to somewhere where it wasn't such a big club and it was difficult for them to motivate themselves. I had to move at a time when a big club wanted me.

Some claimed Clemence was running scared as he felt threatened by Grobbelaar. Clemence says nothing could be further from the truth. 'At the start of my career, I had Tommy Lawrence underneath

me once I got into the side so I had the pressure off him. Frankie Lane came from Tranmere, [Peter] McDonnell came from Bury, [Steve] Ogrizovic came from Chesterfield so I always had somebody putting pressure on me and part of Liverpool's way of getting you to play well was always having somebody to threaten your position. Bruce was no different.'

Clemence moved to Tottenham Hotspur and his first competitive match against his former team-mates was at Wembley on 13 March 1982. Despite his heroics, Liverpool retained the League Cup. A few weeks later Spurs travelled to Anfield with Liverpool needing a win to secure their 13th League Championship. As Clemence ran towards the Kop at the start of the second half he received a fantastic ovation. 'The first half I was playing at the Anfield Road end and they were still chanting: "England's number one" to me, so that was nice. I could never have envisaged when I came out at half-time and ran down to the Kop, the reception I would get. The whole stadium stood up and every single one in the Kop. It's probably the most emotional I have ever been at a football ground. It definitely brought a lump to my throat because I could not believe the reception from them.'

CLEMENCE enjoyed a new lease of life at Tottenham, playing almost until he was 40 and eventually making over 1,000 appearances in total in his fantastic career.

He played 336 games without missing a single match from 9 September 1972 to 4 March 1978. Only two players have made more first-team appearances for the club: Ian Callaghan and Jamie Carragher. In Clemence's distinguished career at Liverpool he kept 323 clean sheets in 665 appearances. Ian Callaghan is a big fan of his talents: 'Ray was one of the best goalkeepers I have ever seen. He is in England's top three alongside Gordon Banks and Peter Shilton. No one dominated the box as well as Clem. He made things look easy, which is the sign of a top keeper. Ray was one of those people who was really enthusiastic in training. He always wanted

people to take shots at him. He defied you to try and put the ball in the net. That's the sign of someone who was always on top of the job and confident in his own ability.'

Clough,
Nigel

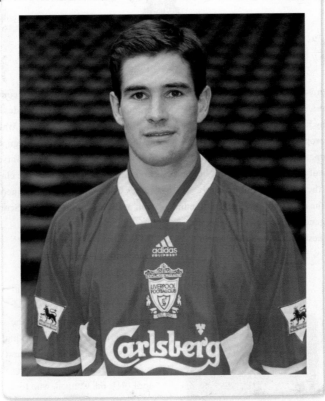

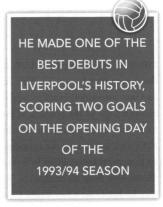
NIGEL CLOUGH was a true stalwart at Nottingham Forest under the management of his legendary father, Brian. In total he made 400 appearances and scored 130 goals in his first spell at the City Ground. When Forest were relegated and his father resigned Nigel moved to Liverpool in 1993. He made one of the best debuts in Liverpool's history, scoring two goals on the opening day of the 1993/94 season against Sheffield Wednesday at Anfield.

Despite his performance *The Times* was not so convinced by Liverpool's new No. 7. 'Clough has neither the pace or purposefulness of Keegan nor the presence of Dalglish, Liverpool's most revered former No. 7s, but an intuitiveness which has rarely been fully exploited by club or country. After a season battling in vain to save his father's job at Nottingham Forest, Clough already seems reinvigorated. His two goals on Saturday were celebrated by a man who appeared content with his new responsibilities. It remains to be seen, however, whether Souness will get the best out of him.'

Clough added two more goals in August 1993 as Liverpool won four of their opening five Premier League games and went top. Things went pear-shaped after that for Souness's Liverpool and the Scotsman was sacked mid-season, with Roy Evans coming in.

After his good start Clough had struggled to make an impact with subdued performances, though on occasion shining like against Manchester United when he was instrumental in turning a 3-0 loss into a 3-3 draw with two great goals. Clough wasn't the type of striker whom you depended on for goals, although the presence of Ian Rush and the up-and-coming Robbie Fowler should have suited him perfectly, playing behind the front men and feeding them with passes. However, Clough only made ten starts in two years under Evans and halfway through the 1995/96 season was offloaded to Manchester City. He settled for a £1,500-a-week reduction in salary to give himself the chance of Premiership football. City boss Alan Ball was impressed: 'The lad has been very sensible. It shows he is prepared to sacrifice something to play first-team football, which is marvellous.'

CLOUGH played in all of City's remaining Premier League matches in the 1995/96 season but City were relegated and an injury sidetracked his career the following season. He was sent out on loan to Nottingham Forest, where he added 13 games and one goal to his total at his old club. Forest didn't want his services once his loan period expired and following an unsuccessful four-week loan to Sheffield Wednesday he returned to City, who were relegated to the third tier at the end of the 1997/98 season.

Clough had not featured at all for City during that campaign and was paid the remaining nine months of his contract and given a free transfer, effectively ending his league career at the age of 32.

In October 1998 Clough accepted the post of player-manager at Burton Albion, then in the Dr Martens League (football's sixth tier). Burton subsequently moved into the Northern Premier League and, as champions of that division in 2002, were promoted to the Conference. Seven years later they won the Conference title and became a Football League club for the first time. However, by the time promotion had been achieved, Clough had replaced Paul Jewell as the manager of Derby County. His arrival brought an improvement in results and the club was able to stave off the threat of relegation. Following two below-par seasons there were no similar fears about relegation in 2011/12. Clough has since signed a new three-year deal with the Pride Park club, and Derby have consolidated their position as a mid-table team.

Season	League		FA Cup		League Cup		Europe		Total	
	App	Goals	App	Goals	App	Goals	App	Goals	App	Goals
1993/94	25 (2)	7	2	0	2	1	-	-	29 (2)	8
1994/95	3 (7)	0	0	0	1	1	-	-	4 (7)	1
1995/96	1 (1)	0	0	0	0	0	0	0	1 (1)	0
Total	**29 (10)**	**7**	**2**	**0**	**3**	**2**	**0**	**0**	**34 (10)**	**9**

Club World Cup

THE INTERCONTINENTAL CUP, which was subsequently renamed the Toyota Cup for sponsorship reasons, ran from 1960 until 2004 and was an annual event recognised by FIFA that was intended to be competed for by the winners of the European Champions' Cup and its South American equivalent, the Copa Libertadores. Confusingly, FIFA also sanctioned the introduction of the Club World Cup, holding its inaugural tournament in Brazil in the year 2000 but inviting contestants from all continents. With the demise of the Intercontinental Cup in 2004, the Club World Cup is generally accepted now as the tournament that decides which is the best club team in the world.

The Intercontinental Cup had a somewhat fractious history, especially in the days when it was a two legs home-and-away format. There were particularly brutal matches between Glasgow Celtic and Racing Club from Buenos Aires in 1967 and between Manchester United and Estudiantes, also from Argentina, a year later. By the time Liverpool first qualified by winning the European Cup in 1977, there were still serious misgivings about travelling to the other side of the world in the middle of a European season. Liverpool's place in 1977 was taken by the club that they beat in the final as was the case a year later when the Reds defended Europe's biggest prize. It wasn't until the format was changed to a single match final in 1980 that a degree of credibility returned to this maligned competition. Nottingham Forest's match against a Uruguayan club passed off peacefully enough in 1980 and this might have persuaded Liverpool's hierarchy to take part after the club won its third European Cup in Paris in 1981. Facing them in Japan was Flamengo from Rio de Janeiro, who included in their line-up one of the best players in the world at that time, Zico. Flamengo led by three goals by the interval and the European champions returned to England a soundly-beaten team. Three years later came Liverpool's second attempt to be crowned world champions. But their bid again ended in disappointment

with a 1-0 defeat by the Argentinian Independiente.

FIFA's Club World Cup reigned from 2005 onwards as the Intercontinental Cup was effectively replaced. This meant that Liverpool, winners of the Champions League in that year, were one of six clubs invited to take part, each one from a different continent. The Champions League winners and the Copa Libertadores winners went directly into the semi-finals. Liverpool comfortably defeated Saprissa from Costa Rica 3-0 while São Paulo had a much closer match against Al-Ittihad from Saudi Arabia, winning 3-2. So, just as in 1981, Liverpool faced a Brazilian club for the right to be called "World Champions". But for the third time they failed, having three goals disallowed in somewhat dubious circumstances. Anyone watching São Paulo's celebrations in 2005 would quickly realise that victory in this match seems to mean a lot more to the South Americans than it does to the Europeans.

Coaches

THERE HAVE BEEN excellent coaches at Liverpool all through the proud history of the club besides the legendary ones during the Bootroom era. Alec Dick and Wally Richardson trained the squad in the club's first ever campaign and a T. Whitway took over for the following five seasons. Tom Watson arrived in 1896 and became the first hands-on manager of the club and two years later he brought in James Chapman who had trained the Scottish international team as well as Hearts, who won the Scottish League in the 1896/97 season.

He kept the players in excellent shape and Liverpool won their first League Championship in 1901. Chapman left Liverpool in 1903 for reasons unknown, said certain to be sorely missed in the club programme. He was working at Leeds City when he took ill and passed away, 56 years of age in April 1911. Bill Connell, who took over in 1903, enjoyed a lengthy association at Liverpool. He had a torrid debut season as the team got relegated, but Liverpool responded with gusto and went on to win the Second Division and First Division in successive seasons. Connell was popular with the players and showed a surprising side to him on the 1913/14 post-season tour during a party in Sweden, raising his voice, not in this instance to berate the players, but in a sing-along. 'Mr Tom Watson was in very good voice and our trainer (Bill Connell). The latter rather surprised the Liverpool players, who had not given him the credit of being a Caruso,' Thomas Fairfoul wrote in his diary in the

*Assistant Liverpool coach
Jimmy Seddon*

Echo. Connell was born on 8 May 1863 in Stockport and stayed at the club until 1928 when he was 65 years old. During his reign he was ably assisted by former players, George Fleming (1907-22) and Joe Hewitt and Charlie Wilson (1922-28). The latter two were joined by another stalwart of the club in Ephraim Longworth when Connell retired. Albert Shelley took over as first-team trainer in 1939 assisted by former England international Jimmy Seddon while Longworth trained the reserves. Shelley could be quite critical of the first-team players, not suffering fools gladly, but he was generally liked. He was also the physio, not really educated as such, but did his best to lessen the suffering of injured players.

BOB PAISLEY, who took over from Seddon as reserve-team trainer in 1954, got to know Shelley quite well. "Trainers had to have hands like leather. There was hardly a player who got by without suffering first degree burns at some time or other. You put the hot towel on and then the cold one,

it was the main treatment,' Paisley said in his autobiography. 'The first person I ever treated was Albert Shelley, our first-team trainer, for a boil on his backside. Albert was one of the old school. He taught me how to harden my hands with the towels. When the physio machines came in I had to show him how to use them, but he never really came to terms with them. He had a common-sense approach to the practical side of it, but he was frightened by the electrical stuff, he even used to put a handkerchief on the leads. So when the machines came in I virtually took over the treatment of all the players.' Shelley was first-team coach until Paisley replaced him in 1957 while Phil Taylor, who had also been involved with the training of the first team from 1954, was promoted from acting manager to full-time manager. Shelley remained a part of the ground staff into the late 1960s taking care of the Bootroom and the dressing rooms as Brian Hall remembers in *The Boot Room Boys*. "Albert Shelley was the old stager in the long white coat or brown coat shuffling around sweeping up after everybody. He could always handle the dressing room banter from all these young lads.' The trio of Paisley, Joe Fagan and Reuben Bennett were kept on in 1959 when Bill Shankly was appointed, later joined by Ronnie Moran and Roy Evans as the basis of the famed Bootroom. Liverpool continued its tradition of appointing former players to the coaching team such as Chris Lawler, Tommy Smith, Doug Livermore, Phil Boersma, Gary Ablett, Phil Thompson and Sammy Lee. The latter two remained Gérard Houllier's and Rafa Benítez's respective links to the Liverpool mentality, but unavoidably foreign influence was exerted on Melwood. Houllier brought in former Lens coach, Patrice Bergues, when he joined in the summer of 1998 and he

Liverpool coaches Sammy Lee and Patrice Bergues

First-team coach Albert Shelley working with Billy Liddell

remained his trusted lieutenant to the end of the treble 2000/01 season. They knew each other well having worked together for the French Football Federation. Bergues brought innovative training techniques to the club while enjoying great respect and popularity among the playing staff and many consider Houllier's downward trajectory from the 2002/03 season owing partly to Bergues' appointment as Lens' general manager. Bergues joined forces with Houllier again in 2005 when he became his assistant at Lyon. Houllier again looked towards a former co-worker at the French FA when he appointed Jacques Crevoisier in 2001. He was known for his psychometric tests on youngsters, to help determine and further their potential. Crevoisier had been a coach since he was 25 years old and had a PhD in psychology. 'English players come across as more committed and aggressive in the test but their self-confidence and concentration is not as good', he told the *Daily Mail* in October 2010. 'If a player has a concentration problem, it is no good just saying 'Concentrate'. So you give them an exercise to hit sharp passes along the ground, no mistakes allowed, and they have to concentrate.

WITH 14-year-olds you ask them to do it for a minute, 18-year-olds maybe two. If you do that three times a week, you will notice the difference. I remember Steven Gerrard doing that exercise and I have never seen anyone do it as well in my life.' Crevoisier left the club in 2003 and later worked for Tottenham's and Arsenal's academy, achieving excellent results. When Benítez was appointed manager in 2004 he brought with him his No. 2 from Tenerife and Valencia, Pako Ayesteran. He looked continually to the future never fully satisfied with his day's work until he could bring Liverpool back to the very top of the English League. 'One of the things I don't like in football is when people say, 'We've done it this way for years,' Ayesteran told Liverpool's official website in 2010. 'My father had a Fiat but at this moment I have a BMW. You have to move on and you have to adapt to new ways.'

Ayesteran was of great value to Liverpool, an excellent trainer who was not simply a 'yes man' and kept Benítez in check, which importantly was missing after he and Benítez parted ways in 2007. 'Pako was much more than a physical trainer, he was my friend and someone I trusted for many years,' Benítez told *The Times* in March 2008. 'Liverpool gave him

autonomy and power and I think that changed him a lot. One day I found out that he had serious contacts with other teams and that seemed to me a betrayal towards me and the club that I couldn't accept.' Ayesteran refuted that statement in April 2013, talking to the *Daily Mail*. 'Things began to change when we arrived at Liverpool and were so successful. In England the people around the game, even for myself, make you feel that you're bigger than you really are. Sometimes you don't take care of the values and principles that made you so successful. Maybe we didn't have as much detail in training. We stopped being critical with ourselves and sometimes we went through the motions. That's the reason I wasn't happy.' As Benítez departed in 2010 Roy Hodgson kept faith with his old Fulham backroom staff while his successor Kenny Dalglish brought in the innovative Steve Clarke. Current boss, Brendan Rodgers, kept his coaching staff from Swansea, but has also recognised it's vital for the identity of the club to have a former Liverpool player around. Mike Marsh was promoted to first-team coach, simply not because of his links to Liverpool's past, but more importantly due to his excellent work with the club's youth squads. Rodgers is certain to keep in mind that while looking to the future don't disregard the past and what can be learnt from it.

Coady, Conor

A PRODUCT of the Liverpool Academy, Conor Coady captained the England Under-17 team that won the 2010 European Championships, beating a much-fancied Spanish side in the final in Liechtenstein.

Coady, whose club team-mate Andre Wisdom was also a member of the winning team, said at the time: 'Lifting that trophy was just unreal. It's everything I've dreamt about.' The experience gained while on international duty certainly helped Coady at club level. In the same calendar year of his international success, Coady moved up to the reserve team after captaining Liverpool's Under-18s throughout the season and was able to help the club's second string to a cup double in the summer of 2010. Coady's achievements were recognised when he was nominated for the BBC Young Sports Personality of the Year.

Coady has already proved to be a confident and assured performer as either a central defender or a

FACTFILE

BORN
Liverpool, 25 February 1993
POSITION
Centre-half / Midfielder
OTHER CLUBS
Sheffield United (loan, 2013)
JOINED
2001
LFC DEBUT
8 November 2012

holding midfielder. He has an imposing physical presence as well as being a good tackler, header and passer. He also has terrific leadership qualities and many are predicting that he could become a future captain for his club. Coady is taking the same path through the ranks at Liverpool as Jamie Carragher and he doesn't mind being compared to him. 'I know Jamie Carragher did a similar thing by playing in midfield for the Under-18s and then moving into defence – if I can do half as well as he has done I'll be delighted.'

In July 2013 Coady signed a six-month loan with Sheffield United in League One.

Season	League		FA Cup		League Cup		Europe		Total	
	App	Goals	App	Goals	App	Goals	App	Goals	App	Goals
2012/13	0 (1)	0	0	0	0	0	1	0	1 (1)	0
Total	0 (1)	0	0	0	0	0	1	0	1 (1)	0

Coates, Sebastian

DESPITE his young age, Sebastian Coates Nion already possesses an impressive CV. After spending a few years in Nacional's youth teams he broke into the first team when he was 18. He had by then already featured in the South American Under-20 Championships where Uruguay finished third.

Coates came into Nacional's side when three months were left of the 2008/09 season, winning the championship and reaching the semi-finals of the Copa Libertadores. His progress was rewarded with the honour of being voted the Uruguayan Championship's 'Revelation of the Season'. Another league title followed in 2011 and he made his international debut only a week before Copa America 2011 when coming on as a substitute in a 3-0 win over Estonia. Coates featured in four out of Uruguay's six matches in Copa America,

HIS PROGRESS WAS REWARDED WITH THE HONOUR OF BEING VOTED THE URUGUAYAN CHAMPIONSHIP'S 'REVELATION OF THE SEASON'

including the 3-0 win over Paraguay in the final. He collected the 'Trophy Claro' for being the Best Young Player of the Tournament.

He was a rock alongside his partner at the centre-half, the legendary Diego Lugano, prompting his nickname 'Luganito' or 'little Lugano'.

THE URUGUAYAN'S reputation was at an all-time high at the time of his arrival in England little more than a week after Liverpool allowed 32-year-old central defender Sotirios Kyrgiakos to move to Wolfsburg. Coates, who is twelve years his junior, was given the Greek's old squad number, 16. Coates himself is a strapping 6ft 6in (196cm), a strong header both in his own area and the oppositions', comfortable on the ball and will never shirk out of a tackle. He has impressive technical ability for a man of his size.

Coates was sought after by many big clubs such as Paris St Germain, AC Milan, Atletico Madrid and Manchester City but he says that his talk with compatriot Luis Suarez made up his mind to join Liverpool. With centre-half being a position for which the first-team squad had adequate cover, Coates only appeared in a dozen matches in 2011/12. He nevertheless showed astonishing agility to score with a stupendous volley at Queens Park Rangers in March 2012. The experience of Daniel Agger, Martin Skrtel and Jamie Carragher has been preferred to the youthful exuberance of the Uruguayan. Coates cut a frustrated figure as he told Uruguayan paper *El Observador* in March 2013 that he sought a loan move in the January transfer window but Brendan Rodgers had denied him that opportunity.

COATES is contracted to Liverpool to 2016 and if he continues to be disregarded he will certainly move to another club sooner rather than later.

FACTFILE

BORN
Montevideo, Uruguay,
7 October 1990
POSITION
Centre-half
OTHER CLUBS
Nacional (2001–11)
SIGNED FROM
Nacional, £4.9million,
30 August 2011
INTERNATIONAL CAPS
12 Uruguay caps (1 goal)
(7 (1) at LFC), 2011–
LFC DEBUT
18 September 2011 /
21 March 2012

Season	League		FA Cup		League Cup		Europe		Total	
	App	Goals	App	Goals	App	Goals	App	Goals	App	Goals
2011/12	4 (3)	1	1 (1)	0	3	0	-	-	8 (4)	1
2012/13	2 (3)	0	2	0	2	0	3	1	9 (3)	1
Total	**6 (6)**	**1**	**3 (1)**	**0**	**5**	**0**	**3**	**1**	**17 (7)**	**2**

Cockburn, Bill

A STRONG defender with a slightly unfortunate surname that would have ensured him merciless stick on and off the field nowadays, Bill Cockburn joined from Second Division Stockport County prior to the 1924/25 season.

BILL COCKBURN
LIVERPOOL

He made his debut covering for centre-half Walter Wadsworth in successive matches against Bury and Nottingham Forest early in the season, but it was as replacement for right-half Jock McNab that he made the majority of his 19 appearances that year.

COCKBURN missed only six of the 42 First Division fixtures during the 1925/26 season. Following three consecutive defeats in early 1926/27 he and half-back Albert Shears made way for Tom Reid and David Pratt, but that change failed to fix the leaky defence. Cockburn's appearance against West Ham United at Anfield seven days before Christmas in 1926 was his last for the club. After spending the 1927/28 season in the reserves Cockburn joined Queens Park Rangers in the Third Division South.

The *Derby Daily Telegraph* praised his qualities in 1926: 'He's a tall man, now in his prime, great in breaking up, and wonderfully accurate with his long swinging passes to the wings.'

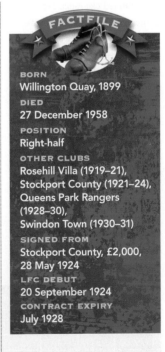

FACTFILE

BORN
Willington Quay, 1899
DIED
27 December 1958
POSITION
Right-half
OTHER CLUBS
Rosehill Villa (1919–21),
Stockport County (1921–24),
Queens Park Rangers
(1928–30),
Swindon Town (1930–31)
SIGNED FROM
Stockport County, £2,000,
28 May 1924
LFC DEBUT
20 September 1924
CONTRACT EXPIRY
July 1928

Season	League		FA Cup		Total	
	App	Goals	App	Goals	App	Goals
1924/25	18	0	1	0	19	0
1925/26	36	0	3	0	39	0
1926/27	9	0	0	0	9	0
Total	**63**	**0**	**4**	**0**	**67**	**0**

Cohen,
Avi

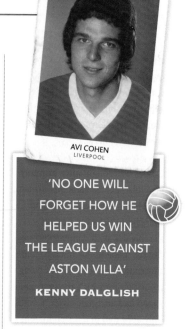

AVI COHEN
LIVERPOOL

ABRAHAM 'AVI' COHEN was the first foreign player to represent Liverpool since South African Doug Rudham arrived 24 years earlier. His transfer successfully concluded six months of the club's interest in the defender. In February 1979 he spent a week training with Liverpool under the watchful eye of manager Bob Paisley. He joined the club in the summer and, due to Ray Kennedy's absence, was given an early debut at Leeds on 15 September 1979 on the left side of midfield.

Cohen didn't feature again until the end of the season as the champions had a fairly settled side. He played in the game against Aston Villa that sealed Liverpool's second consecutive League Championship. It was a day of mixed fortunes for the Israeli left-back. After David Johnson had given the Reds an early lead, Cohen had the misfortune to slice an attempted clearance over Ray Clemence's head into his own goal. But five minutes after the interval, he made up for his error by driving a low shot into the Kop goal to give Liverpool a lead they didn't surrender.

COHEN PLAYED in 14 league matches the following season when Alan Kennedy was out injured. He stirred up controversy when he decided to play against Southampton on 20 September 1980, a day that coincided with the Jewish holiday of Yom Kippur, and was lambasted by the Israeli

media. He didn't feature from February onwards as Liverpool went on to win their third European Cup, and he returned to Israel in October.

He moved back to Britain in May 1987 to play one season for his old team-mate Graeme Souness at Rangers. Cohen managed several teams in Israel from 1990–2001 and the former Israeli captain was the chairman of the Israel Professional Footballers' Association for over five years. Avi tragically died aged only 54 on 28 December 2010 from brain injuries following a motorcycle accident in Israel.

Kenny Dalglish remembered his old colleague: 'Avi was a lovely man who will be remembered fondly by everyone at Liverpool who knew him. He quickly integrated himself into the football club when he joined us and spent a lot of time learning English, which really made him popular. He was well liked by all the lads and although he didn't spend a long time at the club, he certainly left his mark and no one will forget how he helped us win the League against Aston Villa.'

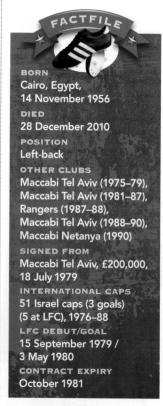

FACTFILE

BORN
Cairo, Egypt,
14 November 1956
DIED
28 December 2010
POSITION
Left-back
OTHER CLUBS
Maccabi Tel Aviv (1975–79),
Maccabi Tel Aviv (1981–87),
Rangers (1987–88),
Maccabi Tel Aviv (1988–90),
Maccabi Netanya (1990)
SIGNED FROM
Maccabi Tel Aviv, £200,000,
18 July 1979
INTERNATIONAL CAPS
51 Israel caps (3 goals)
(5 at LFC), 1976–88
LFC DEBUT/GOAL
15 September 1979 /
3 May 1980
CONTRACT EXPIRY
October 1981

Season	League		FA Cup		League Cup		Europe		Other		Total	
	App	Goals	App	Goals	App	Goals	App	Goals	App	Goals	App	Goals
1979/80	3 (1)	1	1	0	0	0	0	0	0	0	4 (1)	1
1980/81	13 (1)	0	1	0	1	0	2 (1)	0	0	0	17 (2)	0
Total	**16 (2)**	**1**	**2**	**0**	**1**	**0**	**2 (1)**	**0**	**0**	**0**	**21 (3)**	**1**

Cole, Joe

AN ENGLAND international with 56 full caps at the time of his move to Anfield, Cole was already well known by Liverpool supporters as someone who had been a thorn in their side on several occasions, having scored the winning goal for Chelsea against the Reds in both Premier League matches during the 2004/05 season, and also the opening goal in the Champions League semi-final tie two seasons later.

Born in London, Cole was one of a number of fine young English players who came through West Ham United's youth system in the 1990s. At the start of 2003 Hammers manager Glenn Roeder made Cole his captain at the young age of 21. But West Ham were soon relegated from the Premier League and it was pretty much inevitable that Cole, who had just been named 'Hammer of the Year', would move on. Cole joined Chelsea and settled quickly into life at Stamford Bridge, playing in 97 of the maximum 114 Premier League matches in his first three seasons, winning the Premier League title twice.

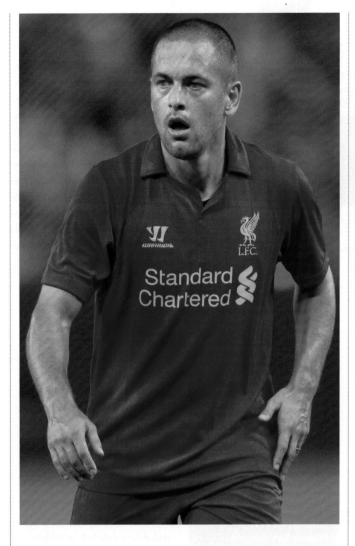

FACTFILE

BORN
Islington, London,
8 November 1981
POSITION
Midfielder
OTHER CLUBS
West Ham United
(1997–2003),
Chelsea (2003–10),
Lille (loan, 2011–12),
West Ham United (2013–)
JOINED
Bosman free transfer,
21 July 2010
INTERNATIONAL CAPS
56 England caps (10 goals),
2001–10
LFC DEBUT/GOAL
5 August 2010 /
16 September 2010
CONTRACT EXPIRY
4 January 2013

COLE ARRIVED AT ANFIELD WITH PROBABLY MORE WINNERS' MEDALS THAN ANY PLAYER WHO HAS PREVIOUSLY SIGNED FOR LIVERPOOL

Injury restricted Cole's club and international appearances in 2006/07 as he needed surgery on his foot at the start of 2007, but he recovered in time to claim an FA Cup-winners' medal. By the middle of 2008, he had reached a crucial stage of his career, playing under new managers – Luis Felipe Scolari and Fabio Capello – for both club and country. Unfortunately, Cole required knee surgery. Even though his appearances were restricted, he scored a crucial goal at Old Trafford late in the 2009/10 season that ultimately saw the Blues regain the Premier League trophy they had relinquished to Manchester United in 2007.

COLE arrived at Anfield with probably more winners' medals than any player who has previously signed for Liverpool. Still the right side of 30, he was expected to be of good use to the squad with 300-plus Premier League appearances and over 50 England caps to his name.

It's fair to say that Cole's debut season as a Liverpool player was far from being the success anticipated when he became Roy Hodgson's first signing (the Milan Jovanovic deal had been instigated by the previous

manager). Cole's Premier League debut lasted only 45 minutes before he was sent off against Arsenal at Anfield. His next home appearance saw him miss a penalty against Trabzonspor in the Europa League. Cole only started 19 of Liverpool's 54 competitive matches and was a substitute in 13 more. Kenny Dalglish gave him his first start in over two months on the final day of the 2010/11 season at Aston Villa but Cole failed to impress.

COLE was loaned to French Ligue 1 champions Lille for the 2011/12 season. He had a good loan spell, even though Lille were unable to successfully defend their title, scoring four times in 32 Ligue 1 matches. Cole, who was, according to Brendan Rodgers, signed for an 'astronomical amount of money' (reportedly £90,000 a week), returned to West Ham on a free transfer in January 2013 with a rumoured pay-off of £3million, but the club is said to have saved itself at least £3.5million in wages for him for the remaining 18 months of his contract.

Season	League		FA Cup		League Cup		Europe		Total	
	App	Goals	App	Goals	App	Goals	App	Goals	App	Goals
2010/11	9 (11)	2	0	0	0	0	10 (2)	1	19 (13)	3
2012/13	0 (6)	1	0	0	1	0	3	1	4 (6)	2
Total	9 (17)	3	0	0	1	0	13 (2)	2	23 (19)	5

Collins, Jimmy

AFTER going back and forth between amateur and professional clubs with modest success Jimmy Collins made seven First Division appearances in Liverpool's forward line during the middle of the 1930s, making his debut at West Bromwich Albion on the opening day of February 1936.

HE WAS picked for the next four matches and also once more before the end of that 1935/36 season. Collins was only to play for the first team on one more occasion a year later, as replacement for centre-forward Fred Howe in the home 1-1 draw with Preston North End. Cardiff in the Third Division South was Collins' next destination. He scored a hat-trick on his home debut and was a popular figure at the club, scoring 41 goals in 76 league games.

He was so described while playing for Cardiff: 'Short, fair-haired and fast (though built like a barrel), Jimmy Collins along with Bert

Turner really began to make things hum after so long in the doldrums. Strong and fearless, he was also mustard with both feet.'

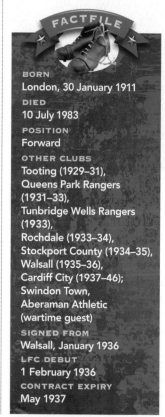

FACTFILE

BORN
London, 30 January 1911
DIED
10 July 1983
POSITION
Forward
OTHER CLUBS
Tooting (1929–31),
Queens Park Rangers (1931–33),
Tunbridge Wells Rangers (1933),
Rochdale (1933–34),
Stockport County (1934–35),
Walsall (1935–36),
Cardiff City (1937–46);
Swindon Town,
Aberaman Athletic (wartime guest)
SIGNED FROM
Walsall, January 1936
LFC DEBUT
1 February 1936
CONTRACT EXPIRY
May 1937

Season	League		FA Cup		Total	
	App	Goals	App	Goals	App	Goals
1935/36	6	0	0	0	6	0
1936/37	1	0	0	0	1	0
Total	**7**	**0**	**0**	**0**	**7**	**0**

Collymore, Stan

STAN COLLYMORE was rejected by both Walsall and Wolves before he was given a chance with Conference club Stafford Rangers. Collymore's first boss, Tommy Coakley, who had him as a Walsall YTS trainee, was as so many enamoured with his talents but worried they might go to waste. 'Even at 16 Stan was very much his own man, with his own ideas about absolutely everything. I felt from day one that he'd either be one of the best players in the world or that he'd have a very short career and finish up as a nothing.' Collymore signed for Crystal Palace in January 1991. Palace were promoted to the Premier League after his first full season but after only a handful of starts in 18 months Collymore dropped a division to join Barry Fry's Southend United where he was a revelation, scoring 18 goals in 33 games.

In 1993, Nottingham Forest paid £2.2million for Collymore's services. He was a tremendous success at Forest, scoring 19 goals in 28 league games and earning them a return to the Premier League. A huge asking price was put on his head, which frightened off potential buyers like Manchester United, who bought Andy Cole instead. Collymore was doing excellently on the field but off the field the situation wasn't ideal, as his former Forest boss Frank Clark later revealed. 'I'm not sure I will live long enough to understand exactly how the boy's brain works. Stan didn't really get close to his team-mates. There was often a certain cool in the air. I remember him decking Alf Inge Haaland with a left hook during training. I described it as a Henry Cooper special.'

Forest finished third in the Premier League and Collymore scored 22 league goals. In the summer of 1995 he made his England debut and a month later he joined Liverpool for a British record fee of £8.5million.

Collymore rifled in a 25-yard winner on his debut against Sheffield Wednesday. 'I've had my ups and downs over the last three years, but now to come to a club like this, where they all want you to do so well, it was a bit emotional,' Collymore told the press. 'When the ball went in, it felt as if my

head exploded. This is just why I wanted to be a footballer. Obviously there is going to be some modification in our play because my trademark is to get in behind people and to get in quite early. The way we play, sometimes we keep the ball and as the season goes on, there will be a bit of compromise between the two styles.'

However, Collymore only scored two goals in his first seven matches and Ian Rush returned to the side to play alongside main striker Robbie Fowler. It wasn't until the start of December, when Rush was recovering from a cartilage operation, that Collymore's partnership with Fowler flourished.

New Year's Day brought the much anticipated reunion of Collymore and Nottingham Forest at Anfield. Forest went 2-0 up inside 20 minutes and cries of 'Judas' and 'What a waste of money' were directed by Forest fans towards their former idol. Collymore responded by setting up three goals and scoring one in a 4-2 victory, and made little effort to hide his joy in front of the Forest fans.

This performance showed his strength of character and was seen as a vital turning point in his Liverpool career. After registering only four goals in the first half of the season Collymore scored 15 goals in 24 games from

January onwards. The most memorable moment in his career, which was later voted as the highlight of Sky Sports' ten-year coverage of the Premier League, came at Anfield on 3 April 1996. Liverpool's former talisman Kevin Keegan had brought his Newcastle team to town and watched as a six-goal thriller came to a close. In the second minute of added time John Barnes spotted Collymore coming in from the left, passed him the ball and he blasted it into the net to drive Anfield wild! Liverpool's lethal partnership of Fowler and Collymore scored a total of 55 goals in the 1995/96 season and hopes were high that the Reds could build on their third-place finish and capture the elusive Premiership trophy next term.

At the end of September 1997 Liverpool were top of the league with six wins and two draws from their opening eight games, but no thanks to Fowler's and Collymore's scoring prowess, as they had only scored one apiece. Patrik Berger, who had come from Borussia Dortmund, was the talk of town with four in four. Rumours circulated of unrest relating to Collymore's attitude towards other players and his refusal to move to Liverpool so he could be near his mother 80 miles away in Cannock. Collymore was honest about his struggles. 'I fully admit that my form so far this season could be better,' he said. 'I'm not about to go into the ground and start banging on the manager's door. Shouting your mouth off about being dropped is a big mistake.'

COLLYMORE was linked with a move to Aston Villa but, ironically, facing Forest again reignited Collymore's scoring touch.

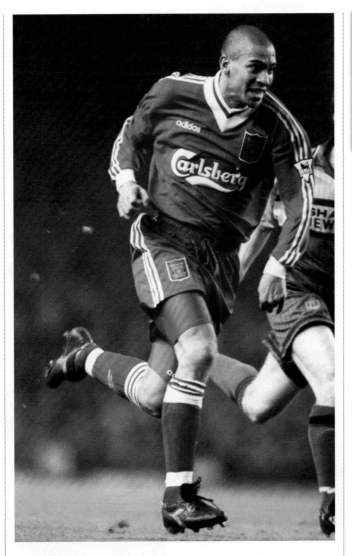

On 17 December he netted two in a 4-2 win over his old club as Liverpool went back to the top of the Premier League. Seven goals in ten games followed and Collymore seemed to have finally realised what it took to be a success on Merseyside. Yet Stan's inconsistency reared its ugly head again, although he was far from the only Liverpool player who suffered from that condition as the club's promising season faded away.

Collymore and Fowler scored a respectable total of 47 goals in their second season together, but Collymore's mood swings and stuttering form finally exhausted Roy Evans' patience and he was sold to Villa in a £7million deal. Evans still had only good things to say about Collymore when interviewed for *royevans.net* in 2003: 'Stan was a great lad, still is a great lad and I've always said that in his time at Liverpool, particularly the first season, he and Robbie were brilliant together. Even now if you look through Robbie's career, the best partner he's ever had was Stan. Stan did a lot of things we didn't want him to do but he had the ability to do a lot of things no one else could.'

> 'HE HAD THE ABILITY TO DO A LOT OF THINGS NO ONE ELSE COULD'
> **ROY EVANS**

Collymore scored one goal in his first 17 matches for Villa and left as an expensive flop three years later with only 15 goals to his name in just over 60 appearances. After a short loan spell at Fulham in 1999 he was allowed to move to Leicester City on a free transfer. It wasn't long before he was on the move again, first to Bradford City in October 2000 and then to Real Oviedo in Spain in January 2001. He played only three times for the Spanish club before announcing his retirement as a player at the age of 30. Since ending his playing career, Stan has had a very public battle against depression, had a bit-role with Sharon Stone in Basic Instinct 2 and found himself a highly successful role as a football pundit.

FACTFILE

BORN
Stone, 22 January 1971

POSITION
Centre-forward

OTHER CLUBS
Stafford Rangers (1990–91), Crystal Palace (1991–92), Southend United (1992–93), Nottingham Forest (1993–95), Aston Villa (1997–2000), Fulham (loan, 1999), Leicester City (2000), Bradford City (2000–01), Real Oviedo (2001)

SIGNED FROM
Nottingham Forest, £8.5million, 1 July 1995

INTERNATIONAL CAPS
3 England caps, 1995–97

LFC DEBUT/GOAL
19 August 1995 / 19 August 1995

CONTRACT EXPIRY
13 May 1997

Season	League		FA Cup		League Cup		Europe		Total	
	App	Goals	App	Goals	App	Goals	App	Goals	App	Goals
1995/96	30 (1)	14	7	5	2 (2)	0	1 (1)	0	40 (4)	19
1996/97	25 (5)	12	2	2	0	0	4 (1)	2	31 (6)	16
Total	**55 (6)**	**26**	**9**	**7**	**2 (2)**	**0**	**5 (2)**	**2**	**71 (10)**	**35**

Colvin,
Bobby

BOBBY COLVIN'S three league appearances for the club go right back to the 1897/98 First Division season when the Reds finished in ninth position.

The small forward's debut came when he was selected for the 2-1 defeat at Blackburn on 8 January 1898. Two months later he played twice more for the first team in consecutive games against Bury. *The Cricket and Football Field* wondered at the end of the 1897/98 season: 'Will Robert Colvin, of Liverpool, ever rise to First league football form? He is young, can sprint and centre, but little men in the attacking line are severely handicapped, and he lacks in physique.'

FACTFILE

BORN
Kirkconnel, Scotland,
5 December 1876
DIED
1906
POSITION
Forward
OTHER CLUBS
Maxwelltown Thistle,
Oldham County,
Glossop North End
(1898–99),
New Brighton Tower
(1899–1901),
Luton Town (1901–02),
Queens Park Rangers
(1902–03),
Swindon Town (1903–04),
Maxwelltown Volunteers,
Carlisle United,
African Royal
SIGNED FROM
Oldham County,
6 November 1897
LFC DEBUT
8 January 1898
CONTRACT EXPIRY
1898

Season	League		FA Cup		Total	
	App	Goals	App	Goals	App	Goals
1897/98	3	0	0	0	3	0
Total	3	0	0	0	3	0

Consecutive

Wins in all competitions

Total	Started	Ended
14	15 March 2006	13 August 2006*
11	18 February 1989	11 April 1989
10	25 August 1990	9 October 1990
10	31 March 1986	10 May 1986
10	1 January 1983	12 February 1983
10	20 March 1982	1 May 1982
10	17 September 1904	19 November 1904
10	2 December 1893	10 February 1894

Home wins in all competitions

Total	Started	Ended
22	31 December 1892	14 April 1894
19	19 February 1972	24 October 1972
18	10 April 1985	26 November 1985
16	26 October 1982	12 February 1983

Liverpool's 3-3 draw in the FA Cup final is a penalty shoot-out win

Away wins in all competitions

Total	Started	Ended
7	19 March 2006	7 May 2006
7	23 January 1988	13 March 1988
6	21 September 2011	29 November 2011
6	19 March 2006	7 May 2006
6	5 May 1990	9 October 1990
6	18 February 1989	11 April 1989
6	16 December 1964	6 February 1965
6	24 September 1960	19 November 1960
6	24 September 1904	19 November 1904

Defeats in all competitions

Total	Started	Ended
9	29 April 1899	14 October 1899
6	17 January 1948	28 February 1948
6	14 September 1912	14 October 1912
6	13 March 1909	10 April 1909
6	27 December 1902	7 February 1903

Home defeats in all competitions

Total	Started	Ended
4	24 November 1923	25 December 1923
3	*13 runs of 3 home defeats, most recent* 2 September 2012	4 October 2012

Away defeats in all competitions

Total	Started	Ended
21	7 March 1953	16 January 1954
7	24 April 1954	16 October 1954
7	25 October 1952	24 January 1953
7	4 September 1926	13 November 1926
7	1 April 1899	14 October 1899

Without win in all competitions

Total	Started	Ended
15	12 December 1953	20 March 1954
12	8 November 1952	24 January 1953
12	18 November 1933	13 January 1934
11	20 January 1912	30 March 1912

Without home win in all competitions

Total	Started	Ended
9	12 February 1955	24 August 1955
7	27 October 1951	5 January 1952
7	25 November 1933	20 January 1934
	Liverpool played 6 home games without a win 26 August 2012 - 7 October 2012	

Without away win in all competitions

Total	Started	Ended
25	7 March 1953	13 March 1954
19	4 January 1936	7 November 1936
16	5 February 1992	19 September 1992
16	27 September 1967	9 March 1968

Without defeat in all competitions

Total	Started	Ended
30	18 February 1893	10 February 1894
25	20 March 1982	28 September 1982
24	3 January 1989	23 May 1989
24	1 November 1987	16 March 1988
22	2 March 1986	30 August 1986
22	30 August 1980	22 November 1980

Without home defeat in all competitions

Total	Started	Ended
85	7 February 1978	3 January 1981
46	17 March 1976	26 October 1977
34	26 November 1989	17 February 1991
32	19 February 2008	22 March 2009
32	29 January 1972	3 February 1973
31	29 January 1966	7 April 1967

Without away defeat in all competitions

Total	Started	Ended
21	9 May 1987	16 March 1988
17	7 January 1989	14 October 1989
16	16 September 1981	2 February 1982
15	15 December 1984	20 May 1985
13	30 November 1994	12 April 1995

League home wins

Total	Started	Ended
21	29 January 1972	30 December 1972
14	9 September 1893	14 April 1894
13	20 April 1985	16 November 1985
11	30 October 1982	12 March 1983
11	26 December 1963	2 September 1964

League away wins

Total	Started	Ended
6	22 January 2002	13 April 2002
6	27 February 1982	24 April 1982
6	31 December 1904	11 March 1905
6	24 September 1904	19 November 1904

League home defeats

Total	Started	Ended
4	24 November 1923	25 December 1923
3	*11 runs of 3 home league defeats, most recent*	
	28 August 1963	14 September 1963

League away defeats

Total	Started	Ended
20	7 March 1953	16 January 1954
7	24 April 1954	16 October 1954
7	4 September 1926	13 November 1926
7	1 April 1899	14 October 1899

League games without win

Total	Started	Ended
14	12 December 1953	20 March 1954
13	18 November 1933	1 February 1934
11	9 November 2002	11 January 2003
11	8 November 1952	24 January 1953

League games without defeat

Total	Started	Ended
31	4 May 1987	16 March 1988
30	2 September 1893	3 September 1894
23	31 March 1990	24 November 1990
23	9 March 1982	25 September 1982
23	11 March 1978	21 October 1978

Scorer in all competitions

Total games	Total goals	Player	Started	Ended
8	11	John Aldridge	14 January 1989	14 March 1989
8	10	Dick Forshaw	8 November 1924	15 December 1924
7	15	Jack Balmer	9 November 1946	21 December 1946
7	10	Dick Forshaw	13 January 1926	27 February 1926
7	7	Steven Gerrard	6 November 2007	11 December 2007
7	7	John Aldridge	9 May 1987	20 September 1987

Scorer at Anfield in all competitions

Total games	Total goals	Player	Started	Ended
8	13	Gordon Hodgson	17 September 1927	3 March 1928
7	12	George Allan	25 January 1896	25 April 1896
7	11	Fernando Torres	23 February 2008	13 April 2008

Scorer in away games in all competitions

Total games	Total goals	Player	Started	Ended
7	11	John Evans	18 December 1954	8 April 1955
7	8	John Aldridge	14 January 1989	26 March 1989
7	8	Sam English	9 September 1933	2 December 1933

Scorer in league games

Total games	Total goals	Player	Started	Ended
10	**12**	John Aldridge	9 May 1987	17 October 1987
8	**10**	John Aldridge	14 January 1989	26 March 1989
8	**10**	Dick Forshaw	8 November 1924	15 December 1924
7	**15**	Jack Balmer	9 November 1946	21 December 1946

Scorer in league home games

Total games	Total goals	Player	Started	Ended
8	**13**	Roger Hunt	16 December 1961	7 April 1962
8	**13**	Gordon Hodgson	17 September 1927	3 March 1928
8	**12**	Fernando Torres	2 February 2008	4 May 2008
7	**10**	Gordon Hodgson	17 November 1928	9 March 1929
7	**9**	Kevin Lewis	10 December 1960	11 March 1961

Scorer in league away games

Total games	Total goals	Player	Started	Ended
7	**8**	Sam English	9 September 1933	2 December 1933
6	**8**	John Barnes	12 December 1987	5 March 1988
6	**8**	John Barnes	11 April 1990	22 September 1990
6	**7**	David Johnson	16 April 1979	1 September 1979
6	**6**	Gordon Hodgson	10 March 1934	29 August 1934

Cooper, Tom

TOM COOPER is considered one of England's greatest full-backs. He was an excellent tackler and a quality passer of the ball. He joined Liverpool late in his career, aged 29, having played 15 internationals for England and captained his country twice from 1927–1934.

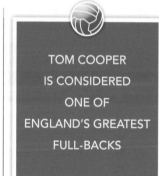

TOM COOPER IS CONSIDERED ONE OF ENGLAND'S GREATEST FULL-BACKS

The right-back surely would have more caps to his name but for injuries that caused cartilages from both knees to be removed. The club programme certainly seemed very pleased he had joined the Liverpool ranks, proclaiming it 'The event of the season', before continuing: 'His fee is a record one for a full-back. Cooper is a back who, although on the robust side, is one of the fairest men in the game. He is "fair" in a double-sense being silvery thatched – "Snowball" some of the fans call him. With Cooper

and Blenkinsop in the side Liverpool will possess the most distinguished pair of backs in the land. Well done, Liverpool!'

THE FORMER CAPTAIN of Derby from 1931–34 shared the skipper's duties at Liverpool with Ernie Blenkinsop in the 1934/35 and 1936/37 seasons before assuming the captain's role on his own from 1937–39.

'SNOWY', as he was more commonly known at Liverpool, made his debut for the Reds when he replaced right-back Billy Steel at Chelsea on 8 December 1934 and only missed two more league matches for the rest of that season. He played in 127 of the 168 games that comprised the next four league seasons. He made nine appearances for Liverpool in the wartime 1939/40 season, the last of which came on 6 April 1940 against Stoke City in the Western Division. Cooper was better than any footballer in the north on the golf course, as proved by him winning the Merseyside Professional Association Footballer's Golf Championship for the third year running in October 1938.

Having joined the King's Regiment Liverpool, Sergeant Tom Cooper died in a motorcycle accident when serving with the military police in Aldeburgh on 25 June 1940. He collided with a double-decker motor bus and an enquiry took place into his death, with the outcome that despatch riders were no longer allowed to ride their motorcycles without wearing a crash helmet.

TOM 'SNOWY' COOPER
LIVERPOOL

FACTFILE

BORN
Fenton, Stoke-On-Trent,
9 April 1905
DIED
25 June 1940
POSITION
Right-back
OTHER CLUBS
Longton, Trentham,
Port Vale (1924–26),
Derby County (1926–34),
Wrexham (wartime guest)
SIGNED FROM
Derby County, £7,500,
4 December 1934
INTERNATIONAL CAPS
15 England caps, 1927–34
LFC DEBUT
8 December 1934

Season	League		FA Cup		Total	
	App	Goals	App	Goals	App	Goals
1934/35	23	0	2	0	25	0
1935/36	26	0	2	0	28	0
1936/37	39	0	1	0	40	0
1937/38	26	0	5	0	31	0
1938/39	36	0	0	0	36	0
Total	**150**	**0**	**10**	**0**	**160**	**0**

Cormack,
Peter

PETER CORMACK first attracted
Bill Shankly's attention as a
20-year-old Scottish international
with Hibernian some five years
earlier. He entertained fans with
his brilliant tricks on the ball,
and his experience and creativity
added something extra to
the Liverpool squad that
had narrowly missed out on
the Championship in 1971/72.

Cormack had a few weeks of
pre-season training behind him
at Forest when he arrived at
Liverpool in the summer of 1972,
mainly consisting of running
through the woods. When he
told Shankly how he had been
preparing for the season Shankly
looked incredulously at him
and said: 'Snooker champions
don't go swimming every day.'

Cormack was an important part
of Shankly's 'new' team that won
not only the First Division title for
the first time in seven years but
also the club's first ever European
trophy, the UEFA Cup. Cormack
had to wait until the seventh game
of the season at Derby's Baseball
Ground before being handed his
debut, but he scored in his first
game at home against Wolves
the following week. His highlight
came in his first Merseyside derby
three months into his Liverpool
career when he headed the winner
with 13 minutes to go.

'SNOOKER CHAMPIONS DON'T GO SWIMMING EVERY DAY'
BILL SHANKLY

'When you score the winner against Everton you're a hero for life,'
Cormack told *LFC Magazine*. 'Larry Lloyd picked me up as we
celebrated and said: "You've made it now." It was a terrific feeling and
I didn't spend much money that night.' Cormack never looked back
after that, finishing with 10 goals in 52 games in his debut campaign.

THE 1973/74 SEASON was another successful one for Cormack.
He figured in all 42 league matches and added an FA Cup winners'
medal to his collection. He was again a regular the following season
and, aged 29 when the 1975/76 season began, he looked to have a few
years of success ahead of him at Anfield, but his campaign finished in
December. 'I've always had this problem with my knee,' Cormack said.
'My cartilage was cracked. I was told I could keep playing, but that
eventually it would give way. One day it did just that, after a game against
Manchester City, and I never played for Liverpool again.'

While Cormack was recuperating Bob Paisley converted Ray Kennedy
from a lumbering forward into a left-sided midfielder so successfully that

on Cormack's return he was
surplus to requirements; he moved
on to Bristol City, then playing
in the top flight, in November
1976. Aged 34, Cormack left
Bristol in 1980 when they were
relegated and returned to
Hibernian. After a brief spell he
moved to Partick Thistle, where
he was manager for four years.
His managerial career subsequently
took him to faraway places like
Cyprus and Botswana.

FACTFILE

BORN
Edinburgh, Scotland,
17 July 1946
POSITION
Midfielder
OTHER CLUBS
Hibernian (1962–70),
Toronto City (loan, 1967),
Nottingham Forest (1970–72),
Bristol City (1976–80),
Hibernian (1980),
Partick Thistle (1980)
SIGNED FROM
Nottingham Forest,
£110,000, 14 July 1972
INTERNATIONAL CAPS
9 Scotland caps, 1966–71
LFC DEBUT/GOAL
2 September 1972 /
9 September 1972
CONTRACT EXPIRY
November 1976
HONOURS
League Championship
1972/73, 1975/76;
FA Cup 1974;
UEFA Cup 1973

Season	League App	League Goals	FA Cup App	FA Cup Goals	League Cup App	League Cup Goals	Europe App	Europe Goals	Other App	Other Goals	Total App	Total Goals
1972/73	30	8	4	1	8	0	10	1	-	-	52	10
1973/74	40 (2)	9	8	1	6	1	1	0	-	-	55 (2)	11
1974/75	33 (3)	3	2	0	3	0	1 (2)	1	1	0	40 (5)	4
1975/76	16 (1)	1	0	0	3	0	3 (1)	0	-	-	22 (2)	1
Total	**119 (6)**	**21**	**14**	**2**	**20**	**1**	**15 (3)**	**2**	**1**	**0**	**169 (9)**	**26**

Cotton,
Charles

CHARLES COTTON started 1903/04 in West Ham's goal after joining pre-season from Reading. He played nine games for the Hammers before his differences with the club's directors led to his transfer to Liverpool.

HE MADE 13 league appearances in a season which was to end in relegation to the Second Division. Peter Platt had been first-choice keeper at the start of that season but Cotton came into the side for the away fixture against Wolves

CHARLES COTTON
[LIVERPOOL]

on 28 December 1903 and kept his place until the Goodison derby on April Fools' Day. Everton thrashed

Liverpool 5-2 and even though Cotton had conceded just a goal a game on average in the 11 matches that preceded the Goodison humiliation, Platt was brought back for the last three matches of the season. Ned Doig was given the goalkeeper's jersey at the start of 1904/05, by which time Cotton had returned to West Ham. Cotton started the 1909/10 season in goal for Southend in the Southern League but developed Bright's Disease, an infection of the kidneys, and he died on 3 January 1910.

FACTFILE

BORN
Plymouth, 1881
DIED
3 January 1910
POSITION
Goalkeeper
OTHER CLUBS
Sheppey United (1897–1900),
Reading (1900–03),
West Ham United (1903),
West Ham United (1904–06),
Southend United (1906–10)
SIGNED FROM
West Ham United,
4 December 1903
LFC DEBUT
28 December 1903
CONTRACT EXPIRY
April 1904

Season	League		FA Cup		Total	
	App	Goals	App	Goals	App	Goals
1903/04	13	0	0	0	13	0
Total	13	0	0	0	13	0

Coutinho,
Philippe

IN JANUARY 2013, Phillippe Coutinho became the fifth player of Brazilian birth to sign for Liverpool Football Club. Coutinho was born in Rio de Janeiro and joined the youth system of one of the city's most prominent clubs, Vasco da Gama. His potential was quickly spotted and Inter Milan made a successful bid for him in 2008 when Coutinho was still only 16 years old. Inter did, however, allow him to remain with Vasco until he had passed his 18th birthday in the middle of 2010.

The youngster's arrival in Italy coincided with that of Rafa Benítez, who was appointed Inter Milan's head coach. Both Benítez and Inter's long-standing president, Massimo Moratti, were enthusiastic about Coutinho but a quotation attributed to them that 'Coutinho is the future of Inter' possibly placed unnecessary pressure on the teenager.

THE BRAZILIAN made his debut for the European champions as a second-half substitute for Wesley Sneijder during the 2010 European Super Cup final against Europa League winners Atletico Madrid in Monaco. Inter were in the end comfortably defeated by the Spanish club. Coutinho only appeared in 11 of Inter's 38 Serie A matches in 2010/11 as the Nerazzurri finished runners-up to their city rivals AC Milan; and he had only played in a handful of matches by the halfway point of the following season when he was loaned to Espanyol. The change of scenery worked well for him as he scored five times in 16 La Liga matches in helping the Barcelona club to move clear of the threat of relegation. At the end of a fairly successful loan spell Coutinho returned to Italy but again had difficulty holding down a regular place at Inter.

COUTINHO took over the No. 10 shirt vacated by Joe Cole at Liverpool. Brendan Rodgers is excited by Coutinho's potential: 'I love players who can make the difference at the top end. I've known about him since he was 15 years of age and watched him come through for Brazil. It was a real coup for us because Inter Milan didn't want to sell him, but when we thought he could become available we did everything we could to get him in. He's a wonderful talent and a great technician, he's got pace, strength and power. He's flexible – he can play in midfield or off the sides. I got a good insight into him last year when he was at Espanyol, he's a real talent and a good, young, exciting player – but also a real good professional and that's key as well.' Coutinho had a sensational start being voted Standard Chartered's player of the month for March and April by fans on the club's official website. The little magician is the first Brazilian to join Liverpool who really fits the stereotype of the Brazilian player with plenty of tricks up his sleeve to drive the crowd wild with excitement. Coutinho has been a magnificent coup for Liverpool.

FACTFILE

BORN
Rio de Janeiro, Brazil
12 June 1982
POSITION
Attacking midfielder
OTHER CLUBS
Vasco da Gama (1999–2010),
Inter Milan (2010–13),
Espanyol (loan, 2012)
SIGNED FROM
Inter Milan, 30 January 2013
INTERNATIONAL CAPS
1 Brazil cap, 2010
LFC DEBUT/GOAL
11 February 2013 /
17 February 2013

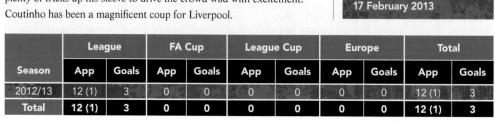

Season	League		FA Cup		League Cup		Europe		Total	
	App	Goals	App	Goals	App	Goals	App	Goals	App	Goals
2012/13	12 (1)	3	0	0	0	0	0	0	12 (1)	3
Total	12 (1)	3	0	0	0	0	0	0	12 (1)	3

Cox, Jack

AFTER ONE SEASON with Blackpool in the Second Division, where he scored 12 goals in 17 games, Jack Cox was transferred to Liverpool for the considerable sum of £150, enabling the Lancashire club to announce a loss of £441 as opposed to over £1,000 for the previous campaign. The 20-year-old scored on his debut three months after his arrival in a 2-0 win over Notts County on 12 March 1898 as Liverpool sought to establish themselves as a top flight club.

Cox was in the line-up in the first game of the 1898/99 season as well as newcomer Alex Raisbeck. They quickly became key components of Tom Watson's side that seemed finally ready to challenge for the League Championship and the FA Cup. Their heroics didn't, however, guarantee them silverware as Liverpool were knocked out of the semi-finals of the FA Cup by Sheffield United in a second replay and defeated 5-0 by Aston Villa in the last league game of the season when a win would have guaranteed Liverpool the title instead of Villa. The 1899/1900 season was a terrible anticlimax for Cox. Liverpool lost their first eight games of the season, then Cox got injured in the middle of November and was out for two months. Liverpool won eight out of their final ten games but only finished a disappointing tenth.

The arrival of centre-forward Sam Raybould in January 1900 gave the team much needed firepower. Cox only missed two games in the 1900/01 season when Liverpool were incredibly only twice top of the league, after the first game and, crucially, the last! Cox contributed 10 goals in 32 games, a fantastic goal ratio for a winger. Despite his success Cox 'wanted a change', but since Liverpool

Jack Cox
LIVERPOOL
&
ENGLAND

offered him the maximum wage when his contract was renewed for the following season the Football League refused his application.

At the beginning of the 1902/03 season Cox moved from right to left-wing as future legend Arthur Goddard, who had joined seven months earlier, established himself on the opposite flank. Liverpool played well below

	League		FA Cup		Other		Total	
Season	App	Goals	App	Goals	App	Goals	App	Goals
1897/98	2	1	0	0	-	-	2	1
1898/99	27	5	6	2	-	-	33	7
1899/1900	25	5	4	1	-	-	29	6
1900/01	32	10	2	0	-	-	34	10
1901/02	31	4	3	0	-	-	34	4
1902/03	29	9	1	0	-	-	30	9
1903/04	33	9	1	0	-	-	34	9
1904/05	32	10	2	0	-	-	34	10
1905/06	28	8	4	0	1	0	33	8
1906/07	25	7	4	1	-	-	29	8
1907/08	35	2	4	3	-	-	39	5
1908/09	28	2	2	1	-	-	30	3
Total	**327**	**72**	**33**	**8**	**1**	**0**	**361**	**80**

expectations following their 1901 triumph and were relegated in 1904.

The club programme described Cox in 1904 as: '[a] brilliant, but erratic genius. His great weakness is a tendency to over elaboration when in possession of the ball, but when the mood is on him, there is no hesitation; no finessing to discover the way towards goal. This is Cox, in his International humour, and when such is the case, the opposing defence know about it. On his day there is no cleverer outside-left in the kingdom than Cox.'

> **'ON HIS DAY THERE IS NO CLEVERER OUTSIDE-LEFT IN THE KINGDOM THAN COX'**

LIVERPOOL fans were shocked to hear that Cox had signed for Fulham of the Southern League on 2 May 1904 but again 'failed to satisfy the Football Association Council as to his reasons for transferring his services to the Fulham Football Club'. Cox had once more been offered the wage limit at Liverpool as well as the privilege of residing at home in Blackpool from where he could commute on a complimentary railway season ticket. He refused those terms, preferring to go to London as he objected to playing in the Second Division.

Merseyside rivals Everton were a big fan of Cox and tried to tempt Liverpool to cash in on him. Everton certainly had a stronger team at the time, having finished the season in third place in the First Division while Liverpool had been relegated. Everton offered £400 for his services, but the Anfield club wanted a minimum of £500 so the Blues were priced out of the move.

FINALLY, Cox re-signed for Liverpool on 29 June 1904. It would have been a disaster for Liverpool to lose Cox to their neighbours as he was subsequently instrumental in Liverpool's remarkable achievement of winning the Second and First Division in consecutive seasons in 1905 and 1906. Cox was missing through injury in the 2-0 semi-final defeat to Everton in the FA Cup in 1906 and in the last six league matches of the 1905/06 season. He had by that point scored eight goals in 28 league games and, while Liverpool's form suffered, three wins in six games were still enough to bring the League Championship back to Anfield.

In May 1909 Cox returned as player-manager to Blackpool, where he had already achieved legendary status after just one season at the start of his career. The tricky and speedy winger gave Liverpool fantastic service for over 11 years despite being unsettled at times, and certainly deserves his place in the club's Official Hall of Fame.

FACTFILE

BORN
Liverpool, 21 December 1877
DIED
11 November 1955
POSITION
Right/left-winger
OTHER CLUBS
South Shore Standard,
South Shore (1896–97),
Blackpool (1897),
Blackpool (1909–11)
SIGNED FROM
Blackpool, £150,
24 December 1897
INTERNATIONAL CAPS
3 England caps, 1901–03
LFC DEBUT/GOAL
12 March 1898 /
12 March 1898
CONTRACT EXPIRY
May 1909
HONOURS
League Championship
1900/01, 1905/06;
Second Division
Championship 1904/05

Craik, Herbert

Herbert Craik

HERBERT CRAIK arrived from Morton in exchange for Donald McCallum in May 1903.

He made just a single first-team appearance for Liverpool as a left-half in a 3-1 defeat at West Bromwich Albion during a depressing spell of five defeats at the start of the 1903/04 season.

Season	League		FA Cup		Total	
	App	Goals	App	Goals	App	Goals
1903/04	1	0	0	0	1	0
Total	1	0	0	0	1	0

FACTFILE

BORN
Greenock, Scotland, 1880
POSITION
Left-half
OTHER CLUBS
Morton (1900–03),
Hearts (1904–05),
Paisley Academicals,
Newton Swifts
SIGNED FROM
Morton, exchange for
McCallum, 15 May 1903
LFC DEBUT
26 September 1903
CONTRACT EXPIRY
1904

Crawford, Bob

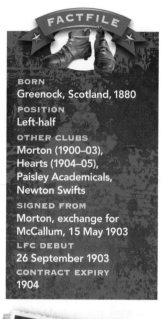

BOB CRAWFORD made his debut in a 4-1 home win over Leicester City on 13 February 1909 and played in the following 5-0 defeat against Arsenal. Crawford returned six weeks later against Everton when Liverpool lost 5-0 again, hardly inspiring confidence in the defenders in question. Crawford survived and made four more appearances before the end of that season when Liverpool narrowly escaped relegation. The highest total of games he played in a single campaign was 33 in the 1910/11 season.

Left-back Tom Chorlton lost his place in the team following Liverpool's terrible start to that

BOB CRAWFORD MADE HIS DEBUT IN A 4-1 HOME WIN OVER LEICESTER CITY ON 13 FEBRUARY 1909 AND PLAYED IN THE FOLLOWING 5-0 DEFEAT AGAINST ARSENAL

season and Crawford, who had played the first three games as right-back, was moved to the left as newcomer Ephraim Longworth became first-choice right-back. Crawford shared left-back duties with Bob Pursell for the next couple of seasons but only played 13 games in the 1913/14 and 1914/15 seasons. As with so many players World War One put a definite end to his career. Crawford was discharged in 1919 from the Royal Engineers with War and Victory medals and became a plumber.

Season	League		FA Cup		Total	
	App	Goals	App	Goals	App	Goals
1908/09	7	0	0	0	7	0
1909/10	20	0	0	0	20	0
1910/11	31	0	2	0	33	0
1911/12	15	0	0	0	15	0
1912/13	23	0	4	0	27	0
1913/14	7	1	0	0	7	1
1914/15	6	0	0	0	6	0
Total	109	1	6	0	115	1

FACTFILE

BORN
Blythswood, Scotland,
4 July 1886
POSITION
Right/left-back
OTHER CLUBS
Arthurlie (1905–09)
SIGNED FROM
Arthurlie, 20 January 1909
LFC DEBUT/GOAL
13 February 1909 /
4 October 1913
CONTRACT EXPIRY
1915

Crawford, Ted

Ted Crawford

TED CRAWFORD made his name in his home town of Filey in North Yorkshire where he set a local league record by scoring 141 goals in 73 matches. He was picked up by Liverpool after scoring 20 goals in 29 matches in the Third Division North with Halifax Town, his first professional club, where former Liverpool favourite Alex Raisbeck was in charge.

Crawford made an impressive start to the 1932/33 league campaign with Liverpool, scoring four goals in his first three matches but drawing a blank in the following four. Crawford's eighth appearance, against West Brom at Anfield on 29 April 1933, proved to be his last in a Liverpool shirt. Crawford played 211 games for Clapton Orient in the Third Division South and the FA Cup, scoring 73 goals. After World War Two he embarked on a managerial career that took him to Degerfors in Sweden, Bologna and Livorno in Italy, AEK Athens in Greece and Barnet in London.

RENOWNED football writer Brian Glanville remembered his good friend in *The Times* in 2003: 'A Yorkshireman from Filey, when it was a fishing village rather than a holiday camp, Crawford was the quintessence of the prewar pro: lean, tough, resilient and undemanding, with a talent for coaching that would emerge after he had retired from playing. Characteristically, he discovered that he had played his last six years as a forward for Clapton Orient with an undiagnosed broken ankle.'

CRAWFORD MADE AN IMPRESSIVE START TO THE 1932/33 LEAGUE CAMPAIGN WITH LIVERPOOL, SCORING FOUR GOALS IN HIS FIRST THREE MATCHES

FACTFILE
BORN
Filey, Yorkshire, 31 October 1906
DIED
13 December 1977
POSITION
Centre-forward / Inside-left forward
OTHER CLUBS
Filey Town (1922–23), Scarborough Penguins, Scarborough Town, Filey Town (1929–31), Halifax Town (1931–32), Clapton Orient (1933–39); Watford, Brighton & Hove Albion (wartime guest)
SIGNED FROM
Halifax Town, £1,200, July 1932
LFC DEBUT/GOAL
27 August 1932 / 27 August 1932
CONTRACT EXPIRY
July 1933

Season	League		FA Cup		Total	
	App	Goals	App	Goals	App	Goals
1932/33	8	4	0	0	8	4
Total	8	4	0	0	8	4

Crossley, Russell

RUSSELL CROSSLEY has the worst average of all goalkeepers in Liverpool's history having conceded 139 goals in 73 matches or 1.9 goals a game, if keepers who have made over 30 appearances are only considered.

CYRIL SIDLOW started the 1950/51 season as Liverpool's main keeper but Crossley had taken his place by late October. The irony was that Sidlow himself had alerted Liverpool to Crossley, who had been the Welshman's stand-in in his army team during the war. Charlie Ashcroft finished the season in goal after Crossley conceded four goals against Huddersfield Town on 31 March 1951; Crossley didn't reclaim the goalkeeper's jersey until the middle of December and kept hold of it until early February 1952. He featured in 36 league games in the following two seasons, with Liverpool finally being relegated.

FACTFILE
BORN
Hebden Bridge, Yorkshire, 25 June 1927
POSITION
Goalkeeper
OTHER CLUBS
Shrewsbury Town (1954–59), Kettering Town (1959–61)
JOINED
On release from Army, June 1947
LFC DEBUT
21 October 1950
CONTRACT EXPIRY
July 1954

Season	League		FA Cup		Total	
	App	Goals	App	Goals	App	Goals
1950/51	24	0	1	0	25	0
1951/52	8	0	2	0	10	0
1952/53	18	0	1	0	19	0
1953/54	18	0	1	0	19	0
Total	68	0	5	0	73	0

Crouch,
Peter

A TOWERING 6ft 7in (201cm) forward who started his career as a trainee at Tottenham in 1998, Peter Crouch was an unexpected signing after the 2005 Champions League win. Following two loan spells at Dulwich Hamlet and in Sweden he was sold for £60,000 to QPR in the Second Division, where he scored 12 goals in 47 games. He left for Portsmouth in the First Division only a year later and blossomed under the guidance of Harry Redknapp, scoring 18 league goals in his eight months at the club. Aston Villa paid £5million in March 2002 for his services; however, Crouch failed to impress at Villa and after 43 games and six goals he was sold to Southampton in July 2004 for £2million.

CROUCH finally took to life in the Premier League, scoring 12 goals in 27 games, but could not prevent Southampton's relegation. His performances didn't go unnoticed by Sven Göran Eriksson, who handed him his international debut, nor Rafa Benítez, who fought a powerful campaign with Liverpool's hierarchy to get his player.

Crouch famously had considerable trouble in scoring his first goal for the Reds. He finally broke the deadlock with a fluke goal against Wigan on 3 December 2005, by which time he had played 1,229 minutes without scoring. He added a second against Wigan and scored five more goals in

December. After netting the winning goal against West Brom on New Year's Eve, he didn't score for another eight games until he knocked Manchester United out of the FA Cup fifth round with a powerful header.

Crouch gained more confidence in his scoring ability in his second season at Liverpool, but curiously Rafa started him in only 30 games, compared to 42 the previous season. 'Crouchinho' has unusual skill for such a tall player and scored two acrobatic goals against Galatasaray and Bolton and a sensational hat-trick against Arsenal in the league on 31 March 2007, scoring with his head, right foot and left foot.

Crouch's Anfield future was constantly questioned as the 2007/08 season unfolded, with his manager electing to start him in only nine league games, coming on as a substitute a further 12 times. He still managed to score 11 goals during the season, including the first and last in the 8-0 mauling of Besiktas in the Champions League.

IT WAS inevitable that most discussions about Crouch revolved around his height and in that respect he was something of a 'specialist' striker. Fernando Torres' arrival at Liverpool meant that Crouch was no longer first choice and Redknapp brought Crouch back to Portsmouth in July 2008. His second spell on the south coast with Pompey could not be considered a failure as he scored 16 goals in 48 first-team matches. Redknapp left to become Tottenham's new boss and he signed Crouch in July 2009 for £9million.

Crouch enjoyed an excellent 2009/10 season with Tottenham, appearing in all 38 Premier League matches but only scoring eight times, including the priceless goal away to Manchester City near the end of the season that ensured Spurs would finish fourth in the table. Crouch continued to be a regular in the England squad under Fabio Capello, just as he had been under his predecessor, Steve McLaren, but despite being so prolific

for the international side he was given only two appearances as a late substitute in England's disastrous 2010 World Cup. Curiously, Crouch hasn't featured for England since he scored in a 2-1 defeat to France on 17 November 2010, having scored a total of 22 goals in 42 internationals. Crouch played in 34 Premier League matches for Tottenham in 2010/11 and was very prolific in Europe, but embarked on yet another adventure when he moved to Stoke City on the last day of the 2011 summer transfer window. In his first season at the Britannia Stadium he scored 10 times in 32 Premier League matches and scored the 'Goal of the Season' against Manchester City on 24 March 2012, juggling the ball before releasing an unstoppable shot from outside the penalty area. Crouch's 'spidery limbs' have done themselves proud at the highest level against all odds.

FACTFILE

BORN
Macclesfield, 30 January 1981
POSITION
Centre-forward
OTHER CLUBS
Tottenham Hotspur
(1997–2000),
Dulwich Hamlet (loan, 2000),
IFK Hässleholm (loan, 2000),
Queens Park Rangers
(2000–01),
Portsmouth (2001–02),
Aston Villa (2002–04),
Norwich City (loan, 2003),
Southampton (2004–05),
Portsmouth (2008–09),
Tottenham Hotspur (2009–11),
Stoke City (2011–)
SIGNED FROM
Southampton, £7 million,
20 July 2005
INTERNATIONAL CAPS
42 England caps (22 goals)
(27 (14) at LFC), 2005–10
LFC DEBUT/GOAL
26 July 2005 /
3 December 2005
CONTRACT EXPIRY
11 July 2008
HONOURS
FA Cup 2006

Season	League		FA Cup		League Cup		Europe		Other		Total	
	App	Goals	App	Goals	App	Goals	App	Goals	App	Goals	App	Goals
2005/06	27 (5)	8	5 (1)	3	1	0	8	0	1 (1)	2	42 (7)	13
2006/07	19 (13)	9	1	0	1	1	8 (6)	7	1	1	30 (19)	18
2007/08	9 (12)	5	4	2	3	0	5 (3)	4	-	-	21 (15)	11
Total	55 (30)	22	10 (1)	5	5	1	21 (9)	11	2 (1)	3	93 (41)	42

Cunliffe, Daniel

DANIEL CUNLIFFE scored more than 40 goals for Oldham County of the Lancashire League in the 1896/97 season before he arrived at Anfield to try to soften the departure of George Allan back to Scotland. Cunliffe made 14 First Division appearances for Liverpool during the 1897/98 season and scored five times.

Numerous changes were made to the club's forward line during that season and Cunliffe only featured in three of the games played during the second half of the campaign. He also played in four FA Cup ties for Liverpool, scoring the winner in their 2-1 second round replay with Newton Heath in the middle of February 1898.

DANIEL CUNLIFFE is a well-known name in Portsmouth's history. He was 'very fast and tricky, clever with both his feet and head, and a thorough worker,' according to the *Portsmouth Evening News*. He joined Pompey before their first season, 1899/1900, and impressed so much that he was chosen to represent England against Ireland

in his only international on 17 March 1900 after helping Portsmouth to finish runners-up in the Southern League. Cunliffe played a total of 284 matches for Portsmouth in two spells and scored 157 goals.

Season	League		FA Cup		Total	
	App	Goals	App	Goals	App	Goals
1897/98	14	5	4	1	18	6
Total	**14**	**5**	**4**	**1**	**18**	**6**

FACTFILE

BORN
Bolton, 11 June 1875
DIED
28 December 1937
POSITION
Forward
OTHER CLUBS
Bolton Orlando,
Oldham County (1896–97),
New Brighton Tower
(1898–99),
Portsmouth (1899–1900),
New Brighton Tower
(1900–01),
Portsmouth (1901–06),
New Brompton (1906–07),
Millwall Athletic (1907–09),
Heywood United (1909–12),
Rochdale (1912–14)
SIGNED FROM
Oldham County, April 1897
INTERNATIONAL CAPS
1 England cap, 1900
LFC DEBUT/GOAL
4 September 1897 /
9 October 1897
CONTRACT EXPIRY
August 1898

Cunningham, Bill

BILL CUNNINGHAM made his debut in the First Division fixture with Middlesbrough as a left-winger at Anfield on 12 March 1920 and then figured on the right wing in the penultimate game of the season, away to Arsenal on 2 May. Both games finished in goalless draws.

LIVERPOOL F.C. 1920-21

His third and final appearance for the Reds was as a replacement for left-half Tom Bromilow in a 2-0 home defeat against Bolton

Wanderers on 18 March 1922. Cunningham, a miner, was killed while working in Shilbottle Colliery in Northumberland on 28 June 1934.

Season	League		FA Cup		Other		Total	
	App	Goals	App	Goals	App	Goals	App	Goals
1920/21	2	0	0	0	-	-	2	0
1921/22	1	0	0	0	0	0	1	0
Total	**3**	**0**	**0**	**0**	**0**	**0**	**3**	**0**

LIVERPOOL
1920/21

FACTFILE

BORN
Radcliffe, Lancashire,
27 October 1899
DIED
28 June 1934
POSITION
Defender / Forward
OTHER CLUBS
Blyth Spartans (1919–20),
Barrow (1924–25),
Mid-Rhondda United
(1925–27)
SIGNED FROM
Blyth Spartans, £50, May 1920
LFC DEBUT
12 March 1921
CONTRACT EXPIRY
January 1924

Curlett Cup

ONE OF THE Liverpool FC museum's proudest possessions is the so-called Curlett Cup. While Liverpool won the League Championship in 1964 and 1966 at Anfield the League trophy was not present at the ground in either instance, but due to the foresight of the Curlett brothers the players still had a trophy to parade. How did a homemade cup became the focal point of these watershed moments in Liverpool's history?

THE MOTHER of the Curlett brothers had a dressing table with a set of vases on top. The one got broken so their mother was going to throw them both away. 'My youngest brother Terry had other plans,' Peter Curlett told the *LFC Magazine*. 'He took the intact vase up to his room and started decorating it. Being a Liverpool fan he naturally painted it red and white. He also cut out pictures of the players from newspapers and football magazines and stuck them on it. It was the day of the Arsenal game and we didn't know the

Roger Hunt signing the cup for the Curletts in 1966

Championship trophy wasn't going to be there.' On 18 April 1964 the brothers brought their cup to the Kop and as Ron Yeats had no trophy to lift they handed it to him and he took off on a lap of honour with it and all the players and Shankly took turns in lifting this priceless title-substitute. When the same scenario developed two years later the brothers also came to the rescue. Liverpool beat Chelsea 2-1 at Anfield on 30 April 1966 and Peter Curlett recollects that as the team were standing in the middle of the pitch applauding the supporters 'Terry ran on and gave our cup to Ron Yeats. My brother immediately disappeared back into the crowd while the players did a lap of honour with it and then got their medals.'

WHEN YEATS went up to get his medal on the podium he banged it down on the table and broke the base of the trophy. After the celebrations my two brothers went back into the dressing room with the team and each player signed under their own photo on the cup.' The curator of the LFC museum, Stephen Done, underlined the trophy's importance to the history of the club: 'When the family brought the Curlett Cup to the museum I was amazed,' he told the *LFC Magazine*. 'This was a part of Liverpool history that I thought had been lost forever. I'd seen it in pictures but never thought I would find it again. This trophy was synonymous with Shanks. His hat-trick of First Division titles was special but on two occasions the team celebrated with this Curlett Cup. So really the League Championship trophy isn't part of Shanks' legacy, but this cup is.'

> 'THIS WAS A PART OF LIVERPOOL HISTORY THAT I THOUGHT HAD BEEN LOST FOREVER'
>
> STEPHEN DONE

Curran, John

JOHN CURRAN shared the right-back position with the legendary Andrew Hannah in 1894/95, playing 14 times to Hannah's 16 as Liverpool were immediately relegated back to the Second Division.

The next year, when Liverpool won the Second Division again, he was first choice at the beginning of the season but was replaced for good in October 1895 by Archie Goldie.

Season	League		FA Cup		Other		Total	
	App	Goals	App	Goals	App	Goals	App	Goals
1894/95	14	0	3	0	1	0	18	0
1895/96	6	0	0	0	0	0	6	0
Total	20	0	3	0	1	0	24	0

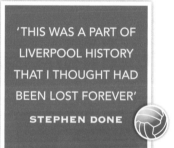

FACTFILE

BORN
Bellshill, Scotland, March 1864
POSITION
Right-back
OTHER CLUBS
Benburb (1890–92), Celtic (1892–94), Hibernian (loan, 1895), Motherwell (1896–97)
SIGNED FROM
Celtic, 1894
LFC DEBUT
3 November 1894
CONTRACT EXPIRY
1896

Dabbs, Ben

ALTHOUGH BEN DABBS made the line-up for the opening day of the 1933/34 season, that appearance at Wolverhampton was the defender's only one of the league campaign and he had to wait until April 1935 before being selected again.

It wasn't until the 1936/37 season that he received an extended run in the side at left-back, figuring in 32 of the last 36 matches, with former England captain Ernie Blenkinsop unavailable through injury. Dabbs played in six consecutive First Division fixtures early in the 1937/38 season but after he conceded an unnecessary penalty in the home derby with Everton on 2 October 1937 he was not chosen again. Dabbs joined Watford in the Third Division South in the summer of 1938.

BEN DABBS' mother and England captain Billy Wright's grandmother were sisters.

FACTFILE

BORN
Oakengates, Shropshire,
17 April 1909

DIED
1980

POSITION
Right/left-back

OTHER CLUBS
Oakengates Town (1930–32),
Watford (1938–46)

SIGNED FROM
Oakengates Town, June 1932

LFC DEBUT
26 August 1933

CONTRACT EXPIRY
June 1938

Season	League		FA Cup		Total	
	App	Goals	App	Goals	App	Goals
1933/34	1	0	0	0	1	0
1934/35	2	0	0	0	2	0
1935/36	13	0	2	0	15	0
1936/37	32	0	0	0	32	0
1937/38	6	0	0	0	6	0
Total	**54**	**0**	**2**	**0**	**56**	**0**

Dalglish, Kenny

KENNETH MATHIESON DALGLISH was born in Dalmarnock in the east of Glasgow only a short distance from Celtic's Parkhead. The family lived there only briefly and moved to an apartment house in Milton, which had a good view over the Rangers training ground. Dalglish's supreme football talent was soon obvious in the YMCA boys' team he played in. He was picked for the Scottish Under-15 national team and played his first game against Northern Ireland, sealing the win with two goals.

DALGLISH was aged just 15 when he played his first game in a Liverpool shirt. He was given a week-long trial and played one game with the B-team against Southport in a 1-0 win on 20 August 1966. 'Liverpool wanted me to stay on a couple of days, but I told them that I needed a couple of days at home because I was going to West Ham for a trial at the weekend,' Dalglish remembered. 'The real reason was that Rangers were playing Celtic at Ibrox that night. I caught the train back up from Lime Street and went straight to the match. I soon saw Shanks again.

Liverpool's first team were due to play West Ham the same weekend as my trial. As I walked through to the players' area at Upton Park, Shanks came along in the other direction. I was overwhelmed with embarrassment. I couldn't speak to him. I just kept my head down and hurried past. I heard his voice shouting, 'Kenny, Kenny', but I said to myself, just keep walking, just keep walking. I regret not talking to Shanks, but I was only 15 and very shy. If anybody spoke to me, I'd blush.'

Shankly always regretted that Liverpool didn't buy Dalglish

when he was handed to them on the proverbial silver platter. Former Liverpool player and Kenny's friend Ian Ross said: 'I remember meeting Shanks one day outside Anfield as I came back from training. He and Reuben Bennett were in Shanks' car. He wound the window down as I walked past. "Hey, Ian!" he shouted. "We're off to Derby to see your pal playing in an Under-23 international." It was February 1972. Scotland drew 2-2 and Dalglish scored both goals. The next day I saw Shankly, so I thought I would tease him a bit. "How did you go on last night? How was Dalglish?" "Don't talk to me about Dalglish. The only man on the pitch. Christ, what a player!"'

> 'WHEN I WAS GROWING UP MY HERO WAS DI STEFANO. KENNY FOR ME WAS ON A PAR WITH DI STEFANO. THAT IS THE BEST COMPLIMENT I CAN PAY HIM'
>
> **GEORGE BEST**

Despite Dalglish's interest in joining his boyhood team, Rangers, he accepted Celtic's offer in July 1967. Celtic had just become the first British team to win the European Cup, with a team widely known as the 'Lisbon Lions'. Dalglish went on loan to Cumbernauld United, one of the teams Celtic used to mould their players. He scored four goals in his first game and had scored 37 goals by the end of the season. Dalglish wanted to turn professional right away, but Stein wanted him to play another season with Cumbernauld. The kid held his ground and after asking his father to talk to Stein the boss caved in.

Dalglish was raised in the dominant Celtic's reserve side, known as the 'Quality Street Gang', named after 'the chocolates'. He finally made his breakthrough into the first team on 14 August 1971 at Ibrox, the ground at which he had once dreamed of playing regularly in Rangers' colours. In the 70th minute Celtic won a penalty. The ball was thrown to Dalglish who started his run-up but stopped midway and tied his shoelaces; he started the run-up again and scored into the opposite corner to the goalkeeper. The press were overwhelmed the next day: 'He was so calm. It was like he was playing a practice match.' Celtic continued their domestic dominance by winning their seventh consecutive league title. Dalglish scored 23 goals in 49 games and one of the major newspapers in Scotland voted him 'Player of the Season'. He played his first senior game for the national team on 10 November 1971 in a 1-0 win over Belgium in a European Championship qualifier.

DALGLISH was by now a hero to the Celtic fans but he kept a low profile off the pitch. He did, though, make an album with one of his Scotland team-mates, Sandy Jardine. Songs from the album didn't reach the top ten, but it did sell, even though they were kindly asked not to make another album! In 1972/73 Celtic won the title again and Dalglish had his best ever season at Celtic in terms of goalscoring, netting 41 goals in 53 games. 'Clubs would need to start bidding in telephone numbers,' Jock Stein replied when asked how much Celtic would want for Dalglish if he was to leave. Rangers ended Celtic's dominance in the league in the 1974/75 season. Dalglish had been moved back to midfield, orchestrating Celtic's play. The *Scottish Sunday Express* predicted that he would soon 'become a midfield mastermind in the Cruyff mould, dictating play, making matches run to his pattern'. The 24-year-old Dalglish was made captain before the 1975/76 season, but the situation at Celtic became progressively worse when their manager, Jock Stein, was seriously injured in a car accident. The title was lost again, but Dalglish was voted the Player of the Year in Scotland by the Players' Association. Dalglish was becoming restless at Celtic and Bob Paisley checked on his availability. He agreed to stay one more campaign during which Jock Stein came back and Celtic retrieved the title. In his Celtic

career Dalglish played 322 games and scored 167 goals. He won four Scottish League titles, four Scottish Cups, a League Cup and earned 47 Scotland caps.

LIVERPOOL had just won the European Cup but now they needed somebody to replace Kevin Keegan, who was leaving for Hamburg SV. Manchester United offered Dalglish more money but he preferred Liverpool. Stein had told Paisley that he'd be the first he would contact if he couldn't talk Dalglish out of leaving and he kept his promise. As Liverpool and Celtic finally sat down for discussions the Reds initially offered £300,000. In the end Liverpool's offer reached £400,000 after Stein had refused both £330,000 and £360,000. Stein said that if Liverpool were to offer 10 per cent more they would reach an agreement. Liverpool chairman John Smith nodded his head and £440,000 was agreed, which was then the record transfer fee between two British clubs.

There was no doubt in Dalglish's mind: Liverpool was the best team in Europe and Anfield was where he wanted to be. 'Old Bob would just pick the players he wanted to bring to Anfield and John Smith and Peter Robinson would sort out the deals,' Kenny said. 'So I walked into the boardroom to meet my next employers. Bob was there as well because new players like to talk to the person who is going to be looking after them. They informed me that the two clubs had agreed a fee. We talked for a couple of minutes. After two years of wanting a move, it was all happening in minutes.'

Bill Shankly was in disbelief when he heard the news. 'I understand that like Kevin Keegan, Dalglish wants to get on, but I would have moved heaven and earth to keep him. I would rather have quit and got out of the game altogether than sold a player of his brilliance,' he said. Only three days later,

on 13 August 1977, Dalglish played his first game for the Reds against Manchester United in the Charity Shield, which finished in a goalless draw. The Liverpool fans were excited, but kept in mind that many good players had come from Scotland and hadn't succeeded south of the border.

Dalglish stepped into the most illustrious team in Liverpool's history: Ray Clemence was the keeper, Phil Neal and Joey Jones full-backs, Phil Thompson and Emlyn Hughes central defenders, in front of them Ian Callaghan and Terry McDermott, Ray Kennedy and Steve Heighway on the wings and up front David Johnson and David Fairclough. Promising defender Alan Hansen waited for his chance in the first team.

Dalglish made his home debut, remembering vividly: 'My Anfield debut came against Newcastle, who counted Tommy Craig amongst their number. I had grown up with Wee Tam, playing Glasgow Schools, Scottish Schools and Scottish Youth with him. Before kick-off, I found Tam looking up at the sign that declares "This Is Anfield". "How are you?" he asked. "I'm all right, I think," I told Tam, "but you see that sign there? It's supposed to frighten the opposition. I'm terrified by it and it's my home ground."' Fortunately for Kenny he settled his nerves by scoring the first goal of the game at the start of the second half. 'The goal was at the Kop end and I nearly finished up in amongst them,' Kenny said. 'Their appreciation was magnificent. It really touched me. That was the start of the relationship between the Kop and me. It was a special relationship, hard to articulate how strong the bond was.'

Paisley strengthened in January by buying Souness, who fitted seamlessly into the team, and while the Reds were not in ideal

Terry Mac congratulates Dalglish on his debut goal at Anfield

form domestically they were clearly determined to defend their European title. The European Cup final marked a fairytale ending for Kenny's debut season. Halfway through the second half a brilliant through ball from Souness let in Dalglish who chipped the ball expertly into the net past the advancing Danish keeper, Birger Jensen. 'Each of the two times Terry Mac ran through and shot low, Jensen dropped down to block the ball,' Kenny said. 'So when Graeme Souness played me in, Jensen came out as he had for Terry and I knew he was going to go down early. I dummied to play it, Jensen fell for it, allowing me the opening to lift the ball over the top of him. As the ball fell sweetly into the net, I continued my run, leaping the hoardings to go and salute the Liverpool supporters who seemed to have taken over Wembley.' Liverpool had won the European Cup for the second consecutive year. Dalglish could be pleased with his first season at Anfield: 31 goals in 62 matches, League and League Cup runner-up and a European champion.

Liverpool started the 1978/79 season by scoring 35 goals and conceding only four in 10 wins out of 11 league games. Dalglish had scored 10 including a brace when Liverpool beat Tottenham 7-0 at Anfield, which is still today

considered one of the greatest games in the club's history. But only two weeks later they lost 2-0 to the English champions, Nottingham Forest, in the first round of the European Cup, followed by a goalless draw in the second leg at Anfield. An early exit for the double European champions. This shock didn't knock Liverpool out of their stride and from Christmas they only lost two games for the rest of the campaign; against Manchester United in an FA Cup semi-final replay and to Aston Villa in the league. Dalglish wore the captain's armband briefly as Emlyn Hughes was no longer a regular. The Scot, however, didn't feel comfortable as captain and Paisley appointed Phil Thompson in his place. Liverpool won the title with eight more points than runners-up Nottingham Forest. Dalglish scored 21 league goals and combined well with David Johnson, who scored 16.

Once more Bob Paisley's judgement of players hadn't failed him. 'I'd seen Kenny playing for Scotland, watched him on television, and the more I saw of him the more I became convinced that he was what I called a Liverpool-type player. It was his attitude to the game. He wasn't flashy. He did the simple things and he was consistent too.

He was rarely out through injury either. His timing was immaculate and his head ruled his feet.' Dalglish had scored 56 goals in 116 games in his first two seasons at Liverpool and his contribution had won over the media, who voted him Football Writers' Player of the Year in 1979.

LIVERPOOL clinched their second consecutive title with a 4-1 win at Aston Villa in the penultimate game of the 1979/80 season, but only managed to come fifth in 1980/81, their worst placing for ten years. Johnson and Dalglish weren't producing goals. Remarkably, Dalglish had played 180 games in a row since joining Liverpool in August 1977 until he was out injured against Bradford City in the League Cup on 27 August 1980. Dalglish went 16 games without a league goal from late November until the end of the season.

Liverpool did, on the other hand, reach the finals in the League Cup and the European Cup. Dalglish netted the first of two in the replayed League Cup final victory over West Ham. He started the European Cup final against Real Madrid even though he had been out injured since the second leg of the semi-final against Bayern in Munich. He played a little deeper in the second half, seeking to draw defenders so that maximum use could be made of McDermott's long runs deep into Real's defence. Alan Kennedy's goal secured another European Cup.

Dalglish failed to score in the first nine league games of the 1981/82 season but finally ended an 11-month drought in the league against Brighton on 17 October 1981. His new strike partner, Ian Rush, scored 17 goals in 32 league matches as Liverpool recaptured the Championship.

DALGLISH was the architect of Liverpool's League Championship win in 1982/83. Rush benefited

from playing up front with him since many of his goals came after a brilliant pass from the Scot. Dalglish was voted Player of the Year by both the FWA and PFA.

Bob Paisley quit at the end of the 1982/83 season, leaving Joe Fagan in charge. Dalglish reached a milestone in his Liverpool career on 26 November 1983 when he scored his 100th league goal for the club with a fantastic shot into the top corner against Ipswich.

KING KENNY

Bill Shankly and Bob Paisley both consider King Kenny to be the best player who has ever worn the Liverpool shirt. Paisley said: 'Of all the players I have played alongside, managed and coached in more than forty years at Anfield, he is the most talented. When Kenny shines, the whole team is illuminated.'

1984 didn't start too well for Dalglish when Kevin Moran broke his cheekbone with the support brace on his wrist in a game against Manchester United on 2 January. Souness said Dalglish looked like the Elephant Man after the clash. Dalglish describes Joe Fagan's and his team-mates' hospital visit: 'When they walked in the door all their faces fell. When Mark Lawrenson saw my face he had to be taken to a side-room for a cup of tea. It didn't bother me my face was a mess. When Joe came in with the players he obviously got a fright as well. "There's the papers," he said, "I'll leave them there. I can't stay, thanks, bye."' Dalglish missed 14 games, but made his recovery in time for the quarter-finals of the European Cup against Benfica on 7 March. The last weekend in March proved to be a big one for Dalglish. The 33-year-old was pleasantly surprised to be offered a four-year contract, he was

included in the PFA Team of the Year along with four of his team-mates, and he played at Wembley as Liverpool and Everton drew 0-0 after extra time in the League Cup final (the Reds went on to win the replay).

The enigmatic Scot was busy smashing European records. Dalglish surpassed Denis Law's scoring record when he scored his 15th goal in the European Cup against Odense Boldklub in the second leg of the first round. He had now played more games, 54 in total, and scored more goals in Europe's premier competition than any other British player. Dalglish played in his third European Cup final, this time against Roma on their turf. The game went into a penalty shootout, but Dalglish had by then been substituted since he couldn't quite cope with the heat in Italy and was carrying a slight injury. Alan Kennedy was the hero, like three years previously, and scored the decisive penalty. Dalglish had won his third consecutive league title, fourth consecutive League Cup and the European Cup for the third time in seven seasons.

In 1984/85 Dalglish was dropped for the first time in his Liverpool career when the Reds faced Tottenham in a live televised match on 12 October. Liverpool lost 1-0 and Fagan admitted it had been his most stupid decision as manager; he put him straight back in the team. Dalglish missed more games after receiving a three-match ban for being sent off for the first time in his career against Benfica in Lisbon on 7 November. A week later he scored his 30th and final goal for Scotland in a game against Spain, equalling Denis Law's record. A great honour was bestowed upon him in the 1985 New Year Honours List when he was awarded an MBE for services to football.

The week before the European final against Juventus at the Heysel stadium Kenny received a phone call from Peter Robinson, Liverpool's secretary, who asked if he and John Smith could pay him a visit. 'Yes, no problem,' was Dalglish's reply. He recalls: 'I thought the conversation was going to finish then but Peter added: "Don't you want to know what we want to see you for?" "Yes," I replied, "If you want to tell me." "Well, we'd like to offer you the manager's job."' Dalglish replied drily, 'That's no problem, Peter, you can still come to the house.' Dalglish accepted the offer on the condition that Bob Paisley would be by his side for the first two years.

Liverpool returned to England in the middle of a media frenzy after 39 people died at the Heysel stadium and held a press conference later that day presenting Dalglish as the new boss. He couldn't have imagined worse circumstances, as Liverpool were facing exclusion from European football for the foreseeable future. Smith told the gathering: 'Kenny is entering the managerial side for the first time and we have every reason to believe he will have a successful period in office. We feel we have a man of great ability on the field who has got an old head on young shoulders.' Dalglish admitted in his autobiography *My Liverpool Home* that he was rather tense towards the press on this fateful day: 'My ability to handle the press was never a noted strength of my managerial career.' 'You know nothing about football and I know nothing about journalism, so we should get on well,' Dalglish told a bemused Ian Hargreaves at the *Liverpool Echo*.

MANY questioned Liverpool's decision to make Dalglish the first player-manager in the English First Division. One of his closest friends, Souness, had said in an interview with Scottish journalist Gerry McNee the year before that he had a feeling the next manager of Liverpool would be Dalglish. 'People are a bit frightened of him. He growls at them, he makes them jump.'

DALGLISH soon replaced the victorious full-backs of the Paisley era, Neal and Kennedy, with Steve Nicol and Jim Beglin. He made Jan Mølby his playmaker and signed midfield enforcer Steve McMahon from Aston Villa, and gave Craig Johnston and Paul Walsh a chance in his position. After a slow start to the season, in which Manchester United had won their opening ten matches, by the end of November Liverpool had reduced United's lead from nine to two points. Liverpool subsequently fell behind neighbours Everton but when Dalglish the manager needed an inspiration for his side Dalglish the player came in handy! The 35-year-old's presence in the team transformed Liverpool's form. Six wins in a row in the league set up a thrilling finish. In the final match of the season at Stamford Bridge Dalglish controlled the ball on his chest and a moment later wheeled away in celebration, having secured the League Championship with his brilliant goal.

Seven days later Liverpool faced Everton at Wembley in the 1986 FA Cup final, going into half-time 1-0 down. 'I remembered something Old Bob had told me: "In times of trouble, the best way to get players' attention is to speak softly because they have to concentrate on what you're saying,"' Dalglish revealed. 'Half-time in a cup final with a group of shattered players slumped on chairs in front of me was not the moment for verbal fireworks.' Dalglish told his troops, 'When we come back in here, I don't want any regrets. The FA Cup final is not a rehearsal.' They responded by securing the club's first League and Cup double with three goals in the second half. Manager of the Year King Kenny really had the golden touch.

Dalglish knew it would be difficult to repeat this feat and by the turn of the year Liverpool trailed first-place Arsenal by nine points,

in third. But Liverpool took 1987 by storm and won nine of the first 11 league games, and had by mid-March gained a few points' lead on Everton with Arsenal falling by the wayside. The Reds then lost three league games in a row as well as the League Cup final to Arsenal. In the end Everton won the League Championship with a comfortable nine-point margin. Liverpool finished a season empty-handed for only the third time in 15 years. Dalglish explained Liverpool's failure. 'The board had approached me at Christmas 1986 and said there was money available for players. I gave them the names of five players and I got four of them – Barnes, Beardsley, Houghton and Aldridge. It took time to buy these four. That was instrumental in 1986/87 being such a fruitless season at Anfield.'

Key changes were made to the team as Rush departed, with Aldridge benefiting from the service of John Barnes on the left and Peter Beardsley's link-up play. Kenny was developing his own team with a different identity from the ones governed by his predecessors. Paisley was no longer by his side and had retired to the boardroom. Barnes was the new talisman, making Liverpool a more potent attacking force. The Reds started the season with three away games as a collapsed sewer under the Kop needed repair. Liverpool ripped Coventry City apart following an opening day 2-1 win over Arsenal. *The Times* recognised the power of Kenny's new army. 'Over the years, the loss of Keegan, Souness, and, in effect, Dalglish, have each supplied excuses for backing someone else. But, somehow, they have nearly always plugged the gap. Such facts were overlooked at the start of this season and Rush's departure to Juventus. I have news for the non-believers: "Liverpool are dead, long live Liverpool".'

LIVERPOOL were on a rampage, netting four goals in four consecutive league games; against Newcastle, Derby, Portsmouth and Queens Park Rangers. Aldridge thrived up front, having scored in ten league games in a row, still a Liverpool record. The Reds' fear factor was overwhelming opponents, even Queens Park Rangers who led the First Division before their clash at Anfield on 17 October. When Rangers' manager Jim Smith was asked how his team had prepared for the match he quipped: 'We got down on our knees and prayed.' QPR lost 4-0, thanks partly to an astonishing double from Barnes.

There was no big secret to Liverpool's success, as John Barnes revealed in his autobiography: 'Liverpool practiced small-sided games every day and it was high-intensity stuff. There was no tactical work, none whatsoever. Liverpool believed that everything we faced in five-a-sides would be encountered again on match day. Liverpool's training characterised Liverpool's play – uncomplicated but devastatingly effective.'

On 28 December Liverpool netted a quadruple against Newcastle for a second time that season and *The Times* waxed lyrical. 'Visiting Anfield is like stepping back in time. Yesterday the gates were closed 50 minutes before kick-off. Stanley Park car park had the "full" notices up 75 minutes beforehand – and both the style of football and the size of the excited audience, 44,647, recalled the game's halcyon days.' From 19 December 1987 to 16 March 1988 Liverpool conceded one goal and scored 31 in 15 games in all competitions! Everton prevented Liverpool from improving Leeds' record from 1974 of 29 league games unbeaten when Wayne Clarke netted the only goal of the game at Goodison on 20 March. Nottingham Forest then inflicted a second league defeat on Liverpool on 2 April in the first game in a series of three between the sides in 11 days. Liverpool beat Forest 2-1 in the FA Cup semi-final and then annihilated Brian Clough's men at Anfield 5-0 in a showcase of all the talent on offer at Liverpool that Sir Tom Finney claimed was 'the finest exhibition I've

seen the whole time I've played and watched the game'. Maurice Roworth, the Forest chairman, was mesmerised. 'Liverpool are the best team in Europe, which is why they are not in Europe. They are too good.' Captain Alan Hansen was proud of his men and said the performance was the 'best since I've been here'. High praise indeed from the Scotsman who was playing his 564th game for the Reds. Nine points separated Liverpool and second-placed Manchester United at the end of this dazzling campaign. The only blot on the landscape was a surprising 1-0 defeat to Wimbledon in the FA Cup final, which prevented a second double in just three seasons.

> 'A WONDERFUL PLAYER, SUCH SKILL, SO BRAVE. PROBABLY THE BEST COMBINATION OF GOALSCORER AND GOALMAKER I'VE EVER SEEN'
> **DIXIE DEAN**

Dalglish had got it right when signing players during the previous summer. Aldridge scored 29 goals in 45 games, Beardsley 18 in 48 and John Barnes 17 in 48, the latter voted the Player of the Year by both the media and the players. It didn't come as a surprise that Dalglish was voted the Manager of the Year. Liverpool won the title in style and the way they played reflected their manager. This side played a more offensive football than previous teams and was more about individual play of great players, even though team spirit was high. This was Kenny Dalglish's team.

On 18 August, two days before Liverpool played Wimbledon in the Charity Shield, the press was stunned; Dalglish had just

announced that Ian Rush had returned to Liverpool. The excitement before the season was great and the fans wondered how he was going to use Barnes, Beardsley, Aldridge and Rush in the same side. On 26 October Liverpool suffered their third defeat of the season, one more than all of the season before. After ten league rounds Liverpool were fourth, eight points behind Norwich. Following a 3-1 defeat to Manchester United on New Year's Day Dalglish locked his side inside the dressing room and what followed was a verbal attack of a calibre that none of his players had seen before.

DALGLISH'S outburst worked like a charm as his team went undefeated in the next 18 league matches, of which 15 were won. But in the semi-finals of the FA Cup against Nottingham Forest football was given a whole new meaning for Kenny Dalglish. This was the third time Dalglish had witnessed a tragedy in a football stadium. When he was in the Celtic squad at the age of 19, 66 died at Ibrox, in 1985 39 died at Heysel, and 96 Liverpool supporters died from injuries received at Hillsborough. The press and the supporters saw a new side to Dalglish as he united the club and city in their grief. As Dalglish visited the bedside of victims of the disaster at North General Hospital in Sheffield he saw 14-year-old Lee Nicol hooked up to a life-support machine.

Kenny looking on in horror at Hillsborough

'I stared at him, not understanding why somebody without a mark or a bruise on him could be clinically dead. It just didn't make sense. The medical experts said this is what happens with asphyxiation. The brain becomes starved of oxygen and just cuts out.' Lee became Hillsborough's 95th victim. Hillsborough was Lee's first away game.

During the same visit one boy woke up from a coma when a doctor told him Kenny Dalglish was by his bed. The harrowing scenes Dalglish witnessed at Hillsborough and in its aftermath, and the care he showed to the victims' families without seeking help to deal with the mental anguish he was experiencing came back to haunt him. Liverpool were rushed to action by the Football Association for the rematch. Liverpool were victorious and symbolically the Reds faced the Blues in the final on an emotional day. Kenny's old mate, Rush, proved to be worth his weight in gold, ensuring a 3-2 win. The last league game was between the two top teams at Anfield. Liverpool had 76 points but Arsenal 73. The goal difference for Liverpool was 65-26 (+39) and Arsenal's 71-36 (+35). A two-goal win in favour of Arsenal would win them the League Championship on goals scored. In the final minute Michael Thomas scored Arsenal's second that grabbed the title away from the hosts. Liverpool had been 45 seconds away from a second double. 'I once watched a clip of that Michael Thomas goal and heard that great commentator Brian Moore say: "Dalglish just stands there." I did. The shock froze me on the spot. I was numb, the fuel gauge empty as dejection set in,' Dalglish said.

Come mid-October 1989 Liverpool had only lost one game for the past seven months, which was, crucially, the title decider in May. Yet Liverpool's form proved to be far less convincing for the rest of the season. They had only a one-point lead when the Israeli Ronny Rosenthal

arrived on loan from Standard Liege in Belgium. He scored seven goals in eight games, the Reds won their 18th league title and Dalglish was named Manager of the Year for the third time in five seasons. He hadn't picked himself for the team on a regular basis since October 1986 and made his last ever appearance when he came on against Derby in the penultimate game of the season. One of the greatest players in the history of football had retired after playing a total of 837 games – at the time he was the most successful player in the history of British football.

BEFORE DALGLISH went on his summer holiday he was brought in for discussions by chairman Noel White and Peter Robinson over a new contract. 'I need a break,' Dalglish told the surprised executives. Another meeting was held in which Dalglish said he wanted shares in the club instead of outright payment if he signed a new deal, as he wasn't sure about his future at the club. Robinson told him that was not possible. 'Get yourself a good holiday. You'll be fine for the start of the season,' were Robinson's parting words to Kenny.

It's fair to say that the press went over the top in their treatment of Dalglish and his team in the 1990/91 season. Kenny was criticised left, right and centre. His team was getting old, his new signing, Jimmy Carter, didn't bed in, Liverpool were too defensive and Dalglish himself was called 'boring', 'miserable' and 'sulky'. By 9 February 1991, following a 3-1 win over Everton in the league, Liverpool had a three-point lead on Arsenal at the top of the table. The Reds had scored 62 goals in 24 games, 2.58 on average, hardly the performance of a team frightened to attack!

LIVERPOOL were to meet the Blues again, in the sixth round of the FA Cup, and a goalless draw

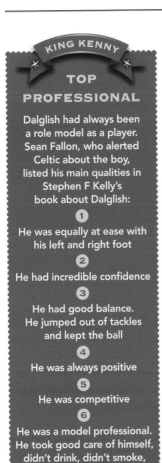

TOP PROFESSIONAL

Dalglish had always been a role model as a player. Sean Fallon, who alerted Celtic about the boy, listed his main qualities in Stephen F Kelly's book about Dalglish:

1 He was equally at ease with his left and right foot

2 He had incredible confidence

3 He had good balance. He jumped out of tackles and kept the ball

4 He was always positive

5 He was competitive

6 He was a model professional. He took good care of himself, didn't drink, didn't smoke, went to bed early and pushed himself in practice.

at Anfield forced a replay at Goodison Park. Liverpool took the lead three times, but Tony Cottee equalised one minute from normal time. In extra time Liverpool were in front once more, but another goal from Cottee in the 113th minute meant a second replay had to take place. Dalglish told reporters: 'If there has ever been any better cup ties than that, then I wish that someone would send me a video of them. I have never been involved in a game like that before.' The press didn't know that Dalglish had already come to the conclusion that this would be his last game as manager of Liverpool Football Club.

'Five hours before kick-off in the FA Cup fourth round derby at Everton, I made up my mind. Whatever happened at Goodison, I would tell the chairman I had to go,' Dalglish revealed in his autobiography. 'The pressure was too much. Driving home after games, I was nipping away at

my kids Kelly and Paul. The atmosphere at home wasn't good and I was to blame. I was a mess. The previous December, I'd come out in big red blotches all over my body. I went to the office Christmas party covered in blemishes. To ease the rash, Liverpool's doctor pumped me with Piriton at Anfield every other day, alternating the cheeks on my backside, so in a fortnight I felt like a pin cushion. As Piriton made me drowsy, I'd fall through my front door then slump into a deep sleep on the couch for hours. My nerves were shredded long before February 20, 1991.'

THE NEXT MORNING Dalglish attended a meeting that was held every month with Noel White and Peter Robinson. Twenty minutes in Dalglish stunned them into silence by saying: 'I want to resign.' 'Why?' asked White finally. 'I've had enough. I need a break. I just feel as if my head is exploding. I want to go now. Today.' Robinson offered him a sabbatical but Kenny had made his mind up. At 4pm Liverpool held an emergency board meeting at which they reluctantly accepted his resignation and shortly after 11am on 22 February 1991 White said to the disbelieving press:

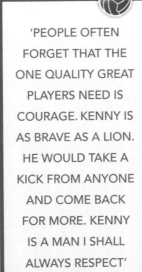

'PEOPLE OFTEN FORGET THAT THE ONE QUALITY GREAT PLAYERS NEED IS COURAGE. KENNY IS AS BRAVE AS A LION. HE WOULD TAKE A KICK FROM ANYONE AND COME BACK FOR MORE. KENNY IS A MAN I SHALL ALWAYS RESPECT'

ALEX FERGUSON

'Thank you for coming on such short notice. I'm going to read a short statement: With great regret I have to say that Kenny Dalglish has requested to the board of Liverpool to resign as manager.'

A little while later at the Lime Street train station in Liverpool the announcer read the typical announcements about the delays of the trains then added apologetically: 'Kenny Dalglish has resigned as Liverpool manager, I just thought you'd like to know that.' Dalglish admitted later that he would have returned to work at Liverpool at the end of the summer. 'If Liverpool had asked me to carry on as manager the moment I returned from Florida, I'd have jumped at the chance because my batteries were recharged. Sadly, they never asked. While in Orlando, I received a phone call to tell me Graeme Souness had got the job and I felt a twinge of regret.'

Eight months after leaving Liverpool, Dalglish was back in football as the manager of Blackburn Rovers. He led Rovers into the newly formed Premier League and in April 1993 Peter Robinson hinted at Kenny returning when he met him at Ewood Park as he picked up his tickets for the Blackburn–Liverpool game taking place the following day. 'Kenny, when are you coming home?' Robinson asked. 'What do you mean?' Dalglish responded. 'When are you coming back to Liverpool, Kenny?' 'Peter, you just have to ask.' 'OK,' he said. 'It's up to yourselves,' Kenny added. 'You just need to phone.' Kenny waited for a call that never came.

PRIOR to the 1994/95 season Dalglish rejected a new contract at Blackburn, hoping that Liverpool would come calling, which did happen while Kenny was on holiday. 'We just want to know whether you would be interested in coming back to the club,'

Robinson said over the phone. 'Of course I am interested,' Kenny replied. 'I couldn't pack fast enough, jumping on a plane and, once back in England, hurtling up to David Moores' house,' Dalglish said in *My Liverpool Home.*

PBR [Robinson], Roy Evans, Tom Saunders and David were already there. Scarcely had I sat down when Peter announced, 'We don't think the time's right for you to come home.' I was taken aback. 'Why phone me and ask me to come back if you don't think the time's right?' I was furious. 'I want to come back to Liverpool. I wouldn't be sitting here now otherwise. I did a good job the first time.' Liverpool's logic baffled me then, and still does now. Never before in all my life have I felt such anger. My stomach was churning as I got in the car and sped off to Anfield, of all places, because Paul was playing some game for Liverpool reserves.

Dalglish signed a new contract at Rovers and, ironically, on a memorable afternoon back at Anfield in the middle of May 1995, despite losing 2-1 to Liverpool on the day, Rovers were crowned English champions.

Shortly after that success, Kenny became Blackburn's director of football with Ray Harford replacing him as team manager. It was not a successful move. The team's performances at home and abroad started to decline and eventually Kenny left Blackburn. In the middle of January 1997 Dalglish was unveiled as Newcastle United's new manager. He steered the Northeast club to runners-up in the Premier League in 1997 and also took them to an FA Cup final the following year. But the real success he had enjoyed at Liverpool and Blackburn was elusive and after starting the 1998/99 season with draws in the opening two

league matches, Dalglish was replaced by Ruud Gullit.

KENNY became Glasgow Celtic's director of football in June 1999 with John Barnes appointed at the same time as head coach. But Barnes was sacked in February 2000 and Kenny took over the manager's responsibilities and guided the Celts to a Scottish League Cup final success over Aberdeen. Despite that trophy, Kenny himself was soon replaced as manager by Martin O'Neill.

FACTFILE

BORN
Glasgow, Scotland,
4 March 1951
POSITION
Midfielder / Forward
OTHER CLUBS
Celtic (1967–77),
Cumbernauld United
(loan, 1967–68)
OTHER CLUBS AS MANAGER
Blackburn Rovers (1991–95),
Newcastle United (1997–98),
Celtic (2000)
SIGNED FROM
Celtic, £440,000,
10 August 1977
INTERNATIONAL CAPS
102 Scotland caps (30 goals)
(55 (14) at LFC), 1971–86
APPOINTED MANAGER
30 May 1985 / 8 January 2011
**LFC DEBUT AS PLAYER
GAME/GOAL**
13 August 1977 /
20 August 1977
LFC DEBUT AS MANAGER
17 August 1985
CONTRACT EXPIRY
21 February 1991 / 16 May 2012
HONOURS AS PLAYER
League Championship
1978/79, 1979/80, 1981/82,
1982/83, 1983/84, 1985/86;
FA Cup 1986;
League Cup
1981, 1982, 1983, 1984;
European Cup
1978, 1981, 1984;
FWA Footballer of the Year
1979, 1983;
PFA Player of the Year 1983
HONOURS AS MANAGER
League Championship
1985/86, 1987/88, 1989/90;
FA Cup 1986, 1989;
League Cup 2012;
Manager of the Year
1986, 1988, 1990

On 3 July 2009 the club officially announced Kenny's return to Anfield, where he was going to 'assume a senior role at the Liverpool Academy and will also act as a Club ambassador working with the commercial side of the business around the world'. Dalglish was asked to help the club find a replacement for Rafa Benítez as manager. Despite wanting the post himself, the job eventually went to Roy Hodgson. But a wretched start to the Premier League season saw the Reds in the unfamiliar territory of the relegation zone after losing at home to Blackpool in October. When results failed to improve, Hodgson left the club and Kenny

'I HAVE COME TO THE CONCLUSION THAT KENNY DALGLISH HAS BEEN PUT ON THIS EARTH BY GOD TO BE A WINNER AT EVERYTHING. I HONESTLY BELIEVE HE HAS BEEN BLESSED'

FORMER LEEDS AND ENGLAND MANAGER DON REVIE

was appointed on 8 January 2011 to replace him until the end of the 2010/11 season.

After successfully leading Liverpool from the bottom half of the table to challenging for a spot in the Europa League Dalglish was appointed permanent manager on 12 May, signing a three-year contract. John Henry, Liverpool's new principal owner, recognised Dalglish's importance to the club. 'Kenny is a legendary Liverpool figure both as a supremely gifted footballer and successful manager. It was obvious to us very early on that the atmosphere surrounding the club had been transformed by

As a Player

Season	League App	League Goals	FA Cup App	FA Cup Goals	League Cup App	League Cup Goals	Europe App	Europe Goals	Other App	Other Goals	Total App	Total Goals
1977/78	42	20	1	1	9	6	9	4	1	0	62	31
1978/79	42	21	7	4	1	0	4	0	-	-	54	25
1979/80	42	16	8	2	7	4	2	0	1	1	60	23
1980/81	34	8	2	2	8	7	9	1	1	0	54	18
1981/82	42	13	3	2	10	5	6	2	1	0	62	22
1982/83	42	18	3	1	7	0	5	1	1	0	58	20
1983/84	33	7	0	0	8	2	8 (1)	3	1	0	50 (1)	12
1984/85	36	6	7	0	1	0	7	0	2	0	53	6
1985/86	17 (4)	3	6	1	2	1	-	-	2	2	27 (4)	7
1986/87	12 (6)	6	0	0	4 (1)	2	-	-	1 (1)	0	17 (8)	8
1987/88	0 (2)	0	0	0	0	0	-	-	-	-	0 (2)	0
1988/89	0	0	0	0	0 (1)	0	-	-	0 (1)	0	0 (2)	0
1989/90	0 (1)	0	0	0	0	0	-	-	0	0	0 (1)	0
Total	**342 (13)**	**118**	**37**	**13**	**57 (2)**	**27**	**50 (1)**	**11**	**11 (2)**	**3**	**497 (18)**	**172**

his presence. We didn't need nor want to look elsewhere for the right man to manage the team.' King Kenny's smile lit up Anfield and the fans' faces once again and, most importantly, Liverpool had reclaimed its long-lost identity.

DESPITE WINNING Liverpool's first trophy for six years, the League Cup, and coming close to a cup double by reaching the FA Cup final, Dalglish was sacked following the end of the 2011/12 season. It followed Liverpool's worst league campaign since the start of the Premier League. Liverpool's managing director, Ian Ayre, said even though it was difficult to let Kenny go the reason was simple. 'If you don't believe the results are right, and feel 37 points off the champions and 17 points off Champions League pace is a long distance you have to make a change,' Ayre said bluntly. 'The history the club was built on was about success and that means success in the League, which leads to Champions League football, and also winning trophies. No one is saying we didn't enjoy winning the Carling Cup and getting to the FA Cup final but ultimately the backbone of football now is the Premier League and European football at the highest level.'

* Dalglish resigned on 21 February 1991 with Liverpool in 1st position
** Dalglish appointed on 8 January 2011 with Liverpool in 12th position

As a Manager in Europe

Season	Champions League	Europa League
2010/11	-	Round of 16

As a Manager

Season	Division	P	W	D	L	GF	GA	Pts	Pos	Win %	FA Cup	League Cup
1985/86	1st Division	42	26	10	6	89	37	88	1	61.90	Winners	Semi-Final
1986/87	1st Division	42	23	8	11	72	42	77	2	54.76	3rd Round	Runners-Up
1987/88	1st Division	40	26	12	2	87	24	90	1	65.00	Runners-Up	3rd Round
1988/89	1st Division	38	22	10	6	65	28	76	2	57.89	Winners	4th Round
1989/90	1st Division	38	23	10	5	78	37	79	1	60.53	Semi-Final	3rd Round
1990/91*	1st Division	24	16	6	2	46	19	54	1	66.67	5th Round	3rd Round
2010/11**	Premier League	18	10	3	5	35	17	33	6	55.56	3rd Round	-
2011/12	Premier League	38	14	10	14	47	40	52	8	36.84	Runners-Up	Winners
Total	-	280	160	69	51	519	244	549	-	57.14	-	-

Dalla Valle, Lauri

LAURI DALLA VALLE spent three months at Inter Milan when he was 15, but after failing to settle in his father's homeland returned to Finland. Dalla Valle was on trial at Liverpool in 2006 and offered a four-year contract but he felt it wasn't the right time to move to England.

A year later Liverpool's chief executive Rick Parry finalised a deal with the Finnish striker, which is rather unusual when signing a youth player. A natural finisher, he scored 20 goals in 28 appearances for Liverpool's Under-18 team in the 2008/09 season which resulted in him being promoted to the reserves. Dalla Valle made his first-team debut for Liverpool as a substitute in the Europa League third qualifying round against FK Rabotnicki on 29 July 2010.

A month later Dalla Valle left for Fulham as part of the deal that brought Paul Konchesky to Anfield. Dalla Valle made a short stop at Fulham and Molde before joining Sint-Truiden in the Belgian second division.

FACTFILE

BORN
Kontiolahti, Finland,
14 September 1991
POSITION
Centre-forward
OTHER CLUBS
JIPPO Joensuu (2006–07),
Fulham (2010–13),
Bournemouth (loan, 2011),
Dundee United
(loan, 2011–12),
Exeter City (loan, 2012),
Crewe Alexandra
(loan, 2012–13),
Molde (2013),
Sint-Truiden (2013–)
SIGNED FROM
JIPPO Joensuu, £600,000,
8 November 2007
LFC DEBUT
29 July 2010
CONTRACT EXPIRY
31 August 2010

Season	League		FA Cup		League Cup		Europe		Other		Total	
	App	Goals	App	Goals	App	Goals	App	Goals	App	Goals	App	Goals
2010/11	0	0	0	0	0	0	0 (1)	0	-	-	0 (1)	0
Total	0	0	0	0	0	0	0 (1)	0	0	0	0 (1)	0

Darby, Stephen

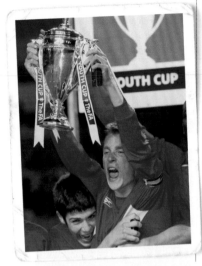

RIGHT-BACK Stephen Darby was captain of the victorious Liverpool side in the FA Youth Cup in 2006.

HE MADE two substitute appearances in the 2008/09 season; in the closing minutes of a defeat at Tottenham in the League Cup and in a European fixture at PSV Eindhoven when he replaced Álvaro Arbeloa. The official Liverpool Supporters Club handed Stephen Darby the 'Ian Frodsham young player of the year' award in recognition of both the progress he had made on the pitch during 2009 and the excellent way he conducted himself off it. He signed a new contract with the club in July 2009, but following only three appearances in the

THE OFFICIAL LIVERPOOL SUPPORTERS CLUB HANDED STEPHEN DARBY THE 'IAN FRODSHAM YOUNG PLAYER OF THE YEAR' AWARD

ensuing season he was loaned to Swindon Town in League One in March 2010. He played in 12 league games as Swindon finished 5th and qualified to meet Charlton Athletic in the playoffs. Each club won its home leg 2-1 and the tie went to a penalty shootout in

which Darby secured Swindon's progress into the playoff final. Darby came on as a substitute for Swindon Town in the League One final against Millwall, but the Wiltshire club lost 1-0. The 23-year-old was released by Liverpool in the summer of 2012 and signed a two-year deal with Bradford City in League Two.

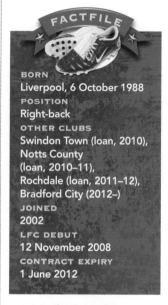

FACTFILE

BORN
Liverpool, 6 October 1988
POSITION
Right-back
OTHER CLUBS
Swindon Town (loan, 2010), Notts County (loan, 2010–11), Rochdale (loan, 2011–12), Bradford City (2012–)
JOINED
2002
LFC DEBUT
12 November 2008
CONTRACT EXPIRY
1 June 2012

Season	League		FA Cup		League Cup		Europe		Other		Total	
	App	Goals	App	Goals	App	Goals	App	Goals	App	Goals	App	Goals
2008/09	0	0	0	0	0 (1)	0	0 (1)	0	-	-	0 (2)	0
2009/10	0 (1)	0	1	0	0	0	1	0	-	-	2 (1)	0
2010/11	0	0	0	0	0	0	0 (1)	0	-	-	0 (1)	0
Total	0 (1)	0	1	0	0 (1)	0	1 (2)	0	0	0	2 (4)	0

Davidson, David

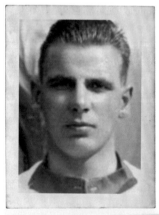

DAVID DAVIDSON was a fierce-tackling central defender who only missed six of the 42 league matches during the 1928/29 season, in which he scored once, the second-half winner against West Ham at Anfield on 13 March 1929.

He played in the first 21 league fixtures of the following season before being replaced by Tom Bromilow for three games

and (after returning for two appearances) then Tiny Bradshaw who played in the remaining 17 league games. Davidson added a second career goal for Liverpool, in a 3-3 draw at Portsmouth on 2 November 1929. Davidson played 142 games for Newcastle, where he won the FA Cup in 1932 but was also relegated to the Second Division in 1934.

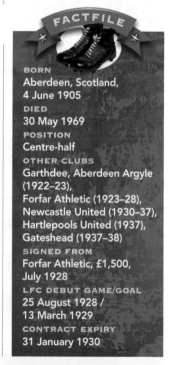

FACTFILE

BORN
Aberdeen, Scotland, 4 June 1905
DIED
30 May 1969
POSITION
Centre-half
OTHER CLUBS
Garthdee, Aberdeen Argyle (1922–23), Forfar Athletic (1923–28), Newcastle United (1930–37), Hartlepools United (1937), Gateshead (1937–38)
SIGNED FROM
Forfar Athletic, £1,500, July 1928
LFC DEBUT GAME/GOAL
25 August 1928 / 13 March 1929
CONTRACT EXPIRY
31 January 1930

LIVERPOOL FOOTBALL CLUB SEASON 1929-30 PLAYERS, DIRECTORS AND OFFICIALS.

Season	League		FA Cup		Total	
	App	Goals	App	Goals	App	Goals
1928/29	36	1	3	0	39	1
1929/30	22	1	1	0	23	1
Total	58	2	4	0	62	2

Davies,
John

JOHN DAVIES' debut was as a replacement for experienced winger Jack Cox in a home game with Wolves on 9 March 1901, but that was the only time he figured that season. Nine more appearances followed in the next two seasons, his selection for the visit of Notts County on 18 October 1902 being his last as a Liverpool player.

FACTFILE

BORN
Liverpool, July 1881
POSITION
Forward
OTHER CLUBS
Blackpool (1903–04)
JOINED
October 1900
LFC DEBUT
9 March 1901
CONTRACT EXPIRY
July 1903

Season	League		FA Cup		Total	
	App	Goals	App	Goals	App	Goals
1900/01	1	0	0	0	1	0
1901/02	6	0	1	0	7	0
1902/03	2	0	0	0	2	0
Total	9	0	1	0	10	0

Dawson,
Jimmy

ALL OF JIMMY DAWSON'S 14 first-team games for the club came during the 1913/14 season. One press report noted that the inside-forward was 'artistic but needed to infuse more devil into his work at close quarters'. There was certainly a devil present when Dawson got sent off along with Stoke's Joe Jones in a wartime match on 18 September 1915. The pair collided and 'angry words ensued'. They squared up to each other but no blows were struck. The referee was going to overlook their differences but the players wouldn't let go of the matter so he had no alternative than to dismiss them.

FACTFILE

BORN
Edinburgh, Scotland,
13 August 1890
POSITION
Inside-right forward
OTHER CLUBS
Leith Athletic (1910–12),
Edinburgh Emmett
SIGNED FROM
Leith Athletic, December 1912
LFC DEBUT GAME/GOAL
1 November 1913 /
29 November 1913
CONTRACT EXPIRY
1916

Dawson was suspended for two weeks by the Football Association.

Season	League		FA Cup		Total	
	App	Goals	App	Goals	App	Goals
1913/14	13	3	1	0	14	3
Total	13	3	1	0	14	3

Defeats

Biggest defeat

	Opponent	Competition	Date
1-9	Birmingham City	2nd Division	11 December 1954
0-8	Huddersfield Town	1st Division	10 November 1934
2-9	Newcastle United	1st Division	1 January 1934
1-8	Bolton Wanderers	1st Division	7 May 1932
1-8	Arsenal	1st Division	1 September 1934
0-7	Sunderland	1st Division	7 December 1912
0-7	West Ham United	1st Division	1 September 1930
0-6	Sunderland*	1st Division	19 April 1930
0-6	Arsenal	1st Division	28 November
0-6	Manchester City	1st Division	11 September 1935
0-6	Charlton Athletic	1st Division	26 September 1953

All away except Sunderland on 19 April 1930

Biggest defeat at Anfield

	Opponent	Competition	Date
0-6	Sunderland	1st Division	19 April 1930
1-6	Manchester City	1st Division	26 October 1929
0-5	Everton	1st Division	3 October 1914
0-5	Manchester City	1st Division	26 March 1937

Biggest defeat in the Premier League

	Opponent	Competition	Date
1-5	Coventry City	Highfield Road	19 December 1992
0-4	Chelsea	Stamford Bridge	16 December 2001
0-4	Manchester Utd	Old Trafford	5 April 2003

Biggest defeat at Anfield in the Premier League

	Opponent	Date
1-4	Chelsea	2 October 2005

The only Premier League game at Anfield that Liverpool have lost by three goals. The Reds have lost by a two goal margin on 13 occasions

Biggest defeat in Europe

	Opponent	Competition	Date
1-5	Ajax	European Cup	7 December 1966
0-3	Inter Milan	European Cup	12 May 1965
0-3	Dinamo Tbilisi	European Cup	3 October 1979
0-3	Paris St Germain	European Cup Winners' Cup	10 April 1997
0-3	Strasbourg	UEFA Cup	21 October 1997

All defeats away

Biggest defeat in the Champions League

	Opponent	Round	Date
2-4	Bayer Leverkusen	2nd Group Phase (A)	9 April 2002
1-3	Barcelona	2nd Group Phase (H)	20 November 2001
1-3	Chelsea	Quarter-final 1st leg (H)	8 April 2009
0-2	Benfica	1st knockout round 2nd leg (H)	8 March 2006
0-2	Valencia	1st Group Phase (A)	17 September 2002
0-2	Fiorentina	1st Group Phase (A)	29 September 2009

Biggest defeat in the FA Cup

	Opponent	Round	Date
0-5	Bolton Wanderers	4th round 1st leg (A)	26 January 1946
1-5	Derby County	3rd round replay (H)	2 March 1898

Biggest defeat in the League Cup

	Opponent	Round	Date
3-6	Arsenal	5th round (H)	9 January 2007
1-4	West Ham United	4th round (A)	30 November 1988

Biggest aggregate defeats

	Home	Away	Opponent	Competition	Dates
-4	0-2	2-4	Spartak Moscow	European Cup Winners' Cup 2nd round	22 October - 4 November 1992
-4	2-2	1-5	Ajax	European Cup 2nd round	7 -14 December 1966
-3	0-2	0-1	Benfica	Champions League 1st knockout round	21 February - 8 March 2006
-3	0-1	1-3	Celta Vigo	UEFA Cup 3rd round	24 November - 8 December 1998
-3	1-2	0-2	Genoa	UEFA Cup 4th round	4 - 18 March 1992
-3	2-0	0-5	Bolton Wanderers	FA Cup 4th round	26 - 30 January 1946

Most defeats in a league season

		League	Games	Position
1953/54	**23**	1st Division	42	22
1952/53	**20**	1st Division	42	17
1936/37	**19**	1st Division	42	18
1906/07	**18**	1st Division	38	15
1933/34	**18**	1st Division	42	18

Fewest defeats in a league season

		League	Games	Position
1893/94	**0**	2nd Division	28	1
1987/88	**2**	1st Division	40	1
2008/09	**2**	Premier League	38	2
1904/05	**3**	2nd Division	34	1
1978/79	**4**	1st Division	42	1
2007/08	**4**	Premier League	38	4

Most defeats at Anfield in a league season

		League	Games	Position
1906/07	**8**	1st Division	19	15
1913/14	**7**	1st Division	19	16
1911/12	**7**	1st Division	19	17
1937/38	**7**	1st Division	21	11

Fewest defeats at Anfield in a league season

		League	Games	Position
1979/80	**0**	1st Division	21	1
1978/79	**0**	1st Division	21	1
1976/77	**0**	1st Division	21	1
1970/71	**0**	1st Division	21	5
1961/62	**0**	2nd Division	21	1
1987/88	**0**	1st Division	20	1
2008/09	**0**	Premier League	19	2
1904/05	**0**	2nd Division	17	1
1895/96	**0**	2nd Division	15	1
1893/94	**0**	2nd Division	14	1

Most away defeats in a league season

		League	Games	Position
1953/54	**17**	1st Division	21	22
1952/53	**15**	1st Division	21	17
1936/37	**15**	1st Division	21	18

Fewest away defeats in a league season

		League	Games	Position
1893/94	**0**	2nd Division	14	1
1987/88	**2**	1st Division	20	1
2008/09	**2**	Premier League	19	2
1975/76	**3**	1st Division	21	1
1981/82	**3**	1st Division	21	1
2007/08	**3**	Premier League	19	4
1988/89	**3**	1st Division	19	2
1904/05	**3**	2nd Division	17	1

Degen, Philipp

Very few had heard of Philipp Degen before he signed for Liverpool and even fewer after he had left. The right-back won the league title two years in succession in his homeland with Basel before joining Borussia Dortmund in 2005. Injuries hampered his progress and he only made 10 league appearances in the 2007/08 season. His contract expired in the summer of 2008 and he joined Liverpool on a Bosman free transfer. Rafa Benítez was quite happy with signing Degen: 'I am confident he will be prove to be a quality addition to our squad. Sometimes you can find these players on the market.'

Degen proved to be quite unlucky at the start of his Liverpool career, hardly being able to step out of the house without getting injured. He broke two ribs on his debut against Crewe Alexandra in the League Cup and when he made his second appearance against Spurs in November 2008 he injured his foot. To the surprise of many, Degen figured in as many as 11 of Liverpool's 56 competitive matches during the 2009/10 season, six from the start and five as a substitute. One of those starts ended with an unfortunate red card at Fulham in October. He didn't start another match until the New Year when he was part of the team that capitulated horribly to Reading in the FA Cup. Although frequently in the 18-man match-day squad, Degen only made five more appearances by the end of the season.

Degen wanted to get his career back on track and moved to Stuttgart on a season-long loan in the summer of 2010, but he only appeared eight times in the 2010/11 season. His Liverpool contract was cancelled at the end of August 2011. On 20 November Degen was offered a contract with his first club, Basel. His contribution to Basel winning both the Swiss Championship and the Swiss Cup in 2012 was only minimal.

FACTFILE

BORN
Hölstein, Switzerland, 15 February 1983
POSITION
Right-back
OTHER CLUBS
Basel (1995–2005), Aarau (loan, 2002–03), Borussia Dortmund (2005–08), Stuttgart (loan, 2010–11), Basel (2011–)
JOINED
Bosman free transfer, 3 July 2008
INTERNATIONAL CAPS
32 Swiss caps, 2005–09
LFC DEBUT
23 September 2008
CONTRACT EXPIRY
31 August 2011

Season	League		FA Cup		League Cup		Europe		Total	
	App	Goals	App	Goals	App	Goals	App	Goals	App	Goals
2008/09	0	0	0	0	2	0	0	0	2	0
2009/10	3 (4)	0	1	0	2	0	0 (1)	0	6 (5)	0
Total	3 (4)	0	1	0	4	0	0 (1)	0	8 (5)	0

Devlin, Willie

WILLIE 'DEMON' DEVLIN
LIVERPOOL

WILLIE 'DEMON' DEVLIN was top scorer in the Scottish League from 1924–26 with 33 and 40 goals respectively in 68 matches with Cowdenbeath, and earned himself a big-money £4,200 move to Huddersfield Town in February 1926.

Huddersfield had won the League Championship for two consecutive seasons and Devlin contributed to their third by scoring four goals in four games in his debut campaign. He scored 10 goals in 28 appearances as the Terriers

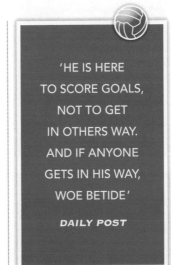

'HE IS HERE TO SCORE GOALS, NOT TO GET IN OTHERS WAY. AND IF ANYONE GETS IN HIS WAY, WOE BETIDE'

DAILY POST

failed to add a fourth consecutive title, finishing second five points behind Newcastle in 1926/27.

DICK FORSHAW had been controversially sold from Liverpool to Everton in March 1927 and the Reds needed a replacement. Devlin was given his Liverpool debut in the final fixture of the 1926/27 season in a visit to West Ham and scored the second goal in a 3-3 draw. He was picked for the first 15 First Division matches the following year and scored 14 times, that figure including four strikes against both Bury (5-1) and Portsmouth (8-2). He then missed three matches before being recalled for a further

three in which he failed to score, and Tom Reid took over as centre-forward for most of the rest of the season.

The *Daily Post* reported on Liverpool's 5-1 win over Bury on 31 August 1927:

When Hodgson opened his account for the evening, Devlin had already scored FOUR goals in the game. One with his left, two with his right and a bullet header to round off a fine display. Could Devlin fill the boots of Forshaw? On this occasion his toes were bursting out the front of his boots. Here was a player who was ill-fitted at Huddersfield, so off he trotted to Anfield. And in just three games, he's posed a new question. How many goals will this player score when getting service like he got tonight? Devlin takes up his position, hangs around the backs, works at will and earnestly, but does not do a jot when it comes to tracking back or helping out those behind him. He is here to score goals, not to get in others way. And if anyone gets in his way, woe betide.

Send it in high, he'll head home.

Send it in low, he'll drive the ball home.

Send it in waist high, he'll volley the ball home.

And by far the most bizarre, send it in behind him and he'll overhead kick it into the goal.

DEVLIN, who could shoot on the run with either foot, scored well over 250 goals in his eventful career.

After stints in various local amateur leagues he joined the French exodus in their newly formed semi-professional national league. Devlin didn't stay too long at Marseille before departing to Switzerland. Willie's brother, Tom, played for Liverpool's reserves in the 1926/27 season and featured later for Switzerland's Zurich just like his sibling.

FACTFILE

BORN
Bellshill, Lanarkshire, Scotland, 30 July 1899
POSITION
Centre-forward
OTHER CLUBS
Vale of Clyde, Clyde (1921–23),
King's Park (loan, 1921–22),
Cowdenbeath (1923–26),
Huddersfield Town (1926–27),
Hearts (1927–28),
Macclesfield (1928–29),
Cowdenbeath (1929–30),
Mansfield Town (1930–31),
Burton Town (1931),
Shelbourne (1931–32),
Bangor City (1932–33),
Boston Town (1933–34),
Ashton National (1934–35),
Olympique Marseille,
Zurich
SIGNED FROM
Huddersfield Town,
6 May 1927
LFC DEBUT GAME/GOAL
7 May 1927 /
7 May 1927
CONTRACT EXPIRY
29 December 1927

Dewhurst, Gerard Powys

GERARD POWYS DEWHURST, who was on the books of the great amateur side, Corinthians, at the time, offered his services to Liverpool for one game against Crewe Alexandra on 24 March 1894.

The Corinthians initially only played friendly matches, although later they did compete for the Sheriff of London Charity Shield, as they were charity matches, and after World War One entered the FA Cup. The Corinthians toured the world and the Brazilian team Corinthians Paulista were so named in their honour. Dewhurst made a total of 32 appearances for the Corinthians and scored 18 goals.

DEWHURST was given permission to feature for Liverpool and it was reported that he didn't think it was beneath his dignity 'to dress along with professionals. Others we could mention might learn a lesson of honesty of purpose from the Cambridge amateur.' According to the *Liverpool Echo* the appearance of Dewhurst, was an 'event eagerly looked forward to'. Liverpool beat Crewe 2-0 and guaranteed the Second Division Championship with four games to go.

Dewhurst joined his family cotton trading firm, Geo. & R. Dewhurst Ltd, becoming chairman and managing director. He was also chairman of the Vulcan Insurance

Company of Manchester and later became chairman of Williams Deacon's Bank and a director of the Royal Bank of Scotland. Dewhurst greatly benefited from the cotton trade and lived in a house with 33 rooms. A 1911 census reveals he lived there with his wife, two sons, two nieces and ten servants! A passenger steam engine was even named after him in 1920, as he was a Great Central Railway director.

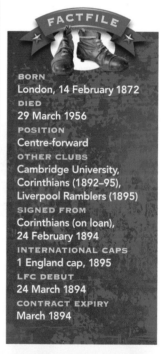

FACTFILE

BORN
London, 14 February 1872
DIED
29 March 1956
POSITION
Centre-forward
OTHER CLUBS
Cambridge University,
Corinthians (1892–95),
Liverpool Ramblers (1895)
SIGNED FROM
Corinthians (on loan),
24 February 1894
INTERNATIONAL CAPS
1 England cap, 1895
LFC DEBUT
24 March 1894
CONTRACT EXPIRY
March 1894

Season	League		FA Cup		Other		Total	
	App	Goals	App	Goals	App	Goals	App	Goals
1893/94	1	0	0	0	0	0	1	0
Total	**1**	**0**	**0**	**0**	**0**	**0**	**1**	**0**

Season	League		FA Cup		Total	
	App	Goals	App	Goals	App	Goals
1926/27	1	1	0	0	1	1
1927/28	18	14	0	0	18	14
Total	**19**	**15**	**0**	**0**	**19**	**15**

Gerard Powys Dewhurst
Great Central Railway class 11F 4-4-0 507 - LNER class D11 5507
at Guide Bridge - 8.3.1924

Diao heads in the fourth against Spartak Moscow

Diao, Salif

SALIF DIAO trained at Monaco's academy in Dakar, Senegal, and impressed enough to be moved to Monaco's first team in 1995. He spent three seasons at Monaco but struggled to win a place in the starting XI as the club enjoyed great success. He was transferred to Sedan in the 2000/01 season where he caught Gérard Houllier's attention.

Diao signed for Liverpool after the 2002 World Cup where he scored for Senegal and was sent off in the group stages against Denmark but was back in the starting line-up in the quarter-final defeat to Turkey. The boss of Senegal, Bruno Metsu, was a big fan of his midfield general. 'He is a monster,' Metsu said. 'I call him the extra-terrestrial one. Salif is a player who makes matches complete. There was no doubt he would be one of the Senegal players to move on to a big club.'

Diao was no monster success at Liverpool. He made 22 starts and 18 substitute appearances in the 2002/03 season, his highlight being a goal against Leeds on 19 October that sent Liverpool to the top of the table. He had also scored in a 5-0 drubbing of Spartak Moscow two weeks earlier, which was quite a novelty for the defensive midfielder who didn't score a single goal in 77 league games in France. Despite early promise Liverpool failed to capitalise on 2002's second-place finish and finished 16 points worse off than in the previous campaign.

> ### 'HE IS A MONSTER, I CALL HIM THE EXTRA-TERRESTRIAL ONE'
> **BRUNO METSU**

DIAO had nevertheless acclimatised better than Liverpool's other summer buys – his compatriot El Hadji Diouf and Frenchman Bruno Cheyrou – by showing he was a tough player who played with his heart on his sleeve. Although Houllier initially had faith in Diao's ability it was clear that Steven Gerrard did not: 'With Salif, I knew after a week of training that he wasn't going to be good enough,' Gerrard said in his autobiography. The Senegalese admitted his situation was bleak in February 2004. 'Houllier has changed his tactics and uses one ball-winner in midfield. It's fair to say this has been a blow to my chances.'

After Houllier left in the summer Rafa Benítez loaned Diao to Birmingham City and Portsmouth, but injury problems made it easy for respective sides not to sign him. Diao joined Stoke City on loan in October 2006 and eventually signed an 18-month deal with them in December 2007. Diao was by no means a regular at Stoke, but convinced his boss to sign him on again and again, also becoming an ambassador for the club to improve its links with African countries.

Diao passed his 35th birthday during the 2011/12 season, at the end of which he left Stoke, having turned down an offer to join their coaching staff. Diao runs "Sport 4 Charity" that brings together sporting personalities with the desire to raise money to help a broad range of charities throughout the world. His primary aim is to encourage children to attend school and be rewarded, by being involved in a sporting programme.

FACTFILE

BORN
Kedogou Tallie, Senegal, 10 February 1977
POSITION
Midfielder
OTHER CLUBS
Monaco (1996–2000), Epinal (loan, 1996), Sedan (2000–02), Birmingham City (loan, 2005), Portsmouth (loan, 2005–06), Stoke City (loan, 2006–07, permanent 2007–12)
SIGNED FROM
Sedan, £4.7million, 6 August 2002
INTERNATIONAL CAPS
39 Senegal caps (4 goals), 2000–09
LFC DEBUT GAME/GOAL
28 August 2002 / 2 October 2002
CONTRACT EXPIRY
25 January 2007

Season	League		FA Cup		League Cup		Europe		Other		Total	
	App	Goals	App	Goals	App	Goals	App	Goals	App	Goals	App	Goals
2002/03	13 (13)	1	1 (1)	0	3 (1)	0	5 (3)	1	0	0	22 (18)	2
2003/04	2 (1)	0	0	0	1	0	2 (1)	0	-	-	5 (2)	0
2004/05	4 (4)	0	0	0	3	1	1 (2)	0	-	-	8 (6)	1
Total	**19 (18)**	**1**	**1 (1)**	**0**	**7 (1)**	**1**	**8 (6)**	**1**	**0**	**0**	**35 (26)**	**3**

Dick,
Douglas

THE VERSATILE Douglas Dick
figured in 11 games as Liverpool
won their first Second Division
title, at the first time of asking.

He played seven consecutive
games from late October to early
December 1893 but was only
chosen to play on four occasions
in the second part of the season
when he had finally been played
in one position; on the right wing.

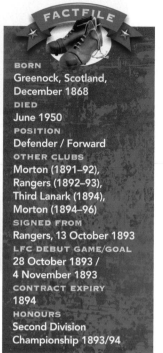

FACTFILE

BORN
Greenock, Scotland,
December 1868
DIED
June 1950
POSITION
Defender / Forward
OTHER CLUBS
Morton (1891–92),
Rangers (1892–93),
Third Lanark (1894),
Morton (1894–96)
SIGNED FROM
Rangers, 13 October 1893
LFC DEBUT GAME/GOAL
28 October 1893 /
4 November 1893
CONTRACT EXPIRY
1894
HONOURS
Second Division
Championship 1893/94

Season	League		FA Cup		Other		Total	
	App	Goals	App	Goals	App	Goals	App	Goals
1893/94	11	2	0	0	0	0	11	2
Total	11	2	0	0	0	0	11	2

Dicks,
Julian

IN SEPTEMBER 1993 Graeme
Souness wanted to add steel to
Liverpool's defence and signed
West Ham hard man Julian Dicks,
who had made 203 appearances
and scored 40 goals for the
London club from 1988–93 and
was voted 'Hammer of the Year'
twice by their supporters' club.
His left foot was lethal from
dead-ball situations.

The left-back turned out to be
the last player Souness brought
to Anfield as manager. Dicks
struggled for fitness and his poor
attitude and weight problems did
not impress new boss Roy Evans.
Dicks returned to the Hammers
after only one season, unhappy
with his stay at the Reds. He
recalled: 'The weight thing was
just an excuse. Evans barely talked
to me in the time I was there.
He just didn't want me. I have
nothing to prove to Liverpool or
anybody. I was training with the
kids and playing with the reserves.
Evans bombed me out altogether.'

Dicks' second spell at West Ham
saw him score 25 goals in 123
matches and clinch the 'Hammer
of the Year' award in 1996 and
1997. West Ham finished 10th in
the 1995/96 season, their highest
final position for a decade. But the
following season they struggled
against relegation, with Dicks
scoring twice in a crucial 4-3
home win over Tottenham
that helped save them from the
dreaded drop.

DICKS injured his knee in
March 1997; he did not play
at all in 1997/98 and in only
nine Premier League matches
in the 1998/99 season, at the
end of which he announced his
retirement at the relatively young
age of 30 after eight operations
on his left knee.

Dicks tried to come to terms
with life outside football, as he
told FourFourTwo. 'When I quit
West Ham I had enough money
in the bank to never work again.
Then, in 2001, I got divorced and
my wife took it all. We'd set up
professional kennels and were
looking after other people's dogs.
I had 13 of them at one time and
two young girls and there was
never any problem. When the
wife left she took the dogs too.'

Dicks tried golf, but had to quit
that sport as well because of his
dodgy knees. He made a brief
return to the game in 2001 when
he signed for non-league Canvey
Island but only made four

appearances for the Essex club. It was a short spell but he tried to make the most of it. 'I launched into a few, had a row with the ref, the linesmen and the crowd... I was in too much pain to carry on.'

'I DON'T ever regret joining Liverpool. I still scored the last ever Liverpool goal in front of the old standing Kop and that will be in the record books for ever,' Dicks told the press while on tour with the Liverpool 'Legends' team in Thailand in 2012. 'The Terminator', as Dicks was called, was even considered too violent on the field by Liverpool's legendary hard man, Tommy Smith. 'I would never criticise players for getting stuck in. But this lad seems to think if he gets within a yard of somebody he's got to either stamp on them, kick them or maim them for life.' Dicks was sent off no fewer than nine times in his career!

'I STILL SCORED THE LAST EVER LIVERPOOL GOAL IN FRONT OF THE OLD STANDING KOP AND THAT WILL BE IN THE RECORD BOOKS FOR EVER'

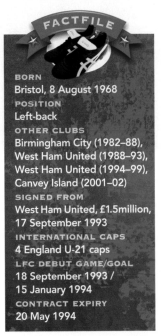

FACTFILE

BORN
Bristol, 8 August 1968
POSITION
Left-back
OTHER CLUBS
Birmingham City (1982–88),
West Ham United (1988–93),
West Ham United (1994–99),
Canvey Island (2001–02)
SIGNED FROM
West Ham United, £1.5million,
17 September 1993
INTERNATIONAL CAPS
4 England U-21 caps
LFC DEBUT GAME/GOAL
18 September 1993 /
15 January 1994
CONTRACT EXPIRY
20 May 1994

Season	League		FA Cup		League Cup		Total	
	App	Goals	App	Goals	App	Goals	App	Goals
1993/94	24	3	1	0	3	0	28	3
Total	**24**	**3**	**1**	**0**	**3**	**0**	**28**	**3**

Dickson,
Joe

LIVERPOOL-BORN Dickson signed professional forms for his home-town club in June 1952 when he was 18 years old but the England youth international had to wait four years for his first-team opportunity.

DICKSON made his debut on the right wing, but played as inside-right and left as well, scoring four goals in six games in the 1955/56 season. He only featured for the reserves in his last two seasons before he moved to Headington United, who changed their name to Oxford United in 1960. Dickson was top scorer at the Oxford club in the 1958/59 season with 27 goals.

FACTFILE

BORN
Liverpool,
31 January 1934
DIED
1992
POSITION
Forward
OTHER CLUBS
Headington United
(1958–60)
JOINED
November 1951;
signed professional
June 1952
LFC DEBUT GAME/GOAL
29 February 1956 /
3 March 1956
CONTRACT EXPIRY
April 1958

Season	League		FA Cup		Total	
	App	Goals	App	Goals	App	Goals
1955/56	6	4	0	0	6	4
Total	**6**	**4**	**0**	**0**	**6**	**4**

LIVERPOOL PLAYERS SEASON 1912–1913

Dines,
Joe

CENTRE-HALF amateur Joe Dines featured just once in the third match of the 1912/13 season away to Chelsea, which Liverpool won 2-1. *The Staffordshire Sentinel* reported on his move on 24 August 1912: 'The news that Joe Dines, the English amateur international footballer, has signed forms for Liverpool caused some dismay out Ilford way, as he had been one of the mainstays of the Ilford FC for some years. Dines will not altogether desert his old club.'

Dines played 27 games for England's amateur side and won a football gold medal at the 1912

Olympic Games. He played in all three of Great Britain's matches in Stockholm where the team beat Hungary 7-0 and Finland 4-0 before conquering Denmark 4-2 in the final on 4 July 1912.

He was described as 'the smiling footballer', a thoughtful young man, a commanding half-back and 'master of the art of dribbling'.

Dines was a second lieutenant in the King's Liverpool Regiment and was killed in Pas de Calais on 27 September 1918. He is buried in the Grand Ravine British Cemetery in Havrincourt, France.

FACTFILE

BORN
King's Lynn, 12 April 1886
DIED
27 September 1918
POSITION
Centre-half
OTHER CLUBS
King's Lynn,
Queens Park Rangers,
King's Lynn (second spell),
Ilford,
Millwall,
Walthamstow Avenue
SIGNED
May 1912
LFC DEBUT
9 September 1912
CONTRACT EXPIRY
1913

	League		FA Cup		Total	
Season	App	Goals	App	Goals	App	Goals
1912/13	1	0	0	0	1	0
Total	1	0	0	0	1	0

Diomede,
Bernard

BERNARD DIOMEDE was part of France's 1998 World Cup winning squad and although he did not feature from the quarter-finals onwards, the fact remains he is one of a select few who have been on Liverpool's books who can call themselves a world champion.

Diomede arrived at Anfield with decent credentials after eight years at Auxerre. He had made a valid contribution to Auxerre's league and cup double in the 1995/96 season, but after playing 175 league games and scoring 30 goals had fallen out with the management and wanted a fresh challenge. Diomede only made four starts for Liverpool in the treble-winning season of 2000/01 and the only thing he did of note was to 'score' with a wonderful

> THE FACT REMAINS HE IS ONE OF A SELECT FEW WHO HAVE BEEN ON LIVERPOOL'S BOOKS WHO CAN CALL THEMSELVES A WORLD CHAMPION

FACTFILE

BORN
Saint-Doulchard, France,
23 January 1974
POSITION
Left-winger
OTHER CLUBS
Auxerre (1992–2000),
Ajaccio (2003–04),
Creiteil (2004–05),
Clermont Foot (2005–06)
SIGNED FROM
Auxerre, £3million,
7 June 2000
INTERNATIONAL CAPS
8 France caps, 1998
LFC DEBUT
14 September 2000
CONTRACT EXPIRY
1 July 2003

overhead kick against Sunderland in his second game, but the ball was adjudged not to have crossed the line, which replays showed to be a wrong decision. He was loaned out to Ajaccio in his final season and they snapped him up when his contract at Anfield expired in 2003.

AFTER DIOMEDE'S contract at Ajaccio came to an end he was invited on a week's trial to Bryan Robson's West Bromwich Albion in January 2005: 'He is at the peak of his career and we are going to look at him for the week,' Robson said. 'While he was at Liverpool, I saw him play a couple of times but he never really had

a good chance there.' Robson, however, did not offer Diomede a contract and he later joined Ligue 2 Creiteil and then Clermont Foot in the Championnat National, the French third division. In January 2008 Diomede retired after being without a club for the past 18 months and established a football academy just south of Paris.

The left-winger was dismayed when the French 2003 Rugby World Cup squad named a live cockerel, its lucky mascot, after him. 'At first I thought it was a joke,' Diomede said not all appreciating this 'honour'. 'My first reaction was that before using someone's name they should ask.

There aren't many Diomede's in the world. I've got a sense of humour, but I would have liked to have been told about it. It's less funny when you're the one concerned.' Diomede, the cockerel that is, was flown home to France for medical tests early on in the World Cup as his crest was turning from red to black. Much like his namesake's career at Liverpool, he had faded after a promising appearance.

Season	League		FA Cup		League Cup		Europe		Other		Total	
	App	Goals	App	Goals	App	Goals	App	Goals	App	Goals	App	Goals
2000/01	1 (1)	0	0	0	0	0	2	0	-	-	3 (1)	0
2001/02	0	0	0	0	0	0	1	0	0	0	1	0
Total	1 (1)	0	0	0	0	0	3	0	0	0	4 (1)	0

Diouf,
El Hadji

EL HADJI DIOUF had a tough upbringing on the streets of Senegal before he emigrated to France and played solitary seasons for Sochaux and Rennes from 1998–2000. After 18 goals in 54 league games in two seasons for Lens and coming close to winning the title in his second season Liverpool's £10million offer prior to the 2002 World Cup was accepted.

Liverpool had finished second in the Premier League the previous season and Gérard Houllier saw Diouf as the player who could get them the elusive Premiership title, rather than Nicolas Anelka who had been on loan at Liverpool for five months. Diouf was the key player in Senegal's team that reached the quarter-finals of the World Cup in South Korea and Japan and was voted the Best African Player in 2002. His Anfield career seemed quite promising as he scored two goals on his home debut against Southampton on 24 August 2002 but the next goal didn't come until November.

More accustomed to the bench than being in the first XI, he got a regular run in the second half of the 2002/03 season but on the right wing instead of as an out-and-out striker. 'He has got incredible potential,' Phil Thompson enthused. 'What has warmed him to everyone is his work rate. It is astonishing.' Houllier stroked Diouf's ego as well and he liked what he was hearing. 'I feel that I have become an international star, but less so than if I were European. African players are always less highly regarded. Gérard Houllier says that I would be one of the best players in the world if I was French or Brazilian.'

Steven Gerrard is, however, not a big fan of the Senegalese star. 'As Gérard started playing him on the right, I knew he was a poor signing. I wasn't Diouf's number one fan. Being around Melwood and Anfield I knew which players were hungry, which players had Liverpool at heart. I felt he wasn't really arsed about putting his body on the line to get Liverpool back at the top,' Gerrard said in his autobiography.

Prior to a fifth round showdown against Celtic in the UEFA Cup, Thompson was very complimentary about Diouf. 'El Hadji is a lovely lad

'BY 14, I'D GOT INTO ALL THE TROUBLE THERE IS. EVERYONE KNEW ME TO BE A THUG, AND THEY WERE ALL SCARED OF ME'

and can play an important part in the rest of the season.' What then happened in that match was not the act of a pristine boy. Diouf disgraced Liverpool's shirt by spitting on a Celtic fan after full-time at Celtic Park. UEFA gave him a two-match ban and he was fined two weeks' wages by the club.

DIOUF was a regular in the first half of the 2003/04 season that cost Houllier his job and the Senegalese didn't get on the scoresheet at all that season, as Jamie Carragher emphasised later.

'He thinks he's a bit of a star, doesn't he?' Carragher said, clearly unimpressed by his former team-mate. 'But he has one of the worst strike rates of any forward in Liverpool history. He's the only number nine ever to go through a whole season without scoring, in fact he's probably the only number nine of any club to do that. He was always the last one to get picked in training.'

Diouf joined Bolton on loan in 2004/05 and quickly scored nine league goals for them, which led to a permanent deal in the summer of 2005. Diouf's summary of his Liverpool career maybe reveals what his main motivation is in football. 'I went to Liverpool, I don't regret playing there, I won matches, I played for a great club, I played with great players, and I also earned a lot of money.'

DIOUF spent four relatively successful seasons at the Reebok, scoring 23 goals in 136 games, before joining Sunderland in the summer of 2008. He scored no goals in 16 games for Roy Keane's men before rejoining Allardyce at Blackburn mid-season for £2million, where he scored a solitary goal in 15 appearances in his debut season. Without a single goal in 2010/11 in 21 matches for Rovers, Diouf moved to Rangers on loan in January 2011. His colourful past did not prevent Doncaster Rovers from offering him a lifeline in October 2011 and he made 23 appearances and scored six times as Rovers were relegated to League One. Diouf's career took another strange turn in August 2012 when he accepted a non-contract deal with Neil Warnock's Leeds. The move was very interesting because Warnock and Diouf had a public row in January 2011 after Diouf abused QPR's James Mackie as he lay on the ground with a broken leg. 'I was going to call him a sewer rat but that might be insulting to sewer rats,' Warnock said and added, 'I hope he goes abroad because I won't miss watching him.' Diouf responded: 'Nobody has heard of him outside of this country so who cares what he thinks about me.' Diouf was a regular under Warnock until the Yorkshireman was sacked on 1 April 2013.

Season	League		FA Cup		League Cup		Europe		Other		Total	
	App	Goals	App	Goals	App	Goals	App	Goals	App	Goals	App	Goals
2002/03	21 (8)	3	3	0	5	3	5 (4)	0	-	0	35(12)	6
2003/04	20 (6)	0	1	0	2	0	3 (1)	0	-	-	26 (7)	0
Total	**41 (14)**	**3**	**4**	**0**	**7**	**3**	**8 (5)**	**0**	**-**	**0**	**61 (19)**	**6**

Doig, Ned

NED DOIG started as a right-winger for amateur side St Helena in Arbroath. Recruited by Arbroath Football Club in 1884, he played as a keeper for about two seasons in the reserve side until he made his first official appearance for the Maroons in February 1886 when he was 19 years old.

Doig had high expectations and taught himself to punch a ball swinging from a crossbeam until he could make it swing twice over the bar, while others could do this only once. By running back and forth, lifting dumbbells placed at either goalpost, he built up his strength, agility and speed. In the early days of football only he and the giant William 'Fatty' Foulke could throw a ball over the halfway line.

In November 1889 Doig was lured south to play for Blackburn Rovers in the English League. However, he had a disagreement with the club after one game and returned home. As he had taken part in a professional game Doig was no longer selected to play for amateurs Arbroath. Sunderland were elected to the Football League in 1890 and Doig was recruited to replace their amateur goalkeeper. Unfortunately his first game was marred by the fact that the Football League deemed him ineligible as he had not been registered with the club for seven days, and Sunderland became the first club to be fined and have points deducted for this offence.

SUNDERLAND, with Doig an ever-present in goal, won the title four times with 'The Team of All the Talents'. Doig completed 14 years' service with Sunderland, at that time a record.

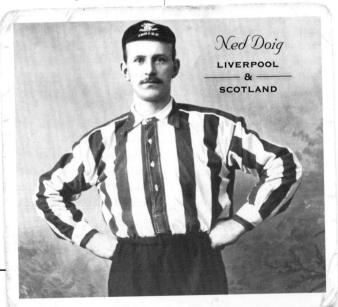

Ned Doig
LIVERPOOL
&
SCOTLAND

He played in 417 league games, missing only thirteen, 35 FA Cup games and a further 216 representative and friendly games.

Liverpool, who were relegated to the Second Division in 1904, signed Doig on 12 August 1904 for £150 after the clubs had spent two months arguing over his transfer fee. Doig's old Sunderland boss, Tom Watson, was now in charge at Liverpool and certainly knew that he was getting a quality keeper. Doig became the oldest player to make a debut for the club aged 37 years and 307 days on 1 September 1904. Liverpool promptly won the Second Division Championship in his first season. Ever-present Doig conceded only 25 goals in 34 games and kept 16 clean sheets.

Doig was highly praised for his performances by the club programme in November 1904. 'The defence of the Livers away from home has been wonderful. This speaks well for Doig whose advent into the team was a master stroke. The veteran has displayed all his old ability, and although he has seen so many years' service he is as agile and clever as ever. To have such a player between the posts must give those in front of him every confidence, and if he keeps fit and well there is no doubt but that at the end of the season it will not be his fault if the team does not go top.'

In 1905/06 Doig lost his place to future England international Sam Hardy after only eight games of the season when Liverpool won their second League Championship. Doig was suffering from rheumatism and he only played in nine more First Division games in the next two seasons. His age of 41 years, 165 days when he played his last game on 11 April

	League		FA Cup		Other		Total	
Season	App	Goals	App	Goals	App	Goals	App	Goals
1904/05	34	0	2	0	-	-	36	0
1905/06	8	0	0	0	0	0	8	0
1906/07	4	0	0	0	-	-	4	0
1907/08	5	0	0	0	-	-	5	0
Total	**51**	**0**	**2**	**0**	**0**	**0**	**53**	**0**

1908 is still a record for the club. Liverpool told Doig his Anfield career had ended by having a postcard delivered to his door which stated, 'Your services are no longer required'. His son Stanley, then aged six, remembered taking the card to his father who upon reading it flew into a rage, sweeping crockery from the table, and all the children scuttled up the stairs to keep out of the way.

Doig played a couple of years for St Helens Recreationals in the Lancashire League, clocking up a further 85 games, before retiring in the summer of 1910. In a career spanning 25 seasons, Ned Doig played in at least 1,055 games of football. He died on 7 November 1919 from Spanish flu at the age of 53.

Done, Cyril

CYRIL Done was a strong centre-forward, who was feared by opposing defences and built more like a boxer than a football player.

The *Daily Mirror* focused on his rise through the ranks at Liverpool prior to his debut at Anfield when Chelsea were the visitors on 2 September 1939:

FACTFILE

BORN
Liverpool, 21 October 1920
DIED
24 February 1993
POSITION
Centre-forward
OTHER CLUBS
Tranmere Rovers (1952–54),
Port Vale (1954–57),
Winsford United (1957–59),
Skelmersdale United
JOINED
January 1938
LFC DEBUT GAME/GOAL
12 October 1946 /
12 October 1946
CONTRACT EXPIRY
May 1952
HONOURS
League Championship 1946/47

Three games at centre-forward... then right into First Division football. This is the strange experience of Cyril Done, eighteen-year-old Liverpool player who today leads their forwards against Chelsea. Not until the opening practice game this season had Done had any experience of centre-forward play. He scored a hat-trick in that match against the first team defence. Done is referred to at Anfield as 'Gordon Hodgson the second'. The two are similar in style, exceptionally strong on the ball and possessing a terrific shot in either foot. Liverpool have every reason to be well pleased with young Done, for he did not cost them a penny piece. For years Liverpool have been trying to solve their centre-forward problem. They have made enough experiments, goodness only knows, but Done stands out as the best proposition of them all.

Done netted the only goal of the game against Chelsea, but the outbreak of World War Two meant that this was the final competitive fixture for several years. Done's goal was excluded from his career total as the three league games played in the 1939/40 season were expunged from Football League records. Done was highly prolific in wartime games with Liverpool and scored 147 goals in 137 games, which was no mean feat. When league football resumed Done made an important contribution by scoring 10 times from 17 appearances, including hat-tricks against Huddersfield and Grimsby, as the Reds marched on to the First Division Championship. Done hardly featured the following season

but 13 goals in his first eight reserve games of the 1948/49 season were hard to ignore and he continued his excellent form with the first team and reached double figures again with 13 goals from 28 appearances.

DONE was not as prolific for the last three seasons of his Liverpool career and he missed out completely on the FA Cup run which took the club to its first Wembley final in 1950. Done moved to Tranmere Rovers in the Third Division North in 1952 and scored 61 goals in 87 league games for them, and 34 goals in 52 games for Second Division Port Vale. Done came back to haunt Liverpool on 8 April 1955 when Port Vale beat the Reds 4-3 at Vale Park. Done scored all four for Vale!

	League		FA Cup		Total	
Season	App	Goals	App	Goals	App	Goals
1946/47	17	10	6	2	23	12
1947/48	4	0	2	0	6	0
1948/49	24	11	4	2	28	13
1949/50	16	5	0	0	16	5
1950/51	24	3	1	0	25	3
1951/52	10	3	2	1	12	4
Total	**95**	**32**	**15**	**5**	**110**	**37**

CYRIL DONE
CENTRE FORWARD
LIVERPOOL

NE

Done, Bob

FULL-BACK Bob Done came to Liverpool as an amateur on 18 February 1926 and signed professional forms two months later. He first appeared in Liverpool's side at Bolton on New Year's Day 1927 but that was one of only two occasions he

played for the first team during that season and only four more appearances followed the next year, deputising for either Tommy Lucas or Donald Mackinlay.

His breakthrough came in 1928/29, when he took over as left-back from Mackinlay, whose legendary career was winding down. He was

replaced by Tommy Lucas after a dozen or so matches in the following season and was in and out of the first team until February 1934. Done featured for the reserves for the last 15 months of his Liverpool career, except in one first-team game on 17 November 1934 when Liverpool defeated Leicester 5-1. Done was a very

hard kicker of the ball and scored 13 goals for Liverpool, six of them from the penalty spot.

Season	League		FA Cup		Total	
	App	Goals	App	Goals	App	Goals
1926/27	2	0	0	0	2	0
1927/28	4	0	0	0	4	0
1928/29	37	5	3	0	40	5
1929/30	13	0	0	0	13	0
1930/31	14	2	0	0	14	2
1931/32	26	3	0	1	26	3
1932/33	29	1	1	0	30	1
1933/34	21	2	4	0	25	2
1934/35	1	0	0	0	1	0
Total	**147**	**13**	**8**	**0**	**155**	**13**

FACTFILE

BORN
Runcorn, 27 April 1904
DIED
6 September 1982
POSITION
Right / Left-back
OTHER CLUBS
Runcorn (1922–26),
Reading (1935–37),
Chester City (1937–38),
Accrington Stanley (1938),
Bangor City (1938–39)
SIGNED FROM
Runcorn, 18 February 1926
LFC DEBUT GAME/GOAL
1 January 1927 /
8 September 1928
CONTRACT EXPIRY
15 May 1935

Doni, Alexander

DONIÉBER Alexander Marangon had been on the books of five different clubs in his homeland before moving to Europe in 2005. He had, however, only played competitive matches for three of those clubs so was relatively inexperienced when he joined Roma at the age of 25. In the 2005/06 season Doni played in 28 of Roma's 38 Serie A matches as the club from the capital finished runners-up to Inter Milan. He missed only seven league matches over the next two seasons as he established himself firmly as the club's first-choice goalkeeper.

Internationally, Doni was first capped in 2007 and later in the same year won the Copa America with Brazil, where he played a big part in the semi-finals, saving two spot kicks in the penalty shootout against Uruguay.

Reds' director of football Damien Comolli said of Doni's capture: 'I spoke to Lucas about Doni and he was very complimentary about him as a person and as a goalkeeper. When you play for Roma for years and years, the pressure at that club in that city is tremendous, so the fact he can handle that shows he can take anything.' Although Doni was on

the substitute's bench when Pepe Reina was sent off at Newcastle early in April 2012, Dalglish had already made his three changes at the time of the dismissal. With Reina's suspension being for three matches, the Brazilian was expected to play in league matches against Aston Villa and Blackburn Rovers as well as the Wembley FA Cup semi-final against Everton. However, he was himself dismissed at Blackburn and that ruled him out of the important cup tie the following weekend.

DONI had not been part of Liverpool's plans in 2012/13 due to 'personal issues', which he finally shed some light on in January 2013 when he had moved back to his first club, Botafogo de Ribeirão Preto (not to be confused with Rio's Botafogo), determined to play in the fourth division of the 2014 Paulista championship. 'I almost ended up on the other

side. I had a heart attack for about 25 seconds,' Doni revealed. 'I always had an arrhythmia and during some tests in Liverpool suffered a cardiac arrest.' Unfortunately, Doni had to retire from the game in August 2013 due to cardiovascular disease.

FACTFILE

BORN
Jundiaí, Brazil,
22 October 1979
POSITION
Goalkeeper
OTHER CLUBS
Botafogo de Ribeirão Preto
(1999–2001),
Corinthians (2001–03),
Santos (2003–04),
Cruzeiro (2004–05),
Juventude (2005),
AS Roma (2005–11),
Botafogo de Ribeirão Preto
(2013)
SIGNED FROM
AS Roma, free transfer,
15 July 2011
INTERNATIONAL CAPS
10 Brazil caps, 2007–10
LFC DEBUT
7 April 2012
CONTRACT EXPIRY
31 January 2013
HONOURS
League Cup 2012

Season	League		FA Cup		Other		Total	
	App	Goals	App	Goals	App	Goals	App	Goals
2011/12	4	0	0	0	0	0	4	0
Total	**4**	**0**	**0**	**0**	**0**	**0**	**4**	**0**

Donnelly,
Willie

ANYONE who got a penalty against Clyde in the 1890s could not be too optimistic as Willie Donnelly faced 21 spot kicks in their goal over two spells and saved 19!

In May 1896 he moved south to England and was Liverpool's second-choice goalkeeper during the 1896/97 season. Harry Storer played in the first 19 games from August up to and including Christmas Day 1896 when he got

WILLIE DONNELLY FACED 21 SPOT KICKS IN CLYDE'S GOAL OVER TWO SPELLS AND SAVED 19!

injured. Donnelly did so well in his absence that when Storer was fit in January he was loaned mid-season to Hibernian.

WILLIE DONNELLY
[LIVERPOOL]

DONNELLY took over on Boxing Day at Burnley and conceded 16 goals in eight matches until Storer returned from Scotland.

FACTFILE

BORN
Edinburgh, Scotland, 1872
DIED
December 1934
POSITION
Goalkeeper
OTHER CLUBS
Vale of Clyde,
Hibernian (1893–95),
Clyde (1895–96),
Clyde (1898–1900),
Celtic (1900–01),
Belfast Celtic (1901–03)
SIGNED FROM
Clyde, May 1896
LFC DEBUT
26 December 1896
CONTRACT EXPIRY
22 June 1898

Season	League		FA Cup		Total	
	App	Goals	App	Goals	App	Goals
1896/97	6	0	2	0	8	0
Total	**6**	**0**	**2**	**0**	**8**	**0**

Dossena,
Andrea

ANDREA DOSSENA claimed to be an English-style rugged defender who took no prisoners and was also a powerful attacker. He started his professional career at Verona, who were relegated to Serie B in his second season. Dossena joined Treviso in the 2005/06 season, but following the club's relegation from Serie A Udinese became his co-owners in 2006. Dossena featured at Udinese in 2006/07, joining the club permanently in 2007. His excellent form earned him a call-up to the Italian national team. When John Arne Riise departed for Rome, Rafa Benítez saw Dossena as his replacement.

Yet the Italian looked woefully out of sorts in his debut season with

Liverpool and confessed to struggling playing further upfield than he was used to in Italy. He did impress in attack when he came on as substitute against Manchester United and Real Madrid and added Liverpool's fourth on each occasion. Dossena was linked with moves to Juventus and Napoli in the summer of 2009

but stayed to fight for his place at Liverpool. However, after making only three starts for the first team in the 2009/10 season, it came as no surprise when he moved to Napoli on a four-year deal in the January transfer window.

DOSSENA nailed a regular spot in Napoli's team and played in both

Europa League matches against his previous employers in 2010/11, his errant back-pass at Anfield allowing Liverpool to equalise through Steven Gerrard. In 2011/12 Dossena appeared in the Champions League six times as Napoli reached the knockout stage of the competition, heading a tough group that included Bayern Munich and Manchester City before being eliminated by the eventual winners, Chelsea.

FACTFILE

BORN
Lodi, Italy, 11 September 1981
POSITION
Left-back
OTHER CLUBS
Verona (2001–05),
Treviso (2005–07),
Udinese (2006–07,
permanent 2007–08),
Napoli (2010–)
Palermo (loan, 2013)
SIGNED FROM
Udinese, £7million,
4 July 2008
INTERNATIONAL CAPS
10 Italy caps (9 at LFC),
2007–09
LFC DEBUT GAME/GOAL
13 August 2008 /
10 March 2009
CONTRACT EXPIRY
8 January 2010

Season	League		FA Cup		League Cup		Europe		Other		Total	
	App	Goals	App	Goals	App	Goals	App	Goals	App	Goals	App	Goals
2008/09	12 (4)	1	2	0	1	0	4 (3)	1	-	-	19 (7)	2
2009/10	1 (1)	0	0	0	1	0	1 (1)	0	-	-	3 (2)	0
Total	**13 (5)**	**1**	**2**	**0**	**2**	**0**	**5 (4)**	**1**	**0**	**0**	**22 (9)**	**2**

Downing,
Stewart

LIVERPOOL needed more than one attempt to secure Downing's services. There were strong rumours about a move to Anfield following Middlesbrough's relegation in 2009, but the then 24-year-old elected to join Aston Villa. In early July 2011 Liverpool made a bid believed to be £15million. This was immediately rejected by the Midlands club, but when Liverpool came back with a higher offer, Villa allowed Downing to leave.

Downing was a boyhood Middlesbrough fan and graduated from Boro's Academy. He flourished under the managership of Steve McLaren and played in three Premier League matches towards the end of the 2001/02 season. His opportunities were limited to begin with but he made 27 league appearances in 2003/04, seven of which came during a loan spell with Sunderland in the Championship. Downing became much more of a regular first-team player once his loan spell on Wearside was over, only once failing to make over 30 Premier League appearances in each of the next five seasons at Boro. The exception was the 2005/06 season, when a knee injury caused him to miss five months of football, although he had recovered in time to take his place in the UEFA Cup final of 2006, in which Middlesbrough were outclassed by Sevilla. McLaren left to take on the England job but his replacement, Gareth Southgate, had similar faith in Downing. When McLaren

was replaced following England's failure to qualify for the 2008 European Championships, Downing continued to be a regular member of the squads named by Fabio Capello.

Even though he was under contract to Aston Villa, Downing had become one of the footballers most expected to move on during the summer of 2011. The *Guardian's* Barney Ronay referred to him as 'the most undervalued of English footballers: intelligent, scuttlingly forceful and with some refined touches in his versatile left foot.' Kenny Dalglish was prepared to return early from Liverpool's tour of the Far East with the purpose of finalising the Downing deal.

Yet Downing's first season as a Liverpool player can hardly be hailed as a success as he delivered no goals and no assists from the 36 Premier League matches he appeared in. Admittedly, he delivered a few brilliant goalscoring opportunities that were pitifully wasted, usually by Andy Carroll. Given an opportunity to open his league account for the club in the last home match, he placed a penalty kick against the woodwork, something he and his team-mates had bad luck with during the whole season. Downing had better luck in the FA Cup, netting against Oldham in the third round and then scoring the winner in the sixth round against Stoke. But on the whole it was a season the winger will look back on with only regret, even though he picked up his second League Cup winners' medal.

Brendan Rodgers' comment on young winger Raheem Sterling in August 2012 seemed to sum up perfectly Downing's performance for the club up to that point: 'Young players will run through a barbed-wire fence for you. Older players will look for the hole in the fence or just turn back and not even go through it.' Rodgers was looking to move the experienced England international on, but the boss revealed that he'd had heart-to-heart discussions with Downing that clearly paid off as he had a much improved second season in which he performed to the best of his ability and finally got some assists to his name and a league goal, which was probably quite a relief in the unforgiving Anfield spotlight. Downing was once again linked with a move away from Anfield in the summer of 2013 and in the same week as the new season started he moved to West Ham United to rekindle his partnership with Andy Carroll who had made a permanent move to Upton Park two months earlier. Downing was reportedly sold for £6million so Liverpool took a massive hit on the player bought from Aston Villa two years previously.

FACTFILE

BORN
Middlesbrough, 22 July 1984
POSITION
Right / Left-winger / Left-back
OTHER CLUBS
Middlesbrough (2000–09),
Sunderland (loan, 2003),
Aston Villa (2009–11),
West Ham United (2013-)
SIGNED FROM
Aston Villa, £18.5million,
15 July 2011
INTERNATIONAL CAPS
34 England caps (7 at LFC),
2005–12
LFC DEBUT GAME/GOAL
13 August 2011 /
6 January 2012
CONTRACT EXPIRY
13 August 2013
HONOURS
League Cup 2012

Season	League		FA Cup		League Cup		Europe		Total	
	App	Goals	App	Goals	App	Goals	App	Goals	App	Goals
2011/12	28 (8)	0	5 (1)	2	3 (1)	0	-	-	36 (10)	2
2012/13	25 (4)	3	1 (1)	0	2	0	11 (1)	2	39 (6)	5
Total	53 (12)	3	6 (2)	2	5 (1)	0	11 (1)	2	75 (16)	7

Draws

Biggest draws

	Opponent	Competition	Date	
5-5	Sunderland	1st Division	19 January	1907
4-4	Sheffield United	FA Cup	23 March	1899
4-4	Arsenal	1st Division	27 October	1928
4-4	Portsmouth	1st Division	11 March	1939
4-4	Manchester United	1st Division	22 August	1953
4-4	Luton Town	2nd Division	2 April	1955
4-4	Aston Villa	2nd Division	30 March	1960
4-4	Everton	FA Cup	20 February	1991
4-4	Chesterfield	League Cup	22 September	1992
4-4	Chelsea	Champions League	14 April	2009
4-4	Arsenal	Premier League	21 April	2009

Most draws in a league season

		League	Games	Position
1951/52	19	1st Division	42	11
1970/71	17	1st Division	42	5
1980/81	17	1st Division	42	5
1925/26	16	1st Division	42	7
1991/92	16	1st Division	42	6
1920/21	15	1st Division	42	4

Fewest draws in a league season

		League	Games	Position
1895/96	2	2nd Division	30	1
1902/03	4	1st Division	34	5
1904/05	4	2nd Division	34	1

Most draws at Anfield in a league season

		League	Games	Position
1951/52	11	1st Division	21	11
1970/71	10	1st Division	21	5
1948/49	10	1st Division	21	12
2011/12	9	Premier League	19	8

Fewest draws at Anfield in a league season

		League	Games	Position
1963/64	0	1st Division	21	1
1893/94	0	2nd Division	14	1
1956/57	1	2nd Division	21	3
1895/96	1	2nd Division	15	1

Most away draws in a league season

		League	Games	Position
1980/81	12	1st Division	21	5
1991/92	11	1st Division	21	6
1973/74	11	1st Division	21	2
1956/57	10	2nd Division	21	3

Fewest away draws in a league season

		League	Games	Position
2011/12	1	Premier League	19	8
1908/09	1	1st Division	19	16
1904/05	1	2nd Division	17	1
1902/03	1	1st Division	17	5
1899/00	1	1st Division	17	10
1895/96	1	2nd Division	15	1

Drummond, John

SHEFFIELD UNITED'S decision to invest in John Drummond in 1891 paid dividends when his goal in the Test match at the end of the 1892/93 season against Accrington saw the Blades promoted to the First Division for the first time in their history. The pitch was in a terrible state and Drummond was practically the only player to be able to stay on his feet, which he attributed to painting the soles of his boots with black lead to prevent the mud from sticking.

Drummond made 89 appearances for the Yorkshire club and scored 24 goals before joining Liverpool in the summer of 1894. He played in 14 of 30 league matches in Liverpool's first ever season in the First Division, battling with fellow Scot Hugh McQueen for a place on the left wing. The team struggled to come to terms with the top flight and was immediately relegated.

DRUMMOND'S only goal for the club came in the FA Cup, when he got the second in a 4-0 first round replay win over Barnsley St Peter's. He joined Barnsley in the Midland League at the end of his career. Drummond had been an apprentice shipyard carpenter as a youth and returned to work in the Dumbarton shipyards after his retirement from football.

FACTFILE

BORN
Edinburgh, Scotland,
15 March 1869
POSITION
Left-winger
OTHER CLUBS
Partick Thistle (1887–90),
Preston North End (1890–91),
Sheffield United (1891–94),
Barnsley St Peter's
SIGNED FROM
Sheffield United, 1894
LFC DEBUT GAME/GOAL
1 September 1894 /
11 February 1895
CONTRACT EXPIRY
1895

Season	League App	Goals	FA Cup App	Goals	Other App	Goals	Total App	Goals
1894/95	14	0	3	1	1	0	18	1
Total	14	0	3	1	1	0	18	1

Dudek,
Jerzy

'THE BIG POLE IN OUR GOAL' will forever be remembered for playing a vital part in Liverpool's history. Jerzy Dudek played regularly for Polish third-division Concordia Knurów since he was 18 years old, gaining valuable experience from a young age and making a total of 119 first-team appearances in four years. He moved to Sokól Tychy in the 1995/96 season and played 15 games in Poland's top flight. Feyenoord saw his great potential and he moved to the Netherlands in 1996. When Ed De Goey was sold to Chelsea the No. 1 shirt was up for grabs and in the championship 1998/99 season Dudek was voted the best keeper in the Eredivisie. His coach Leo Beenhakker described Dudek as 'the best goalkeeper I've seen in 30 years'. In his last campaign in Holland Dudek was awarded the 'Golden Shoe' as the best player of the season.

Dudek almost joined Arsenal instead of Liverpool but the move thankfully fell through, as he was simply outstanding in his first season when the Reds finished second in the league. 'He has been brilliant, absolutely sensational. People talk about him being the best since Clemence and I wouldn't disagree,' former boss Roy Evans said admiringly. 'I was surprised when they sold Westerveld, but Dudek has been a great signing.'

YET DUDEK struggled in his second campaign, having a particular horror show against Manchester United at Anfield on 1 December 2002, gift-wrapping a goal for Diego Forlan. Houllier revealed Dudek broke down in tears after the game and his team-mate Jamie Carragher was very sympathetic. 'We are all disappointed for Jerzy. He was distraught in the dressing room afterwards and apologised to us all,' Carra said. 'I think it's hurting the lads even more because he's such a nice fella as well as being a top-class goalkeeper.' Following this debacle Dudek lost his place to Chris Kirkland, who had been bought by Liverpool on the same day as Dudek, and had been waiting patiently for a chance.

One of the many injuries that Kirkland had at Liverpool allowed Dudek back into the side in late January 2003. Dudek played 38 games to Kirkland's 12 in 2003/04, Houllier's final season. The goalkeepers fought hard for a starting place, but their rivalry was friendly, although Kirkland had one complaint. 'He's the loudest snorer you'll ever hear. It's unbelievable. We were away at Southampton and I think someone sleeping in Newcastle complained about the noise. What you see is what you get with Jerzy though. He's a great man and a brilliant professional.'

Dudek lost his place to Kirkland from October to December 2004 but as Liverpool proceeded to the elimination stages of the Champions League the Pole only missed one game. Whatever had transpired in Dudek's career at Liverpool was taken to another level in Istanbul, where he gained legendary status. His wobbly legs impression of Bruce Grobbelaar in the shootout will be remembered as long as his double save from Shevchenko two minutes from the end of extra time from just a few yards that seemed completely incomprehensible.

'My brother phoned me in the morning and said: "Have you seen it on TV again?"' Dudek recalled afterwards. 'I said no, I hadn't, and he said, "You need to see it; the rebound, the second Shevchenko shot was the Hand of God because from nowhere came your hand to save the goal." I said I didn't know how I did it.' Dudek received valuable inspiration from Carragher before the penalty shootout. 'Carra came up to me like he was crazy – as always! He said: "Jerzy, Jerzy – remember Bruce."' Dudek's

Season	League		FA Cup		League Cup		Europe		Other		Total	
	App	Goals	App	Goals	App	Goals	App	Goals	App	Goals	App	Goals
2001/02	35	0	2	0	0	0	12	0	0	0	49	0
2002/03	30	0	1 (1)	0	2	0	11	0	1	0	45 (1)	0
2003/04	30	0	3	0	1	0	4	0	-	-	38	0
2004/05	24	0	1	0	6	0	10	0	-	-	41	0
2005/06	5 (1)	0	0	0	0	0	0	0	0	0	5 (1)	0
2006/07	2	0	1	0	2	0	1	0	0	0	6	0
Total	**126 (1)**	**0**	**8 (1)**	**0**	**11**	**0**	**38**	**0**	**1**	**0**	**184 (2)**	**0**

penalty save from Shevchenko clinched the European trophy for the fifth time in the club's history.

The monumental Istanbul heroics seemed in the distant past as Dudek went from hero to zero in a couple of months; Rafa Benítez brought in Pepe Reina in the summer and once the 2005/06 season started the Pole was effectively his reserve. Disappointed with the lack of first-team opportunities at Liverpool, Dudek rather curiously chose Real Madrid as his next destination, where he had even less chance to become first choice with Spain's number one, Iker Casillas, in goal rather than Spain's number two, Pepe Reina. 'From being happy to play here and press Pepe, I knew I had to go somewhere to play every week,' Dudek said.

Yet after moving to Spain in 2007 he appeared just twice for Madrid's first team in La Liga and only a dozen times in total in four years! He made his final appearance for Los Merengues on 21 May 2011, in an 8-1 home win over Almería, and was substituted in the 77th minute to a guard of honour from his Real Madrid team-mates which showed his popularity within the squad.

FACTFILE

BORN
Rybnik, Poland,
23 March 1973
POSITION
Goalkeeper
OTHER CLUBS
Concordia Knurów (1985–95),
Sokół Tychy (1995–96),
Feyenoord (1996–2001),
Real Madrid (2007–11)
SIGNED FROM
Feyenoord, £4.85million,
31 August 2001
INTERNATIONAL CAPS
59 Poland caps, 1998–2009
LFC DEBUT
8 September 2001
CONTRACT EXPIRY
1 July 2007
HONOURS
League Cup 2003;
Champions League 2005;
FA Cup 2006

Dundee, Sean

SEAN DUNDEE has become a running joke among Liverpool supporters, considered by many as the worst striker in recent times to wear the red shirt. Whether he fully deserves that title or not, he arrived with a good goalscoring reputation from Germany and was so highly rated that the Germans put pressure on him to become a citizen so he could play for their national team. Dundee startled the South African coach by pulling out of a friendly against Germany in December 1995 literally minutes before kick-off. A month later South Africa lifted the African Cup of Nations and Dundee had missed his chance. Once he did become a German citizen, however, he never played for Germany, pulling out with injury after his only call-up. Dundee's last season in the Bundesliga before joining Roy Evans' troops was disappointing as he struggled in front of goal and Karlsruher were relegated. In two seasons prior to that he scored a respectable tally of 33 goals in 61 Bundesliga games.

Dundee's form at Liverpool was shocking to many and he was already being linked with a move to Auxerre in September, only three months after his arrival. He injured his knee in November and while he was recovering Gérard Houllier told reporters he was waiting for Dundee to make a quick exit. 'He knows there is no future for him at this club,' he said. 'Strasbourg have shown great interest in him, and I've told him it would be a great boost for his career to be playing somewhere, because he's behind Robbie Fowler, Michael Owen and Karl-Heinz Riedle.'

Dundee was upset when he left Liverpool after only 13 months. 'It seems that from day one Houllier never liked me. When I joined the club I thought it was a dream move and I was determined to be a success,' Dundee said. 'But even when there were only two strikers fit – myself and Karl-Heinz Riedle – I never got a look-in. I tried to speak to the manager but I'm not sure he wanted to speak to me. I had a lot of fun, the players are a great bunch and I love the city. But the final straw came when I was told to report back for pre-season training three days later than everyone else. Then it turned out all the other players were leaving on a club trip. Myself and Paul Ince were left to train alone.' Five substitute appearances for the first team was all Dundee could pride himself on

in 14 months at Anfield, but give him credit... he did score three goals in 12 games for the reserves!

FACTFILE

BORN
Durban, South Africa,
7 December 1972
POSITION
Centre-forward
OTHER CLUBS
Bayview (1990),
D'Alberton Callies (1991–92),
Stuttgarter Kickers (1992–93),
Ditzingen (1993–95),
Karlsruher (1995–98),
Stuttgart (1999–2003),
Austria Wien (2003–04),
Karlsruher (2004–06),
Kickers Offenbach (2006–08),
Stuttgarter Kickers
(loan, 2007),
AmaZulu (2008–09)
SIGNED FROM
Karlsruher, £1.8million,
5 June 1998
LFC DEBUT
27 October 1998
CONTRACT EXPIRY
30 July 1999

Season	League		FA Cup		League Cup		Europe		Other		Total	
	App	Goals	App	Goals	App	Goals	App	Goals	App	Goals	App	Goals
1998/99	0 (3)	0	0	0	0 (1)	0	0 (1)	0	-	-	0 (5)	0
Total	0 (3)	0	0	0	0 (1)	0	0 (1)	0	0	0	0 (5)	0

Dunlop, Billy

SCOTTISH-BORN left-back Billy Dunlop first appeared in Liverpool's first team towards the end of the 1894/95 season and stayed at the club for no less than 15 years! Dunlop was a regular the following season but was out of action with an ankle injury from late October to the end of February; despite his absence Liverpool were promoted back to the First Division.

TOM WILKIE and Archie Goldie, the latter incidentally born in the same suburb of Kilmarnock as Dunlop, proved to be a sound full-back pair, but Dunlop finally reclaimed his first-team place from Wilkie for the last seven matches of the 1896/97 season and became a regular in the side for the next decade and a prominent member of the squad that won Liverpool's first ever League Championship in 1901, a feat repeated five years later. Before Dunlop was appointed assistant trainer at Sunderland in July 1911 he lived on Walton Breck Road just outside Anfield working as a tobacconist. 'Billy Dunlop had his lolly shop in Walton Breck Road and used to pass out paper shields with 'Play up Liverpool' to us kids. What a kick we got!' Bill Smith remembered in the *Kop* in March 1967. When future legend Donald Mackinlay was starting

> 'ON HIS DAY, THERE IS NO MORE BRILLIANT PLAYER THAN THIS SAME DUNLOP. A BETTER SERVANT NO CLUB EVER POSSESSED'
>
> **LIVERPOOL MATCH PROGRAMME**

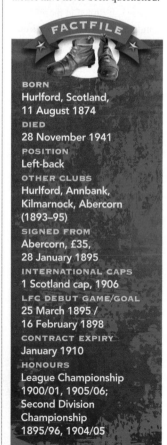

Dunlop second from left in front row when the 1906 champions regrouped in 1922

his career at Liverpool in 1910 he stayed at Dunlop's home as well as his team-mate and fellow defender John McConnell, getting used to their new surroundings after moving from Scotland.

According to Liverpool's match programme from 17 September 1904: 'Dunlop plays a characteristic full-back game and the familiar cry on the Anfield ground of "Boot it, Dunlop" is fairly suggestive of his method of defence. There can be no two opinions of his ability to kick the ball from almost any position. Always keen and watchful on the field, he betrays his over-anxiety to repel the invader by his terrific lunges, and on his day, there is no more brilliant player than this same Dunlop. A better servant no club ever possessed, and though we may occasionally differ from him as to the methods he employs on the field, on one point we must all agree, that for downright single-mindedness of purpose Dunlop's tactics have never been questioned.'

Season	League App	League Goals	FA Cup App	FA Cup Goals	Other App	Other Goals	Total App	Total Goals
1894/95	4	0	0	0	1	0	5	0
1895/96	13	0	0	0	0	0	13	0
1896/97	5	0	2	0	-	-	7	0
1897/98	20	0	5	1	-	-	25	1
1898/99	33	0	6	0	-	-	39	0
1899/1900	34	0	4	0	-	-	38	0
1900/01	33	0	2	0	-	-	35	0
1901/02	33	0	3	0	-	-	36	0
1902/03	28	0	1	0	-	-	29	0
1903/04	21	1	1	0	-	-	22	1
1904/05	32	1	2	0	-	-	34	1
1905/06	31	0	5	0	1	0	37	0
1906/07	23	0	4	0	-	-	27	0
1907/08	2	0	0	0	-	-	2	0
1908/09	13	0	1	0	-	-	14	0
Total	**325**	**2**	**36**	**1**	**2**	**0**	**363**	**3**

FACTFILE

BORN
Hurlford, Scotland,
11 August 1874
DIED
28 November 1941
POSITION
Left-back
OTHER CLUBS
Hurlford, Annbank,
Kilmarnock, Abercorn
(1893–95)
SIGNED FROM
Abercorn, £35,
28 January 1895
INTERNATIONAL CAPS
1 Scotland cap, 1906
LFC DEBUT GAME/GOAL
25 March 1895 /
16 February 1898
CONTRACT EXPIRY
January 1910
HONOURS
League Championship
1900/01, 1905/06;
Second Division
Championship
1895/96, 1904/05

Durnin, John

JOHN DURNIN scored on a regular basis for the reserves, 62 goals in 90 Central League matches from 1986–89, but wasn't considered good enough for the first team. Ian Rush, John Aldridge, Paul Walsh and Peter Beardsley stood firmly in his way.

DURNIN made his first-team debut against Fulham in the second round of the League Cup on 7 October 1986 but had to wait almost two years for his second appearance against Arsenal in the Football League Centenary semi-final. He came on as a substitute at West Ham two months later, which turned out to be his final appearance for the Reds' first team. After he left Liverpool he played for a variety of lower-league clubs and the majority of his career was spent at Oxford and Portsmouth, where he scored 76 goals in 342 league matches from 1989–99. Durnin missed the first month of the 1999/2000 campaign with Pompey after dislocating his elbow when he drove a golf buggy into a fairway hollow! He is a regular member of the Liverpool Legends' team.

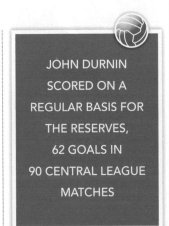

JOHN DURNIN SCORED ON A REGULAR BASIS FOR THE RESERVES, 62 GOALS IN 90 CENTRAL LEAGUE MATCHES

FACTFILE

BORN
Bootle, Liverpool, 18 August 1965
POSITION
Centre-forward
OTHER CLUBS
Waterloo Dock (1981–83), West Bromwich Albion (loan, 1988), Oxford United (1989–93), Portsmouth (1993–99), Blackpool (loan, 1999), Carlisle United (1999–2000), Kidderminster Harriers (2000–01), Rhyl (2001), Port Vale (2001–03), Accrington Stanley (2003–04)
SIGNED FROM
Waterloo Dock £500, 1983; signed professional 29 March 1986
LFC DEBUT GAME/GOAL
7 October 1986
CONTRACT EXPIRY
10 February 1989

DVD

History

Liverpool FC,
Anfield's European Nights (2008);
Liverpool FC,
100 Greatest Moments of The Kop (2006);
Liverpool FC,
501 Goals (2003);
Liverpool,
Team of the Seventies (2011);
Liverpool FC,
3 Great Managers (2007);
Liverpool FC,
Official Updated History (2007);
Steven Gerrard,
My Story (2005).

Great Games

Classic Liverpool Matches,
A Shot Through History (2011);
FA Cup Final: 2006,
The Gerrard Final;
Liverpool FC,
FA Cup Finals (2004);
Liverpool FC,
Champions League Final & The Road To Istanbul (2005);
Liverpool Football Club,
Champions of Europe (2004).

Season Reviews

Liverpool FC,
The Treble - League and Cup Season Review 2000/2001;
Liverpool FC,
End of Season Review 2004/2005;
Liverpool,
Season Review 2007/2008;
Liverpool FC,
End of Season Review 2008/2009.

Classics

15 Minutes That Shook the World, (2009);
Reds & Blues,
The Ballad of Dixie & Kenny (Red edition) (2010);
Scully (2006).

Season	League		FA Cup		League Cup		Other		Total	
	App	Goals	App	Goals	App	Goals	App	Goals	App	Goals
1986/87	0	0	0	0	1	0	0	0	1	0
1988/89	0	0	0	0	0 (1)	0	1	0	1 (1)	0
Total	**0**	**0**	**0**	**0**	**1 (1)**	**0**	**1**	**0**	**2 (1)**	**0**

Easdale,
John

FACTFILE

BORN
Dumbarton, Scotland,
16 January 1919

POSITION
Centre-half

OTHER CLUBS
Brighton & Hove Albion
(wartime guest),
Stockport County (1948–49)

JOINED
Free transfer, February 1937

LFC DEBUT
25 December 1946

CONTRACT EXPIRY
1948

A CENTRE-HALF, who had to wait nine years for his Liverpool debut because of World War Two, Easdale made two league appearances for the club during the 1946/47 League Championship winning season, deputising for regular Laurie Hughes.

Season	League		FA Cup		Total	
	App	Goals	App	Goals	App	Goals
1946/47	2	0	0	0	2	0
Total	**2**	**0**	**0**	**0**	**2**	**0**

Billy McConnell, Liverpool's chairman, with the 1947 league title

Eastham,
Harry

HARRY EASTHAM

HARRY'S FATHER played professionally for Blackpool and he was also related to the better known George, who had a marvellous career with Newcastle, Arsenal and Stoke.

Harry shared the inside-right position with Phil Taylor in the 1936/37 season. He played in the first 12 games of the following campaign before losing his regular spot. Harman van den Berg's cartilage injury gave Eastham a run of six games from January to February 1939 on the left wing. He only featured in three other games during that season as Taylor kept him firmly out of the side. After the long absence of league football due to the war, Eastham returned to Anfield and qualified for a League Championship medal by appearing in 19 of the 42 games that took Liverpool to their fifth First Division title in 1947. He did not play for the first XI at all in 1947/48 and was eventually transferred to Tranmere Rovers in May 1948, making 154 league appearances for them before finishing his league career with Accrington Stanley.

FACTFILE

BORN
Blackpool, 30 June 1917

DIED
1998

POSITION
Forward

OTHER CLUBS
Blackpool (1934–36);
New Brighton,
Southport,
Brighton & Hove Albion,
Bolton Wanderers,
Leeds United,
Newcastle United,
Blackpool (wartime guest),
Tranmere Rovers (1948–53),
Accrington Stanley (1953–55),
Netherfield (1955–56),
Rolls Royce (1956–58)

SIGNED FROM
Blackpool, 3 February 1936

LFC DEBUT GAME/GOAL
31 October 1936 /
21 November 1936

CONTRACT EXPIRY
May 1948

HONOURS
League Championship
1946/47

Season	League		FA Cup		Total	
	App	Goals	App	Goals	App	Goals
1936/37	21	2	1	0	22	2
1937/38	15	0	1	0	16	0
1938/39	7	1	2	1	9	2
1946/47	19	0	2	0	21	0
Total	**62**	**3**	**6**	**1**	**68**	**4**

Eccleston, Nathan

THE England youth international was promoted to Melwood full-time in the summer of 2009.

The striker only made one start while at Liverpool and eight substitute appearances while on relatively unsuccessful loan spells at various clubs. Eccleston moved to Blackpool on the final day of the summer 2012 transfer window. Eccleston was loaned by Blackpool to Tranmere Rovers in October 2012 but played in just one match for Rovers before being injured in training and returning to his parent club.

Season	League		FA Cup		League Cup		Europe		Total	
	App	Goals	App	Goals	App	Goals	App	Goals	App	Goals
2009/10	0 (1)	0	0	0	0 (1)	0	0	0	0 (2)	0
2010/11	0 (1)	0	0	0	0 (1)	0	1 (4)	0	1 (6)	0
Total	**0 (2)**	**0**	**0**	**0**	**0 (2)**	**0**	**1 (4)**	**0**	**1 (8)**	**0**

Edmed, Dick

DICK EDMED was a stylish right-winger who arrived at Anfield in the summer of 1926, hardly missing his old day job at the Chatham Dockyards where he had worked while at Gillingham.

HE WENT STRAIGHT into the first team, missing only four of the 42 league games in his debut season. He was one of two ever-presents (the other being Tom Bromilow) the following season and netted 14 goals in the league, a high total for a winger, although he had also taken on the role of the club's penalty-taker by this time, scoring three times from the spot. Fair-haired Edmed was rather short and light in weight, but 'speedy, clever and direct'. He only missed three league games in 1928/29 and added a further 16 goals, a very impressive total considering that Bob Done was now taking the penalties. 'Will Dick Edmed, of Liverpool, play for England in international

> **'IT IS DOUBTFUL IF THERE IS A MORE EFFECTIVE RIGHT WINGER IN THE GAME TO-DAY ANYWHERE'**
>
> *DERBY DAILY TELEGRAPH*

games this season? It is doubtful if there is a more effective right winger in the game to-day anywhere,' claimed the *Derby Daily Telegraph* in September 1929. Unfortunately, Edmed's fine form was not rewarded with an England cap. Although Edmed figured in two-thirds of the club's league fixtures in 1929/30, a cartilage injury curtailed his availability for the team and he was no longer sure of his place by the end of that season. He made just 12 appearances in his final season before being replaced by Harold Barton.

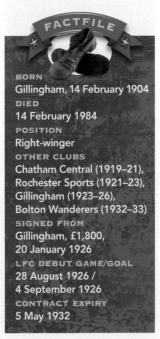
Season	League		FA Cup		Total	
	App	Goals	App	Goals	App	Goals
1926/27	38	6	4	1	42	7
1927/28	42	14	2	1	44	15
1928/29	39	16	3	0	42	16
1929/30	29	4	1	0	30	4
1930/31	12	4	0	0	12	4
Total	**160**	**44**	**10**	**2**	**170**	**46**

El Zhar, Nabil

NABIL EL ZHAR was voted the second-best player of the 2005 Youth World Championships and made his reputation as an attacking midfielder who liked to play just behind the forwards.

His performances for Liverpool were nevertheless disappointing. After making just three first-team appearances in both 2006/07 and 2007/08, El Zhar was called on 19 times in 2008/09, although only three of those appearances were from the start of a match.

Benítez's confidence that the young Moroccan still had a part to play at Anfield was shown in 2009 when El Zhar signed a two-year extension to his contract that tied him to the club until 2012. However, 2009/10 did not turn out to be a big breakthrough season for the young prodigy either. He started just one match, the final Premier League fixture at Hull, and made six appearances as a substitute.

He was loaned to PAOK in Greece on the last day of the transfer window in January 2010 and released from his Liverpool contract in August 2011. He signed a two-year contract with Spanish club Levante, where he became more of a regular.

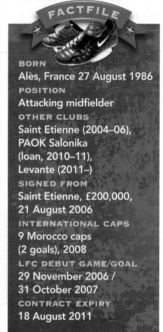

FACTFILE

BORN
Alès, France 27 August 1986
POSITION
Attacking midfielder
OTHER CLUBS
Saint Etienne (2004–06),
PAOK Salonika
(loan, 2010–11),
Levante (2011–)
SIGNED FROM
Saint Etienne, £200,000,
21 August 2006
INTERNATIONAL CAPS
9 Morocco caps
(2 goals), 2008
LFC DEBUT GAME/GOAL
29 November 2006 /
31 October 2007
CONTRACT EXPIRY
18 August 2011

Season	League		FA Cup		League Cup		Europe		Other		Total	
	App	Goals	App	Goals	App	Goals	App	Goals	App	Goals	App	Goals
2006/07	0 (3)	0	0	0	0	0	0	0	0	0	0 (3)	0
2007/08	0	0	0 (1)	0	1 (1)	1	0	0	-	-	1 (2)	1
2008/09	1 (14)	0	0	0	2	0	0 (2)	0	-	-	3 (16)	0
2009/10	1 (2)	0	0	0	0	0	0 (4)	0	-	-	1 (6)	0
Total	**2 (19)**	**0**	**0 (1)**	**0**	**3 (1)**	**1**	**0 (6)**	**0**	**0**	**0**	**5 (27)**	**1**

FACTFILE

BORN
Aghadowey, Coleraine,
Northern Ireland,
18 August 1908
DIED
12 April 1967
POSITION
Centre-forward
OTHER CLUBS
Port Glasgow Athletic Juniors,
Old Kilpatrick,
Yoker Athletic (1929–31),
Rangers (1931–33),
Queen of the South
(1935–36),
Hartlepools United (1936–38)
SIGNED FROM
Rangers, £8,000,
24 July 1933
INTERNATIONAL CAPS
2 Northern Ireland caps
(1 goal), 1932
LFC DEBUT GAME/GOAL
26 August 1933 / 30 August
1933
CONTRACT EXPIRY
30 July 1935

English, Sam

SAM ENGLISH was a powerful centre-forward who joined Liverpool from Rangers before the start of the 1933/34 season. He achieved legendary status at Rangers as he broke the club's scoring record in his debut 1931/32 season, scoring 44 goals in 35 league games, a record that still stands to this day!

It is a more incredible feat considering that all his goals came from open play. English could dispatch the ball into the net easily with both feet, was lightning fast and a brilliant header of the ball. He scored five goals in only his second league game for Rangers in a 7-3 win over Morton and had scored a total of 12 goals in six league games that historic season when his collision with Celtic's goalkeeper, John Thomson, on 5 September 1931 at Ibrox changed English's existence.

THOMSON'S head hit English's knee after the striker had struck the ball that the keeper deflected past the post. An artery ruptured in Thomson's right temple, which led to the 22-year-old's death. English, who was just five months older than Thomson, was on many occasions afterwards mercilessly taunted by rival fans and players for this horrible accident, and his family suffered abuse as well, even though an official enquiry cleared English of any blame. Rangers finished runners-up that season but English's nine goals in seven matches helped them win the Scottish Cup. English scored only 11 goals in 30 league and cup matches in his second season but Rangers still won the Championship.

SAM ENGLISH
LIVERPOOL

English made a blistering start to his Anfield career and by the midway stage of the 1933/34 season he had already scored 16 times. But he only started eight matches during the second half of the season, scoring a further four times. Although not selected on the opening day of the following season, he then had a run of 11 consecutive matches, in which he hit the back of the net three times, before losing his place in the side.

DESPITE being in and out of the team, English still finished with a good goals-per-game record of 26 strikes from exactly 50 matches.

The Northern Irishman returned to Scotland with Queen of the South before moving back to England in 1936 to play for Hartlepools United in the Third Division North. After scoring 31 goals in 75 matches for the club, he retired at the end of the 1937/38 season disillusioned with football. He said that his career since the Thomson accident had been 'seven years of joyless sport'.

He died in the Vale of Leven Hospital in Alexandria, West Dunbartonshire, on 12 April 1967 after battling motor neurone disease. His Rangers team-mate, Bob McPhail, paid English the ultimate praise: 'Though I never played with the great Dixie Dean of Everton, I did play against him. I would have taken English before him.'

Season	League		FA Cup		Total	
	App	**Goals**	**App**	**Goals**	**App**	**Goals**
1933/34	28	18	3	2	31	20
1934/35	19	6	0	0	19	6
Total	**47**	**24**	**3**	**2**	**50**	**26**

Enrique,
Jose

'EL TORO' or 'The Bull' is a nickname Jose Enrique earned for his quickness and physical play while he was in the Spanish Under-21 team.

Enrique made his breakthrough at Villareal before joining Newcastle for £6.3million after just one season with the Yellow Submarine. Enrique was selected as Newcastle's official Player of the Season for 2009/10 and named in the Championship's PFA Team of the Season as the Magpies won promotion to the Premier League. He impressed on his return to the top flight and two days before the start of the 2011/12 Premier League season Liverpool purchased the Spanish left-back. Although Enrique still had one year left on his Newcastle contract, a move away from Tyneside was always likely after he had criticised the club's transfer policy earlier in the summer.

Kenny Dalglish was confident enough in his latest acquisition to

put him straight into the first team on the opening day of the Premier League. By the turn of the year his defensive stability and attacking surges upfield had ensured that he had played in all 19 of the Premier League matches up to that time. His form dipped alarmingly towards the end of the season, but he was still a regular. He picked up a winners' medal in the League Cup and also had an unexpected seven minutes in goal against his old club Newcastle United after Pepe Reina had been sent off at a time when Liverpool had used all their three substitutes. In Brendan Rodgers' era Enrique has returned to the excellent form he showed initially for Liverpool, mostly used as a left-back but also featuring on occasion as a left-winger.

FACTFILE

BORN
Valencia, Spain,
23 January 1986
POSITION
Left-back / Left-winger
OTHER CLUBS
Levante (2004–05),
Valencia (2005–06),
Celta Vigo (loan, 2005–06),
Villareal (2006–07),
Newcastle United (2007–11)
SIGNED FROM
Newcastle United,
£6million, 12 August 2011
LFC DEBUT GAME/GOAL
13 August 2011 /
17 November 2012
HONOURS
League Cup 2012

Season	League		FA Cup		League Cup		Europe		Total	
	App	**Goals**	**App**	**Goals**	**App**	**Goals**	**App**	**Goals**	**App**	**Goals**
2011/12	33 (2)	0	4	0	3 (1)	0	-	-	40 (3)	0
2012/13	25 (4)	2	0	0	0	0	6	0	31 (4)	2
Total	**58 (6)**	**2**	**4**	**0**	**3 (1)**	**0**	**6**	**0**	**71 (7)**	**2**

Europe

IN 1955 the UEFA Congress approved a proposal to introduce a knockout competition, Coupe des Clubs Champions Européens, in which all the domestic champion clubs of their member countries could participate. The Inter-Cities Fairs Cup also began in 1955 but the European Cup Winners' Cup did not start until 1960. UEFA did not recognise the Fairs Cup because it was not a tournament that it had organised itself. UEFA was, however, happy to put its name to the tournament which replaced the Fairs Cup in 1971, the UEFA Cup.

The English football authorities had serious misgivings about allowing its clubs to participate in these competitions in their early years, partly through fear that it would disrupt their domestic schedules. The Football League refused to allow Chelsea to enter the inaugural European Cup. Football League secretary Alan Hardaker had to reverse his original opinion that he was 'terrified of fixture congestion and foreign contamination' and from 1956 the English champions took part.

Leeds United, twice Fairs Cup winners, weren't the only British success story of Europe's early years. Tottenham won the third running of the Cup Winners' Cup in 1963 and Rangers reached the same final four years later but lost to Bayern Munich only to

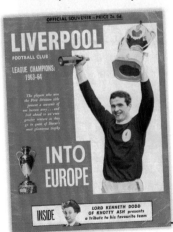

KR Reykjavik captain Ellert Schram greets Liverpool captain Ron Yeats before Liverpool's first European game in 1964

make another final in 1972 which this time they won. Additionally Celtic, Manchester United, Chelsea, Arsenal and West Ham United all had their names on European trophies before Liverpool won their first big continental prize in 1973.

BY THE TIME Liverpool first qualified for Europe by winning the English Championship in 1964, all three competitions were in a healthy state (and a European Super Cup match would be introduced by UEFA from 1972 to be contested annually between the winners of the European Cup and the European Cup Winners' Cup). Although the concept of playing competitive matches in Europe was new to Liverpool in 1964, playing matches outside the British Isles was not. Ten matches were played in North America only weeks before the club was

due to play its first European Cup tie in Iceland; and numerous friendly matches had been played in other European countries. The preliminary round trip into the unknown to Reykjavík was successful and Bill Shankly's team, playing in an all-red strip for the first time, then beat the Belgian champions Anderlecht home and away to move into the quarter-final. With the 'away goals' rule not coming into force until later in the decade and penalty shoot-outs much later still, two draws with Cologne meant a third match in neutral Rotterdam where, despite Liverpool taking a two-goal lead, the Germans hit back to equalise. Progress into the last four was bizarrely decided by the toss of a coloured disc, which had to be flicked into the air twice by the referee before it landed in Liverpool's favour. If that was the slice of luck that Liverpool needed, it was paid back with interest in the semi-final when the Reds had a goal controversially

disallowed in a 3-1 victory at Anfield before losing 3-0 in the cauldron of hate that was the San Siro to defending European champions Inter Milan, whose first two goals were definitely suspicious when it came to their legality.

The prestige of doing well in Europe, particularly in the main competition, the European Champions' Cup, was great but there was a certain naïveté about the way the first European campaign had been conducted. Lessons would be learned that would stand the club in good stead in future years. In 1966 the Cup Winners' Cup final was reached but a freak Borussia Dortmund goal in extra-time brought some sort of German revenge for the way Liverpool had beaten Cologne a year before. Another stab at the European Cup saw a crushing defeat against Ajax in the Amsterdam fog and for the next four seasons the club had to settle for qualifying for the Fairs Cup but without managing to progress past the third round until 1971 when the semi-final was reached.

Arsenal's domestic League and FA Cup Double of 1971 saw Liverpool move into the Cup Winners' Cup as beaten FA Cup finalists. After overcoming moderate Swiss opposition, there was no disgrace in losing to a strong Bayern Munich side. Eight members of the Bayern team that beat Liverpool in Munich in November 1971 would win the Champions' Cup in 1974.

THE EUROPEAN CUP had become a kind of Holy Grail for the top European clubs but you had to prove yourself the best in your own country first before you could take on the best from other countries. In 1973 Bill Shankly's men reached the UEFA Cup final after ten tough matches and only one defeat, at Tottenham in the semi-final when the away goals rule worked in Liverpool's favour. A torrential downpour caused the home leg of the final to be abandoned but, when the match was replayed 24 hours later, Liverpool took a commanding three-goal lead to Germany and just held on to it despite a ferocious onslaught by Borussia Mönchengladbach in the first half of the second leg.

SHANKLY'S third attempt to win the main prize in what turned out to be his final season as manager ended in disappointment with home and away defeats by Red Star Belgrade. Bob Paisley had been carefully watching the team's performances and was ready to make a few changes to the way these ties against continental opponents were approached, not least tactically. Paisley's nous paid dividends almost immediately. He led Liverpool to a second UEFA Cup success in 1976 and then masterminded successive victories in the European Cup in 1977 and 1978. Then, stung by first round defeats in the next two seasons Paisley recharged everyone's batteries and saw his team win a third European Cup in Paris, fittingly against Real Madrid who had dominated the competition in its early years. 'The European Cup was harder to win then than it is these days,' Bob Paisley's widow, Jessie, said at the unveiling of the

Paisley gateway at Anfield in 1999. 'You had to win your league in the first place to get into it, not be the second team. And you didn't get second chances, like you do today with groups. Now you can lose and still qualify. In Bob's day it was a simple knockout. Lose and that was it. So for Bob to have won it once, twice, and then a third time, was the jewel in the crown for him.'

Joe Fagan inherited a very strong squad from Bob Paisley, that was still capable of defeating the best that Europe had to offer; and it did that in the hardest way imaginable by having to play the final at the home stadium of its opponents, AS Roma. Full-back Alan Kennedy, whose goal had decided the Paris final three years earlier, was again the hero, this time striking a tidy penalty-kick to win the shoot-out that followed a drawn match after extra-time.

The club was quite capable of moving on to five successes in the main tournament but in 1985 an hour of mayhem and madness before the final against Juventus in Brussels made the headlines for all the wrong reasons. Thirty-nine spectators died, Liverpool Football Club's previously good name was irrevocably damaged and the club was banished into the wilderness for, as it turned out, six long years.

The return to the European fold in 1991 was welcomed by everyone connected with the club but it coincided with the end of the dominance that had been enjoyed in the previous two and a half decades. Before Heysel Liverpool had qualified for Europe in 21 consecutive seasons. But in the 1990s there were seasons when the club couldn't qualify by any means and it took a change of manager and a fresh approach to change that sudden downturn in fortunes from the powerhouse of old. Gérard Houllier took Liverpool through to the 2001 UEFA Cup final in Dortmund,

where a crazy match swung one way and then the other before a Golden Goal near the end of extra-time finally put an end to the brave challenge of Alaves.

HOULLIER narrowly failed to take Liverpool through to the Champions League semi-final a year later, the top tournament having been renamed and rebranded to allow non-champion clubs to enter. But Rafa Benítez who replaced him in 2004 had more luck. Twenty-one years after their last European Cup final success, Liverpool would again know what it was like to stand at the very top of the European tree. An unforgettable campaign through the autumn and spring months that included many moments of great drama culminated in a momentous tussle against AC Milan at the Ataturk Stadium in Istanbul when a team that was out for the count somehow made a miraculous recovery to rescue a situation that had seemed completely lost. A fifth success in UEFA's premier competition gave Liverpool the right to keep the trophy they had just won until the end of time.

It has been an extraordinary adventure that started with nervous steps way back in the 1960s. Five European Cups, three UEFA Cups and three European Super Cups plus a number of

near-misses have put the club in the very top echelon of European football; and the good name that was damaged so badly in Brussels has been restored. Nobody should forget what happened there or why. 'In order to rise from its own ashes, a Phoenix first must burn,' says a famous quote. Liverpool burned in a very public and shameful way in 1985 but recovered to see the Liverbird, in this instance, fly once more and again conquer Europe the way it had done in earlier years.

Memorable European nights at Anfield:

4 May 1965 - European Cup semi-final first leg:
Liverpool 3 Inter Milan 1

Liverpool: *Tommy Lawrence, Chris Lawler, Ronnie Moran, Geoff Strong, Ron Yeats, Willie Stevenson, Ian Callaghan, Roger Hunt, Ian St John, Tommy Smith, Peter Thompson*

Inter Milan: *Giuliano Sarti, Tarcisio Burgnich, Giacinto Facchetti, Carlo Tagnin, Aristide Guarneri, Armando Picchi, Jair da Costa, Alessandro Mazzola, Joaquín Peiró, Luis Suárez, Mario Corso*

'This was the night Liverpool came of age,' Ian St John once said. Roger Hunt opened the scoring against the European champions in the 4th minute, but Alessandro Mazzola equalised only six minutes later. It was a memorable game for Ian Callaghan for many reasons as he revealed to the *Liverpool Echo* in March 2008. 'After 34 minutes I scored the most treasured goal of my career. What made it all the more rewarding was that it came from a free kick plan we had been practising for some time. Peter Thompson was fouled a few yards outside the penalty area. Willie Stevenson and I lined up, then

I dummied to shoot, ran over the ball and kept on running as Willie stroked it through to Roger Hunt, who sidefooted it to me and I hit it into the net. The Kop went berserk. They started singing 'Go back to Italy' to the tune of 'Santa Lucia'.' Ian St John put Liverpool 3-1 ahead in the 75th minute, but even that lead proved insufficient in Italy to reach the European Cup final.

19 April 1966 - European Cup Winners' Cup semi-final second leg: Liverpool 2 Celtic 0

Liverpool: *Tommy Lawrence, Chris Lawler, Gerry Byrne, Gordon Milne, Ron Yeats, Willie Stevenson, Ian Callaghan, Geoff Strong, Ian St John, Tommy Smith, Peter Thompson*

Celtic: *Ronnie Simpson, Ian Young, Tommy Gemmell, Bobby Murdoch, Billy McNeill, John Clark, Bobby Lennox, Joe McBride, Stevie Chalmers, Bertie Auld, Jamie Hughes*

Liverpool lost 1-0 at Celtic five days previously and the score remained scoreless at Anfield until an hour had been played. Tommy Smith's free-kick found the bottom corner of the goal through the sea of mud on the ground. Only six minutes later Geoff Strong headed the ball into the net from Ian Callaghan's pass. As the last minute ticked away Bobby Lennox thought he had equalised and potentially put Celtic through to the final. Lennox's goal was, however, disallowed because of offside and all hell broke loose as the *Evening Times* reported: 'The Celtic end of Anfield erupted with joy, an entire sea of green and white rolled down to the terracing wall but in a second jubilation had

turned to hate. Bottles, beer cans, tumblers rained on the pitch as players, officials, police and photographers ran for their lives. I cannot remember when so many missiles have been thrown at any game inside such a short space of time. It was a match of tremendous endeavour and excitement and the great pity of it all that it had to end in dispute and rage.' Liverpool just escaped into the final which they lost to Borussia Dortmund.

10 May 1973 - UEFA Cup final, first leg: Liverpool 3 Borussia Mönchengladbach 0

Liverpool: *Ray Clemence, Chris Lawler, Alec Lindsay, Tommy Smith, Larry Lloyd, Emlyn Hughes, Kevin Keegan, Peter Cormack, John Toshack, Steve Heighway (Brian Hall 83), Ian Callaghan*

Gladbach: *Wolfgang Kleff, Günter Netzer, Berti Vogts, Rainer Bonhof, Heinz Michallik, Dietmar Danner, Herbert Wimmer, Christian Kulik, Henning Jensen, Bernd Rupp (Allan Simonsen 82), Jupp Heynckes*

The tie was abandoned 24 hours earlier due to torrential rain and Bill Shankly made the key decision to leave out Brian Hall from the line-up and play big target man John Toshack. In the 21st minute Lawler's long pass found the head of Toshack who put the ball across goal where Keegan jumped forward and scored with a superb header in front of the jubilant Kop. Four minutes later Bonhof panicked with Toshack behind him and handled the ball in the penalty area. Keegan stepped up to the spot, but Kleff put his hands to better use than Bonhof and saved his penalty. With just over half an hour gone another header from Toshack created Keegan's second goal. Keegan's corner kick in the 62nd minute was headed in by Larry Lloyd. Heynckes got a glorious opportunity to reduce the

arrears from the penalty spot but Clemence showed great agility when the ball was heading for his right-hand corner and kept the 3-0 lead intact. Liverpool survived an onslaught in Germany and won their first European prize.

28 April 1976 - UEFA Cup final, first leg: Liverpool 3 Bruges 2

Liverpool: *Ray Clemence, Phil Neal, Tommy Smith, Phil Thompson, Ray Kennedy, Emlyn Hughes, Kevin Keegan, David Fairclough, Steve Heighway, John Toshack (Jimmy Case 46), Ian Callaghan*

Bruges: *Birger Jensen, Alfons Bastijns, Edward Krieger, George Leekens, Jos Volders, Julien Cools, René Vandereycken, Daniel de Cubber, Roger van Gool, Raoul Lambert, Ulrik Lefèvre*

Liverpool were 2-0 down inside 15 minutes, but Jimmy Case's introduction in place of John Toshack for the second half turned the game on its head. After 59 minutes Heighway cut the ball back from the left for Ray Kennedy to strike a wonderful shot into the roof of the net from just outside the area. Case stabbed the ball home two minutes later after Kennedy's shot had struck the post. The Reds' comeback was completed in the 64th minute when Keegan sent Jensen the wrong way from the spot. Three Liverpool goals in five minutes guaranteed a tremendous win on

the night. Liverpool drew 1-1 in Belgium a fortnight later to win the UEFA Cup for the second time.

'Throats must have been red-raw with cheering. But you know what? I believe those fans liked to see us with our backs to the wall because they knew we could win,' Liverpool's hero Jimmy Case said right afterwards.

16 March 1977- European Cup quarter-final second leg: Liverpool 3 St Etienne 1

Liverpool: *Ray Clemence, Phil Neal, Joey Jones, Tommy Smith, Ray Kennedy, Emlyn Hughes, Kevin Keegan, Jimmy Case, Steve Heighway, John Toshack (David Fairclough 74), Ian Callaghan*

St Etienne: *Ivan Curkovic, Christian Lopez, Gérard Janvion, Alain Merchadier (Hervé Revelli 75), Gérard Farison, Dominique Bathenay, Jean Michel Larqué, Christian Synaegel, Dominique Rocheteau, Jacques Santini, Patrick Revelli*

Liverpool were beaten 1-0 in France by St Etienne, the runners-up from the previous season's European Cup campaign. Thousands were locked out of Anfield as the teams took to the field to a deafening reception. But even the most ardent Liverpool fan couldn't have expected the home team to wipe out the visitors' narrow advantage with

barely two minutes gone, Keegan floating a centre from the left over Curkovic's head. But the Reds couldn't keep up their early momentum and Ray Clemence had no chance with Bathenay's vicious, swerving shot which put the visitors ahead again on aggregate in the 51st minute. Ray Kennedy drove Liverpool back into the lead on the night eight minutes later. When only six minutes were left on the clock David Fairclough ran on to Ray Kennedy's pass and kept control of the ball despite being challenged heavily; it was as if the whole stadium held its breath waiting for the outcome. A second or two later the ball was in the Kop goal. When the referee finally blew for the end of the game the noise was probably heard several miles away.

12 April 1978 - European Cup semi-final, second leg:
Liverpool 3
Borussia Mönchengladbach 0

Liverpool: *Ray Clemence, Phil Neal, Tommy Smith, Phil Thompson, Ray Kennedy, Emlyn Hughes, Kenny Dalglish, Jimmy Case, Steve Heighway, Terry McDermott, Graeme Souness*

Gladbach: *Wolfgang Kleff, Berti Vogts, Wilfried Hannes, Hans-Jürgen Wittkamp, Horst Wohlers (Winfried Schäfer 71), Rainer Bonhof, Herbert Wimmer (Ewald Lienen 71), Carsten Nielsen, Christian Kulik, Karl Del'Haye, Jupp Heynckes*

Gladbach had lost to Liverpool in the European Cup final last May and were out for revenge, having the upper hand after a 2-1 win in the first leg. Ray Kennedy put Liverpool in front in the 6th minute. Kennedy was in impressive form as he had a hand in Liverpool's other two goals scored by Kenny Dalglish and Jimmy Case, the latter a tremendous piece of finishing. Gladbach never stood a chance as Liverpool secured their place at Wembley.

6 November 1991 - UEFA Cup 2nd round, second leg:
Liverpool 3 Auxerre 0

Liverpool: *Bruce Grobbelaar, Gary Ablett, David Burrows, Mike Marsh, Jan Mølby, Nick Tanner, Steve McManaman, Ray Houghton, Ian Rush, Mark Walters, Steve McMahon*

Auxerre: *Bruno Martini, Frédéric Darras, Zbigniew Kaczmarek, Alain Roche, Stéphane Mahé, Raphaël Guerrerio, Christophe Cocard, Daniel Dutuel, Kálmán Kovács (Didier Otokoré 19 (Stéphane Mazzolini 75)), Jean-Marc Ferreri, Pascal Vahirua*

Liverpool were only four games into their return to European football following the lifting of the Heysel ban. The ground was only half-full but the supporters present created a wall of sound. Liverpool faced a monumental task to recover from a 2-0 first leg deficit, but were encouraged when Jan Mølby gave them an early lead from the penalty spot. After an half an hour's play Mike Marsh equalised the aggregate score with a powerful header following Ray Houghton's pass. Liverpool delivered the killer blow in the 84th minute when Mølby's well-timed pass split the Auxerre defence open and Mark Walters' shot nestled in the far corner. Match winner Walters underlined the importance of the fans' support post match: 'The fans were the vital factor. The noise they created put fear on the faces of the French players. You could see it.'

19 April 2001 - UEFA Cup semi-final, second leg: Liverpool 1 Barcelona 0

Liverpool: *Sander Westerveld, Stephane Henchoz, Markus Babbel, Sami Hyypia, Jamie Carragher, Vladimir Smicer (Robbie Fowler 80), Didi Hamann, Steven Gerrard (Danny Murphy 78), Gary McAllister, Emile Heskey, Michael Owen (Patrik Berger 62)*

Barcelona: *Pepe Reina, Michael Reiziger (Simao Sabrosa 59), Frank de Boer, Pep Guardiola, Carlos Puyol, Philip Cocu, Luis Enrique, Emmanuel Petit, Marc Overmars (Dani 74), Rivaldo, Patrick Kluivert*

A stubborn Liverpool team kept the score goalless in Catalonia. When the game at Anfield approached half-time Patrick Kluivert inexplicably handled in the box and up stepped Gary McAllister to send the up and coming Pepe Reina the wrong way. A titanic performance in the second half kept Barca at bay and Liverpool went on to beat Alaves in the final.

19 March 2002 - Champions League Group Stage Two:
Liverpool 2 Roma 0

Liverpool: *Jerzy Dudek, Jamie Carragher, Abel Xavier, Sami Hyypia, Stephane Henchoz, Steven Gerrard, Danny Murphy, John Arne Riise, Vladimir Smicer (Gary McAllister 89), Emile Heskey, Jari Litmanen (Igor Biscan 87)*

Roma: *Francesco Antonioli, Lima (Vicenzo Montella 46), Aldair, Marcos Assunçao (Antonio Cassano 69), Francesco Totti, Emerson, Christian Panucci, Damiano Tommasi, Walter Samuel, Gabriel Batistuta (Marco Delvecchio 46), Vincent Candela*

Gérard Houllier returned to the dug-out for the first time since his life-saving heart surgery in October 2001 and was greeted by an exuberant Anfield crowd. Liverpool had to defeat Fabio Capello's Roma by two clear goals to reach the quarter finals. Six minutes into the game John Arne Riise took a corner and in the ensuing scramble Danny Murphy teed up a shot just inside the penalty area when he was brought down by Marcos Assunçao. Jari Litmanen was coolness personified when he delivered the ball into the bottom left hand

corner of the Anfield Road goal. Emile Heskey, who was superb on the night, directed a great header into the net after 62 minutes. Liverpool's performance befitted this emotional occasion. 'This was one of the greatest nights in this football club's history,' declared Phil Thompson who took care of the team in Houllier's absence.

8 December 2004 - Champions League Group Stage One:
Liverpool 3 Olympiacos 1

Liverpool: *Chris Kirkland, Steve Finnan (Josemi 85), Sami Hyypia, John Arne Riise, Djimi Traoré (Florent Sinama-Pongolle 46), Jamie Carragher, Harry Kewell, Steven Gerrard, Xabi Alonso, Antonio Nunez, Milan Baros (Neil Mellor 78)*

Olympiacos: *Antonis Nikopolidis, Anastasos Pantos, Giorgios Anatolakis, Gabriel Schürrer, Stylianos Venetidis (Milos Maric 80), Georgios Georgiadis (Ivan Rezic 70), Pantelis Kafes, Ieroklis Stoltidis, Predrag Djordjevic, Rivaldo, Giovanni (Giannakis Okkas 87)*

Liverpool had to win the Greek side by two clear goals to proceed from their Champions League group and Rivaldo's free kick in the 26th minute hardly inspired confidence that they would succeed in doing so. The stage was set for the mother of all fightbacks. Florent Sinama-Pongolle, who had been on the pitch for a couple of minutes, equalised in the 47th minute but Liverpool failed to add to their tally for the next 33 minutes. Another inspired substitution was provided in the form of Neil Mellor. Pongolle's pass went to Antonio Nunez whose header was saved but Mellor was at hand to give Liverpool hope, but the Reds still needed one more goal. Six minutes later Mellor headed the ball out to Steven Gerrard who delivered a rocket into the net that will stay forever in the minds of

Liverpool supporters. 'That's as loud as I've heard the Kop,' said Gerrard triumphant post match.

3 May 2005 - Champions League semi-final, second leg: Liverpool 1 Chelsea 0

Liverpool: *Jerzy Dudek, Steve Finnan, Jamie Carragher, Sami Hyypia, Djimi Traoré, Didi Hamann (Harry Kewell 72), Igor Biscan, Luis Garcia (Antonio Nunez 84), Steven Gerrard, John Arne Riise, Milan Baros (Djibril Cissé 59)*

Chelsea: *Petr Cech, Geremi (Robert Huth 75), Ricardo Carvalho, John Terry, William Gallas, Claude Makelele, Tiago (Mateja Kezman 67), Frank Lampard, Joe Cole (Arjen Robben 67), Eiður Guðjohnsen, Didier Drogba*

119 decibel-charged Anfield rocked Chelsea to their core. George Sephton rates this game as the most amazing in his 40 plus years' career as Anfield's DJ, as he told *Well Red* magazine. 'Some strange things happened on that night; the goal Luis Garcia scored, that Jose Mourinho is still whining about all these years later, and the six minutes added time. If you listen to recordings of that night there's a gap between the fourth official holding his board up and

me saying 'six minutes added time' because I couldn't believe it. I was just gobsmacked when that came up. People were screaming and booing and quite a few approached me in the street after that and said: 'Why did you give the six minutes added time?' But I don't! It's on the board so I can't do anything else. I'd like to have said that there would be one minute but I'd be out of here if I did that!'

1 May 2007 - Champions League semi-final, second leg: Liverpool 1 Chelsea 0 (LFC won 4-1 on penalties)

Liverpool: *Pepe Reina, Steve Finnan, Jamie Carragher, Daniel Agger, John Arne Riise, Jermaine Pennant (Xabi Alonso 78), Steven Gerrard, Javier Mascherano (Robbie Fowler 118), Boudewijn Zenden, Peter Crouch (Craig Bellamy 106), Dirk Kuyt*

Chelsea: *Petr Cech, Ashley Cole, Paulo Ferreira, John Terry, Claude Makelele (Geremi 118), Michael Essien, Frank Lampard, Joe Cole (Arjen Robben 98), John Obi Mikel, Didier Drogba, Salomon Kalou (Shaun Wright-Phillips 117)*

Would José Mourinho fall foul of Anfield again? He tried to upset his counterpart by claiming, 'Three years without a Premiership title? I don't think I would still be in a job.' Benítez in turn anointed Liverpool fans as the 'special ones.' This was going to be an all-mighty battle. Chelsea were one goal to the good from the first leg, but Daniel Agger wiped out that lead as early as the 22nd minute with a first-time shot from inside the penalty area. The teams could not be separated so a tense Anfield had to endure a penalty shoot-out. Bolo Zenden netted the first penalty while Pepe Reina saved from Arjen Robben. Petr Cech

dived the right way but couldn't prevent Xabi Alonso from scoring Liverpool's second penalty. Frank Lampard thumped his spot kick into goal. Steven Gerrard outmaneuvred Cech and put Liverpool 3-1 up. Geremi could only watch on in despair as Reina saved his attempt and punched the air in delight. Dirk Kuyt sealed Liverpool's priceless win.

10 March 2009 - Champions League Last 16, second leg: Liverpool 4 Real Madrid 0

Liverpool: *Pepe Reina, Álvaro Arbeloa, Fábio Aurélio, Martin Skrtel, Jamie Carragher, Javier Mascherano, Xabi Alonso (Lucas Leiva 60), Steven Gerrard (Jay Spearing, 73), Dirk Kuyt, Ryan Babel, Fernando Torres (Andrea Dossena 83)*

Real Madrid: *Iker Casillas, Pepe, Sergio Ramos, Fabio Cannavaro, Gabriel Heinze, Mahamadou Diarra, Fernando Gago, Wesley Sneijder, Raúl, Arjen Robben, Gonzalo Higuaín*

'This is Anfield, so what?' Spanish newspaper *Marca* said mockingly on their cover on the morning of the game. Liverpool outplayed 'Los Merengues' at Anfield. Torres certainly enjoyed opening the scoring right in front of Real's fans who made him the object of their hate when he was Atletico's captain. He turned his back towards the away fans' section while pulling his shirt to emphasise his name written across the shoulders. Gerrard added a second from the spot after 27 minutes and scored a superb third at the start of the second half despatching the ball into the net while running towards the Kop after Ryan Babel's brilliant move down the left flank. Andrea Dossena sealed an incredible win. The next day's *Marca* had a picture of Torres signalling a zero and the headline; 'Madrid totally beaten'.

Evans,
Alun

ALUN EVANS had so much potential as a teenager but his career didn't reach the heights it was expected to. Ron Yeats had struggled to keep up with him when Liverpool met Wolves at Anfield on 25 November 1967. Evans scored Wolves' only goal in Liverpool's 2-1 victory.

Liverpool had been linked to him on several occasions in the newspapers and Bill Shankly and his scouts were quite visible at Wolves' reserve games but the Scot dismissed the rumours. 'They're very careless people who talk about these things,' he said at the time. A few months later Liverpool paid £100,000 for the 19-year-old, making Evans Britain's most expensive teenager after he had only played one full season for Wolves in the First Division, scoring four goals in 20 games. Shankly had great belief in Evans' ability and compared him to Manchester United and Scotland star Denis Law.

FACTFILE

BORN
Kidderminster,
30 September 1949
POSITION
Forward
OTHER CLUBS
Wolverhampton Wanderers
(1965–68),
Los Angeles Wolves
(loan, 1967),
Aston Villa (1972–75),
Walsall (1975–78),
South Melbourne Hellas
(1978–82),
Morwell Falcons (1983)
SIGNED FROM
Wolverhampton Wanderers,
£100,000,
16 September 1968
LFC DEBUT GAME/GOAL
21 September 1968 /
21 September 1968
CONTRACT EXPIRY
9 June 1972

'I was just called into the office at Wolves and told I was going to Liverpool,' Evans recalled on *Wolvesheroes.com* in 2009. 'I jumped in the car with my father-in-law and I signed pretty quickly. Shanks had a growl at me, though, when I said I expected to work my way into the side via the reserves. He said: 'I wouldn't pay £100,000 for you or anybody else unless it was to play in my first team. You're facing Leicester on Saturday.''

EVANS' START to his Liverpool career could hardly have been more sensational with a goal ten minutes into his debut at home to Leicester, and then two more the following week as he returned to Molineux and helped destroy his former club 6-0. He played in every league game from his debut in September until the end of the season, contributing seven goals to a transitional team. At the time he seemed the ideal candidate to be groomed as Roger Hunt's successor, but he made a modest return again the following season, scoring nine times in 25 games. Most of those appearances came after Hunt had departed for Bolton and the expectation and responsibility seemed to weigh heavily on his young shoulders.

Evans did make a bright start to the 1970/71 season with five goals in his first six games, but after that things started to go wrong for the golden-haired handsome young boy who had the world at his feet. He was attacked in a nightclub in Wolverhampton, leaving him badly scarred in the face as he told *Wolvesheroes.com*: 'I was just out with my girlfriend at the Oasis nightclub on the edge of the town. We were watching a cabaret when this guy came at me with one of those beer glasses with the dimples in and smashed it into the side of my face. There was blood everywhere and the bouncer took me to hospital where I was given nearly 70 stitches. I healed OK but was badly scarred. I found out that the guy who attacked me was out of prison on remand at the time.'

To make matters worse Evans was also badly injured during a Fairs Cup game in Bucharest on 4 November 1970 and was out for four months. After such a lengthy lay-off, many expected he would need a few games to regain his fitness. He came on as a substitute against Tottenham, then four days later on 10 March 1971 came his brightest moment in a

Alun Evans scarred after the nightclub attack

Liverpool shirt when he scored a spectacular hat-trick against Bayern Munich at Anfield in the fourth round of the Fairs Cup. He scored three goals in 14 games to the end of the season, including Liverpool's first in a 2-1 win over Everton in the FA Cup semi-final. He featured for 68 minutes in the 2-1 defeat to Arsenal in the final.

By the start of the 1971/72 season, Evans was in his 23rd year and the best he could achieve was to play in eight consecutive games from mid-October to the middle of November, scoring two goals in the process. A new rising star by the name of Kevin Keegan was now on the scene. Evans' last appearance was ironically against his first club Wolverhampton at Molineux on 22 January 1972. In the summer Evans was transferred to Wolves' Midlands rivals Aston Villa, who had just conquered the Third Division.

AFTER 17 GOALS in 71 games for Villa, he left in the middle of the 1974/75 season for Third Division Walsall while Villa won promotion to the First Division. He played 87 league games and scored seven goals for Walsall before transferring to South Melbourne in Australia in 1978, where he stayed for four years before moving to Morwell Falcons in the same league. After his career finished, Evans moved back to Melbourne and settled there.

BILL SHANKLY did not regret signing Evans for one second even though his Reds' career did not

work out. 'I would have done exactly the same thing again. He was very cute for his age, he was quick and he was also very courageous. Everything was going well for him until he went home to Wolverhampton one weekend.

That incident probably changed Alun's whole life. He had a great spirit but what happened retarded his career. We eventually transferred him to Aston Villa, which effectively meant he was going back home. Sometimes

when a player leaves a club there are sour grapes, but soon after I received a letter from Alun. It began: 'Dear Boss...' I was very pleased and proud that Alun had come to me for advice. That letter meant so much to me.'

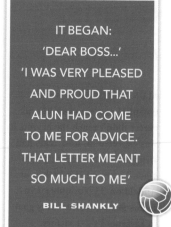

Season	League		FA Cup		League Cup		Europe		Other		Total	
	App	Goals	App	Goals	App	Goals	App	Goals	App	Goals	App	Goals
1968/69	33	7	4	0	1	0	1	0	-	-	39	7
1969/70	17 (2)	3	1 (1)	2	1	1	2 (1)	3	-	-	21 (4)	9
1970/71	21	10	3 (1)	1	3	1	6	3	-	-	33 (1)	15
1971/72	6	1	1	0	2	0	2 (1)	1	1	0	12 (1)	2
Total	**77 (2)**	**21**	**9 (2)**	**3**	**7**	**2**	**11 (2)**	**7**	**1**	**0**	**105 (6)**	**33**

Evans,
John

JOHN EVANS played 90 league matches in three-and-a-half seasons for Charlton Athletic, scoring 38 times in the First Division. He was very prolific against Liverpool, scoring seven goals in five matches including a brace in a 6-0 Charlton win, three months before he was transferred to the Reds. Liverpool were sliding towards relegation after winning only five of their first 24 matches and at least Evans' introduction on Boxing Day 1953 saw a slight improvement, with a draw taken from West Bromwich Albion's visit just 24 hours after the Midlanders had triumphed 5-2 over Liverpool at the Hawthorns. That started a run of 16 successive matches in which Evans scored five times, but the introduction of a number of new players in the second half of the season could not prevent the drop.

EVANS only missed four league games in 1954/55 as Liverpool got used to life in the Second Division, and scored 29 times. He became the first Liverpool player to score five goals in one game for 52 years, as Bristol Rovers were

defeated 5-3 at Anfield on 15 September 1954; a rare feat that only five players have managed in the club's history. Evans was one goal shy of repeating his achievement six months later when Bury were beaten at Gigg Lane, failing to add his fifth in the final 20 minutes of the game.

Evans maintained his record of scoring one goal every two games but only a few weeks into the 1956/57 season he lost his place to Jimmy Melia and was eventually transferred to Colchester United in the Third Division South, where he added 22 league goals.

Season	League		FA Cup		Total	
	App	Goals	App	Goals	App	Goals
1953/54	16	5	1	0	17	5
1954/55	38	29	4	4	42	33
1955/56	31	13	5	0	36	13
1956/57	11	2	0	0	11	2
1957/58	1	0	0	0	1	0
Total	**97**	**49**	**10**	**4**	**107**	**53**

Payne, Arnell, Liddell, Evans and A'Court who scored six against Fulham in 1955

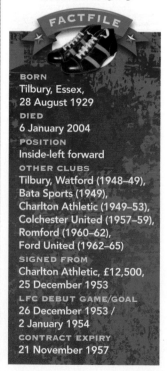

FACTFILE

BORN
Tilbury, Essex, 28 August 1929
DIED
6 January 2004
POSITION
Inside-left forward
OTHER CLUBS
Tilbury, Watford (1948–49), Bata Sports (1949), Charlton Athletic (1949–53), Colchester United (1957–59), Romford (1960–62), Ford United (1962–65)
SIGNED FROM
Charlton Athletic, £12,500, 25 December 1953
LFC DEBUT GAME/GOAL
26 December 1953 / 2 January 1954
CONTRACT EXPIRY
21 November 1957

Evans,
Roy

'I FIRST came on the Kop as an eight-year-old, then I played, coached and now I'm the figurehead. It is special because this is the team I've supported and loved all my life. But it isn't Roy Evans' team. I'm just shaping its destiny for a while.'

Significant words from then-manager Roy Evans, who was at the club for 33 years. Bootle-born Roy was an apprentice at Anfield before signing professional forms when he had turned 17 in October 1965. The England Youth defender didn't see a hint of first-team action until nearly the end of the 1969/70 season when Geoff Strong's injury opened the door for him. The *Liverpool Echo* wanted a quote from local lad Evans after he made his debut against Sheffield Wednesday at Anfield. Evans left quite an impression in print at least when he responded: 'When I told my mum I was in the team, she was so surprised she couldn't eat her tea.' Shankly told the press: 'This boy Evans has the heart and guts to become another Gerry Byrne.' Strong returned in the following game against Everton but was out again for the next two matches in which Evans featured.

Ian Ross started the following season as left-back but three games in Evans got another chance and kept his place for four consecutive games. Evans couldn't have had a better man to learn from than the great Shankly whom, when Evans first started as a player, he used to get changed alongside. 'You never had a conversation with him, he just made statements and threw facts at you,' Evans said. 'Black was black and white was white with him. I don't mean he wasn't friendly because he was very

friendly towards the younger players, but really you just listened to him. He was so enthusiastic about the game. He would say, "It's a great day today" even if it was raining but you knew what he meant. It meant we were about to play football!' When Shankly decided to experiment with winger Alec Lindsay as a left-back against Newcastle on 12 September 1970, Evans was well and truly out of the first-team picture except for two appearances later on in the season. Evans made no first-team appearances in 1971/72 and 1972/73 and featured for Philadelphia Atoms in the USA in the summer of 1973 before playing twice for Liverpool in December in what turned out to be his final season as a player.

BOB PAISLEY, who had just taken over from Shankly, somewhat surprisingly offered the 25-year-old a golden opportunity to join the famous Bootroom by taking control of the club's reserve side. John Smith, who was Liverpool's chairman at the time, made a prediction of Nostradamus' proportions in 1974. 'We have not made an appointment for the present but for the future. One day Roy Evans will be our manager.'

The youngest coach in the Football League proved to be very successful in charge of the reserve team, leading them to victory in the Central League seven times in nine years. When Paisley retired in 1983, Evans was promoted to first-team coach, proving to be of invaluable assistance to first Fagan and then Dalglish. Souness arrived in 1991 with Phil Boersma as his right-hand man and Evans was moved one step down in the pecking order. The writing was on the wall for Souness when before the 1993/94 season, Evans was installed as 'next-in-charge' to the Scot,

obviously being prepared to take over if things didn't work out. When Roy Evans replaced Souness as manager on 31 January 1994, fans were quite optimistic that he would turn Liverpool's fortunes around. Evans seemed to bring some order to the mess Souness had left behind. He inherited a decent squad of players: Fowler and McManaman were exciting young players who were establishing themselves in the first team and there seemed to be a good blend of youth and experience to carry the club forward. His first full season in charge promised brighter times ahead. Liverpool finished the campaign with 74 points, an improvement of 10 points on Souness's best total, but Evans never reached as high a total again. With Collymore signed before the start of the 1995/96 season to join Fowler in a scintillating partnership up front, it heralded two years of, at times, quite breathtaking football, including the two memorable 4-3 victories over Newcastle at Anfield in successive seasons. Evans was celebrated as being at the heart of Liverpool's revival. His man-management had replaced Souness's autocratic style and Liverpool were playing entertaining football. Supporters were concerned, though, that in between the team was well below average and was unable to carry out its Championship threat. In the end the only tangible success came in the 1995 League Cup final at Wembley, where Bolton were beaten 2-1 to record the club's fifth success in the competition.

It could have been so different. Roy's best attempt to bring the League Championship back to Anfield came in the 1996/97 season. Liverpool were top of the league after winning at Southampton in the final match of the calendar year, with a five-point lead on Manchester United and Arsenal, but were gradually overhauled by United. The Reds could have regained the top spot the day after United surprisingly lost to Derby County at Old Trafford early in April. After taking the lead against Coventry, they lost the game in the final few minutes in front of a stunned home crowd. The next home match was also lost, more crucially against United. Roy's time in charge coincided with the rise of 'The Spice Boys', a term given to an unruly group of the club's players, indicating that Evans was maybe too nice to be the manager of such a high-profile club. Team captain John Barnes was unhappy with his team-mates. 'I had no problem with the Liverpool players modelling but I was concerned with their time-keeping, their lack of respect and casual attitude in training.

I ranted and raved at the players to get them going,' Barnes said in his autobiography. 'I became intense and dissatisfied about practices at Liverpool. Melwood was turning from a training ground into a playground. "We've really got to get training sorted out," I often told Roy. I looked at talents like Jamie, Robbie and Macca and felt we could be the best side in the country.'

Manchester United were the thorn in Liverpool's side during Evans' time as manager, just as they were for practically every club in the 1990s. The Reds reserved one of their worst performances under Evans' management for one of the most important matches, the 1996 FA Cup final, remembered as much for the 'men in white suits' who didn't perform once they had changed out of them as it was for Cantona's late goal.

There is a very thin line between success and failure sometimes. Because of everything that had gone on before in the previous three decades, Liverpool were expected to win trophies. When they dried up in the 1990s, there was more pressure on the manager than there would have been at other clubs, where the chairman would have been overjoyed to finish in the top four at the end of a season and win the occasional cup competition. Evans was probably unlucky that he didn't win more than

just the 1995 League Cup. It certainly wasn't for the lack of trying on his part. He was never afraid to face the media when things weren't going to plan and his pride in the job and his enthusiasm and love for the football club he had played for and been associated with for so long was never in doubt. As when Evans was promoted to Souness's assistant in 1993, Houllier was brought to the club during the summer of 1998, but Liverpool's board went one step further and made him joint-manager. How could two managers control the club, having different ideas of how the team were supposed to play? On 12 November 1998, Evans left the club, leaving Houllier in sole charge.

ROY EVANS didn't make a big impression on the Liverpool team as a player and didn't deliver the title as manager, but he remains truly one of Liverpool's greatest servants, as part of the legendary Bootroom.

Evans as Manager in Europe

Season	European Cup	UEFA Cup	European Cup Winners' Cup
1995/96	-	2nd Round	-
1996/97	-	-	Semi-Final
1997/98	-	2nd Round	-

Evans/Houllier as Managers in Europe

Season	European Cup	UEFA Cup	European Cup Winners' Cup
1998/99	-	2nd Round	-

As a Player

Season	League		FA Cup		League Cup		Europe		Total	
	App	Goals	App	Goals	App	Goals	App	Goals	App	Goals
1969/70	3	0	0	0	0	0	0	0	3	0
1970/71	4	0	0	0	1	0	1	0	6	0
1973/74	2	0	0	0	0	0	0	0	2	0
Total	**9**	**0**	**0**	**0**	**1**	**0**	**1**	**0**	**11**	**0**

Roy Evans as Manager

Season	Division	P	W	D	L	GF	GA	Pts	Pos	Win %	FA Cup	League Cup
1993/94*	Premier League	16	5	2	9	15	23	17	8	31.25	-	-
1994/95	Premier League	42	21	11	10	65	37	74	4	50.00	6th Round	Winners
1995/96	Premier League	38	20	11	7	70	34	71	3	52.63	Runners-Up	4th Round
1996/97	Premier League	38	19	11	8	62	37	68	4	50.00	4th Round	5th Round
1997/98	Premier League	38	18	11	9	68	42	65	3	47.37	3rd Round	Semi-Final
Total	-	**172**	**83**	**46**	**43**	**280**	**173**	**295**	-	**48.26**	-	-

* Evans appointed on 31 January 1994 with Liverpool in 5th position

Roy Evans/Gerard Houllier Joint-Management

Season	Division	P	W	D	L	GF	GA	Pts	Pos	Win %	FA Cup	League Cup
1998/99**	Premier League	12	4	4	4	19	14	16	8	33.33	-	4th Round
Total	-	**12**	**4**	**4**	**4**	**19**	**14**	**16**	-	**33.33**	-	-

** Evans resigned on 12 November 1998 with Liverpool in 8th position

FACTFILE

BORN
Bootle, Liverpool,
4 October 1948

POSITION
Left-back

OTHER CLUBS AS PLAYER
Philadelphia Atoms
(loan, 1973)

OTHER CLUBS AS AN ADMINISTRATOR
Fulham (joint-caretaker manager 2000),
Crystal Palace (director of football 2000–01),
Wales (assistant manager 2004–10)

JOINED
1963; signed professional 5 October 1965

APPOINTED MANAGER
31 January 1994

LFC DEBUT AS PLAYER
16 March 1970

LFC DEBUT AS MANAGER
5 February 1994

CONTRACT EXPIRY
12 November 1998

HONOURS AS MANAGER
League Cup 1995

Everpresents

Season	Appearances	Player(s)
1892/93	29	Andrew Hannah, Duncan McLean, Tom Wyllie
1894/95	34	Harry Bradshaw
1896/97	35	John McCartney
1897/98	35	Tom Cleghorn, Harry Storer
1899/1900	38	Billy Dunlop, Tom Robertson
1900/01	36	Bill Goldie, Bill Perkins, Tom Robertson
1901/02	37	Bill Goldie
1902/03	35	Bill Goldie
1904/05	36	Ned Doig
1905/06	44	Arthur Goddard
1909/10	39	Tom Chorlton
1910/11	40	Bobby Robinson
1912/13	42	Bob Ferguson
1913/14	46	Tom Fairfoul
1914/15	40	Jimmy Nicholl
1920/21	45	Walter Wadsworth
1921/	46	Dick Forshaw, Fred Hopkin
1922/23	46	Dick Forshaw, Donald Mackinlay, Elisha Scott
1923/24	47	Elisha Scott
1924/25	46	Danny Shone
1925/26	45	Harry Chambers
1926/27	46	Harry Chambers
1927/28	44	Tom Bromilow, Dick Edmed
1928/29	45	James Jackson, Tom Morrison
1930/31	43	Tommy Lucas, Archie McPherson
1931/32	46	Tom Bradshaw, Gordon Gunson
1932/33	43	Willie Steel
1936/37	43	Alf Hanson
1938/39	45	Jack Balmer, Matt Busby
1948/49	46	Jack Balmer
1950/51	43	Eddie Spicer
1955/56	47	Geoff Twentyman
1956/57	43	Ronnie Moran
1958/59	43	Dick White
1959/60	44	Alan A'Court, Ronnie Moran
1960/61	47	Bert Slater, Dick White
1961/62	47	Alan A'Court, Gerry Byrne, Jimmy Melia, Gordon Milne
1962/63	48	Roger Hunt
1963/64	47	Ian Callaghan, Gordon Milne, Peter Thompson
1965/66	53	Gerry Byrne, Ian Callaghan, Tommy Lawrence, Tommy Smith, Ron Yeats
1966/67	52	Chris Lawler, Tommy Smith, Peter Thompson
1967/68	59	Chris Lawler, Tommy Lawrence
1968/69	51	Ian Callaghan, Chris Lawler, Tommy Smith, Peter Thompson
1969/70	54	Bobby Graham, Chris Lawler

Season	Appearances	Player(s)
1971/72	53	Ray Clemence, Emlyn Hughes, Chris Lawler
1972/73	66	Ian Callaghan, Chris Lawler, Larry Lloyd
1973/74	61	Ian Callaghan, Ray Clemence, Emlyn Hughes, Kevin Keegan
1974/75	53	Ray Clemence, Emlyn Hughes
1975/76	59	Ray Clemence, Phil Neal
1976/77	62	Ray Clemence, Emlyn Hughes
1977/78	62	Kenny Dalglish, Phil Neal
1978/79	54	Kenny Dalglish, Ray Kennedy, Phil Neal
1979/80	60	Kenny Dalglish, Phil Neal, Phil Thompson
1980/81	63	Phil Neal
1981/82	62	Kenny Dalglish, Bruce Grobbelaar, Phil Neal
1982/83	60	Bruce Grobbelaar, Alan Kennedy, Phil Neal
1983/84	67	Bruce Grobbelaar, Alan Hansen, Alan Kennedy, Sammy Lee
1984/85	64	Bruce Grobbelaar, Phil Neal
1985/86	63	Bruce Grobbelaar
1986/87	57	Ian Rush
1987/88	50	Steve Nicol
1989/90	50	Bruce Grobbelaar
1994/95	57	Robbie Fowler, David James
1995/96	53	David James, Steve McManaman
1996/97	52	Stig Inge Bjørnebye, David James

The squad has been rotated to such extent that no one has been everpresent during a single season since 1996/97. The following players have been everpresent in the Premier League from the 1997/98 season onwards.

Season	Appearances	Player(s)
1999/2000	38	Sami Hyypia
2000/01	38	Markus Babbel, Sander Westerveld
2003/04	38	Sami Hyypia
2004/05	38	Jamie Carragher
2007/08	38	Pepe Reina
2008/09	38	Jamie Carragher, Pepe Reina
2009/10	38	Pepe Reina
2010/11	38	Pepe Reina, Martin Skrtel

JACKIE BALMER
LIVERPOOL

PLAYER'S CIGARETTES

T. LUCAS

James Jackson

PLAYER'S CIGARETTES

H. CHAMBERS

Every Other Saturday

'EVERY OTHER SATURDAY' is adjusted from a classic Rangers' song written in the 1960s and is quite popular on matchdays at Anfield. It originates from an era when Rangers supporters finished work on a Saturday morning, a lot from the River Clyde shipyards, and headed to Ibrox for the afternoon fixture.

The first verse of the Rangers song:

Every other Saturday's me half day off
And it's off to the match I go
Happily we wander down the Copland Road
Me and ma wee pal Joe
We love to see the lassies with the blue scarves on
We love to hear the boys all roar
But I don't have to tell you that the best of all
We love to see the Rangers score

```
"Every Other Saturday"
- Liverpool version:

Every other Saturday's me half day off
And it's off to the match I go
We like to take a stroll along the Anfield Road
Me and me old pal Joe
I love to see the lasses with their red scarves on
We love to hear the Kopites roar
But I don't have to tell you that the best of all
We love to see our Liverpool sc-o-o-ore sc-o-o-ore
We've won the English League about a thousand times
And UEFA was a simple do
We've played some exhibitions in the FA Cup
We are the Wembley Wizards too
But... when we won the European Cup in Rome
Like we should have done years before
We gathered down at Anfield
Boys a hundred thousand strong
To give the boys a welcome ho-om-me ho-om-me
(Kenny ohhh Kenny
I'd walk a million miles for one of your goals
ohhh Kenny ohhh Kenny)
```

Family celebrate at Arsenal on 16 March 1963

Supporting the Reds home and away – at the 1965 FA Cup semi-final at Villa Park

King Kenny scoring against Helsinki on 2 November 1982

FA Cup

THE ENGLISH FOOTBALL Association, usually abbreviated to FA was formed in 1863. For the first eight years of its existence, clubs under its control only played friendly fixtures with no prizes at stake. In 1871 the FA's secretary had the idea for a knockout tournament between its member clubs with a trophy being awarded to the winner. Fifteen clubs entered, including the leading Scottish club Queen's Park. Wanderers became the first winners of the FA Cup by defeating the Royal Engineers in the final at the Kennington Oval, now more widely known as the home of Surrey County Cricket Club. Wanderers retained the trophy they first won in 1872 but several other clubs with unusual names to today's followers of the sport also collected the cup in its first decade including Oxford University, the Old Carthusians and the Old Etonians. The first recognisable victor amongst today's clubs was Blackburn Rovers in 1884, by which time there were 100 entrants.

The original trophy presented to Wanderers in 1872 was stolen from a shop in Birmingham in 1895 when Aston Villa were the holders. Villa were fined £25 by the FA so that a replacement could be made. It was an exact replica of the original and was used until 1910 when it was presented to the FA's

president Lord Kinnaird who had won the cup on five occasions, three times with Wanderers and twice with the Old Etonians.

The FA bought a new and larger trophy in time for the 1911 final. Made in Bradford, its first winners were, appropriately, Bradford City. This is the instantly recognisable trophy that is presented to today's winning club, even though the current one is a replica that was made in the early 1990s because the original had become too fragile.

LIVERPOOL Football Club, like many other clubs at the time, competed in the FA Cup before

actually becoming a member of the Football League. Entering the competition at the first qualifying round and being drawn away to Cheshire club Nantwich, Liverpool's first experience of a knockout tournament was a happy one as the team won by four clear goals on 15 October 1892. They did not, however, reach the first round proper because another Cheshire club, Northwich Victoria, knocked them out in the third qualifying round.

Once Liverpool had become a member of the Football League in 1893, they no longer had to qualify. Although the team would initially struggle against established league clubs, it did have a famous victory against Preston North End in 1894, the Lancashire club having been the English champions in both 1889 and 1890. The first run of any note came in 1897 when the club reached the semi-final before being beaten by eventual winners Aston Villa at Bramall Lane. The semi-final would also be reached two years later but there would

On their way to Wembley 1971

again be disappointment after a titanic struggle with Sheffield United that went into a second replay before there was a winner. The first attempt at the second replay was abandoned at Fallowfield, Manchester when Liverpool were leading 1-0, due to a pitch invasion from hundreds of spectators. When the match was replayed three days later, it was Sheffield United who scored the winner five minutes from time.

AS A NEW century dawned, Liverpool teams would continue to struggle to get past the first round but in 1906 the Blues and the Reds were paired in the semi-final. Everton scored twice in the middle of second half and went on to beat Newcastle United in the final at the Crystal Palace ground in south London, which had become the first-choice venue for the final since 1895. It would be another eight years before Liverpool played at that same venue when they eventually reached the final in 1914 after defeating Barnsley, Gillingham, West Ham United, Queens Park Rangers and Aston Villa on their way. Standing between them and the trophy was a strong Burnley

team, also appearing in their first FA Cup final. King George V attended the final, the first British monarch to do so, but Bert Freeman, who spent three years at Everton before joining Burnley, scored the only goal of the game in front of a crowd of nearly 73,000.

When football resumed competitively after World War One, even Liverpool's great Championship-winning teams of 1922 and 1923 could not win the cup; and the 1930s was another barren decade. It wasn't until 1947 that the club reached another semi-final but a different Burnley team again prevailed by a single goal to destroy hopes and dreams of winning the famous cup for the first time.

After reaching the final, which had been held at Wembley Stadium in London since 1923, in 1950 but losing there to Arsenal, the 1950s saw two horrible defeats to lower-ranked opponents; at Third Division North Gateshead in 1953 and then at non-league Worcester City in 1959. Bill Shankly arrived at the end of that calendar year to galvanise the club into a new decade and candidly admitted in his 1976 autobiography: 'Liverpool had never won the FA Cup, and that was a terrible thing.' In 1965 Shankly's men banished seventy-three years of FA Cup pain by defeating Leeds United after extra time at Wembley.

Shankly would have one more FA Cup success in 1974 before handing over the managerial reins to Bob Paisley. Although Paisley was so victorious, the FA Cup eluded him just as it had eluded every other Liverpool manager apart from Shankly. The club would have to wait until 1986 for its third triumph and Kenny Dalglish would lead his men to two more finals before the decade closed; an unexpected defeat to Wimbledon in 1988 being

followed by the emotional post-Hillsborough victory over Everton a year later.

Considering what had been won in the preceding decades the 1990s were barren for Liverpool. But two more FA Cup finals were reached; one being won against Sunderland in 1992 and the other being lost to bitter rivals Manchester United in 1996. Wembley Stadium was pulled down in 2000 and the final moved to the Millennium Stadium in Cardiff for six seasons. Liverpool supporters had referred to the old Wembley Stadium as 'Anfield South' because the team had featured there so often, but Cardiff proved to be a lucky venue too as Liverpool won the first and last FA Cup finals to be played in Wales. Both were dramatic affairs, Michael Owen's two late goals stole the trophy from Arsenal in 2001 and Steven Gerrard's heroics guided his team to a penalty shoot-out success over West Ham United in 2006. Liverpool made it to the new Wembley in 2012 but Chelsea, who have been dominant in the FA Cup in the last few years, were much stronger on the day even though the Reds made an inevitable comeback which came just up short.

There is still something magical about the FA Cup as it remains the oldest knockout competition in the world and its history is littered with great names, fantastic games and many astonishing upsets. Only three clubs; Manchester United (11), Arsenal (10) and Tottenham Hotspur (8) have won the famous trophy more often than seven-fold cup champions Liverpool. The David versus Goliath clash is what makes the FA Cup different from other competitions. Big clubs are pitted against small with exciting regularity and unexpected results. The final is watched all over the

world by people not necessarily with any direct affinity to either finalist.

Memorable FA Cup games

10 February 1894 – second round, Anfield: Liverpool 3 Preston North End 2

Liverpool: *Billy McOwen, Andrew Hannah, Duncan McLean, Matt McQueen, Joe McQue, Jim McBride, Patrick Gordon, Malcolm McVean, David Henderson, Harry Bradshaw, Hugh McQueen*

Preston North End: *Jimmy Trainer, Bob Holmes, Geordie Drummond, William Greer, Moses Sanders, James Sharp, Jack Gordon, John Cunningham, Jimmy Ross, Frank Becton, John Cowan*

This was Liverpool's biggest game to date in their two-year history. The old Preston Invincibles were still a great attraction and many fans were locked out as no more than 18,000 people could squeeze into Anfield. Even though a strong wind prevailed the game as a spectacle did not disappoint. As early as in the fourth minute full-back Jack Holmes' attempted clearance bounced off the legs of Liverpool's David Henderson and into the Preston goal which raised the roof. Malcolm McVean added a second, but Preston stalwart and later Liverpool captain, Jimmy Ross, replied immediately with a shot that crashed into the net.

Preston came out determined in the second half and Frank Becton equalised. Like Ross he later joined Liverpool. The game was 'exceptional' and each side attacked with vigour. Liverpool had the upper hand though and David Henderson delighted the crowd with his second goal which proved to be the winner.

23 March 1899 – Semi-final replay at Burnden Park: Liverpool 4 Sheffield United 4

Liverpool: *Harry Storer, Archie Goldie, Billy Dunlop, Raby Howell, Alex Raisbeck, Bill Goldie, Jack Cox, John Walker, George Allan, Hugh Morgan, Tommy Robertson*

Sheffield United: *Billy Foulke, Harry Thickett, Peter Boyle, Harry Johnson, Tom Morren, Ernest Needham, Walter Bennett, Billy Beer, George Hedley, Jack Almond, Fred Priest*

The teams had already fought out a 2-2 draw at City Ground, Nottingham. Tom Watson had failed at this stage three times with Sunderland and once with Liverpool so he was beyond desperate to reach the final. A brilliant goal by Johnny Walker ensured a 1-0 lead for Liverpool and the second half was only five minutes old when George Allan increased the lead. A man with the wonderful name of Billy Beer cut the deficit in half and soon after the score was 2-2. 'Needham equalised by a shot from the

Supporting the Reds in 1950

touchline, which sailed in the most miraculous fashion into goal,' according to captain Alex Raisbeck in 1915. 'I think that was one of the luckiest goals I ever saw scored, and I have seen a few lucky ones in my day and generation.' An own goal from Peter Boyle put Liverpool ahead again in the 70th minute and two minutes later Liverpool were awarded a penalty. Sheffield United legend 'Fatty' Foulke saved Allan's spot kick but Jack Cox was at hand to put the rebound into the net. As 83 minutes had passed Liverpool looked on their way to Wembley with a 4-2 lead. Robertson thought he had added the fifth after a brilliant solo run but was adjudged to have been offside. 'So sore did we feel over this that it seemed to knock us off our game,' Raisbeck remembered. Two United goals in the 84th and 85th minute by Fred Priest ensured a second replay that Liverpool lost 1-0. 'Storer appeared to lose his nerve,' Raisbeck admitted. The usually reliable Liverpool keeper was heavily criticised for the final two goals and the *Manchester Evening News* reported: 'A great deal of the criticism he was subject to was not altogether too severe.'

**31 March 1906
– Semi-final at Villa Park:
Liverpool 0 Everton 2**

Liverpool: *Sam Hardy, Alf West, Billy Dunlop, Maurice Parry, Alex Raisbeck, James Bradley, Arthur Goddard, Bobby Robinson, Jack Parkinson, John Carlin, Joe Hewitt*

Everton: *Billy Scott, Bob Balmer, Jack Crelley, Harry Makepeace, Jack Taylor, Walter Abbott, Jack Sharp, Hugh Bolton, Sandy Young, Jimmy Settle, Harold Hardman*

The atmosphere was very tense in Birmingham when the Merseyside rivals were about to take the field in their most important derby to date. Twenty excursions trains had been run from Liverpool to the

Midlands' capital and football enthusiasts were attracted from all over the country. It was reckoned that close upon to 50,000 were present to witness this momentous occasion. Liverpool were handicapped in attack by the absence of two of their key players in Jack Cox and Sam Raybould but Everton were at full strength. The latter had scored all three goals for Liverpool against Southampton in the previous round. It was a controversial decision to leave Raybould out as Raisbeck revealed in 1915. On their way in the train to Birmingham the directors had asked Raisbeck to check with Raybould if he was fit and Sam told his skipper that he was ready to play. 'I told the officials what Raybould had said, and it was decided then and there to play him,' Raisbeck said. 'Some of the players, I don't know their names to this day, went to the officials and said they were risking a lot in playing Raybould. The directors were led to understand that I knew everything about it and that I was in agreement with their views. You can imagine my surprise when I learned that Raybould had to stand down.' Everton scored two goals separated by a couple of minutes midway through the second half and returned to a hero's welcome at Lime Street station while Liverpool left their train in solemn mood at Edge Hill.

25 April 1914 – Final at Crystal Palace: Liverpool 0 Burnley 1

Liverpool: *Ken Campbell, Ephraim Longworth, Bob Pursell, Tom Fairfoul, Bob Ferguson, Donald Mackinlay, Jackie Sheldon, Arthur Metcalf, Tom Miller, Bill Lacey, Jimmy Nicholl*

Burnley: *Ronnie Sewell, Tom Bamford, David Taylor, George Halley, Tommy Boyle, Billy Watson, Billy Nesbitt, Dick Lindley, Bertie Freeman, Teddy Hodgson, Eddie Mosscrop*

At last Tom Watson's Liverpool had made it to the final held in London followed by 73,000 eager spectators. The most interesting account of the game was given by a Mr Meredith, who had been blind from birth. According to the *Daily Express* he could 'tell by the interval of time between the sound of a kick and the sound of it bouncing how far and in what direction it has gone' and 'name the player in possession of the ball and describe what he was going to do with it.' According to Mr Meredith 'it was a great game and the play veered pretty evenly.' On Liverpool's side he was most impressed by right-back Ephraim Longworth as 'he kicked and tackled like a Trojan, and saved his goal time after time when it was in great danger.' He also liked right-winger Jackie Sheldon but 'he spoils many a good effort by holding the ball too long, instead of sending it to the centre.' He was, however, very disappointed by forward Tom Miller 'as in many instances he was very slow. I have known Miller at his best, and he was a long way short of it to-day.' Unique observations on a unique day for Liverpool.

**25 March 1950
– Semi-final at Maine Road:
Liverpool 2 Everton 0**

Liverpool: *Cyril Sidlow, Ray Lambert, Eddie Spicer, Phil Taylor, Bill Jones, Bob Paisley, Jimmy Payne, Kevin Baron, Albert Stubbins, Willie Fagan, Billy Liddell*

Everton: *George Burnett, Eric Moore, Jack Hedley, Jackie Grant, David Falder, Peter Farrell, Ted Buckle, Eddie Wainwright, Harry Catterick, Wally Fielding, Tommy Eglington*

Jubilant Liverpool fans before the final in 1914

''Stop Billy Liddell!' Those will be Everton manager Cliff Britton's final words to his players when they leave their dressing-room,' reported the *Liverpool Echo* before the Merseyside teams faced each other in the semi-final for the first time for 44 years. It was though easier said than done to stop the all too powerful Scotsman. Left-half Bob Paisley, who was having his 'best game for seasons,' broke the stalemate with a speculative lob. As Paisley's pass approached the Everton goal Liddell jumped up with Everton keeper George Burnett and two other defenders and the ball went into the goal directly without anybody else touching it. Liddell made sure Liverpool were going to Wembley in the 62nd minute. The match was described as the finest ever between the teams and the crowd was whipped into a frenzy at the final whistle as the *Echo* noted. 'When the players walked off at the end, shaking hands to the accompaniment of a sound which can only be likened to the noise of 10,000 tons of granite chippings dropping on 10,000 Nissen huts (cumulative effect of 10,000 whirling rattles), it was almost a poignant moment for anyone with even the remotest interest in either club.'

15 January 1959 – Third round at St George's Lane: Worcester City 2 Liverpool 1

Liverpool: *Tommy Younger, John Molyneux, Ronnie Moran, Johnny Wheeler, Dick White, Geoff Twentyman, Fred Morris, Jimmy Harrower, Louis Bimpson, Jimmy Melia, Alan A'Court*

Worcester City: *John Kirkwood, Eddie Wilcox, Reg Potts, Sammy Bryceland, Melville, Roy Paul, Tommy Brown, Eddie Follan, Harry Knowles, Bernard Gosling, Tommy Skuse*

'Worcester too Hot for Liverpool' read one Fleet Street headline as Liverpool suffered their most shocking cup defeat. Eight of the players in the non-league side, that had reached the third round for the first time in its history, had been working at the morning of the game and Second Division Liverpool was expected to proceed without great difficulty. Liverpool manager Phil Taylor had seen the City side on one occasion but their game was called off after 45 minutes because of atrocious ground conditions and he expected a tough match even though Liverpool were on a six game winning streak. Worcester went ahead in the ninth minute when John Molyneux's poor back pass allowed 18-year-old winger Tommy Skuse to nip in and put the ball beyond the keeper. Ten minutes from time Dick White scored an own goal, but Geoff Twentyman gave Liverpool hope from the penalty spot couple of minutes later. Liverpool tried in vain to bring a replay to Anfield.

Phil Taylor was gracious in defeat: 'Worcester deserved to win. They outfought us on a pitch that may have reduced the odds against them, but was still as good a playing surface as you can get in England right now. We lost because our forwards refused to fight.'

1 May 1965 – Final at Wembley: Liverpool 2 Leeds United 1

Liverpool: *Tommy Lawrence, Chris Lawler, Gerry Byrne, Geoff Strong, Ron Yeats, Willie Stevenson, Ian Callaghan, Roger Hunt, Ian St John, Tommy Smith, Peter Thompson*

Leeds United: *Gary Sprake, Paul Reaney, Willie Bell, Billy Bremner, Jack Charlton, Norman Hunter, Johnny Giles, James Storrie, Alan Peacock, Bobby Collins, Albert Johanneson*

An amusing sight on this special day was the twelve inches in height that separated the Scottish captains of the day Ron Yeats and Bobby Collins when they shook hands prior to kick-off. The latter was to instigate the most controversial moment of the game when Collins' horror challenge in the opening minutes left Gerry Byrne with a broken collar bone and an injured shin, but the left-back fought on bravely in a display of 'raw courage' as Shankly noted. The first half was terribly disappointing as rain had begun to fall but Liverpool at least woke up from their slumber in the second half and attacked in force while Leeds looked out of sorts concentrated on trying to defend. The deadlock was finally broken in the third minute of extra-time when Byrne's pin-point cross from the left was headed in by Roger Hunt. Leeds equalised in the 102nd minute with a first time volley from Billy Bremner. Ian Callaghan delivered a peach of a pass which Ian St John headed into the net in the 111th minute, a magical moment that will live on forever in the history of the club.

4 May 1974 – Final at Wembley: Liverpool 3 Newcastle United 0

Liverpool: *Ray Clemence, Tommy Smith, Alec Lindsay, Phil Thompson, Peter Cormack, Emlyn Hughes, Kevin Keegan, Brian Hall, Steve Heighway, John Toshack, Ian Callaghan.*

Newcastle United: *Iam McFaul, Frank Clark, Alan Kennedy, Terry McDermott, Pat Howard, Bobby Moncur, Jim Smith (Thomas Gibb), Thomas Cassidy, Malcolm MacDonald, John Tudor, Terry Hibbitt*

This turned out to be the most one-sided final that Liverpool has ever participated in. The Reds really turned on the style with three marvellous goals in the second half. Brian Hall ducked under Tommy Smith's right-wing centre and Kevin Keegan controlled the ball before driving it past McFaul. Clemence's deep punt upfield effectively sealed the result 15 minutes from time. Toshack back-headed the ball into the Newcastle penalty-area and Steve Heighway timed his run perfectly before placing his shot neatly out of the goalkeeper's reach. Shortly before the end, Kevin Keegan added a third goal after a sensational move which involved several players and the ball going from one side of the pitch to the other.

13 April 1985 – Semi-final at Goodison Park: Liverpool 2 Manchester United 2

Liverpool: *Bruce Grobbelaar, Phil Neal, Jim Beglin, Mark Lawrenson, Sammy Lee, Alan Hansen, Kenny Dalglish, Ronnie Whelan, Ian Rush, Kevin MacDonald, John Wark (Paul Walsh 59)*

Manchester United: *Gary Bailey, John Gidman, Arthur Albiston, Norman Whiteside, Paul McGrath, Graeme Hogg, Bryan Robson, Gordon Strachan, Mark Hughes, Frank Stapleton, Jesper Olsen*

Liverpool arrived at this match fresh from a 4-0 victory over Panathinaikos in the European Cup semi-final. Bryan Robson scored from close range in the 69th minute to open the scoring in this classic thriller. There were only three minutes left of normal time when Ronnie Whelan made a short pass to Phil Neal who teed up the ball for the Irishman who curled a sweet volley into the corner of the goal. Frank Stapleton put United in the lead again in the 98th minute when Liverpool were caught on the break. Again Liverpool looked down and out as extra-time was running its course. Dalglish delivered a pass to the far post where Ian Rush headed across Gary Bailey who punched the ball and as it was bouncing in front of the goal Paul Walsh was first on the scene to push it over the line, cue delirious celebrations. United won the replay and beat Everton in the final.

10 May 1986 – Final at Wembley: Liverpool 3 Everton 1

Liverpool: *Bruce Grobbelaar, Mark Lawrenson, Jim Beglin, Steve Nicol, Ronnie Whelan, Alan Hansen, Kenny Dalglish, Craig Johnston, Ian Rush, Jan Mølby, Kevin MacDonald*

Everton: *Bobby Mimms, Gary Stevens, Pat van den Hauwe, Kevin Ratcliffe, Derek Mountfield, Peter Reid, Trevor Steven, Gary Lineker, Graeme Sharp, Paul Bracewell, Kevin Sheedy*

Liverpool's 1986 FA Cup celebrations begin at Wembley

Liverpool were struggling to impose themselves on the first all-Merseyside FA Cup final all throughout the first half. Gary Lineker put Everton in front in the 27th minute, but Jan Mølby, in his finest Liverpool performance to date, set about loosening Everton's grip on the midfield. In the 57th minute he split the Everton defence open to let Ian Rush through who scored despite Craig Johnston's desperate attempt to have the last touch. Six minutes later Johnston had his moment as Mølby created another goal. Liverpool saved the best for last when Ronnie Whelan's sensational pass was touched down by Rush before the Welshman released a trademark shot into the far corner knocking over one of the photographers' cameras in the process. Liverpool had won the League and FA Cup double for the first time in the club's history.

20 May 1989
– Final at Wembley:
Liverpool 3 Everton 2

Liverpool: *Bruce Grobbelaar,*
Steve Nicol, Alan Hansen,
Gary Ablett, Steve Staunton
(Barry Venison 91), Ray Houghton,
Ronnie Whelan, Steve McMahon,
John Barnes, Peter Beardsley,
John Aldridge (Ian Rush 72)

Everton: *Neville Southall, Neil*
McDonald, Pat van den Hauwe,
Kevin Ratcliffe, Dave Watson,
Paul Bracewell (Stuart McCall
58), Pat Nevin, Trevor Steven,
Graeme Sharp, Tony Cottee,
Kevin Sheedy (Ian Wilson 77)

Any bitter rivalry was cast aside on this emotional occasion in wake of the Hillsborough disaster. John Aldridge, who missed a penalty in the defeat to Wimbledon in the 1988 final, struck in the opening exchanges to give Liverpool a perfect start. It looked like it was going to be the only goal of the game until Stuart McCall equalised right at the end from an all-mighty scramble. Ian Rush, who had come on for Aldridge,

proved to be Liverpool's hero in extra-time. Steve Nicol's pass found Rush in the penalty area where he turned his marker and struck the ball into the top far corner. Everton were down, but not out. McCall scored with a beautiful shot to make it 2-2 after 100 minutes. Three minutes later Rush was again found from the left, this time by Barnes. Rush headed the ball neatly into goal. There was to be no comeback for the Blues this time around. No fences were up at Wembley post-Hillsborough which allowed a mass invasion at the final whistle.

20 February 1991 – Fifth round replay at Goodison Park:
Everton 4 Liverpool 4

Liverpool: *Bruce Grobbelaar,*
Glenn Hysén, David Burrows,
Steve Nicol, Jan Mølby,
Gary Ablett, Peter Beardsley,
Steve Staunton, Ian Rush,
John Barnes, Barry Venison

Everton: *Neville Southall,*
Ray Atteveld (Stuart McCall 46),
Andy Hinchcliffe, Kevin Ratcliffe,
Dave Watson, Martin Keown,
Pat Nevin (Tony Cottee 86),
Mike Milligan, Graeme Sharp,
Mike Newell, John Ebbrell

The pace of this derby was unrelenting with Hitchcockian twists and turns. Breathtaking 120 minutes saw eight goals scored by; Peter Beardsley (37 / 1-0), Graeme Sharp (48 / 1-1), Peter Beardsley (71 / 2-1) Graeme Sharp (73 / 2-2), Ian Rush (77 / 3-2), Tony Cottee (89 / 3-3),

John Barnes (103 / 4-3) and Tony Cottee (113 / 4-4). The game took on a whole different meaning when Dalglish handed in his resignation making this the last game he was in charge of at Liverpool for twenty years.

12 May 2001
– Final at Millennium Stadium:
Liverpool 2 Arsenal 1

Liverpool: *Sander Westerveld,*
Stephane Henchoz,
Markus Babbel, Sami Hyypia,
Jamie Carragher, Vladimir Smicer
(Robbie Fowler 77), Danny
Murphy (Patrik Berger 77),
Didi Hamann (Gary McAllister
60), Steven Gerrard,
Emile Heskey, Michael Owen

Arsenal: *David Seaman,*
Lee Dixon (Dennis Bergkamp 89),
Martin Keown, Tony Adams,
Ashley Cole, Freddie Ljungberg
(Nwankwo Kanu 85),
Gilles Grimandi, Patrick Vieira,
Robert Pires, Thierry Henry,
Sylvain Wiltord (Ray Parlour 76)

Did Liverpool deserve to win? Possibly not. Stephane Henchoz handled the ball as Thierry Henry's shot was heading for goal with just quarter of an hour gone and the Swiss international again made good use of his hands in the second half in the penalty area. Freddie Ljungberg finally got the seemingly unavoidable goal for Arsenal in the 72nd minute. The double substitution of Patrik Berger and Robbie Fowler five minutes later proved inspiring.

Following Gary McAllister's high cross into the penalty area the ball fell to Michael Owen who clipped it into net. Only five minutes passed before Owen outran Lee Dixon and put the ball in off the far post. Liverpool got away with Henchoz's misdemeanours and the brilliance of Owen in the closing minutes sealed a memorable victory.

13 May 2006 – Final at the Millennium Stadium:
Liverpool 3 West Ham United 3

Liverpool: *Pepe Reina,*
Steve Finnan, Sami Hyypia,
John Arne Riise, Jamie Carragher,
Harry Kewell (Fernando Morientes
48), Steven Gerrard, Xabi Alonso
(Jan Kromkamp 67),
Momo Sissoko, Djibril Cissé,
Peter Crouch (Didi Hamann 71)

West Ham United: *Shaka Hislop,*
Lionel Scaloni, Anton Ferdinand,
Danny Gabbidon, Paul Konchesky,
Yossi Benayoun, Carl Fletcher
(Christian Dailly 77), Nigel
Reo-Coker, Matthew Etherington
(Teddy Sheringham 85),
Dean Ashton (Bobby Zamora 71),
Marlon Harewood

Liverpool by no means delivered a classic performance in Wales as Jamie Carragher's own goal and Pepe Reina's mistake meant the Reds were 2-0 down within half an hour. Steven Gerrard's long pass into the path of Djibril Cissé in the 32nd minute brought relief. All were mindful of Liverpool's classic Istanbul comeback so it was no real surprise when Gerrard's volley equalised the scores with 53 minutes gone. Paul Konchesky's pass drifted into the Liverpool goal nine minutes later but immediately after the tannoy announcement that there would be a minimum of four minutes added to normal time Gerrard released another special. Reina was the hero in the penalty shoot-out by saving from Bobby Zamora, Paul Konchesky and Anton Ferdinand.

Fagan, Chris

FULL-BACK CHRIS, one of Joe Fagan's five sons, made two appearances for Liverpool. On 22 September 1970 'Kit' made his debut, when coming on as a substitute in extra time in a League Cup second round replay against Mansfield Town at Anfield.

ALUN EVANS had scored Liverpool's winning goal, one minute prior to Fagan's introduction to protect their lead. Fagan moved to Prenton Park in July 1971, and made 97 appearances for Tranmere Rovers over the next four seasons.

FACTFILE

BORN
Manchester, 5 June 1950
POSITION
Right-back
OTHER CLUBS
Tranmere Rovers (1971–75), Bangor City, South Liverpool
JOINED
1966; signed professional 1970
LFC DEBUT GAME
22 September 1970
CONTRACT EXPIRY
July 1971

Season	League		FA Cup		League Cup		Europe		Total	
	App	Goals	App	Goals	App	Goals	App	Goals	App	Goals
1970/71	1	0	0	0	0 (1)	0	0	0	1 (1)	0
Total	1	0	0	0	0 (1)	0	0	0	1 (1)	0

Fagan, Joe

JOE FAGAN spent his childhood in the Litherland area of Liverpool and he watched both Everton and Liverpool play, although he preferred Anfield 'as it had a better boys' pen.' He was educated at St Elizabeth Central School, where he led the 1st XI to victory in the *Daily Dispatch* Trophy in 1935. A reliable centre-half, good in the air and solid on the ground, he then played amateur football for Earlstown Bohemians, where he caught the eye of several clubs. Fagan went on a trial at Liverpool and was offered a chance to join the Reds, but he declined, later explaining, 'There was a feeling at that time that if a youngster joined his local club they would not think as much of him as an outsider.' In October 1938 he opted to join Manchester City. However, as with all his peers, Fagan's playing career was severely hampered by the onset of war in 1939.

During wartime Fagan served his country in the Royal Navy but played in the makeshift wartime league. After the war the City side roared to promotion from the old Second Division with Fagan playing a key part at the heart of

defence. He made his full official debut for City on New Year's Day 1947 and in the following four seasons made 168 appearances, skippering the side for the last three. At the age of 30 Fagan left Maine Road in 1951 to become player-manager of part-timers Nelson, a job he combined with inspecting gas meters in local factories. He then briefly returned to the professional game with Bradford Park Avenue before being appointed trainer under the

management of his old wartime pal Harry Catterick at Rochdale in 1953. It was on Catterick's recommendation, that Fagan joined the Anfield coaching staff as assistant trainer on 30 June 1958 just 18 months before the arrival of Bill Shankly would transform the club from Second Division no-hopers to the best side in Europe. Shankly had long been an admirer of Fagan's and had tried to sign him when he was managing Grimsby and Fagan was playing for City. One of Shankly's first acts on his arrival was to reassure the backroom staff at

Anfield that their positions were safe. It was the start of a footballing dynasty that Joe Fagan was to play a major role in.

FAGAN, an avuncular figure known as 'Uncle Joe', was perhaps the closest of all the backroom staff to the players, acting as adviser and friend as well as coach. If he made a criticism, it was a reasoned one without a hint of malice, and only rarely would he lose his temper. As he once explained: 'I can give anyone the mother and father of a hiding, verbally. You can't let players think you are a soft touch,

not here or at any club.' It wasn't a side of Fagan his players often saw, but they knew they stepped out of line at their own peril. One of Fagan's signings, Republic of Ireland international Jim Beglin, paid his respects to his former boss in 2001. 'Joe was just a very genuine nice man. He was a very humble, down to earth person. He had a lovely way about him and was very gentlemanly. Underneath that soft exterior, there was also a hardened professionalism. Joe had authority and when strong words were needed, Joe could produce them.'

It was Fagan who first kitted out the small bootroom along the changing room corridor at Anfield with upturned empty beer crates so that he, Paisley and Reuben Bennett would have a quiet place to sit and chew the fat. The beer crates came courtesy of Paul Orr, later to become Lord Mayor of Liverpool, who had given Fagan some of the 'black stuff' as a thank you for allowing his amateur team, Guinness Export, to receive treatment at Anfield. 'Elton John told me this story about Joe,' respected journalist John Keith remembered. 'It was Elton John's first visit at Anfield. He was walking down after the match and Joe put his hand out, 'Lad, do you want to come in for a drink?' He goes in the Bootroom. Joe says, 'What do you want, lad?' Elton said, 'Can I have a pink gin?' 'Pink gin, lad?'

> JOE SAYS,
> 'WHAT DO YOU WANT,
> LAD?' ELTON SAID,
> 'CAN I HAVE A PINK GIN?'
> 'PINK GIN, LAD?' 'YOU
> CAN HAVE A BROWN
> ALE, A GUINNESS
> OR A SCOTCH AND
> THAT'S YOUR LOT'

'You can have a brown ale, a Guinness or a scotch and that's your lot.' Fagan began to document the daily goings on at Anfield and Melwood, a system that would build into an encyclopaedic volume of facts and figures referred to over and over again at Anfield in the following 20 years. After a spell looking after the reserves, Fagan was appointed first team trainer in 1971, and stepped up to chief coach in 1974 when the untimely retirement of Shankly forced a coaching staff reshuffle. In 1979 he continued his move up the bootroom hierarchy by becoming assistant manager to Paisley and was instrumental in helping to grow the club's ever increasing pile of silverware. Famously, during the 1981/82 season, when Liverpool were struggling in 12th position and the players were having daily discussions about their loss of form, it was Fagan who put a stop to matters, telling them that they were having more meetings than the United Nations and should just concentrate on playing! 'Joe Fagan sat us all down at Anfield before we went on the bus to train at Melwood,' Phil Neal told *LFChistory.net*. 'Joe had a go at every single player, to Souness, to Dalglish, to me. His finishing words were: 'I've said my piece. We can get on the bus now down to Melwood. I want high tempo in training. At the end of the day we're getting out of this. You're all playing as individuals, start playing as a team. I'm not having another meeting from now till the end of the season.' Joe could look at you and cut you in half. I looked at Smitty, Souness but Joe would take the pair of them. He was such a strength behind Bob.' The team duly went on to win the League Championship.

On 1 July 1983, at the age of 62, Joe Fagan finally became manager of Liverpool FC. This unassuming family man still lived in a modest semi-detached house a few hundred yards from the ground. The difference in the club he would manage from the Second Division outfit he had joined a quarter of a century ago was there for all to see. Fagan's job now was ensuring the club maintained its position amongst Europe's elite. As Paisley had been before him, Fagan was not exactly bursting at the chance to take on the manager's role. In a remarkably self-effacing quote he revealed, 'I took the job because I was in a rut when they offered it to me. Ronnie Moran and Roy Evans were doing the training and I was just helping Bob, putting in my two pennyworth.'

FAGAN had inherited a strong side from Paisley but that's never been a recipe for success. The team needed a strong character to keep it going. Paisley wasn't too worried about his successor, 'You may have found me mean and thirsty in my search for trophies, but the bad news is the man who is taking my place is hungrier than me. Fagan's the name and I don't think he'll need any help from the Artful Dodger!' The omens were not good. One of the strongest characters in the side, captain Graeme Souness had left for Italy. Ronnie Moran was promoted to Fagan's assistant and the 1983/84 season started as so many of the previous seasons with a Charity Shield date at Wembley. Manchester United

comfortably ran out 2-0 winners in a low key affair and typically Joe Fagan hid from no one in his after match analysis telling the assembled press, 'Blame me. It was my fault. I put the substitutes on at the wrong time. You learn something all the time in this game.'

But it was at Molyneux a week later, where the league campaign would get underway against Wolves, that all eyes were really focused. A 1-1 draw meant that Liverpool had gone an incredible nine games without victory as the last seven of Paisley's reign had seen five defeats and two draws as the team wound down after winning the Championship early; a statistical quirk that remained the worst run of the Bootroom era. The team promptly won five of their next six games and the die was cast. The settling in period had been tough initially, but as Fagan explained, it was all about handling expectations, 'The first couple of weeks were a bit rough because my mind was racing everywhere, yet I seemed to be doing nothing,' he said. 'I was frightened to death I would end up like Bob after his first season in charge, without a trophy.'

A fourth round exit at the hands of Brighton in the FA Cup was to be the only other negative aspect of the season. A fourth consecutive League Cup trophy was secured with an historic victory over neighbours Everton. It was the first time the clubs had ever met in the final of a major competition and Liverpool secured a 1-0 victory in a Manchester replay at Maine Road after the first game at Wembley finished in a 0-0 stalemate. A tortuous trek through the earlier rounds, where the Reds were forced into replay after replay, saw them play an incredible 13 games on route to success.

In Europe things were no less dramatic with Liverpool three times having to play second leg games away from home on the

knife edge of a slender first leg lead or on level terms. The first round was routine enough; a 6-0 aggregate score over Danish side Odense but the second round draw was less kind. Spaniards Athletic Bilbao came to Anfield and prised away a 0-0 draw. A solitary Ian Rush goal in Bilbao saw the Reds through to a spring encounter with Benfica where another Rush goal, this time at Anfield, gave the Reds a 1-0 advantage over the Portuguese. On a dramatic night in the Stadium of Light two weeks later, a virtuoso Liverpool demolished Benfica 4-1. The semi-final brought Iron Curtain opposition in the shape of Dynamo Bucharest and again Liverpool struggled to make an impression at Anfield in the first leg. A lone Sammy Lee strike was all they could manage against their physical opponents. In Bucharest however, the team were able to play with more freedom and two more Rush goals helped to secure a 3-1 aggregate score. Liverpool closed in on the league title. A point at Notts County on 12 May took care of that, and incredibly in his first season in charge, Joe Fagan found his side on the brink of a treble never before won in the English game.

But perhaps the most difficult tie of all awaited the Reds in the final of the European Cup. Opponents AS Roma would be playing the game on their home ground, the venue having been decided months in advance by UEFA. Phil Neal put the Reds 1-0 up in the first half only for Pruzzo to equalise in the second half. The game finished in stalemate and went to a penalty shootout in which Liverpool out-psyched their Italian opponents 4-2. The treble was won. Joe Fagan joined the pantheon of greats that night.

What faced Fagan now was how to live up to his own and fans' expectations after such a fairytale season. The 1984/85 season got underway with new signings Paul Walsh and Jan Mølby hoping to make great impressions and they made their bows in the Charity Shield curtain raiser at Wembley. Everton exacted a measure of revenge for their League Cup defeat some months earlier by taking the Shield 1-0. Based on the previous season, a good omen perhaps? No was the answer. Everton were flying under manager Howard Kendall and they romped to the league title with a massive thirteen point margin. Liverpool's grasp on the League Cup was finally loosened by a Spurs side who delivered Liverpool's first knockout in the competition for five years with a 1-0 victory at White Hart Lane.

Liverpool fared better in the FA Cup reaching the semi-final only for Manchester United to put them out in a Maine Road replay. All hopes of silverware rested on the European Cup, a trophy that had started to feel like their private property. The Reds marched impressively into the semi-final after despatching Lech Poznan, Benfica, and Austria Vienna in the earlier rounds. The only real wobble was in the first leg in Austria, a 1-0 reverse that was crushingly overturned 4-1 at Anfield. New signing Walsh had weighed in with a couple of important goals but it was John Wark who had taken the mantle of leading scorer, Ian Rush having spent a lot of the season sidelined with a cartilage injury. The Greeks of Panathinaikos provided the opposition in the semi-final and Liverpool ran out 4-0 winners in the first leg at Anfield to put the tie beyond doubt. A comfortable 1-0 win in Greece tied up the loose ends and Liverpool were into their fifth European Cup final in nine attempts.

Juventus, who had defeated Liverpool in that season's European Super Cup, were to be the opponents in Brussel's Heysel Stadium. In the event, the match on 29 May 1985 carried little relevance. For the record, Juventus won 1-0 with a disputed Michel Platini penalty but none of that mattered. The trouble that erupted before the game and brought the deaths of 39 Juventus supporters was to bring a dark shadow down on the career of the man who had been instrumental in starting the whole Bootroom revolution. Unfortunately it was a shadow Fagan was never able to disassociate himself from. As he was helped across the tarmac of Liverpool's Speke airport the following day by his great friend

Roy Evans, he cut the figure of a disconsolate and broken man. It was a desperately sad end to a glorious career.

EVANS SPOKE movingly about Joe after his passing on 30 June 2001. 'I don't want people to take it the wrong way, and certainly intend no disrespect to Bill Shankly and Bob Paisley, but, to me, Joe was the best, respected throughout football and in life. He was probably the most respected man in football and the guy given the least praise. He was my mentor, from the day I first arrived at the club as a young boy. He was deeply involved in the running of all the great Liverpool teams until the day he left. Of course, he will be remembered by most for winning a treble in 1984, but he was a top coach for 30 years.'

FACTFILE

BORN
12 March 1921, Liverpool
DIED
30 June 2001
OTHER CLUBS
AS MANAGER
Nelson 1951-53
APPOINTED MANAGER
1 July 1983
DEBUT GAME
20 August 1983
CONTRACT EXPIRY
29 May 1985
HONOURS
League Championship 1983/84;
League Cup 1983/84;
European Cup 1983/84;
Manager of the Year 1984

As Manager in Europe			
Season	European Cup	UEFA Cup	European Cup Winners' Cup
1983/84	Winners	-	-
1984/85	Runners-Up	-	-

Season	Division	P	W	D	L	GF	GA	Pts	Pos	Win %	FA Cup	League Cup
1983/84	1st Division	42	22	14	6	73	32	80	1	52.38	4th Round	Winners
1984/85	1st Division	42	22	11	9	68	35	77	2	52.38	Semi-Final	3rd Round
Total	-	84	44	25	15	141	67	157	-	52.38	-	-

Fagan,
Willie

SCOTTISH inside-left forward Willie Fagan was a promising 19-year-old when he joined Preston from Celtic in October 1936. Fagan, along with Bill Shankly, was in Preston's line-up that lost 3-1 in the 1937 FA Cup final against Sunderland. The following October, Fagan joined Liverpool after only one year's stay at Deepdale. He went straight into the Liverpool team, playing 36 consecutive matches until the end of the season and scoring nine times. He only missed three league games in 1938/39, scoring 14 goals, and played in the opening three fixtures of the 1939/40 season before the outbreak of war caused the league programme to be abandoned and Fagan's Liverpool career to be severely curtailed at the age of 22.

Unlike some of his colleagues, Fagan was young enough to re-establish himself at Anfield when league football resumed in 1946. At the time, Fagan was offered a deal by Second Division Bradford Park Avenue but refused to move, which proved beneficial for the player and Liverpool. Fagan scored seven goals in 18 appearances to qualify for a League Championship medal in 1947.

HE WAS called on sporadically (mostly due to injury) in the 1947/48 and 1948/49 seasons

and looked set to be on his way into the Third Division. However, the inside-left position had been problematic for Liverpool, and manager George Kay decided to give Fagan a chance in the opening game of the 1949/50 season. Fagan's Liverpool's career was resurrected once more and his four goals in the FA Cup helped the Reds to the final at Wembley. The *Daily Dispatch* was impressed by Fagan's form and voted him the Outstanding Footballer of 1949. Approaching his mid-30s by the time the next season opened, Fagan's Anfield

career was nearing its end. He played his final game for the club against Huddersfield on the first day of September 1951. If the war hadn't taken so many playing years away from him, there seems little doubt that his fine Liverpool career would have been a great one.

WHILE ON THE transfer list at Liverpool, Fagan played with Distillery in Northern Ireland and was appointed player-manager at Weymouth in the Southern League on 19 July 1952. Press reports show

he was still on Liverpool's books in November 1952, but was available to play for these clubs as they were outside the Football League. Liverpool still held his registration form so no other league club could obtain his signature without their permission. Auburn-haired Fagan revealed in 1950 that he had hoped, from an early age, to be an opera singer. He, however, ended up in prison following the end of his football career! He was not an inmate, but a senior officer at a facility for young offenders on the Isle of Portland, situated in the English Channel.

Celebration time in 1947 – Cyril Done, Fagan and Billy Liddell in good company

Season	League		FA Cup		Total	
	App	Goals	App	Goals	App	Goals
1937/38	31	8	5	1	36	9
1938/39	39	14	3	1	42	15
1945/46	-	-	4	3	4	3
1946/47	18	7	4	0	22	7
1947/48	15	5	0	0	15	5
1948/49	13	2	1	1	14	3
1949/50	35	11	7	4	42	15
1950/51	4	0	0	0	4	0
1951/52	3	0	0	0	3	0
Total	**158**	**47**	**24**	**10**	**182**	**57**

Fairclough, David

LOCAL BOY David Fairclough exploded onto the football scene aged 19, to add some fresh impetus to Liverpool's neck-and-neck battle with QPR for the First Division Championship in 1976. Similar to Ronnie Rosenthal's arrival giving an unpredictable boost to the crucial final leg of the 1989/90 season, Fairclough's seven goals from two starts and six substitute appearances were a big factor in Liverpool ultimately overhauling the Londoners in the final match of the season. The highlight was a mazy, fantastic run from the halfway line with two minutes to go in the early kick-off Anfield derby (on Grand National day), which turned what was looking like a goalless draw into a priceless victory.

Fairclough was living the dream, as he told *LFChistory.net*. 'I grew up about half a mile from the ground and I went to school just 500 to 600 yards away from the stadium. Anfield was very much my patch. I played football in the streets. Comic book stuff really. I remember standing in the street where we lived listening to the crowd in the Inter Milan game in '65. I was only eight and my dad didn't allow me to go to that game. We knew obviously the game was going Liverpool's way and you could hear them singing. We lived, literally, in the shadows of Anfield.'

It was hard for Fairclough to break up the Keegan/Toshack partnership, which was well established, but the Welshman's injury problems did give him a number of opportunities in the second part of the following season when Liverpool were competing for honours at home and abroad. However, there were only a further five goals from 17 starts and 13 substitute appearances.

On 16 March 1977 came the biggest moment in Fairclough's career. The Reds were trailing by an away goal to the French champions Saint Etienne, with time running out in a frenzied atmosphere at Anfield in the second leg of the European Cup quarter-final. Fairclough had come on for Toshack in the 74th minute and with six minutes to go, he latched on to Ray Kennedy's lob and headed for goal. The 'legend' will tell you that he beat several defenders on his way into Merseyside folklore, but the reality is that he kept his eye on the ball, brushed aside any challenge from a defender and then calmly tucked his right-foot shot under Curkovic into the Kop goal. It brought about scenes that those who were there still talk about with a lump in their throat and a shiver down their spine!

FAIRCLOUGH'S ECSTASY was transformed into agony when he discovered he wasn't in the starting line-up for the FA Cup final against Manchester United, or Liverpool's first ever European Cup final. 'I was very disappointed. I played in the FA Cup semi-finals against Everton, started both games and had all the celebrations to go to the cup final. Leading up to the FA Cup final day, Bob Paisley tells me I am going to play in the final. It never happened. "You'll play next week in Rome, I'll need you in Rome." Then in Rome I was sub,' Fairclough disclosed.

Kevin Keegan was certainly impressed by his strike partner, as he revealed in 1977: 'Dave's difficult to play with because you just can't read him, that's what makes him such a dangerous opponent. The best is yet to come from him and in a couple of years' time he'll be a force to be reckoned with. His best asset is his pace coupled with his control. You must remember that he's not a regular yet and, like a lot of youngsters,

might have difficulty in adapting when opponents do get the measure of him. That's when the real test will come, but I'm sure he'll do well. He's got ability you can't coach into a player.'

KEEGAN had been replaced by Dalglish the following season, and Toshack only appeared in a handful of games. This time Fairclough started 34 out of 42 games and scored 15 goals. He was in the starting line-up when the Reds successfully defended their European crown at Wembley. If Fairclough thought he had finally established himself in Paisley's starting XI, he couldn't have been more mistaken. Steve Heighway started as number nine in the 1978/79 season. 'Paisley said: "He'll be burnt out after ten games and then you'll come in. That's your slot,"' Fairclough recalled. 'The team got off like a house on fire and were beating everybody 4-0, 4-1, 5-0 and couldn't stop scoring goals. The first league game I started was against Manchester United on 26 December. We won 3-0 at Old Trafford. I played a couple of games and then I got injured against Everton in March.' The season was over for Fairclough but Liverpool went on to win the Championship.

HIS 'GOLDEN' MOMENT AGAINST SAINT ETIENNE IS ONE WHICH WILL NEVER BE FORGOTTEN

In 1980/81, Fairclough started seven consecutive games from September to October, scoring seven goals and proving he was not just an impact player. Unfortunately he got injured at his most productive and was out until the middle of January. A knee injury finished his season in early February 1981. He didn't play again for Liverpool's first team until October 1982. Fairclough made his comeback in the reserves in September 1981 and was stuck playing for the second-string during the 1981/82 season, scoring 14 goals in 29 matches. What on earth had happened in the meantime? Ian Rush made the number 9 shirt his own with 30 goals in 49 matches. Fairclough had missed his window of

opportunity and he spent the summer of 1982 with Toronto Blizzard in the North American Soccer League to keep his fitness levels up. Fairclough was prolific for Liverpool reserves, scoring 20 goals in as many matches following his spell in America, however he only started three games for the first team in the 1982/83 season. He signed off with three goals in his last four matches for the club in April 1983.

FAIRCLOUGH was not very pleased with Paisley's treatment of him at Liverpool, as he told *LFChistory.net*: 'Down the years, I've had lots of time to think about why I didn't fulfil my potential. Obviously Paisley had to keep 14 to 16 people happy, but he made life difficult for me. I broke into the England squad and I was very much on Ron Greenwood's list of players who were perhaps going to break in. I came back to Anfield and Bob Paisley decided to play me as sub, or leave me out. I had a lot more to offer. I am quite bitter about it, really. It's not one of these things you can go, "Oh well," and be philosophical about it. This is my livelihood and career.' Fairclough's final figures for Liverpool still make impressive reading: 37 goals from 92 starts is a fine achievement but he never quite got rid of the 'Supersub' nickname and that is borne out by the fact that he scored 18 goals in 62 substitute appearances. But his contribution towards the club's success of the late 70s and early 80s should not be underestimated. Maybe he did have a tendency to drift in and out of

some matches, but his pace and unpredictability caused havoc to many a defence and his 'golden' moment against Saint Etienne is one which will never be forgotten.

Season	League		FA Cup		League Cup		Europe		Other		Total	
	App	Goals	App	Goals	App	Goals	App	Goals	App	Goals	App	Goals
1975/76	5 (9)	7	0	0	0	0	2 (3)	1	-	-	7 (12)	8
1976/77	12 (8)	3	4 (1)	1	0 (2)	0	1 (2)	1	0	0	17 (13)	5
1977/78	26 (3)	10	1	0	3 (4)	3	3 (1)	2	1	0	34 (8)	15
1978/79	3 (1)	2	3	0	0 (1)	0	1 (1)	1	-	-	7 (3)	3
1979/80	9 (5)	5	1 (4)	3	1 (4)	5	1 (1)	0	0	0	12 (14)	13
1980/81	6 (3)	4	1	0	3 (1)	1	2	2	0	0	12 (4)	7
1982/83	3 (5)	3	0	0	0 (2)	1	0 (1)	0	0	0	3 (8)	4
Total	**64 (34)**	**34**	**10 (5)**	**4**	**7 (14)**	**10**	**10 (9)**	**7**	**1**	**0**	**92 (62)**	**55**

Fairfoul,
Tom

RIGHT-HALF Tom Fairfoul was an experienced campaigner when he arrived at Liverpool, having spent two seasons at Kilmarnock and seven at Third Lanark, where he featured in 247 matches in the Scottish First Division.

T FAIRFOUL LIVERPOOL

He was a regular for the Liverpool side in the two years that preceded World War One. He played in every one of the 38 First Division matches in 1913/14 and made a further 24 appearances the following season. Nine FA Cup ties over the same period, including the 1914 final defeat by Burnley at Crystal Palace, brought his career total at Liverpool to 71 games. Fairfoul, along with three Liverpool players – Tom Miller, Bob Pursell, Jackie Sheldon – and three United players was found guilty of fixing a game between

Liverpool and Manchester United on Good Friday 1915. Bookies had laid up to 8–1 against United winning 2-0 which is how it ended. The *Liverpool Echo* reported in December 1915 that 'the excuse, if such it can be called, has been made that the players were tempted into the sordid business through the belief that the war would prevent football in 1915/16, and summer wages would not be the rule. But it is too paltry a claim in connection with a grave charge, and can be ignored.' For his

service to his country in the war, Fairfoul's life ban from football was lifted. However, he was too old to return to the game.

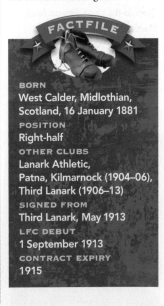

Season	League		FA Cup		Total	
	App	Goals	App	Goals	App	Goals
1913/14	38	0	8	0	46	0
1914/15	24	0	1	0	25	0
Total	**62**	**0**	**9**	**0**	**71**	**0**

Family

THERE HAVE BEEN quite a few occasions in the club's history when close family members have been, either together or in different eras, on the books of Liverpool Football Club. The McQueen brothers, Hugh and Matt, joined Liverpool in October 1892 and spent three seasons together, making their mark on the club's earliest days, and in Matt's instance, well into the 1920s.

The next set of brothers were from Hurlford in Scotland's Ayrshire; defenders Archie and Bill Goldie, joining forces at Liverpool from 1897 to 1900. Charlie Hewitt, the younger brother of Joe, who had been at the club since January 1904, joined Liverpool in May 1907. They appeared together in the club's forward line on 15 occasions in 1907/08 which was Charlie's only campaign at Liverpool while Joe spent six decades at Anfield in various guises. Liverpudlians right-back James and right-winger Sam Speakman only made 34 appearances combined in the early 1910s. Motherwell-native Tom Miller was transferred to Anfield in February 1912 and made 117 appearances for the club before his brother John arrived in 1918. They managed to appear three times in the same line-up from March through April 1920. Harold and Walter Wadsworth played a combined total of 297 games for the first team from 1912 to 1926.

HUGH McQUEEN
[LIVERPOOL]

MATTHEW McQUEEN
[LIVERPOOL]

In fact, the third Wadsworth brother, Charlie, featured in at least one reserve game in the 1919/20 season, scoring a couple of goals in a 5-1 victory over Southport Central. He remained an amateur, employed by their father William's business "Wadsworth Lighterage and Coaling Company" which had a number of barges on the Mersey. One of Liverpool's greatest legends, Elisha Scott, came to the club's attention because of his brother William, who was Everton's former keeper. William featured for Liverpool in the wartime 1918/19 season and was a reserve in 1919/20. A third brother, John, who was two years younger than Elisha, was as well in the reserves in the 1920s. Other great legends such as Alex Raisbeck and Billy Liddell, had a brother at the same time that they were at the club who never made the grade; Andrew and Tommy respectively. Veteran Billy Dunlop enjoyed familiar company in his last season at Liverpool as the club programme on 4 September 1909 revealed: 'J. Dunlop is a brother of our old favourite, W. Dunlop, and he has an excellent opportunity to make as great a name for himself.' James and Billy did appear as a full-back pair in the same line-up but only in the reserves. Harry "Smiler" Chambers had a brother Ben in the reserves in the 1921/22 season. Bolton legend Stan Hanson began as an amateur at Liverpool in the 1932/33 season, never featuring for the first team unlike brother Alf who had arrived a year earlier and made 177 appearances for the first XI. Bill Shepherd who appeared 58 times for Liverpool from 1948 to 1951 had not one, but two brothers; Arthur and Joe, who never went further than the second-string.

Willie Devlin was joined by his younger sibling Tom in 1927. Willie scored 15 goals in 19 games for the first team while Tom was transferred to Swindon the following year without making a name for himself at Anfield. In later years, a set of brothers have rarely been at the club, the exemption being Mark and Chris Seagraves and Alex and Dave Watson.

SONS OF FAMOUS Liverpool players have also tried to follow in their fathers' footsteps at Anfield with various degrees of success. Ned Doig's son, Edward, made a few reserve appearances in the 1919/20 season and the offspring of Gerry Byrne (Peter), Kenny Dalglish (Paul) and Phil Neal (Ashley) left without making a first-team appearance between them. Jon Flanagan failed to make the grade in 1984/85 but Jon Jr. made his debut on 11 April 2011. The son was quick to thank his father for his support: 'My dad was on the books [at Liverpool] and didn't make it. He was up there in the stands and this is for him. He is a great help, always talking and down your ear, telling you what to do.'

Members of the club's coaching staff have also had family

Billy Scott, Elisha's older brother.

representatives. William Connell Jnr. made the reserves in 1918/19 and reserve trainer Jimmy Seddon, who represented England, had his son on his playing staff from 1940 to 1950. Chris Fagan, son of Joe, made a couple of first-team appearances in the 1970/71 season, playing in defence just like his father. Amateur Arthur Berry appeared on four occasions for Liverpool, once during his father Edwin's reign as club chairman from 1904-09. Only two sets of father and son have played for the club's first team. Former England youth international and right-half, Roy Saunders, went close to a century and a half games from 1953 to 1956 and watched on with pride when his son Dean was the focal point of Liverpool's forward line 35 years later. Paul Ince captained Liverpool from 1997 to 1999 and his son, Thomas, featured for 14 minutes in the extra-time of a League Cup defeat to League Two's Northampton Town on 22 September 2010. The Liverpool connection between family members went back one generation further in the Jones family. Bill starred for the Reds as a utility man and was part of the team that won the League Championship in 1946/47. His grandson Rob burst on to the scene in 1991 and would have certainly been a Liverpool and an England regular for years to come if injuries hadn't stopped his career in its tracks. Liverpool FC is one big family in the truest sense of the word.

"Sport Pictures."

WALTER AND HAROLD WADSWORTH

Billy and Tom Liddell relax during a break in training

Fanzines

THE QUARTERLY *Through The Wind And Rain* was Liverpool's first fanzine, established by Bootle boy Steven Kelly in 1989. After publishing 79 issues, selling them on the corner of the Kop and the Centenary stand in all kinds of weather, he decided enough was enough in May 2008.

'In the end, it had just become a group of people moaning about things they have no influence over or can do nothing about,' Kelly told the *Liverpool Daily Post*. Kelly and his friends made sure all four corners around Anfield were covered on matchday and even sold 2,500 copies at the Tottenham home game in the 1995/96 season, but it wasn't always so rosy. 'Sometimes you would be standing there staring into space for hours on end,' he recalled. 'The worst was against Forest in '98. It was like standing in the shower at home. It just bucketed down before the game. What made it worse was that it was the first day of issue. We didn't have a car that day and we were left with all these boxes, then the heavens opened. People were just legging it past you trying not to get wet.'

Red All Over the Land tries to publish as many issues as possible over each season. Its 182nd issue was released in December 2012 and that was the 7th issue in the 2012/13 season. John Pearman started the fanzine back in 1994 and he has touched upon a common problem for fanzines in his editorials. 'Begging people for articles, raiding the odd site, keeping an eye on the BBC weather watch, life could be better you know. I sometimes wonder if we should go quarterly, bi-monthly or go the other way and come out every fortnight. Somebody suggested once a season would be too many. Fanzines of all kinds face the same dilemma and that is the modern world of the media.

When we first hit the streets we'd have about 20-plus writing in venting their anger at something or anything. Now they use phone-ins, drop a tweet to Claire at LFCTV and claim her as a devotee; they can go on any forum. It's not made any easier by the make-up of the Anfield crowd nowadays. The amount of people that have no idea what a fanzine is, keeps on rising. You'd be amazed at the number of people that turn up and think we're selling a programme and how shocked they seem when you tell them the last time a programme cost £2 the Kop was a terrace.' Visit their website *redallovertheland.com* if you want to subscribe.

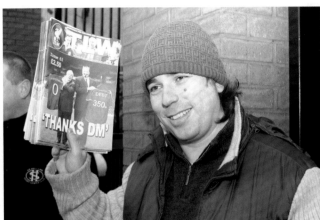

Dave on matchday outside Anfield

DAVE USHER has run the popular monthly *The Liverpool Way* since its inception in 1999 and you can invariably find him selling the latest publication outside the Kop on matchdays. Usher told *ThisIsAnfield.com* in March 2013 how *TLW* came about. 'I've always enjoyed writing but I was always too lazy to do anything about it. Lazy in school, lazy in college, so I didn't have any qualifications of real worth and ended up bouncing around various office jobs. The last job I had was a bit of a doddle, I could have my day's work done by 10am and spend the rest of the day just messing around, so with all that time on my hands I started writing articles for *Through the Wind & Rain* and *Red All Over the Land*. Anyway, I got made redundant and decided to start my own fanzine.' *TLW* is also available from all three WH Smiths in Liverpool City Centre. Postal and digital subscriptions are easily accessible from the fanzine's online store at *liverpoolway.co.uk/shop*. Usher's website offers blogs, podcasts and a forum that is open to all as long as you don't act like a 'tw∗t'.

Well Red is the latest Liverpool fanzine and is arguably the best designed of the lot. Journalist Gareth Roberts launched the 64-page full colour bi-monthly in March 2010 and 'aims to give a true reflection of fans' feelings about happenings at Anfield, free of the commercial and corporate restraints.' Each issue of *Well Red* includes contributions from readers and leading football journalists and authors. '*Well Red* is about quality analysis of the topics the fans are talking about. Of course that includes matters on the pitch, but we're not afraid to tackle matters off the pitch, too,' according to Roberts on robbohuyton.blogspot.com in 2010. 'Spirit of Shankly have close to 5,000 members yet they barely get a mention in the Liverpool press and certainly not in the official publications. There are equally worthy causes like the "Don't Buy The Sun" campaign and of course the "Hillsborough Justice Campaign" which are also underreported in the mainstream press. The magazine is built on quality opinion and analysis – that's the key. There's no bar-room, knee-jerk stuff in *Well Red*.' The magazine is available in newsagents throughout north-west England and in WHSmiths across the UK and you can subscribe from its website *wellredmag.co.uk*.

Ferguson, Bob

BOB FERGUSON was a stalwart of Liverpool's defence, said to be in *Lloyds Weekly News* 'a typical Scottish half-back, neat and clever', who fed his forwards 'beautifully' as well as being 'the tallest man in the team [5ft 10½in – 179cm], and not so slow as he appears'.

FERGUSON made his debut on the opening day of the 1912/13 season and was the club's only ever-present that year, missing just two league games the following season when he no doubt enjoyed playing alongside his former Third Lanark team-mate Thomas Fairfoul in the half-back line. The 1914/15 season was completed despite the outbreak of war, but Ferguson lost his place in the side to future legend Donald Mackinlay.

With a third of the season gone, Ferguson only briefly threatened to reclaim it from the clutches of his compatriot.

The *Liverpool Echo* commented on Liverpool's capture of Ferguson at the time: 'Liverpool made a good stroke when they signed Bob Ferguson. The 3rd Lanark supporters are deeply sorry to lose their favoured centre-half, who is described in Scotland in the following eulogy: "There has never been a more likable player. Honest Bob would

R. FERGUSON, LIVERPOOL.

be the correct title for him for he was always playing the game to the delight of his friends. He was

the sort of man a club manager likes to have under him – dependable, keen for his club's interests and never likely to get himself or the team into disrepute. Mr Watson [Tom Watson, Liverpool's manager] has made a catch and he knows it."'

FACTFILE

BORN
Cleland, Lanarkshire, Scotland, June 1886
POSITION
Centre-half / Left-half
OTHER CLUBS
Cleland Rangers, Third Lanark (1906–12)
SIGNED FROM
Third Lanark, 13 May 1912
LFC DEBUT GAME/GOAL
4 September 1912 / 19 October 1912
CONTRACT EXPIRY
1915

Season	League		FA Cup		Total	
	App	Goals	App	Goals	App	Goals
1912/13	38	1	4	0	42	1
1913/14	36	0	7	1	43	1
1914/15	18	0	0	0	18	0
Total	**92**	**1**	**11**	**1**	**103**	**2**

Ferns, Phil

A RUGGED DEFENDER, whose versatility served Shankly well, Phil Ferns was born in Liverpool and played for youth clubs of the Liverpool Boys' Association.

HE MADE HIS DEBUT for the reserves in the 1957/58 season but wasn't able to force his way into Liverpool's first team until 1962/63, when he covered three times for Tommy Leishman as left-half and twice at left-back for Ronnie Moran on Liverpool's return to the top division. When the club won the League Championship for the sixth time in 1964, Ferns played in enough games (18) to qualify for a winners' medal, filling in for Gerry Byrne, Moran and Willie Stevenson. Ferns went on to make over 100 league appearances for Bournemouth and Mansfield.

FACTFILE

BORN
Liverpool, 14 November 1937
POSITION
Defender
OTHER CLUBS
Bournemouth & Boscombe Athletic (1965–66), Mansfield Town (1966–68), Rhyl
JOINED
September 1957; signed professional 24 March 1958
LFC DEBUT GAME/GOAL
29 August 1962 / 29 August 1964
CONTRACT EXPIRY
August 1965
HONOURS
League Championship 1963/64

Season	League		FA Cup		League Cup		Europe		Other		Total	
	App	Goals	App	Goals	App	Goals	App	Goals	App	Goals	App	Goals
1962/63	5	0	0	0	-	-	-	-	-	-	5	0
1963/64	18	0	1	0	-	-	-	-	-	-	19	0
1964/65	4	1	0	0	-	-	0	0	0	0	4	1
Total	**27**	**1**	**1**	**0**	**0**	**0**	**0**	**0**	**0**	**0**	**28**	**1**

Ferri, Jean Michel

JEAN MICHEL FERRI spent the majority of his career at Nantes, where he played 288 league games and won the French Championship in 1995.

Ferri was Gérard Houllier's first signing, arriving only two weeks after he was left in sole charge of the team, following the departure of Roy Evans. Ferri had endured a nightmare spell in Turkey after signing a 'pay-as-you-play' deal with Istanbulspor a few months earlier. The president of the club told the coach to leave Ferri out of the squad, no matter whether he performed well or not, simply to avoid paying him; so Ferri was happy when Houllier came calling. 'In Turkey, players get big money for appearances. We were still allowed to train but because we were not playing we didn't have the same motivation,' Ferri told the British media on his arrival.

The defensive midfielder was called 'The Machine' because of his work rate. 'Ferri Across the Mersey', the headlines read as he arrived, injured, as cover for Paul Ince in midfield. Ferri made his debut three months later in a 2-1 defeat at Chelsea, replacing Ince

early on in the second half. His second substitute appearance came in the penultimate game of the season, another defeat, this time at Sheffield Wednesday. His team-mates suspected that Ferri was, in reality, Houllier's link to the players, letting his boss know

of any discontent in the dressing room. Ferri played a rough total of 50 minutes in eight months for Liverpool, but left for a similar fee to French Second Division club Sochaux, so no financial harm was done.

FACTFILE

BORN
Lyon, France,
7 February 1969
POSITION
Midfielder
OTHER CLUBS
Nantes (1985–98),
Istanbulspor (1998),
Sochaux (1999–2000)
SIGNED FROM
Istanbulspor, £1.5million,
28 November 1998
INTERNATIONAL CAPS
5 France caps, 1994–95
LFC DEBUT
27 February 1999
CONTRACT EXPIRY
14 July 1999

Season	League		FA Cup		League Cup		Europe		Total	
	App	Goals	App	Goals	App	Goals	App	Goals	App	Goals
1998/99	0 (2)	0	0	0	0	0	0	0	0 (2)	0
Total	**0 (2)**	**0**	**0**	**0**	**0**	**0**	**0**	**0**	**0 (2)**	**0**

The Fields of Anfield Road

THE POPULAR terrace song 'The Fields of Anfield Road' is adopted from an Irish folk ballad written in the 1970s by Pete St. John; 'The Fields of Athenry'. The meaning of the song was totally changed when adapted by Liverpool supporters during the mid-90s as the original is set during the Great Irish Famine in the middle of the 19th century. A man named Michael stole corn for his starving family and is being taken from his home of Athenry in County Galway, Ireland, on board a prison ship heading to Botany Bay, Australia.

The first verse of 'The Fields of Athenry' goes like this:

The Fields of Athenry

FIRST VERSE By a lonely prison wall,
I heard a young girl calling
Michael, they are taking you away,
For you stole Trevelyan's corn,
So the young might see the morn.
Now a prison ship lies waiting in the bay.

And here is the alternative, 'The Fields of Anfield Road' (lyrics by Liverpool fan Edward R. Williams from Wallasey):

'The Fields of Anfield Road'

Outside the Shankly Gates
I heard a Kopite calling
Shankly they have taken you away
But you left a great eleven
Before you went to heaven
Now it's glory round the Fields of
Anfield Road.

Chorus:
All round the Fields of Anfield Road
Where once we watched the King Kenny
play (and could he play)
Stevie Heighway on the wing
We had dreams and songs to sing
Of the glory round the Fields of
Anfield Road

Outside the Paisley Gates
I heard a Kopite calling
Paisley they have taken you away
But you led the great 11
Back in Rome in seventy-seven
And the redmen they are still playing
the same way

Chorus: ...

A third verse was added in 2009 on the 20th anniversary of the Hillsborough disaster, co-written by John Power of the Cast.

Beside the Hillsborough flame
I heard a Kopite mourning
Why so many taken on that day?
Justice has never been done
But their memory will carry on
There'll be glory round the Fields
of Anfield Road

Chorus: ... x 2

Finnan,
Steve

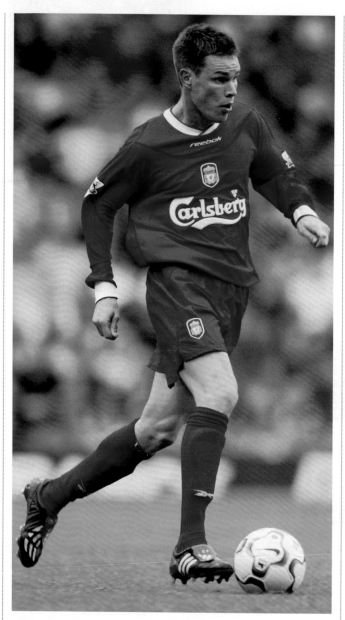

AFTER BEING REJECTED by Wimbledon at the age of 16, Steve Finnan tried his luck with non-league Welling United, contemplating working as a bricklayer for his family's building firm if his football career didn't turn out well. His dreams came true, however, when he signed a professional contract with Birmingham City in Football League One in 1995.

Finnan didn't stay there long, as in March 1996 he was loaned out to Notts County in the third tier of league football, where he stayed until the end of the season. He signed for County in October 1996 and played 80 league games in two seasons before transferring to up and coming Fulham, managed by Kevin Keegan, in November 1998. Fulham and Finnan went from strength to

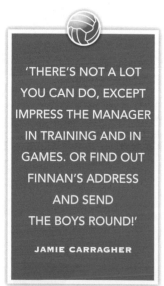

'THERE'S NOT A LOT YOU CAN DO, EXCEPT IMPRESS THE MANAGER IN TRAINING AND IN GAMES. OR FIND OUT FINNAN'S ADDRESS AND SEND THE BOYS ROUND!'

JAMIE CARRAGHER

strength, going up two league levels in three years. Finnan was voted Player of the Year at Fulham in 2002 and received most votes from his fellow professionals in the right-back position in the Premier League's best XI for 2001/02. He excelled in the 2002 World Cup with Ireland and it was time for him to take another step

forward in his career. After 208 games and seven goals with Fulham, he joined Houllier's Liverpool in the summer of 2003. Jamie Carragher, whose place was under threat following the Irishman's arrival, tried to be philosophical about it when put on the spot. 'There's no point sulking about it,' Carragher told Sky

Sports. 'There's not a lot you can do, except impress the manager in training and in games. Or find out Finnan's address and send the boys round!'

FINNAN struggled in his first season, but the 2003/04 season was a low point for many other players: and it turned out to be Houllier's last. Finnan improved considerably after Rafa Benítez took over and proved to be a model of consistency, as he played in 99 of the club's 114 Premier League matches between August 2004 and May 2007. His Spanish boss was very impressed. 'Finnan is a player who will always play at a consistent level,' Benítez said in 2006. 'He will be seven, eight, nine or even ten out of ten every week. Some players find a good level for individual games but

'SOME PLAYERS FIND A GOOD LEVEL FOR INDIVIDUAL GAMES BUT DON'T DO THE SAME EVERY WEEK. FINNAN DOES IT FOR A WHOLE SEASON'

RAFA BENÍTEZ

don't do the same every week. Finnan does it for a whole season.' In 2007/08 Finnan figured in only 35 of Liverpool's 59 competitive matches, as Benítez often preferred Arbeloa and Aurélio as his full-back pairing. Towards the end of January 2008, Finnan announced his retirement from international football after being capped for the fiftieth time by the Republic of Ireland. Giovanni Trappatoni persuaded him back to the Ireland set-up and he returned on 20 August 2008 against Norway, adding three games to his international total before retiring once and for all in September 2008.

Season	League App	League Goals	FA Cup App	FA Cup Goals	League Cup App	League Cup Goals	Europe App	Europe Goals	Other App	Other Goals	Total App	Total Goals
2003/04	19 (3)	0	3	0	0	0	5 (1)	0	-	-	27(4)	0
2004/05	29 (4)	1	0	0	4 (1)	0	12 (2)	0	-	-	45(7)	1
2005/06	33	0	5 (1)	0	0	0	12	0	1	0	51(1)	0
2006/07	32 (1)	0	1	0	0	0	12	0	1	0	46(1)	0
2007/08	21 (3)	0	3	0	1	0	6 (1)	0	-	-	31(4)	0
Total	**134 (11)**	**1**	**12 (1)**	**0**	**5 (1)**	**0**	**47 (4)**	**0**	**2**	**0**	**200 (17)**	**1**

The Irishman signed for La Liga side Espanyol on the last day of the August transfer window in the 2008/09 season. Although he had signed a two-year contract, the Spanish club agreed to release him after just a single campaign. On 28 July 2009 the 33-year-old returned to English football with Portsmouth, incidentally replacing Glen Johnson who had moved to Liverpool. Finnan played 21 times for Portsmouth in the Premier League in 2009/10, taking his cumulative total of league appearances for five English clubs up to the 450 mark. Pompey had a disastrous league season and comfortably finished in last place. The club's salvation came in the FA Cup, when Finnan unexpectedly found himself playing in the final at Wembley four years after representing Liverpool in the Cardiff final against West Ham. Finnan's experience of the final in London was not as happy as it had been in the Welsh capital, Chelsea winning 1-0. The final was Finnan's last appearance in his professional football career.

Finnerhan, Patrick

PATRICK FINNERHAN scored 27 goals in 85 matches for Second Division Manchester City.

He only featured in the 1897/98 season for the Reds when he played five league games as a centre-forward and three FA Cup matches as an inside-right. He scored just one goal for the first team, a winner in the last minute against Wolves at Anfield on 20 November 1897.

In 1901 the *Manchester Courier* reported on Finnerhan's achievements with the birds he had been raising. He was a member of Wittonia Flying Club based in Northwich and his old birds won the Worcester, Swindon and Bournemouth races and his young ones the Worcester and Cheltenham races. Finnerhan secured 'no less than £13 in prize money'.

Season	League App	League Goals	FA Cup App	FA Cup Goals	Total App	Total Goals
1897/98	5	1	3	0	8	1
Total	5	1	3	0	8	1

Finney, Fred

THE RIGHT-HALF was one of 38 players who represented Liverpool during the 1945/46 season, but as this was soon after the end of World War Two when numerous clubs had guest players, the fixtures were not usually recognised in official records.

HOWEVER, the FA Cup continued as usual – although over two legs – and it was in the third round against Chester on 5 January 1946 that Finney made

FRED FINNEY

his only competitive appearances for the club. He featured in ten wartime matches for Liverpool.

Season	League App	League Goals	FA Cup App	FA Cup Goals	Total App	Total Goals
1945/46	-	-	2	0	2	0
Total	0	0	2	0	2	0

Fitzpatrick, Harry

WHILE IN THE ARMY, Harry Fitzpatrick participated in hockey and swimming, and at Liverpool he was still doing gymnastics or just about anything that appealed to this athlete.

HARRY first dreamed of following in his father's (who was the goalkeeper for Bootle) footsteps, but after being tested at centre-half, this became his position in his early career. He developed into an outside-left of note and was more than happy to move from Luton Town to his home town in 1907. Fitzpatrick netted the only goal of the game on his debut, as the Reds beat Sunderland at Anfield on 12 October 1907, and scored again two weeks later, also at Anfield, when Sheffield Wednesday were beaten 3-0. Even though Fitzpatrick scored

two goals in only four games for the first team, he was not as prolific for the reserves, where he spent the majority of his sole season. His main weakness was the gathering of the ball and his distribution, which didn't serve

the tactics of Liverpool who tried to 'place the ball forward and on the ground,' as the club programme noted.

IN DECEMBER 1915, long after he had left the club, Liverpool's

board received a letter asking for 'comforts' for Fitzpatrick, who was a prisoner of war. The club accepted that two parcels of groceries be purchased from Cooper's at about 10/6d each.

FACTFILE

BORN
Everton, Liverpool, February 1880
POSITION
Inside-left forward
OTHER CLUBS
Garston Gas Works Reserves (1897–1900),
Gordon Highlanders (1902–05),
Luton Town (1905–07),
Chesterfield Town (1908–09)
SIGNED FROM
Luton Town, April 1907
LFC DEBUT GAME/GOAL
12 October 1907 / 12 October 1907
CONTRACT EXPIRY
May 1908

Season	League		FA Cup		Total	
	App	Goals	App	Goals	App	Goals
1907/08	4	2	0	0	4	2
Total	4	2	0	0	4	2

Fitzsimmons, Matthew

FITZSIMMONS made just a single league appearance for Liverpool, replacing regular centre-half Fred Rogers in the 3-1 defeat at Bolton on 17 September 1938.

FACTFILE

BORN
Toxteth, Liverpool, 10 December 1913
POSITION
Centre-half
OTHER CLUBS
Mather United;
Ipswich Town (1939);
York City,
Ipswich Town (wartime guest)
SIGNED FROM
Mather United, October 1936
LFC DEBUT
17 September 1938
CONTRACT EXPIRY
June 1939

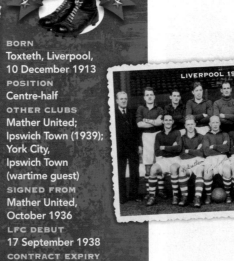

LIVERPOOL 1938/39

Season	League		FA Cup		Total	
	App	Goals	App	Goals	App	Goals
1938/39	1	0	0	0	1	0
Total	1	0	0	0	1	0

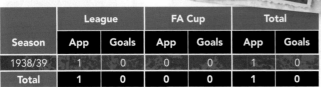

Flag Days

THERE ARE ALWAYS FLAGS and banners present in the Kop, but on specially organised Flag Days Kopites turn back the clock and you will see a sea of Red stretching from one end to the other, a tremendous spectacle.

> 'WE DON'T HAVE TO ORGANISE FLAG DAYS ANYMORE, THEY JUST HAPPEN' IF YOU WANT TO EXPERIENCE A FLAG DAY THEN MAKE SURE TO ATTEND THE LAST HOME GAME OF THE SEASON. YOU WON'T BE DISAPPOINTED!

Kop's last stand 30 April 1994

The first Flag Day was held on 8 May 1993 when Liverpool faced Tottenham in the last fixture of the 1992/93 debut Premier League season. Liverpool were led out by Ronnie Moran as manager Graeme Souness had been sent on a peculiar scouting mission to see Coventry and Leeds meet. The Reds responded in style to the carnival taking place at the Kop end and beat Spurs 6-2 with John Barnes and Ian Rush each netting a brace. Rushie's second was his 300th for the club.

THREE MORE FLAG DAYS were held in the following season before the ultimate occasion, the last game that fans in the Kop were allowed to stand. But, how did this custom come about? 'We were sitting in the Flat Iron on Walton Breck Road, sometime in early 1993,' Kopite Johnny Mackin, told the *LFC Magazine*. 'The campaign to save the old Kop looked doomed so we turned our attentions to seeing it off in style. As a prelude to the final farewell to the Kop we decided to organise a series of Flag Days so

that by the time the final one came around against Norwich in 1994 everyone would know what to do. The response was amazing.' Thankfully, even though the Kop became an all-seater in 1994 Flag Days survived. They have been used for special occasions like 'Paisley Day' on 16 March 1996 when Liverpool beat Chelsea 2-0. Bob Paisley had passed away a month earlier. The 20th anniversary of the glory that was Rome when Liverpool won their first European Cup was celebrated when Liverpool beat Tottenham 2-1 on 3 May 1997. Mackin has a special favourite, 'The Kop's last stand was very emotional, but it has to be Flag Day II on 4 January

1994, that 3-3 with Manchester United on a freezing Tuesday night. It had the lot; noise, colour, flags and flares. We don't have to organise Flag Days anymore, they just happen.' If you want to experience a Flag Day then make sure to attend the last home game of the season. You won't be disappointed!

Flagpole Corner

A FEW YEARS into the 20th century there was a small, wooden terrace at the southern end of the Anfield stadium, known locally as the Oakfield Road Embankment or the Walton Breck Bank, Walton Breck Road being the thoroughfare which ran behind that terrace and branched off into Oakfield Road in a south-easterly direction. But what was suitable for a club at the turn of the century was unsuitable for a club which has already won the English League Championship twice in the six seasons that followed. The exposed wooden terrace was not big enough to hold a successful club's ever-increasing fan base and was replaced by a massive sloping mound of soil and cinders that was surrounded by a simple, white picket fence. It became known as the Spion Kop.

On the last day of January 1858 an enormous six-masted iron steamship was launched into the river Thames in London. Its designer was the famous British engineer Isambard Kingdom Brunel. At the time of its launch the 'SS Great Eastern' was the biggest ship ever built. After a somewhat chequered history the ship was broken up for scrap at Rock Ferry right at the end of the 19th century, a massive task that took a year and a half to complete. Officials of Liverpool Football Club had been looking for a flagpole to erect at the stadium and bought the Great Eastern's top mast from a local scrap merchant for the sum of twenty guineas. The mast was floated across the river Mersey to Garston on the Liverpool side

Kopites in 1914

and transported up Everton Valley by two wagons that were pulled by a team of three horses. To commemorate the opening of the new Kop terrace, the flagpole

was erected at that end of the stadium at the junction of Walton Breck Road and Kemlyn Road. Each mast of the Great Eastern was named after the days in the

The flagpole corner from the same angle in ca. 1912, October 1981 (flag at half mast for Shankly's funeral) and in February 2013

week and the mast at Anfield is named Thursday. The flagpole has stood there ever since, proudly flying a flag bearing the club's crest and also, on many occasions, the pennant awarded to the English champions by the Football League.

It can be seen from distance and has been described as a kind of spiritual magnet for thousands of the club's supporters, so much so that the area where it stands is known as 'Flagpole Corner' and has become a regular meeting-place for many supporters both before and after home matches, a place where people can congregate safely away from the hustle and bustle of the busy streets and hostelries around the stadium on match-days.

ANFIELD STADIUM has changed considerably since Everton vacated it in 1892. But for over a hundred years there has been one constant to go with all the glorious things that have been achieved there and that is the flagpole from Brunel's colossal ship of the 19th century.

Flanagan,
Jon

JON FLANAGAN became one of the youngest players in Liverpool's history to be allocated a first-team squad number after being given the number 38 shirt for the 2010/11 season when he was still several weeks short of his 18th birthday.

Like his fellow defender Jack Robinson, Flanagan had impressed in Rodolfo Borrell's Under-18 team at the Academy. Tony Barrett, who was then at the *Liverpool Echo*, predicted big things for the young Liverpudlian, as the step up to the reserves did not faze Flanagan in the slightest and he 'just got on with the job in hand with the minimum of fuss, defending with a characteristic zeal but never missing the chance to get forward and get crosses into the box whenever the opportunity presented itself'. The right-back played with great confidence and maturity from the start against Manchester City at Anfield in April 2011, as he did only six days later in an equally tough encounter with Arsenal in London. At the Emirates he accidentally knocked out his captain Jamie Carragher, but did not let that affect the level of his performance. At Fulham in early May, he was asked to play on the left so that Glen Johnson could be accommodated on the right. Despite being in a position he was not accustomed to, he still played with great assurance.

Despite the positive impact he made following his introduction into the first team towards the end of the 2010/11 season, Flanagan

only made eight senior appearances in 2011/12. He played at Blackburn in April, but didn't complete the match: already cautioned, he was fortunate not to be dismissed for another foul,

and was then substituted after his error compelled Doni to concede a penalty, as a result of which the goalkeeper was sent off. Brendan Rodgers relegated Flanagan to the reserves for a spell in 2012/13

and the youngster knows that much remains to be done before he can expect to feature in the first team in the same way as other locally born defenders like Gerry Byrne or Jamie Carragher have.

> JON FLANAGAN BECAME ONE OF THE YOUNGEST PLAYERS IN LIVERPOOL'S HISTORY TO BE ALLOCATED A FIRST-TEAM SQUAD NUMBER AFTER BEING GIVEN THE NUMBER 38 SHIRT FOR THE 2010/11 SEASON WHEN HE WAS STILL SEVERAL WEEKS SHORT OF HIS 18TH BIRTHDAY

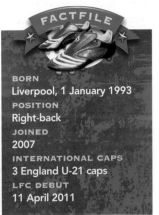

FACTFILE

BORN
Liverpool, 1 January 1993
POSITION
Right-back
JOINED
2007
INTERNATIONAL CAPS
3 England U-21 caps
LFC DEBUT
11 April 2011

Season	League		FA Cup		League Cup		Europe		Total	
	App	Goals	App	Goals	App	Goals	App	Goals	App	Goals
2010/11	7	0	0	0	0	0	0	0	7	0
2011/12	5	0	0 (1)	0	1 (1)	0	-	-	6 (2)	0
2012/13	0	0	0 (1)	0	0	0	1	0	1 (1)	0
Total	**12**	**0**	**0 (2)**	**0**	**1 (1)**	**0**	**1**	**0**	**14 (3)**	**0**

Fleming, George

GEORGE FLEMING
[LIVERPOOL]

AFTER FEATURING in 187 matches for First Division Wolves from 1894 to 1901, George Fleming spent five years at Liverpool when the club's contrasting fortunes were quite dramatic. When Fleming played his first game, Liverpool were defending their first Football League Championship, yet would be relegated just three years later. Liverpool bounced straight back by winning the Second and then the First Division in successive seasons. Fleming played in a number of different positions, making him the utility player of his time, but he preferred the centre-half role.

Fleming had his best season in 1904/05 when, after missing the opening five Second Division fixtures, he played in the remaining 29. He started the 1905/06 Championship season in the first team but lost his place after three matches to newcomer James Bradley. Fleming never featured for Liverpool again, but stayed on to become assistant trainer at the club until his death in August 1922. The club programme in 1904 captured the

essence of Fleming. 'The old wolf. Never a star, but ever a worker. Can still do good service if called upon. Never gives up.'

FACTFILE

BORN
Bannockburn, Scotland, 20 May 1869
DIED
August 1922
POSITION
Defender / Forward
OTHER CLUBS
Broxburn,
East Stirlingshire (1893-94),
Wolverhampton Wanderers (1894–1901)
SIGNED FROM
Wolverhampton Wanderers, 2 May 1901
LFC DEBUT GAME/GOAL
21 September 1901 /
8 February 1902
CONTRACT EXPIRY
1906
HONOURS
Second Division
Championship 1904/05

Season	League		FA Cup		Other		Total	
	App	Goals	App	Goals	App	Goals	App	Goals
1901/02	25	1	2	1	-	-	27	2
1902/03	4	0	0	0	-	-	4	0
1903/04	18	4	0	0	-	-	18	4
1904/05	29	0	2	0	-	-	31	0
1905/06	3	0	0	0	0	0	3	0
Total	**79**	**5**	**4**	**1**	**0**	**0**	**83**	**6**

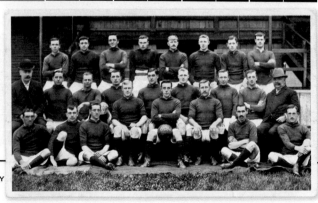

Foreign players

DURING its long and illustrious history, less than 600 British citizens have represented Liverpool Football Club in competitive matches; although it is perhaps surprising, considering its close proximity to the British mainland, and the port of Liverpool in particular, that only two dozen have come from Ireland. In the early days of its existence, the club made a quite deliberate attempt to raid Scotland to find 'a first class player for every position on the pitch.' Their concentrated efforts led to Liverpool's team of the time being nicknamed 'The team of the Macs'. Scottish players would continue to arrive regularly at Liverpool for decades and, unsurprisingly, because Wales was so close to the city, club scouts were also keeping track of young talent there as well as looking across the Irish Sea.

But it wasn't until the 1920s that the club first actively chased a player of non-British descent. Two 20-year-olds stood out when a touring team from South Africa met Liverpool at Anfield on 1 October 1924. Arthur Riley, a goalkeeper, and Gordon Hodgson, a forward, impressed the watching public and, more importantly, Liverpool's board of directors. Riley would eventually replace the legendary Irishman Elisha Scott in the late 1920s and would retain his place for most of the following decade too. Hodgson, who was in fact an Englishman born in South Africa, started scoring goals immediately and didn't stop until he had reached 233 in the First Division alone.

South Africans Lance Carr and Berry Nieuwenhuys arrived in 1933 on the recommendation of Arthur Riley's father and racked

up almost 300 appearances for the Reds and a few more of their compatriots wore Liverpool's colours. These players were effectively amateurs so their recruitment made economic sense. Cape Town native Harman van den Berg tried to impress as World War Two was about to stop all Football League activity. Bob Priday made 40 appearances while giant defender Hugh Gerhardi became homesick. Goalkeeper Doug Rudham joined Liverpool in 1954. But, then incredibly quarter of a century passed before the Reds searched beyond the British Isles to strengthen their squad. Avi Cohen became the first Israeli to feature in the English league, arriving from Maccabi Tel Aviv in 1979. He departed in October 1981, but eight months previously Zimbabwean Bruce Grobbelaar was bought from Vancouver Whitecaps in Canada and Australian Craig Johnston was obtained from Middlesbrough. The first Scandinavian to represent Liverpool was Dane Jan Mølby, signed by Kenny Dalglish from Ajax Amsterdam in 1984 and five years later Swedish World Cup captain Glenn Hysén was brought from Fiorentina.

When the Premier League debuted on 16 August 1992 only 11 'foreign' players featured in the starting line-ups on display. Israeli Ronny Rosenthal, Grobbelaar, Hysén, Mølby, Hungarian Istvan Kozma and John Barnes, who was born in Jamaica, were the only players born outside the British Isles in Liverpool's squad during that campaign. In the second Premier League season the club's increased scouting in Scandinavia produced Torben Piechnik from Denmark and Stig Inge Bjørnebye from Norway. Roy Evans had special fondness for the professional attitude of the Norwegians proved by his acquisition of Bjørn Tore Kvarme, Øyvind Leonhardsen and Vegard Heggem. He also looked further ahead to Germany to find

Karl-Heinz Riedle, Czech Patrik Berger and South African Sean Dundee and the USA to force a working permit for Brad Friedel. As Gérard Houllier moved in the club's squad was invaded by foreign players from all over the globe, forever changing its identity, although Liverpool were by no means an exception as other top flight clubs utilised the freedom of movement and labour.

Unsurprisingly France and Spain have been the biggest provider of imported football talent to Liverpool over the years, considering the nationality of managers Houllier and Rafa Benítez. The Spanish imports comfortably top any 'worth-what-we-paid-for' list with the likes of Xabi Alonso, Luis Garcia, Pepe Reina and Fernando Torres. Maybe it is something to do with

the Gallic disposition but even decent enough footballers like Djibril Cissé and Florent Sinama-Pongolle never had the same success as the Spaniards on the pitch or the same rapport with the supporters off it. Plus sadly there have been some dreadful misfits amongst Liverpool's French Connection in Bruno Cheyrou, Charles Itandje and Bernard Diomede as well as the Senegalese pair Salif Diao and El Hadji Diouf who came from the French league. Although the influx of players from South Africa was primarily condensed into a thirty-year period separated by World War Two the rest of the continent would later provide rich pickings of talent for British clubs looking to the new African nations that had shaken off the shackles of colonial rule and become independent states in their own right. Momo Sissoko (Mali), Rigobert Song (Cameroon) and the popular Titi Camara (Guinea) had some degrees of success.

From south of the Panama Canal there has been a steady stream since the Millennium of men born in Brazil, Argentina and Uruguay with the most successful being Luis Suarez, Lucas Leiva, Maxi Rodriguez and Javier Mascherano. Others like Diego Cavalieri, Gabriel Paletta, Sebastian Leto and the injury-prone Fabio Aurelio are unlikely to be mentioned in the same breath.

EUROPE continued to fragment and new countries were formed. Three years after Berger arrived in the aftermath of his successful showing in the 1996 European Championships for the Czech Republic,

his countryman Vladimir Smicer arrived. Croatian Igor Biscan achieved cult status as well as Pole Jerzy Dudek. Slovakian Martin Skrtel wears his heart on his sleeve and has a steely resolve forged in his upbringing in what used to be known as the Eastern Bloc.

They have come from all corners of the Earth, from countries whose flags bear all the colours of the spectrum. They have one common aim; to prove that they were worthy of wearing the colours of Liverpool Football Club. They are welcome if they prove to have the talent necessary to further enhance the club's rich history.

A best XI of foreign stars to represent Liverpool Football Club

Bruce Grobbelaar

Markus Babbel

Sami Hyypia

Daniel Agger

John Arne Riise

Berry Nieuwenhuys

Xabi Alonso

Jan Mølby

Dirk Kuyt

Fernando Torres

Luis Suarez

Substitutes: **Pepe Reina, Álvaro Arbeloa, Stephane Henchoz, Didi Hamann, Patrik Berger, Luis Garcia, Craig Johnston**

Forshaw,
Dick

DICK FORSHAW joined Liverpool after serving for four years in Ceylon (now Sri Lanka) with the Royal Garrison Artillery. Introduced into the Liverpool first XI after the opening three fixtures of the 1919/20 season, Forshaw played in 23 First Division games and scored seven times, including a hat-trick against Derby County, helping his club finish the season in fourth place.

Another fourth-place finish followed a year later when Forshaw's contribution was nine goals from 27 appearances. It was during the next two years that Forshaw really came to prominence, not missing a single game as the club won the league title in consecutive seasons, 1921/22 and 1922/23, and scoring 36 times in those 84 appearances. Although Forshaw only missed three games when Liverpool unsuccessfully went

for a Championship hat-trick, his goal tally was down to five. His 'normal service' was resumed however in 1924/25 when he was easily the club's leading scorer with 19, and he bettered that in what was to prove his final full season at Anfield with 27 from only 32 league games in 1925/26.

FORSHAW was portrayed by the *Derby Daily Telegraph* in 1921 as 'a brainy, unorthodox lad, who does the unexpected thing, but that has been his secret of success. An opponent never knows what Forshaw will do. He never forgets his partner, but is not bound hand and foot to him. Has a powerful shot in either foot.'

In March 1927 Forshaw, now aged 31, had weighed in with 14 goals when he made the short trip across Stanley Park to continue his career with Everton. A quote from Everton's minute books reveals: 'Forshaw – Secy. reported having asked the L'pool Club if they were prepared to part with this player & the result was an interview with the L'pool club after our match today at which it was agreed to obtain this player at a fee of £3750 & an engagement up to 5th May 1928 at limit wage & £10 signing on bonus.' It was very surprising that Liverpool's board accepted Blues' offer, and the move came not least as a surprise to Forshaw himself, who came home to find the respective secretaries of the clubs waiting for him to inform him of their agreement. His wife, who was a staunch Liverpool supporter, was not at all pleased and declared: 'I have never been an Evertonian and I don't know what I shall do about it.' Forshaw starred alongside the great Dixie Dean at Everton, picking up his third League Championship in his first full season in 1928, becoming the first player to win the title with both Liverpool and Everton.

It certainly wasn't due to lack of form that Forshaw was sold, but to fill the Anfield cashier's coffers. Supporter 'Red Dingle' was shocked to see Forshaw go and composed 'A Supporter's Lament'.

It's all very well for directors
To say we shouldn't cuss;
They think of nowt but £.s.d.
But blimey – what price us?
For there isn't a man in
the thousands
That occupy Spion Kop
Who agrees with the transfer
of Dickie,
The boy with the twinkling hop.

Supposing you've been
a supporter
For more years than you
care to tell:
And owing to treatment in
years gone by
Wished the Everton club in …
Division Two:
Would you like to see your
favourite sold
Without as much as a wink?
It's enough to drive us up
a pole.
You'll agree with me, I think.'

Forshaw made the news for less desirable reasons in April 1932 when he was charged with theft. He had been given £100 by one Richard Green of Alexandra Drive, Liverpool, to place on long-shot Grand Salute to win the Royal Hunt Cup at Ascot in June 1931. The horse won and Green was entitled to £2,050. Forshaw disappeared with the winnings to be later tracked down in Kilburn, London. Forshaw pleaded guilty to four charges of theft but asked for leniency as he had been pressed for money. The court heard that since he retired from football in 1931 he had been a failed commission agent and ran a fish and chip business in London with his wife. He was deemed to have acted with 'peculiar meanness' and was sentenced to 12 months' hard labour.

FACTFILE

BORN
Preston, 20 August 1895
POSITION
Forward
OTHER CLUBS
Gateshead St Vincent;
Nottingham Forest,
Middlesbrough
(wartime guest),
Everton (1927–29),
Wolverhampton Wanderers
(1929–30),
Hednesford Town (1930),
Rhyl Athletic (1930),
Waterford (1930–31)
JOINED
Free transfer, 31 July 1919
LFC DEBUT GAME/GOAL
8 September 1919 /
20 September 1919
CONTRACT EXPIRY
3 March 1927
HONOURS
League Championship
1921/22, 1922/23

Season	League		FA Cup		Other		Total	
	App	Goals	App	Goals	App	Goals	App	Goals
1919/20	23	7	0	0	-	-	23	7
1920/21	27	9	0	0	-	-	27	9
1921/22	42	17	3	3	1	0	46	20
1922/23	42	19	4	1	-	-	46	20
1923/24	39	5	5	1	-	-	44	6
1924/25	37	19	3	0	-	-	40	19
1925/26	32	27	3	2	-	-	35	29
1926/27	24	14	3	0	-	-	27	14
Total	**266**	**117**	**21**	**7**	**1**	**0**	**288**	**124**

Fowler, Robbie

ROBERT BERNARD FOWLER was born and raised in Toxteth in Liverpool, an area where unemployment was rife. Fowler was an Everton supporter in his childhood and loathed Ian Rush's achievements with Liverpool, especially since Rushie was very prolific against Everton. Fowler was chosen to play for the Under-14 team at his school, where he was spotted by Jim Aspinall, a Liverpool scout. 'He knew when and where to put the ball away, and run into space,' Aspinall said. 'He had such a lovely touch on the ball.' Everton also had their eye on him at the time and Fowler featured in a few games for them when he was aged 14 in their Under-17 team. Fowler settled in at Liverpool, though, and signed his professional contract on his 17th birthday. 'Kenny Dalglish was manager when I signed for Liverpool,' Fowler said. 'When I was training there as a schoolboy, Kenny would sometimes drop me off at home. I couldn't wait to get into school the next morning to tell everyone what had happened!' Fowler got his initial taste of the first team at the end of the 1992/93 season, when he was twice put on the bench: against Bolton in the FA Cup, and in the final league match when Liverpool beat Tottenham 6-2.

His international breakthrough came that summer with England's Under-18 team, who won the European title. Fowler started the tournament on the bench but ended up as top scorer, with five goals in four games. Each goal was spectacular and highlighted his incredible talent. Fowler scored in his first match for Liverpool against Fulham in a 3-1 victory in

the League Cup on 22 September 1993, and in the second leg against the Cottagers he scored all five goals in a 5-0 win! Fowler was only the fifth player in Liverpool's history to achieve that feat. He scored his first hat-trick against Southampton in only his fifth league match and no fewer than 13 goals in his first 15 games for Liverpool. It was obvious that he was a goalscoring phenomenon. He also made progress in the international set-up, scoring on his Under-21 England debut against San Marino in November.

A broken ankle in the FA Cup against Bristol City on 19 January sidelined Fowler until the beginning of March, and he only scored three goals in his remaining 11 games, but nevertheless boasted a great record in his first season. Fowler was only one goal behind Ian Rush, with 18 in total, but Fowler had started 33 games compared to Rush's 48.

FOWLER started the 1994/95 season by scoring five goals in the first three games, including an incredible Anfield hat-trick against Arsenal in only four minutes and 35 seconds, which to date is a Premier League record. 'I didn't really have a clue today's goals came so quickly,' Fowler said perplexed after the match. 'I thought they were 15 minutes apart.' With half of the season gone he had already scored 20 league goals. Roy Evans, who by now had succeeded Graeme Souness as boss, was ecstatic with his young genius. 'Robbie has immense talent. He can be frightening,' Evans said enthusiastically. 'As long as he learns from players

like Ian Rush, who knows how far he can go?' Fowler enjoyed playing alongside legend Ian Rush. 'He knows everything about defenders and has told me about the strengths and weaknesses of everyone we've played against and that's made a big difference to me,' Fowler said about his mentor. 'In the games it's the same. He never stops talking, keeps on at me non-stop and that's helped me to develop this season. I'm learning from the best and if you don't learn from the likes of Ian then who can you learn from?'

> IN THE SECOND LEG AGAINST THE COTTAGERS HE SCORED ALL FIVE GOALS IN A 5-0 WIN!

Fowler scored the winner in both legs against Crystal Palace in the semi-finals of the League Cup. He was looking forward to playing at Wembley for the first time in his career. 'I've never been nervous before a game, but Sunday might be different. I'm sure that when I walk out of that tunnel and hear the roar of the crowd the hairs on the back of my neck will stand up.' Fowler and Rush started up front as Liverpool beat Bolton 2-1 in the final. Fowler's best friend, Steve McManaman, was outstanding on the day and scored both goals for the club. Fowler then received a nice birthday present when he was chosen as Young Player of the Year in the Premier League. He was also the only player who had featured in all of Liverpool's games that season, and was the team's top scorer with 25 league goals in 42 matches, and 31 goals in total.

Fowler had dyed his hair peroxide blond at the start of the 1995/96 season. He also had a new partner

up front, Stan Collymore. But in the first two league games Evans used Rush and Collymore, and the top scorer from last season had to settle for being a substitute until Collymore got injured and Fowler was back in again. He was slow out of the blocks but came into his own with a quadruple against Bolton on 23 September 1995. Evans was adamant that it had been the right decision. 'I left Robbie out at the start of the season. He didn't like it at the time, but he realises now that it did him good. There will be times over the next couple of years when I need to boot him up the backside again.'

Fowler was surely one of the most in-form strikers in Europe, and scored two memorable goals at Old Trafford on 1 October 1995. The spotlight was on Eric Cantona, who was returning from an eight-month absence after his misadventures at Selhurst Park. Fowler's equaliser was struck with such incredible venom from the edge of the box that United keeper Peter Schmeichel never saw the ball. Fowler scored his second when he bumped Gary Neville out of the way and cheekily chipped the Dane. Cantona then equalised from the penalty spot in a pulsating 2-2 draw. Fowler scored a hat-trick for the second season in a row against Arsenal on 23 December and at the beginning of March scored two of Liverpool's three goals in the opening eight minutes against Aston Villa. At the end of the month, Villa faced his wrath again when Liverpool beat them 3-0 in the FA Cup semi-final. Mark Bosnich was becoming the best authority on Fowler's skills. He was in awe of the young striker. 'He often shoots early, he doesn't mind where he shoots from, but he seems to get late fade on his shots like a golfer,' the Villa keeper said. 'He usually gets ten out of ten shots on target, and with nine out of ten he hits the corners.' Fowler's second goal in the cup semi-final was spectacular, a shot from the right corner of the

penalty area into the upper-left corner in off the post. Fowler also played his part in the 4-3 thriller against Newcastle on 3 April 1996, two goals from Fowler and the winning goal from Collymore in the final seconds securing a spectacular victory.

A tremendous occasion to showcase his talents waited at Wembley in an FA Cup final against Manchester United. The game was terribly disappointing, ending in a 1-0 defeat, only memorable because it was Ian Rush's last game for the Reds. Rush said goodbye to his young protégé: 'I leave it in good hands. Robbie will probably eclipse all that I have achieved at Liverpool.' Yet another great season for Fowler was at an end. He was again chosen the Young Player of the Year, becoming the second player in history (after Ryan Giggs) to achieve that honour twice. He had improved his scoring record from the previous season and scored 36 goals in all competitions, as well as forming a promising partnership with Collymore.

FOWLER played his first senior international when he came on as a substitute against Bulgaria on 27 March 1996. Souness, who contributed to Fowler's meteoric rise by giving him his first chance in Liverpool's first team, was not surprised. 'Robbie has more natural ability than Ian Rush,' Souness said. 'Rushie had an incredible ability to sniff out a chance. Fowler has got that but has also got the ability to take the ball outside the box and do something great. Rushie relied on the ball to come into the box, whereas Robbie can go and do things on his own. He'll never have the craft of Kenny Dalglish, but if you're talking about being a goal-getter then he could be the best.'

Fowler was included in Terry Venables' England team in Euro 96 on home soil that summer. Venables preferred Shearer and Sheringham up front, but Fowler finally made an appearance in his country's third game of the tournament in one of the best England internationals ever, when the Netherlands were beaten 4-1. Sheringham, who had scored two goals, was

substituted for Fowler 15 minutes from time. Fowler also made a substitute appearance against Spain in the quarter-finals in the 110th minute. England survived that penalty shootout but not the one against Germany in the semi-finals.

Fowler wore the number 9 shirt for the first time instead of number 23 at the start of the 1996/97 season. He had a back injury and only scored two goals in his first eight matches. Collymore wasn't scoring much either, but there was a new kid on the block who kept the worries away for Evans. Patrik Berger scored two goals against Leicester and another double in a 5-1 victory over Chelsea. Fowler soon returned and scored 17 goals in his next 15 matches, including four against Middlesbrough on 17 December 1996. His second goal in that match was his 100th for Liverpool in 165 games. By comparison Rush reached this goalscoring landmark in 166 games. When Fowler broke the record he revealed a T-shirt underneath his Liverpool shirt which said: 'God's Job's A Good 'Un', a cheeky reference to his 'God' nickname bestowed by his admirers.

It is said that lightning never strikes twice, but it did happen in the match against Newcastle at Anfield on 10 March. Another 4-3 victory was the result and this time it was Fowler who scored the winning goal in the last seconds. He owned all the headlines in March. He won rave reviews from FIFA Secretary General Sepp Blatter for trying to prevent a penalty against Arsenal which the referee gave Liverpool after Seaman had been judged to have taken Fowler down. Fowler dived and admitted it as soon as he got up. He took the penalty himself and missed, but Jason McAteer followed up to score. His love affair with the football authorities didn't last long. Two days later,

Fowler was fined for wearing a T-shirt urging people to support 500 sacked dockers in a match against Brann in Bergen. UEFA rules had stated that you can't show any political support in European matches, and Fowler got a small fine. If Fowler wasn't a working-class hero before, he certainly was now. He scored his first goal for the national team on 29 March against Mexico, and was back in the headlines in April when his league season was suddenly cut short after, in a moment of madness, he was sent off in the Merseyside derby when he clashed with David Unsworth. Fowler scored his last goal of the season in the 2-0 victory against Paris St Germain when the Reds crashed out of Europe and was suspended for the last three games of the season. Liverpool's campaign ended on a disappointing note once again. Fowler scored 'only' 18 league goals, compared to 28 the previous season, but his overall total for the season was 31.

LIGAMENT damage in Fowler's right knee, received against a Norwegian XI in Oslo on 31 July 1997, kept him out for the first six matches of the 1997/98 season. Michael Owen was now the focus of attention, after getting his chance at the end of the previous season due to Fowler's ban. They finally played together for the first time against Aston Villa on 22 September at Anfield. Fowler opened the scoring with a well-struck penalty and in the following league game against West Ham he scored one of the best goals of his career. Bjørnebye's cross was headed out towards Fowler who wasted no time and lashed it in when the ball was still in the air. Fowler's temperament was back in question against Bolton on 1 November. He scored after only 48 seconds but in the 75th minute he elbowed Per Frandsen and was sent off. Fowler admitted he was in the wrong. 'I had received a few nasty

challenges, had just missed a one-on-one with their goalkeeper and then Frandsen had a kick at me. I caught him with my arm but it was not that bad and he made a meal of it. I'm still learning all the time and I've got to get stupid things like that out of my game.'

On Boxing Day, Fowler scored two goals in as many minutes against Leeds in a 3-1 victory, and netted a further two in seven matches in January, both in the League Cup, the first against Newcastle in the quarter-finals and the second against Boro in the semi-finals. Fowler had set himself a high standard and not scoring a goal every two games was unacceptable. He was relieved after his Middlesbrough goal. 'They chanted my name throughout the game. My head has dropped a couple of times because forwards rely on confidence. This has probably been the worst run I've had since I started playing, not as regards scoring, but in terms of my form.' Thirteen goals in 23 games was Fowler's record when he scored his last goal of the season on 27 January. He had gone four games without a goal when on 23 February a catastrophic collision with Everton's goalkeeper Thomas Myhre five minutes from time resulted in torn cruciate knee ligaments which kept him out of action for the next seven months. 'After the season I have had so far, it is a shocking blow. What makes it worse is that I felt I was just coming back to top form, after I had gone through a bad patch. I tried to get up and run, but I was wobbling all over the place and couldn't stand up. I got to the hospital on Monday night, but didn't sleep a wink because the pain was so bad.'

Fowler had learned a lot from this season both on and off the field. 'Our fame away from football is frightening and, if I'm honest, I hate it,' Fowler confessed. 'When I was young it wasn't that

bad, but today it's got completely out of hand. At the moment, I'm "taking drugs", everything. It's frightening what people say about you. It hurts. We get tested at Liverpool every week, yet people still write to the club and claim they've seen me doing drugs. Even taxi drivers are going around Liverpool spreading them. "Robbie Fowler, he's doing coke, isn't he?"' Things had certainly changed over the summer at Anfield. Fowler started finally, seven games into the season, eager to impress new joint-boss Gérard Houllier, who had arrived to dictate things alongside Evans. Fowler scored two goals in a 3-3 draw with Charlton.

Ten days later, another two followed against Kosice in the UEFA Cup. Fowler didn't score in the next three matches and was put on the bench as he needed the rest. Evans resigned in November to leave Houllier as sole manager with Phil Thompson as his assistant. The first game under their management was against Leeds at Anfield. Fowler scored the only goal for Liverpool from a penalty, but Leeds ran out 3-1 winners. Fowler shone brightly in the following match when he ran Villa ragged, not for the first time in his career, and a brilliant hat-trick signalled his intentions. Houllier was happy. 'It's difficult to say if Robbie is back to his best but that was certainly an important reference game for him. He went through a mental barrier and he now knows he can do it again. For the first time, he was dropping off, taking part in the

build-up, he was strong and shielding the ball well and also good in the air. What we have had to do is to give him confidence by encouraging him, by trusting him and being patient with him.' Fowler had to wait seven matches for his next goal. Two matches later, on 16 January, he scored his second hat-trick for Houllier in a 7-1 victory against Southampton. Further good news from the Fowler camp followed in January when he signed a new five-year contract with Liverpool. If January was all about the positives, the contrary was looming on the horizon. Two controversial incidents against Chelsea and Everton got Fowler into trouble.

The date: 27 February 1999
Venue: Stamford Bridge
Opponents: Chelsea

Fowler decided to follow up rumours about Graeme Le Saux's sexual orientation by turning his backside towards him and shaking it about. Le Saux's retribution came swiftly when he pole-axed Fowler from behind. Incredibly enough, Fowler got a two-match ban while Le Saux was banned for just one.

The date: 3 April 1999
Venue: Anfield
Opponents: Everton

Fowler 'snorted' the line after scoring the first of his two goals in the 3-2 victory. He said his actions were in response to the 'smackhead' taunts he'd endured at Goodison Park the previous October and on the streets of

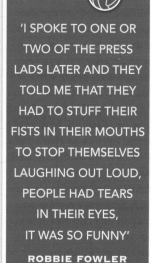

'I SPOKE TO ONE OR TWO OF THE PRESS LADS LATER AND THEY TOLD ME THAT THEY HAD TO STUFF THEIR FISTS IN THEIR MOUTHS TO STOP THEMSELVES LAUGHING OUT LOUD, PEOPLE HAD TEARS IN THEIR EYES, IT WAS SO FUNNY'

ROBBIE FOWLER

Liverpool. Houllier made a miserable attempt to cover it up in front of the disbelieving press, by claiming that this was Fowler's tribute to Rigobert Song, who had brought this celebration over from Cameroon where it was quite common for players to get down and eat the grass after they had scored. 'I spoke to one or two of the press lads later and they told me that they had to stuff their fists in their mouths to stop themselves laughing out loud,' Fowler said. 'People had tears in their eyes, it was so funny.'

Fowler received a two-match ban for the Chelsea incident and four for the snorting. Following the Everton game, he featured in three matches without scoring and was then forced to sit out the remaining six matches of the campaign. Fowler scored in the first game of the 1999/2000 season against Sheffield Wednesday as well as hitting one of the goals of the season on 28 August, a pile-driver from 30 yards that went in off the bar at Highbury. Fowler had felt pain in his ankle before the match against Everton on 27 September but decided to play. He only lasted an hour before being replaced, and then underwent an operation and was expected to be out for three months.

Fowler made three substitute appearances in December, and scored his third goal of the season against Wimbledon on 28 December. He had now scored 150 goals in total for Liverpool: 95 goals scored with his left, 30 with the right and 25 headers; 127 goals were from inside the box, including 11 from the penalty spot, and 23 outside. His ankle was sore after the Wimbledon game but he wasn't prepared for the earth-shattering news that he had to be operated on again. He didn't play for four months until he came on against Everton on 21 April.

FOWLER made a few more substitute appearances before being given a chance in the starting line-up in the penultimate game of the season against Southampton. He was desperate to prove his worth but was replaced after 59 minutes, which made him furious. 'Houllier dragged me off. I was gutted. Just destroyed,' Fowler said. 'I went off down the tunnel boiling, unable to speak. I got showered, still livid, still feeling cheated.' Fowler didn't sit in for the post-match discussions in the dressing room, which angered Houllier, and he was left out of the final game of the season against Bradford with Champions League qualification in the balance. Fowler, who was listening to the game at his nephew's christening (having had a few), decided to leave a message on Houllier's answering machine after Bradford had beaten Liverpool 1-0. 'I'm gutted you cost me the Champions League, I hope you're f****** satisfied in leaving me out now.' Fowler was predictably called to Houllier's office, where they seemed to settle their differences. Fowler says Houllier tried to undermine his position from that day forward. 'Houllier used the local paper, the *Liverpool Echo*, to feed stuff to the fans, questioning my form and ability,' Fowler claimed in his autobiography. 'From the start of the 2000/01 season, there was a pretty concerted campaign against me conducted by Houllier. They used to give marks for each player in the paper, and if ever [reporter] Chris Bascombe marked me up then Houllier was on him, asking why he'd given me that rating. In public he always claimed he had supported me, had gone out of his way to stand by me. In private he was working out how best to see the back of me.'

Fowler was carried off in a 2000/01 pre-season match against Glentoran, following a freakish collision with the goalkeeper, and was out for six weeks. He scored in his tenth game of the season against Chelsea in the fourth round of the League Cup, a dramatic winner in extra time, and was again in the headlines for all the right reasons when he scored a hat-trick in an 8-0 win against Stoke in the League Cup (which was his most prolific competition, having scored 25 goals in 29 matches). That didn't please the French boss one bit, as Fowler reveals. 'Straight after the game, Houllier went in to the press room and he was boiling, really animated. He absolutely tore into me, said I was unfit, overweight, out of shape, and not up to it. After I had just scored a hat-trick in our best performance of the season to take my tally to four in three matches.' Chelsea made a £12million bid for Fowler in December 2000 that Liverpool refused. Fowler was the star of the show when he scored a sensational goal against Birmingham in the League Cup final on 25 February which

resulted in a penalty shootout victory for the Reds. A lob, from far outside the box, ended in the net. 'It was one of those shots which can either end up in the crowd or in the back of the net,' Fowler said. 'It is up there with the best goals I have scored, especially when you consider it was in a major final.' Fowler had been in and out of the starting line-up in Liverpool's successful treble season, but proved a valuable player in the final run-in. He scored a great free kick against Wycombe Wanderers in the FA Cup semi-final.

He was a substitute in the UEFA Cup final against Alaves but scored Liverpool's fourth goal that almost proved the winner, before the Reds clinched victory in extra time. He only played for the last 13 minutes against Arsenal in the FA Cup final win, but Michael Owen scored two goals following Fowler's introduction into the game. One crucial match was left of the season, against Charlton at the Valley. Fowler was sensational and scored two goals, which clinched Liverpool's best ever Premier League finish and a place in the Champions League.

Fowler got into trouble with Phil Thompson at Melwood in August 2001 when Tommo was behind the goal, and Robbie hit a well-placed shot into the goal that caused the net to billow out a bit, the ball going near him. Seen as a threat to Thompson's authority, Fowler was dropped from the squad to face Arsenal in the Charity Shield. After issuing an apology, he was back in the first-team fold and scored his first goal of the season against Haka in the second leg of the Champions League qualifier. Fowler started in the defeats against Bolton and Aston Villa, but was back on the bench for the next three matches. He talked about his problems in October. 'If I pick up a paper seven days a week, I can guarantee I'll probably be in at

least five times. I'm not saying it's an excuse for how I'm playing but when you go out and feel you have to try and prove people wrong all the time you can end up trying too hard. Maybe I'm trying too many fancy things, passes and stuff which won't come off.' In October 2001 his nemesis, Houllier, was taken ill and needed an emergency heart operation, so Thompson was now taking care of business. Certainly though, Houllier was still pulling the strings behind the scenes. A true Fowler highlight was a hat-trick against Leicester on 20 October 2001, but those were his first goals in five starts and two substitute appearances that had passed since his Haka goal. In November, Leeds chairman Peter Ridsdale contacted Liverpool with an £8million bid. The fee in the end came close to £12million, during anxious weeks for Fowler who wanted to experience a different atmosphere where he could enjoy his football and would be backed by the manager. 'After so long at Liverpool, the club where I believed I belonged, I was like a lost soul in those first few

days with my new club. I was thinking, "What have I done letting Houllier beat me like that?"' Fowler said in his book. Roy Evans once famously said he would rather jump in the Mersey than sell Fowler. Nobody at the club jumped into the Mersey on 29 November 2001.

AGAIN, the unthinkable happened in 2006 when Robbie Fowler, like the prodigal son, returned to Liverpool in a sensational move, over four years after he had left Merseyside for Leeds. He scored 14 goals in 33 matches over a 14-month period at Leeds before moving to Manchester City, where he stayed three years, scoring 27 goals in 92 matches. Five days after re-signing for the Reds, he came on as a substitute for Peter Crouch in a home game with Birmingham City. Liverpool had just taken the lead when he entered the pitch, but he was unable to add to the score, although he did have an acrobatic, injury-time overhead kick disallowed for offside. The goals started to come again. Five in the league before the end of the

season was enough to ensure him an additional year's contract at Rafa's Reds. Fowler scored seven goals during what would turn out to be his final season at Anfield; three penalties against Sheffield United, two against Galatasaray in the Champions League and strikes against Reading and Arsenal in the League Cup. That took his final total for Liverpool up to 183 goals from 369 games. Denied the chance to say a proper farewell to the Anfield public by the sudden move to Leeds in 2001, Robbie and his young family proudly walked around the pitch at the end of the final league game of 2006/07 to say goodbye.

On 21 July 2007, Fowler signed for Cardiff City in the Championship. His two League Cup goals at West Bromwich Albion in the third round of the competition led to Cardiff being paired with Liverpool in the next round. He played the whole 90 minutes for Cardiff at Anfield and received a rapturous reception from the home supporters, but was unable to prevent a 2-1 defeat. The recurrence of a hip injury, plus damaged ankle ligaments sustained in a training-ground incident with his captain Darren Purse, meant that his first-team opportunities were limited for the rest of the season. He was not fit enough to be considered for a place in Cardiff's FA Cup final squad for the big match against Portsmouth at the new Wembley. Fowler signed a three-month deal with Paul Ince's Blackburn before the 2008/09 season, but only made three starts and three substitute appearances without scoring a goal. He then signed a two-year contract with Australian side North Queensland Fury in February 2009. Fowler was said to have dubious motives for his move to Australia, but answered his critics by releasing a short statement to the local newspaper in Townsville: 'I'm not here for a holiday. I'm prepared to work hard and get on that pitch.'

> FOWLER'S GENIUS FOR GOALS WILL NEVER BE FORGOTTEN, STILL A DARLING OF THE KOP

The club had severe financial problems, and after one season Fowler was released from his contract to become a free agent again. Towards the end of April 2010, it was Western Australia club Perth Glory who signed 35-year-old Fowler as their 'foreign marquee player', which meant that his wages would be excluded from the club's salary cap.

In July 2011, Fowler made an unexpected move from Australia to Thailand's Muang Thong United, and at the start of October 2011 he was made caretaker coach of the Thai club. In early 2012, he quit the team and moved back to Liverpool, as his wife wanted to go back home. Prior to the launch of a new Indian League, Fowler was one of a few big-name stars sold at an auction, going for £338,000 to Kolkata, but said himself he wasn't sure if he would play there. In the end nothing came of it.

FOWLER trained with Blackpool for a while towards the end of the 2011/12 season. He was, however, unable to agree personal terms with the club and retired from playing. He re-ignited his association with Liverpool by being part of the club's entourage during their 2012/13 pre-season tour in America. Fowler's genius for goals will never be forgotten, still a darling of the Kop.

FACTFILE

BORN
Toxteth, Liverpool, 9 April 1975
POSITION
Centre-forward
OTHER CLUBS
Leeds United (2001–03), Manchester City (2003–06), Cardiff City (2007–08), Blackburn Rovers (2008), North Queensland Fury (2009–10), Perth Glory (2010–11), Muang Thong United (2011)
JOINED
1991; signed professional 9 April 1992 / Manchester City, free transfer, 27 January 2006
INTERNATIONAL CAPS
26 England caps (7 goals) (22 (5) at LFC), 1996–2002
LFC DEBUT GAME/GOAL
22 September 1993 / 22 September 1993
CONTRACT EXPIRY
29 November 2001 / 1 July 2007
HONOURS
FA Cup 2001; League Cup 1995, 2001; UEFA Cup 2001; PFA Young Player of the Year 1995, 1996

Season	League App	League Goals	FA Cup App	FA Cup Goals	League Cup App	League Cup Goals	Europe App	Europe Goals	Other App	Other Goals	Total App	Total Goals
1993/94	27 (1)	12	1	0	5	6	-	-	-	-	33 (1)	18
1994/95	42	25	7	2	8	4	-	-	-	-	57	31
1995/96	36 (2)	28	7	6	4	2	3 (1)	0	-	-	50 (3)	36
1996/97	32	18	1	1	4	5	7	7	-	-	44	31
1997/98	19 (1)	9	1	0	4	3	3	1	-	-	27 (1)	13
1998/99	23 (2)	14	1 (1)	1	2	1	5 (1)	2	-	-	31 (4)	18
1999/2000	8 (6)	3	0	0	0	0	-	-	-	-	8 (6)	3
2000/01	15 (12)	8	3 (2)	2	5	6	6 (5)	1	-	-	29 (19)	17
2001/02	8 (2)	3	0	0	0	0	2 (5)	1	0	0	10 (7)	4
2005/06	9 (5)	5	0	0	0	0	1 (1)	0	0	0	10 (6)	5
2006/07	6 (10)	3	0	0	3	2	1 (3)	2	0	0	10 (13)	7
Total	**225 (41)**	**128**	**21 (3)**	**12**	**35**	**29**	**28 (16)**	**14**	**0**	**0**	**309 (60)**	**183**

FACTFILE

BORN
Sheffield, 1874
POSITION
Centre-forward
OTHER CLUBS
Tinsley, Gainsborough Trinity (1897–99), Queens Park Rangers (1900–01), Woolwich Arsenal (1901-02), Kettering (1902), Roundell (1903), Gainsborough Trinity (1903-06), Grantham (1906)
SIGNED FROM
Gainsborough Trinity, September 1899
LFC DEBUT
7 October 1899
CONTRACT EXPIRY
April 1900

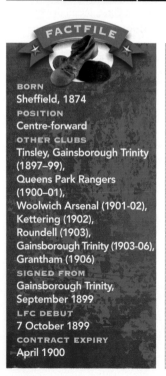

Foxall,
Abe

ABE FOXALL made a single appearance in Liverpool's first team when he was selected as a centre-forward in a home defeat to Derby County in a First Division fixture on 7 October 1899. It was one of the rare occasions when centre-half Alex Raisbeck played up front.

Season	League App	League Goals	FA Cup App	FA Cup Goals	Total App	Total Goals
1899/1900	1	0	0	0	1	0
Total	**1**	**0**	**0**	**0**	**1**	**0**

"Now, Miss Liverpool, you must get up a few more steps or you will drop it, like you did the English Cap. If you do, General Public will sack us with a bad character."

Liverpool went after the double in the 1899-1900 season ("Now Miss Liverpool, you must get up a few more steps or you will drop it, like you did the English Cup. If you do, General Public will sack us with a bad character.")

Friedel,
Brad

BRAD FRIEDEL started his European career with Brøndby in the spring of 1995, after his appeal for a work permit to play for Newcastle United was denied. He was on loan from the United States Soccer Federation, where he had signed a contract to play exclusively with the US national team as it prepared for the 1994 FIFA World Cup and beyond. After ten appearances in the Brøndby goal, his next stop was Galatasaray in Turkey, where he moved permanently in September 1995. He lasted there about ten months before moving back to his dear old US of A, joining Columbus Crew.

The following year he was named MLS Goalkeeper of the Year. Roy Evans wanted him to join Liverpool, but had problems in getting him a work permit. The Department of Employment stated that a foreign player must have played in 'approximately' 75 per cent of his country's internationals in the past two years. 'Brad's percentage is 71 per cent, so how approximate is that?' asked Friedel's agent, Paul Stretford. Liverpool appealed the decision, but meanwhile both Glasgow giants, Celtic and Rangers, offered him the opportunity to join them, but Friedel had set his hopes on a move to Merseyside.

LIVERPOOL won their appeal, and Friedel sealed his deal with the Reds on 19 December 1997. David James was their first-choice keeper and Friedel had to warm

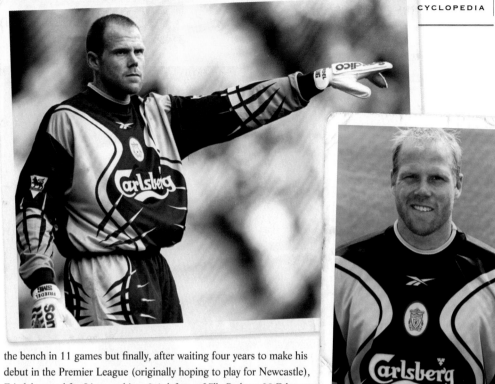

the bench in 11 games but finally, after waiting four years to make his debut in the Premier League (originally hoping to play for Newcastle), Friedel started for Liverpool in a 2-1 defeat at Villa Park on 28 February 1998. He played in Liverpool's final 11 games of the 1997/98 season, winning five, drawing three and losing three, assuring the club of a UEFA Cup place. Gérard Houllier was named joint-manager to Evans in the summer, but Friedel kept his place. Sloppy performances, however, culminating in a disaster against Manchester United at Old Trafford on 24 September 1998, cost him his starting berth after an eight-game run. Friedel got the occasional chance in the League Cup and eventually replaced James in the last five games of the 1998/99 season. Sander Westerveld came in, and James went out in the summer of 2000. It soon became apparent that the best Friedel could hope for was being a reserve keeper at Liverpool.

FRIEDEL moved to Blackburn Rovers on 3 November 2000, regained his confidence, and established himself as one of the top goalkeepers in the Premier League. He had a sensational World Cup in 2002 when the USA reached the quarter-finals and he became the first keeper since 1974 to save two penalties in regular time in a World Cup tournament. In the summer of 2008 Friedel joined Aston Villa, where he stayed for the duration of his three-year contract. His Villa boss, Martin O'Neill, sang his praises. 'He is remarkably fit. If we were doing a half-mile run – of all the seniors and young players – Brad would be in the first eight, which is remarkable.' With Friedel being a free agent in the summer of 2011, Liverpool were rumoured to be interested, but surely he would have only been a reserve to Reina, and Heurelho Gomes' inconsistency resulted in Harry Redknapp offering Friedel the opportunity to become number one at White Hart Lane. Shortly after his fortieth birthday, he signed a two-year deal with Tottenham Hotspur and for the eighth season in a row Friedel played in every Premier League match. He only conceded 41 goals in 38 league matches, and this excellent defensive record helped Spurs finish in fourth place. On 21 April 2012, he played his 300th

BRAD FRIEDEL
LIVERPOOL

Premier League game in a row against Queens Park Rangers. He was awarded a Barclays Merit Award for his unique achievement. Friedel's run of 310 consecutive Premier League games was ended on 7 October 2012, when he was placed on the bench against Aston Villa by Andre Villas-Boas and he eventually lost his place to Hugo Lloris.

FACTFILE

BORN
Lakewood, Ohio, USA,
18 May 1971
POSITION
Goalkeeper
OTHER CLUBS
United States Soccer
Federation (1994–95),
Brøndby (loan, 1995),
Galatasaray (1995–96),
Columbus Crew (1996–97),
Blackburn Rovers (2000–08),
Aston Villa (2008–11),
Tottenham Hotspur (2011–)
SIGNED FROM
Columbus Crew, £1million,
19 December 1997
INTERNATIONAL CAPS
82 USA caps, 1992–2005
LFC DEBUT
28 February 1998
CONTRACT EXPIRY
3 November 2000

Season	League		FA Cup		League Cup		Europe		Total	
	App	Goals	App	Goals	App	Goals	App	Goals	App	Goals
1997/98	11	0	0	0	0	0	0	0	11	0
1998/99	12	0	0	0	2	0	1 (1)	0	15 (1)	0
1999/2000	2	0	0	0	2	0	-	-	4	0
Total	**25**	**0**	**0**	**0**	**4**	**0**	**1 (1)**	**0**	**30 (1)**	**0**

Furnell,
Jim

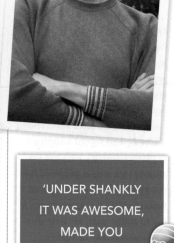

JIM FURNELL had made just three first-team appearances in eight seasons for one of the best teams in the First Division, Burnley, when Everton wanted to purchase him, but he declined their offer. Consequently he was dropped into Burnley's A team, when Bill Shankly made his interest known. Furnell didn't hesitate this time and the 24-year-old moved to Liverpool. Bert Slater was dropped, following 96 consecutive games in the first team, and Furnell played the last 13 games of the 1961/62 season when Liverpool were finally promoted after being stuck in the Second Division for eight long years.

Furnell broke his finger after featuring in the first 13 games of the 1962/63 season, and recalled his twist of fate in the *Lancashire Telegraph* in 1998. 'I went down to collect the ball in a five-a-side and caught the finger on the ground. Shanks took me out of goal and made me complete the match up front. He wouldn't believe that it was broken, but Bob Paisley insisted I should go along to have it checked out by the doctors. I spent a week in hospital, needed a bone graft and didn't play again for months. Didn't realise it at the time, but it was the end for me at Anfield. That's when I saw another side to Shankly. If you were injured it was as though you stopped existing. He didn't come to visit me and more or less ignored me when I reported in at the club for daily treatment.'

Twenty-two-year-old Tommy Lawrence replaced him, having waited patiently for his chance for five years. Lawrence's emergence sealed Furnell's fate at Liverpool, thus enabling Shankly to sell him

to Arsenal in November 1963. Furnell did exceptionally well at the Gunners and played 167 games for the First Division team from 1963 to 1968, until he made way for future legend Bob Wilson.

FURNELL then made 76 league appearances for Third Division Rotherham United before joining fellow Third Division team Plymouth Argyle in 1970. Initially signed as a reserve keeper, he took the number one jersey and was voted Plymouth's Player of the Year in his first season. He had played a total of 206 games for the Pilgrims when he retired in 1976. In 2007 he was named 'Argyle's Greatest Ever Keeper' in a poll on a popular website for Plymouth, so he clearly made a good impression at Home Park. Furnell joined the coaching staff at Plymouth and was then in charge of Blackburn's reserves and youth team development from 1981 to 1998.

'Under Shankly it was awesome, made you understand the real meaning of fanatical,' Furnell told the *Lancashire Telegraph*. 'There's never been an atmosphere to compare with Anfield. We used to get goosebumps running out there, heaven knows what opponents must have felt like. Being in goal in front of 15,000 on the Kop made you feel unbeatable. Tommy Lawrence came up from the reserves to take my place and the team just went from strength to strength. It was the start of the Liverpool domination – two Championships in three years, the European Cup, the FA Cup. You name it, they

won it and, but for the injury, the person wearing the green jersey and picking up the medals would probably have been me. That's fate, that's football and that's life.'

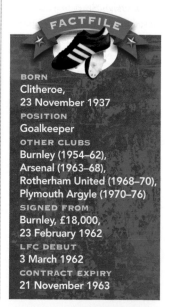

> 'UNDER SHANKLY IT WAS AWESOME, MADE YOU UNDERSTAND THE REAL MEANING OF FANATICAL'

FACTFILE

BORN
Clitheroe,
23 November 1937
POSITION
Goalkeeper
OTHER CLUBS
Burnley (1954–62),
Arsenal (1963–68),
Rotherham United (1968–70),
Plymouth Argyle (1970–76)
SIGNED FROM
Burnley, £18,000,
23 February 1962
LFC DEBUT
3 March 1962
CONTRACT EXPIRY
21 November 1963

Season	League		FA Cup		Total	
	App	Goals	App	Goals	App	Goals
1961/62	13	0	0	0	13	0
1962/63	13	0	0	0	13	0
1963/64	2	0	0	0	2	0
Total	**28**	**0**	**0**	**0**	**28**	**0**

Garcia,
Luis

RAFA BENÍTEZ was in charge of Tenerife in 2000/01 when Luis Garcia starred for the club that got promoted to La Liga, scoring 16 league goals in 40 matches. However, Garcia was only on loan from Valladolid and returned there in 2001/02, playing 29 games, scoring 10 goals. He moved to Atletico Madrid in a €3.6million deal in 2002/03 where he was in sensational form, making 32 appearances and scoring nine. Barcelona activated an option in the player's contract allowing them to re-sign him at a cost of €5million before the 2003/04 season. He had been raised in Barca's B-team from the age of 16 until he was 21. He played 38 games and scored eight goals in his only season in his second spell at Barcelona, coming into his own in the second half of the campaign.

Garcia couldn't resist joining his former boss Benítez at Liverpool, along with his compatriot Xabi Alonso. Both became a hit in their first year in English football. Five vital goals by Garcia in the knockout stages of the Champions League against Bayer Leverkusen, Juventus and Chelsea helped to ensure Liverpool's passage to the glorious final in Istanbul. 'Was it or wasn't it?' is the eternal question about the Chelsea goal in the Champions League semi-final at Anfield, but the scoreboard said 1-0 in Liverpool's favour. Garcia was rather inconsistent in his second season, making 28 starts and coming on as a substitute in

22 games. He was brilliant one game and then wasteful in possession and seemingly careless in the next, frustrating his admirers. Garcia still added 11 goals to his tally of 13 from his debut season, the most important one being Liverpool's second in the FA Cup semi-final victory over Chelsea. Unfortunately for Garcia he was sent off only two minutes after coming on a substitute in the 80th minute in a league game at Upton Park and missed the last three games of the season through suspension, including the FA Cup final victory against West Ham.

GARCIA missed the second half of his third and final season at Liverpool after rupturing the anterior cruciate ligament in his right knee in the 6-3 loss to Arsenal on 9 January 2007. He returned to Spain in the summer of 2007 after rumours that his family was unsettled in Liverpool. Garcia failed to hold down a regular place with Atletico Madrid in his second season in the Spanish capital and lost his place in the national side. In August 2009 Garcia agreed a deal with Racing Santander at the age of 31 after making close to half a century of league appearances for Atletico. He only featured in 15 games, scoring no goals as Santander battled relegation. On deadline day, 31 August 2010, Garcia moved to Panathinaikos on a free transfer. His career was not revitalised in Greece as he played in fewer than half of the defending champions' league matches. The popular Spaniard flew back to England so that he could appear in Jamie Carragher's testimonial match in September, where he scored a cracking goal to remind everyone of his mercurial talent. Garcia has been playing in Mexico for the last couple of years with Puebla and Pumas de la UNAM.

Benítez summed up Luis Garcia perfectly. 'You have to accept Luis for what he is. When he played for me at Tenerife, I tried to change him, but

you have to say OK, he does what he does and provides different things. I have kept trying to remind him – many times – that when he takes the risks he does, he should do it closer to the opposition box. He can give possession away and that can anger the fans. But he also does different things that excite them and he scores goals. I tried to change him in Spain, and he scored 16 goals for me, so you have to accept what he does.' Garcia is still immensely popular on Merseyside as is his song that so many Liverpool supporters have sung at the top of their voices.

Luis Garcia
He drinks Sangria
He came from Barca to
bring us joy!
He's five foot seven
He's football heaven
So please don't take our
Luis away!

Season	League App	League Goals	FA Cup App	FA Cup Goals	League Cup App	League Cup Goals	Europe App	Europe Goals	Other App	Other Goals	Total App	Total Goals
2004/05	26 (3)	8	0	0	2 (1)	0	12	5	-	-	40 (4)	13
2005/06	15 (16)	7	2 (1)	1	0 (1)	0	10 (3)	3	1 (1)	0	28 (22)	11
2006/07	11 (6)	3	1	0	0 (1)	0	4 (3)	3	1	0	17 (10)	6
Total	**52 (25)**	**18**	**3 (1)**	**1**	**2 (3)**	**0**	**26 (6)**	**11**	**2 (1)**	**0**	**85 (36)**	**30**

Gardner, Tommy

FAIR-HAIRED Tommy Gardner, nicknamed 'Gandhi', joined Liverpool as an amateur from Orrell in July 1928, signing professional forms a year later.

He played in five consecutive First Division fixtures in the second half of the 1929/30 season when the regular right-half Tom Morrison was unavailable. Morrison had been an ever-present the season before and would only miss three league matches the following season, so Gardner's opportunities were limited as a result.

THERE was only one victory for the club in the five games Gardner figured in and Liverpool finished the season mid-table. The highlight from his post-Liverpool career was when he gained international honours during his four-year stay at Aston Villa. During Gardner's time at the Villans, the club was relegated to Second Division in 1936 having been runners-up in the First Division three years previously. However, Villa won the Second Division in 1938 in his final season with the club. Gardner was a long-throw expert and once won a *Daily Mail* competition by throwing a ball 32 yards 2 inches.

> GARDNER WAS A LONG-THROW EXPERT AND ONCE WON A *DAILY MAIL* COMPETITION BY THROWING A BALL 32 YARDS 2 INCHES

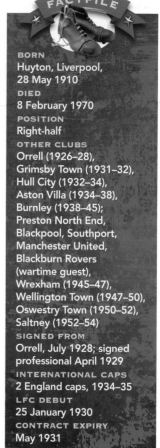

Gardner was nicknamed "Gandhi"

TOMMY GARDNER
[LIVERPOOL]

Season	League		FA Cup		Total	
	App	Goals	App	Goals	App	Goals
1929/30	5	0	0	0	5	0
Total	5	0	0	0	5	0

Garner, James

JUST FIVE Football League matches are recorded for James Garner in Liverpool's colours, spread over two seasons.

He played three consecutive games at right-back as Tommy Lucas was out injured in December 1924 and then appeared in the penultimate game of that season at left-back. His fifth and final appearance came in the 1-1 home draw with Leeds on 10 October 1925, once again standing in for Lucas. Garner featured regularly for Southport in the Third Division North, but a knee injury restricted his progress during his one year at New Brighton.

Liverpool beat Everton 3-1 on 7 February 1925.

Season	League		FA Cup		Total	
	App	Goals	App	Goals	App	Goals
1924/25	4	0	0	0	4	0
1925/26	1	0	0	0	1	0
Total	5	0	0	0	5	0

Garside,
James

James Garside

AFTER IMPRESSING against Liverpool's reserve team for Accrington Stanley, James Garside signed for the 'Livers'. Garside, who had served an apprenticeship as an engine fitter and was considered the best left-winger in the Lancashire Combination, could now focus just on football.

He made five appearances for Liverpool, taking over the centre-forward position from Sam Raybould for the fixture with

Lincoln City in January 1905, one of only two league matches the prolific Raybould missed during

the club's Second Division Championship-winning season. Garside was given four more opportunities the following year in his proper position on the left, when the club managed to achieve the very rare feat of winning the League Championship only one season after being promoted from the Second Division. Garside found his level at Exeter City in the Southern League, playing 110 games and scoring 22 goals from 1909 to 1913.

FACTFILE

BORN
Manchester, 24 January 1885
POSITION
Left-winger
OTHER CLUBS
Darwen,
Accrington Stanley (1903–04),
Accrington Stanley (1906–09),
Exeter City (1909–13)
SIGNED FROM
Accrington Stanley,
10 March 1904
LFC DEBUT
21 January 1905
CONTRACT EXPIRY
1906

Season	League		FA Cup		Other		Total	
	App	Goals	App	Goals	App	Goals	App	Goals
1904/05	1	0	0	0	-	-	1	0
1905/06	4	0	0	0	0	0	4	0
Total	**5**	**0**	**0**	**0**	**0**	**0**	**5**	**0**

Gayle,
Howard

TOXTETH-BORN Howard Gayle's defining moment for his home-town club came when he ran Bayern Munich's defenders ragged in the second leg of the European Cup semi-final on 22 April 1981 at the Olympic Stadium. Kenny Dalglish limped off early on and Gayle impressed for an hour despite being repeatedly fouled before he was replaced by Jimmy Case for fear he would get himself sent off for retaliation. It was a performance of astonishing maturity in such a big game from the young winger and his reward was to play in three of the final four league matches of the season before the European Cup final.

With key players fit again, Gayle knew he would not make the starting line-up in Paris and had to settle for a place on the bench.

Gayle made his debut for Liverpool as a substitute for David Fairclough at Maine Road in October 1980, having signed professional forms with the club three years previously. Gayle never fulfilled the promise he had shown against Bayern and three days later at Tottenham in a performance which prompted *The Guardian* to remark: 'A few more goals of quality by Gayle, who swept Lee's pass into the net after 25 minutes, and Johnson may have more than injury to overcome to regain his place. The impressive pace and timing of Gayle's runs, which bemused Bayern Munich, could well restore a dimension and width to Liverpool's attack missing since the dropping of Heighway.' Gayle spent most of his time at Liverpool in the reserves, where he scored 62 goals in 156 games. He will always be remembered for being the first black player to play for Liverpool, a really incredible fact considering the club had been in existence for 88 years! Gayle

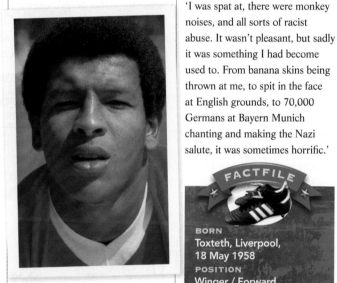

went on to have a successful career with other clubs, most notably Birmingham City, Sunderland and Blackburn Rovers. He even enjoyed a year in the Major Indoor Soccer League in 1986/87 with Dallas Sidekicks.

GAYLE was often on the receiving end of racial abuse from opposing supporters, as he explained in Dave Hill's book *Out of His Skin*.

'I was spat at, there were monkey noises, and all sorts of racist abuse. It wasn't pleasant, but sadly it was something I had become used to. From banana skins being thrown at me, to spit in the face at English grounds, to 70,000 Germans at Bayern Munich chanting and making the Nazi salute, it was sometimes horrific.'

FACTFILE

BORN
Toxteth, Liverpool,
18 May 1958
POSITION
Winger / Forward
OTHER CLUBS
Fulham (loan, 1980),
Newcastle United (loan,1982),
Birmingham City (1983–84),
Sunderland (1984–86),
Stoke City (1987),
Blackburn Rovers (1987–92),
Halifax Town (1992–93),
Accrington Stanley (1993–94)
JOINED
1974; signed professional
November 1977
INTERNATIONAL CAPS
3 England U-21 caps
LFC DEBUT GAME/GOAL
4 October 1980 /
25 April 1981
CONTRACT EXPIRY
6 January 1983
HONOURS
European Cup 1981

Season	League		FA Cup		League Cup		Europe		Other		Total	
	App	Goals	App	Goals	App	Goals	App	Goals	App	Goals	App	Goals
1980/81	3 (1)	1	0	0	0	0	0 (1)	0	0	0	3 (2)	1
Total	**3 (1)**	**1**	**0**	**0**	**0**	**0**	**0 (1)**	**0**	**0**	**0**	**3 (2)**	**1**

Geary, Fred

SMALL AND POWERFUL Fred Geary, barely 5ft 2in (157cm) and weighing 9st 6lb (60kg) at best, is the smallest man to ever play for Liverpool. He was a record-breaking Everton centre-forward of the Victorian era who from 1889 to 1895 scored 86 goals in 99 games. He was the Blues' leading scorer with 20 goals in 23 matches in the 1890/91 season when they won the League Championship.

On 17 January 1891, in a North v. South trial at Nottingham's Town Ground, Geary became the first man to score a goal after a net was put between the frames of the goal, an invention of Liverpudlian John Alexander Brodie, who was also the designer of the Mersey Tunnel. Injuries curtailed three out of Geary's last four seasons at Everton. He was particularly unlucky in an away game at Sunderland in October 1891 when he injured his right ankle, was kicked in the ribs and then had his left ankle so severely

mauled he had to spend the next week in hospital. Geary probably didn't enjoy playing Sunderland, as another incident had occurred in January 1891 when he was striving to equalise to avoid Everton being knocked out of the FA Cup. 'A minute from time he dashed up the field like lightning,' the *Sunderland Daily Echo* wrote some nine years later. 'He came an awful bang against one of the Sunderland backs and down went Fred, his head striking the side post with a sickening thud. They picked him up senseless, and from that shock Geary never fairly recovered. It had knocked all the fight out of him; he grew timorous, shirked a charge, and bye-and-bye Everton got rid of him, and he went over to Liverpool.' Still a rather harsh dismissal of a man who went on to score 45 goals in 59 matches for Everton in the seasons following this incident!

When Geary was 27 years old he joined neighbours Liverpool when they had just been relegated to the Second Division, while Everton were runners-up in the league. Geary made his debut at Notts County on the opening day of the 1895/96 season and, reinvigorated by the move, played in 19 games that year, scoring 11 times as the club won the Second Division. However, he was only selected eight times as Liverpool finished fifth in the top division a year later and would only make a further 12 appearances over the next two seasons; injuries had robbed him of his greatest asset, his pace, which his team-mates had complained about because Geary used to leave them way behind when he took off on his turbo-charged bursts. Two years after playing his last game for Liverpool's first team he was still turning out for the club's reserves in the Lancashire Combination. Alongside his football activities Geary owned a pub and when his career finished he became groundsman at Goodison Park.

Season	League		FA Cup		Other		Total	
	App	Goals	App	Goals	App	Goals	App	Goals
1895/96	19	11	2	0	1	0	22	11
1896/97	8	2	3	0	-	-	11	2
1897/98	11	1	0	0	-	-	11	1
1898/99	1	0	0	0	-	-	1	0
Total	**39**	**14**	**5**	**0**	**1**	**0**	**45**	**14**

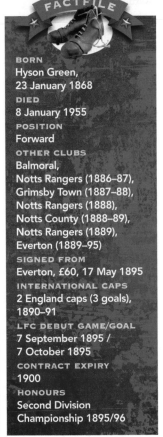

FACTFILE

BORN
Hyson Green,
23 January 1868
DIED
8 January 1955
POSITION
Forward
OTHER CLUBS
Balmoral,
Notts Rangers (1886–87),
Grimsby Town (1887–88),
Notts Rangers (1888),
Notts County (1888–89),
Notts Rangers (1889),
Everton (1889–95)
SIGNED FROM
Everton, £60, 17 May 1895
INTERNATIONAL CAPS
2 England caps (3 goals),
1890–91
LFC DEBUT GAME/GOAL
7 September 1895 /
7 October 1895
CONTRACT EXPIRY
1900
HONOURS
Second Division
Championship 1895/96

Gerhardi, Hugh

HUGH GERHARDI played six league matches for Liverpool mostly in Liverpool's forward line during the latter stages of the 1952/53 season after arriving from Thistle in Johannesburg.

HE MADE his debut at Middlesbrough on 7 February 1953 and played in the next four matches as well, but was only called on once more before the season ended. The *Liverpool Echo* noted: 'His positional play is not expert, his timing is not always good, but by judicious stretching of a long leg he gets results.' Gerhardi is one of the tallest men

ever to feature for Liverpool, at 6ft 4in (194cm). Homesickness made him move back to South Africa after just one season with the club. His story has a tragic ending, as on 12 January 1985 Gerhardi committed suicide in his store in Johannesburg. He had mistakenly believed he had a brain tumour, according to his wife of 30 years, Pauline. She told the *Liverpool Echo*: 'He had been feeling worried for some time but I never dreamed it would come to this. I think what upset him most,

was that because of his blood pressure he had to give up coaching, and that was the most important part of his life.'

FACTFILE

BORN
Johannesburg, South Africa,
5 May 1933
DIED
12 January 1985
POSITION
Inside-right forward
OTHER CLUBS
Thistle (1950–52)
SIGNED FROM
Thistle, August 1952
LFC DEBUT
7 February 1953
CONTRACT EXPIRY
1953

Season	League		FA Cup		Total	
	App	Goals	App	Goals	App	Goals
1952/53	6	0	0	0	6	0
Total	**6**	**0**	**0**	**0**	**6**	**0**

Gerrard,
Steven

STEVEN GERRARD has certainly accomplished nearly everything he envisaged. The Premier League title is the only prize that he lacks to make his Liverpool career complete. Gerrard is a great leader, strong in the tackle, can hit the ball at ferocious speed, has good vision, scores great goals, makes brilliant passes and, simply, has it all. He is the man for the big occasion and the only player to score goals in the finals of the League Cup, FA Cup, UEFA Cup and the European Cup. There is no doubt that 'Stevie G' ranks among the elite of Liverpool FC, right at the top with the likes of Billy Liddell and Kenny Dalglish.

Gerrard's talents were there for all to see at Liverpool; former Liverpool winger and youth coach at the club, Steve Heighway, predicted big things from this boy in the match programme from 6 March 1993. 'Outstanding potential has to be recognised and nurtured and Stephen Gerrard [sic], a gem from Huyton, could be the next on our production line. He attends Cardinal Heenan School and already represents Liverpool Schools Under-14s although he is only 12 years old. He has enormous natural talent and is a Liverpool fan through and through. His attitude towards coaching and personal development is a joy to see and our staff is genuinely excited by his prospects.'

GERRARD started out with his local team, Whiston Juniors, until he was noticed by Liverpool's scouts at eight years of age. He wasn't selected to attend Lilleshall, the national football and sports centre, mainly due to his lack of height. When he was 15, he was the same height as Michael Owen, but his sudden growth caused

problems in his back, which restricted him to only playing 20 games from 14 years of age to 16. Gerrard got his breakthrough into the Liverpool team in 1998 when Jamie Redknapp was injured. New manager Gérard Houllier had inherited the key player to his Anfield revolution. 'One of the things Gérard recently reminded me of is that during that first meeting I told him he wouldn't have to worry about finding a world-class midfielder. I told him there was a young player in our youth team who would be world class within two years,' former chief executive Peter Robinson told the *Liverpool Echo* in 2001.

The first instance that convinced Liverpool fans worldwide that the boy was something special was a heroic display in his first Merseyside derby in only his ninth appearance for the club. He featured as a right-back and made two goal-line clearances as Liverpool successfully protected their lead. Finally the England set-up took notice. He was nominated captain of the Under-18 side and made his debut for the Under-21s in September 1999. Houllier trusted the 19-year-old to begin the 1999/2000 season in the starting line-up alongside Redknapp and promised him at least 20 games. Didi Hamann took his place eight games into the campaign in the Merseyside derby and a disappointed Gerrard came on as a substitute. He lost his composure close to the end of the match and was sent off for an ugly foul and banned for three games. He returned stronger than before, determined to prove himself, and his first goal for the club, against Sheffield Wednesday on 5 December 1999, proved to be spectacular. 'A wonderful talent, a young man with the steel of a Stiles and the style of a Souness' – as Ric George described him in the *Liverpool Echo* – 'side-stepped, danced and dribbled past three defenders before finishing decisively.' He also proved his versatility, as in one year he had played as a left-back, right-back, defensive and offensive midfielder and a right-winger.

> HE IS THE MAN FOR THE BIG OCCASION AND THE ONLY PLAYER TO SCORE GOALS IN THE FINALS OF THE LEAGUE CUP, FA CUP, UEFA CUP AND THE EUROPEAN CUP

On 31 May 2000 Gerrard made his international debut, aged 20 years and one day, in a 2-0 win against Ukraine at Wembley. A relative newcomer to the England squad, Gerrard only made one substitute appearance in Euro 2000 when he came on for Michael Owen in a win over Germany. Kevin Keegan's England team only recorded this one win and failed to qualify from their group. The boy had certainly come far in a short period of time, and his career rose rapidly in the

2000/01 season. He made 50 appearances for Liverpool, won the League Cup and FA Cup and scored a goal, which he ranks as one of his most memorable, in the 5-4 win over Alaves in the UEFA Cup final. Gerrard was named the Professional Footballers' Association's Young Player of the Year. Liverpool, under the guidance of Houllier, continued their progress in the league and finished second in the 2001/02 season, seven points behind Arsenal. Gerrard was ruled out of England's World Cup squad in the summer through injury.

LIVERPOOL'S form dropped considerably the next two years. Despite these setbacks, Gerrard's influence had grown and on 15 October 2003 he was made captain of Liverpool Football Club. Gerrard had many admirers who glanced an envious look at Liverpool's finest. 'Gerrard has become the most influential player in England, bar none. To me, Gerrard is Keane; he is now where Keane was when Roy came to us in 1994,' Alex Ferguson said. 'I've watched him quite a lot, and everywhere the ball is, he seems to be there. He's got that unbelievable engine, desire, determination. Anyone would take Gerrard. You can see Gerrard rising and rising.'

Tommy Smith, Liverpool's legendary 70s stopper, commented in 2004, 'Nobby Stiles once told me that he thought Steven Gerrard was the nearest thing to Duncan Edwards and that is a tremendous compliment for a player. His all-action displays constantly put pressure on the opposition and he must be the best midfielder in the world at present.'

Rafa Benítez took over in 2004 and in a season of reconstruction Gerrard elevated his status in the minds of Liverpool supporters when his tremendous goal against Olympiacos guaranteed his team's process from the group stages of the Champions League in front of

a packed Kop. Gerrard's header nine minutes into the second half in Istanbul inspired an unlikely comeback that can arguably be called the greatest ever. He was quite happy that it never came to pass that he would take Liverpool's fifth penalty in the shootout, as he told *FourFourTwo* magazine. 'I was absolutely s***ting my pants. Terrified. I was very, very nervous, the most nervous I've been on a football pitch. But if someone had offered me a chance to scrub my name off and not take it, I would have told them that I still wanted to take it.' What immediately followed no one could have imagined. Liverpool's chief executive, Rick Parry, had told Gerrard that the club were going to renew his contract in the summer. Liverpool remained too unresponsive in Gerrard's opinion, however, and Chelsea with all their riches tempted him to leave for London. He later said in his autobiography it was the lowest point in his career:

'Madness broke out. I was sitting dazed at home, watching the TV, and when I saw fans burning an old No 17 shirt by the Shankly Gates, it did my head in. I stared at the TV through flowing tears. I was suffocated by stress. My head was banging, and I was eating paracetamol like Smarties. I could see the great possibilities of Chelsea, but my heart wouldn't let me leave. Finally, my mind was made up. At 11pm that night, on July 5, 2005, I called my agent to tell Rick Parry that I wanted to sign.'

Rafa Benítez had no doubt of Gerrard's importance to the club. 'I renew my deal with Liverpool in four or five years and when I do I would like Stevie to be my next coach, assistant manager and maybe even the next manager after me. He can even have the chief scout position if he wants it,' he said in July 2005.

Gerrard scored 20-plus goals for Liverpool for the first time in the 2005/06 season and it was real 'Roy of the Rovers' stuff for him when Liverpool faced West Ham in the 2006 FA Cup final. He scored with a stunning volley in the 54th minute to make it 2-2 and then, when West Ham seemed certain to lift the cup, being 3-2 up with time running out, he scored from a long way out – because, he said, his feet could not carry him any further – an incredibly audacious effort by the captain. Liverpool won the FA Cup after a penalty shootout. Gerrard was recognised by his fellow professionals as the best player in the Premier League that season. If anyone is able to recognise greatness it should be John Barnes, who was voted PFA's top player 18 years earlier. 'He is the most important player that Liverpool have and could be the most important player England has. If you look at attacking midfield players with Zidane and Ronaldinho and if you look at defensive midfield players like Makelele, creative midfield players with the passing of Beckham. He can do it all. For me he is the most complete midfield player in the world.'

> GERRARD'S HEADER NINE MINUTES INTO THE SECOND HALF IN ISTANBUL INSPIRED AN UNLIKELY COMEBACK THAT CAN ARGUABLY BE CALLED THE GREATEST EVER

Eriksson's England in the 2006 World Cup in Germany, playing five games and scoring in two consecutive games against Trinidad & Tobago and Sweden. He missed a penalty as England were eliminated by Portugal in a penalty shootout in the quarter-

finals. Liverpool's talisman had another stunning season in 2006/07, playing in 52 out of a maximum 59 competitive matches. His goal tally reached double figures for the fifth successive season. As autumn turned into winter, Gerrard scored in six successive home matches and during the same period he also scored a stunning free kick up at Newcastle. But his most productive day goal-wise was when Luton Town came to Anfield for an FA Cup third round replay. Gerrard, rested for the original tie in Bedfordshire, scored a hat-trick in 17 second-half minutes in the replay to ensure that there would be no big cup upset.

Like the rest of his club colleagues, Gerrard put the disappointment of losing the Champions League final in Athens behind him as Liverpool prepared for another season. Newspaper speculation again linked Liverpool's skipper with a

big-money move to Chelsea in the summer of 2007. However, as he and Jamie Carragher signed new four-year deals on 4 June 2007, this matter was finally put to rest.

In 2007/08 and 2008/09 Gerrard added another 96 first-team appearances to an already impressive total. He scored twice as Real Madrid were humbled at Anfield in the last 16 in the Champions League, but was unable to prevent Liverpool losing to Chelsea in the next round, the second leg of which he missed because of injury. Costly draws proved Liverpool's downfall in their effort to wrestle the Premier League title from Manchester United in 2009. Gerrard's talent was evident enough for the Football Writers' Association to vote him the best player of the season.

There was something vital missing from Gerrard's game in the 2009/10 season. He knew that the team was expected to 'kick on' from the second place it had achieved in 2009 and win the ultimate prize. His extraordinary ability to get the team out of a hole, something he had done countless times in the previous ten years, was suddenly waning. He only missed seven matches so he was as much a regular in the first team as he had usually been, but his contribution in terms of goals, just 12, was exactly half that of the previous season and his lowest for three years.

LIVERPOOL'S finest was named captain of the England team when injury ruled Rio Ferdinand out of the World Cup in 2010. He responded by netting England's first goal against the United States, but it was a lead he and his colleagues were unable to hold on to. He played in all four of England's matches, including the one in the last 16 when Germany humbled them. In 2010/11 Gerrard played in the fewest number of

competitive matches, just 24 out of 54, since his first full season of 1999/2000. This was partly because of an injury he received against Manchester United at Anfield in March. United were prominent in Gerrard's season. The skipper scored twice at Old Trafford in September, but Berbatov found a late winner. Back at Old Trafford in January in the FA Cup, as Kenny Dalglish returned to the dugout, Gerrard was sent off by Howard Webb.

HE INSISTED that after his successful groin operation he hadn't felt as good for a decade as 2011/12 started. However, injuries restricted Gerrard to only 28 appearances. He still showed glimpses of world-class talent, especially when scoring an Anfield hat-trick against Everton in March, the first player to achieve that feat since Fred Howe in 1935. It was his fifth treble for Liverpool. Asked to summarise

Gerrard's performance, Dalglish said: 'I am not educated enough to add to whatever anyone else has said about Steven. He's been fantastic for this football club. I left school at 15, my vocabulary is not that great. There is no way I could extol the virtues of Steven Gerrard and do him justice.' Gerrard was also fit enough to lead the team out in both the domestic cup finals at Wembley. His joy in lifting Liverpool's first trophy for six years was there for all to see. In the middle of May Roy Hodgson named Gerrard as outright captain of the 23-man squad for the European Championships in which he was his country's key player.

As the 32-year-old embarked on a new season under Brendan Rodgers he claimed he was not yet prepared to play in a deeper role in Liverpool's midfield, aiming to prove he is as dynamic as ever. Lucas' injury at the start of 2012/13, however, forced Gerrard to defend more than attack, being unable to showcase his talents in the final third of the field where he is the most effective.

FACTFILE

BORN
Whiston, Liverpool,
30 May 1980
POSITION
Midfielder
JOINED
1988
INTERNATIONAL CAPS
102 England caps
(19 goals), 2000–
LFC DEBUT GAME/GOAL
29 November 1998 /
5 December 1999
HONOURS
FA Cup 2001, 2006;
League Cup
2001, 2003, 2012;
Champions League 2005;
UEFA Cup 2001;
PFA Young Player of the Year
2001,
PFA Player of the Year 2006,
FWA Footballer of the Year
2009,
PFA Fans' Player of the Year
2001, 2009

On 14 November 2012 Gerrard became the sixth Englishman to reach a century of caps for his country, joining the illustrious group of Billy Wright, Bobby Charlton, Bobby Moore, Peter Shilton and David Beckham. As Liverpool have progressed under Rodgers, Gerrard has been gaining strength and provided quite a few assists for his team-mates as well as netting his fair share of goals. Gerrard reflected on the first half of the 2012/13 season in the *LFC Magazine* in January 2013. 'I've had mixed experiences this season. I've passed some unbelievable landmarks for club and country, getting to the 600 games mark and winning my 100th cap for England. I've played well in some games but I've been disappointed with myself in others. I think my performances are getting closer to where I want them to be so if I can add goals to those performances then maybe people will start saying the old Steven Gerrard is back.' Gerrard had played every single minute of the Premier League season when he was forced off through injury in the 6-0 win over Newcastle in his 35th league match. He sat out the last two games of the campaign as he underwent a shoulder operation.

Season	League		FA Cup		League Cup		Europe		Other		Total	
	App	Goals	App	Goals	App	Goals	App	Goals	App	Goals	App	Goals
1998/99	4 (8)	0	0	0	0	0	1	0	-	-	5 (8)	0
1999/2000	26 (3)	1	2	0	0	0	-	-	-	-	28 (3)	1
2000/01	29 (4)	7	2 (2)	1	4	0	9	2	-	-	44 (6)	10
2001/02	26 (2)	3	2	0	0	0	14 (1)	1	0	0	42 (3)	4
2002/03	32 (2)	5	2	0	6	2	11	0	1	0	52 (2)	7
2003/04	34	4	3	0	1 (1)	0	7 (1)	2	-	-	45 (2)	6
2004/05	28 (2)	7	0	0	3	2	10	4	-	-	41 (2)	13
2005/06	32	10	6	4	1	1	8 (4)	7	2	1	49 (4)	23
2006/07	35 (1)	7	1	0	1	1	10 (2)	3	0 (1)	0	47 (4)	11
2007/08	32 (2)	11	1 (2)	3	1 (1)	1	13	6	-	-	47 (5)	21
2008/09	30 (1)	16	3	1	0	0	8 (2)	7	-	-	41 (3)	24
2009/10	32 (1)	9	2	1	0 (1)	0	13	2	-	-	47 (2)	12
2010/11	20 (1)	4	1	0	0	0	1 (1)	4	-	-	22 (2)	8
2011/12	12 (6)	5	6	2	3 (1)	2	-	-	-	-	21 (7)	9
2012/13	36	9	0 (1)	0	0 (1)	0	6 (2)	1	-	-	42 (4)	10
Total	**408 (33)**	**98**	**31 (5)**	**12**	**20 (5)**	**9**	**111 (13)**	**39**	**3 (1)**	**1**	**573 (57)**	**159**

Fabrice Muamba, Bolton's player who 'died' on the White Hart Lane pitch in March 2012, captured Gerrard's qualities very well in his autobiography:

Steven Gerrard is another leader. He is so quick and such a great athlete, he is like a horse. When he takes off, oh my God ... When he performs there is nobody who can touch him. He can ping the ball serious distances. And I mean really ping the ball. When we played at Anfield on Boxing Day, 2008, Gary Megson made me try and man-mark Gerrard. What? Who does that? I was fit enough for the job and tried to stay with him but he was just too good.... Everywhere he went, I went. I was his shadow. And how did it go? Not very well, let's put it like that.

As it should be, Gerrard – as quoted in his autobiography – has the last word:

I know it sounds hollow talking about dreams and prizes when footballers earn all the money we do, but the things I've got at home, the medals and memorabilia, they mean more to me than extra noughts in my bank account. I whispered to Robbie Fowler that I could picture perfectly the days I stood on the Kop, and literally got carried 20 or 30 yards as the crowd surged forward when he scored a goal. God it was incredible. I never even bothered dreaming that I would ever be captain – that would be too mad – just that I would set foot out on that pitch, just the once. And do you know what, even now, I can't put into words what it feels like to be living that dream.

Gilhespy, Cyril

CYRIL GILHESPY was a right-winger who played in 19 First Division games for Liverpool in the 1920s, spread over four seasons. Billy Lacey was established in the side when the club won the league title in 1921/22 and he only missed three matches that season, with Gilhespy stepping in on two of those occasions.

Lacey missed a number of games in the middle of the following season when Liverpool also finished in first place, but the 10 matches Gilhespy figured in were not enough to qualify him for a Championship medal. Gilhespy was selected for the opening four league fixtures of the 1923/24 season, but hardly had a look-in after that run.

HE WAS a vital part of the Bristol City team that won promotion to Second Division in the 1926/27 season, but after less than stellar progress by the club at this level he moved to First Division Blackburn Rovers after four years at City. Gilhespy wasn't first choice at Rovers and went on a transfer merry-go-round where he never stayed more than 12 months at any club.

FACTFILE

BORN
Fencehouses,
Co. Durham,
18 February 1898
DIED
1985
POSITION
Right-winger
OTHER CLUBS
Chester-le-Street,
Fencehouses,
Sunderland (1920–21),
Bristol City (1925–29),
Blackburn Rovers (1929–30),
Reading (1930–31),
Mansfield Town (1931–32),
Crewe Alexandra (1932–33)
SIGNED FROM
Sunderland, August 1921
LFC DEBUT GAME/GOAL
4 March 1922 /
1 April 1922
CONTRACT EXPIRY
May 1925

Season	League App	League Goals	FA Cup App	FA Cup Goals	Other App	Other Goals	Total App	Total Goals
1921/22	2	1	0	0	0	0	2	1
1922/23	10	2	0	0	-	-	10	2
1923/24	5	0	0	0	-	-	5	0
1924/25	2	0	0	0	-	-	2	0
Total	**19**	**3**	**0**	**0**	**0**	**0**	**19**	**3**

Gillespie, Gary

GARY GILLESPIE was appointed Falkirk's captain in the Scottish Second Division at only 17, the youngest ever skipper in Scottish League history. That responsibility didn't faze the youngster. 'I wasn't overawed,' he said in 1978. 'More surprised. I never had any problems with the players. They accepted me and a rollicking if they needed one!' Gillespie's calculated and cool approach to the game attracted a number of clubs and he wasn't even allowed to finish his debut first-team season before he was snapped up by First Division Coventry in March 1978. Gillespie had his first injury setback of many throughout his career when he tore knee ligaments at Everton after only five reserve-team matches at the Sky Blues. Coventry boss Gordon Milne expected big things of the promising defender. 'He can become a great player. The lad has such a mature head. Obviously he has a lot to learn about our game, but the potential is incredibly exciting.'

Gillespie played six years at Coventry, making around 200 appearances, until he sought more than an annual relegation battle. He had already had talks with Arsenal in the summer of 1983 when he was informed that Liverpool had come in for him. Joe Fagan's first signing had his work cut out for him at Liverpool to split up the successful Lawrenson-Hansen partnership in the centre of defence, and Gillespie spent the 1983/84 season in the reserves apart from a solitary first-team appearance in the first leg of the League Cup semi-final against Walsall on 7 February 1984. He didn't exactly win his team-mates over when

trying to prevent a goal as he hit the ball straight at Phil Neal's backside for an own goal. 'Nealy gave me one of his stares,' Gillespie recalls.

GILLESPIE made the most of his 19 starts in the 1984/85 season as a replacement for the injured Lawrenson and also on occasion as a midfield player. He hadn't featured for the first team in a month when Lawrenson's shoulder injury in the third minute of the 1985 European Cup final at Heysel enabled Gillespie to play in the most important game of his career. His foul on Boniek a good yard outside the box led to a controversial penalty that Platini scored the only goal from on this horrible night. Kenny Dalglish took over as manager in 1985/86 and Gillespie finally got his

breakthrough in the second part of the season when he featured in 24 out of 29 games, again as cover for Lawrenson as well as playing further upfield. He even scored a memorable hat-trick in a 5-0 win over Birmingham at Anfield on 26 April 1986 when playing in defence. He had previously scored one goal for the Reds in 45 appearances, so this goal extravaganza came as a surprise to everybody. Gillespie's second goal started with a run from his own half before exchanging passes with Rush to toe-poke past the keeper. When Liverpool got their second penalty in the game the Kop demanded that Gillespie was given a chance to complete his hat-trick, so Mølby gracefully stepped aside. Gillespie was looking forward to playing in the FA Cup final against Everton when a virus kept him out on the big day. He also missed the 1989 final and the only FA Cup final he played in was not a good memory as Wimbledon beat Liverpool in 1988.

THE SCOTSMAN played a big part in 1986/87 and the incredible 1987/88 season, and the greatest testament to his ability was that Dalglish was forced to move a fully fit Lawrenson to full-back to accommodate Gillespie alongside Hansen. The three also sometimes formed a central defensive unit. Injuries all but ruined the next couple of seasons for Gillespie, but he did manage to play in 35 matches in Dalglish's final season in 1990/91. When Graeme Souness took over he fell out of favour and at 31 years of age

Season	League		FA Cup		League Cup		Europe		Other		Total	
	App	Goals	App	Goals	App	Goals	App	Goals	App	Goals	App	Goals
1983/84	0	0	0	0	1	0	0	0	0	0	1	0
1984/85	10 (2)	1	3 (1)	0	3	0	2 (2)	0	1	0	19 (5)	1
1985/86	14	3	5	0	2	0	-	-	2 (1)	0	23 (1)	3
1986/87	37	0	3	0	9	0	-	-	2	0	51	0
1987/88	35	4	5	0	2	0	-	-	-	-	42	4
1988/89	15	1	2	0	1	1	-	-	3	0	21	2
1989/90	11 (2)	4	1 (1)	0	1	0	-	-	0	0	13 (3)	4
1990/91	30	1	2	0	3	1	-	-	0	0	35	2
Total	**152 (4)**	**14**	**21 (2)**	**0**	**22**	**2**	**2 (2)**	**0**	**8 (1)**	**0**	**205 (9)**	**16**

Gillett and Hicks

HE EVEN SCORED A MEMORABLE HAT-TRICK IN A 5-0 WIN OVER BIRMINGHAM AT ANFIELD ON 26 APRIL 1986 WHEN PLAYING IN DEFENCE

Gillespie joined his boyhood idols Celtic, where he played 82 matches in three years. In the final season of his career, 1994/95, Gillespie featured in four matches for his old club Coventry, managed by former colleague Phil Neal, before he had to retire due to a serious knee injury. Following his retirement he took a coaching position at Coventry. Gillespie was on Dave Jones' coaching staff at Stockport Country when the club were promoted to Football League One in the 1996/97 season. Since then he has drifted into the media side of football. He worked for Radio Merseyside for a number of years and more recently has been employed by Liverpool's official TV channel.

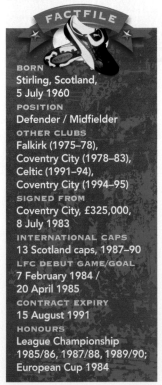

FACTFILE

BORN
Stirling, Scotland,
5 July 1960
POSITION
Defender / Midfielder
OTHER CLUBS
Falkirk (1975–78),
Coventry City (1978–83),
Celtic (1991–94),
Coventry City (1994–95)
SIGNED FROM
Coventry City, £325,000,
8 July 1983
INTERNATIONAL CAPS
13 Scotland caps, 1987–90
LFC DEBUT GAME/GOAL
7 February 1984 /
20 April 1985
CONTRACT EXPIRY
15 August 1991
HONOURS
League Championship
1985/86, 1987/88, 1989/90;
European Cup 1984

AMERICAN BUSINESSMEN George Gillett and Tom Hicks bought Liverpool Football Club from David Moores on 6 February 2007. Their offer valued each share at £5,000 so they paid £174.1m as well as taking on the club's £44.8m debt. On the day of their purchase the pair promised to 'fully acknowledge and appreciate the unique heritage and rich history of Liverpool.' Without even a hint of a sarcastic smile Gillett declared: 'We have purchased the club with no debt on the club.'

The first sign of trouble came the morning after the defeat in the Champions League final in Athens when Rafa Benítez took his employers to task. He suggested he was fighting a losing battle with Manchester United and Chelsea in the transfer market and had lost his patience, having reportedly missed out on Nemanja Vidic, Gareth Bale and Theo Walcott as deals could not be financed. Fernando Torres was bought during the summer to relieve Benítez's anxiety. Benítez revealed to the *Daily Mail* in April 2013 that the American pair did not have a clue even how transfers were done in England. 'Hicks and Gillett would say: 'We will give you money and we will go to the draft.' And I would say: 'It's not a draft! We have to sign players right now!' Another conversation with them was: 'Why can you be relegated?' They didn't understand you could be relegated. It was incredible.' Trouble was brewing and Benítez discovered that the owners had been talking to Jürgen Klinsmann behind his back about him taking over as manager in the summer of 2008. 'In November, when it appeared we were in danger of not advancing in the Champions League, weren't playing well in our Premier League matches, and Rafa and we were having communication issues over the January transfer window, George and I met with Jürgen Klinsmann,' Hicks confessed to the press in January 2008. 'We attempted to negotiate an option, as an insurance policy, to have him become our manager in the event Rafa decided to leave the club for other clubs that were rumoured in the UK Press, or in case our communication spiralled out of control for some reason.' This not only seriously destabilised Benítez's position but was not the way Liverpool fans wanted their club to do business. Club matters had always been private but now everything was out in the open. This was just the calm ahead of the storm.

As the credit crunch paralysed financial markets the game was up for Hicks and Gillett, who had boldly claimed to have bought the club for their own money, but had, in fact, taken out a large loan at the Royal Bank of Scotland and Wells Fargo. It was the quintessential leveraged buyout where the purchase was financed by equity and debt and any cash flow was used to repay the debt, thus ultimately preventing the club to acquire equally strong players to replace the key ones who had left. The club was in serious financial straits as interest payments had been dumped on the club's books, leaving it riddled with debt. In April 2010 the Royal Bank of Scotland wanted to call in their loan but consented to a further grace period of six months. As the deadline moved closer with talks with potential buyers in full swing the American pair announced dramatically that they had removed chief executive Christian Purslow and commercial director Ian Ayre from the board and replaced them with Mack Hicks and Lori Kay McCutcheon who would prevent any sale that they considered to undervalue the club, which was rumoured to be effectively anything below £600million. This was a clear breach of an agreement with the Royal Bank of Scotland which permitted chairman Martin Broughton to lead the sale process and make key decisions such as who would have a seat on the club's board. This sorry mess was finally solved on 15 October 2010 when Hicks and Gillett claimed they were the victims of 'an epic swindle at the hands of rogue corporate directors and their co-conspirators' when the club was sold by the Royal Bank of Scotland to John W Henry's New England Sports Ventures in a £300m deal. Gillett and Hicks threatened legal action but in January 2013 they released a statement that said they had withdrawn all their claims and allegations against the Royal Bank of Scotland, Martin Broughton, Christian Purslow and Ian Ayre, bringing to a conclusion the most turbulent chapter in Liverpool's history with the club having been brought to the brink of administration.

Gilligan, Sam

SAMUAL GILLIGAN was one of four talented brothers who all played professional football both north and south of the border. He moved from Scottish Cup champions Celtic, where he had scored 13 goals in 10 games, to Second Division Bristol City before the 1904/05 season. He was an instant success, scoring 17 goals in 37 games in his debut season and 20 goals in 37 league games as City won the Second Division in the 1905/06 season.

He played for the Bristol City team that lost 1-0 to Manchester United in the 1909 FA Cup final and a year later moved to league runners-up Liverpool. Gilligan made a scoring debut at Manchester City on 24 September 1910 but although he was also selected for the next game at home to Everton, he wasn't picked for the first team again until February, when he started a run

GILLIGAN WAS LIVERPOOL'S HERO ON THE DAY, SCORING THE WINNER IN THE SECOND MINUTE, HIS 11TH GOAL FROM 23 GAMES, TO KEEP HIS CLUB IN THE TOP DIVISION

of 13 matches until the end of that 1910/11 season. His appearances were more frequent the following year, but Liverpool were on the brink of relegation on the last day when the Reds faced Oldham at Boundary Park. Gilligan was Liverpool's hero on the day, scoring the winner in the second minute, his 11th goal from 23 games, to keep his club in the top division. He left for Gillingham the following summer and stayed there two years as player-manager in the Southern League. Gilligan was said to be a bit slow in movement on the field of play, but one contemporary wrote that 'in every match you will find him where the battle rages hottest.'

FOLLOWING World War One Gilligan returned home to Dundee to ship-building, a trade that he knew well from his youth before he had turned professional. What happened to him after that remained a mystery to many for a long time. False sightings and

unconfirmed rumours shrouded him in mystery. What has since come to light is that he migrated to North America in 1923 as unemployment was rife at home. He sailed on the SS Columbia from Glasgow to Boston, ultimately settling in Youngstown, Ohio, the hotbed of the American steel industry. Gilligan worked as an attendant at the Butler Art Institute, joined by his family three years later. He introduced English football to the locals, becoming player-manager of Youngstown's Mahoning Valleys. He later became foreman for the Republican Iron and Steel Company, leading their 'soccer team' until he was 53 years old,

FACTFILE

BORN
Dundee, Scotland,
18 January 1882
DIED
June 1965
POSITION
Forward
OTHER CLUBS
Dalry (1898–1901),
Belmont Athletic (1901),
Dundee Violet (1901-02),
Dundee (1902–03),
Celtic (1903–04),
Bristol City (1904–10),
Gillingham (1913–15),
Mahoning Valleys (1923–32),
Republican Iron and Steel
Soccer Club (1932–35)
SIGNED FROM
Bristol City, 30 April 1910
LFC DEBUT GAME/GOAL
24 September 1910 /
24 September 1910
CONTRACT EXPIRY
21 September 1913

as proved by an article in the *Pittsburgh Press* that said, 'Good old Sam Gilligan' was arriving at Harmarville, Pennsylvania, to play against the local team in 1935. Gilligan moved back to Dundee after his retirement.

Season	League		FA Cup		Total	
	App	Goals	App	Goals	App	Goals
1910/11	15	5	0	0	15	5
1911/12	23	11	0	0	23	11
1912/13	2	0	0	0	2	0
Total	**40**	**16**	**0**	**0**	**40**	**16**

Givens, John

THE FORWARD figured briefly during the first two seasons of Liverpool's Football League existence.

John Givens made a scoring debut at Lincoln City on 17 March 1894, netting a second-half equaliser to earn the Reds a point from a 1-1 draw. He scored three times in the five Second Division matches he played in towards the end of that 1893/94 season but failed to add to his total during the five First Division fixtures he was selected for in 1894/95.

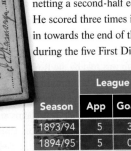

Season ticket from 1893-94

FACTFILE

BORN
Glasgow, Scotland,
January 1870
POSITION
Forward
OTHER CLUBS
Dalry (1890–94), Abercorn
SIGNED FROM
Dalry, 28 February 1894
LFC DEBUT GAME/GOAL
17 March 1894 /
17 March 1894
CONTRACT EXPIRY
1895

Season	League		FA Cup		Other		Total	
	App	Goals	App	Goals	App	Goals	App	Goals
1893/94	5	3	0	0	0	0	5	3
1894/95	5	0	0	0	0	0	5	0
Total	**10**	**3**	**0**	**0**	**0**	**0**	**10**	**3**

Glassey,
Bob

ROBERT GLASSEY
LIVERPOOL

BOB GLASSEY scored after only five minutes of his debut match for Liverpool against Preston North End at Anfield on 7 December 1935. He then added an even earlier strike in the first minute of the victory at Brentford a week later.

He played eight times in the First Division during the 1935/36 season, scoring four goals in all. Glassey had only made one first-team appearance in the following season, on 26 September, when he broke his leg in a reserve game on the last day of October against Aston Villa. He left for First Division Stoke the following month but struggled to gain a regular place at the Potters.

BOB GLASSEY SCORED AFTER ONLY FIVE MINUTES OF HIS DEBUT MATCH FOR LIVERPOOL AGAINST PRESTON NORTH END

Season	League		FA Cup		Total	
	App	Goals	App	Goals	App	Goals
1935/36	8	4	0	0	8	4
1936/37	1	0	0	0	1	0
Total	9	4	0	0	9	4

Glover,
John

JOHN GLOVER
[LIVERPOOL]

JOHN GLOVER was a strong little right-back who was said to be gipsy-like in appearance. He was quiet and unassuming on the field and relied more on skill than brute force.

Glover didn't make the first team at his home-town club, West Bromwich Albion, but managed to play 23 games for Blackburn's first team in his debut season at Ewood Park. Owing to injury and the emergence of future England captain Bob Crompton he moved south to join New Brompton (who in 1912 changed their name to Gillingham) in the Southern League. A step down led to a step up to Championship success at Liverpool in the 1900/01 season, the first of 18 Division One titles for the Reds. Glover played in 10 of the 34 matches that season, replacing John Robertson, who returned for the last three games of the campaign.

GLOVER started the following year as first choice, but was ousted halfway through the season by Robertson. Glover reclaimed his place following Roberton's move in the summer of 1902 and missed only four of the 34 First Division fixtures of 1902/03, which Liverpool finished in fifth place. At the end of the season Glover was caught accepting illegal financial inducements from Portsmouth to sign for the south-coast club. As a result he, along with team-mates Bill Goldie and Sam Raybould, were banned from football until 31 December 1903 and from ever signing for Portsmouth. Glover left Liverpool in January 1904 despite Liverpool's offer of maximum wage for a new contract and played 124 league games for First Division Birmingham until they were relegated in the 1907/08 season.

Season	League		FA Cup		Total	
	App	Goals	App	Goals	App	Goals
1900/01	10	0	0	0	10	0
1901/02	18	0	0	0	18	0
1902/03	30	0	1	0	31	0
Total	58	0	1	0	59	0

Goalkeepers

	Clean sheets	Games	Conceded	Average
Ray Clemence	323	665	488	0.73
Bruce Grobbelaar	267.6	628	534	0.85
Pepe Reina	177	394	335	0.85
Elisha Scott	137	468	645	1.38
Tommy Lawrence	133	390	404	1.04
Jerzy Dudek	76.3	186	177	0.95
Arthur Riley	69	338	608	1.80
Sam Hardy	63	240	341	1.42
Cyril Sidlow	54	165	181	1.10
Harry Storer	45	121	139	1.15
Sander Westerveld	42	103	92	0.89
Bill Perkins	38	117	138	1.18
Ken Campbell	37	142	210	1.48
Tommy Younger	35	127	176	1.39
Bert Slater	29	111	146	1.32
Mike Hooper	23	73	87	1.19
Ned Doig	18	53	68	1.28
Charlie Ashcroft	15	89	159	1.79
Matt McQueen	14	103	129	1.25
Doug Rudham	13	66	111	1.68
Chris Kirkland	12.3	45	47	1.04
Sydney Ross	11	21	18	0.86
Billy McOwen	11	27	22	0.81
Russell Crossley	11	73	139	1.90
Frank Mitchell	8	18	12	0.67
Dave Underwood	8	50	86	1.72
Brad Friedel	7.3	31	40	1.29
Ray Minshull	7	31	55	1.77
Peter Platt	6	44	74	1.68
Brad Jones	5	19	26	1.37
Jim Furnell	5	28	38	1.36
Dirk Kemp	5	33	55	1.67
Diego Cavalieri	4	10	12	1.20
Charles Cotton	4	13	20	1.54
Alf Hobson	4	28	61	2.18
Bill McCann	3	17	41	2.41
Pegguy Arphexad	2.4	6	3	0.50
Harry Wheeler Nickson	2	3	1	0.33
Steve Ogrizovic	2	5	6	1.20
Willie Donnelly	2	8	16	2.00
Scott Carson	2	9	10	1.11
Harry McNaughton	1	1	0	0
Paul Jones	1	2	2	1.00
John Jones	1	4	6	1.50
Charles Itandje	1	7	10	1.43
Augustus Beeby	1	16	28	1.75
Alexander Doni	0.3	4	3	0.75
Patrice Luzi	0.1	1	0	0
Andrew Aitken	0	1	3	3.00
Don Sloan	0	6	13	2.17
John Whitehead	0	3	7	2.33
Stanley Kane	0	6	13	2.17
John Ogston	0	1	1	1.00
Charlie Jowett	0	1	2	2.00
Billy Molyneux	0	1	1	1.00
Frank Lane	0	2	3	1.50
Daniele Padelli	0	1	2	2.00
Bill Marshall	0	1	4	4.00

Notes

16 August 1986
against Everton (1-1):
Bruce Grobbelaar was replaced by Mike Hooper in the 57th minute without conceding a goal and is credited with 2/3 of a clean sheet.

1 May 1993
against Norwich (0-1):
David James got sent off in the 60th minute without conceding a goal and is credited with 2/3 of a clean sheet.

8 December 1998
against Celta Vigo (0-1):
Brad Friedel replaced David James in the 64th minute and is credited with 1/3 of a clean sheet.

9 February 2002
against Ipswich (6-0):
Jerzy Dudek was replaced by Pegguy Arphexad in the 55th minute without conceding a goal and is credited with 2/3 of a clean sheet. Arphexad did not concede either and is credited with 1/3 of a clean sheet.

26 January 2003
against Crystal Palace (0-0):
Jerzy Dudek came on for Chris Kirkland in the 25th minute. Neither Kirkland nor Dudek conceded a goal and they are respectively credited with 1/4 and 3/4 of a clean sheet.

7 January 2004
against Chelsea (1-0):
Jerzy Dudek got injured in the 77th minute without conceding and is credited with 5/6 of a clean sheet. Patrice Luzi came on and kept a clean sheet.

5 February 2006
against Chelsea (0-2):
Pepe Reina was sent off in the 82nd minute. Jerzy Dudek came on, did not concede a goal and is credited with 1/10 of a clean sheet.

Sam Hardy

10 April 2012
against Blackburn (3-2):
Doni was sent off against Blackburn Rovers in the 26th minute without conceding and is credited with 1/3 of a clean sheet.

Penalty Kings

Keeper	Saves
Sam Hardy	15
Bruce Grobbelaar	12
Elisha Scott	12
Ray Clemence	9
Tommy Lawrence	6
Ken Campbell	6
David James	5
Pepe Reina	5
Arthur Riley	4
Ned Doig	3
Augustus Beeby	2
Cyril Sidlow	2
Harry Storer	2
Jerzy Dudek	2
Peter Platt	2
Brad Jones	1
Charlie Ashcroft	1
Chris Kirkland	1
Dave Underwood	1
Mike Hooper	1
Ray Minshull	1
Sander Westerveld	1

Goalkeepers who have saved penalties by Liverpool's opposition. Note that opposition misses especially further back in time have not all been tracked down so this list is still in development.

Goals

Most goals scored in a season

Season	Goals	Games	Average
1985/86	**138**	63	2.19
1981/82	**129**	62	2.08
2000/01	**127**	63	2.02
1982/83	**120**	60	2.00
2007/08	**119**	59	2.02
1983/84	**118**	67	1.76

Most goals scored by LFC at Anfield in the top-flight

Season	Goals	Games	Average
1963/64	**60**	21	2.86
1985/86	**58**	21	2.76
1931/32	**56**	21	2.67
1982/83	**55**	21	2.62
1927/28	**54**	21	2.57

Fewest goals scored by LFC at Anfield in the top-flight

Season	Goals	Games	Average
2011/12	**24**	19	1.26
1903/04	**24**	17	1.41
1948/49	**25**	21	1.19
1896/97	**25**	15	1.67
1913/14	**27**	19	1.42

Most goals scored by LFC away in the top-flight

Season	Goals	Games	Average
1946/47	**42**	21	2.00
1981/82	**41**	21	1.95
1989/90	**40**	19	2.11
1987/88	**38**	20	1.90
1930/31	**38**	21	1.81

Fewest goals scored by LFC away in the top-flight

Season	Goals	Games	Average
1970/71	**12**	21	0.57
1991/92	**13**	21	0.62
1894/95	**13**	15	0.87
1923/24	**14**	21	0.67
1901/02	**14**	17	0.82

Most goals conceded by LFC at Anfield in the top-flight

Season	Goals	Games	Average
1953/54	**38**	21	1.81
1931/32	**38**	21	1.81
1933/34	**37**	21	1.76
1927/28	**36**	21	1.71
1914/15	**34**	19	1.79

Fewest goals conceded by LFC at Anfield in the top-flight

Season	Goals	Games	Average
1978/79	**4**	21	0.19
2006/07	**7**	19	0.37
1979/80	**8**	21	0.38
2005/06	**8**	19	0.42
1987/88	**9**	20	0.45

Most goals conceded by LFC away in the top-flight

Season	Goals	Games	Average
1953/54	**59**	21	2.81
1934/35	**59**	21	2.81
1936/37	**58**	21	2.76
1930/31	**57**	21	2.71
1931/32	**55**	21	2.62

Fewest goals conceded by LFC away in the top-flight

Season	Goals	Games	Average
1975/76	**10**	21	0.48
1978/79	**12**	21	0.57
1971/72	**14**	21	0.67
1970/71	**14**	21	0.67
2008/09	**14**	19	0.74

Liverpool win 1947 title

Goalscorers

Top-scorer in all competitions

Player	Goals	Appearances	Average
Ian Rush	346	660	0.52
Roger Hunt	286	492	0.58
Gordon Hodgson	241	377	0.64
Billy Liddell	228	534	0.43
Robbie Fowler	183	369	0.50
Kenny Dalglish	172	515	0.33
Steven Gerrard	159	630	0.25
Michael Owen	158	297	0.53
Harry Chambers	151	339	0.45
Jack Parkinson	129	219	0.59
Sam Raybould	129	226	0.57
Dick Forshaw	124	288	0.43
Ian St John	118	425	0.28
Jack Balmer	110	309	0.36
John Barnes	108	407	0.27
Kevin Keegan	100	323	0.31

Top-scorer in the League

Player	Goals	Appearances	Average
Roger Hunt	245	404	0.61
Gordon Hodgson	233	358	0.65
Ian Rush	229	469	0.49
Billy Liddell	215	492	0.44
Harry Chambers	135	310	0.44
Robbie Fowler	128	266	0.48
Jack Parkinson	124	199	0.62
Sam Raybould	119	211	0.56
Michael Owen	118	216	0.55
Kenny Dalglish	118	355	0.33
Dick Forshaw	117	266	0.44

Top-scorer in the FA Cup

Player	Goals	Appearances	Average
Ian Rush	39	61	0.64
Roger Hunt	18	44	0.41
John Barnes	16	51	0.31
Harry Chambers	16	28	0.57
Kevin Keegan	14	28	0.50

Top-scorer in the League Cup

Player	Goals	Appearances	Average
Ian Rush	48	78	0.62
Robbie Fowler	29	35	0.83
Kenny Dalglish	27	59	0.46
Ronnie Whelan	14	50	0.28
Steve McMahon	13	27	0.48

Top-scorer in European competitions

Player	Goals	Appearances	Average
Steven Gerrard	39	124	0.31
Michael Owen	22	50	0.44
Ian Rush	20	38	0.53
Roger Hunt	17	31	0.55
Terry McDermott	15	34	0.44

Most goals scored as a substitute

Player	Goals	Appearances	Average
David Fairclough	18	62	0.29
Ryan Babel	12	81	0.15
Steven Gerrard	8	57	0.14
Djibril Cissé	7	36	0.19

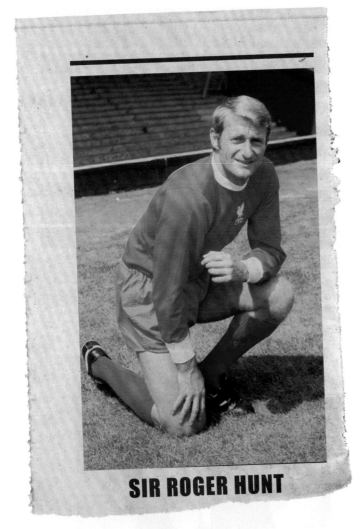

SIR ROGER HUNT

How many minutes for a forward (centre-, inside-left or inside-right) until debut goal

Player	Minutes	Appearances	Date of debut goal	
Peter Crouch	1.229	18	3 December	2005
Arthur Rowley	1.019	11	no goal!	
Ian Rush	813	10	30 September	1981
Michael Robinson	784	10	28 September	1983
Robbie Keane	688	11	1 October	2008
Jack Balmer	531	6	7 December	1935
Kevin Baron	527	6	8 November	1947
Phil Boersma	480	7	4 November	1970
Emile Heskey	436	5	1 April	2000
Les Shannon	382	5	30 August	1948

KEVIN BARON
LIVERPOOL

Most appearances for an outfield player without a goal

Player	Started		Ended		Games	Goals for LFC
Ephraim Longworth	19 September	1910	21 April	1928	370	0
Jamie Carragher	24 January	1999	19 July	2005	305	5
Rob Jones	6 October	1991	25 April	1998	243	0
Jamie Carragher	27 August	2008	19 May	2013	211	5
Ronnie Moran	22 November	1952	26 August	1959	210	17
Stephane Henchoz	21 September	1999	1 December	2004	205	0

Fastest scorers

Player	Time	Date	Opponent	Venue	Result
Paul Walsh	14 seconds	27 August 1984	West Ham United	Anfield	3-0
Kenny Dalglish	21 seconds	21 September 1985	Everton	Goodison Park	3-2
Joe Cole	27 seconds	16 September 2010	Steaua Bucharest	Anfield	4-1
Robbie Fowler	29 seconds	14 December 1996	Middlesbrough	Anfield	5-1
Jack Balmer	30 seconds	16 February 1938	Everton	Goodison Park	3-1
Alan Arnell	30 seconds	3 September 1955	Blackburn Rovers	Ewood Park	3-3
Berry Nieuwenhuys	30 seconds	28 September 1935	WBA	Anfield	5-0
Tom Reid	30 seconds	29 October 1927	Blackburn Rovers	Anfield	4-2
Maxi Rodriguez	32 seconds	9 May 2011	Fulham	Craven Cottage	5-2
Stan Collymore	33 seconds	23 November 1996	Wimbledon	Anfield	1-1

Fastest scorers on their debut

Player	Time	Date	Opponent	Venue	Result
Billy Millar	50 seconds	25 August 1928	Bury	Anfield	3-0
Bill White	2 minutes	14 September 1901	Everton	Anfield	2-2
Mark Gonzalez	3 minutes	9 August 2006	Maccabi Haifa	Anfield	2-1
Bob Glassey	5 minutes	7 December 1935	Preston North End	Anfield	2-1
Daniel Sturridge	7 minutes	6 January 2013	Mansfield Town	Field Mill	2-1
Tom Reid	8 minutes	1 May 1926	Sheffield United	Anfield	2-2
Billy Watkinson	9 minutes	26 April 1947	Aston Villa	Villa Park	2-1
Tony McNamara	9 minutes	21 December 1957	Bristol City	Anfield	4-3
Cyril Done	9 minutes	12 October 1946	Charlton Athletic	Anfield	1-1
Harry Lewis	10 minutes	30 August 1919	Bradford City	Valley Parade	3-1
Alun Evans	10 minutes	21 September 1968	Leicester City	Anfield	4-0

BILLY LIDDELL
LIVERPOOL

GORDON HODGSON
LIVERPOOL

JACK PARKINSON
LIVERPOOL

Players who have scored 30+ goals a season

Player	Season	Goals	Appearances	Average
Ian Rush	1983/84	47	65	0.72
Roger Hunt*	1961/62	42	46	0.91
Ian Rush	1986/87	40	57	0.70
Roger Hunt	1964/65	37	58	0.64
Gordon Hodgson	1930/31	36	41	0.88
Robbie Fowler	1995/96	36	53	0.68
Roger Hunt	1963/64	33	46	0.72
Roger Hunt	1965/66	33	46	0.72
Fernando Torres	2007/08	33	46	0.72
Ian Rush	1985/86	33	56	0.59
John Evans*	1954/55	33	42	0.79
Sam Raybould	1902/03	32	34	0.94
Gordon Hodgson	1928/29	32	41	0.78
Billy Liddell*	1955/56	32	44	0.73
Robbie Fowler	1996/97	31	44	0.70
John Aldridge	1988/89	31	47	0.66
Ian Rush	1982/83	31	51	0.61
Robbie Fowler	1994/95	31	57	0.54
Kenny Dalglish	1977/78	31	62	0.50
Billy Liddell*	1954/55	31	44	0.70
Jack Parkinson	1909/10	30	32	0.94
Luis Suarez	2012/13	30	44	0.68
Ian Rush	1981/82	30	49	0.61
Roger Hunt	1967/68	30	57	0.53

Fastest player to score 50 goals

Player	Games
Albert Stubbins	77
Jack Parkinson	78
Roger Hunt	79
Sam Raybould	81
George Allan	81
Fernando Torres	84
Ian Rush	87
John Aldridge	87
John Evans	90
Luis Suarez	91
Michael Owen	93
Gordon Hodgson	94
Robbie Fowler	94
Harry Chambers	96
Kenny Dalglish	102

Fastest player to score 100 goals

Player	Games
Roger Hunt	144
Jack Parkinson	152
Robbie Fowler	165
Sam Raybould	165
Ian Rush	166
Gordon Hodgson	170
Michael Owen	184
Harry Chambers	186
Kenny Dalglish	241
Dick Forshaw	247

Fastest player to score 150 goals

Player	Games
Roger Hunt	226
Gordon Hodgson	242
Ian Rush	249
Robbie Fowler	261
Michael Owen	280

Fastest player to score 200 goals

Player	Games
Roger Hunt	298
Ian Rush	321
Gordon Hodgson	322
Billy Liddell	485

Fastest player to score 250 goals

Player	Games
Roger Hunt	401
Ian Rush	422

John Evans nets against Everton in the FA Cup in 1955

* Liverpool in the 2nd Division

Goddard, Arthur

ARTHUR GODDARD was a fantastic servant to Liverpool, being a regular scorer from his position on the right wing for over a decade. Goddard played for the Christ Church Club in Stockport from the age of 16 to 19, his talent not going unnoticed, and he started his ascent with Stockport County in the Lancashire League where he played two years, winning the Manchester Cup.

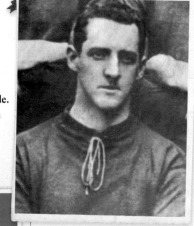

In 1899 Glossop, who had been promoted to the First Division of the Football League for the first time, paid Stockport £260 for his services. This proved to be Glossop's only season in the top flight as they finished last out of 18 teams. Goddard finished fifth with Glossop in the Second Division in the 1900/01 season while Liverpool won their first League Championship. Goddard joined the champions in the second part of the following season and was given his Liverpool debut at Wolverhampton on 8 March 1902, starting a run of eleven successive matches in which he scored twice. Regular right-winger Jack Cox was moved to the left as Goddard established himself in the side over the next two seasons, missing only one league match in each and scoring a total of 17 goals. In 1904/05 he won a Second Division Championship medal and followed that up by being the only ever-present in the team that won the League Championship a year later.

GODDARD continued to play consistently, averaging over 30 league appearances for the next seven years. He was appointed captain of the side in the 1909/10 season and led by example as Liverpool finished second in the league, their best placing for four years. Goddard contributed more to the goalscoring than in previous years, reaching double figures for the first time since 1903. He was so described in the club programme on 29 October 1910: 'By his gentlemanly demeanour on the field, and the genuinely-consistent character of his play since he

> **'I HAVE YET TO SEE A MORE GRACEFUL PLAYER ON THE BALL THAN ARTHUR GODDARD'**
>
> **ALEX RAISBECK**

became associated with the Anfielders, Goddard has deservedly become a great favourite in Liverpool, and he is a typical example of the highest class of footballer. His play is not of the vigorous order; quiet and unassuming, he awaits his opportunity, and then with the embodiment of grace and elegance, he glides down the wing with such ease, that he scarcely seems to be exerting himself. But when we see the half-back and full-back gradually left in the rear, then we tumble to the fact that Goddard is travelling.'

The 1913/14 season proved to be his last at Anfield as he lost his place in the autumn after figuring in 10 of the opening 11 fixtures and only played once more, in April 1914, no doubt disappointed in missing out on Liverpool's first FA Cup final which the Reds lost 1-0 to Burnley. Goddard's contract was not renewed after the season and he went on a free transfer to Cardiff City.

GODDARD played 49 games for Liverpool as a war-time guest, receiving a warm welcome from the *Liverpool Echo* in September 1915. 'A well-preserved, gentlemanly player, I think his play will be all the better suited by the friendly game, because he has not to worry about trips and backs, as in former years.' Goddard was twice chosen for international trials, while at Glossop and Liverpool, and it was predicted he would soon make his full England debut. That

surprisingly never came to fruition, but Goddard was immensely proud to be chosen to represent the English League XI that beat the Irish League 9-0 in 1901.

Arthur Goddard, who is a worthy member of Liverpool's official Hall of Fame, had a fan in his skipper at Liverpool, Alex Raisbeck: 'From the first day I clapped eyes on Goddard I made him out to be a great lad, although he was but a slip of a lad the day he left his home in Stockport,' Raisbeck revealed in the *Weekly News* in 1915. 'Goddard was the finest and most graceful runner it has been my lot to see. He could cover the ground, too, and in his prime I would have backed him against most players. I have played on almost every ground of importance in England and Scotland, and against all sorts and sizes of players, but I have yet to see a more graceful player on the ball than Arthur Goddard. It was a treat to see him cover the ground with such a free and easy movement.'

	League		FA Cup		Other		Total	
Season	App	Goals	App	Goals	App	Goals	App	Goals
1901/02	11	2	0	0	-	-	11	2
1902/03	33	11	1	0	-	-	34	11
1903/04	33	6	1	0	-	-	34	6
1904/05	28	7	2	1	-	-	30	8
1905/06	38	6	5	2	1	0	44	8
1906/07	35	3	4	0	-	-	39	3
1907/08	35	4	4	0	-	-	39	4
1908/09	36	4	2	0	-	-	38	4
1909/10	35	12	1	0	-	-	36	12
1910/11	31	8	2	1	-	-	33	9
1911/12	28	2	1	0	-	-	29	2
1912/13	32	7	4	1	-	-	36	8
1913/14	11	0	0	0	-	-	11	0
Total	**386**	**72**	**27**	**5**	**1**	**0**	**414**	**77**

FACTFILE

BORN
Heaton Norris, Stockport,
14 June 1878

DIED
May 1956

POSITION
Right-winger

OTHER CLUBS
Christ Church Club (1894–97),
Stockport County (1897–99),
Glossop (1899–1902),
Cardiff City (1914–15);
Liverpool (wartime guest)

SIGNED FROM
Glossop, £460,
24 February 1902

LFC DEBUT GAME/GOAL
8 March 1902 /
15 March 1902

CONTRACT EXPIRY
May 1914

HONOURS
League Championship
1905/06;
Second Division
Championship 1904/05

Goldie,
Archie

'SLOW BUT SURE' and comfortable on the ball, right-back Archie Goldie was one of numerous Scottish players to represent the club in its early years.

He was bought to strengthen the squad that had been relegated in 1895 and helped to immediately restore the club to the top division. Goldie played 22 times in that promotion season of 1895/96 and only missed one match the following year as Liverpool

consolidated themselves in the First Division by finishing in fifth place. Goldie's only Liverpool goal also came that season, but his late strike at Sunderland could not prevent a 4-3 defeat at Roker Park. He played regularly for the club in the next three seasons and for over half that period was joined in the side by his brother Bill, also bought from Scottish club Clyde.

Season	League		FA Cup		Other		Total	
	App	Goals	App	Goals	App	Goals	App	Goals
1895/96	22	0	2	0	4	0	28	0
1896/97	29	1	5	0	-	-	34	1
1897/98	28	0	4	0	-	-	32	0
1898/99	25	0	5	0	-	-	30	0
1899/1900	21	0	4	0	-	-	25	0
Total	**125**	**1**	**20**	**0**	**4**	**0**	**149**	**1**

Goldie,
Bill

TOUGH-TACKLING left-half Bill Goldie joined his brother Archie at Anfield in the 1897/98 season and was a firm fixture in the side during the seven years he stayed there. He played 129 consecutive games from 23 December 1899 until 27 April 1903 and picked up a winners' medal as the club won the League Championship title in 1901.

At the end of the 1902/03 season, however, Bill was caught accepting illegal payments from Pompey to sign for them in the Southern League. As a result he, along with team-mates John Glover and Sam Raybould, were banned from football until 31 December 1903. When the suspension was over Bill joined Fulham in January 1904, having played his last game for Liverpool in April 1903. Bill won two Southern League Championships with the Cottagers and featured in the 1907/08 season, which was Fulham's first ever Football League season. This turned out to

be his last, and after 215 games for Fulham he joined Leicester Fosse who had been promoted to the First Division but were relegated a year later. Bill retired from a successful league career in 1911 and ran a pub while occasionally turning out for amateurs Leicester Imperial.

Referee Kingscott charged Bill for 'discourteous language' after the conclusion of the second replay between Sheffield United and Liverpool in the FA Cup semi-finals in 1899. The Liverpool players were furious as they felt that the United goal had been easily yards offside and they had been robbed of a goal when the ball went twice over the line during a melee. Alex Raisbeck, Johnny Walker and Bill Goldie were all called before a league committee. Raisbeck and Walker got off with a stern warning, but Goldie was not so lucky even

though his inquisitors could hardly understand a word he was saying as Raisbeck recounted in the *Daily News* in 1915. 'Willie came from Hurlford and he was excited that night, and moreover, when he was excited he was apt to stutter. Now, when a Hurlford man speaks at any time it is not always quite easy for Scotsmen even to understand what he is saying. And in this case Willie was excited and his stutter was more pronounced than usual. I tell you I laughed myself sore when I heard those English directors examining, cross-examining and re-examining Willie. I am positive to this day that they never made out one word he said, and because poor Willie spoke the braidest o' the braid Scots, accentuated by a slight impediment, he was suspended to the end of the season!'

BILL GOLDIE
[LIVERPOOL]

Season	League		FA Cup		Total	
	App	Goals	App	Goals	App	Goals
1897/98	4	0	0	0	4	0
1898/99	27	2	6	0	33	2
1899/1900	25	1	4	0	29	1
1900/01	34	2	2	0	36	2
1901/02	34	0	3	0	37	0
1902/03	34	1	1	0	35	1
Total	**158**	**6**	**16**	**0**	**174**	**6**

González,
Mark

MARK DENNIS González Hoffman was born to Chilean parents in South Africa, as his father Raul was playing football there at the time.

He was named after Mark Tovey and Dennis Wicks, both former team-mates of his dad while playing for NSL champions

Durban Bush Bucks during the mid-1980s. A coin was tossed to decide whose name would feature first, with 'Mark' being the winner. González moved to Chile when he was 10 years old but failed to get opportunities at top clubs and eventually ended up on the books of Everton! This was, however, a Chilean club called Everton de Viña del Mar. He made his breakthrough at one of Chile's top clubs, Universidad Católica. González was spotted by Liverpool's first-team coach Paco Herrera, a former manager of Albacete, where the Chilean prospect had moved in 2004. Despite his excellent progress, he couldn't prevent Albacete from being relegated from La Liga. A cruciate knee ligament injury in April 2005 threatened the move, but Liverpool's application for his work permit proved a bigger obstacle, as Chile were then outside the top 70 in the FIFA world rankings. The arrival of González at Liverpool was delayed by one year, of which he spent six months on loan at Real Sociedad, proving a great success for the Spanish side. Finally he got his permit in the summer of 2006 and his move to Liverpool became a reality.

His career at Anfield got off to a sensational start. He came on as a late substitute for Steven Gerrard in the home leg of the Champions League qualifier against Maccabi Haifa with the score delicately balanced at 1-1. González received a pass from Alonso and clipped a precise shot past the goalkeeper and into the far corner of the net to ensure a vital victory on the night. Although he played a part in 36 of Liverpool's first-team matches during his one and only full season at Anfield, the goal against Haifa would prove to be the highlight. The Chilean was clearly out of his depth in the Premier League and in July 2007 González signed a contract with Real Betis. He stayed at Betis until the summer of 2009, which

coincided with the Seville club's relegation to the Spanish second tier. CSKA Moscow outbid Olympiacos in August 2009, with González signing a five-year deal with the club from the Russian capital where he has been doing reasonably well, but is not a regular.

FACTFILE

BORN
Durban, South Africa, 10 July 1984
POSITION
Left-winger
OTHER CLUBS
Universidad Católica (2002–04), Albacete (2004–05), Real Sociedad (loan, 2005–06), Real Betis (2007–09), CSKA Moscow (2009–)
SIGNED FROM
Albacete, £1.5million, 20 October 2005
INTERNATIONAL CAPS
46 Chile caps (4 goals), 2003–12
LFC DEBUT GAME/GOAL
9 August 2006 / 9 August 2006
CONTRACT EXPIRY
17 July 2007

	League		FA Cup		League Cup		Europe		Other		Total	
Season	App	Goals	App	Goals	App	Goals	App	Goals	App	Goals	App	Goals
2006/07	14 (11)	2	0	0	2	0	3 (5)	1	1	0	20 (16)	3
Total	14 (11)	2	0	0	2	0	3 (5)	1	1	0	20 (16)	3

Goode,
Bertram

BERTRAM GOODE had scored 13 goals in 17 Lancashire Combination matches for Chester when Liverpool signed him up following the 1907/08 season. Goode only played in seven league matches in his two seasons at Liverpool. His only goal for the club was the first of Liverpool's goals in a 4-2 defeat at the hands of Sheffield United on 28 December 1909.

He joined Wrexham in the Birmingham & District League, where he scored 37 goals in 39 league and cup games including four goals in the 6-1 victory over Connah's Quay in the Welsh Cup final. In 1911 he joined top First Division team Aston Villa, scoring three goals in seven league games, while netting 46 goals for Villa's reserves. He moved to Second Division Hull City the following season, scoring 10 goals in 28 league matches before rejoining Wrexham. Goode scored 136 goals in 276 matches in his three spells at Wrexham and is remembered as one of the greatest strikers in the Welsh club's history.

FACTFILE

BORN
Chester, 11 August 1886
DIED
30 April 1955
POSITION
Forward
OTHER CLUBS
Old St Mary's, Hoole, Saltney, Chester (1907–08), Wrexham (1910–11), Aston Villa (1911–12), Hull City (1912–13), Wrexham (1913–22); Millwall, Southampton (wartime guest), Rhos Athletic (1922), Chester (1922–23), Wrexham (1923–26)
SIGNED FROM
Chester, May 1908
LFC DEBUT GAME/GOAL
7 November 1908 / 28 December 1909
CONTRACT EXPIRY
2 June 1910

	League		FA Cup		Total	
Season	App	Goals	App	Goals	App	Goals
1908/09	6	0	0	0	6	0
1909/10	1	1	0	0	1	1
Total	7	1	0	0	7	1

Tom Miller

Good Friday Scandal

ON GOOD FRIDAY 1915 Liverpool and Manchester United met at Old Trafford. United were one point from the bottom spot occupied by Chelsea, who had played one game less while Liverpool were secure in 13th. United won 2-0 in a game in which 'a more one-sided first half would be hard to witness,' according to the *Liverpool Daily Post*. The second half was not much better as the *Sporting Chronicle* noted: 'The Liverpool forwards gave the weakest exhibition in this half seen on the ground during the season.' George Anderson put United 1-0 up after 40 minutes and the visitors had a golden chance to add their second from the spot after Bob Pursell conceded a penalty by handling the ball in the 48th minute. However, Patrick O'Connell missed the spot-kick by a country mile. Anderson got his second in the middle of the second half after which 'the closing stages were of a scrappy nature with little suggestion of further addition to the score,' as the *Liverpool Courier* noted. The reporter of the *Manchester Daily Dispatch* was not impressed. 'The second half was crammed with lifeless football. United were two up with twenty-two minutes to play and they seemed so content with their lead that they apparently never tried to increase it. Liverpool scarcely ever gave the impression that they would be likely to score.' The two points United received from this game were enough in the end to earn them 18th place and safety, one point ahead of 19th placed Chelsea, who were relegated.

Within a fortnight of the Good Friday match taking place a couple of newspapers implied that the result had been decided beforehand. Bookmakers had laid odds up to 8-1 against United winning 2-0 and a suspiciously large number of bets had been made on that very scoreline, causing the odds to shorten to 4-1. The *Sporting Chronicle* published a notice from a bookmaker called 'The Football King' who promised a substantial reward for information that would lead to punishment of the 'instigators of this reprehensible

conspiracy.' He added: 'We have solid grounds for believing that a certain First League match played in Manchester during Easter weekend was 'squared', the home club being permitted to win by a certain score.'

THIS WAS potentially English football's greatest scandal since Billy Meredith was found guilty of bribing his opponents in 1905. A fight broke out amongst players during a game between Aston Villa and Manchester City on the final day of the 1904/05 season. It eventually transpired that Villa captain Alec Leake had accused Meredith, who played for City, of having offered him £10 to allow City to win. Meredith first refused the claim but later admitted to being 'only the spokesman of others equally guilty.' Meredith was suspended for 12 months after which he joined City's greatest rivals, Manchester United.

After a lengthy investigation, on 23 December 1915 the following verdict was reached by the Football League's Good Friday

Commission: 'It is proved that a considerable sum of money changed hands by betting on the match, and that some of the players profited thereby. Every opportunity has been given to the players to tell the truth, but although they were warned that we were in possession of the facts some have persistently refused to do so, thus revealing a conspiracy to keep back the truth. It is almost incredible that players dependent on the game for their livelihood should have resorted to such base tactics. By their action they have sought to undermine the whole fabric of the game and discredit its honesty and fairness. We are bound to view such offences in a serious light. The honesty and uprightness of the game must be preserved at all costs, and although we sympathise greatly with the clubs, who are bound to suffer seriously, we feel that we have no alternative but to impose the punishments which the players have been warned over and over again would be imposed. We are satisfied that the allegations have been proved against the following: J Sheldon, RR Purcell, T Miller and T Fairfoul (Liverpool), A Turnbull, A Whalley and EJ West (Manchester United), L Cook (Chester) and they are therefore permanently suspended from taking part in football or football management, and shall not be allowed to enter any football ground in the future. There are grave suspicions that

others are also involved, but as the penalty is severe we have restricted our findings to those as to whose offence there is no reasonable doubt.'

The players' bans, except Enoch West's, were lifted when league football resumed in 1919 in appreciation of their service to their country in the war. West, who had not enlisted, continued to maintain his innocence and his ban was not lifted until 1945 when he was 59 years old as a part of general amnesty. Sandy Turnbull was never pardoned as he was killed on the Western Front in 1917.

On 24 December 1915 the *Liverpool Echo* claimed that other players may have been guilty of taking part in the plot. 'There are some lucky fellows connected with the inquiry. That's certain. The commission plainly tells us that other players were under grave suspicion, but that findings of the commission had been restricted. Aye, it is a fact that some fellows have scraped through the inquiry "by the lip of their mouth."'

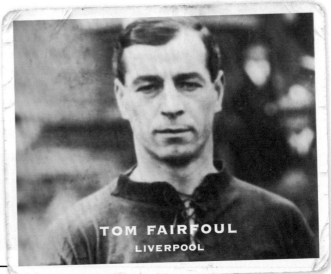

R. PURSELL
[LIVERPOOL]

TOM FAIRFOUL
LIVERPOOL

There were, however, a few players that showed full co-operation with the commission and judging by their performance at Old Trafford did not hold back. Elisha Scott was excellent in goal and forward Fred Pagnam did his utmost to score in the game despite threats from the ringleaders. He hit the crossbar in the second half and was seemingly chastised by a colleague for trying to score. Pagnam revealed that he had been offered £3 by Sheldon in a taxi en route to the match. Ephraim Longworth, who saved once on the line, and Donald Mackinlay both testified that they had been aware of the plot but like Pagnam refused to take part.

JACKIE SHELDON
LIVERPOOL

When Jackie Sheldon testified in Enoch West's case in 1917, he finally confessed his guilt as well as Bob Pursell. Sheldon, who had joined Liverpool from Manchester United in November 1913, told the court that he convinced his team-mates to play along and had met with United players West, Turnbull, and Whalley to decide the outcome of 2-0, with one goal scored either side of half-time.

This was not the first occasion that Liverpool's players had been suspected of match fixing as the *Daily Express* reported on 31 March 1913. 'Mr. Henry George Norris, who is a prominent man in more than the football world, has thrown into the big ball camp a bombshell, the full effect of which none can measure at the present time. He practically accuses Liverpool of allowing Chelsea to win a game on Easter Monday.' Mr Norris was a successful businessman, the mayor of Fulham and a member of the Management Committee of the Football League. Before the game Chelsea were 3rd from bottom with 20 points, Notts County had 17 points but had played one game less and Arsenal was bottom with 15. Chelsea's win over Liverpool was crucial to saving the East London club from the clutches of relegation with four matches to go. Notts County and Arsenal were relegated in the spring, Chelsea finishing three points above County. It is worth noting that in Liverpool's previous outing to the Chelsea game they lost 3-0 at Notts County.

MR NORRIS published his complaint about 'the worst game of football it has ever been my misfortune to see' in the *Fulham Times*. 'It was early apparent to me what was happening, and the final result of a win for Chelsea by the odd goal in three occasioned no surprise either to me or the many thousands who left the field in disgust. I have no hesitation in saying that many matches played as this one would effectually kill professional football in this country as surely as professional running and cycling were killed in the olden days. I was told by certain Chelsea officials that I was talking nonsense and was prejudiced. Was I prejudiced and was I talking nonsense? If I am prejudiced, is the same charge to be levelled at the critic of the Lancashire "*Sporting Chronicle*"? This is what he wrote on Tuesday morning: 'Liverpool terminated their Easter holiday engagements by one of the worst exhibitions of football during their career in the premier league. They allowed Chelsea to defeat them by the odds goal of three, after a display which must assuredly cause their faithful followers much food for genuine complaint. It was not merely the fact that they were beaten that aroused dissatisfaction, but the manner in which their defeat was brought about that led to universal condemnation of their methods. Never before have the Liverpool first team been guilty of such palpable inefficiency as was the case in this game, and Chelsea's success was due not to their superiority, but to the pandering of their opponents, who practically added to their own discomfiture by their crude unintelligence and utterly feeble efforts. In the early stages, Campbell, Longworth, and Tosswill were sterling strivers, but even during this period there were palpable passengers in the Liverpool ranks, who seemed determined to give the Chelsea men every chance of making headway. Liverpool never appeared desirous of obtaining a goal, whereas they allowed their opponents every opportunity of so doing. Never in their career have they given a worse exhibition, and few of the team will emerge from the contest with added reputation. Genuine performers on the Liverpool side could be numbered on the fingers of one hand. Their opponents were feeble in the extreme, yet they won.'

Liverpool had won ten and drawn three of their home matches since 5 October so their capitulation to Chelsea was no ordinary performance. 'The Easter Monday match with Chelsea proved a very disappointing affair, and I should imagine not one of the thirty thousand persons present went away satisfied with what they had witnessed,' the scribe at the club programme wrote. 'The forwards gave their feeblest display of the season; at times they afforded glimpses of what they were capable of accomplishing, but all their efforts ended up in smoke.' This accusation of course created a great stir in the football world and John McKenna, who was the chairman of Liverpool as well as president of the Football

League promised to investigate. 'In the interests of the game and of the clubs concerned I shall at once ask the Football League Management Committee to inquire into the grave charges. I am determined that the obnoxious matter shall be sifted to the bottom.' Neither McKenna nor manager Tom Watson had been present at the game, but two of the three directors who had been there had claimed to McKenna that 'they had never seen such a display before.' Certain players were called before McKenna to answer to the charges, but their reply was an emphatic denial that they had done other than their best. Four of the five forwards who played in the Chelsea game; Arthur Goddard, Jack Parkinson, Tom Gracie and Bill Lacey were dropped for the following home game against Manchester United that was promptly lost as well. 'I have reason to believe that certain forwards were not dropped because of their want of form, but because the directors feared the crowd might become restive,' 'Bee' concluded in the *Liverpool Echo*.

A joint Commission from the Football Association and the Football League was appointed to inquire into the allegations. On 11 April 1913 the following statement was released to the press. 'The Commission is satisfied that no inducement was offered to the Liverpool players to influence the result of the match. Indeed, Mr. Norris assured the Commission that he did not suggest any corrupt or ulterior motive. There is evidence that the form displayed by the Liverpool players was unsatisfactory, but the Commission is satisfied that the allegation that they did not desire to win the match is unfounded.'

Gordon, Patrick

PATRICK GORDON was 'sacked' by Everton, as it was termed in the papers at the time, and offered to neighbours Liverpool, who snapped the Scotsman up. Winger Gordon played in Liverpool's first ever season in the Football League, the victorious Second Division campaign of 1893/94. He featured in 21 of 28 matches and scored six times as the club went undefeated. Although he played in the opening five fixtures of Liverpool's initial season in the First Division, he lost his place in September 1894 and joined First Division Blackburn Rovers the following month.

Gordon replaced Jamie Haydock in the Rovers team, prompting one supporter to publicly complain that Gordon was basically not fit to tie Haydock's laces. Gordon had scored two goals in 12 games when Haydock reclaimed his place. Gordon refused to play for the reserve team and in May 1895 he was

evidently up to no good again and his contract with Rovers was terminated for what was described as 'refractory conduct' during a tour of Scotland. Gordon ended up playing for non-league Liverpool South End.

Season	League		FA Cup		Other		Total	
	App	Goals	App	Goals	App	Goals	App	Goals
1893/94	21	6	3	0	1	1	25	7
1894/95	5	1	0	0	0	0	5	1
Total	26	7	3	0	1	1	30	8

Gorman, James

CENTRE-HALF James Gorman didn't get a lot of chances at Liverpool as Alex Raisbeck's understudy. He made his league debut on the final Saturday of the 1905/06 season, playing his part as an inside-left in a 3-1 home win over Sheffield United. However, he wasn't picked again until the second half of the following season, when he played in nine of the last 14 First Division fixtures when Raisbeck was out injured. He also figured nine times in his final season at Anfield.

This 'undoubtedly very smart player' was sought after by a number of First Division clubs and left for Leicester Fosse at the end of the 1907/08 season. He was dreadfully unlucky as he was so badly injured on his debut against Manchester City on 3 October 1908 that he was out for most of the season, in which newcomers Leicester were relegated straight back to the Second Division. Gorman never really recovered after this incident and only played two more games for the Foxes before joining Hartlepools United in the North Eastern League.

Season	League		FA Cup		Other		Total	
	App	Goals	App	Goals	App	Goals	App	Goals
1905/06	1	0	0	0	0	0	1	0
1906/07	9	0	3	0	-	-	12	0
1907/08	9	0	1	1	-	-	10	1
Total	19	0	4	1	0	0	23	1

Gracie,
Tom

FORWARD TOM GRACIE had been highly rated in Scotland before his transfer to Everton, where he struggled for two seasons with only a solitary goal to show for 13 league appearances. Gracie and Bill Lacey were transferred to Liverpool from the Blues for a combined fee of £300 and Harold Uren, who went the opposite way.

Gracie made a scoring debut at Bury on 24 February 1912 but that was his only goal from six matches that season. When Gracie had only scored once in the first five games of the following season he was dropped from the first team and the *Daily Express* concluded that 'it has been proved over and over again that the Scottish style of play is much slower than the English game, and

a player who is regarded as a star artist over the border may not shine in England. A case in point is that of Tom Gracie, the present Liverpool forward. When he joined Everton there was a great flourish of trumpets, for Gracie was regarded as almost the best centre in Scotland at the time. He never rose to the same height with Everton, however, the pace being too fast.'

GRACIE returned to Scotland with Hearts in 1914 and was the joint leading scorer in the Scottish League in the 1914/15 season with 29 goals in 37 games. As well as playing with Hearts at the time he served as a corporal with the 16th Royal Scots, combining military training with his football duties. He was promoted to

sergeant in May 1915. Sadly, Gracie was diagnosed with leukaemia in March 1915 but continued to play for Hearts, showing great bravery. His coach at Hearts was apparently the only one who knew about the severity of his illness. Tom Gracie passed away in his hometown of Glasgow, aged just 26, on

23 October 1915. Tom's brother had died three and a half weeks earlier in the great World War One offensive at Loos in France.

Season	League		FA Cup		Total	
	App	Goals	App	Goals	App	Goals
1911/12	6	1	0	0	6	1
1912/13	13	1	1	0	14	1
1913/14	14	3	0	0	14	3
Total	**33**	**5**	**1**	**0**	**34**	**5**

Graham,
Bobby

HIS LEAGUE DEBUT
12 DAYS LATER
WAS ONE OF THE
BEST EVER
IN THE HISTORY OF
THE CLUB,
GRAHAM SCORING A
HAT-TRICK AS
LIVERPOOL THRASHED
ASTON VILLA 5-1
AT ANFIELD TWO
MONTHS BEFORE HIS
TWENTIETH BIRTHDAY

BOBBY GRAHAM had three seasons in Liverpool reserves, scoring 16 goals in 40 matches in 1963/64, before scoring in his long-awaited first-team debut for the club in Liverpool's first European home game against KR Reykjavik on 14 September 1964. His league debut 12 days later was one of the best ever in the history of the club, Graham scoring a hat-trick as Liverpool thrashed Aston Villa 5-1 at Anfield two months before his twentieth birthday. He scored in the following game as well against Sheffield United but his explosive start fizzled out and he only played 12 matches in the next three seasons.

Graham finally won a regular place in the side in April 1969 when Roger Hunt and Ian St John were disappearing into the sunset, and played all 54 games in the

1969/70 season. After a promising start to the 1970/71 season, he fell awkwardly on the Anfield turf when Chelsea were the visitors early in October and

was carried off with a broken leg. John Toshack was signed from Cardiff City only weeks later and Kevin Keegan arrived from Scunthorpe the following spring.

GRAHAM'S days at Liverpool were numbered and he moved on to Coventry City where he stayed 18 months, playing only 19 games and also being loaned out to Tranmere, before joining his home-town club Motherwell, signing for his former team-mate, Ian St John. Graham enjoyed much success on his return north of the border and scored 37 goals in 132 league matches for Motherwell between 1973 and 1977. He was signed by neighbours Hamilton Academical for a club record fee of £15,000 in 1977 and added 42 goals in 115 league matches in four years, as well as being the club's assistant manager.

FACTFILE

BORN
Motherwell, Scotland,
22 November 1944
POSITION
Forward
OTHER CLUBS
Coventry City (1972–73),
Tranmere Rovers (loan, 1973),
Motherwell (1973–77),
Hamilton Academical
(1977–81),
Shotts Bon Accord
JOINED
Motherwell Bridge Works
(youth), 1960
LFC DEBUT GAME/GOAL
14 September 1964 /
14 September 1964
CONTRACT EXPIRY
9 March 1972

Season	League App	League Goals	FA Cup App	FA Cup Goals	League Cup App	League Cup Goals	Europe App	Europe Goals	Other App	Other Goals	Total App	Total Goals
1964/65	14	4	0	0	-	-	1	1	0	0	15	5
1965/66	1	0	0	0	-	-	0	0	0	0	1	0
1966/67	3	1	0	0	-	-	2	0	0	0	5	1
1967/68	3 (2)	1	0 (1)	0	0	0	0	0	-	-	3 (3)	1
1968/69	11 (2)	5	0 (1)	0	1	0	1	0	-	-	13 (3)	5
1969/70	42	13	6	4	2	1	4	3	-	-	54	21
1970/71	13 (1)	5	0	0	2	0	2 (2)	1	-	-	17 (3)	6
1971/72	10 (1)	2	1 (1)	0	2 (1)	1	3	0	1	0	17 (3)	3
Total	**97 (6)**	**31**	**7 (3)**	**4**	**7 (1)**	**2**	**13 (2)**	**5**	**1**	**0**	**125 (12)**	**42**

Gray, Jimmy

JIMMY GRAY played for Transvaal in South Africa for five years before joining Liverpool in 1926.

The fearless Scottish left-back made just one appearance for Liverpool's first team in the third league fixture of the 1928/29 season when a late goal by Dick Edmed was not enough to prevent the Reds going down 2-1 at home to Sheffield United.

GRAY is remembered as one of Exeter's best ever players, part of the side that finished runners-up in the Third Division South in 1932/33. He played 221 games for Exeter from 1930 to 1936 and was granted a testimonial match on 1 May 1935, when Liverpool faced Exeter.

FACTFILE

BORN
Glasgow, Scotland,
16 September 1900
DIED
10 May 1978
POSITION
Left-back
OTHER CLUBS
Transvaal (1921–26),
Exeter City (1930–36)
SIGNED FROM
Transvaal, 1926
LFC DEBUT
5 September 1928
CONTRACT EXPIRY
January 1930

Grayer, Frank

FRANK GRAYER was the last of the 27 men Liverpool used during the 1913/14 league season.

He was picked as a replacement for regular right-back Ephraim Longworth for match 36 of a 38-game season at home to Manchester United on 15 April 1914. United won the game 2-1 and it was Grayer's only selection for Liverpool's first team. He was so badly wounded during the war at Ypres that he never played football again.

FRANK GRAYER
[LIVERPOOL]

FACTFILE

BORN
Southampton,
13 February 1890
DIED
21 January 1961
POSITION
Right-back
OTHER CLUBS
St Mary's Athletic,
Southampton (1908–12)
SIGNED FROM
Southampton, £100,
July 1912
LFC DEBUT
15 April 1914
CONTRACT EXPIRY
1915

Season	League App	League Goals	FA Cup App	FA Cup Goals	Total App	Total Goals
1928/29	1	0	0	0	1	0
Total	**1**	**0**	**0**	**0**	**1**	**0**

Season	League App	League Goals	FA Cup App	FA Cup Goals	Total App	Total Goals
1913/14	1	0	0	0	1	0
Total	**1**	**0**	**0**	**0**	**1**	**0**

Green, Thomas

THOMAS GREEN made seven league appearances for Liverpool during 1901/02 and 1902/03.

His only goal for the club was scored in the second minute of his final match, away to Blackburn Rovers on 3 January 1903. Despite his early strike, Liverpool went down 3-1.

Green was a success at Stockport County where he scored 16 goals in 23 appearances in the 1904/05 season in the Midland League and made 61 appearances and scored 12 goals from 1907 to 1909 in the Second Division.

FACTFILE

BORN
Rock Ferry, 25 November 1883
POSITION
Forward
OTHER CLUBS
Tranmere Rovers,
New Brighton Tower,
Swindon Town (1903–04),
Stockport County (1904–05),
Middlesbrough (1905–06),
Queens Park Rangers
(1906–07),
Stockport County (1907–09),
Exeter City (1909–10),
St Helens Town,
Rossendale United
SIGNED FROM
New Brighton Tower,
4 September 1901
LFC DEBUT GAME/GOAL
1 February 1902 /
3 January 1903
CONTRACT EXPIRY
April 1903

Season	League		FA Cup		Total	
	App	Goals	App	Goals	App	Goals
1901/02	4	0	0	0	4	0
1902/03	3	1	0	0	3	1
Total	**7**	**1**	**0**	**0**	**7**	**1**

Griffin, Michael

MICHAEL GRIFFIN only made four appearances for the club. His debut saw a convincing 4-1 home win over Woolwich Arsenal on 15 February 1908 and his fourth and final league appearance almost exactly a year later saw the same scoreline again at home, this time against Leicester City.

GRIFFIN played 34 games for Palace in the Southern League's first division, then joined non-league Hartlepools United before returning to league football with Barnsley in the Second Division, where he made 69 appearances and scored seven goals.

FACTFILE

BORN
Middlesbrough, 1886
POSITION
Left-winger
OTHER CLUBS
Darlington St Augustine's
(1904–06),
Crystal Palace (1909–10),
Hartlepools United (1910–12),
Barnsley (1912–15)
SIGNED FROM
Darlington St Augustine's,
1906
LFC DEBUT
15 February 1908
CONTRACT EXPIRY
May 1909

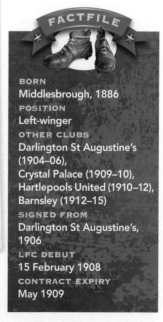

Season	League		FA Cup		Total	
	App	Goals	App	Goals	App	Goals
1907/08	3	0	0	0	3	0
1908/09	1	0	0	0	1	0
Total	**4**	**0**	**0**	**0**	**4**	**0**

Griffiths, Harry

THE ONLY TIME Harry Griffiths figured in the 1905/06 season was as replacement for regular right-back Alf West at Sheffield Wednesday on 14 October, the only one of the 38 First Division fixtures that West missed that season.

Griffiths was called on four times in 1906/07, this time as a left-back, and made his sixth and final appearance for the first team in a 3-0 defeat at Preston on

21 March 1908. He later appeared with former Liverpool players Alex Raisbeck and Maurice Parry at Partick Thistle in Scotland.

Season	League		FA Cup		Other		Total	
	App	Goals	App	Goals	App	Goals	App	Goals
1905/06	1	0	0	0	0	0	1	0
1906/07	4	0	0	0	-	-	4	0
1907/08	1	0	0	0	-	-	1	0
Total	**6**	**0**	**0**	**0**	**0**	**0**	**6**	**0**

FACTFILE

BORN
Middlesbrough,
1 February 1886
POSITION
Right/left full-back
OTHER CLUBS
Wednesbury Old Athletic,
Chesterfield (1908–09),
Partick Thistle (1909–12)
SIGNED FROM
Wednesbury Old Athletic,
17 September 1905
LFC DEBUT
14 October 1905
CONTRACT EXPIRY
June 1908

Grobbelaar, Bruce

BRUCE GROBBELAAR was an athletic goalkeeper who kept virtually unstoppable shots at bay and is remembered as one of the greatest number ones in Liverpool's history. After earning plaudits in South Africa the 20-year-old was given a trial in the summer of 1978 at Ron Atkinson's West Bromwich Albion.

He couldn't get a work permit and was due to return back home five months later when he heard that Tony Waiters, Vancouver Whitecaps' manager, was holding trials in Derby. Grobbelaar impressed and in November 1978, having travelled through three continents in four days and played in two trial games in as many days, he signed a one-year contract with the Canadian side, initially as a reserve keeper to former West Ham star Phil Parkes. Unable to oust him from his starting place, Grobbelaar was loaned to the bottom club of the Fourth Division, Crewe Alexandra, making his league debut at Christmas 1979 and featuring regularly for the Railwaymen until the spring, saying his goodbyes by scoring from the penalty spot in his last ever game! With Parkes

gone, Grobbelaar was finally a regular for the Whitecaps in the 1980/81 season, attracting a host of admirers from England, most notably Bob Paisley. Grobbelaar was playing in the Fourth Division for Crewe Alexandra at Doncaster in April 1980 when Paisley scouted him.

'BEFORE THE GAME, HE HAD THREE OF HIS TEAM-MATES LINED UP ON THE EDGE OF THE PENALTY AREA FIRING IN SHOTS AT HIM. BRUCE WAS DANCING ABOUT LIKE A CARTOON CHARACTER, STOPPING EVERY ATTEMPT'

BOB PAISLEY

'I will never forget going to see Bruce Grobbelaar play for the first time,' Paisley said in *Bob Paisley's personal view of the First Team Squad of 1986-87*. 'Before the game, he had three of his team-mates lined up on the edge of the penalty area firing in shots at him. Bruce was dancing about like a cartoon character, stopping every attempt. I turned to Tom Saunders, who was sitting next to me and said, "We can go, I've seen enough." Saunders and Paisley saw him once more in Canada before he became the understudy to Ray Clemence. Grobbelaar was not put off by Clemence's reputation. 'Bruce walked into Anfield and told the world he was after Ray's jersey. And he said it so Ray could hear!' Paisley said.

CLEMENCE left Liverpool for Tottenham five months after Grobbelaar's arrival and two weeks before the start of the 1981/82 season. The Zimbabwean was thrown in at the deep end, having only featured in three reserve games for Liverpool. Grobbelaar made some errors along the way, but grew slowly into his role as Liverpool's custodian. Grobbelaar remembers it as a baptism of fire. 'One old man wrote to me regularly. He said that he had been watching top-class football for 32 years and if Tommy Smith had still been captain he would have already broken my legs three times. That was one of the more pleasant letters. I also began to hear the obscenities yelled from certain sections of the crowd and I took them to heart. It hurt that they were from our own supporters.' It speaks volumes for Grobbelaar's talent that he kept his place in goal from his Liverpool debut on 29 August 1981 to 16 August 1986, playing 310 consecutive games in the most successful team in England. With half of Grobbelaar's debut season gone, Paisley took the newcomer aside for a serious talk. 'We ended up at Boxing Day 13th in the league, 13 points behind the leaders,' Grobbelaar said. 'That Boxing Day we lost 3-1 to Manchester City and Bob Paisley pulled me into the bath area in the dressing room and he just said to me: "How do you think your first six months have gone?" I said: "It could have been better." And he said: "Yes, you're right. If you don't stop all these antics you'll find yourself playing for Crewe again." And he walked out. It dawned on me I couldn't do all these things I used to do; sit on the crossbar and walking around the pitch on my hands and mess about. He made me realise my mistakes and made sure I put them right.'

Liverpool fans can no doubt easily recollect their favourite Grobbelaar moment, whether it was a moment of madness, showboating or a save that displayed his breathtaking ability. Grobbelaar was a man for the big occasion, as proved in the 1986 FA Cup final when Alan Hansen's clearance was headed straight at goal with him hopelessly out of position. 'I got back as quick as I could and made a real kangaroo leap to reach the ball. It's something Craig Johnston taught me. If I'd tried to catch the ball I would have gone into the net with it,' Grobbelaar said. Johnston certainly appreciated that moment. 'Brucie was a great goalkeeper and that save was out of this world,' the Australian said. An all-time favourite among the Reds faithful is no doubt when Grobbelaar's antics on the goal-line in the penalty shootout of the European Cup final in 1984 put off the most experienced of players. 'Joe Fagan had his arm around me when I was going to the goal and said: "Listen, myself and the coaches, the chairman and the directors, your fellow colleagues and the fans are not going to blame you if you can't stop a ball from 12 yards,"' Grobbelaar revealed. 'That gave me the great lift, there was great weight off my shoulders. As I walked away he said: "Try to put them off." So that's what I did. There were two players that I tried to put off and they were both Italian internationals, Bruno Conti and Graziani.'

UNLESS HE WAS out injured or suffering from meningitis, as in the 1988/89 season, Grobbelaar was a regular fixture in Liverpool's goal until England's Under-21 goalkeeper David James took his place in 1992/93. Grobbelaar went out on loan to Stoke in the last couple of months of the season but reclaimed his place at the start of the following campaign. James made the number one jersey his own from February 1994 onwards and Grobbelaar left for Southampton before the start of the

1994/95 season. He moved to Plymouth Argyle in League Two, where Neil Warnock was in charge, and later joined Warnock at Oldham and Bury, continuing to play league football into his forties.

After being released by Southampton at the end of the 1995/96 season his life was overshadowed by allegations of match fixing. Grobbelaar was alleged to have been paid £40,000 by a Far East betting syndicate for throwing a match against Newcastle in November 1993, which Liverpool lost to an Andy Cole hat-trick, and was also accused of trying to influence games after he moved to Southampton in 1994. Among the evidence was a secret video recording of a hotel room meeting between Grobbelaar and his former business partner, Christopher Vincent. Arsenal great and television soccer expert Bob Wilson was brought in to review tapes of the Newcastle game as well as Liverpool v. Manchester United in January 1994, Norwich v. Liverpool in February 1994, plus two Southampton games. At Grobbelaar's trial Wilson told the jury he had seen no evidence of match fixing, as in the Newcastle game Grobbelaar had virtually no chance with the three goals and had made three excellent saves. In the Manchester United game, which resulted in a 3-3 draw, Grobbelaar had made two saves that were of the highest order at any level in the world, which had kept his side in the game. He could not have saved the two goals scored against him by Norwich and made a 'truly outstanding' save. Grobbelaar was found not guilty on all counts. In July 1999 Grobbelaar was awarded £85,000 after suing *The Sun* for libel over match fixing allegations. In January 2001 Grobbelaar was stripped of the libel award and branded corrupt in the Appeal Court. In October 2002 the House of Lords reinstated Grobbelaar's

LIVERPOOL 1983
LEAGUE CUP WINNERS
Back row - **Lawrenson,**
Fairclough, Hansen,
Whelan, Rush, Grobbelaar,
Paisley (Manager)
Front - **Johnston, Dalglish,**
Neal, Souness, Lee, Kennedy

libel victory on a technicality, but said he had 'undermined the integrity of the game' and reduced the award to £1.

GROBBELAAR'S clownish antics made him lovable but some felt that he was too light-hearted on the field, leading to him occasionally making incredible mistakes. In fact, Grobbelaar took his craft seriously and was furious

with himself if he made an error. He had acquired a different perspective on life when he was fighting in the jungles of Africa. 'I never did get used to killing other men, even if they were hell bent on doing me as much harm as possible,' Grobbelaar revealed about his two years' national service in his autobiography *More Than Somewhat*.

I still dream about another encounter which happened shortly before the end of my first year while we were supporting a Dad's Army unit (made of 35–55-year-old reservists) when we were fed the information that a dozen terrorists were close at hand. We selected the killing ground and laid our claymore mines in the rocks and then set our two sticks of four in ambush positions. The mines killed the first three and the rest we caught in lethal crossfire. There was just enough moon for me to see the white teeth bared in horrific screams that still ring in my ears when I have those awful dreams. Nightmares really are made of that sort of stuff as my wife and a few footballer roommates will testify having seen me wander around in the middle of the night before a big game. If war teaches you anything it is an appreciation of being alive and I will never apologise for laughing at life and enjoying my football.

PAISLEY was in no doubt that Liverpool found a worthy successor to Ray Clemence. 'Bruce is a natural between the posts. When you consider his reflexes, his agility and his co-ordination, you wouldn't swap him for any keeper you care to name past or present,' Paisley noted when assessing Liverpool's squad in the 1986/87 season in Clive Tyldesley's book. 'Liverpool defenders have always had a greater appreciation of him than anybody else. Brucie's record with Liverpool speaks for itself, and his handling skills, his athleticism, his alert distribution and quickness off his line have all become shining examples that future Anfield goalkeepers will be hearing plenty about.'

FACTFILE

BORN
Durban, South Africa,
6 October 1957
POSITION
Goalkeeper
OTHER CLUBS
Durban City,
Vancouver Whitecaps
(1978–81),
Crewe Alexandra (loan,
1979–80),
Stoke City (loan, 1993),
Southampton (1994–96),
Plymouth Argyle (1996–97),
Oxford United (1997),
Sheffield Wednesday (1997),
Oldham Athletic (1997–98),
Chesham United (1998),
Bury (1998),
Lincoln City (1998),
Northwich Victoria (1999),
Hellenic (2001),
Glasshoughton Welfare (2007)
SIGNED FROM
Vancouver Whitecaps,
£250,000, 17 March 1981
INTERNATIONAL CAPS
32 Zimbabwe caps (plus
1 cap for Rhodesia), 1980–98
LFC DEBUT
29 August 1981
CONTRACT EXPIRY
11 August 1994
HONOURS
League Championship
1981/82, 1982/83, 1983/84,
1985/86, 1987/88, 1989/90;
FA Cup 1986, 1989, 1992;
League Cup
1982, 1983, 1984;
European Cup 1984

Season	League		FA Cup		League Cup		Europe		Other		Total	
	App	Goals	App	Goals	App	Goals	App	Goals	App	Goals	App	Goals
1981/82	42	0	3	0	10	0	6	0	1	0	62	0
1982/83	42	0	3	0	8	0	6	0	1	0	60	0
1983/84	42	0	2	0	13	0	9	0	1	0	67	0
1984/85	42	0	7	0	3	0	10	0	2	0	64	0
1985/86	42	0	8	0	7	0	-	-	6	0	63	0
1986/87	31	0	3	0	9	0	-	-	2	0	45	0
1987/88	38	0	5	0	3	0	-	-	-	-	46	0
1988/89	21	0	5	0	0	0	-	-	2	0	28	0
1989/90	38	0	8	0	3	0	-	-	1	0	50	0
1990/91	31	0	7	0	3	0	-	-	1	0	42	0
1991/92	37	0	9	0	4	0	5	0	-	-	55	0
1992/93	5	0	2	0	2	0	2	0	1	0	10	0
1993/94	29	0	2	0	5	0	-	-	-	-	36	0
Total	**440**	**0**	**62**	**0**	**70**	**0**	**38**	**0**	**18**	**0**	**628**	**0**

Gunson,
Gordon

AFTER impressing with 11 goals in 18 league games for First Division Sunderland in the 1929/30 season, Liverpool invested in this flying winger at the start of the 1930s.

FACTFILE

BORN
Chester, 1 July 1904
DIED
8 September 1991
POSITION
Right/left-winger
OTHER CLUBS
Nelson (1923–26),
Wrexham (1926–29),
Sunderland (1929–30),
Swindon Town (1934–35),
Wrexham (1935–36),
Bangor City (1936)
SIGNED FROM
Sunderland, 12 March 1930
LFC DEBUT GAME/GOAL
15 March 1930 / 22 March 1930
CONTRACT EXPIRY
7 June 1934

LIVERPOOL 1931-1932

He was probably easy to spot on the field of play as he was somewhat 'Shrek-like' in appearance. Gunson signed in March 1930 and made ten consecutive appearances until the end of the season, rotating between the right and left wing, again deputising for regulars Fred Hopkin and Harold Barton the following season. With Hopkin gone in the 1931/32 season Gunson was one of only two ever-presents in the league and scored 17 times in those 42 games. His run of successive appearances increased to 61 by early November

1932, but he then lost his place briefly to Harold Taylor before reclaiming it for another shorter run. Gunson struggled in his post-Liverpool career because of a troublesome knee injury he had picked up while at Anfield, and he retired in 1936 aged 32.

	League		FA Cup		Total	
Season	App	Goals	App	Goals	App	Goals
1929/30	10	1	0	0	10	1
1930/31	8	1	1	0	9	1
1931/32	42	17	4	2	46	19
1932/33	21	5	1	0	22	5
Total	**81**	**24**	**6**	**2**	**87**	**26**

Guthrie,
Danny

DANNY GUTHRIE was released by Manchester United at the tender age of 15 and joined the Liverpool youth set up. He made steady progress at Liverpool and finally was rewarded by a first-team debut against Reading in the League Cup in October 2006.

He impressed as a good passer of the ball and a very attack-minded player, but five of his seven appearances for Liverpool were as a substitute. After spending March to May 2007 with Southampton in the Championship, Guthrie was loaned to Bolton in the 2007/08 season and showed he was Premier League class in his

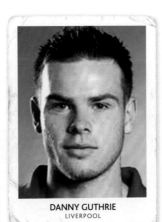

DANNY GUTHRIE
LIVERPOOL

25 appearances, convincing Newcastle to buy him in the summer of 2008 for £2.25million. Guthrie made 24 Premier League appearances, scoring twice,

as Newcastle were relegated to the Championship at the end of the 2008/09 season. He was, however, more prominent as the Geordies made an immediate return to the top division as champions. Guthrie missed the start of 2010/11 because of a knee injury, but was fit enough for a return in the middle of October.

However, he only made 14 league appearances by the end of the season and after being on the fringes of the team again he was released by the Magpies at the end of the 2011/12 season. Still only 25 years old, he signed for Premier League newcomers Reading.

FACTFILE

BORN
Shrewsbury, 18 April 1987
POSITION
Midfielder
OTHER CLUBS
Southampton (loan, 2007),
Bolton Wanderers (loan, 2007–08),
Newcastle United (2008–12),
Reading (2012–)
JOINED
2002; signed professional 8 December 2004
LFC DEBUT
25 October 2006
CONTRACT EXPIRY
14 July 2008

	League		FA Cup		League Cup		Europe		Other		Total	
Season	App	Goals	App	Goals	App	Goals	App	Goals	App	Goals	App	Goals
2006/07	0 (3)	0	0	0	1 (2)	0	1	0	0	0	2 (5)	0
Total	**0 (3)**	**0**	**0**	**0**	**1 (2)**	**0**	**1**	**0**	**0**	**0**	**2 (5)**	**0**

Hafekost,
Charlie

**CHARLIE HAFEKOST moved
to Liverpool following his
performance against the Reds
in the second round of the
FA Cup at Anfield where his
club, Gillingham, lost 2-0 on
31 January 1914.**

The forward came highly
recommended by Sam Gilligan,
Gillingham's manager, who
featured for Liverpool from 1910 to
1913. Hafekost made just a single
appearance for Liverpool's first
team when he was selected as a
makeshift right-half in place of Tom
Fairfoul for a home First Division
fixture with Middlesbrough on
14 November 1914.

FACTFILE

BORN
Sunderland, 22 March 1890
POSITION
Right-half
OTHER CLUBS
Sunderland Royal Rovers,
Gillingham (1912–14);
Tranmere Rovers
(wartime guest),
Darlington Forge Albion,
Hartlepools United (1919–20)
SIGNED FROM
Gillingham, May 1914
LFC DEBUT
14 November 1914
CONTRACT EXPIRY
September 1915

Season	League		FA Cup		Total	
	App	Goals	App	Goals	App	Goals
1914/15	1	0	0	0	1	0
Total	**1**	**0**	**0**	**0**	**1**	**0**

*The Liverpool team with manager
Don Welsh in New York in on 22 May 1953*

Haigh,
Jack

**JACK HAIGH was a
Yorkshireman who signed for
Liverpool in October 1949 when
he was 21 years old, having only
been on the books of Midland
League side Gainsborough
Trinity for three months.**

Haigh made a Boxing Day debut
in 1950 as an inside-right when
Blackpool visited Anfield for a
First Division fixture. He scored in
his next match, a 2-1 victory at
Derby County, playing alongside
luminaries such as Billy Liddell,
Jack Balmer and Albert Stubbins.
Following a 2-0 defeat to Everton
he lost his place but returned two
months later to score twice in five
games. Don Welsh had now taken
over from George Kay and
evidently the new boss and Haigh
didn't see eye to eye. Haigh made
three further appearances towards
the end of the 1951/52 season
without adding to his goals total
and was transferred to Scunthorpe
in the Third Division North before
the start of the following season.

HAIGH is remembered as one
of Scunthorpe's finest players,
playing 364 games and scoring
72 goals from 1952 to 1960.
He was nicknamed the 'Iron Man'
after a brave performance in the
3-1 FA Cup fourth round win over

Newcastle United on 25 January
1958. He was knocked out during
the match as well as being injured
twice more, but refused to give in
and even managed to score a goal.

FACTFILE

BORN
Rotherham,
10 September 1928
DIED
17 September 2007
POSITION
Inside-right/left forward
OTHER CLUBS
Rawmarsh Welfare,
Gainsborough Trinity (1949),
Scunthorpe United (1952–60),
Doncaster Rovers (1960–62),
Buxton (1962–65)
SIGNED FROM
Gainsborough Trinity,
October 1949
LFC DEBUT GAME/GOAL
26 December 1950 /
13 January 1951
CONTRACT EXPIRY
August 1952

Season	League		FA Cup		Total	
	App	Goals	App	Goals	App	Goals
1950/51	8	3	0	0	8	3
1951/52	3	0	0	0	3	0
Total	**11**	**3**	**0**	**0**	**11**	**3**

Hall, Brian

ALL BRIAN HALL wanted in his teens was to go to Liverpool, but not to play football. He wanted to study maths at the university, and graduated three years later. Hall was an industrious player who always gave his all for Liverpool. Small in stature, but clever and a very efficient footballer, he became a vital part of the team Shankly rebuilt in the early 1970s. After three years of reserve football and studies Hall made two brief appearances as a substitute towards the end of the 1968/69 season.

Ian Callaghan's injury in September 1970 gave him his breakthrough. Hall performed so well in Callaghan's absence on the right wing that when Cally returned, Shankly moved him into a central midfield role to accommodate them both. Hall's

most memorable moment came in the 1970/71 season when he scored the dramatic winner in the FA Cup semi-final against Everton at Old Trafford which took Liverpool to Wembley for the first time since 1965. It was also his first-ever goal for Liverpool. Hall had to settle for a runners-up medal on that occasion but he was a member of the side that lifted the trophy three years later against Newcastle to add to the League Championship and UEFA Cup winners' medal he had from the previous season. Hall played a big part in the FA Cup fortunes of Liverpool in 1974. Liverpool and Leicester City drew 0-0 at Old Trafford in the semi-final and the replay was set at Villa Park. Hall scored Liverpool's first goal soon after the interval. He had just finished celebrating when Glover equalised, but Kevin Keegan and John Toshack guaranteed a 3-1 victory and Newcastle were an easy prey in the final.

HALL got on well with Shankly most of the time but did get the hump when Liverpool reached the final of the UEFA Cup in 1973 and faced German side Borussia Mönchengladbach in a two-legged affair, the first being at Anfield. The first match only lasted 30 minutes because the pitch was waterlogged and the game was rescheduled for the following night. Shankly had spotted a weakness in the air in the German back line and for the rematch brought in the aerial supremacy of John Toshack at the expense of Hall's attacking midfield play. 'My reaction was

childish,' Hall told *LFChistory.net*. 'I wasn't really in the best frame of mind to be on the subs bench. Of course we won the match 3-0 and it was viewed as a masterstroke by Shanks but I was still unhappy. It rumbled on to the end of the season where it finally came to a head when I was dropped for the final game against Leicester City. We only needed a draw for the title and Shanks decided to blood a young Phil Thompson at my expense. That incident hit me far harder than the UEFA Cup final one had done.'

Hall played in all but seven of the league matches in 1974/75 but his midfield position was taken over by Jimmy Case before the halfway stage of the following season. He moved on to Plymouth Argyle in the summer of 1976 before returning to the north west and finishing his league career at Burnley. He later felt he had made a 'big mistake' leaving Liverpool

FACTFILE

BORN
Glasgow, Scotland,
22 November 1946
POSITION
Midfielder
OTHER CLUBS
Plymouth Argyle (1976–77),
Burnley (1977–80),
Northwich Victoria (1980–85)
JOINED
1966;
signed professional July 1968
LFC DEBUT GAME/GOAL
7 April 1969 / 27 March 1971
CONTRACT EXPIRY
July 1976

so soon and should have fought harder to reclaim his place. Hall took up teaching for a while but returned to Anfield in 1991 as Public Relations Manager, a post he held until 2011 when he had to retire due to health reasons. A special presentation was made to Hall before Liverpool's Premier League match against Fulham at Anfield on 1 May 2012 to officially mark his retirement.

Hall of Fame

LIVERPOOL FC's official Hall of Fame was first unveiled in 2002 when Ian Callaghan, Phil Thompson, Brian Hall and Alan Hansen discussed the merits of each candidate and sought opinions from supporters groups before selecting two players from each decade. Kenny Dalglish joined this elite group of experts in 2010 when two members were added to the Hall of Fame to represent 2000-2010.

The inductees are:

1892-1900	**Harry Bradshaw**
1892-1900	**Matt McQueen**
1900-1910	**Alex Raisbeck**
1900-1910	**Jack Cox**
1910-1920	**Ephraim Longworth**
1910-1920	**Arthur Goddard**
1920-1930	**Elisha Scott**
1920-1930	**Donald Mackinlay**
1930-1940	**Gordon Hodgson**
1930-1940	**Jimmy McDougall**
1940-1950	**Albert Stubbins**
1940-1950	**Jack Balmer**
1950-1960	**Billy Liddell**
1950-1960	**Alan A'Court**
1960-1970	**Ron Yeats**
1960-1970	**Roger Hunt**
1970-1980	**Ray Clemence**
1970-1980	**Ian Callaghan**
1980-1990	**Kenny Dalglish**
1980-1990	**Alan Hansen**
1990-2000	**Ian Rush**
1990-2000	**John Barnes**
2000-2010	**Steven Gerrard**
2000-2010	**Jamie Carragher**

Season	League App	League Goals	FA Cup App	FA Cup Goals	League Cup App	League Cup Goals	Europe App	Europe Goals	Other App	Other Goals	Total App	Total Goals
1968/69	0 (2)	0	0	0	0	0	0	0	-	-	0 (2)	0
1969/70	0 (1)	0	0	0	0	0	0	0	-	-	0 (1)	0
1970/71	32 (3)	1	7	1	3	0	8	0	-	-	50 (3)	2
1971/72	24 (2)	1	1	0	2	1	3	0	1	0	31 (2)	2
1972/73	17 (4)	2	0	0	1 (1)	0	4 (4)	1	-	-	22 (9)	3
1973/74	20 (2)	4	7 (1)	2	1	0	2 (1)	1	-	-	30 (4)	7
1974/75	35	5	2	0	3	0	4	0	1	0	45	5
1975/76	12 (1)	2	0 (1)	0	2	0	6 (3)	0	-	-	20 (5)	2
Total	**140 (15)**	**15**	**17 (2)**	**3**	**12 (1)**	**1**	**27 (8)**	**2**	**2**	**0**	**198 (26)**	**21**

Hamann,
Didi

**DIETMAR 'DIDI' HAMANN
grew up in Bavaria where
Bayern snapped him up from
Wacker Munich when he was
16 years old. He enjoyed
tremendous success with Bayern,
winning two Bundesliga titles,
the UEFA Cup, the German
Cup and the German League
Cup. He played 106 Bundesliga
games, scoring six goals for
Bayern before opting to test
himself in English football.**

After starring for Germany
in the 1998 World Cup he was
transferred to Newcastle United
for £5.5million. Hamann had
a single season at Newcastle,
playing 31 league and cup
matches and scoring five goals
and losing an FA Cup final against
Manchester United. Hamann's
two matches against his future
employers were a disaster. At St
James' Park a bone-crunching
tackle from Jamie Carragher
ensured that Hamann was six
weeks on the sidelines with
damaged medial ligaments and
the German was sent off at
Anfield. A goal up at the time of
his dismissal, Newcastle increased
their lead before Liverpool hit
back with four second-half goals
of their own.

HAMANN was one of several
new signings unveiled by Gérard
Houllier during the summer of
1999. He made his league debut

for the Reds at Sheffield Wednesday on the opening day of the
1999/2000 season, as did Titi Camara, Sami Hyypia, Vladimir Smicer,
Sander Westerveld and Erik Meijer. The German's debut lasted only
24 minutes, as he ruptured his ankle ligaments. Fortunately he healed
quickly, was back in seven weeks and represented Liverpool in another
29 matches by the end of the season.

Didi missed very few matches over the next three seasons as he cemented
his place in the team as a defensive midfielder with an occasional eye
for a beautiful goal. He could always be relied upon, although Jamie
Carragher, who was one of his many friends at the club, nominated him
as the worst trainer. In 2000/01 Hamann won his first winners' medals
in English football by appearing in all three of Liverpool's successful
cup finals. A second League Cup winners' medal would follow in 2003,
a medal he offered to one of the younger players who had appeared in
earlier rounds. Didi explained: 'Valuing everyone who had made an effort
for us was more important to me than personal gratification.'

It was soon apparent that new manager Rafa Benítez saw the tall German
as an equally important member of the squad as Houllier had. Hamann
played in 43 of Liverpool's 60 competitive matches in 2004/05 but
probably his most important contribution came in the final game of
the season, that astonishing Champions League final in Istanbul. His
half-time substitution for Steve Finnan was one of the catalysts for
Liverpool's truly amazing comeback. He also proved typically cool when
scoring a penalty in the shootout, later discovering that he actually took
that kick with a fractured foot! A year later he would again successfully
cope with the same pressure when the FA Cup final against West Ham

in Cardiff was settled in the same
way. But 2005/06 was a season
in which Hamann's influence
was waning as Momo Sissoko's
influence grew. At the age of
32 he was told by Benítez that he
was surplus to requirements and
he signed a contract with Bolton
Wanderers in the summer of 2006.
He changed his mind but it was
too late to cancel his deal and in
one of the most bizarre transfers
ever he moved from Bolton to
Manchester City 24 hours later.
Hamann explained: 'I had the
offer from Bolton for a few weeks
and thought it was the right thing
to do. But after going on holiday
I felt it wasn't the right decision.
It is something I have got to live
with and they allowed me to speak
to other clubs. As soon as I heard
Man City was interested I made
my mind up pretty quickly.'

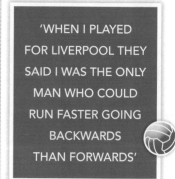

'WHEN I PLAYED
FOR LIVERPOOL THEY
SAID I WAS THE ONLY
MAN WHO COULD
RUN FASTER GOING
BACKWARDS
THAN FORWARDS'

HAMANN had three seasons
at Eastlands, during which he
continued to show that his ability
to perform at a high level was
undiminished. Fifty-four Premier
League and 17 cup appearances
for City took his combined club
total in Germany and England
past the 500 mark. As he revealed
in his autobiography *The Didi
Man: My Love Affair with
Liverpool* he turned to drink and
gambling as his wife moved with
their two daughters to Germany
while he was a City player. "One
night, the Aussies were playing
South Africa in a Test match.
Australia collapsed for 237. It is
a score I remember well. It cost
me £288,400. The next day when
I looked at the mess that was me

Season	League		FA Cup		League Cup		Europe		Other		Total	
	App	Goals	App	Goals	App	Goals	App	Goals	App	Goals	App	Goals
1999/2000	27 (1)	1	2	0	0	0	-	-	-	-	29 (1)	1
2000/01	26 (4)	2	5	1	2 (3)	0	13	0	-	-	46 (7)	3
2001/02	31	1	2	0	1	0	13	0	1	0	48	1
2002/03	29 (1)	2	1	0	1	0	7 (2)	0	1	0	39 (3)	2
2003/04	25	2	4	0	0 (1)	0	5	1	-	-	34 (1)	3
2004/05	23 (7)	0	0	0	3	0	8 (2)	1	-	-	34 (9)	1
2005/06	13 (4)	0	1 (1)	0	1	0	8 (3)	0	0 (1)	0	23 (9)	0
Total	**174 (17)**	**8**	**15 (1)**	**1**	**8 (4)**	**0**	**54 (7)**	**2**	**2 (1)**	**0**	**253 (30)**	**11**

in the mirror I said, "Didi, things have got to change."' After a year out of the game when he got his life back on track, Hamann signed a one-year deal on 20 May 2010 to become player-coach with the Milton Keynes Dons in League One. On 3 February 2011 the German left the Dons to join Leicester City as a first-team coach under the management of

Sven-Göran Eriksson. Five months later Hamann became manager of Stockport County, where he faced a massive task trying to lead the club immediately back into the Football League. Unfortunately, Stockport made a very poor start to the 2011/12 Conference season and with the team having won just three of its opening 19 league fixtures, Hamann resigned from his post on 7 November 2011.

Didi was immensely popular among the Liverpool players and was considered an adopted Scouser after his seven years at the club. Steven Gerrard had plenty of praise for his midfield partnership with Hamann. 'He allowed me to go forward, score and set up goals, and he did all my

defensive work and tackling for me,' Stevie enthused. 'At the time we had him, he was in his prime and he was up there with the best holding midfielders in the world. There's no Liverpool fan, player or coach at Anfield who wouldn't love him to be 26 or 27 now and still doing his stuff because that's how good he was.'

Hancock,
Ted

E. HANCOCK

A FORWARD who played in the last nine league matches of the 1931/32 First Division campaign and made one more appearance the following season, Ted Hancock made his debut on 28 March 1932 when Huddersfield Town won 3-0 at Anfield and he made his final appearance in the 2-1 defeat to Middlesbrough at Anfield on 1 February 1933.

In between those two defeats, Hancock had scored twice, an 88th-minute winner against Chelsea at Anfield on 6 April and the first goal in a 2-1 victory over Arsenal, also at Anfield, three days later. Hancock had a successful career at Burnley under the guidance of former Red Tom Bromilow from 1932 to 1936, playing 109 Second Division games and scoring 20 goals.

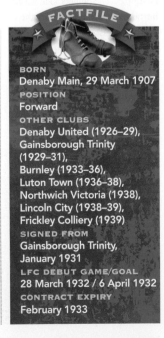

Season	League		FA Cup		Total	
	App	Goals	App	Goals	App	Goals
1931/32	9	2	0	0	9	2
1932/33	1	0	0	0	1	0
Total	**10**	**2**	**0**	**0**	**10**	**2**

Hannah,
Andrew

ANDREW HANNAH was captain of the tremendous Renton team from a small town of 5,000 inhabitants in West Dunbartonshire in central Scotland. Renton beat Cambuslang 6-1 in the Scottish Cup final in 1888, having scored 42 goals against seven conceded in the previous seven rounds!

Cup winners Renton played English FA Cup holders West Bromwich Albion in a game dubbed by the press no less as the 'Championship of the United Kingdom and the World'. Renton were victorious 4-1 and placed a sign on the door of their pavilion at their home ground, Tontine Park, that said, 'Renton FC, Champions of the World'. Renton then proved their superiority over the English by conquering 'the Invincibles' of Preston North End, who had won the Championship in England without losing a single game. *The Evening Telegraph* described Hannah as a 'man to be respected by opponents, for he could break up an attack either by skilful tackling or robust charging'. The penalty kick wasn't introduced in Scotland until the 1891/92 season so a big part of half-back's duties was to protect the goalkeeper, who hardly got any sympathy from the referee. Forwards were allowed to 'go for the goalie' and if a high dropping shot came into the penalty area Hannah forgot about the ball if it was out of his reach and focused on preventing the forwards (by any means possible) from charging his keeper.

WEST BROM were impressed by Hannah and the Scotsman left the amateurs at Renton for the professional football in England in 1888. That move was not kindly looked upon by Scotland's

international selectors and after having made his debut for his country earlier that year he was omitted from future squads. Hannah was homesick in England and returned to Renton after only a few weeks, but went back to England a year later to join Everton, receiving a £100 signing-on fee and £3 a week, no doubt a significant raise for Hannah as the average weekly pay in Renton was around 13 shillings. Hannah was appointed Everton's captain, winning the League Championship in 1891 and being rated as one of the best full-backs in the country. Meanwhile Renton and couple of other clubs had been thrown out of the Scottish League for payments to their players at a time when professionalism was outlawed in Scotland. The payments were hidden under 'Chicken Bree' in their accounts, a diet that the club's players did take nourishment from consisting of port, mixed egg-yolk and egg-white on dry toast, but complemented by a few illegal pounds. When Renton were reinstated to the League in 1891 Hannah left champions Everton for his third spell with the Scottish club.

SCOTTISH SPORT reported on 16 May 1892 that Andrew Hannah was once more going to England, this time to the newly created Liverpool AFC. He received a £150 signing-on fee and was paid £5 a week. The *Birmingham Daily Post* was impressed by Liverpool's capture. 'Hannah will act as captain and his power of developing players is so well known that the Liverpool club are fortunate in having secured the man who did so much towards improving the all-round play of the Everton team.' Right-back Hannah was Liverpool's first captain and undoubtedly one of the club's greatest legends. After Lancashire League success he was one of the eleven men who represented Liverpool in their first Football League fixture on 2 September 1893. He played in 24 of the 28 matches that year and won a Second Division Championship medal, but also experienced relegation a year later when he shared the right-back spot with John Curran, as he hardly featured in the second half of the season due to knee and ankle injuries.

Hannah was a great all-round athlete who won prizes at the prestigious Highland Games. He was also courageous on and off the field, as reported by the *Blackburn Standard* on 25 November 1893. 'On Friday evening Andrew Hannah, captain of the Liverpool Football Club, entered the den of forest-bred lions and lionesses in Wombwell's Royal Menagerie. The daring act was to decide a wager, and Messrs Wombwell, upon Hannah completing his daring enterprise, handed to him the wager deposited with them, and also presented him with a gold medal, value £5.'

> **RIGHT-BACK HANNAH WAS LIVERPOOL'S FIRST CAPTAIN AND UNDOUBTEDLY ONE OF THE CLUB'S GREATEST LEGENDS**

As Liverpool were relegated to the Second Division in 1895 Hannah went back north of the border, finishing his career in the 1896/97 season with Clyde in the First Division. The 32-year-old wasn't as solid as in the 'old days' but his 'reputation still lives green both at Anfield and Goodison Park, Liverpool,' reported the *Dundee Courier*. Hannah had decided to retire but 'money, however, is a very powerful lover in men's lives'. The *Courier* noted that 'he has a lot of adipose [fat] hanging about him. His heading lacks none of its old accuracy, and his long connection with the football ring gives him judgment second to none in the football realm. He looked uncomfortable now and again, but in the hands of the trainer he should even yet be able to give us a sample of his former greatness.'

The Scotsman was a tremendous servant for Liverpool and *Field*

	League		FA Cup		Other		Total	
Season	App	Goals	App	Goals	App	Goals	App	Goals
1892/93	-	-	3	0	22	0	25	0
1893/94	24	1	3	0	1	0	28	1
1894/95	16	0	0	0	0	0	16	0
Total	**40**	**1**	**6**	**0**	**23**	**0**	**69**	**1**

Sport claimed that 'his mature judgement, together with excellent defensive tactics, makes him most invaluable'. His displays were on a number of occasions applauded by newspapers, none more so than when Liverpool faced their biggest challenge to date, a second round FA Cup tie against Preston who still had players that were part of the 'Invincibles' who won the inaugural Football League title without losing a match in 1888/89. Hannah was considered the star performer in Liverpool's famous 3-2 victory on 10 February 1894. 'McOwen was so well shielded by his captain [Hannah] and McLean that he had the occasion to use his hands only once throughout the game. Hannah's display was almost perfection, and that, too, against two of the finest forwards in England (Becton and Cowan). Against the wind it was a treat to see his coolness, now covering the impetuosity of McLean, and anon making virtually a second goalkeeper with his foot and head.'

Hannah, David

'DAVY' HANNAH arrived from the successful Sunderland side that had won the League Championship twice in his four years at the club from 1890 to 1894. Hannah had made a significant contribution by scoring roughly a goal every third game over around 90 appearances.

Although Sunderland were initially unwilling to part with him the club's board wished him well and gave him a marble clock and bronze ornaments as a farewell gift. Hannah was bought in November 1894 to strengthen Liverpool's attacking options as they were on a serious slide down the First Division. He scored in his second game in a 2-2 draw against Everton at Anfield with a 'grand shot' which was so magnificent it 'almost sent the crowd frantic, even the Evertonians applauding the home team for their gallant play'. He put Liverpool 2-0 up just before half-time in the following game against his old club, Sunderland, but the champions-elect showed their class by winning 3-2. Hannah scored six goals in 17 matches but his contribution was not enough to prevent an immediate return to the Second Division. He was called on 11 times the following season as the club won the Second Division Championship for the second time in three years and made a further four appearances during the 1896/97 season, one of which saw him score two goals against

Sunderland. Tom Watson, his old Sunderland boss, was by then in charge of Liverpool. Hannah scored 17 goals in 46 Second Division matches for Arsenal. In 1900 he reflected on the differences between football in the North and South in the *Tamworth Herald* and was 'astonished at the rapid strides of improvement the South has made during the last few years. It is in the forward work that Southern elevens are behind the Northern combinations, the method of passing in the South being so widely different to those in the North.'

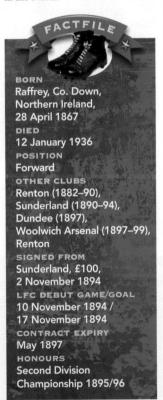

FACTFILE

BORN
Renton, Dunbartonshire, Scotland, 17 September 1864
DIED
29 May 1940
POSITION
Right-back
OTHER CLUBS
Renton (1883–88),
West Bromwich Albion (1888),
Renton (1888–89),
Everton (1889–91),
Renton (1891–92),
Rob Roy (1895–96),
Clyde (1896–97)
SIGNED FROM
Renton, May 1892
INTERNATIONAL CAPS
1 Scotland cap, 1888
LFC DEBUT GAME/GOAL
3 September 1892 /
14 April 1894
CONTRACT EXPIRY
October 1895
HONOURS
Lancashire League 1892/93;
Second Division
Championship 1893/94

FACTFILE

BORN
Raffrey, Co. Down,
Northern Ireland,
28 April 1867
DIED
12 January 1936
POSITION
Forward
OTHER CLUBS
Renton (1882–90),
Sunderland (1890–94),
Dundee (1897),
Woolwich Arsenal (1897–99),
Renton
SIGNED FROM
Sunderland, £100,
2 November 1894
LFC DEBUT GAME/GOAL
10 November 1894 /
17 November 1894
CONTRACT EXPIRY
May 1897
HONOURS
Second Division
Championship 1895/96

Season	League		FA Cup		Other		Total	
	App	Goals	App	Goals	App	Goals	App	Goals
1894/95	17	6	1	0	0	0	18	6
1895/96	11	3	0	0	0	0	11	3
1896/97	3	2	1	1	-	-	4	3
Total	**31**	**11**	**2**	**1**	**0**	**0**	**33**	**12**

Hansen, Alan

'ALAN HANSEN is the defender with the pedigree of an international striker. He is quite simply the most skilful centre-half I have ever seen in the British game. He is a joy to watch. Alan has always been an excellent footballer, a beautifully balanced player who carries the ball with control and grace. He has a very measured, long stride and is much faster than he looks. I can't think more than a couple of players who could beat him over 100 metres. He has both the ability and the patience to launch attacks from deep positions.' Bob Paisley's opinion speaks volumes of this terrific defender who still keeps Geoff Twentyman's letter that says he didn't meet Liverpool's requirements when he went there on trial in 1971.

His lack of physical prowess contributed to him not being seen as a future star at Liverpool. Six years later he was back, an astute £100,000 signing by Paisley in May 1977. He was still only 11½ stone (73kg) when he joined so the club put him on a body-building regime based on Guinness and a 'see-food diet' – whenever he saw food he had to eat it!

Alan Hansen was not just an accomplished footballer. He was good enough to represent his country at junior level in golf, volleyball and squash. Two years after watching a Partick Thistle team that included his brother John beat firm favourites Glasgow Celtic in a Scottish League Cup final at Hampden Park, Alan was playing for Partick himself and would make over a century of league appearances for the Jags, helping them win promotion to the Scottish Premier League in 1976.

Hansen was one of the triumvirate of Scottish players, the other two being Kenny Dalglish and Graeme Souness, signed by Paisley within a 12-month period that would help to ensure that Liverpool's domination of the domestic and European scene in the mid-1970s would continue. An article in *Shoot!* shortly after his arrival said: 'Hansen faces a tough battle for a first-team spot with the established Anfield back-four men. But whoever he replaces, Liverpool fans can look forward with confidence to seeing one of soccer's most talented young men in action. The big occasion brings out the best in Hansen and he says: "I'm really looking forward to life as a Liverpool player and I'm determined not to let them down." It's unlikely he will do so...'

HANSEN made his first-team debut for Liverpool against Derby County at Anfield towards the end of September 1977, prompting journalist Don Evans to note, 'The man of the match, the lad who made his debut for Liverpool and came off a new Spion Kop hero, was the young Scot, Alan Hansen,' giving him a nine out of ten. With the central-defensive pairing of Phil Thompson and Emlyn Hughes already established, Hansen's opportunities were limited during his first full season on Merseyside. But he still appeared in nearly half of all

league matches as well as a number of cup ties. If disappointed to miss out on the League Cup final team narrowly defeated by Nottingham Forest after a replay, his consolation came in being picked in the starting line-up that would successfully defend the

European Cup at Wembley against Bruges. Hansen played left-back in that final but replaced Hughes in the centre of defence early in the 1978/79 season. After Hughes left for Wolves in 1979 Hansen started to make the position his own. 1979 also saw the first of Hansen's eight League Championship medals.

THE SCOTSMAN'S team-mates often remarked how calm he seemed before games, a demeanour that was reflected in his cool and calculated play on the field. Hansen admits he suffered terribly from pre-match nerves, making multiple trips to the toilet, but once he got on the field he was in his element. He became known for dribbling the ball out of defence with style rather than hoof it upfield, prompting Paisley to remark: 'He has given me more heart attacks than any player I have ever known.' Problems with his knees curtailed that aspect of his game from the 1985/86 season onwards, as he was forced to subject himself to cortisone injections to be able to play. Hansen scored 13 goals for Liverpool but he only once got on the scoresheet in his last six years at the club as he was less inclined to attack. He was hardly a battering ram of a central defender, but his vision allowed him to stay on his feet instead of crashing into attackers. 'There are no prizes for guessing I was never sent off and hardly ever booked – most managers would say that this is a ridiculous record for a central defender.'

Much cup success would come his way too as Liverpool twice won the European Cup, in 1981 and 1984, and domestically lifted the Football League Cup four years in a row from 1981 to 1984, although Hansen missed the second of those successes in 1982 through injury after scoring the winner in the previous season's final against West Ham. He had to wait longer to be part of a

Season	League		FA Cup		League Cup		Europe		Other		Total	
	App	Goals	App	Goals	App	Goals	App	Goals	App	Goals	App	Goals
1977/78	18	0	0 (1)	0	3	0	3 (1)	1	0	0	24 (2)	1
1978/79	34	1	6	1	0	0	2	0	-	-	42	2
1979/80	38	4	8	0	5	0	1	0	1	0	53	4
1980/81	36	1	0	0	8	1	9	1	1	0	54	3
1981/82	35	0	3	1	8	0	5	1	1	0	52	2
1982/83	34	0	3	0	8	0	6	0	1	0	52	0
1983/84	42	1	2	0	13	0	9	0	1	0	67	1
1984/85	41	0	7	0	2	0	10	0	2	0	62	0
1985/86	41	0	8	0	7	0	-	-	4	0	60	0
1986/87	39	0	3	0	9	0	-	-	2	0	53	0
1987/88	39	1	7	0	3	0	-	-	0	0	49	1
1988/89	6	0	2	0	0	0	-	-	0	0	8	0
1989/90	31	0	8	0	2	0	-	-	1	0	42	0
Total	**434**	**8**	**57 (1)**	**2**	**68**	**1**	**45 (1)**	**3**	**14**	**0**	**618 (2)**	**14**

successful team in the FA Cup. In 1986, he lifted the cup as Dalglish's new club captain. By then he had a new partner in central defence, Mark Lawrenson, who had replaced Phil Thompson in the 1982/83 season. Lawrenson and Hansen complemented each other perfectly but the Scot says that of the three central defenders he played with at Liverpool, the third being Gary Gillespie, he and

Thompson had the best understanding. Pundits might joke they were hardly a conventional central pair as it was perceived that neither of them could tackle, but their superior ability in reading the game made their communication almost telepathic. Hansen feels Lawrenson lacked positional sense whereas that was Thompson's greatest strength, as well as being a great header of the ball.

HANSEN played in the infamous 1985 European Cup final against Juventus in Brussels and was also selected on the day of the Hillsborough tragedy. Out with a knee injury for most of the 1988/89 season and having watched Ronnie Whelan take over the captain's role, Hansen was dramatically recalled for the semi-final in Sheffield that ended in such tragic circumstances. He played in the rearranged match against Nottingham Forest at Old Trafford three weeks later and also in the emotional Wembley final against Merseyside rivals Everton, although it was Whelan who was given the honour of collecting the trophy after Liverpool's 3-2 extra-time success.

Hansen was 34 years old by the time a new season started and remained relatively injury-free to captain the club to yet another League Championship title in

1990. The wear and tear on his knees didn't allow him to make a single first-team appearance in 1990/91. He played five reserve games from October to December 1990 but was advised that if he wanted to be able to walk properly in the future he should pack it in. Hansen was offered a coaching position at Liverpool which he tried out for a couple of months, but he didn't feel comfortable as a coach and told Liverpool he wanted a clean break from the game. He announced his retirement as a player shortly after Dalglish stood down as manager, in March 1991. Hansen was tipped by many to take over the manager's job at Anfield but despite his enormous affection for Liverpool Football Club, he has no interest in returning to the sport. 'Dalglish and Souness live and breath football in a way that I never have. In my last season as captain, I wasn't getting any sleep at night, worrying about three points here and three points there,' he said. 'And at 2.15 on a Saturday I used to go back and forth to the toilet 45 times. So I knew management wasn't for me.' What he has done, though, is to emerge as a knowledgeable football analyst, principally for the BBC as part of regular Match of the Day team.

Hansen ought to have received far more than the 26 senior caps he was given by Scotland. He went to the 1982 World Cup in Spain but despite being at or close to his peak as a player was left out of the Scottish squad that went to Mexico four years later. It is doubtful if he has too many regrets at his lack of international opportunities, though. As a club player, he was one of the most accomplished and decorated footballers of his generation as well as one of the best defenders to ever play in the English League. His impact and influence on the club's phenomenal success during the 13 seasons he represented Liverpool can never be understated.

Hanson, Alf

'A SLIP OF A LAD, he was not entirely a one-footed player but it was that left boot which put fear into the hearts of goalkeepers when they saw Alf prancing down the wing,' wrote the *Liverpool Echo* of local left-winger Alf Hanson.

HANSON, who spent one season in Everton's A-team and reserves, first appeared in Liverpool's reserve line-up in 1931/32 before finally making his first-team bow in the middle of the 1932/33 season. He featured regularly for Liverpool save for an injury-hit 1935/36 season. Liverpool received a club record fee of £7,500 when Hanson joined Chelsea in the summer of 1938. He played 46 games and scored nine goals for them, but his professional career was effectively over with the outbreak of World War Two. Hanson was player-manager of a few amateur teams after the war: South Liverpool,

ALF HANSON
LIVERPOOL

FACTFILE

BORN
Sauchie, Scotland,
13 June 1955
POSITION
Centre-half
OTHER CLUBS
Partick Thistle
SIGNED FROM
Partick Thistle, £100,000,
5 May 1977
INTERNATIONAL CAPS
26 Scotland caps, 1979–87
LFC DEBUT GAME/GOAL
24 September 1977 /
19 October 1977
CONTRACT EXPIRY
1 March 1991
HONOURS
League Championship
1978/79, 1979/80, 1981/82,
1982/83, 1983/84, 1985/86,
1987/88, 1989/90;
FA Cup 1986, 1989;
League Cup
1981, 1983, 1984;
European Cup
1978, 1981, 1984

FACTFILE

BORN
Bootle, Liverpool,
27 February 1912
DIED
October 1993
POSITION
Left-winger
OTHER CLUBS
Everton (1930–31),
Chelsea (1938–46);
New Brighton, Wrexham,
Manchester City, Chester,
Bolton Wanderers,
Crewe Alexandra, Rochdale,
Tranmere Rovers, Southport,
Liverpool (wartime guest),
South Liverpool (1946–48),
Shelbourne (1948–49),
Ellesmere Port Town
(1949–50),
Penmaenmawr (1950)
SIGNED FROM
Everton, November 1931
LFC DEBUT GAME/GOAL
21 January 1933 /
1 February 1933
CONTRACT EXPIRY
6 July 1938

Shelbourne and Ellesmere Port Town. Alf says that he was actually born 'Hansen' because his father was a Norwegian mariner, but he was always reported in the newspapers as Hanson. He featured for Liverpool in 16 wartime games where he did his best to hide his real christian name, Adolf!

Season	League		FA Cup		Total	
	App	Goals	App	Goals	App	Goals
1932/33	11	2	0	0	11	2
1933/34	36	12	3	1	39	13
1934/35	35	9	2	0	37	9
1935/36	5	0	0	0	5	0
1936/37	42	13	1	0	43	13
1937/38	37	14	5	1	42	15
Total	**166**	**50**	**11**	**2**	**177**	**52**

Hardy,
Sam

'HARDY, I consider the finest goalkeeper I played against. By uncanny anticipation and wonderful positional sense he seemed to act like a magnet to the ball. I never saw him dive full length to make a save. He advanced a yard or two and so narrowed the shooting angle that forwards usually sent the ball straight at him.' Legendary player and later co-founder of the Football Writers' Association, Charlie Buchan, had plenty of praise for Sam Hardy's abilities.

Born a miner's son on Highfield Lane, Sam first came to Chesterfield's attention as a member of the Newbold White Star side that beat their reserves in the 1902 Byron Cup final. Legend has it that when manager Jack Hoskin was tipped off about Derby's reported interest in him, he rushed to sign Hardy, finally

getting his signature under a lamp-post in Newbold, but not before he had been forced to increase his offer of five shillings a week to eighteen shillings. Hardy's on-field performances reflected his character off it, for he was an even-tempered, down-to-earth man. Considering his great talents it was only a matter of time before he moved to a bigger club. Liverpool put six past Hardy while he was in goal for Chesterfield in January 1905, but remembered that, but for Hardy, it would have been closer to 20 on the day. Accordingly, four months later the Reds came in with an offer of £300 plus a friendly, and the 22-year-old Hardy was on his way to greatness after keeping 30 clean sheets in 71 league appearances for Chesterfield. The friendly never took place, and Liverpool topped the fee up with another £40.

HARDY replaced Ned Doig, who had been the club's main keeper for the opening eight fixtures of the 1905/06 season. Liverpool had been struggling for consistency until that point, but Hardy's debut saw Forest

beaten 4-1 and the Reds went on a terrific run, beating Middlesbrough 5-1 and conquering champions Newcastle at St James' Park 3-2, while first-placed Aston Villa were buried 3-0 at Anfield, Hardy saving a penalty. After only four games for the first team the club programme afforded Hardy the following praise: 'Judging from the cool, yet effective, methods which he adopts in clearing his goal, we feel pretty well assured in prognosticating a successful future for this young player. He is fearless in stopping a rush, and remarkably agile in covering the goal space, and is equally at home with both high and low shots. When his first gruelling afternoon comes, we trust Hardy will show himself a master of his craft.' After winning nine out of ten games, Liverpool were top of the table at Christmas, didn't falter and won the League Championship for the first time in Hardy's debut season.

A 10-year-old by the name of Walter Dutton was so impressed by Hardy's performances in goal

that he put together a little poem for publication in the *Liverpool Football Echo* in April 1906.

> *I know a good goalie called Hardy*
> *And when the ball comes he's not tardy*
> *He belongs to the 'Pool*
> *And he's been to school*
> *Has that jolly good goalie called Hardy*

Walter was not the only youth in Liverpool whose imagination Hardy had captured, as T. Ellis' story records in the same issue as the poem above: 'While walking through one of our parks the other day I met a youngster about the age of three walking along by his father's side. "Eh, daddy," said he, "there's Hardy." "Where and what Hardy?" asked the parent. "There he is, daddy – him as keeps goal for the Reds." The father looked and I looked in the direction indicated by the youngster's pointed finger, and there stood, between two piles of coats and caps, a ragged barefoot lad, about ten, engaged might and main in resisting the earnest attempts of other lads to force a penny soft indiarubber ball between the said piles of coats and caps. This is true.'

On 17 April 1911 Hardy got his much-deserved benefit game when Liverpool faced Woolwich Arsenal at Anfield. The club and the Anfield crowd showed him their appreciation. 'Twenty thousand throats cheering the silent custodian to the echo. The band departed decorously, and the rival captains took the centre, Hardy proving fortunate with the coin, at which the generous crowd cheered again,' the *Liverpool Echo* noted. Hardy was firmly first choice at Anfield for seven years until the 30-year-old was replaced by Scotsman Ken Campbell, ten years his junior, at the end of the 1911/12 season. The *Echo* agreed with the management.

'The change has been beneficial for the club, for whereas Hardy was beginning to show signs of inability to get to a shot with that electric speed that made him famous.' Hardy's last game for Liverpool was on 6 April 1912 against Aston Villa. Campbell's success and Hardy's reluctance to move into the city of Liverpool signalled the end of his Reds' career. Two months later he joined the Villans. Following his move Liverpool's board said they 'were going to insist in future that their players should reside in the district'. As in his debut season at Liverpool, Hardy was victorious in his first season with Villa as they beat Sunderland 1-0 in the 1913 FA Cup final. Villa finished four points behind Sunderland in second place, but Liverpool with Campbell in goal finished a disappointing 12th. The following season Hardy suffered FA Cup heartache at the hands of his former team in the semi-final. Jimmy Nicholl scored two goals past Hardy, but Liverpool lost the final to Burnley. Hardy won a second FA Cup winners' medal in 1920, when Villa beat Huddersfield 1-0. A year later he was on the move again after 183 games for the Villans.

In 1921 he took over the pub the Gardener's Arms on Glumangate in Chesterfield. His return to town fuelled fierce speculation that Chesterfield were going to sign him for their impending return to the Football League, but Villa, who had upset the player by insisting that he travel every day to Birmingham to train, were not

taken in by Chesterfield's suggestion that a free transfer might be a fitting reward for his services. Villa managed to get £1,000 from Nottingham Forest for him as the season started, which was a gamble considering Hardy was a few days short of his 39th birthday. Of course, Hardy became a key member of the Forest team that was promoted to the First Division in his first season. Hardy paid scrupulous attention to his fitness, which allowed him to keep playing in the top flight until just before his 43rd birthday, in an era when most players were clapped out at 30. Hardy played 109 games for Forest before retiring in May 1925. He played 551 league games and would have played many more if World War One had not intervened, where he served in the Navy. He won one Championship medal and two FA Cup winners' medals in his brilliant career.

'Safe and Steady Sam' was one of the outstanding English goalkeepers of his time. He made 21 international appearances between 1907 and 1920, at a time when England usually played only three games a season and the nation went to war for four years. Any keeper enjoying a 14-year spell as his country's first choice at the end of the 20th century would have earned around 140 caps, knocking Peter Shilton's record easily off its perch. Hardy won his 21st and last international cap for England against Scotland on 10 April 1920. England beat the Scots 5-4.

SAM HARDY was a man of strong principles and was aware of the good that a man of his profile could do towards improving the lot of his fellow professionals; accordingly, he became a prominent member of the PFA. He was also a hotelier in Chesterfield and ran his own billiard hall in Alfreton in Derbyshire. Sam died in Chesterfield on 24 October 1966.

FACTFILE

BORN
Newbold, Chesterfield,
26 August 1882
DIED
24 October 1966
POSITION
Goalkeeper
OTHER CLUBS
Newbold White Star
(1899–1902),
Chesterfield (1902–05),
Aston Villa (1912–21);
Plymouth Argyle,
Nottingham Forest
(wartime guest),
Nottingham Forest (1921–25)
SIGNED FROM
Chesterfield Town,
£340, May 1905
INTERNATIONAL CAPS
21 England caps (14 at LFC),
1907–20
LFC DEBUT
21 October 1905
CONTRACT EXPIRY
9 June 1912
HONOURS
League Championship
1905/06

Season	League		FA Cup		Other		Total	
	App	Goals	App	Goals	App	Goals	App	Goals
1905/06	30	0	5	0	1	0	36	0
1906/07	34	0	4	0	-	-	38	0
1907/08	33	0	4	0	-	-	37	0
1908/09	32	0	2	0	-	-	34	0
1909/10	32	0	1	0	-	-	33	0
1910/11	27	0	2	0	-	-	29	0
1911/12	31	0	2	0	-	-	33	0
Total	**219**	**0**	**20**	**0**	**1**	**0**	**240**	**0**

Harkness,
Steve

STEVE HARKNESS was a centre-forward at Carlisle when he impressed Kenny Dalglish in an FA Youth Cup tie against Liverpool. He had only played 13 games for Carlisle's first team when Liverpool snapped him up in July 1989.

Harkness was considered a big prospect and was appointed captain of the England Under-18 team. Injuries in the reserves meant he was tried as a left-back and he stayed in that position for the majority of his Liverpool career. David Burrows was Liverpool's first choice in that position and Harkness didn't make his competitive debut until on his 20th birthday in a 1-0 win over Queens Park Rangers. Aside from Burrows, Harkness had to fight for a place at one time or another with Julian Dicks, Steve Staunton and Stig-Inge Bjørnebye. Harkness made six appearances for First Division Southend United from February to March 1995 and was free to move there but Ronnie Whelan's Shrimpers couldn't afford the transfer fee. An injury crisis at Liverpool gave Harkness a second chance at the club at the end of the 1994/95 season. He signed a new three-year contract and was first choice for the first half of 1995/96, playing as a left wing-back in Evans' 3-5-2 formation.

FACTFILE

BORN
Carlisle, 27 August 1971
POSITION
Left-back, Left wing-back
OTHER CLUBS
Carlisle United (1987–89),
Huddersfield Town
(loan, 1993),
Southend United (loan, 1995),
Benfica (1999),
Blackburn Rovers (1999–2000),
Sheffield Wednesday
(2000–02),
Chester City (2002)
SIGNED FROM
Carlisle United, £75,000,
17 July 1989
LFC DEBUT GAME/GOAL
27 August 1991 /
29 April 1995
CONTRACT EXPIRY
9 March 1999

Harkness was pleased that his patience had paid off, as he told *90 Minutes* in September 1995: 'Sometimes I would be in the A-team and wondering what I was doing there when I could have been playing in someone's first team. There were times when I was on the verge of packing it in but I had a change of luck and one last chance to prove myself, and I grabbed it.'

Come January 1996 Harkness got suspended for receiving too many bookings, and that cost him his place as the team prospered without him. He was in the starting line-up on 6 April against Coventry, however, disaster struck following an hour's play. John Salako, who had just come on as a substitute two minutes earlier, launched into a scything tackle that broke Harkness's leg. He was out for 11 months, returning to the team when it was unfortunately struggling following a promising first half of the 1996/97 season. Harkness was again a regular from December onwards in 1997/98. He landed in the midst of a race storm when his former team-mate, Stan Collymore, accused him of racially abusing him at Villa Park in February 1998. Collymore had reportedly told him that he would properly break his leg this time, which incensed Harkness. The players threatened to sue each other and no truce was made despite the PFA's attempts. Nine months later when the sides met again, only 12 minutes in Collymore made a horrific tackle on Harkness that could have easily broken his leg. The Liverpool player was stretchered off while Collymore escaped with a yellow card. Collymore

later received a second yellow for an altercation with Michael Owen. Thankfully Harkness was only out of action for three weeks.

HARKNESS was one of the first players Gérard Houllier got rid of in his first season, after he had only started two games in 1999. Graeme Souness, who was manager at Benfica, persuaded Harkness in March 1999 to move to Portugal where former Liverpool players Dean Saunders and Michael Thomas were plying their trade. Souness was sacked a month later and Harkness was banned from first-team participation for arguing with the club's president following Souness's sacking. Brian Kidd at Blackburn offered Harkness a way out of his Portuguese nightmare in August 1999. Souness then replaced Kidd as boss in March 2000 but Harkness was sold six months later to Sheffield Wednesday, who had just been relegated from the Premier League. He spent two years at struggling Wednesday before joining former team-mate Mark Wright at Nationwide Conference side Chester City. Four months later, at the age of 31, Harkness called it quits following a series of injuries.

Season	League		FA Cup		League Cup		Europe		Other		Total	
	App	Goals	App	Goals	App	Goals	App	Goals	App	Goals	App	Goals
1991/92	7 (4)	0	1	0	2 (1)	0	3 (1)	0	-	-	13 (6)	0
1992/93	9 (1)	0	0	0	0	0	1 (1)	0	0	0	10 (2)	0
1993/94	10 (1)	0	1	0	2 (1)	0	-	-	-	-	13 (2)	0
1994/95	8	1	0	0	0	0	-	-	-	-	8	1
1995/96	23 (1)	1	1	0	4	1	4	0	-	-	32 (1)	2
1996/97	5 (2)	0	0	0	0	0	3	0	-	-	8 (2)	0
1997/98	24 (1)	0	0	0	3 (1)	0	1	0	-	-	29 (2)	0
1998/99	4 (2)	0	1 (1)	0	0 (1)	0	1 (1)	0	-	-	6 (5)	0
Total	**90 (12)**	**2**	**5 (1)**	**0**	**11 (4)**	**1**	**13 (3)**	**0**	**0**	**0**	**119 (20)**	**3**

Harley,
Jim

SCOTSMAN 'Big Jim' Harley was one of the toughest customers to have played for Liverpool Football Club. The natural left-back, who could play on either side, established himself in the team in the 1937/38 season after being on the fringes of the first team for a couple of years, only being 17 when he signed for the club.

During wartime he won Scotland international honours and the Royal Navy commando was also decorated for his role at Dunkirk after operating on a destroyer that made repeated trips across the Channel, bringing soldiers home while under fire from German planes. Harley made 17 appearances as a member of the 1946/47 Liverpool squad that secured the club's fifth First Division Championship. But he had passed his 30th birthday during that season and would only be selected on

JAMES HARLEY
LIVERPOOL F.C.

another 21 occasions in his final campaign at Anfield.

HARLEY was a great sprinter and at 18 years of age won the famous Powderhall Handicap, a New Year sprint in Scotland which has been around since 1870. He competed under the pseudonym 'J. H. Mitchell' so Liverpool would not find out about this extracurricular

activity. The *Liverpool Echo* wrote: 'Besides a Charles Buchan chest and shoulders he had the strong, but slim undercarriage of the sprinter. Woe betide the speeding winger who thought he could make a race of it and take the ball, Harley took both.' Former Reds goalkeeper Charlie Ashcroft told historian Gary Shaw that Harley was one of a kind. 'Charlie revealed that Harley would often come into training covered in cuts and bruises on his face and knuckles,' Gary said. 'He'd been out fighting the night before but not just with one man. That was a waste of time for Harley, who'd prefer to take on two, three or even four at a time. He got arrested for brawling on a number of occasions, which the

club took steps to cover up. Apparently there were few harder than Harley. He was fearless.'

Season	League		FA Cup		Total	
	App	Goals	App	Goals	App	Goals
1935/36	8	0	0	0	8	0
1936/37	5	0	1	0	6	0
1937/38	33	0	5	0	38	0
1938/39	31	0	3	0	34	0
1945/46	-	-	3	0	3	0
1946/47	17	0	4	0	21	0
1947/48	21	0	0	0	21	0
Total	**115**	**0**	**16**	**0**	**131**	**0**

Harrington,
Chris

CHRIS HARRINGTON made four appearances in Liverpool's forward line during the 1920/21 season. He was picked for three consecutive matches in February 1921 against Manchester United (twice) and Bradford City, and then again when Tottenham Hotspur visited Anfield on 25 March 1921.

The winger later made 48 appearances and scored seven goals in the Third Division North for Wigan Borough, Southport and Crewe Alexandra. On 28 July 1928 he headed for New York to play for the Giants along with former Red David McMullan in the American Soccer League.

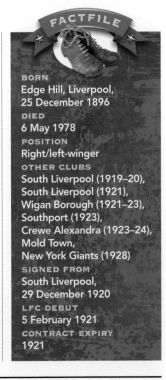

Season	League		FA Cup		Total	
	App	Goals	App	Goals	App	Goals
1920/21	4	0	0	0	4	0
Total	**4**	**0**	**0**	**0**	**4**	**0**

Harrop,
Jimmy

'HEADS UP' HARROP, as he was known in Liverpool, was tagged as legend Alex Raisbeck's successor in the middle of the Liverpool defence.

Harrop started out as a forward, but was moved to centre-half with Rotherham Town where he was appointed captain. He was playing

for Town in the Midland League when a Liverpool director went to watch a player called Foster, who later joined Bristol City, but discovered Harrop. The club programme liked the look of him when he was still a relative newcomer to the Liverpool ranks. 'Our early impressions of Harrop have been distinctly pleasing, for he uses his head to advantage in a double sense, and seems imbued with a determination to play the game intelligently and fairly.'

The *Sunday Chronicle* gave its approval on 16 January 1910: 'The Liverpool club have the gift of discovering men who have the genius to play centre half-back. Who would ever have thought that the legitimate successor to Alec Raisbeck could be found at the first attempt? James Harrop has followed the great Scot with such felicitous feet and such

harmonious heading that he is unquestionably building a lasting reputation. Raisbeck was fresh in complexion, with lint locks, and sturdy build. Harrop is sallow as a son of Romany, has jet-black hair, and is slim of both body and mind.'

HARROP was a cool, methodical player who quickly established himself at the heart of the club's defence for the next four years. Liverpool were in the bottom half of the First Division table for three out of the four seasons Harrop was a regular in the side, but managed to finish second behind Aston Villa in the 1909/10 season when his 'raven locks' had replaced Raisbeck's 'golden crown'. Harrop and goalkeeper Sam Hardy left Liverpool for Aston Villa in the summer of 1912. They had formed a sound friendship and were called 'The Liverpool twins'. Villa had finished

sixth in the First Division, while Liverpool had been close to relegation. The dynamic duo won the FA Cup in their debut season at Villa and the club finished second in the league in their first two seasons. Harrop stayed at Villa Park until 1921, playing 170 league and cup matches and scoring four goals.

Season	League		FA Cup		Total	
	App	Goals	App	Goals	App	Goals
1907/08	8	0	0	0	8	0
1908/09	30	1	1	0	31	1
1909/10	32	1	1	0	33	1
1910/11	34	1	2	0	36	1
1911/12	29	1	2	0	31	1
Total	**133**	**4**	**6**	**0**	**139**	**4**

Harrower,
Jimmy

A TALENTED but inconsistent attacking midfielder, whose vast array of skills simultaneously delighted and frustrated the Anfield crowd, Jimmy Harrower signed from Edinburgh club Hibernian in January 1958 when he was 22 years old. Liverpool had tried to purchase him two years earlier but to no avail.

He had played 12 matches in the First Division by the end of his debut season, scoring twice. He only missed five league fixtures the following season and added another six goals to his total. Bill Shankly arrived halfway through the 1959/60 season and for a while the new manager

couldn't seem to decide between Harrower or Jimmy Melia for the inside-left position. But before the end of the following season, Melia was established in the side and it was clear that Harrower's future lay elsewhere. He moved on to Newcastle United in March 1961 where he only stayed 10 months, featuring in five league games, before returning to Scotland.

Jimmy Harrower passed away on 29 August 2006 and was fondly remembered by Liverpool fans on internet forums. 'Jimmy Harrower was my first favourite player,' wrote 'Longtimered' on the *RAWK* forum. 'He was a real bundle of tricks – and, I'm sure he wouldn't mind me saying, a real

dirty bugger. A typical Scottish inside-forward of his day. Full of tricks and flicks with a mean streak to go with it. If only he'd had a little more pace and consistency I'm sure he'd have made a longer career at Anfield. On his day though he had the crowd drooling in admiration at his skill. Favourite memory. We had a tiny youngster playing – Willie Carlin – who got booted by an opponent. Jimmy ran the length of the field and planted one on him. Instant hero status!'

Phil Taylor welcomes Jimmy Harrower to Anfield in January 1958

Season	League		FA Cup		League Cup		Total	
	App	Goals	App	Goals	App	Goals	App	Goals
1957/58	12	2	2	0	-	-	14	2
1958/59	37	6	1	0	-	-	38	6
1959/60	26	5	2	0	-	-	28	5
1960/61	21	8	1	1	3	0	25	9
Total	**96**	**21**	**6**	**1**	**3**	**0**	**105**	**22**

FACTFILE

BORN
Alva, Scotland,
18 August 1935
DIED
29 August 2006
POSITION
Forward
OTHER CLUBS
Bo'ness United, Alloa Athletic, Hibernian (1954–58), Newcastle United (1961–62), Falkirk (1962–63), St Johnstone (1963–65), Albion Rovers (1965–66)
SIGNED FROM
Hibernian, £11,000, 3 January 1958
LFC DEBUT GAME/GOAL
11 January 1958 / 29 March 1958
CONTRACT EXPIRY
March 1961

Harston,
Ted

TED Harston was a late bloomer who joined Liverpool in 1937 after scoring no fewer than 81 goals in 70 games for Mansfield in the Third Division North, including 55 out of the club's total of 91 in the 1936/37 season!

HARSTON only played for Liverpool on five occasions during the first half of the 1937/38 season. He scored after 13 minutes of his debut at Chelsea on the opening day of the season but Liverpool were thrashed 6-1. He then scored twice in the next game when Portsmouth visited Anfield but lost his place in the side to Fred Howe after four matches had been played of the campaign. Harston's only other appearance for the first XI came when he replaced Howe at Blackpool towards the end of November 1937, a fixture the visitors won 1-0. Harston unfortunately broke his leg in the 1938/39 season, which effectively finished his professional career. He joined amateurs Shorts Football Club in the Kent League in August 1939. Harston was so described in 1936: 'Speed belies his sturdy build, and apart from his deadly shooting, can work the ball well and feed his wings.'

FACTFILE

BORN
Monk Bretton, Barnsley,
27 February 1907
DIED
1971
POSITION
Centre-forward
OTHER CLUBS
Barnsley Co-op, Cudworth Village, Ramsgate Town, Ramsgate Press Wanderers, Sheffield Wednesday (1928–30), Barnsley (1930–31), Reading (1931–34), Bristol City (1934–35), Mansfield Town (1935–37), Shorts
SIGNED FROM
Mansfield Town, £3,000, 18 June 1937
LFC DEBUT GAME/GOAL
28 August 1937 / 28 August 1937
CONTRACT EXPIRY
8 August 1939

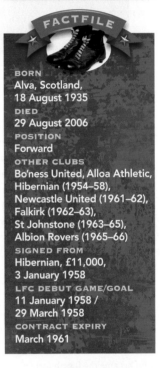

Season	League		FA Cup		Total	
	App	Goals	App	Goals	App	Goals
1937/38	5	3	0	0	5	3
Total	**5**	**3**	**0**	**0**	**5**	**3**

Hartill, Billy

DUBBED 'Artillery Billy' after his stint as a bombardier in the Royal Horse Artillery and also due to his awesome shooting power with both feet, Hartill was a sensational goalscorer for his first club, Wolves, scoring 170 goals in 234 games and grabbing 16 hat-tricks. For a long time he was Wolves' all-time leading scorer (he is now third in the list behind John Richards and Steve Bull). He scored 30 out of Wolves' 115 goals on their way to the Second Division title in 1932.

Hartill, who specialised in the 'hook shot', joined Everton in July 1935, but the 30-year-old never settled there and joined Liverpool six months later. The *Liverpool Echo* commented on the Reds' capture of Hartill, who became the fourth former Blue on Liverpool's books along with Tosh Johnson, Jack Balmer and Alf Hanson: 'He is a player admirably suited to the more open style of Liverpool. He is fast, can shoot with either foot, is good with his head, and takes up excellent position.'

HARTILL'S brief Liverpool career was condensed into four games between 18 January and 22 February 1936. His introduction into the team coincided with a terrible goal drought in which only two goals were scored in seven matches, both by Balmer. Hartill disappeared almost as quickly as he had arrived. He became part of the deal that brought future

legend Phil Taylor to the Reds from Third Division Bristol Rovers in March 1936. Hartill scored 19 goals in 36 games for Rovers before leaving the club in 1937, playing for amateur side Street until his retirement in 1940.

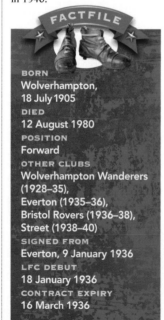

FACTFILE

BORN
Wolverhampton,
18 July 1905
DIED
12 August 1980
POSITION
Forward
OTHER CLUBS
Wolverhampton Wanderers
(1928–35),
Everton (1935–36),
Bristol Rovers (1936–38),
Street (1938–40)
SIGNED FROM
Everton, 9 January 1936
LFC DEBUT
18 January 1936
CONTRACT EXPIRY
16 March 1936

Season	League		FA Cup		Total	
	App	Goals	App	Goals	App	Goals
1935/36	4	0	0	0	4	0
Total	**4**	**0**	**0**	**0**	**4**	**0**

Hartley, Abraham

DUMBARTON won the first two seasons of the Scottish Football League from 1890–92, but only finished fifth, ten points behind Celtic, in Abraham Hartley's only season at the club in which he played eight games and scored five goals. He moved south of the border to Everton where he never played more than 15 games a season but scored in almost every other game in his 61 appearances.

HARTLEY joined neighbours Liverpool in December 1897 after he had scored three goals in as many games for Everton that season. He was picked for seven First Division matches for Liverpool during the 1897/98 season but scored just once, the winning goal at Sheffield United on 29 December 1897. Hartley also figured in five FA Cup ties that year, including the day Liverpool were thrashed 5-1 by Derby County at Anfield in a third round replay, after they had seemingly done the hard part by earning a 1-1 draw at Derby a week before. In May 1898 Hartley joined the Southern League's Southampton, who won the title for the third consecutive season, to which he contributed 14 league goals. He made a short stop at Second Division Woolwich Arsenal, scoring once in five appearances, before joining Burnley. His five goals from 13 appearances were unable to prevent Burnley being relegated to the Second Division at the end of the 1899/1900 season.

The story goes that Hartley had the habit of placing a rolled-up

cigarette behind one ear prior to kick-off, somehow keeping it tucked up there for 45 minutes and then smoking it at half-time! Hartley died at only 37 years of age on 9 October 1909 after collapsing due to heart failure outside the pay office of the London and South Western Railway at the Southampton docks.

FACTFILE

BORN
Dumbarton, Scotland,
8 February 1872
DIED
9 October 1909
POSITION
Forward
OTHER CLUBS
Artizan Thistle,
Dumbarton (1892),
Everton (1892–97),
Southampton (1898–99),
Woolwich Arsenal (1899),
Burnley (1899–1900)
SIGNED FROM
Everton, £175,
17 December 1897
LFC DEBUT GAME/GOAL
25 December 1897 /
29 December 1897
CONTRACT EXPIRY
May 1898

Season	League		FA Cup		Total	
	App	Goals	App	Goals	App	Goals
1897/98	7	1	5	0	12	1
Total	**7**	**1**	**5**	**0**	**12**	**1**

Hateley, Tony

LIVERPOOL paid Chelsea a club record fee of £96,000 to secure the services of this powerful, towering centre-forward. Tony Hateley had already scored over 150 league goals for Notts County, Aston Villa and Chelsea when he arrived at Anfield as a 26-year-old and looked like he had the best years of his career ahead of him.

HIS MAIN strength was his heading although he was somewhat lacking in the technical department as Tommy Docherty, his boss at Chelsea, put so eloquently: 'Hateley's passes should be labelled "To whom it may concern".' He also quipped, 'This boy can trap a ball further than I could kick it.' He scored a hat-trick in only his third league match for the Reds and missed only four First Division fixtures during his debut season, netting 16 times in all. He added another eight goals as Liverpool reached the FA Cup quarter-finals, including four in one game as Walsall were thrashed 5-2 in a fourth round replay on Merseyside. Three goals in Europe meant he had scored no fewer than 27 goals in his first season.

Hateley never managed to repeat the success of that first season and his career at Anfield was to be only a brief one. He was substituted at Leeds on the last day of August 1968 and was never to pull on the famous red shirt again. Liverpool's pass-and-move style did not seem to suit his game and only 15 months after his arrival he was on the move. Shankly bought Alun Evans and the youngster from the West Midlands took over the number 9 shirt. Tommy Smith, Hateley's former team-mate, revealed why he was sold despite his impressive goal tally. 'Tony was a nice fella and a good player in the right team. However, his arrival changed our style of play. From being a passing team, we suddenly started launching the long ball up to the big man. It is not something you plan. It's just that a centre-forward who is good in the air becomes a magnet for the long, high ball.' Hateley never regained the spark that had made him such an asset and he drifted down the Football League. He had a happy return to his first club, Notts County, in the 1970/71 season when he scored 22 goals in 29 games as the Fourth Division title was won. Tony, who is the father of former England international Mark, eventually played for 12 clubs in his career and scored 209 goals in 429 league appearances.

FACTFILE

BORN
Derby, 13 June 1941
POSITION
Centre-forward
OTHER CLUBS
Notts County (1956–63),
Aston Villa (1963–66),
Chelsea (1966–67),
Coventry City (1968–69),
Birmingham City (1969–70),
Notts County (1970–72),
Oldham Athletic (1972–74),
Boston Minutemen (1974),
Bromsgrove Rovers
(1974–75), Barrow (1976),
Prescot Town (1976–78),
Keyworth United (1978–79)
SIGNED FROM
Chelsea, £96,000, 5 July 1967
LFC DEBUT GAME/GOAL
19 August 1967 /
26 August 1967
CONTRACT EXPIRY
19 September 1968

This boy scored ten trebles for the Reds

Hat-trick Kings

17	Gordon Hodgson
16	Ian Rush
12	Roger Hunt
10	Robbie Fowler
10	Michael Owen
8	Dick Forshaw
7	Jack Parkinson
6	Sam Raybould
5	Harry Chambers
5	Steven Gerrard
5	Joe Hewitt
5	Billy Liddell
4	George Allan
4	John Miller*
4	Fernando Torres
3	John Aldridge
3	Jack Balmer
3	Yossi Benayoun
3	Kenny Dalglish
3	Tony Hateley
3	Fred Howe
3	Bobby Robinson
3	Albert Stubbins
3	Luis Suarez
3	John Toshack
3	John Wark

Only those who scored three hat-tricks or more are included.

* Miller scored 3 of his hat-tricks in the Lancashire League.

Hodgson hat-trick king

	League		FA Cup		League Cup		Europe		Total	
Season	App	Goals	App	Goals	App	Goals	App	Goals	App	Goals
1967/68	38	16	7	8	2	0	5	3	52	27
1968/69	4	1	0	0	0	0	0	0	4	1
Total	**42**	**17**	**7**	**8**	**2**	**0**	**5**	**3**	**56**	**28**

GORDON HODGSON
LIVERPOOL

Heggem,
Vegard

THE ONLY PLAYER brought to Liverpool when Roy Evans and Gérard Houllier were joint-managers in 1998, Vegard Heggem arrived with a wealth of experience having played 20 matches in the Champions League with Rosenborg. He scored the winning goal at San Siro when AC Milan were defeated 2-1 in the 1996/97 season. Rosenborg's win qualified the Norwegian team for the quarter-finals ahead of Milan, which is still considered one of the biggest events in Norwegian footballing history.

Roy Evans was quite fond of Norwegian players and there were already three former Rosenborg players at the club when Heggem arrived: Bjørnebye, Kvarme and

Leonhardsen. Heggem couldn't participate in the 1998 World Cup because of a groin injury but his move to Liverpool helped ease that disappointment. Evans wanted to improve the service to the strikers. 'He is good at delivering quality balls into the box and that is something we are looking for. We want good deliveries because with players like Karl-Heinz Riedle and Sean Dundee, it will add another aspect to our game.'

HEGGEM had an excellent debut season at Liverpool, going straight into the team at right-back. The Norwegian liked to break forward and scored his first goal with a thrilling mazy run against Middlesbrough on Boxing Day. He had started 33 games and been a substitute in two when he was injured in a 3-2 win over Everton on 3 April that was overshadowed by Fowler's infamous cocaine-sniffing celebration. Heggem was out for six weeks and only returned in the last five minutes in the last game of the season in which Liverpool finished a disappointing seventh. He had difficulty getting a prolonged run in the 1999/2000 season because he had a knack of picking up hamstring injuries, and only started 11 matches, coming on as a substitute on no fewer than 14 occasions. He scored another wonder solo goal against Bradford on 1 November 1999 but sadly his talent was too rarely on display.

After featuring in only four matches in the successful 2000/01 season Heggem limped off with a hamstring injury in the sixth minute of Liverpool's 4-0 win at Derby on 15 October 2000 and that was his last game for Liverpool's first team. He featured 16 times for the reserves in 2001/02 and made the first-team bench three times but he lacked a yard of pace and the necessary sharpness to make a return. He played in a few friendlies ahead of the 2002/03 season but was struck down with an Achilles

tendon injury that required surgery. In March 2003 Heggem confessed his career might be over and Houllier was realistic in his assessment. 'I'm not sure if Vegard will be able to play top-class football again,' he revealed. 'He had the potential to be a very good player and he is a particularly nice guy.' Heggem left Liverpool when his contract expired in the summer of 2003, his footballing days finished instead of enjoying what could have been the best years of his career. He has since run a very successful salmon fishing lodge in Norway, called Aunan Lodge.

Height

LIVERPOOL PLAYERS have come in all shapes and sizes but these are the ones who have stood out because of their height or lack thereof.

Tallest

6ft 7ins - 201cm
Peter Crouch
6ft 6ins - 198cm
**Sebastian Coates,
Chris Kirkland**
6ft 5ins - 195.5cm
**Steve Ogrizovic,
Frode Kippe, David James**
6ft 4ins - 193cm
**Hugh Gerhardi, Sami Hyypia,
Mauricio Pellegrino**

Smallest

5ft 2ins - 157.5cm
Fred Geary
5ft 4ins - 162.5cm
**Mervyn Jones, Robert Neill,
Sammy Lee, Bob Glassey,
Bobby Colvin**

FACTFILE

BORN
Trondheim, Norway,
13 July 1975
POSITION
Right-back
OTHER CLUBS
Rennebu (1982–91),
Orkdal (1992–94),
Rosenborg (1995–98)
SIGNED FROM
Rosenborg, £3.5million,
21 July 1998
INTERNATIONAL CAPS
20 Norway caps (1 goal)
(19 (0) at LFC), 1998–2000
LFC DEBUT GAME/GOAL
16 August 1998 /
26 December 1998
CONTRACT EXPIRY
1 July 2003

Season	League		FA Cup		League Cup		Europe		Other		Total	
	App	Goals	App	Goals	App	Goals	App	Goals	App	Goals	App	Goals
1998/99	27 (2)	2	1	0	1	0	4 (1)	0	-	-	33 (3)	2
1999/2000	10 (12)	1	0	0	1 (2)	0	-	-	-	-	11 (14)	1
2000/01	1 (2)	0	0	0	0	0	1	0	-	-	2 (2)	0
Total	**38 (16)**	**3**	**1**	**0**	**2 (2)**	**0**	**5 (1)**	**0**	**0**	**0**	**46 (19)**	**3**

Heighway, Steve

STEVE HEIGHWAY often took the 'highway' up the left wing, riding tackles, showing perfect ball control at breakneck speed, delivering great passes. He was one of the greatest entertainers who has ever worn the Liverpool shirt.

Heighway was spotted playing for non-league Skelmersdale United by Bob Paisley's sons, Graham and Robert. Bob himself decided to have a look and was very impressed. 'When I first saw him he almost took my breath away because he had "Star" written all over him and he was playing for Skelmersdale against South Liverpool,' Bob said. 'I even told one of our coaches that here was the best amateur footballer I'd ever seen.' Heighway signed for Shankly's Liverpool in May 1970 when he was 22 years old. Like his team-mate Brian Hall, Heighway was a university graduate, with a degree in economics, a very different background to most professional sportsmen. The club had a fairly settled side at the start of the 1970/71 season as Shankly rebuilt his team. Bobby Graham broke his leg in the home match with Chelsea in early October and that was the start of a long run of success for Heighway as a Liverpool player for the rest of the 1970s and into the 80s.

TOMMY SMITH recalls one incident that showed Heighway could stand up for himself, even when facing the frightening Bill Shankly. 'Shortly after Steve Heighway first joined we were at a meeting with Shanks. Now Steve in those days was still an amateur player in his mind as well as having a university degree, and he would take offence pretty quickly. He's a great lad, terrific fella, but I remember a time when Shanks called him out for not helping a team-mate in a situation where he could have

helped. Shanks said: "Tell me, son, if your neighbour's house was on fire what would you do? Would you get a bucket of water and help him put it out, or would you watch it burn down?" I don't know how everybody kept a straight face, because Steve in his wisdom gets up and says, "Well, all I can say is till you ask me a serious question, I can't answer. If you ask me silly questions, all you're going to get is silly answers." That knocked Shanks back on his heels and set the place rocking, I can tell you.'

> HE WAS ONE OF THE GREATEST ENTERTAINERS WHO HAS EVER WORN THE LIVERPOOL SHIRT

The Dubliner had an unorthodox style and his pace caused many a problem for defenders. Heighway's first chance to impress came in Gerry Byrne's testimonial on 8 April 1970. Heighway confessed that his new club was so unfamiliar to him that he had to ask when taking his position on the pitch which end the Kop was at. Lifelong Red, John Martin, vividly remembers his performance that day:

'It was raining at 7 o'clock in the morning and it never stopped all day. A strange name appeared on the Liverpool teamsheet when the sides were announced. At outside-left would appear not P. Thompson but S. Heighway. My seat was near the front of the Kemlyn Road Stand (now the Lower Centenary Stand) towards the Kop end so I was ideally placed to get a close-up of our new man. The full-back who was marking him was Jimmy Armfield who, although well past his best, was still a formidable opponent. The young Heighway ran him

Season	League App	League Goals	FA Cup App	FA Cup Goals	League Cup App	League Cup Goals	Europe App	Europe Goals	Other App	Other Goals	Total App	Total Goals
1970/71	29 (4)	4	7	2	2	0	7	1	-	-	45 (4)	7
1971/72	40	5	2	0	3	2	4	1	1	0	50	8
1972/73	38	6	4	0	8	2	12	2	-	-	62	10
1973/74	35 (1)	5	6	2	6	1	4	0	-	-	51 (1)	8
1974/75	32 (3)	9	2	1	4	2	4	1	1	0	43 (3)	13
1975/76	39	4	2	0	2	0	11	2	-	-	54	6
1976/77	39	8	7	3	2	0	9	3	1	0	58	14
1977/78	28	5	1	0	8	0	8 (1)	1	0	0	45 (1)	6
1978/79	26 (2)	4	2 (3)	0	1	0	2 (1)	0	-	-	31 (6)	4
1979/80	2 (7)	0	0	0	0	0	0 (1)	0	0	0	3 (8)	0
1980/81	4 (2)	0	0	0	0	0	1 (2)	0	0	0	6 (4)	0
Total	**312 (19)**	**50**	**33 (3)**	**8**	**38**	**7**	**62 (5)**	**11**	**3**	**0**	**448 (27)**	**76**

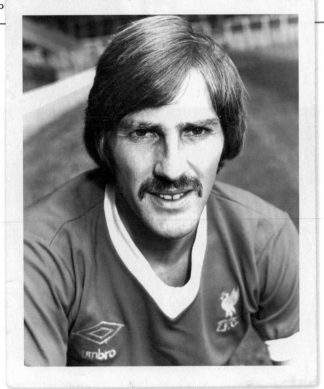

Henchoz,
Stephane

LIVERPOOL'S move for Stephane Henchoz initially raised many eyebrows, with Gérard Houllier utilising a relegation clause in his contract that guaranteed him an immediate release if Blackburn received an offer of £3.5million.

ragged and put over a succession of centres and other passes that had our forwards queuing up to convert them. It subsequently turned out that he wasn't even on the club's books at the time but Shankly wasted no time in tying him to a contract.'

HEIGHWAY turned out in one of the most memorable Merseyside derbies in history in November 1970. Liverpool were two goals down to the defending champions at Anfield when he received the ball out on the left wing after a raking pass from Tommy Smith. Side-stepping John Hurst's attempt to cut him in half, he made his way into the penalty area and, with everyone expecting a cross, squeezed the ball past Andy Rankin at the near post. Seven minutes later his pin-point cross from the left landed on John Toshack's head and Liverpool were level. Chris Lawler scored the winner for the Reds a few minutes from time.

Shankly's young side reached the FA Cup final that season and Heighway scored a similar goal past Bob Wilson but, despite taking the lead, Liverpool suffered the heartbreak of an extra-time defeat to Arsenal. Like a number of his colleagues that day, Heighway would return to Wembley three years later as a winner and again he scored, this time against Newcastle. By then he was an established and important member of the side and had many caps as a regular international with the Republic of Ireland to add to the Championship and UEFA Cup medals he had won with Liverpool in 1973.

Heighway reached double figures three times as a goalscorer but his main role was to create openings for players like Keegan and Toshack and, later on, for the likes of Dalglish, Johnson and Fairclough. Heighway added another UEFA Cup winners' medal in 1976 before being part

of the team that won the greatest prize of all in Rome in 1977, and he added a second European Cup winner's medal a year later when he came on for Jimmy Case against Bruges. He couldn't be absolutely sure of his place after that but still made 28 league appearances in 1978/79 as he collected the fourth of his First Division Championship medals. He was hardly called on at all during the next two years and left England for the United States in 1981 after playing 475 first-team matches in all competitions for Liverpool.

1981 was not a happy time for the popular Irishman, who was affected by severe financial problems at his American club, Minnesota Kicks. After leaving Minnesota he featured for Philadelphia Fever in the Major Indoor Soccer League in the 1981/82 season. He pioneered the role of director of coaching in the United States at the Clearwater Chargers Youth Soccer Club. In 1989 Kenny Dalglish appointed Heighway to the key role of youth development officer at Anfield. He was at the forefront of Liverpool's School of Excellence and then the Academy that was established in Kirkby in 1998, until his retirement in the summer of 2007. A number

of Liverpool stars benefited from working with Heighway, such as Robbie Fowler, Michael Owen and Steven Gerrard.

Bob Paisley was Heighway's boss for seven years and couldn't praise him enough. 'I've never seen a footballer move more gracefully than him,' he said. 'He should have been an Olympic athlete because he was so beautifully balanced.'

FACTFILE

BORN
Dublin, Ireland,
25 November 1947
POSITION
Left-winger
OTHER CLUBS
Skelmersdale United
(1966–70),
Minnesota Kicks (1981)
SIGNED FROM
Skelmersdale United,
1 April 1970
INTERNATIONAL CAPS
34 Ireland caps, 1970–81
LFC DEBUT GAME/GOAL
29 August 1970 /
17 October 1970
CONTRACT EXPIRY
1981
HONOURS
League Championship
1972/73, 1975/76, 1976/77,
1978/79;
FA Cup 1974;
European Cup 1977, 1978;
UEFA Cup 1973, 1976

Houllier saw Henchoz complementing Sami Hyypia's strengths and how right he proved to be. Henchoz was an extremely good man-marker, a brilliant tackler and reader of the game, and had a never-say-die attitude that inspired others around him. His face was as red as an apple after five minutes' play and he would be huffing and puffing, but despite his appearance he had vast amounts of energy.

Henchoz began his career as a midfielder with Neuchatel Xamax in his homeland, making his debut at Santiago Bernabeu against Real Madrid at only 17 years of age when coming on as a substitute in the 84th minute on 11 December 1991 in the UEFA Cup. After four years at Xamax, Henchoz had a difficult two-year stay at Hamburg SV in the German Bundesliga where he said every man suffered because of tyrannic coach Felix Magath. After a defeat the team had to do six one-kilometre sprints, all in under three-and-a-half minutes! Henchoz still had three years left of his contract when he was offered a four-year deal at Manchester United in the summer of 1997. Their discussions stalled over United's doubts over Henchoz's fitness, as he was recovering from surgery after breaking his ankle, an injury that kept him out for four months. The 22-year-old Swiss international instead opted for Blackburn Rovers. The fact that Roy Hodgson was in charge,

who had been Henchoz's coach at Xamax in the 1991/92 season as well as the coach of the Switzerland side, undoubtedly played a part in his decision. Henchoz proved a key player in the Blackburn side and only missed six Premier League matches in two seasons. Rovers finished sixth in his first season but were relegated in his second in which he was chosen 'Player of the Year' by the team's supporters.

HENCHOZ missed the first three months of the 1999/2000 season following a groin operation but settled quickly alongside Hyypia in Houllier's improving side. Henchoz credited Houllier for bringing much-needed discipline to the club: 'When the team is preparing for a match and we're in a hotel, Gérard goes into all the players' rooms at around 10.30pm to make certain everyone is where they should be. No one is allowed to drink alcohol before or after games – and if he finds out you have had even one small beer, you are OUT of the team immediately,' Henchoz told *The People*. 'If the manager is not satisfied that you have come with a good T-shirt and thinks that you are too scruffy, you are fined for that too. If you forget to switch off your mobile phone once you are at the training ground, it means a fine – and if it went off during a team meeting you'd be in major trouble.' Liverpool had a terrific 2000/01 season and Henchoz played a big role in the FA Cup final against Arsenal in 2001 when he earned the nickname 'Handchoz' after using his hand to prevent a certain goal

from Thierry Henry in the first half and then handling while lying on the ground in the second half. Liverpool went on to win 2-1 courtesy of a Michael Owen double. The H & H partnership at the heart of Liverpool's defence was still going strong in 2001/02 as Liverpool finished second in the Premier League. Henchoz was very much in the role of the unsung hero as Hyypia earned all the plaudits but the Swiss defender's team-mates certainly appreciated his worth to the team.

Houllier's Reds finally went off the boil and Henchoz's lengthy absences through injury surely contributed to their defensive frailties. Djimi Traore in 2002/03 and Igor Biscan in 2003/04 deputised in his absence. When fit again in January 2004 after a succession of groin and ankle injuries Henchoz was no longer automatic choice for centre-half but was included in the team at right-back. The 29-year-old, whose contract was due to expire in the summer of 2005, was then dropped in March 2004. 'Even if it's for the good of the team, I still don't understand why I have been left out. I'm not used to sitting on the bench. The Liverpool fans don't understand it, either,' he complained. When Rafa Benítez took over in 2004/05 it became immediately obvious that Henchoz didn't feature in his long-term plans. He joined Celtic in January 2005 but struggled for fitness. Former Liverpool reserve striker Paul Jewell came to his rescue and he joined newly promoted Wigan in the Premiership where he went straight into the starting XI and made 32 appearances in the 2005/06 season. He rejoined Blackburn in 2006/07 but only featured in 16 games before being released in the summer of 2008. In October 2008 the 34-year-old announced that he had retired as a player. In the 2009/10 season Henchoz was manager of third-division Bulle in Switzerland

where he had started his career as a youth player. He is currently studying for his coaching badges.

Henchoz famously never scored a goal in a competitive match for the first team but he did get on the scoresheet for Liverpool in a 5-1 win over Celtic in a friendly at Rentschler Field in East Hartford, Connecticut, on 27 July 2004. A monumental moment for Henchoz and all involved! Phil Thompson certainly appreciated Henchoz's contribution to his and Houllier's initial success. 'If there's a block to be made in the area and you see a red shirt flying in to prevent a goal, you can be fairly sure it will have a number two on the back of it,' he said. 'Head, foot, whatever it takes to prevent a goal.'

Season	League		FA Cup		League Cup		Europe		Other		Total	
	App	Goals	App	Goals	App	Goals	App	Goals	App	Goals	App	Goals
1999/2000	29	0	2	0	2	0	-	-	-	-	33	0
2000/01	32	0	5	0	6	0	10	0	-	-	53	0
2001/02	37	0	2	0	0	0	16	0	1	0	56	0
2002/03	19	0	2	0	4	0	6	0	1	0	32	0
2003/04	15 (3)	0	4	0	1	0	3 (1)	0	-	-	23 (4)	0
2004/05	0	0	0	0	3	0	1	0	-	-	4	0
Total	**132 (3)**	**0**	**15**	**0**	**16**	**0**	**36 (1)**	**0**	**2**	**0**	**201 (4)**	**0**

Henderson, Alastair

ALASTAIR HENDERSON was a half-back who made five appearances for Liverpool during the 1931/32 First Division season.

Tom Morrison was the club's regular right-half at the time, but Henderson replaced him for four successive matches in the autumn. His only other first-team game for the Reds came towards the end of the season, taking over from left-half Jimmy McDougall when Portsmouth were the visitors on 23 April 1932.

Season	League		FA Cup		Total	
	App	Goals	App	Goals	App	Goals
1931/32	5	0	0	0	5	0
Total	5	0	0	0	5	0

Henderson, David

FORWARD David Henderson played in 20 of the 28 league games in the 1893/94 season and scored 10 times as the club won the Second Division without losing a single match.

His highlights during his sole campaign at the club included a brace against Sheffield Wednesday in a 5-1 win at Anfield in which, according to the *Liverpool Mercury*, 'the Liverpool forwards put in some really clever passes, Henderson in particular playing the passing game with rare judgment,' and his two goals in the historic 3-2 cup win over Preston on 10 February 1894 that was the club's most famous victory at the time. Henderson returned to Scotland in November 1894 as Liverpool were trying unsuccessfully to hold on to their new status in the top division.

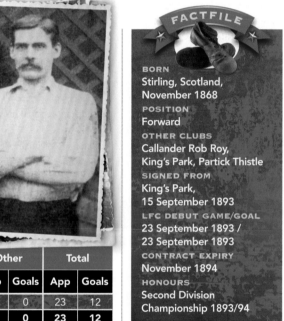

Season	League		FA Cup		Other		Total	
	App	Goals	App	Goals	App	Goals	App	Goals
1893/94	20	10	2	2	1	0	23	12
Total	20	10	2	2	1	0	23	12

Henderson, Hugh

HUGH HENDERSON was only called on twice to represent Liverpool as the central figure in their forward line.

Liverpool lost 5-0 at Aston Villa on his debut on 27 October 1894 and a week later were defeated 3-0 by Burnley at Anfield. Maybe not surprisingly, Henderson never played for the club again. Second-from-bottom Liverpool's 4-0 win over West Bromwich Albion on New Year's Day did offer hope in their first campaign in the First Division. A 5-0 defeat in the following game to Sheffield Wednesday failed to dampen their spirit and Liverpool won three league games on the trot, scoring 11 goals and conceding only one. Three defeats, however, in the last five sealed their fate.

Season	League		FA Cup		Other		Total	
	App	Goals	App	Goals	App	Goals	App	Goals
1894/95	2	0	0	0	0	0	2	0
Total	2	0	0	0	0	0	2	0

Henderson, James

CENTRE-FORWARD James Henderson signed from Annbank in August 1893, but only played one game for Liverpool in the Second Division before heading back north of the border to the town of Broxburn, situated almost halfway between Edinburgh and Glasgow.

Broxburn was a thriving mining and oil-shale community where football was a popular pastime. At one point there were four senior football teams in the area.

It was common practice for football agents to come to Broxburn from Edinburgh and the north of England to sign players. Henderson was probably spotted by one such agent as he moved next to Edinburgh Thistle.

FACTFILE

BORN
Scotland 1870
POSITION
Centre-forward
OTHER CLUBS
Annbank, Broxburn,
Edinburgh Thistle
SIGNED FROM
Annbank, 22 August 1893
LFC DEBUT
2 September 1893
CONTRACT EXPIRY
1894

Season	League		FA Cup		Other		Total	
	App	Goals	App	Goals	App	Goals	App	Goals
1893/94	1	0	0	0	0	0	1	0
Total	1	0	0	0	0	0	1	0

Henderson, Jordan

JORDAN HENDERSON'S breakthrough into the first team at Sunderland came as an 18-year-old in the 2008/09 season but he had actually been associated with his local Premier League club since he was only seven years old. As he progressed through different age groups he played as a striker and a right-winger before moving back into the midfield role which he played in when he helped Sunderland's Under-18 team win successive titles. Henderson was loaned to Coventry City in the Championship for the second half of the 2008/09 season but a metatarsal injury restricted him to only 10 appearances.

His consistent performances brought him successive awards as Sunderland's 'Young Player of the Year' in the 2009/10 and 2010/11 seasons in which he was absent from only six Premier League matches. Sunderland boss Steve Bruce had great expectations for his young midfield dynamo after the first couple of months of the 2010/11 season. 'Jordan has got a very, very bright future,' he said. 'The sky's the limit for him. Jordan has everything you need from a modern-day player – he has a lovely feel for the ball, but he is also 6ft 2in already and has terrific energy.' Henderson made his full international debut on the

same occasion as Andy Carroll, against France at Wembley in November 2010.

There was one aspect of Henderson's game that needed

improving as he admitted in April 2011. Six goals in 92 appearances for Sunderland and Coventry was not a goals-per-game ratio he took much pleasure in and he confessed that 'it has been a weakness in my

FACTFILE

BORN
Sunderland, 17 June 1990
POSITION
Midfielder, Right-back
OTHER CLUBS
Sunderland (2006–11),
Coventry City (loan, 2009)
SIGNED FROM
Sunderland, £16million,
9 June 2011
INTERNATIONAL CAPS
5 England caps
(4 at LFC), 2010–
LFC DEBUT GAME/GOAL
13 August 2011 /
27 August 2011
HONOURS
League Cup 2012

game. Top midfielders score goals. It is a vital part of the modern game.' After being signed by Kenny Dalglish in June 2011, Henderson played in more first-team matches in 2011/12, 48 out of 51, than any other player at Liverpool. At times he seemed a little lost, which was understandable as he was at times played out of position on the right. He did score two goals during his debut season at Anfield, against Bolton in the second home match and Chelsea in the last, finishes of supreme accuracy and confidence. At the end of May Henderson was called up into England's Euro 2012 squad following an injury to Chelsea's Frank Lampard, adding vital experience to his career by coming on as twice as substitute.

Henderson was given the option to leave the club in August 2012, but he wanted to prove himself at Anfield. He seemed rejuvenated as Brendan Rodgers took over at Liverpool, finally showing what he is capable of. 'This season the gaffer told me what he wanted from me, what I needed to improve, and I took it on board. He said I had to be better tactically,

for example. He's been brilliant,' Henderson said in January 2013. He scored in consecutive league matches against Norwich and Arsenal in January and scored a total of six goals, easily his best season total in his career so has has improved considerably in that aspect of his game.

He was voted England's Under-21s Player of the Year and as captain led the side to the European U-21 Championships in Israel.

Season	League		FA Cup		League Cup		Europe		Total	
	App	Goals	App	Goals	App	Goals	App	Goals	App	Goals
2011/12	31 (6)	2	4 (1)	0	6	0	-	-	41 (7)	2
2012/13	16 (14)	5	1 (1)	0	2	0	10	1	29 (15)	6
Total	47 (20)	7	5 (2)	0	8	0	10	1	70 (22)	8

Henry and Werner

AMERICAN SPORTS investment company New England Sports Ventures was founded in 2001 to purchase baseball institution Boston Red Sox. The company assumed a new corporate name: Fenway Sports Group [FSG] on 22 March 2011 to reflect its worldwide ambition. FSG's principal owner is Illinois native John Henry, a son of soybean farmers who got wealthy through his hedge fund 'J.W. Henry & Company' and according to *Forbes Magazine* worth $1.5b which leaves him as the 1000th or so richest man in the world according to its exclusive list. FSG's chairman Tom Werner, who also chairs Liverpool FC's board, co-founded the Carsey-Werner Company, a film and TV production company, in 1982. The most successful shows he has produced are The Cosby Show, Roseanne, 3rd Rock From the Sun and That 70's Show which made his fortune.

FSG's other owners include a number of 'prestigious individuals' according to its website and The New York Times. FSG is also the parent company of the Boston Red Sox and owns 80 per cent of the New England Sports Network and 50 per cent of NASCAR team, Roush Fenway Racing.

When FSG purchased Liverpool FC in October 2010 for £300million it was handed a team with a man at the helm whose ideas of how football should be played had outraged Liverpool fans. John Henry's email account was filled by voices of great concern in the ensuing months. To FSG's credit it reacted decisively when needed by dismissing Roy Hodgson in January 2011, only four months into its ownership, even though it came at a cost estimated to be £8.4million to get rid of the manager and his coaching staff. FSG turned to Kenny Dalglish in the hope of recapturing the Liverpool spirit that had been diluted by the boardroom brawling of the previous regime. However, it is safe to say that its blueprint for success in appointing Damien Comolli as director of football, whose policy was to target established players in the Premier League and purchase them for an absolute fortune, was a disaster. The prices for Andy Carroll (£35m), Jordan Henderson (£16m), Charlie Adam (£6.75m) and Stewart Downing (£20m) turned heads in English football. 'The red carpet into one of Europe's greatest football clubs was rolled with awed reverence for FSG as Moneyball adherents, stats based, scientific, value-for-money player acquirers,' as David Conn described FSG's policy in the *Guardian* in 2012. The £22.8m acquisition of Luis Suarez has though proved to be worth every penny and should not be forgotten that Carroll's price rose with the size of Chelsea's bid for Fernando Torres. The difference was always going to be £15m so as Chelsea bid £50m, Liverpool paid £35m for Carroll. The £16m Liverpool received for the sale of Raul Meireles to Chelsea and David N'Gog to Bolton in August 2011 proved excellent business.

FSG CONFESSED to its ignorance of 'soccer' and has learned the ropes in English football the hard way. In the spring of 2012 another reshuffle forced Comolli and Dalglish and his coaching staff out of the club – a move that relieved FSG's coffers reportedly of another £9.6million

– after underwhelming results in the Premier League. Brendan Rodgers was appointed, a brave young manager who wants his team to entertain. The focus is on bringing young players to the club, 'getting maximum value for what is spent so that we can build quality and depth', according to Henry in 2012. FSG's expenditure in the first 20 months of its ownership meant that Rodgers did not have big funds to spend on new players and his first transfer window in the summer of 2012 left the team woefully short of attacking options. At this point John Henry wrote an open letter to fans to calm the situation. 'Spending is not merely about buying talent. Our ambitions do not lie in cementing a mid-table place with expensive, short-term quick fixes that will only contribute for a couple of years. Much thought and investment already have gone into developing a self-sustaining pool of youngsters imbued in the club's traditions. That ethos is to win.' Henry's letter was predictably full of superlative words regarding FSG's future vision, but was refreshingly self-effacing as well. 'We are still in the process of reversing the errors of previous regimes. It will not happen overnight. It has been compounded by our own mistakes in a difficult first two years of ownership. It has been a harsh education, but make no mistake, the club is healthier today than when we took over. This club should never again run up debts that threaten its existence.'

Heskey,
Emile

EMILE IVANHOE HESKEY made his Premiership debut as a 17-year-old for Leicester City against QPR in March 1995. Leicester were relegated that spring but under the guidance of new manager Martin O'Neill came straight back up to the top division. Heskey scored 10 goals in 35 games in his first whole season in the Premier League in 1996/97 and boasted exactly the same stats the following season.

Liverpool's name was linked constantly with him in the press. Roy Evans has since gone on record to say that he had wanted to sign him around this time. Heskey's contract was due to expire in the summer of 1999, but O'Neill managed to convince the player to sign up for one more year. O'Neill had immense faith in Heskey and he repaid it as halfway through the 1998/99 season he had already scored nine goals compared with the ten he had scored in the whole of the previous season. But Heskey had scored his last goal of that campaign and went 20 games without a goal. Kevin Keegan gave Heskey his England debut on 28 April 1999 against Hungary and despite intense speculation about his future another year was added to his club contract.

HESKEY began the 1999/2000 season strongly, scoring five goals in his first four Premier League games. It seemed to be an open secret that Liverpool would buy him before the season was over. O'Neill replied to the speculation in his own unique style. 'If Liverpool were to come in with £7million and we get double that offer from Barcelona, I will taxi him over to Spain myself.' Heskey made his first England start on 22 February

2000 and he was voted man of the match against Argentina. A few days later he won the League Cup for the second time in his Leicester career. He scored his ninth goal of the season against Sunderland on 5 March and signed a contract with Liverpool a few days later, becoming their most expensive player at £11million. Heskey left the Foxes with a contribution of 197 games and 46 goals.

Gérard Houllier had seen Owen and Heskey play together up front for the England Under-18 team in France and there's no denying he was clearly a favourite of his new boss. 'He's a diamond of a player, he embodies all the right qualities of a professional footballer,' Houllier said. 'He's very hard-working, sacrifices himself for the team. He's always decisive because he's so strong.' Heskey was in the best form of his career in his first full season at Liverpool, netting 22 goals from 56 matches in the historic 'Treble' campaign. He terrorised defences with his pace and power, using his body as a battering ram. Houllier still, nevertheless, demanded more from Heskey. 'He has to keep pressing the pedal because, if he does that, he has great potential and can become a

fantastic player,' he said. 'I believe Emile is showing only 50 or 60 per cent of what he can do. At times he should probably have more self-belief and confidence in front of goal. Yes, he has scored 20 goals for us and one goal for England this season. But he has missed a lot of chances as well – it should be more.' Heskey started the 2001/02 season promisingly but a dry spell of one goal in 32 matches was hardly worthy of an England international and the club's record buy. However, Liverpool were still going strong in the league and finished second. The 2002/03 and 2003/04 were

Season	League		FA Cup		League Cup		Europe		Other		Total	
	App	Goals	App	Goals	App	Goals	App	Goals	App	Goals	App	Goals
1999/2000	12	3	0	0	0	0	-	-	-	-	12	3
2000/01	33 (3)	14	3 (2)	5	3 (1)	0	9 (2)	3	-	-	48 (8)	22
2001/02	26 (9)	9	1 (1)	0	0 (1)	0	17	5	1	0	45 (11)	14
2002/03	22 (10)	6	2 (1)	0	2 (3)	0	10 (1)	3	1	0	37 (15)	9
2003/04	25 (10)	7	3 (1)	1	2	2	4 (2)	2	-	-	34 (13)	12
Total	**118 (32)**	**39**	**9 (5)**	**6**	**7 (5)**	**2**	**40 (5)**	**13**	**2**	**0**	**176 (47)**	**60**

seasons better forgotten for Heskey, and his once-promising Liverpool career ended when he was sold to Birmingham City in May 2004 for £6million. Heskey did have all the attributes, but ultimately his apparent lack of self belief let him down.

HESKEY showed consistency with Birmingham in his debut season but in his second campaign he only contributed four goals from 34 league appearances as the Blues were relegated. Some of the fans seemed to turn against him and all these factors led to a move to Wigan Athletic in July 2006. His stay there followed a by-now familiar pattern: he had a promising debut season, then faded away. Heskey rejoined his

old boss, Martin O'Neill, at Leicester's foes, Aston Villa, in 2009. Heskey was a regular in England's senior international squad during his Liverpool days but was often left out when he was playing for less fashionable clubs. Although he was named in the England squad for Euro 2004, he did not make the trip to Germany for the World Cup two years later. In 2010 he played in his sixth League Cup final; he had appeared in three for Leicester, two for Liverpool and was now representing Aston Villa. This time around Manchester United deprived him of a fifth winner's medal. On 3 December 2011 Heskey made his 500th Premier League appearance, becoming only the sixth player to have

reached that milestone, after Ryan Giggs, David James, Gary Speed, Sol Campbell and Jamie Carragher. For the five English clubs Heskey represented, he scored about 150 goals, but still it is a question what could have been as he never fulfilled his enormous potential. 'Emile is someone who needs his own confidence to be up, and at the moment it is suffering a bit. But you have to accept that the players are human beings,' Houllier said once as he revealed the crux of the problem with Emile. At the end of the 2011/12 season Aston Villa announced that they would not be renewing his contract. So the striker, now 34 years old, became a free agent and joined Newcastle Jets in Australia's A-League.

Hewitt, Charlie

CHARLIE HEWITT, who was known as 'Captain' because of his days as a naval skipper, joined Tottenham Hotspur from Middlesbrough in May 1906. It was a curious transfer at the time as it was fully expected he would sign for the Reds. However, Hewitt only heard of Liverpool's £400 bid for him after he had signed for Tottenham, and before even making an appearance for the London club wished to go to Anfield.

Spurs wouldn't let him go and the Football Association ruled that Hewitt would have to honour his one-year contract. Hewitt featured regularly for Spurs during the 1906/07 season, scoring 12 goals in 43 appearances before leaving for Liverpool immediately as his contract expired. His older brother, Joe, was already in Liverpool's forward line. Charlie scored six times in 16 First Division appearances during his solitary campaign at the Reds. He scored on his debut on the opening day of the 1907/08 season at Nottingham Forest but Liverpool went down by three

goals to one. Charlie figured in 13 of the first 14 matches before losing his regular spot to Bobby Robinson. So having fought hard for a move to Anfield, Charlie only lasted 12 months before signing for West Brom.

After retiring as a player in 1919, Hewitt had a somewhat successful career as manager, promoting Chester to the Football League and taking Millwall out of the Third Division South in 1938. He also got Millwall as far as the FA Cup semi-finals in 1937. World War Two intervened and Charles and the Lions went their

separate ways, until 1948 when he was reappointed manager. He did not achieve as much success in his second spell and was sacked in 1956 after failing to get Millwall out of the Third Division.

HEWITT seemed to be a bona fide guardian angel, according to the *Manchester Courier* that claimed

when he joined Liverpool in 1907 that he had 'achieved fame apart from football' as he had been awarded several Humane Society medals for saving lives, 11 in total!

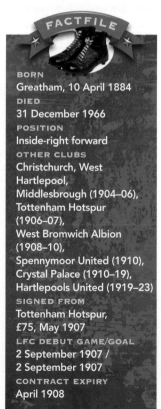

Season	League		FA Cup		Total	
	App	Goals	App	Goals	App	Goals
1907/08	16	6	0	0	16	6
Total	16	6	0	0	16	6

Hewitt,
Joe

JOE HEWITT made his name in his local Chester & District League, originally with Chester Locos where he was 12 months before returning to Newtown Rangers where he had played youth football.

Hewitt was finally recommended to Sunderland where he won the league title in his debut season, but being a newcomer he only played five games and contributed one goal. The inside-left was signed by Liverpool during the 1903/04 season and quickly won a place in the side, playing in the last 10 First Division fixtures but being unable to stop the club's slide into the Second Division. He only figured nine times in 1904/05, as Liverpool came straight back up. Hewitt was moved to centre-forward with devastating effect in the 1905/06 season. The First Division title was won and Hewitt was easily Liverpool's top scorer in the

league with 24 goals from 37 appearances. Injury and illness kept him on the sidelines the following year and he made a few appearances as an outside-left as Sam Raybould re-established himself in the centre. Once Raybould left the club Hewitt returned to centre position, netting 34 times from 75 games in the 1907/08 and 1908/09 seasons. In 1910 Hewitt was transferred to Second Division Bolton Wanderers where he stayed only one season before leaving for Reading in the Southern League.

The *Dundee Courier* reports a harrowing experience for Hewitt in March 1907 when he tried to save his next-door neighbour, Sarah Ann Sweeney, from being

JOSEPH HEWITT
[LIVERPOOL]

burned to death. Mrs Sweeney, who lived at 12 Finchley Road, Anfield, was getting out of bed when her nightdress caught fire. She rushed downstairs and into

Hewitt's house. Hewitt managed to put out the flames, but the unfortunate woman died from the shock. 'Accidental death' was the verdict in Liverpool's Coroner's Court. Hewitt was a member of Liverpool's staff after his retirement in 1911; as coach, club steward and press-box attendant for nearly 60 years.

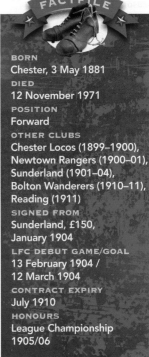

Season	League		FA Cup		Other		Total	
	App	Goals	App	Goals	App	Goals	App	Goals
1903/04	10	1	0	0	-	-	10	1
1904/05	9	1	0	0	-	-	9	1
1905/06	37	24	5	1	1	3	43	28
1906/07	23	8	0	0	-	-	23	8
1907/08	36	21	4	0	-	-	40	21
1908/09	33	12	2	1	-	-	35	13
1909/10	4	2	0	0	-	-	4	2
Total	**152**	**69**	**11**	**2**	**1**	**3**	**164**	**74**

Heydon,
John

HALF-BACK John Heydon signed for Liverpool in January 1949 when he was 20 years old after spending three years in Everton's reserves. He had to wait until October 1950 before making his first-team debut and played a total of 13 times in the league that season, mostly as a cover for left-half Phil Taylor.

Heydon was a regular for the first half of the 1952/53 season but then lost his place in the side. He was eventually transferred to Third Division South club Millwall in May 1953 and had a couple of years in London before returning to Merseyside to finish his playing

career with Tranmere Rovers, also in the third tier of league football, becoming one of three players to have been on the books of all three major Merseyside clubs: Everton, Tranmere and Liverpool.

Season	League		FA Cup		Total	
	App	Goals	App	Goals	App	Goals
1950/51	13	0	1	0	14	0
1951/52	27	0	2	0	29	0
1952/53	23	0	1	0	24	0
Total	**63**	**0**	**4**	**0**	**67**	**0**

Heysel

AS THE middle part of the 1980s loomed, life for a Liverpool supporter was good. The Reds had regained the European Cup and were bidding to become only the second club to win it on five occasions. In the 1984/85 season, Juventus were still looking for their first European title after being beaten in the finals of 1973 and 1983. Liverpool beat Panathinaikos easily in the semi-finals, but Bordeaux fought like tigers in France to erode two-thirds of the Juventus lead from the first leg of the other semi. The Italian team held on so Liverpool v. Juventus it would be at the Heysel stadium in Brussels.

Liverpool's Peter Robinson, one of the most respected administrators in the football world, openly voiced his concerns, only 12 months after a similar showdown had ended in such terrible brutality after Liverpool had won in Rome. Robinson knew from his own assessment and reports that the 55-year-old Heysel stadium had been crumbling for years. The stadium's capacity was around 50,000 but instead of giving each finalist nearly 50 per cent of the capacity each, a decision – catastrophic as it turned out – was made to have a supposedly neutral area in one corner of the Liverpool end. Tickets for this Z section, alongside areas X and Y that were allocated to the English club, were meant for neutral Belgians but most were inevitably snapped up by members of the large Italian community in Belgium.

Large holes in the perimeter of the stadium gave ticketless fans an opportunity to enter free of charge and this meant that Liverpool's two blocks, X and Y, soon became overcrowded. The boundary

between X/Y and Z was only very thin, temporary fencing and beyond the 'No Man's Land' that had been created to keep rival supporters apart, it was clear that spectators in block Z had plenty of space to move about in. There was no history of animosity between the two clubs or sets of supporters. But many Liverpool supporters present in Brussels had been victims of the unprovoked and indiscriminate attacks on them after the 1984 final in Rome. It wasn't long before the opening verbal exchanges became more physical, with missiles being lobbed from one side of the divide to the other. Several people moved from the Liverpool blocks to join those who were already in the neutral/Juventus block. As this large group increased in size, many Italians in Z moved en masse to get away from it. As they tried to move over a side wall to get out of the terrace altogether, that wall could not hold the force of people pressing against it and collapsed.

Thirty-nine died in the crush and hundreds more were injured. Juventus supporters in blocks M, N and O at the other end of the stadium could see that something serious was happening and hundreds of them confronted the Liverpool supporters. Although the police did their best to keep the two sets of fans apart, there were still some serious clashes and these continued while UEFA officials, in tandem with officials of the two clubs, tried to make sense of all the madness. Probably correctly, a decision was made that the final should go ahead. To abandon the match would almost certainly have led to even more violence.

This had become a match Liverpool could not win, not with any pride and honour intact. Swiss referee André Daina made an outrageous decision to award Juventus a penalty-kick for a foul that was well outside the penalty-area. He later turned down a much more justifiable appeal for a Liverpool penalty. Michel Platini scored the penalty that was awarded and Juventus held on for the remaining half hour to win the match 1-0. As Juventus celebrated on the pitch, Liverpool's players, officials and supporters could not get away from the stadium quickly enough. A proud club's name and reputation had become tarnished and sullied overnight.

RECRIMINATIONS were swift. Two days after the final, British Prime Minister Margaret Thatcher urged the Football Association to withdraw English clubs from European competitions. Two days later UEFA banned all the English clubs for 'an indeterminate period of time'. That ban lasted for five years with Liverpool having to serve an extra year before being re-admitted in 1991. Fourteen Britons were later given three-year sentences for 'involuntary manslaughter'.

The stadium unwisely selected to hold the 1985 European Cup final was renovated and re-opened as the King Baudouin Stadium ten years later. A year later Juventus won their second European Cup and nine years after that Liverpool won their fifth. The two clubs remain giants of the European game but their names will always be linked by a terrible and avoidable tragedy.

When Juventus and Liverpool met at Anfield in 2005 in the quarter-finals of the Champions League for the first time since Heysel the club honoured the memory of the 39 victims with a number of commemorative gestures in the lead-up to the match, including a fans' match at the Academy and a banner carrying the theme 'In Memoria e Amicizia' carried by Phil Neal and Michel Platini, captains back in 1985, from the Kop to the away end prior to kick-off. An 'Amicizia" mosaic with the Liverbird at the end was revealed in the Kop. However, when the banner was presented inside the ground the Juventus fans turned their backs in a show of solidarity that indicated that Liverpool hadn't fully apologised in the past and this was too little, too late. The message from the Juve crowd was, though, directed at the hierarchy of Liverpool as relations between the two sets of fans were respectful. On 26 May 2010 a plaque was unveiled at the entrance to Anfield's Centenary stand in remembrance of the 39.

Hickson,
Dave

DAVE HICKSON'S 1959 move from Everton to Liverpool caused an uproar among supporters on both sides. Hickson, with his signature blond quiff, was a big star at Everton and their fans were disgusted with the club for selling him to Liverpool, and Reds' fans were horrified that the club's board would even contemplate signing a player from Everton.

Hickson first signed professional forms with Everton in 1948 having honed his striking skills under the tutelage of goalscoring great Dixie Dean. Hickson's enthusiasm for the game sometimes got the better of him and he was no stranger to suspensions after being sent off twice. He was prolific in front of goal and scored 71 goals in 151 games for the Blues from 1951 to 1955, the majority of the games being played in the Second Division. Everton were promoted in 1954, but after only one season in the top flight, Hickson moved to First Division Aston Villa. He only stayed two months there before joining Huddersfield, where a certain Bill Shankly coached the reserves and took over as manager a year later in November 1956. Liverpool could have snapped him up in 1957 but decided against paying £6,000 for him so Everton moved in and he scored a further 40 goals in 92 games on his return.

'The Cannonball Kid' certainly took a bold decision when he had just passed his 30th birthday when he crossed Stanley Park. Liverpool manager Phil Taylor hoped Hickson would be the man whose goals would take Liverpool back into the First Division. Hickson was relieved after signing

the contract. 'I am very pleased indeed that I have signed for Liverpool after a week of uncertainty and I know my wife and family share my feelings. It has been an anxious time for me recently, but everything is all right now. I am delighted. I just want the Liverpool fans to know that I will always do my best for them and the club as I have done at Everton.' It was a strange coincidence that Hickson played his last senior game for Everton at Anfield defeating Liverpool 2-0 in the Floodlight Cup on 28 October before making his Liverpool debut on the same ground against Aston Villa on 7 November. Hickson had a night to remember as he was given a big kiss by a Liverpool supporter before the game started, which proved a good-luck charm. His second goal of the game in Liverpool's 2-1 win was a tremendous flying header that showed his bravery and as the *Liverpool Daily Post* reported: 'With victory in the air, Anfield erupted. Dave had found a new home, where adulation, spontaneous and overwhelming, promised to outdo anything he had known before.' A month after signing for Liverpool, in December 1959, Hickson was again playing under Shankly. He made a slow start under his former manager but from the middle of February he scored 15 goals in 15 games as Liverpool came up short again. Hickson was less effective in his second season, like his strike partner, Roger Hunt. Shankly brought in Ian St John in 1961, which signalled the end of Hickson's

Anfield adventure. Hickson is the best known of the trio who has been at all three of Merseyside's major clubs: Liverpool, Everton and Tranmere Rovers. The other two players are John Heydon and Frank Mitchell.

HICKSON returned to Ellesmere Port Town as player-coach in 1965 and proved he had lost none of the fire in his belly. A Cheshire League Cup game against Macclesfield Town on 11 September 1965 had to be abandoned after 84 minutes as Hickson refused to leave the pitch after being sent off. The tie was subsequently awarded to Macclesfield. Hickson was a tour guide and a member of the matchday hospitality staff at Goodison Park from the mid-1990s until late in life and played charity football until he was 77 years old! Hickson is truly revered as a legend at his former clubs, having earned the respect of fans, opponents and team-mates alike during his historic career.

FACTFILE

BORN
Ellesmere Port,
30 October 1929
DIED
8 July 2013
POSITION
Centre-forward
OTHER CLUBS
Ellesmere Port Town
(1945–47),
Everton (1947–55),
Aston Villa (1955),
Huddersfield Town (1955–57),
Everton (1957–59),
Cambridge City (1961–62),
Bury (1962),
Tranmere Rovers (1962–64),
Ballymena United (1964–65),
Ellesmere Port Town (1965),
Northwich Victoria (1966),
Winsford United (1967–69),
Fleetwood
SIGNED FROM
Everton, £12,000,
6 November 1959
LFC DEBUT GAME/GOAL
7 November 1959 /
7 November 1959
CONTRACT EXPIRY
July 1961

Season	League		FA Cup		League Cup		Total	
	App	Goals	App	Goals	App	Goals	App	Goals
1959/60	27	21	2	0	-	-	29	21
1960/61	33	16	2	0	3	1	38	17
Total	**60**	**37**	**4**	**0**	**3**	**1**	**67**	**38**

Hignett, Alan

LIVERPOOL-BORN Alan Hignett's solitary first-team appearance came in the final league fixture of the 1964/65 season, when Bill Shankly played largely a reserve side at Wolverhampton only five days before the FA Cup final with Leeds United.

HIGNETT moved for free to Chester in the summer of 1966 along with John Sealey, who also made his only Liverpool appearance against Wolves.

Hignett only played six games for Chester in the Fourth Division

before continuing his career in the New South Wales League in Australia. He joined Pan-Hellenic Soccer Club, formed in 1957 to represent the Greek community in New South Wales. Hignett played into the 1970s with Pan Hellenic and was team captain. After a colourful history that included pitch invasions and heart-stopping relegation battles the club went bankrupt in 1976 and is now known as Sydney Olympic.

FACTFILE

BORN
Liverpool, 1 November 1946
POSITION
Right-half
OTHER CLUBS
Chester (1966),
Pan-Hellenic Soccer Club
JOINED
April 1962; signed
professional November 1963
LFC DEBUT
26 April 1965
CONTRACT EXPIRY
August 1966

Season	League		FA Cup		Europe		Other		Total	
	App	Goals	App	Goals	App	Goals	App	Goals	App	Goals
1964/65	1	0	0	0	0	0	0	0	1	0
Total	1	0	0	0	0	0	0	0	1	0

Hignett, Samuel

THE RIGHT-HALF position was shared by no less than five players in the first eight games of the 1907/08 season.

Jock McNab tips his hat in the 1920s

Samuel Hignett made his only appearance as a right-half in a 1-0 win at home to Sunderland on 12 October 1907. He replaced Bobby Robinson who had been chosen as a reserve for the English League team that would face the representatives of the Irish League. The club programme said

Liverpool's defence had been shaky in the game but Hignett was 'distinctly promising. At first he was nervous and anxious but afterwards he controlled his wing admirably.' However, Robinson played right-half in the following game and Hignett went back into the reserves.

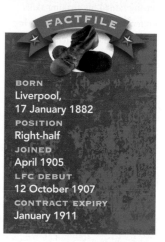

FACTFILE

BORN
Liverpool,
17 January 1882
POSITION
Right-half
JOINED
April 1905
LFC DEBUT
12 October 1907
CONTRACT EXPIRY
January 1911

Season	League		FA Cup		Total	
	App	Goals	App	Goals	App	Goals
1907/08	1	0	0	0	1	0
Total	1	0	0	0	1	0

Shankly, of course with a red suitcase en route to Wembley in 1971

Hillsborough

HILLSBOROUGH. A 12-letter word to send a chill down the spine of any follower of the sport of football. An accident waiting to happen. A tragedy of immense proportions that could have happened to any English club of the time taking thousands of supporters to a big cup-tie at a neutral venue; the home stadium of Sheffield Wednesday Football Club that had already been used many times for the FA Cup semi-finals. A stadium that was considered safe, practical and appropriate until the 1980s.

An increase in hooliganism in the English game in the first half of the 1980s had led to standing spectators being 'penned in' like cattle and at most English stadia in the top division high perimeter fencing had been installed to produce a very visible barrier between spectators and the field of play. The Leppings Lane End at Sheffield Wednesday's stadium had originally been a single terrace, above which was a seated area. Dreadful crushing at the 1981 semi-final between

Tottenham Hotspur and Wolverhampton Wanderers led to Sheffield Wednesday dividing the lower terrace immediately behind the goal into separate pens to prevent sideways movement. Hillsborough was not chosen as a semi-final venue again until 1987 but matters had not improved in the intervening six years. Many of Leeds' massive travelling support experienced similar crushing to the one in 1981 and, in an ominous sign of what would happen in 1989, many of them had to be hauled to safety by people in the seats above the terrace.

Liverpool and Nottingham Forest met in the Sheffield semi-final of 1988 and Liverpool supporters complained about crushing in the Leppings Lane End. It was so bad that Liverpool urged the Football Association to make different arrangements when, remarkably, the same two clubs were again paired at the semi-final stage of the competition in 1989 and again told that the venue would be in Sheffield. Part of Liverpool's

argument was that the club with by far the smaller fan base of the two clubs had been allocated by far the bigger of the two standing terraces, the Hillsborough Kop. The FA was intransigent. What had worked in 1988 would work again in 1989, it decided.

MORE Liverpool supporters crossed the Pennines by road in 1989 than in 1988 because only one special train ran from Merseyside in the second year compared to three the year before. There were roadworks on the motorway on the way to Yorkshire that caused dozens of vehicles to be delayed and this resulted in a huge bottleneck on the outskirts of Sheffield. These delays caused massive congestion outside the Leppings Lane turnstiles about half an hour before the match was due to start. Many hundreds were still outside as kick-off time got closer and this created a huge safety issue and resulted in the police opening a large exit gate to relieve the pressure outside the stadium. Two smaller gates were also opened and hundreds of supporters streamed through anxious to see the start of the match.

Once inside the stadium most of these latecomers made their way down a narrow tunnel that led to the pens. They did not know that the middle pens were already completely full or that there was no police or stewarding presence to direct them to the side pens where there was still room. The force of hundreds of bodies pressing into the back of the already-full central pens caused those already in the pens to press into those in front of them until people at the very front were squashed against the perimeter fencing.

Referee Ray Lewis started the match on time but within a few minutes a lot of spectators had started to clamber up and over the perimeter fencing to get away from the crush. Some fans also managed to open a small gate in the fencing and this enabled others to move pitchside too. On police advice Lewis stopped the match at six minutes past three and instructed the teams to return to their dressing rooms. The police attempted to stop this pitch-invasion but by now it was obvious that things had gone seriously wrong because many spectators at the back of the pens were being pulled up into the seated area of the West stand by Liverpool supporters who could see the full horror of what was unfolding in front of them.

Ninety-four Liverpool supporters died at the stadium or shortly afterwards, the youngest just ten years old, the oldest sixty-seven. The 14-year-old Lee Nicol had his life-support machine turned off four days later and the 21-year-old Tony Bland, who remained in a persistent vegetative state for nearly four years, subsequently died in 1993, making the final death toll ninety-six.

The *Sun* newspaper decided to print a story under what it described as 'The Truth', in which it claimed that Liverpool

supporters had stolen from the dead and dying and urinated on police officers who were trying to save lives. These allegations were immediately and strenuously denied and caused enormous offence, particular to the families of those who had perished so needlessly.

WHAT became known as The Taylor Inquiry, overseen by Peter Taylor, a man who would become the Lord Chief Justice of England in 1992, sat for 31 days. Its conclusion was that failure of police control was the primary cause of the disaster. He criticised Chief Superintendent David Duckenfield for 'failing to take effective control' and South Yorkshire Police, which blamed supporters for arriving at the ground 'late and drunk'. Taylor also published a report which had widespread recommendations about safety at football grounds. The police closed ranks and tried to deflect the blame. The police not only dealt with the chain of events prior to kick off with deadly consequences but also once the game had been stopped. The only professional ambulance attendant to reach the Leppings Lane end, 'Tony', bears testament to the astonishing incompetence of the police, as he revealed to the *Guardian* in March 2009.

'We were at the Northern General when we got a 3-9 call to an incident. They told us there was a fatality, but when we got to the ground there were ambulances from everywhere, even Derbyshire. As we pulled up a policeman came to my window and said: 'You can't go on the pitch, they're still fighting.' As we went along, the police were starting to form a wall across the pitch. We went through them and then saw people running towards us. As we got to the goal there was an absolute sea of people. I'll never forget the sound... it was like a large swimming pool; there was screaming and shouting, it was deafening. People were

banging on the side of the ambulance, shouting 'Help!' and 'Over here!' I was being pulled in different directions, people were shouting for oxygen, all sorts of demands. And I thought: 'I can't help everybody.' I was looking back up the pitch for other ambulances, but nobody was coming. I asked again to be put in touch with ambulance control, but the radio wasn't working. I went to get my oxygen mask and bag, but they were gone. We weren't doing any good. You're used to having one casualty in the back, but there were too many bodies to deal with. We just didn't do a very good job that day. We left people on that pitch who were being worked on, and there were no professionals there to help them. There were 44 ambulances waiting outside the stadium - that means 80-odd staff could have been inside the ground. But they weren't allowed in. There was no fighting! The survivors were deciding who was the priority, who we should deal with. The police weren't. We weren't. Can you imagine a rail accident where all the ambulances wait on the embankment while the survivors bring the casualties up? I know I dealt with it wrong. I know that. But I should never have been put in that position.'

Two groups have amongst others fought the good fight for justice for the 96. Margaret Aspinall heads the 'Hillsborough Family Support Group' [HFSG] that was founded in May 1989 by families who lost loved ones in the Hillsborough disaster. 'The Hillsborough Justice Campaign' [HJC] was formed out of some members' dissatisfaction that survivors were excluded from HFSG. According to HJC's homepage (contrast.org/ hillsborough) only the bereaved could be members. 'It is a sorry state of affairs that two groups have to exist and cannot co-exist,' notes HJC whose shop is at 178 Walton Breck Road, right opposite Anfield. HFSG has its own website at hfsg.co.uk/1.html and its headquarters are at Anfield Sports and Community Centre at Lower Breck Road. Reds should support both parties so they can continue on their road to justice.

AFTER A CHANGE of government, the Labour Home Secretary ordered a further investigation in 1997. This determined that there was no good reason to re-open Lord Justice Taylor's Inquiry or have any sort of other Judicial Inquiry. But pressure was mounting, principally from the HFSG, with one of their demands being fresh inquests because they strongly opposed Lord Justice Stuart-Smith's conclusion that anything that happened after 3.15pm on the day of the disaster was 'inadmissible' as evidence.

The Hillsborough Independent Panel of 2012 went through nearly half a million pages of documents collected over a two-year period and concluded that nearly fifty of the victims were almost certainly still alive

after the 3.15pm cut-off previously laid down and that some of them might have been saved. The panel also found that dozens of statements had been altered or removed if they were unfavourable to the South Yorkshire Police. Much of what had been published as 'Truth' in 1989 was now exposed as 'Lies' and almost immediately apologies were made by the prime minister, the leader of the opposition, South Yorkshire Police and Sheffield Wednesday Football Club. The IPCC (Independent Police Complaints Commission) announced that it would investigate many aspects of police behaviour on the day and afterwards. Most importantly for the families, the High Court quashed the original inquest verdicts and ordered new inquests to be carried out. It is a matter for prosecutors to decide whether or not any individuals or organisations should be charged with any offence but certainly the Football Association and Sheffield Wednesday Football Club need to explain why the stadium's safety-certificate became invalid in 1981 and was never renewed by the time of the disaster.

This should never have happened. Nearly a hundred people died because of their love for a football club. The word Hillsborough will always be synonymous with tragedy. The blackest day in Liverpool's history will never be forgotten and nor will the 96, who had their memories tarnished but finally got at least some form of justice twenty-three and a half years after their lives were taken.

> THE BLACKEST DAY IN LIVERPOOL'S HISTORY WILL NEVER BE FORGOTTEN AND NOR WILL THE 96

Hillsborough memorial

THE HILLSBOROUGH memorial is an emotional reminder of the frailty of human existence. It was unveiled by Nessie Shankly, Bill's widow, on 15 April 1990, the one-year anniversary of the Hillsborough disaster. The memorial is made of marble bearing the names of those who died engraved in gold. The two lists are split by a glass case withholding an eternal flame. The inscription on top of the memorial says: 'Liverpool memorial – Dedicated to those who lost their lives at the F.A. Cup semi-final Hillsborough 15th April 1989.'

'LIVERPOOL MEMORIAL – DEDICATED TO THOSE WHO LOST THEIR LIVES AT THE FA CUP SEMI-FINAL HILLSBOROUGH 15TH APRIL 1989'

You'll Never Walk Alone

John Alfred Anderson	(62)
Colin Mark Ashcroft	(19)
James Gary Aspinall	(18)
Kester Roger Marcus Ball	(16)
Gerard Bernard Patrick Baron	(67)
Simon Bell	(17)
Barry Sidney Bennett	(26)
David John Benson	(22)
David William Birtle	(22)
Tony Bland	(22)
Paul David Brady	(21)
Andrew Mark Brookes	(26)
Carl Brown	(18)
David Steven Brown	(25)
Henry Thomas Burke	(47)
Peter Andrew Burkett	(24)
Paul William Carlile	(19)
Raymond Thomas Chapman	(50)
Gary Christopher Church	(19)
Joseph Clark	(29)
Paul Clark	(18)
Gary Collins	(22)
Stephen Paul Copoc	(20)
Tracey Elizabeth Cox	(23)
James Philip Delaney	(19)
Christopher Barry Devonside	(18)
Christopher Edwards	(29)

Vincent Michael Fitzsimmons	(34)
Thomas Steven Fox	(21)
Jon-Paul Gilhooley	(10)
Barry Glover	(27)
Ian Thomas Glover	(20)
Derrick George Godwin	(24)
Roy Harry Hamilton	(34)
Philip Hammond	(14)
Eric Hankin	(33)
Gary Harrison	(27)
Stephen Francis Harrison	(31)
Peter Andrew Harrison	(15)
David Hawley	(39)
James Robert Hennessy	(29)
Paul Anthony Hewitson	(26)
Carl Darren Hewitt	(17)
Nicholas Michael Hewitt	(16)
Sarah Louise Hicks	(19)
Victoria Jane Hicks	(15)
Gordon Rodney Horn	(20)
Arthur Horrocks	(41)
Thomas Howard	(39)
Thomas Anthony Howard	(14)
Eric George Hughes	(42)
Alan Johnston	(29)
Christine Anne Jones	(27)
Gary Philip Jones	(18)
Richard Jones	(25)
Nicholas Peter Joynes	(27)
Anthony Peter Kelly	(29)
Michael David Kelly	(38)
Carl David Lewis	(18)
David William Mather	(19)
Brian Christopher Mathews	(38)
Francis Joseph McAllister	(27)

John McBrien	(18)
Marion Hazel McCabe	(21)
Joseph Daniel McCarthy	(21)
Peter McDonnell	(21)
Alan McGlone	(28)
Keith McGrath	(17)
Paul Brian Murray	(14)
Lee Nicol	(14)
Stephen Francis O'Neill	(17)
Jonathon Owens	(18)
William Roy Pemberton	(23)
Carl William Rimmer	(21)
David George Rimmer	(38)
Graham John Roberts	(24)
Steven Joseph Robinson	(17)
Henry Charles Rogers	(17)
Colin Andrew Hugh William Sefton	(23)
Inger Shah	(38)
Paula Ann Smith	(26)
Adam Edward Spearritt	(14)
Philip John Steele	(15)
David Leonard Thomas	(23)
Patrick John Thompson	(35)
Peter Reuben Thompson	(30)
Stuart Paul William Thompson	(17)
Peter Francis Tootle	(21)
Christopher James Traynor	(26)
Martin Kevin Traynor	(16)
Kevin Tyrrell	(15)
Colin Wafer	(19)
Ian David Whelan	(19)
Martin Kenneth Wild	(29)
Kevin Daniel Williams	(15)
Graham John Wright	(17)

Hoare,
Joseph

JOSEPH HOARE made seven league appearances for Liverpool during the 1903/04 season but Billy Dunlop and Alf West were firm favourites in the full-back positions.

Hoare trained as a carpenter and joiner and was playing amateur football at Southampton Oxford when Southern League Southampton took a liking to him. He only played occasionally in his three spells at the Saints. Hoare ran a tobacconist's shop in Woolston, Southampton, and eventually returned to amateur football.

JOSEPH HOARE
[LIVERPOOL]

FACTFILE

BORN
Southampton,
November 1881
DIED
24 March 1947
POSITION
Right/left-back
OTHER CLUBS
Southampton Oxford
(1897–1902),
Southampton (1902–03),
Southampton (1904–05),
Bitterne Guild (1905–08),
Southampton (loan, 1907),
Salisbury City (1908–09),
Bitterne Guild (1909–12),
Woolston (1912–14)
SIGNED FROM
Southampton, £75,
25 May 1903
LFC DEBUT
24 October 1903
CONTRACT EXPIRY
1 May 1904

Season	League		FA Cup		Total	
	App	Goals	App	Goals	App	Goals
1903/04	1	0	0	0	1	0
Total	1	0	0	0	1	0

Hobbs,
Jack

JACK HOBBS is the youngest ever player to feature for Lincoln City in the Football League. He was 16 years and 149 days when he came on as substitute against Bristol Rovers on 15 January 2005. The central defender joined the Reds from Lincoln City in August 2005 following a successful trial spell at Melwood and became the captain of the reserves. Because of a long-term injury to Daniel Agger, Hobbs got an opportunity when he came on as a late substitute for Lucas in the League Cup at Reading in September 2007. He played the whole 90 minutes of the next round against Cardiff and made his full league debut five weeks later away to Reading.

The arrival of Martin Skrtel diminished Hobbs' chances of a long run in the first team. He was loaned to Leicester City for the 2008/09 season and performed so well his move was made permanent. He played in 44 matches for Leicester in 2009/10 as the Foxes

reached the Championship playoffs. Hobbs, who was voted Leicester's Player of the Year, was made captain for both legs of the semi-final with Cardiff City but the Welsh club progressed.

LEICESTER signed a number of new defenders for the 2010/11 season which meant that Hobbs was, surprisingly considering his player award from the previous campaign, no longer certain of his place in the team. In February 2011 he made a loan move to Hull City and appeared in 13 matches for the Tigers in the Championship before signing a permanent three-year deal. Hobbs was named captain in Nicky Barmby's side and was an exceptional performer for the club, but ruptured his anterior cruciate ligament in April 2012. Hobbs returned seven months later and regained his spot in Hull's first XI. After Steve Bruce had clinched a Premier League spot for Hull in the 2013/14 season, Hobbs moved on a season-long loan to Nottingham Forest.

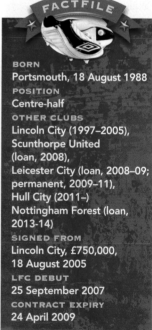

FACTFILE

BORN
Portsmouth, 18 August 1988
POSITION
Centre-half
OTHER CLUBS
Lincoln City (1997–2005),
Scunthorpe United
(loan, 2008),
Leicester City (loan, 2008–09;
permanent, 2009–11),
Hull City (2011–)
Nottingham Forest (loan,
2013-14)
SIGNED FROM
Lincoln City, £750,000,
18 August 2005
LFC DEBUT
25 September 2007
CONTRACT EXPIRY
24 April 2009

Season	League		FA Cup		League Cup		Europe		Other		Total	
	App	Goals	App	Goals	App	Goals	App	Goals	App	Goals	App	Goals
2007/08	1 (1)	0	0	0	2 (1)	0	0	0	-	-	3 (2)	0
Total	1 (1)	0	0	0	2 (1)	0	0	0	0	0	3 (2)	0

Hobson,
Alf

ALF HOBSON was Liverpool's goalkeeper at the start of the 1936/37 season and played in the first 26 games of that campaign before being replaced by Arthur Riley after the club's worst run of the season, a single league point being gained from seven matches during December and January.

Hobson had to pick the ball out of his net 17 times. His final game in this terrible run was a 3-0 defeat to Norwich where he conceded a disastrous goal. He kicked the ball upfield where Scott, who was in the centre circle, returned it straight back to him. As Hobson was struggling to recover, the ball went through his legs and, at a 'snail-like pace', rolled over the line as poor Hobson could only watch on, being stuck in the mud. South Africans Arthur Riley and Dirk Kemp shared the goalkeeping duties the next season, with Hobson playing just once. Hobson played 171 games for Liverpool in wartime and returned to Liverpool's first team in an FA Cup fourth round tie at Burnden Park, Bolton, eight years after

making his previous competitive appearance for Liverpool. Sadly it was not a happy experience for him or his colleagues as Liverpool were thrashed 5-0. FA Cup matches were played over two legs in the first season after the war and by the time Bolton visited Anfield just four days later, Harry Wheeler Nickson was in goal.

HOBSON passed away on 21 February 2004 and was at that point the oldest surviving Liverpool player, aged 90. *LFC.tv* had made contact with Hobson's family up in the north east and was in the process of arranging an interview when his daughter

Susan informed them of their sad loss. Susan said her father was very proud of his connections with Liverpool Football Club. 'There was only one Alf Hobson. He was a great man who followed Liverpool right to the end. He never forgot his days at Anfield and through all the years he'd proudly kept his club blazer with the Liver Bird emblem on it,' she

said. 'He would always look out for Liverpool's result and he was delighted to know that someone from the club had been in touch just before he passed away. His funeral is on Friday and he'll be surrounded by red and white.'

FACTFILE

BORN
Co. Durham,
9 September 1913
DIED
21 February 2004
POSITION
Goalkeeper
OTHER CLUBS
Ferryhill Athletic,
Shildon Colliery,
Chester (1938–41);
Southport,
Burnley (wartime guest),
South Liverpool (1946–47)
SIGNED FROM
Shildon Colliery, April 1936 /
Chester, 1941
LFC DEBUT
29 August 1936
CONTRACT EXPIRY
October 1938 / 1946

Season	League		FA Cup		Total	
	App	Goals	App	Goals	App	Goals
1936/37	25	0	1	0	26	0
1937/38	1	0	0	0	1	0
1945/46	-	-	1	0	1	0
Total	**26**	**0**	**2**	**0**	**28**	**0**

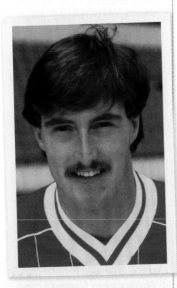

Hodgson,
David

DAVID HODGSON arrived as an England Under-21 international, seemingly having a bright future ahead of him in the game.

He was hardly a proven goalscorer, though, having only scored 20 times in 140 matches for Middlesbrough. He scored four goals in his first six games for Liverpool, flourishing alongside Dalglish and Rush, and played a

total of 37 matches in his first season, scoring nine goals. His main attribute was his pace, but he lacked skill and composure. When fellow striker Michael Robinson arrived at the club, Hodgson's chances were few and far between and he demanded a move. Sunderland were interested but boss Joe Fagan had told Hodgson to speak to him first before signing anything. However, Hodgson went to Sunderland and signed. When he returned Fagan was not best pleased and told Hodgson: 'You've just made the biggest mistake of your life, son.' Fagan felt Sammy Lee wouldn't be a regular for much longer

and had envisaged Hodgson taking his place on the right side of midfield.

HODGSON received a European Cup medal for the win in Rome in 1984, but shortly prior to that Liverpool had travelled to Israel to strengthen the team bond. Hodgson knows a story or two and remembers that trip well: 'We'd been playing Fizzbuzz, one of those drinking games. There was Alan Hansen, Kenny [Dalglish], Bruce Grobbelaar, Stevie Nicol, myself, Ronnie Whelan, Ian Rush, Sammy Lee, all drinking in the square in Tel Aviv,' Hodgson told *LFC Magazine*.

Things got said and a fight started. Me and Rushie were quite close so it's us back to back against everybody else. Somehow it calmed down and I went to the hotel with Rushie and Alan Kennedy, who fell on the ground and couldn't get up. The old Liverpool director Mr Moss was coming out of the hotel just at that moment. So I've got down to pick up Alan Kennedy and I couldn't get up either. And Mr Moss is stood above us frowning. He says: 'Gentlemen, this is Liverpool Football Club.' So I grabbed hold of his trousers and pulled myself up his body. And I put my arm around him and said: 'Mossy, you old bugger, you might be a director but I think you're a great fella.' After breakfast the next morning, they call this big meeting upstairs and around the table there's Bob, Joe Fagan, Moran, Evo and Mr Moss, who stands up. 'I've been at this club for over 20 years and I've never witnessed anything like last night in my life. I've had many accolades passed on to me, but never have I received one so touching than from David Hodgson.' Then they lift the tablecloth and underneath it's piled high with beer! After that meeting, Bob Paisley turned to me and said: 'You're a good Geordie, son. That's what you are.'

AFTER the move to Sunderland Hodgson was on the losing side to Norwich in the 1985 League Cup final and suffered relegation at the end of the season. After only five goals in 40 league games in two seasons Hodgson got a free transfer to Norwich, choosing the Canaries over a similarly lucrative move to Sweden's IFK Gothenburg who then went on to win the UEFA Cup! He was loaned unsuccessfully to old club Middlesbrough in February 1987 and departed for Spain in the summer, which started a long trek between clubs in different countries.

Hodgson went into management and had no fewer than three spells as Darlington's manager from 1995 to 2006. Hodgson still has fond memories of his time at Liverpool: 'When I left Liverpool for Sunderland Roy Evans sent me a glass trophy and they'd inscribed on it: "Good luck, you old bugger!"'

Season	League		FA Cup		League Cup		Europe		Other		Total	
	App	Goals	App	Goals	App	Goals	App	Goals	App	Goals	App	Goals
1982/83	20 (3)	4	3	1	4 (1)	2	3 (2)	2	0 (1)	0	30 (7)	9
1983/84	1 (4)	0	0	0	2 (2)	1	0 (2)	0	0 (1)	0	3 (9)	1
Total	**21 (7)**	**4**	**3**	**1**	**6 (3)**	**3**	**3 (4)**	**2**	**0 (2)**	**0**	**33 (16)**	**10**

Hodgson, Gordon

GORDON HODGSON was one of Liverpool's and indeed the Football League's greatest ever goalscorers; only Roger Hunt has scored more league goals for Liverpool, but all of Hodgson's 233 league strikes came in the First Division from 358 games, a fantastic goals-per-game ratio. Hodgson came to England as one of the youngest members of a South African touring side, with players chosen from across the country: Transvaal, the Western Province, Orange Free State and Natal. The amateurs arrived in Ireland, facing Bohemians in their first game on 30 August 1924, before playing a number of teams in London, usually winning convincingly with Green scoring the majority of the goals.

On 1 October Hodgson's hat-trick in a 5-2 win over Liverpool caught the eye of their board members as well as the *Echo's* Bee. 'The inside right, who took my eye from the first moment, is only nineteen, but plays like a seasoned professional,' he wrote in the local paper. The South Africans played attractive football, 'passing along the ground from the backs to the forwards' and 'there was no roaming and no dribbling across the field. Each player was bent solely on attack.' The tour took them to Wales and Scotland as well as to Holland and Belgium and then back to England again, concluding their exhausting schedule of 25 matches in three months in Liverpool where they beat Everton 3-1, their 15th win. They returned to South Africa on 5 December 1924, but the tour changed the lives of two men in the party; two men that Liverpool fans would cherish for years to come; Hodgson and Arthur Riley.

HODGSON signed for Liverpool on 14 December 1925, having agreed to the move while in South Africa the month previous. He made his debut in February 1926 and featured in 12 matches in the 1925/26 season, scoring four times, just a taste of what was to come. The goalkeeper of the South African touring side, Riley, had already made his debut for Liverpool in October 1925. Hodgson, who is still Liverpool's hat-trick king with 17 to his name, scored his first treble for the club against Sheffield United on 11 September 1926 in his seventeenth game. The *Liverpool Echo* was impressed:

Based on this performance, I would suggest it will not be the last we see from this very talented South African... Chambers (Inside Left) had proven to Liverpool over many years now that 20–30 goals a season was well within his scope. Forshaw (Centre Forward) scored hat-tricks for fun and also weighed in with 20–30 goals a season. With the addition of the South African, Hodgson (Inside Right), I fail to see how any opposition will keep a clean sheet when all three play in the same side. A good striker is a necessity in the game. A brace of good strikers is very rare indeed. The Liverpool side now contains triplets of awesome power, that's just downright greed. God help the first division when Liverpool come to town.

OVER the next nine seasons, Hodgson missed very few games in the league or cup and scored prolifically throughout that period. It was a shame that this golden run coincided with a barren period for the club because his contribution to the Liverpool cause was massive and he deserved to end up with more than the handful of England and Football League representative honours he received. Hodgson, who played twice for the South African international team, also qualified for England as both his parents were born in 'Old Blighty'. South Africa was part of the Commonwealth so he was allowed to feature for both countries.

The 36 league goals Hodgson scored in the 1930/31 season beat Sam Raybould's 1902/03 club record total of 31. His feat would not be equalled for over 30 years, until Roger Hunt came onto the scene. Hodgson scored three hat-tricks that season at Anfield but perhaps it was the four goals he scored in an away match at Hillsborough that gave him most satisfaction of all. He was top scorer in seven out of the nine whole seasons he played at Liverpool. Hodgson's popularity among the crowd prompted an ingenious biscuit seller to name his home-made ginger nuts, that he sold in a quantity of five for a penny on matchdays at Anfield, in his honour. 'Hodgson's Choice! Hodgson's Choice!' he would call. The same shrewd character, mind you, was at Goodison the following week shouting, 'Dixie's Choice! Dixie's Choice!' Never has Merseyside boasted such great goalscorers simultaneously as Gordon Hodgson and Dixie Dean.

HODGSON moved to Aston Villa in January 1936 at the age of 31. He was relegated to the Second Division with Villa and left the Midlands for Yorkshire where he joined struggling First Division Leeds United in the second half of the 1936/37 season, scoring six

goals in 13 games, helping the club to beat the drop. Leeds improved the following season in which Hodgson continued to impress, at 33 years of age, with 25 goals in 36 league games, three goals away from being top scorer in the league. He remained admirably focused despite the loss of his 27-year-old wife on 8 March 1938, leaving Hodgson a widower with two children. He was still as prolific as ever in the final season of his career, scoring five times as Leeds beat Leicester City 8-2 in October 1938. Hodgson scored 51 goals in 81 league games for Leeds in the First Division and could have undoubtedly added to his tally if World War Two hadn't intervened.

Hodgson was an all-round sportsman, playing 56 first-class cricket matches as a fast bowler for Lancashire. But football was his first love and it was no surprise that he progressed from player to manager by taking charge of team

affairs at Port Vale in October 1946. He was there for over four years and saw them move to their current stadium, Vale Park, in 1950. Port Vale legend Roy Sproson had Hodgson as his first boss. 'Gordon Hodgson was a fair chap. He would give you a rollicking one minute and then it would be forgotten. Everybody liked him and his loss was so sad.' Following George Kay's resignation in January 1951 due

to health reasons, Hodgson was among the hopefuls who were interviewed for the manager's job at Liverpool. Don Welsh was eventually appointed, while Hodgson was admitted to hospital a couple of months later where his 'throat complaint' was deemed inoperable. He returned to his home in Burslem after a month in hospital and a few days later, with a promising managerial career still in its infancy, he died of cancer on 14 June 1951 at the early age of 47.

FACTFILE

BORN
Johannesburg, South Africa, 16 April 1904
DIED
14 June 1951
POSITION
Inside-right forward
OTHER CLUBS
Benoni (1919–21), Rustenburg (1921–22), Pretoria (1922–24), Transvaal (1924–25), Aston Villa (1936–37), Leeds United (1937–39); Hartlepools United, York City (wartime guest)
SIGNED FROM
Transvaal, 14 December 1925
INTERNATIONAL CAPS
2 South Africa caps, 1924; 3 England caps (1 goal), 1930–31
LFC DEBUT GAME/GOAL
27 February 1926 / 10 March 1926
CONTRACT EXPIRY
8 January 1936

Season	League		FA Cup		Total	
	App	Goals	App	Goals	App	Goals
1925/26	12	4	0	0	12	4
1926/27	36	16	4	2	40	18
1927/28	32	23	0	0	32	23
1928/29	38	30	3	2	41	32
1929/30	36	14	1	0	37	14
1930/31	40	36	1	0	41	36
1931/32	39	26	4	1	43	27
1932/33	37	24	1	0	38	24
1933/34	37	24	3	1	40	25
1934/35	34	27	2	2	36	29
1935/36	17	9	0	0	17	9
Total	**358**	**233**	**19**	**8**	**377**	**241**

Hodgson, Roy

ROY HODGSON'S journey to Merseyside was definitely a 'long and winding road'. Before his 30th birthday he had left British shores for the first but certainly not the last time and moved to Sweden. His impact was instant as Halmstads won the Swedish championship in both 1976 and 1979. Even more than three decades later, this achievement is still ranked as one of the biggest-ever success stories in the Swedish domestic game.

He was appointed as Bob Houghton's assistant manager at Bristol City in 1980, serving as caretaker manager for four months from January to April 1982, relieved of his duties when the club was relegated to the Fourth Division. In 1983 Hodgson returned to Sweden to manage Örebro SK for two years and Malmö FF where he led the club to the Swedish championship in 1986 and 1988. Hodgson came to other countries' attention by defeating Inter Milan 2-1 on aggregate in the European Cup. So impressed were Malmö by Hodgson's ability that they offered him a lifetime contract. But the wanderlust that was evident in his later managerial career was still apparent in his 40s. He moved to Neuchatel Xamax in Switzerland where he oversaw famous European victories over Glasgow Celtic and Real Madrid, before he agreed to take over the Swiss National team in 1992. Despite being in a strong qualifying group that included both Italy and Portugal, Hodgson led Switzerland to the 1994 World Cup Finals in America, where they reached the last 16. Switzerland qualified just as comfortably for the 1996 European Championships in England but between qualifying

and the tournament finals starting Hodgson had become Inter Milan's manager. In 1997 he improved Inter's league position to third, and they also reached the 1997 UEFA Cup final, which they lost on penalties to Schalke 04. Hodgson was tempted back to England by Blackburn Rovers' millionaire owner Jack Walker in the 1997 close season. Only two years after winning the League Championship, Rovers were struggling at the wrong end of the table. Although Hodgson took Blackburn into a UEFA Cup place, his second season was beset with injuries, strange purchases and dressing room unrest. Marooned at the bottom of the Premier League table as 1998 turned into 1999, the manager was inevitably dismissed.

Having now passed his 50th birthday, Hodgson returned to Scandinavia to take control of Copenhagen's biggest team in May 2000. Shortly after securing the Danish Superliga title in 2001, he took charge of Udinese in Italy but despite a promising start only lasted six months before he was dismissed, allegedly for saying that he regretted taking the job in the first place! In April 2002 he agreed to manage the national team of the United Arab Emirates but was again dismissed after only a short period in charge. Despite these setbacks Hodgson was in as much demand as ever and added to his international curriculum vitae by taking over as coach of Finland in August 2005. Finland failed to qualify for the Euro 2008 finals and Fulham came calling a few days before the end of 2007. Hodgson's 2½ years at Craven Cottage can only be regarded as successful, despite the absence of a worthwhile trophy. Threatened by relegation as his tenure as Fulham boss began, he masterminded a 'Great Escape' that saw survival ensured with a victory at Portsmouth on the final day of the Premier League season. A year later Hodgson led Fulham to 7th in the league, their best ever position. In 2009/10 Fulham marched on to the Europa League final. Liverpool were knocked out in the semi-finals by Atletico Madrid, the team that would break Fulham's hearts in the final.

The cosmopolitan Hodgson was voted the League Managers' Association's Manager of the Year for 2010 by a record margin and at the age of 62 was hired by Liverpool's board headed by Martin Broughton to steady the ship as the club was in the process of changing owners. 'I like a high-tempo passing game,' Hodgson proudly announced on 4 July. 'I was influenced by the Liverpool team which dominated the 70s with all its great players and playing the football they played.' Following Liverpool's 2-0 defeat to Everton on 17 October, two days after Fenway Sports Group's takeover had been realised, the club was second from bottom in the league with one win in eight. Hodgson was by no means worried judging by his post-game comments. 'In my opinion the way we played the game was as good as I've seen us play this season. I think it's a bit unfortunate that after such a good game of football, everything revolves around the fact that Liverpool didn't win it. The shape of our team was good; the quality of our passing was good. We didn't score goals and Everton did, but I refuse to sit here and accept we were in any way outplayed or were in any way inferior.' Liverpool fans hung their heads in shame as they could hardly believe that this was Liverpool's manager speaking after being comprehensively beaten by the club's biggest rivals. At the start of October Hodgson had defended his so-far unimpressive record at Liverpool that only made him an object of ridicule. 'What do you mean, do my methods translate? They have translated from Halmstad to Malmö to Örebro to Neuchatel Xamax to the Swiss national team.' The comparison of these teams to Liverpool's standing in world football hardly was a convincing argument. The two players who Hodgson had brought into the club based on his previous experience working with them;

Christian Poulsen and Paul Konchesky were clearly not of Liverpool quality. The Reds did win three league games in a row following the Goodison Park debacle and during that run beat Napoli 3-1 in a crucial game in their Europa League group that they were eventually promoted from. Hodgson's men were soon on the slide again, losing three out of their next six league games, now in mid-table mediocrity; a familiar spot for Hodgson when he was in charge of his previous English clubs. As Liverpool lost 3-1 to Newcastle United Hodgson seemed on a different planet. His attempts to offer optimism to Liverpool fans were outlandish. 'The only team with better results than us over the past five or six games is Arsenal or Manchester United. If you take the last five or six games we are right up there in terms of results.' In fact Liverpool had won seven points from last 18 possible and were 10–11th in the form table while United had picked up 14 points and Arsenal 12.

> **HE WAS ALWAYS GOING TO BE UP AGAINST IT AT LIVERPOOL AS REDS' FOLLOWERS PINED FOR THE RETURN OF KENNY DALGLISH**

The pressure that was piling up on Hodgson reached breaking point. Liverpool were booed off Anfield after a 1-0 defeat against Wolves to which Hodgson responded: 'The fans have left angry and that's understandable. We've let them down. I am getting used to it, that is the way it is. We've had to live with that for quite a long time now as ever since I came here the famous Anfield support has not really been there.' Three days after a miserable defeat at his former club, Blackburn Rovers, Hodgson left

the club and Kenny Dalglish took charge until the end of the season.

On 11 February 2011, slightly more than a month after being relieved of his responsibilities at Anfield, Hodgson succeeded Roberto Di Matteo at West Bromwich Albion. To be fair to Hodgson he did an excellent job at West Brom, a club which he clearly was more suited to, one who was just happy to be in the top half of the table. To, at least, Liverpool fans' incredulity Hodgson was appointed England manager on 1 May 2012. He had been first linked with the post at the close of the twentieth century as Glenn Hoddle's possible successor, but the post went to Kevin Keegan.

ROY HODGSON'S name is respected in a number of countries where he has coached. He was always going to be up against it at Liverpool as Reds' followers pined for the return of Kenny Dalglish.

Season	Division	P	W	D	L	GF	GA	Pts	Pos	Win %	FA Cup	League Cup
2010/11*	Premier League	20	7	4	9	24	27	25	12	35.00	-	3rd Round
Total	-	**20**	**7**	**4**	**9**	**24**	**27**	**25**	-	**35.00**	**-**	**-**

* Hodgson left on 8 January 2011 with Liverpool in 12th position

Holden,
Ralph

THE HALF-BACK'S first game was as a member of the side that crashed 4-1 at Manchester City on 18 January 1913 and his second match was a goalless draw with West Bromwich Albion at Anfield on 27 September 1913.

RALPH HOLDEN lost a leg in World War One and on 3 May 1919 Liverpool and Tranmere played a testimonial game for him where each Liverpool player donated £2 to the fund, 2lb bags of sugar were auctioned off several times and a pipe raised £15.

Season	League		FA Cup		Total	
	App	Goals	App	Goals	App	Goals
1912/13	1	0	0	0	1	0
1913/14	1	0	0	0	1	0
Total	**2**	**0**	**0**	**0**	**2**	**0**

Holmes,
John

BROTHER of Preston North End's 'Invincibles' legend and England international, Bob Holmes, John made his debut for Liverpool as centre-half in a 5-1 win over Newcastle on 14 September 1895.

According to the *Liverpool Mercury* Holmes 'opened in a very faltering manner. Judgment and speed were both wanting, but as the game proceeded he gradually improved, and at the close of the contest was supporting the forwards in true North-Ender style.' Nineteen of his 44 league and cup appearances came in his debut season in 1895/96 when the club won the Second Division Championship for the second time. He made 25 appearances over the next couple of years as Liverpool consolidated their First Division place after an absence of just one year from the top flight.

John Holmes

Season	League		FA Cup		Other		Total	
	App	Goals	App	Goals	App	Goals	App	Goals
1895/96	17	0	2	0	0	0	19	0
1896/97	13	0	0	0	-	-	13	0
1897/98	12	0	0	0	-	-	12	0
Total	**42**	**0**	**2**	**0**	**0**	**0**	**44**	**0**

FACTFILE

BORN
Preston, 1869
POSITION
Half-back
OTHER CLUBS
Preston North End (1889–95),
Burton Swifts (1898–99),
New Brighton Tower
(1899–1901)
SIGNED FROM
Preston North End,
June 1895
LFC DEBUT
14 September 1895
CONTRACT EXPIRY
1898
HONOURS
Second Division
Championship 1895/96

Honours

First Division Championship

1900/01, 1905/06, 1921/22, 1922/23, 1946/47, 1963/64, 1965/66, 1972/73, 1975/76, 1976/77, 1978/79, 1979/80, 1981/82, 1982/83, 1983/84, 1985/86, 1987/88, 1989/90

Second Division Championship

1893/94, 1895/96, 1904/05, 1961/62

FA Cup

1965, 1974, 1986, 1989, 1992, 2001, 2006

League Cup

1981, 1982, 1983, 1984, 1995, 2001, 2003, 2012

European Cup

1977, 1978, 1981, 1984, 2005

UEFA Cup

1973, 1976, 2001

European Super Cup

1977, 2001, 2005

Charity Shield

1964 (shared), 1965 (shared), 1966, 1974, 1976, 1977 (shared), 1979, 1980, 1982, 1986 (shared), 1988, 1989, 1990 (shared), 2001, 2006

Screen Sport Super Cup

1987

Lancashire League

1892/93

Lancashire Senior Cup and Liverpool Senior Cup honours are listed in their own separate entries.

FA Youth Cup

1996, 2006, 2007

Central League

1956/57, 1968/69, 1969/70, 1970/71, 1972/73, 1973/74, 1974/75, 1975/76, 1976/77, 1978/79, 1979/80, 1980/81, 1981/82, 1983/84, 1984/85, 1989/90

Hood,
Billy

BELFAST-BOY Billy Hood played one amateur international for his country in a 5-1 win over England on 13 February 1937, during his only season at Cliftonville. The following month Hood signed for Liverpool. He made three consecutive league appearances for the Reds during the 1937/38 season as a replacement for the regular right-back, Tom Cooper.

Those three fixtures, against Huddersfield, Blackpool and Derby, resulted in one win and two defeats. At the time Liverpool were struggling close to the bottom of the First Division, having lost 10 out of 18 games. The club finished the season in the middle of the table. Hood returned to Northern Ireland with Derry City after just one season at Liverpool.

FACTFILE

BORN
Belfast, Northern Ireland,
3 November 1914
POSITION
Right-back
OTHER CLUBS
Ballycarry,
Crusaders (1935–36),
Cliftonville (1936–37),
Derry City
SIGNED FROM
Cliftonville, March 1937
LFC DEBUT
20 November 1937
CONTRACT EXPIRY
1938

Season	League		FA Cup		Total	
	App	Goals	App	Goals	App	Goals
1937/38	3	0	0	0	3	0
Total	**3**	**0**	**0**	**0**	**3**	**0**

Hooper,
Mike

AFTER IMPRESSING with Fourth Division Wrexham, as well as receiving a degree in English Literature at Swansea University, Mike Hooper joined Liverpool in 1985 as a reserve to Bruce Grobbelaar who hadn't missed a game for four years. Grobbelaar got injured ten months later in the Charity Shield at Wembley against Everton and Hooper made eight appearances in his absence.

FACTFILE

BORN
Bristol, 10 February 1964
POSITION
Goalkeeper
OTHER CLUBS
Mangotsfield United,
Bristol City (1983–85),
Wrexham (1985),
Leicester City (loan, 1990),
Newcastle United (1993–96),
Sunderland (loan, 1995)
SIGNED FROM
Wrexham, £40,000,
25 October 1985
LFC DEBUT
16 August 1986
CONTRACT EXPIRY
23 September 1993

His longest spell in goal was for 25 consecutive games from September 1988 until January 1989. Hooper had initially come into the side as Grobbelaar had meningitis but when he was ready again in November, Dalglish was happy enough to keep Hooper in goal until shaky performances resulted in him losing his place.

New manager Graeme Souness preferred him to Grobbelaar and David James from November to January in the 1992/93 season, adding 15 games to his tally. Hooper was an able understudy although not competent enough to become Liverpool's first-choice keeper for good. He signed for Kevin Keegan's Newcastle in September 1993, after being on bench duty at Liverpool for eight solid months, and suffered a similar fate at the Magpies as inconsistency crept in when given a proper chance. Hooper dropped out of the game for good in the summer of 1996 aged only 32.

A LITTLE-KNOWN fact about Hooper is that he is a bird enthusiast, as noted by former Manchester City player Paul Lake in his autobiography *I'm Not Really Here*.

Lilleshall's vast gardens were a haven for wildlife – rabbits, foxes and badgers were a frequent sight but it was our feathered friends that held the biggest novelty value for me. I was used to the occasional tweeting sparrow or screeching starling in Manchester, but never had heard anything remotely like the stereophonic Shropshire birdsong that greeted me every morning. Mike Hooper, the Liverpool goalkeeper and fellow Lilleshall inmate, was a keen birdwatcher who never tired of reminding us that we were in a twitcher's paradise. Whenever he heard an unusual chirrup he would stop in his tracks, even if it was slap-bang in a middle of a training session. 'Sshhhh, that's a lesser-crested house-warbler,' he'd say with a whisper, cupping his ears to listen as the ball flew past him into the top corner. 'Yeah, and there's a great tit between the posts,' was one memorable riposte.

	League		FA Cup		League Cup		Europe		Other		Total	
Season	App	Goals	App	Goals	App	Goals	App	Goals	App	Goals	App	Goals
1986/87	11	0	0	0	0	0	-	-	1 (1)	0	12 (1)	0
1987/88	2	0	2	0	0	0	-	-	-	-	4	0
1988/89	17	0	1	0	6	0	-	-	1	0	25	0
1990/91	7	0	0	0	0	0	-	-	0	0	7	0
1991/92	5	0	0	0	1	0	3	0	-	-	9	0
1992/93	8 (1)	0	2	0	3	0	1	0	0	0	14 (1)	0
Total	**50 (1)**	**0**	**5**	**0**	**10**	**0**	**4**	**0**	**2 (1)**	**0**	**71 (2)**	**0**

Hopkin,
Fred

FRED HOPKIN was signed by Liverpool from Manchester United in 1921. He had made 74 appearances and scored eight goals in two post-war seasons at United, where his career began in earnest.

United were given a fine of £350 at the time for paying Hopkin more than the maximum wage and for promising to give him a cut of his transfer fee, which was illegal. Left-winger Hopkin was an ever-present during Liverpool's 1921/22 Championship season. Another title followed a year later when Hopkin missed just two matches and scored his first goal for the club against Bolton Wanderers on 3 March 1923. The goal was followed by a fire in the Anfield Road stand. The joke was that Hopkin was to blame as people were so shocked he had actually scored in his 78th appearance for the club.

The smoke clouded the field of play, but the fire brigade put the fire out and the game finished with a 3-0 win for Liverpool.

HOPKIN was not renowned as a goalscorer, just 12 in 10 seasons, but was certainly a provider from his position on the wing for the likes of Harry Chambers and Dick Forshaw and later for Gordon Hodgson. Hopkin was an excellent sportsman who used his speed to go past defenders and also to win several hurdling competitions. He was so described in the *Derby Daily Telegraph* in 1926: 'Hopkin has turned out to be one of the best investments Liverpool have ever made. His head is now losing its hair, and he may not be as fast as he was, but he can still pull out a rare turn of speed, while as a dribbler he can be elusive. Clings to the touch-line, drops perfect centres, and rarely scores a goal.'

> 'HOPKIN HAS TURNED OUT TO BE ONE OF THE BEST INVESTMENTS LIVERPOOL HAVE EVER MADE'
> *DERBY DAILY TELEGRAPH*

Season	League		FA Cup		Other		Total	
	App	Goals	App	Goals	App	Goals	App	Goals
1921/22	42	0	3	0	1	0	46	0
1922/23	40	1	4	0	-	-	44	1
1923/24	33	0	5	0	-	-	38	0
1924/25	26	1	4	1	-	-	30	2
1925/26	33	1	0	0	-	-	33	1
1926/27	36	0	4	1	-	-	40	1
1927/28	36	3	2	0	-	-	38	3
1928/29	22	0	0	0	-	-	22	0
1929/30	31	3	1	0	-	-	32	3
1930/31	36	1	1	0	-	-	37	1
Total	**335**	**10**	**24**	**2**	**1**	**0**	**360**	**12**

FACTFILE

BORN
Dewsbury, Yorkshire, 23 September 1895
DIED
5 March 1970
POSITION
Left-winger
OTHER CLUBS
Darlington (1912–19); Tottenham Hotspur (wartime guest), Manchester United (1919–21), Darlington (1931–32)
SIGNED FROM
Manchester United, £2,800, May 1921
LFC DEBUT GAME/GOAL
27 August 1921 / 3 March 1923
CONTRACT EXPIRY
August 1931
HONOURS
League Championship 1921/22, 1922/23

Houghton, Ray

HURTFUL rejections shaped Ray Houghton's early club and international career. West Ham let him go after only one game and Under-18 Scotland manager Andy Roxburgh said he wasn't good enough.

Houghton went on to star for Ireland, as his father was born in Donegal. He was born in Glasgow, but moved to London when he was 10. Second Division Fulham snapped him up after West Ham rejected him in 1982 and he made 145 appearances and scored 21 goals in a four-year spell. Houghton won the League Cup in his first season at First Division newcomers Oxford United, scoring one goal in the 3-0 win in the final against QPR. Oxford were placed 18 out of 22 First Division teams in both the two full seasons the Glaswegian spent at the club.

Houghton had a monumental international career with a strong

Irish side, scoring two of the most important goals in the Irish national team's history. He grabbed the winner in the sixth minute in the opening game in Group B between Ireland and England in the European Championships in 1988. He was the hero again in the group stages of the

> HOUGHTON WAS THE LAST PLAYER IN THE DALGLISH JIGSAW OF THE SIDE THAT WALKED AWAY WITH THE TITLE IN 1987/88

World Cup in 1994 when Ireland defeated Italy with Houghton's 12th-minute goal. Ireland reached the last 16, one stage less than in 1990 when Houghton played in all Ireland's five games on the road to the quarter-finals in the World Cup before being knocked out by Italy.

HOUGHTON was the last player in the Dalglish jigsaw of the side that walked away with the title in 1987/88, a season that saw Oxford relegated in bottom place. In the first home game of the season against Oxford, Kenny Dalglish wrote in his diary: 'I was impressed, and not for the first time, by Ray Houghton's performance in Oxford's midfield. He looks a fine player and is a

good competitor.' Six weeks later he was a Liverpool player. Craig Johnston made way and Houghton made an immediate impact, scoring in his second appearance against Wimbledon two minutes after coming on as substitute at Plough Lane. Houghton was an industrious player whose energetic runs inspired others and was a great team player. He suited Liverpool's style perfectly and was a vital cog in their machine. Houghton slotted in smoothly on the right side of midfield with John Barnes on the opposite side, Steve McMahon and Ronnie Whelan or

Nigel Spackman in the engine room and Peter Beardsley and John Aldridge up front. Houghton was Liverpool's hero when his header knocked out Everton in his first Merseyside derby in the fifth round of the FA Cup at Goodison Park. A surprising defeat to Wimbledon in the final prevented another domestic double.

Houghton played 52 out of 53 games the following season as Liverpool lost the league title to Arsenal on the last day of the season. Liverpool reclaimed the title in 1990 but although Houghton had an injury-hit

season he featured in half of 50 matches played. He was a key player in Souness's first full season, scoring a career-best 12 goals, therefore making the Scotsman's decision to sell him to Aston Villa in the summer, at the age of 30, all the more puzzling. Steve McManaman was emerging as a promising right-winger but Houghton still had a couple of good years in him and could have been easily accommodated elsewhere in the team. Houghton made 105 Premier League appearances for Villa and Crystal Palace until the Eagles were relegated in the 1994/95 season.

FACTFILE

BORN
Glasgow, Scotland,
9 January 1962
POSITION
Right-winger
OTHER CLUBS
West Ham United (1979–82),
Fulham (1982–85),
Oxford United (1985–87),
Aston Villa (1992–95),
Crystal Palace (1995–97),
Reading (1997–99),
Stevenage Borough
(1999–2000)
SIGNED FROM
Oxford United, £825,000,
19 October 1987
INTERNATIONAL CAPS
73 Ireland caps (6 goals)
(34 (3) at LFC), 1986–97
LFC DEBUT GAME/GOAL
24 October 1987 /
4 November 1987
CONTRACT EXPIRY
28 July 1992
HONOURS
League Championship
1987/88, 1989/90;
FA Cup 1989, 1992

Season	League		FA Cup		League Cup		Europe		Other		Total	
	App	Goals	App	Goals	App	Goals	App	Goals	App	Goals	App	Goals
1987/88	26 (2)	5	7	2	0	0	-	-	-	-	33 (2)	7
1988/89	38	7	5	0	6	0	-	-	3	1	52	8
1989/90	16 (3)	1	3 (1)	0	2	0	-	-	0	0	21 (4)	1
1990/91	31 (1)	7	3	1	3	2	-	-	1	0	38 (1)	10
1991/92	36	8	8	1	3	1	4	2	-	-	51	12
Total	147 (6)	28	26 (1)	4	14	3	4	2	4	1	195 (7)	38

Houldíng
John

JOHN HOULDING'S story is of a local boy of ordinary means who grew up to be a wealthy brewery owner, the mayor of his city and president of two football teams. His father, cow-keeper Thomas, taught him and John's two brothers, Thomas and William, early about the value of hard work.

John was born at 15 Tenterden Street just off Scotland Road in Liverpool and baptised on 4 August 1833 at the St Martin in the Fields Church nearby. He left school at only eleven years of age to work in the office of Liverpool shipbrokers Miners & Rae. His father was forced to get a job a local brewery to make ends meet when his livestock suffered from cattle plague. John quit his job to

stay at home to look after the rest of the livestock with his brother William and sold milk door-to-door. John became interested in the ale business around 16 years of age when he filled in for his father at the brewery, as he had broken his collar bone. In 1853 John started working as a drayman at Green & Clarkson's brewery in Soho Street. He delivered beer to pubs in the local area by driving a low flat-bed wagon that was pulled by horses. John was very ambitious and didn't rest until he was the company's chief brewer three years later and engineer and book keeper to boot. He opened up a couple of pubs before he realised his dream in 1871 of opening his own brewery, Houlding's Brewery Co. Ltd. in Tynemouth Street. His prime products; 'Beacon Ale' and 'Amber Ale' made him a fortune. When the company was liquidated in 1939 by Ind Coope & Allsop Ltd. it owned 21 public houses.

As a member of the Conservative Party Houlding made his presence felt in political life. He was voted as the Tories' representative in Everton in 1872 and was Councillor for Everton and Kirkdale from 1884. Houlding was very concerned about the well-being of Stanley hospital in his constituency in Kirkdale and was on its management committee. After he established Liverpool Football Club the team played a number of friendly games in aid of the hospital. In 1895 he was raised to the bench of Aldermen. The increasingly influential John Houlding became known as 'King John of Everton' in the Press. He was an Orangeman and Grand Master, second in Freemason seniority only to the King himself. He fought hard to improve the plight of the poor and elderly and gained much recognition for his work on their behalf.

Houlding took an active interest in sports of all kinds and was the second President of The Anfield Bicycle Club as well as President of the English

Baseball Association. In 1876 he moved to Stanley House at Anfield Road, close to Stanley Park where Everton, formed in 1878, were to play their football. In 1881 he was appointed President of Everton Football Club. Three years later the club moved to a land even closer to home, just down the street, in fact, between Anfield Road and Walton Breck Road. Everton's new ground became known simply as Anfield after the district it was situated in. Less than 12 months passed before Houlding had bought the Anfield ground from Joseph Orrell Jr. for a tidy sum of £5,400 that with legal costs amounted to £6,000. The contract stipulated that the land on the perimeter of the Anfield ground that Joseph's uncle, brewer John Orrell, owned should be left alone in case of a future construction of an access road that Houlding should partake in building. This contractual clause later played a big role in the split between Houlding and Everton.

In 1888 a dispute arose between Houlding and the rest of the board, that had concerns about the size of the rent for the use of the ground, which had until then only been £100 per year. Houlding claimed one of the conditions he made when he bought the ground in 1885 was that 'the committee pay me what rent they could until a maximum was reached of about 4 per cent on the cost.' £240 would amount to 4 per cent of the original £6,000 Houlding had to pay for acquiring Anfield. At the general meeting in July 1888 the board consented to pay Houlding £150 per year, and the extra £90 he wanted if money would be available at the end of the season, which in fact proved to be.

HOULDING already proposed in May 1889 that Everton would change into a limited company and buy Anfield, but the board decided against it and agreed to pay him £250 in rent per year. Things really came to head in the summer of 1891 when John Orrell wanted to utilise his right to build his access road that unfortunately meant league champions Everton would have to tear down the stand that had been built on that land. At a special general meeting on 15 September 1891 Houlding reiterated his long-standing desire that Everton would become a limited company. Everton would need to sell approximately 12,000 £1 shares so the club could buy Anfield as well as Orrell's land for £10,875 plus interest. Houlding felt he had done right by the club and since 1886 he had given the club £2,330 that had been thankfully repaid with gate receipts. He felt unfairly treated by the club's delegation that wanted to resolve this matter and his stance had always been 'that so long as football was played on the ground I would not interfere and if at any time they could not pay me my maximum rent they were to pay me what they could.

John Houlding
by Wasan Sotthikason For E.F.C.S.A

I have not interfered. It is Mr Orrell and some members of the Committee who have during the non-playing season.'

Boardmember William Robert Clayton claimed after consulting a land agent that the land was by no means worth as much as Houlding claimed, evaluating it at 4s. 6d. per yard instead of Houlding's 7s. 6d. per yard. Houlding then offered the alternative of Everton continuing to rent Anfield from him for £250 per year and Orrell would be paid £120 a year in rent for his land that could be used as a training ground. Another member of the board George Mahon was very vocal in his opposition to Houlding and didn't consider it financially viable for the club to pay a total of £370 a year. In comparison other First Division teams were paying a lot less to their grounds' landlords. Preston North End, who finished two points behind Everton in the league, paid £30, while Notts County paid £185 (with stands included), Aston Villa £175, Bolton Wanderers £85, Burnley £75, Blackburn Rovers £60, Wolves £50, Sunderland £45, Accrington £40 and West Brom, the bottom team of First Division, £35. It was no wonder that the Everton board was unhappy with paying £250 for their ground and then be forced to fork out an extra £120 for a potential training ground.

A month passed until another meeting was held in the lecture hall of the College at Shaw Street where a letter from Houlding stated that Everton would have no further use of his ground from 30 April 1892 onwards. Mahon had already made plans to rent a land just across the park that would later become Goodison Park, for only £50 rent per year. In the ensuing months the Everton board made efforts to stay at Anfield, substantiated by notes from its meetings, but was only prepared to offer £180 per year for Houlding's ground, but he had no interest in lowering his demands. Everton decided on 25 January 1892 to register a limited company with a capital of £500 to purchase Goodison Park. However, when the board sent the club's registration it was temporarily rejected as Houlding had calculatingly registered his own company in Somerset House on 26 January with a very similar name to 'The Everton Football Club Limited', namely 'The Everton Football Club and Athletic Grounds Company Limited'. Its prospectus stated: 'This Company had been formed for the purpose of carrying on a Football and Athletic club in all its branches, and for acquiring the valuable freehold property known as the Everton football ground, containing about 13,600 square yards of land, and also about 9,700 square yards of freehold land adjoining to the

North and West, owned by Mr. John Orrell which it is acknowledged will together make one of the finest Football Grounds in the United Kingdom.' The price was said to be £8,737 10s. The gloves were off and clear to both parties that parting of the ways was inevitable.

A general meeting was held at the Presbyterian School in Royal Street on 15 March 1892 where president John Houlding arrived cheered by his followers. Chairman George Mahon who was occupying the president's chair offered Houlding his rightful place but, as the *Liverpool Echo* reported, Houlding replied: 'I am here on trial, and a criminal never takes the chair, he stops in the dock,' to which one person shouted 'Best place for him!' Mahon sat down again in the president's chair and informed Mr Houlding that the Football Association had forbidden Houlding to use the word Everton in his new company's title 'which practically knocked the new company on the head.' At the end of the meeting during which Houlding claimed he had acted in the best interests of the club Mahon stated that Houlding was not 'worthy of holding the position of president of this club', a proposal that 382 out of the 400 present agreed with. Houlding was no longer president of Everton Football Club.

On 30 March 1892 Houlding formally approved the rules of his new enterprise. Rule 1 stated: 'That the club be called the Liverpool Football Club and shall play under the rules of the Football Association.' Its formal name that was given when it was officially registered on 3 June 1892 was: 'Liverpool Football Club and Athletic Grounds Company, Limited.'

LIVERPOOL won the Lancashire League in their first season, before winning the Second Division at

first attempt in 1893/94. Their success was a testament to Houlding's capabilities as an administrator and the wise counsel he kept. Houlding took on the dual role of president and chairman in the first four years of the club's existence as Edwin Berry, who was appointed chairman, had to resign within a couple of months due to other business interests. In 1896 William E Houlding, John's son, was appointed chairman as John became more involved in local politics. On 9 November 1897 John was elected Lord Mayor of Liverpool 'there being no opposition' as the *Liverpool Mercury* reported. The Lord Mayor was only voted for a 12-month term and Houlding

served 'in a way that was above criticism and gained for him much esteem.' Houlding's health was starting to fail at the end of the 1890s and the *Liverpool Mercury* reported on 10 March 1900 that 'John Houlding, who for some time past has been in indifferent health, is at present staying at Nice, and his many friends will be gratified to learn that he has derived considerable benefit from his sojourn in that south of France retreat.' Houlding's dream finally came true on 29 April 1901 when Liverpool won the League Championship. John Houlding died at a hotel in Cimiez, a neighbourhood of Nice in the south of France, on 17 March 1902. Since their acrimonious split 10 years ago the management

of Liverpool and Everton had been on friendly terms. Three Everton and three Liverpool players acted as pallbearers at his funeral, flags were flown at half-mast at Goodison Park and the Everton players wore black armbands in memory of Houlding when they took the field. 'His place can never be filled and the Liverpool club is staggering under one of the heaviest blows it has ever received. The future of the Anfielders seems far from reassuring now that their leading spirit has passed away,' the *Liverpool Mercury* wrote a week after his passing.

ON 24 JANUARY 1905 the *Manchester Courier* reported: 'An application was made at the Lancashire Court of Chancery at

Liverpool yesterday, by the executors of the late Alderman Houlding for sanction to an arrangement entered into between them and the Liverpool Club, whereby the executors surrendered all their interest in the club. The sanction was granted. The shares will now be thrown open to the public.' The club was effectively no longer in the possession of the Houldings. When John's son, William, sold Anfield to the club for £10,000 on 19 January 1906 John's final link with Liverpool Football Club was severed. True to his vision and ambition he had built the club from scratch to become one of the leading clubs in England.

Houllier,
Gérard

HOULLIER won the French Ligue 1 title in 1986 as manager of Paris St Germain which was the club's first league title and indeed for any team in the capital for 50 years.

Following a run of bad results Houllier was replaced in 1987, but brought back temporarily to the club in 1988 as his successor, Erick Mombaerts, only won one out of his eight games. In 1988 Houllier was appointed assistant to the French national team to manager Michel Platini. Houllier succeeded him in 1992 and France looked on its way to qualifying for the 1994 World Cup with two games to go in the group stages, but lost surprisingly 3-2 in Israel and needed a draw against Bulgaria at Parc des Princes. The scores were 1-1 until the final minute when David Ginola's misplaced pass launched an attack for the Bulgarians who promptly went up field and scored the winner, securing their place in the

finals. Houllier blamed Ginola for 'committing a crime against the team,' which created an infamous long-standing feud between the pair. Houllier stepped down but continued to work for the French football federation as a technical director and coached its under 18 team ensuring the country's young stars would reach their full potential. When Aime Jacquet led the French team to their World Cup win in 1998 he dedicated the victory to Houllier as the pair had worked closely together when preparing for the tournament.

In the summer of 1998 Liverpool's chief executive, Peter Robinson, heard that his old friend, Houllier, whom he had known for almost 20 years,

was in talks with Sheffield Wednesday and Celtic. Houllier struck a firm friendship with Robinson when he spent a year in Liverpool from 1969-70 as an assistant schoolteacher at Alsop Comprehensive School, writing a thesis on inner city deprivation for his Master's degree. The first Liverpool game he attended was a 10-0 thrashing of Dundalk at Anfield on 16 September 1969. 'I suppose going to the game with Patrice that day was a touch of destiny,' Houllier once recalled. He went with his good friend, Patrice Bergues, who later became his assistant at Liverpool FC. 'We were on the Kop, and it was fantastic to see the unconditional support of the fans. I was also impressed by the energy which was shown in the game, and the stamina of the players. I think 15 minutes before the end of the match the score was 8-0 and still Liverpool went looking for goals.' Robinson suggested to the board that Houllier could strengthen the coaching staff. 'I picked up the phone and said 'I'm just ringing to congratulate you on wherever you go.' I was fishing, of course, and then told Gérard that whatever club he was going to, it was the wrong one. I told him he should be coming to Liverpool,' Robinson told the *Liverpool Echo* in 1999. Robinson boarded a plane the following morning and later brought with him David Moores, Rick Parry and Roy Evans for further discussions. 'The result was we came up with a joint managership idea. I must say that wasn't my idea and I did have reservations,' Robinson added in hindsight. Evans said in Derek Dohren's biography *Ghost on the Wall* that initially he 'understood Gérard was coming in to replace Ronnie Moran, who had retired in the summer.' He soon discovered Houllier wanted a bigger role than being a first-team coach and Evans said he 'swallowed any reservations I had and agreed.' Many regarded Houllier's appointment as a demotion for Evans, as it indicated that he wasn't up to running things on his own. The pair had different ideas on how Liverpool should play or as David James later said: 'When the two systems clashed it was like Halley's Comet hitting the Earth.' Evans stepped aside only four months into their partnership.

As one Bootroom boy moved on, another one was brought in. Phil Thompson didn't know Houllier personally, but he knew what was

needed to bring success back to Anfield. Evans' side had lacked in discipline and he was going to put it right. The players' diet was scrutinised and discipline was the key word as mobile phones were to be switched off at Melwood at all times, the players would be fined for wearing scruffy clothing and alcohol consumption during a playing week was forbidden. When Houllier came to England he was aghast by the drinking culture amongst top-flight footballers. 'What stuns me here: a young player comes into the game, looks the part,' Houllier noted. 'He's not a drinker, looks after himself. Then, as soon as he gets into the first team, he thinks that to show he's a man he has to drink. In probably every other country, the young player actually becomes more serious about the game. He'll do anything he can to improve and stay in the team. The game demands so much more now, not just physically but mentally because of greater tactical awareness.' The rest of the campaign revolved around saving face. Whereas Liverpool were 8th with four wins in their first 12 league games, Houllier's Reds collected 11 wins out of the remaining 26, but lost 10 to finish in 7th place.

HOULLIER gave Liverpool a continental flavour by his summer signings. He clearly felt the team needed an overhaul and brought in a new goalkeeper, Sander Westerveld and made arguably his best ever signing when he purchased unknown Sami Hyypia from Willem II and paired him with Stephane Henchoz from Blackburn in the centre of defence. Didi Hamann was bought from Newcastle United to protect the back four and Vladimir Smicer and Titi Camara added creativity to the attack, trying to make up for the loss of key player Steve McManaman. Erik Meijer was a short-term solution until Houllier got the big man up front he wanted in Emile Heskey. A decent second half to the season which included a run of 1 defeat in 18 league matches saw the team climb the table with a realistic chance of claiming a place in the lucrative Champions League, but Liverpool failed to score in the final five fixtures. The Reds had gained 13 more points than the previous season and boasted the best defence in the Premier League, conceding only 30 goals, but lack of goals was a concern. Injuries to Robbie Fowler, Michael Owen and Vladimir Smicer had contributed to Liverpool scoring only 51 in the league.

Houllier wanted experienced campaigners and brought in two more German internationals to join Hamann. Markus Babbel had a sensational campaign at right-back while left-back Christian Ziege failed to impress.

As Manager in Europe		
Season	Champions League	UEFA Cup
1998/99	-	3rd Round
2000/01	-	Winners
2001/02	Quarter-Final	-
2002/03	1st Phase Group	4th Round
2003/04	-	5th Round

Nick Barmby made valuable contributions to his debut campaign. Liverpool fans thought that Houllier had lost the plot when he brought in veteran Gary McAllister, but he proved to be a key signing. Igor Biscan and Jari Litmanen arrived mid-season to offer more options in what was to be a marathon campaign. Liverpool invested wisely and were to reap the benefits in a truly remarkable season. By the turn of the year Liverpool were 5th with 36 points, four points better off than last season. Liverpool had won nine out of 11 home games but lost six away. The question was whether the team would keep its nerve and guarantee a Champions League spot. A 4-0 win over Charlton at the Valley on the final day of the season secured 3rd place. Liverpool had only added two more points to their total compared to the previous campaign, but they proved crucial. The goals were flowing; twenty more in the league than in the 1999-2000 season. Michael Owen netted 24 in all competitions, Emile Heskey 22, Fowler 17 and Steven Gerrard had scored 10, the future captain's influence on the team increased by each campaign.

HOULLIER'S men were very focused for each task at hand in the domestic cups and the UEFA Cup. It took penalties to beat a stubborn Birmingham City side in the League Cup final and the team certainly enjoyed some huge slices of luck in the FA Cup final with Arsenal before Michael Owen's two late strikes at last saw some sort of revenge for three previous final defeats by the Gunners. But perhaps the UEFA Cup adventure was the most praiseworthy. The club certainly had some favourable draws in the two domestic knock-out competitions but the same could not be said of the final stages of the European equivalent, where Roma, Porto and Barcelona had to be faced in consecutive rounds. Gary McAllister's confident penalty was

As Manager												
Season	Division	P	W	D	L	GF	GA	Pts	Pos	Win %	FA Cup	League Cup
1998/99*	Premier League	26	11	5	10	49	35	38	7	42.31	4th Round	-
1999/2000	Premier League	38	19	10	9	51	30	67	4	50.00	4th Round	3rd Round
2000/01	Premier League	38	20	9	9	71	39	69	3	52.63	Winners	Winners
2001/02	Premier League	38	24	8	6	67	30	80	2	63.16	4th Round	3rd Round
2002/03	Premier League	38	18	10	10	61	41	64	5	47.37	4th Round	Winners
2003/04	Premier League	38	16	12	10	55	37	60	4	42.11	5th Round	4th Round
Total	-	216	108	54	54	354	212	378	-	50.00	-	-

* Houllier appointed on 12 November 1998 with Liverpool in 8th position

the only goal of the semi-final tie with Barcelona and he was voted man of the match in Dortmund where Liverpool prevailed over Alaves with a 'golden' own-goal in the closing minutes of extra time. Liverpool scored 127 goals in 63 matches during the 2000/01 campaign, the third highest total in the club's history.

The arrival of John Arne Riise from Monaco brought fresh impetus on the left side. The European Super Cup and the Charity Shield were added to Liverpool's trophy haul at the beginning of the 2001/02 season but Houllier's team had suffered two defeats in its opening three league games. Sander Westerveld contributed to the defeat at Bolton and Houllier wielded his axe, bringing in two goalkeepers; Jerzy Dudek and Chris Kirkland. A 3-1 win over Everton at Anfield kick-started Liverpool's league campaign and Tottenham and Newcastle were defeated in the ensuing games. Liverpool were 6th with five points less than Leeds United, who were at the top of the league, when they visited Anfield on 13 October 2001. Harry Kewell had scored the only goal of the game for Leeds when the half-time whistle went. Houllier had just begun his team-talk when he felt chest pains. He had, in fact, suffered from exhaustion since August and underwent heart tests while in Paris. He headed to the treatment room where Doctor Mark Waller gave him oxygen. Houllier wanted to return to the dugout for the second half but Waller told him the only place he was going was hospital. Houllier was rushed by ambulance to Royal Liverpool Hospital and soon transferred to the Cardiothoracic Centre at Broadgreen where he underwent an 11-hour emergency heart surgery that saved his life. Houllier had suffered a dissection of the aorta that can quickly lead to death even with optimum treatment. 'We knew it was very

serious, but not for one single moment did I feel I was going to die,' Houllier told the *Daily Post* in November 2001. 'But the people around me knew I had been very lucky. If I had felt those symptoms two hours after the game, I would have told myself again that I was just tired and almost certainly I would have gone to bed. I was in the right place with the right people with the right expert hands.'

Phil Thompson did an admirable job in Houllier's absence, keeping Liverpool on track in the Premier League and the Champions League. Before a crucial match against Roma on 19 March 2002 which Liverpool had to win by two clear goals to reach the quarter-finals of the Champions League Houllier made his long-awaited return. 'He gave the players a pep talk at the hotel this afternoon and we talked about it. Gérard said: 'I fancy this!'' Thompson told the press after Liverpool's 2-0 win. Liverpool beat Chelsea 1-0 in the following game and were in 1st position, but Arsenal, who were a couple of points behind had played two games less. Leverkusen lost 1-0 at Anfield in the 1st leg of the Champions League quarter-finals and as the scores were level 1-1 in Germany Houllier controversially substituted Hamann for Smicer after an hour's play and within seven minutes the German team was 3-1 up. Jari Litmanen's goal in the 78th minute would have put Liverpool through, but Lucio had the final say for Leverkusen, the tie lost 4-3 on aggregate. Liverpool hoped Arsenal would falter as the Reds finished impressively with 13 wins out of the last 15 league games, but the Gunners kept their nerve. Eighty points might have won the title in other seasons but it wasn't enough to beat Wenger's men.

LIVERPOOL kept their momentum for the first three months of the following season. The Reds opened with a 1-0 win over Villa and the Saints were put to the sword, 3-0. Liverpool drew the next three, all 2-2, but then went on a winning run that secured them a seven point lead at the top of the league with 12 games played. Liverpool had though been outplayed twice already that season in the Champions League group phase by Rafa Benítez's Valencia. Plenty of goals were on offer as Liverpool scored freely, but they were also conceding too many. All of a sudden Liverpool's season crumbled. From 9 November 2002 to 11 January 2003 the Reds did not have a league win to celebrate, losing six and drawing five. El Hadji Diouf was bought in the summer to add firepower, but he had only scored twice in the league, against Southampton in August. Liverpool had spent a total of £18.5m on Diouf, his compatriot Salif Diao and Frenchman Bruno Cheyrou in the summer which had proved effectively money down the drain. In comparison £24.5m had purchased Sami Hyypia, Vladimir Smicer, Titi Camara, Stephane Henchoz, Sander Westerveld and Didi Hamann in the summer of 1999. Houllier claimed the team's lack of experience was to blame for Liverpool's worst slump in 50 years. The first 11 he was turning out at the time were on average 25 years of age, but nobody had forced his hand to pick this team. Following a home draw against Blackburn at Anfield on 26 December Houllier voiced his concerns to the press. 'It's frustrating. It's a team that is young, but we have to be patient. When you go through a period like this, you either get stronger or you sink.' 'Right now they are sinking fast,' was the *Telegraph's* retort to Houllier's worries. Liverpool dropped into the UEFA Cup where they were knocked out by Celtic, similar rejects from the Champions League. Houllier's second League Cup success in three years when Manchester United were beaten in the final in Cardiff brought temporary relief. Four league wins on the bounce in April did bring fresh hope that Liverpool would qualify for the Champions League. Ironically two goals from Nicolas Anelka defeated Houllier's Reds in the penultimate league game and on the last day of the campaign they capitulated to Chelsea, which guaranteed the

HE BUILT UP A DISCIPLINED TEAM THAT CAPTURED A UNIQUE TREBLE IN LIVERPOOL'S HISTORY

Stamford Bridge outfit a place among Europe's elite at Liverpool's expense.

The signing of Leeds' talisman Harry Kewell was not enough to ignite the Liverpool team in the 2003/04 season. Houllier's regime had already been written off and arguably he should have left in the summer of 2003, but chairman David Moores was always fiercely loyal to his managers. Houllier stuck to his guns, as he believed Champions League qualification would save his job. In the end, it did not matter. What effect Houllier's life-threatening condition had on him is open to conjecture, but the team's form collapsed in the last two campaigns of his reign.

Patrice Bergues' decision to leave Liverpool in 2001 was no doubt a significant factor in Houllier's downfall. The only significant trophy won at Liverpool since his departure was the League Cup in 2003. 'Gérard Houllier replaced him with Jacques Crevoisier and then Christiano Damiano, neither of whom commanded the same respect from players and other members of staff,' Ian Rush noted in the *Liverpool Echo* in 2007. 'It's impossible for a manager to be a friend of the players. He needs to keep a distance, and that's where assistants play a crucial role. Quite often, if they're not providing this link or are simply causing more irritation, they're having a counter -productive role and making life even tougher for the manager than it already is. I'm sure this happened in the last few years of Gérard's reign after Bergues left.'

Houllier had certainly every reason to be proud of his first four years at Liverpool. He built up a disciplined team that captured a unique treble in Liverpool's history and made a strong challenge for the Premier League title. He demanded the very best of and for his players, convincing the club's hierarchy to build Millennium Pavilion, a state-of-the-art training facility, designed in part by himself. He led Liverpool to their first European success since the club emerged from the six year Heysel ban. 'Houllier replaced Roy Evans after the last of the bootroom boys had been cruelly betrayed by a shiftless bunch of big heads who had high opinions of their lowly efforts,' *Liverpool Echo's* Phil McNulty wrote in his article: '21st century Liverpool is Houllier's legacy' just before Houllier left the club. 'He performed a footballing enema on the club, ridding it of this cancerous attitude and re-affirming a code of professionalism that had been lost by the 'Spice Boy' culture. Those of us who witnessed the antics of those players will perhaps always appreciate more what Houllier did to revive Liverpool.'

PHIL THOMPSON told *LFChistory.net* in 2008 what Houllier had said to him at the end of their time together: 'Phil, if you ever go to another football club in your work, first thing you must do, because you run the club, is to think: "What is your legacy?"' Thompson continued: 'We brought the club back from the players. We left one of the best training grounds in Europe. New people who come in will say: 'What a good job they did' and we did. In the *Liverpool Echo* when we finished they had: '10million pounds of cost to get rid of us.' They had pictures of us in the newspaper like we were criminals. That was absolutely dreadful. We put the smiles back on the faces of the Liverpool fans. People had only heard of the legends of European

finals. We were going down to Cardiff on a regular basis so it wasn't a failure. If people think that we took the club as far as we can, no problem, maybe it was.'

A year after leaving Liverpool, Houllier signed a two-year contract with Lyon who had won four consecutive Ligue 1 championships. He increased that run to six but was unable to convert Lyon's dominance of their domestic game on to the European stage. Towards the end of May 2007 Houllier said he needed a break after the stress of managing the club. Three years later he returned to England to take over Aston Villa. On 20 April 2011 Houllier was taken to hospital after falling ill in the night. He left Villa in June after being advised that a return to the dugout could cause further health issues. The Villains had only won eight of the 28 league games Houllier was in charge. On 1 July 2012 Houllier was appointed as Global Sports Director for Red Bull Soccer that owns academies in Brazil and Ghana as well as FC Salzburg, RB Leipzig and New York Red Bulls.

Howe, Fred

FRED HOWE was recommended to Liverpool by former Red Tommy Johnson who saw him feature for Hyde United in the Cheshire League. Forward Howe made his debut on 6 April 1935 against Derby and figured in six of the final seven First Division fixtures of that season, scoring in successive matches against Aston Villa, Stoke City and Chelsea.

He was the club's leading scorer for the next two seasons with 17 goals from 36 appearances in 1935/36 and 16 from 41 matches in 1936/37. He only figured 11 times in 1937/38, which turned out to be his final season at Liverpool, and failed to add to his goal tally. Howe was a prolific scorer for his later teams through all three levels of the Football League: 15 goals in 29 league games for First Division Grimsby Town, five in six games for Second Division Manchester City, and 20 goals in 30 games as a 34-year-old for Third Division Oldham.

HOWE'S biggest moment in a Liverpool shirt came when he scored four goals in the club's biggest win over their eternal rivals Everton, 6-0, on 7 September 1935. Three of his goals were headers, the last of which came in the 89th minute at an 'express speed'. Only three Liverpool players before him had managed a hat-trick against Everton: Harry Chambers in 1922, Dick Forshaw in 1925 and Harold Barton in 1933. Another 77 years passed before Steven Gerrard joined this exclusive group of men in 2012.

FRED HOWE,
Liverpool F.C.   Topical Times.

Still nobody has equalled Howe's quadruple against Liverpool's rivals at Anfield, so for that alone he deserves to go down in Merseyside folklore.

Season	League		FA Cup		Total	
	App	Goals	App	Goals	App	Goals
1934/35	6	3	0	0	6	3
1935/36	34	17	2	0	36	17
1936/37	40	16	1	0	41	16
1937/38	9	0	2	0	11	0
Total	**89**	**36**	**5**	**0**	**94**	**36**

Howell,
Rab

THE FIRST GYPSY to play for Liverpool and represent England, Rabbi 'Rab' Howell was born in a Romany caravan in Wincobank, Sheffield. The 5ft 5in (165cm) right-half made his debut for Liverpool in their final First Division fixture of the 1897/98 season.

He arrived after featuring in 24 out of 30 league games for Sheffield United, who had finished their league programme as champions before Howell's departure. Howell missed only four league games in his full debut season as the Reds finished second to champions Aston Villa. He was also a first-team regular for most of the last season of the 1890s but played just twice more for the first team after that, midway through the 1900/01

Championship season, not surprising given he was 33 years of age. His Roma heritage and talent was described as follows by his Sheffield United team-mate Ernest Needham:

'A gypsy by birth, perhaps owes some of his inexhaustible vitality to his lucky parentage. Certain it is that no man is more untiring. In his right-hand position this light-weight player always excels. He rejoices at meeting the best of forward wings, and should the outside man indulge in dribbling he sticks to him like a leech. Many duels have I seen between him and Spiksley [of Sheffield Wednesday], and generally Howell has come off best. Unfortunately he is a little too

fond of keeping the ball too long, and loses many opportunities.'

HOWELL made his England debut as a Sheffield United player, scoring in a 9-0 win over Ireland on 9 March 1895, but had to wait four years for his second and final

international against Scotland, by which time he was on Liverpool's books. Liverpool played in a benefit for Howell against Preston North End on 30 September 1904. He had retired a year earlier after breaking his leg, playing at Preston.

FACTFILE

BORN
Sheffield, 12 October 1867
DIED
21 July 1937
POSITION
Right-half
OTHER CLUBS
Ecclesfield,
Rotherham Swifts (1888–90),
Sheffield United (1890–98),
Preston North End (1901–03)
SIGNED FROM
Sheffield United, £200,
6 April 1898
INTERNATIONAL CAPS
2 England caps (1 goal)
(1 (0) at LFC), 1895–99
LFC DEBUT
16 April 1898
CONTRACT EXPIRY
June 1901

Season	League App	League Goals	FA Cup App	FA Cup Goals	Total App	Total Goals
1897/98	1	0	0	0	1	0
1898/99	30	0	6	0	36	0
1899/1900	26	0	2	0	28	0
1900/01	2	0	0	0	2	0
Total	**59**	**0**	**8**	**0**	**67**	**0**

Hughes,
Emlyn

EMYLN HUGHES was one of the most enthusiastic players ever to pull on a Liverpool jersey, fiercely strong and with immense stamina. Bill Shankly saw Hughes play in one of his first games for Blackpool and offered £25,000 for him immediately. Blackpool were not keen on selling him but manager Ron Suart promised Liverpool first refusal if Hughes ever became available. Shankly phoned Hughes every Sunday morning to tell him he'd be a Liverpool player soon.

'I'd be just about to make short work of a plate of eggs, bacon and black pudding when the phone would ring. It would be Shanks,' Hughes said. '"Hey, Emlyn, son,

don't eat that stuff you've got on your plate there. I'll be signing you shortly. I want you lean and hungry, son. Lean and hungry!" Today, thirty years later, I still associate the smell of bacon frying with the telephone ringing at 8.30 sharp on a Sunday morning.' Legendary Blackpool player and journalist Jimmy Armfield interviewed the young Emlyn when he had been a professional footballer for 12 months and was very impressed by his dedication. 'This boy, Emlyn Hughes, is a first class example of how all young lads should set about learning the game at professional level. He knows that there is a big difference between being a schoolboy star and playing professionally and is willing to learn from every source of advice open to him. He really lives for football and doesn't complain about the rigid self-discipline he

has had to impose upon himself in his private life away from the ground. All the best players have started like that, and, most important, have kept it up all their playing days. To get to the top you cannot do the job half-heartedly.'

When Suart was sacked in February 1967 Liverpool knew they had to react quickly. Suart

wasted no time in serving as an intermediary between Shankly and Hughes, contacting his former player the day after his sacking to advise him to join Liverpool. Shankly finally got his man but for a considerably higher fee of £65,000. Hughes recalled the most important day of his career in an interview with *Shankly.com* in 1999.

We had to get to Lytham St Anne's to complete the signing so I could play straight away in Liverpool's next match and Shanks drove us both down there. It's only about ten minutes from Bloomfield Road, but he was the worst driver in the world. He had this old brown Corsair and just as we left the ground he half went through a set of lights and a woman shunted into the back of us and smashed all the lights in. Next thing, a police car flags us down and the young officer comes up to the car and Shanks winds down the window. 'What is it, officer?' he asked, 'I'm sorry, sir, you can't continue the journey in that car as you've got no lights.' said the policeman. 'Do you know who's in this car?' said Shanks, and I thought he was doing the old 'Do you know who I am?' routine. 'No,' said the officer, 'I don't recognise you.' 'No, not me, you fool,' he said, 'I've got the future captain of England alongside me.'

Shankly threw Hughes straight into the side and he played ten First Division games before the end of that 1966/67 season, mostly at left-back. The Kop took him quickly to their hearts and he got the nickname 'Crazy Horse' after he rugby-tackled Newcastle's forward Albert Bennett, who was slipping through his grasp, in his fifth game for Liverpool. Hughes revealed in his autobiography that Shankly had inspired him to do something special in this game. 'Shanks took me to one side and said, "The crowd are looking for a new name to take to. They need a new hero after the sixties side. They want someone to take over as their own. Go out and give them something to remember you by."' Hughes duly obliged!

HUGHES took over Willie Stevenson's left-half position in the following season and was not only a hit with the Anfield crowd, but also with the girls as he was voted the most attractive Football League player at the end of the 1968/69 season, polling 5,000 more votes than second place, receiving 36,000 votes in total! Hughes' strong runs from midfield made numerous openings for his colleagues, although he possessed a venomous shot which brought him nearly 50 goals as a Liverpool player. His goal celebrations were usually a sight to behold as he ran the length of the field like a wild man, displaying his great love for the game.

Hughes' Liverpool career started alongside most of the names that had brought the club so much success in the mid-60s like Ian St John, Ron Yeats and Roger Hunt, but he was never going to be one of the casualties in Shankly's 1970s clearout. Shankly knew what a gem he had found and his was one of the first names on the teamsheet. The 1972/73 season was the big breakthrough for Hughes and Liverpool. After narrowly missing out on honours the previous two seasons, beaten

by Arsenal in the cup final and being deprived of the League Championship, again by Arsenal, in the final fixture of 1971/72, the Reds gained ample compensation by winning the title after a seven-year absence and also collecting their first European trophy, the UEFA Cup. Hughes played in an astonishing 65 competitive games for Liverpool that season but never openly displayed any signs of real tiredness. In fact, his enthusiasm knew no bounds. 'I have played at Spurs on a Saturday afternoon, caught the train to Liverpool and then driven north to Barrow late on Saturday night in order to turn out for a Sunday League team,' Hughes said in his book *Crazy Horse*. 'I did that run when I was a current England international. If the authorities would have found out I would have been in terrible trouble, but I had so much extra energy that after those Sunday morning matches I was looking for a game of tennis in the afternoon.'

Hughes played in midfield until 1973/74 when he moved to centre-half alongside Phil Thompson. They formed an innovative partnership, building Liverpool's attacks from the back by passing to the midfield instead of hoofing the ball upfield. In 1973 Hughes was made captain instead of Tommy Smith, a fact that Smith resented. 'It was my club. I'd been there a damn sight longer than him,' Smith told the *Daily Telegraph* in March 2008. 'Everything in my life was football, especially Liverpool, so why should I let this two-faced little so-and-so spoil my football life? But I did not entertain him, or speak to him off the pitch. Never.' Bob Paisley didn't seem too fond of Hughes either but obviously rated him as a player. 'Emlyn always struck me as a player who could have been an even better one if he had been a slightly different personality. He always liked to be King of the Roost,' Paisley said in *My 50 Golden Reds*.

They called him Crazy Horse on The Kop. But that was one of the more complimentary nicknames that Emlyn Hughes won for himself during his time at Anfield. I'm not giving away any great secrets of the Boot Room when I say he wasn't – and still isn't – the most popular former player to have left Liverpool. Some of his team-mates weren't that fond of him and one of them, Tommy Smith, absolutely hated him. Smithy and Hughes never spoke to each other. I had to speak to them both when all the trouble was brewing up but it never mattered to me if players got on like a house on fire or if they couldn't stand the sight of each other, as long as they didn't let their personal feelings spill over onto the pitch.

The honours kept coming: the FA Cup in 1974, another League / UEFA Cup 'double' in 1976 and then finally in 1977 the biggest prize of all, the European Cup won in Rome and collected – as so aptly put by commentator Barry Davies at the time – by the man wearing 'the smile of the season'. Hughes was honoured by the sportswriters as their Footballer of the Year in 1977.

EMLYN was a versatile player, equally at home in a full-back position, where he was often used by England, or as a central defender, and maybe his best years at Anfield were when he was surging through from a midfield position.

Hughes was still skipper when the European Cup was retained at Wembley in 1978 but as his 30th birthday approached he could no longer be sure of his place in the side. Alan Hansen had taken the centre half spot, but Hughes could also feature at left-back in Alan Kennedy's absence. In August 1979, after 12 wonderful years as a Liverpool player, he made the decision to move to

Wolverhampton Wanderers, receiving a rapturous welcome when he returned to Anfield with his new club. He also finished his first season at Molineux by receiving the Football League Cup, just about the only trophy he hadn't won as a Liverpool player.

HUGHES moved on to Rotherham as player-manager and proudly brought his team over to Anfield for a League Cup tie in November 1982, which the Reds only won thanks to Craig Johnston's late

strike. He also had brief spells with Hull City, Mansfield Town and Swansea City but never approached the success as a manager that he had enjoyed as a player. Emlyn was a larger than life character who enjoyed great popularity as team captain on BBC's A Question of Sport from 1979 to 1982. Very few men ever reached the heights that Emlyn Hughes did as a footballer and there is no doubt that he deserves to be in any 'Hall of Fame' for what he achieved for the club

Liverpool v. Borussia Mönchengladbach 27th March 1979 20p

he served so loyally and for so long. Hughes passed away on 9 November 2004, at the age of 57, from a brain tumour.

Season	League		FA Cup		League Cup		Europe		Other		Total	
	App	Goals	App	Goals	App	Goals	App	Goals	App	Goals	App	Goals
1966/67	10	0	0	0	-	-	0	0	0	0	10	0
1967/68	39	2	9	0	2	0	6	0	-	-	56	2
1968/69	40	3	4	1	3	0	2	1	-	-	49	5
1969/70	41	7	6	0	2	0	4	0	-	-	53	7
1970/71	39	2	7	0	3	1	10	2	-	-	59	5
1971/72	42	8	3	0	3	0	4	1	1	0	53	9
1972/73	41	7	4	0	8	2	12	3	-	-	65	12
1973/74	42	2	9	0	6	0	4	0	-	-	61	2
1974/75	42	1	2	0	4	0	4	1	1	0	53	2
1975/76	41	2	2	0	3	0	11	0	-	-	57	2
1976/77	42	1	8	0	2	0	9	0	1	0	62	1
1977/78	39	0	1	0	9	0	9	1	1	0	59	1
1978/79	16	0	7	0	1	0	4	1	-	-	28	1
Total	**474**	**35**	**62**	**1**	**46**	**3**	**79**	**10**	**4**	**0**	**665**	**49**

Hughes,
James

BOOTLE BOY James Hughes made Liverpool sit up and take notice when he won the Prince's Park League title with Bootle amateur side Hertford Albion.

Hughes played 15 games for Liverpool during the first decade of the twentieth century, but as these were spread over five seasons he was never a regular member of the first team during any of those years. Most of his appearances came as a

replacement for the regular left- and right-half pairing of that time, James Bradley and Maurice Parry. The club programme said in November 1907 that 'he only requires wider experience in first class football to broaden his ideas and increase his ability to baffle more by skill and deft footwork, than by sheer vital force.' After leaving Liverpool, Hughes made 209 appearances for Crystal Palace in the Southern League.

Season	League		FA Cup		Total	
	App	Goals	App	Goals	App	Goals
1904/05	4	0	0	0	4	0
1906/07	4	0	0	0	4	0
1907/08	4	0	1	0	5	0
1908/09	2	0	0	0	2	0
Total	**14**	**0**	**1**	**0**	**15**	**0**

Hughes,
John

JOHN HUGHES was born in Wales, but moved quite young with his parents to Liverpool, so he could be termed a local player. Fellow Welshman and Liverpool player Maurice Parry recommended John 'Geezer' Hughes for a trial at Liverpool and he must have impressed.

HUGHES played usually as a half-back, only missing three of the 34 league matches in the 1903/04 season, an unsuccessful campaign that ended with relegation. A report in 1904 commented on the Welshman: 'Hughes is about the hardest working player at present figuring in league football. He never tires

and is seldom beaten. One thing he lacks, however, is judgement and a little more of this and Hughes could be classed among the best "middies" in the country.' Hughes only made one appearance for Plymouth, on 10 October 1906, still carrying an injury from his Liverpool days and retired from football in January 1907.

Hughes was also a lightweight boxing champion. He was a brave man and boasted a certificate from the Royal Humane Society for life-saving, having saved four people from drowning. Two of these were rescued from the River Mersey and he also rescued a child who had fallen into a clay pit.

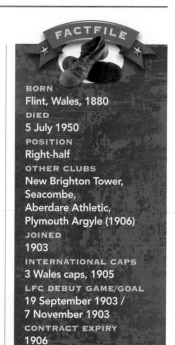
Season	League		FA Cup		Total	
	App	Goals	App	Goals	App	Goals
1903/04	31	2	1	0	32	2
Total	31	2	1	0	32	2

Hughes,
Laurie

A CLASSY centre-half who had great heading ability and a positional sense and overall reading of the game second to none, Laurie Hughes was a late developer physically and, according to his own account, Liverpool and Everton 'didn't want to know me!' when his father wrote a letter asking for a trial for his son at Liverpool's two biggest teams as they felt he was too small to become a successful professional. The local lad, born just off Everton Road in Liverpool, signed amateur terms for Tranmere Rovers after impressing them with his performances for the Liverpool Boys team. Many players were serving their country in the army so Hughes was playing first-team football at the tender age of 17.

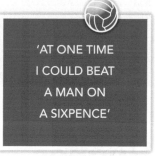

'AT ONE TIME
I COULD BEAT
A MAN ON
A SIXPENCE'

Hughes started out as a wing-half or inside-forward but as he grew taller he was used as a centre-half. 'At one time I could beat a man on a sixpence but when I grew taller I became gangly and never had the same skill I had as a little boy,' he said. Hughes was still impressively skilful and after performing for Tranmere's wartime team since 1941, having faced the Reds on a few occasions, he joined Liverpool with no fee involved in February 1943 and played regularly for the Reds during the remaining war years. He gained immediate success after the resumption of league football as the club won the first post-war Championship. 'That was the best Liverpool squad I played with,'

Hughes told the *LFC Magazine*. 'Great defensively, but we could also bang them in.'

FURTHER success never came, although he did have the honour of playing in the 1950 FA Cup final against Arsenal. His selection was rather controversial as he had missed the semi-final victory over Everton with a broken toe, in which his replacement Bob Paisley had scored the opening goal. But it was Paisley who was left out when the Wembley team was announced.

When the immaculate Stoke centre-half, Neil Franklin, decided to take his talents to the lucrative fields of Colombia in the outlawed Bogotá league in 1950, he declared himself unavailable for the England team. This gave Hughes, who was previously uncapped, an unexpected opportunity to represent England three times in the World Cup that summer in Brazil, against Chile, United States and Spain, becoming the first Liverpool

player to take part in the World Cup. England's 1-0 loss to the USA is still considered one of the most unexpected results in the country's proud football history. 'As a team, we simply never got going,' Hughes recalled sixty years later. 'Whatever we threw at them, they had an answer.' Hughes would have certainly been chosen to represent England against Ireland in the first competitive fixture following the World Cup in October 1950 had he not been badly injured in the annual Football Association's charity match, at Stamford Bridge in September. He landed awkwardly, twisted his knee and was out of action until late January. According to his former team-mate, Bob Paisley, the injury 'was largely responsible for him disappearing from the international scene'. Hughes' only goal in his Liverpool career salvaged a draw two minutes from the end of the home fixture with Stoke on 8 December 1951. But the club's fortunes were dwindling rapidly and, after narrowly avoiding relegation in 1952/53, Liverpool did go down in bottom place a year later. Hughes continued to play regularly and he only missed one league match in 1956/57. Approaching his mid-thirties by then, he only featured once for the first team in the following season, making way for Dick White who had been waiting patiently for his chance for a couple of years. Hughes soldiered

on in the reserves for a couple of years, making his final appearance for the second-string in October 1959, a couple of months before the arrival of Bill Shankly.

Hughes commented on the relatively tame lifestyles led by footballers of his era in 1950: 'As one of the few single men in the team, maybe I have more spare time than my married colleagues. My hobbies are tennis, golf and swimming, with stamp collecting an additional side-line.'

FACTFILE

BORN
Liverpool, 2 March 1924
DIED
9 September 2011
POSITION
Centre-half
OTHER CLUBS
Tranmere Rovers (1941–43)
SIGNED FROM
Tranmere Rovers,
19 February 1943
INTERNATIONAL CAPS
3 England caps, 1950
LFC DEBUT GAME/GOAL
5 January 1946 /
8 December 1951
CONTRACT EXPIRY
1959
HONOURS
League Championship
1946/47

Season	League		FA Cup		Total	
	App	Goals	App	Goals	App	Goals
1945/46	-	-	3	0	3	0
1946/47	30	0	1	0	31	0
1947/48	32	0	2	0	34	0
1948/49	12	0	0	0	12	0
1949/50	35	0	6	0	41	0
1950/51	24	0	0	0	24	0
1951/52	25	1	1	0	26	1
1952/53	11	0	0	0	11	0
1953/54	27	0	1	0	28	0
1954/55	26	0	3	0	29	0
1955/56	39	0	5	0	44	0
1956/57	41	0	1	0	42	0
1957/58	1	0	0	0	1	0
Total	**303**	**1**	**23**	**0**	**326**	**1**

Hughes, Bill

BILL HUGHES was captain of Second Division Bootle when they dropped out of the Football League because of financial difficulties and left a place to be filled by Liverpool.

He made just a single appearance for Liverpool's first team when he played as left-half in a 4-0 win against Northwich Victoria on 3 February 1894. He was a replacement for Jim McBride who was not selected for this match as he had evidently done something to displease the club's board. This victory was one of 22 during the league season, the other six matches being drawn, as the club won the Second Division title with ease at the first time of asking.

FACTFILE

BORN
Liverpool, 1865
POSITION
Left-half
OTHER CLUBS
Oakfield Rovers,
Bootle (1892–93)
SIGNED FROM
Bootle, 16 September 1893
LFC DEBUT
3 February 1894
CONTRACT EXPIRY
1894

Season	League		FA Cup		Other		Total	
	App	Goals	App	Goals	App	Goals	App	Goals
1893/94	1	0	0	0	0	0	1	0
Total	**1**	**0**	**0**	**0**	**0**	**0**	**1**	**0**

Hunt,
Roger

ROGER HUNT signed for Liverpool after attracting scout Bill Jones' attention playing for Stockton Heath in the Mid-Cheshire League. Hunt had only played six reserve matches, scoring eight goals, before making his Liverpool debut against Scunthorpe at Anfield in place of Billy Liddell on 9 September 1959. He played like a seasoned pro and fondly remembers this occasion, as he told *LFC.tv* in February 2009.

'The game was a lot quicker than what I was used to. We were one-nil up when we got a free kick around the hour mark. Jimmy Melia spotted me and played a short pass into my stride. I looked up and hit it instinctively. I knew it was in as soon as I struck it and I can't describe how good it felt to see it smash in off the crossbar.' Hunt was praised by the media, and the *News Chronicle* and *Daily Dispatch* said: 'They do find 'em at Golborne: Peter Kane, world fly-weight champion, Bert Llewellyn, goal-scoring Crewe player... and now Roger Hunt, 21, who had a dream debut for Liverpool. Hunt, stand-in for Billy Liddell, may not be an orthodox centre-forward, but by lying deep he emphasised his footballing ability, creative artistry and control.'

Hunt immediately showed all his greatest strengths. He was quick, strong, skilful and possessed a rocket of a shot. More importantly, he never gave up and worked his socks off for the team. 'I knew perfectly well that I wasn't an out-and-out natural, the sort who can make a ball talk, so it was down to me to compensate for it in other ways,' Hunt said. 'I made up my mind that if I didn't succeed at Anfield it wouldn't be for the lack of determination.

From the first day I threw myself into training, ran and tackled for everything and practised my ball skills at every opportunity.'

In only his fourth appearance for the club, a 4-1 win against Plymouth Argyle on 26 September 1959, the *Liverpool Daily Post* declared him 'a star in the making'. Hunt's third goal in his fledgling career, which was Liverpool's third against Plymouth produced a roar of approval that 'few players outside Liddell have earned'. Hunt joined a club that had been agonisingly close to gaining promotion to the top division again, twice finishing third and twice fourth in the previous four seasons. There would be disappointment again in 1959/60 with another third place in Shankly's first season as manager. Hunt's partnership with former Everton star Dave Hickson worked well but when Hickson departed and Ian St John arrived in the 1961/62 promotion season Hunt started to fire on all cylinders. He scored no fewer than 41 goals in 41 league matches, including five hat-tricks. 'Ian and I gelled straight away,' Hunt said in *Sir Roger: The Life and Times of Roger Hunt*, published in 1995. 'He was a terrific, unselfish player and we seemed to be able to read each other's minds. The fact that he tended to drift back into midfield to pick up the ball early meant I was more an out-and-out striker than a conventional inside-forward, but with two wingers offering super service – Alan A'Court on one side and either Kevin Lewis or Ian Callaghan on the other – that was no hardship.'

HUNT made his England debut against Austria on 4 April 1962, without having featured for the schoolboy, youth or the Under-23 international side. He went to the World Cup in 1962, but did not play a single match. The next few years were golden ones for Liverpool and for Hunt. He scored 129 times in 160 games during the next four seasons, a period in which the club twice won the League Championship and had good cup runs at home and in Europe. His greatest personal achievement at club level was certainly the FA Cup final of 1965 against Leeds. Hunt's header broke the deadlock early in extra time before St John scored the winner. 'The ball reached me at about waist height. At first, I didn't know whether to head it or side-foot it. I went for the header, having to stoop slightly, and I was absolutely overjoyed to see it go in.'

Hunt certainly enjoyed playing under Bill Shankly. 'He was a great communicator and some of his team talks were fantastic. I remember one when we were about to play to his old team, Huddersfield Town – it was hilarious. He went through their team player by player, pulling each individual apart. Then he got to Denis Law, whom he glossed over because Denis was always his favourite player. At the end of it all we were left wondering how he could ever have managed such a bad team!'

THE WORLD CUP was held on English soil in 1966 and Hunt played in all six games, scoring three goals as England lifted the game's biggest prize. Hunt was preferred to Jimmy Greaves in the final in which Hunt had the best view of one of the most controversial World Cup moments in history when Geoff Hurst's shot rocketed off the crossbar towards the goal line. 'I was running in, sniffing for rebounds and was about six yards out when the ball hit the ground. I saw the ball cross the line and I turned instantly to celebrate the goal. I believed at the time that it was over the line and I believe it now. If there had been the slightest shred of doubt in my mind I'd have followed it in to make sure,' Hunt said in his biography. Often criticised by the southern press that preferred the more flamboyant Greaves, Hunt's international record speaks for itself – he was on the losing side only twice in 34 internationals. Sir Bobby Moore knew all about his qualities, 'Roger Hunt is a player's player. He is possibly appreciated more by those who play with him and against him than by those who watch him.'

HUNT was Liverpool's top goalscorer every season from 1962 to 1969 and on 7 November 1967 he broke Gordon Hodgson's record at the club by netting his 242nd goal against TSV Munich. Despite his scoring prowess he could not please all people, as Tommy Smith remembers: 'We used to call him "Over-the-bar Hunt". Everyone used to get mail, praising you, calling you names or simply asking for an autograph. Roger used to get a letter on a regular basis from a lad, who clearly didn't like him. It always

used to start, "Dear Over-the-bar-Hunt. I see you missed another couple of sitters on Saturday."' In March 1969 the normally mild-mannered Hunt caused a sensation when he was substituted in a cup replay at Anfield against Leicester by taking his shirt off and angrily throwing it in the direction of the dugout. Although he started 1969/70 still as first choice, he lost his place to Phil Boersma in the autumn. There would be one final day to remember in front of the supporters who had always given him such great encouragement. With time running out and a 1-1 scoreline against Southampton on 25 October 1969, Shankly brought on Hunt to replace Alec Lindsay and he responded by scoring twice in two minutes! Those were his last league goals for Liverpool and seven weeks later he signed for Bolton Wanderers.

Ian Rush broke Hunt's overall scoring record for Liverpool on 18 October 1992 but Hunt's league tally of 245 goals is still a club record. He was awarded an MBE in 2000. Whether he will be knighted one day remains

to be seen but he has been called 'Sir Roger' by the Kop for more than half a century.

Season	League		FA Cup		League Cup		Europe		Other		Total	
	App	Goals	App	Goals	App	Goals	App	Goals	App	Goals	App	Goals
1959/60	36	21	2	2	-	-	-	-	-	-	38	23
1960/61	32	15	1	1	3	3	-	-	-	-	36	19
1961/62	41	41	5	1	-	-	-	-	-	-	46	42
1962/63	42	24	6	2	-	-	-	-	-	-	48	26
1963/64	41	31	5	2	-	-	-	-	-	-	46	33
1964/65	40	25	8	5	-	-	9	7	1	0	58	37
1965/66	37	30	1	1	-	-	7	2	1	0	46	33
1966/67	39	14	3	1	-	-	5	3	1	1	48	19
1967/68	40	25	9	2	2	0	6	3	-	-	57	30
1968/69	38	13	4	1	3	2	2	1	-	-	47	17
1969/70	15 (3)	6	0	0	2	0	0 (2)	1	-	-	17 (5)	7
Total	**401 (3)**	**245**	**44**	**18**	**10**	**5**	**29 (2)**	**17**	**3**	**1**	**487 (5)**	**286**

Hunter,
John

'SAILOR HUNTER' was a forward who scored five times in 20 First Division appearances in 1899/1900 and played his part in the following season's triumph when Liverpool won their first-ever League Championship.

He replaced inside-left Charles Satterthwaite for six games from the middle of March to mid-April and his brace in a 3-0 win over Newcastle on 30 March 1901 kept Liverpool in touching distance with the top sides. His final selection for the first team came towards the end of March 1902. Hunter then moved for a combined fee of £300 along with team-mate Tom Robertson to Hearts where he played two years, scoring 14 goals in 42 games. He went back south for a brief spell at First Division debutants Woolwich Arsenal before transferring to Portsmouth in the Southern League. His most prolific season was at Dundee when he scored 28 goals in 31 league games.

At only 32 years of age Sailor was appointed manager of Motherwell in 1911, the club's first such appointment since their founding in 1886. After 35 years in charge he left his post due to failing eyesight but continued to attend to administrative affairs at the club from 1946 to 1959, until he was 80. He is Motherwell's longest-serving manager, guiding the team in 1,064 games and to victory in the Scottish League in the 1931/32 season when the team scored an astonishing 119 goals in 38 league games.

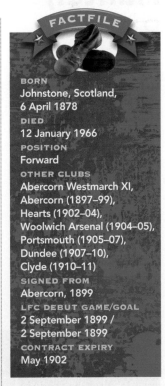

Season	League		FA Cup		Total	
	App	Goals	App	Goals	App	Goals
1899/1900	20	5	4	1	24	6
1900/01	8	3	1	0	9	3
1901/02	9	1	3	2	12	3
Total	**37**	**9**	**8**	**3**	**45**	**12**

Hunter,
Thomas John

T. J. HUNTER
[LIVERPOOL]

'HUNTER is only 19 years of age but is said to give promise of proving an even finer centre-half than Alex Raisbeck,' reported the *Manchester Evening News* on his signing from Beith in September 1899. 'He is spoken of as one of the likeliest men who has left Scotland for some time. His nominal terms are £3 per week winter and summer; but this transfer has cost the Liverpudlians a good deal.'

Hunter, however, never came close to being the incredible servant Raisbeck was at the club. He did feature as a right-winger on his debut in a 1-1 draw with Wolves on 25 November 1899 as Liverpool struggled having only won two out of 14 games in the campaign. Hunter was Raisbeck's replacement once in the successful 1900/01 season, helping Liverpool to a 3-0 win over Newcastle on their way to the title. Hunter moved to Preston in May 1902 before returning to Scotland. Hunter did move back to Preston where he ran a pub called the Skeffington Arms from 1913 until his death in 1928.

Season	League		FA Cup		Total	
	App	Goals	App	Goals	App	Goals
1899/1900	1	0	0	0	1	0
1900/01	1	0	0	0	1	0
1901/02	2	0	0	0	2	0
Total	4	0	0	0	4	0

FACTFILE

BORN
Beith, Scotland, 1880
DIED
13 March 1928
POSITION
Centre-half / Right-winger
OTHER CLUBS
Beith (1898-99),
Preston North End,
Ayr Parkhouse, Ayr United
SIGNED FROM
Beith, 27 September 1899
LFC DEBUT
25 November 1899
CONTRACT EXPIRY
16 May 1902

Hunter,
Bill

BILL HUNTER, a burly forward, made his only appearance for Liverpool in a First Division match at Preston North End on 20 March 1909.

For the record, the hosts won 2-0. Liverpool were on a miserable run of six defeats and consequently dragged into a relegation battle. Four goals from Ronald Orr in the final three games saved Liverpool from the clutches of the Second Division. Hunter played for a number of other professional and amateur clubs, most notably Manchester United for whom he played three games in the First Division in 1913. Indeed he made his United debut against Liverpool and celebrated a 2-0 win at Anfield. He scored two goals in his final game for United against Newcastle before departing for Second Division Clapton Orient.

Season	League		FA Cup		Total	
	App	Goals	App	Goals	App	Goals
1908/09	1	0	0	0	1	0
Total	1	0	0	0	1	0

FACTFILE

BORN
Sunderland, 1888
POSITION
Inside-right forward
OTHER CLUBS
Sunderland West End (1908),
Airdrieonians (1908),
Sunderland (1909),
Lincoln City (1909–11),
Wingate Albion (1911–12),
South Shields (1912),
Barnsley (1912–13),
Manchester United (1913),
Clapton Orient (1913–14),
Exeter City (1914–18)
SIGNED FROM
Airdrieonians, December 1908
LFC DEBUT
20 March 1909
CONTRACT EXPIRY
May 1909

Hurrah for the Reds

The 7 September 1907 edition of the *Liverpool Echo* featured Liverpool FC's first known supporters' song 'Hurrah for the Reds' composed by W. Seddon at 4 Radnor Place in Tuebrook, who had written it a week earlier. Composed only 15 years after the club was founded, it even came with notes attached.

TODAY'S SONGS tend to focus on the biggest heroes in the team like Jamie Carragher, Steven Gerrard and Luis Suarez. This song was no different really; Hewitt and Mac in attack are right-winger Bill McPherson and centre-forward Joe Hewitt. Goddard and Cox are Hall-of-Famers Arthur Goddard and Jack Cox. 'Raisbeck the fox' is Liverpool's talisman at time, pivot Alex Raisbeck, and Hardy who holds the fort is England international Sam Hardy.

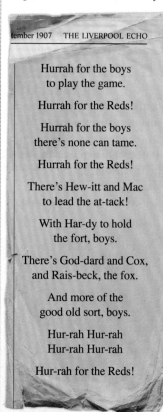

...ember 1907   THE LIVERPOOL ECHO

Hurrah for the boys
to play the game.

Hurrah for the Reds!

Hurrah for the boys
there's none can tame.

Hurrah for the Reds!

There's Hew-itt and Mac
to lead the at-tack!

With Har-dy to hold
the fort, boys.

There's God-dard and Cox,
and Rais-beck, the fox.

And more of the
good old sort, boys.

Hur-rah Hur-rah
Hur-rah Hur-rah

Hur-rah for the Reds!

Hutchison,
Don

DON HUTCHISON had a good spell in Graeme Souness's team in 1992/93, playing 42 games and scoring 10 goals. He was a good passer of the ball, a fierce competitor and possessed enough skills up his sleeve to impress the most ardent fan. However, a long list of unsavoury off-the-field incidents ended his Liverpool career, perhaps his crowning achievement being the displaying of his 'crown jewels' in a city centre bar.

Hutchison played for three other sides in the Premier League, averaging about 30 league games in four solid seasons with Everton from 1998 to 2000, Sunderland in 2000/01 and West Ham in 2001/02. He later gained international recognition with Scotland; his most famous moment scoring the winner against England in the second leg of the Euro 2000 play-off at Wembley on 17 November 1999. However, England won the first leg 2-0 at Hampden Park and went to the finals. In the summer of 2009 Hutchison participated in the "Celebrity Soccer Six" tournament at Stamford Bridge. *The Sun* was represented and Reds were shocked to see one Don Hutchison in their side and on the twentieth anniversary year of the Hillsborough disaster, to boot.

FACTFILE

BORN
Gateshead, 9 May 1971
POSITION
Midfielder
OTHER CLUBS
Hartlepool United (1989–90),
West Ham United (1994–96),
Sheffield United (1996–98),
Everton (1998–2000),
Sunderland (2000–01),
West Ham United (2001–05),
Millwall (2005),
Coventry City (2005–07),
Luton Town (2007–08)
SIGNED FROM
Hartlepool United, £175,000,
27 November 1990
INTERNATIONAL CAPS
25 Scotland caps (6 goals),
1999–2003
LFC DEBUT GAME/GOAL
31 March 1992 /
22 September 1992
CONTRACT EXPIRY
30 August 1994

Season	League App	League Goals	FA Cup App	FA Cup Goals	League Cup App	League Cup Goals	Europe App	Europe Goals	Other App	Other Goals	Total App	Total Goals
1991/92	0 (3)	0	0	0	0	0	0	0	-	-	0 (3)	0
1992/93	27 (4)	7	1 (1)	0	5	2	3	1	0 (1)	0	36 (6)	10
1993/94	6 (5)	0	0 (1)	0	2 (1)	0	-	-	-	-	8 (7)	0
Total	**33 (12)**	**7**	**1 (2)**	**0**	**7 (1)**	**2**	**3**	**1**	**0 (1)**	**0**	**44 (16)**	**10**

Hysén,
Glenn

GLENN HYSÉN first came to prominence at IFK Gothenburg, with whom he won the UEFA Cup in 1982. He spent a couple of years at PSV Eindhoven before returning to Gothenburg in 1987. He moved abroad again in 1989 to Fiorentina in Italy, playing under his former boss at Gothenburg, Sven Göran-Eriksson.

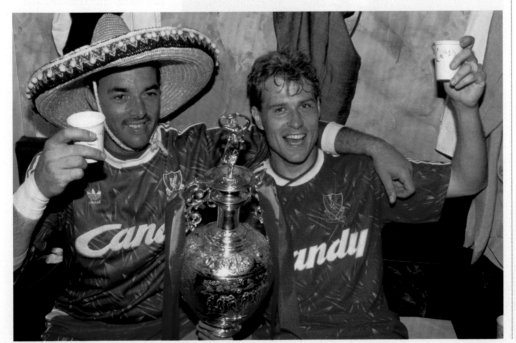

Hysén earned rave reviews for his displays against England in two 1990 World Cup qualification matches prompting great interest in him from English clubs. Liverpool stole him from under the nose of Alex Ferguson at Manchester United who thought they had his transfer signed, sealed... but forgot the deliver bit. Ferguson and United chairman Martin Edwards flew out to Florence to conclude the transfer that was stalling but were then told by Hysén's agent that his client had already signed for Liverpool.

> HYSÉN WAS
> 'MAN OF THE MATCH'
> ON HIS LIVERPOOL
> DEBUT IN THE
> 1989 CHARITY SHIELD

By the time of his arrival on Merseyside, Hysén had been captain of the Swedish national team for many years and voted one of the 10 best players in Europe when *France Football* announced their Golden Ball winner in 1987. Hysén was 'Man of the Match' on his Liverpool debut in the 1989 Charity Shield against Arsenal at Wembley. He had an excellent first season and was an important member of the club's League Championship-winning squad. However despite making 40 appearances his cool and calculated performances seemed to evaporate the following season. When Graeme Souness replaced Kenny Dalglish in the spring of 1991, it was clear that

the Scot and the Swede didn't see eye to eye. Souness picked Hysén in the starting XI only five times in 1991/92, with two further substitute appearances.

In 1992 Hysén returned to Sweden and signed for IFK Gothenburg's city rivals, GAIS, where his contract proved too expensive for the club, causing him great unpopularity among the fans. GAIS promised to build Hysén a house as a signing-on fee but in the end the club didn't fulfil its promise due to financial struggles. GAIS was relegated to the second tier of the Swedish league at the end of his debut season and Hysén was blamed for the club's demise by many fans.

He played on for another two seasons before finishing his career with Gothenburg's Skogens.

Hysén is one of Sweden's most well-known and respected sportsmen. He represented his nation 68 times, scoring seven goals. In club football, he made over 450 appearances for four Gothenburg clubs, PSV Eindhoven, Fiorentina and Liverpool. Hysén's grandfather, great-uncle and father played professionally for IFK Gothenburg. Another generation, Glenn's son Tobias, also signed for IFK in 2007. The Hysén name has truly become synonymous with the history of Sweden's most successful club.

FACTFILE

BORN
Gothenburg, Sweden, 30 October 1959
POSITION
Centre-half
OTHER CLUBS
Warta (1977),
IFK Gothenburg (1977–83),
PSV Eindhoven (1983–85),
IFK Gothenburg (1985–87),
Fiorentina (1987–89),
GAIS (1992–94),
Skogens (1994–97)
SIGNED FROM
Fiorentina, £600,000,
1 June 1989
INTERNATIONAL CAPS
68 Sweden caps (7 goals), 1981–90
LFC DEBUT GAME/GOAL
12 August 1989 /
12 September 1989
CONTRACT EXPIRY
1 May 1992
HONOURS
League Championship 1989/90

Season	League App	League Goals	FA Cup App	FA Cup Goals	League Cup App	League Cup Goals	Europe App	Europe Goals	Other App	Other Goals	Total App	Total Goals
1989/90	35	1	8	0	2	1	-	-	1	0	46	2
1990/91	32	0	5	0	2	0	-	-	1	0	40	0
1991/92	3 (2)	1	0	0	2	0	0	0	-	-	5 (2)	1
Total	**70 (2)**	**2**	**13**	**0**	**6**	**1**	**0**	**0**	**2**	**0**	**91 (2)**	**3**

Hyypia, Sami

SAMI HYYPIA'S performances reminded fans of the good old days of legendary giant Ron Yeats, who was Bill Shankly's pillar in defence. Hyypia was Gérard Houllier's tower and later fulfilled the same role for Rafa Benítez. The word 'legend' is often overused when it comes to sporting achievement. There can, however, be no doubt that the word can justifiably be used to describe the fantastic service Sami Tuomas Hyypia gave to Liverpool Football Club.

Hyypia signed for his local club Kumu, then in the Finnish second division, at the age of 17, after having spent 10 years at Voikkaan Pallo-Peikot for whom he had made three appearances in the

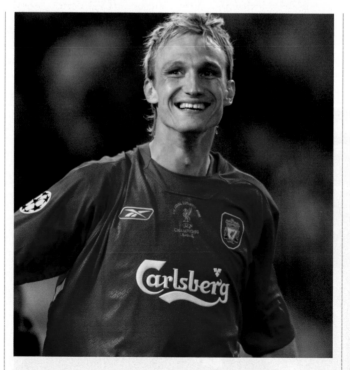

third division in 1989. He made a decision to undertake his period of national service sooner rather than later because it might become a problem if he were to be playing in another country. On his return to football after 11 months in the army, Hyypia impressed the watching

MyPa-47 manager and this led to a transfer to a bigger club in Finland's first division. Hyypia spent four seasons with MyPa, during which they finished league runners-up three times and won the Finnish Cup twice, with Hyypia's header being the only goal of the 1995 final in his last match for the club. That victory put MyPa into the 1996/97 Cup Winners' Cup, where they would be drawn against Liverpool; but by then Hyypia had already moved to the Netherlands. Hyypia might have been plying his trade in England even earlier, because he was twice invited to train with Newcastle for a few days, something he also did in Turkey and Germany with Samsunspor and Werder Bremen respectively. Scotsman Jimmy Calderwood signed Hyypia for the Tilburg club Willem II but not long afterwards Calderwood was replaced by Dutchman Co Adriaanse, whose

nickname was 'Psycho Co' because of his alternative ideas about fitness and training. Despite Adriaanse's gruelling regime Hyypia believes that the whole Tilburg experience was positive because when he adjusted to Melwood 'it was like going back to normal'. Dutch clubs struggled to cope with the extreme fitness of the Willem II players and Adriaanse was able to give Tilburg European football for the first time after finishing fifth in the Dutch league at the end of the 1997/98 season. Although Real Betis ended their European hopes, an even stronger season in the league saw Willem II finish runners-up and gain automatic qualification for the group stage of the following season's Champions League.

Liverpool have a TV cameraman to thank that Hyypia came to Liverpool as Peter Robinson reveals: 'It was midway through the 1998/99 season when there was a knock on the door of my office at Anfield. I had never met the chap. He came in and introduced himself as a cameraman who covered football in Europe. He knew we were looking for a strong defender and recommended we take a look at Sami, who was playing for Willem, one of the smaller Dutch clubs. That is how it all started. I passed the message on to Gérard and, over the next few months, members of the staff went to Holland to watch him on several occasions.'

Ron Yeats was Liverpool chief scout at the time and of all the signings he contributed to he was the proudest of the Great Finn,

'WHEN I WAS TOLD HOW LITTLE MONEY LIVERPOOL HAD SPENT ON SAMI, I NEARLY FELL OFF MY CHAIR!'
RON YEATS

as he told *LFChistory.net*. 'I was glad we signed big Sami Hyypia. I went to see him after he was recommended. I thought this boy looks a good player. At centre-half he was a great passer of the ball, which is unusual for centre-halves. I was really taken with Sami and I put in a report that either the boss or a coach should go over and see this man. They did and then signed him a few weeks after the recommendation.' As a former centre-half Yeats could easily identify with Hyypia: 'They say he hasn't got any pace. I didn't have great pace but I could read what players were going to do. You put them in a corner more or less.' Liverpool didn't waste any time. Houllier preferred if possible to have potential summer signings agreed and signed up before the end of the previous campaign. So Sami travelled to Liverpool and signed a contract on 19 May 1999 with the fee being £2.5million, an incredible bargain in view of what was to come over the next ten years. Ron Yeats later admitted, 'When I was told how little money Liverpool had spent on Sami, I nearly fell off my chair!'

The flamboyant football played under Roy Evans meant that although plenty of goals were scored, far too many were conceded. It was clear that, especially in defence, there needed to be changes. Hyypia was part of that change under the Houllier/Thompson management team, as was the man who would become his reliable partner in defence, Stephane

Henchoz. It was clear from the very beginning that Liverpool had signed a player of great stature and ability who was a leader on the pitch. Even in Hyypia's first season at Anfield, he was asked to deputise as captain for the injured duo of Robbie Fowler and Jamie Redknapp; and when those players moved on in 2001 and 2002 respectively, Houllier had no hesitation in handing the Finn the captain's armband permanently. He had already worn it proudly for most of the historic 2000/01 campaign, being modest and humble enough to 'share' the cup presentations with Redknapp in Cardiff and Fowler in Dortmund. Hyypia's game was so immaculate he did not receive a booking for 87 matches in a row from January 2000 to October 2001. However, this consistent performer was not his usual self in 2003 and in October of that year Houllier made Steven Gerrard captain instead of the mighty Finn. Hyypia accepted the decision with typical dignity and was soon back to his best.

Hyypia's main responsibilities were, of course, in defence, but he still often found time to be effective at the other end of the field, with his contribution to Liverpool's cause in goals scored being very commendable in comparison to some of his illustrious predecessors in the same position. Hyypia netted 35 times in his 10 years at Anfield, compared to Hansen (14), Lawrenson (18), Thompson (13) and Yeats (16). Hyypia never scored more than five goals in a season, but he scored at least twice in each of his 10 seasons as a Liverpool professional, the first coming at home to Manchester United in September 1999 and the last coming in the 5-1 drubbing of Newcastle in front of their own supporters three days after Christmas 2008. In between were numerous strikes of varying importance, but probably none more important than the three goals he scored in the Champions

League quarter-finals: in 2002 against Leverkusen, 2005 against Juventus and 2008 against Arsenal. He rates the sweet left-footed strike against Juventus as his best goal. It was crucial in eventually ensuring a narrow aggregate victory as Liverpool moved on towards Istanbul.

Hyypia was a key player in Liverpool's European triumph in 2005 as he had been the previous seasons, emphasised by the fact that he played every minute in 57 consecutive European games for Liverpool between November 2001 and February 2006. Hyypia formed a superb partnership with Henchoz, bettered only by the Hyypia and Carragher combination under Benítez. It is testament to his ability that through two different Anfield regimes, Hyypia remained as solid and dependable as ever, and having won every other trophy, only needed a Premier League winner's medal to complete his set. Daniel Agger's emergence in the 2006/07 season forced Hyypia out of the first XI, but when called upon he was still a class act. Hyypia was linked with other clubs during the summer of 2007 but nothing came of it. He started his ninth season, the 2007/08 campaign, at Liverpool less sure of his place in the team than at any time since his arrival in 1999. This was partly due to his advancing age but also because of strong competition for places. Agger's long-term injury then gave Hyypia a more prominent

role in the team and he didn't disappoint. In total Hyypia added another 44 appearances to his already impressive total that season.

In April 2008 Hyypia signed an extension to his Liverpool contract that would keep him at the club until the summer of 2009. He only played 19 times for the first team in his tenth and final season. Eventually Liverpool fans and the great Finn had to part ways. Hyypia had been sitting firmly on the bench in the previous four league matches, but there was huge expectation that he would play some part in his final match at Anfield against Tottenham on 24 May 2009. A number of fans were disappointed not to see him lead out the team and Benítez kept everybody waiting until the 84th minute, despite frequent chants of 'Sami, Sami, Sami, on, on, on!' all around the stadium. Steven Gerrard was substituted; he in turn took off the captain's armband and handed it to Hyypia, who proudly wore it for the final time as the match reached its conclusion. Hyypia became extremely emotional when the referee blew the final whistle and the ovation he received from all parts of Anfield reflected not just what a terrific servant he had been for Liverpool, but also what a genuinely nice guy he is.

After he left Liverpool went on a downward spiral and the inferior performance of the club's defenders can be attributed to Hyypia's absence. He had been vital on the field as well as off it, as Fernando Torres pointed out. 'Sami may not have played every week but he was a 10 out of 10 on and off the pitch, bringing calm to the ground and having everyone's admiration.' Liverpool wanted to keep him on the coaching staff but Hyypia felt that he could play regularly for a couple of years more, which he promptly did with Bayer Leverkusen. Roy Hodgson even tried to re-sign him for Liverpool in 2010 but couldn't get him released from his contract. The reason for Hodgson's eagerness to bring Hyypia back was simple. 'He's one I would also put in the Jamie Carragher and Steven Gerrard mould, Liverpool for life.'

Hyypia was Finland's captain when he played his 100th game for the Finnish national side on 12 August 2009 against Sweden. He made five more appearances before retiring from the international scene after a 2-1 loss to Hungary in a Euro 2012 qualifying match on 12 October 2010. On 1 May 2011 Hyypia announced at a press conference in Finland that he would be retiring as a player at the end of the current season. Eleven months later Hyypia was named as caretaker-coach at Leverkusen. In the 2012/13 season Sami worked alongside the club's Under-19 coach, Sascha Lewandowski. After they delivered third place in the Bundesliga Hyypia took sole charge of the team. 'I've been saying it for years, Sami will go down in history alongside the likes of Ron Yeats, Alan Hansen and Emlyn Hughes,' said Jamie Carragher of his long-term

defensive partner. 'When you think of the foreign players who have played in this country, for me Sami is up there with Dennis Bergkamp and Gianfranco Zola. Not many players have come to the Premiership from abroad and played for just one club for as long as Sami has, and in all the time he's been at Liverpool you could probably count his bad performances on the fingers of one hand.'

> BENÍTEZ KEPT EVERYBODY WAITING UNTIL THE 84TH MINUTE, DESPITE FREQUENT CHANTS OF 'SAMI, SAMI, SAMI, ON, ON, ON!' ALL AROUND THE STADIUM

FACTFILE

BORN
Porvoo, Finland,
7 October 1973
POSITION
Centre-half
OTHER CLUBS
Voikkaan Pallo-Peikot
(1980–89),
Kumu Kuusankoski (1989–92),
Mypa-47 (1992–95),
Willem II (1995–99),
Bayer Leverkusen (2009–11)
SIGNED FROM
Willem II, £2.5million,
19 May 1999
INTERNATIONAL CAPS
105 Finland caps (5 goals)
(71 (5) at LFC), 1992–2010
LFC DEBUT GAME/GOAL
7 August 1999 /
11 September 1999
CONTRACT EXPIRY
1 June 2009
HONOURS
FA Cup 2001, 2006;
League Cup 2001, 2003;
Champions League 2005;
UEFA Cup 2001

Season	League		FA Cup		League Cup		Europe		Other		Total	
	App	Goals	App	Goals	App	Goals	App	Goals	App	Goals	App	Goals
1999/2000	38	2	2	0	2	0	-	-	-	-	42	2
2000/01	35	3	6	0	6	1	11	0	-	-	58	4
2001/02	37	3	2	0	1	0	16	2	1	0	57	5
2002/03	36	3	3	0	4	0	12	2	1	0	56	5
2003/04	38	4	4	0	1	0	8	1	-	-	51	5
2004/05	32	2	1	0	1	0	15	1	-	-	49	3
2005/06	35 (1)	1	6	1	1	0	14	0	2	0	58 (1)	2
2006/07	23	1	0	0	1	1	5	1	0	0	29	3
2007/08	24 (3)	1	4	1	0	0	12 (1)	2	-	-	40 (4)	4
2008/09	12 (4)	1	1	0	2	1	0	0	-	-	15 (4)	2
Total	310 (8)	22	29	2	19	3	93 (1)	8	4	0	455 (9)	35

Ibe, Jordon

LONDON-LAD Ibe came off the bench in extra-time in Wycombe's League Cup win over Colchester on 9 August 2011, aged just 15 years and 244 days.

IBE'S milestone is only bettered by Kevin Keen who was 35 days younger when he turned out for Wanderers in 1982. Ibe made his first start two months later against Sheffield Wednesday and scored a superb solo goal, becoming the youngest ever Wanderers' goalscorer in the Football League. The left-winger made his Liverpool debut against Queens Park Rangers in the final fixture of the 2012/13 season, claiming an assist for Philippe Coutinho's winner.

FACTFILE

BORN
London, 8 December 1995
POSITION
Left-winger
OTHER CLUBS
Wycombe Wanderers
SIGNED FROM
Wycombe Wanderers,
£500,000, 20 December 2011
LFC DEBUT
19 May 2013

Season	League		FA Cup		League Cup		Europe		Total	
	App	Goals	App	Goals	App	Goals	App	Goals	App	Goals
2012/13	1	0	0	0	0	0	0	0	1	0
Total	1	0	0	0	0	0	0	0	1	0

Ince, Paul

AFTER 93 appearances and 12 goals for the Hammers, Paul Ince's pace, stamina, tackling (once claiming: 'I love tackling, it's better than sex!'), and good passing ability had caught the eye of Alex Ferguson. His £1million move to Manchester United infuriated West Ham fans as Ince had been photographed in a United kit before the transfer was complete as he had to go abroad on a holiday. His United picture was accidentally used in the *Daily Express* and 'all hell broke loose,' as Ince recollects.

After trophy-laden years at Old Trafford Ince was transferred to Inter Milan in 1995 in a £7million move. Manchester United had first option on him if he ever decided to come back to England, but when Ince returned in 1997 so his two sons could be raised in England Ferguson waived his rights to sign the self-styled 'Guv'nor' and Roy Evans secured his services for Liverpool. His new captain was finally in place, ready to take over the reins from the fading John Barnes in the 1997/98 season. It surprised many to see an ex-United player join Liverpool and Ince admitted:

'It will be strange walking on to the pitch as a Liverpool player. Normally, when I walk out at Anfield, I get slaughtered.' Only Steve McManaman and Michael Owen made more appearances than Ince's 40 in his debut season. Ince was heavily involved again in the 1998/99 season but Roy Evans' once-promising team failed to deliver. Ince's two years at Anfield can probably be considered as neither success nor failure. He had the experience and determination to do well but that was not enough to see his new employers win any silverware. Undoubtedly Ince's sweetest moment in a Liverpool shirt was when he equalised to make it 2-2 in the 89th minute at Anfield after the Reds had been 2-0 down against Manchester United. Stung by their refusal to re-sign him when he returned from Italy, and also hearing the abuse directed at him by United's supporters all throughout the match, Ince certainly enjoyed denying United the win and potentially damaging their Championship hopes.

Ince's relationship with new manager Gérard Houllier turned sour and he left for Middlesbrough in 1999. He let Phil Thompson and Houllier know in no uncertain terms what he thought of the pair in an interview with the *Sunday People* following his move. 'I want Houllier to get the sack and take Thompson down with him. If they think people are no longer any use to them they treat those people like dirt,' fumed Ince. 'It's okay coming out with all this technical stuff about the game but when it comes to managing players off the field as people he certainly doesn't seem to know how to.' Ince admitted he wanted to cause Houllier physical harm when he told him that he wanted him out of the club. 'I thought to myself, "I can't believe I'm hearing this." And I said to him: "You've had months to tell me but you decided you were going to do it just before pre-season. I can't believe this – it's total c**p!" I just wanted to punch Houllier in the face. If I was younger I would have. He would have deserved it.'

Season	League		FA Cup		League Cup		Europe		Total	
	App	Goals	App	Goals	App	Goals	App	Goals	App	Goals
1997/98	31	8	1	0	4	0	4	0	40	8
1998/99	34	6	2	1	2	1	3	1	41	9
Total	65	14	3	1	6	1	7	1	81	17

INCE WAS CAPTAIN of Bryan Robson's Middlesbrough for three years in the Premier League. In 2002 he joined Wolverhampton Wanderers, where he spent four years and experienced both promotion to the Premier League and relegation from it. Ince finished his playing career at Swindon Town, where he was player-coach, and Macclesfield Town, the latter also being the club that gave him his first step on the managerial ladder. In June 2007 Ince was appointed manager of Milton Keynes Dons where he won the League Two title. In June 2008 Ince took charge of Premier League's Blackburn Rovers, but lasted less than six months following a truly appalling run of results. Although Ince agreed a two-year deal on his return to MK Dons he left at the end of the first year because of budget cutbacks. In October 2010 Ince returned to football management with League One club Notts County. After five successive league defeats, Ince was sacked in April 2011. In February 2013 Ince signed as manager of Blackpool following Paolo Di Canio's appointment at Sunderland.

Ince, Tom

THE SON of former Liverpool captain Paul Ince, Tom can play as a left-winger or just off the striker in the 'hole'. He made his only appearance for Liverpool's first team on 22 September 2010, coming on as a substitute in the 106th minute in a shocking defeat to League Two's Northampton Town in the third round of the League Cup.

WHEN his father was appointed manager of Notts County towards the end of October 2010 he brought his son to Meadow Lane on a loan that lasted until 3 January 2011. Tom played in eight matches, scoring twice. Paul lost his job at Notts County, thus ruining any chance of his son joining the club. Tom was frustrated at the lack of first-team opportunities at the Reds and

signed for Blackpool in the Championship before the 2011/12 season with Liverpool pocketing a measly £250,000 compensation

and a 30 per cent cut of his next transfer. Tom has been a key player at Blackpool and is continually linked with a return to Liverpool. The club tried to buy him in January 2013, but Blackpool are, as evident in Charlie Adam's case, not willing to lose key players mid-season, unless for a hefty fee.

FACTFILE

BORN
Stockport, 30 January 1992
POSITION
Left-winger
OTHER CLUBS
Notts County (loan, 2010–11), Blackpool (2011–)
JOINED
2003
INTERNATIONAL CAPS
6 England U-21 caps (2 goals)
LFC DEBUT
22 September 2010
CONTRACT EXPIRY
3 August 2011

Season	League		FA Cup		League Cup		Europe		Total	
	App	Goals	App	Goals	App	Goals	App	Goals	App	Goals
2010/11	0	0	0	0	0 (1)	0	0	0	0 (1)	0
Total	0	0	0	0	0 (1)	0	0	0	0 (1)	0

FACTFILE

BORN
Ilford, 21 October 1967
POSITION
Midfielder
OTHER CLUBS
West Ham United (1981–89), Manchester United (1989–95), Inter Milan (1995–97), Middlesbrough (1999–2002), Wolverhampton Wanderers (2002–06), Swindon Town (2006), Macclesfield Town (2007)
SIGNED FROM
Inter Milan, £4.2million, 10 July 1997
INTERNATIONAL CAPS
53 England caps (2 goals) (12 (0) at LFC), 1992–2000
LFC DEBUT GAME/GOAL
9 August 1997 / 13 August 1997
CONTRACT EXPIRY
30 July 1999

Individual honours

**Football Writers'
Footballer of the Year**

1974   Ian Callaghan
1976   Kevin Keegan
1977   Emlyn Hughes
1979   Kenny Dalglish
1980   Terry McDermott
1983   Kenny Dalglish
1984   Ian Rush
1988   John Barnes
1989   Steve Nicol
1990   John Barnes
2009   Steven Gerrard

**PFA
Player of the Year**

1980   Terry McDermott
1983   Kenny Dalglish
1984   Ian Rush
1988   John Barnes
2006   Steven Gerrard

**PFA
Young Player of the Year**

1995   Robbie Fowler
1996   Robbie Fowler
1998   Michael Owen
2001   Steven Gerrard

**Manager
of the Year**

Bill Shankly   1973
Bob Paisley   1976, 1977, 1979, 1980, 1982, 1983
Joe Fagan   1984
Kenny Dalglish   1986, 1988, 1990

**Top-flight
Top Scorer**

1902/03   Sam Raybould
1909/10   Jack Parkinson
1983/84   Ian Rush
1987/88   John Aldridge
1997/98   Michael Owen
1998/99   Michael Owen

**European
Golden Boot**

1984   Ian Rush

**European Footballer
of the Year**

2001   Michael Owen

JOHN BARNES
PFA PLAYER OF THE YEAR 1988

Insúa,
Emiliano

EMILIANO INSÚA was a promising left-back who was brought initially on loan from Boca Juniors on 11 January 2007. Seven months later Liverpool made the transfer permanent for an eventual cost of £1.68million as well as being entitled to 50 per cent of any future transfer fee for Gabriel Paletta who moved the opposite way to Boca. Insúa started two league matches, at Portsmouth and Fulham, towards the end of the 2006/07 season and a year later he was picked to play in the final three league matches.

His reward was a new three-year contract which would tie him to the club until June 2011. Insúa continued to impress in the 2008/09 season, making 11 starts. He made his international debut for Argentina in a dramatic World Cup qualifier against Peru on 10 October 2009 which Argentina won in the 93rd minute, keeping their hopes on track. In 2009/10 Insúa made a big breakthrough in terms of competitive matches played, 44.

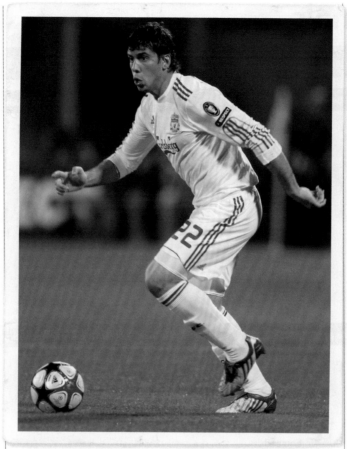

He would have played more games if he hadn't tore quadriceps in his thigh on 4 April against Birmingham. Insúa had started to struggle a bit in games in the second part of the season and was criticised by fans and media. He should perhaps have been rested when his confidence was low but Liverpool lacked cover in the left-back position as Fabio Aurélio was out injured most of the time.

Many saw a bright future ahead for Insúa, who was still only 21 years old but had already featured in 62 games for the first team. New boss Roy Hodgson reportedly wanted to keep him at Liverpool and Insúa wanted to stay but Liverpool and Fiorentina agreed a fee believed to be

£5million on 17 July 2010. However, early in August the Italian club's sporting director revealed that the deal had fallen through because they had been unable to agree terms with the Argentinian. On the final day of August 2010 Insúa joined Turkish club Galatasaray on loan for the 2010/11 season. Meanwhile Liverpool had brought in Hodgson's former player at Fulham, Paul Konchesky, to play at left-back as well as re-signing the injury-prone Aurélio. Few could make sense of the club's transfer policy at the time and no wonder!

INSÚA PLAYED 16 Super Lig matches for Galatasaray, but team manager Gheorghe Hagi, who

replaced Frank Rijkaard in October 2010, did not take the option to buy him. Before the start of 2011/12 Jose Enrique was brought in as first-choice left-back while Insúa left Liverpool permanently in the last week of August 2011 to sign a five-year contract with Portuguese club Sporting Lisbon. Insúa had an adventurous first season in Portugal, playing in 24 league fixtures and 12 Europa League matches as Sporting topped Group D before progressing to the semi-final stage, where they were beaten by Athletic Bilbao. Insúa scored four times during this excellent continental campaign, whereas he had scored just a single goal at his previous European clubs; Liverpool and Galatasaray. Insúa moved to high-flying Atlético Madrid in January 2013.

> FEW COULD
> MAKE SENSE OF
> THE CLUB'S
> TRANSFER POLICY
> AT THE TIME
> AND NO WONDER!

FACTFILE

BORN
Buenos Aires, Argentina,
7 January 1989
POSITION
Left-back
OTHER CLUBS
Boca Juniors (1997–2007),
Galatasaray (loan, 2010–11),
Sporting Lisbon (2011–2013),
Atlético Madrid (2013–)
SIGNED FROM
Boca Juniors – loan,
11 January 2007; permanent,
£1.68million, 26 August 2007
INTERNATIONAL CAPS
4 Argentina caps, 2009–11
LFC DEBUT GAME/GOAL
28 April 2007 /
28 October 2009
CONTRACT EXPIRY
27 August 2011

Season	League		FA Cup		League Cup		Europe		Other		Total	
	App	Goals	App	Goals	App	Goals	App	Goals	App	Goals	App	Goals
2006/07	2	0	0	0	0	0	0	0	0	0	2	0
2007/08	2 (1)	0	0	0	0	0	0	0	-	-	2 (1)	0
2008/09	9 (1)	0	1	0	1 (1)	0	0	0	-	-	11 (2)	0
2009/10	30 (1)	0	2	0	1	1	10	0	-	-	43 (1)	1
Total	**43 (3)**	**0**	**3**	**0**	**2 (1)**	**1**	**10**	**0**	**0**	**0**	**58 (4)**	**1**

Internationals

Most caps

Top 10 internationals who have been on Liverpool's books

Player	Caps	Nation
Jari Litmanen	137	Finland
Rigobert Song	137	Cameroon
Robbie Keane	127	Ireland
John Arne Riise	110	Norway
Xabi Alonso	107	Spain
Fernando Torres	106	Spain
Sami Hyypia	105	Finland
Steven Gerrard	102	England
Kenny Dalglish	102	Scotland
Steve Staunton	102	Ireland

Top 10 English internationals who have been on Liverpool's books

Player	Total	Starts	(sub)
Steven Gerrard	102	99	(3)
Michael Owen	89	77	(12)
John Barnes	79	65	(14)
Kevin Keegan	63	62	(1)
Emlyn Hughes	62	59	(3)
Emile Heskey	62	40	(22)
Ray Clemence	61	60	(1)
Peter Beardsley	59	46	(13)
Joe Cole	56	31	(25)
Paul Ince	53	50	(3)
David James	53	43	(10)

Top 10 active internationals while at Liverpool

Player	Caps	Nation
Steven Gerrard	102	England
Sami Hyypia	71	Finland
Ian Rush	67	Wales
John Arne Riise	64	Norway
Michael Owen	60	England
Emlyn Hughes	59	England
Ray Clemence	56	England
Kenny Dalglish	55	Scotland
Phil Neal	50	England
Xabi Alonso	49	Spain

Top 10 active English internationals while at Liverpool

Player	Caps
Steven Gerrard	102
Michael Owen	60
Emlyn Hughes	59
Ray Clemence	56
Phil Neal	50
John Barnes	48
Phil Thompson	42
Jamie Carragher	38
Emile Heskey	35
Roger Hunt	34
Peter Beardsley	34

ROGER HUNT
LIVERPOOL & ENGLAND

Most goals

Top 10 internationals who have been on Liverpool's books

Player	Goals	Caps	Average
Robbie Keane	59	127	0.46
Milan Baros	41	93	0.44
Michael Owen	40	89	0.45
Fernando Torres	36	106	0.34
Luis Suarez	35	69	0.51
Jari Litmanen	32	137	0.23
Kenny Dalglish	30	102	0.29
Ian Rush	28	73	0.38
Fernando Morientes	27	47	0.57
Vladimir Smicer	27	81	0.33

Top 10 active internationals while at Liverpool

Player	Goals	Caps	Average
Michael Owen	26	60	0.43
Ian Rush	26	67	0.39
Milan Baros	23	38	0.61
Dirk Kuyt	20	64	0.31
Luis Suarez	19	30	0.63
Steven Gerrard	19	102	0.19
Roger Hunt	18	34	0.53
Peter Crouch	14	27	0.52
Kenny Dalglish	14	55	0.25
Fernando Torres	12	40	0.30

272 internationals who have represented 45 nations have been on Liverpool's books (as of 1 July 2013). Outside the British Isles most of them have come from Spain (7), France (7), Norway (6) and the Netherlands (6).

Five Liverpool player have won the World Cup: Roger Hunt, Ian Callaghan and Gerry Byrne (England 1966) and Fernando Torres and Pepe Reina (Spain 2010). Four Reds have won the European Championships, all with Spain in 2008: Fernando Torres, Xabi Alonso, Álvaro Arbeloa and Pepe Reina.

THE LIVERPOOL ENCYCLOPEDIA | 303

Ireland,
Bob

WHEN IRELAND left Scotland to go to England it must have been confusing at the time. Bob Ireland played only 18 league games for Rangers from 1924 to 1929 before heading south of the border to Liverpool.

A day out at Lewis's in the 30s

HE MADE just one first-team appearance for the Reds, replacing regular right-half Tom Morrison in the home First Division fixture with Grimsby Town at Anfield on Boxing Day 1930. Ireland ran a billiards saloon and a number of shops in Perth, the home of St Johnstone football club, where he served two spells in the 1930s.

FACTFILE

BORN
Darvel, Ayrshire, Scotland,
22 July 1900
POSITION
Right-half
OTHER CLUBS
Darvel, Rangers (1923–29),
Peebles Rovers (loan, 1929–30),
St Johnstone (1931–34),
Brechin City (loan, 1933–34),
Workington (1934–36),
Airdrie (1936),
St Johnstone (1936)
SIGNED FROM
Rangers, 21 November 1929
LFC DEBUT
26 December 1930
CONTRACT EXPIRY
27 July 1931

	League		FA Cup		Total	
Season	App	Goals	App	Goals	App	Goals
1930/31	1	0	0	0	1	0
Total	1	0	0	0	1	0

Irvine,
Alan

ALAN IRVINE'S longest spell at one club was at Falkirk in the Scottish top division from 1982 to 1987 where he made 110 league appearances and scored 15 goals.

HE WAS ALSO THE VICTIM OF ONE OF THE CRUELLEST PRACTICAL JOKES EVER COMMITTED AT LIVERPOOL

THIS TALL centre-forward hardly got a look-in at Liverpool as too many good strikers were above him in the pecking order. All four of Irvine's appearances came as a substitute during the 1986/87 season. He was also the victim of one of the cruellest practical jokes ever committed at Liverpool. When Liverpool's FA Cup game against Luton was called off Irvine wasn't told the news. He climbed on the team bus in his best suit ready for match day, not noticing others were in tracksuits. 'He thinks that the game is on,' Hansen said to Dalglish. Kenny called for Irvine to come to his seat. 'We've got some injuries. How would you like playing centre-back?' 'I'm not sure, gaffer,' Irvine replied. 'Would you be more comfortable in midfield?' Kenny asked, to which Irvine said 'Yes.' 'Just don't tell anybody

ALAN IRVINE

you're playing,' were his final instructions. Poor Irvine still hadn't made his debut. The players were let in on the joke and took their seats in the dressing room at Anfield as if the game was on. They were told by Kenny to sort their match tickets out, knowing that would leave Alan alone in the dressing room with him as he was the only one without a ticket. Alan was left waiting in the dressing room for some considerable time until

FACTFILE

BORN
Broxburn, Scotland,
29 November 1962
POSITION
Centre-forward
OTHER CLUBS
Hibernian (1980–83),
Falkirk (1983–86),
Dundee United (1987–88),
Shrewsbury Town (1988–89),
Mazda (1989–90),
St Mirren (1990–92),
Portadown (1992–93),
East Fife (1993–95)
SIGNED FROM
Falkirk, £75,000,
1 October 1986
LFC DEBUT
20 December 1986
CONTRACT EXPIRY
28 August 1987

Kenny finally said: 'The game's off,' to which poor Alan could only mutter: 'I know.'

	League		FA Cup		League Cup		Europe		Other		Total	
Season	App	Goals	App	Goals	App	Goals	App	Goals	App	Goals	App	Goals
1986/87	0 (2)	0	0 (1)	0	0 (1)	0	-	-	0	0	0 (4)	0
Total	0 (2)	0	0 (1)	0	0 (1)	0	0	0	0	0	0 (4)	0

YOU'LL NEVER WALK ALONE

Irwin,
Colin

COLIN IRWIN proved an able deputy for Alan Hansen or Phil Thompson at the centre of defence or for Alan Kennedy at left-back. Liverpool-born Irwin came through the junior ranks at Anfield and made his league debut at home to West Bromwich Albion on 25 August 1979. A promising start continued in the next league match with a headed goal at Southampton, even though Liverpool lost 3-2. But after starting against Dinamo Tbilisi at the beginning of October, Irwin didn't feature in the first team again until six months later.

He came close to making his debut a couple of years earlier when he was still a part-timer at the club, training three times a week, while still working at a Kirkby factory. The electrician was on standby for the 1977 FA Cup semi-final replay against Everton as Tommy Smith was nursing a bruised thigh. The veteran passed his fitness test, though, and was part of a 3-0 win.

IN 1980/81 Irwin only missed one match from 22 November to 28 March, mainly filling in for the injured Thompson. He fought valiantly in the second leg of the European Cup semi-final against Bayern Munich but had to settle for a place on the bench in the final against Real Madrid in Paris, just as three years earlier at Wembley when Liverpool defeated Bruges. When Mark Lawrenson arrived from Brighton in August 1981, Irwin was longer needed at the club and he joined John Toshack's Swansea for a club record fee of £340,000. Irwin was made captain of the Swans, who had a season to remember when they finished sixth in the First Division. Irwin played 37 out of 42 league games, but unfortunately knee injuries curtailed his progress and he only made 11 appearances in the following two seasons when Swansea had been relegated. Irwin emigrated to Australia in the summer of 1984 where he featured for Perth Azurri. When Phil Neal was appointed as Bolton's player-manager in December 1985 he hired Irwin as a first-team coach. He remained with the club until the end of the 1986/87 season. Irwin later returned to Perth in Western Australia as a distribution manager for a wine and spirits wholesaler.

FACTFILE

BORN
Liverpool, 9 February 1957
POSITION
Defender
OTHER CLUBS
Swansea City (1981–84),
Perth Azurri (1984–85)
JOINED
November 1974
LFC DEBUT GAME/GOAL
25 August 1979 /
1 September 1979
CONTRACT EXPIRY
August 1981
HONOURS
European Cup 1978, 1981;
League Cup 1981

Season	League		FA Cup		League Cup		Europe		Other		Total	
	App	Goals	App	Goals	App	Goals	App	Goals	App	Goals	App	Goals
1979/80	7 (1)	2	2	0	2	0	2	0	0	0	13 (1)	2
1980/81	19 (2)	1	2	0	4	0	2 (1)	0	0	0	27 (3)	1
Total	**26 (3)**	**3**	**4**	**0**	**6**	**0**	**4 (1)**	**0**	**0**	**0**	**40 (4)**	**3**

Itandje,
Charles

CHARLES ITANDJE played 170 matches in the French first division for Lens. He first attracted Liverpool's attention when Gérard Houllier was boss.

He was supposed to meet Houllier at the eve of Liverpool's 2001 UEFA Cup final against Alaves but was a no-show. 'I had an appointment but I didn't go,'

Itandje remembered. 'I almost pretended to be dead. I had just signed a pre-contract with Lens, where I was set to become number one, and I did not want to turn it down.' Itandje played in seven cup ties during the 2007/08 season, conceded eight goals and never seemed to instil a lot of confidence in his defenders. His performance in his final game for the club in the humbling defeat by Barnsley was hardly convincing.

ITANDJE was made available for transfer after Liverpool signed Diego Cavalieri in the summer of 2008 but he turned down a move to Turkish club Galatasaray. He didn't appear in Liverpool's first team at all in 2008/09 but he did manage to attract the wrong sort of attention by sniggering and bothering Damien Plessis, who sat next to him, during the 20th anniversary service of the Hillsborough disaster at Anfield in April 2009. He was disciplined by the club for this incident and it was clear that his future lay elsewhere. 'My behaviour was clumsy and awkward, but I am disappointed that the club did not support me,' he said. 'The club told me: "Don't even walk in the street or you will be attacked."' In December 2010 Itandje joined Greek club Atromitos on a free transfer, where he played regularly until he joined PAOK in January 2013.

FACTFILE

BORN
Bobigny, France,
2 November 1982
POSITION
Goalkeeper
OTHER CLUBS
Red Star 93 (1997–2001),
Lens (2001–07),
Kavala (loan, 2009–10),
Atromitos (2011–13),
PAOK (2013-)
SIGNED FROM
Lens, 9 August 2007
INTERNATIONAL CAPS
3 France U-21 caps
LFC DEBUT
25 September 2007
CONTRACT EXPIRY
8 December 2010

Season	League		FA Cup		League Cup		Europe		Total	
	App	Goals	App	Goals	App	Goals	App	Goals	App	Goals
2007/08	0	0	4	0	3	0	0	0	7	0
Total	**0**	**0**	**4**	**0**	**3**	**0**	**0**	**0**	**7**	**0**

Jackson,
Brian

WALTON-BORN Brian Jackson was on Arsenal's books as an amateur before moving on to Leyton Orient where he won the admiration of many clubs by creating a number of goals for the struggling Third Division South club. He was signed by Liverpool in November 1951 when still aged only 18.

He was in the army at the time doing his national service in Hampshire but his commanding officer granted his release to Liverpool. The Reds had been on his trail for some time but Orient were unwilling to do business without finding an adequate replacement, hence Liverpool reserve Donald Woan moved in the opposite direction in addition to the £6,500 fee. Jackson scored on his Liverpool debut against Bolton Wanderers but that was the

BRIAN JACKSON
LIVERPOOL

only time he hit the net in the 15 league games he played that season. Although Jackson was very much part of the Liverpool squad of the time, he never really became a firm 'regular' in the side, with 27 being the highest number of league appearances he made in any single season (1953/54).

Jackson moved on to Port Vale in July 1958 and played 178 games, scoring 34 goals for the Potteries club before signing for Peterborough United in July 1962. He ended his Football League playing career with Lincoln City.

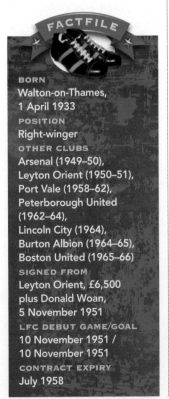

FACTFILE

BORN
Walton-on-Thames,
1 April 1933
POSITION
Right-winger
OTHER CLUBS
Arsenal (1949–50),
Leyton Orient (1950–51),
Port Vale (1958–62),
Peterborough United
(1962–64),
Lincoln City (1964),
Burton Albion (1964–65),
Boston United (1965–66)
SIGNED FROM
Leyton Orient, £6,500
plus Donald Woan,
5 November 1951
LFC DEBUT GAME/GOAL
10 November 1951 /
10 November 1951
CONTRACT EXPIRY
July 1958

> JACKSON SCORED ON HIS LIVERPOOL DEBUT AGAINST BOLTON WANDERERS BUT THAT WAS THE ONLY TIME HE HIT THE NET IN THE 15 LEAGUE GAMES HE PLAYED THAT SEASON

Season	League		FA Cup		Total	
	App	Goals	App	Goals	App	Goals
1951/52	15	1	1	0	16	1
1952/53	5	0	0	0	5	0
1953/54	27	4	1	0	28	4
1954/55	23	2	3	0	26	2
1955/56	15	0	0	0	15	0
1956/57	19	2	0	0	19	2
1957/58	22	2	2	0	24	2
Total	**126**	**11**	**7**	**0**	**133**	**11**

Jackson,
James

Jackson, who was 'all grit and determination', joined Aberdeen in June 1923 for a club record fee of £2,000 from Motherwell. After plying his trade in the homeland of his parents, the Newcastle-born right-back controversially signed for Liverpool in May 1925. Aberdeen's original asking price was £4,500, which Liverpool were not ready to pay. Jackson had been officially signed for the Dons' next season, but requested to be sold to Liverpool, which Aberdeen finally agreed to for only £1,750.

Jackson established himself at Liverpool towards the end of the decade and only missed four out of 126 First Division games from August 1927 until May 1930. He was Liverpool's captain from 1929-31 and led by example as revealed by vice-captain Tommy Morrison in the *Exeter and Plymouth Gazette* in January 1931. 'Let me give you my impression of the ideal captain. He is my present captain Jimmy Jackson, a great footballer, a great gentleman, the perfect skipper. He never attempts to govern or rule, but rallies the boys around him by his very genuineness. Now Liverpool have become famous as the team which is never beaten. I do not say this with any idea of swank, but results have shown that we do fight like bulldogs to the last gasp. Jimmy Jackson is chiefly responsible for that. In numerous matches we have been losing every time and Jackson has rolled up his sleeves, gone here to help the half backs, gone up among the forwards urging them on, and all the time he is shouting words of encouragement to his men. It makes you play. It is very

like an officer encouraging his soldiers in a charge. He has that spirit which imbues you with the desire to save the day. Times out of number we have done it. Jackson has the happy knack of never upsetting his colleagues by continually shouting unnecessary instructions to them. When he speaks it is something worth saying. You must select the right man, the most experienced man, the person who knows human nature. A level head, a stout heart, and a happy temperament will make a good skipper.' Jackson tore a knee ligament in the club's tour of Scotland at the end of 1929/30 and missed the last game of the season as well as the first two months of the following campaign after ill-advisedly playing in the first game. His father, also called James, was Arsenal's captain in the club's inaugural First Division season, so James Jr was always popular among Gunners fans and is said to have received 'the biggest ovation any visiting player ever gained at Highbury'.

> 'JUST AFTER I HAD SCORED THE THIRD GOAL JIMMY TURNED TO ME AND SAID, "WILLIAM, I SHALL NEVER PLAY IN FRONT OF THIS MAN AGAIN"'
>
> **DIXIE DEAN**

Jackson started divinity studies at Aberdeen University and finished them at Cambridge while still featuring for Liverpool. One dumbfounded football writer asked after a game: 'Is Jackson really going to be a minister? If so, if he prays as hard as he plays he ought to be Archbishop of Canterbury in record time!'

When Jackson left the club he was ordained as a minister in the Presbyterian Church and inducted into the charge of St Andrew's Church, Douglas, Isle of Man, on 29 June 1933.

JACKSON was not at all comfortable playing in front of Liverpool's Irish keeper, Elisha Scott, as Everton great Dixie Dean later explained: 'Elisha's language was unbelievable and the things he called me. Jimmy Jackson, who was called the Parson, was one of the Liverpool full-backs that day and he just couldn't stand Elisha's lingo and the words he came out with. Just after I had scored the third goal Jimmy turned to me and said, "William, I shall never play in front of this man again."'

Season	League		FA Cup		Total	
	App	Goals	App	Goals	App	Goals
1925/26	12	0	2	0	14	0
1926/27	19	0	0	0	19	0
1927/28	40	1	2	0	42	1
1928/29	42	0	3	0	45	0
1929/30	40	0	1	0	41	0
1930/31	28	0	1	0	29	0
1931/32	17	0	3	0	20	0
1932/33	14	1	0	0	14	1
Total	**212**	**2**	**12**	**0**	**224**	**2**

In November 1930, Jackson spoke in defence of football at the Great George's Street Congregational Church, Liverpool. According to the scribe at the *Nottingham Evening Post*, Jackson denied that swearing was ever learned at a football match, and declared that on an eight-hour journey with the team he did not hear one offensive word (Elisha must have been gagged and bound in the trunk!). Jackson also stated it was not football that caused men to gamble, but the fact that men and women would gamble on anything. As for the charge of drinking laid against footballers, the professional player realised he must keep fit and must be a total abstainer. Jackson also defended his own status as footballer and preacher. 'A man wrote to me to point out the unapostolic proceedings of being a professional footballer, and, at the same time, a professional preacher of the Gospel. There is still an idea abroad that sport, and football in particular, are wiles of the Devil, used to seduce young men from the straight and narrow path. I am convinced that my ability to play football is just as much a gift from God as any talent that man possesses.'

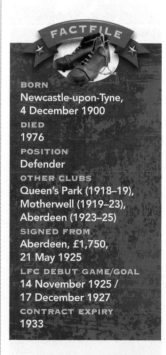

FACTFILE

BORN
Newcastle-upon-Tyne,
4 December 1900
DIED
1976
POSITION
Defender
OTHER CLUBS
Queen's Park (1918–19),
Motherwell (1919–23),
Aberdeen (1923–25)
SIGNED FROM
Aberdeen, £1,750,
21 May 1925
LFC DEBUT GAME/GOAL
14 November 1925 /
17 December 1927
CONTRACT EXPIRY
1933

James, David

DAVID JAMES was considered one of England's best and brightest goalkeepers when he was establishing himself at Watford.

Arriving at Liverpool aged 21 he vowed to become Liverpool and England's first-choice keeper inside two years. James didn't start his Liverpool career very promisingly and critics were happy to write him off after he seemed to fail at the first hurdle. Grobbelaar recaptured his place, but even with him out later through illness, Mike Hooper was preferred to James in the 1992/93 season. Before the season was out, though, James was again handed the number one jersey. He had to settle for bench duty again the following season until 19 February 1994 when Grobbelaar was injured. From that point on James made 213 consecutive appearances until Brad Friedel took his place on 28 February 1998. James got back into the side in the 1998/99 season but that turned out to be his last at Anfield.

James was too prone to make mistakes, but that was a fact that Liverpool's fans had grown quite accustomed to after watching Grobbelaar's wild antics. But unlike Grobbelaar's golden era, Liverpool were not winning each game despite the goalkeeper's errors, and when James made a mistake, it was often the reason behind Liverpool's defeat on a particular evening. Contrary to people's expectations, James seemed to become less confident as the years passed, even earning the nickname 'Calamity James'. One high pass into the penalty area was essentially what was needed because the opposition knew he would have trouble controlling it. James once attributed his lack of concentration

to playing Nintendo games long into the night!

DESPITE his Liverpool career having its ups and downs, James had a very successful career with a number of clubs and a healthy number of international caps to his name. On 14 February 2009 he achieved the all-time Premier League appearance record of 536 games, overtaking Gary Speed. He held the record until Ryan Giggs broke it in 2011. James won the FA Cup with Portsmouth in 2008, which proved third time lucky, as he had lost with Liverpool in the 1996 final to a late Eric Cantona goal and with Aston Villa in 2000. James reached the FA Cup final again

with Portsmouth in 2010 but he was denied a winners' medal. Pompey were relegated at the end of the season after finishing well clear at the bottom of the table. After being part of every season of the Premier League since its inception in 1992/93, James moved to Bristol City in the Championship for the 2010/11 season. He appeared regularly in the Championship for a couple of seasons, then the 41-year-old goalkeeper was released. Towards the end of September 2012 James joined his eighth different English League club when he signed for AFC Bournemouth until the end of the 2012/13 season. James joined Icelandic side IBV Vestmannaeyjar in April 2013,

becoming player-coach under boss Hermann Hreidarsson, his former team-mate at Portsmouth.

In 2004 James looked back at his Liverpool career. 'I have taken stock of what I am about. A lot of people believed I was capable of becoming England's number one and I took it for granted that I was going to do that without having to do the hard stuff, which was working at it. The worst point was the "Calamity James" time of my career when I was 26/27 and I was trying to equate how I would be able to get back into the England team. The move to Aston Villa was the right move at the right time.'

FACTFILE

BORN
Welwyn Garden City,
1 August 1970
POSITION
Goalkeeper
OTHER CLUBS
Watford (1984–92),
Aston Villa (1999–2001),
West Ham United (2001–04),
Manchester City (2004–06),
Portsmouth (2006–10),
Bristol City (2010–12),
AFC Bournemouth (2012–13),
IBV Vestmannaeyjar (2013-)
SIGNED FROM
Watford, £1million,
6 July 1992
INTERNATIONAL CAPS
53 England caps (1 at LFC),
1997–2010
LFC DEBUT
16 August 1992
CONTRACT EXPIRY
17 June 1999
HONOURS
League Cup 1995

Season	League App	League Goals	FA Cup App	FA Cup Goals	League Cup App	League Cup Goals	Europe App	Europe Goals	Other App	Other Goals	Total App	Total Goals
1992/93	29	0	0	0	1	0	1	0	0	0	31	0
1993/94	13(1)	0	0	0	0	0	-	-	-	-	13 (1)	0
1994/95	42	0	7	0	8	0	-	-	-	-	57	0
1995/96	38	0	7	0	4	0	4	0	-	-	53	0
1996/97	38	0	2	0	4	0	8	0	-	-	52	0
1997/98	27	0	1	0	5	0	4	0	-	-	37	0
1998/99	26	0	2	0	0	0	5	0	-	-	33	0
Total	**213(1)**	**0**	**19**	**0**	**22**	**0**	**22**	**0**	**0**	**0**	**276(1)**	**0**

James, Norman

TINY BRADSHAW was the regular Liverpool centre-half when he missed seven of the 42 First Division fixtures in the 1930/31 season and Norman James covered for him. James was pivot, with Tommy Morrison on the right and Jimmy McDougall on the left, on his debut; a 5-2 win over Blackpool. Liverpool were 6th in the table but as he exited the team the Reds were down to 9th, having lost three out of the last four and conceded 10 goals in those defeats. Bradshaw came in for the only remaining game of the season in which Liverpool beat West Ham 2-0.

JAMES wasn't selected at all during 1931/32 as Bradshaw was an everpresent, and he made just one more appearance when Sunderland drew 3-3 at Anfield on 3 December 1932.

FACTFILE

BORN
Liverpool, 25 March 1908
DIED
12 October 1985
POSITION
Centre-half
OTHER CLUBS
Bootle St James',
Braby's Athletic,
Bradford City (1933–36),
Queens Park Rangers
(1936–39)
SIGNED FROM
Braby's Athletic,
April 1929
LFC DEBUT
28 February 1931
CONTRACT EXPIRY
May 1933

Season	League		FA Cup		Total	
	App	Goals	App	Goals	App	Goals
1930/31	7	0	0	0	7	0
1932/33	1	0	0	0	1	0
Total	**8**	**0**	**0**	**0**	**8**	**6**

Jenkinson, Bill

BILL JENKINSON was a full-back who made 13 league appearances during the 1919/20 season having joined the club from South Liverpool during World War One.

HE PLAYED in 12 of the first 14 games of the first league campaign after the 'Great War'

but was dropped following a 3-3 draw with Bradford Park Avenue on 15 November 1919. Liverpool were 15th in the table under the leadership of George Patterson, but one month later he was replaced as manager by David Ashworth, who improved Liverpool's form to such an extent they finished 4th. Jenkinson was only used once by Ashworth, near the end of the season for the visit to Derby County on 10 April 1920. With the most potent full-back partnership in the history of Liverpool to deal with in Donald Mackinlay and Ephraim Longworth, and Tommy Lucas also ready to step in, chances were few and far between for Jenkinson.

FACTFILE

BORN
Golborne, Lancashire,
2 March 1892
DIED
3 April 1967
POSITION
Right/left-back
OTHER CLUBS
Golborne United,
Manchester City (1914–15),
South Liverpool (1915–16),
Wigan Borough (1921–23),
Wallasey United (1923–25)
SIGNED FROM
South Liverpool, 1916
LFC DEBUT
30 August 1919
CONTRACT EXPIRY
June 1921

Season	League		FA Cup		Total	
	App	Goals	App	Goals	App	Goals
1919/20	13	0	0	0	13	0
Total	**13**	**0**	**0**	**0**	**13**	**0**

Johnson, David

TWENTY-FOUR-YEAR-OLD David Johnson was already an England international, having scored 46 goals in 187 league matches for Everton and Ipswich, before featuring for Liverpool. The boyhood Red started his career at Everton, which Johnson says came as a 'great shock' to his family who were all Liverpool supporters. He certainly got Liverpool's attention when he scored the winning goal as a 20-year-old against the Reds at Goodison on 13 November 1971, a feat he would repeat for Liverpool at Goodison in 1978. Shankly made two enquiries for Johnson while he was at Everton but Harry Catterick wouldn't let him go across the park. Shankly asked for him on a couple more occasions, while Johnson's career flourished at Ipswich. When Ipswich finally caved in to Liverpool's attentions it was Bob Paisley who welcomed Johnson, who didn't hesitate to put pen to paper for his boyhood idols.

> THE BOYHOOD RED STARTED HIS CAREER AT EVERTON, WHICH JOHNSON SAYS CAME AS A 'GREAT SHOCK' TO HIS FAMILY WHO WERE ALL LIVERPOOL SUPPORTERS

Although picked from the start for the first eight First Division fixtures of 1976/77, many of Johnson's 26 league appearances that year were from the substitute's bench. He had been bought as a long-term replacement for John Toshack, who had scored

that Liverpool sealed the League Championship by beating the Villans. His form earned him further international recognition and he scored twice in a 3-1 win against world champions Argentina at Wembley in May 1980. Ian Rush's emergence in 1981 relegated Johnson to the bench but not before he finally achieved his dream by being part of the side that lifted the European Cup for the third time at the Parc des Princes in 1981. Johnson re-signed for his first club Everton in August 1982 where he stayed for a couple of years before going down the league ladder. He also sampled life in the USA and Malta.

> DAVID JOHNSON WAS KNOWN AS 'THE DOC', AS HE USED TO SUFFER FROM A REGULAR SORE THROAT, SO ALWAYS KEPT COUGH SWEETS IN HIS BAG ALONG WITH HEADACHE TABLETS

'The Doc' examines King Kenny

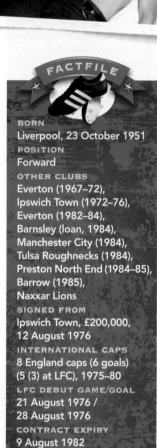

a Liverpool career-high total of 23 goals in the previous season, but was now struggling with injury. Johnson was more often than not on the wing rather than up front, but still easily qualified for the first of his four League Championship medals. He scored in the final league match of the season, away to Bristol City, and that was enough to earn him a place in the FA Cup final team to meet Manchester United. He was substituted for Ian Callaghan during the final and 'Cally' kept his place for the European Cup final in Rome four days later. Johnson, along with the other four substitutes, had to watch Liverpool triumph from the bench. Stuck in the reserves for much of the next season, Johnson started the first leg of the European Cup semi-final against Borussia Mönchengladbach and scored Liverpool's goal in Germany. When he finally seemed to be establishing himself, he tore his knee ligaments against Leicester on 8 April 1978 and missed out again on a European Cup final.

The following season was a bit stop-start, having suffered such a bad injury; Johnson made his long-awaited breakthrough in the second half of 1978/79. He had his best season in 1979/80, scoring 27 goals and forming a powerful partnership with Kenny Dalglish. Johnson scored two goals in a 4-1 win over Aston Villa, the second consecutive year

DAVID JOHNSON was known as 'the Doc', as he used to suffer from a regular sore throat, so always kept cough sweets in his bag along with headache tablets. 'Everyone used to go to my bag to use my gear,' Johnson explained. 'Terry Mac went in there one time and took out all these pills and stuff and said: "It's like a flippin' doctor's bag" and after that it just stuck.'

FACTFILE

BORN
Liverpool, 23 October 1951
POSITION
Forward
OTHER CLUBS
Everton (1967–72),
Ipswich Town (1972–76),
Everton (1982–84),
Barnsley (loan, 1984),
Manchester City (1984),
Tulsa Roughnecks (1984),
Preston North End (1984–85),
Barrow (1985),
Naxxar Lions
SIGNED FROM
Ipswich Town, £200,000,
12 August 1976
INTERNATIONAL CAPS
8 England caps (6 goals)
(5 (3) at LFC), 1975–80
LFC DEBUT GAME/GOAL
21 August 1976 /
28 August 1976
CONTRACT EXPIRY
9 August 1982
HONOURS
League Championship
1976/77, 1978/79,
1979/80, 1981/82;
League Cup 1982;
European Cup 1977, 1981

Season	League		FA Cup		League Cup		Europe		Other		Total	
	App	Goals	App	Goals	App	Goals	App	Goals	App	Goals	App	Goals
1976/77	19 (7)	5	3 (1)	0	2	0	4 (2)	3	0	0	28(10)	8
1977/78	7 (5)	3	1	1	1	0	0 (3)	1	0	0	9 (8)	5
1978/79	26 (4)	16	4	2	0	0	1 (2)	0	-	-	31 (6)	18
1979/80	37	21	8	3	6	2	2	1	1	0	54	27
1980/81	29	8	1	0	5	4	5	1	1	0	41	13
1981/82	10 (5)	2	0 (1)	0	1 (4)	3	3 (1)	2	0 (1)	0	14 (12)	7
Total	**128 (21)**	**55**	**17 (2)**	**6**	**15 (4)**	**9**	**15 (8)**	**8**	**2 (1)**	**0**	**177 (36)**	**78**

Johnson,
Dick

FACTFILE

BORN
Gateshead, June 1895
DIED
3 January 1933
POSITION
Forward
OTHER CLUBS
Felling Colliery;
Sunderland (wartime guest),
Stoke City (1925–29),
New Brighton (1929–31),
Connah's Quay (1931–33)
JOINED
27 January 1920
LFC DEBUT GAME/GOAL
5 April 1920 /
11 September 1920
CONTRACT EXPIRY
20 February 1925
HONOURS
League Championship
1922/23

DICK JOHNSON was a cunning and skilful forward who averaged a goal every other game from the 26 First Division appearances he made during the 1920/21 season, including a hat-trick as Preston North End were thrashed 6-0 at Anfield on 25 September 1920. But injury meant that he had to watch the whole of the following season from the sidelines as his colleagues won the club's third League Championship in 1922.

However, he was a key figure a year later when the title was retained, scoring a hat-trick in the opening 5-2 win over Arsenal, only missing five league games and scoring 14 times.

Johnson was a popular player with his party trick always being met with great applause as the *Liverpool Echo* reported in 1923: 'Johnson met with one of those overhead cycle kicks, very entertaining and becoming much loved by the Anfield fans.' Johnson only played two games in 1923/24 as he seriously injured his knee in the opening game of the season. He also struggled with injury the following campaign before departing for Second Division Stoke in February 1925.

Season	League App	League Goals	FA Cup App	FA Cup Goals	Total App	Total Goals
1919/20	1	0	0	0	1	0
1920/21	26	13	1	0	27	13
1922/23	37	14	4	2	41	16
1923/24	2	0	0	0	2	0
1924/25	11	1	0	0	11	1
Total	**77**	**28**	**5**	**2**	**82**	**30**

Johnson,
Glen

GLEN JOHNSON began his career under Harry Redknapp at West Ham but after just 16 appearances and a loan spell at Millwall the 18-year-old became the first signing for new Chelsea owner Roman Abramovich in 2003 for £6million. Johnson made his Chelsea debut against Liverpool on 17 August 2003, which Chelsea won 2-1 with Johnson playing 73 minutes before being replaced by William Gallas. Only three months later he played his first game for England against Denmark and Johnson's stock was rising high.

He was a regular in the 2003/04 season that turned out to be Claudio Raineri's last and featured in the second half of the 2004/05 Premiership-winning season under Jose Mourinho. Johnson played rarely in the following campaign and spent the whole of 2006/07 on loan at Portsmouth. After four years at Stamford Bridge, Pompey purchased Johnson for £4million in August 2007. Johnson won the FA Cup with Portsmouth in 2008 and was selected as right-back in the PFA Team of the Year 2008/09. His screaming left-foot volley against Hull on 22 November 2008 was the BBC's Match of the Day 'Goal of the Season'.

In June 2009 Johnson joined Liverpool for a colossal £17.5million fee and although he appeared in 35 of the club's 56 competitive matches his first campaign was a mixed success. He scored in two of the opening four league matches to enhance his reputation as an attacking full-back. Defensively he maybe wasn't quite as sound, but that is an accusation that could be levelled at a number of his colleagues too. Johnson was injured in the closing stages of Liverpool's victory against Aston Villa between Christmas and New Year and did not play again until coming on as a substitute at Wigan in March. With fitness as well as form being an important factor for him before England's World Cup squad was announced in May 2010, Johnson came safely through the final league matches of the season. Like his club captain Steven Gerrard, Johnson played from the start in all four of England's matches in South Africa, being substituted only towards the end of the 'last 16' defeat by Germany.

JOHNSON figured in 28 of the 38 Premier League matches in 2010/11 and added a further seven appearances in the Europa

Season	League App	League Goals	FA Cup App	FA Cup Goals	League Cup App	League Cup Goals	Europe App	Europe Goals	Total App	Total Goals
2009/10	24 (1)	3	0	0	0 (1)	0	9	0	33 (2)	3
2010/11	28	2	0	0	0	0	7	0	35	2
2011/12	22 (1)	1	3	0	3	0	-	-	28 (1)	1
2012/13	36	1	0	0	0	0	7	1	43	2
Total	**110 (2)**	**7**	**3**	**0**	**3 (1)**	**0**	**23**	**1**	**139 (3)**	**8**

Johnson,
Tommy

THOMAS Clark Fisher Johnson was a Manchester City legend, whose club record of scoring 38 goals in 39 First Division games in the 1928/29 season still stands.

Johnson scored 158 league goals for City, a club record shared with all-time leading scorer Eric Brook. After 12 years at City 29-year-old Johnson was sold to Everton, who subsequently won the Second Division. His departure sparked protests by City fans, resulting in a drop of 7,000 in the club's attendances. He contributed 22 goals in 41 matches, linking well with Dixie Dean, as Everton won the League Championship in 1931/32. He won the FA Cup with the Blues in 1933 when they beat Manchester City 3-0 in the final. A tricky player on the left wing, Johnson played 159 games and scored 64 goals for Everton before switching to Liverpool at 32 years of age. Everton were very angry at how a document sent only inside football circles – offering Johnson along with seven other players – was made public, prompting their chairman, William C. Cuff, to complain that 'unless there is confidence in football', clubs would no longer 'send out lists naming players they wanted to sell'.

JOHNSON played in the last 11 matches of the 1933/34 season and scored twice, a period in which six games were won and only three lost. This contrasted greatly with the depressing run of 17 games before Johnson was

signed, when only one match resulted in maximum points; so his introduction made a significant difference to the club's fortunes at a crucial stage of the season and it narrowly avoided relegation. Johnson played in nearly half the league games a year later as Liverpool finished in a much more respectable position, seventh, but the longest run of successive games he had was the last 10 matches of the season. The Manchester City and Everton great had seen the back of his best days when he arrived at Liverpool, but his fantastic experience paid off handsomely when the Reds avoided the dreaded drop.

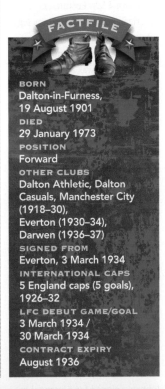

FACTFILE

BORN
Dalton-in-Furness,
19 August 1901
DIED
29 January 1973
POSITION
Forward
OTHER CLUBS
Dalton Athletic, Dalton
Casuals, Manchester City
(1918–30),
Everton (1930–34),
Darwen (1936–37)
SIGNED FROM
Everton, 3 March 1934
INTERNATIONAL CAPS
5 England caps (5 goals),
1926–32
LFC DEBUT GAME/GOAL
3 March 1934 /
30 March 1934
CONTRACT EXPIRY
August 1936

League. Towards the end of the season he was sometimes asked to switch to the left to accommodate the emergence of Jon Flanagan on the right. He won his first winners' medal with the club and scored a tidy penalty in the shootout that followed the drawn League Cup final with Cardiff City. Johnson featured for the England team at Euro 2012 that reached the quarter-finals.

Since Brendan Rodgers replaced Kenny Dalglish as manager at Liverpool Johnson has been in the best form of his Reds' career. He has played a number of games as a left-winger where he can attack at will, and has shown a tremendous desire to succeed.

FACTFILE

BORN
Greenwich, London,
23 August 1984
POSITION
Right/left-back, Left-winger
OTHER CLUBS
West Ham United (2000–03),
Millwall (loan, 2002),
Chelsea (2003–07),
Portsmouth (loan, 2006–07;
permanent, 2007–09)
SIGNED FROM
Portsmouth, £17.5million,
26 June 2009
INTERNATIONAL CAPS
48 England caps (1 goal)
(33 (1) at LFC), 2003–
LFC DEBUT GAME/GOAL
16 August 2009 /
19 August 2009
HONOURS
League Cup 2012

Season	League		FA Cup		Total	
	App	Goals	App	Goals	App	Goals
1933/34	11	2	0	0	11	2
1934/35	19	5	0	0	19	5
1935/36	6	1	2	0	8	1
Total	36	8	2	0	38	8

Johnston,
Craig

A TIRELESS RUNNER who always gave 100 per cent for the team, Craig Johnston was born in South Africa but brought up in Australia. Confident enough in his own ability to write to several English clubs as a 15-year-old asking for a trial, Middlesbrough were the only ones to reply, so he borrowed the £632 return air fare from his father and was signed after a four-month trial.

It could have been so different, as he told *Shoot!* in 1978. When Johnston was only six he got a kick on the leg and suffered from a bone disease. A doctor recommended amputation of the left leg. 'I still remember the horror I felt. Fortunately an American specialist saved my leg,' Johnston recalled. When he was 14 there was a recurrence of leg trouble and he was advised to pack up football. After his first trial game, Boro manager Jack Charlton told Johnston to go back to Australia on the first plane because he would never make a footballer in a million years, in fact, he thought he was the worst footballer he had ever seen. Graeme Souness, whose shirt Johnston inherited when the Scot went to Liverpool, gave the Australian great support and with typical dedication Johnston set about proving Charlton wrong. Charlton was soon replaced by John Neal, who gave Johnston his breakthrough in the First Division in the 1979/80 season.

Johnston signed for Liverpool in April 1981, still aged only 20 but with over 60 league appearances to his credit already. When he watched his new club win the European Cup in Paris only weeks after his arrival, he must have dreamed of being part of similar

successes. After being a substitute in three of the first four league matches in 1981/82 he was subsequently overlooked, however his fortunes started to change on a freezing December night when Arsenal visited Anfield for a fourth round League Cup replay. His first goal for the club five minutes into extra time helped see the Reds through to the quarter-final, although Johnston failed to play any further part in the competition as his team went on to retain the trophy. But he did contribute six goals as Liverpool regained the League Championship from Aston Villa.

JOHNSTON quickly became a crowd favourite because supporters recognised that he would run until he dropped and his courage and strength were never in doubt. He would himself admit that he lacked a certain finesse to be a top player and just ran around the field like a 'lunatic'.

When John Wark arrived, Johnston lost his place in the starting line-up following a win in the replay of the League Cup final against Everton in March 1984. Wark was ineligible for the European Cup as he hadn't signed before the UEFA deadline, so Johnston featured in the successful European Cup final in Rome. When Joe Fagan stepped down after two seasons in charge, Johnston was given fresh hope and encouragement from

his former team-mate Kenny Dalglish. 'Craig was his own worst enemy,' Dalglish said. 'He just didn't believe in his footballing abilities, and I could see that, when his form deserted him, Craig became depressed and the dark cycle continued. Several times during the season I had to beat away this black dog of depression chasing Craig.' Johnston played 61 games in the 'Double' season of 1985/86, again reaching double figures in the scoring stakes as in 1982/83. The joy of scoring in an FA Cup final was plain to see as Johnston netted Liverpool's second goal in a 3-1 win over Everton at Wembley. 'At least Liverpool had one

	League		FA Cup		League Cup		Europe		Other		Total	
Season	App	Goals	App	Goals	App	Goals	App	Goals	App	Goals	App	Goals
1981/82	13 (5)	6	0 (1)	0	0 (2)	1	0 (1)	0	1	0	14 (9)	7
1982/83	30 (3)	7	2 (1)	1	6	1	4	1	0	0	42 (4)	10
1983/84	28 (1)	2	2	1	11 (1)	0	8	1	0 (1)	0	49 (3)	4
1984/85	11	0	0	0	1	0	1 (3)	0	1	0	14 (3)	0
1985/86	38 (3)	7	6 (2)	1	7	1	-	-	5	1	56 (5)	10
1986/87	27 (1)	3	3	0	5	0	-	-	1	0	36 (1)	3
1987/88	18 (12)	5	1 (2)	1	2	0	-	-	-	-	21 (14)	6
Total	**165 (25)**	**30**	**14 (6)**	**4**	**32 (3)**	**3**	**13 (4)**	**2**	**8 (1)**	**1**	**232 (39)**	**40**

magnificent season out of Craig Johnston,' Dalglish concluded.

After a promising start to the 1986/87 season, the recurrence of a back injury kept him on the sidelines. But worse news was to come that Christmas. Craig's younger sister, Faye, nearly died in a gassing accident caused by a faulty heater in her hotel room in Morocco, and he rushed immediately to be at her side. All this was kept from the press at the time and the supporters had no idea of the tragedy that was unfolding in his private life. His mind was elsewhere and although he never gave up when he had a Liverpool shirt on, it was natural that his family came first.

Further injuries meant a reduced number of appearances in 1987/88 and Johnston left England after the (best-forgotten) FA Cup final against Wimbledon to return to Australia to care for his sister, who was brain-damaged as a result of the gassing incident. Years after he quit Liverpool, Johnston was continually being linked with top clubs. He made one thing clear at the time to Liverpool fans all over the world – that he would only return for one club. 'I'd never play for anyone else but Liverpool. The

only other team I'd play for would be Liverpool reserves!'

A year later, devastated by what had happened at Hillsborough, Johnston not only raised £40,000 in his own country for the families of the 96, but also flew halfway across the world to attend the memorial service at Anfield seven days after the disaster and stayed on to help counsel the bereaved families, a wonderful gesture which endeared him to Liverpool fans everywhere.

JOHNSTON is also a true entrepreneur. He designed the Adidas Predator football boot, his own brand of surfboards, became a full-time photographer, was a music producer … his list of accomplishments is endless. The title of his autobiography, *Walk Alone*, was apt because in many ways he was a refreshing change from the 'typical' professional footballer. And the fact that his book was written 'In Memory of the Victims of Heysel and Hillsborough' showed

how much he cared about the community that had accepted him as one of their own and who will always have fond memories of a player who ran himself into the ground for the Liverpool cause.

'I loved playing for Liverpool, especially the atmosphere in the city,' he told the *Guardian* in 2004. 'It was a place where one minute a total stranger would come up to me, hug me and say "I love you", and five minutes later someone would wind down

their car window, give you the finger and shout "I hate you!"' Johnston remains humble about his Liverpool career, maybe underplaying his great achievements. 'You have no idea how crap I was. Even when I was playing for Liverpool, I was the worst player in the best team in the world.'

> 'YOU HAVE NO IDEA HOW CRAP I WAS. EVEN WHEN I WAS PLAYING FOR LIVERPOOL, I WAS THE WORST PLAYER IN THE BEST TEAM IN THE WORLD'

Jones, Allan

ALLAN JONES
[LIVERPOOL]

A FULL-BACK who later made a name for himself at Brentford, playing 280 matches. Allan Jones was a Welsh schoolboy international who joined Liverpool in 1955, signing professional forms for Liverpool two years later.

WHEN regular right-back John Molyneux was unavailable for the visit of Cardiff City a few days before Christmas 1959, Jones stepped in to replace him. The Welshmen won 4-0 but it was a significant day in the club's history as it was the first game Bill Shankly was in charge of Liverpool. The new manager only called on Jones on four more occasions, the only games that Gerry Byrne missed during the club's return to the First Division in 1962/63.

Season	League		FA Cup		Total	
	App	Goals	App	Goals	App	Goals
1959/60	1	0	0	0	1	0
1962/63	4	0	0	0	4	0
Total	5	0	0	0	5	0

Jones,
Barry

A FORMER AMATEUR with Prescot Cables in the North West Counties League, Barry Jones was an apprentice painter and decorator obtained by Liverpool for a £500 donation.

Jones only featured once as a substitute in a European game at Kuusysi Lahti when David Burrows limped off with knee damage in the 15th minute. Burrows joined a lengthy injury list that had prevented Liverpool from having the allowed five substitutes on the night, with only four on the bench. Liverpool had beaten the Finnish side 6-1 in the first leg in the Reds' return to European football after the Heysel ban, but lost the game in Finland 1-0 due to a mistake by Bruce Grobbelaar. Jones had a decent game and prevented a goalbound

shot to hit the net. Jones played around 350 games for lower-league Wrexham and York City before moving into non-league football and finishing his career in the Welsh Premier League.

FACTFILE

BORN
Prescot, 30 June 1970
POSITION
Centre-half
OTHER CLUBS
Prescot Cables,
Wrexham (1992–98),
York City (loan, 1997–98;
permanent, 1998–2001),
Southport (2001–04),
Runcorn Halton (2004–05),
Prescot Cables (2005–06),
Bangor City (2006–07)
SIGNED FROM
Prescot Cables, £500,
19 January 1989
LFC DEBUT
2 October 1991
CONTRACT EXPIRY
10 July 1992

Season	League		FA Cup		League Cup		Europe		Total	
	App	Goals	App	Goals	App	Goals	App	Goals	App	Goals
1991/92	0	0	0	0	0	0	0 (1)	0	0 (1)	0
Total	0	0	0	0	0	0	0 (1)	0	0 (1)	0

Jones, Bill

BILL JONES joined Liverpool as a teenager in 1938 and by the time the Football League resumed 'normal service' following World War Two, he was 25 years old.

He immediately made up for lost time by helping his club win the League Championship, playing in 26 of the 42 league matches in 1946/47 and scoring twice. Although the club would never reach such heights again

for nearly 20 years, Jones was a regular member of the side for the next seven seasons. He featured most often as a centre-half but was extremely versatile and could play – and play well – in several different positions. Jones was capped by his country twice at centre-half and played in Liverpool's first ever Wembley cup final against Arsenal in 1950, but had to settle for a runners-up medal. Unfortunately Liverpool never built on the success they had enjoyed in the immediate post-war years and from 1950 onwards their final league placing got steadily worse until in 1953/54, which proved to be Jones' last season at Anfield, relegation became a reality. It was a sad end to a fine Anfield career.

'Had Liverpool not rescued me from the obscurity of a minor Derbyshire club, I should probably have tried to earn a living at cricket or golf,' Jones said in the souvenir brochure for the 1950 FA Cup final. 'My leaning was towards the latter, and golf is still my main hobby. I plead guilty to being one of the most superstitious fellows in our side. I always avoid being third behind the skipper on leaving the dressing room. Why? I have not the faintest idea.'

BILL IS the grandfather of Liverpool's 1990s right-back Rob Jones and he followed his grandson's career closely. 'We are very proud of his achievements and I have to admit he is a better player than I was,' he would say. 'He is a lot faster for a start.'

WHEN former Liverpool captain and legend Donald Mackinlay was asked in 1955 about who he thought were the best ever players at Liverpool, he singled out Bill. 'One of the finest centre-halves I have ever seen. I would have loved to have played behind him. What a tragedy it was he was moved about such a lot.'

FACTFILE

BORN
Whaley Bridge,
13 May 1921
DIED
26 December 2010
POSITION
Forward / Defender
OTHER CLUBS
Hayfield St Matthews;
York City,
Leeds United,
Reading (wartime guest),
Ellesmere Port Town
SIGNED FROM
Hayfield St Matthews,
September 1938
INTERNATIONAL CAPS
2 England caps, 1950
LFC DEBUT GAME/GOAL
31 August 1946 /
7 September 1946
CONTRACT EXPIRY
May 1954
HONOURS
League Championship
1946/47

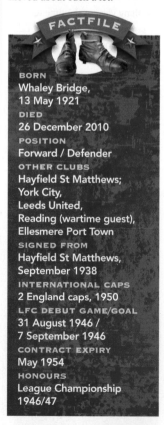

Season	League		FA Cup		Total	
	App	Goals	App	Goals	App	Goals
1946/47	26	2	6	0	32	2
1947/48	41	1	2	0	43	1
1948/49	38	0	4	0	42	0
1949/50	26	0	3	0	29	0
1950/51	38	4	1	0	39	4
1951/52	36	2	3	0	39	2
1952/53	26	2	1	0	27	2
1953/54	25	6	1	0	26	6
Total	256	17	21	0	277	17

Jones,
Brad

WITH ADEQUATE, if relatively inexperienced, back-up to Pepe Reina (in the form of Diego Cavalieri and Peter Gulacsi), Liverpool made a move for Middlesbrough's Brad Jones in the opening week of the 2010/11 Premier League season. With Reina signing a long extension to his contract that would keep him at Anfield until 2016, Jones knew when he signed for Liverpool that only injury, suspension and the occasional cup match would see him being named in his new club's first team from the start.

Brad Jones was born in Armadale, a city close to Perth in Western Australia, but his mother was actually from Maghull on Merseyside so he had connections with Liverpool right from the start. He was offered a professional contract at Middlesbrough on his 17th birthday in March 1999. But it would be five long years before he made his senior debut in goal for the club from Teesside due to Mark Schwarzer's fitness and consistency. This resulted in four loan spells with English clubs, as well as one in Ireland.

When Schwarzer joined Fulham at the end of the 2007/08 season, Jones found himself in the spotlight. He was, though, unable to prevent Middlesbrough's relegation to the Championship in 2009 nor help them back into the top division a year later. At international level, Jones was first called up by his country to

replace Schwarzer in a friendly match in February 2007, with his first senior start coming against Uruguay in the middle of the same year. He was named as one of three goalkeepers in Australia's 23-man squad for the South Africa World Cup, but withdrew as his young son had been diagnosed with cancer.

JONES only played twice for Liverpool's first team during the whole of the 2010/11 season, against Northampton Town in the League Cup at Anfield in September and against Utrecht in December when the club had already qualified for the knockout stage of the Europa League. On 24 March 2011 Jones moved to Derby County in an 'emergency loan' deal, during which he featured seven times. Tragically in November 2011 Jones lost his five-year-old son Luca to cancer.

Jones was propelled unexpectedly into the spotlight at Blackburn's

Ewood Park only a few days after his partner, Dani, had given birth to a son called Nico. Jones came on when Alexander Doni was sent off after conceding a penalty. Jones saved Yakubu's penalty and immediately thrust his arms skywards. 'Luca is with me every day,' Brad said. 'His picture is in my wash bag, his toys are in my travel bag. I take him everywhere. In that sense, I've definitely got someone watching over me. It was nice to save the penalty as it has been a difficult time with losing my son. Maybe he gave me that good fortune.' Jones kept goal splendidly as Liverpool beat Everton 2-1 in the FA Cup semi-final at Wembley, but that was his last first-team appearance of the season. As a sign of his progress, Jones signed a new long-term contract in December 2012. Brendan Rodgers was very pleased with the custodian, who had his fair share of games in the 2012/13 season. 'Brad, who was a No. 3 or No. 4 keeper here, has

really kicked on since the summer and in the games he has played since the summer, showed he is [a] very loyal and supportive No. 2.'

JONES is a lifelong Liverpool supporter: 'There were two things I said when I was eight years old; one was that I was going to play for Australia, which I have, and the other was playing for Liverpool.'

FACTFILE

BORN
Armadale, Australia,
19 March 1982
POSITION
Goalkeeper
OTHER CLUBS
Middlesbrough (1999–2010),
Shelbourne (loan, 2001),
Stockport County
(loan, 2002–03),
Rotherham United
(loan, 2003),
Blackpool
(loan, 2003, 2004–05),
Sheffield Wednesday
(loan, 2006),
Derby County (loan, 2011)
SIGNED FROM
Middlesbrough, £2.3million,
18 August 2010
INTERNATIONAL CAPS
3 Australia caps (1 at LFC),
2007–11
LFC DEBUT
22 September 2010

Season	League		FA Cup		League Cup		Europe		Total	
	App	Goals	App	Goals	App	Goals	App	Goals	App	Goals
2010/11	0	0	0	0	1	0	1	0	2	0
2011/12	0 (1)	0	1	0	0	0	-	-	1 (1)	0
2012/13	7	0	2	0	2	0	4	0	15	0
Total	7 (1)	0	3	0	3	0	5	0	18 (1)	0

Jones,
Harold

INSIDE-LEFT HAROLD JONES made just a single appearance on 5 September 1953 when the Reds lost 5-1 to Preston North End at Anfield. The star of the show was Preston and England legend, Tom Finney, who scored a hat-trick. This was Liverpool's third defeat in their 6th game of the campaign that ended in relegation to the Second Division.

FACTFILE

BORN
Liverpool, 22 May 1933
DIED
6 September 2003
POSITION
Inside-left forward
OTHER CLUBS
Rhyl (1954–57)
JOINED
January 1952
LFC DEBUT
5 September 1953
CONTRACT EXPIRY
June 1954

Season	League		FA Cup		Total	
	App	Goals	App	Goals	App	Goals
1953/54	1	0	0	0	1	0
Total	**1**	**0**	**0**	**0**	**1**	**0**

Jones,
Joey

AN ENTHUSIASTIC and tough-tackling left-back whose uncompromising style quickly endeared him to the Liverpool crowd, Joey Jones was a charismatic Welshman who became a 'cult figure' on the Kop even though he only played for the club during three different seasons.

WREXHAM manager John Neal was furious when Jones was sold to Liverpool in July 1975. 'The directors went over my head. Now I'll have to consider if I have any future with the club.' The former self-confessed youth delinquent was 20 years old when Bob Paisley signed him and was still a bit 'raw'. Even though Jones started the season as first choice he only appeared in 13 First Division matches in total, due to the gulf in class between the Third Division he left behind and the First Division becoming too apparent in his performance.

'When Liverpool signed players from lower divisions, 98 per cent of them went into the reserves and then the first team. I did the opposite,' Jones told *LFChistory. net* in 2011. 'I went straight from

here into the first team. I didn't have that settling down process of going to play in the reserves. In many respects I was playing on adrenaline. Eventually it caught up with me in that first season. After about 15 or 16 games I started to dip.' Jones was a faithful Liverpool

fan, who was living his dream. 'I was actually on the pitch with my heroes… with players, believe it or not, I had pictures of on the walls in the council house in Llandudno, back home in the bedroom I shared with my brother, who is a big Liverpool fan. I now

[found] myself in the dressing room getting changed next to them.'

The left-back role was also covered by Phil Neal and Alec Lindsay in 1975/76 but a year later Jones had established himself in the first team and only missed three of the 42 league fixtures. His exploits on the road to victory in the European Cup in 1977 were immortalised in a banner that read: 'JOEY ATE THE FROGS LEGS, MADE THE SWISS ROLL, NOW HES MUNCHING GLADBACH'. Only Manchester United's victory in the FA Cup final prevented it from being possibly the greatest ever season in the club's history. However, the European victory seemed to be the beginning of the end for Jones, who lost his place in the team in January the following season to the ageing but still dependable Tommy Smith.

JONES ADMITS to being like a madman on the pitch, and never shirked a challenge. A clenched fist towards the Kop when he

ran onto the field became his trademark and got the crowd going, but he got in serious trouble at other clubs when displaying the same passion. 'In my home debut against West Ham, I ran out at Anfield and I remember the Kop chanting my name. Because I knew where I used to stand and I knew where my mates were, my cousins, I was putting my fist up to them, not to cause trouble,' Jones explains. 'Eventually as my career moved

> 'I ALWAYS HAD A GOOD RAPPORT WITH THE FANS. I THINK THEY KNEW THAT DEEP DOWN, I WAS JUST ONE OF THEM'

along, that got me into trouble at various clubs. The opposition thought it was to cause trouble. By the time I had gone to Chelsea I got arrested a couple of times [for] inciting riots. One of them was a bad one, it was on the TV. Two days later I was arrested at Derby County and got arrested at Newcastle. Yet when I was at Liverpool I didn't get arrested once.'

'Joey just loves to be happy and gets enthusiastic about the slightest thing. He's just the sort of player every team needs, because he'll make you forget those tensions with one of his terrible jokes,' Ray Clemence said about Jones in 1977. 'He makes a joke about anything and everything.'

Jones rejoined Wrexham and had spells at Chelsea and Huddersfield before finally returning to his first club before the 1987/88 season and when his playing career ended he has continued to work at the Racecourse Ground as a coach with the same enthusiasm that he had always displayed as a player.

JONES was capped over 70 times by his country and is still fondly remembered by Liverpool fans as one of the most colourful characters ever to pull on the famous red shirt. 'To be honest, I couldn't believe it when Liverpool came in for me in 1975. Talk about a dream come true,' Jones said. 'I'd gone fishing with a couple of mates from Llandudno. We were making our way back to shore after catching a couple of fish when I saw my dad standing on the beach waving his arms. I thought something was wrong at home, but when he told me Wrexham had phoned to say Liverpool wanted to sign me I almost fell back into the sea.

I had three great years and while I was never one of the household names like Keegan, Clemence, Hughes or Smith, I always had a good rapport with the fans. I think they knew that deep down, I was just one of them.'

Season	League		FA Cup		League Cup		Europe		Other		Total	
	App	Goals	App	Goals	App	Goals	App	Goals	App	Goals	App	Goals
1975/76	13	0	0	0	0	0	1	0	-	-	14	0
1976/77	39	3	8	0	2	0	9	0	1	0	59	3
1977/78	20	0	1	0	2	0	3	0	1	0	27	0
Total	**72**	**3**	**9**	**0**	**4**	**0**	**13**	**0**	**2**	**0**	**100**	**3**

Jones, John

JOHN JONES was Liverpool's reserve goalkeeper during the 1924/25 season.

Elisha Scott had been firmly established as the club's last line of defence for many years, but when he got injured against Manchester United in the Lancashire Senior Cup, the big Irishman missed three matches, having featured in the previous 121 league games. Jones stepped in and conceded six goals in those three November games but kept a clean sheet in his fourth and final

appearance for the club, a 1-0 home victory over Tottenham Hotspur on 18 April 1925.

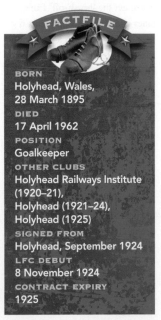

Season	League		FA Cup		Total	
	App	Goals	App	Goals	App	Goals
1924/25	4	0	0	0	4	0
Total	**4**	**0**	**0**	**0**	**4**	**0**

Jones, Lee

LEE JONES was a striker, who scored a number of goals for the youth team and the reserves at Liverpool despite breaking his leg twice.

He was loaned out to his first club, Wrexham, in 1995/96, scoring in almost every other game in 20 appearances in the Second Division. He made a total of four substitute appearances for Liverpool before being loaned again to Wrexham. He was eventually sold to John Aldridge's Tranmere Rovers in the 1996/97 season. After a successful three-year stay at Rovers, Jones returned to Wrexham for his fourth spell in 2002 before playing for and managing Caernarfon Town and NEWI Cefn Druids in the Welsh League. Jones retired due to a knee injury in 2008.

FACTFILE

BORN
Wrexham, Wales,
29 March 1973
POSITION
Centre-forward
OTHER CLUBS
Wrexham (1989–92),
Crewe Alexandra (loan, 1993),
Wrexham (loan, 1996, 1997),
Tranmere Rovers
(1997–2000),
Barnsley (2000–02),
Oswestry Town (2002),
Wrexham (2002–04),
Caernarfon Town (2004–06),
NEWI Cefn Druids (2006–08)
SIGNED FROM
Wrexham, £300,000,
12 March 1992
INTERNATIONAL CAPS
2 Wales caps (1 at LFC), 1997
LFC DEBUT
5 October 1994
CONTRACT EXPIRY
30 May 1997

Season	League		FA Cup		League Cup		Europe		Total	
	App	Goals	App	Goals	App	Goals	App	Goals	App	Goals
1994/95	0 (1)	0	0	0	0 (1)	0	-	-	0 (2)	0
1996/97	0 (2)	0	0	0	0	0	0	0	0 (2)	0
Total	0 (3)	0	0	0	0 (1)	0	0	0	0 (4)	0

Jones, Mervyn

MERVYN JONES was primarily known as one of the smallest men ever to feature at Liverpool, being only 5ft 4in (162cm), although he stood two inches taller than Fred Geary!

The *Liverpool Echo* feared Jones might get the 'brush-off' from taller and stronger opponents if they could 'get down low enough' to administer their shoulder charge, but were impressed by his 'lively, almost cheeky' debut against Fulham in March 1952. Bangor-born Jones figured three times towards the end of the 1951/52 season and then made one further appearance in November 1952. He also played in one FA Cup tie for the Reds, the ignominious third round defeat at Third Division North's Gateshead in January 1953. Jones was transferred to Scunthorpe United in July 1953 and totalled 392 league games and 51 goals in his career.

JONES WAS
PRIMARILY KNOWN AS
ONE OF THE
SMALLEST MEN EVER
TO FEATURE AT
LIVERPOOL,
BEING ONLY 5FT 4IN

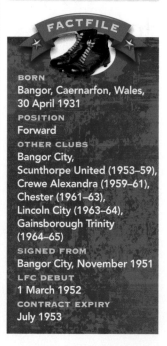

FACTFILE

BORN
Bangor, Caernarfon, Wales,
30 April 1931
POSITION
Forward
OTHER CLUBS
Bangor City,
Scunthorpe United (1953–59),
Crewe Alexandra (1959–61),
Chester (1961–63),
Lincoln City (1963–64),
Gainsborough Trinity
(1964–65)
SIGNED FROM
Bangor City, November 1951
LFC DEBUT
1 March 1952
CONTRACT EXPIRY
July 1953

Season	League		FA Cup		Total	
	App	Goals	App	Goals	App	Goals
1951/52	3	0	0	0	3	0
1952/53	1	0	1	0	2	0
Total	4	0	1	0	5	0

Jones,
Paul

PAUL JONES was an experienced Premier League goalkeeper loaned from Southampton through January 2004, as Chris Kirkland and Jerzy Dudek were both on the injury list.

JONES is the oldest player to make his debut for Liverpool since World War Two, aged 36 years, 8 months and 23 days. He kept a clean sheet against Aston Villa at Anfield but conceded two goals in his second and final game at White Hart Lane. Funnily enough, Jones turned up for the Liverpool 'Legends' team in 2012 as it toured Thailand. 'I was a fanatical Liverpool supporter growing up and I still am a fan today,' Jones told *LFC.tv* in 2012. 'Everyone in North Wales supported Liverpool when I was younger so to get the chance to emulate my boyhood hero Ray Clemence and play in

goal for Liverpool was a real dream come true. I'd never touched the "This Is Anfield" sign when I was an opposition player – I think that tradition should be reserved for Liverpool players – so to get to touch it and know that I was touching it as a Liverpool player meant everything.'

FACTFILE

BORN
Chirk, Wales, 18 April 1967
POSITION
Goalkeeper
OTHER CLUBS
Kidderminster Harriers (1986–91),
Wolverhampton Wanderers (1991–96),
Stockport County (1996–97),
Southampton (1997–2004),
Wolverhampton Wanderers (2004–06),
Watford (loan, 2004–05),
Millwall (loan, 2005),
Queens Park Rangers (2006–07),
Bognor Regis Town (2007)
LOANED FROM
Southampton, 9 January 2004
INTERNATIONAL CAPS
50 Wales caps, 1997–2006
LFC DEBUT
10 January 2004
CONTRACT EXPIRY
28 January 2004

Season	League		FA Cup		League Cup		Europe		Total	
	App	Goals	App	Goals	App	Goals	App	Goals	App	Goals
2003/04	2	0	0	0	0	0	0	0	2	0
Total	2	0	0	0	0	0	0	0	2	0

Jones,
Rob

ROB JONES was a Red since childhood as his grandfather, Bill Jones, had been on Liverpool's books from 1938 to 1954, playing 277 games. Even though Bill spoke very little about his Liverpool career, it is obvious that Rob had enormous affection for his grandfather. 'I always enjoyed my grandad's company. There was just something about his presence that felt magical.' Even during his days as a fledgling professional at Crewe, Rob still travelled to attend home matches at Anfield as often as he could.

Jones started out at Fourth Division Crewe, a club that is renowned for its youth set-up. Crewe were promoted to the Third Division in the 1988/89 season and Jones became a firm fixture in Crewe's first team in 1990/91, but unfortunately the Railwaymen were relegated. The highlight of the season was undoubtedly when Crewe met Liverpool in the third round of the League Cup. Crewe took a surprising lead in the eighth minute at Anfield but the Reds responded with five goals. The second leg at Gresty Road finished 4-1 in favour of the guests. Jones recalls that he made a pledge to himself that this 'wouldn't be the last time I played on the famous turf'.

Only a couple of months into the 1991/92 season Tom Saunders scouted Crewe's right-back, whom manager Dario Gradi had recommended to Graeme Souness. The player in question wasn't very impressive but when left-back Jones was moved to the right in the second half, Saunders and Souness saw this speedy player as the solution to their problem. Only 48 hours later, Jones was facing Ryan Giggs at Old Trafford and performing admirably. Amazingly, roughly four months after playing in the Fourth Division, Jones made his England debut versus France at Wembley. It was a dream come

true and he won the FA Cup in the spring and was looking forward to playing for England in the 1992 European Championships. But unfortunately it didn't work out as planned. Shin splints caused him to miss the competition and he had to undergo surgery only six games into the following season. Nevertheless, he was only out for six weeks and recaptured his place in the starting line-up on his return.

ROB JONES was undoubtedly Liverpool's most exciting full-back for years, using his skill and speed to cause trouble in opposing ranks. He was included in the PFA Team of the Year in the 1991/92 and 1994/95 seasons. Jones remained in the starting XI until 1996 when injuries stopped his career again. Jason McAteer was now playing as right wing-back, as Roy Evans had switched Jones to the left where he was equally

> AMAZINGLY, ROUGHLY FOUR MONTHS AFTER PLAYING IN THE FOURTH DIVISION, JONES MADE HIS ENGLAND DEBUT VERSUS FRANCE AT WEMBLEY

able to perform. Only three days after suffering defeat at the hands of Manchester United in the 1996 FA Cup final, Jones received the worst news possible. He had been suffering from back pains and was diagnosed with a cracked vertebrae and advised to rest from football for at least six months, otherwise he could run the risk of ending up in a wheelchair.

He returned at the end of the 1996/97 season and was in and out of the side until February 1998 when he finally seemed to have recaptured his place. Again injuries curtailed his career but this time for good. He had a large swelling in his left knee and had to undergo three major operations to try to fix the problem. By then Gérard Houllier had ruled him out of his future plans and Jones was on his way out.

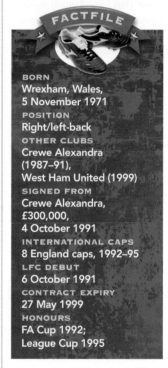

> 'HE HAS TO GO DOWN AS ONE OF THE BEST, IF NOT THE BEST, SIGNING I MADE AT LIVERPOOL. HE SHOULD HAVE BEEN A 15-YEAR MAN FOR THE CLUB BECAUSE HE WAS GOOD ENOUGH TO DO THAT. NOT MANY ARE'
>
> **GRAEME SOUNESS**

> 'HE WAS AS GOOD AS PROBABLY ANYTHING IN EUROPE AT THE TIME'
>
> **JAMIE CARRAGHER**

He trained with West Ham to get a contract there before the 1999/2000 season but he only played in one Intertoto Cup game before the knee started to swell up again. Jones' promising career finished at the age of just 28.

JAMIE CARRAGHER was a big fan and reflected on what could

have been. 'I played with Rob Jones a few times and he was a bit unfortunate with injuries and his best form was probably before I got into the team, when he was as good as probably anything in Europe at the time,' Carragher stated. 'He was playing out of his skin and I think if he'd have stayed

fit he probably would have gone on to win 70 or 80 caps for England instead of Gary Neville.' The manager who signed Jones for the Reds, Graeme Souness, was in no doubt of his qualities. 'He has to go down as one of the best, if not the best, signing I made at Liverpool. He should have been

FACTFILE

BORN
Wrexham, Wales,
5 November 1971
POSITION
Right/left-back
OTHER CLUBS
Crewe Alexandra
(1987–91),
West Ham United (1999)
SIGNED FROM
Crewe Alexandra,
£300,000,
4 October 1991
INTERNATIONAL CAPS
8 England caps, 1992–95
LFC DEBUT
6 October 1991
CONTRACT EXPIRY
27 May 1999
HONOURS
FA Cup 1992;
League Cup 1995

a 15-year man for the club because he was good enough to do that. Not many are.'

Season	League		FA Cup		League Cup		Europe		Other		Total	
	App	Goals	App	Goals	App	Goals	App	Goals	App	Goals	App	Goals
1991/92	28	0	9	0	0	0	2	0	-	-	39	0
1992/93	30	0	2	0	2 (1)	0	2	0	0	0	36 (1)	0
1993/94	38	0	2	0	5	0	-	-	-	-	45	0
1994/95	31	0	7	0	8	0	-	-	-	-	46	0
1995/96	33	0	7	0	3	0	4	0	-	-	47	0
1996/97	2	0	0	0	1	0	0	0	-	-	3	0
1997/98	20 (1)	0	0	0	2	0	3	0	-	-	25 (1)	0
Total	**182 (1)**	**0**	**27**	**0**	**21 (1)**	**0**	**11**	**0**	**0**	**0**	**241 (2)**	**0**

Jones,
Ron

RON JONES made five appearances in Liverpool's forward line just before World War Two. He scored on his debut in a 2-0 win against Manchester City at Anfield towards the end of March 1938.

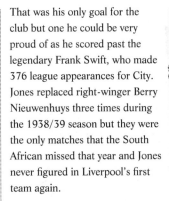

> HIS ONLY GOAL FOR THE CLUB BUT ONE HE COULD BE VERY PROUD OF AS HE SCORED PAST THE LEGENDARY FRANK SWIFT

That was his only goal for the club but one he could be very proud of as he scored past the legendary Frank Swift, who made 376 league appearances for City. Jones replaced right-winger Berry Nieuwenhuys three times during the 1938/39 season but they were the only matches that the South African missed that year and Jones never figured in Liverpool's first team again.

ACCORDING to some sources Jones was killed in action in World War Two, but that is untrue – he passed away 20 March 2010.

FACTFILE

BORN
Mold, Flintshire, Wales,
18 June 1918
DIED
20 March 2010
POSITION
Inside-right forward,
Right-winger
OTHER CLUBS
Mold Alexandra,
Wrexham (1935–38);
Crewe Alexandra
(wartime guest),
Wrexham (1944–46)
SIGNED FROM
Wrexham, 10 March 1938
LFC DEBUT GAME/GOAL
26 March 1938 /
26 March 1938
CONTRACT EXPIRY
1944

Season	League App	League Goals	FA Cup App	FA Cup Goals	Total App	Total Goals
1937/38	2	1	0	0	2	1
1938/39	3	0	0	0	3	0
Total	**5**	**1**	**0**	**0**	**5**	**1**

Josemi

JOSEMI was first choice at the start of the 2004/05 season and his displays were quite promising, but as the campaign progressed he struggled more frequently against pacy widemen and was sent off in the 4-2 win at Fulham on 16 October 2004 with a second yellow after fouling Luis Boa Morte.

JOSEMI was injured from December 2004 to May 2005 and Steve Finnan established himself as right-back in his absence. Three starts in a row in the middle of October 2005 was Josemi's best run in the 2005/06 season. The Spaniard returned to Villareal one European Champions' medal richer after warming the bench in Istanbul. Josemi only played one game as the Yellow Submarine

finished second in La Liga. He was transferred to Mallorca where he played more regularly before signing for Iraklis Thessaloniki in Greece. Josemi was relegated with Iraklis in 2011 and suffered the same fate with Cartagena who were relegated to Spain's Third Division. He is now on the books of his second Greek club, Levadiakos.

FACTFILE

BORN
Malaga, Spain,
15 November 1979
POSITION
Right-back
OTHER CLUBS
Torremolinos (1997–98),
Malaga (1998–2004),
Villareal (2006–08),
Mallorca (2008–10),
Iraklis Thessaloniki (2010–11),
Cartagena (2011–12),
Levadiakos (2012–)
SIGNED FROM
Malaga, £2million,
26 July 2004
LFC DEBUT
10 August 2004
CONTRACT EXPIRY
2 January 2006
HONOURS
Champions League 2005

Season	League App	League Goals	FA Cup App	FA Cup Goals	League Cup App	League Cup Goals	Europe App	Europe Goals	Other App	Other Goals	Total App	Total Goals
2004/05	13 (2)	0	0	0	1	0	5 (2)	0	-	-	19 (4)	0
2005/06	3 (3)	0	0	0	0	0	5	0	1	0	9 (3)	0
Total	**16 (5)**	**0**	**0**	**0**	**1**	**0**	**10 (2)**	**0**	**1**	**0**	**28 (7)**	**0**

Jovanovic, Milan

MILAN JOVANOVIC'S big breakthrough came as an 18-year-old in the colours of Vojvodina in the city of Novi Sad, Serbia's second-largest city. After spending a couple of years in Ukraine and Russia he finally found his home at Belgian club Standard Liège and quickly became a crowd favourite there. Jovanovic was voted Belgian Footballer of the Year at the end of the 2007/08 season and received the Golden Shoe for his league performances in 2009.

He won the Belgian league title twice with Standard. During his third season he came on as a substitute against Liverpool in the Champions League third qualifying round at Anfield late in normal time but Standard were defeated 1-0 after extra time. Jovanovic was Serbia's top scorer in the 2010 World Cup qualifying matches and that led to his inclusion in the 23-man squad that would travel to South Africa for the finals. He quickly made his mark with the goal that defeated Germany in Port Elizabeth. However, Serbia lost to both

Ghana and Australia and failed to reach the knockout stage of the tournament.

JOVANOVIC had made an agreement to join Liverpool on a free transfer before Rafa Benítez left the club and joined the Reds in the summer of 2010. The Serbian had a difficult first season at Anfield and didn't seem to receive much support from Benítez's replacement, Roy Hodgson. Jovanovic started only

13 competitive matches and in eight of those he was substituted. He played in the opening five Premier League matches but after that was more often found on the substitutes' bench than on the pitch, if he figured in the match-day squad at all. He seemed rather one-dimensional, looking more like a Fiat Multipla rather than a race car.

Jovanovic made the pitch only a couple of times under Kenny Dalglish and netted just twice for Liverpool, the opener in the humiliating League Cup defeat

to Northampton Town and the goal in Bucharest that earned a precious Europa League point against Steaua.

JOVANOVIC had been a star in the Belgian League and was considered by Anderlecht as a marquee signing when they obtained his services in August 2011. It was immediately clear that the Serbian was happy to be back in Belgium after his short and unhappy spell in England. Jovanovic scored nine times in 35 league matches as Anderlecht became domestic champions for the 31st time in their history in 2012.

FACTFILE

BORN
Bajina Bašta, Serbia,
18 April 1981
POSITION
Forward
OTHER CLUBS
Vojvodina (1999–2003),
Shakhtar Donetsk (2003–04),
Lokomotiv Moscow
(2004–06),
Standard Liège (2006–10),
Anderlecht (2011–)
JOINED
Bosman free transfer,
8 July 2010
INTERNATIONAL CAPS
44 Serbia caps (11 goals)
(7 (0) at LFC), 2007–12
LFC DEBUT GAME/GOAL
29 July 2010 /
22 September 2010
CONTRACT EXPIRY
5 August 2011

Season	League		FA Cup		League Cup		Europe		Other		Total	
	App	Goals	App	Goals	App	Goals	App	Goals	App	Goals	App	Goals
2010/11	5 (5)	0	0	0	1	1	7	1	13 (5)	2	15 (7)	5
Total	5 (5)	0	0	0	1	1	7	1	13 (5)	2	15 (7)	5

Jowett, Charlie

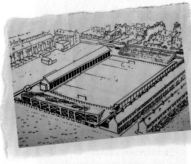

Anfield in the mid 1890s

A GOALKEEPER who was on an amateur trial from a local club called Liverpool Leek, so he never had a contract at Liverpool. Charlie Jowett made a single first-team appearance for the club during the 1896/97 season.

Harry Storer was first-choice keeper at the time and was

selected for 23 of the 30 First Division matches that season. Willie Donnelly made six appearances during the winter months and Jowett's only outing came in the penultimate fixture of the season, a 2-2 draw with Sheffield Wednesday at Anfield on 3 April 1897.

FACTFILE

BORN
Liverpool, 1872
POSITION
Goalkeeper
OTHER CLUBS
Liverpool Leek
ON TRIAL
13 March 1897
LFC DEBUT
3 April 1897
TRIAL EXPIRY
April 1897

Season	League		FA Cup		Total	
	App	Goals	App	Goals	App	Goals
1896/97	1	0	0	0	1	0
Total	1	0	0	0	1	6

Kane,
Stanley

DUE TO Arthur Riley's great consistency in goal Stanley Kane only made three appearances in each of his two seasons, in which he conceded 13 goals.

Kane made his debut in the most difficult circumstances in a Merseyside derby on 20 March 1935 at Anfield. Dixie Dean, who was known to shoulder-charge keepers – as was the habit of strikers in those days – was impeded by Jack Tennant in an attempt to stop Dean making his way to Kane. A disputed penalty

STAN KANE
[LIVERPOOL]

was awarded which Kane got a hand to, but Dean's powerful kick ended up in the back of the net, half-crippling Kane in the process. He thwarted Dixie on other occasions and certainly impressed the *Liverpool Echo*. 'It was a nice tribute of Bradshaw and Tennant, who had done so much grafting work, that they should publicly against Dean's header and his flying shot – a great shot and a greater save. Liverpool has always been renowned for its goalkeepers, and now a new name cannot

be forgotten. Yes, Kane was able.' Once his footballing career was finished Kane became a policeman in Liverpool.

Season	League		FA Cup		Total	
	App	Goals	App	Goals	App	Goals
1934/35	3	0	0	0	3	0
1935/36	3	0	0	0	3	0
Total	**6**	**0**	**0**	**0**	**6**	**0**

Kay,
George

GEORGE KAY was born in Manchester and played for local club Eccles before joining Bolton Wanderers in 1911, with whom he had a brief spell before moving across the Irish Sea to play in Belfast.

When competitive football resumed after World War One Kay joined West Ham United and was their captain in the first FA Cup final to be staged at Wembley

in 1923. The Hammers lost that day to Kay's former club Bolton, but had the ample consolation of a place in the top league as runners-up in the Second Division. Towards the end of the 1920s Kay moved to Stockport County and then on to Luton Town, initially as their player-coach in 1928 before taking on the role of manager a year later at the age of 38. He held that post until the end of the 1930/31 season before being attracted by the opportunity of managing a club in a higher division, Southampton. The Saints had been promoted as Division Three South champions in 1922 and were anxious to taste life at the very top. But during the five full seasons that Kay was in charge at The Dell, the club never made the top-half of the table. All the same, Kay was respected within the game and was clearly knowledgeable and not afraid to try out new ideas. He was also experienced and probably a combination of all those qualities brought him to Liverpool's attention when it was clear that George Patterson would be unable to continue the managerial side of his role as secretary-manager. Although appointed on 6 August 1936 Kay stayed at Southampton to fulfil his duties and started working for Liverpool on 21 August.

KAY had only been at Anfield a couple of years when another world war broke out, a conflict that would interrupt and in some cases end the careers of many a fine footballer. The League was on hiatus but regional competitions took their place. Many of the club's players served their country and Kay was hard at work to find men to represent Liverpool's eleven. Billy Liddell noted when he paid his respects to him in the *Liverpool Echo* soon after his passing that 'with players in the forces stationed all over the country, Mr Kay wrote thousands of letters and must have spent many hours on the phone to commanding officers. Such was his personality that his own players and guest players would willingly make long journeys to play for the Reds.' One of those men was a certain Bill Shankly who was impressed by Kay. 'I played for Liverpool against Everton during the war in the Liverpool Senior Cup, as a guest from Preston. All the players were in the passageway including Billy Liddell and myself. But George Kay, the Liverpool manager, didn't speak. He just went round touching

people on the shoulder. If he touched you then you were playing.' With the war over, the club took the unusual step of touring North America and Canada. It is quite likely that George Kay was the instigator of this trip; he felt that the climate and diet in a part of the world that hadn't been affected by food rationing the way European countries had would be extremely beneficial. The schedule was punishing; 10 matches at various venues between 12 May and 11 June, but it benefited the Reds who started the first post-war season in far better physical shape than many of their competitors as Kay claimed himself in a note to the *Echo* while in America. 'The players are 25 per cent above par in football, due in my opinion to the quality, quantity and variety of food.'

Bob Paisley was full of praise for his former boss George Kay and his importance in the club's history. 'He took Liverpool through the war to come out a bit like West Ham did after the First War. He was one of the people who laid the ground for the way Liverpool teams would play in the

FRIDAY 7 AUGUST 1936

future... keeping the ball on the ground and passing it well, but being strong on the ball as well.'

LIVERPOOL went on to win the League Championship in 1947 but it was a mighty close thing. A hard winter meant that a season which had begun at the end of August didn't finish until the start of June. Liverpool, Manchester United, Wolverhampton Wanderers and Stoke City were all in with a chance of taking the title as the season reached its climax. Liverpool's final fixture was against Wolves at Molineux. The hosts had 56 points, the visitors 55. Liverpool had to win and then wait and hope. They did their part of the job by winning 2-1, other results went their way and the Reds were champions of the Football League for a fifth time. It was George Kay's finest moment as a football manager. One of his key players was Albert Stubbins who told the *LFC Magazine* in 2001: 'George Kay was a first-class manager and a

very big influence on me. He was a lovely man, quiet and a deep thinker. He'd read books about psychology and he knew how to get the best out of his players,' the ginger-haired Geordie said. 'George's first thought was always for his players. He'd never tear a strip off us or criticise a Liverpool player in the press. That's where the psychology came into play. If we were trailing at half-time he'd come into the dressing room and although he'd point out our errors he'd always say, 'Well played, lads'. He knew and we knew, that we weren't playing well, but because he was so understanding we felt we had to play extra well to repay his faith in us.'

The club didn't come close to another championship and the nearest it came to additional success was in 1950 when the Reds reached the FA Cup final for the first time in 36 years. Kay was intent on using his cup experience. 'When I played in the first Cup final ever staged at Wembley, as captain of West Ham United, we did not win the trophy, but I am hoping that my second visit there, as manager of Liverpool will see us successful,' Kay said in Liverpool FC's souvenir brochure for the 1950 final. 'We have a splendid lot of players, grand sportsmen every one of them. No manager ever had charge of a happier team.' Sadly, the big day out at Wembley ended in disappointment with the defeat to Arsenal. Kay travelled to London and led the team out but he was far from being a well

George Kay is welcomed from Southampton by the players and staff on 6 August 1936

man. Still his Liverpool contract was renewed for a further five years in June 1950. He retired in January 1951 a few months short of his 60th birthday and fought his continuing illness with strength and courage. He died in Liverpool on 18 April 1954. Liddell knew how much Kay's job had taken out of him: 'He told me often of the times he had lain in bed, unable to sleep, pondering over the manifold problems that beset every manager... if any man gave his life for a club; George Kay did so for Liverpool.'

FACTFILE

BORN
21 September 1891, Manchester
DIED
18 April 1954
OTHER CLUBS
Luton Town (1929-31), Southampton (1931-36)
SIGNED FROM
Southampton, 6 August 1936
DEBUT GAME
29 August 1936
CONTRACT EXPIRY
30 January 1951
HONOURS
League Championship 1946/47

Season	Division	P	W	D	L	GF	GA	Pts	Pos	Win %	FA Cup
1936/37	1st Division	42	12	11	19	62	84	35	18	28.57	3rd Round
1937/38	1st Division	42	15	11	16	65	71	41	11	35.71	5th Round
1938/39	1st Division	42	14	14	14	62	63	42	11	33.33	5th Round
1946/47	1st Division	42	25	7	10	84	52	57	1	59.52	Semi-Final
1947/48	1st Division	42	16	10	16	65	61	42	11	38.10	4th Round
1948/49	1st Division	42	13	14	15	53	43	40	12	30.95	5th Round
1949/50	1st Division	42	17	14	11	64	54	48	8	40.48	Runners-Up
1950/51*	1st Division	27	9	7	11	34	41	25	13	33.33	3rd Round
Total	-	**321**	**121**	**88**	**112**	**489**	**469**	**330**	-	**37.69**	-

* Kay retired on 30 January 1951 with Liverpool in 13th position

Kaye,
Harry

HARRY KAYE made 169 wartime appearances for Liverpool but made his proper debut in a 5-0 defeat to Bolton in the FA Cup. His solitary league game was a 3-2 defeat by Blackpool at Anfield on 5 April 1947. Liverpool were leading 2-0 against Blackpool with less than an hour to go but lost 3-2. Blackpool were top of the table with a five-point lead on the Reds, but Liverpool had played four games less and went on to win the league. Kaye was transferred to Third Division South's Swindon Town for whom he made 189 league and cup appearances.

	League		FA Cup		Total	
Season	App	Goals	App	Goals	App	Goals
1945/46	-	-	1	0	1	0
1946/47	1	0	0	0	1	0
Total	**1**	**0**	**1**	**0**	**2**	**0**

FACTFILE

BORN
Liverpool, 19 April 1919
DIED
1992
POSITION
Right-half
OTHER CLUBS
Bradford City (wartime guest), Swindon Town (1947-53)
JOINED
1940
LFC DEBUT
26 January 1946
CONTRACT EXPIRY
May 1947

Keane,
Robbie

ROBBIE KEANE is Republic of Ireland's record goalscorer and most capped player. He was Britain's most expensive teenager when Coventry paid Wolves £6million in 1999 and has a total cost of £74million in transfer fees.

HE STARTED his career at Wolverhampton Wanderers in 1997 where he scored 29 goals in 87 games in the First Division. Keane only played one year for Premier League Coventry before a surprising move to Inter Milan for £13million. He had a torrid six months there as he fell out of favour when Italy's World Cup-winning coach, Marcello Lippi, was sacked and replaced by Marco Tardelli. His escape from Italy was David O'Leary's Leeds. However, he struggled for form at a time that Leeds were facing a financial meltdown. Keane was one of a number of Elland Road stars who were sold to pay off debts. He was only 22 years old, but Spurs was his fifth club. Spending six years at White Hart Lane, Keane finished each of his first four seasons as one of the club's top scorers. In both of his last two seasons he went past the 20-goal mark and became the 13th player to score 100 Premier League goals, on Boxing Day 2007.

KEANE is well known for scoring great goals as well as being a goal creator and no doubt Rafa Benítez hoped that Fernando Torres would benefit from being his strike partner as Dimitar Berbatov had. His former manager at Tottenham, Martin Jol, was very surprised when Spurs decided to sell him to Liverpool in the summer of 2008: 'He symbolised Spurs. He was the most influential player in the dressing room. I really thought Robbie Keane would have stayed

there for the rest of his career.' Great things were expected of Keane and he was a regular starter in the early weeks of the season but his first Liverpool goal did not arrive until his 11th first-team appearance, after 688 minutes without scoring, in the home Champions League fixture against PSV Eindhoven. Like Peter Crouch three years earlier, he just couldn't find the net in a Premier League match; and that lasted until West Bromwich Albion came to Anfield on the second weekend in November, when he scored twice. Keane got another brace against Bolton on Boxing Day to follow a superb equaliser at Arsenal just before Christmas.

In February 2009 Keane re-signed for Spurs for significantly less than Liverpool had paid seven months earlier. Many believed former Liverpool chief executive Rick Parry had initially overruled Benítez and bought Keane, but the Spaniard later put that matter straight. Keane certainly hadn't been forced upon him, he said, and it was just a simple matter of 'a good player sometimes cannot perform in a different team'.

Keane's second spell at White Hart Lane was not a particularly happy one. He added only another 11 league goals by the time another January transfer window opened in 2010. Keane moved on

loan to Celtic where he scored 12 goals in 16 league games and added another four goals in three Scottish Cup matches. Despite being at Celtic Park for a relatively short period of time, he made enough impact to be voted the Fans' Player of the Year. Keane was loaned out again in January 2011, this time to West Ham. The Hammers had an option to extend his stay by two years if they avoided relegation. However, the Hammers went down, so Keane returned to Tottenham after scoring twice in nine Premier League matches during his brief stay. In August 2011 he signed for Los Angeles Galaxy. During the off-season in the MLS Keane joined the claret and blue of Aston Villa on a two-month loan, scoring three times in six Premier League matches. On his return to Los Angeles he won the MLS title.

FACTFILE

BORN
Dublin, Ireland, 8 July 1980
POSITION
Centre-forward
OTHER CLUBS
Wolverhampton Wanderers (1995–99),
Coventry City (1999–2000),
Inter Milan (2000–01),
Leeds United (loan, 2000–01; permanent, 2001–02),
Tottenham Hotspur (2002–08),
Tottenham Hotspur (2009–11),
Celtic (loan, 2010),
West Ham United (loan, 2011),
Los Angeles Galaxy (2011–),
Aston Villa (loan, 2012)
SIGNED FROM
Tottenham Hotspur,
£19million, 28 July 2008
INTERNATIONAL CAPS
127 Ireland caps (59 goals) (4 (2) at LFC), 1998–
LFC DEBUT GAME/GOAL
13 August 2008 / 1 October 2008
CONTRACT EXPIRY
2 February 2009

Season	League		FA Cup		League Cup		Europe		Total	
	App	Goals	App	Goals	App	Goals	App	Goals	App	Goals
2008/09	16 (3)	5	1	0	0 (1)	0	6 (1)	2	23 (5)	7
Total	**16 (3)**	**5**	**1**	**0**	**0 (1)**	**0**	**6 (1)**	**2**	**23 (5)**	**7**

Keech,
Bill

BILL KEECH represented Liverpool in six successive Second Division matches in the club's third season as members of the Football League in 1895/96.

HE PLAYED in Liverpool's half-back line, an area of the team where numerous changes were made during the course of that season. Keech later played as forward for Leicester Fosse, scoring five goals in 15 league games, before returning to the half-back line with QPR in the Southern League. Keech was an all-round sportsman and won honours for skating and boxing. Keech was quite a showman and in 1899 he competed in a penalty-shootout with an elephant from Lord John Sanger's travelling show. Keech and the elephant were to have five tries

Bill keech

each and take turns in goal. Unfortunately we do not know who won!

	League		FA Cup		Other		Total	
Season	App	Goals	App	Goals	App	Goals	App	Goals
1895/96	6	0	0	0	0	0	6	0
Total	6	0	0	0	0	0	6	0

FACTFILE

BORN
Irthlingborough,
22 February 1872
POSITION
Half-back
OTHER CLUBS
Wellingborough, Finedon,
Kettering Hawks,
Irthlingborough Wanderers,
Barnsley St Peter's (1894–95),
Barnsley St Peter's (1897),
Blackpool (1897–98),
Leicester Fosse (1898–99),
Loughborough Town
(loan 1899),
Queens Park Rangers
(1899–1902),
Brentford (1902–03),
Small Heath,
Kensal Rise United
SIGNED FROM
Barnsley St Peter's,
10 September 1895
LFC DEBUT
26 October 1895
CONTRACT EXPIRY
1897

Keegan,
Kevin

KEVIN KEEGAN joined Scunthorpe as an apprentice in 1968 and made his name as a midfield player in the Fourth Division, playing 120 league games. He was signed when Liverpool were busy preparing for their FA Cup final date with Arsenal at Wembley. Andy Beattie, Bill Shankly's former team-mate at Preston and the man he ultimately replaced as manager of Huddersfield Town, drummed Keegan's name into the famous Scot time and again and eventually, as Bill later recalled in his autobiography, 'I decided to sign him. I had to, because Andy was so sure about Kevin.'

SHANKLY knew he had signed a player of exceptional potential but the 20-year-old Yorkshireman was left behind when Liverpool flew off on their traditional pre-season tour. Four days before the 1971/72 season was due to open, Shankly

picked Keegan for the first team in a full-scale practice match at Melwood, normally a game where fitness is more important than the result. But Keegan created havoc that day and Shankly had no hesitation in giving him his debut against Nottingham Forest at Anfield the following Saturday when the league season opened. The new player was greeted by the Kop in a traditional way. 'The self-appointed representative of the Kop came on the field to greet me. He gave me a kiss, and the smell of booze on his breath

'I DECIDED TO SIGN HIM. I HAD TO, BECAUSE ANDY WAS SO SURE ABOUT KEVIN'
BILL SHANKLY

almost knocked me off my feet,' Keegan remembers. 'He needed a shave as well as his beard was rough. The police accepted this ritual whenever there was a new player. This Kopite was a nice old fellow with no harm in him. He kissed me, then kissed the grass in front of the Kop and went back to join his mates in the crowd.' Keegan scored after 12 minutes and netted three times in the opening five league fixtures. It was clear that he was in the first team to stay and, in fact, Keegan never played in a single reserve fixture during the whole of his seven seasons at Anfield! Shankly could see straight away he had signed a true gem, as he revealed in late August 1971. 'I was just as sure of

Keegan as I was of Denis Law and I never had cause to think again about Denis,' Shankly said. 'These two players are so much alike in a number of ways. Keegan is an exciting boy all right.'

Defeat at Derby and a controversial draw at Arsenal in the last two First Division games of Keegan's debut season cost Liverpool the title. But he only had to wait another 12 months to lift the title and added a UEFA Cup winners' medal too when his early strikes in the re-arranged home leg of the final against Borussia Mönchengladbach were the platform for the club's eventual aggregate victory. He also received the first of numerous international caps during that season when picked for a World Cup qualifier with Wales in Cardiff on 15 November 1972. In 1973/74 Keegan played in every single one of the 61 competitive matches Liverpool had in the league and three cup competitions, contributing 19 goals. Six of those came in the successful FA Cup run, including two crucial strikes against his home-town club Doncaster Rovers, bottom of the old Fourth Division at the time, who threatened to make one of the biggest upsets in the Cup's history when they took a 2-1 interval lead at Anfield. Ever the man for the big occasion, Keegan produced a sensational volley past Peter Shilton in the replayed semi-final victory over Leicester City at Villa Park and then netted two goals in the one-sided Wembley showdown with Newcastle United.

The 1974/75 season started badly for Keegan, perhaps the lowest point of an illustrious career. He was sent off during a pre-season match against Kaiserslautern in West Germany and also received his marching orders four days later after clashing with Billy Bremner in the Charity Shield at Wembley. Both he and Bremner took off their shirts as they left the field and received lengthy bans;

although Keegan was allowed to play in the opening league match at Luton, he didn't play in the First Division again until October. But he quickly found his old form and played in the remaining 33 league fixtures as the Reds finished runners-up to Derby County. With goals hard to come by that season, how crucial his absence was, especially considering the team was beaten three times in four games during September. In 1976 Liverpool repeated their League and UEFA Cup 'double' of 1973 and again Keegan was prominent, only missing one First Division game and scoring in both legs of the European final against Bruges. 'Mighty Mouse' was voted the FWA Footballer of the Year in 1975/76, and then gave a season's notice, announcing he was moving to West Germany. Keegan had his reasons. 'I'm not a Scouser and I've never pretended to be,' he explained. 'I've never made out to feel as passionate about, for example, derby matches as true Scousers do but at the same time I still hold the club very close to my heart. The fans are brilliant, they always supported me and even when I decided to move abroad I think they understood my reasons for doing so. Bill Shankly had gone and I just felt there was another mountain for me to climb somewhere. As it happens they didn't do too badly out of it because they went out and bought Kenny Dalglish, having sold me for £500,000 and then paying £440,000 for Kenny. They banked £60,000 which was a great piece of business.'

At a time when it was almost unheard of for English players to try their luck abroad, this caused some friction, but nobody could doubt Keegan's commitment to the cause in his farewell season. He was the club's leading scorer in the league and contributed valuable goals as the team reached the finals of both the FA and European cups. With the Championship clinched in the penultimate league match, a historic treble triumph beckoned, but Manchester United ruined that dream and it was just a question of whether the players could lift themselves for one last effort in the European Cup final only four days later. In Rome, Keegan played his heart out and ran himself and Berti Vogts into the ground. Eight minutes from time, he started a typical run from 40 or so yards out, which was only ended by Vogts' foul in the penalty area. Phil Neal converted the spot kick. Keegan bowed out on a high as he told reporters post-match: 'The lap of honour was fantastic. This was the perfect ending for me. I have only stayed on for this season because the club chairman asked me to stay to help to try to win the European Cup. I have kept my side of the bargain.'

£500,000 was a record fee for a British footballer and Keegan was the most expensive player in West Germany. He soon stamped his authority on the Bundesliga, winning the championship in his second season at Hamburg SV and, incredibly, winning two consecutive European Footballer of the Year awards, after being the runner-up in his last season at Liverpool. In his farewell season at Hamburg Keegan featured in the European Cup final against Nottingham Forest but lost 1-0. After three years in Germany the 29-year-old Keegan was on his

Season	League		FA Cup		League Cup		Europe		Other		Total	
	App	Goals	App	Goals	App	Goals	App	Goals	App	Goals	App	Goals
1971/72	35	9	3	2	1	0	3	0	0	0	42	11
1972/73	41	13	4	0	8	5	11	4	-	-	64	22
1973/74	42	12	9	6	6	1	4	0	-	-	61	19
1974/75	33	10	2	1	3	0	3	1	1	0	42	12
1975/76	41	12	2	1	3	0	11	3	-	-	57	16
1976/77	38	12	8	4	2	0	8	4	1	0	57	20
Total	230	68	28	14	23	6	40	12	2	0	323	100

way home. Liverpool had first option on him but he moved to Southampton for £420,000. 'If he does not want to play for Liverpool then we can forego the option. If he had been keen to come back to Liverpool then we would have thought about it,' Bob Paisley said. In Keegan's second season at the Dell he was the First Division's top scorer with 26 goals in 41 games and was voted Player of the Year by his fellow professionals. After two years at Southampton he was on his way to Second Division Newcastle for £100,000, where he stayed until his retirement in 1984, after playing 85 matches and scoring 49 goals for the Magpies.

Eight years later Keegan became manager of Newcastle, leaving after a five-year spell during which he won the First Division title and finished runners-up in the Premier League. Keegan was one year in charge at Fulham, before taking over as England's manager in February 1999. He was England's supremo for one and a half years until, after a poor showing in Euro 2000, he resigned impetuously after a Wembley defeat to Germany. In May 2001, Keegan was appointed manager of Manchester City, winning the First Division title; even though he never reached the heights he had hoped for with City he still tried to entertain the audience as he had as a player. Keegan left City in the 2004/05 season, then made an unexpected return to Newcastle in January 2008, a highly popular appointment as the Geordie fans saw him as their Messiah. Only eight months later Keegan left his beloved club, claiming owner Mike Ashley wasn't providing him with the financial support that he had promised.

IN MARCH 2010 Keegan was honoured by the Bill Shankly award at the *Liverpool Echo* Sports Personality of the Year night. Shankly had been a father figure to Keegan and on this emotional occasion he said: 'He was an inspiration to me from the day I first walked into the club. When he left, for me, a little bit of the club died because he meant that much to everyone.' Their relationship was special and Keegan revealed that he always carries a picture of Shanks. Keegan was an incredible player, tireless in showing off his talents, and his enthusiasm invariably made his team-mates more determined to succeed. He was a smashing success at every club he played. Dangerous in the air despite a comparative lack of height, he had a wonderful understanding with big John Toshack during his early seasons at Anfield and his speed of thought created numerous goals for his colleagues. He was the first pin-up boy Liverpool had really ever had and made the number 7 shirt so famous. Kevin Keegan should rightly be remembered as one of the finest players ever to wear a Liverpool shirt.

FACTFILE

BORN
Armthorpe, 14 February 1951
POSITION
Centre-forward
OTHER CLUBS
Scunthorpe (1967–71),
Hamburg SV (1977–80),
Southampton (1980–82),
Newcastle United (1982–84),
Blacktown City Demons
(1985)
SIGNED FROM
Scunthorpe, £33,000,
3 May 1971
INTERNATIONAL CAPS
63 England caps (21 goals)
(29 (7) at LFC), 1972–82
LFC DEBUT GAME/GOAL
14 August 1971 /
14 August 1971
CONTRACT EXPIRY
3 June 1977
HONOURS
League Championship
1972/73, 1975/76, 1976/77;
FA Cup 1974;
European Cup 1977;
UEFA Cup 1973, 1976;
FWA
Footballer of the Year 1976

Keetley, Joe

JOE KEETLEY was living a dream when he signed for Liverpool in November 1923. He had only joined Third Division North's Accrington Stanley five months earlier on a free transfer and after scoring eight goals in 13 appearances he was sold to league Champions Liverpool for a four-figure sum.

The *Accrington Observer* described him as a 'player of the artistic type, clever in ball-control and artful in beating an opponent'.

Keetley made nine appearances in Liverpool's first team during the 1923/24 season. He was first selected for an away game at Ninian Park, Cardiff, on the Saturday before Christmas and then kept his place for the next four matches, scoring his first goal for the club in a 2-1 defeat at

Newcastle on Boxing Day and then netting against Chelsea at Anfield on New Year's Day. Despite the 3-1 win over Chelsea the double league champions were struggling in 15th place, giving in to Huddersfield Town's dominance in the league.

Keetley had ten brothers, eight of whom played league football. Maybe Joe's rise to stardom was too rapid for his own good, and he left Liverpool after 18 months and went through three league clubs in eight months before going into non-league football.

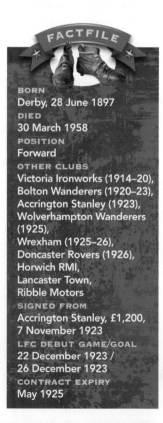

FACTFILE

BORN
Derby, 28 June 1897
DIED
30 March 1958
POSITION
Forward
OTHER CLUBS
Victoria Ironworks (1914–20),
Bolton Wanderers (1920–23),
Accrington Stanley (1923),
Wolverhampton Wanderers
(1925),
Wrexham (1925–26),
Doncaster Rovers (1926),
Horwich RMI,
Lancaster Town,
Ribble Motors
SIGNED FROM
Accrington Stanley, £1,200,
7 November 1923
LFC DEBUT GAME/GOAL
22 December 1923 /
26 December 1923
CONTRACT EXPIRY
May 1925

Season	League		FA Cup		Total	
	App	Goals	App	Goals	App	Goals
1923/24	9	2	0	0	9	2
Total	9	2	0	0	9	2

Kelly,
Martin

LOCAL BOY MARTIN KELLY has successfully come through Liverpool's Academy, which hasn't produced too many starlets since the turn of the century. Only seven years old when he caught the eye of the Liverpool scouts, Kelly started out as a central midfielder, but is essentially a centre-half, tall and elegant on the field of play, who has made most of his first-team appearances as right-back.

He missed almost two years of his development due to a back problem but graduated to Melwood in the summer of 2007 and was a part of Gary Ablett's reserve team that won the league in the 2007/08 season. He made his first-team debut when he came on for Jamie Carragher in the 82nd minute against PSV Eindhoven on 9 December 2008. Kelly was loaned to Huddersfield Town in League One from March until the end of the 2008/09 season and made seven league appearances for the Yorkshire club.

KELLY finally made his first Liverpool start against Lyon at Anfield in the Champions League on 20 October 2009. He turned in a man-of-the-match performance and might have had a good run in the side, but injured his groin in the game and was sidelined for four months. Kelly made two more substitute appearances before another injury put him out for the season. Kenny Dalglish was confident enough in Kelly's ability to start him regularly at the beginning of his second spell as

boss at Anfield. Kelly stood firm in the daunting FA Cup tie at Old Trafford on 9 January 2011 as well as in the next seven Premier League matches. His final appearance of the 2010/11 season came in a miserable 3-1 defeat at Upton Park on 27 February when he was forced off shortly before the interval after injuring his left hamstring. It was a nasty injury that kept him out for the remainder of the campaign during which he had made 23 appearances. Kelly continued to make good progress in 2011/12, was a regular in match-day squads and scored his first senior goal with a header in the League Cup tie at Chelsea at the end of November. He earned his first senior cap in an England friendly against Norway in Oslo that was part of the build-up to Euro 2012. When Chelsea's Gary Cahill was ruled out of Euro 2012 a week later, Kelly replaced him in England's squad. His bad luck with injuries continued in 2012/13 when he ruptured his anterior cruciate ligament against Manchester United on 23

September. A couple of weeks earlier he had told the *Guardian* he was back to his best. 'I've played three games in eight days recently; for me that's a fantastic achievement, because in the past I've struggled and been unlucky with injuries. I feel like I've settled in to my body now. I'm feeling good and raring to push on.' Hopefully Kelly will enjoy better luck in the future, as the Liverpool Academy can be very proud of its graduate.

FACTFILE

BORN
Whiston, Liverpool,
27 April 1990
POSITION
Right-back / Centre-half
OTHER CLUBS
Huddersfield Town (loan, 2009)
JOINED
1997
INTERNATIONAL CAPS
1 England cap, 2012
LFC DEBUT GAME/GOAL
9 December 2008 /
29 November 2011
HONOURS
League Cup 2012

Season	League		FA Cup		League Cup		Europe		Total	
	App	Goals	App	Goals	App	Goals	App	Goals	App	Goals
2008/09	0	0	0	0	0	0	0 (1)	0	0 (1)	0
2009/10	0 (1)	0	0	0	0	0	1 (1)	0	1 (2)	0
2010/11	10 (1)	0	1	0	1	0	10	0	22 (1)	0
2011/12	12	0	3	0	4 (1)	1	-	-	19 (1)	1
2012/13	4	0	0	0	0	0	2 (1)	0	6 (1)	0
Total	**26 (2)**	**0**	**4**	**0**	**5 (1)**	**1**	**13 (3)**	**0**	**48 (6)**	**1**

Kelly,
Philip

PHILIP KELLY played three games in the Lancashire League for Liverpool in the 1892/93 season.

Kelly benefited from goalkeeper's Sidney Ross's injury in the middle of March as Matt McQueen was

moved from the forward line to play in goal which gave Kelly a chance to prove himself. Liverpool beat Fairfield 5-0 but Kelly did not keep his place. Right at the end of the season Kelly was attacked by two of the opposing team, resulting in a leg injury

which ended his brief playing career. However, he maintained an active interest in football, working as a trainer for various amateur teams. He made a career of scouting talented players and also had his hands full with 13 children!

FACTFILE

BORN
Liverpool, 1869
POSITION
Left-winger /
Inside-left forward
JOINED
1892
LFC DEBUT
26 November 1892
CONTRACT EXPIRY
1893

Season	League		FA Cup		Other		Total	
	App	Goals	App	Goals	App	Goals	App	Goals
1892/93	-	-	0	0	3	0	3	0
Total	**0**	**0**	**0**	**0**	**3**	**0**	**3**	**0**

Kelso,
James

RIGHT-HALF JAMES KELSO played just one game for Liverpool Football Club in the club's inaugural season, on 24 September 1892 against Bury.

Both teams played football of 'sterling quality' according to the *Liverpool Mercury* but Liverpool led 4-0 at half-time, and Kelso and his team-mates kept a clean sheet, not adding to the score in the second half. This was only

Liverpool's second league game, having won their first 8-0 against Higher Walton. Liverpool used three different right-halves in their first three games before settling for John McCartney for the remainder of this successful season. Kelso was a promising player and *Field Sport* gave this account of him in 1892: 'Young Kelso is as like his older brother, Bob, in play as he is in features, and great things are expected

from him.' James' brother, Bob, was a famous footballer with Renton, Everton and Dundee, but for some reason James failed to fulfil his potential. On 25 July 1900 James and family had just returned home to Renton from a holiday on the Isle of Man. James, who had always had a steady job and never had a drinking problem, according to the media, seemed in good spirits. Later that day he committed suicide, aged only 31.

	League		FA Cup		Other		Total	
Season	App	Goals	App	Goals	App	Goals	App	Goals
1892/93	-	-	0	0	1	0	1	0
Total	0	0	0	0	1	0	1	0

FACTFILE

BORN
Cardross, Scotland,
8 January 1869
DIED
25 July 1900
POSITION
Right-half
OTHER CLUBS
Renton (–1892),
Renton (1893–?)
SIGNED FROM
Renton, 1892
LFC DEBUT
24 September 1892
CONTRACT EXPIRY
1893

Kelvin,
Andrew

'KELVIN, who will play outside, is a second [Fred] Geary, having the speed of a deer and dogged persistency to score,' claimed *Field Sport* in 1892.

ANDREW KELVIN'S greatest achievement at Kilmarnock was

scoring five goals in the club's 7-1 win over Hurlford in the 1891 Ayrshire Cup final. Kelvin played Liverpool's first five competitive games in the Lancashire League and the FA Cup. The left-winger lost his spot when Hugh McQueen was signed in October

1892. Kelvin made one more appearance for the club in a 2-1 cup defeat to Northwich Victoria on a pitch that was described by the *Liverpool Mercury* as a 'perfect quagmire, with pools of water, intermixed with sawdust and mud.'

	League		FA Cup		Other		Total	
Season	App	Goals	App	Goals	App	Goals	App	Goals
1892/93	-	-	2	0	4	0	6	0
Total	0	0	2	0	4	0	6	0

FACTFILE

BORN
Kilmarnock, Scotland, 1869
DIED
23 October 1911
POSITION
Left-winger
OTHER CLUBS
Kilmarnock
SIGNED FROM
Kilmarnock, 1892
LFC DEBUT
3 September 1892
CONTRACT EXPIRY
1893

Kemp,
Dirk

SOUTH AFRICAN Dirk Kemp was on Liverpool's books as a goalkeeper at the same time as his fellow countryman Arthur Riley. But whereas Riley made over 300 Football League appearances for the club, Kemp had to settle for just 30.

ALF HOBSON started the 1936/37 season as first-choice between the posts and although the experienced Riley took over from him towards the end of January 1937, it was Kemp who was selected for the last seven matches of that campaign.

Kemp played in 13 of the first 14 league matches in 1937/38, but Riley had re-established himself in the side by the halfway stage of the season. It was somewhat unfortunate when Riley left Anfield at the end of the 1938/39 season, leaving his compatriot free to make his mark, that war should deprive the South African of featuring regularly in the Football League, although he did continue to represent the club during the non-competitive war years.

DIRK KEMP
[LIVERPOOL]

	League		FA Cup		Total	
Season	App	Goals	App	Goals	App	Goals
1936/37	7	0	0	0	7	0
1937/38	13	0	0	0	13	0
1938/39	7	0	3	0	10	0
Total	27	0	3	0	30	0

FACTFILE

BORN
Cape Town, South Africa,
15 October 1913
DIED
1983
POSITION
Goalkeeper
OTHER CLUBS
Arcadia (1931–34),
Transvaal (1934–36);
York City,
Brighton,
Southport (wartime guest)
SIGNED FROM
Transvaal, 7 December 1936
LFC DEBUT
27 March 1937
CONTRACT EXPIRY
1945

Kennedy,
Alan

A GREAT attacking left-back who had the knack of scoring vital goals for Liverpool that brought further glory to the club, Alan Kennedy embodies Liverpool's history in the early 1980s. No one can forget when he scored the winning goal in Paris against Real Madrid in the 1981 European Cup final and everyone will remember the look on his face when he celebrated the deciding spot kick in Rome in 1984. Kennedy was a 19-year-old full-back for Newcastle United on the day that Liverpool destroyed his FA Cup final hopes in 1974 by outplaying the Geordies 3-0 at Wembley. Although he would never collect a winners' medal in the FA Cup, he would win more trophies than he could ever have dreamed possible after his transfer from the Northeast to Merseyside just before the start of the 1978/79 season.

KENNEDY was an England B-international and the most expensive full-back in England when he signed for Liverpool for £330,000 in August 1978. Bob Paisley was quite pleased with his latest addition, obtained two days before the European deadline: 'He will be a first-class capture. He is fast, likes to move up to attack and should fit into our side very quickly. There will be seven men challenging for the back four

positions – Hughes, Thompson, Hansen, Neal, Jones, Kennedy and Irwin. I wanted Kennedy because I wanted more competition for places.' Paisley then added: 'If this lad doesn't play for England I'll throw myself in the Mersey...when the tide is out.'

The left-back position had been a bit of a problem area for Liverpool in 1977/78 with Joey Jones, Tommy Smith and Alan Hansen all wearing the number 3 shirt at some stage of that season. Kennedy came across Bill Shankly of all people before his debut, as he told *LFChistory.net*. 'Shankly looked at me: "Hi ya, son. How you're doing?" "I am alright, Mr Shankly. I am a little bit nervous." He went into his pocket and pulled out...and I don't know what he had given me, but he gave me a couple of tablets. I thought, "What has he given me here?" but it's Mr Shankly and whatever he says is right. All of a sudden my mind was going back to the World Cup of '78 where there was a Scottish player who had taken some kind of drug, Willie Johnston, and so in the end... He might have given me drugs, like. I'd better have a little look. When I brought them out there were two sweets there and that's all they were, just two sweets. I thought if Mr Shankly had given me them they must do me good so I ate the sweets.' Kennedy's first game was against Queens Park Rangers and even though Liverpool won 2-1 he didn't have an ideal debut. 'Early on I miskicked with my right foot – the one I use for standing on – and knocked a policeman's helmet off. I also conceded a couple of corners and made a few errors. I just wanted half-time to come to get some reassurance from the manager but when I got back to the dressing room, Bob said to me, "I think that they shot the wrong Kennedy!"'

Kennedy eventually adapted to the side and played 37 league games in each of his first two seasons at Anfield, winning League Championship medals on both occasions. He missed large parts of the 1980/81 season through injury but still contributed two priceless goals to keep the club's run of success going into the 80s. His extra-time goal narrowly failed to beat West Ham in the League Cup final at Wembley but he was a member of the team that beat the Hammers in the Villa Park replay 18 days later. On an unforgettable night in Paris his blistering shot fizzed past the Real Madrid keeper in a blur to bring the European Cup to Anfield for the third time in five seasons. His astonishing record of scoring in big games continued as he struck a second-half equaliser against Manchester United in the 1983 League Cup final and then a year later came the most dramatic moment of all, the decisive penalty kick in the shootout that followed the 1-1 draw with the Italian champions from Rome. This was no doubt the biggest moment of Kennedy's career, one which he was happy to share with *LFChistory.net*. 'To this day I've got no idea why Fagan gave me the opportunity to take a penalty. He may have panicked. He may have looked at the rest of the team and thought, "Why not Ronnie Whelan, Michael Robinson," or whoever was still on the pitch at the time?' Kennedy recalled:

And then to say: 'Alan, how are you feeling?' And I said: 'I'm fine,' because I hadn't been picked. He said: 'OK' and then he walks off. Then he pointed to Graeme Souness and Ian Rush. Phil Neal was always going to take one. But the two others, Steve Nicol and me, thought 'no chance'. He picked Steve Nicol, the youngest man of the team, and all of a sudden... I didn't realise he had picked me at the time. It suddenly sinks in and I panicked. I didn't want it to happen. I hadn't had a bad game in the 120 minutes, but in that situation you have to stand up and be counted. No player had any confidence in me. In the end they were looking at themselves and thinking to themselves, 'He's bound to miss this one. Who's going to take the next one?' That didn't obviously give me the confidence I needed when I am walking up there. You put the ball down... I thought of my family, my girlfriend at the time... I just felt I can't let these people down... We were so bad the week before we had to abandon the practice. The kids beat us in the penalty shoot-out. They say you should be clear, be focused and never change your mind. I didn't have any of those three in my mind. I opened up my body at the end... I didn't know why I did it... Tancredi the goalkeeper went to his left-hand side and I got the ball into the right-hand side. You can't imagine the relief I had at that particular moment. I just wanted to be with all my family, all my friends, all the players and just to say a big thank you. What a relief it was. And I saw all the players afterwards and they were telling me, 'We can't believe you scored that goal.' I said, 'I know!'

Kennedy played in most of the following season's First Division fixtures but got injured at the end

Season	League App	League Goals	FA Cup App	FA Cup Goals	League Cup App	League Cup Goals	Europe App	Europe Goals	Other App	Other Goals	Total App	Total Goals
1978/79	37	3	2	0	1	0	3	0	-	-	43	3
1979/80	37	1	5	0	7	0	1	0	1	0	51	1
1980/81	19	2	1	0	7	1	6	1	1	0	34	4
1981/82	32 (2)	3	3	0	6	0	4	0	0	0	45 (2)	3
1982/83	42	3	3	0	8	1	6	2	1	0	60	6
1983/84	42	2	2	0	13	0	9	0	1	0	67	2
1984/85	32	1	5	0	3	0	7	0	2	0	49	1
1985/86	8	0	0	0	0	0	-	-	0	0	8	0
Total	**249 (2)**	**15**	**21**	**0**	**45**	**2**	**36**	**3**	**6**	**0**	**357 (2)**	**20**

of March, which helped Jim Beglin establish himself in his place. Kennedy did play in the opening eight league matches of the 1985/86 season but an own goal in the last of those games at Oxford was the final straw for the new player-manager, Kenny Dalglish. Kennedy never played for the club again and Phil Neal, his full-back partner for so long and with whom he had enjoyed so much success, would only last a few more games before he too was replaced by Steve Nicol. Kennedy had spells in Belgium, Denmark and Sweden and also with Hartlepool and Wrexham in the lower divisions of the Football League before continuing to play non-league football into his 40s. 'My greatest strengths were pace and attitude. I would never give up and always give 100 per cent. I really thought that coming to Liverpool made me feel I could play football because if you could get into that team you could get into any team. They were so strong and so good and I felt comfortable in the team. There were quite a few players who tried to take my position. I felt I was good enough to beat all of them.'

FACTFILE

BORN
Sunderland, 31 August 1954
POSITION
Left-back
OTHER CLUBS
Newcastle United (1971–78),
Sunderland (1985–87),
Husqvarna (1987),
Beerschot (1987),
Hartlepool United (1987),
Grantham Town (1987),
Wigan Athletic (1987–88),
Sunderland (1988),
Colne Dynamos (1988–90),
Wrexham (1990),
Morecambe (1991),
Netherfield (1991–92),
Northwich Victoria (1992),
Radcliffe Borough (1992–93),
Netherfield (1993–94),
Barrow (1994–95)
SIGNED FROM
Newcastle United, £330,000,
13 August 1978
INTERNATIONAL CAPS
2 England caps, 1984
LFC DEBUT GAME/GOAL
19 August 1978 /
9 September 1978
CONTRACT EXPIRY
September 1985
HONOURS
League Championship
1978/79, 1979/80, 1981/82,
1982/83, 1983/84;
League Cup
1981, 1982, 1983, 1984;
European Cup 1981, 1984

Kennedy,
Mark

KENNEDY hit the headlines when his goal helped the Lions knock out Arsenal from the FA Cup in January 1995 and a couple of months later he became the most expensive teenage footballer in British history when he signed for Liverpool.

He was four times in the starting line-up in his first season at Anfield, but was only given one chance in the starting XI over the next three years. It was a mystery why Liverpool spent a fortune on the boy and then never gave him a proper chance. Kennedy struggled to impress in the Premier League but seemed at his right level when playing in the First Division. He joined Ipswich's coaching staff at the end of the 2011/12 season.

FACTFILE

BORN
Dublin, Ireland, 15 May 1976
POSITION
Midfielder
OTHER CLUBS
Millwall (1992–95),
Queens Park Rangers (1998),
Wimbledon (1998–99),
Manchester City (1999–2001),
Wolverhampton Wanderers
(2001–06),
Crystal Palace (2006–08),
Cardiff City (2008–10),
Ipswich Town (2010–12)
SIGNED FROM
Millwall, £1.5million,
21 March 1995
INTERNATIONAL CAPS
34 Ireland caps (4 goals)
(17 (0) at LFC) 1995–2002
LFC DEBUT
9 April 1995
CONTRACT EXPIRY
26 March 1998

Season	League		FA Cup		League Cup		Europe		Total	
	App	Goals	App	Goals	App	Goals	App	Goals	App	Goals
1994/95	4 (2)	0	0	0	0	0	-	-	4 (2)	0
1995/96	1 (3)	0	0	0	0 (1)	0	0 (1)	0	1 (5)	0
1996/97	0 (5)	0	0 (1)	0	0 (1)	0	0 (1)	0	0 (8)	0
1997/98	0 (1)	0	0	0	0	0	0	0	0 (1)	0
Total	**5 (11)**	**0**	**0 (1)**	**0**	**0 (2)**	**0**	**0 (2)**	**0**	**5 (16)**	**0**

Kennedy,
Ray

RAY KENNEDY was a striker at Arsenal, scoring 71 goals in 212 games in five years, and in his first full season as a professional was a vital part of the triumphant side that won the League and FA Cup double in 1970/71. Kennedy's arrival at Anfield on 12 July 1974 was completely overshadowed by the shock news on the same day that Bill Shankly, the man who had signed him from Arsenal, decided to step down from the manager's chair with immediate effect.

> 'MAYBE IT WILL BE SAID THAT ONE OF THE LAST THINGS I DID AT THIS CLUB WAS TO SIGN A GREAT NEW PLAYER'
> **BILL SHANKLY**

SHANKLY was happy with his last task as manager. 'There is no doubt Kennedy will do a good job for Liverpool,' he declared to the press. 'He is big, brave and strong. His signing means that we now have the greatest strength in depth that we have ever had. Kennedy will cause plenty of trouble to defences. He fights all the way and he was at the top of my list of my wanted men. Maybe it will be said that one of the last things I did at this club was to sign a great new player.' Kennedy was physically very strong and that impressed Shankly, who was still around Melwood. 'I've seen him in training and he looks good. He reminds me of Rocky Marciano.' Kennedy scored in each of his first three games for Paisley's Liverpool and netted a total of eight goals in his

first 13 matches but two goals in his next 11 was less impressive. John Toshack's move to Leicester fell through and he resurrected his partnership with Keegan. Kennedy was back in the starting line-up in February but didn't get on the scoresheet in nine games for the rest of the season. Five goals in 25 league games was a meagre return from a young striker who had enjoyed such a good reputation in London, and he was being linked with a move to Wolves.

KENNEDY'S start to the following season was less than impressive and he had been out of the starting XI for six weeks when Peter Cormack got injured. Kennedy replaced him on the left side of midfield against Middlesbrough on 1 November and the *Daily Post* was concerned about his performance. 'With poor Kennedy looking a most temporary left-half, the nimble Armstrong, Souness and Mills outnumbered the loyally-working

Callaghan.' Paisley hadn't played him there just on a whim, though. 'One of my old friends told me that before Ray went to Arsenal he had played much deeper. I then knew I could back my instinct and see if he could recapture his spark.' Kennedy netted two goals in the following 6-0 win over Real Sociedad and two goals in the next four games. The former cumbersome forward was playing with renewed vigour in his new position. The move was so successful that it saw off Cormack, who had played in that position for the last two seasons. Kennedy had made the number 5 shirt his own and won England recognition at last in 1976. By the end of the season he had added League Championship and UEFA Cup winners' medals to the haul he already had from his Arsenal days. Over the next five seasons he only missed five First Division games and could boast three winners' medals in the European Cup. His success with Liverpool brought him nearly 20 full England caps to add to the six he had gained at Under-23 level as a youngster in the Arsenal team. He also contributed a marvellous total of 49 goals for the Reds in all competitions during those amazing five years and his runs from midfield into scoring positions brought him almost as many goals as he created for others with his astute vision and distribution of the ball.

One of the most important goals Kennedy ever scored came in the semi-final of the European Cup in 1981 when the odds were stacked against Liverpool after Bayern Munich had ground out a 0-0 draw on Merseyside. An already depleted Liverpool team suffered an early setback when Dalglish limped off injured but Kennedy's experience and composure finally told when seven minutes from time he strode forward to collect David Johnson's pass and stroked a firm right-foot shot away from the home keeper for the priceless away goal that would take the club to the final. Kennedy was 30 that summer and 20-year-old Irishman Ronnie Whelan was ready to take over from him on the left. Kennedy could be happy with his Liverpool career but undoubtedly it would have been even more impressive if the early stages of Parkinson's disease hadn't affected his physical condition.

> KENNEDY COULD BE HAPPY WITH HIS LIVERPOOL CAREER BUT UNDOUBTEDLY IT WOULD HAVE BEEN EVEN MORE IMPRESSIVE IF THE EARLY STAGES OF PARKINSON'S DISEASE HADN'T AFFECTED HIS PHYSICAL CONDITION

Since moving to Liverpool he had felt exceptionally tired after training and was sweating profusely. 'At Liverpool I could never understand why I was the odd man out, particularly after a match,' Kennedy revealed in his autobiography. 'Usually the adrenaline is pumping and most of the lads would be talking about what happened on the pitch, grabbing a Coke or chicken leg. They were always doing something, all except me. I used to slump hunched in my seat too tired to move. I tried to kid myself

I was more tired because I had worked harder than the others during a match, yet I knew it was not the case. The odd thing was I could always perform for the full ninety minutes and was rarely the one to be substituted.'

KENNEDY JOINED his former team-mate John Toshack at Swansea in January 1982. Liverpool went on to take the title as the Swans finished fifth, but Kennedy received a fifth League Championship medal, having played enough games for Liverpool to qualify for one. Toshack made Kennedy captain for the following season that ended in relegation. Kennedy was struggling for fitness because of Parkinson's disease (unbeknown to Toshack). Toshack stripped him of the captaincy and complained that he wasn't trying hard enough, was lazy and overweight. Shortly after, troubled Swansea sacked Toshack and Kennedy was given a free transfer in September 1984 after 49 games for the club in two-and-a-half years. In a desperate move to play regular football Kennedy joined the bottom club of the Football League, Hartlepool United, which enabled him to move back to his native Northeast, but by this time the onset of the terrible disease he had been suffering from became more acute. Kennedy managed 23 games in the 1983/84 season then during the summer of 1984 he had a surprising opportunity to move to Cyprus to become Pezopolikos' player-coach. Kennedy enjoyed living there but

the team struggled under him and he was not coping either mentally or physically and resigned in January 1985.

In November 1986 Kennedy was finally diagnosed with Parkinson's disease. He coped bravely with increased lack of mobility and dependence on medication to control his condition and became a public figure to provide funds for research. In 1991 his loyalty to both Arsenal and Liverpool was rewarded with a well-attended testimonial match at Highbury, an emotional experience for him and his family, and all the supporters. Arsenal and Liverpool fans paid the ultimate tribute to Ray Kennedy's great service to both clubs at Anfield on 21 April 2009 before the Premier League match

between the two teams. Kennedy's number at Liverpool, '5', was held up by coloured cards at the Kop and his Gunners' number '10' at the away section in the Anfield Road lower. Kennedy stayed on to watch the game, a thrilling 4-4 draw.

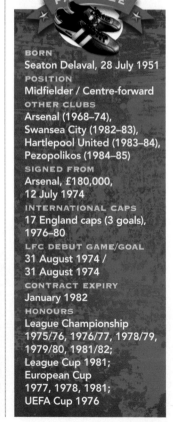

FACTFILE

BORN
Seaton Delaval, 28 July 1951
POSITION
Midfielder / Centre-forward
OTHER CLUBS
Arsenal (1968–74),
Swansea City (1982–83),
Hartlepool United (1983–84),
Pezopolikos (1984–85)
SIGNED FROM
Arsenal, £180,000,
12 July 1974
INTERNATIONAL CAPS
17 England caps (3 goals),
1976–80
LFC DEBUT GAME/GOAL
31 August 1974 /
31 August 1974
CONTRACT EXPIRY
January 1982
HONOURS
League Championship
1975/76, 1976/77, 1978/79,
1979/80, 1981/82;
League Cup 1981;
European Cup
1977, 1978, 1981;
UEFA Cup 1976

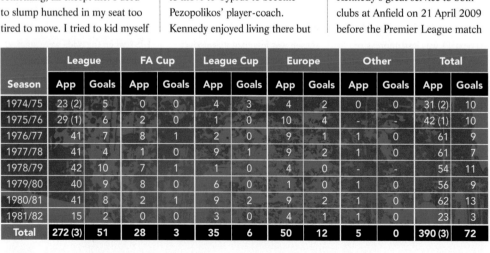

Season	League		FA Cup		League Cup		Europe		Other		Total	
	App	Goals	App	Goals	App	Goals	App	Goals	App	Goals	App	Goals
1974/75	23 (2)	5	0	0	4	3	4	2	0	0	31 (2)	10
1975/76	29 (1)	6	2	0	1	0	10	4	-	-	42 (1)	10
1976/77	41	7	8	1	2	0	9	1	1	0	61	9
1977/78	41	4	1	0	9	1	9	2	1	0	61	7
1978/79	42	10	7	1	1	0	4	0	-	-	54	11
1979/80	40	9	8	0	6	0	1	0	1	0	56	9
1980/81	41	8	2	1	9	2	9	2	1	0	62	13
1981/82	15	2	0	0	3	0	4	1	1	0	23	3
Total	**272 (3)**	**51**	**28**	**3**	**35**	**6**	**50**	**12**	**5**	**0**	**390 (3)**	**72**

Kerr, Neil

NEIL KERR scored 20 goals in 58 league appearances for Rangers before joining Liverpool.

FACTFILE

BORN
Bowling, Dunbartonshire, Scotland, 13 April 1871
DIED
5 December 1901
POSITION
Right-winger
OTHER CLUBS
Cowlairs (1887–89), Rangers (1889–94), Nottingham Forest (1895–96), Falkirk (1896–97), Rangers (1897–99)
SIGNED FROM
Rangers, 4 June 1894
LFC DEBUT GAME/GOAL
13 September 1894 / 6 October 1894
CONTRACT EXPIRY
5 September 1895

He played on the right flank in Liverpool's forward line on 12 occasions during the club's first season in the First Division. Kerr's longest run were seven games from September to November 1894 during which Liverpool lost five and conceded 19 goals on their way to relegation. Kerr died in 1901, aged just 30.

Liverpool on the attack in 1895

Season	League App	League Goals	FA Cup App	FA Cup Goals	Other App	Other Goals	Total App	Total Goals
1894/95	12	3	0	0	0	0	12	3
Total	12	3	0	0	0	0	12	3

Kettle, Brian

BRIAN KETTLE was captain of Liverpool's reserve team for three years, winning the Central League on seven occasions, but the left-back only made four first-team appearances in seven years at the club.

> BRIAN KETTLE WAS CAPTAIN OF LIVERPOOL'S RESERVE TEAM FOR THREE YEARS, WINNING THE CENTRAL LEAGUE ON SEVEN OCCASIONS

HE MADE his debut in place of Joey Jones in Liverpool's 6-0 win over Real Sociedad in November 1975. Kettle replaced Jones in two consecutive games in the 1976/77 season, conceding a penalty in the 14th minute in a 2-1 defeat to Norwich in which turned out to be his last appearance for the first team. Kettle was sold to Wigan where he played 14 games before going into non-league football.

He did confront Paisley over his lack of first-team opportunities in 1977, as he told the official Liverpool site. 'As I made my way along the corridor to his office I was running through what I was going to say in my mind and felt really sure of myself as I knocked on the door. But as I went in, arms behind my back like a little school-kid, all my best-laid plans went to pot. "Excuse me, boss," I said. "Yes, son." "What's my future?" "Your future? You're only 21! Who do you think I am – Patrick flaming Moore?"

FACTFILE

BORN
Prescot, Lancashire, 22 April 1956
POSITION
Left-back
OTHER CLUBS
Dallas Tornado (loan, 1978), Wigan Athletic (1980–81), Burscough, Barrow (1985–86)
JOINED
1972; signed professional May 1973
LFC DEBUT
4 November 1975
CONTRACT EXPIRY
August 1980

"Oh, erm, okay," I said sheepishly, turned round and walked out. That was that!'

Season	League App	League Goals	FA Cup App	FA Cup Goals	League Cup App	League Cup Goals	Europe App	Europe Goals	Other App	Other Goals	Total App	Total Goals
1975/76	1	0	0	0	0	0	1	0	-	-	2	0
1976/77	2	0	0	0	0	0	0	0	0	0	2	0
Total	3	0	0	0	0	0	1	0	0	0	4	0

Kewell,
Harry

HARRY KEWELL was on tour with the Australian soccer academy in England in 1995 when he was spotted by the Leeds United manager Howard Wilkinson. Kewell was voted PFA Young Player of the Year in 2000 and was a prominent player for the club that reached the Champions League semi-finals in 2000/01. Leeds subsequently suffered financial ruin and sold off their key players, including Kewell. He had always been a true Red and showed his allegiance by turning down more lucrative financial offers to go to his beloved Liverpool.

Kewell began his career at the Reds in promising fashion, playing 49 games in the 2003/04 season and scoring 11 goals. Nine of those goals came in the first half of the season, which turned out to be his best spell for the club. Gérard Houllier left with Rafa Benítez taking over, but injuries and subsequent loss of form hindered

Kewell's progress. Benítez seemed puzzled by his injury problems. 'One day Harry is okay, and the next he says he is unfit. We don't know exactly what the problem is. It changes each day. One day he says it's the groin, then it's the ankle.' It wasn't until the latter half of the 2005/06 season that Kewell seemed to approach his best form. He was quite unlucky at Liverpool, proved by the astounding fact that he was forced to be substituted in three successive finals: against Chelsea in the League Cup in 2005, Milan in the European Cup in 2005 and West Ham in the FA Cup in 2006!

AUSTRALIA qualified for the World Cup in Germany 2006, their first finals appearance since 1974. Kewell hoped for an injury-free spell and played in the opening 3-1 win against Japan. He scored Australia's second goal in a 2-2 draw against Croatia and guaranteed his team a place in the last 16 where the Aussies faced the Italians. But once again he was out of action as he was struck down by septic arthritis, a bacterial infection in his left foot. Australia lost 1-0 to Italy. Kewell's injuries kept him out for most of the 2006/07 season and the player that turned out in the 2007/08 season was just a pale imitation of the one who used to terrorise defenders with his skills. When Kewell's contract expired in July 2008 he departed Liverpool for Turkish champions Galatasaray, where he signed a two-year contract. Twenty-two goals from 63 Süper Lig matches in three seasons in Turkey represented a decent goals-per-game ratio that Liverpool supporters never came remotely close to witnessing. Kewell's agent, Bernie Mandic, delivered a damning verdict of the Liverpool medical team. 'Kewell lost three-and-a-half years of his career at Liverpool because the guys over there in England had, quite literally, no idea what they were talking about,' alleged Mandic in the *Sydney*

Morning Herald in 2010. 'It was a disgrace the way Harry was treated.' Kewell survived the South African World Cup without adding to his lengthy injury history but he was sent off for deliberate handball in Australia's group match with Ghana and with that went his 'World Cup dream'.

KEWELL signed a three-year contract with A-League club Melbourne Victory in 2011 and scored eight times in 25 league matches. Sadly, Kewell was forced to return to England after just one year in Australia because his mother-in-law was seriously ill. On 12 July 2012, Harry Kewell was named Australia's greatest ever football player, voted by Australian fans, players and media.

Kewell had a short spell in 2013 at UAE Pro League club Al Gharafa where he played just three games. In June he signed for A-League club Melbourne Heart, returning to Melbourne but with a rival to his former club, Victory.

> HE WAS QUITE UNLUCKY AT LIVERPOOL, PROVED BY THE ASTOUNDING FACT THAT HE WAS FORCED TO BE SUBSTITUTED IN THREE SUCCESSIVE FINALS

FACTFILE

BORN
Smithfield, Australia,
22 September 1978
POSITION
Winger
OTHER CLUBS
Leeds United (1995–2003),
Galatasaray (2008–11),
Melbourne Victory (2011–12),
Al Gharafa (2013),
Melbourne Heart (2013-)
SIGNED FROM
Leeds United, £5million,
9 July 2003
INTERNATIONAL CAPS
58 Australia caps (17 goals)
(22 (7) at LFC), 1996–2012
LFC DEBUT GAME/GOAL
17 August 2003 /
30 August 2003
CONTRACT EXPIRY
1 July 2008
HONOURS
FA Cup 2006;
Champions League 2005

Season	League		FA Cup		League Cup		Europe		Other		Total	
	App	Goals	App	Goals	App	Goals	App	Goals	App	Goals	App	Goals
2003/04	36	7	3	0	0 (2)	1	8	3	-	-	47 (2)	11
2004/05	15 (3)	1	0	0	1	0	7 (5)	0	-	-	23 (8)	1
2005/06	22 (5)	3	4 (2)	0	1	0	2 (4)	0	1	0	30 (11)	3
2006/07	0 (2)	1	0	0	0	0	0 (1)	0	0	0	0 (3)	1
2007/08	8 (2)	0	0 (1)	0	0 (1)	0	1 (2)	0	-	-	9 (6)	0
Total	**81 (12)**	**12**	**7 (3)**	**0**	**2 (3)**	**1**	**18 (12)**	**3**	**1**	**0**	**109 (30)**	**16**

Kewley, Kevin

KEVIN KEWLEY made one substitute appearance in six years at Liverpool, against Middlesbrough at Anfield.

He replaced Terry McDermott who was injured after just ten minute's play. Liverpool beat Boro 2-0 with goals from David Johnson and Steve Heighway. The Reds finished the campaign in 2nd place, losing their title to Nottingham Forest. In March 1978 Kewley left for good for USA side Dallas Tornado where he had been on loan from Liverpool for two consecutive summers. Kewley featured for Tornado until 1979 before going into the Major Indoor Soccer League with Wichita Wings until 1989.

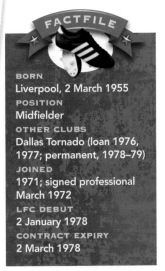

Season	League		FA Cup		League Cup		Europe		Other		Total	
	App	Goals	App	Goals	App	Goals	App	Goals	App	Goals	App	Goals
1977/78	0 (1)	0	0	0	0	0	0	0	0	0	0 (1)	0
Total	**0 (1)**	**0**	**0**	**0**	**0**	**0**	**0**	**0**	**0**	**0**	**0 (1)**	**0**

Kinghorn, Bill

THE LEFT-WINGER played for Liverpool during the last full season before the outbreak of World War Two.

The club had an extremely settled side at the time, with no fewer than 10 players making at least 30 league appearances during that 1938/39 season. Kinghorn shared the left wing for most of the season with Harman van den Berg and Harry Eastham. He started the season in the first XI and featured in 8 of the final 12 games of the campaign. He scored his fourth goal for Liverpool in a 1-1 draw against Sunderland in his last appearance for the club on 22 April 1939.

Season	League		FA Cup		Total	
	App	Goals	App	Goals	App	Goals
1938/39	19	4	0	0	19	4
Total	**19**	**4**	**0**	**0**	**19**	**4**

The lads take a break during training in the 1930s

Roy Saunders, Hugh Gerhardi and Joe Maloney in the early 1950s

Kippax,
Peter

BURNLEY native Peter Kippax made just one appearance for Liverpool after signing for the Reds one week after his contract with Burnley was cancelled. That one game was at home to Birmingham City in a First Division fixture on 12 March 1949. Kippax did not have much of a chance of dislodging the team's regular left-winger, who was none other than Billy Liddell.

On this occasion Liddell was moved to inside-left forward and Kippax enjoyed his debut on the left wing in a 1-0 win. Kippax had previously 'guested' in one wartime match for Liverpool in which he scored in a 2-2 Bolton draw on 29 August 1945. Kippax never signed professional forms for Liverpool but his amateur status allowed him to represent Great Britain in the 1948 Olympics where he featured in all of his side's games. Great Britain beat the Netherlands 4-3 in the first round that secured a quarter-final against France which was won 1-0. Yugoslavia outmaneuvered Kippax and his fellow internationals in the semi-finals, 3-1.

	League		FA Cup		Total	
Season	App	Goals	App	Goals	App	Goals
1948/49	1	0	0	0	1	0
Total	**1**	**0**	**0**	**0**	**1**	**0**

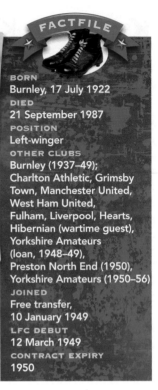

FACTFILE

BORN
Burnley, 17 July 1922
DIED
21 September 1987
POSITION
Left-winger
OTHER CLUBS
Burnley (1937–49);
Charlton Athletic, Grimsby Town, Manchester United, West Ham United, Fulham, Liverpool, Hearts, Hibernian (wartime guest), Yorkshire Amateurs (loan, 1948–49), Preston North End (1950), Yorkshire Amateurs (1950–56)
JOINED
Free transfer, 10 January 1949
LFC DEBUT
12 March 1949
CONTRACT EXPIRY
1950

Kippe,
Frode

'FRODE is young and raw material at the moment and not ready for the first team yet. But he will be in 18 months or so,' said Houllier when he signed Frode Kippe.

The Norwegian was tall and athletic but lacked the necessary pace to succeed in the English top flight. He was one of number of players given a chance in a 4-2 win against Hull in the League Cup on 21 September 1999. Kippe came on in the 67th minute, shortly after Liverpool had taken a 3-2 lead, in place of Vladimir Smicer to tighten at the back. Kippe was loaned to Second Division Stoke from December 1999 to March 2000 and again from October 2000 to May 2001 before making his second

appearance for Liverpool, against Grimsby Town in October 2001. He replaced Gregory Vignal who broke his ankle in the 21st minute in a surprising 2-1 League Cup defeat at Anfield. On his return to Lillestrøm in 2002, Kippe was appointed captain of the club and

Frode and Øyvind Leonhardsen

voted 'Defender of the Year' in 2007 in the Norwegian top division. Kippe still features for Lillestrøm, a rock in the heart of their defence.

FACTFILE

BORN
Oslo, Norway, 17 January 1978
POSITION
Centre-half
OTHER CLUBS
Kolbotn (1996–97), Lillestrøm (1997–99), Stoke City (loan, 1999–2000, 2000–01), Lillestrøm (2002–)
SIGNED FROM
Lillestrøm, £700,000, 6 January 1999
INTERNATIONAL CAPS
8 Norway caps, 2003–08
LFC DEBUT
21 September 1999
CONTRACT EXPIRY
1 March 2002

	League		FA Cup		League Cup		Europe		Other		Total	
Season	App	Goals	App	Goals	App	Goals	App	Goals	App	Goals	App	Goals
1999/2000	0	0	0	0	0 (1)	0	-	-	-	-	0 (1)	0
2001/02	0	0	0	0	0 (1)	0	0	0	0	0	0 (1)	0
Total	**0**	**0**	**0**	**0**	**0 (2)**	**0**	**0**	**0**	**0**	**0**	**0 (2)**	**0**

Kirkland,
Chris

A TOWERING goalkeeper who graduated from Coventry's youth academy and made his first-team debut for the Sky Blues on 22 September 1999, Chris Kirkland played his second game a year later, showing so much promise that he replaced Swedish international Magnus Hedman for good and was voted Young Player of the Year by Coventry's supporters.

His progress was further rewarded when he made his England Under-21 debut on 24 May 2001 against Mexico. After only 28 appearances for Coventry he was signed by Liverpool on the same day Feyenoord goalkeeper Jerzy Dudek was brought to Anfield. Kirkland only started four games in his debut season but after Dudek's clanger against Manchester United at Anfield on 7 December 2002 he was finally given a proper chance. Houllier challenged Kirkland to fulfil his potential. 'Chris is a good shot-stopper and is good at getting down quickly for a big keeper, but what I like best about him is that he is brave. These days talent does not wait. Look at Tiger Woods in golf and how Martina Hingis was in tennis, as well as at Michael Owen here at Liverpool.' Kirkland helped Liverpool into the League Cup final before suffering a serious knee injury in the fourth round of the FA Cup that enabled Dudek to go back into the starting line-up. Another below-par performance by Dudek against United at Anfield, where Giggs scored a couple, gave Kirkland another run in the side in the 2003/04 season. He held on to his starting berth for a month before breaking his finger against Bolton at Anfield. The goalkeepers were playing their own version of hokey-cokey and Paul Jones was

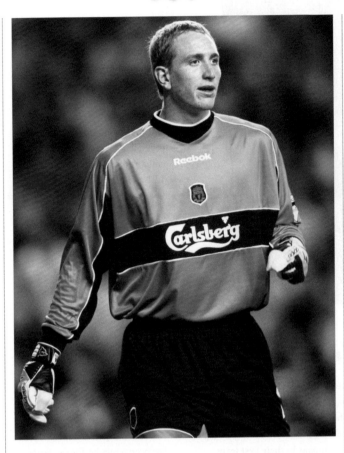

even brought in as an emergency keeper in January 2004 when both Kirkland and Dudek were out injured. Kirkland's second spell in the first XI that campaign only lasted five games before another injury ended his season in March.

KIRKLAND had his longest spell as Liverpool's number one from October to December 2004 before a series of mistakes led to him being axed from the side. The arrival of Scott Carson from Leeds in January 2005 finally ended Kirkland's once-promising Anfield career. His career was resurrected at Wigan Athletic. Kirkland made his full England debut in August 2006, to justify a bet his father had made years earlier that his son would play for

England before reaching the age of 30. Eddie Kirkland was delighted. 'He was 14 or 15 at the time and my family, friends and work colleagues put a bet of £100 at 100/1 and it has come good tonight. Absolutely fantastic.' Bookmakers William Hill confirmed Eddie had staked £98.10 with the firm at 100/1, and would receive a cheque for £9,908.10.

The injury-prone Kirkland would still get niggles as he played regularly for four seasons with Wigan until he lost his place to the Omani Ali Al-Habsi following two heavy defeats at the start of the 2010/11 season. His injury jinx struck again when he was carried off on a stretcher after a collision

with Bolton's Johan Elmander early in January 2011. In October 2011 Kirkland was loaned to Championship club Doncaster Rovers, but, unsurprisingly perhaps, he suffered a back injury on his debut! The 31-year-old goalkeeper joined Sheffield Wednesday prior to the 2012/13 season and was in the headlines when he was struck in the face and knocked to the ground by an invading Leeds fan in the Yorkshire derby on 19 October 2012 at Hillsborough. Leeds had just equalised in the 77th minute. 'I thought he was going to give me some abuse but then suddenly he came at me with both hands and I was stunned, you never know what could have been in his hands,' Kirkland said. 'Later on I thought of my family watching something like that and it was not nice to think my daughter saw me assaulted like that.'

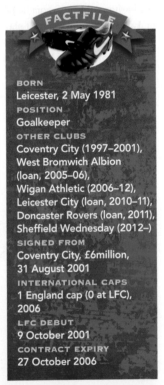

FACTFILE

BORN
Leicester, 2 May 1981
POSITION
Goalkeeper
OTHER CLUBS
Coventry City (1997–2001),
West Bromwich Albion
(loan, 2005–06),
Wigan Athletic (2006–12),
Leicester City (loan, 2010–11),
Doncaster Rovers (loan, 2011),
Sheffield Wednesday (2012–)
SIGNED FROM
Coventry City, £6million,
31 August 2001
INTERNATIONAL CAPS
1 England cap (0 at LFC),
2006
LFC DEBUT
9 October 2001
CONTRACT EXPIRY
27 October 2006

Season	League		FA Cup		League Cup		Europe		Other		Total	
	App	Goals	App	Goals	App	Goals	App	Goals	App	Goals	App	Goals
2001/02	1	0	0	0	1	0	2	0	0	0	4	0
2002/03	8	0	2	0	4	0	1	0	0	0	15	0
2003/04	6	0	1	0	1	0	4	0	-	-	12	0
2004/05	10	0	0	0	0	0	4	0	-	-	14	0
Total	**25**	**0**	**3**	**0**	**6**	**0**	**11**	**0**	**0**	**0**	**45**	**0**

Konchesky, Paul

UNTIL HIS MOVE to Merseyside, Paul Konchesky had spent his entire professional career in London, a journey that had taken him to four different clubs in the capital. That journey began in his mid-teens at Charlton Athletic, whom he joined as a trainee before becoming in August 1997 the youngest player to appear in their first team at the age of 16 years and 93 days, an achievement subsequently surpassed by his later Liverpool team-mate Jonjo Shelvey.

It took Konchesky until the 2000/01 season to become a regular in the first XI at the Valley but his opportunities were nevertheless limited and he went out on loan to Tottenham Hotspur. At the end of 2003 Charlton recalled him because of an injury crisis and he re-established himself in the side. In 2005 Konchesky joined West Ham United and stayed at Upton Park for two seasons, the first of which was by far his best as the Hammers finished in a creditable ninth place as well as reaching the FA Cup final. Konchesky certainly had a final to both remember and forget; his 63rd-minute cross drifted over Pepe Reina's head to put his team 3-2 ahead, but then he was one of three Hammers players whose spot kicks were saved by Reina as Liverpool won the cup on penalties.

In July 2007 Konchesky was on the move again, this time to west London club Fulham. He played in nearly 100 Premier League matches for them and helped the Cottagers to the inaugural Europa League final. In August 2010 Liverpool paid £5million for the left-back; £3.5million in cash plus transferring youngsters Lauri Dalla Valle and Alex Kacaniklic to Fulham. That Roy Hodgson had secured the services of a player he already knew well from their days together at Fulham could seemingly only be a good thing for Liverpool, and Hodgson picked Konchesky regularly during his brief spell at Anfield. However, Liverpool fans concluded right away that Konchesky had no business being in the club's first team. The fans' criticism had an especially profound effect on Paul's mum, Carol, who vented her frustration on her Facebook page after Liverpool's embarrassing defeat at Stoke on 13 November 2010: 'To all you Liverpool Scouse scum, take a real look at your team,' Mrs Konchesky wrote. 'Stop living in the past. The team are crap. Never should have left Fulham.' Hodgson's successor, Kenny Dalglish, didn't have the same faith in the left-back as the erstwhile Fulham boss. On the last day of the January 2011 transfer window Konchesky went on loan to Nottingham Forest in the Championship, before making a permanent move to Sven-Göran Eriksson's Leicester City. The Swede has departed but Konchesky has been a regular for the Foxes.

FACTFILE

BORN
Barking, Greater London, 15 May 1981
POSITION
Left-back
OTHER CLUBS
Charlton Athletic (1997–2005), Tottenham Hotspur (loan, 2003), West Ham United (2005–07), Fulham (2007–10), Nottingham Forest (loan, 2011), Leicester City (2011–)
SIGNED FROM
Fulham, £3.5million plus Dalla Valle and Kacaniklic, 31 August 2010
INTERNATIONAL CAPS
2 England caps, 2003–05
LFC DEBUT
12 September 2010
CONTRACT EXPIRY
13 July 2011

Kop

WHEN ANFIELD was purchased by the club from the Houlding family in 1906 the ground was overhauled and that included the cinder embankment at Walton Breck Road.

The 'Oakfield Road Embankment' or 'Walton Breck Bank' were among the names suggested for the new 50 foot high terrace. An impressed scribe at the club programme commented on the work in progress: 'The first thing that strikes one on entering the ground is the huge terracing which is rising at the west end.

> 'I'M JUST ONE OF THE PEOPLE WHO STAND ON THE KOP. THEY THINK THE SAME AS I DO, AND I THINK THE SAME AS THEY DO. IT'S A KIND OF MARRIAGE OF PEOPLE WHO LIKE EACH OTHER'
>
> **BILL SHANKLY**

ALREADY there are forty steps completed, but eventually there will be one hundred, and it will accommodate about 20,000 people. The terracing is continued along the two sides, but, of course, it does not rise to anything like the height at the west end.' *Liverpool Daily Post* and *Echo Sport* editor Ernest 'Bee' Edwards suggested that the new terrace should be named the 'Spion Kop' in memory of the 340 soldiers, many of whom were from Lancashire, who died in the battle of the spy hill, Spioenkop, in the Second Boer War in South Africa on 23-24 February 1900. The Spioenkop offered a view from the summit for hundreds

Season	League		FA Cup		League Cup		Europe		Total	
	App	Goals	App	Goals	App	Goals	App	Goals	App	Goals
2010/11	15	0	0	0	0	0	3	0	18	0
Total	15	0	0	0	0	0	3	0	18	0

Difficult to get a decent view from the back of the Kop in 1914

of miles all around so it was a very important military target. This splendid huge terrace was quite impressive, offering a fantastic viewpoint all over Liverpool. The club programme noted on 2 September 1907 when it was completed and had withstood a whole season: 'Spion Kop is a sight for the gods when covered with humanity, and its appearance from Oakfield Road is equally admirable. The green at the back makes it quite an oasis in the midst of a wilderness of bricks and mortar.'

> 'WHEN THEY START SINGING 'YOU'LL NEVER WALK ALONE' MY EYES START TO WATER. THERE HAVE BEEN TIMES WHEN I'VE ACTUALLY BEEN CRYING WHILE I'VE BEEN PLAYING'
>
> **KEVIN KEEGAN**

THE KOP was a great vantage point but desperately needed cover to provide shelter from the elements. The largest covered terrace in the country, 425ft (130m) wide and 80ft (24m) high, was opened on 25 August 1928. 'It is a new stand in entirety, only the cinder hill beneath the centre portion and three post-war concrete staircases now remain of

the old Kop of two years ago,' reported the club programme on this momentous day. 'Two thirds of its possible 28,000 spectators can see the game without a single intervening stanchion.' Its outward appearance was dramatic; cream-painted pillars and fancy red bricks adorned the building and twelve feet wide stairs led to the entrance. Kopite Harry Wilson was interviewed by Stephen F. Kelly for his excellent book about the Kop and he had some great tales for future generations to treasure from the

time he began frequenting the Kop in 1927. 'There was no singing in those days, I can tell you that. But there was lots of chanting. We used to chant the names of the players. When Harry Chambers, our centre-forward, scored we'd all chant: 'Cham-bers, Cham-bers!' And then there was Elisha Scott, the greatest goalkeeper of them all. We called him 'Lisha'. He was idolised by the Kop. Before the game started, men would walk around the pitch carrying billboards advertising things like Ovaltine or cocoa and

Queuing at the Kop in the 1950s

especially the boxing contests at the stadium which were very popular in those days. It was a very working class crowd at the Kop, mainly dockers and the like.' There was no tannoy at the ground and enforced changes to the line-up that had been printed in the match programme were written on a chalkboard that was carried around the stadium.

THE LIVERPOOL team that dominated the league in the early 1920s faded away and the club had a rather disappointing 1930s. The war put a temporary stop to the league, but once it recommenced Liverpool won the title again, but were soon on a downward spiral that ended in relegation in 1954. Five years later Bill Shankly arrived and resurrected the fans' spirit.

The singing and swaying to the latest Beatles' hit or any top of the charts tune began in the 1960s when the crowd had to find something to do instead of counting down the hours to

Kopites in 1906

kick-off as they had to come in early to make sure they could get their regular place to watch the game and not to be locked out of the stadium when it was full. The Kop achieved worldwide fame when BBC's Panorama programme recorded the Kopites' fervour and rendition of the Beatles' 'She Loves You' as Liverpool clinched the League Championship on 18 April 1964 by beating Arsenal 5-0. BBC's reporter stood enamoured in front of the Kop: 'I've never seen anything like this Liverpool crowd. The Duke of Wellington before the battle of Waterloo said of his own troops: 'I don't know what they do to the enemy, but my god they frighten me' and I am sure some of players here in this match this afternoon must be feeling the same way.' You could be swept away by the tide of humanity and returned to your original position as by some divine intervention. The Kop had become an institution; a part of the Liverpool legend; a living, breathing entity which, spontaneously, could erupt into song, or chant a chorus which demonstrably spurred on the Reds and was calculated to strike fear into the opposition.

Following the Hillsborough disaster in 1989 the Kop's capacity was reduced to 21,500 for safety reasons and the famous terrace was torn down in 1994 and replaced by a grandstand as

> 'THE FANTASTIC ATMOSPHERE AT ANFIELD WAS LIKE AN ELECTRIC SHOCK FOR LIVERPOOL'S PLAYERS, WHO STARTED THE MATCH AT AN ASTONISHING TEMPO. THEY SEEMED UNSTOPPABLE'
>
> **FABIO CAPELLO**

all-seater stadia had been made compulsory as a result of the Taylor Report. The atmosphere suffered, but had done so even before 1994 as fans began to feel a bit blasé about their ongoing success; when that success had started in the 1960s, by contrast, it was greatly appreciated as it had been a long time coming, and this appreciation continued into the 1970s. The Kop is still a magical place that has retained its humour and can frighten the opposition to death. European nights seem especially to bring the Kopites' might to the fore and precious home victories have been secured that would have been impossible without the fantastic support often instigated by the crowd behind the goal at Walton Breck Road. Fabio Capello, Juventus' coach, whose team lost in the quarter-finals of the Champions League at Anfield in 2005 could certainly vouch for how vital the home support was to his opposition and detrimental to his own team. 'The fantastic atmosphere at Anfield was like an electric shock for Liverpool's players, who started the match at an astonishing tempo. They seemed unstoppable. At Anfield, even experienced players can have a bad start because of the excitement of playing in such a stadium. We were constrained, almost in a daze at the start. Pushed by their fans, the Liverpool players were extremely motivated and aggressive.'

KOPITES have often been called Liverpool's 12th man and that is not without proper reason. The intensity that is created within the confines of the Kop can virtually suck the ball into the net. Liverpool still prefer to attack the Kop in the second half as they know they can always rely on their most vociferous followers in their hour of need.

The unofficial Kop pledge

Always support the team, no matter how bad they are playing.

If the team is doing badly, cheer even louder as they need your support more.

If a player is struggling, sing his name louder and more often as he needs it.

If the opposition are the better side and perform well, appreciate it and give them the credit they are due.

Kozma, Istvan

GRAEME SOUNESS could have been a more successful manager at Liverpool if he had taken the advice of one Michel Platini, who dropped in at his office after Liverpool's victory over Auxerre in November 1991.

'Michel Platini said he had a player for me, a player who'd had some problems back in France but who would love to come and play for Liverpool,' Souness said. 'That player was Eric Cantona. But at that time we didn't really need any more problems, so that was one that got away.' The Frenchman

joined Leeds the following February while at the same time Souness was more than ready to take a chance on Istvan Kozma! The Hungarian's ball-juggling skills were not suited to the pace and competitiveness of the English Premiership. His only shining moment came in the second round of the League Cup when he turned around a 3-0 half-time deficit into a 4-4 draw against Third Division newcomers Chesterfield. He had two assists against a side that was closer to his level of talent. Completely out of his depth in the top flight, Kozma didn't play enough games to be granted a new work permit and returned to Hungary after only two seasons at Liverpool. Kozma is though considered a Dunfermline Athletic legend, and

made 267 league appearances for (the frequently renamed) Újpesti in four different spells at the club.

FACTFILE

BORN
Paszto, Hungary,
3 December 1964
POSITION
Midfielder
OTHER CLUBS
Újpesti Dózsa (1982–89),
Dunfermline Athletic
(1989–92),
Újpesti Torna Egylet
(1993–95),
APOEL (1995–97),
Újpest (1997–98),
Videoton (1998–99),
Lombard FC Tatabánya
(1999–2000),
Újpest (2000–01)
SIGNED FROM
Dunfermline, £300,000,
10 February 1992
INTERNATIONAL CAPS
40 Hungary caps (1 goal),
1986–95
LFC DEBUT
16 February 1992
CONTRACT EXPIRY
1 June 1993

Season	League		FA Cup		League Cup		Europe		Other		Total	
	App	Goals	App	Goals	App	Goals	App	Goals	App	Goals	App	Goals
1991/92	3 (2)	0	0 (2)	0	0	0	0	0	-	-	3 (4)	0
1992/93	0 (1)	0	0	0	0 (1)	0	0	0	0 (1)	0	0 (3)	0
Total	**3 (3)**	**0**	**0 (2)**	**0**	**0 (1)**	**0**	**0**	**0**	**0 (1)**	**0**	**3 (7)**	**0**

Kromkamp, Jan

JAN KROMKAMP started out as a midfielder with Go Ahead Eagles in the 1998/99 season in the Dutch second division. He was sold to first division AZ Alkmaar before the 2000/01 season, where he was transformed into a right-back. His exploits in the UEFA Cup in the 2004/05 season when AZ reached the semi-finals caught the attention of Villareal.

He had trouble adjusting to Spain and after only 11 games and five months into his five-year contract

he went to Liverpool in a straight swap for Josemi. Kromkamp couldn't dislodge Steve Finnan from his position but he did finish his debut season in a blaze of glory as a 67th-minute substitute for Xabi Alonso in the 2006 FA Cup final which went to penalties. Seven months after his arrival a homesick Kromkamp returned to Netherlands on the last day of the transfer window without having made a real impression at Liverpool. He won the Eredivisie two years in a row at PSV (2007 and 2008). After missing 18

months due to injuries he rejoined his first club, second division Go Ahead Eagles, in February 2011.

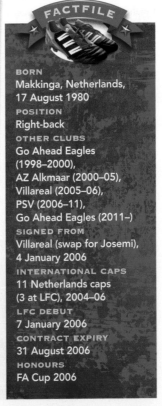

FACTFILE

BORN
Makkinga, Netherlands,
17 August 1980
POSITION
Right-back
OTHER CLUBS
Go Ahead Eagles
(1998–2000),
AZ Alkmaar (2000–05),
Villareal (2005–06),
PSV (2006–11),
Go Ahead Eagles (2011–)
SIGNED FROM
Villareal (swap for Josemi),
4 January 2006
INTERNATIONAL CAPS
11 Netherlands caps
(3 at LFC), 2004–06
LFC DEBUT
7 January 2006
CONTRACT EXPIRY
31 August 2006
HONOURS
FA Cup 2006

Season	League		FA Cup		League Cup		Europe		Other		Total	
	App	Goals	App	Goals	App	Goals	App	Goals	App	Goals	App	Goals
2005/06	6 (7)	0	1 (3)	0	0	0	0	0	0	0	7 (10)	0
2006/07	1	0	0	0	0	0	0	0	0	0	1	0
Total	**7 (7)**	**0**	**1 (3)**	**0**	**0**	**0**	**0**	**0**	**0**	**0**	**8 (10)**	**0**

Kuyt, Dirk

DIRK KUYT was born in Katwijk aan Zee, a small fisherman's town on the North Sea coast. He was the third of four children and raised mainly by his mother, while his father was often out on the open sea. When he was 12 Kuyt had to choose between aspiring to become a fisherman or a footballer. He turned down the offer of an apprenticeship as a fisherman because while at sea he would miss most of the midweek football training sessions.

In March 1998, after several years in the youth team, Kuyt made his debut for amateurs Quick Boys and scored three goals in six matches. He was on an unlikely road to stardom. 'In Holland, you start at the age of five at an amateur club and at that age I was doing fine,' he told the *Daily Mail* in 2009. 'I was with Quick Boys and I was enjoying myself. But, by the time boys reach 14 or 15, the good ones go off to the academies of clubs like Feyenoord, PSV Eindhoven and Ajax. At that stage, though, nobody was showing an interest in me. By then I thought that, even if I did eventually make it into the professional ranks, I was never going to play for one of the bigger clubs. I just had one dream. To play in the first team for my amateur club.' Kuyt became a household name in the 2002/03 season when he scored 20 goals in 34 games for Utrecht in the Eredivisie. In his final match for Utrecht, the Dutch Cup final

against Feyenoord, he contributed one goal in a 4-1 victory. After 67 goals in 184 matches for Utrecht, Bert van Marwijk, later coach of the Dutch national team, brought him to Feyenoord even though the technical director of the club did not believe Kuyt was good enough. Kuyt repaid van Marwijk's confidence by scoring 83 goals in 122 games. He was top scorer in the Eredivisie in 2005 with 29 goals in 34 games and captained Feyenoord in the 2005/06 season.

IN AUGUST 2006 Kuyt took his tremendous work ethic and bags of talent to Anfield. He hit the ground running in England, and played like he had been at

Liverpool for a decade. The Dutchman scored 14 goals in his debut season, including Liverpool's goal in the Champions League final in Athens. He struggled for consistency in his second season. The death of his dearly beloved father, who had followed his son's progress with intensity, no doubt contributed to Kuyt's erratic form. He was finally back to his best in the last part of the 2007/08 campaign, though playing on the right flank instead of up front. He only scored three league goals during the campaign but netted seven goals in the Champions League and was particularly important in the latter stages of the competition, scoring in the last 16 against Inter Milan, the

quarter-finals against Arsenal and in the semi-finals against Chelsea.

Ever the scorer of important goals, Kuyt found the net in the 118th minute against Standard Liege in the second leg of the Champions League third qualifying round at the start of the 2008/09 season. He equalled his league total of 12 goals from his first season and added three in the Champions League, including Liverpool's fourth goal in the second leg of the exciting 4-4 quarter-final against Chelsea at Stamford Bridge. Kuyt continued to be one of his manager's favourite players in 2009/10 as he only missed three of Liverpool's 56 competitive matches during the season. Similar affection was not always shown towards him by some supporters, as Kuyt was never blessed with the best first touch ever seen nor is he the quickest – he runs 'like he has a parachute on', as Jamie Carragher noted. Whatever his shortcomings, nobody could criticise the Dutchman's work-rate or enthusiasm.

THAT 'The Energizer Bunny' loved being a Liverpool player has never been beyond question. Kuyt worked as hard as he ever had during the 2010/11 season, missing only five Premier League matches, and his 13 league goals was his best return as a Liverpool player. Kuyt achieved the rare feat, not seen by a Liverpool player since 2001, of scoring in five consecutive league matches towards the end of the season. He also netted a hat-trick against Manchester United at Anfield on 6 March 2011, having failed to score in his previous nine encounters against them. Six years of hard work and honest endeavour finally brought tangible reward for Kuyt when he collected a League Cup winners' medal in 2012 after putting his team ahead in extra time of the final against Cardiff City at Wembley and then scoring in the shootout that

Season	League		FA Cup		League Cup		Europe		Other		Total	
	App	Goals	App	Goals	App	Goals	App	Goals	App	Goals	App	Goals
2006/07	27 (7)	12	1	1	0 (2)	0	10 (1)	1	0	0	38 (10)	14
2007/08	24 (8)	3	2 (2)	1	0	0	10 (2)	7	-	-	36 (12)	11
2008/09	36 (2)	12	2	0	0	0	10 (1)	3	-	-	48 (3)	15
2009/10	35 (2)	9	2	0	1	0	13	2	-	-	51 (2)	11
2010/11	32 (1)	13	1	0	0	0	6 (1)	2	-	-	39 (2)	15
2011/12	22 (12)	2	1 (4)	1	2 (3)	2	-	-	-	-	25 (19)	5
Total	**176 (32)**	**51**	**9 (6)**	**3**	**3 (5)**	**2**	**49 (5)**	**15**	**0**	**0**	**237 (48)**	**71**

followed. (Kuyt's 100 per cent success rate from eight penalties had ended though when he missed from the spot against Everton in October 2011.) The late Anfield winner against Manchester United in the FA Cup was another reminder that he could still be a man for the big occasion.

At the start of June 2012 the popular 31-year-old signed a three-year contract with Istanbul club Fenerbahce. Kuyt was very emotional leaving Liverpool. 'After six years, I just had a feeling I needed to change something in my career, a new experience, a new country, new people around me, and that's why I made the decision to leave,' he said. 'The club was great, the people were great and the people from Liverpool – the text messages, the phone calls, the e-mails, all the tweets I had on my Twitter account – it's unbelievable how much respect they showed me and it's also a bit emotional.' More than just a footballer, Kuyt is a humanitarian who runs a foundation that supports and organises events for people with disabilities.

FACTFILE

BORN
Katwijk, Netherlands,
22 July 1980
POSITION
Centre-forward / Right-winger
OTHER CLUBS
Quick Boys (1985–98),
Utrecht (1998–2003),
Feyenoord (2003–06),
Fenerbahce (2012–)
SIGNED FROM
Feyenoord, £9million,
18 August 2006
INTERNATIONAL CAPS
Netherlands caps 94 (24 goals)
(64 (20) at LFC), 2004–
LFC DEBUT GAME/GOAL
26 August 2006 /
20 September 2006
CONTRACT EXPIRY
3 June 2012
HONOURS
League Cup 2012

Kvarme, Bjørn Tore

BJØRN TORE KVARME impressed at Norway's most successful club, Rosenborg, who proved their quality by reaching the quarter-finals of the Champions League in the 1996/97 season. Kvarme was heading for Stabæk, also in Norway, when Liverpool intervened in January 1997.

Kvarme's former team-mate, Stig-Inge Bjørnebye, was excited at the prospect of teaming up with 'Beto' again. 'Bjørn is very quick defensively. I remember training with him at Rosenborg and he was terrible to play against because he's very tough,' Bjørnebye said. 'I also think he'll be popular among the lads.' The centre-half, who could also feature at right-back, had an impressive start to his Liverpool career. Kvarme was in the starting XI for the rest of the 1996/97 season, only missing European games because he had already featured for Rosenborg in Europe.

Kvarme continued to be first choice at the start of the 1997/98 season. The first signs of trouble occurred on 18 October 1997 in a derby match at Goodison Park when Danny Cadamarteri made Kvarme look like an amateur in a 2-0 defeat. Kvarme kept his place but on 6 December another well-highlighted mistake against Manchester United made Roy Evans single him out for criticism after the match. Surprisingly,

Kvarme kept his place throughout December and was happy enough with his first year. 'I knew English football from the telly,' he said. 'I knew it was a quick game over here, but maybe it's even quicker than I thought. It's very physical as well.' The day after this article was published Kvarme had another poor display, coming up against Coventry's Darren Huckerby in the FA Cup in January 1998. This was one game too many for Evans and he dropped the Norwegian. Kvarme was never a regular again and left at the start of the 1999/2000 season after Gérard Houllier had bought the central defensive pairing of Sami Hyypia and Stephane Henchoz.

FACTFILE

BORN
Trondheim, Norway,
17 June 1972
POSITION
Centre-half
OTHER CLUBS
Utleira,
Rosenborg (1990–97),
Saint Etienne (1999–2001),
Real Sociedad (2001–04),
Bastia (2004–05),
Rosenborg (2005–08)
JOINED
Free transfer,
10 January 1997
INTERNATIONAL CAPS
1 Norway cap, 1997
LFC DEBUT
18 January 1997
CONTRACT EXPIRY
30 August 1999

Season	League		FA Cup		League Cup		Europe		Total	
	App	Goals	App	Goals	App	Goals	App	Goals	App	Goals
1996/97	15	0	1	0	0	0	0	0	16	0
1997/98	22 (1)	0	1	0	2	0	4	0	29 (1)	0
1998/99	2 (5)	0	0	0	0	0	1	0	3 (5)	0
Total	**39 (6)**	**0**	**2**	**0**	**2**	**0**	**5**	**0**	**48 (6)**	**0**

Kyle,
Peter

FORWARD Peter Kyle was selected in four of the first five league matches of the 1899/1900 season, but lost his place to Johnny Walker and only made one further appearance in the FA Cup replay with Stoke City at Anfield on 1 February 1900.

KYLE was a much-travelled player who 'when in form is really in the best class of centre forward' (*Evening Telegraph*), but he was beset with disciplinary problems, more than once being thrown out of a club after a dispute with a team-mate. His brief stay at Watford ended because of 'utterly disgraceful and demoralising conduct', according to the *West Herts Post*. Kyle's most prolific spell came at First Division Arsenal from 1906 to 1908 where he scored 23 goals in 60 appearances.

FACTFILE

BORN
Cadder, East Dunbartonshire, Scotland, 21 December 1878
DIED
19 January 1957
POSITION
Forward
OTHER CLUBS
Glasgow Parkhead (1896–98),
Clyde (1898–99),
Leicester Fosse (1900–01),
Wellingborough Town (1901),
West Ham United (1901),
Kettering (1901–02),
Wellingborough Town (1902),
Aberdeen (1902–03),
Cowdenbeath (1903–04),
Port Glasgow Athletic (1904),
Royal Albert (1904–05),
Partick Thistle (1905),
Tottenham Hotspur (1905–06),
Woolwich Arsenal (1906–08),
Aston Villa (1908),
Sheffield United (1908–09),
Royal Albert (1909),
Watford (1909–10),
Royal Albert (1910–11),
Raith Rovers
SIGNED FROM
Clyde, 1 May 1899
LFC DEBUT
2 September 1899
CONTRACT EXPIRY
9 May 1900

Season	League		FA Cup		Total	
	App	Goals	App	Goals	App	Goals
1899/1900	4	0	1	0	5	0
Total	**4**	**0**	**1**	**0**	**5**	**0**

Kyrgiakos, Sotirios

SOTIRIOS KYRGIAKOS, a 6ft 4in (192cm) centre-back, is an experienced Greek international who was signed by Liverpool due to Sami Hyypia's move to Bayer Leverkusen and injuries to Martin Skrtel and Daniel Agger.

KYRGIAKOS played in 12 Champions League games as the Greek giants Panathinaikos reached the quarter-finals in the 2001/02 season, but missed most of the club's double-winning 2003/04 season after sustaining knee-ligament damage in a collision with Rangers' goalkeeper Stefan Klos. The injury kept him out of the victorious Greek team in the 2004 European Championships. Coincidentally his next club turned out to be Rangers. Kyrgiakos signed a loan deal in January 2005 with a view to a permanent deal. He won the Scottish Championship and the League Cup, but tried to find a new club during the summer.

After failing to do so he signed a one-year contract with Rangers that was not renewed at the end of the 2005/06 season, as his performances had been way below par. Kyrgiakos played two years as a regular with Eintracht Frankfurt before he returned to his homeland with AEK Athens. He intended to play out his career in Greece, but couldn't resist Rafa Benítez's tempting offer to join Liverpool.

With Carragher, Agger and Skrtel above him in the pecking order, the big Greek only played 21 matches for Liverpool during the 2009/10 season. Although he started 18 times, he was on the

bench for 25. When he did play, however, he was a commanding and dominant defender, unafraid to put himself at risk of injury in his efforts to claim the ball. The only negative point of his debut season at Liverpool was his sending-off in the Anfield derby with Everton in February after being voted as Liverpool's official 'Player of the Month' by the club's fans in the previous month. Under neither Roy Hodgson nor Kenny Dalglish did 'Soto' seriously threaten the normal central defensive partnership of Skrtel and Carragher. Kyrgiakos

featured in just over half of the club's 54 competitive matches during the 2010/11 season but 11 of those came in the Europa League. A clumsy tackle in Braga conceded the penalty which ultimately despatched Liverpool from the competition and his lack of pace became agonisingly apparent. Kyrgiakos started only four matches under Dalglish and signed for Wolfsburg in 2011, returning to the Bundesliga. He was loaned out to Martin O'Neill's Sunderland on the last day of January 2012, where he featured in four first-team matches.

SO WHY did Liverpool sign Kyrgiakos? Rafa Benítez answered that question very well when he analysed Soto's performance against Bolton in January 2010. 'What has Sotirios brought? Headers. He is strong and he likes the challenge. It is something that we needed and right now he is doing well. His attitude has been contagious. Kevin Davies is very strong and it is not easy to stop him in the air, so Sotirios did really well. He lost one tooth in the game and that shows how hard it can be.'

FACTFILE

BORN
Trikala, Greece, 23 July 1979
POSITION
Centre-half
OTHER CLUBS
Panathinaikos (1996–2005),
Agios Nikolaos (loan,
1999–2001),
Rangers (2005–06),
Eintracht Frankfurt (2006–08),
AEK Athens (2008–09),
Wolfsburg (2011–),
Sunderland (loan, 2012)
SIGNED FROM
AEK Athens, £2million,
21 August 2009
INTERNATIONAL CAPS
61 Greece caps (4 goals)
(11 (0) at LFC) 2002–10
LFC DEBUT GAME/GOAL
29 August 2009 /
16 January 2010
CONTRACT EXPIRY
22 August 2011

Season	League		FA Cup		League Cup		Europe		Total	
	App	Goals	App	Goals	App	Goals	App	Goals	App	Goals
2009/10	13 (1)	1	0	0	2	0	3 (2)	0	18 (3)	1
2010/11	10 (6)	2	0	0	1	0	9 (2)	0	20 (8)	2
Total	**23 (7)**	**3**	**0**	**0**	**3**	**0**	**12 (4)**	**0**	**38 (11)**	**3**

David Ashworth's men looking cool in the 1920s

Lacey, Bill

'AS FOR kicking Lacey as a hobby, I can assure you it's a waste of time, the boy is made from Solid Rock. Dynamite could not shift him off the ball,' said a 1923 match report that captured Bill Lacey perfectly.

He joined Everton from Dublin's Shelbourne in May 1908. Lacey only played 37 league games and scored 11 goals for the Blues in three and a half seasons. Liverpool made one of their shrewdest transfer deals ever when they paid £300 for Lacey and Tom Gracie as well as letting Harold Uren go in exchange in February 1912. 'Was there ever a transfer that turned out so profitable to the Livers!' exclaimed the *Liverpool Echo*. Lacey immediately went into the first team and made his debut in a 1-1 draw against Middlesbrough on 2 March 1912. The scribe for the club programme was impressed. 'I have always had an idea that Lacey would make a better man for Liverpool than Everton. We as a rule play more robust football, due to the fact that our forwards have been bigger men. And Lacey, while he is capable of clever work, is also a dashing, fearless forward. He was distinctly the personality on the home side against Middlesbrough, and had there been another of equal calibre I am sure we must have won.' Lacey played in the last 11 fixtures of that season with one goal to his

credit, against Spurs on 16 March 1912. He never was renowned as a goalscorer, just 29 from 259 appearances for Liverpool, but his tricky wing-play set up numerous chances for his colleagues.

LACEY returned to Ireland to feature for, among others, his first club Shelbourne during World War One and as the English League recommenced he showed his versatility by playing as half-back between 1919 and 1921 (as he had successfully tried for Liverpool in the second part of the 1914/15 campaign). Once he returned to his old role on the wing, now on the right as opposed to the left before the war, he was an important part of the side that won the First Division Championship two years running in 1922 and 1923. You could spot Lacey a mile off as his 'jutting chin was the delight of the cartoonists'. He was also said to have a rounded, lovable

Bill Lacey putting for glory

personality and was very popular with the Liverpool faithful. Lacey was only selected nine times during 1924/25, by which time he was approaching his mid-30s, and he was allowed to move across the Mersey to join New Brighton. He moved back to his native Ireland in 1925 and retired from the game in 1931 at 42 years of age!

FACTFILE

BORN
Wexford, Ireland, 24 September 1889
DIED
30 May 1969
POSITION
Winger / Half-back
OTHER CLUBS
Shelbourne (1906–08), Everton (1908–12); Shelbourne, Belfast United, Linfield (wartime guest), New Brighton (1924–25), Shelbourne (1925–27), Cork Bohemians (1927–31)
SIGNED FROM
Everton, 28 February 1912
INTERNATIONAL CAPS
26 Ireland caps (4 goals) (12 (2) at LFC) 1909–30
LFC DEBUT GAME/GOAL
2 March 1912 / 16 March 1912
CONTRACT EXPIRY
June 1924
HONOURS
League Championship 1921/22, 1922/23

Season	League		FA Cup		Other		Total	
	App	Goals	App	Goals	App	Goals	App	Goals
1911/12	11	1	0	0	-	-	11	1
1912/13	21	3	4	3	-	-	25	6
1913/14	35	6	8	5	-	-	43	11
1914/15	32	2	1	0	-	-	33	2
1919/20	32	3	5	2	-	-	37	5
1920/21	22	1	2	1	-	-	24	2
1921/22	39	1	3	0	1	0	43	1
1922/23	30	1	4	0	-	-	34	1
1923/24	8	0	1	0	-	-	9	0
Total	**230**	**18**	**28**	**11**	**1**	**0**	**259**	**29**

Lambert, Ray

RAY LAMBERT joined Liverpool as an amateur at 13 years and 189 days of age in January 1936, becoming the youngest ever player to join a league club at that time. Although the Welshman had signed professional forms for Liverpool before World War Two he didn't get an opportunity to represent his club in a competitive fixture until 1946.

Regional leagues were still operating in the immediate aftermath of the war but Lambert played in four FA Cup ties that year, by which time he was 23 years old. Lambert was a reliable full-back who became an integral member of the team for the next decade, averaging over 30 league matches per season during that period. He could play on either flank and was a fans' favourite. But his early years at Anfield were a lot more successful than those near the end of his playing career. He was able to celebrate the first post-war League Championship in 1947 and also helped his club reach their first Wembley cup final in 1950. After that, although his own form was as steady as ever, the club's final league placing gradually worsened until relegation to the Second Division was confirmed in 1954. Lambert, who was capped five times by his country, remained on Liverpool's books for a further two seasons

RAY LAMBERT
LIVERPOOL

before he retired a few weeks short of his 34th birthday. He was offered a move to Third Division North's Chester in December 1955, but didn't want to leave the club for which he had already played his last first-team game.

THE WELSHMAN said the following in a souvenir brochure dedicated to the Liverpool players who fought for the FA Cup in the 1950 final: 'I have been with Liverpool since joining the

groundstaff at fourteen. They have been very happy years. I would not change them for anything. Being a bachelor, I haven't much to worry about except when I come up against Stanley Matthews. Then, if you're a full-back, you get plenty to worry about. I know

from experience! Cricket and golf are my close-season games, and I prefer biographies to any other form of reading matter. Had I not been a professional footballer, I think I should have chosen to make a living as an electrician.'

> THEY HAVE BEEN VERY HAPPY YEARS. I WOULD NOT CHANGE THEM FOR ANYTHING

FACTFILE

BORN
Bagillt, Flintshire, Wales,
18 July 1922
DIED
22 October 2009
POSITION
Right/left-back
OTHER CLUBS
New Brighton, Reading
(wartime guest)
JOINED
1936; signed professional
18 July 1939
INTERNATIONAL CAPS
5 Wales caps, 1946–49
LFC DEBUT GAME/GOAL
5 January 1946 /
8 October 1949
CONTRACT EXPIRY
1956
HONOURS
League Championship
1946/47

Season	League		FA Cup		Total	
	App	**Goals**	**App**	**Goals**	**App**	**Goals**
1945/46	-	-	4	0	4	0
1946/47	36	0	6	0	42	0
1947/48	30	0	2	0	32	0
1948/49	41	0	4	0	45	0
1949/50	41	1	7	0	48	1
1950/51	34	0	1	0	35	0
1951/52	32	0	3	0	35	0
1952/53	36	0	1	0	37	0
1953/54	20	1	1	0	21	1
1954/55	28	0	4	0	32	0
1955/56	10	0	0	0	10	0
Total	**308**	**2**	**33**	**0**	**341**	**2**

Lancashire Competitions

LIVERPOOL featured in the local Lancashire League in their first campaign in 1892/93 after their application for a spot in the Football League was rejected.

The team of Scotsmen assembled by the club's board won 17, drew two and lost three. Liverpool's 3-0 and 2-0 defeats to Blackpool over the season looked as if they were going to cost them the title as their rivals faced Southport Central in the final match. Southport had lost 13 out of their 21 games and Blackpool only needed a draw. Surprisingly Blackpool lost 1-0 and were equal on 36 points with Liverpool. Even though Blackpool had a better goal difference of +51 versus Liverpool's +47, positions were decided by goal average; the number of goals scored divided by goals conceded.

		P	W	D	L	F	A	Avg	Pts
1	Liverpool	22	17	2	3	66	19	3.4	36
2	Blackpool	22	17	2	3	82	31	2.6	36

Liverpool were presented with the 200 ounce Lancashire League trophy at the club's headquarters, the Sandon hotel, owned by the club's president John Houlding. The local association's treasurer Mr Smith spoke of the 'unexampled success which had been obtained by Liverpool in the first year of its existence.' When this handsome trophy was on display in Mr Charles Gibson's pawnshop in Paddington it was stolen as well as the Liverpool Senior Cup trophy that Liverpool had won. The club had to pay £130 to replace the trophies!

LIVERPOOL also took part in the local association's cup competition, continuing to participate beyond the 1892/93 season even though they had by then left the Lancashire League for the Football League's Second Division. The Lancashire Senior Cup was obviously not as popular as the Football League games but local pride was strong. A lot of stir was

created before Liverpool's 2-2 draw with Bolton Wanderers on 23 January 1897 as three of the Reds' first teamers; Tom Wilkie, Robert Neill and George Allan were conspicuously absent. The *Liverpool Review* revealed a trio of players were left out of side for insubordination, 'so called enjoyment!' The three Scotsmen who had tasted a bit too much of the good life had returned to the side by the time the replay took place but Liverpool lost 2-0 at Burnden Park.

Liverpool, in fact, did not win the Lancashire Senior Cup until 1919 when the club was also featuring in the Lancashire section of the Football League. The regular league divisions were put on hold during World War One. Liverpool

were victorious once in the principal tournament of the Football League's Lancashire section, in 1916/17.

By the time Bill Shankly had arrived in 1959, Liverpool had won the Senior Cup twice in the last four years, but always fielded weakened teams until the final when it really mattered. Ultimately it has become a competition primarily for Liverpool reserves. Liverpool won the Lancashire Senior Cup last time in 2010 when Andre Wisdom lifted the trophy after a 3-0 win over Oldham Athletic.

> **Lancashire Senior Cup has been won by Liverpool in the following years:**
>
> **1919, 1920 (shared), 1924, 1931, 1933, 1944, 1947, 1956, 1959, 1973, 2010.**

Lane,
Frank

GOALKEEPER Frank Lane was signed from Merseyside neighbours Tranmere Rovers in September 1971 as a cover for Ray Clemence.

A RARE injury to the club's first-choice keeper meant that Lane was thrown in at the deep end for his league debut at Derby County on 2 September 1972. However, he unfortunately distinguished himself for all the wrong reasons by safely catching a deep cross from Alan Hinton and then stepping backwards over his own goal-line! Despite this 'howler', the injury situation with Clemence meant that Lane kept his place for the League Cup tie at Carlisle United three days later. There were no further mishaps in a 1-1 draw but Lane never played a first-team match for the club again.

Season	League		FA Cup		League Cup		Europe		Total	
	App	Goals	App	Goals	App	Goals	App	Goals	App	Goals
1972/73	1	0	0	0	1	0	0	0	2	0
Total	1	0	0	0	1	0	0	0	2	0

Latham,
George

IN WORLD War One George Latham was a captain in the 7th Royal Welsh Fusiliers, which turned out to be a useful football team that won the British Forces Football League Cup in 1919.

Latham was awarded the Military Cross for his gallantry on the Turkish Front in 1917 and the Bar in 1918 for further bravery. He served in the Boer War in 1901 where he featured for a couple of South African sides. The club programme assessed the half-back's first-team chances on 8 April 1905 prior to his Liverpool debut. 'Latham is an untiring worker on the field, and his ceaseless energy more than compensates of any deficiency in point of ability. In feeding his forwards he has shown considerable improvement recently, and with experience he should quickly remedy these failings, which at present keep him from being regarded as a League player of the first water.' Burslem Port Vale were thrashed 8-1 at Anfield in the only appearance he made during the 1904/05 season. He was called on occasionally over the next three years and played in a total of 18 league games for the Reds, plus a single appearance in the FA Cup.

LATHAM played 10 games for Wales, making his debut against Scotland in 1905 when Maurice Parry, his Liverpool team-mate, had to withdraw from the Welsh squad as Liverpool needed his services in the league. His last international on 18 January 1913 against Ireland in Belfast was a curious one as he had travelled with the team as its trainer, but ended up playing at right-half in a single-goal victory. He is the oldest league debutant in Cardiff's history at 41. When playing away at Blackburn on 2 January 1922, two of Cardiff's players took ill so trainer Latham was pressed into service. Latham later coached the club, masterminding its 1-0 victory over Arsenal in the 1927 FA Cup final. He wrote his name in the history books as the team was the first and so far still the only one to take the FA Cup out of England. Cardiff had lost the final two years previously to Sheffield United. Latham was a highly respected coach who was also in charge of Great Britain's team that participated in the 1920 summer Olympics in Belgium. When Latham was badly injured in a biking accident in 1936 he was forced to give up coaching. He died in Newtown three years later, aged only 58. A number of football luminaries attended the funeral. A Cardiff City cup final souvenir brochure describes Latham as 'probably the most popular and best loved man in football'. As a sign of respect for him in his home town, Newtown AFC's stadium, Latham Park, is named after him.

Season	League		FA Cup		Other		Total	
	App	Goals	App	Goals	App	Goals	App	Goals
1904/05	1	0	0	0	-	-	1	0
1905/06	5	0	1	0	0	0	6	0
1906/07	9	0	0	0	-	-	9	0
1907/08	3	0	0	0	-	-	3	0
Total	18	0	1	0	0	0	19	0

Lawler, Chris

A GREAT goalscoring defender if there ever was one, Chris Lawler boasts an astonishing record of 61 goals in 549 games, especially considering he was neither the club's penalty-taker nor a free-kick specialist. He specialised in ghosting into the opponent's penalty area, having the 'brain of a striker' as termed by Paisley, and coolly dispatching the ball past the keeper.

His most memorable goal of all came in a Merseyside derby in November 1970 when, after being two goals down, Lawler scored the winner for Liverpool six minutes from time. Local lad Lawler came through the junior ranks at Anfield and signed professional forms on his 17th birthday in October 1960. The cultured centre-half had his way into the team blocked by the great Ron Yeats and had to wait patiently until March 1963 before Bill Shankly gave him his debut. Lawler took Yeats' place in all the six matches the Scotsman missed in the 1963/64 Championship season. Thereafter, Lawler's talent was too great to keep him out of the team. Ronnie Moran, who had been playing left-back with Gerry Byrne on the right, was reaching the end of a successful career. Lawler was brought in as right-back and Byrne moved to the left. By the end of the 1964/65 season Lawler was a proud member of the Liverpool team that won the FA Cup for the first time in the club's history. He

played 316 consecutive games from 2 October 1965 to 24 April 1971, a quite remarkable 'attendance record', helping his side win the Championship in 1966, reach the Cup Winners' Cup final the same year and another FA Cup final in 1971.

LAWLER and Tommy Smith were room-mates and despite being very different characters they worked well together on and off the field, as Lawler explained. 'Tommy and I had an understanding. I'd try and force them inside and then Tommy would sort them out! I'd let him do the tackling. There weren't many that got the better of us. Best, Charlton, yes, they were good. But we usually had the beating of them.' Lawler was nicknamed 'The Silent Knight' because of the uncomplicated way he just got on with his job on the field, described in one report as 'sauntering through games with all the apparent urgency of a man out walking his dog'. He was very quiet off the field and a source for one of the best anecdotes concerning Shankly, as told by Paisley. 'Bill used to take training sessions very seriously when it got round to the seven-a-side matches and this day we were playing without proper goals. Bill hit a shot and claimed a goal which everyone else knew would have gone over

the bar. Anyway, to try and get some support for his view that he had scored he turned to Chris and asked him whether it was a goal or not. Chris said that it wasn't and would have gone over the bar and Bill had everyone in stitches when he turned round and told anyone who would listen: "He doesn't say a word for years and then when he does he tells a lie".'

Approaching his 30th birthday Lawler still retained the fitness and stamina to play in every one of the 66 competitive games the club played in four different competitions during the 1972/73 season, his reward being further winners' medals in the Championship and UEFA Cup. Lawler underwent a cartilage operation following an injury sustained against QPR in November 1973 and was never

the same player after that. He had only played one match in the previous five months when Shankly picked him as the 'twelfth man' for the 1974 FA Cup final. Lawler only featured in 17 matches in a season and a half following Paisley's appointment. He moved to Portsmouth in October 1975, who were managed at the time by his former team-mate Ian St John. Lawler was Liverpool's reserve-team coach for years until he was replaced by Phil Thompson in 1986.

FACTFILE

BORN
Liverpool, 20 October 1943
POSITION
Right-back / Centre-half
OTHER CLUBS
Portsmouth (1975–77),
Miami Toros (loan, 1976),
Stockport (1977–78),
Bangor City (1978–80)
JOINED
1959; signed professional
20 October 1960
INTERNATIONAL CAPS
4 England caps (1 goal), 1971
LFC DEBUT GAME/GOAL
20 March 1963 /
5 December 1964
CONTRACT EXPIRY
October 1975
HONOURS
League Championship
1965/66, 1972/73;
FA Cup 1965, 1974;
UEFA Cup 1973

> A GREAT
> GOALSCORING
> DEFENDER
> IF THERE EVER
> WAS ONE

Season	League		FA Cup		League Cup		Europe		Other		Total	
	App	Goals	App	Goals	App	Goals	App	Goals	App	Goals	App	Goals
1962/63	6	0	1	0	-	-	-	-	-	-	7	0
1963/64	6	0	0	0	-	-	-	-	-	-	6	0
1964/65	33	2	8	0	-	-	7	0	0	0	48	2
1965/66	40	5	1	0	-	-	8	4	1	0	50	9
1966/67	42	4	4	1	-	-	5	1	1	0	52	6
1967/68	42	3	9	1	2	0	6	0	-	-	59	4
1968/69	42	3	4	0	3	3	2	1	-	-	51	7
1969/70	42	10	6	0	2	0	4	1	-	-	54	11
1970/71	41	3	7	2	3	0	10	1	-	-	61	6
1971/72	42	6	3	0	3	1	4	1	1	0	53	8
1972/73	42	3	4	0	8	1	12	0	-	-	66	4
1973/74	18	2	0	0	3	0	4	2	-	-	25	4
1974/75	10	0	0	0	3	0	3	0	0	0	16	0
1975/76	0	0	0	0	0	0	1	0	-	-	1	0
Total	**406**	**41**	**47**	**4**	**27**	**5**	**66**	**11**	**3**	**0**	**549**	**61**

Lawrence, Tommy

STRONG, BRAVE and consistent, Tommy Lawrence was a fearless goalkeeper, even if he was affectionately dubbed 'The Flying Pig' by supporters who felt he was carrying a bit too much weight.

Lawrence had signed as an apprentice at Liverpool in 1955, but continued to play for his local amateur team and worked in the Rylands wire factory in Warrington until he signed professional forms at Liverpool on 30 October 1957, a few months after his 17th birthday. Lawrence finally got his opportunity in Liverpool's first season in the top flight for eight years. Jim Furnell got injured 13 games into the 1962/63 season and Lawrence grabbed his chance with both hands.

Football was different back in those days and the keepers usually didn't have the luxury of wearing gloves. 'We could only wear woollen gloves in wet weather,' Lawrence told the *LFC Magazine*. 'We couldn't wear them in the dry, even when it was freezing.' He only missed four league matches in six seasons as Liverpool won the First Division Championship twice as well as the FA Cup. Lawrence's captain at Liverpool, Ron Yeats, told *LFChistory.net* a priceless story about the keeper he played with for nine years:

Tommy Lawrence was frightened to death of Shanks. He was just a young boy. I'll always remember we were playing Arsenal and we were winning 1-0 with 20 minutes to go and I thought, 'What a good win this will be at Arsenal.' Joe Baker hit the ball from 25 yards. I am not joking, but he stubbed his toe first and then hit the ball. It trickled by me and I went 'It's yours, Tommy!' Tommy was on the line and opened his legs and the bloody ball went right through him. I couldn't believe it. They put the pressure on us for the last five minutes, but we held out. I am thinking to myself all this time, 'When we get into that dressing room I am going to get into the bath before Shanks comes in the door.' Little did I know that the ten players I was playing with thought the same thing. When the final whistle went, if we had sprinted that much during the game we would have won it easily. The door opened and in came Shanks. His face was blue and I am thinking, 'Here it goes.' He went: 'Where is he?' I didn't realise but big Tommy Lawrence was behind me. I was three inches bigger than him and didn't know where he was. His finger went up and he said, 'I am here, boss.' 'Where?' 'I am here, boss.' He said, 'Before you say anything, boss, I want to apologise to you and the lads. I should have never opened my legs to that ball.' Shankly went, 'It's not your fault. It's your bloody mother who should have never opened her legs!'

Shankly was reluctant to break up the team that had brought so much success to the club in the middle of the 1960s but a humiliating FA Cup quarter-final defeat to Second Division Watford proved to be Lawrence's penultimate appearance in the Liverpool first team. Ray Clemence was picked for the next league match after the cup exit. Lawrence knew that he would have to move on and made the short trip across the Mersey at the age of 31 to join Tranmere Rovers, shortly to be joined by Ron Yeats. Lawrence added 80 league appearances to his total before moving on to non-league Chorley as player-coach. Twelve months later he returned to the Rylands wire factory in Warrington as a quality controller and worked there until his retirement.

THE STOCKILY BUILT Scotsman was the first sweeper-keeper, as Lawrence explains. 'Shankly said: "Right, Tommy, you're not playing on the six-yard line. When the ball's on the halfway line, you've got to be on the 18-yard line. If the ball shoots through, you've got to be out to kick it – a sort of stopper." At first I was frightened to death. We did it at Melwood a few times, then we tried it at Anfield. Well, I'm standing there and the

AFFECTIONATELY DUBBED 'THE FLYING PIG' BY SUPPORTERS

Kop is giving me some stick. "Get back on your line!" they're all yelling. No goalkeeper did that in those days... But it worked. I'd come out and do like they do today. You didn't get sent off in those days either. So I used to bring them down. If they pushed it past me, I'd just hit them.'

FACTFILE

BORN
Dailly, Scotland,
14 May 1940
POSITION
Goalkeeper
OTHER CLUBS
Warrington Town,
Tranmere Rovers (1971–74),
Chorley (1974–75)
SIGNED FROM
Warrington Town, 1955;
signed professional 30
October 1957
INTERNATIONAL CAPS
3 Scotland caps, 1963–69
LFC DEBUT
27 October 1962
CONTRACT EXPIRY
10 November 1971
HONOURS
League Championship
1963/64, 1965/66;
FA Cup 1965

Season	League App	League Goals	FA Cup App	FA Cup Goals	League Cup App	League Cup Goals	Europe App	Europe Goals	Other App	Other Goals	Total App	Total Goals
1962/63	29	0	6	0	-	-	-	-	-	-	35	0
1963/64	40	0	5	0	-	-	-	-	-	-	45	0
1964/65	41	0	8	0	-	-	9	0	1	0	59	0
1965/66	42	0	1	0	-	-	9	0	1	0	53	0
1966/67	41	0	4	0	-	-	5	0	1	0	51	0
1967/68	42	0	9	0	2	0	6	0	-	-	59	0
1968/69	42	0	4	0	2	0	2	0	-	-	50	0
1969/70	28	0	5	0	2	0	2	0	-	-	37	0
1970/71	1	0	0	0	0	0	0	0	-	-	1	0
Total	**306**	**0**	**42**	**0**	**6**	**0**	**33**	**0**	**3**	**0**	**390**	**0**

Lawrenson, Mark

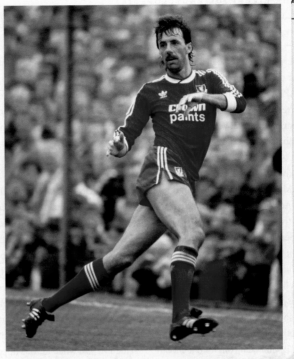

MARK LAWRENSON was playing for his local team, Preston, in the lower half of the Second Division in 1977 when Brighton offered £100,000 for the Irish international.

Alan Mullery, who was Brighton's manager at the time, revealed Liverpool could have signed Lawrenson four years earlier. 'We outbid Liverpool to get him. I phoned the Preston manager, Harry Catterick, and he told me Liverpool had offered £75,000. Mark was only 19, but when I told Mike [Mike Bamber – Brighton's chairman] he said: "Offer £100,000." Liverpool weren't prepared to up their bid so we got him and four years later we sold him for a million.' Brighton were promoted to the First Division in 1979 but a financial crisis in 1981 meant the club had to sell its biggest asset. Mullery wanted to hold on to his best player: 'I'd had four or five First Division clubs on the phone most Fridays wanting to know if he was available and when I was told about our money situation I phoned up Ron Atkinson and sold him to Manchester United. The only trouble was, Mike sold him to Liverpool, which is where he eventually went.' Bob Paisley was especially impressed by Lawrenson's tackling as he revealed in his and Clive Tyldesley's book about the 1986/87 Liverpool squad. 'We nearly bought him from Preston in 1977, but it was playing at the heart of the Brighton defence against Kenny Dalglish in March 1980 that he really caught my eye. Kenny is notoriously difficult to tackle. He is so clever and deceptive and uses his body to shield the ball from opposing defenders. And yet here was a 22-year-old, fresh out of the Second Division, winning the ball from him with sharp, clean challenges.'

Lawrenson was bought for a Liverpool club record fee and also became the most expensive defender in Britain. 'I was nervous as a kitten,' Lawrenson remembers, when he met Paisley. 'I had on my best suit, shirt and tie, my best bib and tucker. I went down to reception and the doorman spotted me and said "Mr Paisley is waiting for you in his car outside." They'd just won the European Cup and there was this fellow, who everyone in football thought was an absolute god, driving me to the ground in his slippers and cardigan! I thought "You'll do for me!"'

LAWRENSON was a great tackler, strong and possessed considerable skill and speed. He started out at Liverpool as a left-back, replacing Alan Kennedy for a while. The 1981/82 Championship had been an unlikely prospect, with many changes in personnel to the squad which had become champions of Europe the previous spring. He figured in 39 of the 42 league games and played a big part in the 3-1 win over Spurs in the penultimate fixture of the season that clinched the title. His towering header past former Anfield favourite Ray Clemence equalised Glenn Hoddle's first-half strike before Lawrenson hooked the ball over his head just four minutes later to lay on a goal for Kenny Dalglish. Ronnie Whelan's late volley ensured that Liverpool could not be caught in the title race. Lawrenson had

played the first part of the 1982/83 season in midfield when he took over the number 4 shirt from Phil Thompson on 28 December 1982 to play alongside Alan Hansen. Lawrenson could play any position in defence, but his partnership with Hansen in the centre was the one he was most admired for. He certainly enjoyed the historic 1983/84 season as Liverpool won their third consecutive league title, fourth consecutive League Cup and the European Cup for the fourth time. Liverpool were soon on their way to their fifth European Cup final following a convincing aggregate win over the Greek champions which was especially enjoyable for Lawrenson. 'One of the best nights we had was after the Panathinaikos semi in 1985. We'd already beaten them 4-0 at Anfield and I scored in the away leg, we strolled it. As it was so far away we stayed overnight and ended up having an impromptu hat party in one of the rooms with all the lads together. It wasn't reported at the time, but, well, you didn't have to wear anything except a hat.' Lawrenson was out injured for three games leading up to the final, and only lasted three minutes against Juventus at Heysel before aggravating his shoulder injury.

Lawrenson was a key member of the 'Double' squad in 1986, although perhaps fortunate to play in the FA Cup final against Everton. He got injured against Oxford towards the end of March and missed the semi-final against Southampton. He then played the full 90 minutes when Liverpool clinched the Championship at Chelsea to stake his claim. Gary Gillespie's late withdrawal from the Wembley squad due to injury made Dalglish's selection headache a lot easier and Lawrenson wore the number 2 shirt at Wembley, adding an FA Cup winners' medal to his achievements. Lawrenson had shown remarkable consistency for

Season	League App	League Goals	FA Cup App	FA Cup Goals	League Cup App	League Cup Goals	Europe App	Europe Goals	Other App	Other Goals	Total App	Total Goals
1981/82	37 (2)	2	3	1	10	0	5 (1)	1	1	0	56 (3)	4
1982/83	40	5	3	0	8	2	3	0	1	0	55	7
1983/84	42	0	2	0	12	0	9	0	1	0	66	0
1984/85	33	1	4	0	2	0	10	1	1	0	50	2
1985/86	36 (2)	3	7	1	7	0	-	-	6	1	56 (2)	5
1986/87	35	0	3	0	8	0	-	-	3	0	49	0
1987/88	10 (4)	0	2	0	2 (1)	0	-	-	-	-	14 (5)	0
Total	**233 (8)**	**11**	**24**	**2**	**49 (1)**	**2**	**27 (1)**	**2**	**13**	**1**	**346 (10)**	**18**

Liverpool, having been chosen four seasons running as part of the PFA Team of the Year. He started the 1986/87 season with seemingly several years of good football still ahead of him at the age of 29, but disaster struck against Wimbledon at Anfield on 28 March 1987 when he ruptured his Achilles tendon and was out for five and a half months. 'I remember standing up to test my right foot and felt as though I was standing on a ramp,' Lawrenson recollects. Lawrenson had started nine games in a row in the 1987/88 season when he limped off against Southampton on 12 December 1987. After being out for one month he played 180 minutes in three days and wanted to play against Arsenal on 16 January to complete three full matches in the space of just one week. Lawrenson booted the ball into the stands in the 51st minute against the Gunners, came off and never played again for Liverpool. 'None of the other players in the Liverpool side had any idea how badly I was struggling,' Lawrenson remembers. 'They were playing so well and winning that their performances masked my weaknesses. When

I got back into the team, I found I couldn't turn and run like I used to be able to do. I was just getting by on my positional play and my experience. When Arsenal's Martin Hayes beat me to the ball over 20 yards twice in a minute, I looked at the bench and knew it was time to pack it in. It came as a complete bombshell to Kenny Dalglish. When the surgeon and I told him, he was speechless. My Achilles is two-and-a-half times bigger in my right leg now.'

LAWRENSON quit Liverpool officially in March 1988 and later that week joined Oxford as manager, where he only lasted seven months because he was furious that the club sold top scorer Dean Saunders to Derby. He threatened Robert Maxwell that he would quit and the following day he was sacked! He moved to Tampa Bay in Florida in 1989 where he was a few months as a player-coach. He was hired as manager of Peterborough in the 1989/90 season but lasted only 14 months before he resigned after a row with the chairman over players' appearance money. Lawrenson took out his boots again with amateur teams Corby Town and Chesham United in the early 1990s. He made a short return to the professional game in 1996 when he was appointed defensive coach at Kevin Keegan's Newcastle. He is now a member of BBC's Match of the Day team.

Bob Paisley had nothing but the highest praise for Lawrenson in *Bob Paisley's personal view of the First Team Squad of 1986-87*. 'Every manager values versatility in a player, but most of the game's jack of all trades are masters of none. Mark is a master wherever he plays. Apart from the all-round ability that he possesses, he has a perfect attitude. He is a very intelligent and easy-going individual. He is not an elegant mover, but he is particularly quick. He possesses very long legs and a correspondingly long stride. He doesn't weigh much over 11 stone, but he's a tough and durable customer. You won't see him being barged or knocked off the ball by bigger, bulkier men. He is steely and hardy. But he times a tackle so precisely that very often there is little or no physical contact between him and the opponent in his sights. The ball is nicked off the toe of the attacker as clean as a whistle, almost without him realising it. Indeed, sometimes you see them run on for a stride or two

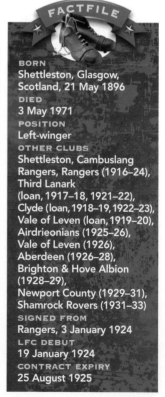

FACTFILE

BORN
Preston, 2 June 1957
POSITION
Centre-half / Left-back / Midfielder
OTHER CLUBS
Preston North End (1971–77), Brighton & Hove Albion (1977–81), Barnet (1988–89), Tampa Bay Rowdies (1989), Corby Town (1991–92), Chesham United (1992–93)
SIGNED FROM
Brighton & Hove Albion, £900,000, August 1981
INTERNATIONAL CAPS
39 Ireland caps (5 goals) (24 (3) at LFC), 1977–87
LFC DEBUT GAME/GOAL
29 August 1981 / 30 September 1981
CONTRACT EXPIRY
March 1988
HONOURS
League Championship 1981/82, 1982/83, 1983/84, 1985/86, 1987/88;
FA Cup 1986;
League Cup 1982, 1983, 1984;
European Cup 1984

as if they've still got it. But, like a thief in the night, Mark has made off with their possession before the alarm can be raised, and they can give chase.'

Lawson,
Hector

Hector Lawson had only made 47 appearances for Rangers in eight years before joining Liverpool in January 1924.

He played 14 games for Liverpool during the 1923/24 season and started his career promisingly, at least according to the *Derby Daily Telegraph*. 'Glasgow Rangers appear to have sent Liverpool a real artiste in Hector Lawson, an outside left who has already made a deep impression in his two games with the ex-champions. Lawson has speed, ball control, and confidence,

and he and Harry Chambers look like becoming a famous wing.' Lawson was only selected twice in 1924/25 and returned to Scotland with Airdrieonians, but never made an appearance for Airdrie as he had developed varicose veins. The blood didn't flow properly through the veins in his legs, causing great pain and skin sores, and he required surgery to strip the swollen areas. The club cancelled his contract and he joined Vale of Leven in March 1926.

Season	League		FA Cup		Total	
	App	Goals	App	Goals	App	Goals
1923/24	10	0	4	0	14	0
1924/25	2	0	0	0	2	0
Total	**12**	**0**	**4**	**0**	**16**	**0**

FACTFILE

BORN
Shettleston, Glasgow, Scotland, 21 May 1896
DIED
3 May 1971
POSITION
Left-winger
OTHER CLUBS
Shettleston, Cambuslang Rangers, Rangers (1916–24), Third Lanark (loan, 1917–18, 1921–22), Clyde (loan, 1918–19, 1922–23), Vale of Leven (loan, 1919–20), Airdrieonians (1925–26), Vale of Leven (1926), Aberdeen (1926–28), Brighton & Hove Albion (1928–29), Newport County (1929–31), Shamrock Rovers (1931–33)
SIGNED FROM
Rangers, 3 January 1924
LFC DEBUT
19 January 1924
CONTRACT EXPIRY
25 August 1925

League Championships

THERE IS GLORY and instant success in winning a cup. But there isn't the satisfaction that comes with being declared champions, of proving yourself to be the best team in the country in front of all the other teams. 'This', said Liverpool manager Bill Shankly as he gently but proudly tapped the famous old trophy presented to Liverpool in 1973, 'is our bread and butter. This is what we want to win all the time.' Shankly was right. If you play home and away to every club in the top division and conquer, that is a very special feeling, one that Liverpool Football Club has known eighteen times between 1901-90.

When the English First Division was founded in 1888, it consisted of a single division of twelve clubs. From 1892, the year Liverpool Football Club was founded, there were two divisions. To win the First Division Championship, as Liverpool did, within ten years of their existence, was a phenomenal achievement, even in a bygone age. The club's early years as a member of the Football League had seen it yo-yo between the top two divisions. Tenth place the year previous gave no hint of what would be achieved under manager Tom Watson in the 1900/01 season. Watson, who had already led Sunderland to the league title three times in the 1890s, masterminded a stunning success that saw his new club pip his old one to the title by two points.

> 'THIS IS OUR BREAD AND BUTTER. THIS IS WHAT WE WANT TO WIN ALL THE TIME'
> **BILL SHANKLY**

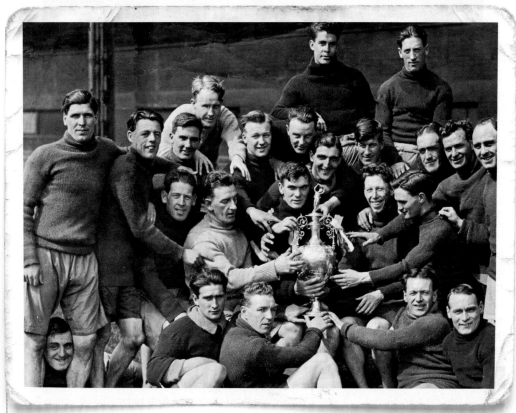

But Liverpool were unable to replicate the success as Sunderland had done a decade earlier and were relegated in 1904 before making an instant return to First Division a year later and then becoming English champions for the second time in 1906. Shortly after competitive football resumed after World War One, David Ashworth was in charge of team affairs and he assembled a strong enough squad to win the First Division in 1922, only three years after taking charge. Only Preston North End, Sunderland, Aston Villa and The Wednesday had previously retained the title and Liverpool were well on the way to becoming the fifth team to accomplish that feat when Ashworth unexpectedly left Liverpool to rejoin Oldham Athletic. Former player Matt McQueen took over as Liverpool manager and steered his team over the line, despite a rocky period at the end of the season when there was only one victory in the final seven league matches.

When Liverpool won their third and fourth title in 1922 and 1923 they still had one title to go before equalling Sunderland's total of five, but Aston Villa was at that point the most successful team in league history with six titles. The Villans hadn't though won since 1910 and wouldn't win their next until 1981.

Two George's, Patterson and Kay, steered the club up to and beyond World War Two and it was the

Liverpool Champions 1923

latter who was in charge when Liverpool won their fifth English title. Liverpool's league season started on 31 August 1946 and the club had to wait until 14 June when Stoke City's defeat at Sheffield United confirmed its title win.

As in 1906 and 1923, the club was unable to build on its success and it was relegated under Don

KODAK FILM

Liverpool Champions 1966

saw his men pip city neighbours Everton to both the First Division title and the FA Cup. Two years later his team made history by winning 22 and drawing 7 of its opening 29 matches before falling to one of only two league defeats that campaign, ironically at Goodison Park. An incredible finish to the next season saw Michael Thomas' late goal rip the trophy from Liverpool's grasp in the final minute of the final match but in 1990 a resilient squad reclaimed top spot and an 18th league title for the club by finishing nine points ahead of second-placed Aston Villa.

SINCE 1990 Liverpool Football Club has failed to add to its eighteen English titles while watching Manchester United equal and then better that total. Second place in 1991, 2002 and 2009 is the best that the club has managed since its last Championship. Hard though it has been to watch a bitter rival dominate, the reality is that the club that finishes first deserves to do so over a long and hard campaign. Eighteen different Liverpool teams of the past have proved that they did have the resilience, discipline, skill and psychology to be better than anyone else.

Welsh in 1954 after a miserable season in which only nine of the 42 league matches were won. It took eight years and another two changes of manager before First Division status was restored under Bill Shankly, the charismatic Scot who had instantly recognised the potential of both the club and its large and loyal fan base. Shrewd purchases of players in key positions and a very settled team saw the 1963/64 Championship clinched with three matches to spare as Arsenal were ripped apart 5-0 at Anfield. The bulk of that squad stayed to reclaim the title two years later, the club's seventh.

If it's hard to get to the top, it is even harder to stay there. Liverpool finished 5th, 3rd, 2nd, 5th, 5th again and 3rd again before Shankly's second great team beat off Arsenal and Leeds United to take the 1973 Championship, a fitting reward for the crushing disappointment of seeing the title ripped from their grasp in the final match of the previous season. Furthermore the club had equalled Arsenal's record of eight Championships. Shankly's was a hard act to follow but his loyal lieutenant, Bob Paisley, did even better and in 1976 he won the first of an astonishing six titles in nine seasons on a dramatic night in Wolverhampton when a flurry of late goals took his team into top place and condemned

Queens Park Rangers to the runners-up spot. Liverpool was finally the most successful club in the history of the English League. To emphasise how difficult the league title was to win at this time, seven different clubs finished runners-up to Liverpool between 1976 and 1984 so the Reds had to fend off so many different challengers whilst still managing to stay at the top of their own game.

KENNY DALGLISH took over from Joe Fagan in the aftermath of Heysel. Already a five-times league winner himself, Dalglish knew exactly what was needed to win the most important prize in English football and a dramatic second half of the 1985/86 season

> LIVERPOOL WAS FINALLY THE MOST SUCCESSFUL CLUB IN THE HISTORY OF THE ENGLISH LEAGUE. TO EMPHASISE HOW DIFFICULT THE LEAGUE TITLE WAS TO WIN AT THIS TIME, SEVEN DIFFERENT CLUBS FINISHED RUNNERS-UP TO LIVERPOOL BETWEEN 1976 AND 1984

Liverpool Champions 1990

League Cup

ALAN HARDAKER became the secretary of the Football League early in 1957. At the same time his counterpart at the Football Association was Sir Stanley Rous. A joint-venture between the two governing bodies in the English game was set up to regenerate interest in the sport, especially as the initial post-World War Two boom in attendances at league matches had gradually declined during the 1950s.

Hardaker encouraged by the early success of the Scottish League Cup then introduced his own version to the English game in 1960. Despite this being a time when British clubs had not started to play regularly in European competitions, which meant that nearly all clubs had few midweek matches, Hardaker's 'baby' was greeted with lukewarm enthusiasm: because participation was not compulsory, many clubs refused to take part in the initial season, 1960/61, and indeed in subsequent seasons. The situation changed for three reasons: a television contract was put in place for the competition's second season which guaranteed extra income; from 1967 the previously two-legged final became a single match at Wembley; and Europe's governing body agreed to allocate a UEFA Cup place to the winners. Stoke City were the first club to benefit from this in 1972.

Liverpool were not one of the absentees in the League Cup's first season but attendances of only 10,000 and 14,000 for the club's first two home matches against Luton Town and Southampton reflected the general lack of interest. The club opted out for the next six years and did not return until the 1967/68 season. With the incentive of a

Wembley final and later a European place for the winners Liverpool would never miss out again.

LONG BEFORE the days of massive squads and player rotation, manager Bill Shankly tended to play his strongest team in the League Cup. That worked until 1970 when, sandwiched between First Division matches against Chelsea and Tottenham Hotspur, Shankly made three changes at Swindon Town from the team that had beaten Chelsea three days earlier. Don Rogers, whose two goals had won the cup for Swindon in 1969, scored twice to dump Liverpool out. Despite this loss, Shankly continued to make changes for League Cup matches during the remaining three years that he was in charge. As did his successor, Bob Paisley, although, initially anyway, he had no more luck in the competition than Shankly. The tide turned in the 1977/78 season when, after never previously reaching the semi-final stage, Paisley took his team all the way to the final at the national stadium, where they would meet First Division newcomers and surprise pace-setters Nottingham Forest. Liverpool were massive favourites because three key Forest players; Peter Shilton, Archie Gemmill and David Needham, could not play in this final because they were cup-tied having played earlier in the competition for other clubs. Maybe this gave the Forest men who did play more belief and determination, especially Shilton's understudy, 19-year-old Chris Woods, who had the game of his life. Former Liverpool player Larry Lloyd played in Needham's place. Forest held out in London and then took the trophy four days later in Manchester after a hugely controversial penalty from John Robertson.

As well as removing Liverpool's hands from the First Division trophy, Forest also eliminated them from the European Cup early in the next season. So a really fierce rivalry had grown up and was festering by the time the two clubs were paired in the semi-final of the League Cup in 1980. Another penalty from Robertson saw Forest take a slender lead from their home leg; and when he added yet another penalty at Anfield the tie was effectively over. So Liverpool's frustration with the League Cup continued but only for a little while longer.

A rule-change prevented Liverpool from severe embarrassment in the season in which they finally put their name on the trophy. The second round stage became a two-legged home-and-away affair. Liverpool's 1-0 defeat at Bradford City would have meant a humiliating exit in earlier years but now they had a second chance at their own stadium, which they took advantage of by four goals to nil. That was the start of a run all the way through to the final, where the soon-to-be-crowned Second Division champions West Ham United were waiting. Once again there was a

controversial goal in a Liverpool League Cup final but this time it was in the Reds' favour. Referee Clive Thomas allowed Alan Kennedy's disputed goal to stand but West Ham equalised with a penalty in the final minute. In the replay at Villa Park eighteen days later Ian Rush made a huge impact on only his second start for the first team. But it was Kenny Dalglish and Alan Hansen who scored the goals that saw the trophy go to Anfield for the first time.

THE REDS won the next three League Cup finals as well, all of which went to extra-time with one going to a replay. Five men; Phil Neal, Alan Kennedy, Kenny Dalglish, Sammy Lee and Ian Rush played in all four victorious finals. Liverpool reached the final again in 1987 but this time lost with Dalglish now the manager. Ian Rush collected a fifth winners' medal in 1995 and the cup as captain, but although the semi-final was reached in 1998, there would not be another final to enjoy until the venue had moved to the Millennium Stadium in Cardiff while Wembley was rebuilt. A nail-biting final in 2001 saw Birmingham City equalise with a penalty in the last minute of normal time. Liverpool took the trophy by winning a penalty shootout 5-4. Two years later bitter rivals Manchester United were beaten in more conventional style with goals from two of the club's brightest young stars, Steven Gerrard and Michael Owen.

The new Wembley Stadium was completed and handed over to the Football Association in March 2007. But it took nearly five years for a Liverpool team to appear there and when the day came, it was equally as dramatic as any of the club's visits to the old Wembley in the 1970s and 1980s. Again, as in 2001, facing a club from a lower division, Liverpool made really hard work of beating Cardiff City and the Reds had to come from behind to take the lead before being pegged back by a late equaliser that would mean another penalty shootout deciding who won the cup. Liverpool missed their first two kicks but Cardiff missed three of their own with Anthony Gerrard's miss meaning that Liverpool took home with them the League Cup for the 8th time in their history.

Alan Hardaker's baby of 1960 was now fully-grown. Hardaker's name is on the trophy that has been presented to the Man of the Match in every League Cup final since 1990. Four Liverpool players appear on that Roll of Honour; Steve McManaman in 1995, Robbie Fowler in 2001, Jerzy Dudek in 2003 and Stewart

Downing in 2012. Liverpool Football Club has won the League Cup eight times, more often than any other club. The League Cup had a difficult birth and childhood but in adulthood it has grown into an essential part of the English football calendar.

> LIVERPOOL FOOTBALL CLUB HAS WON THE LEAGUE CUP EIGHT TIMES, MORE OFTEN THAN ANY OTHER CLUB

Le Tallec,
Anthony

ANTHONY LE TALLEC was an exciting prospect, who had excelled for France at junior level, when he arrived at Liverpool from Le Havre along with his team-mate Florent Sinama Pongolle.

THE HIGHLIGHT of Le Tallec's international career was being voted the second-best player of the Under-17 World Cup which France won in 2001. He possessed good vision and a great range of passing and was a potential superstar in his role just behind the strikers. Le Tallec didn't live up to his promise, however, and his frustration got the better of him at the prospect of limited first-team opportunities at Liverpool. France's Under-21 coach, Raymond Domenech, was displeased with Le Tallec's and Pongolle's progress. 'It is abnormal for boys of their age to play so rarely. When I think their coach is a former coach from the national team! He is not allowed to sign them and not play them. It is a mess.' Le Tallec was sent out on loan in his last few seasons at Liverpool to Saint Etienne, Sunderland, Sochaux and Le Mans. He left Anfield permanently in the summer of 2008 for Le

Mans, where he excelled and earned himself a move to Auxerre in 2010. He made as many substitute appearances as starts, 24 in total, as Auxerre were relegated into the French second division at the end of the 2011/12 season. He started 2012/13 with a bang, clearly way too strong for this level, and moved to Valenciennes in Ligue 1 in September 2012.

LE TALLEC had been excited at the prospect of working with Gérard Houllier, but his move to Liverpool at such a young age stunted his progress, as he explained to *L'Equipe* in 2010: 'Everything started well for me at Liverpool but, unfortunately, the arrival of Rafa Benítez broke my entire career strategy. Even though I was able to get experience, I lost about four years. I arrived at Liverpool as an 18-year-old, but then had to join clubs that were, not weaker, but less rated. It was

strange and sometimes it was difficult. What saved me was my passion for football.'

FACTFILE

BORN
Hennebont, France,
3 October 1984
POSITION
Midfielder
OTHER CLUBS
Le Havre (1995–2003),
Saint Etienne (loan, 2004–05),
Sunderland (loan, 2005–06),
Sochaux (loan, 2006–07),
Le Mans (loan, 2007–08;
permanent, 2008–10),
Auxerre (2010–12),
Valenciennes (2012–)
SIGNED FROM
Le Havre, £1.5million,
1 July 2003
INTERNATIONAL CAPS
14 France U-21 caps (8 goals)
LFC DEBUT GAME/GOAL
13 September 2003 /
15 October 2003
CONTRACT EXPIRY
2 July 2008

Season	League		FA Cup		League Cup		Europe		Other		Total	
	App	Goals	App	Goals	App	Goals	App	Goals	App	Goals	App	Goals
2003/04	3 (10)	0	1 (3)	0	2	0	2 (2)	1	-	-	8 (15)	1
2004/05	2 (2)	0	0	0	0	0	1 (2)	0	-	-	3 (4)	0
2005/06	0	0	0	0	0	0	2	0	0	0	2	0
Total	**5 (12)**	**0**	**1 (3)**	**0**	**2**	**0**	**5 (4)**	**1**	**0**	**0**	**13 (19)**	**1**

Leavey,
Herbert

HERBERT LEAVEY replaced regular centre-forward Jack Parkinson for two games at the end of 1910, the Christmas Eve and Boxing Day fixtures against Aston Villa and Sunderland respectively. Liverpool drew 1-1 with second-placed Villans and lost 2-1 to the Wearsiders who were third.

Tom Watson's men were struggling, only one point off the bottom spot. Liverpool hit a rich vein of form compared to their troubles earlier in the season when Leavey returned to the team for three consecutive games in April 1911. The Reds drew 0-0 with Arsenal and beat Oldham and Bury without conceding a goal, finishing mid-table. Leavey's most productive spell came at Plymouth Argyle in the Southern League where he played 80 games from 1907 to 1910 apart from a four-month spell at Second Division Derby County where he made no appearances before returning to Plymouth.

HE WAS on Barnsley's books when they won the FA Cup in 1912 but missed out on the final

as he broke his leg in the third replay of the quarter-final victory over Bradford City.

Season	League		FA Cup		Total	
	App	Goals	App	Goals	App	Goals
1910/11	5	0	0	0	5	0
Total	5	0	0	0	5	0

Lee,
Sammy

AN ENERGETIC 5ft 4in (162.5cm) midfielder who gained England recognition and was a great servant to the club on and off the pitch, Sammy Lee was immortalised in the song: 'He's fat, he's round, he bounces on the ground.'

It was a loving tribute to the local lad about whom Bob Paisley said, 'With the character and attitude

> 'WITH THE CHARACTER AND ATTITUDE HE SHOWS THEY'D MAKE HIM MAYOR OF LIVERPOOL IF HE WAS A FEW INCHES TALLER'
> BOB PAISLEY

he shows they'd make him Mayor of Liverpool if he was a few inches taller.' Two years after signing a professional contract with Liverpool the 19-year-old made his debut against Leicester in the First Division on 8 April 1978. He came on in the sixth minute for David Johnson, who had torn his knee ligaments. It turned out to be a memorable game for Lee, who scored Liverpool's second goal in a 3-2 win with a fortuitous shot which the Leicester goalkeeper allowed to creep under his body. He only made one more substitute appearance that season and hardly got a chance in the impregnable Liverpool side of 1978/79. An injury to Terry McDermott finally gave him the breakthrough he had been looking for at the end of the 1979/80 season. He featured in all four FA Cup semi-finals against Arsenal that ultimately ended in defeat but played at Anfield when Liverpool clinched the League Championship against Aston Villa. Lee was back in the reserves at the start of 1980/81 season but nine games into the campaign Jimmy Case lost his place on the

wide-right of midfield to the enthusiastic youngster. Liverpool lost the title to Aston Villa but received ample compensation in the knockout competitions. Lee played in the successful League Cup and European Cup finals and his progress in his first full season didn't go unnoticed by Reds' fans as he was the overwhelming winner in Liverpool Supporters Club's Player of the Year poll.

LEE WON three successive League Championships during the next three years, culminating in the glorious 1983/84 season when he played every single game, 67 in total. After the heady achievements of 1984, Lee's form dipped from its usual high standards and he was called on only rarely during the second half of the 1984/85 season, with Craig Johnston and Kevin MacDonald both preferred in his role. He was also in and out of the team in the double season and he agreed to join Queens Park Rangers in the summer of 1986. He left with the best wishes of his team-mates as he had been a big part of the great camaraderie in the Liverpool

dressing room. He has a bubbly personality and is never lost for words, as proven when he created the biggest laugh on-board the plane that carried Liverpool and Everton back home from their 1986 FA Cup final at Wembley where the Reds won the Cup after taking the League Championship from Everton a week earlier. 'During the flight, there was a light-hearted disagreement between the players about the amount of room on the plane,' Jan Mølby remembers. '"Move your fat arse," Everton full-back Pat Van Den Hauwe shouted at little Sammy Lee. "Sorry," replied Sammy, "but what do you expect? I've got two medals in my pocket!"' Lee only had a year in London before seeking a change of fortune in the Spanish first division with Osasuna, where he stayed two years before joining Southampton and then Bolton.

Lee returned to Liverpool as Phil Thompson's replacement as reserve-team coach in 1993. With Houllier's arrival in 1998 Lee moved up to first-team trainer. Following Houllier's dismissal and Benítez's arrival in the summer of 2004 Lee felt a clean break was best for all concerned and he joined England's coaching staff full-time. In June 2005 he joined Bolton as assistant manager to Sam Allardyce and continued coaching the England team on part-time basis.

HE TURNED DOWN the full-time England Under-21 job in 2006 to concentrate on Bolton and took over as the club's manager when Allardyce resigned in April 2007. However, Lee only lasted 14 games in the job after results were well below expectations. Reds rejoiced when Lee returned home to Liverpool once more in May 2008 as Benítez's assistant manager. He survived the managerial changes that saw Hodgson replace Benítez and Dalglish replace Hodgson. However, as pre-season training began ahead of the 2011/12 season, it was announced that Lee would be leaving the club, despite Dalglish saying as recently as May 2011 that Lee was 'a key part of his team'. In February 2012 Lee returned to Bolton as head of coaching at the club's academy.

> 'HE ALWAYS
> APOLOGISED
> FOR ALMOST
> ANYTHING HE DID.
> HE IS A LOVELY
> NATURED PERSON.
> I LOVE HIM TO BITS'
>
> **PHIL NEAL**

'If they are to get into the top three every side needs its hard-working bees. And Sammy was one of those bees,' Phil Neal said. 'He played just in front of me and we formed a really good partnership. I remember Bob Paisley telling him to mark Paul Breitner when we played in the

FACTFILE

BORN
Liverpool, 7 February 1959
POSITION
Midfielder
OTHER CLUBS
Queens Park Rangers (1986–87), Osasuna (1987–90), Southampton (1990), Bolton Wanderers (1990–91)
JOINED
1972; signed professional April 1976
INTERNATIONAL CAPS
14 England caps (2 goals), 1982–84
LFC DEBUT GAME/GOAL
8 April 1978 / 8 April 1978
CONTRACT EXPIRY
August 1986
HONOURS
League Championship 1981/82, 1982/83, 1983/84, 1985/86; League Cup 1981, 1982, 1983, 1984; European Cup 1981, 1984

Munich Stadium and Sammy did a magnificent job. He was always the one who started the singing after we had picked up a trophy – all the old Liverpool songs. We had some great sing-a-longs. He created a really joyous arena. But he was always a very apologetic person. He always apologised for almost anything he did. He is a lovely natured person. I love him to bits.'

Season	League		FA Cup		League Cup		Europe		Other		Total	
	App	Goals	App	Goals	App	Goals	App	Goals	App	Goals	App	Goals
1977/78	0 (2)	1	0	0	0	0	0	0	0	0	0 (2)	1
1978/79	1 (1)	0	0	0	0	0	0	0	-	-	1 (1)	0
1979/80	6 (1)	0	4	0	0	0	0	0	0	0	10 (1)	0
1980/81	37	4	2	0	7	2	9	2	0	0	55	8
1981/82	35	3	2	0	6	0	5	1	1	0	49	4
1982/83	40	3	3	0	8	0	6	0	1	0	58	3
1983/84	42	2	2	0	13	0	9	1	1	0	67	3
1984/85	16 (1)	0	1	0	2	0	4	0	1	0	24 (1)	0
1985/86	13 (2)	0	3	0	3	0	-	-	5	0	24 (2)	0
Total	**190 (7)**	**13**	**17**	**0**	**39**	**2**	**33**	**4**	**9**	**0**	**288 (7)**	**19**

Leishman,
Tommy

TOUGH-GUY Tommy Leishman excelled in the Second Division but was surplus to requirements when Liverpool made the step up to top-flight football.

LEISHMAN was a Scottish left-half who arrived at Anfield as a 22-year-old from St Mirren in November 1959. He figured in 15 of the last 19 league matches of the 1959/60 season and became a regular member of the side for the next two years, missing only three league fixtures during that period. He was a vital part in Shankly's 3-3-4 master plan implemented in the 1960/61 season after a terrible start to the campaign. The manager moved inside-left Jimmy Harrower back as a semi-half-back thus

drawing his opposing half-back out of place and from his position, playing either Leishman or Johnny Wheeler who moved forward supplying the drive and support which the forward line so badly needed. Liverpool won the Second Division title in a season during which, according to

Shankly, 'Tommy Leishman had settled down and having mellowed in his game was playing extremely well.' Leishman proved inadequate for the top flight and was soon replaced by his compatriot Willie Stevenson.

FACTFILE

BORN
Stenhousemuir, Scotland,
3 September 1937
POSITION
Left-half
OTHER CLUBS
St Mirren (1953–59),
Hibernian (1963–65),
Linfield (1965–68),
Stranraer (1968–70)
SIGNED FROM
St Mirren, £10,000,
20 November 1959
LFC DEBUT GAME/GOAL
28 December 1959 /
24 August 1960
CONTRACT EXPIRY
January 1963
HONOURS
Second Division 1961/62

Season	League		FA Cup		League Cup		Total	
	App	Goals	App	Goals	App	Goals	App	Goals
1959/60	15	0	2	0	-	-	17	0
1960/61	40	4	2	0	2	1	44	5
1961/62	41	1	5	0	-	-	46	1
1962/63	11	1	0	0	-	-	11	1
Total	**107**	**6**	**9**	**0**	**2**	**1**	**118**	**7**

Leiva,
Lucas

LUCAS LEIVA is a hard-working box-to-box player who was captain of the Brazilian Under-20 team. In October 2005 he made his debut for Gremio in the Brazilian second division. Gremio were promoted and in Lucas' first season in the top flight in 2006, when his club finished third, he became the youngest ever player to receive Placar magazine's Bola de Ouro (Golden Ball), given to the best player in the Brazilian league, an honour previously won by the likes of Zico, Falcao, Careca, Romario, Kaka and Tevez.

Just before joining Liverpool in May 2007, Lucas went all the way to the two-legged final in the Copa Libertadores where Boca Juniors outplayed the Brazilian team, winning 5-0 on aggregate.

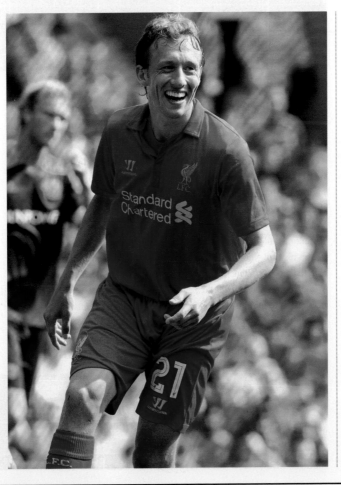

LUCAS TOOK part in 32 competitive matches during his first season in English football. His highlight of the season came when he thundered an equalising goal into the top corner after non-league Havant & Waterlooville had taken a shock early lead in the FA Cup at Anfield in January 2008. Lucas was capped by his country for the first time in August 2007 and played for the Brazil Olympic team in Beijing 2008 that finished third. He was one of two Brazil players who were sent off in the semi-final defeat to Argentina. Alonso and Mascherano continued to be the preferred choice in midfield by Rafa Benítez in the 2008/09 season and Lucas only twice made the starting line-up. He showed his inexperience when he was sent off after 75 minutes for a second booking when he brought down Joleon Lescott against Everton at Goodison Park in a FA Cup fourth round replay.

Following Alonso's move to Real, Lucas featured more than ever before and only Reina, Carragher and Kuyt played in more first-team matches than the previously much-maligned Lucas in 2009/10. Scapegoat for many a poor team performance in the past, the young Brazilian, who turned 23 during the season, won over huge sections of the fan base with assured displays that made him probably the most improved player of any of the first-team squad. Lucas hardly put a foot wrong and was the fourth-most prolific tackler in the Premier League.

At the end of March 2011 the Brazilian signed a new long-term deal that tied him to the club until 2015. His future at Liverpool didn't look bright a couple of years back, even shamefully being booed by his own fans. He admitted to the *Guardian* in March 2011 that he needed some time to settle in. 'Things were not looking good and some supporters were obviously not happy. The move to Liverpool represented a change of country, language and there was also the not so small detail that I was only 20 and arriving at a traditional club in one of the most demanding leagues in the world. Maybe the supporters thought a Brazilian midfielder would do magic. In Gremio I had carte blanche to go forward and participate more in the attacking plays. But things had to change when I arrived in Liverpool, where I am used much more as a holding midfielder.'

MASCHERANO left early in the 2010/11 season and fans wondered if Lucas was ready to take over his mantle. Few could contest that Lucas has developed into an equally strong player as the Argentinian and, crucially, more composed on the field. Lucas was voted Standard Chartered's Player of the Season in 2010/11 as he became one of Liverpool's key players, having made steady progress in the sometimes unforgiving Anfield spotlight. His 2011/12 season came to a shuddering halt when he was stretchered off the Stamford Bridge pitch during the League Cup quarter-final at the end of November, after damaging the anterior cruciate ligament in his left knee. His absence was more keenly felt than anyone else's and Liverpool's midfield fell apart without him in the second half of the campaign when the club lost 11 out of 19 league games. Lucas returned in August 2012, but suffered another setback when he injured his thigh in the warm-up when champions Manchester City visited Anfield. Lucas said he would shake the injury off, but he only lasted five minutes before he was replaced by Jonjo Shelvey. He was sidelined until 1 December and has been getting his match fitness back to normal levels following such a lengthy absence.

FACTFILE

BORN
Dourados, Brazil,
9 January 1987
POSITION
Midfielder
OTHER CLUBS
Gremio (2004–07)
SIGNED FROM
Gremio, £5million,
11 May 2007
INTERNATIONAL CAPS
20 Brazil caps, 2007–
LFC DEBUT GAME/GOAL
28 August 2007 /
26 January 2008

Season	League		FA Cup		League Cup		Europe		Total	
	App	Goals	App	Goals	App	Goals	App	Goals	App	Goals
2007/08	12 (6)	0	3 (1)	1	3	0	2 (5)	0	20 (12)	1
2008/09	13 (12)	1	1 (1)	0	2	1	4 (6)	1	20 (19)	3
2009/10	32 (3)	0	2	0	0	0	12 (1)	1	46 (4)	1
2010/11	32 (1)	0	1	0	1	0	9 (3)	1	43 (4)	1
2011/12	12	0	0	0	3	0	-	-	15	0
2012/13	24 (2)	0	1	0	0	0	2 (2)	0	27 (4)	0
Total	**125 (24)**	**1**	**8 (2)**	**1**	**9**	**1**	**29 (17)**	**3**	**171 (43)**	**6**

Leonhardsen, Øyvind

'I SUPPORTED LIVERPOOL AS A KID. WE SAW ENGLISH GAMES ON NORWEGIAN TV EVERY WEEK, AND LIVERPOOL WERE ALWAYS ON BECAUSE THEY WERE THE BEST'

AFTER Øyvind Leonhardsen was voted the Player's Player of the Year in 1994 while at Rosenborg he moved to Wimbledon, where he impressed during his two-and-a-half years' stay and was twice voted the club's Player of the Year.

Fiorentina and Newcastle were hot on his trail when Leonhardsen rejected a new contract offer from Wimbledon. He needed little persuasion to join his boyhood idols in the summer of 1997. It made the transition easier that he joined fellow Norwegian internationals Stig Inge Bjørnebye and Bjørn Tore Kvarme at Liverpool, especially as they had also been his team-mates at Rosenborg. Leonhardsen was delighted: 'I supported Liverpool as a kid. We saw English games on Norwegian TV every week, and Liverpool were always on because they were the best. My heroes were Kevin Keegan and later Kenny Dalglish. I had Liverpool posters on my bedroom wall.' Roy Evans liked Norwegians because of their work ethic. 'The Scandinavian players in the Premiership often don't have a great deal of flair but Øyvind probably has the most.' Leonhardsen was an industrious midfielder with an eye for a goal,

Season	League		FA Cup		League Cup		Europe		Total	
	App	Goals	App	Goals	App	Goals	App	Goals	App	Goals
1997/98	27 (1)	6	1	0	3 (2)	0	2	0	33 (3)	6
1998/99	7 (2)	1	0	0	1	0	1 (2)	0	9 (4)	1
Total	**34 (3)**	**7**	**1**	**0**	**4 (2)**	**0**	**3 (2)**	**0**	**42 (7)**	**7**

as proved in his first season at the club when he scored six goals in 36 matches. He wasn't, though, first choice when his second season started once Gérard Houllier had moved in by Evans' side, and he only played regularly at the end of the season. He didn't convince Houllier that he would be of any value to his side and he sold him to George Graham's Tottenham. He stayed at Spurs for three years where he played 72 games and scored 11 goals, but was frozen out of the first team following Glenn Hoddle's arrival prior to the 2001/02 season. 'Leo' moved to Aston Villa on a free in 2002 but only lasted a year there before he moved back to Norway. A year later Leonhardsen joined Strømsgodset where he won the Norwegian first division. He retired in 2007 at the age of 37.

FACTFILE

BORN
Kristiansund, Norway,
17 August 1970
POSITION
Midfielder
OTHER CLUBS
Clausenengen (1987–88),
Molde (1989–91),
Rosenborg (1992–94),
Wimbledon (1994–97),
Tottenham Hotspur
(1999–2002),
Aston Villa (2002–03),
Lyn (2004),
Strømsgodset (2005–07)
SIGNED FROM
Wimbledon, £3.5million,
2 June 1997
INTERNATIONAL CAPS
86 Norway caps (19 goals)
(10 (2) at LFC), 1990–2003
LFC DEBUT GAME/GOAL
15 October 1997 / 25
October 1997
CONTRACT EXPIRY
6 August 1999

Lester, Hugh

A NOTED AMATEUR SPRINTER WITH A TIME OF 10.5 SECONDS FOR THE 100 YARDS

AMERICAN-BORN Hugh Lester was a noted amateur sprinter with a time of 10.5 seconds for the 100 yards. He only played twice for Liverpool's first team as an outside-left, or what is now called a left-winger.

When at Oldham he was moved to full-back. He utilised his speed to go up-field but his final touch on the ball was said to lack heartiness. Lester returned to the USA in the 1920s.

	League		FA Cup		Total	
Season	App	Goals	App	Goals	App	Goals
1911/12	1	0	0	0	1	0
1912/13	1	0	0	0	1	0
Total	2	0	0	0	2	0

FACTFILE

BORN
Lehigh, Iowa, USA 1891
POSITION
Left-winger
OTHER CLUBS
Earlestown,
St Helens Recreation (1911),
Oldham Athletic (1913–19),
Reading (1919–20)
JOINED
Unaffiliated, December 1911
LFC DEBUT
8 April 1912
CONTRACT EXPIRY
May 1913

Leto, Sebastian

ATTACKING midfielder Sebastian Leto was sold to Liverpool in the January transfer window in 2007, but played on at Argentinian club Lanús until he officially joined Liverpool on 1 July.

The young Argentinian appeared in four competitive matches in Liverpool's first team during the 2007/08 season. His debut came in the away leg of the Champions League qualifier in Toulouse and a month later he played the full 90 minutes of the League Cup win at Reading. He also featured from the start against Cardiff in the League Cup and Marseille in the Champions League but was substituted on both occasions. Liverpool were denied a work permit for him in the summer of 2008 and he agreed to a two-year loan at Greek side Olympiacos. Halfway through his loan period there was interest from another Athens club in Panathinaikos. This led to the player making a permanent move away from Liverpool on 1 July 2009, with the fee believed to be around £3million. That was good business for Liverpool as Leto had cost them less than £2million two years earlier.

LETO, who made no impact in England, became an instant hero in Greece when he scored the winning goal in the 2010 cup final for Panathinaikos against Aris Thessaloniki. His club also won the Greek Championship.

THIS WAS the second time that Leto had been part of a club that won the Greek League and Cup double because he had achieved the same feat when on loan from Liverpool at Olympiacos in 2009. After two average seasons for Panathinaikos he excelled in the 2011/12 season and scored no fewer than 15 goals in 17 league matches. At the height of his powers he injured his knee in January 2012, and 12 months later terminated his contract with Panathinaikos after he had still not recovered from his injury. A statement released by Panathinaikos said: 'Seba's talent, his contribution to the team, his passion and the bond he formed with the fans has earned him a special place in the history and the heart of the club.' In April 2013 Serie A side, Catania, signed the Argentinian, who is trying to resurrect his career.

FACTFILE

BORN
Alejandro Korn, Argentina,
30 August 1986
POSITION
Midfielder
OTHER CLUBS
Lanús (2005–07),
Olympiacos (loan, 2008–09),
Panathinaikos (2009–13)
Catania (2013–)
SIGNED FROM
Lanús, £1.8million,
1 July 2007
LFC DEBUT
28 August 2007
CONTRACT EXPIRY
1 July 2009

Season	League		FA Cup		League Cup		Europe		Total	
	App	Goals	App	Goals	App	Goals	App	Goals	App	Goals
2007/08	0	0	0	0	2	0	2	0	4	0
Total	0	0	0	0	2	0	2	0	4	0

Lewis,
Harry

SEVENTEEN-YEAR-OLD Harry Lewis created a stir in 1914 for Birkenhead Old Boys in the Merseyside Amateur League when he scored 101 goals of the club's total of 228, including friendlies, in just one season.

LEWIS SCORED 57 goals in 101 wartime marches for Liverpool from 1916 to 1919 before making his proper first-team debut on the opening day of the 1919/20 season. He scored the first of Liverpool's goals in a 3-1 victory away to Bradford City, but also missed a penalty. He scored nine times that season, which turned out to be his best for the club. 'Lewis is not a big chap, but he is skilful in his purveying of the ball, attends to the needs of his wing-man as a mother to her child, but often asserts his individuality in front of goal,'

was a contemporary description of his qualities. Over the next two campaigns he made a further 42 first-team appearances, but his knack of getting the odd goal seemed to have deserted him as he only added three goals to his total of 12. The club programme complained in September 1920 that 'those left-footed drives which were once a feature of his work seem to have vanished'. He did contribute though to Liverpool's Championship win in 1921/22 but missed the 1922/23 league title win due to illness and a subsequent failure to win his place

back. In his absence Harry Chambers and Dick Forshaw had firmly established themselves as inside-forwards and, with Jimmy Walsh as the new centre, Lewis was allowed to leave for Second Division Hull in October 1923.

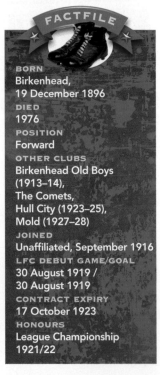

FACTFILE

BORN
Birkenhead,
19 December 1896
DIED
1976
POSITION
Forward
OTHER CLUBS
Birkenhead Old Boys
(1913–14),
The Comets,
Hull City (1923–25),
Mold (1927–28)
JOINED
Unaffiliated, September 1916
LFC DEBUT GAME/GOAL
30 August 1919 /
30 August 1919
CONTRACT EXPIRY
17 October 1923
HONOURS
League Championship
1921/22

Season	League		FA Cup		Other		Total	
	App	Goals	App	Goals	App	Goals	App	Goals
1919/20	23	7	5	2	-	-	28	9
1920/21	17	2	3	0	-	-	20	2
1921/22	19	1	3	0	0	0	22	1
Total	59	10	11	2	0	0	70	12

Lewis,
Kevin

KEVIN LEWIS' timing couldn't have been worse when trying making a name for himself on the wing at Liverpool with the continuous rise of one Ian Callaghan. Born in Ellesmere Port, Lewis returned to the Northwest to play for Liverpool after 23 goals in 62 Second Division appearances for his first club, Sheffield United.

The England youth international became one of Bill Shankly's earliest signings in June 1960. Lewis kept Callaghan out of the side at first, scoring 22 goals in 36 games in his first season, outscoring Roger Hunt by three. Although he started the next season as the team's right-winger, he was displaced by Callaghan. He did find his way back into the side in April, deputising for Ian St John. A win over Southampton was required to secure promotion from the Second Division and Lewis scored both Liverpool's goals in one of the most legendary games in the club's history. He found a way back into the side in 1962/63 after switching to the left, taking over from the fading Alan A'Court. Lewis kept up his average of one goal every two games in his Liverpool career. He had a rocket of a shot and among local fans they were called 'Lewis Expresses'. Once Peter Thompson was purchased from Preston North End in the summer of 1963, however, Lewis' Anfield days were numbered. He returned to Yorkshire in August 1963 but after 45 games and 13 goals in the Second Division with Huddersfield he exited the Football League scene at the very early age of 24. He played football in South Africa, where he settled after a knee injury finished his career at the premature age of 28.

Life could have been very different for Lewis if Shankly hadn't convinced him not to go into the clothing business with fellow Liverpool striker Dave Hickson. The *Liverpool Echo* reported on 3 May 1961:

Two famous players who cost Liverpool more than £20,000 in transfer fees have told the club they are quitting football and taking jobs outside the game. They are centre-forward Dave Hickson, an Ellesmere Port boy who became one of the game's stormy petrels, and Kevin Lewis who learned his football at his native Ellesmere Port and made good with Sheffield United. Hickson has been working for some time with a Liverpool clothing firm and this shock move may well mean a partnership between him and Lewis in the South of England as an extension of the firm's interests there. Shankly said: 'Hickson and Lewis came to see me about this matter a few days ago. The Board were informed of their intention to leave football and to go into industry. There is nothing we can do. I'm sorry Lewis is taking this step because he is such a fine young player, and he is only 20. He has yet to come to his best as a player and his future was very bright.'

SHANKLY evidently blamed Hickson for trying to drive the impressionable Lewis away from football and sold him a couple of months later but kept Lewis, offering him the highest-possible wage available to Liverpool's first-team players at the time.

FACTFILE

BORN
Ellesmere Port, 19 September 1940
POSITION
Winger
OTHER CLUBS
Sheffield United (1955–60), Huddersfield Town (1963–65), Port Elizabeth City (1965–68)
SIGNED FROM
Sheffield United, £13,000, 16 June 1960
LFC DEBUT GAME/GOAL
20 August 1960 / 20 August 1960
CONTRACT EXPIRY
August 1963
HONOURS
Second Division 1961/62

Season	League		FA Cup		League Cup		Total	
	App	Goals	App	Goals	App	Goals	App	Goals
1960/61	32	19	2	1	2	2	36	22
1961/62	21	10	0	0	-	-	21	10
1962/63	19	10	6	2	-	-	25	12
Total	**72**	**39**	**8**	**3**	**2**	**2**	**82**	**44**

Liddell,
Billy

WILLIAM Beveridge Liddell started his career with local teams Kingseat Juveniles and Lochgelly Violet. 'King Billy' came first to Liverpool in July 1938 and signed a professional contract nine months later. Had it not been for a certain Sir Matt Busby, Liverpool's former captain and later Manchester United's manager, Liddell might never have been a Liverpool player. Busby found out that representatives of Manchester City had been to see Billy's parents with a view to getting their son to join the club. After learning that Billy had turned down the invitation to go to City, Busby rang Liverpool manager George Kay and suggested that 'this Liddell lad might be worth an enquiry'.

Liddell spoke about the start of his Reds career in his autobiography.

BILLY LIDDELL
Liverpool and Scotland

The turning point of my young life came after I had been to a Youth Club dance one Saturday night. On returning home shortly before midnight I was surprised to see a light in the living-room. Normally my parents were in bed soon after ten o'clock. Both mother and father were still up and dressed, and were obviously not there to tick me off for being out so late. There was clearly something in the wind, though what it was I couldn't imagine. Certainly I was not prepared for the words which came immediately I had answered their questions about the dance. Mother could not keep silent longer. Neither could she prepare me gradually for the shock to come. Right out without any preliminaries, she asked: 'Willie, how would you like to live in Liverpool?' I could only stand and stare. Football at that moment was far from my thoughts and Liverpool had never been in them at all. When I found words at last all I could say was: 'What on earth do you mean?' Then it came out bit by bit, and as it did I realized that, at the age of sixteen-and-a-half, I was at an important crossroads in my young life.

BEFORE LIDDELL moved south, he was hired as an accountant at Simon Jude & West in Liverpool. His parents had it put into the contract that Billy would be allowed to work there because they wanted him to have something to fall back on if things didn't work out. Liddell trained full-time in pre-season, but only twice a week once the season started, the only Liverpool player who held two jobs. But, he had hardly settled in when World War Two broke out, so Liddell had to wait six years to make his formal debut. Billy enlisted in the RAF and was sent to a training camp in Cambridge and later on to Manitoba in Canada.

Like many professional footballers, Billy tried to play as many games during the war as possible, as Phyllis Liddell, Billy's wife of 55 years,

noted: 'When he was in Canada he went under an assumed name, Bill Tanner, to play. He was just standing on the sidelines watching this match involving a team of Scottish ex-pats called Toronto Scottish. Billy told them he was Scottish, although he didn't tell them he played for Liverpool, and they asked him if he would like a game the next day. He turned up and came on as a substitute. Within ten minutes he'd scored two goals and the other team were asking him if he wanted a rest. He really was football mad!' Liddell finally played his first game for Liverpool on New Year's Day 1940, in a 7-3 win over Crewe. He was said to have given a 'most promising display, his ball control and sense of positioning being features'. Liddell made his amateur international debut against England at Hampden Park on 18 April 1942, four years before making his official debut for Liverpool. Among his team-mates were Bill Shankly and Matt Busby, but it was the young Billy who captured everyone's imagination. 'Maestro Liddell. Ten minutes was sufficient for this boy to play himself into these critical, hard-beating Hampden hearts,' said a press reporter. 'He took the equalizer with a lovely timed header. But it was the way he had in the second goal which put him in the Maestro class. Liddell did the spadework and Dodds did the finishing for what must be one of the greatest goals Hampden has ever seen. The outstripping of the defence, the quick pass with the "wrong" foot, and then Dodds' glorious first-timer. What a goal!' Scotland ran out 5-4 winners. Liddell made 152 appearances in wartime football for Liverpool and scored 82 goals. As early as 1940 a press headline read: 'Liddell is war's best find.'

Liverpool's future talisman played his first official game for the club in the FA Cup against Chester at Anfield on 5 January 1946, Liddell scoring one goal in a 2-0 win. The league competition started in the autumn, but he missed pre-season because he was still in the RAF. Liverpool had already played two games when Liddell made his league debut in a 7-4 win over Chelsea. He scored two goals, the first of which came straight from a corner kick in front of the Kop in the third minute. Despite the 24-year-old left-winger never having turned out in the league previously for Liverpool, he was already viewed as a key player for the side, evident by 'Bee' Edwards' report for the *Liverpool Daily Post*. 'Liddell like Fagan is still not his fittest, and I believe this condition led Chelsea to their great chance in the later stages. Liddell means so much to his side.' In the first post-war season Billy scored seven goals in 34 league games and Liverpool celebrated their fifth league title. But the club couldn't repeat their triumph despite Liddell's brilliance. He twice represented Great Britain against Europe, in 1947 and then in 1955 when Liverpool were playing in the Second Division, which goes to show how highly rated he was. Only Billy and Sir Stanley Matthews were chosen to play both games. Liddell was disappointed to miss out on the FA Cup after being kicked from pillar to post in the 1950 final defeat against Arsenal. He was especially painfully fouled by the Arsenal right-half, fellow Scotsman Alex Forbes. 'I couldn't put my jacket on the next day,' Liddell recalled. A couple of months later he was tempted by two offers from Colombian club Santa Fe in Bogota but refused its agent's advances, claiming 'the disadvantage of leaving home, family and friends outweigh the financial benefits. All my interests are here at Anfield, and I should hate to leave.' Nobody could have blamed him for abandoning ship when after promising seasons that always ended up in mid-table Liverpool were relegated in 1954. Liddell had established himself as

Liverpool's greatest star, the club's top scorer four seasons out of eight in the top flight, but there was only so much one man could do.

Goalkeepers, footballs and goal-nets: none were safe from the power in Liddell's boots. The *Liverpool Echo* reported on Liddell's hat-trick against Tottenham on 1 December 1951: 'Liddell was there at centre-forward again to crack home another cannon round in the 17th minute. This time the goalkeeper was not within close proximity and the net caught another full-blooded shot. This time the referee took a close inspection of the net as it appeared to be ripped off the hooks behind the bar.' Liddell scored the winner after 70 minutes from the spot. 'Liddell took the kick himself and recorded his hat-trick with a shot that Ditchburn could only watch go speeding into the net, at the pace of a bullet. He could have dived and tried to save the shot, but chose to stand still and avoid any injury. At this point you must ask yourself the question, would you get in the way of a Liddell penalty?' Harry Nicholson, Nottingham Forest's keeper, made the

Season	League		FA Cup		Other		Total	
	App	Goals	App	Goals	App	Goals	App	Goals
1945/46	-	-	2	1	-	-	2	1
1946/47	34	7	6	1	-	-	40	8
1947/48	37	10	2	1	-	-	39	11
1948/49	38	8	4	1	-	-	42	9
1949/50	41	17	7	2	-	-	48	19
1950/51	35	15	1	0	-	-	36	15
1951/52	40	19	3	0	-	-	43	19
1952/53	39	13	1	0	-	-	40	13
1953/54	36	7	1	0	-	-	37	7
1954/55	40	30	4	1	-	-	44	31
1955/56	39	27	5	5	-	-	44	32
1956/57	41	21	1	0	-	-	42	21
1957/58	35	22	5	1	-	-	40	23
1958/59	19	14	0	0	-	-	19	14
1959/60	17	5	0	0	-	-	17	5
1960/61	1	0	0	0	0	0	1	0
Total	**492**	**215**	**42**	**13**	**0**	**0**	**534**	**228**

mistake of stopping a Liddell shot. 'From the free kick Liddell hit the keeper with a pile driver and it went over the bar off the keeper's outstretched arm; little did we know at the time but it had fractured Nicholson's right arm.' The *Echo* reporters were privileged to witness the phenomenon of King Billy as in this instance in September 1954: 'When the ball came out of the crowd the referee's attention was drawn to some defect in the ball. Seemingly Billy had burst the ball with his head, so the ref had to call for a new ball. I know I have written many things over the years watching football, but never have I seen a ball burst with the power of a header. Liddell was known for bursting balls with both his right and left feet, but with his head? I guess that's just another bit of footballing history from Liddell, that will eventually have people in the future doubting the power of this man.'

LIDDELL had a number of admirers but felt at home at Liverpool. He was moved to centre-forward and made captain in the 1955/56 season. Goals came easy to him and he scored 114 in five seasons in the Second Division. All careers must to come to an end, however, even Billy Liddell's. At the start of the 1958/59 season Liddell was relieved of the captaincy and on 18 October 1958 he was dropped by Liverpool for the first time in his career against Fulham at Craven Cottage. This was unheard of and created much anger among Liverpool's followers and the press. David Jack at the *Liverpool Echo* made a beeline for Anfield to talk to Liddell himself and the man responsible for this outrage, manager Phil Taylor. Jack pulled no punches and asked Liddell: 'Are you on the way out? Have you seen the red light? Are you thinking of retiring?' Jack reported that 'Gentleman Bill was equally frank, with a firm "No" to each question. When I told manager Phil Taylor that

I intended to write about his star footballer the air could have been cut with a knife. And although I see no reason why a player's relegation should be akin to a keg of dynamite, I respect Mr Taylor's request not to use a single quote from him about Billy Liddell.' Arsenal legend Joe Mercer, who was by then Aston Villa's manager, made a move for the 36-year-old, offering him a chance to return to the First Division in December 1958. 'He'll get goals any time. He's a goal-getter. He always was and will be,' said Mercer at the time. 'Not for £100,000,' said veteran Liverpool president T.V. Williams, adding with foresight, 'There will never be another like him.'

> 'HE IS ONE OF THE GREATEST CLUB MEN EVER TO HAVE PLAYED FOOTBALL'
> **DONALD MACKINLAY**

LIDDELL retired at 39 years of age as the Shankly revolution was about to start. Shankly did enjoy the powers of his compatriot on occasions and certainly wished that Liddell had been 20 years younger. 'Liddell was some player... He had everything,' Shankly enthused. 'He was fast, powerful, shot with either foot and his headers were like blasts from a gun. On top of all that he was as hard as granite. What a player! He was so strong – and he took a nineteen-inch collar shirt!' It was no coincidence that Liverpool became to be known as 'Liddellpool'. Ian Callaghan considers Billy, Kenny Dalglish and Steven Gerrard as Liverpool Football Club's finest and there's no reason to argue with Cally. 'Billy was my idol when I was at school and it was fantastic to take over from him,' Callaghan said. 'I had so much respect for him. **GREAT MAN** – he was a god in

Liverpool. I took over from him on the wing and he finished playing not long after that. When I went to my first professional football match it was Liverpool. When Billy got the ball the anticipation from the crowd was just huge. What is he going to do with it? Is he going to shoot from 30 yards or take it past people? He was wonderful. Billy played with a heavy ball on the heavy pitches. The way he used to kick the ball, wow!'

On 31 August 1960 Liddell made his final appearance for Liverpool in a 1-0 defeat to Southampton in the Second Division. No other player had made more appearances for the club than Billy, his total of 534 eclipsing Elisha Scott's record of 468. Three weeks later Liddell's testimonial took place against an International XI which included several greats such as Bert Trautmann (Manchester City), Stanley Matthews (Blackpool), Nat Lofthouse (Bolton) and Tom Finney (Preston North End). Liverpool won 4-2 with Liddell scoring for the opposition and netting £6,000, with which he bought a house. On the eve of his testimonial Billy revealed once more his affection for his club and the city it was based in. 'It has often been said that there is no sentiment in football, but I believe that my career, at least, has proved that wrong. Every Scot is proud of his heritage, but I am equally proud to know that in the city of my adoption I am accepted as a fellow-Liverpudlian. It hardly seems 22 years since I was being warned about the "terrible" city which has meant so much to me. I cannot recall who said that a city is not just bricks and mortar and fine buildings, it is the people in it, but it expresses what I think. I would like to take the opportunity of thanking the much-maligned Liverpool supporters for the encouragement they have given to me. I have always been happy at Anfield for I know we have the staunchest bunch of supporters in the land.'

EVEN BEFORE the end of his footballing career Billy became a Justice of the Peace in Liverpool, in 1958. He came off the bench in 1992. When he shelved his boots Billy joined the Guild of Students as Deputy Permanent Secretary and Bursar at the University of Liverpool, a post he held until 1984. 'Maccakhan', who was Billy's neighbour for many years, has only good things to say about him.

'I remember speaking to him and his wife, who introduced him to me as a retired accountant! I looked at her in amazement! This was Billy Liddell, not some accountant! I remember Billy looking at me and he gave me a wink and a smile, he could see my amazement at him being described as a retired accountant and my reaction to it. A really lovely fella and a true gentleman.' In his role as a magistrate Billy encountered many of his fans, as he admitted: 'I've been recognised a few times. Once a street seller who traded without a licence shouted hello to me as I walked past and said, "Billy, I was up before you last week!"'

'What can you say about him? Liverpool have had some good club players, but I think he is the finest in their history,' said Donald Mackinlay, Liverpool's captain from the 1920s, in 1955. He added poignantly: '[Stanley] Matthews is a great entertainer, but for me that Liddell man is "It". He is one of the greatest club men ever to have played football.'

FACTFILE

BORN
Townhill, Scotland, 10 January 1922
DIED
3 July 2001
POSITION
Left-winger / Centre-forward
OTHER CLUBS
Lochgelly Violet (1937–38); Chelsea, Linfield, Cambridge Town, Toronto Scottish, Dunfermline (wartime guest)
SIGNED FROM
Lochgelly Violet, £200, July 1938; signed professional 17 April 1939
INTERNATIONAL CAPS
29 Scotland caps (8 goals), 1946–55
LFC DEBUT GAME/GOAL
5 January 1946 / 5 January 1946
CONTRACT EXPIRY
1961
HONOURS
League Championship 1946/47

Lindsay,
Alec

BILL SHANKLY gave Alec Lindsay his first-team debut in a 10-0 Fairs Cup thrashing of Dundalk in September 1969 but he didn't taste any First Division action until the middle of October, when he came off the bench to strike an equaliser against Ipswich Town at Portman Road. That was one of just six league matches he figured in that debut season, being tried all over the forward line.

Shankly was left questioning whether he had bought the right player. 'Listen, son. I want you to take men on, go past them and lash in those shots that brought you the goals when you were playing at Gigg Lane,' Shankly demanded. 'But that wasn't me, boss. That was Jim Kerr,' protested Lindsay. 'Jesus Christ, Bob,' said Shankly to Paisley. 'We've signed the wrong bloody player!' Lindsay became frustrated with life at Liverpool and handed in a transfer request, which was accepted, but then his Reds career changed unexpectedly for the better. He had been a half-back before arriving at Liverpool and Shankly moved the naturally right-footed player to left-back against Newcastle on 12 September 1970, having experimented with Ian Ross and Roy Evans earlier. Despite

Lindsay lacking pace, this decision launched his Liverpool career. Shankly was happy. 'The lad looked as if he had been playing at left-back all his life. He places passes up the touchline with tremendous accuracy.'

Liverpool had moved Lindsay further back but he still put his attacking skills to good use. He was clever at overlapping the defence on the left flank. He always chipped in with a couple of goals himself, possessing a powerful left foot. He only missed four league matches the following season and just five in 1972/73, when he was an important part of the team that won the League Championship and the UEFA Cup. He took over from Kevin Keegan as the club's penalty-taker a year later. That was also the season when he wiped out the disappointment of the FA Cup final defeat to Arsenal in 1971 by being a member of the side that outplayed Newcastle United at Wembley. In that game, with the score still locked at 0-0, his strong run and thunderous shot into Iam McFaul's net was harshly deemed to be offside, when television replays later showed that the ball had come to him not from Kevin Keegan but a Newcastle defender. Lindsay was naturally disappointed. 'It was quite funny because Keegan and me were celebrating on the greyhound track and we turned round to see that the ref hadn't given it. He called Kevin offside, Emlyn Hughes was rowing with him and we had to get back because the game had kicked off again.'

Lindsay lost his place to Phil Neal, Paisley's first signing, midway through the 1974/75 season but remained at Anfield until August 1977, when he was transferred to Stoke City. Paisley was disappointed with how Lindsay's career progressed once Shankly retired and he took over as manager. 'Alec peaked at the end of that successful 1973/74 season but was never the same player again after his life was overtaken by a series of personal problems,' Paisley revealed in his book *My 50 Golden Reds*. 'Unfortunately they badly affected his game and he began to lose heart and it showed in his performances. Sadly Alec was one of those players who wasted a lot of his talent and I am sure he would admit that himself now when he looks back at his career. It all went wrong when he was at the top of his profession.' Lindsay received four international caps, a run which began when Joe Mercer was caretaker England manager and while deliberating on his squad for a forthcoming European summer tour said to one of his colleagues: 'Let's have that Lindsay from Liverpool. He's always smiling!'

LINDSAY'S career at the Potteries didn't work out as he had three managers there in a short space of time. He made a clean break and moved to Oakland, playing in the North American Soccer League and being voted Most Valuable Player in his debut season, but then the club moved lock, stock and barrel to Edmonton, Canada. After four appearances for Toronto Blizzard in 1979 he returned to the Northwest, later turning out for non-league team Newton and becoming a publican at the Foundry Arms in Leigh.

> **'JESUS CHRIST, BOB, WE'VE SIGNED THE WRONG BLOODY PLAYER!'**
> **BILL SHANKLY**

TEAM-MATE Brian Hall was impressed by Lindsay. 'One of the best left foots I've ever seen. Alec was one of those players who had such a lovely sweet movement and motion when he kicked a ball with his left foot that he could kick it three-quarters the length of the pitch and made it look so easy.'

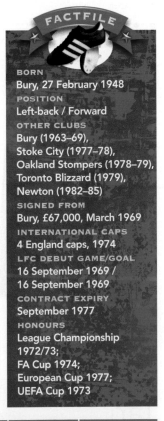

FACTFILE

BORN
Bury, 27 February 1948
POSITION
Left-back / Forward
OTHER CLUBS
Bury (1963–69),
Stoke City (1977–78),
Oakland Stompers (1978–79),
Toronto Blizzard (1979),
Newton (1982–85)
SIGNED FROM
Bury, £67,000, March 1969
INTERNATIONAL CAPS
4 England caps, 1974
LFC DEBUT GAME/GOAL
16 September 1969 /
16 September 1969
CONTRACT EXPIRY
September 1977
HONOURS
League Championship
1972/73;
FA Cup 1974;
European Cup 1977;
UEFA Cup 1973

Season	League		FA Cup		League Cup		Europe		Other		Total	
	App	Goals	App	Goals	App	Goals	App	Goals	App	Goals	App	Goals
1969/70	4 (2)	1	0	0	0	0	1	1	-	-	5 (2)	2
1970/71	21	0	4	0	2	0	8	1	-	-	35	1
1971/72	38	0	3	1	1	0	2	0	1	0	45	1
1972/73	37	4	4	0	7	0	11	1	-	-	59	5
1973/74	36	4	9	0	6	0	3	0	-	-	54	4
1974/75	25	3	2	0	4	0	4	1	1	0	36	4
1975/76	6	0	0	0	3	1	2	0	-	-	11	1
1976/77	1	0	0	0	0	0	0	0	0	0	1	0
Total	**168 (2)**	**12**	**22**	**1**	**23**	**1**	**31**	**4**	**2**	**0**	**246 (2)**	**18**

Lindsay,
John

A SERIOUS knee injury threatened to end John Lindsay's career while at Partick Thistle. He moved to Wales to play with Rhyl Athletic and scored over 60 goals for the Welsh club in the 1927/28 season, an achievement that alerted Liverpool to his talents.

Lindsay played mostly as a left-half or a left-winger in the 16 appearances he made for Liverpool from 1928 to 1929. He scored his first goal at Burnden Park, Bolton, in a fourth round FA Cup replay in January 1929 but Liverpool were eventually knocked out 5-2 after extra time. He also grabbed a couple of league goals, against West Ham at Anfield on 13 March 1929 and the same opposition when they played at Anfield the following season.

Season	League		FA Cup		Total	
	App	Goals	App	Goals	App	Goals
1928/29	10	1	2	1	12	2
1929/30	4	1	0	0	4	1
Total	14	2	2	1	16	3

FACTFILE

BORN
Cardenden, Fife, Scotland, 1900
POSITION
Left-half / Left-winger
OTHER CLUBS
Partick Thistle (1922–27),
Rhyl Athletic (1927–28),
Swansea Town (1930–31),
Rhyl Athletic (1931–32),
Bangor City,
Lochgelly Amateurs
SIGNED FROM
Rhyl Athletic, April 1928
LFC DEBUT GAME/GOAL
1 December 1928 /
30 January 1929
CONTRACT EXPIRY
January 1930

Lipsham,
John

ALTHOUGH LIVERPOOL had been champions the previous year, they slumped alarmingly to 15th position and lost 18 of their 38 league fixtures, failing to score in all three matches for which John Lipsham was selected.

HE HAD three spells at Chester and was one of four brothers who turned out for the club. In his second spell the club's directors felt cheated when he moved to Wrexham at the end of the 1912/13 season after they had given him and Billy Matthews a joint benefit match just two months earlier that raised £82.

Season	League		FA Cup		Total	
	App	Goals	App	Goals	App	Goals
1906/07	3	0	0	0	3	0
Total	3	0	0	0	3	0

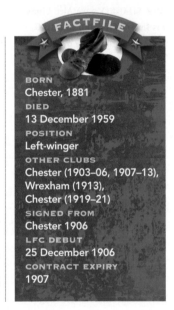

FACTFILE

BORN
Chester, 1881
DIED
13 December 1959
POSITION
Left-winger
OTHER CLUBS
Chester (1903–06, 1907–13),
Wrexham (1913),
Chester (1919–21)
SIGNED FROM
Chester 1906
LFC DEBUT
25 December 1906
CONTRACT EXPIRY
1907

Litmanen,
Jari

JARI LITMANEN became one of Europe's most renowned players with Ajax in Amsterdam. He played five years in the Finnish League before moving to the Netherlands in 1992 to join Ajax.

In his second season, 1993/94, Litmanen scored 26 goals in 30 league games as Ajax won the title. He was the Eredivisie's top scorer and voted Footballer of the Year. Litmanen became European champion with Ajax in 1995 and was third in the vote for Europe's best player. He scored Ajax's goal in normal time against Juventus in the European Cup final a year later, but Ajax lost in a penalty shootout. After 159 league games and 91 goals for Ajax Litmanen answered the call of his former coach Louis Van Gaal to join Barcelona on a Bosman free transfer in the summer of 1999. Litmanen picked up an injury at the beginning of his Barca career and worse was to follow when Van Gaal was sacked in May 2000. Llorenc Serra Ferrer took over and clearly wanted nothing to do with Litmanen. It was then that Gérard Houllier gave him the chance to join up with his boyhood idols. Litmanen's team-mates at Ajax had complained about his constant talking about all things concerning Liverpool Football Club. When he left Ajax for Barcelona he said goodbye by having 'You'll Never Walk Alone' played on the loudspeakers as he walked off the park.

> LITMANEN'S TEAM-MATES AT AJAX HAD COMPLAINED ABOUT HIS CONSTANT TALKING ABOUT ALL THINGS CONCERNING LIVERPOOL FOOTBALL CLUB

This proved to be a case of third time lucky for Liverpool, as they had tried to sign Litmanen twice previously. Roy Evans wanted to sign him in 1998 but didn't have the necessary funds and Houllier tried to sign him in 1999 but he moved to Catalonia. 'We have signed a world-class player. He comes with a massive reputation and I believe he's one of the most exciting signings we have made,' a thrilled Houllier said. Doubts remained over an ankle problem that had dogged Litmanen in the past; injuries did hamper his progress in his debut season and he didn't participate in any of the three finals Liverpool succeeded in. Litmanen left Anfield early on in the 2002/03 season after seemingly being criminally underused by Houllier in his second campaign. Twice he scored in two games in a row only to be left on the bench for the third game. He scored the winning goals against Tottenham and Dynamo Kiev in September 2001, but was substitute against Newcastle. History repeated itself when he netted goals against Arsenal and Aston Villa in December 2001 but was only on the bench against West Ham. The problem was that Litmanen had difficulties in training due to his ankle problems and was hardly able to play for 90 minutes week in and week out. It did come as a surprise when he was considered not useful enough for a starting place when Liverpool had progressed to the Champions League quarter-finals against Leverkusen, as he was the only player of real experience in this competition in the squad. He came on as a substitute in both legs, scoring a goal in the second leg that almost put Liverpool into the semi-final.

LITMANEN was puzzled by Houllier's treatment of him. 'It's strange that he was so pleased when he signed me and then decided to not use me. I cannot explain it myself.' Houllier's

explanations made his reasons even more puzzling. 'I let Jari go because I have always believed he had great potential which could benefit other teams. I really liked the reaction of the Ajax players towards Jari when I sold him!'

JARI returned to Ajax in Holland after leaving Liverpool but, now in his early 30s, he was never able to reproduce the form he had shown during his first spell in Amsterdam. He returned to his homeland to play briefly for Lahti and then had equally short spells with Hansa Rostock in Germany, Malmö in Sweden and Fulham in England.

After two more full seasons at Lahti in 2009 and 2010, Litmanen returned to HJK Helsinki twenty years after he had first arrived there. This meant that he would still be playing competitive football despite passing his 40th birthday, a very rare achievement for an outfield player. Litmanen became Finland's most capped player when he surpassed Ari Hjelm's record by playing his 101st international against Belarus on 1 March 2006. He played his last international in November 2010, which was his 137th appearance in a career that saw 32 goals. Litmanen scored a tremendous goal in extra time of the Finnish Cup final in September 2011 after coming on as substitute in the 80th minute in HJK Helsinki's 2-1 win over KuPs. Helsinki won the Veikkausliiga as well with the team, winning all 18 games Litmanen participated in; a perfect ending to a glorious career.

Didi Hamann appreciated the time he spent with Litmanen at Liverpool. 'I've never seen a player

with such a good eye for the final forward next to him or his team-mates. He never missed a pass, his vision was just unbelievable. He wasn't the quickest when he came to us but his performance on his debut at Aston Villa was one of the best I've ever seen in a Liverpool shirt.'

FACTFILE

BORN
Lahti, Finland,
20 February 1971
POSITION
Attacking midfielder
OTHER CLUBS
Lahden Reipas (1977–90),
HJK Helsinki (1991),
MyPa 47 (1992),
Ajax (1992–99),
Barcelona (1999–2001),
Ajax (2002–04),
Lahti (2004),
Hansa Rostock (2005),
Malmö (2005–07),
Fulham (2008),
Lahti (2008–10),
HJK Helsinki (2011)
SIGNED FROM
Barcelona, free transfer,
4 January 2001
INTERNATIONAL CAPS
137 Finland caps (32 goals)
(10 (4) at LFC), 1989–2010
LFC DEBUT GAME/GOAL
10 January 2001 /
10 February 2001
CONTRACT EXPIRY
30 August 2002

Season	League		FA Cup		League Cup		Europe		Other		Total	
	App	Goals	App	Goals	App	Goals	App	Goals	App	Goals	App	Goals
2000/01	4 (1)	1	1 (1)	1	1 (1)	0	0 (2)	0	-	-	6 (5)	2
2001/02	8 (13)	4	0 (1)	0	1	0	4 (5)	3	0	0	13 (19)	7
Total	**12 (14)**	**5**	**1 (2)**	**1**	**2 (1)**	**0**	**4 (7)**	**3**	**0**	**0**	**19 (24)**	**9**

Liver Bird

THE LIVERBIRD has always been closely associated with Liverpool FC as it is the city's symbol. The city of Liverpool was founded in 1207 by King John. He needed a new port to ship his troops to Ireland and to control the Irish Sea. The new town adopted King John's seal as its own. It showed the eagle of St John holding a sprig of broom in its beak. In 1644 the seal was lost and a new one made. The eagle was replaced by a cormorant, a more familiar bird in the area and in the beak was a piece of seaweed. The cormorant became later known as the mythical 'Liverbird', which is prominent in the city, especially the couple on top of the clock towers on the Royal Liver Building at the Pier Head.

The Liverbird was first referred to in connection with the newly-formed Liverpool FC in September 1892. Liverpool beat Southport 2-0 in the Lancashire Senior Cup on 17 September at Anfield and 'a new man - beg pardon, a flag - floated on the old staff, bearing the letters, L.F.A. surmounted

with the liver. Right proudly did it wave over the field of battle and seemed to beam on its patrons with a hopeful smile.'

When Liverpool's new League Championship flag was unfurled in 1922 it was featured in the *Liverpool Echo* with the players sat above it. It had a giant Liverbird at the forefront with LFC written above it, FIRST and DIVISION on the sides and LEAGUE CHAMPIONS 1900-1, 1905-6 and 1921-22 beneath. The *Echo* was quite confident of the season ahead which turned out to be fully justified. 'The new flag tells the world at large that Liverpool were champions last season and on two other occasions. There is quite a prospect that the flag will have to be brought down and another honour added to it as the result of this season's work. In between the three, how would the words "Winners of the English Cup 1922-23" fit? Very well, we think.'

UNTIL 1961 Liverpool used the city's coat of arms as their crest where the Liverbird is naturally prominent along with Triton and Neptune as well as the city's motto DEUS NOBIS HÆC OTIA FECIT that can be translated as 'God has given us this tranquillity' taken from 'Virgil'. The *Liverpool Echo* reported on 13 December 1961 that the City Council was no longer going to permit Liverpool FC to use the city's coat of arms as their crest. The club's directors were 'surprised and disappointed' not to be able to further increase the city's reputation in England and on the continent. In 2008 Liverpool FC incurred the wrath of the City Council after they attempted to copyright the mythical bird. Negotiations between the two parties continued until an agreement was reached in July 2010 that enabled the club to successfully trademark its design of the fabled Liverbird, a controversial decision to this day. A club spokesman told the press: 'Our position was always to solely seek to protect our specific version of the Liverbird to stop its use in counterfeit Liverpool FC merchandise. We never intended to challenge the usage by the council or other charity or community groups of their version of the Liverbird, and were delighted to work with the local authority on this matter.' The Liverbird is still the centrepiece of the current crest surrounded by the Hillsborough flames, the year of the club's foundation and the Shankly Gates.

A LIVERBIRD badge featured regularly on Liverpool's shirt from November 1955 onwards after making a single appearance at Wembley when Liverpool wore a white shirt with a red badge as they lost 2-0 to Arsenal in the 1950 FA Cup final. There is, though, an image from an unidentified game from 1953 where the players are wearing a badge, but most likely this was also a one-off occasion. The bird was inside an oval-shaped badge from 1955 to 1969 which developed into the club's crest plainly used as its shirt badge. Since Warrior Sports took over as the club's kit manufacturer in 2012 the Liverbird stands on its own on the club's shirt as from 1969 to 1987, a simple, yet elegant design that is classic.

Livermore, Doug

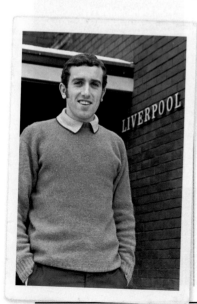

A HARD-WORKING forward who later became Roy Evans' assistant manager at Liverpool, Doug Livermore signed professional forms in November 1965 but over the next five years only appeared for Liverpool's first team on 18 occasions.

He had a brief appearance as substitute when coming on for Tony Hateley at West Ham in April 1968 but wasn't picked again until the second half of the 1969/70 season, when he played in the last 13 league matches of the campaign. After making one start in 1970/71 Livermore knew his future lay away from Merseyside and he was transferred to Norwich City. He was a

midfielder in an eventful Norwich career from 1970 to 1975, during which he won the Second Division title, lost a League Cup final, got relegated from the First Division, broke his wrist and missed a whole year because of two cartilage operations. After featuring in 138 games for Norwich Livermore dropped down a division to third-tier Cardiff City, but the team was

HE WON THE SECOND DIVISION TITLE, LOST A LEAGUE CUP FINAL, GOT RELEGATED FROM THE FIRST DIVISION, BROKE HIS WRIST AND MISSED A WHOLE YEAR BECAUSE OF TWO CARTILAGE OPERATIONS

promoted following his debut season. Livermore then spent two campaigns in the Third Division with Chester.

When his playing days were over Livermore returned to Cardiff as coach and then filled a similar role at Swansea under John Toshack's management. He was also assistant for a time to Mike England when he was in charge of the Welsh national side. Livermore joined the coaching staff at Tottenham in 1987 and was eventually appointed manager following Peter Shreeves' dismissal prior to the 1992/93 season. In the first season of the Premier League Livermore, with first-team coach Ray Clemence by his side, guided Spurs to ninth, an improvement of six places from the prior campaign, and reached the FA Cup semi-final where they lost to Arsenal. In the summer of 1993 Livermore made way for Ossie Ardiles. He returned to Liverpool to assist Roy Evans from January 1994 until November 1998 when Gérard Houllier took sole charge.

Livermore's next appointment was as coach at Nottingham Forest where he worked alongside Shreeves, his predecessor in the manager's chair at Spurs. After returning to Norwich City, Livermore stepped down from his role as assistant manager at the Canaries in February 2007 having spent roughly seven years as a right-hand man to four different managers. One of them was Nigel Worthington, whom Livermore joined at Leicester in the final weeks of the 2006/07 Premiership season.

The pair saved the Foxes from relegation but were not rewarded for their efforts.

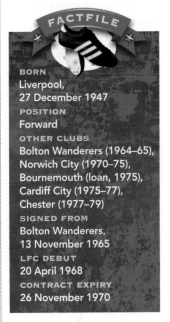

Season	League		FA Cup		League Cup		Europe		Total	
	App	Goals	App	Goals	App	Goals	App	Goals	App	Goals
1967/68	0 (1)	0	0	0	0	0	0	0	0 (1)	0
1969/70	13 (1)	0	0	0	0	0	0	0	13 (1)	0
1970/71	0 (1)	0	0	0	1	0	0 (1)	0	1 (2)	0
Total	**13 (3)**	**0**	**0**	**0**	**1**	**0**	**0 (1)**	**0**	**14 (4)**	**0**

Liverpool Senior Cup

THE LIVERPOOL Senior cup has been competed for by teams in the Liverpool County Football Association since 1882. Liverpool were successful in their debut campaign, beating Everton 1-0, in the first ever Merseyside derby, in the final on 22 April 1893. It was a sweet victory for owner John Houlding who had been thrown out of Everton FC a year prior.

Everton and Liverpool turned out their strongest teams in the competition until the 1960s when their reserves represented them which has not changed since, demoting the Senior Cup in the process. The trophy was evidently still important in the eyes of Liverpool supporters in 1930. The Reds beat Everton 1-0 in the final at Anfield, but were presented the cup in the dressing room which ignited the anger of the Liverpool supporters of the 8,000 present. 'The crowds were rather petulant that they had not been permitted to see the trophy or the representation. The police had a little difficulty in dealing with them and they stayed on needlessly for some time, refusing to take the advice of Superintendent Hughes that there would not be a public presentation,' the *Liverpool Post and Mercury* reported.

THE MOST dramatic final took place on 14 June 1947. Liverpool beat Everton 2-1, but that result was of secondary importance as 15 minutes prior to the game Stoke kicked off their postponed league game against Sheffield United. Liverpool were two points ahead of Stoke at the top of the league but the Potters' superior goal average meant a win would bring them the Championship. Ten minutes from full-time director George Richards announced over the public tannoy at Anfield that Stoke had lost and the league title had been won by Liverpool. 'The crowd didn't care two straws what happened after that. All they wanted was the final whistle, so they could come swarming over the ground from the Kop and Kemlyn Road and carry us off the field,' Billy Liddell remembered in his autobiography. 'The roar which greeted this announcement made the Hampden Park one sound almost like a childish whisper. The crowd threw their hands in the air, many lost their hats and did not bother to look for them after they had tossed them high up in a burst of joyful celebration,' a local scribe noted.

THE LAST FINAL of any note was played on 9 May 1961 a week after Ian St John signed for Liverpool. The Saint made his actual debut in the 4-3 defeat to Everton at Goodison Park in front of more than 51,000 spectators. He netted a hat-trick giving the Reds a taste of what was to come.

Liverpool last won the cup in 2010 when they beat Skelmersdale United 3-2 with the likes of Jon Flanagan, Andre Wisdom and Conor Coady in the team.

Liverpool Senior Cup has been won by Liverpool in the following years:

1893, 1901, 1902, 1903, 1905, 1907, 1909, 1910 (shared), 1912 (shared), 1913, 1915, 1920, 1925, 1927, 1929, 1930, 1936 (shared), 1937, 1939, 1942, 1943, 1946, 1947, 1948, 1951, 1952, 1962, 1964 (shared), 1968, 1977, 1980, 1981, 1982 (shared), 1997, 1998, 2002, 2004, 2009, 2010.

Livingstone, George

GEORGE LIVINGSTONE was an inside-forward who joined Sunderland from Hearts prior to the 1900/01 season and was their top scorer with 11 league goals as the Roker Park outfit finished second in the table, two points behind champions Liverpool. Sunderland went on to win the League Championship the following season but by then Livingstone had moved back north to Celtic. He scored seven goals in 23 matches for the Bhoys and played in the Scottish Cup final, which Hibernian won 1-0; a month later Livingstone joined Liverpool.

He played in 31 of Liverpool's 34 First Division fixtures in 1902/03, the only season he figured in the first team. He scored on his debut in a 5-2 win over Blackburn Rovers at Anfield on the opening day, but would find the net on only three more occasions. Livingstone made his Scotland debut in the ill-fated game against England at Ibrox on 5 April 1902. Twenty-six spectators lost their lives and 517 were injured when the back of the newly built West Tribune Stand

collapsed due to heavy rainfall the previous night. Hundreds of supporters fell up to 40 feet (12 metres) to the ground below. Subsequently, this match was deemed unofficial and caps awarded do not show in official records. Livingstone made his official international debut four years later. Even though he didn't have a particularly successful career at Liverpool, he was certainly popular with his team-mates and was said to have been a great joker in the dressing room.

The highlight of Livingstone's career came after he'd left Liverpool and joined Manchester City. His tremendous pass to Billy Meredith resulted in the winning goal for City against Bolton in the 1904 FA Cup final. After a couple of years at Rangers where he scored 20 goals in 47 league appearances, Livingstone joined Manchester United in 1909.

United won the League in the 1910/11 season in which Livingstone appeared in quarter of the games. He retired in 1914 and later became coach at Rangers (1920–27) and Bradford City (1928–35). The Scotsman played for both Celtic and Rangers and also for Manchester City and Manchester United and could have added the third set of rivals, the Merseyside ones, to his impressive resumé. The future

Red went on trial to Everton in March 1900 when he was registered at Hearts. A note in Everton's minute books on 23 May 1899 reveals that the Blues had resolved to make a £250 bid for Livingstone, but he never joined the Blues as he was sold to Sunderland from Hearts for £175 in May 1900.

FACTFILE

BORN
Dumbarton, Scotland,
5 May 1876
DIED
15 January 1950
POSITION
Inside-right forward
OTHER CLUBS
Sinclair Swifts,
Artizan Thistle, Parkhead,
Dumbarton (1895–96),
Hearts (1896–1900),
Sunderland (1900–01),
Celtic (1901–02),
Manchester City (1903–06),
Rangers (1906–09),
Manchester United (1909–14)
SIGNED FROM
Celtic, £200, 28 May 1902
INTERNATIONAL CAPS
2 Scotland caps, 1906–07
LFC DEBUT GAME/GOAL
6 September 1902 /
6 September 1902
CONTRACT EXPIRY
May 1903

	League		FA Cup		Total	
Season	App	Goals	App	Goals	App	Goals
1902/03	31	4	1	0	32	4
Total	31	4	1	0	32	4

Lloyd, Larry

LARRY LLOYD had already won four England amateur international caps by the age of 17 and only played one season with lower-league Bristol Rovers when he was bought by Bill Shankly to replace Ron Yeats. 'Larry, I have come to the conclusion that you would kick your grandmother for a fiver,' Bill Shankly told Lloyd as their talks began about a move to Liverpool. 'I would actually kick her for half of that,' was Lloyd's droll reply.

Liverpool's interest in Lloyd was aroused when Shankly and chief scout Geoff Twentyman saw him play for Rovers in a fifth round FA Cup tie against Everton at Goodison Park two months earlier. Lloyd lacked pace and skill but he was dominant in the air, strong in the tackle and had the qualities of a leader. He played in two consecutive league games for the Reds in the autumn of 1969 and the last six First Division matches of that season. Yeats filled in occasionally at left-back in the 1970/71 season, leaving the tall Bristolian free to establish himself at the heart of Liverpool's defence. He only missed two league fixtures that campaign and played in the FA Cup final, where Liverpool were beaten in extra time by Arsenal. More disappointment followed a year later when a controversial disallowed 'goal' a few minutes from the end of the final league game cost them the League Championship. But in 1972/73 those near misses were forgotten as Liverpool captured the Championship, with Lloyd featuring in every one of the 66 competitive matches of that draining season; he also headed in the decisive third goal in the first leg of the UEFA Cup final against Mönchengladbach.

Lloyd was still very much first choice at the start of the next season and played in 27 consecutive First Division games up to and including the

home fixture with Norwich City on 2 February 1974. He was substituted by Peter Cormack on that day and the Scot scored the last-minute winner to keep Liverpool in touch with Leeds at the top of the table. While Lloyd was out for the season with a thigh injury Cormack established himself in the middle with fellow midfielder Phil Thompson moving to centre-half in place of Lloyd. Shankly wanted to build more from the back and the partnership of Emlyn Hughes and Thompson fitted the bill – Lloyd didn't. The club was prepared to listen for offers as the 25 year-old Lloyd had demanded to be sold, wanting to play regularly. In August 1974

Coventry City paid £240,000 for Lloyd, which was for that time a very high fee (by comparison Liverpool had paid a club transfer record of £180,000 for Ray Kennedy the previous month).

Lloyd struggled at Coventry and in his third season at the Sky Blues he moved on to Second Division Nottingham Forest, which turned out to be very fortuitous for him and the club. Brian Clough's team was promoted that season in 1976/77, took the league title off Liverpool the following year and prevented a third consecutive European Cup win for the Reds by knocking them out in the first round in 1978/79 and going all the way to win the trophy. Liverpool recaptured the domestic title but in 1979/80 Forest followed in Liverpool's footsteps by winning the European Cup for the second year running. After five exceptional years at Forest Lloyd moved to Wigan as player-manager. Although he took the Lancashire club into the Third Division he was dismissed the following season. He also had a short spell in charge of Notts County, where after his first game a reporter pointed out that nine of his 11 players had been booked

and asked his opinion on this startling fact. Lloyd simply looked straight at him and said, 'Well, I'll have to question the commitment of the other two.'

Lloyd was later candid about suffering depression and falling upon hard times. He was forced to sell his medals at Christie's in 2001, earning a mere £12,000. 'Selling my European medals is the greatest regret of my life,' Lloyd told the *Daily Mail* in 2008. 'I feel sick when I think about it.

FACTFILE

BORN
Bristol, 6 October 1948
POSITION
Centre-half
OTHER CLUBS
Bristol Rovers (1965–69),
Coventry City (1974–76),
Nottingham Forest (1976–81),
Wigan Athletic (1981–83)
SIGNED FROM
Bristol Rovers, £50,000,
23 April 1969
INTERNATIONAL CAPS
4 England caps (3 at LFC),
1971–80
LFC DEBUT GAME/GOAL
27 September 1969 /
26 February 1972
CONTRACT EXPIRY
15 August 1974
HONOURS
League Championship
1972/73,
UEFA Cup 1973

But needs must when the devil drives and the devil was certainly at the wheel then.'

Season	League App	League Goals	FA Cup App	FA Cup Goals	League Cup App	League Cup Goals	Europe App	Europe Goals	Other App	Other Goals	Total App	Total Goals
1969/70	8	0	0	0	0	0	1	0	-	-	9	0
1970/71	40	0	7	0	3	0	10	0	-	-	60	0
1971/72	33	1	2	0	3	0	4	0	1	0	43	1
1972/73	42	2	4	0	8	0	12	1	-	-	66	3
1973/74	27	1	3	0	6	0	4	0	-	-	40	1
Total	150	4	16	0	20	0	31	1	1	0	218	5

Lock,
Frank

AN ELEGANT player who played either at right- or left-back, Frank Lock had played over 200 times for Charlton Athletic when he signed for Liverpool on Christmas Day 1953 along with team-mate John Evans. It was an attempt to bolster an increasingly fragile defence as the club nose-dived towards relegation to the Second Division.

LOCK'S arrival came too late to stop that slide, but at least he had the satisfaction of helping

his colleagues to keep a clean sheet on his debut against West Bromwich Albion at Anfield on Boxing Day, the goalless draw halting a run of three successive defeats in which 15 goals had been conceded! Lock made the line-up at full-back for the first 18 matches of the following season but then lost his place along with fellow full-back Tom McNulty to Ronnie Moran and Ray Lambert.

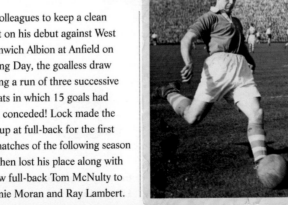

Season	League App	League Goals	FA Cup App	FA Cup Goals	Total App	Total Goals
1953/54	18	0	1	0	19	0
1954/55	23	0	0	0	23	0
Total	41	0	1	0	42	0

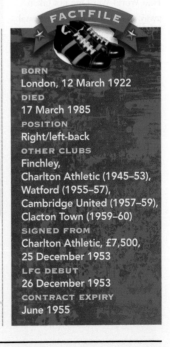
FACTFILE

BORN
London, 12 March 1922
DIED
17 March 1985
POSITION
Right/left-back
OTHER CLUBS
Finchley,
Charlton Athletic (1945–53),
Watford (1955–57),
Cambridge United (1957–59),
Clacton Town (1959–60)
SIGNED FROM
Charlton Athletic, £7,500,
25 December 1953
LFC DEBUT
26 December 1953
CONTRACT EXPIRY
June 1955

Longest Career at Club

	Time	Dates			Games	Rank
Elisha Scott	21 years 1 month 20 days	1 January 1913	-	21 February 1934	468	18
Donald Mackinlay	18 years 4 months 12 days	20 April 1910	-	1 September 1928	434	22
Ian Callaghan	17 years 11 months 13 days	16 April 1960	-	29 March 1978	857	1
Phil Taylor	17 years 9 months 12 days	28 March 1936	-	9 January 1954	343	46
Ephraim Longworth	17 years 7 months 2 days	19 September 1910	-	21 April 1928	370	34
Jack Balmer	16 years 5 months 2 days	21 September 1935	-	23 February 1952	309	55
Jamie Carragher	16 years 4 months 11 days	8 January 1997	-	19 May 2013	737	2
Ian Rush	15 years 4 months 28 days	13 December 1980	-	11 May 1996	660	5
Tommy Smith	14 years 11 months 17 days	8 May 1963	-	25 April 1978	638	7
Billy Liddell	14 years 7 months 26 days	5 January 1946	-	31 August 1960	534	12
Steven Gerrard	14 years 5 months 20 days	29 November 1998	-	19 May 2013*	630	8

Based on active playing career at Liverpool: from date of debut to date of final appearance. Includes rank on Most appearances' list.

* Gerrard is still featuring for Liverpool but his stats in this book are up to 19 May 2013

Longworth,
Ephraim

RIGHT-BACK Ephraim Longworth was one of the most consistent defenders Liverpool have ever had on their books and his career at Anfield from start to finish covered a remarkable 18 years.

Had World War One not taken away so much of his professional career, he would certainly have played in over 500 Football League and FA Cup matches for the club he served so loyally. He was so described in Fulham's match programme ahead of their duel with Liverpool in the FA Cup in February 1912: 'Resourceful to a degree, he combines dash and cleverness with fine effect, and his kicking is always of high standard.' A leading referee at the time, J.T. Howcroft, recommended him to Leyton in 1908 and Longworth made wonderful strides with the London club in his two seasons in the Southern League. Liverpool manager Tom Watson used his extensive contacts in the game and

asked Michael Griffin, who had played under him at Liverpool, who was the best back in the Southern League. Griffin replied: 'Longworth of Leyton.'

LONGWORTH was signed by Liverpool on 9 June 1910 even though he had refused to move

from Leyton a month earlier. Liverpool were said to have paid a club record fee for his services. After his third game for Liverpool, a 2-0 defeat against Everton, he was assessed by the club programme as follows: 'At full-back Longworth showed qualities which were eminently

acceptable. For some seasons we have not been comfortable about our full-backs, and I must say that the Bolton youth is one of the most promising. He is not perfect, but that head save of a sure goal was as good as anything.' Longworth's composed style of play meant that his position at right-back was rarely threatened during his early years on Merseyside. He played in the FA Cup final against Burnley in 1914 and would continue to be a key member of the team for several seasons after the war. He will forever be associated with one of the best defences in Liverpool's history that enabled the club to win the League Championship in 1922 and 1923.

> HE WILL FOREVER BE ASSOCIATED WITH ONE OF THE BEST DEFENCES IN LIVERPOOL'S HISTORY THAT ENABLED THE CLUB TO WIN THE LEAGUE CHAMPIONSHIP IN 1922 AND 1923

Longworth actually lost his place in the team midway through the 1921/22 season to Tommy Lucas and resigned as captain, contrary to the wishes of the board and team-mates. A scribe at the *Derby Daily Telegraph* fully understood his reasons: 'When a captain is left out of the side more often than he plays what can a man do?' Left-back Donald Mackinlay was appointed captain in his place in January 1922. Longworth eventually regained his spot in the first XI, featured in the last dozen matches of Liverpool's victorious season and was an ever-present the following campaign when the title was retained.

Longworth was much beloved by the crowd and the *Liverpool Echo* couldn't speak too highly of him: 'Here is a man who has grown into the favours of the Liverpool people, not by his golden locks, but by his genuine play, his everlasting effort, his sure kick, his deliberate timing of his tackle and his utter thoughtlessness of anything save sport in the truest sense. Longworth is a pillar of the game. He may not have the speed of Duffy, but he has speed of thought and when he cuts across and slides towards the ball with one leg under him and the other edging the ball into touch, he is as sure a defender as we know. In fact we are looking forward to seeing him play for England versus Scotland at Hampden Park in April. Such a thing did not seem possible to some minds, way back last season, but Longworth is no ordinary man; he has given himself great care and his wisdom in being a non-smoker and a teetotaller has been proved over and over again.'

Longworth played five times for England, making his debut at the age of 32 years and 190 days, and is one of a select group of Liverpool players to ever captain England, wearing the captain's armband for the first time against Belgium on 21 May 1921 when

he was aged 33 years and 231 days. Longworth's final selection for Liverpool, at Birmingham on 21 April 1928, came over 17½ years after he had been handed his debut in an away match at Bramall Lane, Sheffield, on 19 September 1910. Remarkably, considering the number of matches he played, he never scored a single goal for Liverpool! Rob Jones and Stephane Henchoz later became famous for never scoring for Liverpool in an official game; Jones played 243 games and Henchoz 205 without getting on the scoresheet, but Longworth managed 370 games without a goal! To be fair to Longworth he did score three goals in 119 war-time matches for Liverpool, but they don't count towards his official total. He revealed in the *Echo* perhaps why he struggled to score goals. 'Some backs love to roam and I am convinced by practical effects that they are wrong. I don't disagree with any full-back going forward when he sees the open door as it were. But as a rule it is wrong for full-backs to wander. There is the vital necessity of defence to be remembered and any defence spreadeagled is asking for a peck of trouble.'

LONGWORTH became a regular columnist for the *Liverpool Echo* in 1919, for a few good years commenting on the game as a whole on and off the field. His first column in the *Echo* on the 'Fallacy of playing football and working', published on 30 August 1919, gives a valuable insight into professional footballers' conditions at the time. 'Others have looked down on us as a lot of money-grabbers with no spirit or sportsmanship. One would imagine that we had no love of the game, all love of money, and were spending nine-tenths of our time filling out football coupons,' Longworth deliberated, continuing:

It is true we are getting a goodish wage for football. A player's life lasts on an average not more than five years. It is a doubtful business full of pitfalls from the first kick-off, when you get your first run with a tip-top side and imagine all sorts of big things, such as benefits, caps and so on. But the outside public forgets that first-team service is necessary for a benefit qualification. A player may be crocked in the first season, he may be crocked in the fourth, and there ends his career as a player. Can you marvel, then, that he demands the best? For a junior starting on the rough ocean of football's life I would say: 'Train hard, learn hard and combine business with playing as long as practicable. Get a trade in your fingers, but when football is THE business of the moment give your whole time to it, and aim as the best.'

E. LONGWORTH
LIVERPOOL

HE IS IN LIVERPOOL FC'S HALL OF FAME, AND RANKS WITH THE GREATEST DEFENDERS THE CLUB HAS EVER HAD

Longworth joined the coaching staff at Liverpool following his retirement as a player. He is in Liverpool FC's Hall of Fame, and ranks with the greatest defenders the club has ever had.

	League		FA Cup		Other		Total	
Season	App	Goals	App	Goals	App	Goals	App	Goals
1910/11	33	0	1	0	-	-	34	0
1911/12	37	0	2	0	-	-	39	0
1912/13	35	0	3	0	-	-	38	0
1913/14	27	0	7	0	-	-	34	0
1914/15	35	0	2	0	-	-	37	0
1919/20	27	0	5	0	-	-	32	0
1920/21	24	0	0	0	-	-	24	0
1921/22	26	0	0	0	1	0	27	0
1922/23	41	0	4	0	-	-	45	0
1923/24	14	0	0	0	-	-	14	0
1924/25	22	0	2	0	-	-	24	0
1925/26	4	0	2	0	-	-	6	0
1926/27	15	0	0	0	-	-	15	0
1927/28	1	0	0	0	-	-	1	0
Total	**341**	**0**	**28**	**0**	**1**	**0**	**370**	**0**

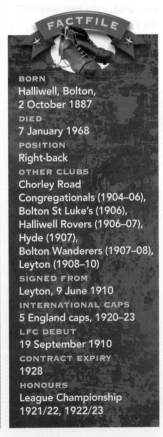

FACTFILE

BORN
Halliwell, Bolton,
2 October 1887
DIED
7 January 1968
POSITION
Right-back
OTHER CLUBS
Chorley Road
Congregationals (1904–06),
Bolton St Luke's (1906),
Halliwell Rovers (1906–07),
Hyde (1907),
Bolton Wanderers (1907–08),
Leyton (1908–10)
SIGNED FROM
Leyton, 9 June 1910
INTERNATIONAL CAPS
5 England caps, 1920–23
LFC DEBUT
19 September 1910
CONTRACT EXPIRY
1928
HONOURS
League Championship
1921/22, 1922/23

Low,
Norman

NORMAN'S FATHER, Scottish international defender Wilf Low, was a certified legend at Newcastle United. Norman was never on the Magpies' books, featuring at Rosehill Villa before he moved to Liverpool when he was only 19.

Tiny Bradshaw was the club's recognised centre-half at that time but Low replaced him for 11 consecutive First Division matches in the first half of the 1934/35 season. In the following season Bradshaw only missed one league

match, Low again deputising for him, and the last of his 13 Football League appearances for Liverpool came on 26 September 1936 in a 2-0 defeat away at Leeds. Low was manager of Third Division Norwich from 1950 to 1955 and Port Vale from 1957 to 1962, where he won the Fourth Division Championship in the 1958/59 season. He was also chief scout at Liverpool for a while before emigrating to North America in 1968.

Season	League		FA Cup		Total	
	App	Goals	App	Goals	App	Goals
1934/35	11	0	0	0	11	0
1935/36	1	0	0	0	1	0
1936/37	1	0	0	0	1	0
Total	**13**	**0**	**0**	**0**	**13**	**0**

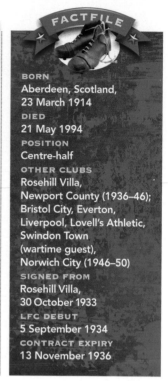

FACTFILE

BORN
Aberdeen, Scotland,
23 March 1914
DIED
21 May 1994
POSITION
Centre-half
OTHER CLUBS
Rosehill Villa,
Newport County (1936–46);
Bristol City, Everton,
Liverpool, Lovell's Athletic,
Swindon Town
(wartime guest),
Norwich City (1946–50)
SIGNED FROM
Rosehill Villa,
30 October 1933
LFC DEBUT
5 September 1934
CONTRACT EXPIRY
13 November 1936

Lowe,
Harry

HARRY LOWE'S display with Gainsborough Trinity against Liverpool in the first round of the FA Cup in January 1911 impressed the Reds. Lowe had built a sound reputation at the Second Division club and was considered one of the best half-backs in the Football League. The *Liverpool Echo* reported in May 1911 that 'a sound judge connected with a South Lancashire club believes that Liverpool have completed an important transfer'.

Tough-tackling and highly consistent half-back Lowe played 29 times in the First Division

during the disappointing 1911/12 season when the club narrowly avoided relegation. Lowe was Liverpool's captain from 1913 to 1915 and was even referred to as 'Captain Courageous' as he set 'a rare example in his men. A man of few words, but great deeds,' according to *Lloyds Weekly News* in 1914. Having featured both at left- and right-half he moved into the centre of defence, playing as 'pivot' as it was called, in 1913/14. He was unfortunately injured in the penultimate league fixture and subsequently missed his club's first ever appearance in an FA Cup final. But he was fit again by the start of the next season and added another 28 appearances to his career total. Lowe, by now aged 33, returned to Anfield when the war was over, but faced a worthy contender for his spot.

'W. Wadsworth's youth, not to mention his zeal and cover-the-ground abilities, could make it difficult even for a Lowe, with all his experience, to claim priority for centre half,' the *Echo* noted. Lowe was only selected for five more games as Walter Wadsworth claimed his place in the team.

Even though Lowe didn't feature in the 1914 FA Cup final he was awarded a runners-up medal following Liverpool's application to the Football Association. The medal is nine-carat gold, about an inch in diameter and minted by J.W. Benson Ltd in Ludgate Hill, London.

FACTFILE

BORN
Whitwell, Derbyshire,
20 March 1886
DIED
25 October 1958
POSITION
Half-back
OTHER CLUBS
Whitwell St Lawrence,
Gainsborough Trinity
(1907–11);
Nottingham Forest
(wartime guest),
Nottingham Forest (1920–21),
Grantham Town,
Mansfield Town (1923–25),
Newark Town (1925–26)
SIGNED FROM
Gainsborough Trinity,
2 May 1911
LFC DEBUT GAME/GOAL
4 September 1911 /
5 April 1912
CONTRACT EXPIRY
March 1920

> HE SET 'A RARE EXAMPLE IN HIS MEN. A MAN OF FEW WORDS, BUT GREAT DEEDS'
>
> *LLOYDS WEEKLY NEWS*

Season	League		FA Cup		Total	
	App	Goals	App	Goals	App	Goals
1911/12	29	1	2	0	31	1
1912/13	34	1	4	0	38	1
1913/14	29	0	5	0	34	0
1914/15	26	0	2	0	28	0
1919/20	5	0	0	0	5	0
Total	**123**	**2**	**13**	**0**	**136**	**2**

Lowry, Tom

Tom Lowry was one of a number of reserve-team players Shankly used in the final meaningless league match of the 1964/65 season away to Wolverhampton, which the Reds won 3-1.

He later became a firm fixture at Fourth Division Crewe, setting the club's appearance record of 475 games between 1966 and1977.

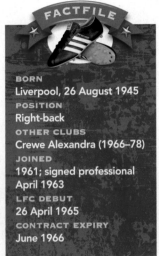
	League		FA Cup		League Cup		Europe		Other		Total	
Season	App	Goals	App	Goals	App	Goals	App	Goals	App	Goals	App	Goals
1964/65	1	0	0	0	-	-	0	0	0	0	1	0
Total	1	0	0	0	0	0	0	0	0	0	1	0

Lucas, Tommy

TOMMY LUCAS was born at St Helens, a stronghold of rugby league, but preferred the round ball to the oval one. Lucas played in Liverpool's defence for nearly a decade and a half between the two World Wars and, although he had spells when he was out of the side, his individual league appearance record for the club can only be bettered by 35 men who have worn the famous red shirt over the years.

As the Football League returned to being a national competition in 1919, the slight-framed Lucas made 16 appearances. There was fierce competition for the full-back positions at that time and even though he played on 27 occasions for the 1921/22 Championship-winning side, he was only called on once the next season due to Ephraim Longworth's and Donald Mackinlay's consistency, despite Lucas by now being an England international! The *Derby Daily Telegraph* noted that Lucas was 'not a big fellow, but sturdily built, strong in tackling, and kicks with a fine discrimination as to length and distance'. He had 'a hefty kick in each boot, and a sound judgment in regard to timing a tackle. And yet he is not a Longworth.'

Undaunted by being virtually ignored as Liverpool retained the title, he would bounce back to make nearly 200 appearances in league and cup over the next five years when Longworth's career faded away. Lucas was selected only occasionally in 1928/29 but again with determination he forced himself back into the first-team picture and was one of two ever-presents, the other being Archie McPherson, during the 1930/31 league campaign.

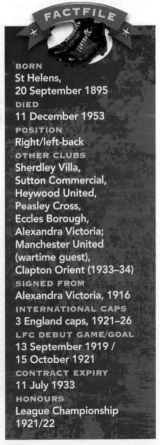
	League		FA Cup		Other		Total	
Season	App	Goals	App	Goals	App	Goals	App	Goals
1919/20	16	0	0	0	-	-	16	0
1920/21	29	0	3	0	-	-	32	0
1921/22	27	2	3	0	0	0	30	2
1922/23	1	0	0	0	-	-	1	0
1923/24	28	0	5	0	-	-	33	0
1924/25	37	0	4	0	-	-	41	0
1925/26	39	0	1	0	-	-	40	0
1926/27	39	1	4	0	-	-	43	1
1927/28	28	0	2	0	-	-	30	0
1928/29	5	0	0	0	-	-	5	0
1929/30	31	0	1	0	-	-	32	0
1930/31	42	0	1	0	-	-	43	0
1931/32	16	0	1	0	-	-	17	0
1932/33	3	0	0	0	-	-	3	0
Total	341	3	25	0	0	0	366	3

Joe Lumsden sitting beside the huge Burton Charity Cup

Lumsden, Joe

A FORWARD who made six First Division appearances for Liverpool plus two in the FA Cup during the 1897/98 season.

JOE LUMSDEN scored twice and created one on his debut in a 3-2 away win at Nottingham Forest on 27 November 1897. After failing to link up in the centre with left-winger Harry Bradshaw in the following game, a 2-1 defeat to Wolves, Lumsden was moved to the left flank where he stayed for a few games, never to appear on the scoresheet again.

FACTFILE

BORN
Derby, 1875
POSITION
Forward
OTHER CLUBS
Burton Wanderers (1896–97),
Glossop North End
(1898–1900)
SIGNED FROM
Burton Wanderers,
June 1897
LFC DEBUT GAME/GOAL
27 November 1897 /
27 November 1897
CONTRACT EXPIRY
1898

	League		FA Cup		Total	
Season	App	Goals	App	Goals	App	Goals
1897/98	6	2	2	0	8	2
Total	**6**	**2**	**2**	**0**	**8**	**2**

Luzi, Patrice

PATRICE LUZI had only made one appearance in the French second division with Ajaccio when he arrived at Liverpool on a free transfer. He featured in a solitary match for the Reds when he came on for the injured Dudek in the 1-0 win against Chelsea on 7 January 2004.

After falling down the pecking order he only played the odd reserve match in the 2004/05 season. He left on a free transfer in June 2005 and went first to Belgium and then to Stade Rennais in France.

FACTFILE

BORN
Ajaccio, France, 8 July 1980
POSITION
Goalkeeper
OTHER CLUBS
Monaco (1997–02),
Ajaccio (loan, 2001–02),
Royal Excelsior Mouscron
(2005–06),
Royal Charleroi (2006–07),
Stade Rennais (2007–10)
JOINED
Bosman free transfer,
29 July 2002
LFC DEBUT
7 January 2004
CONTRACT EXPIRY
1 July 2005

	League		FA Cup		League Cup		Europe		Total	
Season	App	Goals	App	Goals	App	Goals	App	Goals	App	Goals
2003/04	0 (1)	0	0	0	0	0	0	0	0 (1)	0
Total	**0 (1)**	**0**	**0**	**0**	**0**	**0**	**0**	**0**	**0 (1)**	**0**

Liverpool line up against Chelsea on 9 September 1912

Gordon Hodgson – Liverpool's striker extraordinaire

MacDonald, Kevin

THE FORMER Leicester captain Kevin MacDonald was purchased to help fill a part of the huge void left by Graeme Souness's move to Italy. He managed to get a run in the side midway through the 1985/86 double season but a broken arm in a match against Spurs halted his progress. Subsequent injury to Steve McMahon allowed MacDonald back into the side and his excellent form won him a place in the first XI for the FA Cup final ahead of McMahon, who had by then recovered.

MacDonald was Liverpool's unsung hero on the day. 'Headlines were being prepared in salute of Rushie and Jan. In the

dressing room we all rushed to congratulate Kevin MacDonald,' Dalglish said. 'He got in among Everton's midfield, taking the fight to Reidy, reclaiming the ball time after time. Never one of the most celebrated footballers, Kevin Mac will always be remembered fondly for turning the Blue Tide back at Wembley in May 1986.' While MacDonald's qualities were certainly appreciated by his boss he did have one drawback according to King Kenny. '"Albert" grumbled about everything; from the pitch to the weather and the food. He even moaned about other people moaning!'

Disaster struck on 20 September 1986 against Southampton when shortly after coming on as a substitute MacDonald suffered a double leg fracture. He returned to action 15 months later when he was loaned out to his former club, Leicester. He played a few games with Liverpool in 1988/89 before going on another loan spell in Glasgow with Rangers. MacDonald was now out of the first-team picture at Liverpool due to his lengthy lay-off and signed for Coventry City where he played 44 games in two

seasons. He finished his career in the Fourth Division with Walsall.

MacDONALD joined Leicester's coaching staff and was even caretaker manager for four games in late 1994 after Brian Little and Allan Evans quit the Foxes for Villa Park. When Steve Staunton took over as Ireland's manager in January 2006 he appointed MacDonald as his senior coach, albeit on a part-time basis, combining the role with his coaching job at Aston Villa. His contract was terminated along with Staunton's in October 2007. Following the resignation of

Martin O'Neill as Aston Villa manager five days before the 2010/11 Premier League season was due to start, MacDonald was immediately named as caretaker manager of the West Midlands club before Gérard Houllier took over. MacDonald left Villa in June 2012 after being 17 years on the backroom staff, having overseen a steady flow of Academy prospects achieving success in the first team.

On 28 February 2013 MacDonald was appointed as successor to Paulo Di Canio as manager of League One Swindon Town. He steered Swindon to the last of the four play-off positions but they lost to Brentford on penalties in the semi-final. Five months later MacDonald resigned from the Wiltshire club.

> 'KEVIN MAC WILL ALWAYS BE REMEMBERED FONDLY FOR TURNING THE BLUE TIDE BACK AT WEMBLEY IN MAY 1986'
>
> **KENNY DALGLISH**

FACTFILE

BORN
Scotland, 22 November 1960
POSITION
Midfielder
OTHER CLUBS
Caledonian (1976–80),
Leicester City (1980–84),
Leicester City (loan, 1987–88),
Rangers (loan, 1988)
Coventry City (1989–91),
Cardiff City (loan, 1991),
Walsall (1991–93)
SIGNED FROM
Leicester City, £400,000,
November 1984
LFC DEBUT GAME/GOAL
29 December 1984 /
9 October 1985
CONTRACT EXPIRY
13 July 1989
HONOURS
League Championship
1985/86; FA Cup 1986

Season	League App	League Goals	FA Cup App	FA Cup Goals	League Cup App	League Cup Goals	Europe App	Europe Goals	Other App	Other Goals	Total App	Total Goals
1984/85	13	0	7	0	0	0	4	0	0	0	24	0
1985/86	10 (7)	1	2	1	0 (2)	1	-	-	3 (1)	2	15 (10)	5
1986/87	3 (3)	0	0	0	0	0	-	-	2	0	5 (3)	0
1987/88	0 (1)	0	0	0	0	0	-	-	-	-	0 (1)	0
1988/89	3	0	0	0	1 (1)	0	-	-	1	0	5 (1)	0
Total	**29 (11)**	**1**	**9**	**1**	**1 (3)**	**1**	**4**	**0**	**6 (1)**	**2**	**49 (15)**	**5**

Mackinlay, Donald

FEW CAME TOUGHER than Donald Mackinlay, who was Liverpool's captain from 1922 to 1928. He certainly enjoyed his two decades at the Reds. 'If I had 20 years to go again, I would go back to them,' he said in 1955.

Donald was the son of Angus Mackinlay, left-back of Clyde, Greenock Morton and Darwen. He made his debut for Liverpool

at 18 years of age on 20 April 1910 when Liverpool defeated Nottingham Forest 7-3 with Jack Parkinson grabbing four. He only made two appearances as left-half

the following season and featured on the right and left of the half-back line at the close of 1911/12. Mackinlay was slowly making a name for himself but the question remained as to what his best position was. He played mostly as an inside-right in the 1912/13 season, where he was said to be 'as nippy and quick as a jack-in-the-box'. He had quite a magnificent shot in his arsenal and scored six goals in 23 matches that campaign. He was moved back and forth as well in the following season and after only featuring in two out of the last 11 games was given the enormous responsibility of playing as left-half in place of injured captain Harry Lowe in the 1914 FA Cup final, which Liverpool lost 1-0 to Burnley. Mackinlay appeared regularly for Liverpool during World War One, making 136 appearances and scoring 24 goals. Once the league resumed in 1919/20 Mackinlay was a firm fixture in the side and formed probably the best full-back pairing ever in the history of Liverpool with him on the left and Ephraim Longworth on the right. After sharing the captaincy with Longworth in the 1919/20 season he was made sole captain in January 1922 at 30 years of age and held on to this honour until he left Liverpool seven years later.

Mackinlay was the proud general of the Liverpool side that won successive League Championship titles in 1922 and 1923 and had the leadership qualities necessary for such a demanding role, as he explained in 1955. 'Generally today captains do not have sufficient responsibility,' Mackinlay told the *Evening Express*. 'It seems to me that all they do is to take the team out and toss the coin. There's not enough directing and you hardly hear them shout instructions. In my day I had full control on the field and if there was any decision on changing of positions, I took it. I am speaking generally and not individually, but captains today are not what they used to be. I told my players: "If I have to say anything to you, answer me back and don't start sulking."'

Leslie Edwards, the sports editor of the *Liverpool Daily Post and Echo*, saw the Liverpool greats first-hand and he couldn't praise

Mackinlay's abilities highly enough. 'He appeared in half a dozen different positions but the thing I remember most was his skill with a free kick. If I was leaving with a message and Liverpool had been awarded a free kick, I would wait until it had been taken because I knew anything could happen. He hit the ball with terrific power but also had a remarkable touch.'

One such free kick came against Oldham on 26 December 1922 as reported by the *Liverpool Echo*:

McKinlay has specialised in goals from free kicks and has rent asunder many a well-built up defence. McKinlay ran up, and with a fierce drive such as he alone is capable of sent the ball flying into the left hand portion of the goal. In the matter of shooting nothing is more remarkable than the way Donald McKinlay continues to score goals. He has scored from outside left, right back, left back, and left half-back, but in later seasons he has figured at left back, and he has this season piloted a lot of free kicks beyond the goalkeeper. It must be a record for a full back not taking penalty kicks to have scored so many goals in a season in the ordinary run of play.

Mackinlay's shooting prowess gave him a return of 34 goals for Liverpool, of which only four came from the penalty spot. One goal possibly more memorable than the rest came on 16 January 1926 in the 15th minute of a 2-1 league win against West Ham. Mackinlay was a full ten yards inside his own half when he unleashed a shot that hit the back of the Hammers' net. In honour of his 19 years of service for the club Mackinlay received his fourth benefit from Liverpool following the last game of the 1928/29 season against Manchester City at Anfield - a cheque for £468.

Mackinlay next to manager Dave Ashworth.

After leaving Liverpool, he remained in the Merseyside area to play non-league football for Prescot Cables and later became a publican in the city. He was a keen golfer and enjoyed playing the drums. Not surprisingly Donald Mackinlay is a member of Liverpool FC's Hall of Fame.

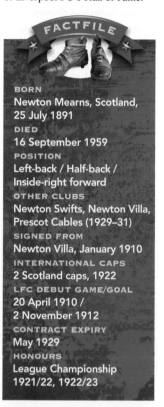

FACTFILE

BORN
Newton Mearns, Scotland, 25 July 1891
DIED
16 September 1959
POSITION
Left-back / Half-back / Inside-right forward
OTHER CLUBS
Newton Swifts, Newton Villa, Prescot Cables (1929–31)
SIGNED FROM
Newton Villa, January 1910
INTERNATIONAL CAPS
2 Scotland caps, 1922
LFC DEBUT GAME/GOAL
20 April 1910 / 2 November 1912
CONTRACT EXPIRY
May 1929
HONOURS
League Championship 1921/22, 1922/23

Season	League		FA Cup		Other		Total	
	App	Goals	App	Goals	App	Goals	App	Goals
1909/10	1	0	0	0	-	-	1	0
1910/11	2	0	0	0	-	-	2	0
1911/12	7	0	0	0	-	-	7	0
1912/13	22	6	1	0	-	-	23	6
1913/14	16	1	6	0	-	-	22	1
1914/15	20	1	2	0	-	-	22	1
1919/20	41	4	5	0	-	-	46	4
1920/21	35	2	3	0	-	-	38	2
1921/22	29	1	3	0	1	0	33	1
1922/23	42	5	4	1	-	-	46	6
1923/24	39	6	5	0	-	-	44	6
1924/25	28	4	2	0	-	-	30	4
1925/26	41	2	3	0	-	-	44	2
1926/27	28	1	4	0	-	-	32	1
1927/28	40	0	2	0	-	-	42	0
1928/29	2	0	0	0	-	-	2	0
Total	**393**	**33**	**40**	**1**	**1**	**0**	**434**	**34**

Maloney, Joe

JOSEPH JOHN Maloney was born in Liverpool and came through the junior ranks at Anfield before signing professional forms in January 1951. The centre-half's opportunities for first-team football were limited and he made six First Division appearances in 1952/53.

LIVERPOOL drew 0-0 against Bolton on his debut but lost the other five games he participated in, conceding four goals on average. He featured in an unfamiliar forward role in the following season at the end of which Liverpool were relegated into the Second Division. Maloney joined Third Division South team Shrewsbury Town and made nearly 250 appearances for the Shropshire club. Norman Low, a former Red, brought Maloney on a free transfer to Port Vale in the summer of 1961. Following a 4-2 opening-day defeat Maloney was released, two days after he made his debut.

FACTFILE

BORN
Liverpool,
26 January 1934
DIED
17 October 2006
POSITION
Centre-half,
Inside-right/left forward
OTHER CLUBS
Shrewsbury Town (1954–61),
Port Vale (1961),
Crewe Alexandra (1961–63),
Winsford United (1963–65)
JOINED
Signed professional
January 1951
LFC DEBUT
4 March 1953
CONTRACT EXPIRY
July 1954

Season	League		FA Cup		Total	
	App	Goals	App	Goals	App	Goals
1952/53	6	0	0	0	6	0
1953/54	6	0	0	0	6	0
Total	**12**	**0**	**0**	**0**	**12**	**0**

Managers

Manager	Reign	
John McKenna / William Barclay	15 March 1892	- 1895
John McKenna / The board	1895	- 27 July 1896
Tom Watson	27 July 1896	- 6 May 1915
George Patterson	14 September 1918	- December 1919
David Ashworth	17 December 1919	- 20 December 1922
Matt McQueen	13 February 1923	- 15 February 1928
George Patterson	7 March 1928	- 6 August 1936
George Kay	6 August 1936	- 30 January 1951
Don Welsh	5 March 1951	- 4 May 1956
Phil Taylor	15 May 1956	- 17 November 1959
Bill Shankly	1 December 1959	- 12 July 1974
Bob Paisley	26 July 1974	- 1 July 1983
Joe Fagan	1 July 1983	- 29 May 1985
Kenny Dalglish	30 May 1985	- 21 February 1991
Ronnie Moran*	22 February	- 15 April 1991
Graeme Souness	16 April 1991	- 28 January 1994
Roy Evans	31 January 1994	- 16 July 1998
Evans / Houllier	16 July	- 12 November 1998
Gérard Houllier	12 November 1998	- 24 May 2004
Rafa Benítez	16 June 2004	- 3 June 2010
Roy Hodgson	1 July 2010	- 8 January 2011
Kenny Dalglish	8 January 2011	- 16 May 2012
Brendan Rodgers	1 June 2012	

* Served as Acting manager

Joe Fagan with Roy Evans and Ronnie Moran

Don Welsh has the lowest winning percentage of all Liverpool managers

George Patterson was twice in charge of Liverpool

Author Arnie Baldursson with Gérard Houllier in October 2001

Manager	Winning %	Games	W	D	L	F	A
John McKenna / Board	69.44	36	25	3	8	116	37
Kenny Dalglish	58.53	381	223	94	64	732	332
Bob Paisley	57.57	535	308	131	96	955	406
John McKenna / WE Barclay	57.14	91	52	17	22	221	118
Rafa Benítez	56.29	350	197	74	79	585	302
Joe Fagan	54.20	131	71	36	24	225	97
Gérard Houllier	52.12	307	160	73	74	516	298
Bill Shankly	51.98	783	407	198	178	1307	766
Roy Evans	51.77	226	117	56	53	375	216
Phil Taylor	50.67	150	76	32	42	294	211
David Ashworth	50.36	139	70	40	29	220	118
Brendan Rodgers	46.30	54	25	15	14	98	64
Tom Watson	44.34	742	329	141	272	1226	1056
Graeme Souness	42.04	157	66	45	46	248	186
Roy Hodgson	41.94	31	13	8	10	41	33
Matt McQueen	40.61	229	93	60	76	354	307
Ronnie Moran	40.00	10	4	1	5	20	16
George Kay	39.55	354	140	93	121	545	508
Evans / Houllier	38.89	18	7	6	5	33	20
George Patterson	37.50	384	144	87	153	688	726
Don Welsh	34.91	232	81	58	93	387	423
Comparison of 1st and 2nd terms							
Kenny Dalglish	60.91	307	187	78	42	617	259
Kenny Dalglish (2nd term)	48.65	74	36	16	22	115	73
George Patterson	38.89	18	7	2	9	23	26
George Patterson (2nd term)	37.43	366	137	85	144	665	700

Marathon

Dalglish training at Melwood in 1984, a year before he was appointed manager

Phil Taylor leading out Liverpool in the early 50s

The longest FA Cup battle				
	Period	Opponent	Round	Results
420 minutes	12 April - 1 May 1980	Arsenal	Semi-final	1-1/1-1/1-1/0-1
300 minutes	17-27 February 1991	Everton	5th round	0-0/4-4/0-1
300 minutes	11-28 January 1987	Luton Town	3rd round	0-0/0-0/0-3
300 minutes	30 March - 18 April 1968	West Bromwich Albion	6th round	0-0/1-1/1-2
300 minutes	17-26 February 1962	Preston North End	5th round	0-0/0-0/0-1
270 minutes	18-30 March 1899	Sheffield United	Semi-final	2-2/4-4/0-1*

* All replays included extra-time except in 1899 against Sheffield United when that rule was not in place. Liverpool were leading 1-0 in the 2nd replay when it was abandoned due to crowd trouble. Sheffield United won 1-0 in the repeated game.

The longest FA Cup run is 9 games				
1967/68	Result	Opponent	Venue	Round
27 January 1968	0-0	Bournemouth & Boscombe Athletic	Dean Court	3rd round
30 January 1968	4-1	Bournemouth & Boscombe Athletic	Anfield	3rd round replay
17 February 1968	0-0	Walsall	Fellows Park	4th round
19 February 1968	5-2	Walsall	Anfield	4th round replay
9 March 1968	1-1	Tottenham Hotspur	White Hart Lane	5th round
12 March 1968	2-1	Tottenham Hotspur	Anfield	5th round replay
30 March 1968	0-0	West Bromwich Albion	The Hawthorns	6th round
8 April 1968	1-1	West Bromwich Albion	Anfield	6th round replay
18 April 1968	1-2	West Bromwich Albion	Maine Road	6th round 2nd replay

The longest FA Cup run is 9 games (continued)

1973/74	Result	Opponent	Venue	Round
5 January 1974	2-2	Doncaster Rovers	Anfield	3rd round
8 January 1974	2-0	Doncaster Rovers	Belle Vue	3rd round replay
26 January 1974	0-0	Carlisle United	Anfield	4th round
29 January 1974	2-0	Carlisle United	Brunton Park	4th round replay
16 February 1974	2-0	Ipswich Town	Anfield	5th round
9 March 1974	1-0	Bristol City	Ashton Gate	6th round
30 March 1974	0-0	Leicester City	Old Trafford	Semi-final
3 April 1974	3-1	Leicester City	Villa Park	Semi-final replay
4 May 1974	3-0	Newcastle United	Wembley	Final

1991/92	Result	Opponent	Venue	Round
6 January 1992	4-0	Crewe Alexandra	Gresty Road	3rd round
5 February 1992	1-1	Bristol Rovers	Twerton Park	4th round
11 February 1992	2-1	Bristol Rovers	Anfield	4th round replay
16 February 1992	0-0	Ipswich Town	Portman Road	5th round
26 February 1992	3-2	Ipswich Town	Anfield	5th round replay
8 March 1992	1-0	Aston Villa	Anfield	6th round
5 April 1992	1-1	Portsmouth	Highbury	Semi-final
13 April 1992	0-0	Portsmouth	Villa Park	Semi-final replay
9 May 1992	2-0	Sunderland	Wembley	Final

The longest League Cup battle

	Period	Opponent	Round	Results
330 minutes	8-29 November 1983	Fulham	3rd round	1-1/1-1/1-0
300 minutes	2-23 November 1988	Arsenal	3rd round	1-1/0-0/2-1

The longest League Cup run is 13 games

1983/84	Result	Opponent	Venue	Round
5 October 1983	4-1	Brentford	Griffin Park	2nd round 1st leg
25 October 1983	4-0	Brentford	Anfield	2nd round 2nd leg
8 November 1983	1-1	Fulham	Craven Cottage	3rd round
22 November 1983	1-1	Fulham	Anfield	3rd round replay*
29 November 1983	1-0	Fulham	Craven Cottage	3rd round 2nd replay*
20 December 1983	1-1	Birmingham City	St Andrews	4th round
22 December 1983	3-0	Birmingham City	Anfield	4th round replay
17 January 1984	2-2	Sheffield Wednesday	Hillsborough	5th round
25 January 1984	3-0	Sheffield Wednesday	Anfield	5th round replay
7 February 1984	2-2	Walsall	Anfield	Semi-final 1st leg
14 February 1984	2-0	Walsall	Fellows Park	Semi-final 2nd leg
25 March 1984	0-0	Everton	Wembley	Final
28 March 1984	1-0	Everton	Maine Road	Final replay

Both Fulham replays included extra-time.

The longest European battle

	Period	Opponent	Round	Results
300 minutes	10 February - 24 March 1965	Cologne	European Cup 2nd round	0-0/0-0/2-2*
270 minutes	28 September - 19 October 1966	Petrolul Ploiesti	European Cup 1st round	2-0/1-3/2-0

A coloured disc, red and white, was used to decide the outcome in the third game after extra-time. Liverpool won the toss up. In 1968 a similar situation came up in the 1st round of the European Fairs Cup but the toss up was at the end of the 2nd game against Athletic Bilbao after Liverpool lost 2-1 in Spain but won 2-1 at Anfield. This time Liverpool lost!

Marsh,
Mike

VLADIMIR SMICER and Mike Marsh shared a similar problem: both players excelled in training sessions but seldom transferred that ability to the Reds' competitive fixtures. Marsh was hardly an internationally known player like Vladi, but possessed enough skill to make people wonder what might have been.

In 1987 Marsh was playing for Kirkby Town and the Railway pub on Sundays, the latter being sponsored by Kirkby native and Liverpool's reserve-team coach, Phil Thompson, who was advised to take a closer look at this promising player. Marsh was a reserve at Liverpool for four years, admitting that he felt unworthy of being in such exclusive company. The players had been his heroes one minute and team-mates the next. He finally got his big break in the 1991/92 season, playing in midfield, and continued his good form into the following season.

> 'WITH THE LIKES OF STEVE MCMAHON, RONNIE WHELAN OR JAN MØLBY ALONGSIDE ME, THINGS WOULD HAVE GONE DIFFERENTLY'

MARSH'S most memorable moment came in the UEFA Cup second round tie versus Auxerre on 6 November 1991 at Anfield. Liverpool had lost the first leg 2-0 but Marsh scored Liverpool's second goal in a 3-0 win. 'I broke into the team at a difficult time,' Marsh explained to the *Liverpool Echo* in 2003. 'Maybe if I'd broken into a settled side with the likes of Steve McMahon, Ronnie

Whelan or Jan Mølby alongside me on a regular basis, things would have gone differently. I ended up playing alongside the likes of Paul Stewart. I actually asked to leave Liverpool. Again, I don't want it to sound as though I'm having a go at someone like Paul Stewart, but I suppose when the manager pays over £2million for a player he's always going to play him.' Marsh was transferred to West Ham along with David Burrows in a swap deal to bring Julian Dicks to Anfield in September 1993.

Marsh later rejoined his former Liverpool boss, Graeme Souness, at Galatasaray for a couple of months in 1995. A knee injury finally ended his professional career at the age of 28. Marsh accepted an insurance payout which meant he wasn't allowed to play in the Football League

again. When Kidderminster Harriers and Boston United were promoted to the Third Division in 1999/2000 and 2001/02 respectively, he had to move on as they were no longer non-league clubs. Marsh joined the Liverpool Academy in July 2009 and coached the Under-16s and Under-18s. In August 2012 he was promoted to Melwood to be a part of the club's first-team coaching set-up. Brendan Rodgers explained: 'Marshy was a terrific young player – he walked out of a pub team into Liverpool, which is an absolutely incredible story. His roots are here at the club, his passion is for the club and he's played for the club. He will help build a bridge between the first team and the Academy.'

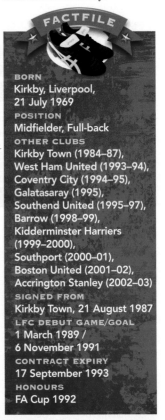

FACTFILE

BORN
Kirkby, Liverpool,
21 July 1969
POSITION
Midfielder, Full-back
OTHER CLUBS
Kirkby Town (1984–87),
West Ham United (1993–94),
Coventry City (1994–95),
Galatasaray (1995),
Southend United (1995–97),
Barrow (1998–99),
Kidderminster Harriers
(1999–2000),
Southport (2000–01),
Boston United (2001–02),
Accrington Stanley (2002–03)
SIGNED FROM
Kirkby Town, 21 August 1987
LFC DEBUT GAME/GOAL
1 March 1989 /
6 November 1991
CONTRACT EXPIRY
17 September 1993
HONOURS
FA Cup 1992

Season	League		FA Cup		League Cup		Europe		Other		Total	
	App	Goals	App	Goals	App	Goals	App	Goals	App	Goals	App	Goals
1988/89	0 (1)	0	0	0	0	0	-	-	0	0	0 (1)	0
1989/90	0 (2)	0	0	0	0	0	-	-	0	0	0 (2)	0
1990/91	1 (1)	0	0	0	1	0	-	-	0	0	2 (1)	0
1991/92	19 (15)	0	4 (2)	0	3 (1)	0	7 (1)	1	-	-	33 (19)	1
1992/93	22 (6)	1	2	0	6	3	4	0	1	0	35 (6)	4
1993/94	0 (2)	1	0	0	0	0	-	-	-	-	0 (2)	1
Total	**42 (27)**	**2**	**6 (2)**	**0**	**10 (1)**	**3**	**11 (1)**	**1**	**1**	**0**	**70 (31)**	**6**

Marshall, Bobby

BOBBY MARSHALL started the 1897/98 season on the right wing and played in the opening 16 fixtures before losing his place to Fred Geary.

He featured in three games in the 1898/99 season but his 'slow movements and aimless passing' in a 2-1 win over Everton in September 1898 did not increase his chances. Also, the 'rasping shots' Marshall was capable of were sadly missing. He scored twice for Liverpool, both goals coming in a 4-2 home win over Derby County on 23 October 1897. Liverpool had been 2-0 up at half-time but with the scores at 3-2 Marshall put the result beyond any doubt near the end with a beautiful header. He moved south to Portsmouth and the *Edinburgh Evening News* reported in March 1903 that since he had left Liverpool 'he has taken part in no fewer than 217 of the 223 matches played by his present club, and during the four seasons he has only missed one Southern League match.' Marshall won the Southern League with Portsmouth in 1901/02.

Robert Grant Marshall

Season	League		FA Cup		Total	
	App	Goals	App	Goals	App	Goals
1897/98	17	2	1	0	18	2
1898/99	3	0	0	0	3	0
Total	**20**	**2**	**1**	**0**	**21**	**2**

Marshall, Bill

THE ONLY MATCH Liverpool's main keeper, Bill Perkins, missed in the 1901/02 season was a sad 'one and only' for William Marshall, as Liverpool were thrashed 4-0 by their neighbours at Goodison Park on 11 January 1902.

The *Liverpool Mercury* criticised Marshall's positioning but was sympathetic towards the custodian who had joined the club the previous month. To be thrown into the lion's den of a Merseyside derby in his first outing led to the 'highest degree of tension' in players, it said.

Season	League		FA Cup		Total	
	App	Goals	App	Goals	App	Goals
1901/02	1	0	0	0	1	0
Total	**1**	**0**	**0**	**0**	**1**	**0**

A commemorative cup given to Bill Marshall by the club

Mascherano, Javier

FROM THE AGE of ten, Javier Mascherano's father Oscar demanded that he should learn the art of the enforcer. Javier clearly mastered that skill and attracted interest for his displays in the 2003 FIFA World Youth Championship when he was on the books of River Plate. He even made his full international debut before playing his first game in the Argentinian league.

In the 2005/06 season Mascherano joined Brazilian club Corinthians for £7.5million. His deal came about after Corinthians signed a controversial deal with London-based investors Media Sports Investments (MSI), headed by the agent Kia Joorabchian. The deal granted MSI a big say in the future of the Brazilian club in exchange for financial investments. This brought many other quality players to the team, such as Carlos Tévez. However, the players in question were not owned by Corinthians but, in fact, MSI. Despite a troubled start to the Campeonato Brasileiro in 2005 the club was eventually crowned League Champions. Unfortunately Mascherano suffered a leg break and didn't contribute a lot to that success. The Argentinian national team flew in their doctor to oversee his rehabilitation so he would be ready for the World Cup in Germany. As it turned out Mascherano played every minute as Argentina reached the quarter-finals only to be knocked out by the hosts after a penalty shootout. The relationship between MSI and Corinthians became increasingly difficult and in 2006 Mascherano and Tévez joined West Ham for an undisclosed fee. The sellers were not Corinthians but, to perfectly muddy the waters, four investment funds: MSI, Just Sports Incorporated, Global Soccer Agencies and Mystere Services Limited – all represented by Joorabchian. Tévez was owned by the former two and Mascherano the latter two.

Quite mysteriously the highly rated Mascherano played only seven games in a struggling Hammers team, sparking rumours about financial clauses that were related to his actual playing time. Mascherano had a particularly memorable game against Spurs when after sliding in on Jermaine Defoe the Spurs striker bit his arm!

Rafa Benítez saw a golden opportunity for Liverpool to acquire a quality player and flew to London to meet him, spending four hours at Canary Wharf talking with Mascherano, using stones to illustrate the role he envisaged him playing in his team. Liverpool had to court FIFA to get him because of FIFA Article 5.3, which states that a player may not sign for more than three clubs, and play for more than two, between 1 July of one year and 30 June of the next. Mascherano had already been a player for Corinthians and West Ham within that time frame. 'There is a big difference between the law and the

rules. A worker cannot be stopped working,' Benítez argued. 'That's the law of the European Community. There are players in the world now who have played for three or four clubs in a season. They have freedom and they need to work.' He had valid reasons for getting Mascherano. 'I knew about this player when he was with River Plate. He was playing in their reserve team but already in the national team. That shows you the quality and the character of the player.'

Liverpool initially paid £1.6million to get Mascherano on loan with a view to a permanent transfer in January 2007, and he certainly impressed the fans, his team-mates and manager. 'Jefecito' or 'Little chief' proved to be a tough-tackling player who distributed the ball well and encouraged others to give their best. In only his 11th game he was Liverpool's best performer in the Champions League final against Milan in Athens. On 29 February 2008 he signed a permanent contract for four years with Liverpool, who paid the required £17million. He soon became a crowd favourite for his commitment and to the tune of White Stripes' 'Seven Nation Army' his name echoed around Anfield, though he was sometimes a bit overzealous.

March 2008 was a mixed month for Mascherano as he scored his first Liverpool goal with a brilliant effort against Reading at Anfield but was then sent off at Old Trafford a week later for confronting referee Steve Bennett at length after a yellow card had been given to Torres just before half-time. Mascherano had to be pushed off the field by Gerrard and Alonso, and Benítez was also forced to plead with him to go to the dressing room. The usual one-game ban for a red card was extended to three games for improper conduct.

FACTFILE

BORN
San Lorenzo, Argentina,
8 June 1984
POSITION
Midfielder
OTHER CLUBS
River Plate (2003–05),
Corinthians (2005–06),
West Ham United (2006–07),
Barcelona (2010–)
SIGNED FROM
Global Soccer Agencies and
Mystere Services Limited,
on loan, 30 January 2007;
permanent, £18.6million,
29 February 2008
INTERNATIONAL CAPS
90 Argentina caps (2 goals)
(41 (2) at LFC), 2003–
LFC DEBUT GAME/GOAL
24 February 2007 /
15 March 2008
CONTRACT EXPIRY
30 August 2010

Mascherano represented Argentina in the Olympic Games in Beijing in August 2008 as one of their over-23 players and became the proud owner of two Olympic gold medals as he was also in Argentina's successful team in Athens 2004. Soon after being appointed head coach of Argentina in November 2008, Diego Maradona appointed Mascherano as team captain. Maradona's decision didn't come as a surprise as he had previously declared that 'Mascherano has the biggest talent of all the young players I have seen in the last years. He is a monster of a player and destined for great things.' The Argentinian was, however, not as dynamic as was expected for Liverpool for the first part of the 2008/09 season and clearly suffered from not getting sufficient rest over the summer because of his international duties. Eventually he got back to his very best and European Champions Barcelona showed strong interest in him during the summer. Mascherano's agent claimed that his client wanted to join Barca, but Liverpool didn't want to sell him under any circumstances.

'I KNOW THAT LIVERPOOL SUPPORTERS AFTER MY EXIT WERE A LITTLE BIT SAD WITH ME SO THIS IS FOR THEM AS WELL'

Argentina's captain took a while to get going in the 2009/10 season, confessing he found it hard to motivate himself after his proposed move to Barcelona fell through. A couple of months into the season he returned to his usual tremendous standards in Liverpool's midfield, only missing four Premier League matches and four cup matches during the

whole campaign. His presence certainly was missed when he was unavailable, but he was, however, the architect of his own unavailability. He received a red card for an unnecessary lunge at United's Edwin Van der Sar at Anfield in October and got another red against Portsmouth just before Christmas. It wasn't surprising that he was ranked number one on the disciplinary list in the 2009/10 Premier League season with nine yellows and two reds. A playing highlight was a fierce drive in the Goodison derby that deflected off Joseph Yobo into the Gwladys Street goal. Mascherano's run and dive in front of the away supporters

showed his passion and his pride in wearing a Liverpool shirt.

THE UNAVOIDABLE happened on the penultimate day of the summer transfer window in 2010 when Mascherano signed a four-year deal with Barcelona, who paid £17.2million for his services. He featured in the 2011

Wembley Champions League final when the Catalans blew Manchester United away. He finally exorcised the demons of his previous final appearance in this competition, in Athens. Mascherano, poignantly, told the watching world: 'I know that Liverpool supporters after my exit were a little bit sad with me so this

is for them as well,' which went down well among the Reds' faithful, but was not received as joyously by fans of Manchester United. Mascherano has been transformed into a centre-half and has been a vital part of Barcelona's success. Reds can hardly fault him for being lured away by the best team in the world.

Season	League		FA Cup		League Cup		Europe		Other		Total	
	App	Goals	App	Goals	App	Goals	App	Goals	App	Goals	App	Goals
2006/07	7	0	0	0	0	0	4	0	0	0	11	0
2007/08	25	1	1 (1)	0	0 (1)	0	13	0	-	-	39 (2)	1
2008/09	27	0	2 (1)	0	0	0	8	0	-	-	37 (1)	0
2009/10	31 (3)	0	0	0	1	0	12 (1)	1	-	-	44 (4)	1
2010/11	1	0	0	0	0	0	0	0	-	-	1	0
Total	91 (3)	1	3 (2)	0	1 (1)	0	37 (1)	1	0	0	132 (7)	2

Matteo,
Dominic

DOMINIC MATTEO was brought to Liverpool when only 11 years old after catching Kenny Dalglish's eye while he was watching his son Paul play for Birkdale United.

It was Graeme Souness who blooded the 19-year-old in October 1993 as a left-midfielder. Matteo was now on the other side of those carefully painted white lines but old habits die hard and he found himself singing along to 'You'll Never Walk Alone' before realising that he was no longer a fan but a player! 'He's a young boy with an awful lot to offer. We just don't yet know his best position,' Souness said following his debut against Manchester City. Matteo, who was making his breakthrough at the same time as Robbie Fowler, got a decent run in the side but once Souness was sacked Matteo only made a few sporadic appearances in Roy Evans' first two full seasons. He did start the first couple of games in the 1995/96 season in a three-man centre-back line but once Neil Ruddock had

recovered from injury Matteo was benched. He finally got his big breakthrough in the 1996/97 season when he featured in two-thirds of the league games when Liverpool were top of the division at the turn of the year but faded away in the last third of the campaign.

In 1999/2000, when Matteo was taking orders from his fourth manager in his time at Liverpool in Gérard Houllier, he played left-back. Matters came to a head when Houllier told Matteo prior to the 2000/01 season that Christian Ziege was on his way from Middlesbrough and going

FACTFILE

BORN
Dumfries, Scotland,
28 April 1974
POSITION
Left-winger / Left-back /
Centre-half
OTHER CLUBS
Sunderland (loan, 1995),
Leeds United (2000–04),
Blackburn Rovers (2004–07),
Stoke City (2007–09)
JOINED
1985; signed professional
27 May 1992
INTERNATIONAL CAPS
6 Scotland caps, 2000–02
LFC DEBUT GAME/GOAL
23 October 1993 /
16 January 1999
CONTRACT EXPIRY
18 August 2000

straight into the first team. Devastated at not even being given a chance to fight for his place, 26-year-old Matteo moved across the Pennines to join Leeds. 'On the Monday, I was signing a five-year deal that, by the standards of the day, was a lucrative one. But, just four days later, I was on my way out of Liverpool,' Matteo revealed in his autobiography. 'I was in shock. How could things change so quickly in just four days? The thought of leaving was an

upsetting one. But, for the good of my career, I needed a fresh start. So, I went. It meant I missed out on all the trophies that Liverpool won the following season. I'll admit that seeing the lads pick up the FA Cup, League Cup and UEFA Cup was difficult.'

MATTEO was made club captain when Rio Ferdinand left Leeds to join Manchester United in the summer of 2002. A few months earlier Matteo had made his Scotland debut. Even though he had English parents he was born in Dumfries and was even eligible for Italy as his grandparents are Italian. He had already played for England's Under-21 team and been called up by Glenn Hoddle to the senior squad, but injuries prevented him from making his full England debut. His former boss Souness persuaded Matteo to join Blackburn Rovers in 2004 and after his time at Ewood Park, where he was captain for a while, he moved to Championship club Stoke City on a free transfer in January 2007. Although Stoke were promoted to the Premier League at the end of the 2007/08 season, Matteo had played little part in that success. Injuries were starting to seriously affect his availability and, with more time on his hands than if he was fully fit, he got dragged into a very serious gambling addiction, on which he squandered a massive sum of money. After an eventful career Matteo called it quits at the end of the 2008/09 season.

'**THE QUESTION** I always ask myself is "Could I have done more with my career, could I have been better?" he reflected in the *Guardian* in 2011. 'And the answer to that is "yes". My age group in football were the last of an era. We were brought up into football having a bevvy, enjoying ourselves, we were out three or four times a week. I think if I'd have lived my life better I might have played for longer, suffered less injuries.'

	League		FA Cup		League Cup		Europe		Total	
Season	App	Goals	App	Goals	App	Goals	App	Goals	App	Goals
1993/94	11	0	0	0	2	0	-	-	13	0
1994/95	2 (5)	0	1	0	0	0	-	-	3 (5)	0
1995/96	5	0	0 (1)	0	0	0	0	0	5 (1)	0
1996/97	22 (4)	0	2	0	3	0	7	0	34 (4)	0
1997/98	24 (2)	0	1	0	4	0	2	0	31 (2)	0
1998/99	16 (4)	1	1	0	0	0	1 (1)	0	18 (5)	1
1999/2000	32	0	1 (1)	1	0	0	-	-	33 (1)	1
Total	**112 (15)**	**1**	**6 (2)**	**1**	**9**	**0**	**10 (1)**	**0**	**137 (18)**	**2**

Matthews, Billy

AFTER HAVING made 13 wartime appearances and scored eight goals in the 1918/19 season, Billy Matthews made his official first-team debut for Liverpool as a centre-half in a 3-0 win over Derby County on 3 April 1920.

Big, burly and boisterous, Billy played as a forward in his other eight appearances for the Reds, who wanted to make him a central defender. He revealed to a reporter at the *Derby Daily Telegraph* in 1922: 'Liverpool think I will make a centre-half, but I know I never shall. It is not in my bones to play there!' Matthews scored three goals in two games at the beginning of the 1921/22 season, in a 3-2 win over Manchester City and a 2-1 win against Sunderland, both at Anfield. The centre-forward position was there for the taking as Liverpool had still not settled for a player to complement inside-forwards Harry Chambers on the left and Dick Forshaw on the right since Dick Johnson's serious injury. In the following five matches Matthews only once got on the scoresheet and lost his place. Danny Shone, Harry Beadles and Harry Lewis also failed to establish themselves as centre-forwards during that campaign that ended with Liverpool lifting the title.

HOWEVER, before the season was out Matthews had moved to Second Division Bristol City. Matthews was a fitness fanatic and a keen cyclist into his nineties and was known as 'Billy white hat' because of the distinctive headgear he wore.

FACTFILE

BORN
Plas Bennion, Wales,
14 April 1897
DIED
18 December 1987
POSITION
Centre-forward
OTHER CLUBS
Colwyn Bay (1916–18),
Bristol City (1922–23),
Wrexham (1923–25),
Northwich Victoria (1925),
Barrow (1925–26),
Bradford Park Avenue
(1926–30),
Stockport County (1930),
New Brighton (1930–32),
Chester (1932),
Oswestry Town (1932),
Witton Albion (1932),
Sandbach Ramblers (1932–33),
Colwyn Bay United (1933),
Rossendale United (1933–36)
SIGNED FROM
Colwyn Bay, 1918
INTERNATIONAL CAPS
3 Wales caps (1 at LFC),
1921–26
LFC DEBUT GAME/GOAL
3 April 1920 /
31 August 1921
CONTRACT EXPIRY
2 March 1922

	League		FA Cup		Other		Total	
Season	App	Goals	App	Goals	App	Goals	App	Goals
1919/20	1	0	0	0	-	-	1	0
1920/21	1	0	0	0	-	-	1	0
1921/22	7	4	0	0	0	0	7	4
Total	**9**	**4**	**0**	**0**	**0**	**0**	**9**	**4**

Maxwell,
Layton

LAYTON MAXWELL was born in St Asaph, the same village as Ian Rush, and probably dreamed of a great Liverpool career. He scored an excellent goal on his debut for Liverpool in the League Cup against Hull which confirmed participation in the third round. 'I scored and you really think you've made it when that happens,' said Maxwell. 'Not many players score at the Kop End on their Liverpool debut. It was some night after that game, but I soon came back down to earth because I was training with the reserves the following week.'

After roughly a year without first-team action the Welshman was loaned to Stockport County for a season when the Edgeley Park club finished bottom in what was then the First Division. Maxwell admitted his future at Liverpool was bleak. 'The trouble is, I like to play in a central role using my pace to come off defenders, but there's someone else at Liverpool who already does that – Owen. That's the competition I've got.'

CARDIFF CITY took Maxwell to his home country but he struggled at the club and his contract was terminated midway through the 2003/04 season. He played a few games for Swansea on a non-contract basis, not doing enough to seal a permanent deal, but enough to disgust his former fans at Cardiff!

FACTFILE

BORN
St Asaph, Wales,
3 October 1979
POSITION
Midfielder
OTHER CLUBS
Stockport County
(loan, 2000–01),
Cardiff City (2001–03),
Barry Town (loan, 2003),
Swansea City (2004),
Rhyl (2004),
Newport County (2004),
Mansfield Town (2004–05),
Carmarthen Town (2005),
Bangor City (2005–06),
Caernarfon Town (2006–08),
ENTO Aberaman Athletic
(2008–09),
Maesteg Park (2009–10),
Barry Town (2010–11),
Pontypridd Town (2011–12)
JOINED
1993; signed professional
1 July 1999
INTERNATIONAL CAPS
14 Wales U-21 caps
LFC DEBUT GAME/GOAL
21 September 1999 /
21 September 1999
CONTRACT EXPIRY
4 July 2001

Season	League		FA Cup		Other		Total	
	App	Goals	App	Goals	App	Goals	App	Goals
1999/2000	0	0	0	0	1	1	1	1
Total	**0**	**0**	**0**	**0**	**1**	**1**	**1**	**1**

McAllister, Gary

DESPITE being linked with a move to Liverpool, 'Gary Mac' joined Leeds in 1990 having played a starring role for Leicester City. McAllister, David Batty, Gordon Strachan and Gary Speed clicked in midfield and with Eric Cantona up front they created the nucleus of the Championship-winning team in the 1991/92 season.

McAllister was voted Leeds United's Player of the Year in 1993/94 but left two years later after a disagreement over contract terms. £3million was considered a high fee for a 31-year-old, but then Coventry boss Gordon Strachan knew his old team-mate wouldn't fail. McAllister became

Coventry's captain and he even captained his national team for a while. In his final season at the Sky Blues he was voted their best player.

Few could believe Gérard Houllier's decision to sign McAllister in July 2000 at the age of 35, not least the man himself. 'This is fairytale stuff for someone at my stage of life. It did surprise me when Liverpool came in for me,' McAllister told the *Liverpool Echo*. 'Liverpool have got three cup competitions next season plus a tough Premiership campaign. The average age of their side last season was under 25, and that's very young indeed for a top-flight club. The manager explained

that there was a need for some experience around the squad, an old head in the side. I've just had my best ever scoring tally in the Premiership with 13 last season, and I'm feeling as fit as ever. It's too early to say just how many games I will play, maybe people will be surprised.'

McALLISTER had only played two games for Liverpool when he received the devastating news that his wife, who was heavily pregnant with their second child, had been diagnosed with breast cancer. McAllister was two months away on compassionate leave from Liverpool. He moved house to Manchester, took care of the new baby and was a source of strength for his wife Denise, whom he had met in the mid-80s and married in 1993. 'You get to travel the world, make money and meet loads of

interesting people. But basically you're pampered and spoiled as an individual until you undergo a life-changing experience, such as the fear of losing your wife,' McAllister told the *Daily Mail* in February 2001. 'I couldn't have made it through that time if it hadn't been for Denise herself and the courage and determination she showed. I had to be strong for her and my son Jake, but I also understood I was gathering strength from watching my wife and listening to her speak about the illness.'

Despite the ongoing issues off the field, McAllister returned in mid-October and led by example as Liverpool marched through all three cup competitions. He ensured his name would be in Liverpool folklore when Everton and Liverpool were heading for

a 2-2 draw in the league at Goodison Park on 16 April 2001. McAllister prepared to take a free kick 44 yards out in stoppage time. Paul Gerrard in the Everton goal expected a cross but McAllister had other ideas and hit a dipping shot into the bottom right-hand corner – 3-2 and delirium for Reds inside the stadium. McAllister was rightly proud of his fantastic goal. 'Just a moment of inspiration. I just went for it and it just managed to creep in the bottom corner. I think they were taken a wee bit by surprise that I went for goal. I think it was even suggested that it was a fluke but no, I've got to tell you that I did mean it, I did mean it!' In the following game McAllister's confident penalty past Barcelona's Pepe Reina at Anfield guaranteed the Reds a place in the UEFA Cup final. He was pulling all the strings in the last third of Liverpool's adventurous season, scoring in five consecutive games. Following his scoring exploits against the Blues and Barca McAllister scored from the penalty spot in a 3-1 win over Tottenham, a beauty of a free kick defeated his former club Coventry, and another exquisite free kick followed against Bradford City. No wonder fans still sing today about Gary Mac's baldy head, his sweet right foot and numerous goals after signing on a free. These were exciting times for a Liverpool supporter.

The League Cup, FA Cup and UEFA Cup were won and McAllister was voted man of the match against Alaves in Dortmund, where he was involved in four of Liverpool's five goals.

McAllister was less influential in his second season at Anfield and was mostly on the bench in the second part of the campaign. Liverpool made a decent title challenge but Arsenal couldn't be conquered. The Kop chanted (tongue firmly in cheek) 'What a waste of money' as McAllister exited Anfield for the last time, leaving behind a whole host of wonderful memories. He couldn't have wished for a better send-off. 'I thought I would get a decent reception but that surpassed all my wildest dreams,' McAllister said. 'That sort of ovation is normally reserved for players who have won European Cups for a club. It was nice to hear the Kop's humour at its best again when they were telling me to go back to Coventry.'

McAllister rejoined the Sky Blues as their player-manager in May 2002. Sadly, his wife's cancer had returned and McAllister resigned from the club in January 2004 so that he could spend more time with his family. Denise passed away in March 2006. After nearly four years out of the game, McAllister was lured back into football management by one of his former clubs, Leeds United, in January 2008. A popular choice with the Elland Road club's supporters, he took Leeds to the League One playoff final at Wembley but they were beaten by Doncaster Rovers. Things did not go well the following season and he was dismissed four days before Christmas 2008 after a bad run of results that included an embarrassing FA Cup exit to non-league Histon. McAllister joined Middlesbrough as first-team coach in May 2010. Four months later he left his post at Boro

to become Gérard Houllier's assistant manager at Aston Villa. When Houllier had to take sick leave in April 2011 McAllister deputised for him until the end of the season, his last game in charge being a 1-0 home victory over Liverpool. When Alex McLeish took over as manager McAllister left Villa.

The 2000/01 season was one of the most memorable in McAllister's distinguished career. 'There was a time when I went into training and we were off to Rome, then on a jet to Cardiff for the League Cup final, then Barcelona, then Portugal, then down to qualify for the Champions League at Charlton. That's what you come into football for, to be involved in the best games against the best players where there's a lot at stake. It was magic.'

FACTFILE

BORN
Motherwell, Scotland, 25 December 1964
POSITION
Midfielder
OTHER CLUBS
Motherwell (1981–85), Leicester City (1985–90), Leeds United (1990–96), Coventry City (1996–2000), Coventry City (2002–03)
JOINED
Bosman free transfer, 1 July 2000
INTERNATIONAL CAPS
57 Scotland caps (5 goals), 1990–99
LFC DEBUT GAME/GOAL
19 August 2000 / 12 November 2000
CONTRACT EXPIRY
13 May 2002
HONOURS
FA Cup 2001; League Cup 2001; UEFA Cup 2001

> THE LEAGUE CUP, FA CUP AND UEFA CUP WERE WON AND MCALLISTER WAS VOTED MAN OF THE MATCH AGAINST ALAVES IN DORTMUND, WHERE HE WAS INVOLVED IN FOUR OF LIVERPOOL'S FIVE GOALS

Season	League		FA Cup		League Cup		Europe		Other		Total	
	App	Goals	App	Goals	App	Goals	App	Goals	App	Goals	App	Goals
2000/01	21 (9)	5	4 (1)	0	2 (3)	0	4 (5)	2	-	-	31 (18)	7
2001/02	14 (11)	0	0	0	1	1	5 (6)	0	1	1	21 (17)	2
Total	35 (20)	5	4 (1)	0	3 (3)	1	9 (11)	2	1	1	52 (35)	9

McAteer,
Jason

JASON McATEER was a bona fide boyhood Red who saw his dream come true when he signed for Liverpool instead of Premier League champions Blackburn. McAteer joined Crosby-based non-league club Marine after being spotted playing Sunday league football on the Wirral. In January 1992 Phil Neal snapped him up for Third Division Bolton. In three seasons the central midfielder helped Bolton to the Premier League and starred for the Republic of Ireland in the 1994 World Cup.

McAteer joined Liverpool at the start of the 1995/96 season. Five months earlier Liverpool had broken his heart when two Steve McManaman goals beat Bolton in the League Cup final. McAteer came as a breath of fresh air, making his mark as a right wing-back. He was always a better attacker than defender, delivering dangerous crosses into the penalty area after energetic runs down the right flank. He was tireless in his efforts and sacrificed himself for the Liverpool team. McAteer was a regular from 1995 to 1997, again suffering Wembley heartbreak in 1996 at the hands of Manchester United. He lost his place in the starting line-up at the start of the 1997/98 season but reclaimed it in November 1997 and played regularly until he broke his leg against Blackburn on the last day of January 1998. Once Roy Evans made way for Houllier to take sole control of the team in November 1998 McAteer's days were numbered.

His post-Liverpool career saw him move to Blackburn Rovers for £4million and he helped Rovers into the Premier League at the end of the 2000/01 season. His highlight in football was scoring the 67th-minute winner

at Lansdowne Road in September 2001 when the ten-man Ireland team beat the Netherlands to put the Irish on course for qualification for the 2002 World Cup. 'The Dutch had already booked their hotels in Japan and Korea so it was lovely to wipe the smiles off their faces. Fantastic, absolutely fantastic time,' McAteer recalled in the *Guardian*.

McAteer moved to Sunderland where he was part of the squad relegated from the Premier League in 2003. Sunderland released him a year later and he moved to his fifth and final English club, Tranmere Rovers. Rovers manager Brian Little made McAteer his club captain and one year following his retirement he became John Barnes' assistant manager at the club. However, Tranmere made a terrible start to the 2009/10

season and both McAteer and Barnes were dismissed by Rovers in October 2009.

McAteer has a reputation for not being the sharpest tool in the box and he gladly confesses to his dimwittedness. 'Sometimes I don't think before I speak – like the time I went into a Dublin pub and asked if they served Guinness,' he once confessed. 'I'm known for being a fool and they called me Trigger.' When McAteer locked himself, Phil Babb and Neil Ruddock out of his brand-new Porsche outside his house, the police asked him to get a coat-hanger so they could pick the lock and McAteer came back with a wooden one. He also can't live down a moment after an Ireland match in Dublin when he was in a pub where snooker legend Jimmy White walked in.

When seeing Jimmy, McAteer shouted: 'Oi Jimmy... One hundred and eighty!'

Above everything else McAteer deserves the highest praise imaginable for organising the 'Tsunami Soccer Aid' charity match which around 38,000 people attended at Anfield on Easter Sunday in 2005. McAteer sprung into action after watching a BBC documentary on the Indian Ocean Tsunami in 2004 that resulted in up to 280,000 deaths, making it the sixth deadliest natural disaster in recorded history. 'I went to bed and thought: "It's easy to put your hand in your pocket, give £20 and forget about it, but I want to do more",' McAteer recollected in the *Guardian*. 'The easiest thing that came to mind was to arrange a Liverpool legends/celebrities match.' His charity event raised over £412,000.

FACTFILE

BORN
Birkenhead, 18 June 1971
POSITION
Left wing-back
OTHER CLUBS
Marine (1988–92),
Bolton Wanderers (1992–95),
Blackburn Rovers
(1999–2001),
Sunderland (2001–04),
Tranmere Rovers (2004–07)
SIGNED FROM
Bolton Wanderers, £4.5million,
7 September 1995
INTERNATIONAL CAPS
52 Ireland caps (3 goals)
(14 (1) at LFC), 1994–2004
LFC DEBUT GAME/GOAL
16 September 1995 /
6 January 1996
CONTRACT EXPIRY
27 January 1999

Season	League		FA Cup		League Cup		Europe		Total	
	App	Goals	App	Goals	App	Goals	App	Goals	App	Goals
1995/96	27 (2)	0	7	3	3 (1)	0	0	0	37 (3)	3
1996/97	36 (1)	1	2	0	4	0	8	0	50 (1)	1
1997/98	15 (6)	2	1	0	3	0	1	0	20 (6)	2
1998/99	6 (7)	0	1 (1)	0	2	0	3 (2)	0	12 (10)	0
Total	**84 (16)**	**3**	**11 (1)**	**3**	**12 (1)**	**0**	**12 (2)**	**0**	**119 (20)**	**6**

McAvoy, Doug

DOUG McAVOY signed for Liverpool from his home-town club in December 1947.

He was 29 years old at the time, struggled to earn a place in the defending champions' team and made only a single appearance for the club in the rest of the season, that debut coming when Stoke City visited Anfield on 3 January 1948, replacing Cyril Done. The same thing happened the following season too; just a solitary appearance against Chelsea in

October 1948. The inside-left forward played his best years in Scotland with Kilmarnock. In 1939 he was sent along with a group of his compatriots by the Scottish FA to tour the USA. They were promoted as 'The Scottish Internationals' even though only seven of the 17 in the squad had ever played for Scotland. Bill Cole, the 'soccer' writer for the *Toronto Star*, blasted the Scottish FA for sending a 'weak team'.

Season	League		FA Cup		Total	
	App	Goals	App	Goals	App	Goals
1947/48	1	0	0	0	1	0
1948/49	1	0	0	0	1	0
Total	**2**	**0**	**0**	**0**	**2**	**0**

McBain, Neil

AYR UNITED'S Neil McBain had trials at Kilmarnock and Third Lanark before joining Manchester United in November 1921. As Liverpool won the league, United were relegated and McBain left Old Trafford in the middle of the 1922/23 season for First Division Everton.

It was a highy controversial move that cost the Blues no less than £4,000 and United fans held public meetings to protest at the transfer as they were losing such a valued player. McBain made 103 appearances for Everton before moving back to Scotland in 1926. Two years later he joined

Liverpool where he replaced long-serving full-back Tommy Lucas for the final stages of the 1927/28 season, when he played in 10 of the last 11 fixtures. He only played twice more for the club, on both occasions replacing Tom Bromilow, in consecutive matches against Arsenal and Birmingham in the late autumn of 1928.

MCBAIN, who was known for his heading ability and elegance on the ball, is the oldest player ever to appear in a league match at the age of 51 years and 120 days. In March 1947 he was the manager

of Third Division North side New Brighton, who were short of a goalkeeper, and put himself in goal, conceding three goals in a 3-0 loss against Hartlepool.

Season	League		FA Cup		Total	
	App	Goals	App	Goals	App	Goals
1927/28	10	0	0	0	10	0
1928/29	2	0	0	0	2	0
Total	**12**	**0**	**0**	**0**	**12**	**0**

McBride, Jim

CENTRE-HALF Jim McBride was a regular member of the Liverpool team that won the Lancashire League in the club's first ever season and the Second Division Championship in the 1893/94 season.

He was thus described: 'McBride makes up by science what he loses by height. He is fearless and bold, and but a stripling.' The Scotsman was a regular in the 1893/94 season but only played five more times the following season as the team finished bottom of the table with 22 points and then losing the decisive relegation/promotion Test match to Bury.

Willie Maley, who was Celtic's manager for no fewer than 43 years, told an amusing story about then Renton players and future Liverpool team-mates, McBride and Andrew Hannah, in the *Evening Times* in 1954. The first international game between the English and Scottish

football leagues took place on 11 April 1892 at Pike's Lane in Bolton with the English equalising 2-2 in the last minute. Hannah and McBride were in the Scottish side along with Maley, who lived to be 90 years old and was in 1954 the sole survivor of this clash. 'The Scottish players' reward for that game was 10s each with a cap and jersey,' Maley recollected. 'On the way home in the usual large saloon carriage, McBride of Renton FC, a young lad of 17, tired out fell sound asleep and Hannah, his

club captain, relieved him of the golden half-sovereign he told us he was taking home "to his mither". When morning came McBride found his gold coin had miraculously turned into a silver sixpence to the astonishment of this "laddie", who was possibly the youngest of internationalists of my experience. Hannah, of course, later "replaced" the gold coin.'

McBRIDE died suddenly at his home in Manchester on 25 May 1899, only 25 years of age.

FACTFILE

BORN
Renton, Dunbartonshire, Scotland,
30 December 1873
DIED
25 May 1899
POSITION
Centre-half
OTHER CLUBS
Renton Wanderers (1889–90),
Renton (1890–92),
Manchester City (1894–97),
Ashton North End (1897–98)
SIGNED FROM
Renton, June 1892
LFC DEBUT GAME/GOAL
3 September 1892 /
3 September 1892
CONTRACT EXPIRY
December 1894
HONOURS
Lancashire League 1892/93;
Second Division
Championship 1893/94

Season	League		FA Cup		Other		Total	
	App	Goals	App	Goals	App	Goals	App	Goals
1892/93	-	-	3	0	20	4	23	4
1893/94	25	3	2	0	1	0	28	3
1894/95	5	0	0	0	0	0	5	0
Total	30	3	5	0	21	4	56	7

McCallum, Don

DON McCALLUM was obtained in June 1901 from Queen's Park, Scotland's oldest football club, founded in 1867.

Liverpool's regular right-back in the 1902/03 season was John Glover and he missed only four of the 34 First Division fixtures during that campaign. On two of those occasions, McCallum stepped in to cover for him, in a 2-1 win over West Bromwich Albion on 11 October 1902 and a 3-1 defeat to Blackburn Rovers on 3 January 1903. He moved to Morton in Greenock, Scotland, prior to the 1903/04 season in exchange for Herbert Craik.

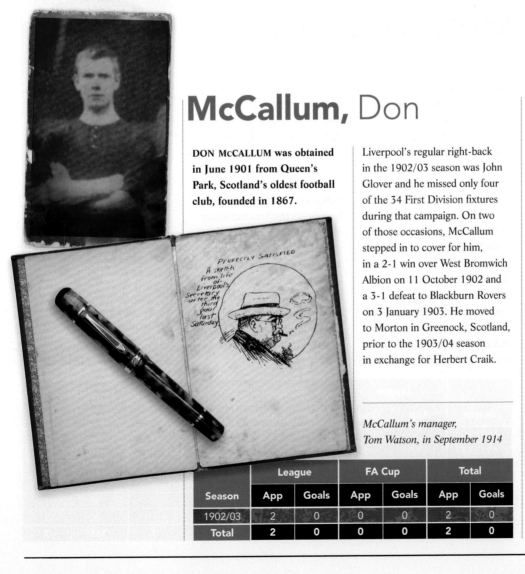

McCallum's manager, Tom Watson, in September 1914

FACTFILE

BORN
Glasgow, Scotland,
June 1880
POSITION
Right-back
OTHER CLUBS
Strathclyde,
Queen's Park,
Morton (1903–04),
Sunderland (1904),
Middlesbrough (1904–06),
Port Glasgow Athletic (1906),
Kilmarnock (1906–08),
Renton (1908–09),
Lochgelly United (1909–12),
East Fife (1912–13),
Mid-Rhondda (1913–14),
East Fife (1914–15)
SIGNED FROM
Queen's Park,
20 June 1901
LFC DEBUT
11 October 1902
CONTRACT EXPIRY
27 May 1903

Season	League		FA Cup		Total	
	App	Goals	App	Goals	App	Goals
1902/03	2	0	0	0	2	0
Total	2	0	0	0	2	0

McCann, Bill

BILL McCANN left blue-and-white-striped Abercorn Football Club in Paisley, Scotland, for the blue and white that Liverpool Football Club played in at that time.

McCann was Liverpool's first-choice goalkeeper for the first half of the 1894/95 season. He lost his place after conceding 11 goals in three successive matches against Aston Villa, Burnley and Stoke. He was replaced by Matt McQueen, a remarkably versatile footballer who was equally at home as an outfield player. McQueen was given seven matches as the club's last line of defence before McCann returned for a 4-0 home win over West Bromwich Albion on New Year's Day 1895. But only four days later Liverpool were thrashed 5-0 at Sheffield Wednesday in a game where McCann was 'very shaky' and it was 'very evident that this fine player was not taking care of himself' according to the *Liverpool Mercury*. The defeat to Wednesday proved to be McCann's final league appearance for the club.

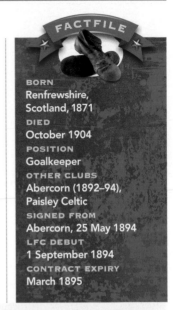

FACTFILE

BORN
Renfrewshire, Scotland, 1871
DIED
October 1904
POSITION
Goalkeeper
OTHER CLUBS
Abercorn (1892–94), Paisley Celtic
SIGNED FROM
Abercorn, 25 May 1894
LFC DEBUT
1 September 1894
CONTRACT EXPIRY
March 1895

Season	League		FA Cup		Other		Total	
	App	Goals	App	Goals	App	Goals	App	Goals
1894/95	15	0	2	0	0	0	17	0
Total	**15**	**0**	**2**	**0**	**0**	**0**	**17**	**0**

JOHN McCARTNEY
LIVERPOOL

McCartney, John

JOHN McCARTNEY was a tough-tackling half-back who was a member of the team that won the Lancashire League and the Second Division in the club's first two seasons.

McCartney missed a number of matches in the 1895/96 season as Liverpool again won the Second Division title but played in all four of the Test matches as the club regained its First Division status. When Liverpool played their first game under the management of Tom Watson and made their debut in red shirts and white pants McCartney was still going strong and one of only a few players who had also featured for the club in 1892. The *Cricket and Football Field* were of the opinion, as reported in September 1896, that McCartney's play was a bit too rough for their liking: 'John McCartney still vexes his own committee by resorting to those tactics which have previously brought the club into bad repute.' McCartney was the victim of rough treatment on 21 November 1896, however, when Alf Milward kicked him deliberately in the Merseyside derby and was sent off. Milward later apologised but pleaded that he had been provoked by the tough Scotsman.

FACTFILE

BORN
Newmilns, Scotland, 1870
POSITION
Left-half
OTHER CLUBS
Newmilns, St Mirren (1890–92), New Brighton Tower (1898–1900)
SIGNED FROM
St Mirren, October 1892
LFC DEBUT GAME/GOAL
15 October 1892 / 29 October 1892
CONTRACT EXPIRY
August 1898
HONOURS
Lancashire League 1892/93; Second Division Championship 1893/94, 1895/96

Season	League		FA Cup		League Cup		Total	
	App	Goals	App	Goals	App	Goals	App	Goals
1892/93	-	-	3	1	18	0	21	1
1893/94	17	1	1	0	1	0	19	1
1894/95	28	0	3	0	0	0	31	0
1895/96	22	1	2	0	4	1	28	2
1896/97	30	1	5	0	-	-	35	1
1897/98	27	2	5	0	-	-	32	2
Total	**124**	**5**	**19**	**1**	**23**	**1**	**166**	**7**

McConnell, John

JOHN McCONNELL made his debut on 18 December 1909 when the Reds lost 3-1 at Villa Park.

He featured in 8 out of the final 10 games of that season, during a run of six victories that secured a runners-up spot to champions Aston Villa. From December 1910 onwards McConnell played regularly in a season which Liverpool failed to reproduce their excellent form from the previous campaign and finished 13th. McConnell played in four of the first five games of the 1911/12 season. Liverpool had conceded 9 goals in those matches so it wasn't surprising that Tom Watson felt a change was needed. McConnell was dropped in place of new signing and future captain, Harry Lowe, from Gainsborough Trinity. McConnell joined Aberdeen at the end of the 1911/12 season.

Season	League		FA Cup		Total	
	App	Goals	App	Goals	App	Goals
1909/10	13	0	1	0	14	0
1910/11	29	0	2	0	31	0
1911/12	8	1	0	0	8	1
Total	**50**	**1**	**3**	**0**	**53**	**1**

McCowie, Andy

FORWARD Andy McCowie made his name in Scotland with Glasgow amateurs Cambuslang Hibernian who won the Glasgow Junior League in 1895/96.

The *Cricket and Football Field* on 31 October 1896 reported on his transfer to Liverpool: 'Tom Watson is reputed to know what a football player is, and in capturing McCowie, of the Cambuslang Hibs, he is said to have secured an inside right who is at present clever enough to shine against the best of our League defenders. A dashing player, who dribbles well and shoots to perfection, is only part of his recommendations, and if only he can hit the target at a decent range, to my mind he will supply what all of our League clubs desire – goals.'

In 1896/97 McCowie played in the final two league fixtures, praised for a 'capital display' in his second game, a goalless draw against Preston. McCowie managed six goals from 19 league games in 1897/98 as the club finished ninth in the First Division and his five goals in 12 matches the following season helped his team climb the table significantly to finish runners-up, just two points behind Aston Villa.

Season	League		FA Cup		Total	
	App	Goals	App	Goals	App	Goals
1896/97	2	0	0	0	2	0
1897/98	19	6	2	0	21	6
1898/99	12	5	0	0	12	5
Total	**33**	**11**	**2**	**0**	**35**	**11**

McDermott, Terry

TERRY McDERMOTT was a spectacular midfield player. He needed two years to settle into the Liverpool side, but when he did, he blossomed.

He scored some truly memorable goals and his wizardry in midfield was justly rewarded in 1980 when he became the first player to win the Football Writers' Association's and Professional Footballers' Association's Player of the Year awards in the same season. His response to the news was understated to say the least. 'I was in the players' lounge and the payphone rang,' McDermott remembered in *LFC Magazine*. 'It was a reporter. He told me and I gave my famous quote: "I can't believe a rag-bag like me has won a trophy like this." Look at all the players before me, like George Best, Billy Bremner and Norman Hunter, who have all won these awards but never done it in the one year.' Kirkby-born McDermott supported Liverpool as a boy but his first professional club was Bury, from where he moved to Newcastle United in February 1973. He played in 56 league matches for the Magpies and, just like Alan Kennedy, played against Liverpool in the 1974 FA Cup final before moving to Anfield. He had made his debut for the England Under-23s at Newcastle and when asked if his next target was a full England cap, he replied: "No, it is to join

Liverpool." McDermott returned to his native Merseyside as one of Bob Paisley's earliest signings in November 1974 when he was a few weeks short of his 23rd birthday. Sir John Smith, Liverpool's chairman, described McDermott as "the quickest big signing ever – two minutes flat." McDermott quipped: "I had to sign as quickly as I could in case Liverpool changed their minds." Phil Thompson explained in his autobiography how he was in his hospital bed when Bob Paisley phoned him and enquired if he knew 'the boy McDermott', who was said to be unhappy at Newcastle. Even though Tommo and Terry were both Kirkby lads they had only met in the Cup final where they swapped shirts. 'Bob said: "I fancy him as a Liverpool player. Can you get in touch with him?" I said: "There is no phone for Macca, but I can write,"' Thompson revealed. 'I sent Terry a letter from my hospital bed and said I understood he was not happy and that Bob Paisley had been talking about him. I explained that Bob felt he had all the attributes to be a Liverpool player, adding: "If you know what I mean." I tried to word it as carefully as I could and soon got a letter back saying: "If you are trying to say would I be interested in Liverpool, it would be my dream." I spoke to Bob who said: "Write and tell him not to do anything daft" (which was hard for Terry Mac!). It was like James Bond with all of these cryptic messages changing hands.'

Three days after his arrival McDermott began a run of six successive league games in place of Brian Hall, but it was then a frustrating time for him as he was in and out of the team. In 1975/76 McDermott was selected in the starting XI for the opening eight games but was stuck in the reserves as Liverpool captured the league title and the UEFA Cup. 'There were many times when I went to see

Bob Paisley and slammed the door so it almost came off its hinges,' McDermott said in *LFC Magazine*. 'On numerous occasions I told him to stick his club where he wanted it. I just felt aggrieved at times because there were days I thought I'd played well and the pop-up toaster would come up showing 8 or 11, or I never played the next game. Maybe that was just a learning curve for me, for them to say to me: "Hey, you think you've made it. You bloody haven't!"'

McDERMOTT'S reward finally came in the memorable 1976/77 season when he started 36 games and was a firm fixture at the business end of the season when Liverpool successfully defended their title. The disappointment of again finishing on the losing side in an FA Cup final was soon forgotten as a typical run into space to collect Steve Heighway's pass saw McDermott fire the Reds ahead in the European Cup final against Gladbach. McDermott would add two more winners' medals to his collection in the world's most prestigious knockout competition. Liverpool's captain at the time, Emlyn Hughes, was happy with McDermott's progress. 'Terry, for my money, must be one of the most improved players in the country since he came into the side. As much as anyone, he has been responsible for getting us to Wembley, to Rome and to the closing stages of the Championship. He just gets better and better!'

McDermott also became a regular member of the England squad and was capped 25 times between 1977 and 1982. He had scored eight goals for two seasons running for Liverpool when he reached double figures in 1979/80 and followed that with a goal spree of 22 and 20 goals in the next couple of seasons, outstanding for a midfielder. He credits a stunning hat-trick in only 16 minutes when Kevin Keegan returned with Hamburg

for the second leg of the Super Cup on 6 December 1977 as the making of him at Liverpool. It wasn't as if his goals were tap-ins either. His first goal of the 1978/79 season on 2 September 1978 was perhaps his most memorable when a sweeping move from one end of the pitch to the other saw him race 70 yards to powerfully head Steve Heighway's cross into the net for the final blow

Season	League		FA Cup		League Cup		Europe		Other		Total	
	App	Goals	App	Goals	App	Goals	App	Goals	App	Goals	App	Goals
1974/75	14 (1)	2	0	0	0	0	0	0	0	0	14 (1)	2
1975/76	7 (2)	1	0	0	1	0	0	0	-	-	8 (2)	1
1976/77	25 (1)	1	5	1	0	0	6 (1)	2	0	0	36 (2)	4
1977/78	36 (1)	4	0	0	8	0	7	4	1	0	52 (1)	8
1978/79	34 (3)	8	7	0	1	0	4	0	-	-	46 (3)	8
1979/80	37	11	6	2	7	1	2	0	1	2	53	16
1980/81	40	13	2	1	9	1	8	6	1	1	60	22
1981/82	28 (1)	14	3	0	10	3	5	3	1	0	47 (1)	20
1982/83	0 (2)	0	0	0	0	0	1	0	0	0	1 (2)	0
Total	221 (11)	54	23	4	36	5	33 (1)	15	4	3	317 (12)	81

in Tottenham's 7-0 humiliation at Anfield. His long-range shooting became a feature of his game to add to his vision and tactical awareness and his chip in the replayed FA Cup semi-final with Everton in 1977 was voted 'Goal of the Season' by the BBC. Emlyn Hughes remembered the goal well. 'We'd talked about Lawson's tendency to come out a long way and Terry kidded him with that chip. We all thought Terry was going to blast it until he pulled it back and floated it in. That, for me, is the hallmark of an exceptional player.' Another awesome strike dumped Spurs out of the FA Cup in 1980 when he

took the ball over his shoulder on the right-hand corner of the penalty box and hit a volley that curved into the far top corner for the only goal of the game. Absolute magic! His runs from deep were very well timed and would often provide the finishing touch to a well-rehearsed attack.

Nevertheless, by the start of the 1982/83 season, it was clear that McDermott would have to look elsewhere for first-team football and he returned to St James' Park in September 1982. He left three years later, but would return twice as assistant manager: to Kevin Keegan in 1992 and Graeme Souness in 2005. He is now Lee Clark's assistant at Birmingham City.

Kenny Dalglish wrote admiringly about McDermott in his autobiography, *My Liverpool Home*: 'As a footballer, Terry was a creature of instinct and intelligence, a killer mix. If I even hinted at darting into a particular area, Terry read my mind. The ball was waiting for me, almost smiling at me. Not only could Terry see a great pass, he could deliver it. Vision and execution are qualities found in only the very best of players and Terry had those strengths.' McDermott was certainly one of the lads at Liverpool. When Alan Kennedy selected him for his best-ever Liverpool

XI he commented: 'I remember him going a week without alcohol so that's good for Terry McDermott. That's why he gets into this dream team of mine.' McDermott was vital to the dressing-room spirit as he was always in an upbeat mood and his partying ways were overlooked as he would always deliver. Bob Paisley didn't mind Terry's antics. 'Off the field Terry was one of the biggest jokers we have had and a man who enjoyed a pint or two. But no matter how well he celebrated he was always in at training the following morning and that is all that mattered to Liverpool Football Club.'

McDevitt, Billy

BILLY McDEVITT arrived as an inside-forward from Belfast, but was transformed into a centre-half at Liverpool.

Three of his appearances came in the 1923/24 season when Walter Wadsworth was unavailable. In his fourth and last game McDevitt was a centre-forward in a 4-1 home win over Sheffield United on 18 October 1924 when all four of Liverpool's goals were

scored by Dick Forshaw. When Forshaw headed his fourth he crashed through United's Milton and his team-mate McDevitt, who both had to be carried off the park semi-conscious, McDevitt sporting a nasty cut above his eye. He joined Exeter City for a club transfer record in 1925, and was appointed the club's manager four years later. He was said to be one of the most popular players ever associated with the club.

FACTFILE

BORN
Northern Ireland,
5 January 1898
DIED
10 January 1966
POSITION
Centre-half
OTHER CLUBS
Glentoran, Swansea Town
(1920–23), Exeter City
(1925–31)
SIGNED FROM
Swansea Town, 1923
LFC DEBUT
17 November 1923
CONTRACT EXPIRY
22 May 1925

Season	League		FA Cup		Total	
	App	Goals	App	Goals	App	Goals
1923/24	3	0	0	0	3	0
1924/25	1	0	0	0	1	0
Total	**4**	**0**	**0**	**0**	**4**	**0**

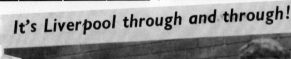

South African imports Gordon Hodgson, Berry Nieuwenhuys and Arthur Riley in the 1930s

Bob Paisley, Reuben Bennett, Bill Shankly and Joe Fagan promoting the new red and white striped Liverpool rock candy!

McDonald, John

SCOTTISH left-winger John McDonald arrived at Anfield before the start of the 1909/10 season to replace old favourite Jack Cox.

He played in 34 of the 38 league matches that year as Liverpool finished runners-up to champions Aston Villa. Although selected for the opening seven games of the following season, he lost his place for a while and was heavily criticised in the club programme: 'MacDonald's performances this season have been completely devoid of skill and determination; even taking into consideration the fact that his inside players have been frail the clever winger of last year has failed in every game in which he has participated. We want to see highly paid professionals exerting themselves to the utmost when taking part in a League game, and not waiting calmly for the ball to be always placed at their toes. Really MacDonald has disappointed all his admirers by his half-hearted endeavours.' The Scotsman returned to the side in January 1911 and only missed one league fixture until the end of the season. Although McDonald was selected

on 20 occasions during his third and final season on Merseyside, the most number of consecutive games he played in were just six.

Season	League		FA Cup		Total	
	App	Goals	App	Goals	App	Goals
1909/10	34	2	1	0	35	2
1910/11	25	1	1	0	26	1
1911/12	19	1	1	0	20	1
Total	**78**	**4**	**3**	**0**	**81**	**4**

McDougall, Jimmy

> SUCH LOYAL SERVICE TO ONE CLUB COINCIDED WITH ONE OF THE LEANEST PERIODS IN LIVERPOOL'S HISTORY

JIMMY McDOUGALL made his name as an inside-left with Partick Thistle and scored 21 goals in 36 league and cup matches in his last season prior to his move to Liverpool.

THE SCOTSMAN had scored seven goals from 23 matches in what was considered as his natural position when Tom Bromilow's absence as left-half in a visit by Aston Villa on 5 January made him a makeshift defender. Liverpool beat Villa 4-0 and by the end of his debut season McDougall had been moved permanently to the half-back line. McDougall was a reliable and uncomplicated defender, a player of great calmness and assurance. He made his debut against Bury on 25 August 1928, which was the premiere of the roofed Kop, bringing the maximum capacity of the ground close to 60,000. McDougall became a fixture in the Liverpool side for a decade from 1928 until 1938, a period when he averaged over 35 games a season. It was a great shame that such loyal service to one club coincided with one of the leanest periods in Liverpool's history.

McDougall arrived on Merseyside five years after the club's fourth League Championship success, a trophy which would not return to Anfield until nineteen years later. The furthest Liverpool got in the FA Cup during McDougall's ten-year stay was the quarter-finals in 1932 and their highest league position was fifth in his first season. McDougall had the honour of being made captain of his country, one of a select band of men to have achieved that while a Liverpool player. He wore the captain's armband on 20 May 1931 in Rome at the National Stadium of the National Fascist Party. Before kick-off he had the dubious honour of accepting a bouquet from Italian dictator Benito Mussolini. Jimmy's older brother, John, was also an international and started out at Port Glasgow before moving south

JIMMY McDOUGALL
LIVERPOOL

to captain Sunderland and Leeds United as a centre-half.

JIMMY STAYED in the Merseyside area once he had made his farewell appearance for the club and played for a while at South Liverpool as well as coaching their youth team. He also managed a successful chandlery business in Liverpool. McDougall scored 12 times for Liverpool in the First Division but eight of those came when he was playing up front before

he was moved into the defence. Perhaps not surprisingly, after eight goals in 25 league games, he then only managed another four in his next 313! Following Liverpool's game against Aston Villa at Anfield on 15 October 1938 McDougall was presented with a £650 cheque for 'his loyalty and fine service as a player'.

Jimmy McDougall is a member of Liverpool FC's official Hall of Fame. Like Alan Hansen, who was on the Hall of Fame's panel, McDougall starred for Partick Thistle in Glasgow and then spent his bulk of his career at Liverpool. 'When we assessed Jimmy as a candidate for the 30s I was looking at his playing record, his consistency and the top-class qualities he brought to the side,' Hansen told *LFC Magazine* in 2003. 'I knew he was a Scottish international, but I did not realise he was

from my old club. Liverpool have bought some tremendous players for virtually nothing and these individuals, like Jimmy McDougall, have become part and parcel of the Anfield success story.'

Season	League		FA Cup		Total	
	App	Goals	App	Goals	App	Goals
1928/29	36	8	3	0	39	8
1929/30	34	1	1	0	35	1
1930/31	40	1	0	0	40	1
1931/32	39	0	4	0	43	0
1932/33	25	0	1	0	26	0
1933/34	32	0	4	0	36	0
1934/35	38	1	2	0	40	1
1935/36	38	1	2	0	40	1
1936/37	39	0	1	0	40	0
1937/38	17	0	0	0	17	0
Total	**338**	**12**	**18**	**0**	**356**	**12**

McDougall, Bob

BOB McDougall was one of 27 different players used during the 1913/14 season and all but one of his league appearances came in the second part of that terrible campaign when Liverpool were close to relegation.

McDougall did start off promisingly and scored the winner on his debut at West Bromwich Albion and the *Dundee Courier* speculated that he was 'doing so well that Parkinson is not quite certain of his place at centre in the Anfield team.' Jack Parkinson's career at Liverpool was virtually over and soon McDougall seemed to be heading for the exit as well

as touched upon in the 3 October 1914 issue of the club programme: 'McDougall was tried at centre-forward, but he was not a success; the young Scot has not got off the mark this season yet, and even in the reserve team has failed to fulfil expectations.' McDougall joined the army in 1915 and had not been away for long when he asked Liverpool trainer Bill Connell to send him his football kit. The *Liverpool Echo* noted when it heard of this request, 'You can't suppress football insticts, even though you ban professional football.' McDougall returned to Scotland with Falkirk in 1916.

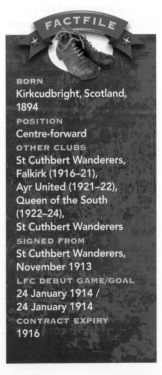

Season	League		FA Cup		Total	
	App	Goals	App	Goals	App	Goals
1913/14	6	1	1	0	7	1
1914/15	1	0	0	0	1	0
Total	**7**	**1**	**1**	**0**	**8**	**1**

McFarlane, John

JOHN McFARLANE scored 80 goals for Aberdeen reserves in the 1927/28 season, but had found it difficult to establish himself in the first team. Soon after scoring a hat-trick for the Dons' second string in a 6-2 win over Montrose, with Liverpool scouts in attendance, he was signed up by the Reds.

McFarlane was the youngest player ever to feature for Liverpool's first team, 17 years and 46 days old, when he was selected for the Anfield derby with Everton on 9 February 1929, which the visitors won 2-1. Gordon Hodgson was missing so the 'Scottish boy who has been doing so well with the Reserves, will lead the attack'.

The *Daily Courier* claimed that he 'led the line with excellent judgement, and was a masterpiece at nipping between the backs with the ball at toe'. McFarlane had to wait until the following September for his second and final appearance, which resulted in another defeat, by three goals to nil at Huddersfield Town.

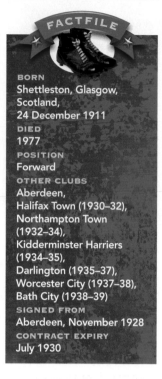

FACTFILE

BORN
Shettleston, Glasgow, Scotland,
24 December 1911
DIED
1977
POSITION
Forward
OTHER CLUBS
Aberdeen,
Halifax Town (1930–32),
Northampton Town (1932–34),
Kidderminster Harriers (1934–35),
Darlington (1935–37),
Worcester City (1937–38),
Bath City (1938–39)
SIGNED FROM
Aberdeen, November 1928
CONTRACT EXPIRY
July 1930

Season	League		FA Cup		Total	
	App	Goals	App	Goals	App	Goals
1928/29	1	0	0	0	1	0
1929/30	1	0	0	0	1	0
Total	2	0	0	0	2	0

McGuigan, Andy

ANDY McGUIGAN was a speedy and tricky forward who was the first player to score five goals in a league game for Liverpool. His extraordinary quintet came against Stoke on 4 January 1902. It did make his task a lot easier that a number of Stoke's players were suffering from food poisoning after having eaten bad fish prior to the match. During the game a number of McGuigan's opponents had to leave the field to throw up and at one point there were only seven Stoke players left!

McGUIGAN made his debut on 6 October 1900 when the Reds visited Derby County and he scored five times in the 14 First Division games he was selected for that year, enough to be eligible for a League Championship medal. Liverpool slumped to eleventh place a year later as they unsuccessfully defended their crown but McGuigan still contributed a goal every other game to give him very respectable final figures for Liverpool. After

struggling with a knee injury he was transferred to Middlesbrough in December 1902. He broke down after only one game and Middlesbrough wanted Liverpool to return the heavy transfer fee paid for him but the Reds refused, providing a doctor's certificate showing McGuigan left with a clean bill of health. In April 1903 McGuigan had a knee cartilage removed, proving, as the *Evening Post* noted that 'a footballer's life is not all beer and skittles!' McGuigan finally left Boro after this single appearance. The Scotsman later became a club director at Liverpool, serving during the club's League Championship wins in 1922 and 1923.

Director McGuigan with Charlie Wilson who is holding the league trophy in 1922

THE FIRST PLAYER
TO SCORE FIVE GOALS
IN A LEAGUE GAME
FOR LIVERPOOL

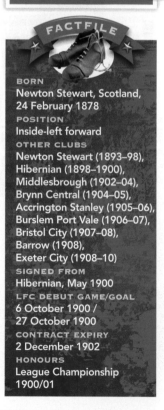

FACTFILE

BORN
Newton Stewart, Scotland,
24 February 1878
POSITION
Inside-left forward
OTHER CLUBS
Newton Stewart (1893–98),
Hibernian (1898–1900),
Middlesbrough (1902–04),
Brynn Central (1904–05),
Accrington Stanley (1905–06),
Burslem Port Vale (1906–07),
Bristol City (1907–08),
Barrow (1908),
Exeter City (1908–10)
SIGNED FROM
Hibernian, May 1900
LFC DEBUT GAME/GOAL
6 October 1900 /
27 October 1900
CONTRACT EXPIRY
2 December 1902
HONOURS
League Championship
1900/01

Season	League		FA Cup		Total	
	App	Goals	App	Goals	App	Goals
1900/01	14	5	2	0	16	5
1901/02	18	9	3	0	21	9
Total	32	14	5	0	37	14

McInnes, Jimmy

JIMMY McINNES arrived at Anfield in time to play in the last 11 First Division fixtures of the 1937/38 season, taking over the left-half position from legend Jimmy McDougall who had served with distinction for nine years.

McInnes made his debut in a 3-1 win over Brentford in west London on 19 March 1938, which included the first of only two goals he scored as a Liverpool player. He scored his second goal at Sheffield United on the opening day of the 1939/40 season, but only three fixtures into the campaign the Football League was suspended due to the outbreak of war and his appearances and goal were expunged from the

records. McInnes never played in a competitive match for Liverpool again, although he did make the team for a number of wartime games in the hastily arranged Western Division of the Football League.

McINNES joined Liverpool's administrative staff after he retired in 1946. He was Liverpool's secretary from 1955 until he took his own life on 5 May 1965, the day after the famous 3-1 win over Inter Milan at Anfield in the semi-final first leg of the European Cup. Four days earlier Liverpool had won the FA Cup for the first time against Leeds at Wembley. Apparently McInnes had been overwhelmed by the size of his task at Liverpool and had resorted to sleeping on a camp bed at Anfield. McInnes had been seen at the ground pulling at some cord earlier in the day, seemingly in quite good humour, but was later found hanging from a beam at the rear of the Kop. Bill Shankly worked with McInnes for five and a half years at Liverpool and got to know him quite well. 'Jimmy was honest and he was also quick-tempered. Sometimes he could be rude to people – some of them needed it, and he was right – but he would be gentlemanly with people he respected,' Shankly revealed in his autobiography.

There were some of us at Anfield with whom he never had a harsh word. Others would find him difficult to deal with and hard to understand. I've heard him calling somebody on the telephone and suddenly, bang! The phone would go down. Jimmy loved a game of snooker, and he was a good player. It was a change from his chores as Secretary. When the club began to be transformed, Jimmy got the lash of the success. There were only a few seats in the stand in those days and when we won the Second Division championship, reached the FA Cup semi-final, won the First Division championship and then won the Cup, Jimmy's work was doubled and everything began to pile up on top of him. He needed help.

> HE TOOK HIS OWN LIFE ON 5 MAY 1965, THE DAY AFTER THE FAMOUS 3-1 WIN OVER INTER MILAN

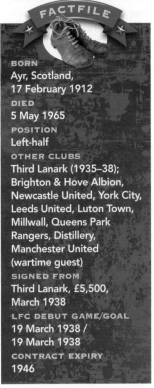

FACTFILE

BORN
Ayr, Scotland,
17 February 1912
DIED
5 May 1965
POSITION
Left-half
OTHER CLUBS
Third Lanark (1935–38);
Brighton & Hove Albion,
Newcastle United, York City,
Leeds United, Luton Town,
Millwall, Queens Park
Rangers, Distillery,
Manchester United
(wartime guest)
SIGNED FROM
Third Lanark, £5,500,
March 1938
LFC DEBUT GAME/GOAL
19 March 1938 /
19 March 1938
CONTRACT EXPIRY
1946

Season	League		FA Cup		Total	
	App	Goals	App	Goals	App	Goals
1937/38	11	1	0	0	11	1
1938/39	34	0	3	0	37	0
Total	**45**	**1**	**3**	**0**	**48**	**1**

McKenna, John

JOHN McKENNA'S one and only appearance for Liverpool's first team came as a replacement for the injured regular right-winger Arthur Goddard when Liverpool beat Birmingham City 2-0 at Anfield on 26 January 1907.

'McKenna gave great satisfaction whenever he came into possession and his greyhound-like tactics usually proved too difficult for either Cornan or Kearns to check easily,' said the *Liverpool Echo*. Goddard's return in the next game signalled the end of McKenna's short Liverpool career.

FACTFILE

BORN
Liverpool, 1882
POSITION
Right-winger
OTHER CLUBS
Old Xaverians
SIGNED FROM
Old Xaverians, 1906
LFC DEBUT
26 January 1907
CONTRACT EXPIRY
1907

Season	League		FA Cup		Total	
	App	Goals	App	Goals	App	Goals
1906/07	1	0	0	0	1	0
Total	**1**	**0**	**0**	**0**	**1**	**0**

McKenna, John

ULSTERMAN John McKenna moved to Liverpool in search of employment and after going through a series of menial jobs he was appointed as vaccinations officer for the West Derby Union. This body was responsible for the upkeep of the Liverpool workhouses, where the desitute were offered housing accommodation in return for work. This awoke his interest in helping those who were less fortunate in the city and he did his utmost to relieve their misery throughout his life.

He later became very concerned about players' welfare and helping out football clubs who were struggling financially. McKenna got to know Everton's president, John Houlding, through the Orange Order, a protestant fraternal organisation that supports a political union between Ireland and Great Britain. They struck up a firm friendship as they also had a shared interest in sports. McKenna, who had been a keen rugby player, was the leading figure in the formation of a regimental rugby club when he was a volunteer in the Lancashire Artillery as a battery sergeant-major. Reportedly he devoted his life to football after seeing a match between Everton and Bootle, as the *Nottingham Evening Post* noted in 1936. 'From that time he become a convert from Rugby and devoted his life to the furtherance and improvement of Soccer football.'

At the denouement of Houlding's fight with Everton's board McKenna was a vociferous spokesman on his behalf. When Houlding was removed as president at the meeting in the Presbyterian School on Royal Street on 15 March 1892 McKenna tried to talk to the assembly in support of Houlding but was met with cries of 'Lie down, McKenna!' and 'Traitor!' It was one of the rare occasions that the strong-willed McKenna had to retreat in battle. McKenna joined the board when Houlding formed Liverpool Football Club. He didn't have the title of Secretary, that was essentially the team manager at the time, as that was taken by former vice chairman of Everton, William Barclay, but as the first eleven were chosen by the board McKenna had more influence over who played than the secretary. Liverpool's application to join the Football League in their first season was rejected. *Field Sports* claimed someone at Liverpool had made an administrative blunder. 'Applicants were asked, according to the printed form circulated by the League, to leave themselves open for elections to the Second Division if not successful in the vote for the First Division. In the Liverpool Club's form handed to the meeting this saving clause was struck out, thus leaving the application for the First Division only. The League would not have them in the premier list, and consequently, as there was no request left for inclusion in the subordinate ranks, Liverpool are out of it altogether.' Most likely this was a mistake on Barclay's behalf as his job entailed taking care of such documentation. Liverpool got the better of all their opponents in the Lancashire League in their first year and when the chance arose to apply again for the Football League John McKenna made sure there would be no mistake this time around and sent a telegram signed 'Barclay' to the Football Association's headquarters in London: 'Liverpool make application to the Second Division of the League.' Imagine Barclay's surprise when he received a telegram that read: 'Liverpool elected. Come to London meeting at three o'clock tomorrow to arrange fixtures.' McKenna, not Barclay, went to the capital as Liverpool's representative. Liverpool were also victorious in the Second Division, but finished bottom of the First Division in the 1894/95 season. Barclay quit as secretary, whether that was due to reasons other than the team's capitulation is difficult to establish. McKenna, who contrary to popular belief, never had the job title 'Secretary' at Liverpool, was no doubt as before influential in the running of the team but was ably assisted by the board. As the 1896/97 season started Houlding had hired the best secretary in the country, Tom Watson, who had won the League

Championship three times with Sunderland's 'Team of all the talents', to take charge of the Liverpool team.

McKenna was elected as chairman of Liverpool in 1909, a post he stayed in until 1914. He became chairman again in 1917 when John Asbury took ill and remained so until 1919. The Ulsterman was known as 'Mr Straight-from-the-shoulder', a hard-nosed businessman who an unnamed Liverpool player noted 'talked like an American. He quoted figures, income, expenditure, gates and liabilities that simply floored those who imagined the clubs were rolling in wealth.' 'Honest John' didn't suffer fools lightly and his 'military bearing and staccato voice' got him far as the *Liverpool Echo* reported when he clashed with a Manchester City director. 'When the director entered the Liverpool boardroom vehemently declaring that City had been robbed of the game, McKenna immediately called for quiet using his well-known phrase; 'A moment, please, a moment.' He then proceeded to ask the director if he knew what the word "robbed" meant. Did he believe the referee was a thief? He promptly proceeded to insist on the director making an apology in the presence of everyone in the room.'

McKENNA was a man of clear vision who in 1917 told Liverpool's annual meeting that the time had passed when big sums of money could buy players. He was rather glad, for it would make them strive to 'grow their own players.' He stayed on as director until July 1921 when he resigned from the directorship as a protest against the shareholders' meeting refusing to re-elect two directors, Matt McQueen and John Keating. He complained that the Liverpool shareholders 'seemed to have quite failed to recognise the ability and genuine hard work done by these men on behalf of the club.

I am certainly not going to be a party to it.' So it was an unhappy end for McKenna at the club that he had been involved with for nearly 30 years.

McKenna was without doubt one of the great early administrators of the English game, a man who was widely admired, respected and occasionally feared. He was president of the Lancashire Combination as well as a member of the Football League's management committee in the early 1900s. He was voted the Football League's vice-president

in 1908 and then president two years later, a position he held for over two decades until his death. In addition to that he had been vice-president of the Football Association since 1928. According to the *Nottingham Evening Post* 'it was not his intricate knowledge of the laws and regulations of the game that influenced the League in their choice, but the fact that by temperament and practical conception Mr. McKenna was particularly created to lead.' He was furthermore eulogised as 'one of the foremost leaders and legislators of the Association football game of all time.'

McKENNA passed away on 22 March 1936 at Walton hospital in Liverpool at 82 years of age. Three weeks earlier he fell badly on the platform when hurrying to catch a train to Manchester. Instead of recuperating fully he went on a trip to Inverness on 14 March to watch an amateur international match between Scotland and England in his capacity as a member of the International Selection Committee of the FA. The shock he suffered since the accident and the arduous journey was more than his health could take. He fell ill on the return journey, feeling poorly at his home at 6 Castlewood Road in Anfield the whole week before he was transferred to hospital in the late evening of 21 March. He died the following morning. A memorial tablet in honour of McKenna was unveiled by William Charles Cuff, vice President of the League and Chairman of Everton Football Club, at Anfield on 27 February 1937. Cuff paid McKenna the following tribute: 'I feel I have lost a lifelong friend. We travelled together on football business many times, and I am not looking forward to taking those journeys alone. Mr. McKenna was a

McKenna's tablet is at the top of the stairs after entering through the main entrance of the Main stand

staunch friend, who beneath his brusque exterior, had a heart of gold. From the Football League and Football Association point of view I think the greatest man in football has gone. He will live long in the memory of all who had anything to do with the governing of football. Fearless, outspoken, and absolutely honest, he was well named "Honest John".'

FACTFILE

BORN
Drumcaw, County Monaghan, Ireland, 3 January 1855
DIED
22 March 1936
SIGNED
15 March 1892
LFC DEBUT GAME
3 September 1892
CONTRACT EXPIRY AS DIRECTOR
July 1921
HONOURS
Lancashire League 1892/93; Second Division 1893/94, 1895/96

As a Manager											
Season	Division	P	W	D	L	GF	GA	Pts	Pos	Win %	FA Cup
1892/93	Lancashire League	22	17	2	3	66	19	36	1	77.27	3rd Qualifier
1893/94	2nd Division	28	22	6	0	77	18	50	1	78.57	3rd Round
1894/95	1st Division	30	7	8	15	51	70	22	16	23.33	2nd Round
1895/96	2nd Division	30	22	2	6	106	32	46	1	73.33	2nd Round
Total*	-	88	51	16	21	234	120	118	-	57.95	-

* Lancashire League excluded from total

McKinney, Peter

PETER McKINNEY was considered a 'dark horse', at least by the *Derby Daily Telegraph's* informant, when he signed from Consett Celtic at the end of the 1919/20 season.

McKinney's debut was against Sheffield United early in October 1920 and he scored Liverpool's first goal in a 2-2 Anfield draw. Still he had to wait six months for another chance in the first team.

HIS THIRD and final appearance was in the last match of the season, a convincing 3-0 home win over Arsenal that secured 4th place for Liverpool, who dominated the league in the two following seasons. A year after leaving Liverpool McKinney emigrated to the United States and joined the New York Giants in the American Soccer League. He played seven years for the Giants, eventually settling down in New York for life.

FACTFILE

BORN
Consett, Co. Durham, 16 December 1897
DIED
23 December 1979
POSITION
Forward
OTHER CLUBS
Consett Celtic, New York Giants (1923–30)
JOINED
Unaffiliated, April 1920
LFC DEBUT GAME/GOAL
9 October 1920 / 9 October 1920
CONTRACT EXPIRY
1922

	League		FA Cup		Total	
Season	App	Goals	App	Goals	App	Goals
1920/21	3	1	0	0	3	1
Total	3	1	0	0	3	1

McLaughlin, John

THE coaching staff at Liverpool believed John McLaughlin was a star in the making. 'His potential is unbelievable. He knows the game, and is very mature for his age,' Bill Shankly declared. 'He is the best schoolboy prospect to be turned up for a very long time.'

Shankly eased him into the First Division scene by picking him for the final game of the 1969/70 season, away to Chelsea. McLaughlin had a hand in Liverpool's only goal, scored by Bobby Graham in a 2-1 defeat. Despite being only 18 years old when the following season opened, Shankly had enough faith in the slightly built teenager to make him an important part of the club's midfield at the time and his faith was rewarded when McLaughlin struck two first-half shots into the Kop goal when Huddersfield Town visited Anfield for the second home fixture of the season.

McLAUGHLIN played in 30 consecutive First Division games but then made way for Alun Evans and only figured in three of the remaining 12 matches. This season turned out to be his only one as a regular during Shankly's rebuilding of his side. Once Shankly had completed the transformation McLaughlin was cast aside. He made the line-up for the opening day of 1971/72

but was only picked on four further occasions, with two of those being as substitute.

The emergence of Brian Hall and the arrival of Peter Cormack made it increasingly difficult for

McLaughlin to break into the first team and he was allowed to leave Anfield to have a loan spell on the south coast with Ian St John's Portsmouth. He also featured in the summer of 1975 and 1976 in the North American Soccer League. A knee injury put McLaughlin out of league football for good when he was only 24.

Season	League App	League Goals	FA Cup App	FA Cup Goals	League Cup App	League Cup Goals	Europe App	Europe Goals	Other App	Other Goals	Total App	Total Goals
1969/70	1	0	0	0	0	0	0	0	-	-	1	0
1970/71	33	2	4	1	1	0	7	0	-	-	45	3
1971/72	3 (2)	0	0	0	1	0	0	0	0	0	4 (2)	0
1973/74	1	0	0	0	0	0	1	0	-	-	2	0
1974/75	0	0	0	0	1	0	0	0	0	0	1	0
Total	**38 (2)**	**2**	**4**	**1**	**3**	**0**	**8**	**0**	**0**	**0**	**53 (2)**	**3**

McLean, Duncan

IN 1890 Duncan McLean left the famed Scottish amateurs Renton, rejoining his former captain Andrew Hannah at Everton in the professional English League.

A year later he won the League Championship but followed former Everton president, John Houlding, out of the club in 1892,

to join his new outfit, Liverpool. The strongly built McLean was a regular in the first team during his distinguished Liverpool career. His adventurous play seemed though to displease the Liverpool directors going by these programme notes for a Cliftonville game in April 1893: 'Why will McLean persist in marring his

'IF MAC WILL GET RID OF THIS ONE FAULT HE WILL BE AS GOOD A BACK AS THERE IS IN ENGLAND TODAY'

FACTFILE

BORN
Renton, Scotland,
20 January 1868
DIED
17 November 1941
POSITION
Left-back
OTHER CLUBS
Renton Union,
Renton (1888–90),
Everton (1890–92),
St Bernard's (1895–99)
SIGNED FROM
Everton, July 1892
INTERNATIONAL CAPS
2 Scotland caps, 1896–97
LFC DEBUT GAME/GOAL
3 September 1892 /
7 October 1893
CONTRACT EXPIRY
October 1895
HONOURS
Lancashire League 1892/93;
Second Division
Championship 1893/94

really brilliant and effective play by getting too far away from his own goal? By all means back up the halves, but a full-back has no business whatever amongst the forwards, except on the defensive. If Mac will get rid of this one fault he will be as good a back as there is in England today.' Liverpool struggled right from the start in their first top-division season in 1894/95, winning just one of their first 17 league matches, and were unsurprisingly relegated back to the Second Division. This proved to be McLean's final season for the club and he joined Scottish Cup winners St Bernard's from Edinburgh, skippering the side and finally gaining international recognition, probably made easier by the fact that he was playing now on the 'right side' of the border.

	League		FA Cup		Other		Total	
Season	App	Goals	App	Goals	App	Goals	App	Goals
1892/93	-	-	3	0	22	0	25	0
1893/94	27	4	3	0	1	0	31	4
1894/95	24	0	2	0	0	0	26	0
Total	**51**	**4**	**8**	**0**	**23**	**0**	**82**	**4**

McLean,
James

JAMES McLEAN, the former amateur captain of Vale of Leven, figured for Liverpool as a right-back in four of the first eight matches in the 1903/04 season.

In McLean's third game Liverpool and Everton drew 2-2 at Anfield on 10 October 1903 and he was 'erratic' and made 'very serious blunders' according to the *Liverpool Echo*.

LIVERPOOL lost three out of the four games he featured in; a pattern which was to become all too familiar during the rest of the season and Liverpool were eventually relegated from the First Division with only 26 points from 34 fixtures.

FACTFILE

BORN
Edinburgh, Scotland, 1880
POSITION
Right-back
OTHER CLUBS
Edinburgh Thistle,
Vale of Leven, Motherwell
SIGNED FROM
Vale of Leven, 21 May 1903
LFC DEBUT
19 September 1903
CONTRACT EXPIRY
3 June 1904

	League		FA Cup		Total	
Season	App	Goals	App	Goals	App	Goals
1903/04	4	0	0	0	4	0
Total	**4**	**0**	**0**	**0**	**4**	**0**

Bathtime in the 50s

Admiring their league title in the 1920s

McLean, John

JOHN McLEAN arrived at Anfield during the 1894/95 season to try to shore up a defence that was leaking goals all over the place; 31 in the first dozen fixtures of a traumatic debut season in the top division.

The *Liverpool Mercury* reported on his debut in a 3-1 loss to Stoke: 'J. McLean turned out a real champion. He is the rough diamond, and only requires polishing to be a really first-class player.' In March 1895 McLean was criticised as he had 'fostered a desire for dribbling and forward work, which is of no earthly use to his side, for, as generally is the case, he is robbed or his final pass interposed, and when the ball is sent to his opposing forwards he is in nine cases out of ten out of his place, and consequently a much larger share of work fell to the backs.' McLean could play as right or left half-back but those

two positions were mostly taken by John McCartney and John Holmes in 1895/96 so he only added a further eight appearances to his total.

Season	League		FA Cup		Other		Total	
	App	Goals	App	Goals	App	Goals	App	Goals
1894/95	18	0	2	0	1	0	21	0
1895/96	8	0	0	0	0	0	8	0
Total	**26**	**0**	**2**	**0**	**1**	**0**	**29**	**0**

McLeod, Tommy

A LEFT-WINGER with a powerful shot who was noticed by the Daily Post reporter Leslie Edwards, who saw him playing Army football in Germany, Tommy McLeod played three times towards the close of the 1946/47 season, the year Liverpool dramatically won the league title by winning their final fixture 2-1 at Wolverhampton on the last day of May.

McLeod had replaced Albert Stubbins in the Good Friday draw at Deepdale against Preston North End and then took over from Cyril Done for the Easter Monday return with Preston and also for the next home match against Sunderland. He wasn't called on at all the next season but had a run of four consecutive matches halfway through the 1948/49 campaign which saw Liverpool finish mid-table for the second season running.

Season	League		FA Cup		Total	
	App	Goals	App	Goals	App	Goals
1946/47	3	0	0	0	3	0
1948/49	4	0	0	0	4	0
Total	**7**	**0**	**0**	**0**	**7**	**0**

McMahon, Steve

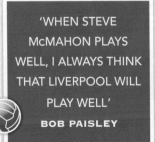

'WHEN STEVE McMAHON PLAYS WELL, I ALWAYS THINK THAT LIVERPOOL WILL PLAY WELL'
BOB PAISLEY

'WHEN STEVE McMahon plays well, I always think that Liverpool will play well.' This compliment from Bob Paisley bears the ultimate testament to McMahon's capabilities.

He started out as a ball boy at Goodison Park and eventually joined his boyhood heroes Everton. He was a regular for the Blues for three seasons and voted the supporters' Player of the Year in his debut campaign. When he felt it was time to move on he chose Aston Villa over Liverpool in a £300,000 deal. He confessed that he didn't dare to do the virtually impossible to move straight from the blue half of Liverpool to the red. His transfer turned out to be a step down as Everton were a club on the rise, winning the League Championship two years after his move, while Aston Villa struggled to follow their 1980/81 title triumph.

Before McMahon eventually joined Liverpool he had certainly had his tussles with their players. 'They set me up. Kenny got me booked and Souey got me sent off,' McMahon told *LFC Magazine* of their Anfield battle on 17 September 1983. 'They were

crafty. I was wound up anyway going back to Merseyside and they did me a treat.' After Souness left Liverpool for Rome in 1984, a playmaker of some force was needed as the Reds lost the title to Everton. When Liverpool came in for McMahon again in September 1985 he turned down one of Liverpool's greatest rivals. 'I had made it clear that I wanted to move back to the north. The manager said: "I think you might like this move." He informed me that Manchester United manager Ron Atkinson had made a satisfactory offer that had been accepted by Villa. I believe it involved a swap deal with Alan Brazil. I think I shocked Tony Barton when I replied: "Thanks but no thanks." There had been a great deal of press speculation that Liverpool would move in, and I was prepared to bide my time for that chance. When the opportunity arose to sign for Liverpool I took it and it was the best decision of my career.'

KENNY DALGLISH took over before the 1985/86 season and McMahon was his first signing. In only his third game McMahon

FACTFILE

BORN
Liverpool, 20 August 1961
POSITION
Midfielder
OTHER CLUBS
Everton (1977–83),
Aston Villa (1983–85),
Manchester City (1991–94),
Swindon Town (1994–98)
SIGNED FROM
Aston Villa, £350,000,
12 September 1985
INTERNATIONAL CAPS
17 England caps, 1988–90
LFC DEBUT GAME/GOAL
14 September 1985 /
21 September 1985
CONTRACT EXPIRY
24 December 1991
HONOURS
League Championship
1985/86, 1987/88, 1989/90;
FA Cup 1986, 1989

faced Everton at Goodison Park and scored Liverpool's third with a thumping shot that proved to be the winning goal. McMahon was ruthless in the middle of the park, putting in strong tackles to say the least. He contributed to the goalscoring as well and displayed sorely missed leadership qualities in the engine room. McMahon got injured at a crucial stage of the season and the only Englishman in Liverpool's troops at Wembley had to settle for the bench when the Reds beat the Blues in the FA Cup final. He played 50 games in his second season in comparison with 36 in his first and scored no fewer than 14 goals, but Everton recaptured their crown.

McMahon's game prospered in 1987/88 and he was one of five shortlisted for PFA's Player of the Year award as Liverpool shattered their opposition. He was a perfect workhorse to support the more glitzy talents of Barnes and Beardsley, though he could conjure up magic on his own.

On 16 January 1988, with the score at 0-0 late in the first half, a promising Liverpool move appeared to have finished when a pass from Ray Houghton was misdirected and seemed to be heading for the paddock. McMahon was having none of it and chased a seemingly lost cause. At full speed he put his foot on the ball to prevent it from going out of play before careering towards the paddock supporters. Somehow he contrived to stop himself from toppling into the crowd, regained his balance and control of the ball, which he then took down the right wing before sliding a brilliant pass across to the onrushing Aldridge who scored the first in a 2-0 victory over Arsenal.

McMahon picked up his third League Championship in the 1989/90 season. Despite his tough demeanour on the field he escaped a sending-off at Liverpool until he received two red cards in a seven-month period in 1991. The first one came when he put

in a late tackle on Liverpool old boy Howard Gayle, receiving a second yellow in an ill-tempered FA Cup clash against Blackburn Rovers in January. The following month McMahon injured his knee after a clash with John Ebbrell in the fifth round of the FA Cup, which meant an early end to his season just a few days before Dalglish's resignation. McMahon's second dismissal came in only his third game of the 1991/92 season when he elbowed Luton Town's Philip Gray when preventing him from taking a quick free kick. Later Vinnie Jones claimed McMahon was his only real rival in the modern-day game for the accolade of 'hardest man in football'. Jones had taken him out in the opening exchanges of the 1988 FA Cup final between Liverpool and Wimbledon but as McMahon fell down from Jones' tackle he caught the Wimbledon man on the face, leaving a decent scar. Jones said McMahon got his revenge by kicking him with his studs in their next game at Anfield, forcing Jones to have stitches in a major cut.

In November 1991 30-year-old McMahon left for Manchester City. McMahon was used to higher standards than were on offer at City at the time and Niall Quinn compared him to Roy Keane in his intensity and will to win. 'Because he expected to win trophies, he could make the

players at City feel bad about themselves... The happy-go-lucky atmosphere in our squad just didn't appeal to him.' McMahon remained at Maine Road until he was tempted away by an offer to become the player-manager of Swindon Town in 1994.

ALTHOUGH unable to save Town from a second successive relegation in 1995, he did steer them to the semi-final stage of the League Cup, where they were defeated by Bolton Wanderers. Swindon won the Division Two title in 1996 but the manager left the club after a dreadful start to the 1998/99 season. In January

2000 McMahon was appointed manager at Blackpool. Halfway through the 2003/04 season he bizarrely interrupted the press conference that had been arranged to announce his resignation, claiming he had withdrawn it after having talked to his chairman. He did eventually resign for real just before the end of the 2003/04 season. McMahon became the manager of Perth Glory in Australia early in January 2005 but that job lasted less than a year. In September 2011 he was hired to

expand Liverpool's brand and scouting into India. The former midfielder is head coach at the facility as a part of the club's ambition to leave its footprint in every continent in the next three years.

Season	League		FA Cup		League Cup		Europe		Other		Total	
	App	Goals	App	Goals	App	Goals	App	Goals	App	Goals	App	Goals
1985/86	23	6	4	1	5	3	-	-	4	0	36	10
1986/87	37	5	1	0	9	8	-	-	3	1	50	14
1987/88	40	9	7	0	2	0	-	-	-	-	49	9
1988/89	28 (1)	3	6	3	3	1	-	-	2	0	39 (1)	7
1989/90	37 (1)	5	8	1	2	0	-	-	1	0	48 (1)	6
1990/91	22	0	4	2	2	1	-	-	1	0	29	3
1991/92	15	1	0	0	4	0	5	0	-	-	24	1
Total	**202 (2)**	**29**	**30**	**7**	**27**	**13**	**5**	**0**	**11**	**1**	**275 (2)**	**50**

McManaman, Steve

'**WE'VE** another boy who's ten and if he sees a tin can on his way to school, he steps over it. Steven was the opposite.' Steve McManaman's father could see that his son was born to play football. Steven grew up as an Everton supporter, but joined Liverpool at 14 years of age.

> THE LEAGUE CUP WAS WON FOR THE FIFTH TIME, McMANAMAN SCORING BOTH GOALS WITH ANOTHER MAN OF THE MATCH PERFORMANCE AT WEMBLEY

Ten days after his first England Under-21 international, the 18-year-old got his first taste of first-team action when he came on against Sheffield United at Anfield on 15 December 1990. He made a couple more substitute appearances before making the starting line-up in the opening game of the 1991/92 season. McManaman had a sensational campaign, willing to run with the ball at length on the right wing armed with an unbelievable stamina, vital as John Barnes was out for most of the season. 'He has the chance to be one of the great players,' Graeme Souness judged after McManaman's first start. His debut campaign ended on a high as he delivered a masterful performance in the 2-0 win over Sunderland in the FA Cup final.

BARNES was impressed by the Red prodigy. 'He's always been a good dribbler and now he's conscious of people around him and how to bring them into the game,' Barnes said. 'Crossing may not be his strongest point, but too many people try to find the perfect player. He appears to be frail, but

that is deceptive. There are a lot of good players around but no one is more exciting than him.' Injuries curtailed McManaman's progress in the next couple of seasons as Souness's disastrous spell as manager came to an end. The 1993/94 season only produced two goals for McManaman and he was criticised for his goalscoring ability. When Roy Evans took over in 1994, McManaman was given a free role and no longer being tied to the wings inspired him to greater heights. Liverpool beat Crystal Palace 6-1 in the first game of the season and McManaman scored twice, his first goals in 363 days. The League Cup was won for the fifth time, McManaman scoring both goals with another man of the match performance at Wembley.

He continued his good form into 1995/96 when Liverpool showed great form at times but disappointed in the end. The summer went well though for McManaman when he starred for England in Euro 96, reaching the semi-finals. He later failed to reproduce his form for his country, drawing comparisons with John Barnes.

Liverpool sparkled again in 1996/97, but weren't the finished product. A number of teams tried to stifle McManaman by having one player chase him around for 90 minutes. Despite the close attention he did well enough to be on the five-man shortlist for PFA's Player of the Year. In 1997/98 McManaman, now the most experienced player in the side, became vice-captain to Paul Ince. He scored 12 goals that season, including two superb solo goals against Celtic and Aston Villa. Rumours had been rife for a while that Juventus and Barcelona were going to offer £12million for him and Liverpool allowed Barca to negotiate with McManaman. However, when he arrived in Spain there was no one to meet him. It seems that he was effectively used as a patsy in Barcelona's quest to secure the signature of Rivaldo.

McMANAMAN'S ninth and last season at Liverpool was not a pleasant one. His contract had been allowed to run into its last year, sparking fears of a Bosman exit. 'Roy and I have talked many times about Steve's position and

what we might do to try and keep him at the club,' said Gérard Houllier shortly after his arrival in July 1998. 'And we are in complete agreement that our next big signing has got to be Steve.' Chairman David Moores is said to have agreed to McManaman's wage demands at Liverpool, but the majority of the board didn't want to sanction that kind of money for fear of sparking a wage explosion.

In January 1999 McManaman announced that he would be leaving for European champions Real Madrid in the summer. 'This was a big, major, important contract and if I were to sign for Liverpool, a three, four, five-year deal, it would've taken me into my early thirties and I don't think I'd have played abroad then,' McManaman explained later. It soon became apparent that Real only wanted to make a quick buck off McManaman as the club tried to sell him for £6million soon after his arrival. Real discovered, however, that the lad could also play and he starred in the Champions League final in his first season, scoring a superb goal in a 3-0 win over Valencia. McManaman won a second Champions League winners' medal with Madrid in 2002 when he came on as a second-half substitute for Luis Figo in Glasgow, but on the whole the amount of playing time he was given was being reduced season by season.

After nearly 150 matches and 16 goals for Real in four campaigns McManaman returned to England in August 2003 with Manchester City, then managed by Kevin Keegan, where he was reunited with former Liverpool team-mates Robbie Fowler, Nicolas Anelka and, later, David James. McManaman stayed with City for two seasons, playing in 44 first-team matches, but failed to score a single goal. Keegan resigned in March 2005 and his successor, Stuart Pearce, released

FACTFILE

BORN
Kirkdale, Liverpool,
11 February 1972
POSITION
Right-winger
OTHER CLUBS
Real Madrid (1999–2003),
Manchester City (2003–05)
JOINED
1987; signed professional
19 February 1990
INTERNATIONAL CAPS
37 England caps (3 goals)
(24 (0) at LFC), 1994–2001
LFC DEBUT GAME/GOAL
15 December 1990 /
21 August 1991
CONTRACT EXPIRY
1 July 1999
HONOURS
FA Cup 1992;
League Cup 1995

'HE WAS SO NATURALLY TALENTED BUT IT WAS EASY TO FORGET HOW MUCH WORK HE GOT THROUGH IN A LIVERPOOL SHIRT'

**TONY BARRETT
JOURNALIST**

the midfielder on a free transfer towards the end of May.

Journalist Tony Barrett rightly considers Steve McManaman one of the best players to grace Liverpool's shirt in the 1990s. 'He comes from Kirkdale and everyone on Scotland Road was talking about Steve McManaman and from the moment he came into the side you could see why,' he wrote. 'He had that ability to beat defenders with ease and with just a drop of the shoulder or a jink he would be away. He was so naturally talented but it was easy to forget how much work he got through in a Liverpool shirt. There was no one who ran more and he was a natural athlete and he ran and ran and ran.'

Season	League		FA Cup		League Cup		Europe		Other		Total	
	App	Goals	App	Goals	App	Goals	App	Goals	App	Goals	App	Goals
1990/91	0 (2)	0	0 (1)	0	0	0	-	-	0	0	0 (3)	0
1991/92	26 (4)	5	8	3	5	3	8	0	-	-	47 (4)	11
1992/93	27 (4)	4	1	0	5	2	3	1	0	0	36 (4)	7
1993/94	29 (1)	2	2	0	1 (1)	0	-	-	-	-	32 (2)	2
1994/95	40	7	7	0	8	2	-	-	-	-	55	9
1995/96	38	6	7	2	4	1	4	1	-	-	53	10
1996/97	37	7	2	0	4	2	8	1	-	-	51	10
1997/98	36	11	1	0	5	0	4	1	-	-	46	12
1998/99	25 (3)	4	0	0	0	0	3	1	-	-	28 (3)	5
Total	**258 (14)**	**46**	**28 (1)**	**5**	**32 (1)**	**10**	**30**	**5**	**0**	**0**	**348 (16)**	**66**

McMullan, David

DAVID McMULLAN made his debut in a home match against Manchester City on 17 October 1925.

He made ten First Division appearances that season as the club finished in seventh place and also made the team for the three FA Cup ties Liverpool were involved in that year. He was only called on twice the following season, both times to cover for left-half Tom Bromilow. Although McMullan had a decent run of 14 consecutive league games in 1927/28, his place in the side was eventually taken by Tom Morrison.

The Belfast boy made an audacious move to New York in the summer of 1928. Ernest 'Bee' Edwards, the *Liverpool Echo* reporter, contacted an American agent and told him McMullan

could prove a useful forward: 'McMullan consulted me about a football job. Here was a man out of work; a married man with a family. He could get no situation in England. I worked to give him a berth of some kind.' On 28 July McMullan left Liverpool on the White Star liner Celtic heading for New York, accompanied by George Moorhouse, the manager of a soccer team named the New York Giants, just as the more renowned baseball team. Also travelling with McMullan were former Everton player C.E. Glover and former Liverpool forward

Chris Harrington, who had both signed for the Giants. McMullan wrote to Bee in October very pleased with his new adventure in New York. 'Just a line about the football over here. You would be surprised if you saw the game they

play over here. It is good and fast, but I think it is the small grounds that make it so fast, and, of course, they have as much grass as one of my old chums at Anfield has hair!'

FACTFILE

BORN
Belfast, Northern Ireland, 1901
POSITION
Half-back
OTHER CLUBS
Forth River,
Distillery (1921–25),
New York Giants (1928),
Belfast Celtic,
Distillery (1928–29),
Exeter City (1929–30)
SIGNED FROM
Distillery, October 1925
INTERNATIONAL CAPS
3 Northern Ireland caps, 1925–27
LFC DEBUT
17 October 1925
CONTRACT EXPIRY
July 1928

Season	League		FA Cup		Total	
	App	Goals	App	Goals	App	Goals
1925/26	10	0	3	0	13	0
1926/27	2	0	0	0	2	0
1927/28	19	0	1	0	20	0
Total	**31**	**0**	**4**	**0**	**35**	**0**

McNab, Jock

FACTFILE

BORN
Cleland, Lanarkshire, Scotland, 17 April 1894
DIED
2 January 1949
POSITION
Right-half
OTHER CLUBS
Bellshill Athletic,
Queens Park Rangers
(1928–30)
SIGNED FROM
Bellshill Athletic,
November 1919
INTERNATIONAL CAPS
1/0, 1923
LFC DEBUT GAME/GOAL
1 January 1920 /
15 April 1922
CONTRACT EXPIRY
June 1928
HONOURS
League Championship
1921/22, 1922/23

JOHN McNAB was a tough customer on the field more commonly known as 'Jock' because of his Scottish background. He made his debut for Liverpool at home to Manchester United on New Year's Day 1920, but hardly got a look-in until right-half John Bamber was struck down with appendicitis four games into the 1921/22 season.

FRANCIS Checkland deputised for Bamber in the next five appearances but McNab came in for the tenth match against Preston North End and only missed four First Division games until the end of the season, picking up a League Championship medal in the process, something he would also experience a year later, when he missed just three of the 42 matches.

McNab continued to be a regular in the club's defence for another four years, but missed two months of the 1923/24 season when he suffered major facial injuries after hitting the windshield of a taxi he was travelling in. McNab moved

JOHN McNAB
LIVERPOOL F.C.

south to join Queens Park Rangers at the end of the 1927/28 season.

The *Derby Daily Telegraph* reckoned McNab's 'robustness is sometimes a mistaken idea, he's so big and strong that he can't help opponents tumbling down when they barge into him'. Evidently his enthusiasm got the better of him on 14 February 1925 when he was sent off for

'HE'S SO BIG
AND STRONG THAT
HE CAN'T HELP
OPPONENTS TUMBLING
DOWN WHEN THEY
BARGE INTO HIM'

*DERBY
DAILY TELEGRAPH*

kicking a Newcastle player. His team-mate Walter Wadsworth was sent off as well, along with Newcastle's Urwin. An amusing postscript to the game was when Wadsworth and McNab were bemoaning their luck after being sent off, there was a knock on the dressing room door. "Who is it?" asked McNab, and was told it was one of the club's directors. "Bloody hell, has the ref started to send the directors off now?" came McNab's response.

Season	League		FA Cup		League Cup		Total	
	App	Goals	App	Goals	App	Goals	App	Goals
1919/20	2	0	0	0	-	-	2	0
1920/21	1	0	0	0	-	-	1	0
1921/22	29	2	3	0	1	0	33	2
1922/23	39	1	4	0	-	-	43	1
1923/24	30	0	4	0	-	-	34	0
1924/25	29	2	2	0	-	-	31	2
1925/26	34	0	3	0	-	-	37	0
1926/27	29	0	4	0	-	-	33	0
1927/28	7	1	1	0	-	-	8	1
Total	**200**	**6**	**21**	**0**	**1**	**0**	**222**	**6**

McNamara, Tony

TONY McNamara made the short journey across Stanley Park to Anfield from Goodison in December 1957 after a number of successful years with Everton, with whom he had scored 22 times in 111 league matches.

McNAMARA went straight into the side for the home game against Bristol City four days before Christmas and scored Liverpool's second goal in a 4-3 victory. That started a run of six successive matches and two more goals for the elegant right-winger, but he wasn't called on much in the final weeks of the campaign and left in the close season. McNamara became the first player to appear in all four divisions of the Football League within 12 months: Everton in the First Division, Liverpool in the Second, Crewe in the Fourth Division and Bury in the Third.

Season	League		FA Cup		Total	
	App	Goals	App	Goals	App	Goals
1957/58	9	3	1	0	10	3
Total	**9**	**3**	**1**	**0**	**10**	**3**

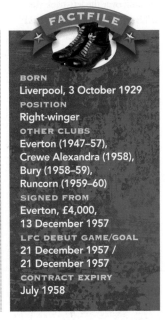

McNaughton, Harry

HARRY McNAUGHTON was a goalkeeper who made just a single appearance in Liverpool's first XI. He replaced the legendary Elisha Scott in the Anfield derby with Everton on 23 October 1920 and kept a clean sheet as the Reds won 1-0, with the winner coming 10 minutes before half-time from Dick Forshaw.

According to the *Liverpool Courier* McNaughton had a relatively quiet first half but was called upon three times in the second 'when he had to be spry to get rid of some awkward drives, and once was well beaten by a shot which hit the crossbar and rebounded into play. What little he had to do the keeper did well, but he was splendidly covered by the backs, and also owed something to the poor shooting of the Everton inside forwards.'

Season	League		FA Cup		Total	
	App	Goals	App	Goals	App	Goals
1920/21	1	0	0	0	1	0
Total	**1**	**0**	**0**	**0**	**1**	**0**

McNulty,
Tom

SALFORD-BORN Tom McNulty made 59 appearances for Manchester United since making his first-team debut at the end of the 1949/50 season and won the League Championship in the 1951/52 season.

He took over the left-back slot at Liverpool that had been held at the start of that year by Eddie Spicer and played in the last dozen First Division games of the 1953/54 relegation season. As Liverpool tried to come to terms with a lower standard of football McNulty, who could play on either flank, failed to nail down

a regular place in the side as John Molyneux and Ronnie Moran developed a good understanding at the back.

Season	League		FA Cup		Total	
	App	Goals	App	Goals	App	Goals
1953/54	12	0	0	0	12	0
1954/55	19	0	0	0	19	0
1955/56	1	0	0	0	1	0
1956/57	2	0	0	0	2	0
1957/58	2	0	0	0	2	0
Total	**36**	**0**	**0**	**0**	**36**	**0**

McOwen,
Billy

BILLY McOWEN was a schoolboy prodigy who featured for Blackburn from the age of 15 until he was 19, being the youngest goalkeeper in the league.

McOwen wasn't a regular in Liverpool's first ever season as Sidney Ross stood in goal, but after he retired through injury he had the honour of being Liverpool's first goalkeeper in a Football League match at

Middlesbrough Ironopolis on 2 September 1893. He played in 23 of the 28 Second Division matches and conceded only 16 goals without losing a single match during the whole campaign! McOwen needed to be a tough character playing in goal at a time when keepers received no protection from referees. They were frequently 'rushed' or charged, and lying on the ground with three or four players on top of them after an attack came with the territory.

McOWEN would try everything to prevent a goal, as reported by the *Blackburn Standard* on 30 December 1893: 'McOwen, the Liverpool Football Club goalkeeper (says Pastime), jumps up and pulls the crossbar down when the ball appears likely to hit it. The Football Association has ruled that in the case of a temporary displacement of the bar the referee may award a goal if, in his opinion, the ball has passed under the place where the bar ought to have been. If a referee will allow a goal when the ball passes just over the bar while McOwen is hanging on to it, it may deter this ingenious player from practising a not very desirable trick. Other goalkeepers with the same trick are Ogilvie (Blackburn Rovers) and Hillman (Burnley). It makes the crowd laugh, but it doesn't look fair.'

McOwen was a dentist and when Liverpool were promoted to the First Division he left the club as he would make a much better living pulling teeth rather than saving shots. He became an amateur again and played with Blackpool and later with Nelson. McOwen was an expert in saving

penalties and during his career faced 13 penalty kicks and saved 12 of them!

Season	League		FA Cup		Other		Total	
	App	Goals	App	Goals	App	Goals	App	Goals
1892/93	-	-	0	0	1	0	1	0
1893/94	23	0	3	0	0	0	26	0
Total	**23**	**0**	**3**	**0**	**1**	**0**	**27**	**0**

McPherson, Archie

BOB CLARK started the 1929/30 season at inside-left for Liverpool but was replaced after only two games by Henry Race for the next 13. Archie McPherson, signed from Rangers in November, then took over the inside-left position and only missed two matches between his debut on 23 November 1929 and the end of that season, scoring five goals in the process.

McPHERSON was one of two ever-presents, the other being Tommy Lucas, in 1930/31 and he contributed 10 goals to that season's league total of 86, scoring a brace on three occasions. Only two goals

Season	League		FA Cup		Total	
	App	Goals	App	Goals	App	Goals
1929/30	25	5	1	1	26	6
1930/31	42	10	1	0	43	10
1931/32	28	2	1	0	29	2
1932/33	24	1	0	0	24	1
1933/34	9	0	0	0	9	0
1934/35	2	0	0	0	2	0
Total	130	18	3	1	133	19

FACTFILE

BORN
Alva, Clackmannanshire, Scotland, 10 February 1910
POSITION
Inside-left forward
OTHER CLUBS
Bathgate, Alva Albion Rovers, Rangers (1929), Sheffield United (1934–37), Falkirk (1937–39), East Fife (1939), Dundee United (1939)
SIGNED FROM
Rangers, 16 November 1929
LFC DEBUT GAME/GOAL
23 November 1929 / 21 December 1929
CONTRACT EXPIRY
20 December 1934

followed a year later when he was restricted to 28 First Division appearances. Although he stayed at Anfield for another three seasons, the number of games he played in reduced each campaign until he made the last of his 133 league and cup appearances for Liverpool as a right-half in a home match with Leicester City on 17 November 1934.

McPherson also played cricket, as a batsman, for Clackmannan County in the Scottish Counties Championship, while he was a player at Sheffield United.

McPherson, Bill

SCOTTISH inside-right forward Bill McPherson arrived at Anfield in 1906 to join a club that had just proudly won the First Division for the second time.

At the start of his Liverpool career the club programme described him as 'slight and wiry in build, but lithe and active in all his

FACTFILE

BORN
Beith, Ayrshire, Scotland, 22 November 1884
POSITION
Inside-right forward
OTHER CLUBS
Beith (1902–04), St Mirren (1904–06), Rangers (1908–11), Hearts (1911–13)
SIGNED FROM
St Mirren, July 1906
LFC DEBUT GAME/GOAL
6 October 1906 / 6 October 1906
CONTRACT EXPIRY
May 1908

movements and there is no fear of his stamina. He is just the type of man to whom the honours fall. He is modest, unassuming, and, like so many others who have adopted professional football as a calling – a gentleman.' Surprisingly the team failed to repeat its impressive form of the previous year and even though McPherson scored on his debut against Woolwich Arsenal, the eventual defeat that day was the fourth in a row which would rise to five after a home loss to Sheffield Wednesday a week later. As McPherson settled the team's fortunes changed dramatically and seven wins came from the next nine matches. Even though the team's performances overall were very inconsistent, McPherson contributed with an excellent total of 11 goals from the 32 games he figured in that season.

McPHERSON only played seven times in the first half of 1907/08 but was picked more frequently from then on, making 20 league appearances in all to take his

career total for Liverpool up to 55. He also represented his club on seven occasions in the FA Cup, with his only goal being enough to beat Oldham in a second round tie on 2 February 1907. McPherson joined Rangers in 1908 and scored in three consecutive rounds as the side progressed to the 1909 Scottish Cup final against Celtic. Rangers had to settle for a 2-2 draw in the first final as their keeper carried the ball over the goal-line for Celtic's second goal eight minutes before the final whistle as he turned away to protect himself from an onrushing forward. Extra time was expected to be played as the teams were level 1-1 after 90 minutes of the second game at Hampden. However, when it was realised a third game was to be played the spectators rioted for several hours, tearing up the goalposts, ripping up parts of the pitch and setting

fire to the wooden barricades and the pay-boxes. The mounted police tried to contain the situation but were fended off with stones, while the fire brigade was repelled by missiles and had its hoses cut. 'I would suggest the withdrawal of all policemen from football matches,' wrote one correspondent in the *Glasgow Evening Times*, 'and substitute a regiment of soldiers with fixed bayonets.' Any plans of a second replay were abandoned and the trophy was withheld!

Season	League		FA Cup		Total	
	App	Goals	App	Goals	App	Goals
1906/07	28	10	4	1	32	11
1907/08	20	6	3	0	23	6
Total	48	16	7	1	55	17

McQue,
Joe

SCOTTISH centre-half Joe McQue was in the Liverpool team that won the Lancashire League in the club's inaugural season. His claim to fame is also scoring in Liverpool's first Football League match, in 1893. He was described as 'a finely built young fellow, with superb tackling powers and excellent judgement of the ball'.

HE ONLY MISSED two games as the club easily won the Second Division title by 12 points from Small Heath in second place. McQue initially struggled with the pace of the First Division. 'Compared with last year's brilliance a great falling off is most noticeable in McQue,' the *Liverpool Mercury* reported. Liverpool weren't strong or experienced enough to cope with life in the First Division, but only Harry Bradshaw made more league appearances for the club than McQue in 1894/95. Liverpool were relegated but came

straight up again as champions. McQue started the 1896/97 season as a regular but six weeks into the campaign the diminutive Robert Neill replaced him. Neill returned home the following

season so McQue got more chances in his final season at Anfield, playing 19 games. McQue had an excellent eye for goal and 14 goals for a defender at that time was a terrific return.

	League		FA Cup		Other		Total	
Season	App	Goals	App	Goals	App	Goals	App	Goals
1892/93	-	-	2	0	18	2	20	2
1893/94	26	2	3	1	1	0	30	3
1894/95	29	1	3	0	0	0	32	1
1895/96	26	5	2	0	4	0	32	5
1896/97	8	0	1	0	-	-	9	0
1897/98	14	2	5	1	-	-	19	3
Total	103	10	16	2	23	2	142	14

FACTFILE

BORN
Glasgow, Scotland,
11 March 1873
DIED
11 June 1914
POSITION
Centre-half
OTHER CLUBS
Pollokshields, Celtic,
Third Lanark
SIGNED FROM
Celtic, August 1892
LFC DEBUT GAME/GOAL
3 September 1892 /
3 September 1892
CONTRACT EXPIRY
September 1898
HONOURS
Lancashire League 1892/93
Second Division
1893/94, 1895/96

McQueen,
Hugh

HUGH McQUEEN arrived from Leith Athletic, along with his older brother by four years, Matt, who played in all positions at Liverpool and later managed the club. Like his brother, Hugh played for West Benhar and Bo'ness before becoming a professional footballer at Leith Athletic.

Hugh was an outside-left whose greatest assets were his speed and pinpoint crosses. Only one month after his arrival at Liverpool, Hugh, as well as Matt, missed the 2-0 win over Rossendale in the Lancashire League as Hugh had the previous day got married to Mary Jane Ross in Edinburgh. They had met at a dancing class where Hugh and his team-mates used to go to help strengthen their leg muscles. On the marriage certificate Hugh is listed as both a hotel waiter and a professional footballer.

McQUEEN only missed one match as the club remained unbeaten throughout its Second Division campaign in 1893/94. He nearly lost his life when he dived off a springboard at Southport baths where the team was relaxing on 27 April 1894, the day before the vital Test match against Newton Heath which would determine if Liverpool would be promoted. He was hauled out of the water,

admitting later that he couldn't swim! Liverpool, with McQueen in the side, were promoted after a 2-0 win but struggled to cope with life in the First Division. McQueen left Anfield for Derby County after the club's relegation back to the Second Division, wishing to remain in the top flight.

Derby had just escaped relegation from the First Division, but greatly improved during McQueen's six seasons at the club, finishing league runners-up in 1895/96 and third in 1896/97. Derby were also a great cup team, reaching the FA Cup semi-finals in 1896 and 1897 and losing the final in 1898 and 1899. Hugh won a gold medal for being the best player on the losing side in the 1898 final, a small consolation for missing out on the big prize. He played 168 games and scored 22 goals from 1895 to 1901 at Derby County.

On 6 February 1909 Hugh returned to Anfield to a standing

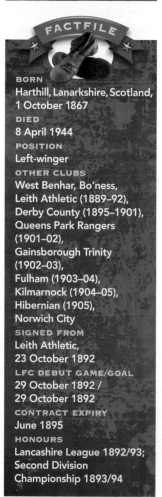

FACTFILE

BORN
Harthill, Lanarkshire, Scotland,
1 October 1867
DIED
8 April 1944
POSITION
Left-winger
OTHER CLUBS
West Benhar, Bo'ness,
Leith Athletic (1889–92),
Derby County (1895–1901),
Queens Park Rangers
(1901–02),
Gainsborough Trinity
(1902–03),
Fulham (1903–04),
Kilmarnock (1904–05),
Hibernian (1905),
Norwich City
SIGNED FROM
Leith Athletic,
23 October 1892
LFC DEBUT GAME/GOAL
29 October 1892 /
29 October 1892
CONTRACT EXPIRY
June 1895
HONOURS
Lancashire League 1892/93;
Second Division
Championship 1893/94

ovation as Norwich City's trainer when the Canaries managed a famous 3-2 victory in the FA Cup. McQueen actually played his last ever game a month later when he featured in a 6-1 defeat to Rotherham in the United League on 15 March 1909. He had officially hung up his boots by that time as he was 41 years old but was called into Canaries' line-up to make up the numbers. McQueen, a lifelong abstainer, was also a well-known cricketer and played for Ipswich. He once played in a charity cricket match with the King, who played with a bat presented to McQueen as a boy and broke it! Hugh and Mary Jane had two sons. The younger son, Neil, fought in both world wars and also played football, winning a medal in the Northumberland League. Hugh Jr moved to Canada and served with the Canadian Overseas Expeditionary Force in World War One; he was tragically killed in action in France on 15 September 1916. After his retirement from the game Hugh became a newsagent and tobacconist in Magdalen Street in Norwich. He passed away on 8 April 1944, five months prior to Matt's death.

Season	League		FA Cup		Other		Total	
	App	Goals	App	Goals	App	Goals	App	Goals
1892/93	-	-	1	1	16	3	17	4
1893/94	27	11	2	0	1	0	30	11
1894/95	12	2	2	1	0	0	14	3
Total	**39**	**13**	**5**	**2**	**17**	**3**	**61**	**18**

McQueen, Matt

MATT McQUEEN, along with his brother Hugh, arrived at Liverpool from Leith Athletic in Scotland only two months into the club's very first season. Matthew, so named after his grandfather, had eight siblings in total, three brothers and five sisters. They lived in Harthill in North Lanarkshire, a small village of only a couple of hundred inhabitants who made their living in the coalmines. Matt's father Peter was a roadman at the pit, preparing and repairing underground passageways. He later became a coal oversman, supervising the safety of the working conditions in the pit. Unavoidably, the boys were put to work at the Benhar Colliery. Hugh was a pony driver and Matt was a miner earning about 4 shillings per day (20p in today's money).

Matt had already been capped by Scotland as a winger, while at Leith Athletic, before moving south to Merseyside. He and Hugh made their debut in a 9-0 win over Newtown in an FA Cup qualifier on 29 October 1892 and the local press was pleased with the new additions. 'At Anfield, the Liverpool Club management are not allowing the grass to grow under their feet, and are kneading together a team which will take more beating than most elevens will be able to give them. The latest captures have been very quietly effected, and in the brothers McQueen they have secured a couple of players far above the average. The debut of the McQueens must be regarded as a decided success, to judge from the lavish applause extended to them.'

MATT featured regularly in his first four seasons at the club, making football history as he was certainly the only man in English football history to win two League medals, albeit in the Second Division, as both an outfield player and a goalkeeper. He featured on 45 occasions in Liverpool's goal and his skills were praised in a *Liverpool Mercury* report after a home 3-3 draw against Wolves on 1 December 1894, 'his clean, sharp and adroit work placing him in the highest rank as a cool custodian'. When Arsenal's Harry Storer arrived to claim Matt's goalkeeper's shirt in December 1895, even his versatility could not guarantee him a place in the side and he was only selected six times during the next three seasons.

After he finished playing, Matt became a qualified referee. He was appointed to Liverpool's board of directors on 16 December 1919

and then in February 1923 was offered the chance to take over as manager of Liverpool when David Ashworth surprisingly left the defending champions to move to Oldham Athletic. McQueen saw

M. McQUEEN, Esq.
Manager

the club safely through to their second successive League Championship. A car accident in November 1923 changed his life, as the club programme commented on in March 1924: 'Our opening note must be one of deep sympathy with the unfortunate and regrettable accident which occurred to Mr Matthew McQueen a little time ago, and which has led to the amputation of a limb. We are certain that all our readers will hope that the popular manager of the Liverpool club will speedily regain health and vigour and that his physical disability will not preclude him from enjoying many years of activity in the football world.'

After the successive Championships of 1922 and 1923, the club's fortunes declined somewhat with finishes of twelfth, fourth, seventh and ninth, and the Reds came close to relegation in 1927/28. Since losing his leg

Matt's health had deteriorated further and he resigned in February 1928. Matt and his wife Florence lived at 32 Kemlyn Road, just a stone's throw from the Anfield stadium; the Centenary Stand now covers the site where

McQueen's house once stood. Matt was a regular and welcome visitor to the club from the day of his retirement until his death at the age of 81 on 28 September 1944.

As a Player

Season	League		FA Cup		Other		Total	
	App	Goals	App	Goals	App	Goals	App	Goals
1892/93	-	-	1	0	16	5	17	5
1893/94	27	2	3	0	1	0	31	2
1894/95	23	0	3	0	1	0	27	0
1895/96	22	0	0	0	0	0	22	0
1896/97	1	0	0	0	-	-	1	0
1897/98	2	0	0	0	-	-	2	0
1898/99	2	0	1	0	-	-	3	0
Total	**77**	**2**	**8**	**0**	**18**	**5**	**103**	**7**

As a Manager

Season	Division	P	W	D	L	GF	GA	Pts	Pos	Win %	FA Cup
1922/23*	1st Division	14	6	5	3	15	9	17	1	42.86	3rd Round
1923/24	1st Division	42	15	11	16	49	48	41	12	35.71	4th Round
1924/25	1st Division	42	20	10	12	63	55	50	4	47.62	4th Round
1925/26	1st Division	42	14	16	12	70	63	44	7	33.33	4th Round
1926/27	1st Division	42	18	7	17	69	61	43	9	42.86	5th Round
1927/28**	1st Division	28	10	8	10	61	54	28	10	35.71	4th Round
Total	**-**	**210**	**83**	**57**	**70**	**327**	**290**	**223**	**-**	**39.52**	**-**

* McQueen appointed on 13 February 1923 with Liverpool in 1st position
** McQueen resigned on 15 February 1928 with Liverpool in 10th position

McRorie, Danny

DANNY McRORIE arrived at Liverpool in controversial circumstances in November 1930, a month after making his international debut for Scotland against Wales. Following an investigation by the Scottish Football League Commission it was confirmed that Morton had made an illegal payment to McRorie when he was transferred to Liverpool.

MORTON was fined £150 and the chairman, Mr Urquhart, was suspended indefinitely from taking any part in football. McRorie had a great reputation as a player as he had been the Scottish First Division's leading scorer with 18 goals in 16 matches in his last campaign at Morton. McRorie played just three times during the 1930/31 season and notched the first of his six Liverpool goals in an amazing game at Roker Park, Sunderland, on 6 December 1930. His strike

just before the interval gave Liverpool hope, reducing Sunderland's lead to 4-3, but in a match with many twists and turns the home side eventually ran out 6-5 winners. Right-winger McRorie didn't make the team during the opening weeks of the following season but then played in 25 of the last 29 First Division fixtures. His third and final season at Anfield saw him selected for first-team action on just five more occasions, in October and November 1932.

Season	League		FA Cup		Total	
	App	Goals	App	Goals	App	Goals
1930/31	3	1	0	0	3	1
1931/32	25	5	2	0	27	5
1932/33	5	0	0	0	5	0
Total	**33**	**6**	**2**	**0**	**35**	**6**

McVean, Malcolm

MALCOLM McVEAN holds the honour of scoring Liverpool's first ever goal in league football during the second half of their Second Division fixture at Middlesbrough Ironopolis on 2 September 1893. After scoring 10 goals in 21 games in the Lancashire League McVean scored nine times in the club's inaugural Football League season but he only managed five the following year as the team struggled to cope with a higher standard of football in the First Division.

The inside-right, who was said to be a 'good shot and rare dodger', remained at Anfield for a further two years, during which he won another Second Division Championship medal in 1896 and helped his side establish itself in the First Division. After five years at Liverpool the 26-year-old left for First Division Burnley in March

> MCVEAN HOLDS THE HONOUR OF SCORING LIVERPOOL'S FIRST EVER GOAL IN LEAGUE FOOTBALL

1897 along with team-mate Jimmy Ross but they were relegated with their new club in the spring. McVean had begun an apprenticeship in Scotland as a shipyard boilermaker when Liverpool signed him from Third Lanark and when he hung up his boots he went back to work in the shipyards. He died in Bonhill, Alexandria, in June 1907, aged

only 36. The *Dundee Courier* reported: 'McVean was of a sociable disposition, and being gifted with a rare fund of dry humour, was a most interesting companion.'

FACTFILE

BORN
Jamestown, Scotland,
7 March 1871
DIED
6 June 1907
POSITION
Forward
OTHER CLUBS
Vale of Leven,
Third Lanark (1889–92),
Burnley (1897),
Dundee (1897–98),
Bedminster (1898–99)
SIGNED FROM
Third Lanark, July 1892
LFC DEBUT GAME/GOAL
3 September 1892 /
3 September 1892
CONTRACT EXPIRY
19 March 1897
HONOURS
Lancashire League 1892/93;
Second Division
Championship 1893/94,
1895/96

Season	League App	League Goals	FA Cup App	FA Cup Goals	League Cup App	League Cup Goals	Total App	Total Goals
1892/93	-	-	3	2	21	10	24	12
1893/94	22	9	3	1	1	0	26	10
1894/95	20	5	3	2	1	0	24	7
1895/96	24	7	0	0	3	1	27	8
1896/97	23	5	2	1	-	-	25	6
Total	**89**	**26**	**11**	**6**	**26**	**11**	**126**	**43**

Meijer, Erik

GÉRARD HOULLIER needed a tall striker and Erik Meijer seemed a sensible acquisition on a free transfer. His only goals for the club came in the League Cup in the inauspicious surroundings of Boothferry Park, Hull. Meijer may have had limited abilities as a footballer but he had a never-say-die attitude that inspired others around him.

Once big Emile Heskey arrived in March 2000 the end was nigh for

Meijer. Jamie Carragher certainly approved of the Dutchman. 'He was just a great fella to have around the place and a great fella to have on the pitch when he did play, a real team player who'd really put himself about. He was just unfortunate at the time that we had so many good strikers and he was probably number four choice before he got the chance to move on. Mad Erik, I think he's definitely a cult hero.'
In 2003 Meijer moved to Aachen, a town on the German/Dutch border. He was a key player as Aachen returned to the 1. Bundesliga for the first time in 36 years. He was named the club's Director of Sport in 2009.

FACTFILE

BORN
Meersen, Netherlands,
2 August 1969
POSITION
Centre-forward
OTHER CLUBS
Fortuna Sittard (1987–89),
Antwerp (1989–91),
Eindhoven (loan, 1989–90),
Fortuna Sittard
(loan, 1990–91),
MVV Maastricht (1991–93),
PSV Eindhoven (1993–95),
KFC Uerdingen 05 (1995–96),
Bayer Leverkusen (1996–99),
Preston North End
(loan, 2000),
Hamburger SV (2000–03),
Alemannia Aachen (2003–06)
JOINED
Bosman free transfer,
1 July 1999
INTERNATIONAL CAPS
1 Netherlands cap, 1993
LFC DEBUT GAME/GOAL
7 August 1999 /
14 September 1999
CONTRACT EXPIRY
11 December 2000

Season	League App	League Goals	FA Cup App	FA Cup Goals	League Cup App	League Cup Goals	Europe App	Europe Goals	Total App	Total Goals
1999/2000	7 (14)	0	0	0	3	2	-	-	10 (14)	2
2000/01	0 (3)	0	0	0	0	0	0	0	0 (3)	0
Total	**7 (17)**	**0**	**0**	**0**	**3**	**2**	**0**	**0**	**10 (17)**	**2**

Meireles,
Raul

BEFORE moving to England, Raul Meireles had played all his club football in his homeland of Portugal, starting his career at Boavista where he was loaned to second-tier Aves for a couple of seasons. After impressing with Boavista's first team in his debut campaign in 2003/04 he was snapped up by European champions Porto, where he needed a couple of years before becoming a regular as a central midfielder. During his six seasons with Porto, Meireles was part of a squad that won the Portuguese title four times and the cup on three occasions. As his reputation grew, international recognition followed with his full debut coming in 2006.

Meireles' only season at Liverpool was a success. He only missed five Premier League matches and also played in eight cup ties. He struggled initially as he was stuck on the right flank as Roy Hodgson obviously didn't realise what his main strengths were. Once he was moved to the centre he started to come into his own. Never a really consistent scorer from midfield

at his previous club Porto, with 15 goals from 137 league matches, he nevertheless showed he was more than capable of hitting the target by netting five times in six matches from 16 January to 12 February 2011. This hot streak included a sweet strike to give the Reds the lead in the Anfield derby against Everton and a sensational volley at Wolverhampton the following weekend which was Liverpool's Goal of the Season. Meireles also netted the second-half winner at Stamford Bridge as the team's revival under Kenny Dalglish gathered pace. During the season the industrious midfielder scored one goal every 509 minutes and had five assists to his name from 66 chances created. Meireles covered more ground than anyone else and never hid. His name was not splashed across the papers, but it suited him perfectly to get on with his work quietly as he claimed:

'As a player I am a team worker, not a star or an individual player.'

THE 28-YEAR-OLD midfielder moved to Chelsea in the summer of 2011. He played in nearly fifty first-team matches for the London outfit in 2011/12. He came on as a substitute 15 minutes from the end of the FA Cup final against Liverpool to earn his first winners' medal in English football, but was suspended for the Champions League final win against Bayern Munich.

Following a move to Fenerbahce in summer 2012, the Portuguese caused uproar in Turkish football in December 2012 when he was sent off in Fenerbahce's game against Galatasaray. He responded to his red card by allegedly spitting at the referee and making a homophobic gesture towards him. The until-then quiet Portuguese international denied

the charges emphatically, but the Turkish FA still suspended him for 11 games, later reduced to four on appeal as it had been 'physically impossible' for Meireles to have spat at the referee as he was speaking throughout when berating the match official.

> A SENSATIONAL VOLLEY AT WOLVERHAMPTON WAS LIVERPOOL'S GOAL OF THE SEASON

FACTFILE

BORN
Porto, Portugal,
17 March 1983
POSITION
Midfielder
OTHER CLUBS
Boavista (1999–2004),
Aves (loan, 2001–03),
Porto (2004–10),
Chelsea (2011–12),
Fenerbahce (2012–)
SIGNED FROM
Porto, £11.5million,
29 August 2010
INTERNATIONAL CAPS
69 Portugal caps (8 goals)
(7 (1) at LFC), 2006–
LFC DEBUT GAME/GOAL
12 September 2010 /
16 January 2011
CONTRACT EXPIRY
31 August 2011
HONOURS
PFA Fans' Player of the Year
2011

Season	League		FA Cup		League Cup		Europe		Total	
	App	Goals	App	Goals	App	Goals	App	Goals	App	Goals
2010/11	32 (1)	5	1	0	0	0	7	0	40 (1)	5
2011/12	0 (2)	0	0	0	1	0	-	-	1 (2)	0
Total	32 (3)	5	1	0	1	0	7	0	41 (3)	5

Melia,
Jimmy

OVER A LONG and distinguished football career, Jimmy Melia played 500 Football League games for five different clubs. Melia was born in the Scotland Road district of Liverpool and had five sisters and five brothers of which he was the only one to pursue a football career.

He was chosen captain of the Liverpool Schools side and made the England schoolboys team starring alongside Bobby Charlton and later played for the England youth team. Melia signed professional forms with his home-town club on his seventeenth birthday in November 1954. Liverpool had just been relegated to the Second Division and were desperate to return to the First, especially as city rivals Everton had passed them on the way down as they returned to the top tier. Melia had to wait until shortly before Christmas 1955

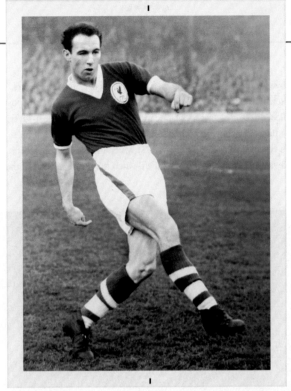

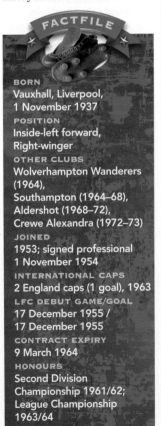

FACTFILE

BORN
Vauxhall, Liverpool,
1 November 1937
POSITION
Inside-left forward,
Right-winger
OTHER CLUBS
Wolverhampton Wanderers
(1964),
Southampton (1964–68),
Aldershot (1968–72),
Crewe Alexandra (1972–73)
JOINED
1953; signed professional
1 November 1954
INTERNATIONAL CAPS
2 England caps (1 goal), 1963
LFC DEBUT GAME/GOAL
17 December 1955 /
17 December 1955
CONTRACT EXPIRY
9 March 1964
HONOURS
Second Division
Championship 1961/62;
League Championship
1963/64

to make his debut where he delivered a man of the match performance, setting up one goal and scoring Liverpool's second in a 5-2 victory over Nottingham Forest. He played in four games out of five before he had to return to his national service. First-team opportunities were curtailed but he settled for appearances with the British Army side as well as Liverpool's reserves.

In the 1956/57 season, at only 19, he broke into the first team, taking over from John Evans. Inside-left Melia flourished and was Liverpool's top scorer in the 1958/59 season, scoring 21 goals in 40 games. He worked hard for the team and possessed a good football brain.

The strain of just missing out on promotion three seasons running finally took its toll on manager and ex-player, Phil Taylor, and it quickly became apparent that Bill Shankly saw in Melia all the qualities that were needed to help the club back to its position among the country's elite. Following two disappointing defeats at the start of his tenure Shankly moved Melia from his natural position at inside-forward to the right wing. Shankly explained: 'This was a case of expediency, as we really had not wings of sufficient experience among the juniors to play in the senior side. The plan was for him to be a deep-lying inside-right/outside-right with Roger Hunt playing the role of a poacher at centre-forward alongside Dave Hickson.' Melia struggled on the wing and was replaced by Billy Liddell, who was fast approaching the end of his career. On his return to the side two months later Jimmy Harrower made way as Melia was put in his old

position. Youngster Ian Callaghan was given a go on the right wing in the last month of the season. Melia played in all 42 league games when the team took the Second Division title in 1961/62.

MELIA had a good debut season in the First Division, missing only three games, but in the middle of December the following season he got injured. It was his first real injury and dented his confidence, in fact he only played three more games for Liverpool before he lost his place to Alf Arrowsmith. He was almost immediately transferred to Wolverhampton Wanderers, who paid a club record fee of £48,000 for his services. The *Daily Mirror* reported that 'recently he has been barracked by the Anfield crowd – a factor in his decision to jump at the chance of joining Wolves.' Melia had played in enough league matches before the transfer to qualify for a Championship medal. Before the end of the year, though, he had moved further south to join Southampton and enjoyed four good years there before moving on to Aldershot as a player-coach, later taking over as manager. In January 1971 he had the enormous thrill of leading his club out for an FA Cup third round tie at Anfield, receiving a wonderful reception from the Liverpool crowd who remembered how tirelessly he had worked when he was one of their own.

After his playing days were over, Melia coached in the United Arab

Season	League		FA Cup		League Cup		Total	
	App	Goals	App	Goals	App	Goals	App	Goals
1955/56	4	1	0	0	-	-	4	1
1956/57	26	6	1	0	-	-	27	6
1957/58	34	10	2	0	-	-	36	10
1958/59	39	21	1	0	-	-	40	21
1959/60	34	14	2	0	-	-	36	14
1960/61	26	3	1	0	0	0	27	3
1961/62	42	13	5	0	-	-	47	13
1962/63	39	5	5	2	-	-	44	7
1963/64	24	4	1	0	-	-	25	4
Total	**268**	**77**	**18**	**2**	**0**	**0**	**286**	**79**

Emirates, Kuwait and USA before being appointed Brighton & Hove Albion's chief scout, becoming their manager in the 1982/83 season. After Brighton's relegation to the Second Division in 1983

he moved to Portugal where he managed Belenenses for three years. He later moved to the USA where he currently resides, filling the post of technical director of Liverpool's Academy in Texas. In his post-Liverpool career he is probably most remembered for being behind Brighton's heroic run to the FA Cup final in 1983, which included a shock fifth round victory over Liverpool at Anfield when they were bottom of the

First Division and their hosts were top. To make matters worse, the winning goal was scored by another Liverpool old-boy, Jimmy Case!

Mellor, Neil

NEIL MELLOR'S father Ian made his name with Manchester City and his son, being on their books, dreamed about wearing the blue of City. However, City felt his services were no longer needed and Neil Mellor joined Liverpool. 'I was 16 when I went to the Academy and they signed me on a three-year scholarship. It was a great experience, great coaches; Steve Heighway, Dave Shannon and Hughie McAuley down there,' he told *LFChistory.net*. 'The key is to improve your skills and try to become a good person. Even though you don't make it as a footballer you want to become a decent person. They put as much emphasis on education as well as footballing skills.'

After struggling with injuries the first year Mellor made rapid progress and became a goalscoring phenomenon. He was top scorer with eight goals in Liverpool's FA Youth Cup run in the 2000/01 season. The following campaign he scored no fewer than 27 goals in 23 games for the Under-19 side and 18 goals in 18 games for the reserves. Mellor made three starts in a row for the first team in January 2003, scoring his debut goal in a 2-1 defeat to Sheffield United in the

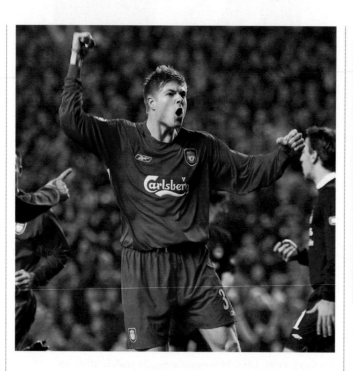

League Cup. Gérard Houllier sent the 20-year-old Mellor on a season-long loan to West Ham in August 2003 but he only appeared in 21 matches in which he scored two goals. He returned to Liverpool's reserves before the end of the 2003/04 season, not being allowed to play for the first team due to FA regulations, and scored 10 goals in four reserve games, bringing his tally to 45 goals in 44 reserve matches. Mellor's former team-mate, Chris Kirkland, commented on his goalscoring prowess: 'When he scores in training, he still celebrates as if it's a league game. He runs off on his own to the corner flag with his hand in the air. The lads call him "Shearer" because of his celebrations and he's definitely one to watch.'

MELLOR'S best spell at the club came in November and December 2004 when he scored a dramatic winner against Arsenal in front of the Kop in the closing seconds of the game and played a big part in a dramatic win over Olympiacos, scoring one and setting up another for Steven Gerrard, as Liverpool were promoted from the group stages of the Champions League. Mellor's heroics against Arsenal ensured he was one of *LFC.tv's* '100 players who shook the Kop' in 2006, prompting Jamie Carragher to comment: 'Mellor is in here? He's had bad knee injuries but I'm not surprised with the weight he's carrying!' Unfortunately Mellor's season finished by January as he had to have a knee operation. He had no

FACTFILE

BORN
Sheffield, 4 November 1982
POSITION
Centre-forward
OTHER CLUBS
West Ham United
(loan, 2003–04),
Wigan Athletic (loan, 2006),
Preston North End (2006–12),
Sheffield Wednesday
(loan, 2010–11)
JOINED
1999
LFC DEBUT GAME/GOAL
4 December 2002 /
8 January 2003
CONTRACT EXPIRY
30 August 2006

alternative, admitting 'there were times when I was in so much pain that I couldn't even run for the ball'.

Mellor had a short spell with Wigan Athletic at the start of 2006 but his injury-ravaged career was revived by a move to Preston North End in the Championship in August 2006. Although he continued to suffer from injuries, particularly to his knee, Mellor proved he had not lost the instinct in front of goal and scored 30 goals from 113 league matches for Preston between August 2006 and April 2010. In July 2010 Mellor's former Preston manager Alan Irvine persuaded Neil to join him at Sheffield Wednesday and he repaid him by scoring 13 goals in 33 League One matches in the city of his birth. Injuries continued to haunt him on his return to Deepdale and as the 2011/12 season reached its conclusion, Mellor announced his retirement as a player at the young age of 29. One can only imagine what could have been for Mellor who had six operations on his legs, three on each.

Season	League		FA Cup		League Cup		Europe		Other		Total	
	App	Goals	App	Goals	App	Goals	App	Goals	App	Goals	App	Goals
2002/03	1 (2)	0	1	0	2	1	0	0	0	0	4 (2)	1
2004/05	6 (3)	2	0 (1)	0	4	2	1 (1)	1	-	-	11 (5)	5
Total	7 (5)	2	1 (1)	0	6	3	1 (1)	1	0	0	15 (7)	6

Phil Taylor with his squad at Melwood

Melwood

LIVERPOOL FC bought the ground which Melwood stands on in West Derby from St Francis Xavier School in 1950. Two of the priests who taught at the school and devoted a great deal of their time to helping students with their football were named Father Melling and Father Woodlock. The training ground was named 'Melwood' in their honour. Facilities like these had long since been necessary for a club the size of Liverpool. 'Before they bought Melwood they trained at Anfield and out in the strip of land that is now the Main stand car park,' Ronnie Moran said. 'There would be a kickabout going around on this rough patch. It was a bit of a mess.'

Don Welsh was Liverpool's manager when the club acquired Melwood, but neither he nor his successor Phil Taylor did much to improve the facilities. It needed a Scotsman with an incredible strength of character to make people sit up and take notice that the club, Anfield and Melwood had been deteriorating throughout the years and if they were going to get out of this sorry mess something radical had to be done. 'When I went to Melwood to take my first training session it was in a terrible state,' Bill Shankly revealed in his autobiography. 'There was an old wooden pavilion and an air-raid shelter, and there were trees, hills and hollows, and grass long enough for Jimmy Melia to hide in standing up. It was a sorry wilderness. One pitch looked as if a couple of bombs had been dropped on it. 'The Germans were over here, were they?' I asked.' Nessie Shankly, Bill's wife remembered well his reaction to the club's training facilities. 'The Liverpool people couldn't have been warmer or more welcoming. The club, however, was a big disappointment to Bill.

The biggest shock of all to him was the training ground at Melwood. I remember we were standing in the middle of the pitch at Melwood and Bill said to me, 'Oh, Ness, have I made a terrible mistake leaving Huddersfield?''

SHANKLY had a battle on his hands. He would go there every day with Bob Paisley, Reuben Bennett, Joe Fagan and the groundsman at Melwood, Eli Wass, and dig up the place with their bare hands. There were bricks, broken glass and stones everywhere. The changing rooms were in an old green wooden pavilion which used to get very cold. Shankly not only cleaned up the training ground but changed the players' training methods. Players were used to meeting and changing for training at Anfield and then board the team bus for the short three-mile trip to Melwood. After training, they would jump on the bus back to Anfield to shower and change and get a bite to eat. Tommy Lawrence remembers how relieved the players were when they learnt about their new boss' football philosophy. 'In pre-season you got in at Anfield and you then put a pair of trainers on. They weren't like trainers like you have today for running on the roads. They were pumps. You needed to run from Anfield to Melwood. Around Melwood three or four times and then run all the way back. Roger Hunt and I used to travel with the train from Warrington and after about three days, we couldn't even go down the steps, the backs of our calves were just gone. As soon as Shanks came he just changed it. 'You play on grass and you will train on grass.' And that was it. Then we actually saw a bag of balls. We had never seen a bag of balls.'

'The pigsty' and 'Wembley' were two of the grounds at Melwood where the Scotsman's disciples honed their skills and focus was on the ball in the legendary five-a-sides, 'pass and move, pass and move.' Running short distances between the numbered boards of the 'sweat box' kept them in shape.

The modern day Melwood is a far cry from those days. In January 2001 Liverpool started work on the Millennium Pavilion, a state-of-the-art facility for players and coaches, designed in part by then manager Gérard Houllier. Architects Atherden Fuller Leng, who had worked on plenty of projects for the club before such as the Hillsborough memorial, the Paisley

Gateway and the Shankly Gates as well as the remodelling of Barcelona's Camp Nou, were brought in to design this modern complex. AFL completed the new Melwood in November 2001 at a cost of roughly £4.5m and the pavilion's structure is so described on the architect's homepage. 'A definitive feature of the building is the double-height, top-lit street. This space defines the three main areas of the building via walls of split-face blockwork, iroko timber cladding and the signature red-rendered wall. All three elements also feature externally combining with the striking metal-clad press lounge to create a building form of considerable note.'

The two storey building has all the modern amenities that a footballer could ever wish for; 15m x 8m swimming pool with jet streams for resistance training, rehabilitation and isokinetic gymnasium on two levels with hypoxic chamber to simulate training at altitude, doctors/ physiotherapy suite with a consultation room and six bed treatment room, changing and dining facilities for 40 first team members, a large gymnasium with a mezzanine floor for specialist equipment, and a separate feature of the complex is a covered 40m x 30m area with a synthetic field-turf surface for the players to perform certain forms of training. There are a number of all-weather pitches on the premises and a small covered area for fans who have been especially invited to watch the players train. There is no excuse for Liverpool players not to be in optimum shape.

Merseyside derby

Willie Fagan challenging Everton's keeper, George Burnett, in the 1950 FA Cup semi-final

LIVERPOOL Football Club was born out of the break-up between John Houlding and Everton in 1892 so it is no wonder Merseyside derbies have taken on such importance. It is a historic fixture that first took place on 22 April 1893 in the final of the Liverpool Senior Cup, in which, to add insult to injury, former Everton player Tom Wyllie scored the winner for Liverpool at Bootle's Hawthorne Ground. The game was not without controversy as Everton thought they deserved a penalty in the closing moments as a Liverpool player punched the ball in the penalty area. The referee ordered a drop-ball which was kicked clear and then he blew for full-time.

Everton complained about 'the general incompetence of the referee' and Liverpool were not presented with their trophy. The Blues' protests were in vain and eventually the Liverpool Senior Cup was presented to the Reds. The teams met for the first time in the league on 13 October 1894. Liverpool had been promoted as Second Division champions but were seriously struggling in the top flight without a single win in eight games while Everton were on top with seven wins out of seven. A neutral observer, a certain Mr John Humphreys, reported on this occasion for the *North Wales Chronicle*. 'I never saw such a crowd. As early as one o'clock all streets, for miles around, leading to Goodison Park began to be thronged with men, women, and boys, all tramping to one place. As far away as the Pier Head every tramcar was loaded with excited intending spectators of the game, and these, together with a heterogeneous assemblage of omnibuses, wagonettes, drays, pony carts, hansom cabs, fourwheelers, and every imaginable description of wheeled

vehicle, formed a huge procession stretching (to take one route alone) from the bottom of Scotland-road right up to the ground.' Liverpool were comprehensively beaten 3-0, but offered a stronger resistance when the teams met for the first time at Anfield five weeks later. The result, a 2-2 draw, 'had not a dull period'. The highlight was David Hannah's equaliser for Liverpool to make the scores 1-1, his grand shot so magnificent it 'almost sent the crowd frantic, even the Evertonians applauding the home team for their gallant play,' according to the *Liverpool Echo*.

mental reservation on the part of each follower that, come what may, their own side may win.' The opposing fans are often, in fact, part of the same family, one sibling Red, the other Blue or for example father and son divided by their loyalties.

Liverpool win the league while Everton lift the cup

Any ill-feeling if there ever was one really between the two sets of supporters seemed to have disappeared when the teams met on 30 September in the 1905/06 season during which Liverpool won the League Championship and Everton took the FA Cup, beating their local rivals in the semi-finals. F.E. Hughes wrote in the *Liverpool Echo*: 'Time was when the feelings between adherents of Reds and Blues ran high as 'twixt Capulet and Montague, but now the vendetta is nothing more serious than a

Kopite Harry Wilson wrote on the rivalry in the 1930s in Stephen F Kelly's *Kop*. 'The derby matches, of course, were the best. Most of the Evertonians would go down the Anfield Road end, but you used to get a few on the Kop. That was the only time there was ever any bother but it wasn't really much. They used to take the mickey. They used to call Chambers 'Toilet' and they'd shout at him. And Elisha Scott was called 'The Baker' because of Scott's bakery. We used to have names for their players as well. It was like a festival, all fun.'

As "G" wrote in the *Liverpool Echo* on 2 April 1913 some fans tried to be a disruptive influence cheering the Reds' or Blues' opponents on the day. 'Everton and Liverpool never play at home on the same day. The Everton crowd go to Anfield to see the visitors win; the Liverpool crowd go to Goodison to see the visitors win; and each lot vent their sarcasm on their rivals. There are no more bitter partisans than the Liverpool crowd at Goodison and vice versa.'

THE MOST anticipated derby for years took place in 1950 when the teams met in the FA Cup semi-final. Everton got the better of Liverpool in the same fixture in 1906 and while the Blues had won the competition twice, the Reds were still chasing the elusive cup. 'Seven people received hospital treatment and more than sixty got first-aid treatment on Everton and Liverpool football grounds yesterday, when more than 40,000 queued for tickets for next Saturday's semi-final,' reported the *Aberdeen Journal*. 'At one time it looked as if a dangerous situation would develop when the 20,000 strong, two-mile-long queue at Everton got out of hand. Police reinforcements on foot, aided by mounted police and St. John's Ambulance Brigade men, rushed to the main gates to keep the crowd in check.' On this occasion Liverpool beat Everton 2-0 but the Reds still had to wait 15 years before they won the cup.

The teams played each other every calendar year from 1896 until

FOR THOSE OF YOU WATCHING IN BLUE AND WHITE, THIS IS WHAT A EUROPEAN CUP LOOKS LIKE....

1951 when Everton were relegated to the Second Division. Liverpool followed suit in 1954 and to make matters worse Everton were promoted at the same time. When news of Liverpool's demise reached the crew and passengers of the Queen Elizabeth a coffin was made carrying wreaths and the club was buried at sea. The Evertonians onboard were the instigators of this ceremony but the Reds' supporters sorrowfully played along. The oration was delivered by the captain of the ship, Sir Ivan Thompson, who was an avid Red. 'We are gathered together at this sad time to bid a sorrowful farewell to a body known as 'The Reds' who through their inability to play football have been forced to make this ignominious descent in the limbo of the Second Division,' were his opening words. His last in a long-winded speech before the body was thrown overboard were:

Ashes to ashes, dust to dust,
The First Division won't
have you, the Second must,
You now go down much
to our disgust,
But you'll be back we hope
and trust,
So, goodbye Reds,
Play in peace down below,
We don't want to lose you but
we think you ought to go.

As a result the teams only met once in the league or the FA Cup during the next eleven years in what turned out to be a momentous occasion. Liverpool were hardly favourites as a Second Division team without an away win during the whole campaign against First Division Everton in the fourth round of the FA Cup on

29 January 1955. The police had to disperse a big crowd outside Goodison Park who had queued up for tickets for hours in vain as cup fever gripped the city. The Blues were simply outclassed by rampant Reds 4-0 in a game that was hailed in the papers as 'probably the most dramatic day in the long history of the famous Merseyside football 'derby'.' Liverpool's key player in the match Billy Liddell revealed manager Don Welsh was so pleased with the win that he gave the players 10 shillings each. Liverpool were promoted in 1962 and went on to win the league in 1964 and 1966 and Everton won the FA Cup in 1966 and the league title in 1970.

As Liverpool dominated the league from 1976 to 1984, winning the title seven out of nine seasons, the teams went their separate ways in terms of success but the Blues were to return with a vengeance under the guidance of Howard Kendall. In 1984 Liverpool won the league while Everton lifted the FA Cup, the third time that had happened, previously in 1906 and 1966. When Everton and Liverpool

battled for supremacy in the league in the mid-1980s their rivalry was re-ignited, but the Hillsborough disaster brought them closer again, culminating in the 'friendly final' on 20 May 1989 when Blues and Reds sat together in harmony at Wembley. Three years previously the Reds proved victorious in the first ever Merseyside FA Cup final, 3-1. Liverpool have had the upper hand in their battles in recent years and in fact David Moyes failed to beat Liverpool at Anfield in his 11 years at Everton. Both teams are well established in the Premier League and it is of utmost importance for the city of Liverpool to have both clubs in the top flight so the Merseyside derby will be a firm fixture in the calendar as it is arguably one of the most thrilling spectacles in English football.

LIVERPOOL have faced each other on 220 occasions in competitive games in the Football League, FA Cup, League Cup, Screen Sport Super Cup and the Charity Shield, that is all games which are counted as official[*]. The Reds have proved victorious in 40 per cent of these games.

Total 220
(Won = 87 / Drawn = 67 / Lost = 66). Goals for/against = 304-252.
Anfield 100
(Won = 41 / Drawn = 35 / Lost = 24). Goals for/against = 149-109.
Goodison Park 108
(Won = 39 / Drawn = 29 / Lost = 40). Goals for/against = 136-132.
Neutral venues 12
(Won = 7 / Drawn = 3 / Lost = 2). Goals for/against = 19-11.
League: Total 188
(Won = 72 / Drawn = 59 / Lost = 57). Goals for/against = 256-220.
Anfield 94
(Won = 40 / Drawn = 31 / Lost = 23). Goals for/against = 142-103.
Goodison Park: 94
(Won = 32 / Drawn = 28 / Lost = 34). Goals for/against = 114-117.
FA Cup total: 23
(Won = 10, Drawn = 6, Lost = 7). Goals for/against = 37-27.
League Cup total: 4
(Won = 2 / Drawn = 1, Lost = 1). Goals for/against = 2-1.
Charity Shield total: 3
(Won = 1 / Drawn = 1, Lost = 1). Goals for/against = 2-2.
Screen Sport Super Cup total: 2
(Won = 2). Goals for/against = 7-2.
Total friendly games: 45
Total wartime games: 52

* These totals do not include games in the Liverpool Senior Cup or the Lancashire Senior Cup because these competitions have been essentially demoted as the clubs eventually turned out their reserves instead of their strongest 11. The Floodlit Challenge Cup is also not included in the official total.

In Memoriam
Treasured Memories of
Everton F.C.
who "Fell Asleep" 29th January, 1955
at Goodison Park.

'Peacefully sleeping, free from all pain
We wouldn't wake them to suffer again'

Sadly missed by all at Anfield Road.

"Dear Departed Friends"

Top 5 biggest wins in official games

7 September 1935	6-0	Anfield	1st Division
25 September 1965	5-0	Anfield	1st Division
6 November 1982	5-0	Goodison Park	1st Division
7 October 1922	5-1	Anfield	1st Division
26 September 1925	5-1	Anfield	1st Division

Top 5 biggest defeats in official games

9 April 1909	0-5	Goodison Park	1st Division
3 October 1914	0-5	Anfield	1st Division
11 January 1902	0-4	Goodison Park	1st Division
19 September 1964	0-4	Anfield	1st Division
1 April 1904	2-5	Goodison Park	1st Division

418 players have featured for Liverpool against Everton's 478.

Top 5 Liverpool players with most appearances

Ian Rush	36
Bruce Grobbelaar	34
Alan Hansen	33
Ronnie Whelan	31
Ian Callaghan	31

Jamie Carragher played Everton on 30 occasions and of the current players Steven Gerrard has faced the Blues most often, 29 times.

Top 5 Everton players with most appearances

Neville Southall	41
Kevin Ratcliffe	32
Graeme Sharp	30
Dave Watson	30
Jack Taylor	29

Top 5 Liverpool players with most goals

Ian Rush	25 in 36 games
Harry Chambers	8 in 13 games
Jack Parkinson	8 in 15 games
Steven Gerrard	8 in 29 games
Dick Forshaw	7 in 12 games

Top 5 Everton players with most goals

Dixie Dean	19 in 17 games
Sandy Young	12 in 22 games
Jimmy Settle	8 in 13 games
Graeme Sharp	7 in 30 games
Bobby Parker	6 in 4 games

Hat-tricks or more

4	Sandy Young	1 April 1904	2-5	Goodison Park
4	Fred Howe	7 September 1935	6-0	Anfield
4	Ian Rush	6 November 1982	5-0	Goodison Park
3	Bobby Parker	3 October 1914	0-5	Anfield
3	Harry Chambers	7 October 1922	5-1	Anfield
3	Dick Forshaw	26 September 1925	5-1	Anfield
3	Dixie Dean	25 February 1928	3-3	Anfield
3	Dixie Dean	19 September 1931	1-3	Anfield
3	Harold Barton	11 February 1933	7-4	Anfield
3	Ian Rush	30 September 1986	4-1	Goodison Park
3	Steven Gerrard	13 March 2012	3-0	Anfield

Sendings-off

21 November 1896	Anfield	Alf Milward
20 October 1979	Anfield	Terry McDermott, Garry Stanley
7 November 1981	Anfield	Eamonn O'Keefe
6 November 1982	Goodison Park	Glenn Keeley
16 April 1997	Goodison Park	David Unsworth, Robbie Fowler
27 September 1999	Anfield	Sander Westerveld, Francis Jeffers, Steven Gerrard
29 October 2000	Anfield	Thomas Gravesen
16 April 2001	Goodison Park	Igor Biscan
19 April 2003	Goodison Park	David Weir, Gary Naysmith
20 March 2005	Anfield	Milan Baros
28 December 2005	Goodison Park	Phil Neville, Mikel Arteta
25 March 2006	Anfield	Steven Gerrard, Andy van der Meyde
20 October 2007	Goodison Park	Tony Hibbert, Phil Neville
27 September 2008	Goodison Park	Tim Cahill
4 February 2009	Goodison Park	Lucas Leiva
6 February 2010	Anfield	Sotirios Kyrgiakos, Steven Pienaar
1 October 2011	Goodison Park	Jack Rodwell

Own goals

30 January 1902	Goodison Park	Bill Balmer	2-0
6 December 1969	Goodison Park	Sandy Brown	3-0
4 March 1972	Anfield	Tommy Wright	4-0
4 March 1972	Anfield	John McLaughlin	4-0
20 October 1979	Anfield	Mick Lyons	2-2
21 March 1981	Anfield	John Bailey	1-0
18 August 1984	Wembley	Bruce Grobbelaar	0-1
16 April 1997	Goodison Park	Claus Thomsen	1-1
18 October 1997	Goodison Park	Neil Ruddock	0-2
25 March 2006	Anfield	Phil Neville	3-1
20 October 2007	Goodison Park	Sami Hyypia	2-1
29 November 2009	Goodison Park	Joseph Yobo	2-0
28 October 2012	Goodison Park	Leighton Baines	2-2

Famous boyhood Blues who played for the Reds

Jamie Carragher, Robbie Fowler, Steve McMahon, Steve McManaman, Michael Owen, Ian Rush

Famous boyhood Reds who played for the Blues

John Bailey, Mike Newell, Leon Osman, Peter Reid, Dave Watson.

Despite the fact that few players have moved between the sides in later years Liverpool have completed more direct transfers with Everton than any other club, 29 in total.

Transfers from Everton to Liverpool

Player	Appearances/Goals	Years at club
Tom Wyllie	21/5, 1890-92	25/15, 1892-93
Duncan McLean	26/0, 1890-92	82/4, 1892-95
Patrick Gordon	22/5, 1890-93	30/8, 1893-94
John Whitehead	2/0, 1894	3/0, 1894-96
Fred Geary	99/86, 1889-95	45/14, 1895-1900
Alex Latta	148/70, 1889-96	No appearances 1896-97
Abraham Hartley	61/28, 1893-97	12/1, 1897-98
David Murray	2/0, 1903-04	15/0, 1904-05
Don Sloan	6/0, 1907-08	6/0, 1908-09
Tom Gracie	13/1, 1911-12	34/5, 1912-14
Bill Lacey	40/11, 1909-12	259/29, 1912-24
Frank Mitchell	24/0, 1913-21	18/0, 1921-23
Alf Hanson	No appearances 1931	177/52, 1931-38
Tosh Johnson	161/65, 1930-34	38/8, 1934-36
Billy Hartill	5/1, 1935-36	4/0, 1936
John Heydon	No appearances 1946-49	67/0, 1949-53
Tony McNamara	113/22, 1951-57	10/3, 1957-58
Dave Hickson	243/111, 1951-55 and 1957-59	67/38, 1959-61
Nick Barmby	133/24, 1996-2000	58/8, 2000-02
Abel Xavier	45/4, 1999-2002	21/2, 2002-04

Transfers from Liverpool to Everton

Player	Appearances/Goals	Years at club
Harold Uren	45/2, 1906-12	24/3, 1912-13
Dick Forshaw	288/124, 1919-27	42/8, 1927-29
Jimmy Payne	243/43, 1942-56	6/2, 1956-57
Johnny Morrissey	37/6, 1955-62	314/50, 1962-72
Kevin Sheedy	5/2, 1978-82	368/97, 1982-91
David Johnson	213/78, 1976-82	105/20, 1971-72 and 1982-84
Alan Harper	No appearances 1976-83	241/5, 1983-88 and 1991-93
Peter Beardsley	175/59, 1987-91	95/32, 1991-93
Gary Ablett	147/1, 1981-92	156/6, 1992-96

Gary Mac beats Everton from 44 yards in 2001

There are also several players who have been on the books of both clubs but were not transferred directly between them. In some instances they did not make grade at their respective club and went on to make a name for themselves across Stanley Park or indeed players who featured regularly for both clubs.

Player	Appearances/Goals	Years at club
Jack Balmer*	309/110, 1935-52	No appearances 1934-35
Benjamin Howard-Baker	No appearances 1920	13/0, 1920-21 and 1926-27
Arthur Berry	3/0, 1906-09 and 1/0, 1912	29/7, 1910-11
Harry Bradshaw	138/51, 1893-98	No appearances 1891-92
David Burrows	193/3, 1988-93	23/0, 1994-95
Edgar Chadwick	45/7, 1902-04	300/109, 1888-99
John Gidman	No Appearances 1970-71	78/3, 1979-81
Andrew Hannah	69/1, 1892-95	44/0, 1889-91
Don Hutchison	60/10, 1990-94	89/11, 1998-2000
Neil McBain	12/0, 1928	103/1, 1922-26
Steve McMahon	277/50, 1985-91	119/14, 1980-83
Dave Watson	No Appearances 1976-80	528/37, 1986-2000
Sander Westerveld	103/0, 1999-2001	2/0, 2005-06 (loan)

* Balmer had been released by Everton when Liverpool signed him so not a direct signing between the clubs.

A time to Remember.........
Date 25th September 1965
Place ANFIELD
Time Five past West

AT THIS TIME OF CHRISTMAS CHEER,
IT IS WRONG OF ME TO JEER,
BECAUSE I THINK YOU'RE CRYING STILL,
FROM WHEN WE BEAT YOU 5-TO NIL!
SO CHRISTMAS EVE WHEN YOU'RE IN BED,
REMEMBER SANTA TOO WEARS RED,
AND HIDE YOUR BLUE & WHITE ROSETTE
OR NIL AGAIN IS WHAT YOU'LL GET
!!!

5.0!

EE-AYE-ADDIO
we also won the cup!
All the best -(from the Best)

Metcalf,
Arthur

ARTHUR METCALF had only played 12 games and scored two goals in three seasons at First Division Newcastle when he arrived at Liverpool aged 23.

This clever and thoughtful player had a good goals-per-game ratio at Liverpool and was the club's top scorer in his debut 1912/13 season, when he netted 18 times from 32 matches, featuring both as an outside-left and inside-right. He also scored a hat-trick in the FA Cup that year in a 4-1 second round victory at Arsenal.

The following season Metcalf was badly injured against Sunderland on 13 September and hardly featured for five months, but played a big part in Liverpool's cup run that got them all the way to their first ever FA Cup final, which they unfortunately lost 1-0 to Burnley. Despite the outbreak of war, the 1914/15 season was completed and Metcalf added another seven goals to his career total, in 16 games. Although he

A. METCALF LIVERPOOL

never played competitive league football for Liverpool again, Metcalf was a prolific scorer for the club in the local Lancashire leagues that were arranged for the duration of the war. The *Lancashire Daily Post* said he was a 'likeable man who knew the whole alphabet of the game'.

METCALF passed away on 9 February 1936, only 46 years of age, after being taken ill while on duty as a gateman at Anfield.

FACTFILE

BORN
Seaham, County Durham, 8 April 1889
DIED
9 February 1936
POSITION
Left-winger /
Inside-right forward
OTHER CLUBS
Herrington Swifts (1907–08),
Hebburn Argyle (1908–09),
North Shields Athletic (1909),
Newcastle United (1909–12),
Stockport County (1919–20),
Swindon Town (1920–22),
Accrington Stanley (1922–23),
Aberdare Athletic (1923–25),
Norwich City (1925–26)
SIGNED FROM
Newcastle United, £150,
24 May 1912
LFC DEBUT GAME/GOAL
28 September 1912 /
14 October 1912
CONTRACT EXPIRY
1919

	League		FA Cup		Total	
Season	App	Goals	App	Goals	App	Goals
1912/13	28	15	4	3	32	18
1913/14	10	2	5	1	15	3
1914/15	14	6	2	1	16	7
Total	**52**	**23**	**11**	**5**	**63**	**28**

Michael,
Bill

LIVERPOOL had previously tried to loan Bill Michael from Hearts in the 1894/95 season when they were seriously depleted for an important Test match that would decide their fate in the First Division. Hearts wouldn't release him and the Reds were relegated.

A scribe at the *Athletic News* had the following first impression of Michael shortly after his arrival at Liverpool: 'He is a very nice player – one of the big ones in a small compass, and can play on the wings or centre.' He was also described as having been 'the battering ram' of Hearts the previous season and 'could charge into a bull elephant and still come off best', so it's pretty evident he made his presence felt. Michael got his chance in the side at outside-left when Becton was suspended by the club for a couple of months after missing training. Michael regained a regular spot in the team in the last eight games of the campaign after Jimmy Ross had been sold to Burnley. The inside-forward scored five times as the club comfortably held on to their First Division status at the second time of asking by finishing in a respectable fifth place. Liverpool wanted to keep Michael and offered him a 'big sum down' and £4 per week for renewing his contract, but he wanted a return

to Scotland and his old club Hearts re-signed him ahead of Hibernian, Celtic and Rangers.

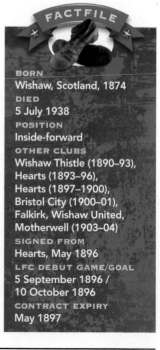

FACTFILE

BORN
Wishaw, Scotland, 1874
DIED
5 July 1938
POSITION
Inside-forward
OTHER CLUBS
Wishaw Thistle (1890–93),
Hearts (1893–96),
Hearts (1897–1900),
Bristol City (1900–01),
Falkirk, Wishaw United,
Motherwell (1903–04)
SIGNED FROM
Hearts, May 1896
LFC DEBUT GAME/GOAL
5 September 1896 /
10 October 1896
CONTRACT EXPIRY
May 1897

	League		FA Cup		Total	
Season	App	Goals	App	Goals	App	Goals
1896/97	19	5	4	0	23	5
Total	**19**	**5**	**4**	**0**	**23**	**5**

Millar, Billy

BILLY MILLAR wrote his name in the history books of the club at only 21 years of age when he scored the fastest ever goal for a debutant, in just 50 seconds!

ON THE opening day of the 1928/29 season Liverpool faced Bury at Anfield. A newspaper report described the action: 'The goal followed directly after kick-off. The ball went to Edmed, who made progress on the right and cleverly forced the Bury defence to concede a corner. Edmed placed it accurately, and Miller [sic] cooly deflected the centre past Richardson.' He added a second 20 minutes from time as the Reds won comfortably 3-0 in the premiere of the new roofed

HE SCORED THE FASTEST EVER GOAL FOR A DEBUTANT, IN JUST 50 SECONDS!

Spion Kop. Despite his excellent start Millar only figured twice more for the club's first team, against Sheffield United at home on 5 September which Liverpool lost 2-1 and in a 3-0 home victory against Newcastle on 13 October. He set a scoring record at Barrow by scoring 30 goals in 30 games in the Third Division North.

FACTFILE

BORN
Ballymena, Northern Ireland, 25 October 1906
DIED
1990
POSITION
Forward
OTHER CLUBS
Lochgelly United (1922–26), Linfield (1926–28), Barrow (1929–33), Newport County (1933–34), Carlisle United (1934–35), Sligo Rovers (1935–37), Cork (1937–38), Drumcondra (1938–39)
SIGNED FROM
Linfield, 1928
INTERNATIONAL CAPS
2 Northern Ireland caps (1 goal), 1931–32
LFC DEBUT GAME/GOAL
25 August 1928 / 25 August 1928
CONTRACT EXPIRY
1929

Season	League		FA Cup		Total	
	App	Goals	App	Goals	App	Goals
1928/29	3	2	0	0	3	2
Total	3	2	0	0	3	2

Miller, John

MILLER DID TURN OUT TO BE A GOALSCORING MACHINE IN HIS ONLY SEASON AT LIVERPOOL, SCORING 25 GOALS IN 24 GAMES

JOHN MILLER was victorious with Dumbarton in the first two seasons of the Scottish Football League from 1890 to 1892.

Following their final game in the 1891/92 season at Abercorn, the champions for the second year running were welcomed by a sizeable crowd at the station with a local band playing Handel's 'See the Conquering Hero Comes'. From early on it was clear that John Miller was a major coup for Liverpool, as *Field Sports* commented: 'J. Miller is an ideal centre, and no man has earned such high praise as Miller has done since he came to Liverpool. He is a most unselfish player, feeding his forwards with remarkable accuracy, and when a chance of scoring presents itself his shots are

sent with a velocity that gives the goalkeeper little chance.'

MILLER did turn out to be a goalscoring machine in his only season at Liverpool, scoring 25 goals in 24 games and writing his name in the club's early history books by netting five goals in one game, a 7-0 win against Fleetwood Rangers on 3 December, a feat only four players at Liverpool have repeated. Once Liverpool entered the Second Division, Miller wanted a pay rise of £100 down and £3 per week, which was a considered an 'exorbitant sum' in the papers at the time, especially considering every Liverpool player got a bonus for being a resounding success in their local Lancashire League. Miller joined First Division side The Wednesday, which the

Athletic News concluded 'must be paying him a heavy sum'. Miller scored seven goals in 13 games for The Wednesday before moving back to Scotland.

FACTFILE

BORN
Dumbarton, Scotland, 1870
POSITION
Centre-forward
OTHER CLUBS
Dumbarton (1888–92), The Wednesday (1893–94), Airdrieonians (1894–95)
SIGNED FROM
Dumbarton, 1892
LFC DEBUT GAME/GOAL
24 September 1892 / 24 September 1892
CONTRACT EXPIRY
June 1893
HONOURS
Lancashire League 1892/93

Season	League		FA Cup		Other		Total	
	App	Goals	App	Goals	App	Goals	App	Goals
1892/93	-	-	3	3	21	22	24	25
Total	0	0	3	3	21	22	24	25

Miller,
John

JOHN MILLER made a limited number of first-team appearances for Liverpool during the 1919/20 season, his debut coming in a 1-0 home defeat to Chelsea on 18 October 1919.

ALTHOUGH he played in the next two matches as well, he had to wait until nearly the end of the season before being recalled for the trip to Sheffield Wednesday. His brother Tom was more successful at Liverpool, making 146 appearances and scoring 56 goals from 1912 to 1920. The two Millers played together on three occasions for Liverpool's first team. While playing only a supporting role at Liverpool, John quickly established himself at Aberdeen after joining for a club record fee from Liverpool, scoring 27 goals in 42 appearances in his debut season at Pittodrie. Unfortunately he broke his leg at the start of the following season and never recaptured his form.

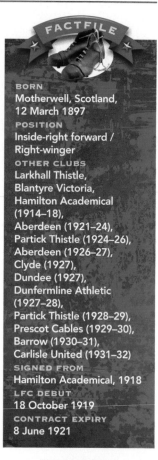

FACTFILE

BORN
Motherwell, Scotland,
12 March 1897
POSITION
Inside-right forward /
Right-winger
OTHER CLUBS
Larkhall Thistle,
Blantyre Victoria,
Hamilton Academical
(1914–18),
Aberdeen (1921–24),
Partick Thistle (1924–26),
Aberdeen (1926–27),
Clyde (1927),
Dundee (1927),
Dunfermline Athletic
(1927–28),
Partick Thistle (1928–29),
Prescot Cables (1929–30),
Barrow (1930–31),
Carlisle United (1931–32)
SIGNED FROM
Hamilton Academical, 1918
LFC DEBUT
18 October 1919
CONTRACT EXPIRY
8 June 1921

Season	League		FA Cup		Total	
	App	Goals	App	Goals	App	Goals
1919/20	8	0	0	0	8	0
Total	**8**	**0**	**0**	**0**	**8**	**0**

Miller,
Tom

TOM MILLER, an electrifying forward, established himself quickly at Anfield following a transfer from Hamilton Academical in February 1912. He helped the club reach their first FA Cup final in 1914, a season in which he scored 20 goals in 40 games.

All his good deeds at Liverpool are sadly overshadowed by the fact that Tom Miller – along with three other Liverpool players, Thomas Fairfoul, Bob Pursell and Jackie Sheldon, and three Manchester United players – was found guilty of fixing a game between the clubs on Good Friday 1915. For his service to his country in the war Miller's life ban from the game was lifted and he was still a Liverpool player after league football resumed. Miller scored 13 goals in 25 games in the 1919/20 season as Liverpool finished fourth. He was described in a contemporary article as having 'a rare burst of speed and a good shot and knows how to hustle the defenders' and that he was 'a rare stamp of forward, intelligent, quick on his toes and skilful in passing and finishing'.

MILLER started the following season well by scoring three goals in his first two games, but funnily enough, considering the Good Friday scandal, he moved to Manchester United in September 1920. Miller scored eight goals in 27 appearances in his only season at United before moving to his native Scotland in July 1921 to play for Hearts, who signed him for a club record fee. The 31-year-old was, however, past his best and was offloaded to Southern League's Torquay United.

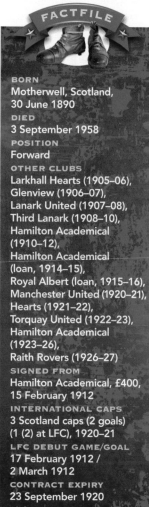

FACTFILE

BORN
Motherwell, Scotland,
30 June 1890
DIED
3 September 1958
POSITION
Forward
OTHER CLUBS
Larkhall Hearts (1905–06),
Glenview (1906–07),
Lanark United (1907–08),
Third Lanark (1908–10),
Hamilton Academical
(1910–12),
Hamilton Academical
(loan, 1914–15),
Royal Albert (loan, 1915–16),
Manchester United (1920–21),
Hearts (1921–22),
Torquay United (1922–23),
Hamilton Academical
(1923–26),
Raith Rovers (1926–27)
SIGNED FROM
Hamilton Academical, £400,
15 February 1912
INTERNATIONAL CAPS
3 Scotland caps (2 goals)
(1 (2) at LFC), 1920–21
LFC DEBUT GAME/GOAL
17 February 1912 /
2 March 1912
CONTRACT EXPIRY
23 September 1920

Season	League		FA Cup		Total	
	App	Goals	App	Goals	App	Goals
1911/12	8	1	0	0	8	1
1912/13	30	8	4	0	34	8
1913/14	32	16	8	4	40	20
1914/15	33	11	2	0	35	11
1919/20	20	11	5	2	25	13
1920/21	4	3	0	0	4	3
Total	**127**	**50**	**19**	**6**	**146**	**56**

Milne,
Gordon

WHEN BILL SHANKLY bought Gordon Milne in his first full season as manager he knew the boy pretty well, having been his dad's team-mate at Preston for a few years. Milne's play was uncomplicated and others prospered around his unselfish and skilful play.

He made the transition from Second Division to the First without any problems and he was a vital part on the right side of Shankly's midfield. He only missed a handful of league fixtures in three seasons as Liverpool won the Second Division in 1962, established themselves in the First Division and then won the League Championship in 1964. Milne's greatest disappointment was without a doubt missing out on the 1965 FA Cup final, just as his father, Jimmy, had missed Preston's cup win in 1938.

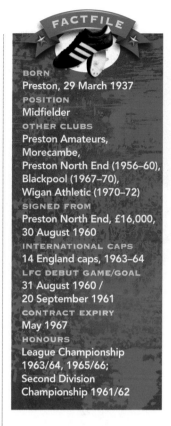

FACTFILE

BORN
Preston, 29 March 1937
POSITION
Midfielder
OTHER CLUBS
Preston Amateurs,
Morecambe,
Preston North End (1956–60),
Blackpool (1967–70),
Wigan Athletic (1970–72)
SIGNED FROM
Preston North End, £16,000,
30 August 1960
INTERNATIONAL CAPS
14 England caps, 1963–64
LFC DEBUT GAME/GOAL
31 August 1960 /
20 September 1961
CONTRACT EXPIRY
May 1967
HONOURS
League Championship
1963/64, 1965/66;
Second Division
Championship 1961/62

ANOTHER LEAGUE title followed in 1966 but he was two months out through injury, which proved a setback to his chances of making the World Cup squad. Milne had played 14 internationals and had hoped to be one of Liverpool's four players with England in the 1966 World Cup, but he wasn't chosen for the final group.

Despite being a regular in the previous season 30-year-old Milne was sold to Second Division Blackpool in May 1967. Three years later he took on the role of player-manager at non-league Wigan Athletic. He was the England youth team manager for nearly 12 months before eight years as manager of Coventry City. After a four-year spell as manager of

Leicester City, he moved abroad to coach Turkish club Besiktas and enjoyed great success with them, helping them to a hat-trick of championship wins in 1990, 1991 and 1992. Following a spell with Grampus Eight in Japan, Milne became the chief executive of the League Managers' Association in 1995 before returning to management in Turkey. He took over as director of football at Newcastle United in 1999, working alongside Sir Bobby Robson until 2004 when he was appointed to the same post at Besiktas, where he stayed until his retirement in 2007.

Season	League		FA Cup		League Cup		Europe		Other		Total	
	App	Goals	App	Goals	App	Goals	App	Goals	App	Goals	App	Goals
1960/61	16	0	1	0	0	0	-	-	-	-	17	0
1961/62	42	2	5	0	-	-	-	-	-	-	47	2
1962/63	41	0	6	0	-	-	-	-	-	-	47	0
1963/64	42	2	5	0	-	-	-	-	-	-	47	2
1964/65	34	5	6	1	-	-	7	0	1	0	48	6
1965/66	28	7	1	0	-	-	6	0	1	0	36	7
1966/67	31 (2)	1	4	0	-	-	3	0	0	0	38 (2)	1
Total	**234 (2)**	**17**	**28**	**1**	**0**	**0**	**16**	**0**	**2**	**0**	**280 (2)**	**18**

Minshull,
Ray

CYRIL SIDLOW was the club's recognised last line of defence in the years immediately following World War Two, but Ray Minshull deputised for him in six matches in the fantastic 1946/47 Championship season.

He earned the distinction of saving a penalty from Bill Shankly when Preston North End visited Anfield on 7 April 1947, 12½ years before he became Liverpool's

boss. Albert Stubbins revealed Minshull's strategy in his newspaper column the following week. 'Before our Easter Monday games with Preston Jack Balmer commented that Bill Shankly, visiting wing-half, always placed penalty kicks to the left side of goalkeepers. During the game when Preston were awarded a spot kick, the wily Shankly ran at the ball as though to slam it – instead he attempted a place shot. Ray

Minshull was prepared, and his clever save ended any hopes Preston had of saving the game – and proved Jack Balmer to be correct.'

Although Minshull was at Anfield for four seasons, he only made 31 appearances for the club and had to leave Merseyside to find regular first-team football, signing for Southport in June 1951, making 217 league appearances for them.

Minshull was Wigan Rovers' player-manager in the Cheshire County League in the 1959/60 season and coached in Gibraltar and Austria. He became a highly popular youth development officer at Everton in the 70s and 80s, unearthing a number of gems such as Gary Stevens, Steve McMahon and former captain Kevin Ratcliffe, who is very grateful to Minshull for bringing him to Merseyside. 'I would have first met Ray when I was 14 years old,' Ratcliffe told Everton's official website. 'He used to come across to my house to speak to my dad before I signed for the club. Ray was a great fellow even though he was also a tough disciplinarian.'

Season	League		FA Cup		Total	
	App	Goals	App	Goals	App	Goals
1946/47	6	0	0	0	6	0
1947/48	13	0	2	0	15	0
1948/49	4	0	1	0	5	0
1949/50	5	0	0	0	5	0
Total	**28**	**0**	**3**	**0**	**31**	**0**

FACTFILE

BORN
Bolton, 15 July 1920
DIED
15 February 2005
POSITION
Goalkeeper
OTHER CLUBS
Southport (–1946),
Southport (1951–57),
Bradford Park Avenue
(1957-59),
Wigan Rovers (1959-60)
JOINED
September 1946
LFC DEBUT
19 October 1946
CONTRACT EXPIRY
June 1951

Mitchell, Frank

GOALKEEPER Frank Mitchell was never likely to displace the great Elisha Scott, but the former Everton player did enjoy a run of 15 consecutive First Division matches in the second half of the 1920/21 season, only being on the losing side three times.

IN DECEMBER 1921 Mitchell featured in two consecutive games as Scott had been knocked unconscious by a shot from Middlesbrough's Bob Pender in Liverpool's 3-1 defeat on 26

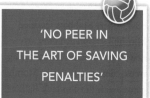

'NO PEER IN THE ART OF SAVING PENALTIES'

November. In 1921 the *Derby Daily Telegraph* said Mitchell was 'quite a dapper figure... this canny Scot from Elgin. The Anfield club think the world of him, and rightly so, for he has a glorious knack of anticipation, and gets to shots in wonderful style.' He was also said to have 'no peer in the art of saving penalties, and one of the amusements of the Liverpool boys when training is to test their shooting powers from the spot

– with Frank in goal.' Mitchell broke his wrist playing for the reserves on 20 January 1923 against Port Vale and joined his third Merseyside team, Tranmere Rovers, in the summer.

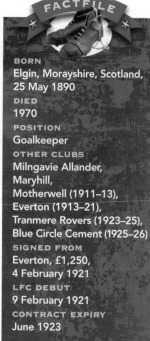

FACTFILE

BORN
Elgin, Morayshire, Scotland,
25 May 1890
DIED
1970
POSITION
Goalkeeper
OTHER CLUBS
Milngavie Allander,
Maryhill,
Motherwell (1911–13),
Everton (1913–21),
Tranmere Rovers (1923–25),
Blue Circle Cement (1925–26)
SIGNED FROM
Everton, £1,250,
4 February 1921
LFC DEBUT
9 February 1921
CONTRACT EXPIRY
June 1923

Season	League		FA Cup		Other		Total	
	App	Goals	App	Goals	App	Goals	App	Goals
1920/21	15	0	0	0	-	-	15	0
1921/22	3	0	0	0	0	0	3	0
Total	**18**	**0**	**0**	**0**	**0**	**0**	**18**	**0**

Mølby,
Jan

WITHOUT a doubt one of the most talented players in Liverpool's history, Jan Mølby fought a hard battle with his weight, but his vision, immense skill, sublime passing and shooting ability more than made up for his lack of mobility. When Graeme Souness left Liverpool, Mølby was invited for a ten-day trial at Anfield. In his first match, against Home Farm in Ireland, he took the ball on his chest, kneed the ball over the defender's head and volleyed it into the net. Joe Fagan signed him two days later.

The great Dane had honed his trade at Ajax in Amsterdam for two and a half years prior to joining the European champions. He was in for a shock when he moved to Merseyside. 'When we arrived at Carrow Road for my first game, we filed into the away dressing room,' Mølby remembered in his autobiography. 'I asked Ronnie Moran, "What do we do now?" "Just get changed," growled Ronnie. "Get yourself ready for the game, son." "What time do we go out to warm up?" I asked. "You don't have time to warm up, save your energy." I couldn't believe what I was hearing. At Ajax, we spent about 25 minutes warming up.'

Despite the lack of preparation Liverpool got the right results. 'I played four European games in the European Cup at Ajax. We'd go to the training camp on Saturday, we'd live like monks, play on a Wednesday, get beat. I came to Liverpool, you get drawn against Benfica, meet up on a Wednesday morning, do an hour's training, go to the hotel and have steak and a few chips, go and have a couple of hours' sleep, go and play and beat them.'

MØLBY was a regular in his first season as a defensive midfielder until he had to make way for Kevin MacDonald halfway through the campaign. Mølby was undoubtedly Liverpool's best player in the 1985/86 Double season as Kenny Dalglish had great belief in him. 'I couldn't believe such a creative player was languishing in Liverpool reserves and I couldn't wait to use him,' Dalglish later said. 'Jan had unbelievable feet and I defied anybody to state categorically which was the stronger, because either foot could propel the ball at unbelievable speed towards goal.' Mølby enjoyed his freedom under Dalglish, playing sweeper on occasion as well as shadow striker behind Rushie. He scored 21 goals in 58 matches and delivered a man-of-the-match performance in the 3-1 win over Everton in the FA Cup final. Mølby's most famous goal came in the fourth round of the League Cup on 26 November 1985. Paul McGrath had put Manchester United 1-0 up but with roughly half an hour to go the Dane took charge at Anfield. 'I took the ball off Norman Whiteside inside our own half. I went on a run past three or four United players and then shot with my right foot from about 20 yards. Gary Bailey, the United keeper, still insists it was the hardest shot he had ever faced. It's true that from the moment it left my boot to the moment it hit the net Gary didn't see it.' A minute later Mølby netted another from the penalty spot, adding to his legend as the most prolific penalty-taker in Liverpool's history, scoring 42 out of 45 penalties. The secret to his spot-kick success was fairly simple: 'If the goalkeeper didn't move before I struck my shot I would always put it low to his right but if he moved I would go the other way. I guess that's not something you can teach somebody, it's just something in their make-up.'

When asked by *LFChistory.net* what went wrong in those three instances he missed from the spot Mølby was quick to reply: 'It was three of the finest saves you have ever seen. I am always disappointed when you talk about Gordon Banks' save against Pele that you don't mention the likes of Martin Hodge from Sheffield Wednesday, Dave Beasant from Chelsea and Paul Barron from QPR.' Mølby proved the difference on more than one occasion that season, as Mark Lawrenson remembers. 'Jan was the

sort of player who could turn a game with one pass. He could disappear for long periods and then pop up with a moment of inspiration,' said Lawrenson. 'With a player like Ian Rush in the side you only need one chance to score a goal. More often than not Mølby was our man to unlock a defence.'

1987/88 turned to be a joyous campaign for Liverpool but a personal disaster for Mølby. He broke his leg after a challenge by John Wark in pre-season training and in February 1988 he was arrested after a high-speed car chase, having given the police the slip as he had been out drinking. The law was waiting for him the following day, having identified him as the perpetrator. Six months later he was put behind bars for six weeks. Mølby had been a regular as a central defender while waiting for his trial, but now faced an uncertain future at the club. His spell in prison was the most harrowing time of his life but had its light-hearted moments, as he revealed in his autobiography. He participated in a five-a-side in Kirkham open prison and found the sports hall packed to witness his talents. 'I enjoyed the run-out but I remember that day because of a bit of an incident with this long-haired fella from Manchester. He'd never been to a five-a-side before, he couldn't play football, and as he came running towards me I nutmegged him. As I tried to run around him, he ran straight into me and pushed me up against the wall. Before I could do anything, a couple of Scousers who were watching from above slipped down the wall and took care of him as the game was going on. He got a real working-over.'

Once Mølby was released Dalglish convinced the club's board to give him another chance at Liverpool. The Scot was a big admirer of Mølby's abilities, but couldn't help being frustrated with him.

'Jan deprived an awful lot of people of an awful lot of enjoyment by not being able to stay in shape,' Dalglish said. 'Jan could have been one of the very best because his ability was unquestioned.' Mølby was soon back playing in January 1989 until another injury cut his season short.

After being on the fringes of the first team in the 1989/90 Championship season Mølby became a regular starter in the second part of 1990/91. Dalglish resigned and Souness took over but Mølby kept his place and on 30 November 1991 he reminded everyone of the fantastic talent he possessed. Only three minutes had passed in Liverpool's league game against Norwich at Anfield when Mølby struck a venomous shot from 30 yards into the top corner. Souness enthused: 'I think the match was worth coming to see for that goal alone.' Mølby won the FA Cup for the second time in the 1991/92 season, which turned out to be his last as a Liverpool regular. Injuries and subsequent lack of fitness restricted him to only 42 games in his last four seasons at Liverpool before being released in 1996.

> MØLBY WAS THE MOST TECHNICALLY GIFTED LIVERPOOL PLAYER I HAVE EVER SEEN
> **BOB PAISLEY**

BOB PAISLEY noted in *Bob Paisley's personal view of the First Team Squad of 1986-87* that Mølby was the most technically gifted Liverpool player he had ever seen and when the legendary Geordie speaks you sit up and listen. 'Certainly when Mølby is allowed the time to play the way he likes, he is a treat to watch. He just seems to flick and jab at the ball and it flies off his foot.

FACTFILE

BORN
Kolding, Denmark, 4 July 1963
POSITION
Midfielder
OTHER CLUBS
Kolding (1979–82),
Ajax (1982–84),
Barnsley (loan, 1995),
Norwich City (loan, 1995–96),
Swansea City (1996–97)
SIGNED FROM
Ajax, £200,000,
22 August 1984
INTERNATIONAL CAPS
33 Denmark caps (2 goals)
(25 (2) at LFC), 1982–90
LFC DEBUT GAME/GOAL
25 August 1984 /
1 December 1984
CONTRACT EXPIRY
21 February 1996
HONOURS
League Championship
1985/86, 1987/88;
FA Cup 1986, 1992

Everything he does is so sweet and crisp,' Paisley wrote. 'He can't get enough of the ball when everything is running for him. He's like a compulsive gambler. No pass is too difficult to try, no shooting chance is allowed to go untaken. He can go through a ten-minute spell when you think he's operating it by remote control. He could go on the stage with his repertoire of party pieces if he ever was short of a few bob. Getting that repertoire to stretch to 90 minutes per game and 60 games per season is the trick that he is bound to find the most difficult to master.'

Season	League App	League Goals	FA Cup App	FA Cup Goals	League Cup App	League Cup Goals	Europe App	Europe Goals	Other App	Other Goals	Total App	Total Goals
1984/85	19 (3)	1	0	0	0 (1)	0	0	0	1	0	20 (4)	1
1985/86	39	14	8	3	5	2	-	-	5 (1)	2	57 (1)	21
1986/87	34	7	3	0	7	5	-	-	2 (1)	0	46 (1)	12
1987/88	1 (6)	0	0 (1)	0	0	0	-	-	-	-	1 (7)	0
1988/89	12 (1)	2	3	0	2	1	-	-	1	1	18 (1)	4
1989/90	12 (5)	1	0	0	2 (1)	0	-	-	0	0	14 (6)	1
1990/91	22 (3)	9	5 (2)	0	1 (1)	0	-	-	0	0	28 (6)	9
1991/92	25 (1)	3	5 (1)	1	3	0	5	1	-	-	38 (2)	5
1992/93	8 (2)	3	0	0	1	0	2	0	0	0	11 (2)	3
1993/94	11	2	0	0	2	1	-	-	-	-	13	3
1994/95	12 (2)	2	0	0	2	0	-	-	-	-	14 (2)	2
Total	**195 (23)**	**44**	**24 (4)**	**4**	**25 (3)**	**9**	**7**	**1**	**9 (2)**	**3**	**260 (32)**	**61**

Molyneux,
John

JOHN MOLYNEUX joined Chester as a 16-year-old in 1947 after being spotted playing football with A. Monk and Co. by one of the directors of Chester who was also a director of the company.

He was a regular in Chester's first team from the 1949/50 season onwards in the Third Division North until he joined up for national service at the age of 21, having been deferred at the usual age of 18 as an apprentice fitter at Monk's. After only being available for 20 league games in two years Molyneux returned from the army to play 46 league games in the 1954/55 season when Chester finished bottom of the league.

Molyneux was a powerful right-back of great physique.

He was an unspectacular player, but solid. His opponents would have one hell of a time trying to pass this ferocious tackler. Molyneux was a regular in the Liverpool side for six of the eight years the club was in the Second Division. In his last season, 1961/62, Shankly had finally found the right mixture of players to take Liverpool to the First Division. As Ron Yeats arrived Dick White was moved from centre-half, taking Molyneux's place at right-back. After featuring in only one game earlier in the season, Molyneux was given a chance in a 1-0 Boxing Day defeat at Rotherham United. Liverpool won the next couple of games but still conceded seven goals in the process and Molyneux was the one who paid the price for the avalanche of goals. Liverpool finally got back into the

First Division but Molyneux returned to Fourth Division Chester, where he played a couple of seasons before cartilage trouble ended his full-time professional football career and he joined New Brighton in the Cheshire County League.

WHEN *LFChistory.net* asked the 81-year-old John Molyneux in the summer of 2012 what was the most abiding memory of his Liverpool career, he said: 'My most outstanding memory when playing at Liverpool was watching the Spion Kop crowd coming down and up the steps like a wave in the sea whenever Billy Liddell was going down the wing towards the Kop.'

FACTFILE

BORN
Warrington, 3 February 1931
POSITION
Right-back
OTHER CLUBS
Chester (1947–55),
Chester (1962–65),
New Brighton (1965–67)
SIGNED FROM
Chester, £5,500,
23 June 1955
LFC DEBUT GAME/GOAL
3 September 1955 /
8 January 1958
CONTRACT EXPIRY
September 1962

Season	League App	League Goals	FA Cup App	FA Cup Goals	League Cup App	League Cup Goals	Total App	Total Goals
1955/56	32	0	5	0	-	-	37	0
1956/57	40	0	1	0	-	-	41	0
1957/58	40	0	5	1	-	-	45	1
1958/59	37	1	1	0	-	-	38	1
1959/60	38	1	2	0	-	-	40	1
1960/61	39	0	2	0	3	0	44	0
1961/62	3	0	1	0	-	-	4	0
Total	**229**	**2**	**17**	**1**	**3**	**0**	**249**	**3**

Molyneux,
Billy

BILLY MOLYNEUX was a small goalkeeper who joined Liverpool as an amateur in 1961 from Earle in the Lancashire Combination.

Tommy Lawrence was Liverpool's number one keeper and Molyneux only made one appearance in the final league game of the 1964/65 season that was won 3-1 against Wolves. Bill Shankly wanted to rest his key players so Alan Hignett, Tom Lowry and John Sealey also made their debuts in this particular game that took place five days prior to the FA Cup final against Leeds.

FACTFILE

BORN
Ormskirk, 10 January 1944
POSITION
Goalkeeper
OTHER CLUBS
Earle (1961),
Oldham Athletic (1967–69),
Wigan Athletic (1969–70)
SIGNED FROM
Earle, April 1961;
signed professional
29 November 1963
LFC DEBUT
26 April 1965
CONTRACT EXPIRY
16 June 1967

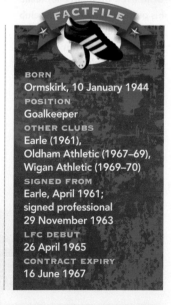

Season	League App	League Goals	FA Cup App	FA Cup Goals	League Cup App	League Cup Goals	Europe App	Europe Goals	Total App	Total Goals
1964/65	1	0	0	0	0	0	0	0	1	0
Total	**1**	**0**	**0**	**0**	**0**	**0**	**0**	**0**	**1**	**0**

Money, Richard

CENTRAL DEFENDER Richard Money had acquired a good reputation in the lower leagues with Scunthorpe and Fulham, for whom he appeared in close to 300 league matches, despite being only 24 years old. Even though 1980/81 was a season when Liverpool's league form was erratic (a final placing

ONE OF THE MOST FAMOUS NIGHTS IN LIVERPOOL'S EUROPEAN HISTORY

of fifth compared with first in the two previous seasons), Money was unable to break through and made only 14 First Division appearances.

Although his Liverpool career was but a brief one, he could at least claim to have been part of one of the most famous nights in Liverpool's European history when he played in the 1-1 draw against Bayern in Munich's Olympic Stadium, a result that took the club through against all the odds to their third European Cup final. Money's performance was praised by Laurie Cunningham, Real Madrid's England winger, who prepared to face Liverpool in the final in Paris. 'I watched Liverpool play in Munich on television and I was very impressed by Richard Money,' Cunningham said.

'I liked the way he kept the forwards supplied with accurate crosses.' Money and Cunningham didn't come face to face in the final as Alan Kennedy had recovered from injury and Money was an unused substitute.

MONEY became Scunthorpe's manager in 1993 and also managed AIK and Västerås in Sweden, Australia's Newcastle United Jets, Walsall and Luton Town. In October 2012, Money was appointed as head coach of Conference club Cambridge United.

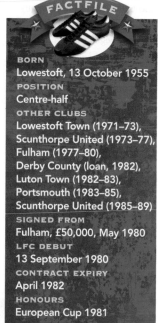

FACTFILE

BORN
Lowestoft, 13 October 1955
POSITION
Centre-half
OTHER CLUBS
Lowestoft Town (1971–73),
Scunthorpe United (1973–77),
Fulham (1977–80),
Derby County (loan, 1982),
Luton Town (1982–83),
Portsmouth (1983–85),
Scunthorpe United (1985–89)
SIGNED FROM
Fulham, £50,000, May 1980
LFC DEBUT
13 September 1980
CONTRACT EXPIRY
April 1982
HONOURS
European Cup 1981

Season	League App	League Goals	FA Cup App	FA Cup Goals	League Cup App	League Cup Goals	Europe App	Europe Goals	Other App	Other Goals	Total App	Total Goals
1980/81	12 (2)	0	1	0	1	0	1	0	0	0	15 (2)	0
Total	12 (2)	0	1	0	1	0	1	0	0	0	15 (2)	0

Mooney, Brian

DUBLINER Brian Mooney made his only appearance for the club when he came on as substitute for his compatriot Jim Beglin during the club's 3-2 League Cup victory over Fulham at Craven Cottage in October 1986.

TWO WEEKS earlier Liverpool had defeated the Cottagers 10-0 in the first leg at Anfield. Mooney's chances of breaking through at Anfield were extremely slim given the club's continued success through the 1980s. He had a loan spell at Wrexham before joining Preston in the 1987/88 season. He spent three seasons at Deepdale, where he played 128 games for the Lancashire club, scoring 20 goals. He was voted Preston's Player of the Year in the 1988/89 season and the 'Moon Man', as he was called at Preston, is considered a legend in those parts.

FACTFILE

BORN
Dublin, Ireland,
2 February 1966
POSITION
Midfielder
OTHER CLUBS
Home Farm (1981–83),
Wrexham (loan, 1985–86),
Preston North End (1987–91),
Sheffield Wednesday
(loan, 1990),
Sunderland (1991–93),
Burnley (loan, 1992),
Shelbourne (1993–95),
Bohemian (1995–99),
University College Dublin
(1999–2001),
Monaghan United (2001–02)
SIGNED FROM
Home Farm, £20,000,
15 August 1983
INTERNATIONAL CAPS
4 Ireland U-21 caps
LFC DEBUT
7 October 1986
CONTRACT EXPIRY
9 October 1987

Season	League App	League Goals	FA Cup App	FA Cup Goals	League Cup App	League Cup Goals	Europe App	Europe Goals	Total App	Total Goals
1986/87	0	0	0	0	0 (1)	0	0	0	0 (1)	0
Total	0	0	0	0	0 (1)	0	0	0	0 (1)	0

Moores, David

THE MONIKER the 'Denim Chairman' could easily be applied to Scouser David Moores who is more comfortable in a denim jacket and trousers rather than a suit.

His uncle, Sir John Moores, created a family fortune with the foundation of the Littlewoods empire in 1923. In 1960 he appointed his brother, Cecil, as chairman of the company as John sought to become chairman of Everton which he succeeded in doing. Cecil's son, David, an heir to the pools empire, became chairman of Liverpool FC on 18 September 1991. He bought 17,850 shares which represented 51.6 per cent of the club, guaranteeing him the status of major shareholder. Undoubtedly this fact would have rankled with 'Honest' John McKenna, chairman of Liverpool in the first quarter of the century who fought tooth and nail as the president of the Football League to keep gambling and football separate. In 2004 Kenny Dalglish argued Moores' importance to the club's history in the wake of the annual general meeting during which Moores said he would review his position at the end of the campaign if results didn't improve. 'David's support for Liverpool started way back when the club was looking for money to redevelop the old Kemlyn Road stand. There was a share issue and he pledged that he would buy up any options that remained. I can't remember too many people coming forward, but David stood by his word and we built the outstanding Centenary stand we see today.' 'The Moores family have been great benefactors to Merseyside football. David's appointment will keep the predators at bay,' said David's predecessor, Sir John Smith,

who is the club's longest-serving chairman in the history of the club. David Moores' tenure lasted 16 years, 12 months shorter than Sir John's. Tony Barrett noted in *The Times* on 26 May 2010: 'Almost two decades on, the predators have not only stormed the Shankly Gates, they have put the future of Liverpool at stake.' What had happened in the meantime?

AN AVID RED, David Moores took over England's most successful club at a point when Kenny Dalglish had seven months previously resigned as manager and Liverpool had lost the league title to Arsenal. The fact that the club has not regained it since leads to many questions regarding Moores' leadership at the club. While Manchester United took giant strides towards domination in the revolutionary Premier League Liverpool tumbled down from their perch and were left behind by other clubs as well. Moores was, to his detriment, fiercely loyal to manager Graeme Souness. Moores' seemingly laissez-faire attitude towards the running of the club was mirrored in the lack of discipline in the squad while Roy Evans served as manager. The team's performances were improving on the pitch, but when it mattered most they caved in and finished up empty-handed. Moores admitted in an open letter to *The Times* in May 2010 that 'in the wake of Euro 96 with the influx of more and more overseas superstars on superstar wages, I was aware the game was changing beyond all recognition and deeply worried, too, about my ability to continue underwriting the financial side. I was from the ever-decreasing pool of old-school club owners, the locally based, locally wealthy supporter like Jack Walker who stuck his money in out of his passion for the club.'

Rick Parry, who was the Premier League's first chief executive, was appointed to the same position at Liverpool in the summer of 1999 having served as Peter Robinson's deputy chief executive for the previous 12 months. Parry was duly told to bring Liverpool into the realities of modern football. Gérard Houllier had been appointed controversially by Roy Evans' side in July 1998, unavoidably taking over as sole manager a few months later. Liverpool's revolution on the administrative side was delivered by a local while a Frenchman revolutionised the training ground, the diet and put paid to the players ruling the roost. The squad was improved by the addition of personnel with various

experience of continental football. Still six years later the club was at crossroads again. Houllier had left following two disappointing seasons where standards had dropped dramatically. A senior Anfield official revealed to Brian Reade in his book *An Epic Swindle* that all had not been well in the boardroom at Anfield for a long time under Moores. 'With David it was all about having an easy life. Not because he was a bad person, and certainly not because he didn't care about Liverpool. But because all he wanted to do was to turn up, park his car, have a smoke in the boardroom, go to the match, be around the players and the club and go back home. If you confronted him with a problem he'd wave you away with the words 'See Rick'.'

> **THE HIGHLIGHT OF THE EVENING IN ISTANBUL WAS SEEING A TEARFUL DAVID MOORES SITTING IN THE DRESSING ROOM CRADLING THE EUROPEAN CUP**
> **STEVEN GERRARD**

In 2004 Moores welcomed the Spanish Armada in the guise of Valencia manager, Rafa Benítez. Moores could hardly have envisaged the impact he would have in his first campaign when he delivered the European Cup, raising the profile of his club worldwide. Steven Gerrard noted in his autobiography that the highlight of his evening in Istanbul was seeing a tearful David Moores sitting in the dressing room cradling the European Cup.

Despite his love for the club Moores had realised in 2003 that he would have to sell his shares as

he simply didn't have the financial means to continue as he risked bankrupting his family. 'In football nowadays, it's not enough to be rich. You need to be super-rich to own a club as big as Liverpool,' he said on the eve of his last match as chairman, against Barcelona at Anfield on 6 March 2007. Offers from local building magnate Steve Morgan and the former Thai prime minister Thaksin Shinawatra were rejected in 2004 and discussions with American Robert Kraft came to nought. Dubai International Capital [DIC], the investment arm of the Dubai government, tabled a £450m offer for the club in December 2006 that would value each share at £4,500, supposedly service the club's debt and fund the new stadium. DIC had first registered its interest in the immediate aftermath of Istanbul. While DIC was doing its seemingly endless due diligence of the club's books Moores grew concerned as he wanted the deal done before the January transfer window so Rafa Benítez could utilise the new investors' wealth to strengthen the team. The club also needed to fund a £12m steel order to keep the plans for the new stadium on schedule. George Gillett, whose former offer was considered insufficient, returned in late January 2007, arm-in-arm with his new best friend Texan Tom Hicks, with an improved offer that valued each share at £5,000. A confidential document from DIC to potential major City investors

revealed that it was going to borrow £300m of the £450m purchase and had devised a seven-year exit strategy, hoping to make a huge profit. The document that was leaked and published in the *Daily Telegraph* on 27 December effectively ended Moores' interest in the Dubai bid.

On 30 January 2007 the board agreed to the offer from Gillett and Hicks. Over 1,700 shareholders voted and the result was 100 per cent in favour. Liverpool fans had expected the DIC deal to go through and some felt that the club was too eager to jump into bed with the Americans. Moores claimed in *The Times* in May 2010 that Gillett's affairs had been looked at in great detail, but he 'took Tom Hicks on trust, on George's say-so' but had 'received assurances from Rothschilds, one of the most respected names in global finance who vouched for both Tom Hicks and George Gillett.' Then he admitted that the deal had indeed been a little too hurried. 'Could we have done more? Probably, though under those circumstances, in that time-frame, probably not.'

'**THE ONLY REGRET** is that we never won the Premiership under my chairmanship, but with the new owners I'm sure the club can win No 19 soon,' Moores told the *Guardian* in 2007. 'I feel I'm leaving it in safe hands. I know I got the best possible deal.' Moores earned just over £89m from the sale of his stake, stayed as lifetime president of the club and a member of the board. 'I made the decision for the good of the club, not myself,' he insisted, claiming he would have benefited more personally from taking DIC's offer.

Moores watched helplessly on as a split developed between Gillett and Rick Parry on one side and Tom Hicks and Rafa Benítez on the other. Moores resigned from the club's board in June 2009 after Parry had been pushed out. Fenway Sports Group sought to purchase the club while Gillett and Hicks tried to hopelessly hang on. Moores wrote a dramatic open letter to *The Times* in May 2010 pleading with the pair to let go.

'Ultimately, the deal we signed up to was laid out in unambiguous terms in the share offer document. It is a matter of fact that the document pledged there would be no debt placed on the club, and significant funds would be made available for investment in the squad and the new stadium. I signed up for that — not money. It has been hard for me, sitting mute on the sidelines as the club I love suffers one blow after another. Since resigning from the board I have not set foot inside Anfield — and it hurts. I hugely regret selling the club to George Gillett and Tom Hicks. I believe that, at best, they have bitten off much more than they can chew. Giving them that benefit of the doubt — that they started off with grand ideals that they were never realistically going to achieve — I call upon them now

to stand back, accept their limitations as joint owners of Liverpool Football Club, acknowledge their role in the club's demise, and stand aside, with dignity, to allow someone else to take up the challenge. Don't punish the club's supporters any more – God knows they've taken enough. Take an offer, be realistic over the price, make it possible. Let the club go. It is a sign of strength, not weakness, to concede for the greater good.' Yours faithfully, David Moores.'

IN OCTOBER 2010 Liverpool got rid of Gillett and Hicks. Moores deeply regretted his hasty decision to sell to the pair, who piled a huge mountain of debt on Liverpool Football Club. It was a terrible burden on the club's books but seemingly an even bigger one on Moores' conscience.

> MOORES DEEPLY REGRETTED HIS HASTY DECISION TO SELL TO THE PAIR, WHO PILED A HUGE MOUNTAIN OF DEBT ON LIVERPOOL FOOTBALL CLUB. IT WAS A TERRIBLE BURDEN ON THE CLUB'S BOOKS BUT SEEMINGLY AN EVEN BIGGER ONE ON MOORES' CONSCIENCE

Moran,
Ronnie

RONNIE MORAN joined Liverpool as a fresh-faced 15-year old, having been recommended by the postman who used to deliver letters to the club chairman!

Moran was an apprentice electrician as well as featuring for

Liverpool's C team. He signed professional forms for his home-town club shortly before his 18th birthday in January 1952. He had played 13 times by the end of the 1953/54 season when Liverpool were relegated to the Second Division. Eddie Spicer's unfortunate leg-break allowed Moran to establish himself as the team's left-back the following season and he would miss only six league matches over the next five

years. Moran was club captain when Bill Shankly arrived in 1959 and was certainly inspired by his arrival. 'I learned more in the first three months than I'd done in the seven years that I'd been a pro. I wish I'd been five years younger.' In Shankly's full debut season, 1960/61, Moran got injured on 1 October, and apart from a brief one-game unsuccessful return in January 1961, he was out injured for 16 months.

He played in enough fixtures to qualify for a Second Division Championship medal in 1962 and only missed seven games when the league title was won two years later. Moran, who took over spot-kick duties in 1960, had scored eight out of ten penalties when he missed four in a row, the last in the quarter-finals of the FA Cup in 1964. Swansea City were leading 2-1 when Moran squandered his spot kick in the

80th minute. It was a harrowing experience for Moran, who despaired: 'I don't think I'll ever forget it.'

During the 1964/65 season, Chris Lawler became established as the club's right-back as Moran lost his place in the side. Moran did return at the end of this historic campaign, playing in both legs against Inter Milan in the European Cup semi-final, but missed out on a place in Liverpool's FA Cup-winning team at Wembley against Leeds as Gerry Byrne returned to the side. A successful playing career had come to an end, but a new career at the club was ahead.

Moran's qualities as a player ensured a longer stay for him at Liverpool. His enthusiasm for the game had always spread around his team. He was totally committed in every game, a quality that prompted Shankly to offer him the chance to join the training staff. Moran recalled the moment his life took a new turn during the 1966/67 preseason, having spent the previous campaign in the reserves. 'Shanks called me to one side. I thought, this is it, he's going to tell me another club's come in for me, and he said to me, "Ronnie, how would you like to join the backroom staff?"' Moran told *LFChistory.net*. 'I went off and discussed it with my wife. We are both from Liverpool and didn't want to leave, and the next day I told Bill, "Yes." We never really discussed specific roles, I guess Shanks and Bob had seen me shouting and talking a lot when I was playing and liked what they'd seen. They just let me get on with it.' Moran's appointment didn't surprise Ian Callaghan. 'I don't know how I would have managed without him. It was a big step up playing in the first team, and I don't know how I would have coped without someone keeping an eye on me and helping me out of difficult situations,' Cally said. 'I soon learned that

at Liverpool, we were essentially part of a team and depended on each other.'

The sergeant major of Melwood was well known for keeping strict discipline at the club and despite Tommy Smith's quote that Moran 'could moan for England' he was a vital part of the Boot Room and the club's success. Robbie Fowler was one of many players who were inspired by Moran. 'At Liverpool we are all taught to keep our feet on the ground and I, for one, have reason to remember

that no one subscribed to that theory more than Ronnie,' Fowler remembers. 'After playing against Fulham and scoring five goals I was feeling well pleased with myself when Ronnie came in the dressing room and said: "I don't know what you're looking so smug about. You should have scored seven." Those words will live with me forever and I think they sum up the greatness of the man.'

MORAN took over temporarily as manager after Dalglish's resignation in 1991. 'I innocently answered the phone at home in

As a Player													
	League		FA Cup		League Cup		Europe		Other		Total	
Season	App	Goals	App	Goals	App	Goals	App	Goals	App	Goals	App	Goals
1952/53	11	0	1	0	-	-	-	-	-	-	12	0
1953/54	1	0	0	0	-	-	-	-	-	-	1	0
1954/55	17	0	4	0	-	-	-	-	-	-	21	0
1955/56	39	0	5	0	-	-	-	-	-	-	44	0
1956/57	42	0	1	0	-	-	-	-	-	-	43	0
1957/58	41	0	5	0	-	-	-	-	-	-	46	0
1958/59	40	0	1	0	-	-	-	-	-	-	41	0
1959/60	42	5	2	0	-	-	-	-	-	-	44	5
1960/61	12	2	0	0	0	0	-	-	-	-	12	2
1961/62	16	1	3	0	-	-	-	-	-	-	19	1
1962/63	33	5	6	2	-	-	-	-	-	-	39	7
1963/64	35	2	4	0	-	-	-	-	-	-	39	2
1964/65	13	0	0	0	-	-	4	0	1	0	18	0
Total	**342**	**15**	**32**	**2**	**0**	**0**	**4**	**0**	**1**	**0**	**379**	**17**

the early spring of 1991. It was Kenny Dalglish. Me and the wife were just on our way out and I asked him what he wanted. "I've packed in," he said. "I've had enough." I thought he was joking, as he was a great practical joker and I told him to stop messing around. He must have filled up because he put the phone down and the line went dead.' The next call Moran took was from Liverpool chairman Noel White, who promptly offered the vacated manager's job to the scarcely believing assistant. 'Of course I accepted, but becoming manager was not something I'd ever envisaged, but then again, neither had Bob nor Joe before me,' Moran said. The 56-year-old Moran was the obvious candidate to come to the rescue in a crisis until a permanent successor to Dalglish could be named. After all, he had been involved at Anfield in one capacity or another since the early 1950s and knew the club inside out. He inherited a team that was top of the table and still very much involved in the race for the Championship with Arsenal. Moran's first task was to lift the gloom around the club and prepare the first team for a visit to Luton the following Saturday.

The whole club still seemed to be in shock after Dalglish's departure, although that can't be used as an excuse for a tame 3-1 defeat at Kenilworth Road. The next two matches were lost as well, the FA Cup second replay at Goodison and, more crucially, the home league fixture with title rivals Arsenal, decided by Paul Merson's second-half goal.

But three defeats were followed by three victories, the third of which was a stunning 7-1 triumph at the Baseball Ground against soon-to-be-relegated Derby County on a day when the Reds went back to the top of the table because of Arsenal's failure to win at Norwich. His last game was an astonishing game at Elland Road against Leeds, which Liverpool won 5-4 after holding a 4-0 lead with less than a third of the match played. It looked as if Graeme Souness would be unveiled as the new manager at the end of the season, but as media interest escalated it made his position at Ibrox almost untenable and he moved south just before Liverpool were due to play Norwich City at Anfield on 20 April 1991. Moran had been a willing deputy for a few weeks but his record was modest; four victories, one draw, five defeats. According to Phil Thompson, who calls Moran his mentor, Moran had, contrary to popular opinion, wanted the manager's job on a full-time basis. 'Kenny left and Ronnie took over. I was with the reserves. I stepped up and helped Ronnie and Roy,' Thompson told *LFChistory.net*.

> *It was the three of us. Ronnie straight away said: 'I don't want this. I can't handle the press. I can do all the things on the training field, but dealing with the media, signings and everything I don't think.' After a few good weeks Ronnie decided that: 'I can handle this.' He went to see Peter Robinson and Sir John Smith and he said: 'I can do this. If you want to offer me the job again I'll take it.' They went: 'Ronnie, I wish you had come last week because we've got a new manager. It's Graeme Souness!' Ronnie's chance of being manager at Liverpool ended then and there.*

When Souness was recovering from his triple by-pass heart surgery in 1992 Moran was happy to deputise again. He was in charge for the final seven league matches of that 1991/92 season plus the FA Cup semi-final replay with Portsmouth before Souness returned for the final, closely watched by a doctor, with Moran having the honour of leading the Liverpool team out on this successful day at Wembley.

MORAN RETIRED in 1998 after 46 years at the club and was rewarded with a well-attended testimonial match against

Glasgow Celtic on 16 May 2000. On this occasion Alex Ferguson paid a glowing tribute to Moran: 'It is fair to say that Manchester United and Liverpool have had their moments over the years. The rivalry between our two clubs is well documented and I wouldn't have had it any other way whilst the game is on,' the United manager said. 'But that is where it ends as far as coaches, managers and players are concerned. Ronnie Moran has always been one of the first to shake the hand of an opponent, whether that be following a win or defeat. I wish that I'd had

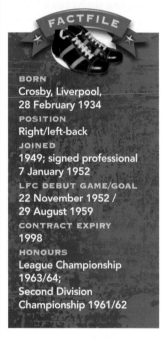

FACTFILE

BORN
Crosby, Liverpool,
28 February 1934
POSITION
Right/left-back
JOINED
1949; signed professional
7 January 1952
LFC DEBUT GAME/GOAL
22 November 1952 /
29 August 1959
CONTRACT EXPIRY
1998
HONOURS
League Championship
1963/64;
Second Division
Championship 1961/62

one pound for every argument I've had with Ronnie, but after the game he was always the first to offer you a drink. There is no question Ronnie Moran is one of Liverpool's all-time greats.'

RON MORAN
Liverpool

'THERE IS NO QUESTION RONNIE MORAN IS ONE OF LIVERPOOL'S ALL-TIME GREATS'

ALEX FERGUSON

As a Manager

Season	Division	P	W	D	L	GF	GA	Pts	Pos	Win%	FA Cup	League Cup
1990/91*	1st Division	10	4	1	5	20	16	13	-	40.00	5th Round	-
Total	-	10	4	1	5	20	16	13	-	40.00	-	-

* Acting manager. Moran's spell as deputy for Graeme Souness is not counted towards his total.

Morgan, Adam

LIVERPUDLIAN Adam Morgan was involved with the first team in 2012/13 after making a big name for himself as Liverpool Under-18s' top scorer during the 2010/11 season with 21 goals as the Reds finished runners-up in their league.

Morgan made two appearances during his loan spell at League Two club Rotherham United from January to February 2013.

FACTFILE

BORN
Liverpool, 21 April 1994
POSITION
Centre-forward
OTHER CLUBS
Rotherham United (loan, 2013)
JOINED
2004
LFC DEBUT
23 August 2012

Season	League		FA Cup		League Cup		Europe		Total	
	App	Goals	App	Goals	App	Goals	App	Goals	App	Goals
2012/13	0	0	0	0	0	0	2 (1)	0	2 (1)	0
Total	**0**	**0**	**0**	**0**	**0**	**0**	**2 (1)**	**0**	**2 (1)**	**0**

Morgan, Hugh

ONE WEEK after making his Scotland debut this skilful, fearless, little forward joined Liverpool from St Mirren for a club record fee of £200.

TOM WATSON saw him feature for the Scottish League against the Irish League at Carolina Port in Dundee and was so taken by his display he signed him.

Hugh Morgan missed just two league fixtures in his second season and was the club's leading scorer with 13 goals as Liverpool finished runners-up, two points behind champions Aston Villa. He joined First Division Blackburn Rovers in the summer of 1900 and, as fate would have it, made his debut against Liverpool on 1 September 1900 at Anfield, losing 3-0 to the Reds. 'As a player he is a master in the art of combination, is most unselfish, and always trying to make openings for his partner,' the *Evening Post* claimed in 1903.

FACTFILE

BORN
Longriggend, Scotland,
7 August 1874
DIED
30 June 1938
POSITION
Inside-right forward
OTHER CLUBS
Longriggend Wanderers,
St Mirren (1896–98),
Blackburn Rovers (1900–03),
Dundee (1903–04),
St Mirren
SIGNED FROM
St Mirren, £200,
25 March 1898
INTERNATIONAL CAPS
2 Scotland caps (1 at LFC),
1898–99
LFC DEBUT GAME/GOAL
2 April 1898 /
16 April 1898
CONTRACT EXPIRY
14 June 1900

Season	League		FA Cup		Total	
	App	Goals	App	Goals	App	Goals
1897/98	4	1	0	0	4	1
1898/99	32	10	6	3	38	13
1899/1900	23	3	3	0	26	3
Total	**59**	**14**	**9**	**3**	**68**	**17**

Morientes, Fernando

FERNANDO MORIENTES became a Real Madrid player in 1997 after scoring 36 goals in two successful years at Real Zaragoza. Morientes blossomed in the Champions League with Madrid and won the competition in 1998, 2000 and 2002; he was also a finalist with Monaco in 2004, scoring nine goals in 12 games en route to the final against Porto, an achievement that saw him named European Striker of the Year.

Real certainly regretted loaning him to Monaco as the French club eliminated Real in the quarter-finals and Morientes scored in both legs against his employers! Morientes scored a total of 99 goals in 261 games for Real Madrid and won two La Liga titles. Ronaldo's arrival in Madrid was the beginning of the end for Morientes, who had been relegated to fourth-choice striker in 2004/05.

MORIENTES' arrival at Liverpool in January 2005 was hailed as a masterstroke by Rafa Benítez. Steven Gerrard was excited at prospect of teaming up with the Spaniard. 'It's good from a symbolic point of view that we've signed someone who's so renowned as a world-class player. I just hope, after all the success he's had and trophies he's won, he's as hungry to do the same for us.' The Spaniard finally netted in his fourth game, a 2-1 away win against Charlton. Two minutes after John Arne Riise's equaliser the ball broke to Morientes who, in a blur of quality, moved the ball from right to left, opening up the chance to shoot. From the edge of the box his left-footed strike arrowed into the top corner. Morientes was also on the scoresheet in the following game against Fulham with a trademark header. However, slight knocks and European ineligibility restricted his progress and he only added one goal before the end of the season, obviously lacking sharpness.

There was no doubt about Morientes' class and experience but sadly he remained primarily a squad player. The Champions League had been kind to Morientes throughout the years and he had his brightest moments in the red of Liverpool in Europe's premier competition. Two goals against CSKA Moscow on 10 August 2005 opened his account for the season and he scored a sensational goal against Anderlecht. However, Morientes was anything but prolific in the Premier League. His best ratio in La Liga was a goal every 1.74 games in the 1998/99 season (19 goals in 33 matches) and 1.83 (18 in 33) in 2001/02 for Real

Madrid, but Morientes only scored five league goals for Liverpool in 28 matches, a ratio of a goal every 5.60 matches. The *Liverpool Echo's* Chris Bascombe delivered a damning verdict on the misfiring striker that, despite its cruelness, raised a smile. 'Morientes is a bit like bird flu. He's been lethal in other countries and we keep getting told it's only a matter of time before he makes his mark here, but there's no sign of it yet.' Morientes won some silverware before his unavoidable departure, when he won the FA Cup with Liverpool after coming on as a substitute in the 48th minute in the final against West Ham.

He joined Valencia in July 2006 after a disappointing 16-month spell at Anfield. The Premier League clearly didn't suit Morientes and he was glad to see the back of England as he revealed to the daily *Sport*.

'I didn't like the physical nature of the game in England or the referees who let more things go. A striker isn't protected from rival defences there, and they gave me a really hard time.'

	League		FA Cup		League Cup		Europe		Other		Total	
Season	App	Goals	App	Goals	App	Goals	App	Goals	App	Goals	App	Goals
2004/05	12 (1)	3	0	0	2	0	0	0	-	-	14 (1)	3
2005/06	20 (8)	5	2 (3)	1	1	0	9 (2)	3	1	0	33 (13)	9
Total	32 (9)	8	2 (3)	1	3	0	9 (2)	3	1	0	47 (14)	12

LIVERPOOL FOOTBALL CLUB 1960/61

LIVERPOOL 1960/61
*Back row - **Wheeler, A'Court, Moran, Slater, White, Molyneux, Harrower***
*Middle - **Lewis, Hunt, Hickson, Campbell, Morrissey***
*Front - **Byrne, Leishman, Callaghan, Melia***

Morris,
Fred

Fred Morris turned professional when he signed for Walsall, for whom he made 227 appearances, scoring 49 goals. He signed for Liverpool shortly before his 29th birthday. Although not selected for the opening two Second Division games of the 1958/59 season, Morris played in the remaining 41 and scored 12 times, a very respectable tally from his position on the right wing. He was in the line-up as the following season commenced but then had a spell on the sidelines before returning and scoring twice in a 4-3 home win against Leyton Orient on 21 November 1959. But only days later, Bill Shankly swept into Anfield and Morris was

one of the early casualties. Shankly's first match in charge of Liverpool turned out to be Morris' last for the club.

Season	League		FA Cup		Total	
	App	Goals	App	Goals	App	Goals
1958/59	40	12	1	0	41	12
1959/60	7	2	0	0	7	2
Total	**47**	**14**	**1**	**0**	**48**	**14**

Morris,
Richard

INSIDE-LEFT Richard Morris was one of the first Newtown natives to volunteer his services at the front in the Boer War. In August 1902 his former team-mates at Newtown sent him a gold medal and watch chain as 'a token of esteem and regret at his leaving their district'.

Although Morris only scored five times in his 38 league appearances for Liverpool, two of them earned a draw in the Merseyside derby in October 1903. Morris was often criticised for wasting good scoring opportunities, but he was 'one of the trickiest players who ever kicked a ball. He is too clever, too fond of arguing I believe is the expression

now current,' noted the club programme in 1904. He was furthermore described as a 'tireless runner and top speed dribbler'. Liverpool had excellent forwards on their books, restricting Morris to only seven games in the 1904/05 season, so he headed to Second Division Leeds City in the summer of 1905.

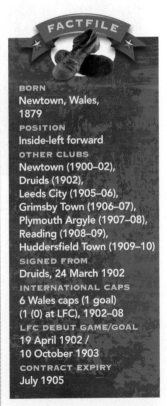

Season	League		FA Cup		Total	
	App	Goals	App	Goals	App	Goals
1901/02	3	0	0	0	3	0
1902/03	11	0	0	0	11	0
1903/04	17	4	1	0	18	4
1904/05	7	1	0	0	7	1
Total	**38**	**5**	**1**	**0**	**39**	**5**

Morrison, Tom

RIGHT-HALF Tom Morrison was at Anfield for eight years between the two world wars. He was one of only two ever-presents in the 1928/29 season and would average 36 league appearances for the next five years before he moved on to Sunderland after losing his place in the team to Ted Savage in 1934/35.

Morrison, who made his final first-team appearance for Liverpool in November 1934, was reported missing by the club in March 1935 after he failed to appear when selected to play in a Central League game on 9 February. Liverpool had imposed two terms of 14-day suspensions, the second of which expired on 12 March. That prompted Liverpool's directors, still without a word of his whereabouts, to report the matter to the authorities. Morrison eventually returned but didn't make another first-team appearance and was

sold in November 1935 to Sunderland, where he won the League Championship in his one and only season at Wearside.

MORRISON was quite a curious character who vanished following Sunderland's title celebration dinner in May 1936, leaving his medal, wife and child behind him. At that time a fellow by the name of Jock Anderson arrived in the ancient village of Gamlingay, near the border of Cambridgeshire and Bedfordshire. He was with a gang of men, who slept in the open and made a living there by pea picking. Anderson wanted to feature for the local village football side and soon his skills were making headlines and many scouts came to watch in view of signing him

for league clubs. The centre-forward's exploits had inspired Gamlingay to reach the top of their division but in the beginning of December 1936 Anderson had departed the village without notification. Gamlingay's form collapsed in his absence. The *Cambridge Independent Press* revealed on 11 December 1936 who Anderson really was. 'Gamlingay Football Club have been playing an international footballer unawares. The man was known as Anderson, but it transpires that he is Tom Morrison, the Scottish international and former Sunderland full back, who mysteriously vanished from his home seven months ago.' Four days before the article was published Morrison was in court in Sunderland as he was charged for leaving his wife and child

'chargeable to the Public Assistance Committee'. After Morrison's solicitor promised that the money paid in relief to Mrs. Morrison would be repaid to the authorities along with costs, the charge was withdrawn. Morrison signed for Ayr United before the start of the 1936/37 season but disappeared again from his home and did not report for training. His contract with the club was terminated in August 1937.

FACTFILE

BORN
Coylton, Ayrshire, Scotland, 21 January 1904
DIED
1973
POSITION
Right-half
OTHER CLUBS
Troon Athletic (1921–24),
St Mirren (1924–28),
Sunderland (1935–36),
Gamlingay (1936),
Ayr United (1937)
SIGNED FROM
St Mirren, £4,000,
9 February 1928
INTERNATIONAL CAPS
1 Scotland cap, 1927
LFC DEBUT GAME/GOAL
11 February 1928 /
13 December 1930
CONTRACT EXPIRY
6 November 1935

	League		FA Cup		Total	
Season	App	Goals	App	Goals	App	Goals
1927/28	15	0	0	0	15	0
1928/29	42	0	3	0	45	0
1929/30	36	0	1	0	37	0
1930/31	39	1	1	0	40	1
1931/32	35	1	4	0	39	1
1932/33	32	1	1	0	33	1
1933/34	33	1	4	0	37	1
1934/35	8	0	0	0	8	0
Total	**240**	**4**	**14**	**0**	**254**	**4**

TOM MORRISON
LIVERPOOL FC

Morrissey, Johnny

JOHNNY MORRISSEY came through the junior ranks at Anfield before signing professional forms in April 1957 shortly after his 17th birthday. Kevin Lewis blocked his way into the team on the right wing but he played regularly from late January onwards in the 1960/61 season.

Roger Hunt's injury opened the door for him as outside-left Alan A'Court was moved to the middle, giving Morrissey a run in the side on the left. With the up-and-coming Ian Callaghan on their books, Morrissey was deemed surplus to requirements by Liverpool's board of directors

that decided to sell him over Shankly's head for a give-away £10,000 in 1962. Shankly threatened to quit over this matter and actually wrote a resignation letter that he never sent to the board. Morrissey, who was a tough customer and uncompromising on the field, played over 250 games in a successful spell for the Blues, and won the League Championship in 1963 and 1970.

MORRISSEY earned the respect of the Anfield Iron, Tommy Smith, in their many battles on Merseyside. 'You don't expect wingers to be the bravest of the brave. However, there was one who you handled

JOHNNY MORRISSEY
LIVERPOOL

with care, simply because he was likely to get the first tackle in and the second one if you let him! His name was Johnny Morrissey and he played for our arch-rivals,' Smith said. 'He was fearless. The Everton fans called him "Mogsy". He looked more like a boxer than a footballer.'

FACTFILE

BORN
Liverpool, 18 April 1940
POSITION
Midfielder
OTHER CLUBS
Everton (1962–72),
Oldham Athletic (1972–73)
JOINED
1955; signed professional
29 April 1957
LFC DEBUT GAME/GOAL
23 September 1957 /
5 September 1959
CONTRACT EXPIRY
1 September 1962

Season	League		FA Cup		League Cup		Total	
	App	Goals	App	Goals	App	Goals	App	Goals
1957/58	2	0	0	0	-	-	2	0
1958/59	2	0	0	0	-	-	2	0
1959/60	9	1	0	0	-	-	9	1
1960/61	23	5	1	0	0	0	24	5
Total	**36**	**6**	**1**	**0**	**0**	**0**	**37**	**6**

Mosaics

A MOSAIC on the Kop is one of the most spectacular sights you can see at Anfield. This multi-coloured piece of art is usually on display to remember a certain occasion or a cause or show support to anyone dear to the Kopites' heart.

The first one took place when Liverpool faced Manchester United on 19 December 1995. A yellow 'LFC' was spelt out on a red background. The mosaics are paid for by the club and their design a collaborative effort headed by Kopite Andy Knott, who initially printed the coloured cards used in his small printing company 'Expressions Offset' that he sold in 2007. It can take up to five hours for the cards to be

placed in their relevant spots on the Kop, but it depends on how intricate the design is and how many are willing to help. Andy explained the origins of the Kop mosaics on the DVD "No Heart As Big", released in 2003. 'I did the first one in 1995 against Man United which came from a meeting that we had with the club. A group of fans got together about getting atmosphere back in the ground. After the Kop had been seated it did dip, but events like the mosaics are helping.'

There have been quite a few mosaics been done since then. The biggest Liverpool mosaic was, in fact, revealed at the Millennium Stadium at the 2001 FA Cup final. 24,000 seats were covered in red and yellow stripes with LFC and the Liverbird behind the goal. The Anfield mosaics are each one a momentous occasion but some of them are particular standouts.

18 December 1999, Coventry 2-0
The 40th Anniversary of Bill Shankly's arrival at Anfield. 'SHANKS' was spelt across the top of the Kop. Below were two images of Shanks' face flanking the Cross of St Andrew. 'Some of the great names from Liverpool's past 40 years were introduced to the fans, the two Scots pipers on the pitch played Shankly's favourite hymn, Amazing Grace. On the Kop the Kopites held up 12,000 coloured cards,' a fan remembered on fanzine's *Red All Over the Land* website. 'Barely a minute into the hymn and the Kop began singing slowly and almost in hushed tones, 'Shankly, Shankly.' I swear it was one of the most moving things I've ever heard; the hairs stood up on the back of my neck. It was difficult to hold back the tears.

The cards were then hurriedly put aside and the massed flags and banners were unfurled. This was the loudest, most passionate YNWA that I've heard in years.'

4 November 2001, Manchester United 3-1
Three weeks after Gérard Houllier underwent a life-saving heart surgery a mosaic with the initials 'GH' within the tricolor French flag was portrayed as Houllier's name echoed around the stadium. Houllier was watching the game at home and in his final interview with Liverpool's official website in 2004 he said this was one of the highlights during his Anfield career.

19 March 2002, Roma 2-0
A mosaic and chants of 'Allez, Allez, Gérard Houllier' rang around L4 to celebrate the return of the Frenchman to the dugout.

LIVERPOOL FC CROWD MOSAIC

Sami Hyypia is rightly hailed as one of the most important players in the history of this great club. Everything Liverpool football Club has achieved since the day he signed, in 1999, he has played a major part in. In a time when the word 'Legend' get used far too easily and far too often, there is no doubt that Sami Hyypia is a true Legend. In every sense of the word.

We would like to take this opportunity to salute Sami Hyypia. A True Anfield hero. A man who's contribution to Liverpool football Club over the past 10 years has been absolutely immense.

As soon as 'You'll Never Walk Alone' finishes this afternoon, hold aloft these cards as a gesture of gratitude to Sami and let him know that it has been an honour, a privilege and a pleasure to support him over the last decade.

Thanks for everything, Sami - Liverpool Legend.

Organised by raotl.co.uk

'As the game got underway the atmosphere was frenzied,' Dan Holland remembers on *ThisisAnfield.com*. 'Emile Heskey scored with a flick header at the Kop end of the ground. The noise that resulted from that goal was immeasurable; the mass hysteria that followed meant you could feel the reinforced concrete structure that is our famous Spion Kop literally move beneath your feet.'

26 August 2006, West Ham 2-1
The Spion Kop made its premiere on 1 September 1906 on a sweltering day when Stoke were beaten 1-0. The current Kop celebrated its 100th anniversary with a 'The Kop 100' mosaic.

6 January 2007, Arsenal 1-3
The Kop held cards that displayed the message 'The Truth' with a Hillsborough flame for the first 6 minutes of the game to signify the 6 minutes played before the game at Hillsborough in 1989 was abandoned. 'The Truth' was a reference to former *Sun* editor Kelvin MacKenzie's repeated lies about the behaviour of Liverpool supporters at Hillsborough.

21 April 2009, Arsenal 4-4
A unique occasion as the fans of the opposition also played their part in the display of the mosaic. Ray Kennedy, who suffers from Parkinson's disease, came onto the field to huge applause from both sets of fans as he was a legend at Arsenal as well as at Liverpool. Kennedy's Gunners' number '10' was at the away section in the Anfield Road lower and Kennedy's Reds' number '5' at the Kop.

24 May 2009, Tottenham 3-1
Sami Hyypia said a tearful goodbye to Liverpool fans.

Never before had a current player of the club been honoured in this way. Disappointed not to see him in the starting line-up the Kop demanded that Benítez should put him on. Hyypia came on in the 84th minute in place of Steven Gerrard, who handed him the captain's armband. 'I told him before the game I wanted to wait until the last minute, but the fans were pushing,' Benítez explained. The Mosaic spelt 'SAMI' on top of the Finnish flag.

23 September 2012, Manchester United 1-2
The visit of Manchester United was Liverpool's first home match since the independent report that revealed the truth behind the Hillsborough disaster was published. Ryan Giggs and Steven Gerrard released 96 balloons and for the first time three of the four stands at Anfield were included in the mosaic. The number '96' was displayed on the Anfield Road end, 'Justice' on the Lower Centenary stand and 'The Truth' on the Kop. 'Whenever a mosaic is to do with Hillsborough it is always special, even more so now that the truth is out and the families can get on and realise that they were right for 20 odd years,' Andy Knott told the media. 'You get a sense of pride, especially when you see the pictures after and anybody who helps just feels proud. It just makes everybody know that we are supporting the families and the survivors.'

Most Successful

		League	FA Cup	League Cup	European Cup	UEFA Cup
Phil Neal	17	8	0	4	4	1
Alan Hansen	16	8	2	3	3	0
Phil Thompson	14	7	1	2	2	2
Kenny Dalglish	14	6	1	4	3	0
Ian Rush	14	5	3	5	1	0
Bruce Grobbelaar	13	6	3	3	1	0
Ronnie Whelan	12	6	2	3	1	0
Ray Clemence	12	5	1	1	3	2
Ian Callaghan*	12	5	2	0	2	2
Graeme Souness	11	5	0	3	3	0
Alan Kennedy	11	5	0	4	2	0
Ray Kennedy	10	5	0	1	3	1
Mark Lawrenson	10	5	1	3	1	0
Terry McDermott	10	4	0	2	3	1
Sammy Lee	10	4	0	4	2	0

ONLY THOSE who have won 10 major honours are included. If players have the same total they are ranked according to league wins and then European Cup wins.

COUPE DES CLUBS CHAMPIONS EUROPEENS 1977

* Callaghan also won a 2nd Division medal that is included in his total.

Muir, Alex

SCOTSMAN ALEX MUIR started his career with Lochgelly Violet, the same club that Billy Liddell came from.

The right-winger, who had worked in Caldwell's paper mill alongside playing for Violet, had to wait until February 1948 to make his debut as Liverpool defended their league crown they had won in such dramatic style. Muir played four times in the league, games which resulted in three defeats and just a single victory, at Blackburn on 10 April 1948.

Season	League		FA Cup		Total	
	App	Goals	App	Goals	App	Goals
1947/48	4	0	0	0	4	0
Total	**4**	**0**	**0**	**0**	**4**	**0**

FACTFILE

BORN
Inverkeithing, Fife, Scotland,
10 December 1923
DIED
4 September 1995
POSITION
Right-winger
OTHER CLUBS
Lochgelly Violet,
South Liverpool (1949–51)
SIGNED FROM
Lochgelly Violet, July 1947
LFC DEBUT
21 February 1948
CONTRACT EXPIRY
1949

Alan Kennedy with the big-eared one

Murdoch, Bobby

BOBBY MURDOCH averaged one goal in every three games throughout his career, and the local boy played in 15 of the last 18 league matches of the 1957/58 season, scoring five times, but was only called on twice more the following season.

Murdoch played twice for Liverpool in the FA Cup, scoring on both occasions: the only goal of the fifth round tie at Scunthorpe United on 15 February 1958 and the club's consolation goal in a 2-1 sixth round defeat at Ewood Park, Blackburn, two weeks later. He played in the opening game of the 1958/59 season but did not feature again until against Cardiff on 14 February 1959, in a 3-0 defeat at Ninian Park, which turned out to be his last appearance for the club.

MURDOCH became a player for South Liverpool in 1965 and the club's player-manager in 1971, remaining at Holly Park until 1976.

FACTFILE

BORN
Garston, Liverpool,
25 January 1936
POSITION
Forward
OTHER CLUBS
South Liverpool (1952–53),
Bolton Wanderers (1953–55),
Barrow (1959–60),
Stockport County (1960–62),
Carlisle United (1962),
Southport (1962–63),
Wigan Athletic (1963–65),
South Liverpool
SIGNED FROM
Bolton Wanderers,
11 May 1955;
signed professional
9 May 1957
LFC DEBUT GAME/GOAL
26 December 1957 /
8 February 1958
CONTRACT EXPIRY
2 September 1959

Season	League		FA Cup		Total	
	App	Goals	App	Goals	App	Goals
1957/58	15	5	2	2	17	7
1958/59	2	0	0	0	2	0
Total	**17**	**5**	**2**	**2**	**19**	**7**

Tommy Younger in action against Blackburn on 22 February 1958

Murphy,
Danny

DANNY 'Super Dan' Murphy was a very experienced 20-year-old, having played 132 matches in the Football League, when he arrived at Roy Evans' Liverpool in July 1997. The attacking midfielder, who was a scorer of spectacular goals, wanted to get off the mark on his Liverpool debut against Wimbledon but was beaten to the spot by another youngster. 'I tried to take that penalty, but Michael Owen took it instead. I don't think I scored again for two-and-a-half or three years!' Murphy complained.

He struggled to find his feet at Liverpool, frequently employed up front, which made his lack of goals the more frustrating, and he was loaned back to Crewe in February 1999. Once Murphy returned he finally got his long-awaited goal and then added another in a 5-1 win over Hull in the League Cup on 14 September 1999. 'Late in 1999 we tried to advertise for him to go, but no club would take him,' said Gérard Houllier when he reflected on this difficult time in Murphy's career. 'So I said to the board, "Well, we will keep him then. He is still young." I am pleased Danny started to do things the right way because then I knew he would become a great player for Liverpool.' In the 2000/01 season Murphy's fortunes turned around and he scored an impressive tally for a

midfielder, 10 goals in 47 matches, and started both in the UEFA and FA Cup finals, having missed the League Cup final through injury. Murphy also made his full international debut against Sweden in November 2001 and altogether made nine international appearances, of which eight were friendlies and only one start. Murphy only missed four league games over the next two seasons and was voted the club's best player by Liverpool fans in 2002/03. Houllier was more than pleased with his progress. 'What I like most about him is the fact that he shows for the ball, asks for the ball, and always wants to be involved. I don't like players who bottle out, and Danny is a fighter.'

THE 2003/04 SEASON was a big disappointment for everyone including Murphy, who started 28 games compared with 55 in the previous campaign. Once Houllier had departed it was clear that Benítez wanted to revitalise the midfield and deemed the 27-year-old surplus to requirements, a harsh treatment of an excellent squad player like Murphy. He will certainly forever be cherished among Reds fans for the three goals he scored at Old Trafford, each resulting in 1-0 victories. In December 2000 his free kick inflicted United's first defeat at home for two years and Liverpool's first away win over United for ten years! The following season Murphy was at it again, ensuring Liverpool's fifth

consecutive win over United five minutes from the end of normal time. Two years later Liverpool were awarded a penalty by Mike Riley at Old Trafford after an hour's play and Murphy stepped up to the spot and scored with confidence. In fact, Murphy scored from all of his eight penalties in his time at Liverpool.

Murphy was a stalwart at Fulham in the five years he stayed there and saved the club from relegation when he scored the only goal of the game at Portsmouth on the final day of the 2007/08 season. His Fulham contract expired at the end of 2011/12 and the 35-year-old joined recently relegated Blackburn. Although he had signed a two-year contract with Rovers, he was released at the end of his first year.

MURPHY has been a co-commentator on Sky Sports for a few years now and seems ideal for the job, as well as being a deep thinker of the game who might go into coaching or management.

FACTFILE

BORN
Chester, 18 March 1977
POSITION
Midfielder
OTHER CLUBS
Crewe Alexandra (1992–97),
Crewe Alexandra (loan, 1999),
Charlton Athletic (2004–06),
Tottenham Hotspur (2006–07),
Fulham (2007–12),
Blackburn Rovers (2012–13)
SIGNED FROM
Crewe Alexandra, £1.5million,
15 July 1997
INTERNATIONAL CAPS
9 England caps (1 goal),
2001–03
LFC DEBUT GAME/GOAL
9 August 1997 /
14 September 1999
CONTRACT EXPIRY
10 August 2004
HONOURS
FA Cup 2001;
League Cup 2003;
UEFA Cup 2001

Season	League		FA Cup		League Cup		Europe		Other		Total	
	App	Goals	App	Goals	App	Goals	App	Goals	App	Goals	App	Goals
1997/98	6 (10)	0	0 (1)	0	0	0	0	0	-	-	6 (11)	0
1998/99	0 (1)	0	0	0	1 (1)	0	0 (1)	0	-	-	1 (3)	0
1999/2000	9 (14)	3	2	0	2	3	-	-	-	-	13 (14)	6
2000/01	13 (14)	4	4 (1)	1	5	4	6 (4)	1	-	-	28 (19)	10
2001/02	31 (5)	6	1 (1)	0	1	0	13 (3)	2	1	0	47 (9)	8
2002/03	36	7	3	1	4	2	12	2	0 (1)	0	55 (1)	12
2003/04	19 (12)	5	1 (1)	1	2	2	6 (1)	0	-	-	28 (14)	8
Total	**114 (56)**	**25**	**11 (4)**	**3**	**15 (1)**	**11**	**37 (9)**	**5**	**1 (1)**	**0**	**178 (71)**	**44**

Murray, Bill

BILL MURRAY'S brief Liverpool career consisted of just four matches. The defender played as a makeshift centre-forward in the last two fixtures of the 1927/28 season.

He had to wait until the middle of November 1929 before he figured for the first team again, this time in an away game with Aston Villa as a replacement for centre-half Jimmy McDougall as well as seven days later at Anfield against Leeds United. Murray later became Barrow's captain in the Third Division North.

FACTFILE

BORN
Alexandria, Scotland,
9 November 1904
POSITION
Centre-forward / Centre-half
OTHER CLUBS
Bowhill Celtic (1920–22),
Vale of Clyde (1922–24),
Clydebank (1924–26),
New Brighton (1926–27),
Clydebank (1927),
Barrow (1930–33),
Bristol Rovers (1933–36),
Folkestone (1936–38)
SIGNED FROM
Clydebank,
28 November 1927
LFC DEBUT GAME/GOAL
28 April 1928 /
16 November 1929
CONTRACT EXPIRY
31 January 1930

Liverpool FC's founder, John Houlding, watching his men

Season	League		FA Cup		Total	
	App	Goals	App	Goals	App	Goals
1927/28	2	0	0	0	2	0
1929/30	2	1	0	0	2	1
Total	**4**	**1**	**0**	**0**	**4**	**1**

Murray, David

LEFT-BACK David Murray arrived from Everton for free after failing to impress in his one year at the Blues, making only two appearances. Twelve of his 15 league appearances for Liverpool came in the 1904/05 season, the year in which the Reds won the Second Division.

But Murray only played three more times the following season when Liverpool stormed to the title in the First Division. Murray joined Leeds City for £150 in December 1905, serving them with distinction for four years, having been made captain of the Second Division side in the 1906/07 campaign. Murray enlisted for the Argyll and Sutherland Highlanders at the

onset of World War One and died, aged just 33, in Loos, France, on 10 December 1915.

FACTFILE

BORN
Busby, Glasgow, Scotland,
4 December 1882
DIED
10 December 1915
POSITION
Left-back
OTHER CLUBS
Leven Victoria (1900–03),
Everton (1903–04),
Hull City (1905),
Leeds City (1905–09),
Mexborough (1909–10),
Burslem Port Vale (1910)
SIGNED FROM
Everton, free transfer,
29 August 1904
LFC DEBUT
1 September 1904
CONTRACT EXPIRY
December 1905
HONOURS
Second Division
Championship 1904/05

Season	League		FA Cup		Other		Total	
	App	Goals	App	Goals	App	Goals	App	Goals
1904/05	12	0	0	0	-	-	12	0
1905/06	3	0	0	0	0	0	3	0
Total	**15**	**0**	**0**	**0**	**0**	**0**	**15**	**0**

Jock McNab, Walter Wadsworth, John Bamber and Tom Bromilow

Neal, Phil

ONE OF THE MOST decorated players in English football history, Phil Neal had made his name with Northampton Town where he played nearly 200 league games for the Cobblers when he was transferred to Liverpool in November 1974 as Bob Paisley's first managerial signing.

Paisley did waste a journey to see him, as Neal told *LFChistory.net*: 'Paisley often used to pay to go through the terraces and talk to people about the players like: "What's that Phil Neal like?" When Bob Paisley saw me for the last time at Northampton he brought a Liverpool director with him, Mr Sidney Reaks. For the first twenty minutes I played at right-back but the rest of the game I played in goal. Bob said: "We came all that way to see you for the last time. I wanted to show my director what a good right-back you were. The keeper got carried off and you put the green jersey on."'

Vastly experienced even at the relatively young age of 23, being thrown into the Goodison derby with Everton just days after his arrival on Merseyside did not bother Neal in the slightest. He missed the next three matches after that goalless debut but then played in the last 22 fixtures of the 1974/75 season, mostly at left-back in place of Alec Lindsay even though he preferred to be on the right. That started a quite astonishing run of consecutive appearances for Liverpool: a total of 417 between 23 October 1976 and 24 September 1983. That is, needless to say, a Liverpool record! Incidentally, he missed three games due to the injury that stopped his record-breaking run before he made another 127 appearances in a row!

Few know better about Neal's value to Liverpool than Ray

Clemence, as he revealed in 1977: 'Most people know that Phil is my room-mate and best friend at the club. Phil adds an extra dimension to the team with his ability to surge forward and set things up,' Clem said. 'It's easy to see when you're playing with him, that he's got a tremendous awareness of every other player in the side and what their job is. I suppose he picked it up in his utility days at Northampton – in fact he often tells me he's a better goalkeeper than I am! Phil has so much skill on the ground that I don't think he'd be lost in midfield. Add to that his defensive qualities and the fact he's no mean performer in the air and you've got a very good player indeed.'

'Zico', so called by the supporters for the number of goals he scored as a defender, won a League Championship medal in his first full season at Anfield in 1975/76, something he would achieve on no fewer than eight occasions. He also played in six European club finals for Liverpool and was the only member of the 1977 European Cup-winning side in Rome to return there seven years later for a similar but much sterner test against the Italian champions. Neal's cool penalty in 1977 sealed that first triumph in the continent's premier club tournament as Neal fondly remembers. 'As I ran up to the ball I then did something I never did and which you should never do – I changed my mind. Instead I hit it low to the other side of the keeper but it went in and up came Cally in delight. I still get a tingle when I see the videos of Bob Paisley and Ronnie Moran and the lads leaping up off the bench with joy.' Neal scored again in a European final – this time from open play – in 1984 before adding another tidy penalty in the shootout that followed the 1-1 draw, setting the scene for Alan Kennedy's dramatic clincher from 12 yards. A year later, having succeeded Graeme Souness as captain, Neal had the chance to emulate the great Real Madrid players, di Stefano and Gento, by picking up a fifth winners' medal in the European Cup. Sadly, on a night of mayhem and madness in Brussels, his European dream was taken away from him on one of the blackest days football has ever known.

Neal played 50 times for England, a clear recognition that he was one of the finest full-backs of his time. Neal approached the 1985/86 season under Kenny Dalglish's leadership at the age of 34, still disappointed that he had been overlooked for the manager's job that he claimed he was practically 'promised'. Dalglish was already looking to the future and it wasn't long before Steve Nicol took Neal's place in the side. Neal accepted an offer from Bolton Wanderers to be their manager. He lost his job at Burnden Park after six and a half years and was shortly afterwards appointed Graham Taylor's right-hand man during his spell in charge of the England team. Neal was manager at Coventry City from October 1993 to February 1995 and following his dismissal had short spells as manager of Cardiff City and assistant manager at Manchester City and Peterborough United. He is especially proud of his time at Bolton as he revealed to *LFChistory.net*:

I took them to Wembley three times in the lower-league cups. I made a profit five out of the six years I was there. I built a club that when Bruce Rioch and Colin Todd took over they said you left a good disciplined club which was easy to kick off from. Then I went to Coventry. We finished eleventh in the Premier League. I sold Phil Babb. I was the one responsible for getting £3.6million for him while Kevin Keegan with Terry McDermott six months before at Newcastle tried to get him for £175,000. Terry Mac was on the phone every day before the deadline in March: 'You'll not get another penny more.' I convinced the chairman to leave him until after the World Cup. Phil Babb had a great World Cup and it was a wonderful boost for Coventry's bank balance.

Phil Neal's record speaks for itself. He played in nearly 700 Football League games for Northampton, Liverpool and Bolton – a staggering tally. Added to that are his cup appearances plus the representative honours he gained, which take his total close to the 1,000 mark, a quite astonishing achievement. He was very much aware that it is the team that counts and not so much individuals, but his own performances throughout his long career were always of a very high standard. Never a flamboyant showman who courted attention or publicity, he just got on with his job through hard work. Neal was lucky never to be seriously injured but he looked after himself and his good positional sense, added to his ability to create openings for colleagues further afield and even be in the right place to score himself, meant that

his position in the team was never threatened until he was in his mid-30s.

The first thing that comes to mind regarding Phil Neal is how is it possible to play 417 games in a row! 'I got over a broken toe, but I had to play for six weeks with size eight-and-a-half on one foot and size seven on the other,' Neal told *LFChistory.net*. 'Ronnie Moran made me a plaster cast on the little toe I had broken. It was uncomfortable with my normal-size shoes.' Before Neal embarked on his record-breaking run he was absent for an away game against Trabzonspor on 20 October 1976. That was, in fact, the first game he had missed since 14 December 1974!

Neal should have been out for at least four weeks when he

fractured a cheekbone in January 1976, but he soldiered on with no protection for his face as was the norm in those days:

Roger Davis the centre-forward at Derby gave me an elbow. I had my cheekbone lifted in line with the rest of my face to put my face back in shape (by the way... it's never recovered [Neal quips]). I chose to play against the specialist's wishes who said that I shouldn't play for a month. There were little incidents when I could have missed a game but I was doubly determined not to. It was so exciting. I didn't miss a day's training in all those years I was there. I wouldn't ring in for a cold. Every day I had a smile on my face.

THE FIRST THING THAT COMES TO MIND REGARDING PHIL NEAL IS HOW IS IT POSSIBLE TO PLAY 417 GAMES IN A ROW!

FACTFILE

BORN
Irchester, 20 February 1951
POSITION
Right-back
OTHER CLUBS
Northampton Town (1967–74), Bolton Wanderers (1985–89)
SIGNED FROM
Northampton Town, £66,000, 9 October 1974
INTERNATIONAL CAPS
50 England caps (5 goals), 1976–83
LFC DEBUT GAME/GOAL
16 November 1974 / 4 November 1975
CONTRACT EXPIRY
December 1985
HONOURS
League Championship 1975/76, 1976/77, 1978/79, 1979/80, 1981/82, 1982/83, 1983/84, 1985/86;
League Cup 1981, 1982, 1983, 1984;
European Cup 1977, 1978, 1981, 1984;
UEFA Cup 1976

Season	League App	League Goals	FA Cup App	FA Cup Goals	League Cup App	League Cup Goals	Europe App	Europe Goals	Other App	Other Goals	Total App	Total Goals
1974/75	23	0	2	0	0	0	0	0	0	0	25	0
1975/76	42	6	2	0	3	0	12	1	-	-	59	7
1976/77	42	7	8	2	2	0	8	4	1	0	61	13
1977/78	42	4	1	0	9	1	9	2	1	0	62	7
1978/79	42	5	7	0	1	0	4	0	-	-	54	5
1979/80	42	1	8	0	7	0	2	0	1	0	60	1
1980/81	42	2	2	0	9	0	9	1	1	0	63	3
1981/82	42	2	3	0	10	1	6	0	1	0	62	3
1982/83	42	8	3	0	8	1	6	2	1	0	60	11
1983/84	41	1	2	0	12	1	8	1	1	0	64	3
1984/85	42	4	7	1	3	0	10	0	2	0	64	5
1985/86	11 (2)	1	0	0	2	0	-	-	1	0	14 (2)	1
Total	**453 (2)**	**41**	**45**	**3**	**66**	**4**	**74**	**11**	**10**	**0**	**648 (2)**	**59**

Neill,
Robert

GLASWEGIAN centre-half Robert Neill was probably our shortest-ever player in that position, at 5ft 4in (165cm). He was loaned to Liverpool from Hibernian as they were missing several regulars for the Test match against Bury in the 1894/95 season. Liverpool lost 1-0 and were relegated to the Second Division.

NEILL continued his career at Hibernian and made his international debut against Wales on 21 March 1896 where he scored two goals in a 4-0 win. Liverpool bought the 20-year-old Neill in May 1896 shortly after Hibs suffered a 3-1 loss to Hearts

in the Scottish Cup final. Following his arrival he was so described by the *Athletic News*: 'Neill is a clever little half-back, quiet and unassuming in style, but very quick and effective.' Liverpool had just made an immediate return to the First

NEIL.

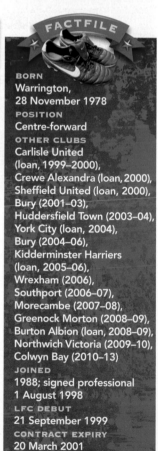

Division and finished in a creditable fifth place in the 1896/97 season.

NEILL finally replaced Joe McQue in the first XI after being in the reserves for the first six weeks of the campaign, said to be certainly the most expensive reserve in Liverpool's ranks.

The Scotsman returned to his homeland after just one season because of family bereavement and had quite a successful career with Rangers where in seven years he won four league titles and one

'MY MOST EXCITING MATCH TOOK PLACE IN 1897, WHEN FOR LIVERPOOL I PLAYED IN THE SEMI-FINAL OF THE ENGLISH CUP'

Scottish Cup. He made 109 appearances for Rangers and scored 28 goals. After retirement, he became a restaurateur. According to the *Dundee Courier*, 'he had a most winsome manner, and he was a prime public favourite. He was beloved by his clubmates, and admired by his opponents for the beauty and fairness of his play.' In 1909 the *Montreal Daily Witness* reported that Neill was, along with other footballers from the British Isles, working on the construction of the new Congregational Church in Pointe St Charles in Montreal. 'Thick-set and sturdy, with the arm of a Hercules, it is easy to understand why Robert Neill occupied a prominent place in the Association game in "Bonnie

Scotland".' The Montreal newspaper conducted an interview, a pretty rare one for a Liverpool footballer from the 19th century. 'I played football for seven years. The dear old Glasgow Rangers was my team, and I also played for Liverpool previous to that. Edinburgh Hibernian also claimed me for some time,' Neill said. 'My most exciting match took place in 1897, when for Liverpool I played in the semi-final of the English Cup. We were defeated by a narrow margin.' Apparently Neill was still turning out for local sides in some capacity. 'I am somewhat tired of football, though I have played for Westmount here and the M.A.A.A. [Montreal Amateur Athletic Association]. Still, I may take it

up again.' Four years later Robert Neill died of chronic alcoholism in his home town of Govan, Glasgow, on 2 March 1913, aged 37.

FACTFILE

BORN
Govan, Glasgow, Scotland, 24 September 1875
DIED
2 March 1913
POSITION
Centre-half
OTHER CLUBS
Ashfield (1891–94), Hibernian (1894–96), Rangers (1897–1904), Airdrieonians (1904–05)
SIGNED FROM
Hibernian – loan, April 1895 / Hibernian, May 1896
INTERNATIONAL CAPS
2 Scotland caps (2 goals), 1896–1900
LFC DEBUT GAME/GOAL
27 April 1895 / 19 December 1896
CONTRACT EXPIRY
April 1895 / April 1897

Season	League		FA Cup		Other		Total	
	App	Goals	App	Goals	App	Goals	App	Goals
1894/95	0	0	0	0	1	0	1	0
1896/97	22	2	4	1	-	-	26	3
Total	**22**	**2**	**4**	**1**	**1**	**0**	**27**	**3**

Newby, Jon

JON NEWBY came to Liverpool at only nine years of age. A quick though slightly built striker, he won the FA Youth Cup with his team-mates Jamie Carragher, David Thompson and Michael Owen in 1996.

After featuring for roughly 30 minutes in four substitute appearances in the 1999/2000 season, Newby signed for Bury in March 2001, the fourth club he had been loaned to while at Liverpool. He finally settled wwat Colwyn Bay in the Northern Premier League Premier Division. At the end of the 2010/11 season the Seagulls were promoted via the playoffs into the Conference North. When manager Dave

Challinor left his post for AFC Fylde in November 2011 Newby took over as the club's player-manager, serving until he was sacked on New Year's Day 2013.

FACTFILE

BORN
Warrington, 28 November 1978
POSITION
Centre-forward
OTHER CLUBS
Carlisle United (loan, 1999–2000), Crewe Alexandra (loan, 2000), Sheffield United (loan, 2000), Bury (2001–03), Huddersfield Town (2003–04), York City (loan, 2004), Bury (2004–06), Kidderminster Harriers (loan, 2005–06), Wrexham (2006), Southport (2006–07), Morecambe (2007–08), Greenock Morton (2008–09), Burton Albion (loan, 2008–09), Northwich Victoria (2009–10), Colwyn Bay (2010–13)
JOINED
1988; signed professional 1 August 1998
LFC DEBUT
21 September 1999
CONTRACT EXPIRY
20 March 2001

Season	League		FA Cup		League Cup		Total	
	App	Goals	App	Goals	App	Goals	App	Goals
1999/2000	0 (1)	0	0 (2)	0	0 (1)	0	0 (4)	0
Total	**0 (1)**	**0**	**0 (2)**	**0**	**0 (1)**	**0**	**0 (4)**	**0**

N'Gog,
David

DAVID N'GOG was snapped up by Rafa Benítez for a relatively cheap fee from Paris St Germain where he made 24 appearances and scored three goals. Although he wasn't often on the scoresheet for PSG it could be attributed to the fact that he played on the wing or came on as substitute.

N'Gog made five starts in his debut season at Liverpool and appeared 14 times as a substitute, earning more chances than might have been expected. He scored three times, his debut goal coming against PSV in the Champions League before he added two goals in the Premier League against Sunderland and Blackburn.

N'GOG was often given the unenviable task of replacing

Fernando Torres when the Spaniard was unavailable in the 2009/10 season. He scored eight goals during a difficult season for the club: five in the Premier League, the winner in the League Cup at Leeds plus two in Europe against Debrecen and Lille. He was also involved in one of the season's most controversial incidents when, according to Birmingham City's Lee Carsley among others, he dived to win a penalty in the Anfield league game. This assured him of a very hot welcome in the return match at St Andrews four months later when he came on as a second-half substitute for Torres.

The young Frenchman celebrated his 22nd birthday shortly before the end of the 2010/11 season, in which he made no fewer than 38 first-team appearances, 20 from the start and 18 as a substitute. But N'Gog only started two matches after Kenny Dalglish took over from Roy Hodgson. Five of his eight goals that campaign came in Europe. On the final day of the 2011 summer transfer window, six games short of a century for Liverpool, N'Gog moved to Bolton Wanderers who were relegated the following spring.

FACTFILE

BORN
Gennevilliers, France,
1 April 1989
POSITION
Centre-forward
OTHER CLUBS
Paris St Germain (2001–08),
Bolton Wanderers (2011–)
SIGNED FROM
Paris St Germain, £1.5million,
24 July 2008
INTERNATIONAL CAPS
17 France U-21 caps (3 goals)
LFC DEBUT GAME/GOAL
31 August 2008 /
9 December 2008
CONTRACT EXPIRY
31 August 2011

Season	League		FA Cup		League Cup		Europe		Total	
	App	Goals	App	Goals	App	Goals	App	Goals	App	Goals
2008/09	2 (12)	2	0	0	2	0	1 (2)	1	5 (14)	3
2009/10	10 (14)	5	1 (1)	0	2	1	5 (4)	2	18 (19)	8
2010/11	9 (16)	2	0 (1)	0	1	1	8 (3)	5	18 (20)	8
Total	**21 (42)**	**9**	**1 (2)**	**0**	**5**	**2**	**14 (9)**	**8**	**41 (53)**	**19**

Nicholl,
Jimmy

J. NICHOLL LIVERPOOL

LIVERPOOL manager Tom Watson said of Jimmy Nicholl that he 'isn't a brilliant forward, but he's a useful one and he can shoot!' Nicholl was crowded out from Middlesbrough's forward line and after making his debut in January 1914 proved to be a valuable player in Liverpool's brilliant cup run that very season.

The hard-fought battle against Sam Hardy's Aston Villa in the FA Cup semi-final produced an unlikely hero in Nicholl. After half an hour's play he headed the ball into the net. In the second half Metcalf struck a powerful shot that thundered off Hardy's

bar with Nicholl pouncing upon the rebound to net the second. He was in Liverpool's line-up in the final but unfortunately didn't get on the scoresheet as the Reds lost 1-0 to Burnley.

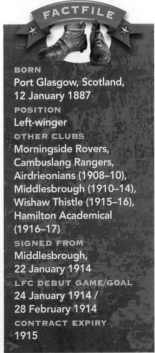

FACTFILE

BORN
Port Glasgow, Scotland,
12 January 1887
POSITION
Left-winger
OTHER CLUBS
Morningside Rovers,
Cambuslang Rangers,
Airdrieonians (1908–10),
Middlesbrough (1910–14),
Wishaw Thistle (1915–16),
Hamilton Academical
(1916–17)
SIGNED FROM
Middlesbrough,
22 January 1914
LFC DEBUT GAME/GOAL
24 January 1914 /
28 February 1914
CONTRACT EXPIRY
1915

Season	League		FA Cup		Total	
	App	Goals	App	Goals	App	Goals
1913/14	14	3	5	2	19	5
1914/15	38	9	2	0	40	9
Total	**52**	**12**	**7**	**2**	**59**	**14**

Nicholson,
John

JOHN Nicholson was Dick White's centre half understudy and only got a look-in for one game; a 2-2 draw against Brighton. Just as White's career was finishing, Ron Yeats arrived at Anfield and it was clear that Nicholson had no future with the club.

In August 1961 Nicholson left for Port Vale where he was appointed captain and made a club-record 208 consecutive appearances. The highlight of his career was when the Valiants drew his former club, Liverpool, in the fourth round of the FA Cup in January 1964. Following a heroic goalless draw at Anfield, reportedly a few thousand fans stormed through the gates at Vale Park, joining the 42,179 capacity crowd to see the replay. The Third Division club was knocked out by Peter Thompson's goal two minutes before the end of extra-time, preventing a second replay. Sadly, Nicholson was killed in a car crash the day after his 30th birthday.

FACTFILE

BORN
Liverpool, 2 September 1936
DIED
3 September 1966
POSITION
Centre-half
OTHER CLUBS
Port Vale (1961–65),
Doncaster Rovers (1965–66)
JOINED
7 January 1957
LFC DEBUT
10 October 1959
CONTRACT EXPIRY
August 1961

	League		FA Cup		League Cup		Total	
Season	App	Goals	App	Goals	App	Goals	App	Goals
1959/60	1	0	0	0	-	-	1	0
Total	1	0	0	0	0	0	1	0

Nickson,
Harry
Wheeler

HARRY WHEELER NICKSON'S career for Liverpool seems unusual in that he only appeared in FA Cup matches for the club.

However, he was also one of Liverpool's representatives during that 1945/46 season in the Football League North, but his 10 games in the competition are not included in official records as most clubs had numerous guest players. In the Cup, Nickson played in both legs against Chester and in the second leg against Bolton, which Liverpool won 2-0. But as they had already lost the first match by five goals, it was the team from Burnden Park that progressed into the fifth round.

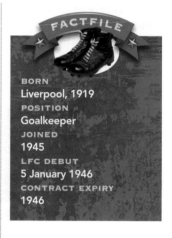

FACTFILE

BORN
Liverpool, 1919
POSITION
Goalkeeper
JOINED
1945
LFC DEBUT
5 January 1946
CONTRACT EXPIRY
1946

	League		FA Cup		Total	
Season	App	Goals	App	Goals	App	Goals
1945/46	-	-	3	0	3	0
Total	0	0	3	0	3	0

Nicol,
Steve

BOB PAISLEY bought 19-year-old Steve Nicol in October 1981 as a long term replacement for right-back Phil Neal. He cost £300,000 from Ayr United where he had been a part-time player and an out-of-work building labourer.

Kenny Dalglish was not so impressed by his arrival as he revealed in his autobiography:

Until then, the three Scots already at Anfield, Al [Hansen], Graeme [Souness] and me had been pretty well able to look after ourselves. We had built up an understanding that the Scots were the master race. We would quote historical facts to the English players to prove it. Some of the most important inventions and discoveries in the world came from Scots, like television, the telephone, penicillin, the steam engine and tarmac. Not to mention those other wonders of the world, golf and whisky. Everything we had built up, he destroyed in 10 minutes because of the photograph that was taken of him when he signed. There he was with a tammy on, a silly Liverpool scarf and sillier grin. Unbelievable. Stevie was a lovely guy, a real one-off.

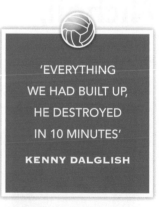

'EVERYTHING
WE HAD BUILT UP,
HE DESTROYED
IN 10 MINUTES'

KENNY DALGLISH

Nicol had his first taste of the first team three weeks after arriving at Liverpool in a friendly against an Irish International XI alongside other hopefuls such as Kevin Sheedy and Craig Johnston. He made 26 appearances in the

Central League side in his first season in 1981/82 and featured four times for the first team in 1982/83. Nicol emerged as quite a player in the glorious 1983/84 season when Liverpool won the League, European Cup and League Cup. Phil Neal was not to be moved from the back four, but Nicol slotted in at right midfield. He started 32 out of 67 games and came second in the PFA's vote for the Most Promising Player of the Year behind Luton's Paul Walsh. His highlight could have so easily been his lowest point after coming on as a substitute for Johnston and playing 47 minutes in the European Cup final in Rome. He blazed over Liverpool's first penalty in the shootout, but thankfully Nicol ended on the winning side. He had still proved his courage in Liverpool's hour of need. Graeme Souness, who was his captain at Liverpool, was very impressed by Nicol and a year after after leaving Liverpool he predicted that Nicol would wear the captain's armband one day. Nicol did indeed revel in the captain's role in the 1990/91 season when club captain Ronnie Whelan was absent through injury. There are numerous stories on Nicol's 'dimwittedness' and his former team-mate David Hodgson knew a couple, as he told the *LFC Magazine*. 'The Nic had size-12 feet. And Billy Mercer, a young goalkeeper, was the same size. The older pros used to give the kids the boots to wear in. So Steve gives those boots to Billy, who tries them on and realises the paper's still in them. He takes the paper out, puts them back on and tells Steve later on that they're great. "You're joking?" says the Nic. "They just won't fit me."'

'Chico' is one of the most versatile players Liverpool has ever seen. As well as playing on the right side at the back or further up the wing, the genuinely two-footed Scot did an excellent job on the left and also had a successful spell in the heart of the defence when Alan

FACTFILE

BORN
Ayrshire, Scotland,
11 December 1961
POSITION
Left-back / Winger
OTHER CLUBS
Ayr United (1977–81),
Notts County (1995),
Sheffield Wednesday
(1995–98),
West Bromwich Albion
(loan, 1998),
Doncaster Rovers (1998–99),
Boston Bulldogs (1999)
SIGNED FROM
Ayr United, £300,000,
26 October 1981
INTERNATIONAL CAPS
27 Scotland caps, 1984–91
LFC DEBUT GAME/GOAL
31 August 1982 /
22 October 1983
CONTRACT EXPIRY
20 January 1995
HONOURS
League Championship
1983/84, 1985/86,
1987/88, 1989/90;
FA Cup
1986, 1989, 1992;
European Cup
1984;
FWA Footballer of the Year
1989

Hansen was injured for the majority of the 1988/89 season. He was a great defender, but also had great attacking prowess. Nicol was quite adept at taking on defenders and an accurate crosser of the ball. He scored some brilliant goals and was even top of the goalscoring charts at the beginning of the 1987/88 season, after scoring six goals in his first six league games, including a superb hat-trick against Newcastle, which Bob Paisley described as a 'masterpiece'. Ronnie Moran told *LFChistory.net* that 'Shanks always preached that we had eleven captains. He wanted to see players think things out and rectify things if they were going wrong. I remember Steve Nicol getting a hat-trick once at Newcastle. Nobody told him

where he had to go and what to do, he just worked it out himself. He got the match ball and I told him it was probably the only one he'd ever get, but nobody told him off for joining in the attack.' Nicol's importance was officially recognised with a Football Writers' Association's Player of the Year award in 1988/89, after filling six different positions that season. He was a regular in Liverpool's first team for 11 years and is a certified club legend.

NICOL had brief spells with other clubs in England – Notts County, Sheffield Wednesday, West Bromwich Albion and Doncaster Rovers – before deciding to try his luck across the Atlantic Ocean when offered a player-coach's role at the Boston Bulldogs in 1999.

He was a lucky man to be alive at that point as he had almost perished at Christmas 1995 when he was dragged from a freezing lake after plunging through the ice. 'I've been getting a bit of stick from the other lads about that,' he said shortly afterwards. 'But I'd rather be taking the flak than not be here at all!' Nicol enjoyed his new surroundings in Boston, though they were a far cry from the hectic English football. 'Playing for Boston Bulldogs in front of 700 to 800 fans was obviously different from playing for Liverpool in front of the Kop and 40,000 passionate Reds,' Nicol told the *Guardian*.

The Bulldogs served the New England Revolution as its feeder club and when coach Walter Zenga was sacked in 1999, Nicol took over on a caretaker basis.

He was appointed assistant coach at the Revolution in January 2002 and later that year became manager. He was named MLS Coach of the Year in 2002 as the Revolution reached the MLS final where they lost to Los Angeles Galaxy. After advancing them to three consecutive MLS Cup finals from 2005 to 2007 their big breakthrough came with the US Open Cup win of 2007, to which they added the North American Superliga title in 2008. In 2010 Nicol failed, for the first time in a league-record eight straight seasons, to guide the Revolution to a playoff berth. After failing again the following year Nicol was sacked as their coach. He is the longest-serving coach with a single club in MLS history with a record of 112 wins, 108 draws and 81 defeats.

ALAN HANSEN played alongside Nicol for a number of years and certainly appreciated his compatriot's enormous capabilities judging by his autobiography.

"When I was switched from the left side to the right of Liverpool back four towards the end of my career, when my knee problems had taken their toll on my running, it made me feel I could light a cigar and read a newspaper to have Steve on the outside. His fitness was astonishing. Dietitians would be horrified at the amount he ate. He could eat for Britain. He and I and our families once were on a Norwegian cruise together and he probably consumed more than the rest of us put together. It was not unusual for him to go through six or eight packs of crisps in one go. But he never carried any excess weight, hardly missed a tackle and gave the impression of being able to bomb up and down that right touchline forever. Suffice it to say that after our first match together on the right, I thought, 'Where have you been all my life?'"

> "AFTER OUR FIRST MATCH TOGETHER ON THE RIGHT, I THOUGHT, 'WHERE HAVE YOU BEEN ALL MY LIFE?'"
>
> **ALAN HANSEN**

Season	League App	League Goals	FA Cup App	FA Cup Goals	League Cup App	League Cup Goals	Europe App	Europe Goals	Other App	Other Goals	Total App	Total Goals
1982/83	2 (2)	0	0	0	0	0	0	0	0	0	2 (2)	0
1983/84	19 (4)	5	2	0	9	2	2 (2)	0	0	0	32 (6)	7
1984/85	29 (2)	5	6	0	2	0	7	2	2	0	46 (2)	7
1985/86	33 (1)	4	4	0	3	0	-	-	6	0	46 (1)	4
1986/87	14	3	0	0	5	1	-	-	2	1	21	5
1987/88	40	6	7	0	3	1	-	-	-	-	50	7
1988/89	38	2	6	0	6	0	-	-	2	0	52	2
1989/90	21 (2)	6	7	3	2	0	-	-	1	0	31 (2)	9
1990/91	35	3	7	0	2	0	-	-	0	0	44	3
1991/92	34	1	8	0	3	0	7	0	-	-	52	1
1992/93	32	0	1	0	4	0	2	0	0	0	39	0
1993/94	27 (4)	1	2	0	2	0	-	-	-	-	31 (4)	1
1994/95	4	0	0	0	1	0	-	-	-	-	5	0
Total	**328 (15)**	**36**	**50**	**3**	**42**	**4**	**18 (2)**	**2**	**13**	**1**	**451 (17)**	**46**

Nieuwenhuys, Berry

'I RATE HIM as being without superior, and I am not excluding Stanley Matthews. He is much more the direct and effective player; a goal-getter and a goal-provider.'
From a newspaper article on Berry Nieuwenhuys.

Berry Nieuwenhuys was born in Kroonstad in the Free State, and after completing his schooling at Bethlehem went to work in the mines in the Transvaal. A keen and natural sportsman, his first love was rugby, but he soon switched to the round-ball game. 'I was once a rugby player and then when I turned over to soccer and joined Germiston I played in only four matches before being chosen for the Transvaal,'

Nieuwenhuys remembered. 'I did so well in that game that I swanked a bit but our trainer gave me such a telling off that I broke down and cried. No more swollen heads for me!'

Imagine this. You're a relative youngster playing a minor club game of football in South Africa when a man dashes onto the field during a lull in play and asks if you'd like to play for Liverpool. You wonder if he's for real, but, of course, accept. A few weeks later, on the other side of the world, you are playing in front of 50,000-plus screaming spectators at Anfield. It sounds like something out of *Boys' Own* magazine, but that's just what happened to Berry Nieuwenhuys

in 1933. Eight years earlier another young South African player, Arthur Riley, had gone to England to keep goal for Liverpool Football Club. His English-born father still lived in South Africa, where he keenly followed the sport. Having been impressed by Nieuwenhuys and another player, Lance Carr, he contacted the management at Liverpool and told them that he'd found a couple of 'likely lads' in South Africa. The club told him to go ahead and hire them. That was the way people did business in those days – no agents, no contracts, no fat commissions; just a shake of the hand.

The eager Nieuwenhuys and Carr arrived in England on 11 September 1933 and were met on the quayside by Walter Cartwright and George Patterson, Liverpool

Football Club's chairman and secretary/manager respectively. After one warm-up game in a junior side Nieuwenhuys was named for the seniors to play against Tottenham Hotspur at White Hart Lane on 23 September. The *Evening Express* headlines told it all. 'A gem from South Africa,' they trumpeted as he set up two brilliant goals for his new club. 'Nivvy's triumph in first big match for Liverpool. Home defeat for Spurs after 2 years.' The English had trouble with his full name and immediately shortened it to something more handy; 'Nivvy' as 'the typewriter won't stand the strain of spelling his name in full'. Nivvy's second game was no less than a Merseyside derby at Anfield. He opened the scoring after roughly half an hour's play in a 'cool and calculating manner' in the best derby for 30 years according to the *Evening Express*. The local papers were full of praise for the newcomer: '"Nivvy" afterwards showed that he has the big game temperament, but he has more – the ability. He moved about smoothly, employed touches of the master craftsman, and his centres were ever thoughtful. He certainly captured the fancy of the "Koppites". He is neatness personified. By no means an individualist, he adopts the easiest path, making some delightful short passes along the ground to his inside partner and next turning over a choice centre. "Nivvy" is anything but flashy, but he has a wonderful turn of speed.'

Nieuwenhuys was interviewed by the *Evening Express* following the 3-2 home win and he was thrilled to have taken part in 'the greatest match in which I have ever had the honour to play'. He continued,

Never before had I seen such a vast crowd, such brilliant football, or such clean football, and it was the thrill of my life when I managed to score the first goal. The point which struck me most was the cleanliness of the game. When we were leaving for England we were told that the game here was rough and dirty. Well, I can assure you that this match was 100 per cent cleaner than anything I have seen in Africa. I did not see one real foul in the entire ninety minutes. I confess I was rather staggered by the size of the crowd at the start but I did my best to forget they were there. That was hard in view of the continuous roar of voices. Still you could play in front of a crowd like that for years. They are such sportsmen. I thank them for the encouragement they gave me and also for the wonderful reception I was accorded when I left the field. I don't mind confessing it touched me.

FACTFILE

BORN
Kroonstad, South Africa,
5 November 1911
DIED
12 June 1984
POSITION
Right-winger
OTHER CLUBS
Boksburg,
Germiston Callies;
Arsenal,
West Ham United
(wartime guest)
SIGNED FROM
Germiston Callies,
11 September 1933
LFC DEBUT GAME/GOAL
23 September 1933 /
30 September 1933
CONTRACT EXPIRY
1947
HONOURS
League Championship
1946/47

Not only was Nivvy a brilliant right-winger, but he could fit into any position without effort, being one of a select few to play in nine different positions in top-level football. The two positions he never filled – left-wing and goalkeeper – he was quietly confident would not have posed a problem had the need arisen. Numerous football writers declared the fleet-footed player to be the best winger in the land.

Nivvy and Jack Balmer relaxing on vacation

'It's our Nivvy, our British Nivvy', the Liverpool fans sang, convinced that their favourite should play for England, but it was not to be. The rules stated that for a player from the Commonwealth to represent England his father had to have been born in the UK, as in the instance of Gordon Hodgson, and this was not the case with Nivvy. The debate was, however, shortened by the unwelcome arrival of Hitler in Poland in September 1939. During the war years Nivvy served as a PT instructor with the Royal Air Force, captaining the RAF side,

and still managed to play quite a number of games for Liverpool. Footballers usually represented the clubs nearest the camps where they were based and Nivvy also played for West Ham in the early 1940s and Arsenal in 1945/46. He was on occasions paid with sweets and cigarettes. Nivvy, a lifelong teetotaller and non-smoker, used to hang on to his sweets and swap his cigarettes for even more delicacies.

NIVVY turned 35 in the first post-war season, 1946/47. He played the first seven games of the campaign and then featured again in eight more in the middle of the successful season when Liverpool triumphed in the First Division. He retired from football in 1948,

Season	League		FA Cup		Total	
	App	Goals	App	Goals	App	Goals
1933/34	34	9	4	1	38	10
1934/35	29	10	2	1	31	11
1935/36	39	10	2	0	41	10
1936/37	40	13	1	0	41	13
1937/38	40	13	5	0	45	13
1938/39	39	14	3	2	42	16
1945/46	-	-	4	1	4	1
1946/47	15	5	0	0	15	5
Total	**236**	**74**	**21**	**5**	**257**	**79**

returning to South Africa to take up a position as assistant coach to golf legend Bobby Locke. In 1946 Nivvy had entered the British Open after hurrying back from Liverpool's tour of the USA, and missed the cut by just two strokes. That same year he played in the Irish Open, figuring among the money winners, and during the last years of his football career he doubled as assistant coach at the West Derby Golf Club. He moved for a spell to Rhodesia and then returned to Johannesburg to work as a golf pro while coaching various premier league soccer teams, including Southern Suburbs and his old club,

Germiston Callies. Nivvy was also a very talented tennis player. King Gustav VI of Sweden once sent an aircraft to the UK to fetch the South African for a knock-up on the royal courts. Nivvy also scouted for talent in England as was reported by the *Daily Mirror* in July 1959:

Instant suspension faces any soccer stars accepting offers from a South African agent, who plans a talent swoop in Britain. In a warning letter to the clubs the FA have revealed that the agent is Berry 'Nivvy' Nieuwenhuys, former Liverpool winger, who now coaches in Johannesburg. Acting for the Transvaal Professional League – a newly formed rebel outfit not affiliated to the South African FA – Nieuwenhuys will approach players here with big-money contracts, a job outside football and free passage to South Africa. But stern action faces any who accept. They would be blacklisted automatically by the FA, and any body associated to FIFA, the international controllers.

THE SOUTH AFRICAN sporting hero passed away in Grahamstown in the Eastern Cape Province of South Africa in 1984. He led an eventful

life filled with the greatest wonder, the biggest of which was moving from his homeland to the hustle and bustle of the English game.

Nunez,
Antonio

ANTONIO NUNEZ was spotted by Real Madrid in 2001 playing for third-division side Las Rozas. He played in the reserve team until 2003/04 when he managed 16 games for Real Madrid as a utility player in their star-studded team, scoring on his debut for Real against Villareal on 2 September 2003. It was a dream come true for the boyhood Real fan, but unfortunately, Real finished empty-handed in the 2003/04 season.

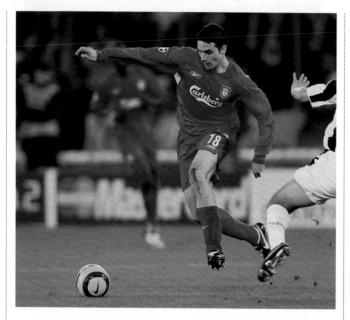

in the 2005 League Cup defeat. Nunez didn't set the world alight at Liverpool, but he won a treasured Champions League medal. He played the full 90 minutes in the crucial group-stage win over Olympiacos and featured for 60 minutes in the goalless draw against Juventus, but had to settle for bench duty in the Istanbul final.

Nunez was valued at £1.5million in Michael Owen's £8.5million move from Liverpool to Real Madrid. It was an exciting prospect for Nunez, who wanted to play more than the odd game. 'Even if Owen hadn't signed for Madrid, I already had an offer from Liverpool and I knew that the manager was keen to sign me,

which is something to be proud of,' Nunez said. The attacking midfielder was one of a quartet of Spanish players signed by Rafa Benítez in his first season as manager: Josemi had already arrived and Xabi Alonso and Luis Garcia soon followed suit. Nunez injured his knee in his first day of training and wasn't ready for

action until three months later. He made three starts in a row following his Arsenal debut and got a fair chance, but more often than not failed to impress. Nunez did make history by becoming the only Liverpool player to score his only goal for the club in a major final when he reduced Chelsea's 3-1 lead to one goal in extra time

FACTFILE

BORN
Madrid, Spain,
15 January 1979
POSITION
Midfielder
OTHER CLUBS
San Federico (1998–99),
Las Rozas (1999–2001),
Real Madrid (2001–04),
Celta Vigo (2005–08),
Real Murcia (2008–09),
Apollon Limassol (2009–12),
Huesca (2012–)
SIGNED FROM
Real Madrid, £1.5million,
17 August 2004
LFC DEBUT GAME/GOAL
28 November 2004 /
27 February 2005
CONTRACT EXPIRY
29 July 2005
HONOURS
Champions League 2005

Season	League		FA Cup		League Cup		Europe		Total	
	App	Goals	App	Goals	App	Goals	App	Goals	App	Goals
2004/05	8 (10)	0	1	0	2 (1)	1	2 (3)	0	13 (14)	1
Total	8 (10)	0	1	0	2 (1)	1	2 (3)	0	13 (14)	1

Ogrizovic,
Steve

STEVE OGRIZOVIC, or 'Oggy', arrived at Anfield from Chesterfield in November 1977 as cover for the outstanding Ray Clemence, after only 18 games in Chesterfield's first team.

The former policeman was a fine goalkeeper in his own right, as witnessed by the remarkable career he subsequently had with Coventry, but his chances of displacing the England international were always going to be very slim. Ogrizovic conceded four goals against Derby on his Reds debut on 8 March 1978. This was the first game Clemence had missed since 9 September 1972, having made 336 appearances in a row! Ogrizovic did keep a clean sheet in the Leeds game three days later, but then Clemence returned. The giant reserve keeper made only three first-team appearances over the next three seasons. His highlight was playing in the second leg of the European Super Cup in which Liverpool beat Anderlecht 2-1 at Anfield on 19 December 1978, having lost 3-1 in Belgium. Ogrizovic won an FA Cup winners' medal in 1987 with the Sky Blues after beating Tottenham 3-2. He played his 600th game for Coventry and his 719th in total against Liverpool on 1 April 2000!

Season	League		FA Cup		League Cup		Europe		Other		Total	
	App	Goals	App	Goals	App	Goals	App	Goals	App	Goals	App	Goals
1977/78	2	0	0	0	0	0	0	0	0	0	2	0
1978/79	0	0	0	0	0	0	1	0	-	-	1	0
1979/80	1	0	0	0	0	0	0	0	0	0	1	0
1980/81	1	0	0	0	0	0	0	0	0	0	1	0
Total	**4**	**0**	**0**	**0**	**0**	**0**	**1**	**0**	**0**	**0**	**5**	**0**

Ogston,
John

JOHN OGSTON
LIVERPOOL

JOHN OGSTON won the Scottish Junior Cup at Aberdeen's Banks O'Dee in 1957, which is still the greatest achievement in the club's history. Shortly after that he joined the biggest club in his native city, Aberdeen. After spending three years as the Dons' reserve goalkeeper he was their number one from 1960 to 1965, making a total of 230 appearances and gaining legendary status.

Nicknamed 'Tubby', as he was a big lad, was signed by Bill Shankly as a deputy to Tommy Lawrence. In four years he only played one game for the Reds in a 3-1 league victory over Newcastle on 7 April 1967. He went initially on loan to Doncaster in August 1968, before being sold to them permanently in July 1969 as Ray Clemence was establishing himself as Liverpool's number one. Ogston played well into his thirties for several teams in the Highland League.

Season	League		FA Cup		League Cup		Europe		Other		Total	
	App	Goals	App	Goals	App	Goals	App	Goals	App	Goals	App	Goals
1966/67	1	0	0	0	-	-	0	0	0	0	1	0
Total	**1**	**0**	**0**	**0**	**-**	**-**	**0**	**0**	**0**	**0**	**1**	**0**

One-Club Men

A promising Eddie Spicer

IT IS VERY RARE at Liverpool or indeed any other club that a player will spend his whole career there. Here are the local heroes whose only club was Liverpool and enjoyed the longest career. The dates are respective player's active career at the club: from first-team debut to final appearance.

	Career	Dates	Games	Rank*
Jamie Carragher	16 years 4 months 11 days	8 January 1997 - 19 May 2013	737	2
Ronnie Moran	12 years 5 months 20 days	22 November 1952 - 12 May 1965	379	31
Gerry Byrne	11 years 6 months 8 days	28 September 1957 - 5 April 1969	333	51
Ray Lambert	9 years 10 months 14 days	5 January 1946 - 19 November 1955	341	48
Eddie Spicer	7 years 10 months 19 days	30 January 1946 - 19 December 1953	168	121

* Rank on the club's All-time top appearances' list.

Opposition

Most goals scored against Liverpool

Goals	Player	Appearances	Average	Clubs
21	**Charlie Buchan**	27	0.78	Sunderland (22/1911-25), Arsenal (5/1925-28)
19	**Dixie Dean**	17	1.12	Everton (19/1925-37)
16	**Bobby Gurney**	15	1.07	Sunderland (16/1930-37)
15	**Harry Hampton**	17	0.88	Aston Villa (16/1905-15), Birmingham City (1/1920)
15	**John Bradford**	24	0.63	Birmingham City (24/1922-34)
14	**Steve Bloomer**	29	0.48	Derby County (20/1895-1906), Middlesbrough (8/1906-09), Derby County (2 1912-13)
14	**Martin Peters**	40	0.35	West Ham United (14/1962-69), Tottenham (15/1970-74), Norwich City (11/1975-1980)
13	**Dave Halliday**	12	1.08	Sunderland (8/1925-29), Arsenal (1/1929), Manchester City (3/1931-32)
13	**Billy Hibbert**	20	0.65	Bury (9/1906-11), Newcastle United (9/1911-19), Bradford City (2/1921-22)
12	**Jimmy Greaves**	19	0.63	Tottenham (16/1963-69), West Ham United (3/1970-71)
12	**Sandy Young**	23	0.52	Everton (22/1902-11), Manchester City (1/1912)

Most appearances against Liverpool

Appearances	Player	Clubs
58	**Peter Shilton**	Leicester City (17/1967-74), Stoke (4/1975-76), Nottingham Forest (14/1977-81), Southampton (15/1982-87), Derby County (8/1987-91)
54	**Pat Jennings**	Tottenham (32/1964-76), Arsenal (21/1977-85), Tottenham (1/1986)
46	**Ryan Giggs**	Manchester United (46/1991-)
45	**David O'Leary**	Arsenal (44/1975-93), Leeds United (1/1994)
44	**Frank Lampard**	West Ham United (7/1997-2001), Chelsea (37/2001-13)
43	**Steve Perryman**	Tottenham (43/1969-86)
41	**Neville Southall**	Everton (41/1982-97)
41	**John Hollins**	Chelsea (23/1965-75), QPR (8/1975-78), Arsenal (10/1979-83)
40	**Martin Peters**	West Ham United (14/1962-69), Tottenham (15/1970-74), Norwich City (11/1975-1980)
39	**Dave Watson**	Norwich (9/1981-86), Everton (30/1987-1999)

Most goals in one game against Liverpool

Goals	Player	Date	Result	Opponent	Competition
5	Charlie Buchan	7 December 1912	0-7	Sunderland	1st Division
4	Andrey Arshavin	21 April 2009	4-4	Arsenal	Premier League
4	Júlio Baptista	9 January 2007	3-6	Arsenal	League Cup
4	Mark Viduka	4 November 2000	3-4	Leeds United	Premier League
4	Jimmy Greaves	15 April 1963	2-7	Tottenham	1st Division
4	Ian Wilson	2 May 1955	1-6	Rotherham United	2nd Division
4	Cyril Done	8 April 1955	3-4	Port Vale	2nd Division
4	Stuart E Leary	26 September 1953	0-6	Charlton Athletic	2nd Division
4	Dennis Westcott	7 December 1946	1-5	Wolves	1st Division
4	Dickie Spence	8 December 1934	1-4	Chelsea	1st Division
4	Jack Milsom	7 May 1932	1-8	Bolton Wanderers	1st Division
4	George Brown	16 January 1932	1-6	Aston Villa	1st Division
4	Jimmy Dunne	4 April 1931	1-4	Sheffield United	1st Division
4	Vic Watson	1 September 1930	0-7	West Ham United	1st Division
4	Bobby Gurney	19 April 1930	0-6	Sunderland	1st Division
4	Thomas Jennings	2 October 1926	2-4	Leeds United	1st Division
4	Frank Roberts	17 January 1925	0-5	Manchester City	1st Division
4	Danny Shea	6 September 1913	2-6	Blackburn Rovers	1st Division
4	Fred Howard	18 January 1913	1-4	Manchester City	1st Division
4	Albert Shepherd	22 October 1910	1-6	Newcastle United	1st Division
4	Albert Shepherd	4 December 1909	6-5	Newcastle United	1st Division
4	Sandy Young	1 April 1904	2-5	Everton	1st Division

FA and League Cup combined

		W	D	L
30	Arsenal	10	8	12
27	Everton	12	7	8
21	Man United	7	4	10
20	Burnley	9	5	6
16	Southampton	9	3	4
16	WBA	6	5	5

European competitions

		W	D	L
10	Benfica	6	0	4
10	Chelsea	2	5	3
8	Barcelona	3	3	2
7	Bayern Munich	2	4	1

Liverpool have faced numerous teams in a number of competitions and by fate certain opponents have faced them on more occasions than others.

Top 10 teams that Liverpool have been most successful against

Team	Win%	Win	Total	Draw	Lost
West Ham United	53.6	67	125	34	24
Derby County	52.63	70	133	29	34
Leeds United	50.88	58	114	29	27
Birmingham City	50.86	59	116	28	29
Stoke City	50.00	64	128	35	29
Nottingham Forest	49.14	57	116	29	30
Wolves	49.00	49	100	17	34
Aston Villa	48.91	90	184	39	55
Manchester City	48.50	81	167	44	42
Newcastle United	47.88	79	165	39	47

Top 10 teams that Liverpool have struggled against

Team	Lost%	Lost	Total	Win	Draw
Manchester United	39.57	74	187	62	51
Leicester City	36.00	36	100	41	23
Arsenal	35.51	76	214	82	56
Chelsea	34.34	57	166	74	35
Wolves	34.00	34	100	49	17
Bolton Wanderers	33.08	44	133	57	32
Sunderland	32.50	52	160	73	35
Sheffield United	31.30	41	131	59	31
Sheffield Wednesday	31.09	37	119	55	27
Everton	30.00	66	220	87	67

Only teams included that have played 100 games or more against Liverpool

Charlie Buchan scored five for Sunderland against Liverpool!

Orr,
Ronald

RONALD ORR was a huge success at Newcastle after he joined in May 1901. He won the League Championship in 1905 and 1907, and played 180 games for the Tynecastle club, scoring 69 goals.

Orr was top scorer at Liverpool in the 1908/09 season with 20 goals from 33 league games, almost single-handedly dragging the club out of relegation trouble. Liverpool and Bury were equal on 33 points in 15th place when they faced each other in the penultimate game of the season. Orr let fly with 'one of his old-time shots' in the sixth minute, but Bury went 2-1 up and the Second Division was looming. Orr equalised right before the interval and the game finished 2-2. Liverpool needed a point from their final game of the season against Newcastle, who had already secured the Championship. In a scrappy game at St James' Orr was again Liverpool's hero, scoring the only goal of the game in the 78th minute.

ORR played two out of the first three games in the 1911/12 campaign before damaging ligaments in his right leg in the Merseyside derby on 16 September 1911. He added two games to his Liverpool total in the middle of December, before returning to his native Scotland with Raith Rovers in January 1912.

Season	League		FA Cup		Total	
	App	Goals	App	Goals	App	Goals
1907/08	7	5	0	0	7	5
1908/09	33	20	2	3	35	23
1909/10	31	5	0	0	31	5
1910/11	30	5	2	0	32	5
1911/12	7	1	0	0	7	1
Total	**108**	**36**	**4**	**3**	**112**	**39**

Otsemobor, Jon

THE BOY from Speke was more frequently in the news due to his misadventures off the field during his stay at Liverpool. In October 2003 Otsemobor was shot in the buttocks by a small-calibre pistol in downtown Liverpool and his car was torched a couple of weeks later near his home.

Thankfully he recovered to make five first-team appearances in December 2003 while Steve Finnan was absent through injury. Phil Thompson, Liverpool's assistant manager, was pleased with his contribution. 'He's a shy and unassuming lad who gets the job done. He's got great pace and is very composed.' When Rafa Benítez took over he sent Otsemobor on loan to Crewe Alexandra in the Championship for the first half of the 2004/05 season, where he made 15 appearances. Despite Crewe's interest, Otsemobor wanted to have a final attempt at making a career at Liverpool but it was soon apparent he was not in Benítez's plans. Otsemobor has acquired hero status at his current club, Milton Keynes Dons, after back-heeling the injury-time winner in MK Dons' grudge

match against AFC Wimbledon in the second round of the FA Cup in December 2012.

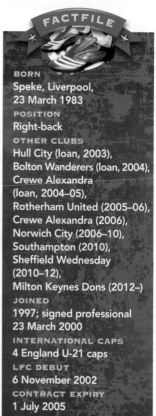

Season	League		FA Cup		League Cup		Europe		Other		Total	
	App	Goals	App	Goals	App	Goals	App	Goals	App	Goals	App	Goals
2002/03	0	0	0	0	1	0	0	0	0	0	1	0
2003/04	4	0	0	0	1	0	0	0	-	-	5	0
Total	**4**	**0**	**0**	**0**	**2**	**0**	**0**	**0**	**0**	**0**	**6**	**0**

Owen,
Michael

TERRY OWEN knew pretty early that his son, Michael, had a gift for goals. 'When he was five or six we used to take him along to the mini club, a kind of kid fun session at the Deeside Leisure Centre. There were all sorts of activities going on, trampolining, table-tennis, but all he was interested in was the football games. And his co-ordination and eye for a ball was quite exceptional for a five-year-old. Most lads of that age just toe punt the ball but Michael was a natural – he was tucking shots into the corner of the net with the side of his foot. You would have thought he was three or four years older than he was. It was remarkable.'

Michael supported his dad's favourites, Everton, as a lad. Terry, who played a couple of games for Everton, left it to Michael to decide. 'The first club to spot him playing for Deeside was Liverpool. Then Brian Kidd came down from Manchester United and there were plenty of others. But Steve Heighway, the Liverpool youth development officer, wrote us a smashing letter and it was love at first sight for Michael, he was impressed from day one.' At eight, Owen was selected for the Deeside Area Primary School's Under-11 team. At nine he was captain and at ten he smashed Ian Rush's 20-year record for the same team by scoring a staggering 97 goals in a single season, improving Rushie's record by 25 goals. His mother remembers: 'He scored 97 in his last season and he broke Gary Speed's appearance record because he'd played in all three seasons for the 11-year-olds since he was eight.' The prodigy attended the FA's School of Excellence at Lilleshall and he was soon playing for England teams

from Under-15 upwards, of course breaking more scoring records with 28 goals in 20 games for the England Under-15s and Under-16s.

In the 1995/96 season Owen played for Liverpool's youth team even though he was still at Lilleshall. Most of the players were 18, but Owen was only 16. He scored a hat-trick against holders Manchester United in the quarter-finals of the FA Youth Cup, netting the winner in added time. Owen scored another hat-trick in a 4-2 win in the first leg of the semi-final against Crystal Palace. Liverpool were 3-0 down after only 50 minutes in the second leg, but Jamie Cassidy reduced the deficit. The scores were level at 5-5 after 90 minutes, with Owen taking control in extra time and scoring two goals. Liverpool faced West Ham in the final, also played over two legs. West Ham hadn't lost in 24 consecutive games, boasting future stars like Rio Ferdinand and Frank Lampard in their team. Owen was missing from the first leg at Upton Park as he was busy scoring both goals for the England Under-16 team against Turkey in the European Youth Finals in Austria. Jon Newby shone in his absence as Liverpool won 2-0. Owen was back for the second leg alongside team-mates such as Jamie Carragher and David Thompson. Liverpool fell behind early but Owen equalised with his 11th goal in five cup matches and Stuart Quinn scored the winner. Liverpool had won the FA Youth Cup for the first time in the club's history.

OWEN celebrated his 17th birthday by signing a professional contract and being handed a place in Roy Evans' senior squad. Steve Heighway had no doubt that a glittering career was ahead. 'He is ready for whatever you throw at him; nothing fazes Michael Owen. If the manager wants a recommendation from me, Michael gets it.' Owen declared his intentions. 'I've scored between 40 and 45 goals this season in 30 to 35 games and now my aim is a first-team place in the next year or so.' Owen got his first taste of first-team football in the last couple of games in 1996/97, scoring on his debut against Wimbledon. Evans' plan was to ease the

young striker into the first team but Robbie Fowler's injury meant he was in the starting line-up for the first game of the 1997/98 season. 'We said before the season started that we would take care of him, nurse him along, but he has changed all that,' said Evans. 'He wants to play all the time.' Owen scored from the penalty spot in the first game of the season against Wimbledon. Regular penalty-taker Fowler was absent and Evans handed the responsibility to his young prodigy. On 16 September Owen made his European debut against Celtic at Parkhead. Did that faze him? No, it took him only six minutes to get on the scoresheet. On 1 October 1997 Owen signed a five-year contract with Liverpool worth a basic £2.5million. His £10,000-a-week deal made him the highest-paid teenager in British football. He became the youngest ever player in the twentieth century to make his debut for England, aged 18 years and 59 days, on 11 February 1998. He was top scorer in his first Premier League season with 18 goals, along with Dion Dublin and Chris Sutton, and voted PFA Young Player of the Year and third in the PFA Player of the Year award. Owen's incredible goal against Argentina in the World Cup in 1998 made him an international star.

'Form is temporary, class is permanent' is a phrase that has often been repeated in Owen's career. He always delivered a fair amount of goals every season when fit. Forty-six goals in 84 matches in Owen's first two full campaigns was way above what could be expected at a time the team was going through a big transition. Owen's hamstring first gave way on 12 April 1999 against Leeds at Elland Road, putting him out of action for almost five months. He returned to again score 20-plus goals in the 2000/01 season when he was crowned the 'Prince of Wales'

after his two late goals against Arsenal won the FA Cup. His ongoing hamstring trouble caused concern because he was so dependent on his burst of pace. Owen crowned a memorable 12 months when he became the first (and so far only) Liverpool player to be voted European Footballer of the Year, in 2001, becoming the first Briton to win the Ballon d'Or since Kevin Keegan in 1979. He received 176 points, 34 more than the formidable Raul, the Real Madrid and Spain forward. Owen was at his most prolific in the 2001/02 season with a goal in every 1.5 games, and made a career-high 54 appearances in the 2002/03 season when he was for the second consecutive season only two goals away from the 30-goal mark. Houllier made way for Rafa Benítez in the summer of 2004 and it also signalled the end for Owen at Liverpool. He wanted to test pastures new.

'Owen can be one of the world's great players and the best players must play for Real Madrid,' said Real Madrid president, Florentine Perez, who started as early as March 2002 to woo Owen. Houllier laughed off any apparent interest then. 'They might be able to afford Ronaldo but they cannot afford Michael Owen. For that kind of money they could only buy his left foot. Michael is Liverpool through and through and he is staying with me.'

In the end, with his contract running down, £8million prised him away from Anfield to Real.

'Since I was 10 I didn't just want to be a footballer, I wanted to be the best footballer in the world. I was taken aback when the first thing some people said was "How's he going to get into the first team?" They didn't say, "Fantastic, he's moving to the biggest club in the world".' Thirteen goals in 20 starts was by no means a bad record in Owen's sole season at the Bernabeu but he was still a fringe player with Raul and Ronaldo firmly first choice.

At the end of the season, Owen held discussions with Liverpool but once Newcastle offered a staggering £17million a return to the Reds was out of the question. Liverpool's chief executive Rick Parry could hardly believe what he was witnessing. 'Michael eventually emerges three coaches later as fifth choice, on a big wage and not happy, and then somebody knocks on the door and offers to double their money,' Parry said. 'I'm sure the first reaction was to rub their eyes in surprise. From our point of view, Michael on the right terms, certainly – but not on the wrong terms.'

NEWCASTLE in total conceded 14 goals to Michael Owen in 11 games when he was a Red so maybe it was no surprise they wanted to have him on their side! However, this risky move only delivered 26 goals in 81 league matches over four seasons. Owen scored an impressive seven goals in 11 matches in 2005/06, and had recovered in time to be selected for England duty in the 2006 World Cup. However, a serious knee injury in the first minute of the group match against Sweden kept him out of action for almost the entirety of the following campaign.

Defending Premier League champions Manchester United dramatically became Owen's third English league club to the dismay of Liverpool supporters. Few can have been surprised that Owen's high-profile and controversial move to Manchester was wrecked by injury. His highlights at United were a very late winner in the Manchester derby, a Champions League hat-trick at Wolfsburg and a Premier League winners' medal in 2011. On 4 September 2012 the 32-year-old signed for Stoke City on a 12-month pay-as-you-play contract. He only made nine appearances for the Potters, including just one start and a single goal, before retiring from football at the end of the 2012/13 season.

IN DECEMBER 2012 Owen reflected on his personal website on his struggle with injuries, having seen former team-mates enjoy lengthy careers into their late thirties. Owen played 316 games for club and country ahead of his 24th birthday – compare that with Ryan Giggs (112), Paul Scholes (123) and David Beckham (184). 'As a youngster, I was considered exceptional and in many ways, that was to my detriment. I would play a full season with Liverpool and then I was jetting off to play for England.' Owen was convinced that his hamstring injury in April 1999 proved a key moment.

My body made me pay for pushing it to the limit too often. My hamstring snapped in two and it was at that point that my ability to perform unimpeded was finished. My rehabilitation was compromised due to our physio leaving the club that summer and not being replaced until the following season. With no regular medical care, a routine injury was destined to restrict me for the rest of my career. People laugh when I say that I am not naturally injury prone. I cringe when I look back on a quote I came out with after Gérard Houllier rested me for a game. 'I will rest when I'm 40.'

Despite his great personal achievements at Liverpool, Owen was never quite beloved on the Kop as might be expected. From the player's point of view, he might always regret stating that he left Liverpool 'to win the big trophies', only to watch from a distance as his new club won nothing and his old club won the biggest trophy of all just a year later.

FACTFILE

BORN
Chester, 14 December 1979
POSITION
Centre-forward
OTHER CLUBS
Real Madrid (2004–05),
Newcastle United (2005–09),
Manchester United (2009–12),
Stoke City (2012–13)
JOINED
1990; signed professional
18 December 1996
INTERNATIONAL CAPS
89 England caps (40 goals)
(60 (26) at LFC), 1998–2008
LFC DEBUT GAME/GOAL
6 May 1997 / 6 May 1997
CONTRACT EXPIRY
14 August 2004
HONOURS
FA Cup 2001;
League Cup 2001, 2003;
UEFA Cup 2001;
PFA Young Player
of the Year 2001,
Premier League top scorer
1997/98, 1998/99,
European Footballer
of the Year 2001

Season	League		FA Cup		League Cup		Europe		Other		Total	
	App	Goals	App	Goals	App	Goals	App	Goals	App	Goals	App	Goals
1996/97	1 (1)	1	0	0	0	0	0	0	-	-	1 (1)	1
1997/98	34 (2)	18	0	0	4	4	3 (1)	1	-	-	41 (3)	23
1998/99	30	18	2	2	2	1	5 (1)	2	-	-	39 (1)	23
1999/2000	22 (5)	11	1	0	2	1	-	-	-	-	25 (5)	12
2000/01	20 (8)	16	4 (1)	3	1 (1)	1	10 (1)	4	-	-	35 (11)	24
2001/02	25 (4)	19	2	2	0	0	11	6	1	1	39 (4)	28
2002/03	32 (3)	19	2	0	3 (1)	2	11 (1)	7	1	0	49 (5)	28
2003/04	29	16	3	1	0	0	6	2	-	-	38	19
Total	**193 (23)**	**118**	**14 (1)**	**8**	**12 (2)**	**9**	**46 (4)**	**22**	**2**	**1**	**267 (30)**	**158**

Own Goals

SINCE DUNCAN McLean 'foolishly headed' in the equaliser after Liverpool had been leading Wolves 2-1 on 1 December 1894 a total of 135 Liverpool players have put the ball in their own net. Here are the ones who are top of that unwanted list.

Jamie Carragher (8)

Date	Opponent	Result
5 December 1998	Tottenham Hotspur	1-2
1 May 1999	Tottenham Hotspur	3-2
11 September 1999	Manchester United*	2-3
13 May 2006	West Ham United	3-3
1 November 2008	Tottenham Hotspur	1-2
13 December 2008	Hull City	2-2
24 October 2010	Blackburn Rovers	2-1

Carragher scored two own goals in the United game.

Ron Yeats (6)

Date	Opponent	Result
2 September 1961	Norwich City	2-1
14 October 1961	Walsall	6-1
26 August 1964	Leeds United	2-4
5 May 1966	Borussia Dortmund	1-2
25 February 1967	Fulham	2-2
13 December 1969	Manchester United	1-4

Dick White (5)

Date	Opponent	Result
15 January 1959	Worcester City	1-2
21 February 1959	Huddersfield Town	2-2
20 March 1959	Stoke City	3-4
7 October 1961	Middlesbrough*	0-2

* White scored two own goals in the Middlesbrough game.

Tiny Bradshaw (4)

Date	Opponent	Result
18 March 1933	Leeds United	0-5
6 May 1933	Sheffield Wednesday	4-1
29 August 1934	Manchester City	1-3
2 May 1936	Stoke City	1-2

Alan Hansen (4)

Date	Opponent	Result
4 December 1984	Coventry City	3-1
2 April 1988	Nottingham Forest	1-2
13 May 1989	Wimbledon	2-1
3 April 1990	Wimbledon	2-1

Sami Hyypia, Mark Lawrenson, Alec Lindsay, Phil Neal, John Arne Riise, Neil Ruddock and Phil Thompson all scored three own goals.

Oxley, Cyril

LIVERPOOL SCOUTS went to watch Chesterfield's goalscoring machine Jimmy Cookson, who scored 256 goals in 292 league matches, but left more impressed by Cyril Oxley whose skills set up a number of chances for his centre-forward.

It was a big step for Oxley to go from the Third Division North to the First Division but the right-winger went straight into Liverpool's first team and kept his place throughout the 1925/26 season. He played in 31 consecutive matches until the season ended, scoring six times, including one in a 3-3 draw with Everton. Following Dick Edmed's arrival in the summer of 1926 Oxley was firmly stuck in the

reserves for the next two seasons before departing for Southend United in the Third Division South in 1928.

FACTFILE

BORN
Worksop, 2 May 1904
DIED
20 December 1984
POSITION
Right-winger
OTHER CLUBS
Whitwell Colliery,
Chesterfield (1924–25),
Southend United (1928–29),
Kettering Town (1929–30),
Morecambe (1930–31),
Southend United (1931–32)
SIGNED FROM
Chesterfield, £2,000,
25 October 1925
LFC DEBUT GAME/GOAL
31 October 1925 /
14 November 1925
CONTRACT EXPIRY
September 1928

John Houlding was kicked out at Everton!

Gordon Hodgson and Dixie Dean on the same side in a cricket team

	League		FA Cup		Total	
Season	App	Goals	App	Goals	App	Goals
1925/26	31	6	3	0	34	6
Total	31	6	3	0	34	6

Pacheco, Dani

IN JUNE 2007, Dani Pacheco arrived from Barcelona's youth set-up where there was an abundance of attacking talent. He was far and away the best player in Liverpool's reserves in the 2009/10 season and finally got his first-team chance when he came on for Alberto Aquilani against Fiorentina in the Champions League on 9 December 2009.

Pacheco's playing style reminds one of Yossi Benayoun and the little Spaniard said he did try to copy the Israeli's moves at Anfield. His career hasn't taken off as expected though and he has only made five starts at Liverpool.

Pacheco moved to Norwich City on an 'emergency loan' move on 23 March 2011. He contributed to their promotion charge by scoring twice in the six Championship fixtures in which he featured. Pacheco went on a season-long loan to Atletico Madrid in August 2011 but curiously Atletico then immediately allowed him to go out on loan to Rayo Vallecano. Their reasoning was to see if he developed further elsewhere and then maybe buy him off Liverpool at the end of the season for a fixed price. Pacheco only played in 11 La Liga matches for Vallecano in 2011/12 and Atletico didn't use their option to buy him outright. On the final day of the January 2013 transfer window, Pacheco moved on loan for the rest of the season to Spanish second-division club Sociedad Deportiva Huesca. Pacheco is still young but it looks increasingly unlikely he will have a prosperous career at Liverpool.

FACTFILE

BORN
Malaga, Spain,
5 January 1991
POSITION
Midfielder
OTHER CLUBS
Norwich City (loan, 2011),
Atletico Madrid
(loan, 2011–12),
Rayo Vallecano (loan,
2011–12), Huesca (loan, 2013)
SIGNED FROM
Barcelona (youth),
30 June 2007
INTERNATIONAL CAPS
2 Spain U-21 caps
LFC DEBUT
9 December 2009

Season	League		FA Cup		League Cup		Europe		Total	
	App	Goals	App	Goals	App	Goals	App	Goals	App	Goals
2009/10	0 (4)	0	0	0	0	0	0 (3)	0	0 (7)	0
2010/11	0 (1)	0	0	0	1	0	2 (3)	0	3 (4)	0
2012/13	0	0	0	0	1	0	1 (1)	0	2 (1)	0
Total	**0 (5)**	**0**	**0**	**0**	**2**	**0**	**3 (7)**	**0**	**5 (12)**	**0**

Padelli, Daniele

A FORMER Italian Under-20 and Under-21 international keeper who was loaned to Liverpool from Sampdoria in the January 2007 transfer window, Daniele Padelli had made his Under-21 debut for Italy against Luxemburg on 12 December 2006, coming on as substitute in a game that turned out to be his only one at that level.

PADELLI returned to Sampdoria after conceding two goals in Liverpool's 2-2 draw with Charlton in the last league game of the 2006/07 season (that was also Robbie Fowler's last appearance for the club).

Parent club Sampdoria continued to loan Padelli to other Italian clubs and following his loan spell at Udinese in the 2011/12 season he made a permanent move there. He featured against Liverpool in the last game of the group stage of the Europa League on 7 December 2012. He conceded one goal to Jordan Henderson but made two tremendous close-range saves from Luis Suarez.

FACTFILE

BORN
Lecco, Italy, 25 October 1985
POSITION
Goalkeeper
OTHER CLUBS
Sampdoria (2004–12),
Pizzighettone (loan, 2005–06),
Crotone (loan, 2006),
Pisa (loan, 2007–08),
Avellino (loan, 2008–09),
Bari (loan, 2009–11),
Udinese (loan, 2011–12;
permanent, 2012–)
LOANED FROM
Sampdoria, 9 January 2007
INTERNATIONAL CAPS
1 Italy U-21 cap
LFC DEBUT
13 May 2007
CONTRACT EXPIRY
8 June 2007

Season	League		FA Cup		League Cup		Europe		Other		Total	
	App	Goals	App	Goals	App	Goals	App	Goals	App	Goals	App	Goals
2006/07	1	0	0	0	0	0	0	0	0	0	1	0
Total	**1**	**0**	**0**	**0**	**0**	**0**	**0**	**0**	**0**	**0**	**1**	**0**

Pagnam,
Fred

ALTHOUGH HIS Liverpool career was a brief one in terms of games, Fred Pagnam was a robust forward who had an outstanding goals-per-game ratio while he was at Anfield. Fred's father had been much averse to his son taking up football as a profession but luckily for Liverpool he didn't get his way.

Old Liverpool stalwart and former Blackpool player-manager Jack Cox recommended Pagnam to Liverpool and according to the *Liverpool Echo* after he had completed his first season he was 'generally recognised as the best find of the year in Division 1 circles'. Pagnam scored on his Liverpool debut at Chelsea on 10 October 1914 and three weeks later hit the net four times as Tottenham were crushed 7-2 at Anfield. Pagnam was easily the club's top scorer that season with 26 goals from 31 appearances.

In 1917, Pagnam gave evidence in the famous match-fixing scandal involving seven Liverpool and Manchester United players who had taken bribes to let their game

end 2-0 in United's favour on Good Friday 1915. Pagnam said he was illegally approached en route to the game and offered £3 by Liverpool's Jackie Sheldon to throw the game, but had refused to participate. Like so many players of his generation, his professional career was cut short by World War One, but he maintained his prolific scoring record for Liverpool in wartime matches, 43 goals in 49 matches.

Pagnam scored four goals in his eight league appearances for Liverpool in the 1919/20 season before joining Arsenal for £1,500, the biggest transfer of the season so far, in October 1919. Pagnam had an impressive scoring record in the First Division with the Gunners: 26 goals in 50 league matches. Despite being the club's top scorer in his second season he was sold, to raise some much-needed funds, to Cardiff City for £3,000, helping the Welsh side gain promotion to the First Division with eight goals in 14 matches. Pagnam only stayed

there for six months after failing to score in his first 13 top-flight games in the 1921/22 season, suffering the only lean spell of his career. He left Cardiff for Watford in the Third Division South in December 1921 and netted 49 goals in 72 matches over a season and a half. His most famous feat at the Hornets was scoring three hat-tricks in a run of five games. According to Watford historians he was 'a non-conformist whose quirky personality was not universally popular'. While still a player he had to apologise to the Watford directors for his behaviour towards his team-mates.

Pagnam must, however, have impressed the hierarchy at Vicarage Road as he was Watford's manager from 1926 to 1929. He also had a spell in charge of the Turkish national team in 1931 and coached in the Netherlands for eight years. His coaching overseas ended when he had to escape the Nazis with his Dutch wife in 1940.

FACTFILE

BORN
Poulton-le-Fylde, Lancashire,
4 September 1891
DIED
1 March 1962
POSITION
Centre-forward
OTHER CLUBS
Lytham,
Blackpool Wednesday
(1909–10),
Huddersfield Town (1910–12),
Southport Central (1912–13),
Blackpool (1913–14),
Arsenal (1919–21),
Cardiff City (1921),
Watford (1921–26)
SIGNED FROM
Blackpool, 21 May 1914
LFC DEBUT GAME/GOAL
10 October 1914 /
10 October 1914
CONTRACT EXPIRY
17 October 1919

Season	League		FA Cup		Total	
	App	Goals	App	Goals	App	Goals
1914/15	29	24	2	2	31	26
1919/20	8	4	0	0	8	4
Total	**37**	**28**	**2**	**2**	**39**	**30**

Paisley,
Bob

'I WAS AGGRESSIVE but I played the game because I loved and enjoyed it. I might have hurt people and I got hurt myself a few times, but not with any malice. When I went on to the field I just wanted to play football,' said Bob Paisley of his playing career.

Paisley established himself in the Liverpool side as an uncompromising left-half when league football resumed at the end of World War Two and immediately won the league title, the first of many championships he would be associated with as player, trainer/coach, assistant manager and eventually manager of the only professional club he served during his long career in the game. Albert Stubbins, who was Paisley's team-mate in the championship team of 1947, was grateful for his inclusion in the side: 'Bob Paisley offered so much energy in the course of a game that I often thought he would be stretchered off when the final whistle sounded.'

Paisley knew everything about hard work from his upbringing. 'Hetton-le-hole is a typical Durham mining village, a close-knit community seven miles from Sunderland where coal was king and football was religion,'

Paisley said. Bob was the third eldest of four brothers, Willie and Hugh being the oldest, and Alan the youngest. Bob's father Sam worked in the local mine, and his mother Emily was the homemaker who kept the family's body and soul together through the days of depression and hardship. During the General Strike in 1926 the seven-year-old Bob was forced to scramble over slag heaps collecting coal dust that could be mixed with water to make a crude fuel, and along with his childhood friends at school he depended on the soup kitchens to supplement a meagre diet. Paisley's precocious talents as a schoolboy footballer were well noted in the County Durham area. His performances as a 15-year-old for Hetton Juniors attracted scouts from further afield. Unfortunately for Paisley his childhood dream of playing for Sunderland was crushed as he was deemed too small by the club. He suffered rejection for the same reason at the hands of Wolves and Spurs and it seemed his footballing ambitions were not to be realised. Bishop Auckland came to Paisley's rescue as they signed him up prior to the start of the 1937/38 season and he was paid the princely sum of three shillings and sixpence per match. The Bishops were one of England's premier non-league clubs and ferried their players to matches in private luxury cars. Quite a stir was caused on match days in Hetton as Paisley was invariably picked up by a hired Rolls-Royce.

In the incredible treble-winning season of 1938/39 Bishop Auckland collected their tenth amateur championship, a non-league record, and Sunderland's interest in signing Paisley was reignited. However, Liverpool were now on the scene, and Paisley had promised Liverpool manager George Kay that at the end of the season he would sign for them. Bishop Auckland won the Amateur Cup at Roker Park when they beat Willington 3-0 after extra time. Paisley played his part in an incredible run-in to the season that saw the team play 11 matches in 14 days. There was still one more cup final for the Bishops to play on 6 May 1939. They beat South Shields to take the Durham Challenge Cup and thus completed their treble. Two days later Paisley boarded a train to Exchange Street station in Liverpool to begin an association that was to last over half a century. He duly signed for Liverpool for a £25 signing-on fee plus £8 a week in season and £6 a week during the summer. 'I was

full of beans that day, but it was very quiet really,' Paisley remembered. 'I was met at the station and after that long trek up Scotland Road in a tramcar I found there were only one or two youngsters at the ground – Billy Liddell, Eddie Spicer and Ray Lambert. The rest had been recruited for the territorials.'

BEFORE being posted abroad in the war in 1941 Paisley made 34 appearances and scored 10 goals for Liverpool, the majority of them coming in the North Regional League. He joined the 73rd Regiment of the Royal Artillery, serving as an anti-tank gunner with Montgomery's Eighth Army, the so-called Desert Rats, in the watershed victory at El Alamein. But there was still time for sport even then and Bob once captained the regimental hockey team and then played football and cricket all in the same day! It was during this time he also began to cultivate an interest in racehorses, an interest that was to endure for

the rest of his life. While Bob was on active service in Italy he was given the news that his younger brother Alan had died back home at the age of 15 from scarlet fever and diphtheria. On hearing this news, Bob wandered aimlessly away from where he had been positioned, understandably dazed and upset by what he had heard; moments later a shell dropped and exploded right where he had been. The tragic news had saved his life. In June 1944 he rode aboard a tank as the Allies liberated Rome. It was a proud moment as the relieving forces were welcomed as heroes by the Italians.

'Paisley went in, was beaten, then had the temerity to go back for more. The result was that Matthews, who had left him yards behind, suddenly found the second tackle the lethal one. Matthews mesmerised Lambert, but he did no such thing to Paisley.' A press report on the battle between Sir Stanley Matthews and Paisley in a Liverpool–Blackpool game.

PAISLEY resumed his Liverpool career in 1945/46, featuring in the FA Cup as well as the temporary North and South Division set up by the Football League. On 31 August 1946, in a team that boasted Jackie Balmer and the great Billy Liddell, Liverpool finally kicked off the new post-war era. Paisley missed the opening two matches but made his full league debut in the third game of the season against Chelsea at Anfield on 7 September. On a dramatic afternoon Paisley helped Liverpool to an incredible 7-4 victory. According to the *Liverpool Echo*: 'Paisley and Liddell transformed the attack.' Four days after the Chelsea goal feast the Reds crashed 5-0 to Matt Busby's Manchester United and manager Kay promptly went out and signed 28-year-old Albert Stubbins from Newcastle United for a club record £13,000. The signing of Stubbins proved a masterstroke and Liverpool marched to the title. Paisley played in 33 of Liverpool's 42 league matches that season and quickly established himself at left-half as a mainstay of the side. He had gained the admiration of others in the squad through his hard work, tenacity and his ability to correctly analyse the game's turning points in the dressing room afterwards. Stubbins remarked: 'The fact that he went on to carve out a successful management career was a big surprise to me because as a player Bob was so quiet. During the week he had never much to say. It was only after a game, when we were relaxing in the hot bath, that Bob would speak and then we couldn't shut him up!' Paisley had won several admirers in the press for his dogged displays. 'Left-half is where he shines and this season his dour, bulldog-like displays have made him a great favourite. Has won a regular place by sheer dogged tenacity, keen tackling and tireless energy. Is one of the best throw-in experts.'

If the success of 1946/47 had been a heady one for Liverpool, the following years were something of an anticlimax for the club. In 1949/50 Liverpool were seemingly marching on to new glories as they ripped through the first 19 league games unbeaten. It set a new record in English football, finally broken by Leeds United in 1973/74. Unfortunately, after losing their first game of the season to Huddersfield on 10 December the wheels began to come off the league campaign and attention turned instead to the FA Cup. The club progressed confidently through to the semi-finals after dismissing Blackpool 2-1 at Anfield. Neighbours Everton provided the opposition at Manchester City's Maine Road in front of 73,000 spectators. Paisley was never renowned as a goalscorer but a lob from the left caught the Everton goalkeeper out after 29 minutes. Liddell added another in the second half as Liverpool celebrated their first FA Cup final participation since 1914. But there was great disappointment in store for the likeable Geordie. He had been absent through a knee injury leading up to the final but was declared fit in the days before the game. 'When people talk of their darkest day this was mine. I read that I wouldn't be playing in a newspaper, and the bottom fell out of my world,' Paisley told Horace Yates in the *Liverpool Echo* in 1979.

Even now I cringe a bit when I think of it, not just because we lost 2-0, but because I lost my place. We had two international centre-halves, Bill Jones and Laurie Hughes. Before the final they were both chosen for England, one in the B team, and I expect that put the directors under some pressure. I was never big-headed and had never taken it for granted that I would be picked, but it was a knockout blow all the same. Wembley was the event of the season, probably even more than it is today. I was offered what was big money in those days to pour out my heart to a newspaper. Thankfully I thought the better of it. That was the only occasion in my lifetime when I was disenchanted with Liverpool. I have lived to bless the day when I bit my tongue and said nothing. I didn't want to move really.

Paisley also said this disappointment helped him when he had to make similarly tough decisions as a manager.

A press report said: 'If I had to choose three outstanding examples of players who can combine non-stop running and boundless energy with effective use of the ball I would choose Paisley, Forrest (Bolton) and Shankly (Preston).' So Paisley was already being mentioned in the same breath as Shankly!

Paisley remained at Liverpool and went on to play 41 of the 42 league games in the 1950/51 season, but Liverpool were now set inexorably on a downward spiral. George Kay stood down as manager in February 1951 through ill health and was replaced by Don Welsh, but the decline was gathering pace. In the following three seasons Liverpool finished ninth, 11th, and 17th. Relegation to the Second Division was avoided only on the last day of the 1952/53 season when the Reds roared to a 2-0 win over Chelsea at Anfield. Inevitably, Liverpool were relegated at the end of the 1953/54 season. Paisley was 35 years old and on 4 May 1954 it was made public in the *Liverpool Evening Express* that 'Bobby Paisley, the tough little North-Easterner who specialises in the long throw and is of the never-say-die order' was not on the retained list of players for the coming season.

PAISLEY had his future mapped out as he revealed in a 1950 FA Cup final souvenir brochure. 'Though I hope to have a few more seasons still in senior football, I am studying to be a physiotherapist and masseur when my playing days are over. We married men have to look to the future, you know.'

Paisley had studied physiotherapy for two years before his retirement as a player and visited local hospitals to sit in on operations and observe medical practices. 'The physio side probably stemmed from the knocks I got as a player,' Paisley said. 'If I was pinned down I'd say that was my greatest asset. I could speak to players and give them examples of injuries and how they heal.' Liverpool offered Paisley the job of reserve-team manager in 1954 and eventually his skill with the new electrical equipment made him the in-house physio. Liverpool struggled to adjust to life in the Second Division. Meanwhile, after finding his feet in his new role, Bob Paisley's reserves, which he inherited from Jimmy Seddon, began to make pleasing headway. In his second term at the helm Paisley guided the reserves to runners-up spot in the Central League. Phil Taylor, who had quit playing for Liverpool at the same time as Paisley, took over essentially as caretaker-manager after Welsh's sacking at the end of the 1955/56 season and having served his

apprenticeship for a whole season he was appointed as manager outright, as the *Liverpool Echo* reported on 1 May 1957. 'While Mr Taylor has been acting manager, the club did not fill the coaching position which he formerly occupied. They have now appointed Bob Paisley, at present second-team trainer, as chief coach. He will take up the duties when the players report for training next season. There was a big difference in the styles of play of Phil Taylor and Bob Paisley; the one stylish and thoughtful; the other rugged and determined. If they work in double harness in such a way as to bring the best out of the player in the same directions Liverpool should benefit considerably.' A series of near-miss promotion attempts ensued as the 1950s turned into a frustrating decade for the Reds that ended with the blessing of Bill Shankly's arrival.

In 1969, after 30 years at Liverpool, Paisley revealed to the readers of the *Liverpool Echo* how to be a successful trainer.

A trainer's life is one of the busiest of all the jobs associated with running a football club. It is a seven-day-a-week affair. I have to go back a long, long time since I last remember a day during which I didn't set foot in Anfield and that includes Sundays. A trainer is a combination of everything. He has to have expert medical knowledge, immense football experience, be quick and alert in summing up any conceivable situation both on and off the field, and when it comes to an injury he must, into the bargain, be something of a psychologist. You have to know your players inside out. Some need encouragement, others need bullying; and you've got to know which are which, otherwise results can be disastrous.

'THAT WAS THE ONLY OCCASION IN MY LIFETIME WHEN I WAS DISENCHANTED WITH LIVERPOOL. I HAVE LIVED TO BLESS THE DAY WHEN I BIT MY TONGUE AND SAID NOTHING'

Bill Shankly to-day praises the Anfield training staff
—Joe Fagan, Bob Paisley and Reuben Bennett.

Paisley also divulged 'old-school' tricks of the trade on how to handle an injured player that makes wonderful reading. 'It's no good telling a player he's going to be off for six weeks, because he becomes lax in his personal life. He might be tempted to stay out late, drinking and smoking. And a few days like that can destroy all the work that had been done in his training for months. In many ways you have to be a con man, [tell him] his injury is only minor and that he could be playing next Saturday. It's not different from faith healing for if a player thinks his injury is minor it often happens it heals quicker.'

In 1971 when Shankly signed what was to be his last contract for Liverpool Paisley was promoted to assistant manager with Joe Fagan replacing him as first-team coach. Three years later, at 55 years of age, Paisley became the successor to Shankly. Some thought that Shankly had made a hasty decision he would later regret. New chairman, John Smith, offered him a contract on an increased salary, but it wasn't about money. Shankly had been at Liverpool for nearly 15 years and it was a terrible wrench to leave. He recalls in his autobiography that he suggested to the directors that 'the only way to make the changeover was to promote the rest of the staff'. He even added that he had 'elevated them earlier with a view to what I was going to do later on'. Having signed professional forms in May 1939,

Paisley had already been at Anfield twice as long as Shankly and, despite his reluctance to take the job, if the job was going to remain in-house, he was the only logical candidate. Paisley knew the club and the game inside out and was a fine judge of a player. He had an almost uncanny ability of being able to correctly diagnose an injury and treat it accordingly. But where personality was concerned Bob was totally opposite to Bill. He had been in the background for so long that the responsibility of dealing with the press was frightening. Paisley knew the enormity of the task at hand and confessed to the press: 'It's like being given the Queen Elizabeth to steer in a Force 10 gale.' Chief executive Peter Robinson confirms Paisley had to be virtually manhandled to accept the responsibility. 'When we approached Bob he said "no". In the end the chairman, directors and I had to gang up on him.'

While Paisley prepared for his first league game against Luton Town on 17 August 1974 Shankly spent his first Saturday afternoon in retirement watching his local home match, Everton v. Derby County. Even though Paisley wasn't the darling of the media like Shankly he showed early on that he was also capable of a one-liner. When the press asked Bob what Shankly was doing this particular afternoon, he replied: 'He's trying to get right away from football. I believe he went to Everton.' Paisley's first season in charge was not a success, not by the high standards set by his predecessor anyway. The team fought hard to reclaim the league title but defeat at Middlesbrough on the penultimate weekend of the season meant their challenge was over. There was disappointment in the cups too, with a late Ipswich goal at Portman Road putting the holders out of the FA Cup and Middlesbrough beating them in the League Cup at Anfield in November. Liverpool enjoyed their biggest ever competitive victory with an 11-0 thrashing of the Norwegian part-timers from Drammen in the opening round of the Cup Winners' Cup, but conceding a last-minute equaliser at home to Ferencvaros in the next round was a blow the team was unable to recover from. As things turned out, that 1974/75 season would be the only one during Paisley's reign that no silverware was won.

CONTINUITY on the pitch was vital to the club's success. The sort of wholesale buying and selling that would be commonplace long after his retirement was not part of Paisley's agenda. Changes were made gradually and the newcomers integrated carefully into an already successful side. Phil Neal arrived in 1974, soon replacing Alec Lindsay, the only change to the regular XI in Paisley's debut season from Shankly's last campaign. Terry McDermott, who had arrived from Newcastle, was having trouble adjusting as well as the final signing of

the Shankly era, Ray Kennedy. In March 1975, following four draws in a row, Paisley did change Shankly's usual formation. 'Earlier in the season, I could not alter the older style of play, because the players would not have accepted it. The players, I think, have matured in the last few months and they played in a very grown-up way against Burnley,' Paisley told the *Echo*. 'Liverpool have never been the team to change tactics, we've always played one way, total commitment to going forward. But so many times this season we have found out to our cost that this method didn't pay. With Kevin Keegan pulled back a little from the front line, the style is changing.'

In 1975/76 the most vital changes to Paisley's side took place in midfield. Peter Cormack's days were numbered following Paisley's successful transformation of Ray Kennedy into a left-sided midfielder and Jimmy Case was promoted from the reserves to replace the industrious Brian Hall. Liverpool's improvement on the road provided Paisley's team with nine more points to win the League Championship in 1976 as well as repeating Shankly's UEFA Cup success from 1973. Prior to the 1976/77 season Liverpool purchased David Johnson, who slowly made his mark on the team, while Joey Jones was preferred to Tommy Smith in defence. Liverpool retained the league title and were unbeaten at home in the league, a feat Shankly only accomplished once in the top division, in 1970/71. Liverpool embarked on a historic run in the European Cup in which young striker David Fairclough proved vital as well as old hand Tommy Smith, who returned to the centre of defence late in the season following Phil Thompson's injury.

Shankly had seen his European dream crushed in 1965 amidst claims of matchfixing, but there was no stopping Paisley's army.

Liverpool faced Crusaders first on their way to Rome. 'I remember the Ulstermen packing their penalty area at Anfield and making it extremely difficult for us to find the space to create chances. One of their players lost a contact lens during the game and I told him, "There's only one place it will be, in the penalty area!"' Paisley quipped. Liverpool were one goal down after the first leg against Trabzonspor, which was a terrible experience as Ray Clemence recalls. 'The pitch had rocks all over it. The hotel was awful and we were woken by the noise of farm animals at 5am.' The Turkish side didn't stand a chance at Anfield as Liverpool scored three in the opening 19 minutes. Again Liverpool made it difficult for themselves by losing the away

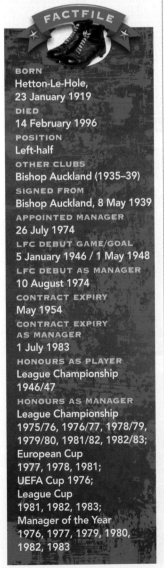

FACTFILE

BORN
Hetton-Le-Hole,
23 January 1919
DIED
14 February 1996
POSITION
Left-half
OTHER CLUBS
Bishop Auckland (1935–39)
SIGNED FROM
Bishop Auckland, 8 May 1939
APPOINTED MANAGER
26 July 1974
LFC DEBUT GAME/GOAL
5 January 1946 / 1 May 1948
LFC DEBUT AS MANAGER
10 August 1974
CONTRACT EXPIRY
May 1954
**CONTRACT EXPIRY
AS MANAGER**
1 July 1983
HONOURS AS PLAYER
League Championship
1946/47
HONOURS AS MANAGER
League Championship
1975/76, 1976/77, 1978/79,
1979/80, 1981/82, 1982/83;
European Cup
1977, 1978, 1981;
UEFA Cup 1976;
League Cup
1981, 1982, 1983;
Manager of the Year
1976, 1977, 1979, 1980,
1982, 1983

match in France in the quarter-finals, but that defeat to Saint Etienne set up a thrilling finale in the match at Anfield where Fairclough raced on to a through ball with six minutes left and, as the *Daily Mirror* reported, a few precious seconds later saw him 'buried under a pile of hugging and kissing team-mates'. Austrian champions FC Zurich were easily dispatched in the semi-final before Paisley put down a marker when Liverpool were triumphant in Rome. Paisley famously declared: 'This is the second time I've beaten the Germans here... the first time was in 1944. I drove into Rome on a tank when the city was liberated. If anyone had told me I'd be back here to see us win the European Cup 33 years later I'd have told them they were mad!'

RON YEATS, Shankly's former captain, saw Liverpool come of age in Europe, as he told *LFChistory.net*. 'Unfortunately for our team, we went to the semi-final of the European Cup and the final of the Cup Winners' without winning it. The team after us won everything, four European Cups. But they had learned from us. You learn from a team's mistakes. In the beginning of Europe we used to be gung-ho. I can remember the away tactics, go at them! Get a goal! Get two goals! We did this at times and it would come off, but sometimes it doesn't. When it doesn't come off, you're out of the competition.'

Arguably the greatest signing Paisley ever made brought a new dimension to the side. Kenny Dalglish replaced Kevin Keegan as the catalyst at Liverpool in 1977. Two months later Paisley made another key signing in Graeme Souness from Middlesbrough. The third Scot, Alan Hansen, had joined in May 1977. Paisley had formed the core of the side that was going to achieve more than any other previous Liverpool team. Amazingly Paisley won the European Cup for the second year running, but lost the league to Nottingham Forest. Winning can become a habit but Liverpool were winning in style, no more so than during the 1978/79 season when they scored 85 goals in their 42 league fixtures with Ray Clemence only conceding 16 at the other end. During the eight years before he stood down in 1983, Paisley's teams won the English Championship six times and also won four European trophies as well as taking the much-maligned League Cup more seriously than before and achieving a hat-trick of victories in his last three seasons as manager, an achievement that would be added to in Joe Fagan's initial year in charge. The domestic success was remarkable on its own but to couple it with unparalleled triumphs in Europe was almost beyond belief. Bob Paisley became the only man to coach teams to the European Champions' Cup on three different occasions.

> PAISLEY'S TEAMS WON THE ENGLISH CHAMPIONSHIP SIX TIMES AND ALSO WON FOUR EUROPEAN TROPHIES AS WELL AS TAKING THE MUCH-MALIGNED LEAGUE CUP MORE SERIOUSLY THAN BEFORE

PAISLEY gave some insight into his way of thinking in the *Liverpool Daily Post* on 21 April 1983 at the end of his career as Liverpool manager.

I have always preferred to liken the Championship to a marathon. You have to know how to start the race, how to take the strain when problems come along and to make sure you don't give any potentially dangerous rivals an advantage. My policy is to ideally have five or six men around the age of 26, a couple of youngsters, a couple round the 28 mark and one or two in their 30s. But the nucleus of the team should be experienced and not too old. You don't just look at the calendar. The medical side is an important yardstick. Our two over-30s are Phil Neal and Kenny Dalglish. Phil is the type of player who doesn't often get injured. Kenny takes more knocks than the others, but he is very strong. They have been outstanding from a stamina point of view as well as in skill. They have kept going as well as anyone. But they still need that help from the younger players.

By the time he retired in 1983, Bob Paisley had been associated with Liverpool Football Club for 44 years. He would continue to offer advice to his successor Kenny Dalglish for a couple of years before becoming a board member.

such devotion and such success? The answer is almost certainly not. Knowing that the 1983 League Cup final would be the last time Paisley would lead his team out as manager at Wembley, the players graciously allowed their boss to climb the famous steps to collect the trophy on their behalf. A man who preferred to stay in the background had a special moment to remember that is one of the most heart-warming sights Liverpool fans have ever seen. A few weeks later Paisley walked out at Anfield for the last time as the man in charge to be presented with the League Championship trophy yet again. Bob Paisley, the man who had to follow a legend, had become one himself. The epitaph on his tombstone says is all: 'He remained an ordinary man amid extraordinary achievements.'

With his mentor by his side Dalglish led the club to the League and FA Cup double in his first season in charge. There was some irony in that because the FA Cup was the one domestic trophy that had eluded Paisley as a manager.

PAISLEY had an uncanny ability to spot players who suited his philosophy and knew how to get the best out of them. 'There are five things generally accepted to be necessary to make a footballer: skill, strength, stamina, speed and flexibility,' Paisley preached. 'You have to bear these factors in mind when you are putting together your training programme. The whole scene is a stamina test, a marathon race. Strength has to be developed from the start. You build that up, giving the player a higher resistance to things. Skill comes next, developed with a constant repetition of pattern. Speed comes after you've run them in. Then you start to get them stretching out. Flexibility is important, and we probably suffer in this country because of our climate. It's a well-known fact that players performing in warmer climates have a wider range of movements.'

THERE WERE as many great games during Paisley's time in charge as there were great players. This can only be a general summary of an astonishing period in the club's history. Will there ever again be one man who serves the club for so long and with

As a Player

Season	League		FA Cup		Total	
	App	Goals	App	Goals	App	Goals
1945/46	-	-	4	0	4	0
1946/47	33	0	6	0	39	0
1947/48	37	1	2	0	39	1
1948/49	36	1	4	0	40	1
1949/50	23	1	5	1	28	2
1950/51	41	1	1	0	42	1
1951/52	37	2	3	1	40	3
1952/53	26	2	0	0	26	2
1953/54	19	2	0	0	19	2
Total	252	10	25	2	277	12

As a Manager

Season	Division	P	W	D	L	GF	GA	Pts	Pos	Win %	FA Cup	League Cup
1974/75	1st Division	42	20	11	11	60	39	51	2	47.62	4th Round	4th Round
1975/76	1st Division	42	23	14	5	66	31	60	1	54.76	4th Round	3rd Round
1976/77	1st Division	42	23	11	8	62	33	57	1	54.76	Runners-Up	2nd Round
1977/78	1st Division	42	24	9	9	65	34	57	2	57.14	3rd Round	Runners-Up
1978/79	1st Division	42	30	8	4	85	16	68	1	71.43	Semi-Final	2nd Round
1979/80	1st Division	42	25	10	7	81	30	60	1	59.52	Semi-Final	Semi-Final
1980/81	1st Division	42	17	17	8	62	42	51	5	40.48	4th Round	Winners
1981/82	1st Division	42	26	9	7	80	32	87	1	61.90	5th Round	Winners
1982/83	1st Division	42	24	10	8	87	37	82	1	57.14	5th Round	Winners
Total	-	378	212	99	67	648	294	573	-	56.08	-	-

As a Manager in Europe

Season	European Cup	UEFA Cup	European Cup Winners' Cup
1974/75	-	-	2nd Round
1975/76	-	Winners	-
1976/77	Winners	-	-
1977/78	Winners	-	-
1978/79	1st Round	-	-
1979/80	1st Round	-	-
1980/81	Winners	-	-
1981/82	3rd Round	-	-
1982/83	3rd Round	-	-

Paisley Gateway

ON 8 APRIL 1999, Liverpool Football Club unveiled the Paisley Gateway, a belated but welcome tribute by the club towards one of its greatest servants, Bob Paisley, four weeks prior to the 60th anniversary of Paisley joining the club on 8 May 1939.

The commemorative gates are in front of the Kop on Walton Breck Road. Bob's widow, Jessie, had taken an instrumental role in the design in tandem with architects Atherden Fuller Leng, who also designed the Shankly Gates and the Hillsborough Memorial. Jessie was the guest of honour, uncovering the gates to a wide and appreciative audience including her family, former players and officials of Liverpool FC.

The gates stand an imposing 14ft (4.5m) high and weigh over two tons (1800kg). Prominent in the design of the gates is the European Cup, appearing in three places across the top archway, one for each of Bob's triumphs in Rome, London and Paris. The gates feature the crests of his birthplace, Hetton-le-Hole, and the liver bird of his 'adopted' city of Liverpool. The Hetton-le-Hole crest is made up of an eye-catching early steam engine,

an acknowledgement of the area's pioneering role in the rail revolution. Four footballs surround each of the crests. On the brick pillars that flank the gates sit two bronze reliefs, one depicting the man himself and the other detailing the list of honours he brought to Liverpool FC.

Other family members present at the unveiling were Bob and Jessie's sons Robert and Graham and daughter Christine, as well

as Bob's brother Hughie and his wife Mary, who had travelled down from Hetton.

JESSIE was presented with a ceremonial key to the gates and paid the following moving tribute to her late husband. 'If this was an Oscar ceremony I would be expected to fling my arms around, burst into tears and say Bob didn't deserve it. But although the tears aren't far away, I'm not going to say that. If you ask me if Bob deserved it, I say, "Yes, 100 per cent".'

A BELATED BUT WELCOME TRIBUTE BY THE CLUB TOWARDS ONE OF ITS GREATEST SERVANTS, BOB PAISLEY

Paletta, Gabriel

GABRIEL PALETTA starred for the Argentinian Under-20 team that won the 2005 FIFA World Youth Championship, alongside starlets such as Lionel Messi and Sergio Aguero. He had come a long way in one year, having established himself at Banfield, a small club in the greater Buenos Aires. Liverpool's scouts were impressed by the towering centre-half and wasted no time signing him.

The BBC's South American expert, Tim Vickery, was impressed by the highly promising defender, but felt at the time Paletta needed 'some more mileage before making the move across the Atlantic'.

VICKERY proved to be correct in assuming that Paletta would struggle. He played eight times in Liverpool's first team in his only season at Anfield and clearly had difficulty in adapting to English football, which was painfully clear

during Liverpool's 6-3 loss to Arsenal at Anfield in the fifth round of the League Cup. Paletta joined Boca Juniors at the start of the 2007/08 season. He helped them reach the semi-final of the 2008 Copa Libertadores, where the Buenos Aires club lost 5-3 on aggregate to the Brazilians from Fluminense. In July 2010 Paletta left for Italian Serie A club Parma. The Argentinian has become a firm fixture in the middle of Parma's defence, clearly more ready when he left Boca to play in Europe.

FACTFILE

BORN
Buenos Aires, Argentina,
15 February 1986
POSITION
Centre-half
OTHER CLUBS
Club Atlético Banfield
(2002–06),
Boca Juniors (2007–10),
Parma (2010–)
SIGNED FROM
Club Atlético Banfield,
£2million, 4 July 2006
LFC DEBUT GAME/GOAL
25 October 2006 /
25 October 2006
CONTRACT EXPIRY
26 August 2007

Season	League		FA Cup		League Cup		Europe		Other		Total	
	App	Goals	App	Goals	App	Goals	App	Goals	App	Goals	App	Goals
2006/07	2 (1)	0	0	0	3	1	1 (1)	0	0	0	6 (2)	1
Total	2 (1)	0	0	0	3	1	1 (1)	0	0	0	6 (2)	1

Palk, Stan

STAN PALK was a right-winger who arrived at Anfield after one of his team-mates put in a good word for him to Liverpool.

One day when he was in the factory where he was working during the war, George Kay, Liverpool's manager, came to talk to him. After impressing at training Palk was signed for one pound ten shillings a week. Palk made six league appearances in the second half of the 1946/47 season, the first post-war championship eventually going to Liverpool. He was called on seven times the following season but then moved

on to Gordon Hodgson's Port Vale in July 1948, as he told *LFC.tv* in 2005. 'I'd just come back from the States [from Liverpool's summer tour] and I got the shock of my life. Tom Bush, a former centre-half, who was then working on the office staff, knocked on my door and said I was wanted down at the ground. I turned up and standing there was Gordon Hodgson, the legendary Liverpool centre-forward, who managed Port Vale. I really wanted to stay

with Liverpool but the opportunity of first-team football was too tempting and I eventually decided to go.' Palk was Vale's skipper for four years and made 159 league appearances, scoring 14 goals.

Season	League		FA Cup		Total	
	App	Goals	App	Goals	App	Goals
1946/47	6	0	0	0	6	0
1947/48	7	0	0	0	7	0
Total	**13**	**0**	**0**	**0**	**13**	**0**

Parkinson, Jack

JACK PARKINSON was a prolific goalscorer and tremendously quick, winning a total of 20 titles in various sprinting competitions. He had a run of 17 consecutive league matches in his debut season, in which he scored six times.

The following season he netted 20 times from just 21 games in the Second Division. Unfortunately Parkinson broke his wrist in Liverpool's opening game in the 1905/06 season but returned in

mid-March to contribute seven goals to the Reds' victorious league campaign (but not playing enough games to qualify for a winners' medal). Parkinson's career continued to be curtailed by injuries but despite his difficulties his goals-per-game ratio remained exceptional apart from the 1908/09 season when he only scored four in 18 games. Twenty-six-year-old Parkinson started the 1909/10 season with a bang and scored 11 goals in his first seven games, including a hat-trick against Nottingham Forest, one goal in a 3-2 victory over Everton and a brace in a 3-2 win against Manchester United. The writer in the club's programme from 13 November 1910 was excited with his progress: 'The Bootle youth has improved beyond measure this season. Here again we are delighted to see the wholesome leaven of intelligence permeating his movements and some of his passes to the wing men are decidedly clever. He has also demonstrated a fondness for baffling the custodian with well-placed shots, and not relying entirely on force to gain goals.' Parkinson continued to terrorise defences and in April 1910 he celebrated finishing the top scorer of the First Division as well as becoming the first Liverpool player since Sam Raybould in 1902/03 to score 30 goals in a season. His progress was also finally recognised by the England selectors as he

made his international debut on 14 March 1910 against Wales. He scored another 43 in the top division over the next three seasons, but by 1913/14 he could no longer be sure of his place in the side and signed for Second Division Bury in August 1914.

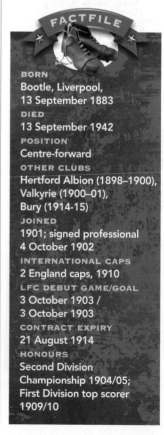

Season	League		FA Cup		Other		Total	
	App	Goals	App	Goals	App	Goals	App	Goals
1903/04	18	6	0	0	-	-	18	6
1904/05	21	20	2	1	-	-	23	21
1905/06	9	7	1	0	1	0	11	7
1906/07	9	7	4	0	-	-	13	7
1907/08	8	6	2	1	-	-	10	7
1908/09	17	3	1	1	-	-	18	4
1909/10	31	30	1	0	-	-	32	30
1910/11	33	19	2	1	-	-	35	20
1911/12	24	12	2	1	-	-	26	13
1912/13	24	12	2	0	-	-	26	12
1913/14	5	1	2	0	-	-	7	1
Total	**199**	**123**	**19**	**5**	**1**	**0**	**219**	**128**

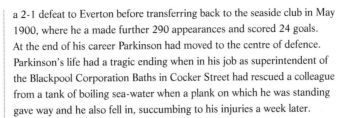

Parkinson,
John

a 2-1 defeat to Everton before transferring back to the seaside club in May 1900, where he a made further 290 appearances and scored 24 goals. At the end of his career Parkinson had moved to the centre of defence. Parkinson's life had a tragic ending when in his job as superintendent of the Blackpool Corporation Baths in Cocker Street had rescued a colleague from a tank of boiling sea-water when a plank on which he was standing gave way and he also fell in, succumbing to his injuries a week later.

Parkinson had been a member of the Blackpool lifeboat crew since his youth and throughout the country he was known as the 'sailor-footballer'. His funeral took place on 23 December 1911 at Christ Church in Blackpool, where he was married the year before.

JOHN PARKINSON played 85 league games and scored 29 goals in his first spell at Blackpool. He only played one game for Liverpool, up front in

FACTFILE

BORN
Blackpool, 27 August 1875
DIED
20 December 1911
POSITION
Centre-forward
OTHER CLUBS
Blackpool (1896–99),
Blackpool (1900–10),
Barrow
SIGNED FROM
Blackpool, 22 May 1899
LFC DEBUT
23 September 1899
CONTRACT EXPIRY
May 1900

Season	League		FA Cup		Total	
	App	Goals	App	Goals	App	Goals
1899/1900	1	0	0	0	1	0
Total	**1**	**0**	**0**	**0**	**1**	**0**

Parr,
Steve

A FULL-BACK, who played on both flanks for Liverpool, Steve Parr signed for the Reds in May 1948 but didn't make his first-team debut until the opening day of the 1951/52 season in which he featured in the first ten matches of the campaign. However, he never seriously threatened Bill Jones, Eddie Spicer or Ray Lambert, who were all preferred to Parr in his time at Liverpool. Parr only played four games in the 1952/53 season of which three were lost and he was sold to Exeter City in Third Division South at the end of the 1954/55 season.

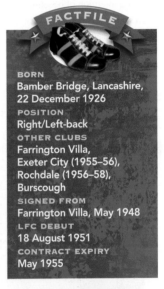

FACTFILE

BORN
Bamber Bridge, Lancashire,
22 December 1926
POSITION
Right/Left-back
OTHER CLUBS
Farrington Villa,
Exeter City (1955–56),
Rochdale (1956–58),
Burscough
SIGNED FROM
Farrington Villa, May 1948
LFC DEBUT
18 August 1951
CONTRACT EXPIRY
May 1955

Season	League		FA Cup		Total	
	App	Goals	App	Goals	App	Goals
1951/52	16	0	0	0	16	0
1952/53	4	0	0	0	4	0
Total	**20**	**0**	**0**	**0**	**20**	**0**

Parry,
Ted

Edward "Ted" Parry was at the ripe old age of 28 when he became a professional footballer, having spent his playing days as an amateur in Colwyn Bay, Wales.

He was an able full-back who was at Anfield for five years in the early 1920s but he only made 13 league appearances in all that time while playing in five internationals for Wales. It was easier said than done to displace Liverpool's outstanding trio of full-backs: Tommy Lucas, Donald Mackinlay and Ephraim Longworth. His Liverpool debut came against Derby County towards the end of the 1920/21 season but he hardly got a look-in as successive League Championships were won in 1922 and 1923. In the second of those title-winning seasons, ten men played in at least 37 of the 42 league games so the team almost picked itself. After spending the majority of his Liverpool career as captain of the Central League side he moved to Third Division Walsall at 33 years of age before returning to Colwyn Bay.

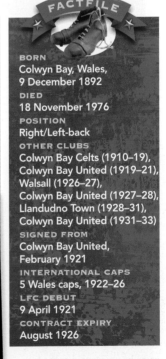

FACTFILE

BORN
Colwyn Bay, Wales,
9 December 1892
DIED
18 November 1976
POSITION
Right/Left-back
OTHER CLUBS
Colwyn Bay Celts (1910–19),
Colwyn Bay United (1919–21),
Walsall (1926–27),
Colwyn Bay United (1927–28),
Llandudno Town (1928–31),
Colwyn Bay United (1931–33)
SIGNED FROM
Colwyn Bay United,
February 1921
INTERNATIONAL CAPS
5 Wales caps, 1922–26
LFC DEBUT
9 April 1921
CONTRACT EXPIRY
August 1926

Season	League		FA Cup		Other		Total	
	App	Goals	App	Goals	App	Goals	App	Goals
1920/21	2	0	0	0	-	-	2	0
1921/22	7	0	0	0	0	0	7	0
1923/24	3	0	0	0	-	-	3	0
1924/25	1	0	0	0	-	-	1	0
Total	**13**	**0**	**0**	**0**	**0**	**0**	**13**	**0**

Parry,
Maurice

'HE IS APT to grow over-enthusiastic, the fault of his Celtic temperament I suppose, but is often unfairly penalised.'

Right-half Maurice Parry was so described by the club programme in 1904. Parry had earlier moved to Leicester to get a job in the engineering trade but signed as a professional for the local club. He admitted he 'went into it blindly as I had no intention of becoming a professional'. Parry was a very clever player who 'could twist and turn and tie the opposing forward in a tangle and then steal the ball

from his toe'. He was called up by his country, Wales, on 16 occasions during his nine years at Anfield. He made his debut early in the 1900/01 season, the year when his club won the league title for the first time. He didn't play enough games to qualify for a medal then but made up for that later in the decade when Liverpool won the Second and First Division in successive seasons, 1904/05 and 1905/06. He wasn't called on for much more than half the fixtures over the next three years and eventually moved to Partick Thistle at the end of the 1908/09 season, soon followed by his old Liverpool team-mate Alex Raisbeck.

PARRY coached and played in South Africa from 1911 to 1913 and later held coaching positions at Barcelona, Frankfurt, Cologne and in the Channel Islands. While serving as a second lieutenant in the South Wales Borderers he proved a popular figure, as reported by one crew member who was on the ship that transported Parry to the Greek island of Lemnos in September 1915. 'Of course, he was a person of no small importance in the eyes of our crew, who are all Liverpool men. He was the life and soul of the party, and it was always he who started the music and singing. In an impromptu concert held on the last night the cry was always "Parry".' The organ-playing teetotaller returned to Liverpool many years after he had left as a player to bring his coaching skills to the club where he had played the majority of his professional career. Having suffered from long-term effects of wartime gassing he died of chronic bronchitis on 24 March 1935.

Season	League App	League Goals	FA Cup App	FA Cup Goals	Other App	Other Goals	Total App	Total Goals
1900/01	8	0	0	0	-	-	8	0
1901/02	12	0	0	0	-	-	12	0
1902/03	31	0	1	0	-	-	32	0
1903/04	29	1	1	0	-	-	30	1
1904/05	30	2	2	0	-	-	32	2
1905/06	36	1	5	0	1	0	42	1
1906/07	19	0	0	0	-	-	19	0
1907/08	21	0	3	0	-	-	24	0
1908/09	20	0	2	0	-	-	22	0
Total	**206**	**4**	**14**	**0**	**1**	**0**	**221**	**4**

Englischer Fußball-Trainer mit allerbesten Referenzen und nachweisbar besten Erfolgen, langjähriger Spieler der engl. Ober-Liga sucht Stellung als **Trainer.** Angebote an Maurice Parry, Frankfurt a. M., Hotel Hansa-Royal, Kronprinzenstraße 54/56.

FACTFILE

BORN
Trefonen, Wales, 7 November 1877
DIED
24 March 1935
POSITION
Right-half
OTHER CLUBS
Newtown (1894–96), Long Eaton Rangers (1896–97), Nottingham Forest (1897), Oswestry United (1897–98), Leicester Fosse (1898–99), Loughborough Town (loan, 1899), Brighton United (1899–1900), Partick Thistle (1909–10), Wrexham (1910–11), South African football (1911–13), Oswestry United (1913–14)
SIGNED FROM
Brighton United, March 1900
INTERNATIONAL CAPS
16 Wales caps, 1901–09
LFC DEBUT GAME/GOAL
13 October 1900 / 1 April 1904
CONTRACT EXPIRY
17 May 1909
HONOURS
League Championship 1905/06; Second Division Championship 1904/05

Parry,
Rick

THE BOYHOOD Liverpool fan and Ellesmere Port native landed his dream job when he was appointed deputy chief executive at Liverpool Football Club in 1998, working beside chief executive Peter Robinson, from whom he would take over 12 months later.

Parry was working as a senior management consultant at giant accounting firm Ernst & Young when he was named as the first

chief executive of the Premier League in February 1992. He negotiated a record-breaking £214million TV deal over five years with Sky and the BBC which guaranteed the Premier League's ensuing success. In turn he became a prime candidate to realise the enormous financial potential of Liverpool, who were ironically struggling in the environment he helped create in comparison with their main rivals who had better utilised the financial windfall from English football's new dawn.

Parry's first significant step to restore Liverpool's reputation was announced on 13 July 1999 when Northwest-based media group Granada paid £22million for a 9.9 per cent stake in the club. Granada would manage Liverpool's commercial interests, utilise possibilities in merchandising, publishing, television rights, catering and corporate hospitality. 'We realised that we can't stand still while the rest of Europe moves forward,' Parry told the press. 'The rightful place for Liverpool is on top of the pile and we felt we couldn't get there on our own. We are the one club who have the worldwide fan base to match United's. And now we have a partnership with Granada aimed at exploiting it.' Liverpool fans were relieved as the club had previously been reluctant to embrace

outside investment and tap their worldwide potential. Unfortunately Granada in their eight-year relationship with the club failed to deliver on most fronts.

Parry completed the club's most successful transfer negotiations for many a season in the summer of 1999 as Gérard Houllier's resurrection of Liverpool gathered pace. Surely nobody complained about the £2.5million Parry negotiated with Willem II for Sami Hyypia and £8million was money well spent on Didi Hamann. The treble won in 2000/01 highlighted Liverpool's sensible spending on players

that sadly evaporated in 2002. Liverpool's abysmal showing in the 2002/03 season fuelled speculation that Houllier's time at Anfield was coming to an end, but Parry supported him publicly, as would be expected of a chief executive. 'After a consistent period of growth and success, you don't throw it all away at the first sign of a blip. It is not simply a case of saying it because we won the Worthington Cup. We want him here for the long haul,' Parry told the press. Worse was to follow in the 2003/04 season. 'We don't accept fourth as being the level where we want to be,' Parry warned Houllier in April 2004.

As Houllier left in the summer of 2004 Rick Parry completed negotiations with Valencia's Rafa Benítez. Success on the field should breed success off the field and Rick Parry could hardly have wished for a better opportunity for Liverpool to spread their wings and conquer new territories when the European Cup was won in Istanbul.

In 2005 Granada was responsible for renewing terms with Carlsberg that had been the club's shirt sponsors since 1992. The new deal was worth a paltry £5million over two years. In comparison Manchester United secured a £56million shirt sponsorship deal with AIG over four years in 2006. 'One suspects a major revamp of Liverpool's virtually non-existent commercial department will be high on the agenda to ensure such a vast difference between the Reds and United is never exposed again,' reported the *Liverpool Echo* in April 2006. Finally in 2007 Granada, that had by then merged into ITV plc, sold its 9.9 per cent stake in Liverpool, at a loss of £4.5million, to Tom Hicks and George Gillett.

Parry told the press that the Americans' takeover was 'great for Liverpool, our supporters and the shareholders, it is the beginning of a new era for the

club. They are bringing to the table tremendous and relevant experience, a passion for sport, real resources and a strong commitment to the traditions of Liverpool. We know that George and Tom want a long-term relationship with Liverpool and that they also understand the importance of investing in our success both on and off the field. They have made clear their intention to move as quickly as practicable on the financing and construction of our proposed new stadium at Stanley Park and also to support investment in the playing squad.'

With Granada out of the loop Rick Parry announced Liverpool's new deal with the Danish brewers in June 2007. 'The Carlsberg and Liverpool partnership is one of the longest and most successful in football, based on trust and mutual respect,' Parry said. The £21.6million agreement trebled the previous deal, guaranteeing Liverpool £7.2million per year for the next three seasons. The Reds' deal was still minuscule compared with United's AIG deal and Chelsea's with Samsung that secured the east London club £50million over five years. Even Spurs' partnership with Mansion House was worth £34million over four years. Liverpool were losing out on major transfer targets that could have been brought in if sufficient money had been available and furthermore there was still no sign of a new stadium that could increase matchday revenue so Liverpool would be able to compete on some level with their neighbours down the M62.

PARRY was hardly working under optimum conditions. Hicks and Gillett's honeymoon was soon over as they could not agree on the design of the new stadium, or anything else for that matter. Parry was not prepared for the bombshell from Tom Hicks in April 2008. In a Sky Sports interview conducted at his home in

Dallas, with the Texan millionaire sitting in a cosy armchair in front of his fireplace, he delivered one knockout blow after another. 'If you look at what has happened under Rick's leadership it's been a disaster. We've fallen so far behind the other top clubs. The new stadium should have been built three or four years ago. We have two sponsors, maybe three, when we should have 12 to 15. We are not doing anything in Asia the way Man U is and Barcelona is. We have still got the top brand in the world of football, we just don't know how to commercialise it and get the money from it to buy great players. Rick needs to resign from Liverpool. He has put his heart into it but it's just time for a change.'

The gloves had really come off and this was open warfare. Parry, who enjoyed Gillett's full backing, told the media: 'Only the Liverpool board can ask me to resign and the board has not done so. There is a Liverpool way, which I understand, but it now appears that there is a Dallas Way.'

Benítez was trying to negotiate a new contract, which Hicks was willing to give him, but the Spaniard was adamant he wanted Parry out as he felt the club had missed out on a number of key players such as Nemanja Vidic, Abou Diaby, Florent Malouda and Gareth Barry because Parry had failed to act decisively when targets had been identified by his scouting team. Parry would no doubt argue that there were a multitude of other reasons why these deals did not happen.

On 27 February 2009 Liverpool announced that Rick Parry would leave the club in May. Parry said his goodbyes, saying the split had been relatively amicable. These words made better sense to supporters when it was revealed a year later that his severance package from Liverpool FC combined two years' pay of £1.5million per year, made up of

salary and bonuses, and £1.3million as a negotiated settlement with Gillett and Hicks, whom he had helped bring to the club.

'I have dealt with Parry over the course of his time at Liverpool and found him to be an honest, hard-working, low-key operator who prefers to go about his business away from the spotlight,' said Phil McNulty, the BBC's chief football writer, when Parry's imminent departure had been confirmed. 'Parry is an advocate of what used to be known as "the Liverpool Way" of doing business without fuss and behind closed doors, not the public airing of dirty linen that has driven a coach and horses through that philosophy in recent years. He is a lifelong Liverpool fan and the image portrayed by some as a man who will procrastinate, almost to the deliberate detriment of Liverpool, is false.'

Four months after Rick Parry left Anfield Liverpool announced a record £80million, four-year shirt sponsorship deal with Standard Chartered Bank.

> HE NEGOTIATED A RECORD-BREAKING £214MILLION TV DEAL OVER FIVE YEARS WITH SKY AND THE BBC WHICH GUARANTEED THE PREMIER LEAGUE'S ENSUING SUCCESS

Partridge, Richie

RICHIE PARTRIDGE, a promising Stella Maris schoolboy, signed a five-year contract with Liverpool in August 1996. Partridge, who had an excellent crossing ability and plenty of tricks, was considered an exciting prospect coming through the Anfield ranks.

The diminutive Irishman, who could 'comfortably limbo dance at full stretch', made his first-team debut when Liverpool ran riot beating Stoke 8-0 in the League Cup on 29 November 2000. The speedy winger was very unfortunate with injuries in his time at the Reds and surely would have made his debut earlier if he had not damaged his left cruciate ligament in 1999. Coventry did get a glimpse of his undeniable talent when he went on loan to Gary McAllister's Sky Blues in the First Division in 2002/03. He flourished and scored truly spectacular goals in his 31 outings, and was also voted the fans' player of the season.

Back at Liverpool Partridge's right cruciate ligament went when he collided with a team-mate in a reserve match in November 2003. He was out of action for ten months. Partridge made a couple of substitute appearances in 2004/05 before he was released on a free transfer on 1 July 2005.

THE DUBLINER enjoyed his football again with The New Saints in the Welsh Premier League as he scored 12 goals in 31 matches in the 2010/11 season, but very early on in the following season he was forced to retire due to a persistent knee injury. He did have a promising career to fall back on as during the latter stages of his playing career Partridge studied physiotherapy at Salford University where he graduated

with a first-class honours degree in 2009. He later worked at Liverpool's medical department from Under-9 to Under-16 level. He is currently a director at the 10 Bridge Physiotherapy Clinic just outside Chester. On a personal note, Richie Partridge

is Michael Owen's brother-in-law as he is married to Lesley, Michael's sister.

Season	League		FA Cup		League Cup		Europe		Total	
	App	Goals	App	Goals	App	Goals	App	Goals	App	Goals
2000/01	0	0	0	0	1	0	0	0	1	0
2004/05	0	0	0	0	0 (2)	0	0	0	0 (2)	0
Total	**0**	**0**	**0**	**0**	**1 (2)**	**0**	**0**	**0**	**1 (2)**	**0**

Paterson, George

GEORGE Longmore Paterson played three times as a left-winger for Liverpool during the last full season before the outbreak of World War Two.

PRIOR TO ANFIELD he featured for the works team of Hall Russell & Company Limited, which was the last of the Aberdeen shipbuilders. He had played in two amateur internationals for Scotland as well as representing Aberdeenshire. Paterson made his Reds debut in a 1-0 home win over Stoke between Christmas and New Year 1938 and his second and last league appearance came in the 2-0 defeat at Aston Villa on 18 February 1939. Paterson also figured once in the FA Cup, scoring Liverpool's second goal in their 3-0 third

round victory over Luton Town at Anfield on 7 January 1939. Paterson later joined Shankly's coaching staff at Liverpool.

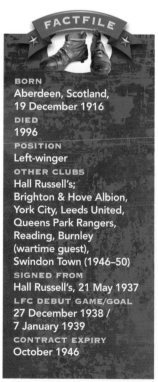

Season	League		FA Cup		Total	
	App	Goals	App	Goals	App	Goals
1938/39	2	0	1	1	3	1
Total	**2**	**0**	**1**	**1**	**3**	**1**

Patterson, George

GEORGE PATTERSON was appointed as assistant to secretary Tom Watson in 1908 and took over the leadership of the Liverpool team following his death in 1915.

He was not officially appointed as his successor until 14 September 1918, as announced by the *Liverpool Echo*. 'I (Bee) am glad that Mr. George Patterson has been appointed secretary of Liverpool F.C. He is a practical man, unobtrusive, and shows wisdom with pen and in football matters. He is following one of the best in the late Tom Watson, but has been well schooled, and will make good. In his football days he played a deal of football with Orrell and other clubs, but from an Army point of view his big frame is useless – he has an extraordinary number of wriggling bones that have been broken. Here's to him!'

Patterson led the Reds through wartime's chaotic local competitions in which, despite the fact that players were stationed all over the country and beyond, he could rely on a few who had performed for the team in the preceding years, even bringing legend Arthur Goddard back to Anfield. He also blooded

youngsters who were to serve Liverpool well throughout the 1920s such as John Bamber (80 games/2 goals), Harry Chambers (339/151), Harry Lewis (70/12) and Tommy Lucas (366/3). The *Liverpool Echo* included an announcement from Patterson on 25 July 1918 looking for personnel to feature for his team. 'LIVERPOOL FOOTBALL CLUB are Prepared to Receive APPLICATIONS from Experienced PLAYERS, who are exempt from military service, for season 1918–19. Apply, stating age, height, weight, position, and club last played for, to George F. Patterson, Walton Breck-rd.' When the league resumed in the 1919/20 season a distinction was made between being a 'Secretary' (that entailed duties performed by a modern 'chief executive'), and 'Manager', the man responsible for the team's results. In fairness the manager didn't manage the team in the strictest sense of the word, as the board chose the first XI. Halfway through the campaign Patterson returned to taking care only of his secretarial duties after Liverpool had won seven out of 18 league games and were 18th in a league of 22. David Ashworth came from Stockport County to take over as manager. Patterson was pleased by his successor's progress as the club scored 18 goals without reply in five wins in the league and three in the FA Cup from the middle of January to mid-February. 'The interest in the club is enormous, and their run of league and cup successes is quite natural under the circumstances,' Patterson said in the *Liverpool Echo*. 'The boys are playing fine football and for long enough the people of Liverpool have recognised this and have stood by the side although we started rather badly. It was one goal against us week by week. We turned the corner in December and confidence and good football have done the rest. The boys fear no team.'

WHEN ASHWORTH'S successor, Matt McQueen, retired in 1928, it was no surprise that Patterson was asked again to take over the reins as manager, which makes him the first man to have two spells as secretary/manager of Liverpool, not Kenny Dalglish as so far has been believed by Liverpool FC historians. Two decades of football administration clearly made Patterson the right candidate to replace McQueen as the club was already carrying out an unwritten policy of 'promoting from within'. As things turned out, the eight full seasons during which Patterson was in charge were some of the quietest years in the club's history, the exception being when, after finishing 7th in 1935, there was an alarming slump the following season with the team being victorious in only three of the last 20 league games. Liverpool eventually escaped relegation by three points but it had been a close call. The pressure of managing a First Division club as well as being an administrator taking care of the bureaucratic side took a lot out of Patterson, who said enough was enough in 1936 as the stress was affecting his health. The board had been happy to have him in this dual role as it was less expensive than having two men on its payroll! So success on the field was clearly not a priority, reflected by the grave

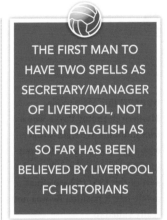

concerns of shareholders at the 1936 annual general meeting who asked the board if the appointment of a new manager would involve an extra salary. 'The directors of the Liverpool Football Club have decided to advertise for a manager or team manager to fill the vacancy caused by Mr. G. Patterson reverting to his original position as secretary,' the *Nottingham Evening Post* reported on 18 July 1936. George Kay was persuaded to leave his post at Southampton and head north to take over at Anfield, while Patterson continued as the club's secretary until 1939.

FACTFILE

BORN
1887
APPOINTED MANAGER
14 September 1918 /
7 March 1928
DEBUT GAME
30 August 1919
CONTRACT EXPIRY
December 1919 /
6 August 1936

GEORGE S. PATTERSON,
Secretary.

Season	Division	P	W	D	L	GF	GA	Pts	Pos	Win %	FA Cup	League Cup
1919/20	1st Division	18	7	2	9	23	26	16	18	38.89	-	4th Round
1927/28*	1st Division	12	2	4	6	16	28	8	16	16.67	-	3rd Round
1928/29	1st Division	42	17	12	13	90	64	46	5	40.48	4th Round	2nd Round
1929/30	1st Division	42	16	9	17	63	79	41	12	38.10	3rd Round	Runners-Up
1930/31	1st Division	42	15	12	15	86	85	42	9	35.71	3rd Round	2nd Round
1931/32	1st Division	42	19	6	17	81	93	44	10	45.24	6th Round	
1932/33	1st Division	42	14	11	17	79	84	39	14	33.33	3rd Round	Semi-Final
1933/34	1st Division	42	14	10	18	79	87	38	18	33.33	5th Round	Winners
1934/35	1st Division	42	19	7	16	85	88	45	7	45.24	4th Round	Winners
1935/36	1st Division	42	13	12	17	60	64	38	19	30.95	4th Round	Winners
Total	-	**366**	**136**	**85**	**145**	**662**	**698**	**357**	-	**37.16**	-	-

* Patterson appointed on 7 March 1928 with Liverpool in 8th position

Payne,
Jimmy

DUBBED the 'Merseyside Matthews', Jimmy Payne was a tricky, diminutive right-winger who would beat man after man for fun, although he did spend part of the 1951/52 season at inside-left, a position he was not really suited to.

Payne, who supported Everton as a kid, made his debut for Liverpool against Bolton Wanderers at Anfield on 11 September 1948, having joined the club six years earlier. After the title win in 1947,

Liverpool's fortunes gradually declined and they were relegated to the Second Division at the end of the 1953/54 season. Payne struggled with injuries in the latter part of his career, lost his form and the Liverpool crowd seemed to turn against him. He eventually signed for Everton in April 1956 but due to injuries his spell there was a brief one, playing only six games and scoring two goals.

DUBBED THE MERSEYSIDE MATTHEWS', JIMMY PAYNE WAS A TRICKY, DIMINUTIVE RIGHT-WINGER WHO WOULD BEAT MAN AFTER MAN FOR FUN

Season	League		FA Cup		Total	
	App	Goals	App	Goals	App	Goals
1948/49	35	3	3	1	38	4
1949/50	31	5	7	2	38	7
1950/51	38	6	1	0	39	6
1951/52	35	9	3	1	38	10
1952/53	33	8	0	0	33	8
1953/54	17	3	1	0	18	3
1954/55	17	2	1	0	18	2
1955/56	16	2	5	1	21	3
Total	222	38	21	5	243	43

FACTFILE

BORN
Bootle, Liverpool,
10 March 1926
DIED
23 January 2013
POSITION
Right-winger /
Left-inside forward
OTHER CLUBS
Bootle ATC,
Everton (1956–57)
SIGNED FROM
Bootle ATC,
May 1942;
signed professional
2 November 1944
LFC DEBUT GAME/GOAL
11 September 1948 /
9 October 1948
CONTRACT EXPIRY
18 April 1956

Peake,
Ernest

TWENTY-year-old Ernest Peake was already a Welsh international before joining Liverpool.

'Standing 5ft 8¾in [175 cm] and weighing 10st 8lb [67 kg] he is not well equipped physically for a League footballer, but his cleverness more than counterbalances any lack in this respect,' wrote the club programme one week after he made his debut at Arsenal, where he looked distinctly nervous in a 5-0 drubbing that, unsurprisingly, was the centre-half's only appearance of the season. It wasn't until the 1912/13 season that Peake enjoyed a regular run in the side after Bobby Robinson and James Harrop had left the club, figuring mainly as left-half in 26 of the last 29 First Division matches when Liverpool finished mid-table.

Season	League		FA Cup		Total	
	App	Goals	App	Goals	App	Goals
1908/09	1	0	0	0	1	0
1909/10	3	0	0	0	3	0
1910/11	8	3	0	0	8	3
1911/12	8	0	0	0	8	0
1912/13	26	2	4	1	30	3
1913/14	5	0	0	0	5	0
Total	51	5	4	1	55	6

FACTFILE

BORN
Aberystwyth, Wales,
May 1888
DIED
19 November 1931
POSITION
Centre-half / Left-half
OTHER CLUBS
Aberystwyth Town (1904–08),
Third Lanark (1914–15),
Blyth Spartans (1919–20)
SIGNED FROM
Aberystwyth Town, May 1908
INTERNATIONAL CAPS
11 Wales caps (1 goal)
(10 (1) at LFC), 1908–14
LFC DEBUT GAME/GOAL
20 February 1909 /
22 October 1910
CONTRACT EXPIRY
1914

Pearson, Albert

LEFT-WINGER Albert Pearson made a scoring debut as Liverpool opened the 1919/20 campaign with a 3-1 victory at Bradford City.

He missed only nine league matches that season and added a further three goals in David Ashworth's first season as Liverpool's manager. But in the second of Pearson's two years on Liverpool's books, Harold Wadsworth was preferred to him. Just as Liverpool embarked on their most successful years to date Pearson moved to Second Division Port Vale. In December 1921 he was so described by the *Derby Daily Telegraph*: 'Dark-haired with sharp features, he is as good with the ball as he is good-looking, and still retains all his trickery, speed and resource.'

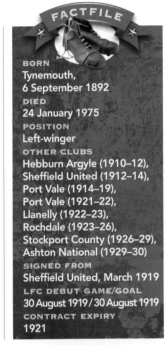
	League		FA Cup		Total	
Season	App	Goals	App	Goals	App	Goals
1919/20	33	4	5	0	38	4
1920/21	10	0	3	0	13	0
Total	**43**	**4**	**8**	**0**	**51**	**4**

Pearson, Joe

Centre-half Joe Pearson played his only game as Liverpool debuted in competitive football in the Lancashire League on 3 September 1892 against Higher Walton, beating them 8-0.

	League		FA Cup		Other		Total	
Season	App	Goals	App	Goals	App	Goals	App	Goals
1892/93	-	-	0	0	1	0	1	0
Total	**0**	**0**	**0**	**0**	**1**	**0**	**1**	**0**

Pellegrino, Mauricio

MAURICIO Pellegrino started his professional career in Velez Sarsfield in Argentina in 1990, staying there for the majority of the 1990s before joining Barcelona on loan in the 1998/99 season, where he won the first of his three Spanish titles.

The tall Argentinian then became a key figure in the heart of Rafa Benítez's defence at Valencia, winning La Liga in 2002 and 2004. Pellegrino acquired a wealth of experience in European football as he competed in two Champions League finals and won the UEFA Cup. In the 2001 final against Bayern Munich Pellegrino suffered the worst nightmare of any footballer when he missed the decisive penalty in the shootout.

BENÍTEZ brought the 33-year-old Beatles fan over in January 2005. 'I could not sleep for several nights after the move was confirmed. The first free weekend I get I plan to visit everything in the city that is connected with the Beatles,' Pellegrino said, who was occasionally referred to as the 'Fifth Beatle' by the Argentinian press. It was painfully clear that he was over the hill when he came to Liverpool and after an uneventful five months he went back to Spain with Alaves. Pellegrino returned to Liverpool in the summer of 2008 as first-team coach and left in 2010 when Benítez was sacked as manager. He followed Rafa to Inter, where he along with his boss only stayed a few months. In the summer of 2012 Pellegrino was appointed manager of his old club Valencia. He only lasted until December 2012, leaving them 12th in the table.

	League		FA Cup		League Cup		Europe		Total	
Season	App	Goals	App	Goals	App	Goals	App	Goals	App	Goals
2004/05	11 (1)	0	0	0	1	0	0	0	12 (1)	0
Total	**11 (1)**	**0**	**0**	**0**	**1**	**0**	**0**	**0**	**12 (1)**	**0**

Peltier, Lee

RIGHT-BACK Lee Peltier made three appearances for Liverpool in the League Cup and featured in an irrelevant Champions League game in Istanbul against Galatasaray during the 2006/07 season.

These turned out to be the only games he ever played for the club. Peltier was loaned out to Yeovil Town in League One in 2007/08 during which he was put under the spotlight in a couple of games by former player Steve Claridge for the *Guardian*. 'He was quick to close down opponents all over the pitch but he maintained that nice balance between stopping his winger and being in touch with his centre-half to utilise the pace he has on the cover,' Claridge wrote. He concluded that Peltier could thrive among better players and have a bright future in the game.

Following his successful loan spell at Yeovil he was sold to the West Country club in January 2008.

AT THE END of June 2009 Huddersfield Town signed Peltier

on a three-year contract. Manager Lee Clark had been impressed by Peltier when he had a trial spell at Norwich where he was assistant manager and was excited by his new signing: 'He is a fantastic athlete and is very accomplished on the ball, as you would expect given he was schooled at Liverpool.' Peltier was voted his team-mates' player of the year at the end of his first season in Yorkshire and was a regular as well in his second year when Huddersfield reached the playoff final, where they lost to Peterborough United. Peltier was signed by Sven-Göran Eriksson at big-spenders Leicester City before the 2011/12 season, moving up a level to the Championship. Eriksson was soon dismissed but Peltier added to his ever-growing reputation. The 25-year-old

Peltier joined Neil Warnock's Leeds United in the Championship in August 2012 and was soon made captain of the Yorkshire side.

FACTFILE

BORN
Liverpool, 11 December 1986
POSITION
Right-back
OTHER CLUBS
Hull City (loan, 2007),
Yeovil Town (loan, 2007;
permanent, 2008–09),
Huddersfield Town (2009–11),
Leicester City (2011–12),
Leeds United (2012–)
JOINED
1997; signed professional
25 November 2004
LFC DEBUT
25 October 2006
CONTRACT EXPIRY
31 January 2008

Season	League		FA Cup		League Cup		Europe		Other		Total	
	App	Goals	App	Goals	App	Goals	App	Goals	App	Goals	App	Goals
2006/07	0	0	0	0	3	0	1	0	0	0	4	0
Total	0	0	0	0	3	0	1	0	0	0	4	0

Penalties

INCLUDED are the top 25 penalty kings. Note that misses by earlier players have not all been found as it is not very easy to spot every single one from press reports so this list is still in development in that respect.

Gary Mac scores past Pepe Reina in the Barca goal in 2001

	Scored	Missed	Taken	Success Rate
Jan Mølby	42	3	45	93.33
Phil Neal	38	13	51	74.52
Billy Liddell	34	7	41	82.93
Steven Gerrard	31	8	39	79.49
Tommy Smith	22	10	32	68.75
Robbie Fowler	20	6	26	76.92
John Aldridge	17	1	18	94.44
Terry McDermott	16	4	20	80.00
Gordon Hodgson	15	1	16	93.75
Michael Owen	13	10	23	56.52
Kevin Keegan	11	6	17	64.71
John Barnes	10	5	15	66.67
Willie Fagan	9	1	10	90.00
Danny Murphy	8	0	8	100.00
Willie Stevenson	8	1	9	88.89
Dirk Kuyt	8	2	10	80.00
Arthur Goddard	8	3	11	72.73
Alec Lindsay	8	3	11	72.73
Ronnie Moran	8	6	14	57.14
Jackie Sheldon	7	3	10	70.00
Sam Raybould	7	5	12	58.33
Mark Walters	6	0	6	100.00
Jack Parkinson	6	1	7	85.71
Robert Done	6	2	8	75.00
Gary McAllister	5	1	6	83.33

Penalty shootouts

Date	Opposition	AET	Result		Competition
10 August 1974	Leeds United	1-1	7 - 6	W	Charity Shield
30 May 1984	AS Roma	1-1	5 - 3	W	European Cup Final
13 April 1992	Portsmouth	0-0	3 - 1	W	FA Cup Semi-final replay
14 December 1993	Wimbledon	2-2	5 - 6	L	League Cup 4th round replay
18 January 1995	Birmingham City	1-1	2 - 0	W	FA Cup 3rd round replay
25 February 2001	Birmingham City	1-1	5 - 4	W	League Cup Final
4 December 2002	Ipswich Town	1-1	6 - 5	W	League Cup 4th round
1 December 2004	Tottenham Hotspur	1-1	5 - 4	W	League Cup 5th round
25 May 2005	AC Milan	3-3	6 - 5	W	Champions League Final
13 May 2006	West Ham United	3-3	6 - 4	W	FA Cup Final
1 May 2007	Chelsea	1-0	5 - 1	W	Champions League Semi-final 2nd leg
22 September 2010	Northampton Town	2-2	4 - 6	L	League Cup 3rd round
26 February 2012	Cardiff City	2-2	5 - 4	W	League Cup Final

Alan Kennedy guarantees victory against Roma in 1984

Penman, James

JAMES PENMAN replaced the regular left-back of the time, Donald Mackinlay, when Bradford Park Avenue came to Anfield on 6 November 1920, a match the visitors won by one goal to nil.

The club programme commented on his debut and only appearance for the Reds' first team: 'He shaped very promisingly in the first half, and his first experience in League football should be beneficial. His kicking was clean, but there was a tendency in the second half towards hesitancy in tackling an opponent.'

Season	League		FA Cup		Total	
	App	Goals	App	Goals	App	Goals
1920/21	1	0	0	0	1	0
Total	1	0	0	0	1	0

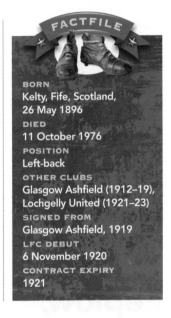

FACTFILE

BORN
Kelty, Fife, Scotland, 26 May 1896
DIED
11 October 1976
POSITION
Left-back
OTHER CLUBS
Glasgow Ashfield (1912–19), Lochgelly United (1921–23)
SIGNED FROM
Glasgow Ashfield, 1919
LFC DEBUT
6 November 1920
CONTRACT EXPIRY
1921

Pennant, Jermaine

JERMAINE PENNANT became the most expensive teenager in English football history when he signed for Arsenal for £2million from Notts County in January 1999.

Arséne Wenger is a master at turning youngsters into fully fledged professional footballers, but couldn't handle the rebellious Pennant, who was brought up in one of the worst neighbourhoods in Nottingham and soon discovered the bright lights of London. He only played 26 games for Arsenal in six and a half years, his highlight a hat-trick in a 6-1 win over Southampton in the Premier League in May 2003. Those three goals turned out to be his only ones for the club. Pennant was shipped out to other clubs and finally impressed Birmingham enough to pay £3million for him on 1 July 2005. He had been on loan at Birmingham since January and during this time turned in some impressive performances, but also served 30 days in jail for driving under the influence with a suspended licence!

RAFA DECIDED to gamble on the right-winger after an impressive 2005/06 season as he thought Pennant was mature enough to star for his boyhood favourites. Pennant made the highest number of appearances by any Liverpool player, 52 in total, in his debut season but there was still room for improvement in terms of number of assists and goalscoring. His only goal up to that point was a tremendous one against Chelsea at Anfield. Pennant started the next season in similar vein, the only blot on his copybook a silly red card against Porto in the Champions League in September. He received an injury in his next group-stage game, at Besiktas, and was sidelined for a couple of months. On his return he didn't start as many games as he was used to. Once the 2008/09 season got under way, it became clear that Pennant was not likely to figure much in the manager's plans. He started only three matches, with one more brief appearance coming as a substitute at Everton at the end of September. On 20 January 2009 he was loaned to Portsmouth for the remainder of the season. Pennant became a free agent on the opening day of July 2009 and a week later he joined Real Zaragoza, who had just been promoted back to Spain's top division.

PENNANT appeared in 25 La Liga matches in a struggling team. After a single season in Spain Pennant returned to English football when he agreed to a four-month loan deal with Premier League club Stoke City, which led to a permanent contract. Pennant's career was revived after joining Stoke and the Potteries reached the final of FA Cup for the very first time in 2011, but were left disappointed at Wembley as Manchester City won the trophy. Pennant had a decent second season, but he still seemed plagued by personal problems that have curtailed his great natural ability. As Tony Pulis had no more use for him at Stoke he was loaned to Wolves in the Championship for the 2012/13 season. Pulis' successor, Mark Hughes, gave Pennant a one-year contract at Stoke in the summer of 2013.

FACTFILE

BORN
Nottingham,
15 January 1983
POSITION
Right-winger
OTHER CLUBS
Arsenal (1999–2005),
Watford (loan, 2002,
2002–03),
Leeds United (loan, 2003–04),
Birmingham City (2005–06),
Portsmouth (loan, 2009),
Real Zaragoza (2009–10),
Stoke City (2010–),
Wolverhampton Wanderers
(loan, 2012–13)
SIGNED FROM
Birmingham City, £6.7million,
26 July 2006
INTERNATIONAL CAPS
24 England U-21 caps
LFC DEBUT GAME/GOAL
9 August 2006 /
20 January 2007
CONTRACT EXPIRY
1 July 2009

Season	League		FA Cup		League Cup		Europe		Other		Total	
	App	Goals	App	Goals	App	Goals	App	Goals	App	Goals	App	Goals
2006/07	20 (14)	1	1	0	2	0	9 (5)	0	1	0	33 (19)	1
2007/08	14 (4)	2	2	0	0	0	2 (3)	0	-	-	18 (7)	2
2008/09	2 (1)	0	0	0	1	0	0	0	-	-	3 (1)	0
Total	**36 (19)**	**3**	**3**	**0**	**3**	**0**	**11 (8)**	**0**	**1**	**0**	**54 (27)**	**3**

Peplow,
Steve

STEVE PEPLOW scored 19 goals for the reserves in the 1968/69 season, but unfortunately he is just another forward who never made the grade at Liverpool. After waiting patiently in the reserves the 20-year-old played in three consecutive first-team matches in November 1969.

He made his debut against West Ham at Anfield in the first game televised in colour by the BBC's Match of the Day. He celebrated a 2-0 victory over the Hammers led by Bobby Moore and the following game was a Leeds draw. His last first-team appearance was an eventful game in the Fairs Cup against Vitoria Setubal at Anfield. Liverpool had lost the first leg 1-0 and, being a goal down at half-time, Peplow was substituted for Roger Hunt. The goalscoring legend scored his last ever goal for the club in the final minute ensuring a 3-2 victory. The players waited around for extra time, but the referee informed them that the away-goals rule came into effect after 90 minutes and since the Portuguese side had scored two goals at Anfield the Reds were out. In typical upbeat mood Bill Shankly refused to acknowledge that the Reds were well and truly conquered. 'We were beaten by a penalty, an own goal and the rules of the competition.'

Peplow played a couple of seasons at Swindon before a fortunate move to Ron Yeats' Tranmere. 'Ron had plans to use me as a

Season	League		FA Cup		League Cup		Europe		Total	
	App	Goals	App	Goals	App	Goals	App	Goals	App	Goals
1969/70	2	0	0	0	0	0	1	0	3	0
Total	**2**	**0**	**0**	**0**	**0**	**0**	**1**	**0**	**3**	**0**

central midfielder but I could not tackle rice pudding,' Peplow told the *Liverpool Echo*. 'He tried me out wide but it was John King, Ron's successor, who converted me to a right-winger.' Peplow established himself finally at Tranmere Rovers where he played 248 Third and Fourth Division games, scoring 44 goals from 1973 to 1981. Peplow recalled a funny story related to his Reds' debut when interviewed by the *Liverpool Echo* in 2007. It was Peplow's wedding day in 1995 and his best man was an old Tranmere team-mate by the name of Barrie Mitchell. The Scot

sprang a surprise on Peplow at the reception, presenting him with a video. 'The cover said something like "Love Techniques for the Beginner". I thought Barrie had got hold of a naughty video by way of a joke, but it turned out to be a specially commissioned recording of my debut for Liverpool,' Peplow revealed. 'Barrie had been in touch with Ray Stubbs at the BBC. Ray got the commentator, John Motson, to dig out the recording of that old Liverpool–West Ham match. It was on film and they managed to get it transferred to video. It was a wonderful surprise.'

Perkins, Bill

HARRY STORER had started the 1898/99 season between the sticks at Liverpool and played in the first 32 fixtures before being replaced by Matt McQueen for the next two.

BILL PERKINS' introduction into the side effectively ended McQueen's playing days. Perkins started the next season but after eight successive defeats he was replaced by Storer in mid-October. Perkins returned at the end of the year and became established as the side's main keeper until the 1902/03 season when he shared duties with Peter Platt. But after Platt was selected for a home game with Sunderland on 30 March 1903, Perkins disappeared out of the scene for good after 117 first-team appearances in league and cup. But he did have the satisfaction of winning a League Championship medal in 1901, when he was an ever-present in the team.

Season	League		FA Cup		Total	
	App	Goals	App	Goals	App	Goals
1898/99	5	0	0	0	5	0
1899/1900	23	0	4	0	27	0
1900/01	34	0	2	0	36	0
1901/02	33	0	3	0	36	0
1902/03	12	0	1	0	13	0
Total	**107**	**0**	**10**	**0**	**117**	**0**

Perry, Fred

RIGHT-BACK Fred Perry played for amateur club Worthing on the south coast before signing for Liverpool in July 1954.

He played just once for the club's first team, as part of the side beaten 2-1 by Blackburn Rovers at Anfield on New Year's Eve in 1955.

Season	League		FA Cup		Total	
	App	Goals	App	Goals	App	Goals
1955/56	1	0	0	0	1	0
Total	**1**	**0**	**0**	**0**	**1**	**0**

Peters,
Keith

KEITH PETERS made a single first-team appearance for Liverpool, replacing regular left-back Jim Harley when the club lost 3-0 at Ayresome Park in a First Division match with Middlesbrough on 2 January 1939.

FACTFILE

BORN
Port Sunlight, 19 July 1915
DIED
1989
POSITION
Left-back
OTHER CLUBS
Brighton & Hove Albion
(wartime guest)
JOINED
July 1936
LFC DEBUT
2 January 1939
CONTRACT EXPIRY
1944

Season	League		FA Cup		Total	
	App	Goals	App	Goals	App	Goals
1938/39	1	0	0	0	1	0
Total	**1**	**0**	**0**	**0**	**1**	**0**

Piechnik,
Torben

TORBEN Piechnik blossomed in his country's victorious Euro 1992 squad, showing considerable man-marking skills against some of the best forwards in the world.

Graeme Souness could have been forgiven for thinking that Piechnik was a quality defender, but he was tormented by Liverpool old boy Dean Saunders on his debut as the Welshman put two past Liverpool. Piechnik made only one appearance the following season, embarrassingly taken off at half-time after Newcastle had run Liverpool ragged. Jan Mølby told *LFChistory.net* why his compatriot failed at Liverpool. 'Torben's biggest problem was he didn't want to listen,' Mølby said. 'It became a problem with the

manager telling him how he wanted him to play and Torben not wanting to play that way. He defended by dropping off, whereas Liverpool squeezed up, pressurised the opposition. It was only a matter of time before they were going to send him back to Denmark.'

FACTFILE

BORN
Copenhagen, Denmark,
21 May 1963
POSITION
Centre-half
OTHER CLUBS
Kjøbenhavns Boldklub
(1979–87),
Ikast FS (1988–89),
B 1903 (1989–92),
FC København
(1992 – KB and B 1903
merged to form FCK),
AGF (1994–99)
SIGNED FROM
FC København, £500,000,
1 September 1992
INTERNATIONAL CAPS
15 Denmark caps (4 at LFC),
1991–96
LFC DEBUT
19 September 1992
CONTRACT EXPIRY
1 June 1994

Season	League		FA Cup		League Cup		Europe		Other		Total	
	App	Goals	App	Goals	App	Goals	App	Goals	App	Goals	App	Goals
1992/93	15 (1)	0	2	0	5	0	0	0	0	0	22 (1)	0
1993/94	1	0	0	0	0	0	-	-	-	-	1	0
Total	**16 (1)**	**0**	**2**	**0**	**5**	**0**	**0**	**0**	**0**	**0**	**23 (1)**	**0**

Pither,
George

GEORGE PITHER had played 16 league matches and scored six goals for Merthyr Town in the Third Division South when he joined Liverpool in the first part of the 1925/26 season.

He played a dozen matches exclusively as replacement left-winger for the established Fred Hopkin, in 1926/27 and 1927/28. Pither's only goal for the club came on the first day of October 1927 when Portsmouth were crushed 8-2 at Anfield, the other scorers being William Devlin with four and Gordon Hodgson who scored a hat-trick. After 18 months at Anfield Pither returned to the third tier of league football with Crewe Alexandra.

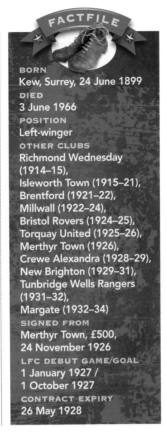
Season	League		FA Cup		Total	
	App	Goals	App	Goals	App	Goals
1926/27	6	0	0	0	6	0
1927/28	6	1	0	0	6	1
Total	**12**	**1**	**0**	**0**	**12**	**1**

Platt,
Peter

LIVERPOOL had to agree terms with First Division Blackburn Rovers for Peter Platt even though he was then playing for Oswaldtwistle Rovers in the Lancashire Combination as Blackburn still held his Football League registration.

PETER PLATT
[LIVERPOOL]

Twenty-year-old Platt took over from Bill Perkins in the Liverpool goal for the last seven league games of 1902/03, having already been picked 15 times earlier in the season. He started the 1903/04 season as first choice but was replaced by Charles Cotton after 18 matches. Platt won his place back for the last three fixtures of that campaign but never represented the club again. When the next season started on the first day of September 1904, Ned Doig was between the sticks. While at Liverpool Platt was said to be still engaged at his trade as a cotton weaver. He passed away at only 38 years of age in a mini flu epidemic in Nuneaton.

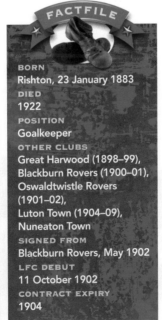
Season	League		FA Cup		Total	
	App	Goals	App	Goals	App	Goals
1902/03	22	0	0	0	22	0
1903/04	21	0	1	0	22	0
Total	**43**	**0**	**1**	**0**	**44**	**0**

Plessis,
Damien

HOLDING midfielder Damien Plessis left Lyon in 2007 claiming that he hadn't had any chances to prove himself at the French club. On securing his signature, Rafa Benítez said: 'He is a good player, big and strong, and we're sure he'll do well for us.'

The Frenchman was a surprise choice to start the league match against Arsenal at the Emirates that was sandwiched between the two Champions League games against the same opponents in April 2008. He played the full 90 minutes, giving an assured and composed display, as he did three weeks later in another away match at Birmingham City. Plessis made two starts at the beginning of the 2008/09 season, but was replaced at half-time against Sunderland

with regular first choice Xabi Alonso, who had been struggling with injury. As expected, Plessis

got his chance mostly in the League Cup with other first-team irregulars. Although named in seven match-day squads in 2009/10, Plessis only figured once, in the League Cup fourth round tie away to Arsenal at the end of October. This turned out to be his last game for Liverpool. At the end of August 2010 Plessis moved to Panathinaikos in Greece for an undisclosed fee. Shortly before Christmas 2011, Plessis was signed on loan by Doncaster Rovers for the remainder of the season, but was not selected for a single fixture as Rovers were relegated from the Championship. Plessis signed for second-division French side Arles-Avignon in July 2012.

FACTFILE

BORN
Neuville-aux-Bois, France,
5 March 1988
POSITION
Midfielder
OTHER CLUBS
Lyon (2003–07),
Panathinaikos (2010–12),
Doncaster Rovers
(loan, 2012),
Arles-Avignon (2012–)
SIGNED FROM
Lyon, 31 August 2007
INTERNATIONAL CAPS
1 France U-21 cap
LFC DEBUT GAME/GOAL
5 April 2008 /
12 November 2008
CONTRACT EXPIRY
31 August 2010

Season	League		FA Cup		League Cup		Europe		Total	
	App	Goals	App	Goals	App	Goals	App	Goals	App	Goals
2007/08	2	0	0	0	0	0	0	0	2	0
2008/09	1	0	0	0	2	1	1 (1)	0	4 (1)	1
2009/10	0	0	0	0	1	0	0	0	1	0
Total	**3**	**0**	**0**	**0**	**3**	**1**	**1 (1)**	**0**	**7 (1)**	**1**

Class of 1899 ready for action!

Points

THE RECORDS are catergorized according to number of games and number of points for a win.

Period: 1894-98 (excludes 2nd Division season 1895/96)

Most points in the First Division with 30 games played				
	W	D	L	Pos.
1896/97	33	12	9	9	5

Period: 1898-1904

Most points in the First Division with 34 games played				
	W	D	L	Pos.
1900/01	45	19	7	8	1

Period: 1905-15

Most points in the First Division with 38 games played					
	W	D	L	Pos.	If 3 points
1905/06	51	23	5	10	1	74

Period: 1919-81 (excludes 2nd Division seasons 1954/55 - 1961/62)

Most points in the First Division with 42 games played (2 for a win)						
		W	D	L	Pos.	If 3 points
1978/79	68	30	8	4	1	98
1965/66	61	26	9	7	1	87
1968/69	61	25	11	6	2	86

Period: 1981-88 and 1991-92

Most points in the First Division with 40-42 games played (3 for a win)					
		W	D	L	Pos.
1987/88	90	26	12	2	1
1985/86	88	26	10	6	1

Period: 1988-91

Most points in the First Division with 38 games played					
		W	D	L	Pos.
1989/90	79	23	10	5	1

Period: 1992-

Most Points in the Premier League					
		W	D	L	Pos.
2008/09	86	25	11	2	2
2005/06	82	25	7	6	3
2001/02	80	24	8	6	2

Period: 1894-98 (excludes 2nd Division season 1895/96)

Fewest points in the First Division with 30 games played					
		W	D	L	Pos.
1894/95	22	7	8	15	16

Period: 1898-1904

Fewest points in the First Division with 34 games played					
		W	D	L	Pos.
1903-04	26	9	8	17	17

Period: 1905-15

Fewest points in the First Division with 38 games played					
		W	D	L	Pos.
1906/07	33	13	7	18	15

Liverpool line up before the 1978/79 season

Period: 1919-81 (excludes 2nd Division seasons 1954/55 - 1961/62)

Fewest points in the First Division with 42 games played (2 for a win)						
		W	D	L	Pos.	If 3 points
1953/54	28	9	10	23	22	37
1936/37	35	12	11	19	18	47
1952/53	36	14	8	20	17	50

Period: 1981-88

Fewest points in the First Division with 40-42 games played (3 for a win)					
		W	D	L	Pos.
1984/85	77	22	11	9	2
1986/87	77	23	8	11	2

Period: 1988-92

Fewest points in the First Division with 38 games (and 42)					
		W	D	L	Pos.
1991/92	64	16	16	10	16

Includes season 1991/92 as it was the worst despite 4 more games played.

Fewest points in the Premier League 1992-					
		W	D	L	Pos.
2011/12	52	14	10	14	8
1998/99	54	15	9	14	7
2010/11	58	17	7	14	6

Poor Scouser Tommy

ONE OF THE most popular songs among Liverpool supporters is 'Poor Scouser Tommy', which is based in part on a sorrowful song called 'Red River Valley' about lovers being torn apart. One is being left in the Red River Valley while the other moves away. It originates from the late nineteenth century.

The first verse of 'Red River Valley' goes:

From this valley they say you are going,
We will miss your bright eyes and sweet smile,
For they say you are taking the sunshine
That has brightened our pathways a while.

'Poor Scouser Tommy' begins as follows:

Let me tell you the story of a poor boy
Who was sent far away from his home
To fight for his king and his country
And also the old folks back home.

So they put him in a Highland division
Sent him off to a far foreign land
Where the flies swarm around in their thousands
And there's nothing to see but the sand.

Well, the battle it started next morning
Under the Arabian sun,
I remember that poor Scouser Tommy
Who was shot by an old Nazi gun

As he lay on the battlefield dying (dying dying)
With the blood gushing out of his head (of his head)
As he lay on the battlefield dying (dying dying)
These were the last words he said...

The second part of 'Poor Scouser Tommy' is based on 'The Sash', a ballad from Ireland commemorating the genocide committed by King William III in the Williamite war in Ireland in 1690–91. It is popular among Ulster loyalists. The lyrics are thought to be around 100 years old, and the melody has been traced back to the early 19th century. The first verse of 'The Sash' goes:

Sure I'm an Ulster Orangeman, from Erin's isle I came
To see my British brethren all of honour and of fame
And to tell them of my forefathers who fought in days of yore
That I might have the right to wear the sash my father wore!

Poor Scouser Tommy continued:

Oh... I am a Liverpudlian
I come from the Spion Kop
I like to sing, I like to shout
I go there quite a lot (every week).
[alternatively: I get thrown out quite a lot (every week)]

We support the team that plays in red
A team that we all know
A team that we call Liverpool
And to glory we will go.

A verse was added after the 5-0 drubbing of Everton on 6 November 1982:

We've won the League, we've won the Cup
We've been to Europe too
We played the Toffees for a laugh
And we left them feeling blue – Five Nil!

One two
One two three
One two three four
Five nil!

Rush scored one
Rush scored two
Rush scored three
And Rush scored four!
La la la la
la la la
la la

All is you need is Rush.... da da dara da.
All is you need is Rush.... da da dara da.
All is you need is Rush ... Rush... Rush is all you need...
Rush is all you need

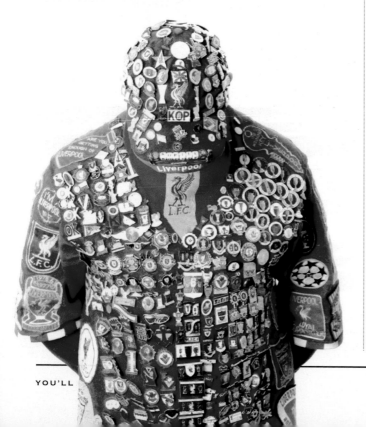

Potter,
Darren

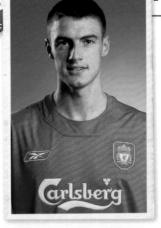

FACTFILE

BORN
Liverpool, 21 December 1984
POSITION
Midfielder
OTHER CLUBS
Southampton (loan, 2006),
Wolverhampton Wanderers
(loan, 2006-07;
permanent, 2007-09),
Sheffield Wednesday
(2009-11),
Milton Keynes Dons (2011-)
SIGNED FROM
Blackburn Rovers (youth),
2001; signed professional
18 April 2002
INTERNATIONAL CAPS
5 Ireland caps, 2007
LFC DEBUT
10 August 2004
CONTRACT EXPIRY
18 January 2007

THE LIVERPUDLIAN Darren Potter, as with many born in this area, had Irish roots and therefore qualified to represent the Republic of Ireland. He was released by Everton when he was 15, but their loss was Liverpool's gain.

He wasn't very optimistic about his chances. 'I am more comfortable in the middle than on the right, but you know that Steven Gerrard, the best player in Europe, Xabi Alonso and Didi Hamann are competing for those places, so it is not going to be easy playing there. But as far as I am concerned, I'd give an arm and a leg just to get a shirt in any position.' Potter's first-team opportunities at Anfield were limited but the midfielder did feature in 17 matches between 2004 and 2006, making 10 starts, mostly in the League Cup or the Champions League qualifying rounds. Potter had a short loan spell at Southampton towards the end of the 2005/06 season and following a successful loan spell at Wolves he was transferred in January 2007. Potter seems to have finally settled at League One club Milton Keynes Dons where he was reunited with Dons manager Karl Robinson, who had been a coach at Liverpool around the time Potter made the first of only two Premier League appearances for the Reds.

Season	League		FA Cup		League Cup		Europe		Other		Total	
	App	Goals	App	Goals	App	Goals	App	Goals	App	Goals	App	Goals
2004/05	0 (2)	0	1	0	3 (1)	0	1 (2)	0	-	-	5 (5)	0
2005/06	0	0	0	0	1	0	4 (2)	0	0	0	5 (2)	0
Total	**0 (2)**	**0**	**1**	**0**	**4 (1)**	**0**	**5 (4)**	**0**	**0**	**0**	**10 (7)**	**0**

Poulsen,
Christian

FACTFILE

BORN
Asnæs, Denmark,
28 February 1980
POSITION
Midfielder
OTHER CLUBS
Holbæk B&I (1995–2000),
FC København (2000–02),
Schalke 04 (2002–06),
Sevilla (2006–08),
Juventus (2008–10),
Evian Thonon Gaillard
(2011–12),
Ajax (2012–)
SIGNED FROM
Juventus, £4.55million,
12 August 2010
INTERNATIONAL CAPS
92 Denmark caps (6 goals)
(7 (0) at LFC), 2001–12
LFC DEBUT
19 August 2010
CONTRACT EXPIRY
31 August 2011

CHRISTIAN POULSEN'S route to Anfield was certainly a circuitous one. His aggressive playing style has seen him involved in a number of controversial incidents over the years. Poulsen was given his first big break as a 20-year-old by Roy Hodgson at FC København at the start of the new millennium and was part of the squad that won the Danish Superliga title in 2001 and ended as runners-up in 2002, when he was voted the club's player of the season.

Poulsen played as an attacking midfielder in Denmark, scoring 10 goals in 45 games for the team from Copenhagen, before moving to Schalke after the 2002 World Cup. After four seasons in Gelsenkirchen he joined reigning UEFA Cup holders Sevilla. Poulsen was the first player to be named as the Danish Player of the Year for two consecutive years in 2005 and 2006, and arrived with a big reputation to protect. He was a phenomenal success at Sevilla and Spanish newspaper *Marca* singled him out as the best buy in Spain over the summer. The Spanish club retained the UEFA Cup in Glasgow after defeating their compatriots Espanyol. Poulsen signed a four-year contract on his arrival at Juventus in 2008, but would only

spend two seasons with the Turin club, featuring in 48 out of their 76 league games. Poulsen had famous battles with Francesco Totti and Kaká, with the former losing his temper and spitting in his face in the 2004 European Championship, earning him a three-match ban in the process. 'He plays his game when the referee is not watching, he starts swinging kicks, pushing his rivals when the official's back is turned.

He is a coward and he shouldn't be playing football,' complained Milan's coach Carlo Ancelotti after one battle.

SIGNED in August 2010, Poulsen clearly struggled to cope with the English game. For a club raised on the likes of Graeme Souness,

Steve McMahon and Javier Mascherano patrolling the midfield, Poulsen's limp play was a sorrowful sight. He signed a one-year deal with French Ligue 2 champions Evian Thonon Gaillard in the summer of 2011. In doing so, he became only the second footballer, after Romanian

Florin Raducioiu, to have played professionally in the top division of all five of the so-called big European Leagues: Germany, Spain, Italy, England and France. Poulsen added the Netherlands to his curriculum vitae when he joined Ajax in August 2012.

Season	League		FA Cup		League Cup		Europe		Total	
	App	Goals	App	Goals	App	Goals	App	Goals	App	Goals
2010/11	9 (3)	0	0	0	0	0	9	0	18 (3)	0
Total	9 (3)	0	0	0	0	0	9	0	18 (3)	0

Pratt,
David

DAVID PRATT established himself as centre-half at Bradford City, who were unfortunately relegated to the Second Division in his debut season. Reports said he was 'the mainstay of the defence' and 'a coming international'.

PRATT SIGNED for Liverpool in January 1923 and became immediately known for the strength of his arms, as the *Liverpool Echo* revealed in the report on his debut: 'Pratt was amazing the crowd with some of his throw-ins, I swear some reached the middle of the field. If he could develop this "Long Throw" it could be a useful asset if further up the field and would almost be like a corner.' Pratt played left-back when Liverpool guaranteed the league title with two games to go against Herbert Chapman's Huddersfield Town. The following season he was an understudy to right-half Tom Bromilow and added 15 games to his total. The highest number of league games Pratt played in during a single season was 26 in the 1924/25 season when he profited from Bromilow's

absence due to injury and Walter Wadsworth's lengthy ban for a dismissal.

Pratt was player-manager of Southern League Yeovil and Petters United when he revealed his musings on 'Sport in relation to everyday life'. 'Sport as a factor in development we welcome as an

ally, but sport as a dominant passion is an enemy of the soul,' concluded Pratt, in what was described as a 'striking address' to the Yeovil Rotary Club. He did admit that there was no question about the value of recreation that was encouraged by most churches, but the difficulty was with professional sports which

thousands of people followed. In industrial cities like Sheffield, Newcastle and Sunderland it had been demonstrated beyond all question that football matches had helped to empty public houses, and many women bought season tickets for their husbands. Watching the game had a psychological and moral as well as social value, 'but when all cultural interests are crowded out by it, there is real danger to the life of the nation'.

FACTFILE

BORN
Lochore, Fife, Scotland,
5 March 1896
DIED
28 July 1967
POSITION
Right-half
OTHER CLUBS
Lochore Welfare (1912–14),
Lochgelly United (1914–17),
Hill O'Beath (1917–19),
Celtic (1919–21),
Bo'ness (loan, 1919–20),
Bradford City (1921–23),
Bury (1927–29),
Yeovil & Petters United
(1929–33)
SIGNED FROM
Bradford City, January 1923
LFC DEBUT GAME/GOAL
17 February 1923 /
25 December 1925
CONTRACT EXPIRY
November 1927

Season	League		FA Cup		Total	
	App	Goals	App	Goals	App	Goals
1922/23	7	0	0	0	7	0
1923/24	15	0	0	0	15	0
1924/25	26	0	4	0	30	0
1925/26	14	1	0	0	14	1
1926/27	14	0	4	0	18	0
Total	76	1	8	0	84	1

Price,
John

ABERYSTWYTH-BORN John Price figured only once in the first team at Anfield.

His opportunity came when he was selected to play at left-back in a Second Division 4-2 defeat at Elland Road in Leeds on 19 November 1955.

Season	League		FA Cup		Total	
	App	Goals	App	Goals	App	Goals
1955/56	1	0	0	0	1	0
Total	**1**	**0**	**0**	**0**	**1**	**0**

FACTFILE

BORN
Aberystwyth, Wales,
22 November 1936
POSITION
Left-back
OTHER CLUBS
Aston Villa (1957),
Walsall (1957–58),
Shrewsbury Town (1958–59)
SIGNED FROM
Fordhouse Youth Club,
October 1954
LFC DEBUT
19 November 1955
CONTRACT EXPIRY
March 1957

Priday,
Bob

THE SOUTH African Bob Priday was a useful winger, who played on both flanks. His signing took place on the liner Capetown Castle at Southampton docks after arriving from Cape Town.

He made four appearances in the 1946 FA Cup competition but the nine games he was selected for when the national leagues resumed in 1946/47 were not quite enough to qualify him for a League Championship medal. However, he made an important impact at the end of that marathon season that turned out to be absolutely priceless. A second-half strike earned a point at Brentford on 17 May 1947 and in the next game he contributed to a late winner that saw off Arsenal. He later moved

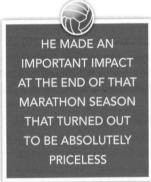

HE MADE AN IMPORTANT IMPACT AT THE END OF THAT MARATHON SEASON THAT TURNED OUT TO BE ABSOLUTELY PRICELESS

back to South Africa where he lived with his wife and six children.

Season	League		FA Cup		Total	
	App	Goals	App	Goals	App	Goals
1945/46	-	-	4	0	4	0
1946/47	9	1	0	0	9	1
1947/48	21	4	2	1	23	5
1948/49	4	0	0	0	4	0
Total	**34**	**5**	**6**	**1**	**40**	**6**

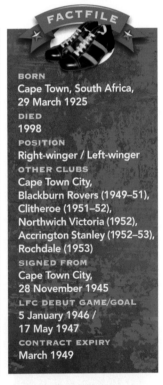

FACTFILE

BORN
Cape Town, South Africa,
29 March 1925
DIED
1998
POSITION
Right-winger / Left-winger
OTHER CLUBS
Cape Town City,
Blackburn Rovers (1949–51),
Clitheroe (1951–52),
Northwich Victoria (1952),
Accrington Stanley (1952–53),
Rochdale (1953)
SIGNED FROM
Cape Town City,
28 November 1945
LFC DEBUT GAME/GOAL
5 January 1946 /
17 May 1947
CONTRACT EXPIRY
March 1949

Programmes

MATCH-DAY programmes have been published for Liverpool's games since their first ever match: a friendly against Rotherham on 1 September 1892.

'These programmes should not be thrown away, but should be preserved, as they will form an interesting record of the doings of both teams, and also contain a list of fixtures, etc, up to date,' was noted in this historic publication.

Liverpool and Everton shared the match-day programme from 1904 to 1935. A typical publication from 1904 was 16 pages at the cost of one penny, which included a spotlight on the respective club's opponents: 'Everton Jottings' and

'Anfield Happenings' detailed their last game and one player was in the spotlight. The centrefold published the line-ups for Liverpool's first-team game and Everton's reserve game or vice versa. There was detailed information on current shows at the Empire Theatre at Lime Street, the Royal Hippodrome at West Derby Road, Picton Hall at William Brown Street and the Lyric Theatre in Everton Valley among various other local halls throughout the issue. The dandelion and burdock stout

The covers of the joint programmes. Blue when Everton was playing at Goodison and Red when Liverpool was at Anfield

'Sunflower', 'Glover's amber ales' as well as the famous old Highland whisky 'Roderick Dhu' were a few of the products

advertised. Finally the previous weekend's results were printed as well as the current league table.

The clubs went their separate ways at the end of the 1934/35 season and produced programmes for matches at their respective grounds only. The first such programme issued for Liverpool was for the opening home game of the 1935/36 season against Manchester City. Apart from the attractive new cover, which emphasised the red of Liverpool, the style of the programme remained very much as it had been in previous seasons: a large

issue of 16 pages. Liverpool have ever since published their own programme and the current one is the A5-sized 'This is Anfield' which numbers 84 pages.

Rare programmes can fetch hundreds of pounds and in order to share information on collectables the Liverpool Programme Collectors Club was formed by Keith Stanton in 1986. Stanton issues a club bulletin four times a season on memorabilia such as programmes, books and match tickets. An offers list for rare and collectable programmes accompanies the bulletin.

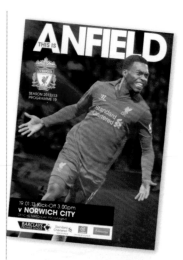

Pursell, Bob

LIVERPOOL were fined £250 and an ex-director of the club, John Fare, was suspended from football for six months (reduced from two years) after buying Bob Pursell for £360 from Queen's Park, because the Reds failed to talk to his club prior to approaching him.

Pursell's main strengths were his physique and speed, and he was a regular in the second half of his debut season, 1911/12. He was in and out of the side during the next two years but did play in all eight of the cup ties which saw Liverpool reach their first FA Cup final in 1914, but it was Burnley who took the famous trophy home after a narrow 1-0 victory. Pursell was so described in the papers: 'On his day a brilliant defender. One of the fastest full-backs playing. Provides the counterfoil to the dash of Longworth, his height standing him in good stead in his defensive work.'

Controversy continued to follow Pursell's career as he along with three other Liverpool players

– Tom Miller, Thomas Fairfoul, Jackie Sheldon – and three United players was found guilty of fixing a game between Liverpool and Manchester United on Good Friday 1915. Incidentally, Pursell was the one who conceded a penalty in the game, most certainly on purpose, which to his dismay Pat O'Connell missed. For his service to his country in the war Pursell's life ban from the game was lifted. World War One had taken the best years of his competitive playing career away, but he did return to Anfield after peace was declared. Pursell fractured his arm in the first practice match of the 1919/20 season and wasn't ready for action until December, when he was picked in consecutive

First Division games against Manchester United and Everton. However, these proved to be Pursell's only first-team appearances that season and he joined Port Vale in May 1920. He featured in 68 games for Vale until breaking his leg in a 1-1 draw against Leicester on 14 April 1922, which finished his career.

FACTFILE

BORN
Campbeltown, Scotland,
18 March 1889
DIED
24 May 1974
POSITION
Left-back
OTHER CLUBS
Aberdeen University,
Queen's Park (1909–11),
Port Vale (1920–22)
SIGNED FROM
Queen's Park, £360,
29 August 1911
LFC DEBUT
30 September 1911
CONTRACT EXPIRY
May 1920

Season	League		FA Cup		Total	
	App	Goals	App	Goals	App	Goals
1911/12	24	0	2	0	26	0
1912/13	21	0	1	0	22	0
1913/14	26	0	8	0	34	0
1914/15	27	0	2	0	29	0
1919/20	2	0	0	0	2	0
Total	**100**	**0**	**13**	**0**	**113**	**0**

Race,
Harry

HARRY RACE made a dramatic debut at Derby County on 15 February 1928, when the Reds made a great fightback after being 2-0 down at the break. His strike early in the second half followed by two from Dick Edmed turned a probable defeat into an unlikely victory.

Race's only other goal in his 11 First Division appearances at the end of that 1927/28 season came in the club's next away fixture, at Arsenal. It was Liverpool's third of the day but Arsenal scored six themselves. Race, who was described as fast and clever on the ball, was in and out of the team

during the next two years but his goals-per-game ratio was very respectable. In August 1930 he was purchased by First Division Manchester City for no less than £3,000, a substantial fee at the time. However, Race only played 11 games in three seasons for City, scoring three goals. He was transferred to Nottingham Forest on 26 June 1933 and had three successful years at the City Ground in the Second Division.

RACE was killed in World War Two at El Alamein in Egypt on 24

October 1942 while serving as a corporal in the Queen's Own Cameron Highlanders.

FACTFILE

BORN
Evenwood, Co. Durham,
7 January 1906
DIED
24 October 1942
POSITION
Forward
OTHER CLUBS
Raby United,
Manchester City (1930–33),
Nottingham Forest (1933–37),
Shrewsbury Town (1937–38),
Hartlepools United (1938–41)
SIGNED FROM
Raby United, October 1927
LFC DEBUT GAME/GOAL
15 February 1928 /
15 February 1928
CONTRACT EXPIRY
1 August 1930

Season	League		FA Cup		Total	
	App	Goals	App	Goals	App	Goals
1927/28	11	2	0	0	11	2
1928/29	13	9	0	0	13	9
1929/30	19	7	0	0	19	7
Total	**43**	**18**	**0**	**0**	**43**	**18**

Raisbeck,
Alex

Alex Raisbeck was commanding on the pitch and had a military air in the way he carried himself at centre-half, certainly not out of place as he was one of seven brothers who either became soldiers or footballers. Only a select few in Liverpool's history have commanded so much respect and admiration and he was undoubtedly the club's first superstar.

THE SCOTTISH international was born in a village called Wallacestone in the Falkirk area of central Scotland, 24 miles west of Edinburgh and 33 miles east of Glasgow. When his family moved to Larkhall in South Lanarkshire Alex featured for a Boys' Brigade team which was sponsored by Livingstone Memorial United Presbyterian Church. Football was his passion, as he recounted in the exclusive articles he wrote for the *Daily News* in 1915. 'The local

shoemaker flourished exceedingly, for young Raisbeck took to playing football. No matter where the leather went – sometimes the leather was of the tin variety and peeping toes brought me many a rebuke.' However, life was not all fun and games for the young 'Alick'. 'I was only twelve years of age when I was given the opportunity of following any particular trade to which I had a fancy, but I followed in my father's and brothers' footsteps and sought for livelihood in the bowels of the earth. Going down the pit at six in the morning, coming up at five, is no joke.'

ONLY A SELECT FEW IN LIVERPOOL'S HISTORY HAVE COMMANDED SO MUCH RESPECT AND ADMIRATION AND HE WAS UNDOUBTEDLY THE CLUB'S FIRST SUPERSTAR

Aged around 13 years of age Raisbeck was performing for Larkhall Thistle's third team, the Gasworks XI. He made the first team the following season but in an unusual position. 'The committee would insist upon me playing at outside-right, although they must have noticed my extraordinary tendency to wander into the middle of the field. In my early days I required no instructions about following the ball. It acted as a magnet to me and hundreds and hundreds of times I was told to "keep my place". I couldn't if it was to be at outside right, and eventually I drifted into the position which I think I may claim to have made my own.' Raisbeck played as outside-right for half a season before he found his place in the half-back line. After a couple of years at Thistle Raisbeck had attracted the attentions of Hibernian and a family friend, Hibs' left-half Judge Murphy, paid his family a visit to reveal his team's interest. Raisbeck did need a bit of convincing from his brother, Willie, but ultimately one thing mattered the most to him. 'I was working in the pits, and you can understand I was not very reluctant to leave the bowels of the earth for a whiff of the open-air.' Raisbeck signed for Hibernian on 30 July 1896 and made his debut in a 2-2 draw with Abercorn on 12 September 1896 at Underwood Park, Paisley. He played nine more games as Hibernian finished second in the league, two points behind Hearts. He made such an impression in his debut season that he was chosen to play left-half in the inter-league game between

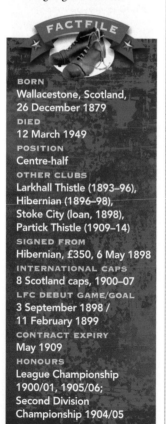

Scotland and Ireland. The *Dundee Courier and Argus* even compared him to Rangers great Neil Gibson, a superb half-back often described as the greatest footballer of his generation in Scotland: 'Raisbeck of the Hibernians, is a second edition of Neil Gibson, only he is bigger, and can stand more knocking about than the Ranger.'

After 29 games and four goals for Hibs the 18-year-old was loaned to Stoke for the last two months of the 1897/98 season to participate in the Potters' Test matches to retain their status in the First Division. Liverpool later used this loan system to strengthen their team temporarily with players from Scotland, like Robert Neill and Barney Battles. Raisbeck played all four games and scored one goal as Stoke won two out of four and finished top of their group, escaping the dreaded drop into the Second Division. Stoke were interested in signing Raisbeck on a permanent basis, but fate would have it differently. 'I had a mind, don't forget, to sign for Stoke, and actually made an appointment to meet Mr Austerberry, the secretary of the club, in Edinburgh. At the appointed hour no Stoke secretary appeared and in Phil Farmer's house I met instead Tom Watson. I had never seen the gentleman before, and I shall never forget him. He made me an offer which I could scarcely refuse. If Mr Austerberry had kept his appointment I would in all probability have been a Stoke, instead of a Liverpool player. It was a fortunate thing for me.'

On 6 May 1898 Watson convinced the young Scotsman to sign for Liverpool, who had finished mid-table in the First Division, four points above Stoke. The *Athletic News* reported on Liverpool's capture of Raisbeck and his compatriot, George Allan: 'Two more important catches for the Anfield club have been effected, and few will say that Allan of the Celts and Raisbeck, of Stoke-cum-Edinburgh Hibs, are not good goods. Raisbeck had a name in Scotland as the best centre half in the country, and for Stoke, where he has shown what he can do. Now with these last additions, they should go on smilingly.'

Raisbeck was welcomed with open arms at Liverpool and the usual hot-pot dinner at a director's house as the custom was for any newcomer at the club. 'I remember when I first went to Liverpool I felt a bit shy and diffident. I was, after all, only a laddie, and a Scottish laddie at that. Although I had a guid Scottish tongue in my head, I did not let it wag too freely, the "gift of the gab" not being mine.' Raisbeck felt at home though with so many Scotsmen in the side and enjoyed a special relationship with Tom Watson. 'From the day I became one of his players he took a particular interest in me; he fathered me, to tell the truth.'

RAISBECK always led by example and was chosen captain of the team after only one season at Liverpool. He was not, however, entirely fond of the responsibility. 'The position of captaincy was none of my seeking, and very often it was not to my liking either. Time and again during my

career I asked to be relieved of the job, but I was told to "go away"; "you're doin' fine". At least that was the meaning of the directors, although that was not, as can readily be understood, the language used.' Despite being 5ft 10in (178cm) Raisbeck's timing and athleticism enabled him to reach the ball before taller opponents. He was an energetic centre-half, a position more similar to a modern-day midfielder than a defender, and was also the instigator of attacks, possessing an impressive stamina. The scribe in the club programme, after Liverpool's and Everton's cup replay at Goodison Park on 8 February 1905, captured his essence as a player. 'Never has Raisbeck shown more wondrous football. He was here, there and everywhere. Now initiating an attack, now breaking up another, and again chasing Sharp when that lithe young man appeared to be all on his own. He dominated the whole field, and was, without question, the one superlative player. I am never inclined to over elaborate praise, but truly, Alec Raisbeck was a giant among pigmies.'

Raisbeck led Liverpool to their first ever First Division Championship title in 1901, clinched in dramatic circumstances on the last day of the campaign with a 1-0 win at West Bromwich Albion. Raisbeck could scarcely believe the reception the Liverpool team got on its return. 'I should imagine there

was a crowd of between 50,000–60,000 packed in front of the Central Station, and right along nearly as far as Lime Street. The street was literally black with people, and in the time-honoured way the horses were dispensed with and our brake practically carried along by willing hands to our headquarters at the Sandon Hotel. As we went along the crowd yelled for me to make a speech from the brake. I was not to be found, however, as I found it convenient to lie low behind some of the others. Speechmaking was never in my line.'

INCREDIBLY, Liverpool were relegated three years later, something that, in fact, prevented Raisbeck from leaving Merseyside, as he revealed in 1915. 'I had a feeling that the sixth season would be my last with the Reds. I was fully prepared for a swop but at the end of the season Liverpool found itself in the unfortunate position of being relegated to the Second Division of the League. I simply could not leave my club in its day of disaster.' Liverpool rebounded straight back into the First Division and won the title straight away in a season that was also 'remarkable', at least to the *Liverpool Echo*, for the fact that 'Alec Raisbeck has taken off his beloved moustache, and has joined the bare-faced brigade'. Raisbeck felt the team did not compare to Tom Watson's Sunderland greats of the 1890s, but this was an incredible feat by any rate. 'We marched right from the Second Division to the leading position of the First in successive years, which will demonstrate to you what sort of side we were. You perhaps expect me to follow on with the suggestion that we were a "Team of all the talents". We were not. Some of us were perhaps better than others, but, taking us all over, we were only a little above the average as a combination. As a team we were as one man, and therein lay the secret of our success.'

Raisbeck missed four months of the 1908/09 campaign with a knee injury and during his enforced absence he started to feel a bit homesick. 'Towards the end of the season the desire to seek fresh quarters haunted me all the more. I then made up my mind to return to Scotland and notified the officials to that effect. They were surprised to hear of my intention, and at first were not willing to let me go, but when they learned that it was for health reasons only they did not stand in my way. I had no club in view, and had not the slightest idea where I would like to land.' Before he could go looking for pastures new he had to ensure that Liverpool would escape relegation. The Reds needed a point in the final game of the season at St James' Park where they faced a Newcastle team who had already won the championship. Ronald Orr scored Liverpool's winner in the 78th minute. Raisbeck was very relieved, 'I never played in a match, full-back by the way, which gave me greater satisfaction. There was a whistle sounded which was music in my ears.'

When Partick Thistle's secretary, George Easton, was in Liverpool to sign Raisbeck's Welsh team-mate Maurice Parry, he asked Alex whether he knew of any more quality players. 'I casually remarked to my friend Easton that I shouldn't mind a shift myself. The Partick secretary did not at first believe me, but when he learned that I was serious on the matter he lost no time in getting in touch with the Liverpool officials.' Raisbeck was leaving his home away from home where he was adored, even though he was characteristically not carried away by it. 'On many an occasion I have been given hero worship when in my own mind I knew that I did not deserve it,' he said in 1915. 'In a very real sense I was one of Fortune's footballers, and probably the luckiest and most profitable of any transaction to

which I was a party was when I shook Tom Watson of Liverpool by the hand, who in turn, in his own peculiar genial way, asked me for a sample of my handwriting, which in effect tied me to Anfield for eleven of the happiest years of my life.'

RAISBECK proudly wore Partick Thistle's colours for five seasons. In 1914 he turned his hand to management at Hamilton Academical where he was in charge for three seasons before he was appointed director at the club for three and a half years. Raisbeck returned to England and took over as manager of Second Division Bristol City on 28 December 1921. City were relegated that spring but bounced straight back as champions of the Third Division South in the 1922/23 season. That very season manager David Ashworth left league champions Liverpool just before Christmas; Raisbeck was tipped as his successor before Matt McQueen took over in mid-February. Raisbeck resigned on 29 June 1929 after Bristol City finished 20th out of 22 teams, narrowly escaping relegation. He managed Halifax Town (1930–36), Chester (1936–38) and Bath City (1938) before returning to Liverpool in 1939, not as manager as he once hoped to, but as a scout. He served Liverpool until his dying day on 12 March 1949.

Victor Hall painted a vivid picture in an article in 1924 called 'Alec Raisbeck, who raised Liverpool's

prestige' in the *Liverpool Echo*, 15 years after Raisbeck left Liverpool to go back to his native Scotland.

What a trier he was! Who that ever saw him play can forget the unmatchable enthusiasm he displayed in the sheer love of the game. He not only put body and dash into individual games he played, but more importantly he helped to create the soul, that inward sacred fire of zeal without which no club can thrive and live. Let us recall his characteristics. Tall, lithe, sinuous, and yet gifted with muscular and physical development beyond the ordinary. Raisbeck was wholeheartedly a destroyer of attacks when it came from the opposing wing. We have never seen in England a speedier half-back, who could tackle a speedy forward, turn with him, and overtake and tackle him again. There may be and may have been others so gifted. We have not seen them. His judgement was sound, his valour outstanding and, naturally for a half-back, his control and placing of the ball was equally confident. During his playing career at Anfield, he had to meet forwards whose names and records were outstanding in the history of the game, and yet of none of them could it be said that they were the superior or master of Raisbeck's defensive play.

When a survey was conducted among Liverpool supporters in 1939 to name the best players Liverpool had ever had in their ranks, Raisbeck, who had left the club three decades earlier, came second only behind the incredibly popular Elisha Scott.

RAISBECK is a member of Liverpool's Official Hall of Fame and certainly deserves to be mentioned in the same breath as Kenny Dalglish, Billy Liddell and Steven Gerrard.

Season	League		FA Cup		League Cup		Total	
	App	Goals	App	Goals	App	Goals	App	Goals
1898/99	32	1	6	1	-	-	38	2
1899/1900	32	3	4	0	-	-	36	3
1900/01	31	1	2	0	-	-	33	1
1901/02	26	0	3	0	-	-	29	0
1902/03	27	1	1	0	-	-	28	1
1903/04	30	1	1	0	-	-	31	1
1904/05	33	2	2	0	-	-	35	2
1905/06	36	1	4	0	1	0	41	1
1906/07	27	4	1	0	-	-	28	4
1907/08	23	2	3	0	-	-	26	2
1908/09	15	2	1	0	-	-	16	2
Total	**312**	**18**	**28**	**1**	**1**	**0**	**341**	**19**

Ramsden,
Bernard

Liverpool on tour in the 1930s

LEFT-BACK Bernard Ramsden made his debut for the club as a 19-year-old at Chelsea on the opening day of the 1937/38 season. He made 15 appearances during his debut season and was only selected for 10 league matches the following year but by the time the 1939/40 season opened he had become first choice.

UNFORTUNATELY, that season was suspended due to the outbreak of war. Ramsden went with the rest of the Liverpool team on a pre-season tour to the USA in 1946 and clearly fell in love with the place, as he had planned to sail back to the States on 7 December, marry a Miss Audrey Clark of New York, whom he met after saving the life of one of her relatives, and open up a florist's shop there. Who knows whether he got cold feet or not, but Ramsden decided to stay put; and on the same date that he was

to originally commence his trip, Liverpool lost 5-1 to Wolves and he lost his place in the team! He made six appearances before the season's end, which qualified him for a League Championship medal. Ray Lambert took over his position and Ramsden moved on to Sunderland in March 1948 before finishing his playing career with their Northeast neighbours Hartlepools United. Ramsden was 'a bit of a vocalist' and had an offer to perform in music halls, but he preferred to stay in football.

HE HAD PLANNED TO SAIL BACK TO THE STATES ON 7 DECEMBER, MARRY A MISS AUDREY CLARK OF NEW YORK, WHOM HE MET AFTER SAVING THE LIFE OF ONE OF HER RELATIVES

FACTFILE

BORN
Sheffield, 8 November 1917
DIED
1976
POSITION
Left-back
OTHER CLUBS
Sheffield Victoria;
Brighton & Hove Albion,
Leeds United,
York City (wartime guest),
Sunderland (1948–50),
Hartlepools United (1950)
SIGNED FROM
Sheffield Victoria,
January 1935
LFC DEBUT
28 August 1937
CONTRACT EXPIRY
15 March 1948
HONOURS
League Championship
1946/47

Season	League		FA Cup		Total	
	App	Goals	App	Goals	App	Goals
1937/38	14	0	1	0	15	0
1938/39	10	0	3	0	13	0
1945/46	-	-	1	0	1	0
1946/47	23	0	1	0	24	0
1947/48	10	0	0	0	10	0
Total	**57**	**0**	**6**	**0**	**63**	**0**

Raven, David

DAVID RAVEN captained England at various youth levels. He was highly rated, but didn't make the progress expected and only featured in four games for Liverpool.

He made his debut in a 1-1 draw at Tottenham on 1 December 2004 in the League Cup and started in another under-strength side in a shocking FA Cup defeat to Burnley two months later. He replaced Sami Hyypia for the last third of the following league game at Southampton, which turned out to be Liverpool's third defeat in a row. His last game was another unsuccessful cup outing, this time at Selhurst Park where

Crystal Palace beat Liverpool 2-1 on 25 October 2005. Raven played 11 games for Tranmere on loan in the 2005/06 season, enjoying his stay at the club for which he played at schoolboy level and had supported as a kid. Raven was sold in the summer of 2006 to Carlisle United, who had just been crowned champions of League Two. The right-back played over 130 league games and earned cult hero status at Carlisle but was released by the club and joined Shrewsbury Town prior to the 2010/11 season. In the summer of 2011 Raven returned once more to Tranmere, before moving to Terry Butcher's Inverness Caledonian Thistle in Scotland.

FACTFILE

BORN
West Kirby, Wirral,
10 March 1985
POSITION
Right-back
OTHER CLUBS
Tranmere Rovers (loan, 2006),
Carlisle United (2006–10),
Shrewsbury Town (2010–11),
Tranmere Rovers (2011–12),
Inverness Caledonian Thistle
(2012–)
JOINED
April 2001; signed
professional 20 May 2002
LFC DEBUT
1 December 2004
CONTRACT EXPIRY
3 July 2006

Season	League App	League Goals	FA Cup App	FA Cup Goals	League Cup App	League Cup Goals	Europe App	Europe Goals	Other App	Other Goals	Total App	Total Goals
2004/05	0 (1)	0	1	0	1	0	0	0	-	-	2 (1)	0
2005/06	0	0	0	0	1	0	0	0	0	0	1	0
Total	**0 (1)**	**0**	**1**	**0**	**2**	**0**	**0**	**0**	**0**	**0**	**3 (1)**	**0**

Rawlings, Archie

THE DUNDEE COURIER described Archie Rawlings' qualities in June 1920 as follows: 'Rawlings depends largely on his great speed for beating his man, but he possesses a deadly right foot, which is as accurate with centres as it is powerful with shots for the net. Rawlings appears eminently suited for the English game, his height and pace being likely to stand him in good stead.'

Tall and powerful right-winger Rawlings joined champions Liverpool in March 1924, after playing 147 games in four years for struggling First Division

Preston, where he had lost his place to Alf Quantrill. The 32-year-old was brought in to replace the club's fantastic servant, Bill Lacey, who was in his last season. Rawlings played in the last 11 matches of the 1923/24 season as Liverpool struggled to follow up to their two consecutive League Championship wins. He only missed two games in 1924/25 as the team's form improved considerably, finishing fourth after languishing in mid-table the previous term. After playing in 10 of the opening 11 games of the 1925/26 season, Rawlings lost his place to Cyril Oxley and only figured twice in the second half of the campaign.

FACTFILE

BORN
Leicester, 2 October 1891
DIED
11 June 1952
POSITION
Right-winger
OTHER CLUBS
Wombwell, Shirebrook,
Darfield United,
Barnsley (1911–12),
Northampton Town (1912–14),
Rochdale (1914–15),
Dundee (1919–20),
Preston North End (1920–24),
Walsall (1926–27),
Bradford Park Avenue
(1927–28),
Southport (1928),
Dick Kerr's XI (1928–29),
Fleetwood (1929–31),
Burton Town (1931–33)
SIGNED FROM
Preston North End,
March 1924
INTERNATIONAL CAPS
1 England cap, 1921
LFC DEBUT GAME/GOAL
15 March 1924 /
27 September 1924
CONTRACT EXPIRY
24 June 1926

Season	League App	League Goals	FA Cup App	FA Cup Goals	Total App	Total Goals
1923/24	11	0	0	0	11	0
1924/25	40	7	4	2	44	9
1925/26	12	1	0	0	12	1
Total	**63**	**8**	**4**	**2**	**67**	**10**

Raybould,
Sam

SAM RAYBOULD established himself quite late on the league scene after playing with a string of amateur sides.

He was 24 years old when he scored 10 goals in 13 games in half a season for Second Division New Brighton Tower, before finding stardom at neighbours Liverpool. Raybould was the first player to score 100 league goals for Liverpool, a feat he achieved in 162 First and Second Division matches between 20 January 1900 and 9 December 1905. He was top scorer with 17 when Liverpool won the League Championship for the first time in 1901. His most prolific period came two years later when he grabbed 32 goals from 34 league and cup games and was top of the scoring charts in the First Division by a good margin of six goals. His abilities were obvious to everyone. 'He is a dangerous player when in possession, and backs who make mistakes might as well concede a goal straight away,' the local press reported admiringly.

> RAYBOULD WAS THE FIRST PLAYER TO SCORE 100 LEAGUE GOALS FOR LIVERPOOL

Having just become the first Liverpool player to score 30 goals in one season Raybould got himself in trouble with the football authorities by agreeing to 'financial inducements' to sign for Southern League Portsmouth on 1 May 1903, along with team-mates John Glover and Bill Goldie. When the Football League was founded in 1888 it was based entirely in the North and Midlands,

with the establishment of County Football Associations in the South being firmly opposed to professionalism. Portsmouth tried to use the lack of regulations of transfers between the leagues to their advantage, but their approach was deemed illegal and Raybould was suspended for six months for agreeing to sign for Pompey. He was also given a lifetime ban on ever signing for the south coast side. His absence proved significant as Liverpool slumped from fifth place a year before to relegation candidates. During the enforced break Raybould was very successful in quarter-mile professional sprints in the Midlands and is said to have run 120 yards (110m) in just over 11 seconds. His ban lasted until 31 December 1903, but he seemed to have been forgiven for wishing to move as he was selected for the first team straight away in January. But even Raybould's four goals from 15 games towards the end of the season could not prevent the dreaded drop into the Second Division.

RAYBOULD was a strong and powerful striker with a wonderful turn of speed and good ball control, and was praised for his daring rushes upfield and judicious distribution of play to the wingers, but first and foremost of his skills was his deadly scoring capacity. He was moved from centre-forward to left wing in the Second Division and struggled

to make an impression in the opening matches. At the time he suffered more abuse from his own fans than any other player, as they had expected him always to score goals. In the end Raybould came good and scored 19 league goals as the club made an immediate return to the First Division. He made a significant contribution when the First Division title was won just a year later by scoring 11 goals in 25 matches. The last of Raybould's 211 league appearances for Liverpool came on the final day of the 1906/07 season at home to Sheffield United and he marked the occasion in typical fashion with a goal, the last of the 130 he scored for the club. Despite being such a sensational goalscorer for

FACTFILE

BORN
Staveley, Chesterfield,
11 June 1875
DIED
17 December 1953
POSITION
Centre-forward / Left-winger
OTHER CLUBS
Seymour Exchange,
Poolsbrook United,
Staveley Colliery,
North Staveley,
Ilkeston Town (1894),
Derby County (1894–95),
Ilkeston Town (1895–97),
Poolsbrook United (1897–98),
Ilkeston Town (1898–99),
Bolsover Colliery (1899),
New Brighton Tower
(1899–1900),
Sunderland (1907–08),
Woolwich Arsenal (1908–09),
Chesterfield Town (1909–11),
Sutton Town (1911–13),
Barlborough United (1913–15)
SIGNED FROM
New Brighton Tower, £250,
3 January 1900
LFC DEBUT GAME/GOAL
13 January 1900 /
20 January 1900
CONTRACT EXPIRY
May 1907
HONOURS
League Championship
1900/01, 1905/06;
Second Division
Championship 1904/05;
First Division top scorer
1902/03

Season	League		FA Cup		Other		Total	
	App	Goals	App	Goals	App	Goals	App	Goals
1899/1900	11	7	0	0	-	-	11	7
1900/01	31	17	2	1	-	-	33	18
1901/02	29	16	0	0	-	-	29	16
1902/03	33	31	1	1	-	-	34	32
1903/04	15	4	1	1	-	-	16	5
1904/05	32	19	2	0	-	-	34	19
1905/06	25	11	4	4	1	1	30	16
1906/07	35	15	4	2	-	-	39	17
Total	**211**	**120**	**14**	**9**	**1**	**1**	**226**	**130**

Raybould worked hard during his ban

Liverpool he never played for the English national team, but featured three times for the Football League XI playing the Scottish League XI.

Thirty-two-year-old Raybould left Liverpool in 1907 for First Division Sunderland. He scored 10 goals in 27 league games in the 1907/08 season, keeping Sunderland just above the relegation places. After only one season he went to fellow First Division team Woolwich Arsenal and scored six goals in 26 league games before going down a couple of divisions to guide Chesterfield Town to the Midland Championship, scoring 14 goals in 47 games in his two years there as well as running the Old Angel Hotel in Chesterfield. The *Derby Daily Telegraph* claimed in 1910 that Sam had been forced to move from Liverpool because his

wife Selina had fallen in with 'some women neighbors of a very undesirable character, and took to drink.' Unfortunately the move to Sunderland did not solve the problem and in February 1910 Sam was granted a divorce from his wife of 12 years and given custody of three of their four children.

Redknapp, Jamie

THE ULTIMATE professional on and off the field, Jamie Redknapp trained as a youngster with Tottenham, but it was at his dad Harry's club, Bournemouth, where he started his professional career. Before he had even started a single game, Kenny Dalglish had already paid a visit.

Harry let Jamie go for two weeks to have a look at Liverpool, but he decided he was better off at least for one more year at Bournemouth. After only 13 first-team matches for Bournemouth Redknapp became the most expensive 17-year-old in football when Liverpool paid £350,000, with the fee later rising to £500,000. Unfortunately Jamie never played under Dalglish, even though he was on the bench against Wimbledon four days after his arrival. Only five weeks after Redknapp had arrived at Liverpool, Dalglish resigned. Graeme Souness had great faith in Redknapp's ability and he became the youngest player to appear for the club in European competition when he played his first game against Auxerre on 23 October 1991. He wore his idol's shirt, Dalglish's number 7. Phil Charnock broke his European record a year later.

SOUNESS liked what he saw from Redknapp saying, 'This young

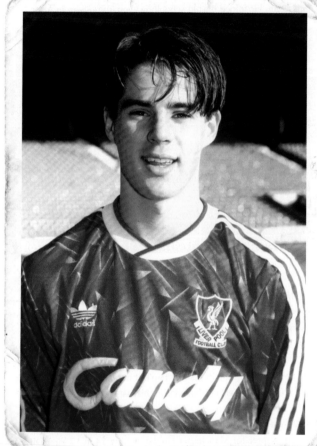

man comes from a footballing background. His father was a very good First Division player and he knows what's expected of him. He has a very big future in front of him.' Redknapp played 146 games over the next three years as Souness's reign descended into chaos and Roy Evans took over. Redknapp was captain of the Under-21 national team that won the Toulon tournament in France in the summer of 1994 and was undoubtedly Liverpool's best player in 1994/95, Evans' full debut season. Redknapp made his full England debut against Colombia on 6 September 1995 when his shot inspired Rene Higuita's legendary scorpion-kick save. At that point Redknapp was in inspired form for Liverpool, scoring with long-distance shots in two games in a row against Spartak Vladikavkaz and Blackburn. He was then chosen for England to face Switzerland on 15 November. Seven minutes into the game, he picked up a hamstring injury. Four months later he was back in the starting line-up, but more disappointment awaited: Liverpool lost to Manchester United in the FA Cup final and then in Euro 1996, Redknapp got injured again playing the Scots.

Liverpool coped well without Redknapp in the first half of the 1996/97 season and he was in and out of the team. His injury jinx struck again, this time in a friendly international game against South Africa on 24 May 1997, and he was out for five months. Redknapp slowly regained his old form and was looking forward to the 1998 World Cup. He got injured against Coventry only two months prior to the competition, and that meant the end of his season and his World Cup ambitions.

In 1998/99 Gérard Houllier came in, initially at Roy Evans' side, and Redknapp's career was soon flying high again. He was in his best form for three years, played 39 matches and scored 10 goals. In the summer of 1999, Houllier made Redknapp captain. On 20 November 1999 he was injured against Sunderland and spent the next four months on the sidelines. Three substitute appearances in succession on his return reached a crescendo when he scored the winning goal against Newcastle. Two days later he played with the reserves against Sheffield Wednesday but got injured once more, this time being out for a month. That begged the question: Why not rest him when Liverpool play teams beginning with the letter S? Redknapp had picked up injuries against Switzerland, Scotland, South Africa, Sunderland and Sheffield Wednesday. The S-curse had struck again.

Redknapp didn't play a single match in 2000/01 due to injury, but lifted the FA Cup on behalf of the Liverpool team, despite his initial apprehension as he explained on Sky's A League of Their Own.

*Before the game I wasn't going to do it. I had missed out all year and Robbie Fowler said: 'You are the club captain and we want you to do it if we win it.' I went: 'Don't be stupid, no chance. It's not my time.' Sami Hyypia was going to be captain on the day. Robbie came on the pitch after we had won the game 2-1. Robbie said: 'Come on, you can do this!' I said: 'No, no. Honestly I don't want to do it.' Out of the corner of my eye I could see Gérard Houllier going to Sami Hyypia: 'You go. You are the captain. You go up there.' I thought: 'Oh, really? I think I will do this!' I thought, 'Houllier, you w*****! Have some of that!'*

REDKNAPP, in turn, refused a testimonial at Liverpool because he didn't feel he had played enough in the previous seasons to deserve it. When Redknapp returned in 2001/02, he lasted only eight games before he was injured again. He joined his old schoolboy team Tottenham in April 2002,

having made his last appearance for the Liverpool first team at the end of October 2001. Redknapp took over the captaincy at Tottenham, playing half a century of games in two and a half years. He went on a free transfer to Southampton in January 2005, but only stayed there for five months under the guidance of his father. Redknapp was forced to retire at 32 in the summer of 2005 and works now as a Sky Sports pundit.

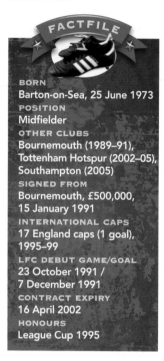

FACTFILE

BORN
Barton-on-Sea, 25 June 1973
POSITION
Midfielder
OTHER CLUBS
Bournemouth (1989–91), Tottenham Hotspur (2002–05), Southampton (2005)
SIGNED FROM
Bournemouth, £500,000, 15 January 1991
INTERNATIONAL CAPS
17 England caps (1 goal), 1995–99
LFC DEBUT GAME/GOAL
23 October 1991 / 7 December 1991
CONTRACT EXPIRY
16 April 2002
HONOURS
League Cup 1995

Season	League		FA Cup		League Cup		Europe		Other		Total	
	App	Goals	App	Goals	App	Goals	App	Goals	App	Goals	App	Goals
1991/92	5 (1)	1	2	0	0	0	1 (1)	0	-	-	8 (2)	1
1992/93	27 (2)	2	1	0	6	1	4	0	0	0	38 (2)	3
1993/94	29 (6)	4	2	0	4	0	-	-	-	-	35 (6)	4
1994/95	36 (5)	3	6	1	8	2	-	-	-	-	50 (5)	6
1995/96	19 (4)	3	2 (1)	0	3	0	4	1	-	-	28 (5)	4
1996/97	18 (5)	2	1	0	1	1	4 (3)	0	-	-	24 (8)	3
1997/98	20	3	1	1	3	1	2	0	-	-	26	5
1998/99	33 (1)	8	2	0	0	0	4	2	-	-	39 (1)	10
1999/2000	18 (4)	3	0	0	1	0	-	-	-	-	19 (4)	3
2001/02	2 (2)	1	0	0	0 (1)	0	1 (2)	1	0	0	3 (5)	2
Total	**207 (30)**	**30**	**17 (1)**	**2**	**26 (1)**	**5**	**20 (6)**	**4**	**0**	**0**	**270 (38)**	**41**

Reid, Tom

THOMAS Joseph Reid played in a number of different positions for Liverpool but was predominantly used in the forward-line.

By no means speedy or graceful, he was the archetypal old-fashioned centre-forward who happened to be a goalscoring machine! Reid made his Liverpool debut on the final day of the 1925/26 season in a home fixture with Sheffield United, scoring after only eight minutes and adding another goal

to help his team secure a point from a 2-2 draw. Reid often scored in 'pairs'; the next season he repeated that two-goal debut performance on no fewer than five separate occasions. Reid was Liverpool's second-highest scorer in the league behind goalscoring legend Gordon Hodgson in 1927/28 with 15 from 25 fixtures. He was only called on six times the following season, scoring in his first two but not adding to his impressive scoring record, 30 goals in 55 games, in his last four appearances.

ONLY 24 years old when he left Liverpool in February 1929, Reid went on a scoring spree for Manchester United, netting 14 in 17 First Division games for the rest of the 1928/29 season, but 22 goals in 43 games in the next two campaigns couldn't prevent United being relegated to the Second Division. Reid added 27 goals in 36 games in two seasons in the Second Division, being described in their match programme as 'somewhat cumbersome in his methods, but he is an opportunist of the first water'. He was loaned to neighbours and fellow Second Division team Oldham Athletic in March 1933 where he scored nine in 13 games in the remainder of the 1932/33 season. His loan was made permanent when the Latics supporters club donated the £400 needed. Reid was Oldham's top scorer

the following season with 16 league goals. In total Reid scored 145 goals in 245 Football League appearances.

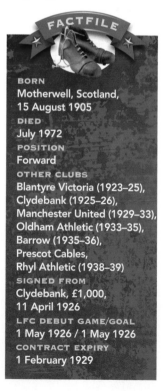

FACTFILE

BORN
Motherwell, Scotland, 15 August 1905
DIED
July 1972
POSITION
Forward
OTHER CLUBS
Blantyre Victoria (1923–25), Clydebank (1925–26), Manchester United (1929–33), Oldham Athletic (1933–35), Barrow (1935–36), Prescot Cables, Rhyl Athletic (1938–39)
SIGNED FROM
Clydebank, £1,000, 11 April 1926
LFC DEBUT GAME/GOAL
1 May 1926 / 1 May 1926
CONTRACT EXPIRY
1 February 1929

Season	League		FA Cup		Total	
	App	Goals	App	Goals	App	Goals
1925/26	1	2	0	0	1	2
1926/27	20	11	1	0	21	11
1927/28	25	15	2	0	27	15
1928/29	5	2	1	0	6	2
Total	**51**	**30**	**4**	**0**	**55**	**30**

Reina,
Pepe

JOSÉ MANUEL 'Pepe' Reina played 30 league games from 2000 to 2002 for Barcelona and was involved in both legs against Liverpool in the semi-finals of the UEFA Cup in the 2000/01 season. Liverpool proceeded to the final after Gary McAllister scored past the 18-year-old Reina from the penalty spot in the second leg at Anfield.

After Louis van Gaal returned to Barcelona for his second spell in charge it soon became clear that he didn't have enough faith in Reina, who joined Villareal in the summer of 2002. Reina played 32 league games in his first season and didn't miss a single La Liga game in either his second or third season, which proved to be his last. He was considered the best keeper in La Liga in 2004/05 as Villareal grabbed third place and a potential spot in the Champions League for the first time in the club's history. Reina was noted for saving seven penalties out of the nine Villareal conceded that season.

The 22-year-old Reina was very experienced for his age with around 175 first-team games under his belt when he arrived at Liverpool in the summer of 2005. Rafa Benítez clearly saw him as his number one for the future and the determined Spaniard didn't disappoint his compatriot. Reina enhanced his reputation as a penalty-stopper when he saved three penalties from West Ham in the shootout of the 2006 FA Cup final and ended his first season as a Cup hero. He didn't make the best of starts in his second season, making a glaring error in the Merseyside derby on 9 September 2006 when Liverpool lost 3-0 at Goodison Park. The Spaniard kept his place in the starting line-up even though he was well below his best. Benítez's faith in

KODAK FILM

him paid off, Reina grew stronger as the season progressed and he kept Jerzy Dudek out of the starting XI. In 2008, amazingly for the third season in succession, Reina was the recipient of the 'Golden Glove' award for keeping the most 'clean sheets' in the Premier League. He also achieved 50 'clean sheets' in the fewest number of league matches, 92, beating the previous record held by Ray Clemence by three matches.

REINA joined club colleagues Álvaro Arbeloa, Fernando Torres and Xabi Alonso in the Spanish squad for the 2008 European Championships held in Austria and Switzerland. Real Madrid's Iker Casillas had been impossible for Reina to dislodge from the number one slot, but he proudly went up to collect a winners' medal even though he had only played an active part in one of the group matches, against Greece. Reina's celebrations once the conquering heroes returned to Spain will never be forgotten as his clownish side really came out in a big way. In the 2008/09 season Reina was again a vital part of the Liverpool team that had seemed likely to bring in the elusive Premier League title. In April 2010, it was revealed that the popular Spaniard had signed a six-year extension to his contract. One of the team's most reliable performers during a turbulent 2009/10 season, Reina was again the 'Golden Glove' winner for most clean sheets in the league, 17 in total, a distinction he shared with Chelsea's Petr Cech. In the 2010 World Cup Reina was as before second-choice for his country behind Casillas and did not see a single minute of competitive action in any of Spain's seven matches as they won the tournament for the first time. He was, as ever, heavily involved in the victory celebrations!

Reina played in all 38 Premier League matches for the fourth successive season in 2010/11, but was clearly way below his best form. He missed four Premier League matches in 2011/12 after being sent off at Newcastle in April following an altercation with home defender James Perch.

Pepe did, however, play in more domestic cup matches than in any previous season as a Liverpool player as the club reached the Wembley finals of both the League and FA Cup. Pepe's performances in the Liverpool goal had been on a downward spiral but he improved in 2012/13, having regained somewhat his sharpness and focus. Reina had planned to join Barcelona in the summer of 2013 so Liverpool searched for a new keeper, which led them to Simon Mignolet at Sunderland. However, keeper Victor Valdes wanted to see out the last year of his contract at Barca and keeping Reina on the bench at Liverpool, being paid supposedly £110,000 a week, made little sense for the club. Instead of returning to his boyhood club, Reina moved on a season-long loan to Napoli, rejoining Rafa Benítez.

Season	League		FA Cup		League Cup		Europe		Other		Total	
	App	Goals	App	Goals	App	Goals	App	Goals	App	Goals	App	Goals
2005/06	33	0	5	0	0	0	13	0	2	0	53	0
2006/07	35	0	0	0	1	0	14	0	1	0	51	0
2007/08	38	0	0	0	0	0	14	0	-	-	52	0
2008/09	38	0	2	0	0	0	11	0	-	-	51	0
2009/10	38	0	1	0	0	0	13	0	-	-	52	0
2010/11	38	0	1	0	0	0	11	0	-	-	50	0
2011/12	34	0	5	0	7	0	-	-	-	-	46	0
2012/13	31	0	0	0	0	0	8	0	-	-	39	0
Total	**285**	**0**	**14**	**0**	**8**	**0**	**84**	**0**	**3**	**0**	**394**	**0**

Richardson, Wally

WALLY Richardson, who played military football with the King's 1st Regiment, featured in only one game in the Lancashire League for Liverpool in 1892/93.

He was in fact the trainer of the team and had to be called upon when Liverpool were missing players for the game against Rossendale on 25 March 1893.

A newspaper report said: 'Liverpool were again short of their regular players (Ross and McCartney), and at the last moment had to turn out the right-half in the person of the trainer (Richardson), who, under the conditions, made a fair show.'

Season	League		FA Cup		Other		Total	
	App	Goals	App	Goals	App	Goals	App	Goals
1892/93	-	-	0	0	1	0	1	0
Total	0	0	0	0	1	0	1	0

Riedle, Karl-Heinz

KARL-HEINZ Riedle was born in East Germany but finally made the grade in the Bundesliga when he joined Werder Bremen in 1987, winning the Bundesliga in his first season.

He won the World Cup with Germany in 1990 and later that summer became one of Europe's most expensive players when he moved to Lazio. Three years later he returned to Germany with Dortmund, who won the Bundesliga title in 1994 and 1995. He arrived at Liverpool a bona fide international star after scoring two goals for Dortmund in the Champions League final win over Juventus a couple of months earlier.

Roy Evans had brought in a trio of experienced players in the summer of 1997 in Riedle, Øyvind Leonardsen and Paul Ince, who he hoped would benefit the less experienced in his squad. Riedle had, however, clearly left his best footballing years behind him in Germany, seemingly strangely unaware, despite all his experience, of the offside rule. His two full seasons at Liverpool followed a similar pattern as he was first choice at the beginning and the end of the campaign, having lost his place before regaining it due to the enforced absence of either Michael Owen or Robbie Fowler.

RIEDLE scored two against Hull in the League Cup in his farewell appearance before joining Fulham in the First Division. He was caretaker manager of the southwest London club in the 1999/2000 season alongside Roy Evans.

Season	League		FA Cup		League Cup		Europe		Total	
	App	Goals	App	Goals	App	Goals	App	Goals	App	Goals
1997/98	18 (7)	6	1	0	2 (3)	0	1 (2)	1	22 (12)	7
1998/99	16 (18)	5	1	0	0 (1)	0	2 (2)	1	19 (21)	6
1999/2000	0 (1)	0	0	0	1	2	-	-	1 (1)	2
Total	34 (26)	11	2	0	3 (4)	2	3 (4)	2	42 (34)	15

Riera, Albert

ALBERT RIERA was part of the side that won the Copa del Rey for the first time in Mallorca's history. His first experience of English football was when he was on loan at Manchester City, where he didn't make a good impression, but on his return to Espanyol he became a key player, scoring one of their goals in the UEFA Cup final in 2007 which was lost to Sevilla on penalties.

Riera made his international debut for Spain against Denmark on 13 October 2007, but didn't make the Spanish squad that conquered in Euro 2008.

Riera had a decent debut season with Liverpool, starting 33 games out of his total of 40, so Rafa Benítez clearly had great faith in him. He showed that he could strike the ball accurately and work hard for the team. Liverpool were in excellent form and Riera seemed to have been a wise addition to the Spanish contingent at the club.

Former Red Mark Lawrenson was certainly impressed. 'Albert Riera fits the stereotype of a continental winger. He can be a bit frustrating, flits in and out of games and yet when he comes good then he is a class act. Just study how many times Fernando Torres drifts in from the left and then goes for goal with his right foot. That is because Riera has been stretching the opposition.'

AFTER RIERA had only started 12 matches in 2009/10 he openly criticised Benítez on Radio Marca in March 2010. 'I've been here two years and I know how he [Benítez] is. He has never sorted out a situation with a player by talking with him. His dialogue with the players is practically nil. My aim is to go to the World Cup and for this I have to be playing. When the coach says nothing to you and you are well, with no physical problems and training well, you cannot help but think it must be something personal,' Riera said, earning himself a two-week suspension.

After Benítez departed Anfield Roy Hodgson made a pledge that

FACTFILE

BORN
Mallorca, Spain, 15 April 1982
POSITION
Left-winger
OTHER CLUBS
Real Mallorca (1999–2003),
Bordeaux (2003–05),
Espanyol (2005–08),
Manchester City (loan, 2006),
Olympiacos (2010–11),
Galatasaray (2011–)
SIGNED FROM
Espanyol, £8million,
31 August 2008
INTERNATIONAL CAPS
16 Spain caps (4 goals)
(11 (3) at LFC), 2007–09
LFC DEBUT GAME/GOAL
13 September 2008 /
18 October 2008
CONTRACT EXPIRY
23 July 2010

he would give every player a chance to prove that they had a future with the club. A knee injury excluded Riera from pre-season training and he joined Greek club Olympiacos on 23 July 2010. He enjoyed a promising first season in Greece, playing in 26 of the 30 Superleague matches and scoring six times. However, it was his only full season in Greece because he signed a four-year deal with Galatasaray in Turkey early in

September 2011. It proved to be a wise choice as the Istanbul-based club won the national championship in 2012.

Season	League		FA Cup		League Cup		Europe		Total	
	App	Goals	App	Goals	App	Goals	App	Goals	App	Goals
2008/09	24 (4)	3	2 (1)	1	0	0	7 (2)	1	33 (7)	5
2009/10	9 (3)	0	0	0	1	0	2 (1)	0	12 (4)	0
Total	**33 (7)**	**3**	**2 (1)**	**1**	**1**	**0**	**9 (3)**	**1**	**45 (11)**	**5**

Riise, John Arne

JOHN ARNE Riise was bought by Monaco for £700,000 from Norwegian second-division side Aalesund in the summer of 1998. After Jean Tigana left Monaco in 2001, Riise wanted also to look for pastures new. Leeds showed an interest but could not broker a deal. Riise was frozen out of the first team but finally it looked like his old mentor Tigana would bring him to Fulham. Liverpool then improved on Fulham's offer after Riise has agreed terms with the London side and hijacked the deal. Riise benefited from his three-year stay in France and combined good technique and power.

He had no trouble in adapting to the English game and was a tremendous success in his debut season. He helped Liverpool bring in the Charity Shield and the European Super Cup to add to their impressive treble from the previous campaign and in only his second start in the Premier League Riise ran half the length of the pitch to score the Reds' last goal in a 3-1 victory over Everton at Goodison Park. Two months later his excellent engine and powerful left foot impressed the club's supporters when he unleashed an incredible shot outside the penalty area that reached 70mph before going in off

the bar against Manchester United at Anfield. Ripping off his shirt in celebration became his trademark.

THE NORWEGIAN delivered on the attacking front, but sometimes his defensive skills left a lot to be desired so he was also used in left midfield. Following a disappointing 2003/04 when Riise was dropped on occasions and drew a blank in the scoring stakes, he played in all but one league game under new boss Rafa Benítez in the 2004/05 season that culminated in the drama that was Istanbul. Riise was actually the only Liverpool player to miss in the penalty shootout, but he did provide the superb cross that enabled Gerrard to head in Liverpool's first goal in their astonishing revival.

Riise made amends a year later for his penalty miss, in the FA Cup final against West Ham. 'I asked the manager to let me take the fourth penalty given what happened in Istanbul last year. I was carrying an injury at the time which meant that I couldn't blast the penalty there which I'd normally do. I had to place it and their keeper (Dida) saved it. That was a nightmare, even though we won the cup, it still left me demoralised but I could use the power now. I blasted it down the middle and it flew in, and as soon as it hit the back of the net, I burst into tears. They were stinging my eyes,' Riise explained.

Riise lost his way at Liverpool in his last two seasons, often exposed by his lack of skill in receiving the ball and delivering it to a team-mate, with his personal nadir being his own goal in the 2008 Champions League semi-final against Chelsea. Liverpool were heading for a priceless 1-0 win in the first leg when Riise dived to head the ball into his own net at the Kop end in the 90th minute.

AFTER SEVEN eventful years of highs and lows at Anfield, Riise left for Roma in 2008. Jamie Carragher said Riise would be missed: 'He can be very proud of what he's achieved with Liverpool. He has played nearly 350 games and scored a lot of goals. He's played at a very high level for a long time now. He's never injured and he's a great professional who has always looked after himself.' Riise had two decent seasons in Rome before joining his brother Björn Helge at Fulham in July 2011, at last joining the Cottagers after snubbing a move there in favour of Liverpool in 2001. John Arne deservedly got a great reception when he returned to Anfield as a visiting player on 1 May 2012 when the Cottagers beat Liverpool 1-0.

FACTFILE

BORN
Molde, Norway,
24 September 1980
POSITION
Left-back / Left-winger
OTHER CLUBS
Aalesund (1994–98),
Monaco (1998–2001),
AS Roma (2008–11),
Fulham (2011–)
SIGNED FROM
Monaco, £4million,
20 June 2001
INTERNATIONAL CAPS
110 Norway caps (15 goals)
(64 (6) at LFC), 2000–13
LFC DEBUT GAME/GOAL
12 August 2001 /
24 August 2001
CONTRACT EXPIRY
1 July 2008
HONOURS
FA Cup 2006;
League Cup 2003;
Champions League 2005

Season	League		FA Cup		League Cup		Europe		Other		Total	
	App	Goals	App	Goals	App	Goals	App	Goals	App	Goals	App	Goals
2001/02	34 (4)	7	2	0	0	0	14 (1)	1	1	0	51 (5)	8
2002/03	31 (6)	6	2 (1)	0	4	0	10 (1)	0	1	0	48 (8)	6
2003/04	22 (6)	0	1	0	1 (1)	0	4	0	-	-	28 (7)	0
2004/05	34 (3)	6	0	0	3 (2)	1	15	1	-	-	52 (5)	8
2005/06	24 (8)	1	6	3	0	0	11 (1)	0	1 (1)	0	42 (10)	4
2006/07	29 (4)	1	1	0	1	1	12	2	1	1	44 (4)	5
2007/08	22 (7)	0	4	0	0 (1)	0	5 (5)	0	-	-	31 (13)	0
Total	**196 (38)**	**21**	**16 (1)**	**3**	**9 (4)**	**2**	**71 (8)**	**4**	**4 (1)**	**1**	**296 (52)**	**31**

Riley,
Arthur

THE VISIT of a South African football team that beat Liverpool 5-2 in a friendly on 1 October 1924 was a remarkable one.

Not only did the guests exhibit 'joyous football, a goal-getting game that showed us that South African football has improved more quickly than our own', but two players in particular caught the attention of the Liverpool board and the *Echo's* correspondent, Bee: Gordon Hodgson and 'the goalkeeper, a tall, keen fellow who has reach,

anticipation and a safe pair of hands, is only twenty, but he looks more like thirty-five'. Riley and Hodgson were signed by Liverpool in the 1925/26 season. The 21-year-old Riley was bought mainly as cover for Elisha Scott, ten years his senior. The Irishman's form and reputation kept the South African mostly out of the first-team picture until he finally started an extended run in the side in October 1927. But it wasn't until near the second part of the following season that he could really feel safe about being first choice. Scott was a hard act to follow but Riley proved a more than capable replacement. Scott, who was now 38 years of age,

reclaimed his spot in the 1931/32 season and held on to it until February 1933 when Riley returned. The 1930s were very mediocre as far as the club's results were concerned and twice, in 1936 and 1937, they flirted

FACTFILE

BORN
Boksburg, South Africa,
26 December 1903
DIED
1978
POSITION
Goalkeeper
OTHER CLUBS
Transvaal
SIGNED FROM
Transvaal, August 1925
INTERNATIONAL CAPS
2 South Africa caps, 1924
LFC DEBUT
24 October 1925
CONTRACT EXPIRY
1940

Matt Busby and George Kay hoping that Riley has a good aim

Season	League		FA Cup		Total	
	App	**Goals**	**App**	**Goals**	**App**	**Goals**
1925/26	3	0	0	0	3	0
1926/27	10	0	0	0	10	0
1927/28	25	0	2	0	27	0
1928/29	20	0	3	0	23	0
1929/30	34	0	1	0	35	0
1930/31	27	0	1	0	28	0
1931/32	5	0	0	0	5	0
1932/33	15	0	0	0	15	0
1933/34	32	0	0	0	32	0
1934/35	39	0	2	0	41	0
1935/36	39	0	2	0	41	0
1936/37	10	0	0	0	10	0
1937/38	28	0	5	0	33	0
1938/39	35	0	0	0	35	0
Total	**322**	**0**	**16**	**0**	**338**	**0**

dangerously with relegation. Although Alf Hobson took over in goal for much of the 1936/37 season, Riley's courage and agility probably turned a number of games which could have left the club's First Division status even more at risk. It was a shame such loyalty was never rewarded by being part of a successful Liverpool team. The highest final league placing during any of the years Riley was at Anfield was fifth in 1929.

Riley,
Arthur

IN **1982 Arthur Riley retired as head groundsman at Anfield, having served the club since 1928, the same year the newly roofed Kop had its premiere! His father Bert was head groundsman from 1908 until 1950 when Arthur succeeded him.**

The family connection didn't end there, as Arthur's younger brother Len helped him out from 1950 to 1970. Arthur was at the time the longest-serving employee at the club, having been there a total

of 54 years. 'My father would only allow the new grass to be hand-cut,' Riley told the 1983 Liverpool Annual. 'It took me two complete days to push a hand mower over the pitch with the blades set high. The following week, I hand-cut it again, another two days' work, with the blades set a little lower. Before there was a roof on the Kop and when it just had a wooden fence around it the wind would dry the pitch.' Arthur, not to be confused with the goalkeeper of the same name, had seen every game at Anfield in his time and rated the championship-winning teams of 1922 and 1923 as the best ever.

Roberts,
John

John Roberts, or 'Nipper' as he was commonly called, played just once for the club, when he was selected to replace Sam English for the visit to Stoke City on 4 September 1933. A 1-1 draw meant that Liverpool's miserable start to the 1933/34 season continued. Roberts was highly successful with Wigan Athletic in the Cheshire League, scoring 54 goals in 57 matches in an 18-month period. 'Nipper' was then very prolific with Port Vale, scoring 56 goals in 95 league games until World War Two finished his league career. He was an all-round sportsman and even featured in England's baseball team. Roberts served with the Irish Guards during the war and was captured in Tunisia. He attracted widespread attention when he escaped from a prisoner-of-war camp in Italy and walked 400 miles to freedom despite a broken neck.

FACTFILE

BORN
Blundellsands, Liverpool,
15 March 1910
DIED
1 June 1985
POSITION
Centre-forward
OTHER CLUBS
Marine, Orrell,
Northern Nomads,
Blundellsands,
Southport (1931–33),
Wigan Athletic (1934–35),
Port Vale (1935–40),
Wrexham (wartime guest)
SIGNED FROM
Southport, May 1933
LFC DEBUT
4 September 1933
CONTRACT EXPIRY
June 1934

Season	League		FA Cup		Total	
	App	**Goals**	**App**	**Goals**	**App**	**Goals**
1933/34	1	0	0	0	1	0
Total	**1**	**0**	**0**	**0**	**1**	**0**

PEDIA

Roberts, Syd

SYD ROBERTS joined Liverpool after growing up at Bootle Junior Ordnance Corps.

ALTHOUGH he was part of Liverpool's squad for six different seasons, he only played in 58 league matches for the club and a large number of those (25) came in 1932/33. He was mostly used as an inside-forward on both the left and right flank. He had been a regular when he got seriously injured in a cup tie against Tranmere at the end of January 1934 and didn't return to action until December that year. At the end of the 1934/35 season he had to undergo an operation on his left knee for cartilage trouble and only featured in eight games during his last two years at Liverpool.

Season	League		FA Cup		Total	
	App	Goals	App	Goals	App	Goals
1931/32	1	0	0	0	1	0
1932/33	25	6	0	0	25	6
1933/34	13	3	2	1	15	4
1934/35	11	1	2	2	13	3
1935/36	6	0	0	0	6	0
1936/37	2	0	0	0	2	0
Total	**58**	**10**	**4**	**3**	**62**	**13**

FACTFILE

BORN
Bootle, Liverpool, March 1911
POSITION
Inside-right/left forward
OTHER CLUBS
Shrewsbury Town (1937–38), Chester (1938–39), Northfleet United (wartime guest)
SIGNED FROM
Bootle JOC (youth), July 1928
LFC DEBUT GAME/GOAL
23 April 1932 / 8 October 1932
CONTRACT EXPIRY
August 1937

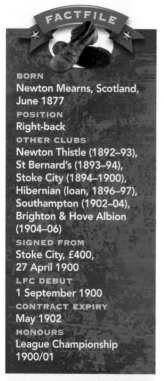

Robertson, Tom

FACTFILE

BORN
Newton Mearns, Scotland, June 1877
POSITION
Right-back
OTHER CLUBS
Newton Thistle (1892–93), St Bernard's (1893–94), Stoke City (1894–1900), Hibernian (loan, 1896–97), Southampton (1902–04), Brighton & Hove Albion (1904–06)
SIGNED FROM
Stoke City, £400, 27 April 1900
LFC DEBUT
1 September 1900
CONTRACT EXPIRY
May 1902
HONOURS
League Championship 1900/01

JOHN THOMAS Robertson was known as Tom while his namesake at the club was referred to as Tommy. The Scottish right-back was brought to England by First Division Stoke and he certainly made an impression, playing 126 games in two spells for the Potters. He was a powerful kicker of the ball and timed his tackles to perfection.

Robertson was only on Liverpool's books for two years but he did win the league title in the first of those seasons, 1900/01, which was also a first for the club too. He made 22 consecutive appearances from the start of the season before John Glover took over for the next nine matches. But Robertson was back in place for the final three fixtures as the title was secured by two points from runners-up Sunderland. Glover started the 1901/02 season but Robertson came back into contention during the second half of the campaign and made a further 17 First Division appearances. Robertson joined the Saints in the Southern League in May 1902. Liverpool were quite annoyed by the transfer, as the *Evening Telegraph* explained: 'It cost them close

upon £400 for his transfer from Stoke, and they have not had two years' service out of him. So far as they are aware, Robertson had no grievance, and as he was offered the maximum rate of wages, some very unpleasant things are being said in Liverpool as to the inducement for him to journey south.' Robertson enjoyed great success with the Saints, winning the Southern League two years in succession from 1902 to 1904. He took the common route of many ex-footballers to run a pub following his retirement. Robertson was described as a quiet guy who would rather walk on hot coals than being interviewed by a football reporter.

Season	League		FA Cup		Total	
	App	Goals	App	Goals	App	Goals
1900/01	25	0	2	0	27	0
1901/02	17	0	3	0	20	0
Total	**42**	**0**	**5**	**0**	**47**	**0**

Robertson, Tommy

TOMMY ROBERTSON won the Scottish Championship with Hearts in 1897 where he was instrumental in clinching the title by scoring four times in a 5-0 victory over Clyde on 20 February.

Four days after Robertson played his only international for Scotland the Edinburgh club suffered as he and team-mate Johnny Walker both moved to Liverpool. Robertson scored on his debut against Sheffield Wednesday

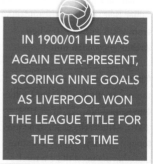

IN 1900/01 HE WAS AGAIN EVER-PRESENT, SCORING NINE GOALS AS LIVERPOOL WON THE LEAGUE TITLE FOR THE FIRST TIME

and only missed a single league match over the next two seasons and contributed 15 league goals, a terrific total from a man in his position. In 1900/01 he was again ever-present, scoring nine goals as Liverpool won the league title for the first time. After adding 25 games and six goals to his league and cup totals in 1901/02 Robertson returned to Scotland to play once again for Hearts. Liverpool's captain in Robertson's time at the club, Alex Raisbeck, said Tommy was one of his best pals at the club and was sorry to see him move to Dundee, in the *Weekly News* in 1915. 'Tommy was a very versatile player. He could play in almost any position in the forward line, and with much credit to himself, too.'

Season	League		FA Cup		Total	
	App	Goals	App	Goals	App	Goals
1897/98	3	2	0	0	3	2
1898/99	33	6	6	1	39	7
1899/1900	34	9	4	1	38	10
1900/01	34	9	2	0	36	9
1901/02	22	5	3	1	25	6
Total	**126**	**31**	**15**	**3**	**141**	**34**

Robinson, Bobby

A hard-working player who gave his all for Liverpool both up front and at the back, Bobby Robinson was a goalscoring sensation in the Sunderland schools' tournaments, in one season scoring 132 out of his school's 156 goals. After 18 months with Sunderland Royal Rovers in the Wearside League Robinson joined Sunderland in the midst of the 1901/02 season in which he contributed one goal in five appearances as his club won the league title. In February 1904 he joined Liverpool shortly after a fellow Sunderland striker, Joe Hewitt, had moved to Anfield.

Robinson made nine First Division appearances, scoring five times, before the end of that debut season but those goals were not enough to stop the club's slide into the Second Division. In his first full season at Anfield he was top scorer with 24 from 32 league matches as Liverpool won the Second Division by two points from Bolton Wanderers. His greatest feat that season was scoring all four goals in a 4-0 home win against Leicester Fosse on 1 October 1904.

ROBINSON and his colleagues coped astonishingly well back in the top division, so much so that they ended the season as champions, four points ahead of Preston North End. Robinson only missed four fixtures and added another 10 goals to his rapidly growing total. During the latter stages of his Liverpool

career, Robinson moved into the half-back line and so his goals-per-game average inevitably suffered, but he prolonged his Anfield stay by three seasons. Prior to the 1909/10 season when Robinson was due to be moved to half-back, being the heaviest man on the team, extreme measures were used to get his surplus fat off. He was made to sit in a small 'hot room' in furnace-like

conditions, and also sprinted, ball-punched, skipped and lifted dumbbells. In a 1912 profile it was said that he 'believes that energy is invaluable in football as in the daily routine of life, and he relies mainly on his bustling tactics, determination, and unlimited energy, combined with a degree of skill for his success at half-back. Is easily distinguished when on the field by reason of his fair hair and well-built figure, and as a forward he has demonstrated his versatility.'

BOBBY struggled with injury in the 1912/13 season but recovered, as the *Liverpool Echo* reported at the end of January 1913: 'I am delighted to inform this legion of friends that "Bobby" Robinson, the Liverpool half-back, has not finished with football, and

under the careful attention of Dr Ferguson, a director of the club, he is making such progress towards health and strength that there is every hope and chance of his playing football; in fact he is training again.' Robinson didn't make another appearance for Liverpool's first team but added a couple of years to his career at Tranmere in the Lancashire Combination.

Season	League		FA Cup		Other		Total	
	App	Goals	App	Goals	App	Goals	App	Goals
1903/04	9	5	0	0	-	-	9	5
1904/05	32	24	1	0	-	-	33	24
1905/06	34	10	4	0	0	0	38	10
1906/07	28	8	4	0	-	-	32	8
1907/08	24	9	2	0	-	-	26	9
1908/09	21	5	1	1	-	-	22	6
1909/10	37	1	1	0	-	-	38	1
1910/11	38	0	2	0	-	-	40	0
1911/12	31	2	2	0	-	-	33	2
Total	**254**	**64**	**17**	**1**	**0**	**0**	**271**	**65**

Robinson, Jack

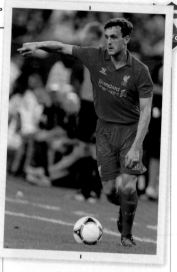

JACK ROBINSON is an attacking left-back who first trained at Melwood ahead of the Europa League clash with Benfica in March 2010.

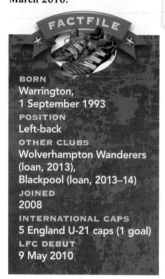

Robinson had been excellent for the Under-18 team and made his first-team debut before even playing for the reserves. At just 16 years and 250 days, he became the youngest ever player to feature for Liverpool's first team when he came on as a substitute at Hull in the final Premier League game of the 2009/10 season on 9 May 2010. Jerome Sinclair has since improved Robinson's record by 244 days on 26 September 2012. Robinson added just two more appearances to his name in 2010/11 in consecutive Premier Leagues matches in April when he replaced the injured Fabio Aurelio at Arsenal and played for nearly 80 minutes against Birmingham. Robinson signed an extension to his contract at the end of October 2011, even though competition for the left-back slot he prefers had been increased by the signing

AT JUST
16 YEARS AND
250 DAYS, HE BECAME
THE YOUNGEST
EVER PLAYER
TO FEATURE
FOR LIVERPOOL'S
FIRST TEAM

of Jose Enrique. He was loaned to Wolves in January 2013 to gain some experience in the Championship. Robinson joined Championship side Blackpool, on a season-long loan deal in 2013/14.

	League		FA Cup		League Cup		Europe		Total	
Season	App	Goals	App	Goals	App	Goals	App	Goals	App	Goals
2009/10	0 (1)	0	0	0	0	0	0	0	0 (1)	0
2010/11	1 (1)	0	0	0	0	0	0	0	1 (1)	0
2011/12	0	0	0	0	2	0	-	-	2	0
2012/13	0	0	2	0	2	0	2	0	6	0
Total	**1 (2)**	**0**	**2**	**0**	**4**	**0**	**2**	**0**	**9 (2)**	**0**

Robinson, Michael

MICHAEL ROBINSON scored 13 goals in 36 games for Preston in the Second Division at only 20 years of age. Malcolm Allison at First Division Manchester City was impressed by his talent and bought him for the considerable fee of £750,000. Robinson failed to live up to expectations and was sold to Brighton only one year later for £400,000.

His career was on the rise again at Brighton where he scored 43 goals in 133 appearances and featured in the 2-2 draw with Manchester United in the FA Cup final, before losing 4-0 in the replay.

When Brighton were relegated in the 1982/83 season, Sevilla, Manchester United and Newcastle all showed interest in Robinson, but once Liverpool came knocking there was only one destination for the boyhood Red.

Joe Fagan was patient with his new signing when Robinson didn't score in his first nine games. He eventually scored two in a 5-0 victory over Odense Boldklub in the first round of the European Cup and a hat-trick in the league against West Ham two weeks later. Robinson credits Fagan's psychological ploy on the morning of the Odense game to his upturn in fortune as he told the *LFC Magazine*.

Ronnie Moran says: 'The boss wants to see you.' I remember walking down the corridor to Joe Fagan's office thinking, 'Well, that's it, I'm not playing.' When I got there, Joe said, 'Michael, lad, I was making a cup of tea this morning and my wife was reading the Echo and saying I was going to leave you out. And I was worried about that because you're worth your weight in gold. Before I go and talk to the press I want you to see the team I'm going to give them.' He handed me a piece of paper with the numbers 1 to 11 blank apart from no. 10, where it said Michael Robinson. 'That's the team, laddie. You and 10 more.' That night I scored twice.

However, Robinson didn't feature regularly on the scoresheet for the rest of the 1983/84 season and didn't play in the last 10 fixtures as Liverpool retained their domestic title. He had been a Wembley substitute in the all-Merseyside League Cup final but didn't figure in the Maine Road replay three days later. The 1983/84 season proved in the end to be an exciting one for

Robinson as it culminated in a substitute appearance in the European Cup final in Rome.

Robinson was by his own admission not very skilful and could have been in better physical shape. Even though he was always going to fade in comparison, playing with Europe's most lethal striker did have its advantages. 'Ian Rush made me look brilliant in the air,' Robinson confessed. 'When I jumped up and headed, the ball would always go to Rushie. He could read my body; the way I jumped up Ian would deduce where the ball would go. He worked it out before I had. Rush never knew which bloody knife or fork to use, but on the

pitch he was a genius.' Robinson's second season at Anfield was an anticlimax and he only made seven starts before he was transferred to Queens Park Rangers in late December 1984. He was in QPR's

line-up when they drew 2-2 with Liverpool in the second leg of the League Cup semi-final at Anfield. QPR had won their home game 1-0 and so progressed to the final, where they lost 3-0 to Oxford.

AFTER SCORING just six goals in 58 matches over three years for Rangers he tried his luck in the Spanish League with Osasuna, where he stayed two-and-a-half years and enjoyed the company of his former team-mate, Sammy Lee, who had joined six months after Robinson's arrival. Robinson remained in Spain and has established himself as a respected and knowledgeable football analyst on his own TV show on the Spanish television network.

Season	League App	League Goals	FA Cup App	FA Cup Goals	League Cup App	League Cup Goals	Europe App	Europe Goals	Other App	Other Goals	Total App	Total Goals
1983/84	23 (1)	6	2	1	8 (1)	3	5 (1)	2	1	0	39 (3)	12
1984/85	3 (3)	0	0	0	3	1	1	0	0	0	7 (3)	1
Total	**26 (4)**	**6**	**2**	**1**	**11 (1)**	**4**	**6 (1)**	**2**	**1**	**0**	**46 (6)**	**13**

Robinson,
Peter

'I SHALL always think back with special happiness to one particular period at my time at Anfield which represented everything I could have hoped for in the organisation and running of a football club. That was when Eric Roberts was the chairman, Eric Sawyer the financial director and Peter Robinson the secretary. We had a wonderful working relationship.' These words of Bill Shankly speak volumes about the brilliant job Robinson did at Liverpool. Appropriately, he was the first winner of the *Liverpool Echo's* prestigious Bill Shankly Memorial Award.

'I saw him every morning, because the players would change at Anfield then get a coach to Melwood.

Then he would have half-an-hour after training with me over a cup of tea, then I would probably get a phone call two or three times every night,' Robinson told the *Liverpool Echo* in 2009 of his close working relationship with Shankly. Robinson's job title changed later from 'Club Secretary' to 'Chief Executive', but entailed more or less the same responsibilities. Before his arrival at Anfield Robinson gained precious experience as assistant secretary at Stockport County and secretary

at his home-town club Crewe Alexandra, Scunthorpe and Brighton and Hove Albion, experiencing life in all four divisions of the Football League.

He first joined Liverpool as club secretary in 1965 following Jimmy McInnes' tragic suicide. The club had just won the FA Cup for the very first time. Liverpool sealed their second League Championship under Shankly's leadership in Robinson's first season, but then went seven years without a trophy to show for their efforts. During the late 1960s, when Shankly and the board were not seeing eye to eye, Sunderland made him a generous offer to become their manager. Shankly asked Robinson if he would go with him to the north east if he were to accept. 'The idea of making them great again appealed to us, but we declined it,' Robinson recalled in the *Liverpool Echo* in 2008.

Robinson explained his role as club secretary in the *Football Monthly* in 1969:

At Anfield on match days alone it is my job to ensure that apart from the permanent staff, 150 part-time workers are engaged and at their various positions be they gatemen, programme sellers, stewards, or in the refreshment bars. We receive several hundreds of letters every week asking for information to settle bets, requesting club badges, players' autographs, back numbers of programmes, from visiting supporters asking directions to Anfield, from home fans asking for directions to away grounds, plus the normal club business letters. They all have to be answered in addition to arranging board meetings and travel for our four teams, including European travel, of course. It is also our job to establish and maintain a close liaison with local and National Press.

BOB PAISLEY brought on Liverpool's golden age as the club dominated Europe. Robinson claims his proudest moment was when Liverpool won the European Cup for first time in 1977.

His most important signing was Kenny Dalglish, who arrived in the wake of the momentous triumph in Rome as Liverpool's talisman, Kevin Keegan, left for Hamburg. Robinson's biggest regret from his time at the Reds was not being able to persuade Keegan to come back to Liverpool and form a partnership with Dalglish.

In the wake of the Heysel tragedy Liverpool turned to Kenny Dalglish to lead the team. The club would suffer considerably financially from its exclusion from European competitions, but fortunately Liverpool had been careful with their money so they were still able to buy the very best and were not forced to get rid of their prize assets. Had the Belgian FA, Belgian authorities and UEFA heeded Robinson's multiple warnings before the European Cup final took place the tragedy would never have occurred. 'Liverpool's secret was that they employed the best; the best tea-ladies, the best players and the best administrator in Peter Robinson, known as PBR and renowned for looking after the players brilliantly,' Kenny Dalglish wrote in his autobiography. Robinson's working relationship with Dalglish lasted for 24 years and he said in the press following the Scotsman's resignation in 1991 that 'watching Kenny Dalglish walk out of Anfield was the saddest moment of my life'.

ROBINSON was generous with player wages and negotiated transfers with utmost skill. 'PBR was actually very canny with money,' Dalglish said in *My Liverpool Home*. 'Before the end of the tax year, he occasionally called me in. 'Kenny, we've got about £250,000 spare if you want to spend it.' Peter had done it before with previous managers, so May signings were not uncommon. Frank McGarvey came in 1979 and Rushie arrived a year later.'

Former chief executive of the Football Association and Liverpool supporter Brian Barwick got to know Robinson in a professional capacity. 'A man of sound judgement, few words and somebody who, mentally and physically, always seemed on the move. Indeed, many was the time I would be holding a telephone conversation with him only to find the man at the other end of the receiver had moved on to the next call!' he recalled in the *Liverpool Daily Post* in 2012.

Liverpool fans recognise Robinson instantly as they have seen him on numerous photos sitting with pen in hand with the Reds' latest signing,

from Kenny Dalglish to Didi Hamann. 'PBR' retired as chief executive in 1999, moving into the boardroom as executive vice-chairman. Robinson knows the inner workings of Liverpool in the last third of the twentieth century better than anyone else and his revelations could probably fill a few bestsellers. But the nature of his job was to keep his cards close to his chest and, being the gentleman he is, he has faithfully remained silent since his retirement in 2000, at the age of 64.

'WATCHING KENNY DALGLISH WALK OUT OF ANFIELD WAS THE SADDEST MOMENT OF MY LIFE'

PETER ROBINSON

Rodgers,
Brendan

'I PROMISE I'll fight for my life and for the people in this city,' a determined Brendan Rodgers said at his unveiling as Liverpool's manager. The Ulsterman is a true visionary.

'My big dream is to be a highly successful football manager whose methods provide innovation for youth and senior footballers and coaches,' he told the *Belfast*

Telegraph in April 2012. 'I started coaching for one reason and that was to make a difference for people, not just as footballers but as human beings.'

RODGERS was a young player with Ballymena United in his home county of Antrim before he was spotted by Manchester United, attending their academy during school holidays. At 16 he moved to London to further his career as youth-team captain of Reading, then in the Third Division. Unfortunately, a genetic knee condition forced Rodgers at

only 20 to terminate any ambitions of becoming a professional footballer, as it had stopped the playing career of two of his four brothers. He put his disappointment aside and worked hard at pursuing a career as a coach. Rodgers became Reading's academy manager at only 22 and travelled far and wide to educate himself. He studied coaching techniques in Spain with Barcelona, Sevilla and Valencia, ultimately becoming fluent in Spanish, and spent time with the legendary Dutchman Rinus Michels whose 'Total Fotball'

appealed to him. He chose those particular clubs as he was fascinated by their playing style and inherit belief in youngsters. José Mourinho made him the manager of Chelsea's academy in 2004 and reserve-team manager two years later, the post a vital link between the academy and the first team. Born exactly ten years to the day before Rodgers, Mourinho saw other characteristics in him which mirrored his own. 'I like everything in him,' Mourinho told BBC Northern Ireland in 2006. 'He has ambition and does not see football very differently from myself.

He is open, likes to learn and likes to communicate. I hope he can progress in his career because he has conditions for that and is a good lad.' 'I had three and a half years with José,' Rodgers told the *Independent* in 2011. 'It was like being at Harvard University.'

In 2008 the Championship's Watford gave Rodgers the chance to become a manager of a first team where he could incorporate his ideas. 'I was brought up in a traditional 4-4-2, kick the ball up the pitch, but when I was a youth international with Northern Ireland we would play France, Spain and Switzerland and we would chase the ball,' Rodgers told the *Daily Mail* in 2011. 'I wanted to play in their team, I liked the ideology. I educated myself by studying, watching and learning.' Rodgers uses a 4-2-3-1 formation when his team does not have the ball, which by his ambitious standards should ideally not be more than 21 per cent of each game. He likes his team to dominate the play and when his players lose the ball they have to apply intense pressure and ideally retrieve it inside five or six seconds as close to the opponent's goal as possible so an attack can be launched immediately. If there's not a possibility of an attack, his team will recycle the ball, catching its breath by passing it patiently at the back, slowly building momentum. In possession the shape of his team is 3-4-3 with the full-backs pushing forward, the central defenders moving in either direction to narrow the space left at the flanks while the defensive midfielder drops between them. Two attack-minded players control the midfield while the wingers push forward either side of the central striker.

RODGERS' teams reflect his father's work ethic, as he explained to BBC Sport Wales in May 2011. 'I used to help Dad paint and decorate to earn pocket money. He instilled in me the value of a

hard day's work. He believes that leads to success in whatever you do. He'd work from dawn to dusk to ensure his young family had everything. I think you can see his philosophies in my team.'

WHEN RODGERS took over at Watford on 24 November 2008 with Frank Lampard Snr as his right-hand man, the Hornets had won five league games out of 18 and were in 21st place out of 24. Rodgers won 11 of the remaining 28 league games, steering Watford to mid-table safety. His first English club were obviously monitoring the Irishman's progress. Steve Coppell stepped down after failing to take Reading back into the Premier League they had left at the end of the 2007/08 season and on 5 June 2009 Rodgers was appointed to replace him. But it was not a happy return to the Madejski Stadium and he was sacked by the Berkshire club on 16 December as Reading sat in a similar position as Watford had when he was called upon to rescue them. This time he was the culprit behind his club's plight. 'I went in thinking, "Right, the club want a new vision, a new philosophy" and I felt if I stripped it down quickly and let it build then that would be okay,' he reflected when he took over at Liverpool. 'But what I realised after that was you are still in the business of winning. You talk about football, creativity and invention, but you have to win games – as simple as that. That six months at Reading over the course of a nearly 20-year period coaching and managing has been great learning for me. Hopefully that will be the defining moment of my career.'

For six months following his sacking Rodgers said he could not even get an interview with a League Two club, but Swansea City chairman Huw Jenkins recognised the superb job he had done with youngsters at Reading and Chelsea and appointed him as the club's manager in the summer of 2010. Rodgers' headquarters were eight miles from the Liberty Stadium in the Glamorgan Health & Racquet Club in a tiny windowless office with just enough space for a desk, a couple of chairs, a computer and a filing cabinet. In a sensational first season Rodgers led the Swans into the promised land of the Premier League, although it took a dramatic playoff final victory against his old club Reading at Wembley to achieve this. Tipped by many to make an immediate return to the Championship, Swansea finished the 2011/12 campaign eleventh in the Premier League, playing courageous football designed to entertain. The Swans had an 85.7 per cent pass completion, only bettered (and by only 0.2 per cent) by champions Manchester City. In comparison Kenny Dalglish's Liverpool had the eighth-best pass completion average of 80.9

per cent. Arsenal boasted 59.6 per cent possession, at the top with a healthy margin, but Swansea came third with 57.5 per cent just behind Manchester City. Liverpool were seventh with 55 per cent possession.

Before the final fixture of the campaign against Liverpool, Rodgers asked Swansea fans to dress up as Elvis at the Liberty Stadium as a response to bookmakers who gave better odds of Elvis being alive than Swansea avoiding relegation at the start of the season. 'Someone from the Valleys drove down to the Liberty Stadium a couple of days after I said it with a cake with a swan dressed as Elvis,' Rodgers told *Wales Online*. 'Football is global, but it's also about fun. It's an entertainment and we must not forget that.' Talking to the press the day before Liverpool's arrival Rodgers did not jump on the bandwagon and displayed a healthy respect for Kenny Dalglish's achievements at Liverpool. 'He renewed the motivation in the group [of players] and the city, and this season he has reshaped the squad. It's the beginning of a process that he hopes in the future will bring success. But that's the problem with being a manager; it's like trying to build an aircraft while it is flying. You don't get time to put it in the hangar and do everything you need and send it out there, you have to try and do it while it's flying.' Three weeks later Rodgers became Liverpool's new pilot.

Rodgers rejected Liverpool's first approach, claiming he was happy at the Liberty. He did not want to be interviewed as just another name on a shortlist of candidates that included Wigan Athletic's Roberto Martínez, potentially unsettling his Swansea career. When he received assurances from Liverpool that in fact he was their first choice, the contract negotiations began. Liverpool's initial idea was to have a director

of football to work closely with the new manager; Louis Van Gaal was the name most connected with the position. Rodgers told Liverpool's hierarchy that he would not work under those circumstances and convinced them to shelve their blueprint for success. Soon after his appointment Rodgers came armed with a 180-page dossier to show owners John Henry and Tom Werner his future vision for Liverpool. He did not need anyone looking over his shoulder. 'I started over 15 years ago, and it's something I've been piecing together for many years since,' he revealed in July 2012. 'Then, when I became a manager, I put it into a format with a philosophy and methodology. It's a document on the culture, philosophy and game plan going forward. It's a model, a shortcut to how I work, the kind of players I want tactically and the personality traits of players.'

'I WANT to use the incredible support to make coming to Anfield the longest 90 minutes of an opponent's life,' Rodgers told the media circus gathered to witness his unveiling at Anfield. 'I want to see this great attacking football with creativity and imagination, with relentless pressing of the ball. I know what it's like because I had a team like that at Swansea. That was with a terrific little club and a terrific group of players. When people came to Swansea it was probably the longest 90 minutes of their life. So after 10 minutes when they hadn't had a touch of the ball they are looking at the clock and seeing only 10 minutes had gone. It's a long afternoon.'

Rodgers had effectively a shoestring budget since the previous regime of Kenny Dalglish and Damien Comolli had emptied Liverpool's coffers. He had to get rid of more players than he was able to bring in to create funds. It soon became apparent that neither Charlie Adam nor Andy Carroll was suited to his game plan. Adam was

offloaded to Stoke while Carroll went on loan to West Ham United with a view to a permanent transfer. Maxi Rodriguez and Craig Bellamy went on their own volition while Dirk Kuyt wanted one last big payday in Turkey. Misfit Alberto Aquilani returned to Italy and Joe Cole moved in January to West Ham, where his career had started. The jury is still out on the biggest purchases Rodgers made in the summer of 2012: Fabio Borini and Joe Allen. They came for a combined fee of £25.4million, which was a considerable total in regards to the size of Rodgers' budget, but they are paid low wages by Liverpool's standards as the club has made great strides in lowering its enormous wage bill. Squad player Oussama Assaidi was purchased for a modest £3million while Nuri Sahin's loan from Real Madrid did not work out as he jumped at the chance to play for his old club, Borussia Dortmund. A failed attempt to get Clint Dempsey on the last day of the transfer window, leaving Rodgers woefully short of attackers, left the manager frustrated and going through the opening months of his debut Liverpool campaign almost with one hand tied behind his back. In turn he was able to give youngsters Raheem Sterling and Suso more playing time than expected.

The rest of Dalglish's recruits, outside of Luis Suarez, knew they were living on borrowed time. Jordan Henderson was offered to other clubs while Rodgers delivered a public flogging to Stewart Downing and Jose Enrique. Great credit to the trio, who responded with improved performances on the pitch, as did Pepe Reina, who had been on a downward spiral. The central pair in defence however, Martin Skrtel and Daniel Agger, who had been secured on new long-term deals in the summer, made plenty of uncharacteristic errors throughout the 2012/13 season which cost Liverpool precious points. Rodgers reinstated Jamie Carragher to the centre of defence in his farewell season instead of the Slovakian.

RODGERS could not celebrate a home win in the league until his fifth attempt when Reading were beaten 1-0. He had not been handed the easiest of starts by having to face Manchester City, Arsenal and Manchester United in his first three league home games, which only delivered a single point. A thrilling 2-2 draw at Goodison Park where Luis Suarez continued his stellar start to the season was followed by a disappointing 3-1 defeat at home to Rodgers' former club, Swansea, in the fourth round of the League Cup. Rodgers gave quite a few fringe players a chance to prove themselves, but regretted his decision after a lacklustre first half and brought on Steven Gerrard and Suarez at half-time.

Another significant failure was the fourth round FA Cup exit against Oldham Athletic, the day after Rodgers had celebrated his 40th birthday. Rodgers put out his youngest side yet with an average age of only 23.21 years. Liverpool had clearly not learned their lesson since an apathetic lucky win at non-league Mansfield in the third round. 'The Reds' line-up still included nine full internationals and should have been good enough to get the job done,' the *Liverpool Echo* reasoned. 'But Rodgers will surely rue his decision to put so much faith in youth. Luis Suarez and Martin Skrtel were

the only outfield players aged over 23 who started and it showed.'

Finally, in the January transfer window Rodgers was able to bring in a striker in the shape of Daniel Sturridge from his old club Chelsea and Liverpool also purchased the exciting attacking midfielder Phillipe Coutinho from Inter Milan. Sturridge was unable to prevent Liverpool's FA Cup exit in his third start for the club, but had until that match netted in all three of his appearances. His fellow newcomer, the diminutive Coutinho, brought his silky skills to the team and weighed in with a couple of goals and impressive assists that bode well for the future. Liverpool again fell short of expectations when they exited the Europa League in the last 32 after a 2-0 defeat at Zenit St Petersburg. A Suarez-inspired Liverpool team almost rescued the tie at Anfield, but a 3-1 win was insufficient.

Each time Liverpool strung a series of good results together and a Champions League place seemed a distinct possibility the team lost its way. Rodgers' debut season was predictably a hit-and-miss affair as he rebuilt the squad in his own image. Rodgers will provide entertainment to the Liverpool fans but he has to ensure stability as well.

FACTFILE

BORN
26 January 1973, Carnlough, Northern Ireland
OTHER CLUBS
Watford (2008–09),
Reading (2009),
Swansea City (2010–12)
SIGNED FROM
Swansea City, 1 June 2012
LFC DEBUT GAME
2 August 2012

As a Manager in Europe		
Season	**Champions League**	**Europa League**
2012/13	-	Group Stage

Season	Division	P	W	D	L	GF	GA	Pts	Pos	Win %	FA Cup	League Cup
2012/13	Premier League	38	16	13	9	71	43	61	7	42.11	4th Round	4th Round
Total	-	38	16	13	9	71	43	61	-	42.11	-	-

Rodriguez, Maxi

MAXI RODRIGUEZ was born and brought up in Rosario by his grandparents and mother as his father had abandoned the family. It was a struggle but Maxi was a strong character and first came to prominence with local club Newell's Old Boys. He played for the club for three seasons, scoring 20 times in 59 league matches, before moving on loan for half a season to second-division Real Oviedo in Spain.

He starred for Argentina in the 2001 World Youth Championship, scoring four goals, including one in the 3-0 win over Ghana in the final. A year later he moved permanently from Argentina to La Liga's Espanyol in time for the 2002/03 season. Maxi's reputation grew in Barcelona and he earned himself a transfer to Atletico Madrid in 2005. He featured in 29 La Liga matches and scored 9 goals in his opening season and was in Argentina's squad for the 2006 World Cup in Germany, where his sensational extra-time winner defeated Mexico in the last 16. Atletico Madrid and Liverpool were placed in the same Champions League group in the 2008/09 season. Maxi scored Atletico's goal in their 1-1 draw at Anfield but Rafa Benítez was already aware of the player's capabilities. Liverpool made their move in January 2010 and Maxi was introduced to his new home public before Liverpool's FA Cup replay with Reading in the middle of the month. The 29-year-old who could operate both in midfield and on the wing proved to be a good squad player. The manager showed great faith in the Argentinian by starting him in 13 fixtures between 6 February and 2 May 2010. In the 2010 World Cup in South Africa Maxi made four starts and one substitute appearance as the double world champions reached the quarter-finals.

Used sparingly by Roy Hodgson, the Argentinian was more of a regular under Kenny Dalglish. He came to prominence towards the end of the 2010/11 season with a flurry of goals, scoring seven times in three successive Premier League matches including hat-tricks against Birmingham City and Fulham. Maxi made twice as many first-team appearances as he had in 2009/10. Ten goals in 35 matches showed his ability to arrive in the nick of time from midfield to finish off a well-worked attack. Even though Maxi only appeared in just over 40 per cent of Liverpool's first-team matches in 2011/12, he again proved that he had an eye for a goal, adding to his League Cup goal against Exeter by scoring twice in away matches at Chelsea in the league and the League Cup in November and then scoring three goals against Blackburn home and away, a total of six goals from 17 starts.

On 13 July 2012 Maxi returned to his first club, Newell's Old Boys, in his home town, Rosario.

On the same day Maxi addressed Liverpool's supporters in an open letter: 'Dear Reds, I am leaving Liverpool FC today. Before signing for LFC, I just saw the club as one of the greatest institutions in football. After my time here I can confirm that this is not just a great club but also a great family. I have tried to give everything every day that I was wearing the LFC crest. It has been a great honour to defend this shirt during two and a half years. I am returning home with a suitcase full of great memories, good friends within the team and also within this great family that works every day in the club. Thanks a lot for your support. You can NOT imagine what a great honour it was for me when the Kop sang, "Maxi, Maxi Rodríguez runs down the wing for me da da da da da da..." Hasta la vista!'

FACTFILE

BORN
Rosario, Argentina,
2 January 1981
POSITION
Midfielder
OTHER CLUBS
Newell's Old Boys
(1999–2002),
Real Oviedo (loan, 2001),
Espanyol (2002–05),
Atletico Madrid (2005–10),
Newell's Old Boys (2012–)
SIGNED FROM
Atletico Madrid, Free transfer,
12 January 2010
INTERNATIONAL CAPS
45 Argentina caps (12 goals)
(6 (2) at LFC), 2003–12
LFC DEBUT GAME/GOAL
16 January 2010 /
25 April 2010
CONTRACT EXPIRY
13 July 2012
HONOURS
League Cup 2012

Season	League		FA Cup		League Cup		Europe		Total	
	App	Goals	App	Goals	App	Goals	App	Goals	App	Goals
2009/10	14 (3)	1	0	0	0	0	0	0	14 (3)	1
2010/11	24 (4)	10	1	0	0	0	4 (2)	0	29 (6)	10
2011/12	10 (2)	4	3 (2)	0	4	2	-	-	17 (4)	6
Total	**48 (9)**	**15**	**4 (2)**	**0**	**4**	**2**	**4 (2)**	**0**	**60 (13)**	**17**

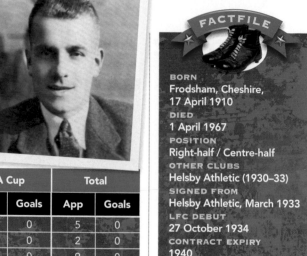

Rogers, Fred

MORE experienced players like Ted Savage, Tom Morrison and Matt Busby restricted Fred Rogers to just seven First Division appearances in his first two years at Anfield and only nine more followed in 1936/37.

Busby became the club's recognised right-half and Rogers moved over to the centre of defence, where he was selected 28 times during the 1937/38 season. Thirty more First Division appearances followed in 1938/39 but, as for so many of his contemporaries, the war took away potentially the best years of his professional career.

Season	League		FA Cup		Total	
	App	Goals	App	Goals	App	Goals
1934/35	5	0	0	0	5	0
1935/36	2	0	0	0	2	0
1936/37	9	0	0	0	9	0
1937/38	24	0	4	0	28	0
1938/39	30	0	1	0	31	0
Total	70	0	5	0	75	0

FACTFILE

BORN
Frodsham, Cheshire, 17 April 1910
DIED
1 April 1967
POSITION
Right-half / Centre-half
OTHER CLUBS
Helsby Athletic (1930–33)
SIGNED FROM
Helsby Athletic, March 1933
LFC DEBUT
27 October 1934
CONTRACT EXPIRY
1940

Rogers, Tom

TOM ROGERS made his debut in a meaningless last-day-of-the-season encounter with Sheffield United at Anfield in April 1907 and played a dozen First Division games the following season.

He started as first choice in the 1908/09 season, but was seriously injured against Nottingham Forest on 1 October 1908 and was out of action for 11 months. Once he returned he was given a run of 14 league matches midway through the 1909/10 season in place of Bob Crawford as Liverpool recovered after a disastrous previous campaign and finished second. The left-back was said to be 'very wild at times' in his play and liable to mistakes.

Season	League		FA Cup		Total	
	App	Goals	App	Goals	App	Goals
1906/07	1	0	0	0	1	0
1907/08	12	0	1	0	13	0
1908/09	6	0	0	0	6	0
1909/10	17	0	1	0	18	0
1910/11	2	0	0	0	2	0
Total	38	0	2	0	40	0

FACTFILE

BORN
Prescot, Lancashire, 1885
POSITION
Left-back
OTHER CLUBS
Rossendale United
SIGNED FROM
Rossendale United, April 1907
LFC DEBUT
7 April 1907
CONTRACT EXPIRY
1912

Roque, Miki

LIVERPOOL scout Paco Herrera discovered Miki Roque at Lleida in the Spanish second division. Roque later commented, 'I don't mind where I play as long as I can play football which I love. I can play centre-half and central midfield and like both positions.'

Roque's progress was rewarded when he came on for Xabi Alonso in Liverpool's Champions League return to the Ataturk Stadium in Istanbul against Galatasaray in December 2006. After two loan spells in his homeland Roque moved to Real Betis where he started ten matches in the 2010/11 season. In March 2011 came the sad news that Roque had been diagnosed with pelvic cancer and he had to suspend his playing career to concentrate on treatment. On 24 June 2012 Miki Roque lost his greatest battle of all at the tragically early age of 23.

Season	League		FA Cup		League Cup		Europe		Other		Total	
	App	Goals	App	Goals	App	Goals	App	Goals	App	Goals	App	Goals
2006/07	0	0	0	0	0	0	0 (1)	0	0	0	0 (1)	0
Total	0	0	0	0	0	0	0 (1)	0	0	0	0 (1)	0

FACTFILE

BORN
Tremp, Catalonia, Spain, 8 July 1988
DIED
24 June 2012
POSITION
Centre-half
OTHER CLUBS
Oldham Athletic (loan, 2007), Xerex (loan, 2007–08), Cartagena (loan, 2008–09), Real Betis (2009–11)
SIGNED FROM
Lleida (youth), 15 August 2005
LFC DEBUT
5 December 2006
CONTRACT EXPIRY
1 July 2009

Rosenthal,
Ronny

RONNY ROSENTHAL became an instant cult hero with his explosive start to his Liverpool career. He had a 10-day trial at First Division Luton Town after a failed medical ruined his move to Udinese. He scored two goals in three reserve games for the Hatters, but they couldn't broker a deal with Liege. The asking price was £500,000. Liverpool asked Liege if they could have a look and after only one reserve appearance he was signed on loan.

> ROSENTHAL'S FULL DEBUT FOR THE FIRST TEAM WAS AGAINST CHARLTON, WHERE HE SCORED THREE TIMES

Rosenthal's full debut for the first team was against Charlton, where he scored three times. He recalled: 'Kenny was disappointed with Peter Beardsley and told me an hour before the game I'd be playing. After 10 minutes I scored with my right foot, then again immediately after half-time with my left and finally with my head after combining with John Barnes. The perfect hat-trick, I believe they call it.' Four goals in the last six games of the season followed, his contribution vital to Liverpool's league triumph. Rosenthal's good form saw his asking price rise by 100 per cent but that didn't deter Liverpool from tying up a permanent deal in the summer.

Rosenthal's dream start did not though secure him a starting place the following season and

Liverpool's club record of eight straight wins from the start of the campaign kept him firmly in the reserves. Rosenthal scored 19 goals that season for the second-string but sadly his opportunities to shine in the first team proved few and far between. He did score a memorable last-minute winner in front of the Kop in the Merseyside derby on 20 March 1993. 'The Rocket Man' stayed at Anfield until January 1994 when Tottenham paid £250,000 to secure his contract. He made 100 first-team appearances for Spurs, scoring 11 goals, including a sensational second-half hat-trick in a cup replay at Southampton in 1995. In August 1997 Rosenthal moved on a free transfer to Watford and helped them win the Second Division Championship. He retired as a player at the end of the 1998/99 season at the age of 35.

ROSENTHAL has continued to live in England following his retirement and is a football

consultant. As of 2013, his younger son Tom is a promising footballer at Watford's academy. Unfortunately, Rosenthal is perhaps most remembered for the often-replayed miss at Villa Park in September 1992 when he somehow managed to hit the crossbar at the Holte End after rounding the home keeper and being presented with the most open of open goals. It has been conveniently forgotten that Rosenthal did score later in that match, although Liverpool lost 4-2. Rosenthal has special memories from his time at Liverpool that are as delightfully quirky as his career was. 'There was one incident I'll never forget. We were warming up on the training field the morning after the Christmas party. Bruce Grobbelaar was leading the pack with Roy Evans behind him as we jogged round the pitch. Without warning Bruce breaks wind and as Roy was right behind him, he was the first to run into it. It was so bad Roy keeled over and actually started

vomiting. All the other players then ran into it and keeled over or tried to escape the poisonous gas. It really was the most incredible sight I've ever seen on a training field.'

FACTFILE

BORN
Haifa, Israel, 11 October 1963
POSITION
Centre-forward
OTHER CLUBS
Maccabi Haifa (1974–86), Bruges (1986–88), Standard Liege (1988–90), Tottenham Hotspur (1994–97), Watford (1997–99)
SIGNED FROM
Standard Liege, £1 million – loan, 22 March 1990; permanent, 29 June 1990
INTERNATIONAL CAPS
60 Israel caps (11 goals), 1984–96
LFC DEBUT GAME/GOAL
31 March 1990 / 11 April 1990
CONTRACT EXPIRY
26 January 1994

Season	League		FA Cup		League Cup		Europe		Other		Total	
	App	Goals	App	Goals	App	Goals	App	Goals	App	Goals	App	Goals
1989/90	5 (3)	7	0	0	0	0	-	-	0	0	5 (3)	7
1990/91	4 (12)	5	3	0	0 (3)	0	-	-	0 (1)	0	7 (16)	5
1991/92	7 (13)	3	1 (2)	0	0 (3)	0	1	0	-	-	9 (18)	3
1992/93	16 (11)	6	1 (1)	0	2 (1)	1	0 (3)	0	1	0	20 (16)	7
1993/94	0 (3)	0	0	0	0	0	-	-	-	-	0 (3)	0
Total	**32 (42)**	**21**	**5 (3)**	**0**	**2 (7)**	**1**	**1 (3)**	**0**	**1 (1)**	**0**	**41 (56)**	**22**

Ross, Ian

IAN ROSS will forever be remembered as Der Kaiser's shadow, when he man-marked Bayern's Franz Beckenbauer to perfection in a European Fairs Cup game on 18 March 1971 in Munich. He even had the time to score Liverpool's goal in a 1-1 draw.

The Glaswegian signed professional forms for Liverpool in August 1965 when he was 17 years old. He'd had trials at both Arsenal and Chelsea, when he'd had to stay in a hotel in London, but when Liverpool came calling the club put him up with a family and that made all the difference.

Ross made his debut at Sheffield Wednesday in the middle of January 1967, coming on for Ian Callaghan, but he didn't figure in another league match until March 1968. The only season in which he became anything like a regular was 1971/72, when he was sold before the end of the campaign. Ross had been filling in for Tommy Smith and Alec Lindsay in defence as well as Brian Hall in midfield when Shankly decided to drop him, which he didn't agree with and demanded to be sold.

Aston Villa, then a Third Division side on the rise, had made inquiries and were willing to pay a club-record fee of £70,000. Villa were promoted in the spring and played in the First Division in Ross's last season at the club. Ross featured in 175 league matches at Aston Villa from 1972 to 1976, creating a formidable partnership with Chris Nicholl at the heart of the Villans' defence and captaining the side as well.

ROSS enjoyed a successful coaching career in Iceland, even playing in his first year for Valur as well as coaching the team in 1984. After four years he moved from league champions Valur to KR Reykjavik, who were incidentally Liverpool's first European opponents back in 1964.

Season	League		FA Cup		League Cup		Europe		Other		Total	
	App	Goals	App	Goals	App	Goals	App	Goals	App	Goals	App	Goals
1966/67	0 (1)	0	0	0	-	-	0	0	0	0	0 (1)	0
1967/68	4	0	2	0	0	0	0	0	-	-	6	0
1968/69	3	0	0	0	0	0	0 (1)	0	-	-	3 (1)	0
1969/70	7	1	4 (1)	1	0	0	1	0	-	-	12 (1)	2
1970/71	8 (4)	0	0	0	0	0	1 (1)	1	-	-	9 (5)	1
1971/72	20 (1)	1	3	0	3	0	3 (1)	0	0	0	29 (2)	1
Total	**42 (6)**	**2**	**9 (1)**	**1**	**3**	**0**	**5 (3)**	**1**	**0**	**0**	**59 (10)**	**4**

Ross, Jimmy

LIVERPOOL showed their intent by paying a club record fee of £75 for double league champion inside-right Jimmy Ross from Preston's 'Invincibles' in 1894.

It was an ambitious signing as Ross was a legend at Preston, scoring 18 goals in the club's undefeated season. He was the league's top scorer in 1889/90 with 24 goals and scored seven goals in Preston's record 26-0

win over Hyde in the 1887/88 season. The transfer didn't go through without a hitch, as the *Liverpool Review* reported on 25 August 1894:

'Since the Liverpool club signed him on from Preston, Jimmy has exhibited a reluctance to carry out his bargain with his new club. A note appeared in the papers the other day that Jimmy was determined not to play for Liverpool on any account, chiefly because his brother, the late famous Nick Ross, had on his deathbed expressed a desire that Jimmy should not desert the North End, for whom they had both been playing for the last ten years. This being the case, the relations of Jimmy Ross towards the Liverpool club are at the time of writing somewhat strained and awkward, but as he has duly 'signed on', and as the Liverpool club have paid some £75 down for his transfer, the probability is that if the Anfield people wish to press their claim Jimmy will be found duly in his place on the fine Anfield sward when Aston Villa opens the season for the Liverpudlians in two weeks' time.

ROSS took over as Liverpool captain from Andrew Hannah midway through his debut season and ran the show, pretty much, at Anfield in his first two years at the club. He had incredible technique, precise passes and was good with both feet. He was a joker on the pitch, an entertainer in every sense of the word. Twelve goals from 27 league matches was not a bad return during a season when the club managed only 51 from 30 games and were relegated straight back to the Second Division. Inside-right Ross banged in 23 goals from 25 league games when the club

made an immediate return to the top division. But in his third campaign, even though Liverpool did finally establish themselves as a first division club by finishing in a very creditable fifth place, Ross only found the net two times from 21 league matches. Late in the 1896/97 season he joined Burnley along with teammate Malcolm McVean and their first match was at Anfield only a week later. Burnley beat Liverpool 2-1 but didn't do enough to prevent their relegation. Burnley won the Second Division the following season with Ross scoring an impressive 23 goals in 27 league matches. Ross only played half a season in First Division before joining Manchester City who were on their way to the Second Division title. Ross scored 21 goals in 67 games for City, but ill-health forced him to retire from the game in the 1901/02 season. Ross contracted an acute skin disease, Erysipelas, succumbed to raging fever and passed away only 36 years of age on 12 June 1902.

His coffin was covered with wreaths and floral tributes, one from Preston North End bearing the following appropriate inscription: 'In memory of one of the old Invincibles'.

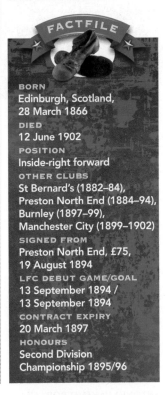

Season	League		FA Cup		Other		Total	
	App	Goals	App	Goals	App	Goals	App	Goals
1894/95	27	12	3	0	1	0	31	12
1895/96	25	23	2	1	4	0	31	24
1896/97	21	2	2	1	-	-	23	3
Total	**73**	**37**	**7**	**2**	**5**	**0**	**85**	**39**

Ross,
Sydney

SYDNEY ROSS was Liverpool's first-choice goalkeeper in the club's only season in the Lancashire League. The majority of the regulars in the side had the prefix 'Mc' in front of their names so the team was known as 'The team of Macs'.

The *Liverpool Echo* noted at the time that 'it was amusing to hear Ross frequently greeted by humorously-inclined spectators behind the goal with cries of "Play up, MacRoss".' Unfortunately for Ross he was badly injured in a Lancashire Cup tie against neighbours Bootle on 11 March 1893 and it was noted in the newspapers at the

time: 'Ross was again an absentee, being an inmate at Stanley hospital till Friday, and it is feared he has received a permanent injury.'

ROSS certainly didn't play for Liverpool again and returned to Scotland where he resumed his career. He played a few matches for Cambuslang in the 1893/94 season before signing for Third Lanark in May 1894. He was mostly a reserve goalkeeper at Lanark before moving in the summer of 1898 to Clyde who also signed Liverpool keeper Willie Donnelly. Ross moved to Australia and died in Brisbane on 4 February 1924.

Season	League		FA Cup		Other		Total	
	App	Goals	App	Goals	App	Goals	App	Goals
1892/93	-	-	3	0	18	0	21	0
Total	**0**	**0**	**3**	**0**	**18**	**0**	**21**	**0**

Rowley,
Arthur

ARTHUR ROWLEY is not to be confused with Antonio (Tony) Rowley. They were together at Anfield for one year, then four years later Arthur followed Tony to Tranmere.

ARTHUR was a little, nippy forward who didn't manage to score a single goal in his 11 matches for Liverpool.

Season	League		FA Cup		Total	
	App	Goals	App	Goals	App	Goals
1952/53	11	0	0	0	11	0
Total	**11**	**0**	**0**	**0**	**11**	**0**

Rowley,
Tony

ANTONIO CAMILIO ROWLEY, who was of Italian descent but born in Wales, scored a hat-trick on the opening day of the 1954/55 season after featuring mostly for the reserves in his debut campaign when Liverpool were relegated to the Second Division.

Rowley didn't score in the following two games and he was back in the reserves as John Evans and Billy Liddell were both scoring plenty of goals. When Rowley did get a chance with the first team he usually scored. His career at Liverpool was bizarre. He didn't play much during the regular season due to injuries or bad form, but always managed to reclaim his place in the starting XI and score more than his fair share of goals. He scored eight goals in 13 matches in his first full season, six goals in seven matches the next, followed by seven in 14 matches in 1956/57.

ROWLEY finally put a run together of 19 games in his final season, scoring eight goals in six consecutive matches, but then injuries prevailed again and he

WHEN ROWLEY DID GET A CHANCE WITH THE FIRST TEAM HE USUALLY SCORED

was sold to Third Division Tranmere when two months were left of the campaign. While at Tranmere Rowley was chosen for the Welsh national side, making his only international appearance against Northern Ireland on 22 April 1959. He continued to score goals for Tranmere, 47 goals in 100 league matches, which is still below his Liverpool average, a goal every 1.6 games, an impressive ratio at any level.

Season	League		FA Cup		Total	
	App	Goals	App	Goals	App	Goals
1953/54	2	1	0	0	2	1
1954/55	13	8	0	0	13	8
1955/56	7	6	0	0	7	6
1956/57	14	7	0	0	14	7
1957/58	24	16	3	1	27	17
Total	**60**	**38**	**3**	**1**	**63**	**39**

Ruddock,
Neil

NEIL 'RAZOR' Ruddock's career before he was transferred to Liverpool was very colourful. He grew up at Millwall where George Graham changed him from a left-winger to a centre-half.

Tottenham purchased Ruddock when he was 17, with Terry Venables replacing David Pleat after his first year at the club. Ruddock made his senior debut against Liverpool at White Hart Lane on 28 November 1987. Disaster struck when Gary Gillespie broke Ruddock's leg. He returned to Millwall in the summer of 1988 after only 11 appearances for Spurs. Ruddock stayed only eight months at Millwall before moving to fellow First Division team Southampton. Razor's career finally took off in earnest at the Dell and he remained there for four successful years. Ruddock and Venables were finally reunited at Spurs in 1992. Twelve months later there were a number of clubs interested in him, as Ruddock revealed to *LFChistory.net*. He was on holiday in Spain when his old mate at Southampton and then reserve coach at Liverpool, Sammy Lee, phoned him up. 'When I came home I had Souness and Liverpool waiting, Glenn Hoddle

at Chelsea, Brian Clough at Forest, Kevin Keegan, Newcastle, Walter Smith, Rangers and Kenny Dalglish, Blackburn. I met Kenny on Monday. Tuesday was Liverpool and I was going to Newcastle on Wednesday. When I met Souness at Liverpool, I thought: "This is it." When I grew up Liverpool were a great team. The old Kop was still there. Nothing is better than this, when I used to run out at Anfield with 25,000 Scousers singing. Going to the ground you could hear the Kop already in there singing. That's the thing I remember most and take away from football.'

CONTROVERSY as ever followed Ruddock around. After only making two appearances for Liverpool he featured in Ronnie Whelan's testimonial against Newcastle. When only two minutes had passed of the match, Peter Beardsley fractured his cheekbone in three places after a clash with Razor, who later scored the only goal of the game. Beardsley said that Ruddock had acted deliberately to prove he was a hard man to the Liverpool fans. Ruddock said in his autobiography that 'If anything the slight rearrangement of his face did Pete a favour...' Liverpool won four out of their opening five games in the 1993/94 season with Mark Wright and Ruddock at the heart of their defence but then lost

three in a row and it was downhill from then on. Ruddock's most memorable moment in a Liverpool shirt came at the start of 1994 when he almost knocked himself out equalising in dramatic fashion against Manchester United and completing Liverpool's fightback from 3-0 down to 3-3. A humiliating FA Cup exit at the hands of First Division Bristol City at Anfield was one defeat too many for the club's hierarchy. Souness, who had been in charge at Liverpool for two full seasons, was sacked only six months after Ruddock's arrival.

In Roy Evans' first full season in charge, 1994/95, Phil Babb and John Scales arrived from Coventry and Wimbledon respectively within 48 hours of each other. Evans played three at the back – Ruddock, Scales and Babb – and claimed 'it's been beneficial for Razor to be guarded by these two guys'. How did Razor like the 5-3-2 formation? 'I liked playing with Mark Wright and then Nicol. He never seemed to have a bad game,' he told *LFChistory.net*. 'Scales and Babbsy... I didn't know what they were gonna do. Half the time Babb didn't know what he was doing anyway.' Ruddock was a success acting as a sweeper, lacking the necessary speed to cope in front of them. After featuring in 52 games in 1994/95

Ruddock struggled with injuries in the following season but as the campaign drew to a close with the FA Cup final on the horizon he completed three games in a row and fully expected to be in the starting line-up facing Manchester United at Wembley. Ruddock had only won the League Cup in his time at Liverpool and felt he would curtail the talents of Eric Cantona. He suffered the biggest disappointment of his career as Evans revealed at training that he was dropping him in favour of Scales. 'I might be a big bloke and have the reputation of being a hard man but I cried like a baby when he dropped that bombshell,' Ruddock confessed. 'Roy admitted after that he made a mistake. At that time I was getting the better of Cantona and he wasn't playing too well against us. It was my birthday as well. What a birthday present!' Ruddock courted controversy again in a reserve game in October 1996 when he broke the ankle of Manchester United's Andy Cole. The United hitman claimed the tackle had been made to hurt him. Ruddock was typically nonchalant and replied: 'I can only assume it was the way he fell.'

The opposition loved to hate this colossus. Ruddock was a tough character who could hit some fantastic passes upfield and was great in the air. However, lack of

> 'GOING TO THE GROUND YOU COULD HEAR THE KOP ALREADY IN THERE SINGING. THAT'S THE THING I REMEMBER MOST AND TAKE AWAY FROM FOOTBALL'

discipline and lack of fitness made life difficult for him at Liverpool where competition for places was fierce. The 1996/97 season was the most successful one in Ruddock's time at Liverpool as the club finally made a decent title challenge, but he was no longer first choice. Ruddock reported for pre-season training having shed a stone but injured his knee only 23 minutes into the 1997/98 campaign. On his return two months later he conceded an own goal against Everton and his terrible display in a 3-0 defeat in Strasbourg was his final performance for the club.

Gérard Houllier arrived at the club in July 1998 to become joint-manager by Evans' side. When Houllier introduced himself to the players Ruddock wasn't impressed as he told *LFChistory.net*. 'Houllier came into the dressing room and he went to Fowler, "Ahh, Robbie Fowler," went to David James: "hello, David," he comes to me and said: "I'm sorry, what is your name?" I said, "Have you been in a coma for 15 years?" Everyone laughed. He didn't get my sense of humour. I think it was about a week later I was gone.' After two seasons at Upton Park he moved down a division to Crystal Palace, owned by the controversial Simon Jordan. Ruddock had a fall-out with Jordan and joined forces with his former Liverpool boss Roy Evans at Swindon Town in August 2001. Evans was boss and Ruddock player-coach, signing a three-year deal. Seventeen months later the money and promises ran out. Ruddock's football career was over.

RUDDOCK could arguably have achieved more in the game had he eschewed some of the more excessive aspects of the footballer's lifestyle. 'I loved the lifestyle. Sometimes I was easily led by my friends. It was my friends. See how I get away with it. My friends led me astray... gladly.'

Season	League		FA Cup		League Cup		Europe		Total	
	App	Goals	App	Goals	App	Goals	App	Goals	App	Goals
1993/94	39	3	2	0	5	1	-	-	46	4
1994/95	37	2	7	0	8	0	-	-	52	2
1995/96	18 (2)	5	2	0	3 (1)	0	2	0	25 (3)	5
1996/97	15 (2)	1	0	0	2	0	2 (1)	0	19 (3)	1
1997/98	2	0	0	0	1	0	1	0	4	0
Total	**111 (4)**	**11**	**11**	**0**	**19 (1)**	**1**	**5 (1)**	**0**	**146 (6)**	**12**

Rudham,
Doug

GOALKEEPER Robert 'Doug' Rudham was on tour with the South African national team when he attracted Liverpool's interest. He had turned down a professional contract offer from First Division Chelsea two years previously.

He signed for the Reds at a time when Liverpool didn't seem to have a regular first-choice keeper. Rudham shared duties with Dave Underwood and Charlie Ashcroft during the 1954/55 season and even managed to keep his place after conceding nine goals at Birmingham in December! Rudham played in the first 17 league matches of the next season but lost his place to Underwood after conceding four goals at Leeds in November. 'Dave has

been doing so well in the reserves that his form simply cannot be ignored,' said Liverpool boss Don Welsh. 'It is up to Rudham to fight his way back.' When Underwood let in three at Fulham in April, Rudham was brought back for the final four games of the season. However, Tommy Younger was brought in from Hibernian during the close season and Rudham made only six appearances in the next three years.

WHEN Younger moved on to Stoke in the 1959/60 season, Rudham was kept out by new signing Bert

Slater but regained his place after three league matches and played in the next 14, bringing his total of appearances in the Football

League to 63. His last game came in a 4-2 defeat at Lincoln, after which Slater won his place back as Bill Shankly took over the reins at the club. Rudham returned to his native Johannesburg in May 1960.

Season	League		FA Cup		Total	
	App	Goals	App	Goals	App	Goals
1954/55	22	0	3	0	25	0
1955/56	21	0	0	0	21	0
1956/57	2	0	0	0	2	0
1957/58	3	0	0	0	3	0
1958/59	1	0	0	0	1	0
1959/60	14	0	0	0	14	0
Total	**63**	**0**	**3**	**0**	**66**	**0**

Rush, Ian

IAN RUSH is simply the greatest goalscorer in Liverpool's history.

He was born and raised with four sisters and five brothers in the village of St Asaph in North Wales. When he was 13 and playing for Deeside primary schools his scoring prowess alerted scouts at Liverpool and Manchester United. He eventually went on trials to Burnley, Wrexham and Chester. Cliff Sear, the youth team manager at Chester, put him at ease and Rush felt at home at the club. Liverpool scout Geoff Twentyman was a regular visitor at Chester's games and come 1980 Bob Paisley was convinced enough about his talent. Rush didn't share his great belief that he would succeed at Liverpool and tried to price himself out of a move by demanding £100 a week from the Reds. In fact Liverpool were more than ready to triple that figure so this cunning plan didn't quite work out. Liverpool paid £300,000 for the 19-year-old Rush, which was the highest fee ever paid for a youngster at the time in the world. What clinched the deal for Rush was that Chester manager Allan Oakes told him: 'If you don't make it, you can always go back to Chester.'

> IAN RUSH IS SIMPLY THE GREATEST GOALSCORER IN LIVERPOOL'S HISTORY

Rush left Chester after scoring 17 goals in 39 matches and made his debut for Liverpool in a 1-1 draw against Ipswich on 13 December 1980, replacing Kenny Dalglish, who was out with an injured ankle. Wearing the famous number 7 at

New arrivals: Richard Money and a certain Ian Rush

Liverpool was quite a responsibility for the youngster, who was raised as an Everton supporter. Paisley was quite calm, as he told *The Times*: 'It was not an easy decision, but what swayed me in the end was that if I had picked anyone else it would have meant playing them out of position. I have replaced a striker with a striker.' Rush's second game was a League Cup final replay no less. He had an impressive game at Villa Park and rattled the crossbar. Liverpool celebrated a 2-1 win courtesy of goals from Dalglish and Alan Hansen. Rush finished the 1980/81 season with nine games for Liverpool but still no goals. He had, however, so far netted 12 goals in 30 reserve appearances.

RUSH didn't get a chance in the first team at the beginning of his first full season. He also had trouble adapting socially to his new surroundings. He was shy and didn't like how Dalglish and the senior players used to wind him and the other new recruits up. Rush knocked on Bob Paisley's door and declared he wanted a chance with the first team or else he would leave. Paisley said he would make him available for transfer and Rush left his office determined to show him he could score an abundance of goals with the reserves that would alert other clubs. He scored five goals in his first four reserve games of the season. Paisley's trick had worked, as he never intended to sell him. The manager did wonder at first if he had made a wise decision to buy him as he revealed in *Bob Paisley's Personal View of the Liverpool First Team Squad of 1986-87*. 'He couldn't score a goal to save his life and what little self-confidence he had started to seep away. Once he started scoring he couldn't stop. At first, they were all walloped in with his right foot. Then he got the odd one with his left foot and we would kid him about it. Soon they were going in so frequently with either foot that we couldn't remember which was his strong one. Before we knew he was heading in goals as if it were going out of fashion too.'

Rush broke his duck on 30 September 1981 at Anfield against Oulu Palloseura from Finland in the European Cup. He came on as a substitute and scored one of Liverpool's seven on the night. Then David Johnson

got injured and Rush had a golden opportunity to establish himself in the side. He scored a brace against Exeter in the League Cup, netted another two goals in the league against Leeds, and didn't stop until he had scored 30 goals that season. The pinnacle was his first goal at Wembley in the League Cup final. Ronnie Whelan scored Liverpool's other two goals in their 3-1 win over Tottenham. Whelan and Rush entered the side at a similar time and became firm friends. Their time had certainly come. Few believed Rush could sustain his current rate of scoring goals the following season, but he proved them all wrong and was voted the Football League's most promising player in the 1982/83 season. Rush and Dalglish had formed a lethal partnership and their understanding of each other's strengths was incredible. Rush was a quick runner and a quick thinker as well. He would make his move long before the opponent had realised. Sure enough, Kenny rewarded his run with a brilliant pass and soon the ball was in the net. Dalglish described their successful partnership in his autobiography. 'Rushie was perceptive and had two good feet. He is one of the most instinctive finishers football has ever seen. My partnership with Rush proved so good because he could run and I could pass. I would just try to put the ball in front of him. Rushie said that he made runs knowing the ball would come to him. That was true but only because his runs were so clever. His run was more important than my pass. Rushie was a good passer himself. He could have been a midfielder because his range of passing was great. Rush was easily the best partner I've ever had. We could have been made for each other.' Rush soon earned the nickname 'The Ghost' for the way he snuck up behind defenders. His most memorable scoring feat that season was without a doubt his four goals in the derby match

against Everton at Goodison Park. His destruction of the Blues was immortalised in song as an extra verse in 'Poor Scouser Tommy'. Liverpool won the same double as the season before, the League Championship and the League Cup.

The 1983/84 season was perhaps Rush's best for Liverpool. He scored a breathtaking hat-trick at Aston Villa and four against Coventry. Just before he went out on the field against Luton on 29 October 1983 he soaked his rock-hard boots in the bath. He scored five goals at Anfield and since then he religiously wet his boots prior to kick-off for every game. Liverpool fans would hardly believe it if 90 minutes passed without Rush scoring. He finished off Dinamo Bucharest in the semi-finals of the European Cup by a couple of goals. The final was a memorable one and Rush was one of four Liverpool players who scored in the penalty shootout in Rome. He had scored no fewer than 47 goals that season and was awarded the Golden Boot for being Europe's top scorer. It was hardly surprising that his fellow professionals in England and the local media would choose him as the best player of the season. He had also destroyed the Liverpool record of Roger Hunt, who had scored 41 goals in one season 20 years earlier.

> HE HAD SCORED NO FEWER THAN 47 GOALS THAT SEASON AND WAS AWARDED THE GOLDEN BOOT FOR BEING EUROPE'S TOP SCORER

Rush was tempted to leave his beloved club for Napoli in 1984, as he revealed to *LFChistory.net*. 'Napoli offered me £1million and I wanted to speak to them just

before the deadline. John Smith, the Liverpool chairman, refused.' Napoli went on to sign Diego Maradona instead.

Rush suffered his first setback when he was sidelined for the first 14 games in the following season. His first game was against Everton but he drew a blank. Only a few days later he was back with a vengeance when he scored a hat-trick against Benfica in the second round of the European Cup. Stuart Jones at *The Times*, like any Liverpool fan, was mesmerised by his treble. 'Rush is an extraordinary predator. The scorer of 47 goals last season was covered with rust and he looked lost outside the penalty area, where the ball seemed a slippery object beyond his control. Inside it, the ball appeared to follow him around and obey instructions that were born more out of instinct than careful thought,' he wrote. 'The man who transformed that tie in the first leg at Anfield last March was Dalglish, also returning from a lengthy absence. The Portuguese hailed him as "a Messiah". Rush personifies the Second Coming.' Rush repeated his feat from a year earlier when he scored two goals in the semi-final against Panathinaikos at Anfield, but the European Cup final at Heysel was a tragedy.

LIVERPOOL captured the double in the 1985/86 season with Rush once again playing a key part, scoring twice in a 3-1 victory over Everton in the first ever Merseyside final, which he rates as his most memorable game. Rush wanted to try pastures new and the club finally had to part with its greatest asset, for which it was going to receive a record fee for a British footballer, £3.2million. Rush was supposed to join Juventus in the summer of 1986, but Juventus president Giampiero Boniperti said to the Welshman's great surprise during the contract negotiations that he was going to be loaned out to Lazio in Serie B for the 1986/87 season, as Michel Platini had decided to play one more season. The French maestro and Michael Laudrup would occupy the two places allowed for foreigners at the Italian club. Rush suggested to Boniperti that he be loaned to Liverpool. He noted that club secretary Peter Robinson, who was representing Liverpool in the negotiations, 'practically grazed his jaw on his shirt buttons at the thought of Liverpool receiving over £3million,

but still having me for another season'. Those who feared Rush wouldn't give 100 per cent for the club in his final season soon calmed down. He scored 21 goals in his first 21 games. Incredibly, Liverpool had never lost a game in which Rush scored. The tally had reached 145 games when Liverpool faced Arsenal in the League Cup final. Rush gave Liverpool the lead but Charlie Nicholas replied with two and Arsenal ran out winners. Everton recaptured the championship from their neighbours but not before Rush made them suffer at Anfield when he scored his 18th and 19th goal in 20 derby matches, equalling Dixie Dean's record. Dixie achieved that feat in 17 matches, but Rushie scored a total of 25 goals against the Blues. Kevin Sheedy, former Red and current Blue, admitted that Everton would 'sleep easier at night' following his move to Italy. Rush said goodbye to Liverpool by scoring six goals in his final eight games.

The magnetic Welshman scored 14 goals for Juventus in the 1987/88 season, of which eight were in Serie A. Diego Maradona was number one in the scoring charts with 14 league goals and Rush scored as many goals as Marco van Basten and more than Rudi Voeller. He showed Juve fans what he was capable of when he scored four goals against Pescara in the cup. But injuries, illness, the defensive nature of Italian football and, most importantly, Michel Platini's decision to quit Juventus all played a part in Rush's failure to deliver the goods on a regular basis. Peter Robinson was relaxing in the Spanish sun in 1988 when he spotted a magazine article that said talented striker Alexander Zavarov was on his way to Juventus, and that meant there would be one foreign player too many at the Turin club. Robinson suspected who would be left out and immediately phoned Dalglish. Rush's return to Liverpool after only one season abroad came as a

surprise to everyone and no one realised until he sat down with the manager in front of the stunned press that he had re-signed for his old club. The majority of the press believed that Liverpool were buying Gary Pallister from Middlesbrough to replace the injured Alan Hansen. The price was £2.7million, so Liverpool had bought him for £500,000 less than they had received. Liverpool had run away with the title in the previous campaign and defences all around England were already quivering in their boots to meet up with Rush again, not least his neighbours across Stanley Park.

Once Rush returned he was clearly not in his best condition, but in January fans started to see glimpses of the old Rush. He scored in three games in a row but then he got injured and a knee operation meant two months on the sidelines. He proved a valuable substitute in the FA Cup final against his old foes Everton. John Aldridge made way for Rush in the second half, having scored the only goal of the game until then. Stuart McCall equalised in the last seconds of normal time. Rush scored Liverpool's second with a brilliant shot in the fifth minute of extra time but that was cancelled out by another McCall equaliser in the 102nd minute. Two minutes later Rushie proved to be the hero of the day when he scored with a deadly accurate header and Liverpool won the Cup.

RUSH was preferred to John Aldridge in the starting line-up the following season and critics got on his back right away. The pressure was greater because Aldridge had been the team's top scorer the previous season. After his third consecutive game without a goal *The Times* reported: 'The selection of Rush, though, is puzzling. There can be no compelling reason for Kenny Dalglish to omit the club's leading scorer for the last two seasons, Aldridge, in favour of a forward

who is still palpably far below his former fearsome form.' However, Dalglish's confidence in his old friend was 100 per cent. Aldridge was not happy and signed for Real Sociedad in Spain, where he continued to score on a regular basis. Rush didn't let Dalglish down and finished the season as top scorer with 26 goals. Like clockwork, he scored the same amount of goals next season but Dalglish's resignation spoiled Liverpool's chances of holding on to their League title. Rush sustained an injury along with other key players in Graeme Souness's first whole season in 1991/92. He got himself fit for the FA Cup final against Sunderland and struck gold as usual at Wembley. He sealed Liverpool's 2-0 win and his fifth goal in a FA Cup final was an unprecedented achievement.

LIVERPOOL struggled in the next two seasons but Rush still delivered 41 goals. On 18 October 1992 Rush made another record his very own. He scored his 287th goal for Liverpool in a 2-2 draw against Manchester United at Old Trafford. Roger Hunt had to step down from his pedestal as Liverpool's greatest goalscorer. Rush was in awe of Sir Roger. 'Obviously I am proud and privileged to have beaten the record of a great player like Roger Hunt. He was my father's hero.' Souness gave Rush the captain's armband he fully deserved in the autumn of 1993. He also received a new and promising strike partner by the name of Robbie Fowler. They connected well and the Welshman took the young striker under his wing. Souness resigned in January 1994 and Roy Evans took over. Rush played his 600th game for Liverpool against Blackburn in the fifth round of the League Cup and celebrated by scoring his thirteenth hat-trick! He went on to score sixteen in total, one less than the club's hat-trick king, Gordon Hodgson. Steve McManaman proved instrumental in the 1995 League Cup final against Bolton and no one was more proud than Rush to lift the cup as captain.

In the summer of 1995 Liverpool bought the striking sensation that was Stan Collymore for a record fee. Rush was approaching his 34th birthday

and the prediction was this was going to be his final season. He continued as captain and figured at the start of the season, but got sidelined through injury. Fowler and Collymore established a good rapport and the writing was firmly on the wall for the legend. One more record gave way before Rushie left Anfield. On 6 January 1996 he scored against Rochdale in the third round of the FA Cup at Anfield. It was his 42nd goal in the competition and put him one above Denis Law, with whom he had shared the record as the competition's greatest goalscorer in the twentieth century. Rochdale manager Mick Docherty was honoured to witness this monumental feat. 'It couldn't happen to a better pro. He is a shining light in the profession because of his work rate, dedication and his great scoring record.'

On 27 April 1996 Ian Rush played his farewell game at Anfield. He came on as a substitute in a 1-0 win over Middlesbrough but couldn't get on the scoresheet. Rush was applauded by both sets of fans. He took his shirt off and threw it into the Kop. 'It was an emotional day but also a fantastic day for me,' Rushie said after the final whistle. 'The reception I got will live with me forever. I'm sorry I didn't score. The fans were willing me to score and I wanted to score as much as they wanted me to. I wanted to stay on the pitch forever.' He played his final league game against Manchester City and scored in a 2-2 draw. He looked forward to his final appearance that was, appropriately enough, at Wembley in the FA Cup final. 'In a perfect world, I would come on and score the winner. But it's the one game where I would happily sit on the bench for 90 minutes until Liverpool had won,' Rush said, waiting for his big moment. Evans was in no doubt he would play some part in the final.

'You don't keep someone with his experience on the bench. Wembley would be a fitting end to his Liverpool career, but I don't think there is a fitting venue in the world for Ian to finish off his career.' Rush came on in the second half but a dull game ended 1-0 in Manchester United's favour.

A few days later Rush joined Leeds United. He was continually played out of position on the wing at Leeds and only recorded three goals for the Yorkshire club. In the summer of 1997 his old mate Dalglish lured him to Newcastle. Rush scored two goals for the Tyneside team and both were historic. He scored his 48th goal in the League Cup, which equalled Geoff Hurst's record, and his last goal of his top-flight career came against Everton in the FA Cup on 4 January 1998. Once more his old favourites were his victims. He was loaned out to Sheffield United in the spring and then hired as player-coach of Wrexham in the 1998/99 season. The legendary striker made a couple of appearances for Sydney Olympic in Australia before retiring in 1999.

IAN RUSH was also a star for his country. He played 73 internationals for Wales and scored 28 goals, which is of course also a goalscoring record. His biggest disappointment was that he never got the opportunity to represent his country in the European Championships or the World Cup. Wales' Ryan Giggs is among his biggest admirers. 'As a schoolboy the three strikers I admired most were Ian Rush, Mark Hughes and Gary Lineker. But Rushie stood out because he was such an inspiring example to youngsters with so many other assets to his game.' Rush has passed his FA coaching badges and travelled around the world to Australia and Iceland among other countries, where he has taught kids to become accomplished goalscorers, trying to pass on the knowledge that he has gained.

Houllier also recognised his coaching ability and added him temporarily to his Liverpool staff to help his strikers score goals.

It's incredible to fathom that before Rush left Liverpool for Juventus he was still living with his parents in St Asaph. He was a global superstar yet extremely well grounded. His Catholic faith was strong and he went to church at 8 o'clock every Sunday morning. Despite all his success Rush has always stayed true to who he is, a village boy from Wales. Rush told *LFChistory.net*: 'My dad brought me up to respect people. One thing he always said was: "If you're nice to people on the way up, they'll be nice with you. If you're not nice with them they'll sit and be waiting for you to come down."' Rush argued he was a better all-round player once he returned from Italy. He had certainly always impressed with his goalscoring talents but what made him stand apart was his defensive work. He was Liverpool's first defender when the opposition had the ball. Joe Fagan was always impressed by Rush's attention to teamwork. 'He set an example to all his colleagues, not only in his scoring, but also in his willingness to tackle back. He wins the ball so often it provides a psychological boost for defenders.' Rush scored 207 goals in 331 appearances in his first spell at Liverpool and added 139 in 329 games in his second phase at the club following his return from Juventus. Ian Rush is a unique striker at a club that prides itself on great forwards and he will never have an equal.

Season	League App	League Goals	FA Cup App	FA Cup Goals	League Cup App	League Cup Goals	Europe App	Europe Goals	Other App	Other Goals	Total App	Total Goals
1980/81	7	0	0	0	1	0	1	0	0	0	9	0
1981/82	32	17	3	3	10	8	3 (1)	2	0	0	48 (1)	30
1982/83	34	24	3	2	8	2	5	2	1	1	51	31
1983/84	41	32	2	2	12	8	9	5	1	0	65	47
1984/85	28	14	6	7	1	0	7	5	2	0	44	26
1985/86	40	22	8	6	6	3	-	-	2	2	56	33
1986/87	42	30	3	0	9	4	-	-	3	6	57	40
1988/89	16 (8)	7	1 (1)	3	4	1	-	-	2	0	23 (9)	11
1989/90	36	18	8	6	3	2	-	-	1	0	48	26
1990/91	37	16	7	5	3	5	-	-	1	0	48	26
1991/92	16 (2)	4	4 (1)	1	3	3	5	1	-	-	28 (3)	9
1992/93	31 (1)	14	1	1	4	1	4	5	1	1	41 (1)	22
1993/94	41 (1)	14	2	1	5	4	-	-	-	-	48 (1)	19
1994/95	36	12	7	1	7	6	-	-	-	-	50	19
1995/96	10 (10)	5	0 (4)	1	2	1	2 (1)	0	-	-	14 (15)	7
Total	**447 (22)**	**229**	**55 (6)**	**39**	**78**	**48**	**36 (2)**	**20**	**14**	**10**	**630 (30)**	**346**

Russell,
Colin

LIVERPOOL-born Colin Russell made one brief appearance for the first team, coming on for winger Howard Gayle in the end-of-season Anfield fixture with Sunderland on 2 May 1981. Liverpool lost 1-0 and was only eighth in the table, finishing fifth in the spring.

It was a time when Bob Paisley had many injury worries to his first-choice players ahead of the European Cup final with Real Madrid.

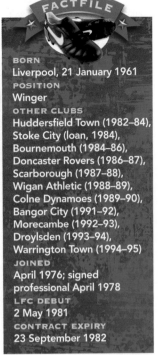

Season	League		FA Cup		League Cup		Europe		Other		Total	
	App	Goals	App	Goals	App	Goals	App	Goals	App	Goals	App	Goals
1980/81	0 (1)	0	0	0	0	0	0	0	0	0	0 (1)	0
Total	**0 (1)**	**0**	**0**	**0**	**0**	**0**	**0**	**0**	**0**	**0**	**0 (1)**	**0**

Rylands,
Dave

DAVE RYLANDS struggled to force his way into the first-team picture as Bill Shankly continued his rebuilding process in the 1970s.

He filled in for injured Larry Lloyd when Doncaster Rovers, bottom of the old Fourth Division at the time, arrived at Anfield for their FA Cup third round tie on 5 January 1974. Only two goals from Doncaster-born Kevin Keegan saved the day and by the time Liverpool travelled to Yorkshire for the replay three days later, Lloyd had been restored to his place at the heart of the defence.

Season	League		FA Cup		League Cup		Europe		Total	
	App	Goals	App	Goals	App	Goals	App	Goals	App	Goals
1973/74	0	0	1	0	0	0	0	0	1	0
Total	**0**	**0**	**1**	**0**	**0**	**0**	**0**	**0**	**1**	**0**

Sahin, Nuri

ALTHOUGH Nuri Sahin was born in Germany, he is of Turkish descent and Turkey is the country he has represented at senior level since 2005.

Earlier that year he and his team-mates won the 2005 UEFA European Under-17 Football Championships in Italy where he was voted the best player of the tournament. When he was 16 the midfielder joined Borussia Dortmund and he quickly became not only the youngest player to appear in the Bundesliga but also its youngest ever scorer. He did not, however, progress as quickly as had been expected, but benefited from a loan move to Feyenoord, where he was reunited with the Dutch coach who had signed him for Dortmund in 2005, Bert van Marwijk. On his return to Germany Sahin played in 88 out of a maximum 102 Bundesliga matches over the next three seasons. The third of those seasons, 2010/11, brought Dortmund their first domestic championship for nine years and

Sahin was voted the Bundesliga's best player. He signed a lengthy six-year contract with Real Madrid in 2011. He was sidelined by injury, and was unable to make his Real debut until November; although his new club won the La Liga title, Sahin only appeared in four of the 38 matches.

WITH A promising career at a kind of stalling-point, a move to Liverpool was considered beneficial to both the player and his new club. The supposed defensive midfielder showed his skill in arriving late into the box to devastating effect, netting three goals in a space of three days in a 2-1 win over West Bromwich Albion in the League Cup and a 5-2 league win at Carrow Road. He desperately needed games to build up his match fitness, though, and did not seem to handle the pace of the Premier League. He was virtually invisible in a few games as if he was hiding on the

field, but hope remained he would prove a valuable member of the team when fully fit. After remaining firmly on the bench for three games running he got a start against Udinese in the final game of the Europa League group stage, but had to bow out in the 12th minute with a broken nose. This turned out to be his final appearance for Liverpool as he returned to his parent club in January 2013 to be loaned back to his first club, Borussia Dortmund, for 18 months. Sahin revealed to Spanish newspaper *AS* in March 2013 that he was bemused by the use of his talents at Liverpool. 'Brendan Rodgers wanted me to play as a

number 10. But I do not play behind the strikers. I talked to him and asked him why he was playing me there. It is not my real position. The coach could not answer me. Thank God I have left Brendan Rodgers.'

FACTFILE

BORN
Lüdenscheid, Germany,
5 September 1988
POSITION
Midfielder
OTHER CLUBS
Borussia Dortmund (2001–11),
Feyenoord (loan, 2007–08),
Real Madrid (2011–), Borussia
Dortmund (loan, 2013-14)
SIGNED FROM
Real Madrid (on loan),
25 August 2012
INTERNATIONAL CAPS
38 Turkey caps (2 goals)
(5 (0) at LFC), 2005–
LFC DEBUT GAME/GOAL
2 September 2012 /
26 September 2012
CONTRACT EXPIRY
11 January 2013

Season	League		FA Cup		League Cup		Europe		Total	
	App	Goals	App	Goals	App	Goals	App	Goals	App	Goals
2012/13	7	1	0	0	1	2	4	0	12	3
Total	7	1	0	0	1	2	4	0	12	3

Salisbury, Bill

BILL SALISBURY was at Anfield for a single season towards the end of the 1920s.

He was brought into the team for the trip to Arsenal on 27 October 1928 but didn't figure on the scoresheet in a 4-4 draw. However, he had more fortune in his second away match for the club, when his second-half strike was the only goal of the game at Portsmouth. Salisbury's only other goal in the 16 First Division games he played for Liverpool came in the 8-0 trouncing of Burnley at

Anfield on Boxing Day, 1928. He also scored in the only FA cup tie he was selected for, a third round win at Bristol City. "Sally" was linked with a transfer back to Scotland or the USA, but Ireland was his next destination, once his transfer fee had been reduced from £500 to £100. After four years on the Emerald Isle he moved back to Partick Thistle. The *Dundee Courier* welcomed his arrival even though he had 'lost some of the fire and fervour which characterised his play in the days before he was transferred to Liverpool.'

FACTFILE

BORN
Glasgow, Scotland,
23 February 1899
DIED
12 January 1965
POSITION
Centre-forward
OTHER CLUBS
St Anthony's,
Partick Thistle (1918–1929),
Bangor (1929–30),
Distillery (1929–30),
Shelbourne (1930–31),
Bangor (1931–33),
Partick Thistle (1933–34)
SIGNED FROM
Partick Thistle,
25 October 1928
LFC DEBUT GAME/GOAL
27 October 1928 /
10 November 1928
CONTRACT EXPIRY
29 August 1929

Season	League		FA Cup		Total	
	App	Goals	App	Goals	App	Goals
1928/29	16	2	1	1	17	3
Total	16	2	1	1	17	3

Sambrook, Jack

JACK SAMBROOK was a forward who deputised twice for Dick Johnson in the middle of the 1922/23 First Division season. On both occasions Chelsea were the opponents, with the Reds sharing the points after a goalless draw at Stamford Bridge on 30 December 1922 before winning 1-0 at Anfield a week later.

Season	League		FA Cup		Total	
	App	Goals	App	Goals	App	Goals
1922/23	2	0	0	0	2	0
Total	**2**	**0**	**0**	**0**	**2**	**0**

FACTFILE

BORN
Wednesfield, 10 March 1899
DIED
30 December 1973
POSITION
Centre-forward
OTHER CLUBS
Willenhall (1917–19),
Wolverhampton Wanderers (1919–22),
Stockport County (1923–24),
Southport (1924–26),
Willenhall, C & L Hills
SIGNED FROM
Wolverhampton Wanderers,
August 1922
LFC DEBUT
30 December 1922
CONTRACT EXPIRY
15 May 1923

Ephraim Longworth and Donald Mackinlay, the powerful full-back pair of the 1920s

Satterthwaite, Charlie

TALL AND strongly built, Charles Satterthwaite scored a hat-trick in only his second appearance against Glossop at Anfield and was considered one of best catches the club had ever made considering his performance in his debut 1899/1900 season.

> SATTERTHWAITE SCORED A HAT-TRICK IN ONLY HIS SECOND APPEARANCE AGAINST GLOSSOP AT ANFIELD AND WAS CONSIDERED AT THE TIME ONE OF BEST CATCHES THE CLUB HAD EVER MADE

'Since the inclusion of Raybould and Satterthwaite in the team, matters have gone ahead with a smoothness which had almost become foreign to the play witnessed before their arrival, and the utility of a decent centre has never been more forcibly exemplified than in the case of the Anfield eleven this season,' reported the *Liverpool Echo*. Satterthwaite played 21 games and scored five goals in the 1900/01 championship-winning season. Although he was selected for the opening two First Division fixtures of 1901/02, he then lost his place and played on only four more occasions for the club's first team. Satterthwaite earned the distinction of being the first player to score a First Division goal in Arsenal's history (they dropped the 'Woolwich' from their name in 1914). He was Arsenal's leading scorer in two of his first three seasons and played a total of 178 games and scored 70 goals in his six-year spell at the Gunners.

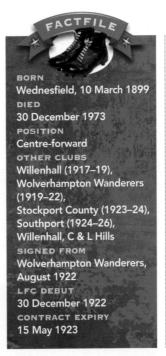

FACTFILE

BORN
Cockermouth, April 1877
DIED
25 May 1948
POSITION
Inside-right/left forward
OTHER CLUBS
Black Diamond (1894–95),
Workington (1895),
Bury (1895–97),
Burton Swifts (1897–99),
New Brompton (1902–03),
West Ham United (1903–04),
Woolwich Arsenal (1904–10),
Workington
SIGNED FROM
Burton Swifts,
8 December 1899
LFC DEBUT GAME/GOAL
16 December 1899 /
23 December 1899
CONTRACT EXPIRY
1902
HONOURS
League Championship
1900/01

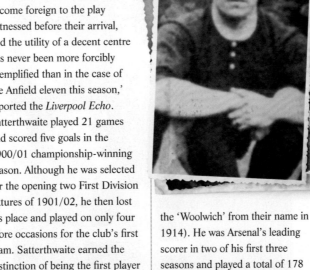

Season	League		FA Cup		Total	
	App	Goals	App	Goals	App	Goals
1899/1900	18	6	0	0	18	6
1900/01	21	5	0	0	21	5
1901/02	6	2	0	0	6	2
Total	**45**	**13**	**0**	**0**	**45**	**13**

Saul, Percy

PERCY SAUL was a full-back who impressed in two seasons at Plymouth Argyle where he featured in 94 matches and scored four goals from 1904 to 1906.

Argyle fans were sorry to see him go to Liverpool prior to the 1906/07 season in which he made 36 appearances as a right-back, taking over from Alf West who was injured four games into the campaign. Saul was inconsistent in his debut season at Liverpool but made progress in his second campaign, as was commented upon in the club programme on 30 September 1907: 'The most improved back in England is Percy Saul. Last season he showed flashes of great brilliance, but these were darkened by a number of unaccountable mistakes. He was most erratic. But this season, while the brilliancy remains, consistency has also been added, and Saul's performances have attracted attention all round. Perhaps he is taking more care in training. He is remarkably speedy, and he kicks with remarkable precision while in the most extraordinary positions.'

ALF WEST had returned to the side in the 1907/08 season but Saul was preferred to Billy Dunlop

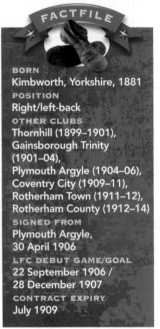

on the left; he made a further 31 appearances and scored his only league goal for the club in a home match against Sheffield United at the end of December 1907.

Saul was picked only 16 times for league and cup fixtures in 1908/09 in what turned out to be his last season at Anfield.

Season	League		FA Cup		Total	
	App	Goals	App	Goals	App	Goals
1906/07	33	0	3	0	36	0
1907/08	27	1	4	1	31	2
1908/09	15	0	1	0	16	0
Total	**75**	**1**	**8**	**1**	**83**	**2**

FACTFILE

BORN
Kimbworth, Yorkshire, 1881
POSITION
Right/left-back
OTHER CLUBS
Thornhill (1899–1901),
Gainsborough Trinity (1901–04),
Plymouth Argyle (1904–06),
Coventry City (1909–11),
Rotherham Town (1911–12),
Rotherham County (1912–14)
SIGNED FROM
Plymouth Argyle,
30 April 1906
LFC DEBUT GAME/GOAL
22 September 1906 /
28 December 1907
CONTRACT EXPIRY
July 1909

Saunders, Dean

DEAN SAUNDERS was on his way to Australia on a free transfer when Brighton manager, Chris Cattlin, spotted him at Swansea reserves. He made rapid progress up the league ladder and after scoring 33 goals in 73 games for First Division Oxford Saunders was sold against the wishes of manager Mark Lawrenson to Derby County.

Former Liverpool favourite Lawrenson handed in his resignation to chairman Robert Maxwell, who owned Derby as well. Saunders scored a decent 57 goals in 131 games before he arrived for a British record fee along with his team-mate Mark Wright at Liverpool. Son of former Liverpool half-back Roy Saunders, Dean played in a struggling side, whose passing game didn't suit him at all.

He was used to Derby's counter-attacking style that enabled him to score plenty of his goals by using his exceptional pace.

Saunders wasn't very prolific in the league at Liverpool with about one goal every four games, but flourished in the UEFA Cup with

FACTFILE

BORN
Swansea, Wales,
21 June 1964
POSITION
Centre-forward
OTHER CLUBS
Swansea City (1980–85),
Cardiff City (loan, 1985),
Brighton & Hove Albion (1985–87),
Oxford United (1987–88),
Derby County (1988–91),
Aston Villa (1992–95),
Galatasaray (1995–96),
Nottingham Forest (1996–97),
Sheffield United (1997–98),
Benfica (1998–99),
Bradford City (1999–2001)
SIGNED FROM
Derby County, £2.9million,
19 July 1991
INTERNATIONAL CAPS
75 Wales caps (22 goals),
1986–2001
LFC DEBUT GAME/GOAL
17 August 1991 /
27 August 1991
CONTRACT EXPIRY
10 September 1992
HONOURS
FA Cup 1992

nine goals in five matches that included a quadruple against Kuusysi Lahti. He contributed two goals to Liverpool's successful 1992 FA Cup run. On 5 September 1992 Saunders scored his second goal in seven matches in the 1992/93 season before being sold to Aston Villa.

THE WELSHMAN felt hard done by leaving the Reds after such a short stay. 'Graeme called me in one day and told me he needed a centre-half [Torben Piechnik], and that he could raise the money by selling me to Aston Villa,' Saunders said. 'I couldn't believe he was prepared to let me go, but he said he didn't think my partnership with Ian Rush had worked out, and Rushie wouldn't be the one going anywhere.' Souness was left to suffer at the hands of Saunders only nine days after his departure from Anfield, when he scored two goals in Villa's 4-2 victory over Liverpool.

Saunders was reunited with Souness twice as a player, with Galatasaray and Benfica, as well as joining the Scotsman's coaching staff at Blackburn Rovers and Newcastle United. Saunders gained managerial experience at Wrexham from 2008 to 2011 before he was appointed manager of Championship club Doncaster Rovers. He was unable to save Rovers from relegation, but when the club was in second place in League One Saunders left for 18th-placed Wolverhampton Wanderers in the Championship in January 2013. Following Wolves' relegation to League One Saunders was sacked by the club four months later.

Dean's family connection with Liverpool from an early age made his decision to join Liverpool an easy one as he told *LFC Magazine*. 'My dad Roy played for Liverpool in the 1950s with Billy Liddell, so I was always keen on the club. He had a bag of Liverpool cuttings and I remember being amazed by pictures of a Goodison derby with 77,000 in the crowd.'

Season	League		FA Cup		League Cup		Europe		Other		Total	
	App	Goals	App	Goals	App	Goals	App	Goals	App	Goals	App	Goals
1991/92	36	10	8	2	5	2	5	9	-	-	54	23
1992/93	6	1	0	0	0	0	0	0	1	1	7	2
Total	**42**	**11**	**8**	**2**	**5**	**2**	**5**	**9**	**1**	**1**	**61**	**25**

Saunders,
Roy

ROY SAUNDERS had to wait nearly five years before getting his chance in Liverpool's first team. After a dreadful run of eight defeats in the previous 11 league games, Liverpool beat Middlesbrough 3-2 at Ayresome Park. Leslie Edwards at the *Liverpool Echo* saw promise in Saunders in his fifth game for Liverpool against Bolton at Anfield on 4 March 1953.

He wrote: 'I have never seen a greater contribution of sheer graft than came from Saunders. He must be as strong in the tackle as any player in the game. And how tireless! Besides his link with the attack when his shot hit the bar, he did sufficient to show that the material he possesses can be developed.' Saunders played in 13 of the last 16 league fixtures as the club narrowly avoided relegation, something which was however only delayed by one more year.

AFTER THE DROP into the Second Division, which coincided with the retirement of regular right-half Phil Taylor, Saunders became more of a fixture in the side. But after making only five first-team appearances in 1957/58 and one fewer the next season, he moved on to Swansea in March 1959 and played in nearly 100 league games for the South Wales club. He later joined Swansea's coaching staff. Roy is the father of Dean Saunders, who also graced the Liverpool shirt.

FACTFILE

BORN
Salford, 4 September 1930
DIED
29 January 2009
POSITION
Right-half
OTHER CLUBS
Hull City (1946–48),
Swansea City (1959–63),
Ammanford Town (1964–69)
SIGNED FROM
Hull City, 24 May 1948
LFC DEBUT GAME/GOAL
10 January 1953 /
25 August 1956
CONTRACT EXPIRY
March 1959

Season	League		FA Cup		Total	
	App	Goals	App	Goals	App	Goals
1952/53	14	0	1	0	15	0
1953/54	20	0	0	0	20	0
1954/55	28	0	4	0	32	0
1955/56	37	0	5	0	42	0
1956/57	27	1	1	0	28	1
1957/58	4	0	1	0	5	0
1958/59	4	0	0	0	4	0
Total	**134**	**1**	**12**	**0**	**146**	**1**

Saunders,
Tom

TOM SAUNDERS was born and bred in Liverpool and was always a fan of the Reds. He joined the Territorial Army at the age of 16 and spent four years in North Africa. He was a teacher for 17 years at Olive Mount secondary school in Wavertree before becoming headmaster at West Derby comprehensive. His main passion was football and he had played amateur football with a few local teams: New Brighton, Burscough, Fleetwood, Marine and Prescot Cables. He managed the schoolboys' team in Liverpool, and England schoolboys for ten years.

Saunders was approached by Tony Waiters, Liverpool's departing youth team coach, in 1970 and became the first youth development officer in football. He was also hired by Bill Shankly to spy, mostly, on the club's European opponents, as he had tremendous insight and sound judgement. Saunders was appointed to the board of directors in 1993 and made vice-president of the club. He was the ideal link between the administration and the staff and he was invaluable to managers Graeme Souness, Roy Evans and Gérard Houllier. 'He was like my father, I chatted to him at our training ground every day,' Houllier said in 2002. 'He was a man of football, not only a figure of the past but a man of the future, a visionary.

'A MAN OF THE FUTURE, A VISIONARY'
GÉRARD HOULLIER

Saunders told Mark Platt at *LFC Magazine*, two months prior to his death in July 2001, how his scouting job for Shankly came about:

Bill Shankly said to me one day, 'Tom, I want you to go and watch Chelsea.' This was my first big assignment. On the following Friday, prior to the game against Chelsea, Shanks held his usual team meeting and he asked me to attend with the dossier I'd compiled. We all gathered around this table, which had a pitch marked out on it and magnetic discs identifying the players. Shanks then starts talking about boxing and Ali. Suddenly, without any warning, he swept the Chelsea counters off the table. 'Don't let's waste time! That bloody lot can't play at all.' With that, the team talk was rapidly brought to a close. I wasn't invited to speak and it left me thinking what had been the point of me going to watch them. It was a salutary lesson to me. Shanks and Bob would always stress that it wasn't about how the opposition played, it was about how we played.

Saunders travelled wide and far, including beyond the Iron Curtain, which entailed some hair-raising adventures. 'One thing I always used to look for was the movement of players off the ball, this was a very revealing exercise,' he said. 'Basically to see what the pattern of a team's play was, how they were organised, whether they were competitive or not and to look out for any outstanding individual performances. I'd only normally watch a team once, especially if there was any distance involved. However, I wouldn't decry the work that goes on nowadays in preparation for a game. The job now is almost like a science. But I am a little bit old-fashioned. I think the ball is round, it bounces and people can make mistakes. No two games are the same and you can't predict the outcome. That is what makes it so fascinating.'

SAUNDERS officially retired in 1986 after he had quintuple-bypass surgery. He was still around the place and when his successor as youth development officer left he was invited to hold the fort. After Kenny Dalglish became manager he asked Saunders to basically sit in his office. Ian Hargreaves at the *Liverpool Echo* was curious about Saunders' role and had a chat with the gentleman:

'You see, Kenny just asked if I'd mind sitting in his office taking the telephone calls,' Saunders said nonchalantly. He said that Kenny asked him things occasionally. I said, 'You mean you're a sort of adviser.' 'Oh no,' he said. 'I never offer any advice, I never say, why don't you do this, because people don't like that. I take messages and he'll occasionally say to me, "Oh, what do you think about this?" And I'll say to him, "It's up to you, boss, but you might just have seen that maybe he doesn't play well when we're playing away or he's a bit left-sided or I think he may have got domestic troubles."' Now, I imagine some of that would be regarded as absolute gold dust as information about people.

Chief executive Peter Robinson revealed that Saunders scouted potential new signings as well. 'Tom was very much the man who made a lot of

decisions about recruitment of new players. Tom would go and see them and Tom's word would be accepted by all of them. I think if there's one man in this club who has not had the praise he deserves it's Tom Saunders. He's always been the unsung hero.'

Saunders died at the age of 80 in the summer of 2001, shortly after fellow Liverpool legends Joe Fagan and Billy Liddell passed away. Houllier revealed Saunders followed Liverpool's fortunes during the treble 2000/01 season despite his failing health. 'Even when he was ill at the end of last season, he was determined to join us in Cardiff, Dortmund and Charlton. I have a photograph of Tom and I with the three trophies we won, which I will always cherish.' These are the words of Liverpool Football Club spokesman after Saunders' death: 'Tom Saunders made a huge contribution to the success enjoyed by Liverpool Football Club over the last 30 years. A man of humility and modesty, Tom never sought the limelight and always put the interests of the club before any want of personal recognition. A gentleman whose wide counsel was greatly appreciated, he had the special gift of being able to move in many different circles. Players, technical staff and directors turned to him for advice, happy to confide in him safe in the knowledge that he would always have the best interests of that individual at heart. Always a welcome visitor at Melwood and in the dressing room after games, Tom will be sadly missed by everyone at Anfield.'

The *Echo's* Ian Hargreaves remembers 'Old Tom' vividly. 'He would always go out in the morning for a strict walk around the pitch half a dozen times, really concentrated. Peter Robinson once said to me, "There's been no man who's done more for this club than Tom Saunders, including Bill Shankly."'

Savage,
Ted

TED SAVAGE made a name for himself in Third Division Lincoln's ranks at the tender age of 17 and played 100 matches for the Imps from 1928 to 1931.

> SAVAGE MADE HIS FIRST DIVISION DEBUT AS AN INSIDE-LEFT WHEN LIVERPOOL FACED GRIMSBY TOWN AT ANFIELD ON 26 SEPTEMBER 1931 AND SCORED TWICE IN A 4-0 VICTORY

AFTER the club just missed out on promotion to the Second Division he was sold to Liverpool. Although primarily a half-back Savage made his First Division debut as an inside-left when Liverpool faced Grimsby Town at Anfield on 26 September 1931 and scored twice in a 4-0 victory. He would never find the net for the club again in the 104 games that followed, but he did play in the vast majority as a defender. The only seasons when Savage could be considered a first-team regular were 1934/35 and 1935/36 when he played in 27 of the 42 league games each campaign. Savage joined Manchester United in December 1937, signed as a

TED SAVAGE
LIVERPOOL

cover, and only made five appearances for the club. After only a ten-month stay he moved to Wrexham where he played 26 league matches in the Third Division North before World War Two ended his professional playing career.

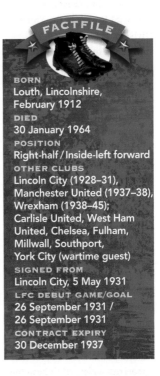

FACTFILE

BORN
Louth, Lincolnshire, February 1912
DIED
30 January 1964
POSITION
Right-half / Inside-left forward
OTHER CLUBS
Lincoln City (1928–31), Manchester United (1937–38), Wrexham (1938–45); Carlisle United, West Ham United, Chelsea, Fulham, Millwall, Southport, York City (wartime guest)
SIGNED FROM
Lincoln City, 5 May 1931
LFC DEBUT GAME/GOAL
26 September 1931 / 26 September 1931
CONTRACT EXPIRY
30 December 1937

Season	League App	League Goals	FA Cup App	FA Cup Goals	Total App	Total Goals
1931/32	7	2	0	0	7	2
1932/33	11	0	0	0	11	0
1933/34	15	0	0	0	15	0
1934/35	27	0	2	0	29	0
1935/36	27	0	2	0	29	0
1936/37	8	0	1	0	9	0
1937/38	5	0	0	0	5	0
Total	**100**	**2**	**5**	**0**	**105**	**2**

Sawyer,
Eric

ERIC SAWYER'S name is not well known among the Reds faithful but it's safe to say they have him to thank that Bill Shankly stuck it out at Anfield when the club's board was reluctant to give him the finances needed to strengthen the squad for Liverpool to make it out of the Second Division.

'There was a minute in the boardroom minutes book that staggered me,' Peter Robinson revealed about the state of affairs in 1959 when Bill Shankly took over as manager. 'It recommended that Liverpool shouldn't pay more than £12,000 for any player, and if you bear in mind the going rate for any top player in the late 50s

was well above that, Liverpool were getting what they were paying for. There was also a minute which stated every player should be seen by at least two directors before he was signed and, if possible, they should be in excess of six feet tall. We paid £37,500 for Ian St John and £22,000 for Ron Yeats. Under the previous regime they simply wouldn't have been bought.' John Moores, head of the Littlewoods empire, persuaded the club to put Eric Sawyer, a brilliant businessman, on the board, where he stayed until 1979. Shankly was grateful for his arrival, as he revealed in his autobiography.

No job is easy, and I stuck to it to the end, until the eventual triumphs, thanks mainly to a man of vision, a director who would only be associated with success and who was sick and tired of sitting in the pigsty we called a ground. That man was Eric Sawyer. When Mr Sawyer, a big man in the Littlewoods organization, joined the Board he knew that we were not good enough. We had lots of discussions together. I told him of players who were available and others who might be available. I told him, 'These could be the foundations of the success we need.' 'Bill,' he said, 'if you can get the players, I'll get the money.' Ron Yeats and Ian St John were still the players on my mind, but when we discussed possible transfer moves at Board meetings the tune was still 'We can't afford them.' That's when Mr Sawyer stepped in and said, 'We cannot afford not to buy them.'

Eric Sawyer can rightfully take his place beside Shankly and Robinson as one of the visionaries who helped transform Liverpool.

Sawyer in the boardroom flanked by Bill Shankly and fellow Liverpool boardmember Harry Latham

> ERIC SAWYER CAN RIGHTFULLY TAKE HIS PLACE BESIDE SHANKLY AND ROBINSON AS ONE OF THE VISIONARIES WHO HELPED TRANSFORM LIVERPOOL

Scales,
John

WHEN JOHN Scales was 19 he
moved on a free transfer after
one season in Leeds' reserves
to Bristol Rovers in the Third
Division. He impressed
sufficiently in his two seasons
there to join the Crazy Gang at
Wimbledon, enjoying a fairy-tale
ending to his debut campaign
by winning the FA Cup at the
expense of Liverpool.

Scales came on as a substitute in
the Wembley final for forward
Terry Gibson in the middle of the
second half. After he plied his
trade at the top level for seven
years with Wimbledon he moved
to Liverpool, arriving the day
after fellow centre-half Phil Babb,
who was signed from Coventry.
Roy Evans was delighted to
capture the central defender whom
he had been tracking for the past
12 months. 'John is big, strong
and a great athlete. He's been the
steadiest defender in the league
for a long time and he'll be a great
asset to us,' Evans predicted.

Scales was of a more skilful nature
than a lot of his fellow defenders

but his lack of aggression sometimes was a cause for concern for the
Reds' fans. He knew his limits, distributed the ball quite sensibly and was
not overambitious. He looked after himself, was very energetic and a
strong header of the ball. In fact, he won medals for high jump in his
teens. Scales lacked the necessary quality to succeed at a top-notch club
like Liverpool and only lasted two years at Anfield. 'The ability in the
team was phenomenal. The discipline was lacking and I'll hold my hands
up at the time,' Scales admitted. 'It's certainly very difficult when you
lose the discipline in a club.' Scales' move to Tottenham caused quite a

controversy as he had already
had a medical for his boyhood
club Leeds. He had a change of
heart at the last moment and
joined Spurs where, because of
injuries, he only played 33 games
in four seasons.

Season	League		FA Cup		League Cup		Europe		Total	
	App	Goals	App	Goals	App	Goals	App	Goals	App	Goals
1994/95	35	2	7	0	7	1	-	-	49	3
1995/96	27	0	7	0	2	1	2	0	38	1
1996/97	3	0	0	0	1	0	2 (1)	0	6 (1)	0
Total	**65**	**2**	**14**	**0**	**10**	**2**	**4 (1)**	**0**	**93 (1)**	**4**

Scott,
Alan

ALAN SCOTT was selected to play in Liverpool's forward line on the
opening day of the 1929/30 First Division season but it was not a
happy debut for him as the team was crushed by five goals to nil at
Middlesbrough. That was his only appearance of that campaign and
he had to wait until 27 December 1930 to be picked again.

This time he had a happier afternoon as Liverpool took a point from
a 3-3 draw at Blackburn Rovers and Scott scored one of the goals,
as he also did on his only other league appearance for the club, against
Manchester United on Easter Monday 1931. Apart from the three
league matches he figured in, Scott also represented Liverpool once in
the FA Cup, the third round defeat at Birmingham on 10 January 1931.

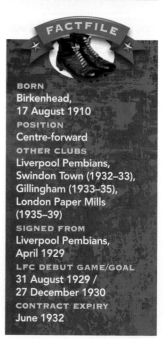

Season	League		FA Cup		Total	
	App	Goals	App	Goals	App	Goals
1929/30	1	0	0	0	1	0
1930/31	2	2	1	0	3	2
Total	**3**	**2**	**1**	**0**	**4**	**2**

Scott, Elisha

QUITE POSSIBLY the greatest goalkeeper in Liverpool's history, the Ulsterman's Anfield career spanned an astonishing 22 years from his arrival in 1912 until he left in 1934. Had World War One not taken away four years of his professional career, Elisha Scott would undoubtedly have made many more than the 468 first-team appearances for his one and only English club.

Elisha wanted to follow in the footsteps of his elder brother, Irish international goalkeeper Billy, who had just finished his eight-year career at Everton. He arranged a trial for Elisha at the Blues, who didn't sign him on account of his small stature. Their loss was Reds' gain as Billy recommended his baby brother to Liverpool. In fact, Billy Scott featured for Liverpool in the wartime 1918/19 season and was a reserve for half of the 1919/20 season.

ELISHA started playing youth football for Belfast's Boys' Brigade in 1909, as a striker. The reason he became a goalkeeper was because of an argument with one of his team-mates at the time. In a match he told his goalkeeper off: 'What's the use of us scoring goals against the other team and you're letting them in, my granny could be a better goalie than you!' The next match Scott was wondering what the team were laughing about until he looked up at the board that had the names and playing positions – it read: 'Goalkeeper: Elisha Scott's Granny.' After that Scott was in goal.

The *Lloyds Weekly News* reported on 25 August 1912 that 'much interest has been created by the announcement that Liverpool will to-morrow in a trial match play a new goalkeeper named Elisha Scott, who hails from Belfast, and is only eighteen years old [he was in fact nineteen]. He is said to be one of the best young goalkeepers in Ireland.' Following his trial Scott signed for Liverpool on 1 September 1912 at 10am on a Sunday morning in the Liverpool office. His last club, Broadway United, who didn't own Scott as such, did complain to his new employers for not receiving a penny and later Liverpool agreed to a small donation towards their pitch. The Ulsterman fractured his wrist early on but finally made his debut for Liverpool on 1 January 1913 in a goalless draw against Newcastle at St James' Park, and the *Liverpool Echo* gave him a good review. 'Hats off to Scott, Liverpool's youthful guardian. His debut was brilliant and a pleasing augury.' Newcastle were so impressed with Scott that they made an offer of £1,000 for his services.

Ten months passed before the 20-year-old got a second chance between the sticks when Liverpool faced Bolton. The *Echo* was again impressed: 'Campbell's excellence has kept Scott back from senior football, but today Scott made his first appearance at Anfield for the first team, and was accorded a hearty welcome. Very much like Hardy in appearance and in his method of clearing Elisha Scott is described by one critic as "more promising at his age than even Hardy was", high praise.' Sam Hardy later said that Elisha Scott was the best goalkeeper in the world at that time. Hardy had been Liverpool's main keeper from 1905 to 1912

but the current incumbent was 20-year-old Kenneth Campbell. Scott displaced him for the last 23 First Division fixtures of the 1914/15 season. Campbell was still between the posts immediately after the war as Scott was recuperating following an operation for varicocele. Scott returned to his old position at the end of March 1920 and within a week Campbell was transferred to Partick Thistle.

'Lisha' was named in the team for the opening game of the 1920/21 season, a position he held on to for many a campaign after that. He only missed three league matches when the League Championship was won in 1922 and was one of three ever-presents when the title was retained a year later. Scott enjoyed unprecedented popularity – a spectator even rushed on to the field in 1924 after his remarkable save to give him a big kiss! He was a colourful character; he once charged up the field to create an attack on his own, but lost the ball before he could get in a shot. Referees did on occasion get on his nerves, as in the instance when he was penalised for carrying the ball.

Scott booted the ball into the stands and was promptly ordered to fetch it by the match official. Scott had no intention of doing so and the matter finally came to a close when one of his team-mates brought the ball back.

SCOTT'S stats are there for all to see but what did his club captain from 1921 to 1928, Donald Mackinlay, think of him? 'A wonderful goalkeeper, the best I have ever seen. I put him above Sam Hardy,' Mackinlay said, and added: 'Stories about him are always coming up, but this one is true. When Jimmy Jackson first played for us I told him Elisha would probably have a few words to say to him during the games. "Don't take too much notice of him though, he doesn't mean it," I said. Jimmy replied, "He won't say anything to me," and I told him, "Won't he? He says them to me and I'm the captain."'

Dixie Dean's and Elisha Scott's duels in the Merseyside derbies were legendary and they might have tried to upset one another on the field, as Dixie recollects. 'My great Liverpool rival was, of course, Elisha Scott. Once we were playing at Anfield and just as I was into the players' entrance I met Elisha. His first words to me were, "You'll get no goals today, you black-headed so-and-so." I said to him: "If I don't lick you today I'm going right back to work on the railway."' They still had mutual respect for each other. 'Although we were enemies on the field we were quite different off it. We used to have a pint together now and again and the first thing Elisha would say to me was, "I received the aspirins all right." I used to send him a tube of aspirins with a note telling him to have a good night's sleep because I'd be there tomorrow to score goals against him. We used to have many a laugh over that.'

When Scott was approaching his mid-30s South African Arthur

Riley was given more playing time. Scott had only made one appearance in four months when Liverpool offered him and £9,000 in exchange for Preston North End's inside-forward Alex James as the 1928/29 season drew to a close. The Liverpool legend would have departed but James rejected the proposal due to his wage demands not being met. Everton had already had one offer for Scott in 1928 rejected but when they came back in January 1930 Liverpool were ready to let him go and secretly accepted a £5,000 bid from the Blues. The deal was thankfully called off when Scott received an ankle injury. Thirty-seven-year-old Scott eventually reclaimed his place in the team in March 1931 and was a regular in the side for the next two years.

Although relatively small for a goalkeeper at 5ft 9½in (175cm), Scott's agility and courage were never in question, nor was his loyalty to the club he served so well for so long. His age and Riley's form restricted him to just ten First Division appearances in his final season on Merseyside, 1933/34. He was transfer-listed in April 1934, available for £250, causing great outrage among the fans. Everton were finally going to land their man as Liverpool's board had agreed to the sale and Elisha was willing to leave to play regularly. Liverpool fans launched a newspaper campaign, flooding the local paper with letters of protest, like the following example published on 24 April 1934: 'To think, the one and only Elisha should have to submit to the indignity of a transfer is unthinkable, especially as it is being proved week in and week out where the weakness is. He is the world's best. The "owld man" could do for me if he came out and played in goal on crutches.' The fans' reaction changed the club's mind.

Such was the aura that surrounded him that the club took the unusual step of allowing Elisha to address the home crowd before the final home match at Anfield against Chelsea: 'We have always been the best of friends

and shall always remain so. I have finished with English association football. Last, but not least, my friends of the Kop. I cannot thank them sufficiently. They have inspired me. God bless you all,' Scott said. The *Liverpool Echo* bade Liverpool's talisman farewell. 'Invariably his work has been that of a master – a master of divination and anticipation, amounting to little less than positive genius. Intuition some people would call it; double sight or perceptive powers we prefer to say; and all due to an instanter reasoning out of "where" the opposition intended to plant that ball. And so it just "happened" that Scott got there first. That's all.'

ELISHA returned to his homeland to join Belfast Celtic as their player-manager, leaving behind an army of admirers and a host of wonderful memories. He was first capped at full international level shortly after the end of World War One and remarkably was still selected to represent his country two years after he left Liverpool. Donald Mackinlay could vouch for the fact that Scott had not forgotten anything even at that age. 'Look at Elisha. I saw him play in goal for the Irish League against the English League when he must have been 44. He played a blinder and when his team won, looked as though he could have jumped over the crossbar.' Scott played his final game for Belfast Celtic in 1936 in his 43rd year. He is Belfast Celtic's most influential manager, guiding the club through a trophy-laden period collecting ten Irish League titles (1936–42, 1944, 1947 and 1948), six Irish Cups, three City Cups, eight Gold Cups and five County Antrim Shields. Sectarian crowd trouble led to Celtic withdrawing from the Irish League in 1949 as the club felt it couldn't protect their players and supporters from further violence.

Scott was asked his opinion on modern goalkeepers in 1955:

'They don't seem to concentrate on the game and agility is not there. To be a good goalkeeper you have to be 100 per cent in every game. A goalkeeper must be keyed up and mentally take part in the game for the whole 90 minutes. It's no use telling yourself not to bother as the ball is at the other end of the field. You know how fast football is. Many of those silly goals we see are due to the goalkeeper being in the wrong position when the opposition forwards swoop suddenly down on the goal.' It is also fascinating to read the great custodian's opinion on the lost art of goalkeeping: 'Punching is an art which goalkeepers these days have not completely learned. Many have of course, but you can hit it further with your cap than

Elisha and Dixie Dean reminisce in 1955

some of them can punch today. To punch a ball properly you must get poise, get set and do it. No half measures. Make up your mind when a ball is coming over what you are going to do with it and don't change it. Many goalkeepers these days are frightened to leave the goal. They forget it will always be there when they get back. Another thing. Any ball in the six-yards area was my bird and it should be for every goalkeeper. If he thinks a full-back or another defender is in the way, tell 'em to get to blazes out of it. I did.'

In 1939 a survey was conducted among Liverpool supporters to name the greatest player Liverpool FC had ever had in their ranks. Elisha Scott's popularity was such that he topped this prestigious list. In the words of Dixie Dean: 'Elisha was the greatest I've ever seen. You can have Swift, Trautmann, Banks, Wilson. You can have them all. I'll take Elisha Scott.'

Season	League		FA Cup		Other		Total	
	App	Goals	App	Goals	App	Goals	App	Goals
1912/13	1	0	0	0	-	-	1	0
1913/14	4	0	0	0	-	-	4	0
1914/15	23	0	2	0	-	-	25	0
1919/20	9	0	0	0	-	-	9	0
1920/21	26	0	3	0	-	-	29	0
1921/22	39	0	3	0	1	0	43	0
1922/23	42	0	4	0	-	-	46	0
1923/24	42	0	5	0	-	-	47	0
1924/25	38	0	4	0	-	-	42	0
1925/26	39	0	3	0	-	-	42	0
1926/27	32	0	4	0	-	-	36	0
1927/28	17	0	0	0	-	-	17	0
1928/29	22	0	0	0	-	-	22	0
1929/30	8	0	0	0	-	-	8	0
1930/31	14	0	0	0	-	-	14	0
1931/32	37	0	4	0	-	-	41	0
1932/33	27	0	1	0	-	-	28	0
1933/34	10	0	4	0	-	-	14	0
Total	**430**	**0**	**37**	**0**	**1**	**0**	**468**	**0**

'ELISHA WAS THE GREATEST I'VE EVER SEEN'
DIXIE DEAN

Scott, James

JAMES SCOTT was selected for the last four fixtures of the 1911/12 season, making his debut as an inside-right at Bradford City on Easter Monday 1912, a game that the visitors won by two goals to nil.

He featured as an inside-left in the following game before moving to centre-half. Scott made the starting line-up on the opening day of the following season playing as right-half in six of the first nine games before losing his place to Ernest Peake. He finished his playing career at New York Giants in the American Soccer League.

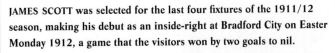

FACTFILE

BORN
Stevenston, Ayrshire, Scotland, 1892
POSITION
Left-half, forward
OTHER CLUBS
Stevenston United, Ardeer Thistle, Dumbarton (1919–1921), Third Lanark (1921–22), New York Giants (1923–25)
SIGNED FROM
Ardeer Thistle, 1910
LFC DEBUT
8 April 1912
CONTRACT EXPIRY
3 June 1919

Season	League		FA Cup		Total	
	App	Goals	App	Goals	App	Goals
1911/12	4	0	0	0	4	0
1912/13	6	0	0	0	6	0
Total	**10**	**0**	**0**	**0**	**10**	**0**

Scott, Tom

TOM SCOTT'S move from Darlington to Liverpool was quite controversial as Everton claimed that they were supposed to sign him along with John O'Donnell, who had been secured by the Blues from Darlington a week earlier.

Darlington claimed that the deals for the two players were supposed to be separate and that the player had no interest in signing for Everton. In the end

Darlington compensated Everton to the tune of £250 for this matter the following August. When interviewed by the *Liverpool Echo's* Bee shortly after his arrival at Liverpool, Scott revealed why he had turned down Everton. 'I did not think I should stand much chance of getting into the first team and the cost of their reserve side, and it put me off them. Besides I had played at Anfield and was impressed by the ground, the people and so on. If Liverpool had not signed me I should have stayed at Darlington. I should never have gone to Everton.'

THE CLEVER FORWARD was on Liverpool's books for four years

> I HAD PLAYED AT ANFIELD AND WAS IMPRESSED BY THE GROUND, THE PEOPLE AND SO ON

in the 1920s but only made 18 first-team appearances in that time. He made his debut at Preston on 14 March 1925 and scored the first of his four goals for the club at Leeds a fortnight later. Scott scored a total of 76 league goals in 204 games in his career.

Season	League		FA Cup		Total	
	App	Goals	App	Goals	App	Goals
1924/25	6	1	0	0	6	1
1925/26	4	1	1	0	5	1
1926/27	4	1	0	0	4	1
1927/28	3	1	0	0	3	1
Total	**17**	**4**	**1**	**0**	**18**	**4**

Seagraves, Mark

MARK SEAGRAVES never played in a league game for Liverpool but deputised for the injured Gary Gillespie in an FA Cup match at York City and in the first leg of the League Cup semi-final at QPR during the 1985/86 season.

> HE PLAYED AGAINST HIS OLD CLUB, LIVERPOOL, IN THE 1995 LEAGUE CUP FINAL, LOSING 2-1 TO A DOUBLE FROM STEVE MCMANAMAN

After a brief loan spell with Norwich City from 21 November to 6 December 1986, where he played just three times in the league, Seagraves returned to Anfield but was eventually given a permanent transfer to Manchester City nine months later. Seagraves certainly enjoyed his time at Bolton where he played 157 league games from 1990 to 1995. At the end of his Bolton career he played against his old club, Liverpool, in the 1995 League Cup final, losing 2-1 to a double from Steve McManaman.

Season	League		FA Cup		League Cup		Europe		Total	
	App	Goals	App	Goals	App	Goals	App	Goals	App	Goals
1985/86	0	0	1	0	1	0	0	0	2	0
Total	**0**	**0**	**1**	**0**	**1**	**0**	**0**	**0**	**2**	**0**

Sealey, John

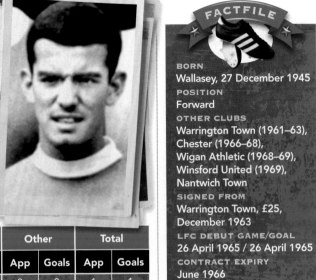

WALLASEY-BORN forward John Sealey was picked for the final league game of the 1964/65 season as regular first-team players were rested before the FA Cup final.

He did have the satisfaction of scoring the Reds' second goal in this meaningless match away to Wolves which Liverpool won 3-1 in front of under 14,000 spectators. Sealey is an avid Liverpool fan and holds a season ticket in the Main Stand.

FACTFILE

BORN
Wallasey, 27 December 1945
POSITION
Forward
OTHER CLUBS
Warrington Town (1961–63), Chester (1966–68), Wigan Athletic (1968–69), Winsford United (1969), Nantwich Town
SIGNED FROM
Warrington Town, £25, December 1963
LFC DEBUT GAME/GOAL
26 April 1965 / 26 April 1965
CONTRACT EXPIRY
June 1966

Season	League		FA Cup		League Cup		Europe		Other		Total	
	App	Goals	App	Goals	App	Goals	App	Goals	App	Goals	App	Goals
1964/65	1	1	0	0	-	-	0	0	0	0	1	1
Total	**1**	**1**	**0**	**0**	**0**	**0**	**0**	**0**	**0**	**0**	**1**	**1**

Sending Offs

Sending offs have become more common since the start of the Premier League, but before players got away with a lot more serious offences. Even legendary hardman Graeme Souness was never sent off while at Liverpool! These are the men who have most often been ejected off the field of play while wearing Liverpool's colours.

101 PLAYERS have been sent off in Liverpool's history. Tom Robertson was the first player dismissed on 9 February 1901.

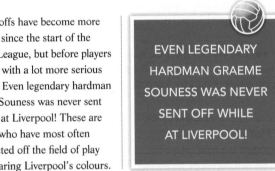

EVEN LEGENDARY HARDMAN GRAEME SOUNESS WAS NEVER SENT OFF WHILE AT LIVERPOOL!

Steven Gerrard (6)

Date	Opponent	Time
27 September 1999	Everton	90 min
13 April 2001	Leeds United	70 min
8 September 2001	Aston Villa	74 min
11 May 2003	Chelsea	89 min
25 March 2006	Everton	18 min
9 January 2011	Manchester United	32 min

Igor Biscan (3)

Date	Opponent	Time
6 January 2001	Rotherham United	61 min
16 April 2001	Everton	78 min
25 March 2004	Marseille	36 min

Jamie Carragher (3)

Date	Opponent	Time
13 February 1999	Charlton Athletic	68 min
27 January 2002	Arsenal	72 min
31 October 2009	Fulham	82 min

Didi Hamann (3)

Date	Opponent	Time
21 August 2000	Arsenal	78 min
25 November 2001	Sunderland	44 min
17 September 2002	Valencia	79 min

Javier Mascherano (3)

Date	Opponent	Time
23 March 2008	Manchester United	44 min
25 October 2009	Manchester United	90 min
19 December 2009	Portsmouth	45 min

Ian St John (3)

Date	Opponent	Time
24 March 1962	Preston North End	49 min
26 February 1966	Fulham	88 min
26 December 1967	Coventry City	31 min

Includes players who have been sent off at least three times.

Sephton,
George

Sephton presented with a recognition of his 40 years of service for the club

BETTER KNOWN as the 'Voice of Anfield', George Sephton has become a Liverpool institution, having been the stadium announcer since 1971. To put the length of his tenure into perspective, his first game was on 14 August 1971 when Kevin Keegan made his Reds debut against Nottingham Forest.

He witnessed Shankly's side secure the club's eighth league title two years into the job in 1973 and since then 10 league titles have been won and 10 managers been in charge of the team.

SEPHTON has always been a Liverpool supporter and his dad even had a trial at the club in 1923.

Sephton was hired after he wrote a letter to chief executive Peter Robinson, dismayed at the incompetence of the Anfield DJ at the time. Liverpool had incidentally just sacked the DJ and were looking for a replacement, so his letter couldn't have come at a more opportune time. The dulcet tones of Sephton's voice have been described as 'having the effect of a warm blanket on a cold match day'. For many years his commentary position was from a precarious perch in the television gantry suspended above the crowd, which he would reach by climbing across the Main Stand roof and down a ladder!

'It was cold and windy but the atmosphere was fantastic,' he told the *Liverpool Echo*. Now he is comfortably seated in the match control room in the corner of the Kop, which he says is warmer but 'with the sound proofing I don't get as much of the atmosphere as I used to'. When forced to name one game that has been more memorable than others in terms of atmosphere he says nothing beats the Champions League semi-final in 2005 against Chelsea, not even the St Etienne game. 'It was one of them nights that live forever.' Sephton has only missed a handful of matches since 1971 and the day he retires will be a sad one indeed, as he has become an inseparable part of Anfield.

Shafto,
John

JOHN SHAFTO was stolen from right under the noses of Everton. The Blues' minute books state that it was decided to offer Shafto '£2/15/- per week & the Club a donation of £125 maximum' to Hexham.

Everton had sent one of their scouts to sign the boy, a certain T. Fleetwood, and he stayed overnight in a hotel, where he mentioned the reason for his visit. A Liverpool fan heard him talking, immediately phoned Anfield, and George Kay went straight away to steal Everton's almost cut-and-dried signing.

The forward was one of 29 players used by Kay during the 1937/38 First Division season. Shafto was introduced into the side during the autumn of 1937 and performed well, scoring seven in 16 games, including two in the last 10 minutes at Goodison to seal a 3-1 win over city rivals Everton. Not a bad start for a 19-year-old! Liverpool had an unusually young forward line on this occasion with Nieuwenhuys the oldest at 26; inside-forwards were Jack Balmer (22) and Willie Fagan (18) and Harman Van den Berg (19) was on the left flank. Balmer scored for Liverpool after 30 seconds, but Tommy Lawton equalised in the eighth minute. Shafto got the ball into the Everton net on three occasions, in fact, but the referee spotted that he actually punched the ball instead of heading it for what would have put Liverpool 2-1 up. His cheeky effort did not count. Shafto guaranteed Liverpool victory in the last ten minutes with two well-placed shots, the second 'as good as goal as I have ever seen', as noted by 'Stork' in the *Liverpool Echo*.

DESPITE his success in those matches, he was only picked on four more occasions the following season. Shafto got most of his opportunities in Balmer's absence in the 1937/38 season, but Balmer was an ever-present in 1938/39 and Willie Fagan was now in the central role. The club had a much more settled team, with no fewer than seven men playing in 35 or more league games compared to just two the previous year.

Season	League		FA Cup		Total	
	App	Goals	App	Goals	App	Goals
1937/38	13	6	3	1	16	7
1938/39	4	0	0	0	4	0
Total	17	6	3	1	20	7

FACTFILE

BORN
Humsbaugh,
8 November 1918
DIED
1978
POSITION
Centre-forward
OTHER CLUBS
Hexham (1934–36);
Brighton & Hove Albion,
Bradford City (wartime guest)
SIGNED FROM
Hexham, November 1936
LFC DEBUT GAME/GOAL
23 October 1937 /
6 November 1937
CONTRACT EXPIRY
1944

Shankly,
Bill

'THE CHANGE that came over the place was incredible. Where there had been the nice approach of Phil Taylor, now there was this bristling, rasping fellow like James Cagney, who was setting out to conquer the world. Everything changed. Suddenly everyone was walking about with a new sense of purpose.' – Roger Hunt.

Bill Shankly's legacy can be seen at Anfield today, but not just in the gates that bear his name or the statue at the back of the Kop. Shankly was the catalyst that Liverpool Football Club needed. Other men carried on the job that he started but he was the father of the modern-day Liverpool and did more than most to turn them into one of the great powers of first English and then European football. The debt the club owes him can never be repaid.

Shankly was a tremendous competitor who made his name as a player at Second Division Preston North End after he arrived from Carlisle United, one division below, in 1933 at twenty years of age. 'Carlisle was only a stepping stone. I knew I was going further than that,' Shankly remembered. 'At the end of the season I was paid £4 10s a week, which was good, because the top rate in English football then was £8.

I was much better off than the coalminer for doing something in the fresh air that I would have done for nothing.' He eventually made his full debut for Preston on 9 December 1933 against Hull City and quickly established himself as a regular and a crowd favourite owing to his whole-hearted attitude and commitment to the side. At the end of the season Preston had gained promotion to the First Division. The newcomer clearly impressed Preston North End's correspondent, Walter Pilkington: 'One of this season's discoveries, Bill Shankly, played with rare tenacity and uncommonly good ideas for a lad of twenty. He is full of good football and possessed with unlimited energy; he should go far.' In an otherwise disappointing season in 1936/37, Preston had the satisfaction of reaching the FA Cup final. At Wembley they came up against Sunderland who ran out 3-1 winners. The following year, Shankly scored his first league goal for Preston in a 2-2 draw against Liverpool at Anfield on 2 February 1938. Preston reached the FA Cup final that season as well. Huddersfield's centre-half, Alf Young, brought down George Mutch inside the penalty area and Mutch scored from the resulting penalty that won Preston the cup.

SHANKLY'S tongue-in-cheek humour after the match probably didn't make Young feel any better: 'I was standing next to Alf Young afterwards. Tears were running down his cheeks. I said to him, "Ay, and that's no' the first one you've given away!"' It was the pinnacle of Shankly's playing career, as the great man himself remembered in his autobiography: 'Tommy Smith, the captain, was carried shoulder-high and we all had our hands on the Cup. The sweat poured off us, even though we had short-sleeved jerseys, having learned from the year before. I've still got that silk jersey, made in Preston.'

Sir Tom Finney, Preston North End legend, was Shankly's team-mate. 'Shanks first set foot in Deepdale in 1933 and within months,

at just 19, he was in the first team. As you may imagine, he wasn't a guy to give up his shirt without a fight and he followed his debut by playing 85 games in a row. A much better all-round player than some might have you believe, Shanks worked tirelessly to improve. After morning training he was always asking if anyone fancied going back for an extra session or a game of head tennis in the afternoon.' When Shankly was at the peak of his powers seven years of his career were lost to World War Two.

While serving in the RAF, he made wartime appearances for Norwich, Luton, Arsenal and Partick Thistle as well as playing a single game for Liverpool in a 4-1 win over Everton at Anfield on 30 May 1942. When full league football resumed for the 1946/47 season Preston still held his registration. Shankly was now viewed as being part of a pre-war generation. Many clubs were throwing in youngsters in an attempt to make a fresh post-war start. In 1949, Shankly was Preston's captain as the side struggled in the First Division and was eventually relegated in the spring. Before the end of the campaign, Shankly's old club, Carlisle United, offered him the chance to become their manager, which he accepted. When Tommy Docherty took his place in the Preston team, Shankly told him, 'Congratulations. You are now the greatest right-half in the world. Just put the number 4 shirt on and let it run round, it knows where to go.'

Shankly could look back on a successful playing career. 'As a player I specialised in tackling, which is an art, and I was never sent off the field or had my name in a referee's book,' he recalled. 'The art of tackling, as with many things, is in the timing – the

Mother, father and the boys. (From left) John, Bill, Bob, Jimmy and Alec

Mother, father and the boys. (*From left*) John, Bill, Bob, Jimmy and Alec.

contact, winning the ball, upsetting the opposition, maybe even hurting them. You're in, you're out, you've won it and you've hurt him and left him lying there, but it's not a foul because you have timed everything right. I played it hard, but fair. No cheating. I'd have broken somebody's leg maybe, with a hard tackle, with a bit of spirit, but that's a different story from cheating.' Sir Stanley Matthews had always believed Shankly would succeed as a coach because he was a natural leader of men. 'If my father was my guiding light in life, Bill Shankly was my football mentor. Has there been anyone with a greater love for the game? If there has, I have yet to meet him. He was an established player when I first encountered him during my days as a junior. He invariably popped along to our matches. Bill would stop off anywhere a game of football was being played and, even at that early stage of his career, you knew he would go into coaching and management and make a damn good job of it.'

SHANKLY was never short of confidence in his own ability. 'I had the knowledge. I had been with people who knew how to train teams and I had my own conception of human beings and psychology.' His methods were

Presented to Mr W. (Bill) Shankly by the lads & dads of the Crosland Road Sunday afternoon club – as a token of their appreciation for the friendship & fellowship during his period of residence in Huddersfield

certainly different from some of his contemporaries. Shankly was prepared to do any job however menial and instead of writing notes in the programme for the supporters to read, he preferred to use the tannoy to speak to them shortly before the start of each home fixture. 'The supporters loved it!' Shankly exclaimed. Carlisle were a struggling Third Division North side who found it hard to attract southern-based players because of their geographic remoteness. Shankly immediately turned this disadvantage on its head and turned Brunton Park into something of a fortress. He would tell his players how tired the opposition must be as they had to travel up to such a remote corner of the country. He dragged a team that finished 15th in the 1948/49 season up to third place. After a squabble with the club who had reneged on a bonus promise should the team finish in the top three, Shankly resigned.

GRIMSBY TOWN had been relegated in 1951 and would be playing in the Third Division North just like Carlisle, but Shankly wanted the job because 'Carlisle did not have the money to make progress and because I thought there was more potential at Grimsby'. Five months earlier Shankly had applied for a post in the First Division. George Kay had to resign from Liverpool due to health reasons and, as Shankly recalled in his autobiography: 'I got a telephone call from Liverpool and was asked if I'd like to be interviewed for the manager's job.' Shankly wanted to put his own stamp on his team, but back in those days the members of the board had a big say in team matters. 'The big snag had cropped up when the Liverpool board had said the manager could put down his team for matches and the directors would scrutinise it and alter it if they wanted to,' Shankly explained. 'So I just said, "If I don't pick the team, what am I manager of?"'

The Blundell Park outfit had been in the First Division in 1948 and were in freefall. The morale of the players and the supporters was low. However, the players who had been at the club when Grimsby were in the top flight were still there, as there was little point in players swapping and changing clubs in those days due to the maximum wage. Shankly was quickly able to use the raw material at his disposal to weld the players into a good side. In 1951/52 Grimsby just missed promotion, despite picking up an incredible 36 points out of a possible 40 in the last 20 matches. The 1952/53 season started with much optimism but the ageing team struggled after a bright start and the season fizzled out. Shankly was given no money to buy new players and was reluctant to blood some promising reserves because of the loyalty he felt to these older stalwarts, a fault that was to surface at Liverpool years later. Disillusioned by events, he quit in January 1954, citing a lack of ambition by the club as his main reason.

'Workington threw out a challenge to me. They were struggling at the bottom of the Third Division North and were threatened with extinction. There was only one man they thought could save them and that was me,

so they offered me a bonus if I saved them,' he said of his next appointment. Shankly was only a few days without a job after leaving Grimsby but had undoubtedly taken a step down the football ladder by taking over as manager at Workington. The fact that he had walked out on two clubs, without actually winning anything tangible, meant that he was still to make an impression in the boardrooms of the wealthy senior clubs. Ever the optimist and, of course, with an unabating self-confidence, Shankly set about reviving the club. Workington had only been a league side for two years and had been forced to apply for re-election at the end of both seasons. At the end of the 1953/54 season, Shankly had lifted them to 20th position, six points clear of re-election. Workington were transformed, playing a delightful brand of football. Season 1954/55 saw them finish a creditable eighth in the Third Division North. Shankly had recharged the batteries that had run so low after his experience at Grimsby and he was looking to step up the managerial ladder again. The realisation that Workington's ambitions were restrained by a chronic financial straitjacket meant there was no real future for him at the club. When he heard his old colleague from his Preston days, Andy Beattie, was in trouble at First Division Huddersfield, he was only too glad to tend his resignation at Workington on 15 November 1955 and help him out.

Shankly became assistant manager and coached the reserves at Huddersfield but on 5 November 1956, after the club had been relegated to the Second Division, Beattie left and Shankly took over as manager. On Christmas Eve 1956, Shankly gave a full first-team debut to one of the rising stars of the club, 16-year-old Denis Law. Shankly was unable to take Huddersfield back into the top division but was

making a mark for himself as a manager. However, he was again frustrated at the lack of finance available to strengthen the team at a club that probably didn't match his own ambition. He went to Scotland to see a non-competitive match and came back enthusing about two players he had watched closely. Those players were Ron Yeats and Ian St John. As Shankly pointed out: 'Yeats and St John were the players Huddersfield needed, but they couldn't afford to buy them.'

On 1 December 1959 Liverpool chairman T.V. Williams issued the following statement: 'Mr Bill Shankly, manager of Huddersfield Town, was last night appointed manager of Liverpool Football Club in succession to Mr Phil Taylor, who resigned on November 17. He has accepted the position, but has agreed to stay on at Leeds Road for another month before coming to Anfield in the early days of the New Year, unless circumstances permit an earlier release.' Few could imagine what impact this man would have but the *Daily Post* reporter knew there was something special on the way. 'The new manager's confidence and firm resolve are infectious. Nobody can be in his company for more than a few minutes and not realise that here is a rare driving force who will spare himself no pains to get the job he has in view. The players will find him fair, friendly, and always willing to help and advise, but in return he will demand a high price – the last possible ounce of effort each player is able to give.'

Shankly arrived for good at Liverpool on 14 December. The press loved his demeanour and the *Liverpool Echo* was under his spell. 'Quite a character this new Liverpool manager is. The thing that most impacts you about him

Liverpool chairman T.V. Williams welcomes Shankly to Liverpool

is his burning zeal for good class football and for supreme fitness. As he says: "Anyone who isn'a fit canna play fitba and he's not much use for anything else." This man if my reading of him is correct is a disciplinarian, a go-getter, a hard-hitter and someone who has enough confidence in himself to come here and say, "Never mind about a contract, give me the team and leave the rest to me."'

LIVERPOOL were in the Second Division and going nowhere. The training ground, Melwood, was a shambles, Anfield was not a pretty sight and the club was overburdened with average players, but with quality players in the reserves. Shankly felt immediately at home as he sensed in the huge crowds a kinship with the supporters from the word go. They were his kind of people. With the backing of Reuben Bennett, Bob Paisley and Joe Fagan and the enthusiasm of the fans behind him he set about rebuilding the team. 'But after only one match I knew that the team as a whole was not good enough,' he would say. 'I made up my mind that we needed strengthening through the middle, a goalkeeper and a centre-half who between them could stop goals, and somebody up front to create goals and score them.' Liverpool conceded seven goals without a reply in Shankly's first two games in charge. He wasn't disheartened after the first one, quite the opposite. 'I told them that this defeat was the best possible thing which could have happened, because in my experience, more is learned from defeats than victories.' Soon enough Liverpool were a changed side. 'They think more, thump less. Chase more, chance less,' the *Liverpool Echo* reported, adding that they were now beating teams with 'almost condescending arrogance'.

As well as improving the club's training conditions Shankly cleared the squad of any dead wood. 'Within a month I had put down 24 names of players I thought should go and they went inside a year.' Shankly tried to convince the directors at the club that Liverpool should spare no expense in strengthening the team. 'I used to fight and argue and fight and argue and fight and argue until I thought: "Is it worthwhile, all this fighting and arguing?" It is bad enough fighting against the opposition to win points, but the internal fights to make people realise what we were working for took me close to leaving many times.' Finally, 18 months after Shankly took over at Liverpool in came Yeats and St John, the two players he had wanted at Huddersfield, thanks to the vision of the club's new financial director, Eric Sawyer.

SHANKLY felt Liverpool were ready for promotion and made sure the players were ready. 'The coaching and training staffs, with the players, had spent a lot of time on tactical plans to suit the type of players we had, and this, together with the great physical fitness of the lads, added up to a feeling of optimism tinged with caution,' Shankly reflected in the *Liverpool Echo* in the summer of 1962. 'I know everybody was looking

forward to the start of the big effort which we had determined to make to win the prize which had been lost to us so often by such narrow margins.' If Liverpool were nervous it didn't show, as they had opened up a seven-point lead in October. Shankly was happy with the solidity of his defence and the attacking prowess of his forwards. Liverpool had been put through their paces by coaches Reuben Bennett and Joe Fagan and the players' stamina was vital. After Liverpool had destroyed Swansea 5-0 on 25 November with a hat-trick from Hunt and a brace from Melia, Shankly remembered a Swansea official's words to him after the game. 'I was really glad when the game was over, even in the closing stages your players were like vultures seeking for prey.' Liverpool lost two games on the trot over Christmas with their lead down to just two points. Shankly had a simple explanation for Liverpool's apparent loss of form. 'Both these games were played on grounds which resembled skating rinks and training on skates was possibly the only item of preparation for the season for which we had not undertaken. I have long held the opinion that no game of any importance should be played on grounds in such a state. All sanity is against it.'

THE REDS were soon back in the swing of things and ensured their long-awaited place in the First Division with five matches to go with a 2-0 win over Southampton. Shankly was amazed by the fans' reaction post-game. 'The crowd waited with commendable patience whilst the players cooled off and changed into their ordinary clothes, but the moment Ronnie Yeats showed himself a tidal wave of humanity swept across the field and engulfed poor Yeats. Behind Yeats came Ian St John and part of the flood detached itself and completely submerged him. Other players who were following had

the good sense to take refuge in the tunnel. This was the proudest moment of my footballing life, and I was delighted that I had had something to do with the return of Liverpool to First Division football.' Yeats told *LFChistory.net* that the 1961/62 season was the most vital one in his and arguably Shankly's career. 'The most successful thing we did, and I'll say this always, was winning the Second Division. Without that nothing else would have happened, because we couldn't progress without winning it. It was the best season I remember at Liverpool Football Club. We won it quite easily. He was building a team. When I first came to the club in '61 we had one international who was then Ian St John. Three years later we had 14 internationals. That's the progress we were making.'

'When we won promotion to the First Division I went to a shareholders' meeting and they were so thrilled about it that they presented us with cigarette boxes,' Shankly told John Roberts in 1976. 'I told them, "We got

promotion, but you don't think that is satisfactory, do you? Next time we come back here for presents we will have won the Big League, the First Division." They looked at me the way the officer in the RAF had done when I told him I wanted leave to play for Scotland against England, as if to say, "We've got a right one here."' A season of consolidation followed in which Liverpool finished eighth, while Everton secured the championship. Liverpool and Everton were about to carve up the domestic honours between them in the next five or six seasons, but as the 1963/64 season started it was Everton who were top dogs on Merseyside, a fact that rankled with Shankly.

THE SCOTSMAN had the nucleus of a side that had gained promotion but with the important addition of left-winger Peter Thompson. After a less than stellar beginning of the season Liverpool finally reached the top spot on 23 November 1963 following a win over Manchester United, their eighth in the previous nine league games. Shankly remembered: 'At Easter I said, "Right, boys, we've jogged along nicely. Let's go out and get it going. Never mind anything that happens, off you go!"' We won seven games on the trot, running through teams and tearing them to pieces, and we rounded things off by drubbing Arsenal 5-0 at Anfield.' Captain Ron Yeats recollects Shankly's satisfaction at having won the league. 'I remember he said to Tommy Lawrence, after we had just won the league but still had a few games to play out the season, "Tom, wouldn't it be great if we could put a deck chair in the middle of the goal, you sitting in it, cigar in your mouth, and when the ball comes, you get out of your deck chair and catch it and say, 'It's a lovely day to play football, isn't it?'"'

The following season Liverpool finished a disappointing seventh in the league with 13 fewer points than the previous season. Liverpool's participation in the European Cup took a lot of energy from them, only denied at the semi-final stage due to a dishonest referee in Milan. Liverpool were also doing brilliantly in the FA Cup, reaching their third final in the club's history. The Reds had lost both their FA Cup finals to date in 1914 and 1950, but Shankly finally managed to bring the Cup home after St John headed in the winner. 'It was a wet day, raining and splashing, and my shoes and pants were covered in white from the chalk off the pitch as I walked up to the end of the ground where our supporters were massed,' Shankly said. 'We had beaten Leeds United and our players had the arena, but I took off my coat and went to the

supporters because they had got the Cup for the first time. Grown men were crying and it was the greatest feeling any human being could have to see what we had done. There have been many proud moments. Wonderful, fantastic moments. But that was the greatest day.'

LIVERPOOL won the title again in 1966 while Everton took the FA Cup. Liverpool lost the final of the European Cup Winners' Cup at Hampden Park to Borussia Dortmund. The great 1960s side had gained promotion from Second Division, won the League Championship twice, the FA Cup once, and progressed in Europe. Now it was a transitional time for the club. After that second title in 1966 Liverpool didn't win the league again in that decade, or any other honour for that matter. Shankly's mistake was to let the side rumble on without any major rebuilding for too long. 'We were all at the same age when we started so around '67 we were all around 30,' Yeats explained to *LFChistory.net*. 'He started to change the side, changing tactics, changing players, it took maybe three years to come together. When you say we weren't successful, we were still a top team, maybe always second or third, getting to the semi-final.' Shankly had been taken aback by the deterioration of his key players, having expected them to last as he did in the game. 'I had told them, "If you are a good athlete, your best seasons will be between twenty-eight and thirty-three." I had my best seasons during that

FACTFILE

BORN
Glenbuck, Scotland,
2 September 1913
DIED
29 September 1981
OTHER CLUBS
Carlisle United (1949–51),
Grimsby Town (1951–54),
Workington (1954–55),
Huddersfield Town (1956–59)
SIGNED FROM
Huddersfield Town,
1 December 1959
LFC DEBUT
19 December 1959
CONTRACT EXPIRY
12 July 1974
HONOURS
League Championship
1963/64, 1965/66, 1972/73;
Second Division
Championship 1961/62;
FA Cup 1965, 1974;
UEFA Cup 1973;
Manager of the Year 1973

period of my life. Maybe the success they had shortened their careers. They had won the League, the FA Cup and the League again, and they had been in Europe so often. Perhaps they were no longer hungry enough.'

One cold afternoon in February 1970 Liverpool were dumped out of the FA Cup at Second Division Watford. 'After Watford I knew I had to do my job and change the team,' recalled Shankly. 'It had to be done and if I didn't do it I was shirking my obligations.' Most of the old guard were phased out and in their place came the likes of Ray Clemence, Larry Lloyd, John Toshack, Steve Heighway and Brian Hall, not to mention the inspirational signing of Kevin Keegan from Scunthorpe United. These newcomers plus the

younger players from the 1960s like Tommy Smith, Chris Lawler, Ian Callaghan and Emlyn Hughes would be the nucleus for his next great team that went on to win the UEFA Cup and the League Championship in 1973 and the FA Cup in 1974. John Toshack learned a lot from Shankly to progress in his own managerial career. 'Bill Shankly used to say: "A football team is like a piano. You need eight men to carry it and three who can play the damn thing."' Newcastle's 3-0 humiliation against the Reds in the FA Cup final turned out to be Shankly's swansong. 'After the FA Cup final I went into the dressing room and I felt tired from all the years. I said to a bloke who was looking after the dressing room, "Get me a cup of tea and a couple of pies, for Christ's sake." When I sat down with my tea and pies, my mind was made up. If we had lost the

final I would have carried on, but I thought, "Well, we've won the Cup now and maybe it's a good time to go." I knew I was going to finish.' Shankly responded to claims that his wife Ness had convinced him to retire. 'Nobody made me pack in. It was worked out between myself and Ness. Deep down I had thought about it the previous season. Ness had said, "How long is this going to go on?" I had said, "I can't tell you." That wasn't even Nessie's business. It was mine and mine alone.' However, Nessie said, at the time, the matter was pretty straightforward. 'Bill has resigned for my sake. He knew that the tension and strain of being married to Liverpool's manager was getting me down. I was highly strung and full of tension. The days the team was playing, whether Bill was home or away, were terrible. He gave so much of himself and you had to feel for him and with him. I wanted him to think about retirement and he did.' The legendary manager Don Revie was a good friend of Shankly and knew how top-flight football could wear you down. 'His retirement was a great loss to the game, but I am glad he got out at the top. The pressures of managing a team like Liverpool or Leeds and keeping them at the top are tremendous.'

The relationship between Shankly and Liverpool became somewhat strained after he left. 'I went to the training ground at Melwood for a while. It is only down the road from where I live,' Shankly said in his autobiography.

As Manager

Season	Division	P	W	D	L	GF	GA	Pts	Pos	Win %	FA Cup	League Cup
1959/60*	2nd Division	21	11	5	5	46	30	27	3	52.38	4th Round	-
1960/61	2nd Division	42	21	10	11	87	58	52	3	50.00	4th Round	3rd Round
1961/62	2nd Division	42	27	8	7	99	43	62	1	64.29	5th Round	-
1962/63	1st Division	42	17	10	15	71	59	44	8	40.48	Semi-Final	-
1963/64	1st Division	42	26	5	11	92	45	57	1	61.90	6th Round	-
1964/65	1st Division	42	17	10	15	67	73	44	7	40.48	Winners	-
1965/66	1st Division	42	26	9	7	79	34	61	1	61.90	3rd Round	-
1966/67	1st Division	42	19	13	10	64	47	51	5	45.24	5th Round	-
1967/68	1st Division	42	22	11	9	71	40	55	3	52.38	6th Round	2nd Round
1968/69	1st Division	42	25	11	6	63	24	61	2	59.52	5th Round	4th Round
1969/70	1st Division	42	20	11	11	65	42	51	5	47.62	6th Round	3rd Round
1970/71	1st Division	42	17	17	8	42	24	51	5	40.48	Runners-Up	3rd Round
1971/72	1st Division	42	24	9	9	64	30	57	3	57.14	4th Round	4th Round
1972/73	1st Division	42	25	10	7	72	42	60	1	59.52	4th Round	5th Round
1973/74	1st Division	42	22	13	7	52	31	57	2	52.38	Winners	5th Round
Total	-	609	319	152	138	1034	622	790	-	52.38	-	-

* Shankly appointed on 1 December 1959 with Liverpool in 10th position

As Manager in Europe

Season	European Cup	UEFA Cup	European Cup Winners' Cup	European Fairs Cup
1964/65	Semi-Final	-	-	-
1965/66	-	-	Runners-Up	-
1966/67	2nd Round	-	-	-
1967/68	-	-	-	3rd Round
1968/69	-	-	-	1st Round
1969/70	-	-	-	2nd Round
1970/71	-	-	-	Semi-Final
1971/72	-	-	2nd Round	-
1972/73	-	Winners	-	-
1973/74	2nd Round	-	-	-

But then I got the impression that it would perhaps be better if I stopped going. I felt there was some resentment – 'What the hell is he doing here?' I would have loved to have been invited to away matches, but I waited and waited until I became tired of waiting. I asked other clubs for tickets, sometimes when Liverpool were the visiting team and sometimes to see other teams play. Tommy Docherty invited me to Old Trafford when Manchester United played Liverpool in a night match. Tommy invited me to have a meal with him in a restaurant at Old Trafford and we enjoyed a wonderful hour of banter before the match. Sidney Reakes, the Liverpool director, said to Tommy, 'I see Bill Shankly's here.' 'Aye,' said Tommy. 'He's welcome here.'

Shankly said he would have been honoured if he had been invited to become a director of the club as he wanted to continue to help in any way he could, but the offer never came. Peter Robinson explained to the *Liverpool Echo* in 2009 what might be the reason why Shankly was not asked to become a director.

Clubs were very much director-run. There was a weekly board meeting attended by nine directors where Bill had to come and give a written report on the first, second, third and fourth teams, then give a verbal report with directors asking all sorts of silly questions. Because the directors changed every three years it was difficult for Bill to build any kind of rapport with them and he hated those meetings. He would have to tell them of his plans and there would be leaks to the press about players he wanted to sign. I used to tell him, 'If you dislike these meetings so much why don't you find a match to go to when they're held?' Gradually he would start attending them fortnightly and then monthly. And I can't tell you how many times I covered for him.

SHANKLY missed his involvement with the club and was quite bitter. 'It was never my intention to have a complete break with Liverpool, but at the same time I wasn't going to put my nose in where it wasn't wanted. Maybe I was an embarrassment to some people,' he concluded in his autobiography; a book that was not looked kindly upon by Liverpool FC at the time, in 1976. Bill Shankly seemed indestructible but he suffered a heart attack in the autumn of 1981 and died shortly afterwards on 29 September. The man who knew Shankly best was his right-hand man, Bob Paisley. 'One man transformed Liverpool from a run-of-the-mill Second Division team into the greatest team in the world,' Paisley said. 'That man, of course, was Bill Shankly. His philosophy was simple: "If you are going to play football, you play to win." While he was the making of Liverpool, there is no doubt that Anfield was the making of Bill Shankly. His character, his own enthusiasm and his will to win were so infectious.'

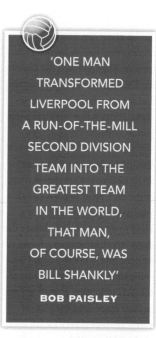

'ONE MAN TRANSFORMED LIVERPOOL FROM A RUN-OF-THE-MILL SECOND DIVISION TEAM INTO THE GREATEST TEAM IN THE WORLD, THAT MAN, OF COURSE, WAS BILL SHANKLY'

BOB PAISLEY

Shankly Gates

HORACE YATES of the *Liverpool Echo* suggested gates at Anfield in honour of their legendary manager, Bill Shankly, in 1972.

NEW GATES were erected at the ground where the main entrance to the car park was. 'The gates, I am told, will be very similar to those at the Lord's cricket ground, which have been named the "W.G. Grace Gates" to commemorate one of the world's most famous cricketers. Surely, here is the spark of an idea for Liverpool. Why not name theirs the "W. Shankly Gates" to perpetuate the name of the man who pulled Liverpool out of the doldrums and led them to the finest phase

of their history? For years Anfield and Shankly have been synonymous.' Ten years later, on 26 August 1982 Shankly's widow, Ness, formally unlocked the Shankly Gates, 11 months after her husband's passing. They were designed by Liverpool fan Kenneth Hall of County Forge in

Frome, Somerset. 'I have followed Liverpool since I was nine years old, attending their many matches where support is needed most. I was delighted when our design was chosen,' he told local papers.

The 14ft gates are on the Anfield Road side, next to the Hillsborough

memorial. They are forged from wrought iron and at the top they bear a heraldic symbol showing the club crest with the liver bird, and the cross of St Andrew and a thistle to denote Shankly's Scottish origins. Across the black and golden gates are the words 'You'll Never Walk Alone'.

THEY BEAR A HERALDIC SYMBOL SHOWING THE CLUB CREST WITH THE LIVER BIRD, AND THE CROSS OF ST ANDREW AND A THISTLE TO DENOTE SHANKLY'S SCOTTISH ORIGINS

Shankly Statue

ON 4 DECEMBER 1997, the statue of Bill Shankly, created from bronze by Liverpool artist Tom Murphy, was unveiled in front of the Kop. A miniature version of the statue was presented to Bill's widow, Nessie, after the day's events. Standing at over 8ft tall, Murphy's creation shows Shankly in familiar pose, taking applause from adoring fans and wearing a fan's scarf around his neck.

THE POSE, chosen specifically by Murphy, is a representation of an incident in 1973 when Shankly

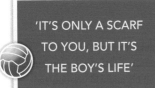

'IT'S ONLY A SCARF TO YOU, BUT IT'S THE BOY'S LIFE'

and his team were parading the League Championship trophy in front of the Kop. A young supporter tossed his scarf onto the pitch in front of Shankly and an over-eager policeman kicked it away before being admonished by the great man. 'It's only a scarf to you, but it's the boy's life,' he said. Shankly then picked up the scarf and tied it round his neck.

'I wanted to make the statue look like a living thing. The pose I chose is one people will immediately recognise, arms straight out and triumphant, saluting victory before his adoring fans,' Murphy said. He studied videos and photographs and spoke with Nessie, ex-Liverpool players, and even Bill's former tailor before starting on the sculpture which weighs in at three-quarters of a ton and stands handsomely on a four-sided plinth

made from Scottish red granite. The statue was commissioned and financed by the club sponsors at the time, Carlsberg. It was unveiled by Ron Yeats, Shankly's captain from 1961 to 1971, who commented: 'There is not enough time in the world to talk about the contribution Bill made to Liverpool Football Club. It is all very well for managers to take over clubs when they are doing well, when all the structures for success are already there, but when Bill came here the whole thing was falling apart – the team and the stands. He took this place by the throat and made it great.'

Shannon, Les

LES SHANNON joined Liverpool as an amateur from Everton at 17 years of age. He made his debut for Liverpool towards the end of the 1947/48 season when he replaced Albert Stubbins for the home fixture with Manchester City, one of only two matches Stubbins missed during that league campaign.

Shannon was selected for the first 10 games of the following season when Stubbins was unavailable because he went on strike, but was then himself replaced by Cyril Done. Shannon's only goal for Liverpool was the first in the 2-1 win at Sheffield United on 30 August 1948.

Two years after joining First Division Burnley in 1949, Shannon came into his own as a deep-lying inside-forward and became a regular in the side, playing 102 games and scoring 31 goals. Following the retirement of Reg Atwell in 1954 he was moved to half-back, where he featured until his retirement. Shannon made in

total 281 appearances and scored 44 goals at Burnley, where he is fondly remembered.

SHANNON joined Everton as youth coach in 1959 and stayed three years before being appointed as Billy Wright's assistant manager at Arsenal, serving the Gunners until 1966. As manager of Bury (1966–69) he swung between the Third and Second Division and as Stan Mortensen's successor at Blackpool (1969–70) he guided the Seasiders to the Second Division title. 1971 signalled the start of his Greek adventure, where he managed four clubs before moving to Norway to coach Brann. He was part of

Luton Town's backroom staff from 1986 to 2001. Les Shannon passed away on 2 December 2007 and 'You'll Never Walk Alone' was played at his funeral. Les is the father of Dave Shannon, former Academy coach at Liverpool.

FACTFILE

BORN
Liverpool, 12 March 1926
DIED
2 December 2007
POSITION
Centre-forward
OTHER CLUBS
Burnley (1949–59)
SIGNED FROM
Everton (youth) 1943; signed professional November 1944
LFC DEBUT GAME/GOAL
17 April 1948 / 30 August 1948
CONTRACT EXPIRY
November 1949

Season	League		FA Cup		Total	
	App	Goals	App	Goals	App	Goals
1947/48	1	0	0	0	1	0
1948/49	10	1	0	0	10	1
Total	**11**	**1**	**0**	**0**	**11**	**1**

Shears,
Albert

ALBERT SHEARS arrived as a striker and scored five goals in his first three reserve games for Liverpool from late September to early October 1924. He finally made his first-team debut two years later as a defender in a 1-0 win over Bury at Gigg Lane.

He spent a total of four seasons at Anfield with his best season appearance total being eight in 1926/27. During that campaign he played five consecutive games as centre-half in Jock McNab's absence. He returned four games later but the team was in terrible form and was in 21st place out of 22. Shears stayed one season at neighbours Tranmere before he was obtained by Wigan Borough in 1931 but three months after his arrival the club folded. His four league appearances for Wigan Borough were expunged and these turned out to be Shears' last as a Football League player despite spells at Barnsley and Aldershot.

Season	League		FA Cup		Total	
	App	Goals	App	Goals	App	Goals
1925/26	2	0	0	0	2	0
1926/27	8	0	0	0	8	0
1927/28	4	0	0	0	4	0
1928/29	2	0	0	0	2	0
Total	16	0	0	0	16	0

Sheedy,
Kevin

KEVIN SHEEDY was born in Wales but through his parents also qualified to play for the Republic of Ireland, which he did with distinction for 10 years. The 18-year-old established himself in the Hereford side that was relegated from the Third Division in the 1977/78 season.

Sheedy signed for Liverpool in July 1978 but had to wait two and a half years for his first-team debut, which came on 14 February 1981 in a 2-2 home league draw with Birmingham City. His only other two appearances in the First Division for the club were both as a substitute the following season.

Sheedy also played in two League Cup ties for Liverpool in 1981/82 and scored in both of them, against Exeter and Middlesbrough.

With his opportunities at Anfield limited particularly due to Ronnie Whelan's emergence, Sheedy decided to make the short trip across Stanley Park and became an Everton great, scoring regularly from his midfield position and winning championship and cup medals along the way. He's considered the best left-footer in Everton's history, playing 368 games and scoring 97 goals for the club from 1982 to 1992. Sheedy has been a coach at Everton's Academy since 2006.

Season	League		FA Cup		League Cup		Europe		Other		Total	
	App	Goals	App	Goals	App	Goals	App	Goals	App	Goals	App	Goals
1980/81	1	0	0	0	0	0	0	0	0	0	1	0
1981/82	0 (2)	0	0	0	2	2	0	0	0	0	2 (2)	2
Total	1 (2)	0	0	0	2	2	0	0	0	0	3 (2)	2

Sheldon,
Jackie

JACKIE SHELDON couldn't get into Manchester United's first team because of superstar Billy Meredith so he tried his luck at neighbours Liverpool. In his debut season he missed only three league fixtures once he had been introduced into the side at the end of November and also played in all eight FA Cup ties, which saw Liverpool reach their first major final.

But there was great disappointment for all concerned at the club after the single-goal defeat by Lancashire rivals Burnley. The right-winger was the smallest man in the team, but 'a terror for his size'. The *Derby Daily Telegraph* described him as 'a red-haired Adonis from Derbyshire, whose neat, natty, and diminutive figure is the joy to his admirers, but a nightmare to his opponents on the field'. He was said to be a 'regular "box o' tricks", full of strange swerves and graces, but does not overdo the fancy work'.

In the 1914/15 season, the last full league season for four years, only Jimmy Nicholl made more appearances and only Fred

Pagnam and Tom Miller scored more goals than Sheldon. His career at Liverpool will, however, always be tainted by the fact that he organised the infamous Good Friday scandal. He convinced players on both sets of teams to help ensure that Manchester United would beat Liverpool 2-0 to ease their relegation worries. Suspicions were raised by bookmakers and the FA proceeded with an extensive investigation. While in the army in France, Sheldon sent a letter to the *Athletic News* published on 10 April 1916 that proclaimed his innocence. 'I emphatically state to you, as our best and fairest critic, that I am absolutely blameless in this scandal and am still open, as I have always been, to give any Red Cross Fund or any other charitable institution the sum of £20 if the FA or anyone else can bring forward any bookmaker or any other person with whom I have had a bet,' he wrote.

In September 1916 Sheldon wanted to go to Anfield to watch Liverpool play Burnley. Even though he was banned he was granted free admittance as a wounded soldier but told to stay away from the dressing rooms. When Sheldon testified in Enoch West's case in 1917, who was one of the accused, he finally confessed to the court that he had convinced his team-mates to play along and met with a trio of United players to decide the outcome of 2-0, with one goal scored either side of half-time. Sheldon was found guilty of match-fixing and banned from football for life. For his service to his country in the war Sheldon's life ban was lifted and he had two more good years at Anfield when the war was over, missing just 12 league fixtures in total.

SHELDON retired from football after he broke his left leg in a sickening collision with Harry Storer Jr, the son of the old Liverpool keeper, against Derby County on 16 April 1921. Sheldon beat Storer the first time he tried to tackle him, but in his second attempt Storer caught him

on the leg so badly that there was 'an ominous crack, and every one of the 28,000 spectators feared a broken bone'. The *Liverpool Echo* called it: 'The most serious happening of the football season.'

FACTFILE

BORN
Clay Cross, 11 February 1888
DIED
19 March 1941
POSITION
Right-winger
OTHER CLUBS
Nuneaton Town (1906–09),
Manchester United (1909–13)
SIGNED FROM
Manchester United, £300,
26 November 1913
LFC DEBUT GAME/GOAL
29 November 1913 /
6 December 1913
CONTRACT EXPIRY
1921

Season	League		FA Cup		Total	
	App	Goals	App	Goals	App	Goals
1913/14	22	5	8	1	30	6
1914/15	35	10	2	0	37	10
1919/20	37	1	5	2	42	3
1920/21	35	1	3	0	38	1
Total	**129**	**17**	**18**	**3**	**147**	**20**

Shelvey,
Jonjo

HARD-WORKING, tenacious, attacking midfielder Jonjo Shelvey was one of Rafa Benítez's last signings at Liverpool.

When Shelvey was only 16 years and 59 days old he became Charlton Athletic's youngest ever player when he featured for the Addicks against Barnsley in the Championship on 26 April 2008. A year later Chelsea came calling but the young East Londoner

rejected the London Blues and stayed loyal to the first club that had offered him a professional contract. Shelvey made 49 appearances for Charlton Athletic and scored eight goals before he accepted a move to Liverpool two years later. The Reds paid an initial £1.7m with further potential payments up to £3m depending on domestic and international appearances.

If it was unsettling that Benítez, who had signed him, left so soon after his own arrival at Anfield, it soon became clear that incoming boss Roy Hodgson was already aware of the midfielder's promise. Still a teenager when his debut season as a Liverpool player finished, Shelvey could look back on 21 first-team appearances, but he only made four starts. Shelvey joined Championship side Blackpool on loan at the end of September 2011, but was recalled to Anfield early the day after Lucas Leiva was stretchered off in the League Cup quarter-final at Stamford Bridge. Shelvey had tremendous success at Blackpool and scored six goals in 10 Championship matches, including a hat-trick in a 5-0 victory at Leeds. He made nine starts for Liverpool in 2011/12 and could be pretty happy with his progress, although he didn't feature in either cup final. In the

final home match of the season, he scored his first Premier League goal with a blistering shot from distance that flew past Chelsea goalkeeper Ross Turnbull like a guided missile. In the second week of July 2012 Shelvey signed a new long-term contract. 'Tactically I have become a lot better and technically too,' Shelvey said. 'When you're working with people like Steven Gerrard and people like that, you're learning things day in, day out and it's an honour.'

An impressive start to 2012/13, which included three goals in two

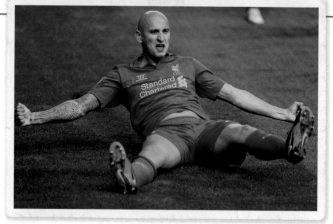

Europa League matches, helped to earn Shelvey his full international debut when he came on as a second-half substitute for Michael Carrick in a World Cup qualifying match against San Marino at Wembley. The midfielder was used on occasion as a makeshift striker by Brendan Rodgers, who emphasised Shelvey's importance to the team in the documentary 'Being Liverpool' as a goalscoring midfielder, but he was in disappointing form as the season progressed. He was sent off at

Anfield in the 2-1 defeat to Manchester United for a two-footed tackle on Johnny Evans, who arguably should have been dismissed as well as he likewise went two-footed into the challenge. Shelvey did lack composure and concentration when involved in the heat of battle in midfield.

RODGERS felt he did not use the opportunities given and he was sold to Swansea.

FACTFILE

BORN
Romford, 27 February 1992
POSITION
Midfielder
OTHER CLUBS
Charlton Athletic (2008–10),
Blackpool (loan, 2011)
Swansea City (2013-)
SIGNED FROM
Charlton Athletic, £1.7million,
10 May 2010
INTERNATIONAL CAPS
1 England cap, 2012
LFC DEBUT GAME/GOAL
22 September 2010 /
6 January 2012
CONTRACT EXPIRY
3 July 2013

Season	League		FA Cup		League Cup		Europe		Total	
	App	Goals	App	Goals	App	Goals	App	Goals	App	Goals
2010/11	0 (15)	0	0 (1)	0	0 (1)	0	4	0	4 (17)	0
2011/12	8 (5)	1	1 (1)	1	0 (1)	0	-	-	9 (7)	2
2012/13	9 (10)	1	1 (1)	0	1	0	7 (3)	4	18 (14)	5
Total	**17 (30)**	**2**	**2 (3)**	**1**	**1 (2)**	**0**	**11 (3)**	**4**	**31 (38)**	**7**

Shepherd, Bill

BILL SHEPHERD made his debut for Liverpool on the opening day of the 1948/49 league season and only missed one of the 42 league matches played that campaign. Although he played in the first four games of the following season, Eddie Spicer's arrival on the scene cost him his place.

Ray Lambert, who had been left-back, took Shepherd's place in the team and Spicer came in at left-back. Bill's brothers, Arthur and Joe, were both on Liverpool's books in the 1940s. Arthur scored 12 goals in 11 games for Liverpool during the war and was a reserve player from 1946 to 1949.

FACTFILE

BORN
Liverpool,
25 September 1920
POSITION
Right-back
OTHER CLUBS
Elm Park,
Wigan Athletic
SIGNED FROM
Elm Park,
December 1945
LFC DEBUT
21 August 1948
CONTRACT EXPIRY
1952

Season	League		FA Cup		Total	
	App	Goals	App	Goals	App	Goals
1948/49	41	0	4	0	45	0
1949/50	6	0	0	0	6	0
1950/51	5	0	0	0	5	0
1951/52	2	0	0	0	2	0
Total	**54**	**0**	**4**	**0**	**58**	**0**

Shield, John

JOHN SHIELD'S solitary first-team selection for the club came when he deputised for regular left-half Jimmy McDougall in a First Division fixture at Deepdale, Preston, on 11 April 1936.

Liverpool lost 3-1 and were struggling in 19th place in a league of 22 teams, finishing only three points away from a relegation spot.

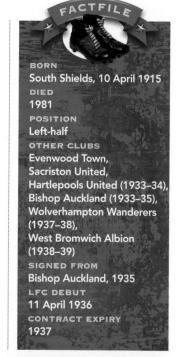

FACTFILE

BORN
South Shields, 10 April 1915
DIED
1981
POSITION
Left-half
OTHER CLUBS
Evenwood Town,
Sacriston United,
Hartlepools United (1933–34),
Bishop Auckland (1933–35),
Wolverhampton Wanderers
(1937–38),
West Bromwich Albion
(1938–39)
SIGNED FROM
Bishop Auckland, 1935
LFC DEBUT
11 April 1936
CONTRACT EXPIRY
1937

Season	League		FA Cup		Total	
	App	Goals	App	Goals	App	Goals
1935/36	1	0	0	0	1	0
Total	**1**	**0**	**0**	**0**	**1**	**0**

Shields, Sam

THE LIVERPOOL handbook from the 1949/50 season claimed Sam Shields was a 'brilliant schemer in addition to having a strong shot'.

However, the tough Scottish centre-forward returned to his native country after a solitary appearance for the club in which Liverpool drew 1-1 with Wolves. Liverpool were top of the league at that time after 18 rounds but only finished 7th at the end of the campaign.

Season	League		FA Cup		Total	
	App	Goals	App	Goals	App	Goals
1949/50	1	0	0	0	1	0
Total	1	0	0	0	1	0

FACTFILE

BORN
Denny, Stirlingshire, Scotland,
21 March 1929
POSITION
Centre-forward
OTHER CLUBS
Cowdenbeath (1947–49),
Airdrieonians (1951–52),
Darlington (1952–53), Horden
Colliery Welfare (1953–55)
SIGNED FROM
Cowdenbeath, April 1949
LFC DEBUT
26 November 1949
CONTRACT EXPIRY
27 July 1951

Shirts

'ONCE A BLUE, always a Red' is a phrase often attached to the likes of Robbie Fowler and Jamie Carragher who grew up as fans of the blue team in Liverpool, but made their career at the Reds. It can also be applied to Liverpool Football Club, as its first shirts were blue and white halves with a buttoned collar; in fact, quite similar to Blackburn Rovers' current strip.

Liverpool also played in a white away shirt similarly designed to the home version. Liverpool did not become the Reds until 1 September 1896. *The Cricket and Football Field* noted the premiere of the club's new colours: 'Liverpool's new dress of red shirts and white knickers is striking, and a contrast to Everton's blue shirts and white knickers.' 'Knickers' was short for knickerbockers. From the 1901/02 campaign onwards the home shirt had a mandarin collar through which a lace could be tied and the away shirt was white with a red shoulder and collar area. Liverpool's black and grey away jersey introduced in the 2012/13 season was a tribute to the 1901 shirt that was designed to remember the city's rich maritime history.

Liverpool made a quite bizarre demand to the Football League in 1904 and again in 1906 that all clubs should wear a red shirt and white knickers while playing at home and a white shirt and dark knickers away. Manchester United supported the idea in 1906, but their demand was refused. Liverpool's colour scheme stayed the same until the 1935/36 season when the team wore a burgundy shirt at home. The red shirts had definitely returned in the first post-war season of 1946/47 and they were numbered as well on the back according to the new Football League regulations.

A WHITE STAND collar was incorporated into the red shirt in 1953 while the white away shirt had a red stand collar. This new design hardly brought any joy as the club was relegated following this disastrous campaign. A V-neck shirt was used for the first time in the 1955/56 season, which changed to a crew-neck when Liverpool returned to the First Division six years later. Also

in 1955 Liverpool began wearing a club badge on their shirts.

THE REDS became 'all red' for the first time when they faced Anderlecht on 25 November 1964. 'Shankly thought the colour scheme would carry psychological impact; red for danger, red for power,' Ian St John said in his autobiography. The white crew-neck, though, still remained. From 1969 the liver bird was embroidered directly onto the team's shirts without a background.

In 1972 the club's strip was made for the first time by an official sports manufacturer. Umbro's diamond-shaped logo was just about visible on the shirts from 1973, but became more prominent from 1976, which also marked the return of the V-neck that would remain until 1987 when it was replaced by a round one. In 1978 Liverpool used for the first time a third kit that was all yellow. Liverpool broke ground in English football in 1979 when they became the first professional club to wear a sponsor's logo on their shirts. The Liverpool players had

the name of Japanese electronics giants Hitachi emblazoned across their chest, except it was not permitted during televised matches and in FA Cup and European ties.

In 1981 Liverpool replaced their white away shirt with a yellow one. It had red pinstripes, a design change that was also used the following season in the home shirts that had white pinstripes and a white collar with a red stripe through it. North west paint manufacturer Crown Paints succeeded Hitachi as kit sponsor, the board delighted to be joining forces with a local company. German sportswear giants Adidas took over from Umbro in 1985, bringing its distinctive design of three stripes on the shoulders and removing the pinstripes across the body. A white kit relegated the yellow one to third choice and Adidas broadened the away shirt's colour palette to grey (1987–91) and several combinations of green and white (1991–96). The home shirt from 1989 to 1991 included red and white flashes that distorted

the previous simple red design. From 1991 to 1993 Adidas's classic stripe design moved from across the shoulders to three distinctive white ones over the shoulder counterbalanced by another three on the shorts.

By this time Italian household appliance company, Candy, had ended its four-year sponsorship of the club's shirt and been replaced by Carlsberg. The club took a lot of heat during the Danish brewers' reign as some did not want their club to promote alcoholic beverages. Standard Chartered bank replaced Carlsberg in 2010 in a ground-breaking deal.

REEBOK took over from Adidas as kit manufacturers in 1996/97 and got off to an inauspicious start by offering an ecru away shirt, an off-white that did not exactly appeal to the eye. This design, though, did not prove as controversial as when BLUE of all colours made its return to the club's shirt in 2011 for the first time since 1896. Adidas claimed the blue on the club's third shirt was in fact cyan. The result was it became the club's best-selling third shirt in history.

The crew-neck had not been a feature of Liverpool's shirts since 1976, but returned on the home shirts in 1998, remaining only until 2000 when a red V-neck stand collar with a white trim was incorporated. A special Champions League shirt was made in 2001 to celebrate

Liverpool's debut campaign in UEFA's flagship competition. The red shirt had a white collar and above the badge were four stars in remembrance of the number of Liverpool's wins in European Cup finals. These special-edition shirts became very popular, especially following the win in Istanbul 2005 that added one more star to the shirt.

THE NEXT BIG change to the club shirts' design was when Adidas returned to the club in 2006, having acquired Reebok. The collar also returned, accented by a white lining leading from it down the sides of shirt. Adidas infused the red home shirt with faint triangle shapes in 2010, but the main differences in the past few years have perhaps not been in the shirts' outward appearance, but in the fabric that has become

more breathable to add to the players' comfort on match day.

In January 2012 Liverpool FC announced a record deal for a Premier League club when Warrior Sports replaced Adidas as the club's kit manufacturer. The Warrior deal was worth £25m a year until 2018, almost twice what the club was getting from Adidas. The club's 2012/13 home kit could not have been more appropriately designed for the Reds, as this is, strictly speaking, the first time Liverpool have actually worn all-red.

Shone,
Danny

DANNY SHONE joined Liverpool from local amateur side Grayson's of Garston, the team of a well-known local shipping company.

Shone was officially employed by the firm, but did very little labour as he was more of interest to them as a footballer! Forward Shone made his Liverpool debut on the opening day of the 1921/22 season, a disappointing 3-0 defeat at Sunderland. Billy Matthews replaced him for the next game and scored twice. Shone had a run of 11 consecutive games in the middle of the season and scored

his debut goal in a 1-1 draw against Everton at Goodison Park as well as grabbing a hat-trick in 36 minutes against Middlesbrough, prompting the *Liverpool Echo* headline: 'The Sun did not shine at Anfield but Shone!' Despite making only two appearances in the second part of the season, he had still made a useful contribution to Liverpool's 1922 league success. But when the title was retained a year later with one of the most settled teams in Liverpool's history, Shone was very much an onlooker and only played once all season.

The 1924/25 season was easily Shone's best at Anfield; he played in every one of the 46 league and cup matches and scored 15 times. The *Derby Daily Telegraph* reported on his progress in January 1925. 'Danny Shone, who registered two goals for Liverpool last week, is one of the most improved players in the Anfield camp. When he originally joined the club from Garston's he was thought to be a centre-forward, but subsequently he deputised at inside-left for Harry Chambers, and later, when Forshaw went to centre-forward, became an inside-right. This is his best position.' Shone was only picked three times the following campaign and after playing solely for the reserves for two seasons he agreed a move to London to resurrect his professional career. He scored five goals in 12 First Division games in his six-month stay at the Hammers before departing for Third Division South Coventry where he only played nine games during his solitary season.

FACTFILE

BORN
West Derby, 22 May 1899
DIED
1974
POSITION
Forward
OTHER CLUBS
Earle, Grayson's of Garston, West Ham United (1928–29), Coventry City (1929–30)
SIGNED FROM
Grayson's of Garston, May 1921
LFC DEBUT GAME/GOAL
27 August 1921 /
5 November 1921
CONTRACT EXPIRY
June 1928
HONOURS
League Championship
1921/22

Season	League		FA Cup		Other		Total	
	App	Goals	App	Goals	App	Goals	App	Goals
1921/22	15	6	0	0	0	0	15	6
1922/23	1	0	0	0	-	-	1	0
1923/24	15	5	1	0	-	-	16	5
1924/25	42	12	4	3	-	-	46	15
1925/26	3	0	0	0	-	-	3	0
Total	**76**	**23**	**5**	**3**	**0**	**0**	**81**	**26**

Y

Sidlow, Cyril

WELSHMAN Cyril Sidlow had just become the main keeper at First Division Wolves in the 1938/39 season when his professional career was stopped in its tracks by the outbreak of World War Two.

After appearing for Wolves during the war Sidlow was deemed surplus to requirements as the league resumed due to the emergence of future England keeper Bert Williams. The 30-year-old jumped straight into the Liverpool team and before the final league game of the 1946/47 season he was in a curious situation. Manchester United, Stoke and Wolves had the chance to win the title along with Liverpool, and fate would have it that Sidlow faced his old Wolves team at Molineux. Sidlow was still living in Wolverhampton and was neighbours with Wolves' goalkeeper, Williams. Bob Paisley recollected Sidlow's 'plight' in his book *My 50 Golden Reds*. 'He trained with Wolves throughout the week, linking up with us on match-days only. So you can imagine what it must have been like for him having to walk down the streets towards Molineux that Saturday afternoon. They were his mates he was playing against and he knew that, unlike us, he would have to suffer whatever the result. If we won – and deprived Wolves of the title – then he knew he wouldn't be able to walk out of the front door of his little house in Wolverhampton without folk pointing at him as the man who had stopped their team becoming champions of the Football League.' Billy Liddell, Liverpool's talisman, was impressed by Sidlow's performance in Liverpool's 2-1 win that eventually sealed the title for the Reds. 'Cyril made save after save when it seemed certain that he

must be beaten.' Sidlow couldn't resist paying a visit to Bert Williams next door. 'After I had received my League Champions' medal, I took it round to Bert to show him. I don't know whether he appreciated that very much!'

Sidlow kept his place for the next three years and helped the club reach its first Wembley Cup final but it ended in disappointment with a 2-0 defeat to Arsenal. He conceded four goals in his final Liverpool appearance in a home First Division game against Newcastle United on 4 November 1950. The much younger Russell Crossley, who replaced Sidlow, had ironically been recommended to the club by the Welshman himself. 'Russell did me a good turn when I was in the Army. When we had matches to play for the Army team he would play so that I could get off and play for Wolves in the wartime leagues,'

Sidlow explained. 'He wasn't as old as I was and when he came out of the Army I told George Kay that he should sign him up and he became my understudy for a season or so before taking over.' Sidlow moved to neighbours New Brighton in the Lancashire Combination before moving back to Wolves in 1953 as emergency cover for Williams. He was registered as a player but never turned out for the first team, although he did a good job of coaching youngsters at the club.

SIDLOW became known for throwing the ball to his team-mates rather than kicking it aimlessly upfield. 'Cyril was another in the long school of accomplished goalkeepers to be at the club,' Bob Paisley said. 'Reading the game was one of his major strengths and while sometimes that isn't quite as flashy as the goalkeeper who is

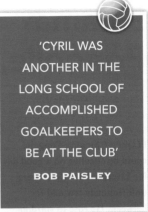

'CYRIL WAS ANOTHER IN THE LONG SCHOOL OF ACCOMPLISHED GOALKEEPERS TO BE AT THE CLUB'

BOB PAISLEY

diving about all the time, I know which style most outfield players prefer in their side. Maybe it was that ability which explained why he was never hailed as being as good as he was by supporters. A goalkeeper who is flinging himself about all over the place catches the eye and people will say: "He's brilliant." In fact, they are making it hard work for themselves whereas goalkeeping was an easy art for the big Welshman.'

FACTFILE

BORN
Colwyn Bay, Wales,
26 November 1915
DIED
12 April 2005
POSITION
Goalkeeper
OTHER CLUBS
Colwyn Bay United (1931–33), Abergele (1933–34), Colwyn Bay United (1934), Flint Town (1934–35), Llandudno (1935–37), Wolverhampton Wanderers (1937–1946); Notts County, Wrexham, Darlington, Burnley, Hartlepools United (wartime guest), New Brighton (1952–53), Wolverhampton Wanderers (1953–55)
SIGNED FROM
Wolverhampton Wanderers, £4,000, 21 February 1946
INTERNATIONAL CAPS
7 Wales caps, 1946–49
LFC DEBUT
31 August 1946
CONTRACT EXPIRY
August 1952
HONOURS
League Championship 1946/47

Season	League		FA Cup		Total	
	App	Goals	App	Goals	App	Goals
1946/47	34	0	6	0	40	0
1947/48	29	0	0	0	29	0
1948/49	38	0	3	0	41	0
1949/50	37	0	7	0	44	0
1950/51	11	0	0	0	11	0
Total	**149**	**0**	**16**	**0**	**165**	**0**

Sinama-Pongolle,
Florent

FLORENT Sinama-Pongolle could be effective on a good day for Liverpool but those were unfortunately few and far between. He rose to stardom when France won the Under-17 World Cup. He was top scorer with nine goals, a record, and voted the best player of the tournament.

He possessed great pace, striking accuracy and seemed certainly one for the future. No player has played as many games, 37, and scored as many goals, 11, for the French Under-21 team. Following their signing in 2002 Pongolle and Anthony Le Tallec were promptly loaned back to Le Havre to gain more experience before finally arriving in July 2003. The 19-year-old Pongolle didn't expect to feature much in his debut season but injuries to Milan Baros and Michael Owen forced Gérard Houllier's hand and he took part in 23 matches, mostly as a substitute.

HOULLIER'S SUCCESSOR, Rafa Benítez, admitted that he had tried

to sign the young Le Havre stars for Valencia but was outbid by the Reds. The Spaniard and Liverpool fans could be thankful for the part Pongolle played in the crucial comeback win over Olympiacos that paved the way for the Istanbul adventure. He came on as a substitute at the start of the second half for Djimi Traore against the Greek side and just a couple of minutes later he had equalised. Liverpool added two late goals to proceed from the group stage. Unfortunately Pongolle missed the rest of the season as he caught his studs in the turf only four minutes after coming on against Watford at Vicarage Road on 25 January 2005. Pongolle also proved vital in Liverpool's comeback against Luton in the third round of the FA Cup in January 2006. Liverpool were losing 3-1 at Kenilworth Road when he got one goal back and added a second and the team's fourth in the 73rd minute. He played no further part in Liverpool's successful FA Cup run

as a few weeks later he was loaned to Blackburn Rovers for the rest of the 2005/06 season. Robbie Fowler had just rejoined Liverpool, pushing Pongolle further down the pecking order.

PONGOLLE moved to Recreativo de Huelva after scoring 11 goals in 28 matches while on loan at the club. His career seemed on a rapid rise after moving to Atletico

FACTFILE

BORN
Saint-Pierre, French overseas department of Reunion, 20 October 1984
POSITION
Forward
OTHER CLUBS
Le Havre (1995–2003), Blackburn Rovers (loan, 2006), Recreativo de Huelva (loan, 2006–07; permanent, 2007–08), Atletico Madrid (2008–10), Sporting Lisbon (2010–12), Real Zaragoza (loan, 2010–11), Saint Etienne (loan, 2011–12), FC Rostov (2012–)
SIGNED FROM
Le Havre, £1.5million, 1 July 2003
INTERNATIONAL CAPS
1 France cap, 2008
LFC DEBUT GAME/GOAL
15 October 2003 / 25 October 2003
CONTRACT EXPIRY
4 May 2007

Madrid, but he has found difficult to settle at his clubs and is currently playing in the Russian Premier League.

Season	League		FA Cup		League Cup		Europe		Other		Total	
	App	Goals	App	Goals	App	Goals	App	Goals	App	Goals	App	Goals
2003/04	3 (12)	2	1 (2)	0	1 (1)	0	1 (2)	0	-	-	6 (17)	2
2004/05	6 (10)	2	1	0	4 (1)	1	0 (4)	1	-	-	11 (15)	4
2005/06	3 (4)	0	0 (1)	2	0 (1)	0	1 (4)	1	0 (2)	0	4 (12)	3
2006/07	0	0	0	0	0	0	0	0	0 (1)	0	0 (1)	0
Total	**12 (26)**	**4**	**2 (3)**	**2**	**5 (3)**	**1**	**2 (10)**	**2**	**0 (3)**	**0**	**21 (45)**	**9**

Sinclair,
Jerome

AT 16 YEARS and six days Jerome Sinclair became Liverpool's youngest ever player when coming on as a substitute against West Bromwich Albion in the third round of the League

Cup on 26 September 2012, beating the record set by Jack Robinson at Hull City in 2010.

Liverpool's history-maker was so unknown that even his name was recorded incorrectly, as Jordan Sinclair, by the club staff on the official team-sheet. Sinclair's first-team debut came only seven days after his first game for

Rodolfo Borrell's Academy side in the NextGen Series against Inter Milan in Italy, after impressing for the Under-18 side.

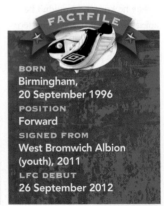

FACTFILE

BORN
Birmingham, 20 September 1996
POSITION
Forward
SIGNED FROM
West Bromwich Albion (youth), 2011
LFC DEBUT
26 September 2012

Season	League		FA Cup		League Cup		Europe		Total	
	App	Goals	App	Goals	App	Goals	App	Goals	App	Goals
2012/13	0	0	0	0	0 (1)	0	0	0	0 (1)	0
Total	**0**	**0**	**0**	**0**	**0 (1)**	**0**	**0**	**0**	**0 (1)**	**0**

Sissoko,
Momo

BORN TO Malian parents in France, Momo Sissoko opted to play for Mali after featuring for the French Under-21 team. He has a biting tackle and is a formidable shield for any defence. Sissoko was nurtured in Auxerre's respected academy, playing as a striker for the reserves and scoring 50 goals in two years according to his website.

RAFA BENÍTEZ brought the youngster over to Valencia in 2003 before he made his first-team debut at Auxerre and developed his game in a new position as a defensive midfielder. Despite his young age Benítez picked him from the start in nine La Liga matches as well as bringing him on as substitute on 12 occasions in his debut campaign. He also featured in nine UEFA Cup matches, so he played an active part in Valencia's double success in La Liga and the UEFA Cup in 2004.

Sissoko continued to impress at Mestalla following Benítez's departure to Liverpool. Everton were about to capture the promising midfielder when Benítez became aware of his availability and 'stole' him straight from under the Blues' noses. Benítez made big claims that 'Momo' would become a better player than Vieira, and Sissoko's hyperactive performances in the middle of the park earned him rave reviews. It was a dramatic first season as an eye injury received against Benfica in the Champions League in February 2006 threatened to end his playing career. When he returned a month later, he had to wear safety goggles, which he soon discarded as they kept steaming up. The season ended on a high as Liverpool beat West Ham in the

FA Cup final. Sissoko played from the start, as he had done in 36 other matches during the season.

SISSOKO was man of the match in Liverpool's win over Chelsea in the 2006 Community Shield. As his second season progressed he wasn't his usual self, whether his eye injury had affected his confidence or not. Sissoko clearly had to improve on the technical aspects of his game, namely his close control and passing. He suffered another bad injury against Birmingham in the fourth round of the League Cup in November 2006, dislocating his shoulder, and was out of action for three months. Javier Mascherano's arrival in February

2007 meant more competition in midfield. As the 2007/08 season began, Sissoko was on the bench for the opening two games against Aston Villa and Toulouse. He wasn't even in the squad for the first home league match against Chelsea but played from the start at Sunderland a week later, where he amazed everyone by scoring his first Liverpool goal with a sweet strike from the edge of the penalty area. He started the League Cup tie at Chelsea a few days before Christmas 2007 but it was the last time he would pull on a Liverpool shirt.

By the end of January 2008 he was a Juventus player having been sold for £8.2million. At least the

club made a decent profit on the reported £5.6million it had paid Valencia in 2005. The very man who sold him to Liverpool, Claudio Ranieri, brought Sissoko over to Italy. They were old acquaintances as Ranieri had been his boss for one season, 2004/05, at Valencia. Sissoko was a regular as Juventus finished league runners-up to Inter Milan in 2009, but the rest of his career in Turin was curtailed by a broken metatarsal and a knee injury. After six months of rehabilitation Sissoko made his debut in September 2011 for the upcoming European giants at Paris St Germain, whom he had joined in the summer. Sissoko had continuing knee trouble in his first campaign in Paris, during which he made 27 starts, and missed the first two months of the 2012/13 season as he injured his left knee in a pre-season friendly. He was loaned to Fiorentina in the January 2013 transfer window.

Season	League		FA Cup		League Cup		Europe		Other		Total	
	App	Goals	App	Goals	App	Goals	App	Goals	App	Goals	App	Goals
2005/06	21 (5)	0	6	0	0	0	8 (3)	0	2	0	37 (8)	0
2006/07	15 (1)	0	0	0	2	0	7 (2)	0	1	0	25 (3)	0
2007/08	6 (3)	1	0	0	2	0	2 (1)	0	-	-	10 (4)	1
Total	**42 (9)**	**1**	**6**	**0**	**4**	**0**	**17 (6)**	**0**	**3**	**0**	**72 (15)**	**1**

Skrtel,
Martin

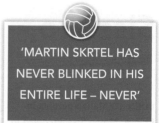

MARTIN SKRTEL'S tough tackling, 'no-nonsense' approach and never-say-die attitude quickly brought him a reputation as a cult figure at Anfield. When he joined Liverpool he became the most expensive defender in the club's history, despite being a relative unknown outside his native Slovakia and Russia, where he won the Russian Championship with Zenit St Petersburg in 2007.

Skrtel made an unimpressive start to his Liverpool career, coming on as a rather nervous-looking substitute for the last 20 minutes against Aston Villa at Anfield and then being credited with an own goal in the FA Cup defeat of non-league Havant & Waterlooville five days later. However, he played in 18 of the remaining 23 first-team matches of the season and won over the supporters. The fans were impressed and even applied quotes formerly only reserved for Chuck Norris to describe him, such as: 'There is no theory of evolution, just a list of animals Martin Skrtel allows to live' or 'Martin Skrtel has never blinked in his entire life – never'.

'THERE IS NO
THEORY
OF EVOLUTION,
JUST A LIST OF
ANIMALS
MARTIN SKRTEL
ALLOWS TO LIVE'

A knee injury suffered against Manchester City on 5 October 2008 disrupted Skrtel's first full season at Liverpool and kept him on the sidelines for two months.

When he was passed fit again he played the majority of Liverpool's games in the second half of the season. Injury restricted Skrtel to just 29 of Liverpool's 56 competitive matches during the 2009/10 season. He broke the metatarsal in his right foot while playing in the 3-1 victory over Unirea Urziceni in Romania on 25 February 2010. After being in the squad for most of the early-season fixtures, this was a big blow for the uncompromising defender, who must have wondered if he would recover in time to represent his country at the World Cup finals in South Africa. To the surprise of many, Slovakia qualified for the knockout stage of the tournament, mainly because of a 3-2 victory over defending champions Italy in the final group match. Skrtel played every minute of all four of his country's games in South Africa. He played in every Premier League match for the first time in 2010/11 and took his total of first-team appearances past the century mark. Skrtel added two goals, opening the scoring in the away matches at Tottenham and West Bromwich, but both matches were eventually lost by the same score, 2-1. However, Skrtel was still lacking finesse, conceding free kicks in dangerous areas with his roughhouse rugby-style tackling.

SKRTEL PLAYED in nearly 90 per cent of Liverpool's first-team matches in 2011/12 and had his best season so far, creating a formidable pairing with Daniel Agger in the centre of defence. He got on the scoresheet four times and had clearly refined the rough edges to his game. Two days after the 2012/13 Premier League season started, Skrtel signed a new long-term contract with Liverpool, but was in disappointing form in the campaign. The Slovakian was in the spotlight in the Reds' first league home game against league champions Manchester City. His tremendous header put his side 1-0 up, but a misplaced backpass by the defender allowed Carlos Teves to equalize 2-2. Skrtel lost his spot in the team to Jamie Carragher in January 2013.

Season	League		FA Cup		League Cup		Europe		Total	
	App	Goals	App	Goals	App	Goals	App	Goals	App	Goals
2007/08	13 (1)	0	1	0	0	0	5	0	19 (1)	0
2008/09	20 (1)	0	2	0	0	0	7	0	29 (1)	0
2009/10	16 (3)	1	1 (1)	0	1 (1)	0	5 (1)	0	23 (6)	1
2010/11	38	2	1	0	0	0	7 (3)	0	46 (3)	2
2011/12	33 (1)	2	5	1	4 (2)	1	-	-	42 (3)	4
2012/13	23 (2)	2	1	0	0	0	7	0	31 (2)	2
Total	**143 (8)**	**7**	**11 (1)**	**1**	**5 (3)**	**1**	**31 (4)**	**0**	**190 (16)**	**9**

Slater,
Bert

BERT SLATER was 23 when he arrived at the club from Falkirk in exchange for Tommy Younger and went straight into the first team at the start of the 1959/60 season.

Despite conceding three goals on his debut against Cardiff he was praised by the *Liverpool Echo*:

The critical spotlight was very much focused on the failure of the men behind to play up to standards which we have come to take so much for granted. From this criticism must be excepted the Scottish debutant goalkeeper, Slater. In no way could he be associated with the defeat. A less capable player would have been beaten more frequently and if Slater can go on improving on this standard Liverpool's worries in goal appear to have been taken care of for many years to come. His spectacular pounces to the extreme ends of his goal did him the greatest credit. What roars of delights would feats such as he achieved produce from an Anfield crowd. He is a worthy successor to Tommy Younger and, unless I am very much mistaken, will prove not only as spectacular as his predecessor but every bit as successful.

Slater did, however, concede two goals in his third outing that he was responsible for and manager Phil Taylor replaced him with South African Doug Rudham, who played in the next 14 Second Division games.

Bill Shankly's arrival in December 1959 saw an improvement in Slater's fortunes. In fact, Slater played in 96 consecutive Football League matches before he was

replaced by Jim Furnell, who had just been signed from Burnley, after Liverpool were knocked out of the FA Cup by Preston in February 1962. It was maybe a bit harsh punishment for only having conceded a solitary goal in three cup ties against Preston, but Peter Thompson's goal in the second replay sealed Slater's fate. Shankly let the keeper know his days at Liverpool were numbered in no uncertain terms, as Slater said in July 2004. 'In the close season Bill Shankly told me I was on my way to Dundee,' Slater recalled. 'I said "no", because I wanted to stay and fight for my place in the First Division. He then named six goalies right down to the Under-12 goalkeeper, and told me I was not even quoted.' Bill sold him in the summer to his brother

Bob who was boss at Scottish champions Dundee.

ALAN A'COURT had some sympathy for his former team-mate as he revealed in his autobiography. 'Slater was rather an unlucky player who often suffered for other people's mistakes. He rarely received due credit for his agility, his excellent reflexes and the bravery he showed diving at the feet of opposing forwards.' A'Court also recollected an amusing incident involving then physio Bob Paisley. 'Bert Slater was knocked unconscious during a goalmouth tussle and Paisley simply could not revive him. He tried everything, smelling salts, cold water, manipulation, the lot, until in desperation, he knelt down by

Bert's side and said: "Bert, give us a kiss." The effect was nothing less than miraculous, for Bert sat bolt upright, glared at Bob and told him to f*** off before scrambling to his feet and playing on.'

> 'BERT, GIVE US
> A KISS'
> **BOB PAISLEY**

Slater's Dundee went all the way to the semi-finals in the European Cup in his debut season, but lost to eventual champions AC Milan. After three years in Scotland he moved to Watford where he played 152 matches for the Hertfordshire club before joining its coaching staff. Slater was nicknamed 'Shorty', because he was unusually short for a goalkeeper; only 5ft 8½in (173cm).

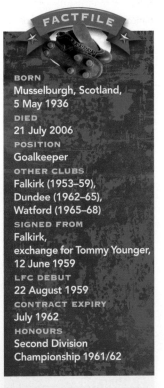

FACTFILE

BORN
Musselburgh, Scotland,
5 May 1936
DIED
21 July 2006
POSITION
Goalkeeper
OTHER CLUBS
Falkirk (1953–59),
Dundee (1962–65),
Watford (1965–68)
SIGNED FROM
Falkirk,
exchange for Tommy Younger,
12 June 1959
LFC DEBUT
22 August 1959
CONTRACT EXPIRY
July 1962
HONOURS
Second Division
Championship 1961/62

Season	League		FA Cup		Other		Total	
	App	Goals	App	Goals	App	Goals	App	Goals
1959/60	28	0	2	0	-	-	30	0
1960/61	42	0	2	0	3	0	47	0
1961/62	29	0	5	0	-	-	34	0
Total	**99**	**0**	**9**	**0**	**3**	**0**	**111**	**0**

Sloan, Don

DON SLOAN was a reserve to goalkeeper Billy Scott at Everton for two years before moving across Stanley Park. He was one of 27 players selected at various stages of the 1908/09 First Division season.

The club's first-choice keeper at that time was Sam Hardy and Sloan stepped in for the six fixtures that he missed that year. Sloan didn't keep a clean sheet in any of those games and conceded 13 goals, finishing on the winning side twice. He left in the summer of 1909 to become player-manager at his old club Distillery in Belfast. Sloan died on New Year's Day 1917 while serving in the Black Watch, an infantry battalion of the Royal Highlanders of Scotland. He was killed on the front in France and is buried at the Faubourg D'Amiens cemetery at Arras.

FACTFILE

BORN
Rankinston, Ayr, Scotland,
31 July 1883
DIED
1 January 1917
POSITION
Goalkeeper
OTHER CLUBS
Distillery (1903–06),
Everton (1906–08),
Distillery (1909–13)
SIGNED FROM
Everton, £300, 2 May 1908
LFC DEBUT
10 October 1908
CONTRACT EXPIRY
July 1909

Season	League		FA Cup		Total	
	App	Goals	App	Goals	App	Goals
1908/09	6	0	0	0	6	0
Total	**6**	**0**	**0**	**0**	**6**	**0**

Smicer, Vladimir

VLADIMIR SMICER was an oustanding success in France with Lens after leaving his native Czech Republic. He was a key player as Lens captured the French title in 1997/98, making 28 appearances and scoring seven goals.

Smicer's progress at Liverpool was certainly not helped by the numerous injuries he picked up that disrupted his run in the side, but on the whole he lacked consistency. Even though he regularly outshone everybody at the training ground he didn't show off his talents at a regular rate in competitive matches. Of the 184 matches he played he was substitute on no fewer than 74 occasions and was taken off in 83 of the 110 matches he started.

SMICER was, nevertheless, in inspired form in the 2000/01 treble season. 'The £3.75million Czech, who has been Mr Meek since his arrival 18 months ago, has suddenly transformed himself into Vlad the Impaler. Confidence shone through his work as he tormented Harry Redknapp's men with his skill, running and energy,' commented the *Sunday Mirror* after Liverpool's 3-0 win over West Ham on 3 February. A memorable highlight of the 2001/02 season was Smicer's sensational last-minute winner against Chelsea on 24 March that sent the Reds top. 'Vladi' seemed totally to have lost his way at Liverpool following the 2002/03 season, when he admitted his future was bleak. 'I would not have been surprised had the manager said there was no place for me. Now I have one more chance – the last one. I think a few of the fans don't like me. Sometimes when you lose the ball you can hear that they are not happy,' Smicer said. As Gérard Houllier departed the following season Smicer hoped for a second chance under Benítez, but he underwent an operation on a fractured cartilage in the summer of 2004 and wasn't ready for action until February 2005. He made only two starts in the 16 matches he featured in under Rafa, but ended his Liverpool career in style in the Champions League final against Milan by reducing the deficit to 3-2 and scoring in the penalty shootout. Smicer enjoyed the moment and lit up a celebratory cigar. 'This one was enormous, it was the biggest in the world,' he said, smiling. 'Every time I went to relight it, it seemed to be the same size, it lasted all night!'

'Vladi was really funny and he is a really good player who did really important things for this club,' Xabi Alonso said after Smicer's departure. 'He was always smiling and despite him being injured for a long time he always had a great attitude and he brought a smile to the changing room.'

As Smicer's Liverpool contract had expired he moved to France

FACTFILE

BORN
Vernerice, Czech Republic,
24 May 1973
POSITION
Right-winger / Midfielder
OTHER CLUBS
Slavia Prague (1987–96),
Lens (1996–99),
Bordeaux (2005–07),
Slavia Prague (2007–09),
Dolni Chabry
SIGNED FROM
Lens, £3.75million,
24 May 1999
INTERNATIONAL CAPS
81 Czech Republic caps
(27 goals) (38 (10) at LFC),
1993–2005
LFC DEBUT GAME/GOAL
7 August 1999 /
15 January 2000
CONTRACT EXPIRY
13 June 2005
HONOURS
FA Cup 2001;
League Cup 2001, 2003;
Champions League 2005;
UEFA Cup 2001

Season	League		FA Cup		League Cup		Europe		Other		Total	
	App	Goals	App	Goals	App	Goals	App	Goals	App	Goals	App	Goals
1999/2000	13 (8)	1	2	0	2	0	-	-	-	-	17 (8)	1
2000/01	16 (11)	2	4 (1)	1	5 (1)	4	6 (5)	0	-	-	31 (18)	7
2001/02	13 (9)	4	1	0	1	0	8 (3)	1	0	0	23 (12)	5
2002/03	10 (11)	0	1	0	4 (1)	0	3 (3)	1	0 (1)	0	18 (16)	1
2003/04	15 (5)	3	1	0	1	1	2 (1)	0	-	-	19 (6)	4
2004/05	2 (8)	0	0	0	0	0	0 (6)	1	-	-	2 (14)	1
Total	**69 (52)**	**10**	**9 (1)**	**1**	**13 (2)**	**5**	**19 (18)**	**3**	**0 (1)**	**0**	**110 (74)**	**19**

with Bordeaux where he also unfortunately struggled with injuries; he had similar problems after his return to his first club in the Czech Republic, Slavia Prague. While Smicer's contribution was minimal, Slavia won the national title two years running. In November 2009 Vladi Smicer announced his retirement as a player at the age of 36 and became the assistant of the Czech

Republic's head coach, Michal Bilek. 'My heart wants to play on, but the body will not have it,' he said. Smicer still enjoys a run-out with his local team, Dolni Chabry, situated in the suburbs of Prague, and plays in the Czech Republic's sixth division. Smicer's role with the national team has since been changed from assistant to sports manager, working alongside coach Bilek.

Smith, Alexander

ALEXANDER SMITH arrived at Liverpool for a trial in February 1937 along with Buckie Thistle team-mate George Calder. Smith impressed sufficiently in the reserves' 2-1 win against Preston to be signed up, but Calder, who scored as well as Smith in the game, returned to Scotland.

The 'stocky, little' forward's only appearance for Liverpool's first team came on 16 October 1937 in a 2-0 away defeat at Wolverhampton. Smith won the

Liverpool Senior Cup, played for the reserves and enjoyed being a part of a cricket team featuring Everton and Liverpool players, including Dixie Dean, that played local clubs in the off-season. Smith had to retire when both cartilages were removed from his knees in 1938. While fighting the Japanese with the 10th Gurkha Rifles in Burma in 1943 he lost his left leg beneath the knee. He died on his 59th birthday in 1974.

FACTFILE

BORN
Buckie, Banffshire, Scotland,
17 January 1915
DIED
17 January 1974
POSITION
Centre-forward
OTHER CLUBS
Buckie Thistle,
Buckie Rovers,
Buckie Wanderers,
Forres Mechanics (1935-36),
Buckie Thistle (1936-37)
SIGNED FROM
Buckie Thistle, £150,
February 1937
LFC DEBUT
16 October 1937
CONTRACT EXPIRY
1938

Season	League		FA Cup		Total	
	App	Goals	App	Goals	App	Goals
1937/38	1	0	0	0	1	0
Total	1	0	0	0	1	0

Smith, Jack

CENTRE-FORWARD
John Thomas Smith, more commonly referred to as Jack, played amateur football for Bromborough on the Wirral before signing professional forms for Liverpool in March 1951 when he was 23 years old.

He scored after 18 minutes of his debut for the club when Derby County were beaten 2-0 at Anfield on 29 September 1951 and in fact netted in three of his first four appearances, but only managed another three goals in the remaining 23 First Division fixtures that he was selected for that season. A year later he scored eight times from the same number of league matches, 27, but after dropping almost altogether out of the first-team picture during the club's relegation year of 1953/54, he was transferred to Third Division South Torquay United.

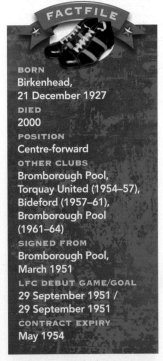

FACTFILE

BORN
Birkenhead,
21 December 1927
DIED
2000
POSITION
Centre-forward
OTHER CLUBS
Bromborough Pool,
Torquay United (1954–57),
Bideford (1957–61),
Bromborough Pool
(1961–64)
SIGNED FROM
Bromborough Pool,
March 1951
LFC DEBUT GAME/GOAL
29 September 1951 /
29 September 1951
CONTRACT EXPIRY
May 1954

Season	League		FA Cup		Total	
	App	Goals	App	Goals	App	Goals
1951/52	27	6	1	0	28	6
1952/53	27	8	1	0	28	8
1953/54	3	0	0	0	3	0
Total	57	14	2	0	59	14

Smith,
James

RIGHT-BACK James Smith played his only game for Liverpool against Reading in the third round of the League Cup in October 2006.

Smith left on a free transfer to Stockport County in December 2007 after a successful loan spell. Smith moved to Southport in the Blue Square Premier League in July 2011 and was appointed the club's vice-captain in the summer of 2012.

FACTFILE

BORN
Liverpool, 17 October 1985
POSITION
Right-back
OTHER CLUBS
Ross County (loan, 2007),
Stockport County (2007–08),
Vauxhall Motors (2008),
Altrincham (2008–11),
Southport (2011–)
JOINED
1993; signed professional
15 May 2006
LFC DEBUT
25 October 2006
CONTRACT EXPIRY
28 December 2007

Season	League		FA Cup		League Cup		Europe		Other		Total	
	App	Goals	App	Goals	App	Goals	App	Goals	App	Goals	App	Goals
2006/07	0	0	0	0	0 (1)	0	0	0	0	0	0 (1)	0
Total	0	0	0	0	0 (1)	0	0	0	0	0	0 (1)	0

Smith,
Jimmy

JAMES TERENCE SMITH is a legendary goalscorer in Ayr United's history and he made the *Guinness Book of Records* for holding the British seasonal record of 72 goals: four in friendlies, two in the Scottish Cup and a phenomenal 66 in 38 matches as Ayr won the Scottish Second Division Championship in the 1927/28 season.

HE MADE THE GUINNESS BOOK OF RECORDS FOR HOLDING THE BRITISH SEASONAL RECORD OF 72 GOALS

Smith was introduced into the Liverpool side for the sixth First Division fixture of the 1929/30 season. He scored twice on his debut against Manchester United and played in 38 consecutive league and cup games before the season ended, scoring 23 goals. Smith grabbed another 14 league goals a year later but lost his place halfway through the season, his position usually filled by Dave Wright, who continued to be selected ahead of Smith when the 1931/32 season opened and Smith was restricted to just three more appearances for the club. His final game was in a defeat at Sheffield United on the last day of October 1931, the last of his 62 appearances for Liverpool, in which he had scored an impressive total of 38 goals.

SMITH'S career took a decidedly downward turn after Liverpool, going from one club to another, but he finally settled once he moved to Dumbarton in the Scottish Second Division. He scored 36 goals in 49 league games and took over as Dumbarton's manager in 1939.

He was appointed as director in 1941 as the club could no longer afford a manager and stayed in that capacity until 1943.

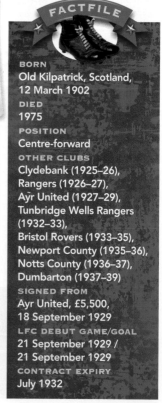

FACTFILE

BORN
Old Kilpatrick, Scotland,
12 March 1902
DIED
1975
POSITION
Centre-forward
OTHER CLUBS
Clydebank (1925–26),
Rangers (1926–27),
Ayr United (1927–29),
Tunbridge Wells Rangers
(1932–33),
Bristol Rovers (1933–35),
Newport County (1935–36),
Notts County (1936–37),
Dumbarton (1937–39)
SIGNED FROM
Ayr United, £5,500,
18 September 1929
LFC DEBUT GAME/GOAL
21 September 1929 /
21 September 1929
CONTRACT EXPIRY
July 1932

Season	League		FA Cup		Total	
	App	Goals	App	Goals	App	Goals
1929/30	37	23	1	0	38	23
1930/31	21	14	0	0	21	14
1931/32	3	1	0	0	3	1
Total	61	38	1	0	62	38

Smith,
Jock

JOHN SMITH, or 'Jock' as he was known because of his Scottish origins, was said to be 'a grand acquisition' for newly formed Liverpool, 'possessing rare speed and good dribbling powers'.

Inside-right Smith played 10 games in the Lancashire League for Liverpool and scored five goals. He later scored 12 goals in

35 games for Second Division Newcastle United, who had been merged from his former club, Newcastle East End, and Newcastle West End in 1892. Jock, who was a fitter by trade, met a tragic end. On 23 January 1911 when Smith was 55 years of age he committed suicide in his back yard two days after one of his children had died. 'Suicide whilst in a depressed state of mind' was the verdict returned at an inquest held at the Newcastle Central Police Station. Newcastle United gave his widow a benefit match at St James' Park.

FACTFILE

BORN
Ayrshire, Scotland, 1866
DIED
23 January 1911
POSITION
Inside-right forward
OTHER CLUBS
Kilmarnock (1885–87),
Newcastle East End (1887),
Kilmarnock (1887–88),
Sunderland (1889–92),
The Wednesday (1893–94),
Newcastle United (1894–96)
SIGNED FROM
Sunderland, 1892
LFC DEBUT GAME/GOAL
3 September 1892 /
3 September 1892
CONTRACT EXPIRY
2 August 1893
HONOURS
Lancashire League 1892/93

Season	League		FA Cup		Other		Total	
	App	Goals	App	Goals	App	Goals	App	Goals
1892/93	-	-	1	0	10	5	11	5
Total	0	0	1	0	10	5	11	5

Smith,
Sir John

'There is something they call the Liverpool Way. We're a very, very modest club. We don't talk. We don't boast. But we're very professional.'

Sir John Smith set the precedent that Liverpool fans wished had been kept since, instead of the club airing its dirty laundry in public. The dapper 53-year-old Smith, who had honed his business acumen as sales director of brewers Tetley Walker Ltd, was appointed chairman of Liverpool Football Club in 1973, having been a director at the club for two years. He hadn't been long in the post when he had to deal with Bill Shankly's refusal to renew his contract. The club thankfully did the 'right thing' at this crucial time and appointed from within the trusted right-hand man of Shankly, Bob Paisley, as it would do when Joe Fagan and Kenny Dalglish were asked to continue the Bootroom tradition.

SMITH ran a tight ship with the experienced chief executive Peter Robinson by his side. The club became the first professional English club to agree a shirt sponsorship deal, signing a contract with Japanese electronics giants Hitachi in 1979. Smith pioneered the deal to fight the rising costs of running a football club, expecting others to follow their lead. 'In terms of commerce and industry we, at Liverpool, are broke but in football terms we are wealthy,' Smith told the press. 'From a turnover of £2.4million last year, Liverpool's profit at the end of the day was a meagre £71,000, this for one of the leading clubs in Europe. The overheads in our game are colossal and we have got to generate more remunerative activity off the field.' Three years later north west paint manufacturer Crown Paints succeeded Hitachi and the Italian household appliance giants Candy followed in 1988, the latter still in place when Smith retired as chairman. Liverpool didn't hesitate in splashing the cash when needed to get the best players available, and paid their squad handsomely to secure their unique success locally as well as on the continent, where Liverpool had unprecedented success for an English

team under Smith's chairmanship. Undoubtedly the club would have had further glories to celebrate were it not for the Heysel ban.

Smith reigned in the most successful era of the club, being the longest-serving chairman in the history of Liverpool, a total of 17 years, before stepping aside for David Moores and taking a director's seat on the board in 1990, incidentally also the year when Liverpool last won the League Championship.

John Smith was knighted in 1989 for his contribution to sport and industry, seven years after being awarded the CBE. Following Sir John's passing on 31 January 1995 Peter Robinson paid his respects. 'He was the outstanding chairman of his time. His record is unparalleled in football. He was a man of firm beliefs, but had a warm working relationship with managers and star players. Sir John was especially proud of the family atmosphere he helped to create and the continuity of managers from within the club during his years of success.'

Smith, Sydney

SYDNEY SMITH was an amateur during his stay at Liverpool, employed as a public schoolteacher.

He led Liverpool's forward line in the opening two games of the 1903/04 season, which would end in relegation to the Second Division after just nine of their 34 league matches were won. Smith scored on his debut at Nottingham Forest but his strike ten minutes from time was not enough to salvage a point as the hosts had scored twice themselves during the opening period. Smith retained his place when Sheffield Wednesday were the visitors to Anfield a week later but after another defeat he was replaced by John Carlin.

FACTFILE

BORN
Liverpool, 1882
POSITION
Centre-forward
OTHER CLUBS
Southport Central (1904–07)
JOINED
16 April 1903
LFC DEBUT GAME/GOAL
5 September 1903 /
5 September 1903
CONTRACT EXPIRY
April 1904

Season	League		FA Cup		Total	
	App	Goals	App	Goals	App	Goals
1903/04	2	1	0	0	2	1
Total	2	1	0	0	2	1

Smith, Tommy

FACTFILE

BORN
Liverpool, 5 April 1945
POSITION
Centre-half / Right-back /
Midfielder
OTHER CLUBS
Swansea City (1978–79)
JOINED
1960; signed professional
5 April 1962
INTERNATIONAL CAPS
1 England cap, 1971
LFC DEBUT GAME/GOAL
8 May 1963 / 29 August 1964
CONTRACT EXPIRY
August 1978
HONOURS
League Championship
1965/66, 1972/73, 1975/76,
1976/77;
FA Cup 1965, 1974;
European Cup 1977;
UEFA Cup 1973, 1976

'I WAS BORN with football in my blood. Red of course, not Blue. There are no half-measures in Liverpool, either in the pubs or in a football sense. My grandfather and father supported Liverpool. There was no debate. No argument. I would also follow the Mersey Reds. Indeed it went a little bit deeper than that with me. I was a fanatic, brought up on a diet of football, football and more football.'

Tommy Smith is Liverpool FC through and through. He worked as a groundsman at Anfield, was a player, captain and coach, and only a handful of players have played more games than him for Liverpool. Bill Shankly summed him up best: 'Tommy Smith wasn't born, he was quarried.' Smith was born only a spitting distance from Anfield and as a 15-year-old in May 1960 his mum brought him to Shankly and told him to take good care of her son. Smithy became one of the toughest customers to ever wear the Liverpool shirt. But there was more to his game than tackling, as he had excellent technique and scored quite a few goals in his time, albeit some of them from the penalty spot. Smith played alongside Billy Liddell up front when he started out with the reserves and played his first five games of the 1964/65 season as a forward, scoring two goals. His team-mate Chris Lawler was amused by his playing style: 'I told him, "Smithy, the opposition would kick-off and you would be straight in to tackle the centre-half. Shouldn't it have been the other way round?"'

SMITH was moved to the centre of defence on 5 December 1964 in a 5-1 league win against Burnley and never looked back. Despite often wearing the number 10 jersey in his early years, Smith was never the inside-forward that his shirt number suggested, something which was to confuse foreign opponents who expected him to venture further up the field than he did. By the end of the season the 20-year-old Smith had become a regular member of the side and featured in the emotional day at Wembley when Liverpool won the FA Cup for the first time. For the next 10 years Smith was a fixture in the team. He only missed 41 out of 420 First Division fixtures and was able to claim the number 4 shirt almost exclusively as his own. Later in his Liverpool career he played as right-back until he lost his place to the up-and-coming Phil Neal.

Smith shared in the remarkable success of the mid-60s but was young enough to survive the changes that inevitably came as the decade ended and Bill Shankly started to rebuild for the future. Shankly saw in Smith the leadership qualities that he knew would help and encourage younger players and new signings, and made him captain in March 1970. Smith revelled in the role and in his first full season as captain Shankly declared: 'If Smith isn't named Footballer of the Year, football should be stopped and the men who picked any other player should be sent to the Kremlin.' Members of the Football Writers' Association disagreed and voted for Frank McLintock.

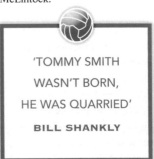

'TOMMY SMITH
WASN'T BORN,
HE WAS QUARRIED'

BILL SHANKLY

Smith held on to the armband until November 1973 following a row with Shankly just prior to kick-off at Highbury, as he had been dropped from the starting XI to face Arsenal. Smith left the stadium and took the next train home to Liverpool. He came close to leaving the club but soldiered on and quickly won his place back. Replaced by Emlyn Hughes as captain, Smith moved to right-back as Chris Lawler's

Anfield career came closer to its end. He only missed one of the remaining 25 league games and collected his second FA Cup winners' medal in the 3-0 win over Newcastle United, the biggest margin of victory in a Cup final since 1960.

John Roberts, whose classic lengthy interviews with Dixie Dean and Bill Shankly comprise two fantastic books about these legends, recalls a great story about Tommy Smith as told to him by Joe Mercer, Dixie Dean's former Everton team-mate. Dixie Dean was obsessed with a quest for an artificial right leg to replace the limb that had been amputated shortly before Christmas 1976.

'He [Mercer] told me of the day he accompanied his old friend to hospital, where Dixie urged a specialist to tell him of any extra exercises he might try to hasten his fitness to obtain a new leg. Dixie would enter the hospital reception area with the aid of a walking frame and look at the artificial limbs in cases on the walls. 'The room was filled with chaps who had limbs missing,' Joe said. 'Dixie took one look at them all and cracked: "Aye-aye ... I see Tommy Smith's been in 'ere!"'

BOB PAISLEY enjoyed having Tommy Smith in his ranks. 'His fearless nature not only unsettled the opposition, it inspired his team-mates. They drew strength from his example. It was little bit like having a big brother around to sort out any trouble you got into. Seeing Tommy racing on to the field after having a couple of stitches inserted into a head wound could put courage into the most cowardly of hearts – as long as you were on his side!' Smith utilised his fear factor to the fullest. 'There was an incident once when I was coming back from injury and had played for the reserves in a match against Preston at Anfield,' Smith told *Shankly.com*.

I was approached by a chap and his wife as I left the ground. I asked if I could help them and they simply thanked me for not kicking their son. He had been playing inside-left for Preston! Again, it showed the value of reputation. I did warn players. When Tottenham striker Jimmy Greaves came out at Anfield one time I handed him a piece of paper. He said: 'What's this?' I said: 'Just open it.' It was the menu from the Liverpool Infirmary. I make no bones about it, that's what I was good at. Some players were good dribblers, others good headers, I was a hard tackler and I used it to gain that 'edge' that Shanks was always looking for.

Smith announced that the 1976/77 season was to be his last. Phil Neal and Joey Jones were regulars at full-back and the young Phil Thompson was proving to be reliable in another position that Smith could cover with equal competence. Smith had only played three times in the league when he won a regular spot following Thompson's injury in March. He played in the last 13 league fixtures, made his fourth FA Cup final appearance for the club and also made the team for the European Cup final in Rome. Expected beforehand to be his last game as a Liverpool player, just playing in such a match in such an arena would have satisfied most men, but not Tommy Smith! With the final tensely balanced at 1-1 and with Gladbach sensing their chances after Simonsen's equaliser, he met Steve Heighway's left-wing corner firmly with his head to send the ball flashing past Wolfgang Kneib. His first goal for two and a half years! Neal's late penalty secured Liverpool's greatest triumph and the team returned to an extraordinary welcome and, as fate would have it, Smith's own testimonial fixture at Anfield two days after the final, at which the giant and coveted trophy was proudly paraded.

SMITH decided to play one more season and made another 34 first-team appearances. An accident in his garden in April 1978, when he dropped a big hammer on his foot, ended his Liverpool career a month too soon. Smith moved to Swansea City, six months after his former team-mate John Toshack had been appointed as player-manager at the Vetch Field. He helped the Swans out of the old Third Division on their meteoric rise from the Fourth to the First.

Tommy Smith can rightly be classed as one of most consistent and influential players ever to have been at Anfield. During his long

Season	League App	League Goals	FA Cup App	FA Cup Goals	League Cup App	League Cup Goals	Europe App	Europe Goals	Other App	Other Goals	Total App	Total Goals
1962/63	1	0	0	0	-	-	-	-	-	-	1	0
1964/65	25	4	8	0	-	-	7	0	0	0	40	4
1965/66	42	3	1	0	-	-	9	1	1	0	53	4
1966/67	42	1	4	0	-	-	5	0	1	0	52	1
1967/68	36	3	7	1	2	1	6	1	-	-	51	6
1968/69	42	6	4	1	3	0	2	0	-	-	51	7
1969/70	36	4	3	0	2	0	4	3	-	-	45	7
1970/71	41	2	7	0	3	1	10	0	-	-	61	3
1971/72	37	6	3	0	1	0	3	0	1	0	45	6
1972/73	33	2	2	0	4	0	10	1	-	-	49	3
1973/74	34	1	7	0	5	0	3	0	-	-	49	1
1974/75	36	2	0	0	4	0	4	1	1	0	45	3
1975/76	24	0	2	0	0	0	9	0	-	-	35	0
1976/77	16	0	4	0	0	0	7	1	0	0	27	1
1977/78	22	2	0	0	6	0	5 (1)	0	0	0	33 (1)	2
Total	**467**	**36**	**52**	**2**	**30**	**2**	**84 (1)**	**8**	**4**	**0**	**637 (1)**	**48**

spell at the club he won four League Championships and played in four FA Cup finals, as well as in the finals of all three European club competitions. Only Borussia Dortmund's bizarre extra-time winner at Hampden Park in 1966 and Liverpool's apathetic attitude towards the

League Cup in its early days probably prevented him from having a medal haul that few other British players could ever match. After retiring as a player, Smith looked after his business interests on Merseyside and later became a respected member of the *Liverpool Echo*'s sports department.

Poor health and a bad car accident affected his journalistic activities, but he coped with those adversities with the same courage and determination that will always be remembered whenever he wore a Liverpool shirt.

Tommy Smith is prettier than Sophia Loren

Smyth,
Mark

MARK SMYTH was on his way from Liverpool when Gérard Houllier was in charge, but Rafa Benítez saw something in him and decided to keep him on. Smyth played a total of 51 minutes for Liverpool in a penalty shootout win over Tottenham in the fifth round of the League Cup on 1 December 2004. He didn't get any further chances to impress and was released in the summer of 2005.

FACTFILE

BORN
Liverpool, 9 January 1985
POSITION
Midfielder
OTHER CLUBS
Accrington Stanley (2005), Vauxhall Motors (2005–06), Bangor City (2006–07), Leigh Railway Mechanics Institute (2007–08), Witton Albion (2008–09), Bangor City (2009–12)
JOINED
2001; signed professional 23 April 2002
LFC DEBUT
1 December 2004
CONTRACT EXPIRY
1 July 2005

Season	League		FA Cup		League Cup		Europe		Other		Total	
	App	Goals	App	Goals	App	Goals	App	Goals	App	Goals	App	Goals
2004/05	0	0	0	0	0 (1)	0	0	0	-	-	0 (1)	0
Total	0	0	0	0	0 (1)	0	0	0	0	0	0 (1)	0

Smyth,
Sammy

BELFAST-BORN forward Sammy Smyth played for his home-town clubs Linfield and Dundela before moving to Wolves in July 1947.

His highlight there was scoring a goal in their 3-1 victory in the 1949 FA Cup final against Leicester City. After four years,

115 appearances and 43 goals at Molineux, he was transferred to Stoke City where he scored 19 goals in 44 games for the struggling First Division club. Smyth joined Liverpool when he was 27 years old and went straight into the team. He made his debut on 3 January 1953 when Liverpool visited the club he had just signed from. But it was no happy return. Stoke won 3-1 and Liverpool lost their next two matches as well to give them an unenviable record of just three points from the last 22 and leave them in very real danger of relegation to the Second Division. After just one league victory in 15 games, Smyth scored in the next three matches, all of which were won. The seven goals he managed to score from 18 games were a big factor in Liverpool just climbing to safety by the end of the season.

BUT a year later, an even better strike-rate, 13 from 26 games, couldn't prevent relegation despite a late rally which saw four victories in six games. The club's proud record of being a First Division club for nearly 50 years was at an end. Smyth wanted to focus on his business in his native Northern Ireland so Liverpool had to cope without their top scorer in the Second Division. Manager Don Welsh was disappointed to lose Smyth but wished him well. 'Sammy is quite rightly looking to his future and we accept

that. We will miss him, but we'll get by without him.' Smyth was a bookmaker and then opened his own sports shop business.

FACTFILE

BORN
Belfast, Northern Ireland, 25 February 1925
POSITION
Inside-left / Centre-forward
OTHER CLUBS
Distillery (1942–44), Linfield (1944–47), Dundela (1947), Wolverhampton Wanderers (1947–51), Stoke City (1951–52), Bangor (1955)
SIGNED FROM
Stoke City, £12,000, December 1952
INTERNATIONAL CAPS
9 Northern Ireland caps (5 goals), 1947–50
LFC DEBUT GAME/GOAL
3 January 1953 / 7 February 1953
CONTRACT EXPIRY
January 1955

Season	League		FA Cup		Total	
	App	Goals	App	Goals	App	Goals
1952/53	18	7	0	0	18	7
1953/54	26	13	0	0	26	13
Total	44	20	0	0	44	20

Song,
Rigobert

RIGOBERT SONG was handed immense responsibility from an early age with his country. When he was only 16 he was the captain of the Cameroon Under-20 side and roughly a year later he was playing for his country in the World Cup finals in the United States.

Coach Henri Michel said he had never known such a self-confident youngster as Song, who was later appointed captain of the senior team. He got a red card against Brazil in the 1994 finals and when he was sent off against Chile during the World Cup in France in 1998, he became the first player to be sent off in two consecutive World Cup finals tournaments. He also featured in the 2002 and 2010 World Cup and played at a record eight Africa Cup of Nations tournaments. Song also

holds the record of the most-capped player in the history of the Cameroon national team with 137 appearances.

SONG was obviously fond of the colour red, because he often played in red shoes, and six months after the World Cup in France he became one of the first players signed by Gérard Houllier for Liverpool. Song was quite a character, but the high-spirited African could not cope with life in the Premier League. He was tough, skilful and brave in battle but lacked discipline and got caught out of position far too many times for the liking of Liverpool's management. Jamie Carragher was not his biggest fan, as he revealed in his autobiography. Song had apparently mocked Carra's defensive skills and the Bootle boy made him pay. 'Song walked on to the training pitch with a smile on his face. He was limping off it with a grimace an hour later,' Carragher said. 'The first chance I got, I did him. Never have I hunted down a 50-50 tackle with greater appetite.' Song only made 38 appearances for Liverpool's first team before being transferred to West Ham in November 2000. But a change of scenery

did not mean a change of fortune and he struggled to hold down a first-team place with the Hammers as well. He was sent on loan to Cologne and subsequently agreed a permanent deal with French club Lens in 2002. After two years in France, Song moved to Turkey where he won the league in 2006 and 2008 with Galatasaray and finished his career with Trabzonspor.

FACTFILE

BORN
Nkenglicock, Cameroon,
1 July 1976
POSITION
Centre-half / Right-back
OTHER CLUBS
Tonnerre Kalara Club de
Yaoundé (1992–94),
Metz (1994–98),
Salernitana (1998–99),
West Ham United (2000–02),
Cologne (loan, 2001–02),
Lens (2002–04),
Galatasaray (2004–08),
Trabzonspor (2008–10)
SIGNED FROM
Salernitana, £2.6million,
26 January 1999
INTERNATIONAL CAPS
137 Cameroon caps (4 goals)
(14 (2) at LFC), 1993–2010
LFC DEBUT
30 January 1999
CONTRACT EXPIRY
28 November 2000

Season	League App	League Goals	FA Cup App	FA Cup Goals	League Cup App	League Cup Goals	Europe App	Europe Goals	Total App	Total Goals
1998/99	10 (3)	0	0	0	0	0	0	0	10 (3)	0
1999/2000	14 (4)	0	0 (1)	0	2	0	-	-	16 (5)	0
2000/01	3	0	0	0	0	0	1	0	4	0
Total	**27 (7)**	**0**	**0 (1)**	**0**	**2**	**0**	**1**	**0**	**30 (8)**	**0**

Songs

SINGING INSIDE Anfield did not start until the 1960s, but long before that supporters had sung in honour of their team while spending their time in the surrounding alehouses before kick-off or while on the road to an away ground where putting their stamp on the foreign surroundings solidified them as a group.

The first song that is known to have been sung in support for Liverpool FC was 'Hurrah for the Reds' in 1907 [see separate entry].

When the Reds' supporters were on their way by train to London for the club's first ever FA Cup Final against Burnley they sang what they hoped would be a prophetic song.

The Burnley men came like the wolves on the fold
And their faces gleamed bright as the Klondyke gold
To the football field they all wended their way
To see their old foes at football to play
But nine and alack, when they got on the field
And saw their opponents, they knew they'd to yield
For they rushed them and pushed until they were sore
And beat them all hollow, as they'd oft done before

On match day you can hear a number of songs or just simple chants before, during and even after a game in the establishments that surround Anfield such as The Albert and The Park, both within touching distance of the Kop on Walton Breck Road. Some songs in this collection are no longer heard regularly or at all, but are well worth recording as they inspired fans and players alike throughout Liverpool's history. The famous songs

THE FIRST SONG THAT IS KNOWN TO HAVE BEEN SUNG IN SUPPORT FOR LIVERPOOL FC WAS 'HURRAH FOR THE REDS' IN 1907

'Every Other Saturday', 'Fields of Anfield Road', 'Poor Scouser Tommy' and 'You'll Never Walk Alone' have their own entries in this encyclopedia. Here are a select few others to enjoy!

Liverbird upon my chest

When 'A Liverbird Upon My Chest' is sung by Liverpool supporters they pound their chests with their fists to emphasise their point. It depends on the lung capacity of each singer at any given time how many verses are belted out. More verses than are listed here have been added so the song is continually in process as such.

A Liverbird upon my chest

(To the tune of Ballad of the Green Berets)

Here's a story about a football team
The greatest team you've ever seen
A team that play Total Football
They've won the league, Europe and all.

A Liverbird upon my chest... upon my chest!
We are the men of Shankly's best
A team that plays the Liverpool way
And wins the Championship in May

With Kenny Dalglish on the ball
He was the greatest of them all
And Ian Rush, four goals or two
Left Evertonians feeling blue

CHORUS:
A Liverbird upon my chest... upon my chest...

Now if you go down Goodison Way
Hard luck stories you hear each day
There's not a trophy to be seen
'Cos Liverpool have swept them clean

CHORUS

Now on the glorious 10th of May
There's laughing Reds on Wembley Way
We're full of smiles and joy and glee
It's Everton 1 and Liverpool 3

CHORUS

Now on the 20th of May
We're laughing still down Wembley Way
Those Evertonians feeling blue
It's Liverpool 3 and Everton 2

CHORUS

And as we sang round Goodison Park
Four Ian Rush goals had made their mark
Those Evertonians are crying still
It's Liverpool 5 and Everton 0.

CHORUS

We remember them with pride
Those mighty reds of Shankly's side
And Kenny's boys of '88
There's never been a side so great.

CHORUS

Now back in 1965
When great Bill Shankly was alive
We're playing Leeds, the score's 1-1
When it fell to the head of Ian St John...

CHORUS

On April 15th '89
What should have been a joyous time
96 friends we all shall miss
And all the Kopites want justice.
Justice.

[96]

Campione

Ohhhhhhhh Campione
The one and only
We're Liverpool!
They said our days were numbered
We're not famous any more
But Scousers rule the country
Like they've always done before

Ohhhhhhhh Campione...

John Barnes

(Tune: 'Buffalo Soldier')

Oh his father was a soldier (repeat)
He couldn't play the football (repeat)
His son he played for Watford (repeat)
But now he play for Liverpool (repeat)
His name is Johnny Barnes (repeat)
He comes from Jamaica (repeat)
And if you read the papers (repeat)
He's going to Italia (repeat)

Oh no no, no no no, no no no, no no no no.

Billy the King

(Tune: 'Lily the Pink')

Oh let's drink, a drink, a drink
To Billy the king, the king, the king
The creator of the greatest team
For he invented professional football
And this year we'll win the league

Now Gerry Byrne
Refused a tourniquet
When he's broken his collar bone
And they just rubbed on medicinal compound
And Gerry goes marching on, on, ON!

Oh let's drink, a drink, a drink *(chorus)*

Bill Shankly from Glenbuck

(Tune: 'Sean South from Garryowen')

'Twas on a cold December's day
Back in 1959
When a man came down from Huddersfield Town
To lead the Anfield line
He bought Yeats from Dundee and St John
And the football world was shook
This man he became a legend
Bill Shankly from Glenbuck

On the Kop we'd sway and sing
Till our hearts would burst with pride
And Shanks he made a pact with us
To build another side
With Keegan, Tosh and Steve Heighway
The great man kept his word
Then in '74 he bade farewell
Our dear old Scottish Laird

Now when Shanks was gone we sang walk on
But feared we'd walk alone
The search was on to find the one
Who could fill the master's throne
The one we crowned became renowned
Throughout the football game
Three European Cups, six championships
Bob Paisley was his name

Now when Bob stepped down he left his crown
Inside his Anfield home
Joe Fagan came and brought new fame
With a treble won in Rome
Though the Heysel year left Joe in tears
The following year he'd sing
When we won the league and FA Cup
And Kenny was our king

When he played in red Bob Paisley said
He's the best he'd ever seen
And the team he built in 88
Ruled the Football League supreme
And when Hillsborough left us all bereaved
And the Kop bedecked in flowers
Kenny proved he truly was a king
In Anfield's darkest hour

Days of ball to feet, of victory sweet
Days of passion, guile and fire
The legacy of one so great
Bill Shankly from Ayrshire

Istanbul Is Wonderful

Oh Istanbul (Oh Istanbul)
Is Wonderful (Is Wonderful)
Oh Istanbul is wonderful
It's full of mosques, kebabs and scousers
Oh Istanbul is wonderful

Red and White Kop

(Tune: 'Yellow Submarine')

On a Saturday afternoon
We support a team called Liverpool
And we sing until we drop
In a red and white Spion Kop

We all live in a red and white Kop
A red and white Kop
A red and white Kop
We all live in a red and white Kop
A red and white Kop
A red and white Kop

In the town where I was born
Lived a man who sailed the seas
And he told me of his pride
They were a famous football team

We all live in a red and white Kop (chorus)

So we trailed to Anfield Road
Singing songs of victory
And there we found the holy ground
Of our hero Bill Shankly

We all live in a red and white Kop (chorus)

A couple of songs for Stevie G

Steven Gerrard is our captain
Steven Gerrard is a Red
Steven Gerrard plays for Liverpool
Scouser born and bred
de de de de de de de de deh (x 4)

Then one night in Turkey
It was 21 years to come
With a liver bird upon his chest
He brought the cup back home
de de de de de de de de deh (x 4)

(Tune: 'Can't Take My Eyes Off You')

You're just too good to be true
Can't take the ball off of you
You've got a heavenly touch
You pass like Souness to Rush
And when we're p***ed in the bars
We thank the Lord that you're ours
You're just too good to be true
Can't take the ball off of you

Oh! Steven, Steven, Steven Gerrard!
Oh! Steven, Steven, Steven Gerrard!
Oh! Steven, Steven, Steven Gerrard!
Oh! Steven, Steven Gerrrrrrrard!

OH! STEVEN GERRARD!

Because he hates Man U
Oh! Steven Gerrard!
He hates the Blue s***e too
Oh! Steven Gerrard!
You're a Red through and through! (repeat)

That's Amore
– Robbie Fowler

When the ball hits the net
It's a fairly safe bet that it's Fowler
Robbie Fowler

And when Liverpool score
You will hear the Kop roar Oh, it's Fowler
Robbie Fowler

Ian Rush, Roger Hunt
Who's the best man up front? Oh, it's Fowler
Robbie Fowler

He's the King of the Kop
He's the best of the lot
Robbie Fowler!

The Reds Are Coming
Up the Hill

The reds are coming up the hill, boys
The reds are coming up the hill, boys
They all laugh at us
They all mock at us
They all say our days are numbered
Born to be a Scouse
Victorious are we
If you wanna win a cup
Then you'd better hurry up
Cos we're Liverpool FC
Victorious and glorious
We took the Gwladys Street
Between four of us
And glory be to God
that there isn't any more of us
Cos we would take the lot!

TWELVE DAYS OF CHRISTMAS

(Tune: Sung in the same way as the beloved Christmas carol so it might take a while to complete; easy to update with current players)

ON THE 12TH DAY OF CHRISTMAS
BOB PAISLEY SENT TO ME

TWELVE DAVID FAIRCLOUGHS,
ELEVEN IAN CALLAGHANS,
TEN JOHN TOSHACKS,
NINE STEVE HEIGHWAYS,
EIGHT JIMMY CASES,
SEVEN KEVIN KEEGANS,
SIX EMLYN HUGHES,
FIVE RAY KENNEDYS,
FOUR TOMMY SMITHS,
THREE JOEY JONES,
TWO PHIL NEALS
AND A CLEMO IN OUR GOAL!

Those Were the Days

(Tune: 'Those Were the Days')

Those were the days my friends
We took the Stretford End
We took the Shed
The North Bank Highbury
We took the Geordies too
We fought for Liverpool
We are the Kop
Of Liverpool FC

We'll Be Coming

We'll be coming
We'll be coming
We'll be coming down the road
When you hear the noise of the Bill Shankly boys

We'll be coming down the road …
(repeat until you basically drop)

We Love You Liverpool

We love you Liverpool we do
We love you Liverpool we do
We love you Liverpool we do
Oh Liverpool we love you

Shankly is our hero, he showed us how to play
The mighty reds of Europe
are out to win today
He made a team of champions,
with every man a king
And every game we love to win and
this is what we sing

We love you Liverpool we do… *(chorus)*

Clemence is our goalie,
the best there is around
And Keegan is the greatest
that Shankly ever found
Heighway is our favourite,
a wizard of the game
And here's the mighty Toshack
to do it once again

We love you Liverpool we do … *(chorus)*

We've won the league, we've won the cup
We're masters of the game
And just to prove how good we are
We'll do it all again
We've got another team to beat
and so we've got to try
'Cos we're the best in all the land
And that's the reason why

We love you Liverpool we do … *(chorus)*

We're the Best Behaved Supporters in the Land

(Tune: 'She'll Be Coming Round the Mountain')

We're the best behaved supporters in the land (when we win) x 2
We're the best behaved supporters
The best behaved supporters
We're the best behaved supporters in the land (when we win)

We're a right shower of b******ds when we lose (but we don't) x 2
We're a right shower of b******ds
A right shower of b******ds
We're a right shower of b******ds when we lose (but we don't)

We're totally noncommittal when we draw! (But we don't) x 2
We're totally noncommittal
Totally noncommittal
Totally noncommittal when we draw! (But we don't)

We've Won It Five Times

We won it at Wem-ber-ley
We won it in gay Paris
In 77 and 84 it was Rome

We've won it five times
We've won it five times
In Istanbul, we won it five times

When Emlyn lifted it high
He lit up the Roman sky
Thommo in Paris
and Souness did it as well

We've won it five times *(chorus)*

At Wembley we won it at home
We had 26,000 in Rome
20,000 in Paris when we
won it again (won it again)

We've won it five times (chorus)

Stevie G's eyes lit up
When he lifted the European Cup
21 years and the cup was coming
back home (coming back home)

We've won it five times (chorus)

We keep it! We keep it! We keep it!

Souness,
Graeme

'BEING SUCCESSFUL has always been more important to me than being popular. I long ago accepted that the name of Graeme Souness would top few popularity polls, regardless of whether the votes were cast by my fellow professionals or by the supporters. In that respect I suppose you could say that I have achieved my ambition for, thanks to Liverpool, I have a cupboard full of memories and scarcely a friend on the terraces or in the dressing room.'

Graeme Souness was a true midfield maestro who is certain to finish on almost everyone's greatest Liverpool XI list. He attracted attention for his part in Tottenham's great run in the FA Youth Cup. When he was 17, he knocked on manager Bill Nicholson's door and demanded a fair chance in the first team. Nicholson didn't agree, Souness stormed out and went back home to Scotland. Souness played 10 games in the North American Soccer League for Montreal Olympique before Tottenham sold him to Middlesbrough in 1973 for £30,000. The only game Souness played for Tottenham's first team was a European match against Icelandic club Keflavík.

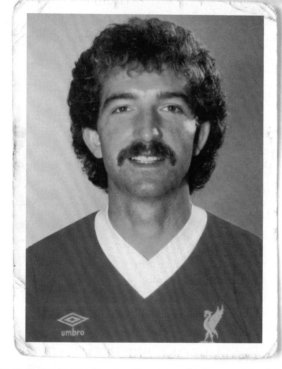

When Jack Charlton took over at Boro soon after Souness joined, he learned from his fellow coaches that the fiery Scot liked the nightlife a bit too much. Charlton reminded him that he could be a very successful football player or his career could be over in just one year if he wasn't careful. Souness took notice of these wise words... for the time being. In 1978, Souness went off the tracks again and broke the club's disciplinary code. 'I am fed up, disenchanted with the game. I feel like a good holiday away from it all,' Souness complained. He nevertheless left a strong impression on Middlesbrough fans as one of the best players to serve the club in the post-war years. Following a week's suspension imposed by Boro he got a call telling him to go to a hotel in Leeds to talk to a certain club. To Souness's delight, the European champions were the party interested. Middlesbrough chairman Charles Amer disclosed: 'There was no argument. John Smith, the Liverpool chairman, accepted our price without a blink. We shook hands and it was all over in about 90 seconds.' Club skipper Stuart Boam seemed relieved this matter had been settled. 'Graeme is a great player, make no mistake about that, but all the publicity and unrest was not good for team morale. It unsettled the rest of the players.' Souness was understandably delighted after signing for the European champions. 'I feel on the top of the world,' he enthused.

'To join a world-class club like Liverpool is marvellous.' Souness was driven in a limousine back home and told to be ready for the next Liverpool match against WBA. The sum Liverpool paid for him was £352,000, which was at that time a transfer record between English clubs, £2,000 more than Manchester United had paid for Leeds' Joe Jordan a week earlier.

SOUNESS'S Liverpool career didn't start very promisingly, as he revealed in his autobiography.

As a kid you usually live in digs where there is someone to keep an eye on you but when I moved from Middlesbrough to Liverpool I was given a room in the Holiday Inn. This was the start of the third period of my life during which I very nearly managed to wreck my own career. I lived there for nine months and it was then I earned the nickname of 'Champagne Charlie'. The routine was quickly established. I would train at Melwood, go back for lunch and a few beers, get involved in a session at the cocktail bar, sleep between 4 and 7pm and then crawl back down for dinner. If that became a little too boring there was always a club open somewhere, where they were only too happy to have a Liverpool player gracing their bar or the dance floor.

SOUNESS also made a serious faux-pas with one of the most experienced campaigners at Anfield. 'That first day at Anfield, 10 January 1978, was a revelation. It seems a long time now but I remember how normal and ordinary it all was, no prima donnas, no superstars. I made only one error on that first morning, I asked Tommy Smith if I could borrow his hairdryer and he turned to Phil Neal and said pointedly: "Everyone is allowed one mistake." I took my own in the future,' he wrote in his autobiography.

Souness's first goal for his new club was voted BBC's Goal of the Season, the recipients of his thunderbolt were Manchester United on 25 February 1978. Souness was in and out of the side, but the end of the season was sweet as his pass released Dalglish to score the winning goal in the European Cup final. 'The nearest I had been to European competition before was watching the Eurovision Song Contest so it was a dream come true when I won a European Champions' medal within four months.' Souness was the driving force in midfield for Liverpool and controlled the play with Terry McDermott when Liverpool won the title in 1979 and 1980. Souness led by example and netted a hat-trick against CSKA Sofia in the quarter-finals on the way to yet another European triumph. 'If Graeme plays until he's 100 he'll never hit three more perfect shots in one match,' former Kop idol Ian St John acclaimed. The trophies kept on

coming and Souness's genius was there for everyone to see. During Christmas 1981 Liverpool lost 3-1 to Manchester City and the team was in 12th place. Bob Paisley felt that he needed to make a serious adjustment to the team. He promoted Souness to captain in place of Phil Thompson, but at the cost of the players' friendship. 'One day, at half-time during a dodgy performance at Villa Park, Bob asked Thommo if maybe the captaincy was not a bit too much for him,' Souness revealed.

Phil, a proud Liverpudlian who treasured the captaincy, gave a very abrupt reply. Bob did not like that one bit and flew back at him. It was a rare sight and, a few days later, I was leaning against a goalpost helping to collect balls at a shooting practice session when he asked me how I would feel about the captaincy. I knew that was what I wanted and I told him that if it was offered I would take it, and sure enough at the next match at Swansea I was captain. It was a great thrill and a great honour even though it ended any pretence of friendship between Phil Thompson and me. He took it as a personal affront and it was a long, long time before he would say even hello to me.

The 1983/84 season turned out to be Souness's last with the Reds, winning the league title for the third year in a row. Souness said his goodbyes to Liverpool in style by securing the League Cup against Everton with a great shot from outside the penalty area and came second in the PFA's Player of the Year voting. The club reached their fourth European Cup final by winning every away leg. In the second leg of the semi-final with Dinamo Bucharest, Souness was attacked verbally and physically by Romanian players, incensed that he had broken the jaw of one of their colleagues in the first meeting at Anfield two weeks previously. He responded, as he usually did when the odds were stacked against him, with a performance of great discipline.

FACTFILE

BORN
Edinburgh, Scotland, 6 May 1953
POSITION
Midfielder
OTHER CLUBS AS PLAYER
Tottenham Hotspur (1969–73), Montreal Olympique (loan, 1972), Middlesbrough (1973–78), West Adelaide Soccer Club (loan, 1977), Sampdoria (1984–86), Rangers (1986–90)
OTHER CLUBS AS MANAGER
Rangers (1986–91), Galatasaray (1995–96), Southampton (1996–97), Torino (1997), Benfica (1997–99), Blackburn Rovers (2000–04), Newcastle United (2004–06)
SIGNED FROM
Middlesbrough, £352,000, 10 January 1978
INTERNATIONAL CAPS
54 Scotland caps (4 goals) (37 (2) at LFC), 1974–86
APPOINTED MANAGER
16 April 1991
LFC DEBUT GAME/GOAL
14 January 1978 / 25 February 1978
FIRST GAME AS MANAGER
20 April 1991
CONTRACT EXPIRY AS PLAYER
12 June 1984
CONTRACT EXPIRY AS MANAGER
28 January 1994
HONOURS AS PLAYER
League Championship 1978/79, 1979/80, 1981/82, 1982/83, 1983/84; League Cup 1982, 1983, 1984; European Cup 1978, 1981, 1984
HONOURS AS MANAGER
FA Cup 1992

THE EUROPEAN Cup final turned out to be Souness's farewell Liverpool appearance and he left on a high. Following Liverpool's win after a penalty shootout, that included one from Souness of the unstoppable variety, he couldn't keep his emotions in check. 'I went berserk. For the first time I wept tears of joy and I was alternately laughing and crying along with a few other professionals and we launched into our famous victory celebration song as we lined up for a team picture. The words are too dirty to

As a Player												
	League		FA Cup		League Cup		Europe		Other		Total	
Season	App	Goals	App	Goals	App	Goals	App	Goals	App	Goals	App	Goals
1977/78	15	2	0	0	0	0	2 (1)	0	0	0	17 (1)	2
1978/79	41	8	7	1	1	0	4	0	-	-	53	9
1979/80	41	1	8	1	7	0	2	0	1	0	59	2
1980/81	37	6	1	0	8	1	8	6	1	0	55	13
1981/82	34 (1)	5	3	0	9	1	6	0	1	0	53 (1)	6
1982/83	41	9	3	0	8	2	6	0	1	0	59	11
1983/84	37	7	2	0	12	5	9	0	1	0	61	12
Total	**246 (1)**	**38**	**24**	**2**	**45**	**9**	**37 (1)**	**6**	**5**	**0**	**357 (2)**	**55**

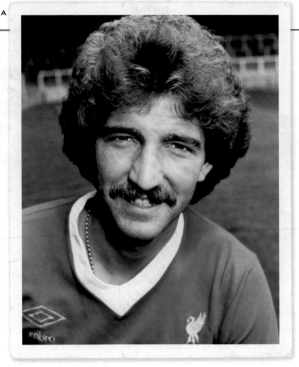

repeat but they seemed to delight the Italian photographers.'

Souness's performance on that memorable night in the Italian capital undoubtedly helped secure his move to Sampdoria shortly afterwards. He received a warm welcome in Italy, as he recollected in his book *No Half Measures*. 'Goodness knows what the other people on the aeroplane must have thought when we touched down for it was like a carnival time with what seemed to be thousands of people on the tarmac. There were flowers for my wife, kisses and hugs from old ladies and a Sampdoria shirt with a number eleven on the back was thrust into my hands.' He helped the club win the Italian Cup and scored in the final. After two successful years in Italy, he returned to his homeland to become player-manager at Glasgow Rangers and immediately set about the task of ensuring that they would become the club to beat in Scotland.

In 1991 Souness followed best mate Dalglish into the managerial hot seat at Anfield after a successful five-year spell at Rangers. Dalglish left an ageing side behind but on the other hand future stars like Fowler, McManaman and Redknapp were coming into their own. Liverpool needed a leader in defence to replace Alan Hansen.

Mark Wright was bought from Derby as well as striker Dean Saunders. Peter Beardsley was off to Everton and the promising Steve Staunton followed him out of the exit door. Rangers wizard Mark Walters was an old acquaintance, and the best purchase Souness ever made, Rob Jones, arrived in October 1991. However, the team was in dire straits early on. At the end of September it was in mid-table and Barnes, Wright and Whelan were all out injured. Mølby missed 10 weeks and Rush was out for 20 games. Rush blamed Souness for Liverpool's lengthy injury list in his autobiography, as he had put the players through a strenuous training programme in pre-season. 'It produced an incredible series of injuries to the lads, before a single ball had even been kicked.'

SOUNESS tried to strengthen his team by purchasing Arsenal's Michael Thomas, and Hungarian Istvan Kozma arrived from Dunfermline. Liverpool were back in Europe after a six-year absence; having pushed Lahti easily out of the way, the Reds lost 2-0 to Auxerre in France, but an impressive performance at Anfield ensured a 3-0 victory. Tirol was an easy prey, but Genoa in the fourth round proved an obstacle that Liverpool could not handle. Steve McManaman proved the catalyst in the 1992 FA Cup final against Sunderland and delivered much-needed silverware, following a disappointing league campaign in which Liverpool finished sixth, 18 points behind champions Leeds. Souness had missed several games in April and May because he had to undergo triple-bypass heart surgery. He was back in charge at Wembley, but could hardly enjoy his only Cup victory as Liverpool's boss.

As a Manager in Europe			
Season	European Cup	UEFA Cup	European Cup Winners' Cup
1991/92	-	4th Round	-
1992/93	-	-	2nd Round

However, the beginning of the end for Souness was already in motion in mid-April when he sold the *Sun*, hated on Merseyside for its misreporting of the Hillsborough disaster, his bypass operation story, on the third anniversary of the tragedy. Liverpool supporters would never forgive him this error. Souness begged forgiveness in the *Liverpool Echo* in 2011.

I agreed to have a picture taken after the FA Cup replay against Portsmouth. That picture was meant to go in on the Tuesday but because it had gone to extra time and penalties, it missed the deadline. So it went in on the Wednesday. The Wednesday was the anniversary of Hillsborough and that killed me. The local journalist for the Sun at the time was Mike Ellis, who was away on holiday and was the one person who could have said to the Sun newspaper's office, you just can't do that. So I hold my hands up. I'm still a Liverpool supporter. They are still my team. I had a great time as a player at Liverpool and I'd like to think I had a great relationship with the supporters at the time, and it hurts me. I can only apologise and it's something I have to live with.

Souness himself admitted that he wanted to change things too quickly at the club. Established stars like Peter Beardsley, Steve McMahon, Barry Venison and Ray Houghton were on their way while he bought players of much lesser talent like Mark Walters, Istvan Kozma, Julian Dicks and Paul Stewart. In the summer of 1992 David James was signed as a future replacement for the ageing Grobbelaar.

In 1992/93 Liverpool made their worst start to a season for 39 years. The alarm bells were seriously ringing. Dean Saunders was sold to help fund the arrival of Torben Piechnik. Liverpool

As a Manager												
Season	Division	P	W	D	L	GF	GA	Pts	Pos	Win %	FA Cup	League Cup
1990/91*	1st Division	5	3	0	2	11	6	9	2	60.00	-	-
1991/92	1st Division	42	16	16	10	47	40	64	6	38.10	Winners	4th Round
1992/93	Premier League	42	16	11	15	62	55	59	6	38.10	3rd Round	4th Round
1993/94**	Premier League	26	12	7	7	44	32	43	5	46.15	3rd Round	4th Round
Total	-	115	47	34	34	164	133	175	-	40.87	-	-

*Souness appointed on 16 April 1991 with Liverpool in 2nd position **Souness resigned on 28 January 1994 with Liverpool in 5th position*

drew 4-4 at Anfield against Third Division side Chesterfield, in which they were 3-0 down for a period. Souness was unable to utilise the talents of John Barnes and Jan Mølby through injury. Nobody seemed up to the task and Souness wasn't even present for the final game of the 1992/93 season against Tottenham at Anfield. He was instead bizarrely sent away to run the rule over Coventry against Leeds United. It was widely expected that Souness would leave before the start of the following season, but the board decided to promote Roy Evans to assistant manager, clearly indicating he would take over from Souness if things didn't work out as planned.

Souness next signed Nigel Clough from Nottingham Forest and Neil Ruddock from Tottenham. Liverpool started the season in emphatic fashion with three wins, but three defeats in a row in September put things into perspective. October and the start of November proved to be fruitful, with five wins and two draws, but Liverpool ended 1993 by drawing four league games in a row. Liverpool were in seventh place with 36 points from 23 games midway through the season. A 1-1 draw away with Bristol City in the FA Cup third round caused concern, which changed to panic

when Liverpool lost the replay at Anfield 1-0. This was totally unacceptable and Souness knew it. He handed in his resignation the following week. He was not present at the mandatory press conference but instead issued a statement confessing: 'This is a sad day for me. After a great deal of soul-searching I have reached the conclusion that the best thing for the club and I is that we should part company. I took this job believing that I could return the club to its former glory but this proved to be more difficult than I anticipated. The fans have been very patient but I feel that their patience is now running out. Liverpool Football Club has, and always will have, a very special place in my heart and I can only wish the club well and every success in the future.' Chairman David Moores was certainly sorry to see his friend leave and cited Souness's heart surgery, his father's death and the unprecedented amount of player injuries not helping him in the job. But no matter what had happened it finally came down to just one thing. 'The results have been well below what is expected by the club and its supporters.'

SOUNESS pulls no punches when he looks back on his managerial career at Liverpool. In his autobiography he cites the legacy of the Hillsborough and Heysel tragedies hanging over his predecessor, Kenny Dalglish, who he suggests held back in clearing out the squad. 'I know I made mistakes, both in my manner and the way in which I tried to change things too quickly,' he wrote. 'But everyone accepted that when I took the job that it was the most difficult period for the club in its recent history. We managed to win the cup in my 2½ years, but my timing was

all wrong. Players like Redknapp, McManaman and Fowler were waiting to flourish, but were still too young.' He added that he'd 'fallen out of love with football.' He wrote: 'From the operation until the day I resigned in April 1994, I didn't enjoy the job.'

PERHAPS unfairly, his record as manager overshadows – in some eyes – his time as a player. 'Forget Souness,' were Joe Fagan's words as Liverpool came together in the 1984/85 season, emphasising the important role he had played in that team. Bruce Grobbelaar, Sammy Lee and Ronnie Whelan all acclaim Souness, not Dalglish, as the best player they ever played with at Liverpool. As a player Souness had many remarkable years of success with numerous trophies and unforgettable performances. He deserves to be remembered as one of the greatest players ever to wear the famous red shirt.

> HE DESERVES TO BE REMEMBERED AS ONE OF THE GREATEST PLAYERS EVER TO WEAR THE FAMOUS RED SHIRT

South, Alex

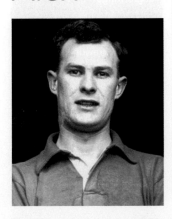

Alex South joined the ground staff at his home-town club Brighton at 15 years of age and made a total of 81 league appearances for the Seagulls before joining his old boss Don Welsh at Liverpool.

South only made seven appearances for Liverpool during the 1954/55 season, the team's

first in Second Division since 1905. He played instead of Laurie Hughes who was absent through injury for the last couple of months of the season but after four consecutive games when the Reds conceded 11 goals in two defeats and two draws he lost his spot. He later made 302 league appearances for Halifax Town and is considered a legend in those parts.

Season	League		FA Cup		Total	
	App	Goals	App	Goals	App	Goals
1954/55	6	1	1	0	7	1
Total	6	1	1	0	7	1

FACTFILE

BORN
Brighton, 7 July 1931
POSITION
Centre-half
OTHER CLUBS
Brighton & Hove Albion (1946–54),
Halifax Town (1956–65)
SIGNED FROM
Brighton & Hove Albion, £5,000, December 1954
LFC DEBUT GAME/GOAL
12 January 1955 / 2 April 1955
CONTRACT EXPIRY
October 1956

Spackman, Nigel

NIGEL SPACKMAN was a powerful midfielder who complemented the more skilful players around him and strengthened any team with his versatility. Former non-league player Spackman made over 300 appearances for Bournemouth and Chelsea before he arrived at Liverpool to further solidify the squad that had just won the League and FA Cup double in 1986.

Spackman deputised for Mark Lawrenson and Gary Gillespie in his debut season, but there was hardly any place for him as Liverpool made a blistering start to the 1987/88 season. He benefited from Ronnie Whelan's injury in January and played an active part as Liverpool ran away with the title during this magical campaign. Spackman started the FA Cup final against Wimbledon even though he had suffered bad

cuts after a clash of heads with team-mate Gary Gillespie against Luton five days earlier. Spackman and Gillespie both played with bandaged heads as Wimbledon caused one of the greatest upsets in FA Cup history, depriving Liverpool of their second Double in three seasons. Halfway through the 1988/89 season, when it was clear that Spackman's chances of being a first-team regular were limited, he returned to London and joined Queens Park Rangers.

AFTER NINE MONTHS at Loftus Road, Spackman moved north of the border to Glasgow giants Rangers, where he became

a part of the club's historic run of winning nine league titles in a row. Spackman returned to Chelsea in the 1992/93 season where he spent three and a half years in the Premier League before his swansong at Sheffield United.

FACTFILE

BORN
Romsey, 2 December 1960
POSITION
Midfielder / Defender
OTHER CLUBS
Andover (1976–80),
Bournemouth (1980–83),
Chelsea (1983–87),
Queens Park Rangers (1989),
Rangers (1989–92),
Chelsea (1992–96),
Sheffield United (1996–97)
SIGNED FROM
Chelsea, £400,000,
24 February 1987
LFC DEBUT
25 February 1987
CONTRACT EXPIRY
2 February 1989
HONOURS
League Championship
1987/88

Season	League		FA Cup		League Cup		Europe		Total	
	App	Goals	App	Goals	App	Goals	App	Goals	App	Goals
1986/87	12	0	0	0	1 (1)	0	0	0	13 (1)	0
1987/88	19 (8)	0	5	0	1	0	-	-	25 (8)	0
1988/89	8 (4)	0	0	0	4	0	0	0	12 (4)	0
Total	**39 (12)**	**0**	**5**	**0**	**6 (1)**	**0**	**0**	**0**	**50 (13)**	**0**

Speakman, James

ALTHOUGH James Speakman was at Anfield for four seasons just before World War One, he only played eight times for the first team. Arthur Goddard was Liverpool's right-winger during the 1909/10 season and missed only three First Division matches that year.

Speakman fared little better the following season, being restricted to just a single appearance, again as cover for Goddard. James was the younger brother of Sam, who was also on Liverpool's books from 1912. James' attributes were so described in the club programme on 25 October 1909: 'He possesses a useful turn of speed, and is much faster than would seem to be the case for when running he moves with little

apparent effort. In controlling the ball and passing it across the goalmouth he greatly resembles Goddard whose understudy he is, and the similarity of style of the two right-wingers is quite convincing.' During 1911/12, numerous changes were made to Liverpool's line-up in a turbulent season that saw them finish just outside the relegation zone. Speakman figured in three consecutive games towards the end of that season, during which he netted his only Liverpool goal at Bradford City. He only played

once more for the club, almost a year later, in a home defeat to Manchester United on 29 March 1913.

FACTFILE

BORN
Huyton, Liverpool,
1888
POSITION
Right-winger
OTHER CLUBS
Huyton Quarry,
Garston North End,
Prescot Wireworks,
South Liverpool
SIGNED FROM
Prescot Wireworks,
February 1909
LFC DEBUT GAME/GOAL
9 October 1909 /
8 April 1912
CONTRACT EXPIRY
August 1913

Season	League		FA Cup		Total	
	App	Goals	App	Goals	App	Goals
1909/10	2	0	0	0	2	0
1910/11	2	0	0	0	2	0
1911/12	3	1	0	0	3	1
1912/13	1	0	0	0	1	0
Total	**8**	**1**	**0**	**0**	**8**	**1**

Speakman, Sam

SAM SPEAKMAN made 14 league appearances at full-back in the 1913/14 season in which Liverpool struggled in the league, although the Reds did reach their first FA Cup final that year.

Speakman deputised for right-back Ephraim Longworth in the last game before the final but, unfortunately for him, Longworth was ready for action on the biggest occasion in the club's history. Despite the outbreak of World War One the 1914/15 league season was completed, but Speakman was only selected seven times during that campaign.

He did continue to represent Liverpool in the regional leagues that replaced the national ones for the next four years and was still at Anfield when the Football League resumed at the end of August 1919. However, although Speakman was selected for the opening four fixtures of that First Division campaign, the away match at Arsenal on 8 September 1919 proved to be his last as a Liverpool player.

FACTFILE

BORN
Huyton, Liverpool,
9 August 1884
POSITION
Right-back / Left-back
OTHER CLUBS
Prescot Athletic, Colne,
South Liverpool (1920–23)
SIGNED FROM
Colne, 1912
LFC DEBUT
September 1912
CONTRACT EXPIRY
1920

	League		FA Cup		Total	
Season	**App**	**Goals**	**App**	**Goals**	**App**	**Goals**
1913/14	14	0	1	0	15	0
1914/15	7	0	0	0	7	0
1919/20	4	0	0	0	4	0
Total	**25**	**0**	**1**	**0**	**26**	**0**

Spearing, Jay

JAY SPEARING was captain of Liverpool's Under-18 team that won the second of their successive FA Youth Cups in 2007 and was also a key player in the side that won the FA Premier Reserve League title in 2007/08.

FACTFILE

BORN
Wallasey,
25 November 1988
POSITION
Midfielder
OTHER CLUBS
Leicester City (loan, 2010),
Bolton Wanderers
(loan, 2012–13;
permanent 2013–)
JOINED
2004
LFC DEBUT
9 December 2008
CONTRACT EXPIRY
9 August 2013
HONOURS
League Cup 2012

SPEARING finally made his long-awaited debut for Liverpool's first team in the Champions League group match away to PSV Eindhoven on 9 December 2008. Another equally brief but impressive substitute appearance came in the same competition against Real Madrid at Anfield three months later. Spearing came on for captain Steven Gerrard with Liverpool already comfortably ahead 3-0 on the night and 4-0 on aggregate. The little midfielder impressed the crowd with his confidence against the famous Spanish club. Spearing started League Cup ties at Leeds and Arsenal as well as at Sunderland in the 'beach -ball' match and made two substitute appearances against Portsmouth and Wolves either side of Christmas, but those were his only first-team appearances in 2009/10. On 23 March 2010 he was loaned out to Championship club Leicester City until the end of the season.

The 2010/11 season was something of a breakthrough for Spearing, who made 16 starts and four substitute appearances for Liverpool. He gained valuable experience, especially in the Europa League competition, in which he figured eight times. Lucas Leiva's unfortunate injury openedthe door for Spearing in 2011/12 and he was picked to start in 24 matches, but the difference in quality between him and Lucas was painfully obvious and he became a target for the boo-boys. Spearing finally got his hands on a senior winners' medal after being a member of the squad that beat Cardiff City at Wembley in the League Cup final. Spearing was loaned to Bolton Wanderers in the Championship for the

2012/13 season where he was voted the club's player of the year by supporters. He moved permanently to Bolton in the summer of 2013.

	League		FA Cup		League Cup		Europe		Total	
Season	**App**	**Goals**	**App**	**Goals**	**App**	**Goals**	**App**	**Goals**	**App**	**Goals**
2008/09	0	0	0	0	0	0	0 (2)	0	0 (2)	0
2009/10	1 (2)	0	0	0	2	0	0	0	3 (2)	0
2010/11	10 (1)	0	0	0	1	0	5 (3)	0	16 (4)	0
2011/12	15 (1)	0	4	0	5	0	-	-	24 (1)	0
2012/13	0	0	0	0	0	0	2 (1)	0	2 (1)	0
Total	**26 (4)**	**0**	**4**	**0**	**8**	**0**	**7 (6)**	**0**	**45 (10)**	**0**

Speedie,
David

FIERY SCOTSMAN David Speedie was a surprising purchase by Kenny Dalglish and proved to be his last signing for Liverpool before he resigned.

Speedie enjoyed great success with Chelsea, winning the Second Division and finishing sixth in two consecutive seasons in the First Division. He formed a lethal partnership with Kerry Dixon at Stamford Bridge and netted 47 goals in 162 league games from 1982 to 1987. Speedie thought that his chance to join a top club had passed him by but when Liverpool came calling he grabbed the opportunity. 'It was the third time Kenny had tried to buy me,' Speedie revealed. 'He had tried before when I was at Chelsea and Coventry. I nearly

joined in 86/87.' Chelsea chairman Ken Bates prevented Speedie from leaving for Anfield, but eventually he moved to Merseyside via Coventry.

Speedie started his Anfield career in explosive fashion. He scored an equaliser at Manchester United on his debut and gained immense popularity by scoring twice in four minutes in the Merseyside derby on his home debut a week later. His brief career at Liverpool can hardly be called a failure because he scored in every other league game, a total of six in 12 matches. Speedie was one of numerous casualties in the early days of the Graeme Souness era.

'I had three years left on my contract and I didn't want to leave, but I wasn't going to stay and train with the kids,' Speedie told the *Irish Independent* in April 2011. 'I'd told Souness what I thought of him on a pre-season tour in Germany.' After hurling a few expletives in Souness's direction that can't be repeated in print, Speedie's Liverpool career was most definitely over and he was sold to Blackburn Rovers. 'When Kenny speaks to you, he gives you advice, you listen. When Graeme Souness speaks to you, and gives you advice, you don't listen. Kenny knows how to treat people,' Speedie added.

DALGLISH followed Speedie a few months later to Blackburn Rovers, becoming his boss for the second time. Speedie's single season at Rovers was a fantastic success. He scored 23 goals in 36 league games as the club was promoted to the Premier League. After he left Leicester at the end of the 1993/94 season, Speedie featured for a number of non-league clubs before retiring as a player to work as a football agent, where his most notable client was Steve Simonsen. He quit his profession after he divorced his wife, giving her his license, later claiming it was the biggest mistake of his life. Speedie played for Harworth Colliery Institute in 2007 and amazingly took out his boots again in 2011 featuring for Francis AFC in the third division of Dublin's United Churches League.

In addition to Speedie's apparent wanderlust, he also had problems with his temperament, which frequently drew him into confrontation with opponents, teammates and officials. 'People sort of look and say, "You were a little b*****ks,"' Speedie says proudly. 'That's mainly what people say, which I think is a compliment. I was always running around,

chasing, giving my all and it's nice to be remembered that way. I never gave anybody a minute.'

FACTFILE

BORN
Glenrothes, Scotland,
20 February 1960
POSITION
Centre-forward
OTHER CLUBS
Barnsley (1977–80),
Darlington (1980–82),
Chelsea (1982–87),
Coventry City (1987–91),
Blackburn Rovers (1991–92),
Southampton (1992–93),
Birmingham City
(loan, 1992–93),
West Bromwich Albion
(loan, 1993),
West Ham United (loan, 1993),
Leicester City (1993–95),
Crawley Town (1995–96),
Atherstone United (1996),
Hendon (1996),
Stamford (1996–97),
Kirby Muxloe (1997),
Guiseley (1997),
Crook Town (1997–98),
Harworth Colliery Institute
(2007),
Francis (2011)
SIGNED FROM
Coventry City, £675,000,
30 January 1991
INTERNATIONAL CAPS
10 Scotland caps, 1985–89
LFC DEBUT GAME/GOAL
3 February 1991 /
3 February 1991
CONTRACT EXPIRY
August 1991

Season	League		FA Cup		League Cup		Europe		Total	
	App	Goals	App	Goals	App	Goals	App	Goals	App	Goals
1990/91	8 (4)	6	1 (1)	0	0	0	0	0	9 (5)	6
Total	8 (4)	6	1 (1)	0	0	0	0	0	9 (5)	6

Spicer,
Eddie

GARSTON LAD Eddie Spicer went to Heath Road school in Allerton where he excelled in football and cricket.

He was the captain of the Liverpool Schoolboys side that won the English Shield in 1936/37 and, as he said himself: 'I had youthful longings to make football my living, though I hardly dared hope ever to appear in Liverpool's first team.' He signed a professional contract with Liverpool in 1939 but World War Two delayed his proper debut for the first team. He joined the Royal

Marines and as a lieutenant had many interesting experiences, of which the most memorable was an encounter with a German footballer, as he wrote in a letter to his mother in 1944. He told her how a German medical corps sergeant-major surrendered to him, shouting: 'Don't shoot. I am a soccer international!' 'He spoke perfect English and said that he was a professional footballer back

in the Fatherland and had played against several English touring clubs,' wrote Spicer. 'He mentioned many well-known English players including Callaghan of Aston Villa, against whom he said he had played in 1937, and with whom he corresponded for a time. We had quite an interesting chat while he was being patched up, and you would have thought we were the best of friends.'

SPICER was only 24 years old when Liverpool won the League Championship in 1947, featuring in 10 matches as either left- or right-half, but was four games short of receiving a winners' medal. In the following couple of seasons he mainly got a chance if either Phil Taylor or Bob Paisley were out injured. Spicer made his long-awaited breakthrough in the 1949/50 season when left-back Ray Lambert was switched to the right. Spicer was a firm fixture on the left in the team that contested the club's first Wembley FA Cup final in 1950 and finished ninth in the table in 1951.

Spicer's career took a tragic turn when he suffered a dreadful leg fracture in a pre-season game against Malmö in Stockholm on 16 May 1951 that caused him to miss the complete 1951/52 season. The tough-tackling Spicer, who was equally comfortable on the right side, fought back bravely from his injury and made 28 appearances in the following season. The 31-year-old was finally having a trouble-free run in the side in 1953/54 when he arrived at Old Trafford on 19 December 1953. Liverpool's new keeper, Dave Underwood, was making his debut. 'We didn't know anything about him [Underwood] and after about 20 minutes I can remember Roger Byrne, who was outside-left that day, going down the wing,' Spicer said. 'I went with Tommy Taylor. Roger hit this ball, hard and low across the penalty box and I went for the ball expecting

'THE SIGHT FROM THE QUEEN MARY AS WE SAILED INTO NEW YORK HARBOUR FOR THE AMERICAN TOUR IN 1946. THAT WAS SOMETHING NEVER TO BE FORGOTTEN'

our goalkeeper to come out and drop on it. That's what our other goalkeepers would have done and that's what I thought Underwood would do. Instead he just took a woof at it with his boot, missed the ball and hit me.' Bob Paisley, who was playing that day, recalled: 'That mighty blow shattered Ted's left leg. It disintegrated just the way a piece of dead wood does if you tread on it. In all he had 19 fractures and he was in and out of hospital for the next 12 months having it

set and reset and it took more than 12 months for him to get over it and to start to walk again.' Suffice to say, Spicer never played professional football again and was indeed lucky to be able to walk properly.

SPICER was granted a testimonial on 19 September 1955 when a combined Liverpool/Everton team played a Lancashire XI, which attracted 41,266 spectators, pocketing Spicer £4,500. Later Spicer became a football correspondent in Wales for the *Liverpool Daily Post* and ran a pub near Ruthin, in North Wales. 'One of the outstanding memories of my football life was the sight from the *Queen Mary* as we sailed into New York harbour for the American tour in 1946. That was something never to be forgotten,' Spicer said in 1950.

FACTFILE

BORN
Garston, Liverpool, 20 September 1922
DIED
25 December 2004
POSITION
Half-back / Left-back
JOINED
1937; signed professional October 1939
LFC DEBUT GAME/GOAL
30 January 1946 / 6 December 1947
CONTRACT EXPIRY
1954

Season	League		FA Cup		Total	
	App	Goals	App	Goals	App	Goals
1945/46	-	-	1	0	1	0
1946/47	10	0	0	0	10	0
1947/48	14	2	1	0	15	2
1948/49	4	0	0	0	4	0
1949/50	37	0	7	0	44	0
1950/51	42	0	1	0	43	0
1952/53	28	0	0	0	28	0
1953/54	23	0	0	0	23	0
Total	158	2	10	0	168	2

Spirit of Shankly

LIVERPOOL FC's first football supporters' union, the 'Sons of Shankly' [SOS], was formed in January 2008 to 'hold whoever owns the football club to account'.

This powerful organisation delivered a clear message to Tom Hicks and George Gillett that they were no longer welcome at the club by frank public discussion, private contact with the owners, and protests around Anfield and inside the stadium.

SOS, that later changed its name to the 'Spirit of Shankly' so as not to appear just exclusively for men, works on behalf of Liverpool fans regarding the many issues they face such as improving the standard and value of travel arrangements and the access to and cost of match tickets. SOS works with relevant agencies to improve the area of Anfield and builds links with grassroots supporter groups both at home and abroad. The union's long-term aim is to bring about supporter representation at boardroom level. SOS pledges on its website to fight on for the fans. 'Tom Hicks and George Gillett have gone, but the loyal supporters remain. Whilst they do, they need a voice. We will continue to be that voice.'

St John,
Ian

IAN ST JOHN would prove to be one of the most significant signings ever made by Liverpool Football Club. St John was a strong and tricky forward whose timing enabled him to outjump much taller defenders.

He had already secured his name in the Motherwell history books by scoring a famous 2½-minute hat-trick against Hibs in 1959. Liverpool had been trying desperately to get out of the Second Division for seven seasons, during which time they had finished 11th, third four times and fourth twice. Bill Shankly had been appointed from Huddersfield two years previously and felt he needed a strong centre-half and a centre-forward. He had not forgotten the two Scotsmen he had watched while he was at Huddersfield, but the Yorkshire club couldn't afford them. 'One Sunday morning in 1961 the *Sunday Post* had the headline "St John wants to go",' Shankly said. 'I was on the phone straight away and we were in Motherwell on the Monday night. Charlie Mitten came on the scene from Newcastle and tried to sign him, but we arranged the fee of £37,500 on the Monday night and signed St John the next day. I said to Mr Sawyer [Eric Sawyer, Liverpool's financial director], "He's not just a good centre-forward, he's the only centre-forward in the game."' St John made an immediate impact by scoring a hat-trick in a 4-3 defeat over Everton in the Liverpool Senior Cup final at Goodison Park. Ron Yeats followed his fellow countryman south of the border in July.

St John and Yeats would prove to be inspirational signings that helped an extremely settled side cruise to the Second Division title by eight points from Leyton Orient.

'**THE SAINT**' only missed two league games, scored 18 league goals and developed a lethal understanding with Roger Hunt. Liverpool coped quite comfortably with First Division football and finished eighth in their first year back in the top league; they were also unlucky to lose to Leicester City in the FA Cup semi-final. A year later Shankly's foresight and tactical shrewdness came to fruition. Liverpool won the First Division Championship for the first time for 27 years and St John contributed 21 league goals, the highest league total he achieved during any single season as a Liverpool player. A year later came his and the club's greatest moment. Shankly had promised Sawyer that with St John and Yeats in the team Liverpool would win the FA Cup for the first time in the club's history. After 73 years of trying it came true when St John's diving header towards the end of extra time at Wembley flew past Leeds United's goalkeeper Gary Sprake and earned the Scotsman immortality on the red half of Merseyside for that one athletic moment.

St John collected a second League Championship medal in 1966 and hardly missed a game for the next three seasons. By then he had dropped further back, using his tactical nous in the middle of the park. As the 1960s closed, Shankly had the difficult task of leaving out some of the players who had served him so well for most of the decade. Now 31 years old, St John became one of the 'casualties'. St John got upset with Shankly when he was dropped for a game against Newcastle on 11 October 1969 when his Liverpool career was drawing to a close. 'Shanks had a little flaw in his make-up, that he couldn't face up to the hard decision that a player was coming to the end of his career,' St John told *LFChistory.net*.

This was the first time in my life as a professional that I'd never played in the team. So it's hard to take. I walked into the dressing room and my boots are under a 12. I said to Shanks: 'We were up there Friday night, Saturday morning. You could have pulled me over.' I was sub for the first time and Bob said: 'Get warmed up. You better get on here.' We were losing the game. I said: 'No, I'm not getting warmed up. If he comes and tells me to warm up I'll warm up,' because Shankly was up in the stand. He never came down and we lost. Shanks never said anything. We just had stony silence after we had that row. Only after a short time we started talking again because we'd had as good as a relationship you can get with your manager. When Shankly packed it in and was retired I used to see him quite a bit. We got back on track again. I was one of the pallbearers when he died.

IAN ST JOHN was hardly any saint and put his considerable boxing skills to the test a few times on the playing field. 'I was sent off six times, but two of those were for mistaken identity. The referees were blind in those days as well,' St John once said tongue-in-cheek. 'I loved boxing and it stood me in good stead because I wasn't frightened in the games no matter how big they were, the centre-halves.' St John was sent off three times in the league while at Liverpool. 'I had a quick temper which was a bad thing. The fact I wasn't frightened of anybody was a good thing.'

The Scot was stuck in Liverpool's reserve team in the 1970/71 season before an unexpected move. 'Shanks put me on the bench against Swansea in the first round of the cup in January. We were struggling at Anfield and he brought me on and I scored a goal. That week Shanks said to me: "How would you like going to South Africa?" I thought that is as far away from Liverpool he can get me.' St John was transferred to Hellenic where he won the league title, joined by former Liverpool teammates Willie Stevenson and Roger Hunt. After a brief stay at Coventry St John returned to Merseyside for Third Division Tranmere Rovers in the 1972/73 season to play for his good friend, Ron Yeats.

St John took over as manager of his home-town club Motherwell in 1973. Four years later he had a brief but fairly unhappy spell as manager of Portsmouth. 'Shanks could sell you everything. He got me a job that was the worst job in football,' St John said. 'He convinced me to go to Portsmouth when I was at Motherwell. I had just missed out on Leeds when Don Revie had left to go to the Emirates. Shanks said: "Ok, son, aye. Go to Portsmouth." I would have money to spend on players, a new ground they were still waiting for. Not a penny. Nothing. I had the worst group of players you have ever seen in your life.'

St John's knowledge and passion for football enabled him to break into the world of television and for several years he was a popular figure on ITV in tandem with his former international adversary Jimmy Greaves. In recent times St John's alarming honesty when commenting on Liverpool's fortunes has on several occasions angered Reds, but he takes it in his stride. Shankly gave his honest opinion on St John in an interview with Brian Reade in 1975: 'My first great buy. Clever, canny, bags of skill, made things happen.

Liked a scrap too. Jesus, did he like a scrap. I sometimes wanted to tie his fists behind his back. Great player, though. Gave you everything on the pitch. Mind you, a lazy bugger at training. He hated it. Always trying to pull one on us. But what a player.'

FACTFILE

BORN
Motherwell, Scotland, 7 June 1938
POSITION
Forward
OTHER CLUBS
Motherwell Bridge Works, North Motherwell, Douglas Water Thistle (1956–57), Motherwell (1957–61), Hellenic (1971), Coventry City (1971–72), Tranmere Rovers (1972–73)
SIGNED FROM
Motherwell, £37,500, 2 May 1961
INTERNATIONAL CAPS
21 Scotland caps (9 goals) (14 (8) at LFC), 1959–65
LFC DEBUT GAME/GOAL
19 August 1961 / 30 August 1961
CONTRACT EXPIRY
February 1971
HONOURS
League Championship 1963/64, 1965/66; Second Division Championship 1961/62; FA Cup 1965

Season	League		FA Cup		League Cup		Europe		Other		Total	
	App	Goals	App	Goals	App	Goals	App	Goals	App	Goals	App	Goals
1961/62	40	18	5	4	-	-	-	-	-	-	45	22
1962/63	40	19	6	1	-	-	-	-	-	-	46	20
1963/64	40	21	5	1	-	-	-	-	-	-	45	22
1964/65	27	4	8	2	-	-	8	5	0	0	43	11
1965/66	41	10	1	0	-	-	9	2	1	0	52	12
1966/67	39	9	4	2	-	-	5	2	1	0	49	13
1967/68	41	5	9	0	2	0	4	1	-	-	56	6
1968/69	41	4	4	0	3	0	2	0	-	-	50	4
1969/70	25 (1)	5	6	1	1	1	2 (1)	0	-	-	34 (2)	7
1970/71	0 (1)	0	0 (1)	1	0	0	0 (1)	0	-	-	0 (3)	1
Total	**334 (2)**	**95**	**48 (1)**	**12**	**6**	**1**	**30 (2)**	**10**	**2**	**0**	**420 (5)**	**118**

Staniforth,
Fred

FRED STANIFORTH originally made his name at First Division Bristol City where he played over 150 games. The highlight of his career was in 1909 when City lost 1–0 to Manchester United in the FA Cup final.

Staniforth's Liverpool debut on the right wing came in a crushing 4-1 home defeat by Sheffield Wednesday on 4 October 1913. He missed the next five games but returned for consecutive matches against Preston (1-0 win) and Newcastle (0-0 draw) in November of the same year. Liverpool legend Arthur Goddard was finishing his career at the club passing the torch on the right wing to Jackie Sheldon, with no place for Staniforth in the team.

FACTFILE

BORN
Kilnhurst, Yorkshire, 1884
DIED
23 May 1955
POSITION
Right-winger
OTHER CLUBS
Kilnhurst Town, Rotherham Main, Mexborough, Bristol City (1906–11), Grimsby Town (1911–13)
SIGNED FROM
Grimsby Town, May 1913
LFC DEBUT
4 October 1913
CONTRACT EXPIRY
1914

Season	League		FA Cup		Total	
	App	Goals	App	Goals	App	Goals
1913/14	3	0	0	0	3	0
Total	**3**	**0**	**0**	**0**	**3**	**0**

Staunton, Steve

OVER TWO SPELLS with the club, Steve Staunton's versatility proved useful for Liverpool as he could play in a number of different positions. Although he played as a left-back more often than not, he actually struck a second-half hat-trick when he replaced Ian Rush in a League Cup tie against Wigan in October 1989 and even made a brief starring appearance in goal in a Merseyside derby ten years later when Sander Westerveld was sent off a few minutes after Liverpool had made their third and final substitution.

'Stan' first arrived from Dundalk in 1986 and made his breakthrough two years later when he was nineteen. Barry Venison and David Burrows had earlier featured at left-back in 1988/89, but Staunton made the position his own in the last three months of the season. He started 22 matches in the following campaign when Liverpool won the title, usually selected when players were missing throughout the team. In 1990/91 Staunton had his longest stay in the team as Kenny Dalglish resigned and Graeme Souness arrived. Unfortunately for him

Staunton also proved to be a useful keeper!

he became a victim of the rule restricting the number of non-English players at each club. Souness decided unwisely the defender was dispensable and sold him to Aston Villa in August 1991. Staunton subsequently developed into one of the best left-backs in the country.

Once Roy Evans had taken over at Anfield in 1994, Staunton was linked with a return to Liverpool almost every single year. When he finally arrived in July 1998 he had obviously left his best years behind him at Villa. The experienced campaigner was used only

sparingly in Gérard Houllier's first full season in charge in 1999/2000. In the following season, he appeared only twice for the first team, both times as substitute. Two weeks after his final appearance away to Olympiacos in the UEFA Cup, Staunton returned to Villa. His final game as a professional footballer came on New Year's Eve 2005.

IN JANUARY 2006, three days before his 37th birthday, Staunton was surprisingly named as Brian Kerr's successor to manage the Republic of Ireland's full international team. It was quite a

shock because more high-profile candidates had been mentioned and Staunton only had a brief spell as assistant coach at Walsall on his CV. His short-term aim was to ensure qualification for the 2008 European Championship finals. Despite Ireland's failure to qualify Staunton refused to resign, but was finally replaced by Giovanni Trapattoni. Staunton served as Gary McAllister's assistant at Leeds United in 2008 and had a disastrous five-month spell as boss of Darlington, who suffered 26 league defeats in 32 matches.

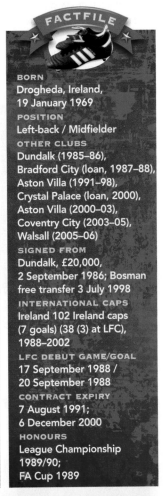

FACTFILE

BORN
Drogheda, Ireland, 19 January 1969
POSITION
Left-back / Midfielder
OTHER CLUBS
Dundalk (1985–86), Bradford City (loan, 1987–88), Aston Villa (1991–98), Crystal Palace (loan, 2000), Aston Villa (2000–03), Coventry City (2003–05), Walsall (2005–06)
SIGNED FROM
Dundalk, £20,000, 2 September 1986; Bosman free transfer 3 July 1998
INTERNATIONAL CAPS
Ireland 102 Ireland caps (7 goals) (38 (3) at LFC), 1988–2002
LFC DEBUT GAME/GOAL
17 September 1988 / 20 September 1988
CONTRACT EXPIRY
7 August 1991; 6 December 2000
HONOURS
League Championship 1989/90; FA Cup 1989

Season	League		FA Cup		League Cup		Europe		Other		Total	
	App	Goals	App	Goals	App	Goals	App	Goals	App	Goals	App	Goals
1988/89	17 (4)	0	3	0	4	0	-	-	1	1	25 (4)	1
1989/90	18 (2)	0	4 (2)	0	0 (2)	3	-	-	0	0	22 (6)	3
1990/91	20 (4)	0	7	1	2	1	-	-	0	0	29 (4)	2
1998/99	31	0	1	0	2	0	5 (1)	0	-	-	39 (1)	0
1999/2000	7 (5)	0	1	0	3	1	-	-	-	-	11 (5)	1
2000/01	0 (1)	0	0	0	0	0	0 (1)	0	-	-	0 (2)	0
Total	**93 (16)**	**0**	**16 (2)**	**1**	**11 (2)**	**5**	**5 (2)**	**0**	**1**	**1**	**126 (22)**	**7**

Steel,
Willie

WILLIE STEEL made his debut at right-back six days before Christmas 1931 in a 1-1 home draw with Derby County. He only missed one league fixture for the rest of the season, was the club's only ever-present a year later and missed just three games in 1933/34.

He lost his place following the arrival of England international Tom Cooper in the 1934/35 season. Evidently his £2,000 transfer to First Division Birmingham City took a number of people by surprise as he had been, according to Liverpool's programme, 'a popular man here, a model professional and a most consistent performer'. Steel was manager of Airdrie in his native Scotland from 1954 to 1963.

Willie Steel on the left with Elisha Scott and James Parson Jackson

Season	League App	League Goals	FA Cup App	FA Cup Goals	Total App	Total Goals
1931/32	22	0	4	0	26	0
1932/33	42	0	1	0	43	0
1933/34	40	0	3	0	43	0
1934/35	16	0	0	0	16	0
Total	**120**	**0**	**8**	**0**	**128**	**0**

Sterling,
Raheem

RAHEEM STERLING joined Liverpool as a 15-year-old from the youth set-up at Queens Park Rangers on 27 February 2010. His family had moved from Jamaica when he was seven, following in the footsteps of another Liverpool legend, John Barnes.

Sterling lacks the physical strength that Barnes had, but he is not afraid of his opponents. 'I was mocked by the crowd at a youth game in Germany once for my height. I've always played above my age group, with bigger guys,' Sterling told the *Daily Mail* in January 2013. 'With the physicality, I had to learn new tricks, learn to outsmart my opponent.' There is a tendency to exaggerate the potential of young promising players like Sterling and the hype machine certainly went into full swing when he scored five goals for Liverpool's youth side in a 9-0 FA Cup win over Southend in February 2011. Following his performance he was included in the club's senior squad that travelled to Prague ahead of their Europa League contest on 17 February 2011. Sterling, who had to have a guardian following him to Prague as he was so young, ultimately didn't make the bench but the experience was valuable. Sterling has strong faith in God and says he gains strength from above. 'When the time is right, I will fully be

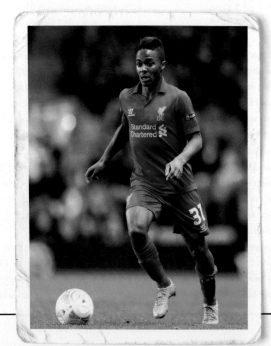

Christian. My mum is a big help, a big influence in that. Faith is an important thing for me. Every match day I put faith in God. It's not part of a pre-match ritual or anything, but I pray at home the day and night before.'

Finally, after much speculation, Sterling made his Liverpool first-team debut when he came on as a late substitute against Wigan Athletic at Anfield in a 2-1 Premier League defeat on 24 March 2012. Two more substitute appearances followed in the end-of-season matches against the west London clubs Fulham and Chelsea. Since Brendan Rodgers took over as boss at Liverpool Sterling has become a vital part of the first-team set-up. His rapid progress earned him a call-up to the England Under-21 team in October and on 14 November 2012, at 17 years and 332 days, he became the fifth-youngest England player in

history when he made his debut against Sweden in Stockholm.

STERLING SIGNED a five-year contract with Liverpool just before Christmas 2012. The 18-year-old made more appearances than expected in the 2012/13 season,

as Liverpool lacked depth in the squad. He has caused opposing teams quite a lot of problems and has felt the consequences. 'It is annoying trying to get to sleep with your legs in pieces. I know I get kicked a lot. I didn't know I was one of the most fouled players in the league. If that's what it takes and we get free kicks, I will take getting the kicks.' Once Daniel Sturridge and Philippe Coutinho arrived in January 2013 Sterling was more sparingly used and then a thigh injury cut his season short. He is still young and has a lot of time to develop as a player.

Season	League		FA Cup		League Cup		Europe		Total	
	App	Goals	App	Goals	App	Goals	App	Goals	App	Goals
2011/12	0 (3)	0	0	0	0	0	-	-	0 (3)	0
2012/13	19 (5)	2	1	0	0 (1)	0	2 (8)	0	22 (14)	2
Total	19 (8)	2	1	0	0 (1)	0	2 (8)	0	22 (17)	2

Stevenson, General

GENERAL STEVENSON'S father must have had a strong affinity with the military, as he named two of his sons General and Admiral.

ON 9 DECEMBER 1897 the *Sheffield Evening Telegraph* announced that 'Mr Tom Watson, on behalf of the Liverpool F.C., has signed on General Stevenson, full back of the Padiham Club, who is considered one of the best backs in the Lancashire Combination, and last season captained the Hapton team when they won the Lancashire Junior

Cup. Both the Blackburn Rovers and Burnley clubs were after him, but he decided to go to Liverpool.' Nearly a year passed before the right-back made his first-team debut. He went on to play 22 games for Liverpool at the end of the 19th century before being replaced by Archie Goldie. Stevenson featured in 318 games at Millwall in the Western League, which the Lions won twice, in 1908 and 1909.

Season	League		FA Cup		Total	
	App	Goals	App	Goals	App	Goals
1898/99	8	0	1	0	9	0
1899/1900	13	0	0	0	13	0
Total	21	0	1	0	22	0

Stevenson, Willie

WILLIE (or 'Billy') Stevenson was the dressing room joker and a big favourite with the Liverpool fans. When Kenny Dalglish went on trial at Liverpool at 15 years of age he became the victim of Stevenson's humour. Dalglish asked for Stevenson's autograph when the players were relaxing in the changing room. 'I went to Billy Stevenson and said: "Would you please sign this, Billy?" He said: "No." As I walked away all the players burst out laughing. Billy was only kidding.'

Stevenson arrived on Merseyside in October 1962 having lost his place in the Rangers line up to legend Jim Baxter. Bill Shankly outbid Preston North End for his services. Stevenson took over the left-half spot from Tommy Leishman. Liverpool consolidated their First Division status after eight years away by finishing eighth and then, with one of the most settled sides in the club's history, took the League Championship a year later.

LIVERPOOL had reached the semi-final of the FA Cup in 1965 and were leading 1-0 against Chelsea with just over ten minutes

to go when the Reds were awarded a penalty. Liverpool had missed six penalties in a row, Tommy Smith and Gordon Milne being the latest culprits, and it would need a brave soul to assume this responsibility. 'Suddenly Billy Stevenson stepped forward. Casually he picked up the ball and placed it on the spot,' said Ian St John, who was impressed by his compatriot's courageousness. 'No one said anything despite the fact that he had never taken a penalty before. With his belief that he was a little bit better than the rest of us, propped up by his liking for fine suits and the best cognac, he might have been saying, "Step aside, you peasants, and let me do the job." No one complained or challenged his decision. It came to him that he couldn't really miss and nor did he.' Liverpool reached the final and the FA Cup finally made its way into Liverpool's trophy cabinet for the first time.

Stevenson was a skilful midfielder with an eye for a sensational pass. He won a second League Championship medal in 1966 but suffered great disappointment when Liverpool lost to Borussia Dortmund in the final of European Cup Winners' Cup at Hampden. 'We should have won that game but on the night we were awful. All us Scots had all our families and friends there,' Stevenson said. 'I was so disappointed that in the shower room I picked up my medal and hurled it through the window.

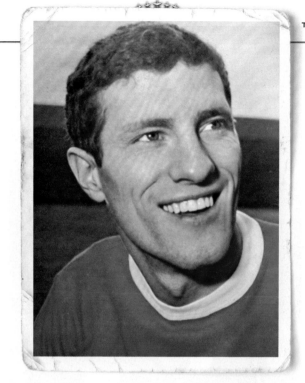

IT MUST have fallen somewhere in the car park below.' *LFChistory.net* asked St John about this incident to which the Saint replied, quick as a flash: 'He spent years looking for that medal!' Stevenson was also a regular member of the side in the first few exciting years of European club competition, which complemented his passing style and poise. When the 1967/68 season opened it was Emlyn Hughes who had taken his place. Stevenson was only picked once more for the first team, in a

home fixture with Wolves on 25 November 1967 in which he scored with a late and decisive penalty. Still only 28 years old, he was far too good a player to be languishing in a reserve team and he accepted Stoke City's offer in December 1967. Stevenson made 82 league appearances for Stoke before returning to Merseyside with Tranmere.

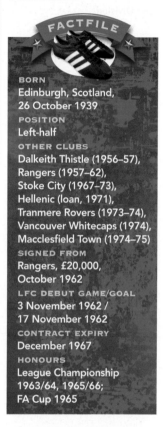

FACTFILE

BORN
Edinburgh, Scotland,
26 October 1939
POSITION
Left-half
OTHER CLUBS
Dalkeith Thistle (1956–57),
Rangers (1957–62),
Stoke City (1967–73),
Hellenic (loan, 1971),
Tranmere Rovers (1973–74),
Vancouver Whitecaps (1974),
Macclesfield Town (1974–75)
SIGNED FROM
Rangers, £20,000,
October 1962
LFC DEBUT GAME/GOAL
3 November 1962 /
17 November 1962
CONTRACT EXPIRY
December 1967
HONOURS
League Championship
1963/64, 1965/66;
FA Cup 1965

Season	League		FA Cup		League Cup		Europe		Other		Total	
	App	Goals	App	Goals	App	Goals	App	Goals	App	Goals	App	Goals
1962/63	28	2	6	0	-	-	-	-	-	-	34	2
1963/64	38	1	5	0	-	-	-	-	-	-	43	1
1964/65	39	3	8	1	-	-	9	1	1	0	57	5
1965/66	41	5	1	0	-	-	9	0	1	1	52	6
1966/67	41	3	4	0	-	-	5	0	1	0	51	3
1967/68	1	1	0	0	0	0	2 (1)	0	-	-	3 (1)	1
Total	**188**	**15**	**24**	**1**	**0**	**0**	**25 (1)**	**1**	**3**	**1**	**240 (1)**	**18**

Stewart, Jimmy

JIMMY STEWART started out on the left flank north of the border but it was as an inside-right forward that the solidly built Scotsman played for Liverpool.

He made his debut on the opening day of the 1909/10 season and only missed one match as the club finished runners-up to First Division champions Aston Villa. Stewart had a wonderful season and was the second-highest scorer with 18 league goals behind the prolific Jack Parkinson with 30.

That debut campaign was easily Stewart's best in a Liverpool shirt. He was only called on a further 25 times over the next four seasons. Stewart was a trainer at Hamilton Academical for nine years before becoming coach at Hearts, Blackpool, Dundee and Portsmouth.

FACTFILE

BORN
Dumbarton, Scotland, 1885
POSITION
Inside-right forward
OTHER CLUBS
Ashfield, Motherwell
(1907–09),
Hamilton Academical
(1914–17),
Dumbarton (1917–18),
Hamilton Academical
(1918–19)
SIGNED FROM
Motherwell, April 1909
LFC DEBUT GAME/GOAL
4 September 1909 /
11 September 1909
CONTRACT EXPIRY
29 January 1914

Season	League		FA Cup		Total	
	App	Goals	App	Goals	App	Goals
1909/10	37	18	1	0	38	18
1910/11	11	4	1	0	12	4
1911/12	6	3	0	0	6	3
1912/13	4	1	0	0	4	1
1913/14	3	0	0	0	3	0
Total	**61**	**26**	**2**	**0**	**63**	**26**

Stewart,
Paul

PAUL STEWART established himself in the lower leagues with Blackpool from 1981 to 1987, earning himself a place in the club's Hall of Fame before joining Manchester City in the First Division.

City were immediately relegated, but Stewart blossomed in his first full season, scoring 24 goals in 40 matches. Tottenham Hotspur brought him back to the top flight, developed Stewart into a midfielder and he gained England recognition. Liverpool clearly rated Stewart highly as they spent £2.3million on the 27-year-old prior to the 1992/93 season. In his first two years at Liverpool Stewart's sluggish demeanour continued to frustrate fans and defy belief. He played as a striker on a few occasions but failed to capture the imagination up front as in the middle of the park. Stewart didn't play a single game in his last two years at Liverpool, being loaned out to other clubs or struggling with injuries.

FACTFILE

BORN
Manchester, 7 October 1964
POSITION
Midfielder / Centre-forward
OTHER CLUBS
Blackpool (1978–87),
Manchester City (1987–88),
Tottenham Hotspur (1988–92),
Crystal Palace (loan, 1994),
Wolverhampton Wanderers
(loan, 1994),
Burnley (loan, 1995),
Sunderland (loan, 1995;
permanent, 1996–97),
Stoke City (1997–98),
Workington (1998–2000)
SIGNED FROM
Tottenham Hotspur,
£2.3million, 29 July 1992
INTERNATIONAL CAPS
3 England caps, 1991–92
LFC DEBUT GAME/GOAL
8 August 1992 /
19 August 1992
CONTRACT EXPIRY
5 March 1996

Season	League		FA Cup		League Cup		Europe		Other		Total	
	App	Goals	App	Goals	App	Goals	App	Goals	App	Goals	App	Goals
1992/93	21 (3)	1	1	0	3	0	2	2	1	0	28 (3)	3
1993/94	7 (1)	0	0	0	3	0	-	-	-	-	10 (1)	0
Total	**28 (4)**	**1**	**1**	**0**	**6**	**0**	**2**	**2**	**1**	**0**	**38 (4)**	**3**

Storer,
Harry

GOALKEEPER Harry Storer starred for Arsenal for 18 months in the Second Division and made 76 appearances before he joined Liverpool at the age of 25 in 1895.

At Liverpool he replaced Matt McQueen, a versatile player who was just as comfortable in goal as he was in an outfield position. The *Liverpool Mercury* liked the look of Storer: 'The new goalkeeper is cool, daring and exceedingly safe with his hands, and these qualities constitute all

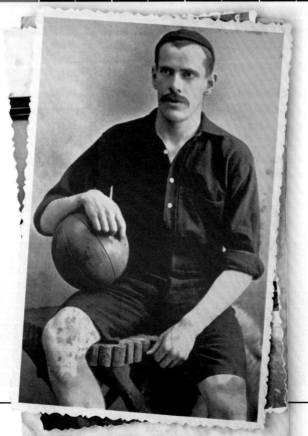

that is best in a first-class goalkeeper.' He played in the last 11 league matches of that season, conceding only eight goals, and helped his new club make a swift return to the First Division. Storer missed only seven of the next 87 league fixtures before McQueen took over again in goal for two games and then Bill Perkins for the last five matches of the 1898/99 season. Storer's absence from the team from late December 1896 to late February 1897 was because he was initially injured, with Willie Donnelly taking his place. But once Storer was fit Liverpool loaned him to Hibernian, whose main keeper was out injured. Hibernian had a cup tie against Rangers coming

up and as 'the Scottish Cup rules provide for little qualification, membership alone enabling a player to be eligible,' as the *Edinburgh Evening News* reported, 'Liverpool have accordingly assisted the Hibernians out of a difficulty.' Despite Storer's presence in Hibs' goal Rangers beat them 3-0.

PERKINS was between the sticks at Liverpool at the start of the 1899/1900 season and although Storer did get a run of 11 successive games during the autumn and into the winter of 1899, it was Perkins who finished the season in goal, signalling the end of the Derbyshire native's

Liverpool career. Storer's only fault in the goal was said to be he got a little careless if he hadn't been busy during the match, though he was far from being the only keeper with that weakness. He would lose concentration and let in an easy goal. Storer augmented his income by running a pub. When he was going to renew his licence in September 1899 it was objected to on the grounds that 'hero-worship attached to professional footballers made it desirable that footballing and public-house management should be disassociated', reported the *Manchester Evening Post*. The chairman of Liverpool Licensing Sessions ruled that Storer was simply providing another means of livelihood for himself and his family when his football career would be over and a renewal was granted. Following the end of his league career Storer kept himself in shape by turning out on occasion for part-timers Holloway in Derbyshire. Harry's brother Bill was a footballer as well and an excellent cricketer who played six Tests for England. Harry was also a good cricketer and played six first-class matches for Derbyshire during the 1895 season. Harry Jnr inherited his father's football and cricket skills, featuring for Derby County and Derbyshire, and later became a football manager in charge of Coventry, Birmingham and Derby in the Second Division and Third Division North from 1931 to 1963. Harry Storer Snr died of consumption aged only 37 on 25 April 1908.

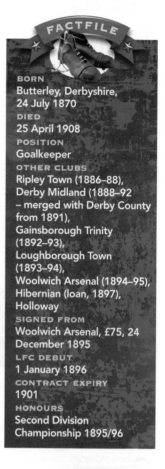

Season	League		FA Cup		Other		Total	
	App	Goals	App	Goals	App	Goals	App	Goals
1895/96	11	0	2	0	4	0	17	0
1896/97	23	0	3	0	-	-	26	0
1897/98	30	0	5	0	-	-	35	0
1898/99	27	0	5	0	-	-	32	0
1899/1900	11	0	0	0	-	-	11	0
Total	**102**	**0**	**15**	**0**	**4**	**0**	**121**	**0**

Storton,
Trevor

TREVOR STORTON was signed from Tranmere Rovers at the start of the 1972/73 season after he had featured in over 100 games for Rovers from 1968.

Bill Shankly was still in the process of rebuilding his team but it was quickly evident that centre-half Storton was not one of the players he expected to be a big part of that. Storton was given his league debut at Leeds at the end of September 1972 but only made another three league appearances that season, and just one the following season before he returned to the lower divisions with Chester for whom he made 468 appearances in all competitions until 1984. 'Trevor Storton was a legend in the true sense of the

word,' his former team-mate, keeper Grenville Millington, told the *Chester Leader*. 'He was a person you didn't mess with. When I got into the Chester team Trevor was an experienced player, but he was always experienced, even when he was young. I always felt safe as a goalkeeper with Trevor in front of me in defence.' Storton was Bradford Park Avenue's manager from 1997 to 2004 and was working as assistant manager at Halifax Town when he was diagnosed with cancer. He passed away on 23 March 2011, at 61 years of age.

Season	League		FA Cup		League Cup		Europe		Total	
	App	Goals	App	Goals	App	Goals	App	Goals	App	Goals
1972/73	4	0	0	0	4	0	1 (1)	0	9 (1)	0
1973/74	1	0	1	0	0	0	0	0	2	0
Total	**5**	**0**	**1**	**0**	**4**	**0**	**1 (1)**	**0**	**11 (1)**	**0**

Stott,
Jimmy

JIMMY STOTT was only at Anfield for one season in 1893/94, but distinguished himself by being the club's top scorer that year, netting 14 goals in just 17 appearances as the club was promoted to the top division at the first time of asking.

He played in 12 of the first 14 games but only made a further five appearances during the second half of the season.

The highlight was a hat-trick in the 6-0 trouncing of Middlesbrough Ironopolis at Anfield in October 1893. Stott was Newcastle United's captain from 1896 to 1898, the club gaining promotion from the Second Division at the end of his captaincy. He made 125 appearances for the Magpies in four years, earning the reputation of being a tough customer on the field. In 1896 he was censured by the Newcastle board for 'continual fouling of his opponent'. Sadly he contracted a brain tumour and died in a 'lunatic asylum' (as a mental institution was so crudely named in those days) on 8 October 1908.

JAMES STOTT
LIVERPOOL

FACTFILE

BORN
Darlington, 6 November 1870
DIED
8 October 1908
POSITION
Inside-left forward
OTHER CLUBS
Cambuslang (1889-90),
South Bank (1890-92),
Middlesbrough (1892-93),
Grimsby Town (1894-95),
Newcastle United (1895-99),
Middlesbrough (1899-1900)
SIGNED FROM
Middlesbrough,
6 August 1893
LFC DEBUT GAME/GOAL
2 September 1893 /
16 September 1893
CONTRACT EXPIRY
29 July 1894
HONOURS
Second Division
Championship 1893/94

Season	League		FA Cup		Other		Total	
	App	Goals	App	Goals	App	Goals	App	Goals
1893/94	15	14	2	0	0	0	17	14
Total	**15**	**14**	**2**	**0**	**0**	**0**	**17**	**14**

Strong,
Geoff

GEOFF STRONG scored 69 goals in 125 league matches for Arsenal so he was an experienced professional when he arrived at Liverpool in November 1964 to replace the seriously injured Alf Arrowsmith. Strong had already scored for Arsenal at Anfield on the opening day of the 1964/65 season.

Strong had been all set to join Aston Villa a week previously, but couldn't agree on personal terms. Shankly used Strong to great effect in many different positions and his versatility was a key part of Liverpool's continued domination of domestic football in the mid-1960s. Ron Yeats was happy with his arrival, as he didn't have to deal with him any more. 'I wasn't surprised Bill Shankly signed him because he used to give me a lot of problems,' Yeats said. A few days after experiencing Shankly's training

KODAK FILM

SHANKLY USED STRONG TO GREAT EFFECT IN MANY DIFFERENT POSITIONS AND HIS VERSATILITY WAS A KEY PART OF LIVERPOOL'S CONTINUED DOMINATION OF DOMESTIC FOOTBALL IN THE MID-1960S

regime Strong was physically sick and complained: 'What have I joined here, a bloody commando course?!' He was in and out of the side during the first half of the season but he did pick up an FA Cup winners' medal when the unlucky left-half Gordon Milne missed the final through injury, and he featured as well in the dramatic European Cup semi-finals against Inter Milan. The fact that Liverpool couldn't find a forward spot for a player

who had scored 31 goals in 46 matches for Arsenal in the previous campaign is a testament to Liverpool's strength in depth up front.

STRONG wasn't much more of a regular the following season either, starting exactly half of the 42 league matches, filling in mostly for Milne again but also up front in Roger Hunt's absence. He produced a moment to remember in the semi-final of the Cup Winners' Cup against Celtic at Anfield when, despite being badly affected by a leg injury, he climbed to meet Ian Callaghan's right-wing centre and head the ball past Ronnie Simpson for the goal that took Liverpool through to the final. 'The cripple has scored!' was perhaps Kenneth Wolstenholme's second most-famous utterance as a commentator. Strong only missed six league matches in 1966/67 as he found a firm place on the left flank, scoring 12 goals. Despite his success he was more in the role of a 'seat-filler' in the following campaign. Gerry Byrne's injuries had caught up with him in 1968, which opened the door initially for Peter Wall, but Strong made the left-back position his own in his last two years at Anfield. Even though he was more of a squad player than a regular in the Liverpool side, Strong was a very popular player and when he led his new team, Coventry City, out at Anfield in November 1970 he received a wonderful ovation from the Liverpool crowd in tribute to the service he had given the club for nearly six years.

Season	League		FA Cup		League Cup		Europe		Other		Total	
	App	Goals	App	Goals	App	Goals	App	Goals	App	Goals	App	Goals
1964/65	13	3	1	0	-	-	2	0	0	0	16	3
1965/66	21 (1)	5	0	0	-	-	4	2	1	0	26 (1)	7
1966/67	36	12	3	0	-	-	5	0	1	0	45	12
1967/68	18 (1)	5	9	1	0	0	1	0	-	-	28 (1)	6
1968/69	28 (3)	2	4	0	2	0	0 (1)	0	-	-	34 (4)	2
1969/70	34	3	6	0	2	0	4	0	-	-	46	3
Total	**150 (5)**	**30**	**23**	**1**	**4**	**0**	**16 (1)**	**2**	**2**	**0**	**195 (6)**	**33**

Stuart, William

Stuart.

WILLIAM STUART made his debut for struggling First Division Liverpool against Manchester City in the middle of the 1911/12 season, when the Reds were close to being relegated.

Stuart scored in a 3-2 win and played in the next four games that were all lost but one. In Liverpool's 3-1 defeat to Everton on 20 January 1912 the *Liverpool Daily Post and Mercury* noted that 'Stuart's methods were admired by many for their grace and cleverness, but he was not an effective force.'

Season	League		FA Cup		Total	
	App	Goals	App	Goals	App	Goals
1911/12	3	1	2	0	5	1
Total	**3**	**1**	**2**	**0**	**5**	**1**

Stubbins, Albert

CENTRE-FORWARD Albert Stubbins was one of Liverpool's most popular players in the period immediately following the end of World War Two and is rightly remembered as a legend at Anfield as well as at Newcastle United.

He scored a record of 244 goals in wartime for Newcastle that included 23 hat-tricks! Everton's and Liverpool's representatives were in United's boardroom, both having offered £1,000 less than the record £14,000, paid by Arsenal to Wolves for Bryn Jones. Stubbins was, however, nowhere to be found. He had evidently gone to the movies so the notice: 'Would Albert Stubbins please report to St James' Park,' was flashed on cinema screens.

He did not realise what was going on until he returned home, whence he took a taxi to his club's home ground where the Merseyside rivals had been waiting almost for four hours.

Stan Seymour, the Newcastle director, said: 'Which representative would you like to see first?' I said: 'Let's flip a coin. Heads Liverpool. Tails Everton.' It came down heads – Liverpool. Bill McConnell, the Liverpool chairman, and George Kay and myself discussed matters and I was impressed with them both, and with the possibilities of Liverpool, so said I would go to Anfield. I also knew several of the Liverpool players at the time like Willie Fagan and Jack Balmer. That probably gave Liverpool the slight edge and in the end I never spoke to Everton because I had been so impressed with Liverpool's offer.

STUBBINS scored on his Reds debut at Bolton and only missed two more league fixtures for the rest of the season as Liverpool won the League Championship. He was equal top scorer at the club with Jack Balmer with 24 goals each. Stubbins scored his most memorable goal against Birmingham on 1 March 1947 in the quarter-finals of the FA Cup, here described by Liverpool's talisman at the time, Billy Liddell. 'When I put the ball over it was going a bit off course, but Stubbins literally threw himself through the air to meet it with his head when parallel with the ground, about two feet above the turf. It went in like a rocket, giving Gil Merrick absolutely no chance, and Albert slid on his stomach for several yards on the frozen pitch before coming to a stop.' Stubbins was, of course, very proud of this astonishing goal that displayed his bravery. 'It was an icy ground and both of my knees were lacerated and bleeding but it was certainly worth it.'

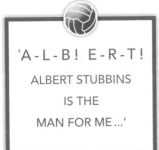

'A-L-B! E-R-T!
ALBERT STUBBINS
IS THE
MAN FOR ME...'

Stubbins again scored 24 league goals in 1947/48, which included four, two in each half, when Huddersfield Town visited Anfield on 6 March 1948, even though he had been threatened before the game. 'On the morning of the match I received a telegram and although I can't remember the exact wording, the general consensus was if I scored, my legs would be broken. I didn't want to worry the rest of the team so I kept it to myself. It was obviously meant to frighten me, but it didn't work. I never did find out who sent it. Perhaps it was George Kay's way of geeing me up!'

The Geordie became embroiled in a contractual dispute with his employers in the 1948/49 season. He had already planned for the future and wanted to become a journalist when his career was over. Chairman Bill McConnell had arranged for him to write a column in the *Football Echo* when he signed his Liverpool contract. 'When Bill died, the board felt they weren't responsible for his promise,' Stubbins told Mark Platt at *LFC Magazine*. There was some confusion and that's why I delayed signing on. It was all very amicable and at no time did the club and myself ever fall out. It was a private matter and that's why so few people knew the real reason behind the dispute. It was widely assumed that my family was unsettled on Merseyside.' Partly because of this dispute and partly because of injury problems, Stubbins only played 18 games that season. Ever the professional, he didn't let his personal feelings affect his commitment to the club that was paying his wages and he again reached double figures in the league in the 1949/50 season despite missing 14 First Division matches and was

Stubbins' incredible goal in the snow against Birmingham

Season	League		FA Cup		Total	
	App	Goals	App	Goals	App	Goals
1946/47	36	24	6	4	42	28
1947/48	40	24	2	2	42	26
1948/49	15	6	3	1	18	7
1949/50	28	10	7	1	35	11
1950/51	23	6	1	0	24	6
1951/52	12	5	0	0	12	5
1952/53	5	0	0	0	5	0
Total	**159**	**75**	**19**	**8**	**178**	**83**

FACTFILE

BORN
Wallsend, 13 July 1919
DIED
28 December 2002
POSITION
Centre-forward
OTHER CLUBS
Whitley & Monkseaton (1934–35),
Sunderland (1935),
Newcastle United (1936–46),
Sunderland (wartime guest),
Ashington (1953–54)
SIGNED FROM
Newcastle United, £13,000, 12 September 1946
LFC DEBUT GAME/GOAL
14 September 1946 / 14 September 1946
CONTRACT EXPIRY
September 1953
HONOURS
League Championship 1946/47

also a member of the team defeated by Arsenal in the 1950 FA Cup final. By now in his early 30s, Stubbins' name was less frequently on Liverpool's teamsheet and the last of the 178 first-team appearances he made for the club came at Stoke on 3 January 1953. He had kept up his record of scoring a goal almost every other game. 'Even if I had a bad game the crowd would never crucify me like they would some players.' Stubbins enjoyed a great following among Reds that was reflected in the formation of 'The Albert Stubbins Crazy Crew', an appreciation society set up by the sons and grandsons of Kopites who adored him. 'My son, Eric, says they'd never have started a fan club if they had seen me play,' Stubbins quipped in an interview with the *Independent* in 1996.

STUBBINS became immortalised when his image was put on the cover of The Beatles' album *Sergeant Pepper's Lonely Hearts Club Band*, looking over the shoulder of Marlene Dietrich. Paul McCartney sent Stubbins the album along with a telegram which read: 'Well done Albert for all those glorious years of football. Long may you bob and weave.'

Manchester City's academy in 2003. Three years later, still only 16 years old, his goals helped City reach the FA Youth Cup final where his brace against Liverpool gave the Blues hope in the second leg as they tried to claw back a three-goal deficit from the first leg at Anfield. Although Liverpool's youngsters took the trophy home after a 3-2 aggregate victory, Sturridge had announced himself as someone to be watched.

However, his opportunities for playing in City's first team were limited and shortly before his 20th birthday he signed a four-year deal with Chelsea. The Londoners won the Premier League title at the end of his first full season, but his contribution was not massive, just one goal from 13 league matches. He was more prominent in the FA Cup that season, netting four times and coming on as a very late substitute at Wembley in the final as Chelsea beat Portsmouth. Halfway through the following season, Sturridge had a very successful loan spell at Bolton Wanderers. Eight goals from 12 appearances was a very creditable goals-per-game ratio, but still wasn't enough to get him a regular starting spot in the Chelsea team under new manager Andre Villas-Boas. The young striker was an unused substitute in both the FA Cup final against Liverpool and the Champions League final against Bayern in Munich, but he did score eleven league goals, including an equaliser at Stamford Bridge against the club who would eventually sign him from Chelsea.

Sturridge only appeared in seven league matches for Chelsea in the first half of the 2012/13 season before he joined Liverpool. He hit the ground running and became the first player since Ray Kennedy in 1974 to score in his first three appearances for Liverpool. Jim Cassell, who was head of Manchester City's academy during Sturridge's time there, hopes the striker will realise his full potential. 'Hopefully Liverpool will get the best from Daniel as he has the potential to be a top-class international striker. Daniel was exceptional, even as a 13-year-old. He had great pace, fantastic feet and magnificent vision. He trained hard, was respectful and always

immaculately turned out – I thought he was great. We knew he could go on and achieve great things.' Sturridge has plenty of skill on the ball, has great vision and is a pleasure to watch. Importantly, he bonded instantly with the team on and off the pitch and his career could finally flourish after showing immense promise at Manchester City and Chelsea.

Sturridge,
Daniel

WITH Liverpool's lack of strikers to support Luis Suarez coming under intense scrutiny during the first half of the 2012/13 season, the name of Daniel Sturridge kept resurfacing as a new transfer window got closer. Having been thwarted in an attempt to sign an adequate replacement or foil for Suarez in the summer, it was clear that the same mistake could not be made twice.

STURRIDGE was born in the Midlands and played at youth level for both Aston Villa and Coventry City before heading north to join

FACTFILE

BORN
Birmingham,
1 September 1989
POSITION
Centre-forward
OTHER CLUBS
Manchester City (2003–09),
Chelsea (2009–13),
Bolton Wanderers
(loan, 2011)
SIGNED FROM
Chelsea, £12million,
2 January 2013
INTERNATIONAL CAPS
6 England caps (1 goal)
(2 (1) at LFC), 2011–
LFC DEBUT GAME/GOAL
6 January 2013 /
6 January 2013

Season	League App	League Goals	FA Cup App	FA Cup Goals	League Cup App	League Cup Goals	Europe App	Europe Goals	Total App	Total Goals
2012/13	11 (3)	10	2	1	0	0	0	0	13 (3)	11
Total	11 (3)	10	2	1	0	0	0	0	13 (3)	11

Suarez,
Luis

'THE PLAYERS in the Premier League are lucky they only have to test themselves against him twice a season,' Steven Gerrard said of Luis Suarez in January 2013 to *Liverpoolfc.com*.

'They should be very glad of that because he's running rings around us every day all year round. We have to put up with it every day. He's a warrior. It's very rare to see in a centre-forward that

mentality – that they never give up and fight for every ball. Even when you are 3-0 up, he's the same. It's kids in the street stuff. He's the same every day in training.'

Luis Alberto Suarez Díaz was born in Salto, the second-most populous city in Uruguay. He was raised by his mother and grandmother and has six siblings, of which three brothers play professional football. Luis began his professional career with Nacional in Montevideo and helped them to win the Primera División in 2005/06 while still a teenager. He credits his girlfriend at the time, Sofia, who is now his wife, for keeping him away from the troublemakers he had been hanging out with and start to apply himself at the age of 14. Inevitably, as with many other promising players from South America, Suarez came to the attention of a number of European clubs and this led to a move to Groningen in Holland when he was still only 19. However, he only had one season in the Dutch Eredivisie at Groningen before big-city club Ajax signed him in August 2007. Suarez's 81 goals from 110 league matches in three and a half seasons at Ajax was a rate that few strikers in world football could match. Inevitably, he became a star on the international stage too.

The way Suarez performed in the 2010 World Cup in South Africa catapulted him to the watching world's attention in a big way. He started all three group matches and scored the only goal of the final group match against Mexico that ensured Uruguay would top Group A. He then scored twice in a 3-0 victory over South Korea that led to a quarter-final with Ghana. Unfortunately, Suarez then received much negative publicity for a deliberate handball that led to a penalty (which was missed) and a red card that ruled him out of the World Cup semi-final with the Netherlands.

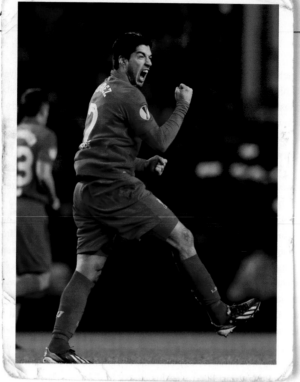

Not long after he became one of only a handful of players to score a century of first-team goals for Ajax his club punished him with a two-match ban and a heavy fine after he had bitten PSV Eindhoven's Ottman Bakkal. The Dutch Football Association extended this ban to cover seven Eredivisie matches. This controversial incident led to much speculation that the Ajax captain's time in Holland was coming to an end. Liverpool had scored only 31 times from their opening 24 league matches of the 2010/11 season and Suarez had already proved that he could make the transition from one continent to another as a 19-year old.

SUAREZ was an instant hit at Anfield, scoring from an almost impossible angle at Sunderland, and his performances in the convincing home win over Manchester United in March and the away thrashing of Fulham in May were mesmeric. Suarez had a sensational Copa America in the summer of 2011. In six matches he had 16 shots at goal, eight on target, resulting in four goals, including the opening goal of the final against Paraguay. Uruguay won the Copa America and Suarez was named the best player

of the tournament. The first full season in English football for Luis Suarez could hardly be described as trouble-free. Although his goals-per-game ratio was good and his technical brilliance was there for all to see, he missed eight matches in the middle of the season after being found guilty of racially abusing Manchester United defender Patrice Evra during the Anfield league meeting in the middle of October. In the return fixture at Old Trafford, the pair avoided shaking each other's hand and that inevitably led to more headlines and constant abuse from opposing supporters, not that it really affected the level of his performance – it seemed to spur him on.

'What matters most to me is my family, playing for Liverpool, the Liverpool fans and the team,' Suarez told the *Daily Mail*. 'Anything else that goes on is not my problem. I don't read the papers or watch TV. But I also know that if they boo me, it's not only because of anything I've supposedly done, but also because they're afraid, because they know I'm a player who is a threat to their team.'

On some days Suarez was practically unplayable but on others he seemed to spend a lot of time moaning and falling over. His close control and quick-footed brilliance far outweighed the bad, the sort of brilliance that enabled him to score a number of stunning goals, especially the first of his League Cup brace at Stoke in October and the third of his amazing hat-trick at Norwich in April. When Suarez returned to Melwood following Uruguay's elimination from the 2012 Olympic Games football tournament, he quickly signed a new long-term contract.

Suarez didn't waste time in validating his boss's superlative description of his powers as he scored a hat-trick at Carrow Road for the second consecutive season. He had been criticised in the past for being wasteful with his plethora of chances, but now they were going in left, right and

centre; he reached the 20-goal mark by January. Suarez had also clearly been told not to dive, and complained a lot less to officials, saving his energy to do what he does best. The swallow-dive celebration in front of David Moyes at Goodison Park, however, after he had scored in the Merseyside derby in October, was a perfect riposte to the Everton manager's complaints of his diving prior to the game. Suarez scored a breathtaking goal against Newcastle when he balanced a long pass from Jose Enrique before slotting it past the keeper. Undoubtedly one of the best goals ever seen at Anfield. If you take away Suarez's fantastic enthusiasm you wouldn't have half the player, but this flawed genius has a temperamental issue he has to deal with. Suarez came second in the vote for the PFA's Player of the Year award and rebuilt his reputation as he scored a total of 30 goals for Liverpool in the 2012/13 season. He threw it all away in a moment of madness on 21 April 2013 when, in a match against Chelsea he bit Branislav Ivanovic in the arm in front of the Kop, which resulted in a 10-game ban from the FA. Liverpool resolved to stick by him as he was a key player for their future, but this proved to be a shameful final chapter in his otherwise magnificent campaign for the Reds.

FACTFILE

BORN
Salto, Uruguay,
24 January 1987
POSITION
Centre-forward
OTHER CLUBS
Nacional (2003–06),
Groningen (2006–07),
Ajax (2007–11)
SIGNED FROM
Ajax, £22.8million,
31 January 2011
INTERNATIONAL CAPS
69 Uruguay caps (32 goals)
(30 (19) at LFC), 2007–
LFC DEBUT GAME/GOAL
2 February 2011 /
2 February 2011
HONOURS
League Cup 2012

Season	League		FA Cup		League Cup		Europe		Total	
	App	Goals	App	Goals	App	Goals	App	Goals	App	Goals
2010/11	12 (1)	4	0	0	0	0	0	0	12 (1)	4
2011/12	29 (2)	11	4	3	4	3	-	-	37 (2)	17
2012/13	33	23	1 (1)	2	0 (1)	1	6 (2)	4	40 (4)	30
Total	**74 (3)**	**38**	**5 (1)**	**5**	**4 (1)**	**4**	**6 (2)**	**4**	**89 (7)**	**51**

Suso

JESÚS Joaquín Fernández Sáez de la Torre, or simply 'Suso', showed exceptional promise as a youngster but refused to consider moving away from his home-town club Cadiz until he was in his mid-teens. He had once been on the first-team's bench at only 15 when Cadiz played Real Madrid and ended up with David Beckham's shirt.

Spanish giants Real Madrid and Barcelona were both monitoring his progress and it seemed that the club from the capital would be successful, as Real was Suso's favourite team, until a telephone call from Rafa Benítez persuaded him to consider England as an alternative destination. Although Benítez left his post as manager in June 2010, he made sure that the 16-year-old had agreed to join Liverpool before he departed. The Cadiz manager described his protégé as 'a boy with great quality, a good shot, his vision is great and his passing is outstanding', and once the backroom staff at Liverpool could see evidence for themselves Suso was fast-tracked to the reserve team, bypassing the club's Academy. He was

immediately successful at the level that had been chosen for him, scoring regularly for the reserves in addition to making a number of appearances in the NextGen competition. Kenny Dalglish didn't bring Suso into his first-team picture as expected and the youngster came close to leaving. Ulsterman Brendan Rodgers, however, decided to take Suso on the club's pre-season tour of North America and he ultimately made his full debut as part of the team that won a thrilling Europa League match in Switzerland in September 2012. The 18-year-old signed a new long-term contract with the club in October 2012. Rodgers was delighted with his progress. 'At 18, he has demonstrated outstanding technical qualities but also shown

very good temperament to play for such a prestigious club.' Suso has represented Spain at different youth levels and started all five matches in the 2012 European Under-19 Championships in Estonia, which Spain won by defeating Greece 1-0 in the final in Tallinn. He made his Under-21 international debut against Italy on 14 November 2012. Suso joined La Liga newcomers, Almeria, on a season-long loan deal in 2013/14.

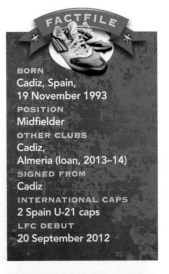

FACTFILE
BORN Cadiz, Spain, 19 November 1993
POSITION Midfielder
OTHER CLUBS Cadiz, Almeria (loan, 2013–14)
SIGNED FROM Cadiz
INTERNATIONAL CAPS 2 Spain U-21 caps
LFC DEBUT 20 September 2012

Season	League App	League Goals	FA Cup App	FA Cup Goals	League Cup App	League Cup Goals	Europe App	Europe Goals	Total App	Total Goals
2012/13	8 (6)	0	1	0	0 (1)	0	3 (1)	0	12 (8)	0
Total	8 (6)	0	1	0	0 (1)	0	3 (1)	0	12 (8)	0

Shankly's men at Lime Street station in 1971 on their way to London to play in the FA Cup final

Liverpool signing the Championship brochure at Lewis's in 1964

Tanner, Nick

BRISTOLIAN Nick Tanner joined a club that had just won its seventeenth League Championship. He finally made his competitive debut for the Reds, as a central defender, in an away match with Manchester City 18 months after joining Liverpool.

He figured in three more First Division matches that Championship-winning season. At a time when only two substitutes could be named, Tanner made Liverpool's bench just three times in 1990/91 but his career was revived by a change of manager

when Graeme Souness was appointed to replace Kenny Dalglish. With Alan Hansen now retired and Gary Gillespie moving to Glasgow Celtic, Tanner played from the start in 32 of 42 First Division games. In the 20th of those matches he scored his only Liverpool goal, a close-range effort at Goodison Park that crept over the line despite the claims of Everton defenders that it had not.

TANNER only made 10 appearances in the 1992/93 season in a turbulent time at Anfield when big questions were asked about Souness's style of management. Unfortunately, a persistent back problem forced Tanner into early retirement as a player in 1994. This must have been a huge disappointment for

someone who was still 'the right side of 30'. Tanner told *LFChistory.net* that he is proud of his time at Liverpool. 'I only cost £20,000! I can honestly say I did my best in every game and feel I gave good value for money at a very difficult time for the club.'

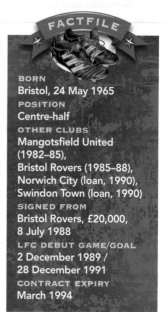

Season	League		FA Cup		League Cup		Europe		Other		Total	
	App	Goals	App	Goals	App	Goals	App	Goals	App	Goals	App	Goals
1989/90	2 (2)	0	0	0	0	0	-	-	0	0	2 (2)	0
1991/92	32	1	2	0	5	0	5 (1)	0	-	-	44 (1)	1
1992/93	2 (2)	0	0	0	1 (2)	0	1 (1)	0	1	0	5 (5)	0
Total	**36 (4)**	**1**	**2**	**0**	**6 (2)**	**0**	**6 (2)**	**0**	**1**	**0**	**51 (8)**	**1**

Taylor, Harold

HAROLD TAYLOR
LIVERPOOL

HAROLD TAYLOR was purchased by the club in 1932 after he had completed his best season at Stoke, scoring nine goals in 17 league matches as the Potters finished third in the Second Division.

In five seasons during the 1930s Taylor made 70 league appearances out of a possible 210 for Liverpool. Taylor usually played in the forward line but in his first campaign he was used as a left-half as legend Jimmy McDougall was absent during the second part of the

season in which Liverpool struggled. These were mediocre times for the club when the team was far from settled and only once during his five years on Liverpool's books did they finish in the top half of the table, when they were seventh in 1935. Taylor only

scored six goals for Liverpool, one of which came in the highest-scoring Merseyside derby ever; a 7-4 victory on 11 February 1933.

Season	League		FA Cup		Total	
	App	Goals	App	Goals	App	Goals
1932/33	22	2	0	0	22	2
1933/34	19	3	2	0	21	3
1934/35	14	1	0	0	14	1
1935/36	14	0	0	0	14	0
1936/37	1	0	0	0	1	0
Total	**70**	**6**	**2**	**0**	**72**	**6**

Taylor, Phil

A PROMISING forward converted into a classy right-half who took over the captaincy from Jack Balmer in the 1949/50 season, Phil Taylor harboured ambitions to become a county cricketer if his football career didn't work out.

HE PLAYED for his home-town club Bristol Rovers before joining Liverpool in March 1936. Taylor scored a last-minute goal at Derby on his debut on 28 March 1936 to save a point in a 2-2 draw and made a further six First Division appearances before the season closed, also netting against Blackburn Rovers. Liverpool finished in 19th place that year but had climbed to mid-table respectability by the end of the decade as World War Two drew ever closer. Liverpool won the first post-war League Championship and Taylor, by now approaching his peak at 29 years old, played in 35 of the 42 league matches and made three appearances for the England team in the autumn of 1947.

'It was a very different world back then for a player,' Taylor noted in Alan A'Court's autobiography. 'When I first played for Liverpool we didn't even have our own training ground, because the club didn't buy Melwood from St Francis Xavier School until the early '50s. Most of our training on Tuesday, Wednesday and Thursday consisted of running with virtually no work on individual skills or team tactics at all. I think a modern player would have ten fits wearing the kind of boots we wore. Ours were so heavy, with solid toecaps that could murder you if you were kicked. I can remember sitting with my boots in a tub of water, so they would shrink to fit my feet.'

TAYLOR would continue to be a key member of the team for the next four years. He captained Liverpool through their run to the club's first ever Wembley Cup final in 1950. Once he had passed his 30th birthday, Taylor was selected less frequently. He remained at Anfield when he retired as a player in 1954, serving as chief coach before he replaced Don Welsh as manager in May 1956 on a temporary basis, before signing a long-term contract a year later.

Taylor found the pressure of getting Liverpool back into the top division almost intolerable, which eventually led to his resignation in November 1959. A terrible FA Cup defeat at non-league Worcester City earlier in the year had enraged the fans. When none of the five league fixtures Liverpool played in October 1959 were won, his position at the club was no longer tenable. It was over 23 years since he had first arrived at Anfield as an 18-year-old player. A sorrowful Phil Taylor spoke to the *Liverpool Daily Post* about his decision: 'No matter how great has been the disappointment of the directors at our failure to win our way back to the First Division, it has not been greater than mine. I made it my goal. I set my heart on it and strove for it with all the energy I could muster.' He later reflected on his time in the hot seat in Alan A'Court's autobiography published in 2003.

Looking back, one of the biggest differences with today was the position of the manager. At that time, teams at almost all clubs were picked by the board of directors, though they usually did ask the advice of the secretary or coach. I know both Don Welsh and myself had to present our teams to full board meetings, often involving eight or nine directors. If you had been winning, the directors were unlikely to object to your team, but it was much harder when you wanted to make changes, and I can remember times when the side that ran out was not really the one I had wanted to play. I was probably not a strong enough personality to be a good manager, because you really need to insist on being in charge if you are going to be successful.

Taylor passed away on 1 December 2012, aged 95.

As a Player

Season	League App	League Goals	FA Cup App	FA Cup Goals	Total App	Total Goals
1935/36	7	2	0	0	7	2
1936/37	14	3	0	0	14	3
1937/38	29	6	5	0	34	6
1938/39	39	14	3	0	42	14
1945/46	-	-	1	0	1	0
1946/47	35	1	6	0	41	1
1947/48	34	0	2	0	36	0
1948/49	30	1	4	0	34	1
1949/50	37	0	7	0	44	0
1950/51	36	2	0	0	36	2
1951/52	24	1	2	0	26	1
1952/53	21	2	0	0	21	2
1953/54	6	0	1	0	7	0
Total	**312**	**32**	**31**	**0**	**343**	**32**

As a Manager

Season	Division	P	W	D	L	GF	GA	Pts	Pos	Win %	FA Cup
1956/57	2nd Division	42	21	11	10	82	54	53	3	50.00	3rd Round
1957/58	2nd Division	42	22	10	10	79	54	54	4	52.38	6th Round
1958/59	2nd Division	42	24	5	13	87	62	53	4	57.14	3rd Round
1959/60*	2nd Division	17	6	5	6	35	31	17	11	35.29	-
Total	**-**	**143**	**73**	**31**	**39**	**283**	**201**	**177**	**-**	**51.05**	**-**

* Taylor resigned on 17 November 1959 with Liverpool in 11th position

FACTFILE

BORN
Bristol, 18 September 1917
DIED
1 December 2012
POSITION
Right-half /
Inside-right forward
OTHER CLUBS
Bristol Rovers (1932–36);
Bristol Rovers,
Brighton & Hove Albion,
Newcastle United,
Leeds United (wartime guest)
SIGNED FROM
Bristol Rovers, £5,000 plus
Ted Hartill, March 1936
APPOINTED MANAGER
15 May 1956
INTERNATIONAL CAPS
3 England caps, 1947
LFC DEBUT GAME/GOAL
28 March 1936 /
28 March 1936
FIRST GAME AS MANAGER
18 August 1956
CONTRACT EXPIRY
17 November 1959
HONOURS
League Championship
1946/47

Team of the Macs

WHEN John McKenna secured players for the newly formed Liverpool Football Club he searched high and low in Scotland, where there was a plenty of talent and, more importantly, it came cheap.

THE MOST common XI that season were all Scotsmen: Sidney Ross, Andrew Hannah, Duncan McLean, John McCartney, Joe McQue, Jim McBride, Matt McQueen, Tom Wyllie, Malcolm McVean, John Miller and Hugh McQueen.
The team, originally known as 'The Anfielders', came to be known as 'Team of the Macs'. McKenna probably encountered similar problems as his successor

LIVERPOOL FOOTBALL CLUB
SEASON 1892-93

J.McQUE J.McCARTNEY A.HANNAH S.H.ROSS M.McQUEEN D.McLEAN J.McBRIDE A.PICK [TRAINER]
T.WYLLIE J.SMITH J.MILLER M.McVEAN H.McQUEEN

at Liverpool, Tom Watson, did when he was obtaining new recruits north of the border around the same time for the Newcastle clubs and Sunderland. Three years after joining Liverpool Watson gave readers of the *Leicester Chronicle* and the *Leicestershire Mercury* an invaluable glimpse into the inner workings of being a football secretary in the late 19th century. '"My Hunting for Men" has been that of a football secretary anxious to secure the best kickers for his club. Then it meant forays into Scotland, conducted at the risk, if not of life, at any rate of limb. The English football agent was received pretty much as an English army of invasion used to be received in the olden times, for the Scots were thoroughly roused against the poaching of their best football players by southern clubs, and they were not sparing of the horse-pond or rotten eggs when they caught the hated Sassenach poacher.'

This Is Anfield

THE 'THIS IS ANFIELD' sign hangs above the stairs that lead down from the dressing rooms to the Anfield pitch as Bill Shankly wanted to remind the men in red shirts who they were playing for and also remind the opposition who they were playing against. 'Our maintenance foreman, Bert Johnson, had it painted, white letters on a red background: THIS IS ANFIELD. A form of intimidation,' Shankly wrote in his autobiography. He encouraged his players to touch the sign as they walked down those steps. This tradition has continued through the ensuing decades.

LIVERPOOL faced Newcastle in the first game after the 'This Is Anfield' sign was put up, on 18 March 1972. "We see we are in the right place, boss", Malcolm 'Supermac' Macdonald told his boss, Joe Harvey, when the Newcastle players were in the passageway. Shankly, quick as a flash, quipped: "You'll soon find out, son, when you get on that pitch." Liverpool beat Newcastle 5-0! Shankly later said: 'Malcolm Macdonald took it very well. He was quoted in the papers as saying how quickly I had replied to what he said before the game.'

Newcastle United weren't the only visiting team to be affected by having to walk past that sign

Tennant, Jack

JACK TENNANT spent four years at Second Division Stoke, only making one appearance before he was released on a free transfer to Torquay United.

He was ever-present at right-back in his only campaign at Torquay in the Third Division and made his

debut for Liverpool in the autumn of the 1933/34 season. Ernie Blenkinsop started 1934/35 as first-choice left-back but his cartilage injury opened up a spot for Tennant, who moved to the opposite side and played for the remaining 26 games of the season.

WHEN Blenkinsop got injured again at the turn of the year Tennant must have expected to deputise again but the speedy full-back was sold to Bolton, where he helped consolidate the newcomer's place in the First Division. He made a total of 105 appearances for the Trotters before the outbreak of World War Two. Tennant was later a guest player for Liverpool during the war.

FACTFILE

BORN
Newcastle-upon-Tyne,
3 August 1907
DIED
1978
POSITION
Left-back
OTHER CLUBS
Washington Colliery,
Newcastle United (1926–27),
Washington Colliery (1927),
Stoke City (1927–32),
Torquay United (1932–33),
Bolton Wanderers (1936–38),
Stoke City (1938–46);
Wrexham, Liverpool,
Southport (wartime guest)
SIGNED FROM
Torquay United, May 1933
LFC DEBUT
9 September 1933
CONTRACT EXPIRY
2 January 1936

Season	League		FA Cup		Total	
	App	Goals	App	Goals	App	Goals
1933/34	13	0	1	0	14	0
1934/35	26	0	2	0	28	0
Total	39	0	3	0	42	0

as they made their way onto the pitch. In the last four seasons of Shankly's reign as manager, Liverpool played 84 home matches in the First Division, winning 63, drawing 18 and losing just three. Many teams were beaten in their heads even before the match began. It wasn't a question of 'Can we win here today?' It was a question of 'How many might we lose by today?' A total of 157 goals

scored compared to only 56 conceded in those four years showed the power of Anfield, the Kop and perhaps that sign. The figures prove that Anfield was indeed a most intimidating venue for the visiting team.

THOUSANDS of players and many fans touched the original sign until eventually it was replaced as it was slightly damaged. It now resides in a hotel on the Isle of Man. The fourth version of the This is Anfield sign had been in use since 1998 when Brendan Rodgers arrived at the club in the summer of 2012. Shortly before Rodgers' arrival, the curator of the Liverpool museum, Stephen Done, had tracked down the whereabouts of the second sign that was in the possession of one of the publishing and advertising agencies that the club dealt with. So, only a month after Rodgers' appointment the oldest surviving intact 'This Is Anfield' sign was restored

to its rightful place in the tunnel. 'When you come into a football club, you need to have a real sense of the past, a sense of the present and a sense of the future,' Rodgers said on this occasion. 'And the nostalgia around this football club is immense. We're very much in the modern era but I think it's very important to remember the great past of this football club and the "This Is Anfield" sign is a massive part of that.'

Thomas,
Michael

MANY Liverpool fans got the shock of a lifetime when Michael Thomas, the Arsenal player who ruined the club's title dreams in the most dramatic fashion possible in May 1989, joined the Reds in 1991. If you ever wanted to run on to Anfield and rugby-tackle somebody as a last resort it was when Thomas slipped past the Liverpool defence in the very last minute to secure the League Championship for the Gunners.

FACTFILE

BORN
Lambeth, 24 August 1967
POSITION
Midfielder / Right-back
OTHER CLUBS
Arsenal (1982–91),
Portsmouth (loan, 1986–87),
Middlesbrough (loan, 1998),
Benfica (1998–2000),
Wimbledon (2000–01)
SIGNED FROM
Arsenal, £1.5million,
16 December 1991
INTERNATIONAL CAPS
2 England caps, 1988–89
LFC DEBUT GAME/GOAL
18 December 1991 /
18 January 1992
CONTRACT EXPIRY
1 August 1998
HONOURS
FA Cup 1992;
League Cup 1995

> IF YOU EVER WANTED TO RUN ON TO ANFIELD AND RUGBY-TACKLE SOMEBODY AS A LAST RESORT IT WAS WHEN THOMAS SLIPPED PAST THE LIVERPOOL DEFENCE IN THE VERY LAST MINUTE TO SECURE THE LEAGUE CHAMPIONSHIP FOR THE GUNNERS

A DREAM come true for Thomas who had joined Arsenal as a schoolboy in 1982. After making over 200 appearances for the Gunners, the unthinkable happened. Thomas joined Liverpool who suffered at his hands two and half years previously. 'I was born and bred in London and I think anybody who's scored the winning goal against any team that cost them the Championship would be

apprehensive joining that team,' Thomas told *LFChistory.net*. 'I was surprised that Liverpool came in for me. At the time I didn't want to stay in England. I wanted to go to Italy or Spain but George Graham wouldn't let me go. Liverpool consistently wanted me to come to the club. In the end, why would I turn down a great club like Liverpool?' Thomas made some amends when he scored a fantastic goal for Liverpool in the 2-0 win over Sunderland in the FA Cup final at the end of his first season. He also provided the killer pass for Liverpool's second in the 67th minute, scored by Ian Rush. Graeme Souness liked his versatility, as Thomas was able to play as a right-back or a midfielder. His Liverpool career came to a halt when he snapped his Achilles tendon in January 1993 and was effectively out for a season and a half. Thomas played 29 games in the 1994/95 season in an improving Liverpool side under the management of Roy Evans. Liverpool won the League Cup by

beating Bolton but unfortunately for Thomas he sat firmly on the bench during the final. Thomas' best season at Liverpool was in 1996/97, when he displayed his box-to-box athleticism and played a holding role in midfield, allowing Barnes the freedom to attack and there was even talk of an England recall for Thomas, who featured twice for his country while at Arsenal. Thomas lost his place in the team to Øyvind Leonhardsen in the 1997/98 season and rejoined Souness at Benfica in August 1998.

Season	League		FA Cup		League Cup		Europe		Other		Total	
	App	Goals	App	Goals	App	Goals	App	Goals	App	Goals	App	Goals
1991/92	16 (1)	3	5	2	0	0	0	0	-	-	21 (1)	5
1992/93	6 (2)	1	2	0	1	0	2	0	0	0	11 (2)	1
1993/94	1 (6)	0	0	0	0	0	0	0	-	-	1 (6)	0
1994/95	16 (7)	0	2 (1)	0	1 (2)	0	0	0	-	-	19 (10)	0
1995/96	18 (9)	1	5 (1)	0	0 (1)	1	2 (1)	0	-	-	25 (12)	2
1996/97	29 (2)	3	1	0	4	0	5 (1)	0	-	-	39 (3)	3
1997/98	10 (1)	1	0	0	1	0	1	0	-	-	12 (1)	1
Total	**96 (28)**	**9**	**15 (2)**	**2**	**7 (3)**	**1**	**10 (2)**	**0**	**0**	**0**	**128 (35)**	**12**

Thompson, Charlie

SOUTH AFRICAN Charlie Thompson made five league appearances and one in the FA Cup for Liverpool in the early-1930s. His league debut came in a goalless draw against Newcastle at Anfield on 21 April 1930 as a replacement for Tom Bromilow at centre-half.

He featured in in five consecutive games in the 1930/31 season, filling in for Tom Morrison at right-half and Jimmy McDougall on the left. The final appearance of Thompson's brief Liverpool career was a 2-1 defeat at Huddersfield on 17 January 1931.

FACTFILE

BORN
Johannesburg, South Africa,
April 1909
DIED
1979
POSITION
Half-back
OTHER CLUBS
Wallsend (1926–29),
Blackpool (1931–32),
Barrow (1932–33)
SIGNED FROM
Wallsend, May 1929
LFC DEBUT
21 April 1930
CONTRACT EXPIRY
1931

Season	League		FA Cup		Total	
	App	Goals	App	Goals	App	Goals
1929/30	1	0	0	0	1	0
1930/31	4	0	1	0	5	0
Total	5	0	1	0	6	0

Thompson, David

DAVID THOMPSON, a tenacious winger, was a favourite among the Liverpool crowd as he was a local boy always willing to give 100 per cent. The diminutive terrier made two starts in a row in November 1998 as Roy Evans departed Liverpool leaving Gérard Houllier in sole charge.

In January 1999 Thompson was sent off in a reserve game against Blackburn and following a row with Houllier was sent to train with the kids at the Academy for two weeks. Three months later Fowler's six-game suspension forced Houllier's hand and as Steve McManaman was pushed up front to fill the void Thompson made three consecutive starts on the right wing. Houllier made wholesale changes to the squad in the summer of 1999 but thankfully for Thompson he was very much

involved and enjoyed his best run in the side. He contributed to the scoring, netting the winner against Chelsea in October. In the 4-1 win over Sheffield Wednesday, mostly noted for Steven Gerrard's debut goal, Thompson rounded off a brilliant solo run with a left-foot shot that floated into the far corner.

More trouble was, however, around the corner. In January 2000 Thompson was sent off again while playing for the reserves for punching Leeds United's David Hopkin in an off-the-ball incident. 'If he wants to make it at the top he has got to control himself, I'm very angry,' Houllier told the *Liverpool Daily Post*.

THOMPSON was sold to Coventry City before the start of the 2000/01 season as Houllier's

revolution continued apace. When Markus Babbel was loaned to Blackburn Rovers in 2003 Thompson quipped: 'Once you fall out with the Liverpool manager, you're finished at the club,' to which Houllier replied: 'I'm glad David Thompson is not at the club any more.' Ironically the Liverpool team was crying out for years following Thompson's departure for a player similar to his style who was able to run the length of the field. In August 2002 Thompson was given the opportunity to re-establish himself in the Premier League with Blackburn Rovers. He even earned himself a call-up to the England squad in October 2002 but unfortunately had to withdraw through injury. Thompson never reached the same heights again after the 2002/03 season and towards the end of 2007 he retired from football because of constant injury problems, particularly to his cartilage.

FACTFILE

BORN
Birkenhead,
12 September 1977
POSITION
Right-winger
OTHER CLUBS
Swindon Town (loan, 1997–98),
Coventry City (2000–02),
Blackburn Rovers (2002–06),
Wigan Athletic (2006),
Portsmouth (2006–07),
Bolton Wanderers (2007)
JOINED
1992; signed professional
8 November 1994
INTERNATIONAL CAPS
7 England U-21 caps
LFC DEBUT GAME/GOAL
19 August 1996 /
13 April 1998
CONTRACT EXPIRY
3 August 2000

Season	League		FA Cup		League Cup		Europe		Total	
	App	Goals	App	Goals	App	Goals	App	Goals	App	Goals
1996/97	0 (2)	0	0	0	0	0	0	0	0 (2)	0
1997/98	1 (4)	1	0	0	0	0	0	0	1 (4)	1
1998/99	4 (10)	1	0	0	2	0	2	0	8 (10)	1
1999/2000	19 (8)	3	0 (1)	0	3	0	-	-	22 (9)	3
Total	24 (24)	5	0 (1)	0	5	0	2	0	31 (25)	5

Thompson, Max

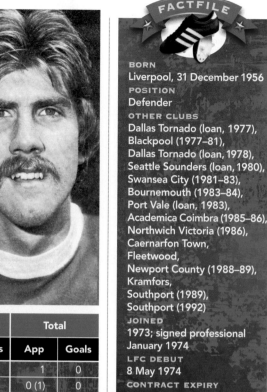

IN 1974 Max Thompson was the second youngest player ever to feature for Liverpool's first team, at 17 years and 129 days, 83 days older than John McFarlane who made his debut in 1929.

THOMPSON came in for John Toshack in the final league fixture of the season in an otherwise unchanged team that had trounced Newcastle at Wembley four days earlier. Liverpool fans did not suspect then, that this would be the last time Bill Shankly ever picked a team to play a league match. Thompson made a brief appearance against Real Sociedad in the 1975/76 UEFA Cup, which turned out to be his last game for the club. He left Anfield for Blackpool in December 1977 after spending the summer on loan at Dallas Tornado in the NASL. Thompson played for a variety of teams in many countries such as the USA, Portugal and Sweden. He returned to Liverpool Football Club as a physiotherapist in the 1990s.

FACTFILE

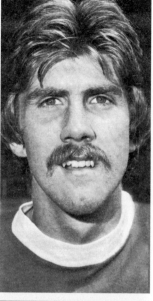

BORN
Liverpool, 31 December 1956
POSITION
Defender
OTHER CLUBS
Dallas Tornado (loan, 1977),
Blackpool (1977–81),
Dallas Tornado (loan, 1978),
Seattle Sounders (loan, 1980),
Swansea City (1981–83),
Bournemouth (1983–84),
Port Vale (loan, 1983),
Academica Coimbra (1985–86),
Northwich Victoria (1986),
Caernarfon Town,
Fleetwood,
Newport County (1988–89),
Kramfors,
Southport (1989),
Southport (1992)
JOINED
1973; signed professional
January 1974
LFC DEBUT
8 May 1974
CONTRACT EXPIRY
December 1977

Season	League		FA Cup		League Cup		Europe		Total	
	App	Goals	App	Goals	App	Goals	App	Goals	App	Goals
1973/74	1	0	0	0	0	0	0	0	1	0
1975/76	0	0	0	0	0	0	0 (1)	0	0 (1)	0
Total	**1**	**0**	**0**	**0**	**0**	**0**	**0 (1)**	**0**	**1 (1)**	**0**

Thompson, Peter

PETER THOMPSON was the great schoolboy star of his day and was pursued by almost every top club in the country when the time came for him to leave school.

He became a regular First Division player at 17 for Preston, making his debut against Arsenal on 30 August 1960. Chairman Nat Buck was one of the many who raved about him. 'I've lost count of the number of clubs who want him, but how could we sell?' England manager Walter Winterbottom was another fan of his natural instincts on the football field. 'Those who have seen the boy pressed me to watch him and I was tremendously impressed with both his skill and maturity. He had so much of Finney about him and seems certain to go straight to the top.'

Bill Shankly had been impressed by the speed and trickery of the young winger during a marathon fifth round FA Cup tie between Liverpool and Preston in February 1962 which went to a second replay at Old Trafford. After two goalless draws the deadlock was finally broken by Thompson when the ball fell invitingly for him and he hit it straight back past keeper Bert Slater to claim a famous win. Thompson was a regular for three seasons at Preston before he moved to Liverpool for £37,000. He almost messed up his transfer to the Reds when he was given the pen to sign his contract in Shankly's office, as he told *LFChistory.net*. "Actually, Mr Shankly, I would like a signing-on fee," I said. "You what? I am giving you the chance to play in the greatest city in the greatest team that is going to be in the world and you want illegal money. Get out!" "Give me the pen," I said. So I signed. Best thing I ever did.'

The Preston lad was an amazing right-footed left-winger, who tormented full-backs having spent countless hours on the training ground perfecting crossing with his left. Which way was Tommo going to go? His opponents didn't have a clue and most of the time his team-mates didn't know what to expect either. Liverpool was envied by other teams for possessing such a powerful pairing on opposing flanks as Thompson and Callaghan.

THOMPSON went straight into Liverpool's first team on his arrival and he played in all 42 league games as the club won the

title by four points. He won another championship medal in 1966 as well being part of the first Liverpool team to win the FA Cup the year before. Thompson came to Alf Ramsey's attention and would surely have won more than just 16 caps had the then England boss not decided to axe traditional wing-play in favour of his own tactics. Who can argue with him after England's World Cup win in 1966? Thompson was desperately unlucky at international level, first in 1966 and then again in 1970, being named in the initial World Cup squad of 28 players before losing out both times as one of the 'unlucky six' axed before the tournament.

BOB PAISLEY knew him better as a player than most. 'He was always a very good winger but I don't think he ever exploited his skills the way he should have done. He was probably too nice a person, too even tempered. If he had a little bit more venom he would have got more caps for England than he did. He wasn't a gentle build, in fact he was the perfect build for racing along and using his strength but it's something he wouldn't do. We tried to get him to do it on so many occasions but

we could never convert him to our way of thinking.' 'I tried to change from being a little boy who used to beat players,' Thompson said. While he was at Preston the press would criticise him for being greedy but his idol Tom Finney encouraged him not to change. 'You've got one great ability. Take that away, what are you left with?' the Preston great told Thompson. When Thompson was at Liverpool Roger Hunt wanted the winger to be more direct, as Thompson told *LFChistory.net*:

The problem was when I got the ball I got my head down and off I went. On the Friday we had a meeting. Roger never said anything. Shankly said: 'Meeting finished', but Roger said, 'Actually, Peter beats his full-back about four or five times and we don't know where to run. Why don't you just beat your man and cross it?' Shankly said: 'That is a good idea.' We played against West Brom at Anfield, I pushed it past the full-back, crossed it, Roger smashed it into the net. Roger said: 'That's what I want.' I said: 'That's boring. I am not doing that. Let Ian Callaghan do that.' Ian and I were completely different. I was an individualist. Ian was straightforward, boring, pushing it down the line, cross it, boom 1-0! How boring is that?

THOMPSON had avoided any major injuries and only missed twelve league games in seven and a half seasons until he suffered an injury in December 1970 and was out until March 1971. He recovered in time to come off the bench to replace Alun Evans in the 1971 FA Cup final against Arsenal and provided Steve Heighway with the opening goal in the third minute of extra time. Unfortunately, that was not enough to win the game.

Thompson with author Arnie Baldursson

Thompson started the first seven league games of the 1971/72 season but an injury forced him out and once he was match-fit again he only appeared sporadically in the first team for the rest of the season. Thompson languished in the reserves in his last two years at the club. He suffered from serious knee injuries and was ignored by his boss Shankly, who famously had no time for injured players. 'When my day was up Shankly was horrible. He treated me like a son for about nine years,' Thompson revealed to *LFChistory.net*. 'I had two operations on my left knee. When I had my second operation the specialist said: "You'll never play again." I got upset. I was only thirty. So when I went back to Liverpool, the boss said: "You are knackered. You are finished." "Who are you talking to, me?" I responded. That's how he was. "People are working on the docks to pay you money," he told me. "You are a cripple!"' Shankly

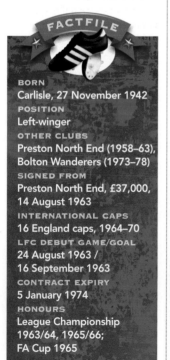

FACTFILE

BORN
Carlisle, 27 November 1942
POSITION
Left-winger
OTHER CLUBS
Preston North End (1958–63), Bolton Wanderers (1973–78)
SIGNED FROM
Preston North End, £37,000, 14 August 1963
INTERNATIONAL CAPS
16 England caps, 1964–70
LFC DEBUT GAME/GOAL
24 August 1963 / 16 September 1963
CONTRACT EXPIRY
5 January 1974
HONOURS
League Championship 1963/64, 1965/66; FA Cup 1965

wouldn't pay Thompson's contract up and in the end the Liverpool idol couldn't motivate himself to go to training. 'I am not going in having Shankly swear at me,' Thompson explained to Bob Paisley, who pleaded with him to return to Melwood. Jimmy Armfield at Second Division Bolton took a chance on Thompson and acquired him on loan in December 1973. He signed for Bolton a month later for £18,000 and is considered one of the best bargain buys in the club's history. Thompson retired in April 1978 after Bolton won the Second Division title, having played 132 matches in his Indian summer.

RARELY has a footballer with as much natural ability worn the shirt of Liverpool and Peter Thompson is in a class only reserved for a select few. Shankly didn't have a problem with his former talisman after he left Liverpool, as he was no longer a burden on the club's payroll, and sang his praises in Thompson's testimonial brochure:

If Peter Thompson would not have taken up football he could have competed in the Olympic Games. That's how good an athlete he was. He could run forever, but more importantly in football he could run with the ball – probably the hardest thing to do. He could run every minute of every game, every week, every year better than anybody else. His work rate was outstanding, his fitness unequalled, his balance like a ballet dancer. I have no hesitation in placing Peter up among the all-time greats – alongside such players as Tom Finney, Stanley Matthews and George Best. They say he didn't score enough goals, they said his final pass wasn't telling enough. Well, if he had scored goals as well as everything else he did, he would have been in the same category as Jesus Christ!

Season	League App	League Goals	FA Cup App	FA Cup Goals	League Cup App	League Cup Goals	Europe App	Europe Goals	Other App	Other Goals	Total App	Total Goals
1963/64	42	6	5	2	-	-	-	-	-	-	47	8
1964/65	38	5	8	1	-	-	8	0	1	0	55	6
1965/66	40	5	1	0	-	-	9	1	0	0	50	6
1966/67	42	10	4	0	-	-	5	1	1	0	52	11
1967/68	41	2	9	1	2	1	6	1	-	-	58	5
1968/69	42	8	4	0	3	1	2	0	-	-	51	9
1969/70	39	3	4	1	2	0	4	3	-	-	49	7
1970/71	24 (4)	2	1 (1)	0	1	0	6 (2)	0	-	-	32 (7)	2
1971/72	9 (1)	0	1	0	1	0	0 (2)	0	0 (1)	0	11 (4)	0
Total	**317 (5)**	**41**	**37 (1)**	**5**	**9**	**2**	**40 (4)**	**6**	**2 (1)**	**0**	**405 (11)**	**54**

Thompson, Phil

PHIL THOMPSON is one of the greatest characters who has graced Liverpool's shirt and one of the most decorated players in English football history.

He started as an apprentice at the club he had fervently supported as a boy and Liverpool's coach, Ronnie Moran, knew they had a player of great potential on their hands. 'I still remember Tommo's first morning with us when he arrived with a batch of other kids. Sometimes you can instantly spot players who are going to make it all the way to the top. He was the Liverpool prototype, who did the right things without being prodded along all the time. You don't make them, they make themselves.'

Thompson signed professional forms in January 1971 and made his debut at Old Trafford on Easter Monday 1972, coming on as a substitute for John Toshack after the big Welshman had put

Liverpool into a commanding 2-0 lead. Thompson gained some useful experience during the 'double' League and UEFA Cup triumph year of 1972/73. He started out as a midfielder in the team and just qualified for his first championship medal by making 14 First Division appearances. By the opening day of the next season, which was Bill Shankly's last as Liverpool manager, he had become an established part of the team's centre of defence. Thompson's style was more continental than that of Larry Lloyd and most of his fellow British professionals. His distribution from defence was first class and he fitted well beside Emlyn Hughes, adding a new dimension to Liverpool's play. Thompson added to his already impressive medal collection when he was in the Liverpool side that conquered Newcastle 3-0 at Wembley in the 1974 FA Cup final. Fired up by Malcolm MacDonald's boasts about how he would terrorise Liverpool's defence, Thompson showed astonishing maturity and

composure at the tender age of
20 to effectively neuter the twin
threat that Super Mac and his
strike partner John Tudor posed.
'Tommo' was lucky to get a gold
medal for his efforts as the police
weren't going to let him go up
the hallowed steps to receive his
prize. He had swapped shirts with
Newcastle's Terry McDermott
and had a Newcastle hat on as
well. 'The policemen thought
I was a Newcastle player and they
were trying to sort of ease me
away and wouldn't allow me to
go up the steps. I think they were
trying to put me in my place.
"You go up second".' He had
already played 70 games for
Liverpool, but was clearly not a
familiar face. Winning the FA Cup
was a dream come true for the
local boy who along with his mum
was busy making Liverpool flags
before the game for his brothers
to take to Wembley!

THE REDS finished league
runners-up to Derby County in
1974/75 as Bob Paisley came to
terms with managing a top club
side. In 1975/76 the club repeated
its 1973 success at home and in
Europe. Thompson only missed
one league match and scored the
winning goal from close range in
the UEFA Cup semi-final against
Barcelona that took the club
through to the final with Bruges,
whom they narrowly beat 4-3
on aggregate to secure the giant
trophy. To top off a remarkable
year of personal success,
Thompson was capped at full
international level by England for
the first time. He would eventually
go on to win 42 caps at senior
level and captain the team on
six occasions. By now firmly
established in the Liverpool team,
Thompson won his third First
Division Championship medal in
1977 but missed out on the club's
great triumph in Rome due to a
cartilage operation. Disappointed
though Thompson must have
been, nobody could argue that
the man who replaced him in the
team, Tommy Smith, didn't do

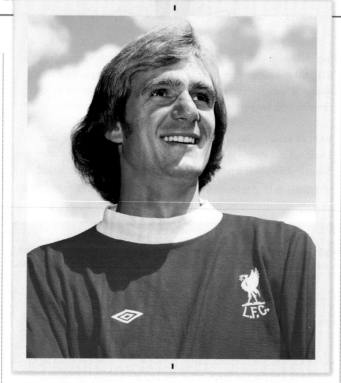

his bit to help secure the prestigious trophy! A year later it was Smith
who missed the European Cup final due to injury, but it was Alan Hansen
who replaced him in the team for the showdown with Bruges at Wembley.
After an uncharacteristic error by Hansen near the end of the game
when his woeful back-pass had goalkeeper Ray Clemence in all sorts
of trouble, it was Thompson who protected Liverpool's narrow lead by
clearing the ball off the line. Emlyn Hughes was a big fan of Thompson,
as he revealed in 1977. 'Phil is the best back-four player in the country.
He reads the game brilliantly and never panics no matter what.'

In April 1979 the Kirkby lad was given the ultimate honour of captaining
the team. Emlyn Hughes was coming to the end of his career at
Liverpool, but then Paisley made Kenny Dalglish captain, a role he was
accustomed to from his Celtic days. 'Kenny was captain for about five
or six games and then we were playing Arsenal at home and Bob said:
"I'm changing the captain. Phil is going to be captain." I was so pleased
and thrilled. I can always remember Phil Neal's words to me: "Tommo,
that shouldn't even have been an issue. There is only one person who
has the divine right to be captain at this moment in time and that's you."'

THOMPSON'S first game as captain was against Arsenal at Anfield on
7 April 1979. His team-mates made sure he would never forget the
occasion. 'I went down the steps at Anfield, touched the sign,' Thompson
revealed in his autobiography. 'I came up the steps. I go out on the pitch,
straight over to the edge of the penalty area. What I had in my mind
was that my brother, Owen, was on the Kop. I was looking for my
brother. I hear everybody laughing. Clapping first and then laughing.
I am thinking: "What's going on here?" I am waving to my brother and
I turned round and the players were still in the tunnel. They allowed me to
walk out on my own. They were killing themselves laughing.' Thompson's
biggest moment in his Liverpool career came two years later when he
walked up the steps first in Paris to collect the club's third European Cup
after the 1-0 victory over Real Madrid. However, later that year he lost
the captaincy to Graeme Souness. 'I was absolutely devastated. Bruce
Grobbelaar had just come to the club and Ray Clemence had moved on.
We'd had a great understanding. It was the most difficult time I'd had
as a player. Bob thought the captaincy was part of it. In fairness he had
a point. I was disappointed because I felt Graeme Souness in the

background was pushing for the
captaincy himself,' Thompson
admitted to *LFChistory.net*.

Thompson won his sixth and
seventh championship medals
in 1982 and 1983, as well as
winning another League Cup
winners' medal in 1982, but
missed the 1983 final with
Manchester United because of
injury. Thompson was by now
approaching his thirtieth birthday
and the younger Mark Lawrenson
had become Hansen's partner in
defence. Thompson eventually
brought the curtain down on
a wonderful playing career at
Anfield by agreeing to join
Sheffield United in March 1985,
after being on loan at Bramall
Lane for four months. He
returned to Liverpool as reserve
coach in 1986, replacing Chris
Lawler. Robbie Fowler noted in
his autobiography that Thompson
was a strict taskmaster.

*Phil Thompson was a coach
who would push youngsters to
see how tough they were, and
a lot of the young lads coming
through despised him for it.
I'm amazed he never got
properly sparked out there. One
time I thought it was really
going to kick off in the dressing
room when he was the reserve
boss, when he started having
a right go at a young striker
called Wayne Harrison, who
Liverpool had bought from
Oldham and had high hopes
for. Wayne answered back, so
Tommo starts about putting
your medals on the table. So
Wayne snapped back at him,
'No, let's put our damn toes on
the table.' Tommo has only got
four on one foot, so you can
imagine how ballistic he went.
Everyone else in the dressing
room was p***ing themselves
and trying to push their fists
in their mouths to muffle the
noise, because obviously he
wasn't the sort of coach you
wanted to do that with.*

A Tribute to
Phil Thompson
Liverpool and England

official testimonial brochure

THOMPSON had been raised on Ronnie Moran and followed in his footsteps, saying, 'Ronnie was my mentor and he was very, very hard at times, but it was the Liverpool way.' Thompson stayed on as coach until Souness sacked him infamously in 1993, but returned as assistant manager in 1998. Houllier wanted more discipline from his camp than any Liverpool player had been used to and Thompson made sure everybody was on their toes. Thompson had filled every role at the club except manager, but was left to lead Liverpool when Houllier recuperated from his heart operation, guiding the club to a respectable second in the league in the 2001/02 season. Thompson left after the Frenchman's reign finished at the end of the 2003/04 season.

'I regard Phil as one of the best possible examples of a true professional. His greatest asset as a player is his ability to read the game, he showed that gift even as a teenager. He is not the biggest man physically for his role in defence but his football brain is outstanding.' – Bob Paisley.

FACTFILE

BORN
Kirkby, Liverpool,
21 January 1954
POSITION
Centre-half / Midfielder
OTHER CLUBS
Sheffield United (loan, 1984–85;
permanent, 1985–86)
JOINED
April 1970; signed
professional 22 January 1971
INTERNATIONAL CAPS
42 England caps (1 goal),
1976–82
LFC DEBUT GAME/GOAL
3 April 1972 /
4 September 1973
CONTRACT EXPIRY
March 1985
HONOURS
League Championship
1972/73, 1975/76, 1976/77,
1978/79, 1979/80, 1981/82,
1982/83;
FA Cup 1974;
League Cup 1981, 1982;
European Cup 1978, 1981;
UEFA Cup 1973, 1976

Season	League		FA Cup		League Cup		Europe		Other		Total	
	App	Goals	App	Goals	App	Goals	App	Goals	App	Goals	App	Goals
1971-72	0 (1)	0	0	0	0	0	0	0	0	0	0 (1)	0
1972-73	12 (2)	0	2	0	0 (1)	0	2 (1)	0	-	-	16 (4)	0
1973-74	35	2	9	0	4	0	2 (1)	0	-	-	50 (1)	2
1974-75	32	0	2	0	1	0	1	2	1	0	37	2
1975-76	41	0	2	0	3	0	11	2	-	-	57	2
1976-77	26	2	4	0	2	0	3	0	1	0	36	2
1977-78	27	3	1	0	7	0	7	1	1	0	43	4
1978-79	39	0	6	0	1	0	3	0	-	-	49	0
1979-80	42	0	8	0	7	1	2	0	1	0	60	1
1980-81	25	0	1	0	6	0	7	0	1	0	40	0
1981-82	34	0	1	0	7	0	5	0	1	0	48	0
1982-83	24	0	0	0	4	0	4 (1)	0	1	0	33 (1)	0
1983-84	0	0	0	0	0	0	0	0	1	0	1	0
Total	**337 (3)**	**7**	**36**	**0**	**42 (1)**	**1**	**47 (3)**	**5**	**8**	**0**	**470 (7)**	**13**

Thompson,
Bobby

FULL-BACK Bobby Thomson was signed by Liverpool from Partick Thistle in December 1962 and made five league appearances for the club towards the end of the 1962/63 season, filling in for Ronnie Moran.

He was competing for a spot with the more experienced and established trio of Moran, Gerry Byrne and Phil Ferns and eventually left Anfield for Luton in August 1965 after making only three appearances during the 1963/64 title-winning season. He made 74 league appearances for the Hatters in the Third and Fourth Division before moving to Australia.

Liverpool's usual formation in 1964/65

FACTFILE

BORN
Menstrie, Scotland,
21 November 1939
POSITION
Right/left-back
OTHER CLUBS
Partick Thistle (1957–62),
Luton Town (1965–67)
SIGNED FROM
Partick Thistle, £5,000,
6 December 1962
LFC DEBUT
18 April 1963
CONTRACT EXPIRY
August 1965

Season	League		FA Cup		Total	
	App	Goals	App	Goals	App	Goals
1962/63	5	0	0	0	5	0
1963/64	2	0	1	0	3	0
Total	**7**	**0**	**1**	**0**	**8**	**0**

Tomley, Fred

LIVERPOOL-BORN Fred Tomley made two league appearances for the Reds in consecutive games in March 1955.

Liverpool beat Bury 4-3 but then lost 4-2 to Lincoln City so Tomley as pivot of the defence was replaced, but that did not prevent the team from leaking goals. The Reds were in rapid decline after being relegated the previous season and finished mid-table in the Second Division. Tomley was transferred to Chester in July the same year but the towering defender quickly moved back into amateur football.

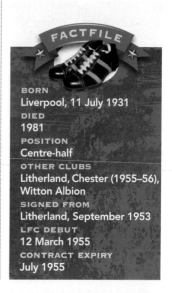

FACTFILE

BORN
Liverpool, 11 July 1931
DIED
1981
POSITION
Centre-half
OTHER CLUBS
Litherland, Chester (1955–56), Witton Albion
SIGNED FROM
Litherland, September 1953
LFC DEBUT
12 March 1955
CONTRACT EXPIRY
July 1955

Season	League		FA Cup		Total	
	App	Goals	App	Goals	App	Goals
1954/55	2	0	0	0	2	0
Total	2	0	0	0	2	0

Torres, Fernando

FERNANDO TORRES' great talent was obvious to everyone as he made his progress through the youth ranks at Atletico Madrid after joining the club in 1995. Torres starred for Spain in the 2001 European Under-16 Championships, scored the only goal in the final against France and finished as the leading goalscorer with seven goals in six games; he was voted the best player of the tournament. The following season Torres scored six goals in 36 matches as he established himself in the Atletico team that won promotion to La Liga. Torres shone on the international stage in the summer of 2002 at the European Under-19 Championship where he again scored the only goal in the final, was the tournament's leading goalscorer with four goals in four games and was voted the best player.

Torres showed his promise by scoring 13 goals in 29 games in his first season in the top flight, but it was in the 2003/04 season when he became a 19-year-old superstar. He scored 19 league goals in 35 games and made his full international debut on 6 September 2003 against Portugal. 'I was captain in Atletico at 19, playing in the same team as Demetrio Albertini, who won three Champions Leagues, and Sergi Barjuan from Barcelona, who had won everything, and they were 32, 33,' Torres said. He proved his worth in his first World Cup in 2006 with three goals in four matches, but the Spanish team were on their way home after losing 3-1 to France in the last 16. Torres had been a key player at underachieving Atletico Madrid his whole career and needed a new challenge. He had scored on average a goal every 2.6 games in 244 appearances for the club, a total of 91 goals. Rafa Benítez and Liverpool's new American owners showed their intent for the 2007/08 season by splashing out a club record fee of £20.2million for the exciting Spaniard. It was surely a coincidence he was paraded at Anfield on 4 July, USA's independence day. A lot of responsibility was placed on Torres' young shoulders in Madrid, but at Liverpool he wasn't the only one responsible for the success or lack thereof. It is hard to know which adjectives or superlatives to use to describe his first season in English football. He announced himself to the Anfield public by scoring a beautifully taken goal against Chelsea. He would score similar goals at Marseille and at Tottenham, by dropping his shoulder and easing past a defender before placing his shot immaculately into the far corner of the goal.

Benítez was criticised for 'resting' Torres early in the season but the facts suggest such criticism was unjustified. He was involved in 33 of the 38 league matches and even if he didn't play so frequently in the domestic cup games, he still found time to score a sublime hat-trick in the League Cup tie at Reading. He was indispensable in Europe. He scored a wonderful winner in the San Siro to see off the challenge of Inter Milan and then scored against Arsenal and Chelsea in the quarter-final and semi-final. Torres wasn't prolific enough in away matches, as just three of his 24 league goals came away from Anfield. At home he was absolutely sensational. His strike against Sunderland on 2 February 2007 started a run of eight home league matches in which he scored 12 times, including successive hat-tricks against Middlesbrough and West Ham United as well as the winner in his first Merseyside derby. He scored at White Hart Lane on the final day of the league season and overtook a record previously held by Ruud van Nistelrooy for the most number of league goals scored by a non-British player

during his debut season in England's top division. He was runner-up to Cristiano Ronaldo in the vote for the Football Writers' Player of the Year and also came second when the votes were cast by his fellow professionals.

TORRES did not finish his debut season with a winners' medal for his club, but on the international scene, however, it was quite a different story. Torres travelled to the European Championships in Austria and Switzerland as part of a talented squad that included his Liverpool team-mates Xabi Alonso, Pepe Reina and Alvaro Arbeloa. Torres played in all five matches as his country progressed to the final in Vienna. He proved he was the man for the big occasion by scoring a brilliant winner in the first half. He had now scored winning goals in European Championships' final at three different levels, Under-16, Under-19 and now senior, an incredible record. Liverpool's new favourite 'Number 9' had a stop-

start season in 2008/09. Niggling injuries curtailed his progress and at the turn of the year Torres had only scored five goals in 16 matches, including a brace in away victories against Everton and Manchester City. Torres was determined to make up for lost time in the second part of the season and scored 11 goals in 22 matches when the title was Liverpool's to lose, which they unfortunately did.

In 2009/10 Fernando's goals-per-game ratio in Premier League matches was his best yet, 18 from 22 matches. In so doing, he became the fastest Liverpool player to reach 50 league goals. Frustratingly, he missed almost as many matches as he played in, as Liverpool gained 23 fewer points in the league compared to the previous season. The major test of whether Liverpool could match Torres' ambitions did not come with a change of ownership or even a change of manager. It came when Chelsea tried again to prise him away from Anfield in the January 2011 transfer window. It hardly came as a surprise when Torres handed in a transfer request, as he had been looking very unhappy in the red shirt over the last few months. On the day the window closed Torres was at Melwood in the morning but in the evening he was in London signing for defending Premier League champions Chelsea. It was a most unsatisfactory end to Torres' three and a half years in L4. His quip of never having kissed the Liverpool badge left a bitter taste.

MANY ONLOOKERS suspected that Chelsea would find it difficult to accommodate Drogba, Anelka and Torres in the same team and so it proved. Torres would have to wait until 23 April to score his first Chelsea goal and by the end of the season it was still his only goal from 14 Premier League and four Champions League matches. The massive transfer fee seemed to be a real millstone around his neck and his performances for Chelsea in the second half of the season were really no different to those for

Liverpool in the first half of the season. Torres has continued to struggle, looking a shadow of the player who brought such delight to the Anfield crowd. At Liverpool 69 per cent of Torres' goals, a total of 56, were engineered by defence-splitting passes, in most instances from Steven Gerrard or Xabi Alonso. The Spaniard was no doubt comforted in seeing Rafa Benítez replacing Roberto Di Matteo as Chelsea's manager in November 2012, but that has failed to bring a real spark to his game considering the immense talent he possesses.

FACTFILE

BORN
Madrid, Spain, 20 March 1984
POSITION
Centre-forward
OTHER CLUBS
Atletico Madrid (1995–2007),
Chelsea (2011–)
SIGNED FROM
Atletico Madrid, £20.2million,
4 July 2007
INTERNATIONAL CAPS
106 Spain caps (36 goals)
(40 (12) at LFC), 2003-
LFC DEBUT GAME/GOAL
11 August 2007 /
19 August 2007
CONTRACT EXPIRY
31 January 2011

Season	League		FA Cup		League Cup		Europe		Total	
	App	Goals	App	Goals	App	Goals	App	Goals	App	Goals
2007/08	29 (4)	24	1	0	1	3	10 (1)	6	41 (5)	33
2008/09	20 (4)	14	2 (1)	1	1 (1)	0	9	2	32 (6)	17
2009/10	20 (2)	18	2	0	0	0	7 (1)	4	29 (3)	22
2010/11	22 (1)	9	1	0	0	0	1 (1)	0	24 (2)	9
Total	**91 (11)**	**65**	**6 (1)**	**1**	**2 (1)**	**3**	**27 (3)**	**12**	**126 (16)**	**81**

Toshack,
John

JOHN TOSHACK made his name as a striker with his home-town club Cardiff City, signing professional forms on his 17th birthday in March 1966. He gave Cardiff fine service for over four years, during which time he scored 86 goals from 193 appearances.

Liverpool tried to sign Frank Worthington from Huddersfield Town but the player failed a medical and Bill Shankly turned his attention instead to the 21-year-old Welshman who arrived for a club record of £110,000. 'Tosh' endeared himself to the home public in only his second match when he thumped a headed equaliser into the Kop goal in the cauldron of a Merseyside derby against Everton. Although Toshack only scored seven times in 33 matches in his debut season at Anfield, it was clear that his aerial power would be an important part of Liverpool's attack for years to come.

The arrival of Kevin Keegan before the 1970/71 season was a godsend for Toshack and Liverpool. 'Myself and Kevin Keegan worked up a good understanding and as a partnership we flourished,' Toshack enthused. 'We seemed to hit it off from almost day one and then got better and better

as time went by.' They became the quintessential big target man and the smaller forward playing off him. A typical Liverpool attack was a pass from the wing, headed down by Tosh for his smaller accomplice, to score. Keegan was thankful for his strike partner at Liverpool. 'Tosh was a wonderful player to play alongside. His aerial ability was fantastic and I always knew that he was going to win the high balls. From then on it was just a question of me reading which way the ball was going to go and from those situations we created many chances.'

LIVERPOOL hadn't won a trophy under Shankly since 1966 but came close in 1971 and 1972 in the FA Cup and the League Championship respectively. Liverpool and Arsenal drew 0-0 in the final league game of the 1971/72 season when Liverpool needed a win to snatch the title away from Derby and seal a record eighth League Championship. Toshack scored a legitimate goal against the Gunners but the offside flag was up to Shankly's disgust.

Toshack was unlucky with injuries during his time at Anfield. He didn't suffer serious long-term injuries but usually niggling ones that meant he only once played in 30 or more league matches in any of the six full seasons that he was a Liverpool player.

TOSHACK missed 20 league games in 1972/73 but still scored 13 vital goals as the title was won after a tense struggle with Leeds and Arsenal. But it was in the UEFA Cup final of that year that Toshack made perhaps his most telling contribution. Left out of the starting line-up against Mönchengladbach on an evening when torrential rain caused the home leg to be abandoned after less than half an hour, he was brought in to replace Brian Hall 24 hours later and caused havoc in the German defence, laying on two first-half goals for Keegan. He also played for the whole of the second leg in Germany two weeks later when Liverpool just held on to take their first European trophy 3-2 on aggregate.

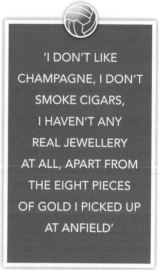

'I DON'T LIKE CHAMPAGNE, I DON'T SMOKE CIGARS, I HAVEN'T ANY REAL JEWELLERY AT ALL, APART FROM THE EIGHT PIECES OF GOLD I PICKED UP AT ANFIELD'

The Reds were unable to retain their domestic crown in 1974 but ample compensation was achieved in the FA Cup when eight of the players who had tasted defeat against Arsenal three years earlier were named in the side to face Newcastle United. Toshack had already scored the only goal of a difficult quarter-final trip to Second Division Bristol City and the important third goal which sealed the semi-final replay victory against Leicester City at Villa Park. At Wembley it was his flicked header from Ray Clemence's long kick downfield that allowed Steve Heighway to run on and put Liverpool into a commanding 2-0 lead with only 15 minutes left.

Following Ray Kennedy's arrival and Shankly's retirement in the summer of 1974 Toshack lost his place in the starting line-up. His frustration boiled over and on 21 November 1974 the club accepted a £160,000 bid for him to move to Leicester City. Toshack was reluctant to move and told reporters, 'Nothing would please me more than to be running out on the field with Liverpool against West Ham on Saturday. No disrespect to Leicester but this club is out on its own... they are the best bunch of players I've ever been with.' Paisley was sorry to see him go: 'My position is that I don't want any player to leave Anfield, but when Leicester's interest was known John felt he wanted to go. John felt he was not prepared to wait for his chance. It was a straight battle between him and Ray Kennedy.' Toshack was expected to make his Leicester debut the following day, but he failed his medical and returned to Liverpool, which was a blessing in disguise.

Three weeks later he recovered his place in the team and scored in three consecutive games on his return. 1975/76 was Toshack's most productive and injury-free season on Merseyside. He only missed seven league matches and again won League Championship and UEFA Cup winners' medals in the same season. He passed 20 goals in a season for the only time as a Liverpool player, scoring a hat-trick of headers against Hibernian in the UEFA Cup and also the goal which brought a famous win in Spain against Barcelona in the first leg of the semi-final. At 27 years of age,

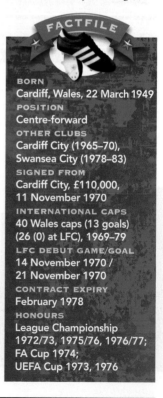

FACTFILE

BORN
Cardiff, Wales, 22 March 1949
POSITION
Centre-forward
OTHER CLUBS
Cardiff City (1965–70),
Swansea City (1978–83)
SIGNED FROM
Cardiff City, £110,000,
11 November 1970
INTERNATIONAL CAPS
40 Wales caps (13 goals)
(26 (0) at LFC), 1969–79
LFC DEBUT GAME/GOAL
14 November 1970 /
21 November 1970
CONTRACT EXPIRY
February 1978
HONOURS
League Championship
1972/73, 1975/76, 1976/77;
FA Cup 1974;
UEFA Cup 1973, 1976

Season	League App	League Goals	FA Cup App	FA Cup Goals	League Cup App	League Cup Goals	Europe App	Europe Goals	Other App	Other Goals	Total App	Total Goals
1970/71	21	5	7	1	0	0	5	1	-	-	33	7
1971/72	28 (1)	13	1	0	1	0	1 (1)	0	0 (1)	0	31 (3)	13
1972/73	22	13	4	2	6	1	6 (2)	1	-	-	38 (2)	17
1973/74	19	5	6	3	2	2	3	1	-	-	30	11
1974/75	20 (1)	12	2	0	0	0	0 (2)	0	-	-	22 (3)	12
1975/76	35	16	2	1	2	0	10 (1)	6	-	-	49 (1)	23
1976/77	22	10	2	1	1	0	4	1	1	1	30	13
1977/78	2 (1)	0	0	0	1	0	1	0	0	0	4 (1)	0
Total	**169 (3)**	**74**	**24**	**8**	**13**	**3**	**30 (6)**	**10**	**1 (1)**	**1**	**237 (10)**	**96**

he should have been approaching his peak as a player but injury meant that he missed the last part of the 1976/77 season and he could only watch and admire as his colleagues won the European Cup for the first time.

It is maybe a little known fact to many Liverpool supporters that Toshack has tried his hand at poetry. 'Gosh it's Tosh' is one of his creations. You be the judge.

```
"GOSH IT'S TOSH"

On Wednesday Shankly names a team,
But for one player a shattered dream.
His season's finished, blown away,
But he is still to have his say.

The Gods are angry.
They send rain, in torrents, and smite the game.
Then just by chance it really pours,
Twenty-two players on all fours.

The Referee says, 'That's enough',
Will Liverpool call the German bluff?

A day passes and, from the deluge,
I emerge, to rise above Mönchengladbach.
'The Welshman kills them in the air,
Toshack and Keegan, what a pair!!'

Europe fears me. Gosh it's Tosh. It is 1976.
The Nou Camp belongs to me.
A Goalden night and what a thrill,
It's Liverpool one, Barcelona nil.
```

After only making five appearances for Liverpool the following season, Toshack decided to return to South Wales in February 1978 to become player-manager at Swansea City. He supervised the club's meteoric rise from the Fourth Division to the First. He proudly led his team out at Anfield on 3 October 1981, an afternoon of mixed emotions after the recent passing of Bill Shankly who had brought him to Merseyside nearly 11 years before. As the teams lined up for a minute's silence in memory of Shanks, Toshack took off his Swansea tracksuit to reveal underneath a red Liverpool shirt with his number 10 on the back. It was a moment which endeared him to the Liverpool supporters but not so to the Swansea faithful, who were bemused by his sense of loyalty.

Although Swansea returned to the lower divisions almost as quickly as they had risen from them, Toshack's name and reputation had been noticed outside the United Kingdom and in the summer of 1984 he was named as the new manager of Sporting Lisbon. Although that post lasted less than a year, he later achieved success in Spain with both Real Sociedad and Real Madrid and is one of very few Britons to have won both league and cup competitions in another European country.

Toshack, who earned 40 caps for his country, was appointed manager of Wales for the first time in 1994, but only spent 41 days in the post, resigning after a 3-1 defeat to Norway. He took charge of the Welsh national team again in November 2004. Toshack left the Wales post after his country's defeat to Montenegro in a European Championship qualifier in September 2010. Slightly less than a year later he was unveiled as the new manager of FYR Macedonia, but roughly 12 months later his contract was terminated, apparently because he refused to relocate to Macedonia. In March 2013 Toshack took over as manager of Khazar Lankaran of the Azerbaijan Premier League.

Tosswill, John

JOHN TOSSWILL scored on his debut in a 2-0 win against Oldham and played in the first six matches of the 1912/13 season before he lost his place. He wasn't recalled until March 1913 and played a further five games before the end of the season. He was on the winning side in his first three games but then lost seven out of eight as Liverpool finished mid-table.

Tosswill was very deaf and would on occasion score a brilliant goal only to find that some seconds before, the game had been stopped for offside or a foul. He was a corporal in the Royal Engineers and passed away after illness aged only 25 on 28 September 1915 in the Eastbourne Military Hospital in Sussex.

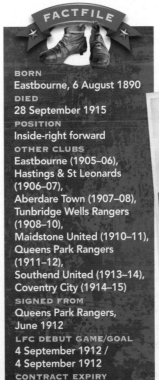

FACTFILE

BORN
Eastbourne, 6 August 1890
DIED
28 September 1915
POSITION
Inside-right forward
OTHER CLUBS
Eastbourne (1905–06),
Hastings & St Leonards (1906–07),
Aberdare Town (1907–08),
Tunbridge Wells Rangers (1908–10),
Maidstone United (1910–11),
Queens Park Rangers (1911–12),
Southend United (1913–14),
Coventry City (1914–15)
SIGNED FROM
Queens Park Rangers, June 1912
LFC DEBUT GAME/GOAL
4 September 1912 /
4 September 1912
CONTRACT EXPIRY
20 August 1913

Elisha Scott visiting Liverpool in 1955

Season	League		FA Cup		Total	
	App	Goals	App	Goals	App	Goals
1912/13	11	1	0	0	11	1
Total	**11**	**1**	**0**	**0**	**11**	**1**

Transfers

The five most expensive players bought by the club

Fee	Name	Club	Date
£35million	Andy Carroll	Newcastle United	31 January 2011
£22.8million	Luis Suarez	Ajax	31 January 2011
£20.2million	Fernando Torres	Atletico Madrid	4 July 2007
£19million	Robbie Keane	Tottenham	28 July 2008
£18.6million	Javier Mascherano	GSA & MSL*	29 February 2008

* Mascherano's third-party owners were Global Soccer Agencies and Mystere Services Limited.

JIMMY ROSS

The five most expensive players sold by the club

Fee	Name	Club	Date
£50million	Fernando Torres	Chelsea	31 January 2011
£30million	Xabi Alonso	Real Madrid	5 August 2009
£17.25million	Javier Mascherano	Barcelona	30 August 2010
£16million	Robbie Keane	Tottenham	2 February 2009
£12million	Robbie Fowler	Leeds United	29 November 2001

Record buys in club history

Fee	Name	Club	Date
£75	Jimmy Ross	Preston North End	3 August 1894
£100	Frank Becton	Preston North End	18 March 1895
£200	Hugh Morgan	St Mirren	26 March 1898
£350	Alex Raisbeck	Hibernian	6 May 1898
£460	Arthur Goddard	Glossop	24 February 1902
£500	Alf West	Barnsley	3 November 1903
	Ephraim Longworth**	Leyton	9 June 1910
£900	Wilf Bartrop	Barnsley	13 May 1914
£1,250	Frank Mitchell	Everton	4 February 1921
£2,800	Fred Hopkin	Manchester United	May 1921
£8,000	Tiny Bradshaw	Bury	January 1930
£13,000	Albert Stubbins	Newcastle United	12 September 1946
£16,000	Gordon Milne	Preston North End	30 August 1960
£37,500	Ian St John	Motherwell	2 May 1961
£65,000	Emlyn Hughes	Blackpool	27 February 1967
£96,000	Tony Hateley	Chelsea	5 July 1967
£100,000	Alun Evans	Wolves	September 1968
£180,000	Ray Kennedy	Arsenal	12 July 1974
£200,000	David Johnson	Ipswich Town	12 August 1976
£440,000	Kenny Dalglish	Celtic	10 August 1977
£650,000	Craig Johnston	Middlesbrough	3 April 1981
£900,000	Mark Lawrenson	Brighton & Hove Albion	August 1981
£1.9million	Peter Beardsley	Newcastle United	14 July 1987
£2.9million	Dean Saunders	Derby County	19 July 1991
£8.5million	Stan Collymore	Nottingham Forest	1 July 1995
£11million	Emile Heskey	Leicester City	10 March 2000
£14.5million	Djibril Cissé	Marseille	1 July 2004
£20.2million	Fernando Torres	Atletico Madrid	4 July 2007
£35million	Andy Carroll	Newcastle United	31 January 2011

** Longworth was said to be 'a club-record buy' in the region of £500 to £900.

IAN ST. JOHN
[LIVERPOOL & SCOTLAND]

Traoré, Djimi

DJIMI TRAORÉ seemed nervous when his big chance arrived at the start of the 2000/01 season as he was put in the unfamiliar role of left-back. He was loaned to France the following season and gained valuable experience with El Hadji Diouf's Lens and almost won the French Championship. He found his feet when he was moved to his natural centre-half position when Stephane Henchoz got injured in the 2002/03 season.

Traoré fell out of favour with Houllier in 2003/04 in what proved to be his last campaign as boss. Traoré welcomed a change at the top. 'A lot of the French players didn't have a chance to play and express themselves. We had to work twice as hard to play. In the end, I didn't trust him any more. I was upset. So many times I knocked on his door saying I wanted to leave the club.' Rafa Benítez showed a lot of faith in Traoré in his inaugural season

in English football, using him as a left-back opting for the centre-half pairing of Sami Hyypia and Jamie Carragher. On 18 January 2005 Traoré dumped Liverpool out of the third round of the FA Cup with a disastrous own goal but didn't lose his focus and was a part of Liverpool's victorious team in Istanbul where he played the whole 120 minutes. Traoré was used less by Benítez the following season as it was painfully clear he wasn't up to the high standard required at Liverpool.

DURING the summer of 2006, Traoré was sold to Charlton Athletic. He was sent off on his debut against West Ham on the opening day of the 2006/07 season. In June 2009 he left England for good and played in 29 league and three cup matches for Monaco in 2009/10. His career seemed resurrected,

however, a cruciate ligament rupture ruined the following season for him. He signed a one-year contract with Marseille in August 2011 but only made 14 first-team appearances and left when his contract expired in the summer of 2012. In February 2013 Traoré signed for MLS club Seattle Sounders.

FACTFILE

BORN
Laval, France, 1 March 1980
POSITION
Left-back / Centre-half
OTHER CLUBS
Laval (1997–99),
Lens (loan, 2001–02),
Charlton Athletic (2006–07),
Portsmouth (2007–09),
Rennes (loan, 2008),
Birmingham City (loan, 2009),
Monaco (2009–11),
Olympique Marseille (2011–12),
Seattle Sounders (2013-)
SIGNED FROM
Laval, £550,000,
18 February 1999
INTERNATIONAL CAPS
10 Mali caps (1 goal),
2004–05
LFC DEBUT GAME/GOAL
14 September 1999 /
6 November 2003
CONTRACT EXPIRY
9 August 2006
HONOURS
FA Cup 2006;
League Cup 2003;
Champions League 2005

Season	League		FA Cup		League Cup		Europe		Other		Total	
	App	Goals	App	Goals	App	Goals	App	Goals	App	Goals	App	Goals
1999/2000	0	0	0	0	2	0	-	-	-	-	2	0
2000/01	8	0	0	0	1	0	2 (1)	0	-	-	11 (1)	0
2001/02	0	0	0	0	0	0	1	0	0	0	1	0
2002/03	30 (2)	0	2	0	2 (1)	0	10 (1)	0	1	0	45 (4)	0
2003/04	7	0	0	0	2	0	2	1	-	-	11	1
2004/05	18 (8)	0	1	0	5	0	10	0	-	-	34 (8)	0
2005/06	9 (6)	0	1 (1)	0	0 (1)	0	5	0	1	0	16 (8)	0
Total	**72 (16)**	**0**	**4 (1)**	**0**	**12 (2)**	**0**	**30 (2)**	**1**	**2**	**0**	**120 (21)**	**1**

Twentyman, Geoff

WHEN CARLISLE UNITED player Geoff Twentyman had reached National Service age he had no choice but to go. At one point Private Twentyman was summoned to his CO's office and was told, 'The War Office has been approached by a Mr Shankly who says that if you could be released Carlisle would win the Third Division Championship.'

He was duly made available for 32 appearances, but United only managed third spot in the 1950/51 season. Bill Shankly left Carlisle United to take over at Grimsby Town in the summer and in December 1953 Twentyman left for Anfield. Carlisle manager Fred Emery said that the destruction of their stand by fire

earlier that year forced their hand. 'We have to build up our finances, so we had to let Geoff go.' Grimsby manager Shankly wished Twentyman well in a letter dated 18 December 1953. 'Congratulations on your stepping up to the big stuff, it's taken these people a long time to make a move for you. However, Geoff, it has been worth

it for you, because you have gone to probably the finest club in the game, with the most ardent supporters ever, behind you.'

The presence of England centre-half Laurie Hughes, and later Dick White, meant Twentyman was switched to left-half at Liverpool. Unfortunately he had joined in the club's lean years. Just four months later Liverpool were relegated to the Second Division after finishing rock bottom of the top flight. After a mid-table finish in 1955, Liverpool were always challenging for promotion back to the top division but third-place finishes in

1956 and 1957 were not quite good enough. Twentyman was not best pleased at being unable to feature in his ideal centre-half position and threatened to leave the club in February 1957. He played 15 games per season on average during his last three years at the club. Towards the end of the decade, Ballymena United wanted him as a player-manager and, despite the pleading of the recently arrived Bill Shankly, Twentyman moved across the Irish Sea. A relatively successful period of management followed until Twentyman wanted to focus again just on the playing side; he returned to the North of England for the

he became a widely respected and welcomed figure in football. His presence on the pitch was a steadying influence for both players and fans. His talent-spotting became almost legendary on Merseyside, unearthing some of the game's real giants like Ian Rush, Phil Neal and Alan Hansen, and he is fondly remembered at both Anfield and Brunton Park. Twentyman worked also under Paisley, Fagan and Dalglish before leaving his post after 19 years in 1986 to become Graeme Souness's chief scout at Rangers.

FORMER team-mate Alan A'Court remembered him with great fondness in his autobiography: 'Geoff Twentyman was typical of that old Liverpool side, a hard grafting half-back, who could hold his own with anyone and never stopped working. Geoff used to love a bottle of Guinness, especially at half-time when he needed to replace lost body fluid, as he perspired

a lot. Another man would have been a fool to drink a bottle like that, but it did him good, and simply emphasised that people's metabolism can be very different!'

1963/64 season, rejoining a strong and ambitious Carlisle United. He played only a small part as United went on to win promotion, finishing second in the Fourth Division. He went on to manage Morecambe, Hartlepool and Penrith before accepting Shankly's offer of the post of chief scout at Anfield in 1967. Twentyman was the model professional in every sense of the word. Unhurried and unflappable on the pitch, hardworking and dignified off it,

Season	League		FA Cup		Total	
	App	Goals	App	Goals	App	Goals
1953/54	20	0	0	0	20	0
1954/55	35	3	4	0	39	3
1955/56	42	7	5	0	47	7
1956/57	30	3	1	0	31	3
1957/58	7	1	3	0	10	1
1958/59	25	4	1	1	26	5
1959/60	11	0	0	0	11	0
Total	**170**	**18**	**14**	**1**	**184**	**19**

Underwood, Dave

LIVERPOOL had been shipping goals in the 1953/54 season and goalkeeper Dave Underwood was brought in mid-campaign to stop the rot along with a few more new arrivals. Underwood would never forget his debut for all the wrong reasons as he accidentally shattered the left leg of his team-mate Eddie Spicer, thus ending his career.

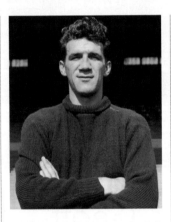

Liverpool were relegated and Underwood hardly had a look-in until he played 26 consecutive league and cup games from November 1955 to April 1956. The South African Doug Rudham had reclaimed his place just before the end of that season so Underwood demanded to be sold.

Underwood had three spells at Watford and was a very popular figure at the club. Despite being a part-timer, working for a haulage

contractor, Underwood's performances impressed and he was voted Watford's Player of the Year in 1962 and landed a move to First Division Fulham. Following an injury to Fulham's number one, Underwood made 16 appearances in the 1963/64 season, a great comeback for the keeper.

In 1977 Underwood was appointed chairman of Barnet. In his five-year tenure at the club Barnet signed footballing great

Jimmy Greaves, who later thanked Underwood for helping him to overcome his much-publicised alcohol addiction. 'Dave was manager and goalkeeper with a face like an old-time prize fighter; a broken nose, swollen lips,' a former player of his at Hastings, Ricky George, told legendary commentator John Motson. 'He also talked with a lisp. I was always notoriously late for games and I remember one Sunday we were playing the inmates of Ford Open Prison and Dave told me the kick-off was two o'clock. At five to two on the dot I rushed in breathlessly to find an empty

dressing room. About a quarter of an hour later, big Dave strolled in with the rest of the players grinning fit to burst: "Whoopth-a-daithy," he says, "I've thuthed you out, Ricky, alwayth late. Kick-off'th at free." I loved the man, I truly did.'

Season	League		FA Cup		Total	
	App	Goals	App	Goals	App	Goals
1953/54	18	0	0	0	18	0
1954/55	6	0	0	0	6	0
1955/56	21	0	5	0	26	0
Total	**45**	**0**	**5**	**0**	**50**	**0**

Uren, Harold

AFTER progressing through the local leagues Harold Uren made his Liverpool reserves debut in April 1906.

The amateur still featured with Wrexham in the Birmingham League, but finally made a couple of first-team appearances for Liverpool in November 1907. Uren could play both on the right and left flank and the scribes at the club programme expected greater things of him in the future: 'Standing 5ft 10in and weighing

12st, he is a promising specimen of a well built athlete and in his recent trials he has shown that his football abilities are of no mean order. He can centre the ball splendidly, especially when playing on the left wing, and is in command of a few tricks that enable him to baffle the attentions of the opposing defence. To reach the highest flights, however, it will be necessary for him to increase his speed, and a study of the methods of such a graceful player as Goddard, whose course of actions is determined upon before the ball reaches him, would exercise a beneficial effect also.'

HOWEVER, it wasn't until the middle of October 1910 that Uren had an extended run in the side. His best season for the club was also his final one, 1911/12, when he played in 24 of the 38 league fixtures and registered his only two Liverpool goals. In February 1912 Everton exchanged Bill Lacey and Tom Gracie for Harold Uren plus £300. The *Liverpool Echo* reckoned his lack of success at Liverpool was due to his peculiar playing style and 'that the other forwards could not make headway from his ideas'. However, his Blues career didn't prove a success either as he only made 24 appearances in 15 months. Harold's sons, Harold jnr and Richard, were both England internationals in rugby.

	League		FA Cup		Total	
Season	App	Goals	App	Goals	App	Goals
1907/08	2	0	0	0	2	0
1908/09	1	0	0	0	1	0
1909/10	3	0	0	0	3	0
1910/11	12	0	1	0	13	0
1911/12	24	2	2	0	26	2
Total	**42**	**2**	**3**	**0**	**45**	**2**

FACTFILE

BORN
Clifton, Bristol,
23 August 1885
DIED
7 April 1955
POSITION
Right/left-winger
OTHER CLUBS
New Brighton Wesleyans,
West Kirby (1903–06),
Harrowby (1906),
Wrexham (1906–07),
Everton (1912–13),
Wrexham (1913),
Lochgelly United
JOINED
Amateur, April 1906
LFC DEBUT GAME/GOAL
16 November 1907 /
28 October 1911
CONTRACT EXPIRY
27 February 1912

Van den Berg, Harman

HARMAN van den Berg (literally, 'Harman from the mountains' in Afrikaans) was born in Observatory, a suburb of Cape Town, and was skilful in many sports.

Before arriving at Liverpool in October 1937 he had been prominent at football, cricket and rugby, even capped for Western Province, the South African rugby union team. As soon as he stepped off the Union Castle liner, *Carnarvon Castle*, George Kay was at the docks in Southampton to finally secure the South African's signature on a professional contract.

THE LEFT-WINGER made his first-team debut as a replacement for the injured Alf Hanson in the Goodison derby on 16 February 1938. Fellow South Africans Arthur Riley and Berry Nieuwenhuys were also in the first XI that day when Everton were beaten 3-1. The *Daily Post* concluded: 'One would have thought Van Den Berg had been playing in senior football for years instead of making his debut.' The *Liverpool Echo* had plenty of praise as well for the 19-year-old: '...nicely built, speedy, good ball control, accurate with his centres, and a good shot, he made a most encouraging debut'. Hanson returned after an absence of three games and Van den Berg didn't add to his total until he made 12 consecutive appearances in the first half of the following season before succumbing to a serious cartilage injury that kept him out until four weeks were left of the campaign. Van den Berg was in the line-up when the 1939/40 season started but the outbreak of war meant that league football was suspended. Of the three league goals that Van den Berg scored for Liverpool, two were particularly dramatic: an equaliser in the last minute to save a point at Leicester in October 1938 and a first-minute strike in the 3-3 Anfield draw with Huddersfield Town three weeks later. In 1941, Van den Berg's fiancée, Miss Lavina Ainley from Anfield, Liverpool, was sailing overseas to marry the South African airman when a Nazi u-boat torpedoed the liner. She spent 21 hours on a lifeboat before being rescued by an American flying boat.

	League		FA Cup		Total	
Season	App	Goals	App	Goals	App	Goals
1937/38	3	0	0	0	3	0
1938/39	16	3	0	0	16	3
Total	**19**	**3**	**0**	**0**	**19**	**3**

FACTFILE

BORN
Cape Town, South Africa,
21 March 1918
DIED
7 June 1977
POSITION
Left-winger
OTHER CLUBS
Peninsular
SIGNED FROM
Peninsular, 18 October 1937
LFC DEBUT GAME/GOAL
16 February 1938 /
8 October 1938
CONTRACT EXPIRY
1941

Venison,
Barry

BARRY VENISON first attracted nationwide attention when he led Sunderland out in the 1985 League Cup final, the youngest ever captain in a Wembley final, aged 20 years and 220 days. Sunderland lost 1-0 to Norwich on the big day and he suffered further disappointment when the Roker Park club was relegated at the end of the season.

After one campaign in the Second Division Venison promoted himself to Liverpool's management and other First Division clubs by writing a letter to them asking if they were interested in his services. Kenny Dalglish signed Venison, who was just turning 22 but had already made 205 appearances for Sunderland. Venison began the 1986/87 season as a right-back with Jim Beglin playing on the left. Venison switched to the left when Beglin broke his leg halfway through the season. Injuries hampered Venison's progress in the successful 1987/88 campaign,

FACTFILE

BORN
Consett, 16 August 1964
POSITION
Right/left-back
OTHER CLUBS
Sunderland (1979–86),
Newcastle United (1992–95),
Galatasaray (1995),
Southampton (1995–97)
SIGNED FROM
Sunderland, £200,000,
31 July 1986
INTERNATIONAL CAPS
2 England caps, 1994–95
LFC DEBUT GAME/GOAL
16 August 1986 /
29 August 1988
CONTRACT EXPIRY
31 July 1992
HONOURS
League Championship
1987/88, 1989/90;
FA Cup 1989

allowing Gary Ablett to settle into the team. He was out injured for the majority of the second part of the 1988/89 season but made a substitute appearance at the start of extra time in the 3-2 win over Everton in the FA Cup final. Venison did manage to get an injury-free run in the side in the 1989/90 championship season, but suffered with injuries in his last two campaigns at the club.

HE JOINED Newcastle in the summer of 1992. Kevin Keegan's Magpies conquered the Second Division in Venison's debut season and then took the Premier

League by storm. In September 1994 Venison made his full England debut after excelling in Newcastle's midfield. At the end of the 1994/95 season Venison rejoined former Reds boss Graeme Souness at Galatasaray. Five months later he moved to Southampton in the Premier League, followed by Souness who took over at the Saints prior to the 1996/97 campaign. Venison only featured in two games, in the second of which he was sent off against Leicester, which proved to be his last ever career appearance as he was forced to retire due to a back injury.

Season	League App	League Goals	FA Cup App	FA Cup Goals	League Cup App	League Cup Goals	Europe App	Europe Goals	Other App	Other Goals	Total App	Total Goals
1986/87	31 (2)	0	2	0	4 (2)	0	-	-	2 (1)	0	39 (5)	0
1987/88	18	0	2	0	2	0	-	-	-	-	22	0
1988/89	14 (1)	0	0 (1)	0	4	0	-	-	2	1	20 (2)	1
1989/90	25	0	7 (1)	0	2 (1)	0	-	-	1	0	35 (2)	0
1990/91	6	0	4 (1)	0	2	0	-	-	1	0	13 (1)	0
1991/92	9 (4)	1	1 (2)	0	0	0	0 (3)	1	-	-	10 (9)	2
Total	**103 (7)**	**1**	**16 (5)**	**0**	**14 (3)**	**0**	**0 (3)**	**1**	**6 (1)**	**1**	**139 (19)**	**3**

Vignal,
Gregory

WHEN Markus Babbel contracted Guillain-Barré syndrome in 2001, Jamie Carragher was moved to the right flank allowing Gregory Vignal to slot in on the left.

The Frenchman linked up well with John Arne Riise in front of him and showed some attacking prowess. Unfortunately Vignal fractured his foot when Liverpool got dumped out of the League Cup by Grimsby on 9 October 2001. Vignal made four appearances for the side in the 2002/03 season, but was clearly far away from being match fit. He eventually joined Portsmouth after he was released from his Liverpool contract a year early in the summer of 2005.

Season	League		FA Cup		League Cup		Europe		Other		Total	
	App	Goals	App	Goals	App	Goals	App	Goals	App	Goals	App	Goals
2000/01	4 (2)	0	0 (1)	0	0	0	0	0	-	-	4 (3)	0
2001/02	3 (1)	0	0	0	1	0	4	0	0	0	8 (1)	0
2002/03	0 (1)	0	0	0	2	0	0 (1)	0	0	0	2 (2)	0
Total	**7 (4)**	**0**	**0 (1)**	**0**	**3**	**0**	**4 (1)**	**0**	**0**	**0**	**14 (6)**	**0**

Voronin,
Andriy

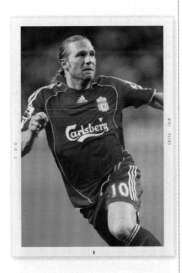

ANDRIY Voronin has plied his trade in Germany for the majority of his career after leaving childhood club, Chornomorets Odesa, aged 16.

Voronin impressed Rafa Benítez when Bayer Leverkusen faced Liverpool in the Champions League in 2005 and the Reds manager didn't waste any time to snap him up on a free once his contract expired in the summer of 2007. Voronin's first season at Anfield could neither be called a success nor a failure. His first 'start', in the Champions League qualifier in Toulouse, saw a thrilling goal which won the match and set the team up nicely for a place in the lucrative group stage of the competition. League goals soon followed at Sunderland and at home to Derby. He was outstanding in the 8-0 annihilation of Besiktas even though he didn't end up on the scoresheet himself. Early in the New Year, he injured his ankle during a training session and was sidelined for several weeks. He returned to the first-team picture again towards the end of the season, was a scoring substitute against Blackburn and repeated that feat at Tottenham on the final day of the league season. Benítez wanted to move him on after only 12 months at the club and he was loaned to Hertha Berlin for the 2008/09 season.

Voronin was a great success at Hertha, who finished fourth in the Bundesliga. He scored 11 goals in 20 league matches, but Hertha couldn't afford his wages so he returned to Liverpool. Voronin was a peripheral figure at Liverpool in the 2009/10 season and finally left for Moscow in the 2010 January transfer window.

Season	League		FA Cup		League Cup		Europe		Total	
	App	Goals	App	Goals	App	Goals	App	Goals	App	Goals
2007/08	13 (6)	5	0 (1)	0	1	0	4 (3)	1	18 (10)	6
2009/10	1 (7)	0	0	0	1	0	1 (2)	0	3 (9)	0
Total	**14 (13)**	**5**	**0 (1)**	**0**	**2**	**0**	**5 (5)**	**1**	**21 (19)**	**6**

Waddle,
Alan

A TALL FORWARD who was a deputy to John Toshack, Alan Waddle only scored once in 22 appearances but it was a memorable goal; the winner in the Merseyside derby at Goodison Park on 8 December 1973. Even though he was the toast of the red half of the city, on the day he went unnoticed when he took a train home the same evening, as he told the *Liverpool Daily Post*.

'I'd arranged with our manager Bill Shankly before the game to have a couple of days off to go visit my father back in the north east. The media spotlight wasn't as intense as it is now and I didn't do any interviews after the match, I just had a quick shower and slipped away.' A solitary goal for the club was less than what was expected of him but he naturally wonders what could have been. 'I "scored" on my debut in front of the Kop but the goal was disallowed,' he told the *Daily Post*. 'I remember a midweek afternoon match against Coventry when I could've had a hat-trick but I hit the post and the crossbar and the ball just wouldn't go in. I sometimes think what would have happened if some of those chances had fallen for me.'

A COUSIN of former England player Chris Waddle, Alan played for a lot of clubs in his career. His most prolific spell came when he scored 34 goals in 90 appearances

for Swansea from 1978 to 1980 as John Toshack's side climbed up from the Third Division to the Second. He featured alongside former Reds such as Ian Callaghan, Tommy Smith and Phil Boersma. Waddle moved to Australia in 2009 to be closer to his daughter, and was appointed technical advisor of amateur Australian side Demon Knights before taking over as the club's head coach during the 2012 campaign.

FACTFILE

BORN
Wallsend, 9 June 1954
POSITION
Centre-forward
OTHER CLUBS
Halifax Town (1971–73),
Leicester City (1977–78),
Swansea City (1978–80),
Newport County (1980–1981),
Gloucester City (1981–82),
Mansfield Town (1982),
Happy Valley (1982–83),
Hartlepool United (1983),
Peterborough United
(1983–85),
Hartlepool United (1985),
Swansea City (1985–86),
Barry Town (1986),
Al Wakrah (1986–1987),
Barry Town (1987–88),
Llanelli (1988),
Port Talbot Athletic (1988),
Maesteg Park Athletic
(1988–89),
Bridgend Town (1989),
Llanelli (1989–93)
SIGNED FROM
Halifax Town, £40,000,
22 June 1973
LFC DEBUT GAME/GOAL
27 November 1973 /
8 December 1973
CONTRACT EXPIRY
September 1977
HONOURS
European Cup 1977

Season	League		FA Cup		League Cup		Europe		Other		Total	
	App	Goals	App	Goals	App	Goals	App	Goals	App	Goals	App	Goals
1973/74	11	1	2	0	3	0	0	0	-	-	16	1
1974/75	0 (5)	0	0	0	0	0	0	0	0	0	0 (5)	0
1976/77	0	0	0	0	0	0	0 (1)	0	0	0	0 (1)	0
Total	**11 (5)**	**1**	**2**	**0**	**3**	**0**	**0 (1)**	**0**	**0**	**0**	**16 (6)**	**1**

Wadsworth, Harold

HAROLD WADSWORTH'S older brother Walter was already at Anfield when he arrived in 1918 but Harold found stiff competition for his left-wing position from Albert Pearson and was restricted to just nine league appearances in his debut season.

He was selected more frequently in 1920/21 and was applauded for his 'splendid turn of speed' on his reintroduction into the side but his fault was still said to be 'a desire to delay crossing the ball which allows a defence to take up position again'. He only made four league appearances during the two seasons when Liverpool first won and then retained the league title. Wadsworth played mostly on the right wing in 1923/24, which proved to be his last season as a Liverpool player. Wadsworth was an ever-present in Leicester's team that won the Second Division. After 106 games and

seven goals for the Foxes he left for Second Division Nottingham Forest in April 1927. Wadsworth

played 35 games and scored 10 goals before helping Millwall establish themselves in the Second Division for three years.

FACTFILE

BORN
Bootle, Liverpool,
1 October 1898
DIED
2 November 1975
POSITION
Right/left-winger
OTHER CLUBS
St Matthew's,
Tranmere Rovers (1914–1918),
Leicester City (1924–27),
Nottingham Forest (1927–28),
Millwall (1928–32)
SIGNED FROM
Tranmere Rovers, January 1918
LFC DEBUT GAME/GOAL
4 October 1919 /
25 September 1920
CONTRACT EXPIRY
24 June 1924

Season	League		FA Cup		Other		Total	
	App	Goals	App	Goals	App	Goals	App	Goals
1919/20	9	0	0	0	-	-	9	0
1920/21	25	3	0	0	-	-	25	3
1921/22	1	0	0	0	0	0	1	0
1922/23	3	0	0	0	-	-	3	0
1923/24	17	0	0	0	-	-	17	0
Total	**55**	**3**	**0**	**0**	**0**	**0**	**55**	**3**

Wadsworth, Walter

BEFORE the likes of Gerry Byrne, Ron Yeats, Tommy Smith and Jamie Carragher, the defender who had opponents shaking in their boots was Walter Wadsworth from Bootle. After reading through several match reports at the time it becomes quite evident that Wadsworth was the quintessential tough man who referees had to give a talking to on quite a few occasions because of the severity of his challenges.

Wadsworth was also quite an accomplished footballer. He was at the heart of one of the best back-five formations in the history of the club with full-backs Ephraim Longworth and Donald Mackinlay, and his fellow half-backs Jock McNab and Tom Bromilow. Equipped with this excellent quintet, and with goalkeeper Elisha Scott as a last line of defence, Liverpool first won and then retained the League Championship in 1922 and 1923.

Waddy greeted by King George V in 1920

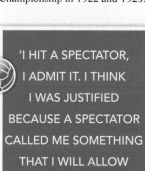

'I HIT A SPECTATOR, I ADMIT IT. I THINK I WAS JUSTIFIED BECAUSE A SPECTATOR CALLED ME SOMETHING THAT I WILL ALLOW NO MAN TO CALL ME'

WADSWORTH'S temper tended to boil over on the field, mainly aimed at opposition players, but the fans of his adversaries also had to watch out. Spectators gave the players an ear-bashing as well back then and in one particular game against Sheffield United on 1 December 1923 at Bramall Lane Wadsworth snapped when goaded by a United fan. He was unrepentant about this incident, as evidenced by his article in the *Topical Times*, which was published the following week. 'I hit a spectator, I admit it. I think I was justified because a spectator called me something that I will allow no man to call me. It must not be imagined that because a spectator has paid his

bob that he can, willy-nilly, help himself in the epithets department. I hope the action I took will lead to the offenders realising that they cannot lean over the railings and offer vile insults at footballers.'

Wadsworth's career low came on 14 February 1925 at Anfield. Newcastle's Urwin threw mud at Wadsworth, who in return punched him in the face. Wadsworth was banned by the Football League for the remainder of the season and only made a further four appearances for Liverpool before signing in May 1926 for Alex Raisbeck's Bristol City at the ripe old age of 36. He was Bristol City's captain when they won the Third Division South and also featured in 27 Second Division games. He played into his forties with Oswestry Town and was a tremendous competitor who never gave in for Liverpool's or any other team's cause! Sunderland legend and England player Charlie Buchan described Wadsworth as the most difficult half-back he had faced. 'You never know what he's going to do next. He's so unorthodox and seems to "get there" without disclosing his intentions.'

When 63-year-old Donald Mackinlay, former captain of Liverpool, looked back at his

career in an interview in 1955 he remembered Wadsworth as the toughest guy he had ever come across. 'I remember one match in the early twenties when Wadsworth injured a leg and I saw blood coming out of his boot. I told him to get some attention to it and his reply was: "Whose blood is it, yours or mine?" and went on playing.'

FACTFILE

BORN
Bootle, Liverpool,
7 October 1890
DIED
12 October 1951
POSITION
Centre-half
OTHER CLUBS
Lingdale, Ormskirk (1911–12),
Bristol City (1926–28),
Flint Town (1928–29),
New Brighton (1929–30),
Oswestry Town (1930–31)
SIGNED FROM
Ormskirk, April 1912
LFC DEBUT GAME/GOAL
20 March 1915 /
28 August 1920
CONTRACT EXPIRY
14 May 1926
HONOURS
League Championship
1921/22, 1922/23

Season	League		FA Cup		Other		Total	
	App	Goals	App	Goals	App	Goals	App	Goals
1914/15	1	0	0	0	-	-	1	0
1919/20	33	0	5	0	-	-	38	0
1920/21	42	5	3	0	-	-	45	5
1921/22	38	0	3	1	1	0	42	1
1922/23	37	2	4	0	-	-	41	2
1923/24	37	0	5	0	-	-	42	0
1924/25	25	0	3	0	-	-	28	0
1925/26	5	0	0	0	-	-	5	0
Total	**218**	**7**	**23**	**1**	**1**	**0**	**242**	**8**

Walker,
Johnny

JOHNNY WALKER and Tommy Robertson signed for Liverpool from Edinburgh club Hearts at the end of the 1897/98 season for a combined fee of £350.

Walker had been a tremendous success at Hearts, winning the Scottish League in 1895 and 1897 and lifting the Scottish Cup as captain in 1896. He made his Scotland debut against Ireland on 30 March 1895, scoring twice in a 3-1 win. In his full debut season at Liverpool Walker missed just two league and cup games, scoring 11 goals in 32 First Division matches as the Reds finished runners-up to Aston Villa. Walker did get into trouble in November 1898 along with team-mates Hugh Morgan and George Allan when they were charged with a breach of the peace and obstructing the police. They were being a little too lively in the street and a constable arrived to settle down matters. Walker shouted: 'Let's show him

some Scotch blood!' In the end the constable took Allan into custody while Morgan and Walker tried to prevent his arrest. The inside-right started the following campaign in great form, scoring seven goals in the opening 10 games, but only got three goals in the remaining 21. Despite the fact that Walker's goals dried up he continued to be a key player for the Reds, who now relied on the goalscoring talents of centre-forward Sam Raybould. Liverpool's last game of the 1900/01 season was against relegation-doomed West Bromwich Albion. A draw would suffice for the Reds to topple Sunderland, who were equal on points with a superior goal average, but had already played all their games. Walker was the hero of the day, as the *Daily Express* reported: 'Robertson only just missed

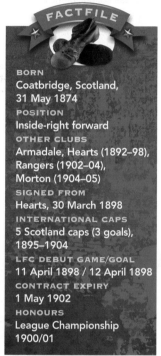

scoring for Liverpool and at the other end Garfield was charged off the ball just when about to shoot at an almost open goal. At last, however, Liverpool got away and Walker scored.' Walker played one more season for Liverpool before returning to his native Scotland to play for Rangers.

WALKER was very popular among his team-mates, not least with Alex Raisbeck. 'Johnnie, I make bold to say, was the most splendid fellow I met during the whole of my professional career,' he said in

the *Daily News* in 1915. Walker was the practical joker of the pack. Whether locking out his team-mates from their hotel rooms (much to the chagrin of the coach who wanted every player early to bed) or decorating Billy Dunlop's 'swanky' brown man-bag with wallpaper and paste, 'he was simply unique and up to all manner of tricks', according to skipper Raisbeck.

	League		FA Cup		Total	
Season	App	Goals	App	Goals	App	Goals
1897/98	3	2	0	0	3	2
1898/99	32	11	6	1	38	12
1899/1900	27	10	4	0	31	10
1900/01	29	6	1	0	30	6
1901/02	18	1	0	0	18	1
Total	**109**	**30**	**11**	**1**	**120**	**31**

FACTFILE

BORN
Coatbridge, Scotland,
31 May 1874
POSITION
Inside-right forward
OTHER CLUBS
Armadale, Hearts (1892–98),
Rangers (1902–04),
Morton (1904–05)
SIGNED FROM
Hearts, 30 March 1898
INTERNATIONAL CAPS
5 Scotland caps (3 goals),
1895–1904
LFC DEBUT GAME/GOAL
11 April 1898 / 12 April 1898
CONTRACT EXPIRY
1 May 1902
HONOURS
League Championship
1900/01

Walker,
Willie

INSIDE-FORWARD Willie Walker was a regular in Liverpool's side in September and October of the 1897/98 season.

During his brief stay with the club the transfer system came into operation, and a sum of £100 was put on his head. Through a singular mistake in the list Liverpool sent to FA headquarters his name read 'J. Walker' instead of 'W. Walker'. It was only a slip, but the wrong initial was made to stand, and the Scotsman was allowed to re-join his old club, Leith Athletic, for free!

On 12 January 1907 Walker played inside-right in Leith Athletic's

match against Vale of Leven at Logie Green, Edinburgh. While Walker was shooting for goal, Barr, one of the Leven backs, put up his foot to stop the ball, but struck Walker in the stomach. Walker went off the field but resumed for a few minutes. At the end of the game he went to hospital where he was kept for a week. He was discharged as he seemed to be recovering, but soon returned to the Edinburgh Royal Infirmary where he passed away the following day on 23 January 1907.

	League		FA Cup		Total	
Season	App	Goals	App	Goals	App	Goals
1897/98	12	3	0	0	12	3
Total	**12**	**3**	**0**	**0**	**12**	**3**

FACTFILE

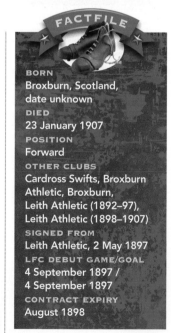

BORN
Broxburn, Scotland,
date unknown
DIED
23 January 1907
POSITION
Forward
OTHER CLUBS
Cardross Swifts, Broxburn
Athletic, Broxburn,
Leith Athletic (1892–97),
Leith Athletic (1898–1907)
SIGNED FROM
Leith Athletic, 2 May 1897
LFC DEBUT GAME/GOAL
4 September 1897 /
4 September 1897
CONTRACT EXPIRY
August 1898

Wall, Peter

PETER WALL, or 'Max' as he was christened by players and supporters alike after the famous comedian, arrived at Liverpool as a 22-year-old when Shankly paid £35,000 for him and his fellow Wrexham full-back Stuart Mason, who lasted two years at Anfield without making a first-team appearance.

Liverpool had previously missed out on Huddersfield's defender Bob McNab, who moved to Arsenal and played 365 games for the Gunners, but Wrexham couldn't refuse Liverpool's offer for the promising pair greatly valued by manager Jack Rowley. 'It grieves me to lose these players,' he said. 'I might get back to Wales and find my windows have been smashed. But the fans must realise that this deal has been done to benefit the club and the players.' Wall had difficulty in breaking the monopoly that Chris Lawler and Gerry Byrne had in the two full-back positions, until towards the end of the 1967/68 season. Wall was first-choice left-back for the first 13 league matches the following season, but then the more experienced and versatile Geoff Strong took over the number 3 shirt. Wall made over 190 appearances as Crystal Palace dropped from the First Division to the Third. He faced his old team, Liverpool, at Selhurst Park on

19 August 1972, but unfortunately broke his leg in a tackle by Tommy Smith. Wall joined NASL's California Surf in 1978 and finished his career in the States.

Season	League		FA Cup		League Cup		Europe		Total	
	App	Goals	App	Goals	App	Goals	App	Goals	App	Goals
1967/68	9	0	0	0	0	0	0	0	9	0
1968/69	13	0	0	0	2	0	2	0	17	0
1969/70	9	0	6	0	0	0	1	0	16	0
Total	**31**	**0**	**6**	**0**	**2**	**0**	**3**	**0**	**42**	**0**

Wallace, Gordon

GORDON WALLACE made his first-team debut in the club's first season back in the top division after an eight-year absence. A year later when Liverpool won the League Championship no fewer than 10 men made at least 33 league appearances, but Gordon Wallace's only league game came at Burnley towards the end of the season, when he replaced the injured Roger Hunt.

WALLACE was the toast of the town in an eight-day period in the 1964/65 season when he scored five goals. He scored once as Liverpool drew 2-2 with West Ham in the Charity Shield and then made history when he scored Liverpool's first goal in the European Cup after only three minutes against KR in Reykjavík. He added another in the game after an hour's play. Wallace scored twice at Anfield against Arsenal on the opening day of the league campaign, the first ever game covered by the BBC as their *Match of the Day*. Following three consecutive defeats Shankly brought in Bobby Graham in Wallace's place and he had to wait

> HE SCORED
> LIVERPOOL'S FIRST
> GOAL IN
> THE EUROPEAN CUP
> AFTER ONLY
> THREE MINUTES
> AGAINST
> KR IN REYKJAVÍK

GORDON WALLACE
LIVERPOOL

over five months for his next league outing. Wallace called it quits at Anfield in October 1967 after a succession of injuries and two frustrating years in Liverpool's reserve team. He made just over 100 appearances in five years at Fourth Division Crewe, scoring 22 goals.

Season	League		FA Cup		Europe		Other		Total	
	App	Goals	App	Goals	App	Goals	App	Goals	App	Goals
1962/63	7	1	0	0	-	-	-	-	7	1
1963/64	1	0	0	0	-	-	-	-	1	0
1964/65	12	2	0	0	1	2	1	1	14	5
Total	**20**	**3**	**0**	**0**	**1**	**2**	**1**	**1**	**22**	**6**

Walsh,
Jimmy

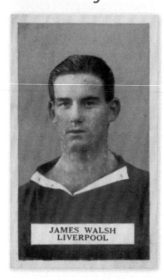

JAMES WALSH
LIVERPOOL

CENTRE-FORWARD Jimmy Walsh got his first-team chance when Dick Johnson seriously injured his knee in the opening game of the 1923/24 season.

Walsh scored twice on his league debut, a thumping 6-2 home win against Birmingham City on 29 August 1923, and finished the campaign as the club's top scorer with 19 from 42 matches. His star turn was scoring a hat-trick in a 4-1 FA Cup second round victory at Burnden Park against Bolton Wanderers in February 1924. After this exceptional season it was all downhill for Walsh as far as his Liverpool career was concerned. He only made a further 35 appearances for the club over the next four seasons.

Season	League		FA Cup		Total	
	App	Goals	App	Goals	App	Goals
1923/24	37	16	5	3	42	19
1924/25	4	3	1	0	5	3
1925/26	12	3	0	0	12	3
1926/27	7	0	0	0	7	0
1927/28	9	2	2	0	11	2
Total	**69**	**24**	**8**	**3**	**77**	**27**

FACTFILE

BORN
Stockport, 15 May 1901
DIED
1971
POSITION
Forward
OTHER CLUBS
Stockport County (1919–22), Hull City (1928–31), Colwyn Bay United (1931), Crewe Alexandra (1931–32), Colwyn Bay United (1932–33), Rhyl Athletic
SIGNED FROM
Stockport County, 20 May 1922
LFC DEBUT GAME/GOAL
29 August 1923 / 29 August 1923
CONTRACT EXPIRY
June 1928

Walsh,
Paul

PAUL WALSH was voted the PFA's most promising player of the year in 1983/84 and was at the centre of a bidding war between Manchester United and Liverpool. Walsh opted for a move to Merseyside, seemingly a ready-made poster boy destined for greatness.

Ian Rush was sidelined at the start of the 1984/85 season so Walsh went straight into the first team

> WALSH WENT STRAIGHT INTO THE FIRST TEAM AND SCORED JUST 14 SECONDS INTO HIS HOME DEBUT AGAINST WEST HAM, WHICH IS STILL THE QUICKEST EVER GOAL SCORED BY A LIVERPOOL PLAYER

and scored just 14 seconds into his home debut against West Ham, which is still the quickest ever goal scored by a Liverpool player. His injury in his 10th league game coincided with Rush's return to full fitness and he was in and out of the team for the rest of the season. Walsh did score three times in Liverpool's successful run in Europe and played in the ill-fated final against Juventus in Brussels. A great run of 18 goals in 25 matches in the 1985/86 Double season was a testament to Walsh's ability, but then disaster struck when he ruptured his ligaments. One wonders what might have been, as this was the most important spell of

his Liverpool career. Walsh started his scoring spree in a 2-1 defeat to QPR in the league, netted in the Screen Sport Super Cup against Southampton, scored two against his old club Luton in the league and a hat-trick against Brighton in the League Cup. He failed to score against

FACTFILE

BORN
Plumstead, London, 1 October 1962
POSITION
Centre-forward
OTHER CLUBS
Charlton Athletic (1977–82), Luton Town (1982–84), Tottenham Hotspur (1988–92), Queens Park Rangers (loan, 1991), Portsmouth (1992–94), Manchester City (1994–95), Portsmouth (1995–97)
SIGNED FROM
Luton Town, £700,000, 21 May 1984
INTERNATIONAL CAPS
5 England caps (1 goal), 1983–84
LFC DEBUT GAME/GOAL
18 August 1984 / 27 August 1984
CONTRACT EXPIRY
16 February 1988
HONOURS
League Championship 1985/86

Leicester, but managed one against Coventry and then ripped West Brom apart by setting up three and scoring Liverpool's fourth. Tottenham and Aston Villa were added to his victims, with Walsh having scored 12 goals in 12 games.

Kenny Dalglish was a big fan of his talents. 'When we brought the ball in to his feet Walshy danced around defenders. I was well aware that many centre-halves, particularly the old-school ones, found it tricky dealing with small strikers such as Walshy. He buzzed around as they swatted away at him ineffectually. They also discovered to their surprise, and cost, that Walshy could climb into the air, hang there and head the ball.' Liverpool's 14-match unbeaten run fell apart against Arsenal on 14 December 1985. Dalglish chopped and changed the squad while Liverpool struggled, only drawing three of their next four games. Walsh scored two goals in Liverpool's 3-2 win over Watford on 12 January and had

firmly established himself in the first team when Kevin Moran's tackle on 9 February ruined his season. He returned seven weeks later, obviously being hurried back too soon, and his name then didn't appear on the teamsheet until the penultimate game of the season. Meanwhile, with Dalglish back in the team Liverpool strung together a remarkable 11 wins from the final dozen First Division fixtures to climb over neighbours Everton. Liverpool secured the league and cup double, Walsh watching from the stands as Liverpool beat Everton 3-1 in the FA Cup final.

WALSH returned to the starting line-up on 25 October 1986 and scored a hat-trick against Norwich

a week later. He was a regular in the side until late April 1987, but wasn't even included in the squad in the last three games. He had only scored three goals since the Norwich game. The arrival of John Aldridge and Peter Beardsley in 1987 meant that Walsh was surplus to requirements at Anfield so he joined Tottenham. He made 28 starts for Spurs in the 1988/89 season but was less involved following the arrival of Gary Lineker and had to become accustomed to the role of a substitute. He won the FA Cup at Spurs in 1991, coming on in the 82nd minute against Nottingham Forest in the final and playing the whole of extra time in which Des Walker scored a decisive own goal. In June 1992

Walsh went the opposite way along with a tidy sum when Darren Anderton was brought in from Portsmouth. Walsh was popular at First Division Pompey and was voted the fans' Player of the Year in his debut season. In March 1994 Walsh was on the move again, this time to Manchester City in the Premier League. Again he proved a popular acquisition as his elegance and all-action style delighted the fans. Walsh made a somewhat surprising return to Pompey in September 1995 after featuring in 39 league matches and scoring 12 goals in the previous season. A cruciate ligament injury in 1996 finished his career after only 22 appearances in his second spell at Portsmouth.

Season	League		FA Cup		League Cup		Europe		Other		Total	
	App	Goals	App	Goals	App	Goals	App	Goals	App	Goals	App	Goals
1984/85	22 (4)	8	1 (2)	2	2	0	7	3	0 (1)	0	32 (7)	13
1985/86	17 (3)	11	2	1	4	4	-	-	6	2	29 (3)	18
1986/87	23	6	3	0	4 (1)	0	-	-	0 (1)	0	30 (2)	6
1987/88	1 (7)	0	0	0	0 (1)	0	-	-	-	-	1 (8)	0
Total	**63 (14)**	**25**	**6 (2)**	**3**	**10 (2)**	**4**	**7**	**3**	**6 (2)**	**2**	**92 (20)**	**37**

Walsh, Sheila

IN MAY 2005 Rafa Benítez made his private secretary, Sheila Walsh, the centre of attention when opinions varied on whether Luis Garcia's effort in the Champions League semi-final had actually crossed the line or not.

'After the game my secretary Sheila, who was sitting right in line in the Main Stand, said to me that the ball had crossed the line,' Benítez said. 'She is a very honest person and that was good enough for me. It was a goal.'

Sheila had been a valued employee at the club since becoming Bob Paisley's secretary in 1981 and went on to serve every manager since. She was a joy to deal with for the various international fan clubs that wanted to gain access to Melwood, greeting them with a big smile upon their entry to the

SHEILA HAD BEEN A VALUED EMPLOYEE AT THE CLUB SINCE BECOMING BOB PAISLEY'S SECRETARY IN 1981

training ground. She passed away on New Year's Day 2008 after losing her brave battle against cancer. A whole host of Liverpool

players and managers past and present paid their respects at her funeral at the church of St Mary the Virgin in Waterloo.

Benítez was emotional to lose a trusted friend. 'During my time as the manager here, I found Sheila to be professional, committed, warm, friendly and above all courageous in the face of her suffering.' Roy Evans, whom Sheila worked for as well, put on record his appreciation. 'Sheila was brilliant, both as a person and as a colleague. She was a real unsung hero. When you are manager of Liverpool, you have a lot of demands placed on you, but Sheila was brilliant at sorting out what we needed to do immediately and what could wait. She was fantastic at taking the pressure off people, but she also had a wonderful personality

and a great sense of humour. One thing which I am sure people can appreciate is there is a great need for privacy when you are managing a club like Liverpool. You don't want little snippets of information getting out here and there, and Sheila was one of the most discreet people you could ever meet.'

Walters, Mark

MARK WALTERS made a name for himself in the Aston Villa team in the 1982/83 season at the tender age of 18. Unfortunately for him Villa were on a slow decline after winning the League Championship in 1981 and the European Cup in 1982 and were eventually relegated in 1987.

Villa came straight up again but halfway through their first season back in the top flight Walters was enticed to Graeme Souness's Rangers. Walters joined the likes of Trevor Steven, Gary Stevens, Terry Butcher, Chris Woods and Ray Wilkins, and the former Villa star was a tremendous success but suffered terrible racial abuse. Walters' Rangers debut was on 2 January 1988 in an Old Firm derby at Parkhead. Monkey noises were aimed at him and bananas thrown on to the field. He was also pelted by all kinds of objects at Hearts' Tynecastle. 'That was the worst place of all. It wasn't just the abuse because I can handle that,' Walters said. 'It was all the objects that were being thrown.'

Souness envisaged Walters doing same amount of damage to English defenders in a Liverpool shirt. Walters had only been at

Liverpool for three months when he became the darling of the Kop when Auxerre came to town in the first season that the Reds were back in Europe. Liverpool had lost 2-0 in the first leg but were 2-0 up at Anfield and heading for extra time when Jan Mølby's magnificent pass split the French defence in the 84th minute. Walters raced through and clipped a shot just inside the far post. Delirium followed and Liverpool were through to the third round. Walters' best season was 1992/93 when he scored 13 goals in 44 games and scored a tremendous double after coming on as a substitute against Kenny Dalglish's Blackburn Rovers on 13 December 1992 at Anfield. In the 77th minute Jamie Redknapp laid the ball into the path of Walters, who cut inside a tiring David May and unleashed a drive that he described as the best goal of his Anfield career. Walters netted the winner eight minutes later.

HOWEVER, his blessed step-over worked way too seldom. He was very inconsistent and tended to fade out of games. He was loaned

out to Stoke after making almost as many appearances for Liverpool reserves in the Pontins League Division One in the 1993/94 season as for the first team in the Premier League. His free transfer to Southampton in January 1996 was hardly a surprise. The middle name of Mark Walters, Everton, always comes up and is of course highlighted considering his association with the Reds. Asked by a Red if he would ever consider changing his middle name, Walters said: 'No, well

unfortunately my mother told me that if I change any part of my name she'll disown me, so that one's for life.'

FACTFILE

BORN
Birmingham, 2 June 1964
POSITION
Right/left-winger
OTHER CLUBS
Aston Villa (1978–87),
Rangers (1987–91),
Stoke City (loan, 1994),
Wolverhampton Wanderers
(loan, 1994),
Southampton (1996),
Swindon Town (1996–99),
Bristol Rovers (1999–2002),
Ilkeston Town (2002),
Tividale (2002),
Willenhall Town (2002–03),
Dudley Town (2003–05)
SIGNED FROM
Rangers, £1.25million,
13 August 1991
INTERNATIONAL CAPS
1 England cap, 1991
LFC DEBUT GAME/GOAL
17 August 1991 /
7 September 1991
CONTRACT EXPIRY
17 January 1996
HONOURS
FA Cup 1992;
League Cup 1995

Season	League App	League Goals	FA Cup App	FA Cup Goals	League Cup App	League Cup Goals	Europe App	Europe Goals	Other App	Other Goals	Total App	Total Goals
1991/92	18 (7)	3	2 (1)	0	4	2	4 (1)	1	-	-	28 (9)	6
1992/93	26 (8)	11	1	0	5	2	3	0	1	0	36 (8)	13
1993/94	7 (10)	0	1	0	0 (2)	0	-	-	-	-	8 (12)	0
1994/95	7 (11)	0	2 (2)	0	1	0	-	-	-	-	10 (13)	0
Total	**58 (36)**	**14**	**6 (3)**	**0**	**10 (2)**	**4**	**7 (1)**	**1**	**1**	**0**	**82 (42)**	**19**

Wark, John

JOHN WARK burst onto the scene in 1975 as a part of Ipswich's successful FA Youth Cup-winning team and the centre-half who had been fifth choice at the beginning of the season was by now starring in the first team.

He benefited from the guidance of Bobby Robson, developing into a free-scoring midfielder and reaching the pinnacle of his career in the 1980/81 season when he was voted PFA Player of the Year as well as Young European Player of the Year, having netted 14 goals in Ipswich's successful UEFA Cup campaign, equalling the European record set by Jose Altafini of AC Milan in the 1962/63 European Cup. He scored a total of 36 goals

in this outstanding campaign when Ipswich finished runners-up in the league to Aston Villa. Wark had his brush with Hollywood in the role of Arthur Hayes, a prisoner of war held by the Nazis in *Escape to Victory*. Among his co-stars were Sylvester Stallone, Michael Caine, Bobby Moore and Pele.

Wark scored 46 goals in his last two seasons at Ipswich, but after

Robson's departure the club was on the slide and the player who Robson once claimed to be 'the finest goalscoring midfielder of his generation' wanted a change of scenery. 'I felt that I deserved to be paid more but Ipswich refused and that prompted me to ask for a transfer,' Wark admitted.

THE SCOTSMAN made a high-profile move to Anfield with the impending departure of inspirational skipper Graeme Souness. Wark was staggered by how uncomplicated his medical at Liverpool was. 'I was rather taken aback when the doctor entered the Anfield bootroom,' Wark said in his autobiography:

He was small in stature and I couldn't help but detect the smell of alcohol on his breath as he introduced himself to me. I was even more surprised when he announced we would stay put to conduct the medical examination. He took my blood pressure, looked at the reading and muttered 'that's fine'. Then something happened that to this day I still cannot get over. He asked me to bend down and touch my toes. Trying not to show my surprise, I did exactly as he asked and as I lifted my head he spoke again, this time to announce 'you've passed'.

Wark was certainly one of the lads and an unnamed team-mate described him as 'a total mad-cap with an unnerving habit of roaring with laughter without prior warning'. On his arrival on Merseyside Wark was placed at the same hotel as summer arrivals Jan Mølby and Paul Walsh. Almost inevitably because of the culture at the time, the trio didn't waste time finding out what the city of Liverpool had to offer in terms of nightlife. Mark Lawrenson referred to Wark as 'our champion beer-drinker'. Wark scored on his debut at Watford and made nine First Division appearances as the championship was won for a third successive year, but he was ineligible to play in the European Cup that ended in victory in Rome.

Not everybody was convinced as to Wark's usefulness to Liverpool, but prior to the 1984/85 season he declared, 'People feel Joe Fagan made a mistake buying me but I'm determined to make them eat their words!' Wark was Liverpool's leading goalscorer with 27 goals

in his first full season. He scored 18 goals in 40 league games, continued his incredible striking rate in Europe with five in 10 games, scored four in seven FA Cup games, netted three hat-tricks and scored his 100th league goal in a game against Ipswich. Wark was number 11 in Liverpool's starting line-up at Heysel on a fateful night in the biggest game of his career, but looking back, he admitted, it was 'as if I am staring at a blank page in a book'. A damaged Achilles suffered in training and a broken ankle when back in first-team action were heavily responsible for the low number of matches Wark played in the glorious Double season of 1985/86 and the following fruitless campaign.

The emergence of Jan Mølby, settling in while Wark was out injured, restricted his chances further. Mølby was a big fan of Wark and analysed

him as a player for *LFChistory.net*. 'John is probably along with Bryan Robson the greatest goalscoring midfielder there has ever been. My strength was to read the game, but I still didn't have that ability he had of knowing exactly when to arrive in the penalty area. John was an exceptional player. His biggest problem at Liverpool was he wasn't enough of a Liverpool player. His game was doing the job in the opposition's penalty box and maybe he didn't take enough part in the rest of the game.'

Wark's mentor, Bobby Robson, advised him: 'Money isn't everything. Go where you will be happiest.' That place was Ipswich Town, even though by then they were in the Second Division following relegation in 1986. During his second spell at

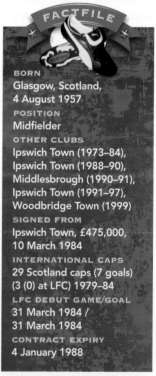

FACTFILE

BORN
Glasgow, Scotland,
4 August 1957
POSITION
Midfielder
OTHER CLUBS
Ipswich Town (1973–84),
Ipswich Town (1988–90),
Middlesbrough (1990–91),
Ipswich Town (1991–97),
Woodbridge Town (1999)
SIGNED FROM
Ipswich Town, £475,000,
10 March 1984
INTERNATIONAL CAPS
29 Scotland caps (7 goals)
(3 (0) at LFC) 1979–84
LFC DEBUT GAME/GOAL
31 March 1984 /
31 March 1984
CONTRACT EXPIRY
4 January 1988

Season	League		FA Cup		League Cup		Europe		Other		Total	
	App	Goals	App	Goals	App	Goals	App	Goals	App	Goals	App	Goals
1983/84	9	2	0	0	0	0	0	0	0	0	9	2
1984/85	40	18	7	4	2 (1)	0	10	5	2	0	61 (1)	27
1985/86	7 (2)	3	2 (2)	2	2 (1)	1	-	-	0 (2)	0	11 (7)	6
1986/87	8 (3)	5	2	0	1 (2)	2	-	-	1	0	12 (5)	7
1987/88	0 (1)	0	0	0	1	0	-	-	-	-	1 (1)	0
Total	**64 (6)**	**28**	**11 (2)**	**6**	**6 (4)**	**3**	**10**	**5**	**3 (2)**	**0**	**94 (14)**	**42**

Portman Road, Wark's eye for a goal remained as strong as ever, as did his competence as a penalty-taker after being successful with 38 out of 43 spot kicks during his first spell with the East Anglian club. A poor contract offer by his standards prompted him to go to Middlesbrough in 1990 after being voted the club's Player of the Year in two successive seasons. Wark returned 'home' one year later for his third spell, this time returning to his old position of centre-half. He soon made an emotional return to Anfield in the FA Cup in 1992. He was forced to come off with severe cramp towards the end of a pulsating match that Liverpool won 3-2 after extra time. 'The fans gave me a standing ovation. They gave me one of best feelings I have ever known in football. I was almost in tears,' Wark said.

Wark played six more years for Ipswich until his retirement at 40. He made more than 820 appearances and scored a staggering total of 223 goals, not bad for a midfielder! Wark became one of four inaugural inductees into Ipswich Town's Hall of Fame. Bob Paisley has the last word: 'How many times have you heard it said that goalscoring is all about being in "the right place at the right time?" Most footballers know where the right "place" is, but relatively few can sense when the time is "right". John Wark has great timing. You could set your watch by him.'

> 'MOST FOOTBALLERS KNOW WHERE THE RIGHT "PLACE" IS, BUT RELATIVELY FEW CAN SENSE WHEN THE TIME IS "RIGHT". JOHN WARK HAS GREAT TIMING. YOU COULD SET YOUR WATCH BY HIM'
>
> BOB PAISLEY

Warnock, Stephen

LEGENDARY left-back Alan Kennedy had a hand in bringing Stephen Warnock to Liverpool. 'I remember Stephen being at one of my soccer schools and he really stood out as being a brilliant prospect. I got on the phone to Steve Heighway and Roy Evans and said you have got to take a look at this boy.'

Warnock overcame three leg breaks as he made his way from the Liverpool Academy into professional football but showed great character and determination to survive these ordeals and make a name for himself. Academy director and former Liverpool star Steve Heighway witnessed Warnock's struggles. 'Watching him go through six months of rehabilitation from a broken leg, then watching him break his leg immediately again and go through a further six months rehab and then get another slight break after that. I don't think people realise what he has achieved.' Warnock has always played football at full blast, which his former Liverpool team-mate Danny Guthrie can attest to: 'Stevie Warnock is the hardest tackler. He's mean in the tackle, even in training.'

Before he made his first-team debut Warnock impressed when on loan at Coventry in the 2003/04 season, voted the fans' Player of the Season. Warnock made 30 appearances for Liverpool in Rafa Benítez's first season at the club. Despite finally making progress 2004/05 was a heartbreaking season for Warnock as he missed out on a League Cup and European Cup medal. 'I spent the summer getting over that,' he reflected. Warnock made six more starts the following season but he wasn't too happy with Benítez's modus operandi. 'Even if you'd played really well one week, you never thought you would play the next. People were being rested in September and October and I just think that's crazy. It was comical sometimes. No one would have a clue why certain people weren't included but the manager would keep his reasons to himself.'

After making only six appearances in the first half of 2006/07 Warnock was sold to Blackburn, where he made the left-back position his own and also featured in midfield. Warnock was in inspired form and was voted Blackburn's Player of the Year in the 2008/09 season. On 11 April 2009, before Blackburn Rovers' match against Liverpool, Warnock laid a floral tribute with the numbers '96' in front of the Kop on the 20th anniversary of the Hillsborough disaster. This was greeted with chants for Warnock from the Kop. Warnock had a successful 2009/10 season with Aston Villa and made Fabio Capello's squad for the 2010

FACTFILE

BORN
Ormskirk, 12 December 1981
POSITION
Left-back
OTHER CLUBS
Bradford City (loan, 2002), Coventry City (loan, 2003–04), Blackburn Rovers (2007–09), Aston Villa (2009–13), Bolton Wanderers (loan, 2012), Leeds United (2013–)
JOINED
1996; signed professional 27 April 1999
INTERNATIONAL CAPS
1 England cap, 2008
LFC DEBUT GAME/GOAL
10 August 2004 / 15 March 2006
CONTRACT EXPIRY
22 January 2007

World Cup, but didn't see a single minute of action. Warnock played in most of Villa's first-team matches in 2011/12, but clearly wasn't fancied by Paul Lambert as he started his reign at Villa Park. Following his release from his Villa contract Warnock signed a three-year contract for Leeds United.

Season	League		FA Cup		League Cup		Europe		Other		Total	
	App	Goals	App	Goals	App	Goals	App	Goals	App	Goals	App	Goals
2004/05	11 (8)	0	1	0	3 (1)	0	2 (4)	0	-	-	17 (13)	0
2005/06	15 (5)	1	1 (1)	0	1	0	5 (1)	0	1	0	23 (7)	1
2006/07	1	0	0	0	3	0	2 (1)	0	0	0	6 (1)	0
Total	**27 (13)**	**1**	**2 (1)**	**0**	**7 (1)**	**0**	**9 (6)**	**0**	**1**	**0**	**46 (21)**	**1**

Watkinson, Billy

BILLY WATKINSON was described by Liverpool's handbook in 1949 as 'a strong type of player, possessing a good shot'. Liverpool won the first post-war League Championship in 1946/47 and Watkinson played in the last six matches of that seemingly endless season.

THE FOLLOWING campaign he played in the first seven league games before losing his place to Bob Priday. It was always going to be hard to keep a spot in a forward line with the experience and goalscoring abilities of men like Billy Liddell, Albert Stubbins and Jack Balmer. Watkinson was transferred to Accrington Stanley in January 1951 for a club record fee of £3,000. He scored an impressive 45 times in 105 league matches for Stanley in the Third Division North, and had a two-year spell in the same division with Halifax, where he scored 24 goals in 60 appearances.

Season	League		FA Cup		Total	
	App	Goals	App	Goals	App	Goals
1946/47	6	1	0	0	6	1
1947/48	11	0	0	0	11	0
1948/49	6	1	0	0	6	1
1949/50	1	0	0	0	1	0
Total	24	2	0	0	24	2

FACTFILE

BORN
Prescot, Lancashire,
16 March 1922
DIED
2001
POSITION
Right/left-winger
OTHER CLUBS
Prescot Cables (1939–46),
Accrington Stanley (1951–54),
Halifax Town (1954–56),
Prescot Cables (1956–58)
SIGNED FROM
Prescot Cables,
February 1946
LFC DEBUT GAME/GOAL
26 April 1947 /
26 April 1947
CONTRACT EXPIRY
20 January 1951

Watson, Alex

THE YOUNGER brother of former Everton player Dave Watson, Alex's highlight was a starting place in the Charity Shield side against Wimbledon in the 1988/89 season.

Alex Watson made his league debut for Liverpool in a 1-0 win at Loftus Road in March 1988. The strength of Liverpool's squad at the time meant that he was competing with established international players and it was no surprise when he left Anfield.

Watson enjoyed a good career with a number of clubs, most notably Bournemouth and Torquay, and played over 500 matches in total.

FACTFILE

BORN
Liverpool, 5 April 1968
POSITION
Centre-half
OTHER CLUBS
Derby County (loan, 1990),
Bournemouth (1991–95),
Gillingham (loan, 1995),
Torquay United (1995–2001),
Exeter City (2001–03),
Taunton Town (2003–04),
Clevedon Town (2004–05)
JOINED
May 1984; signed
professional 18 May 1985
LFC DEBUT
5 March 1988
CONTRACT EXPIRY
18 January 1991

Season	League		FA Cup		League Cup		Europe		Other		Total	
	App	Goals	App	Goals	App	Goals	App	Goals	App	Goals	App	Goals
1987/88	2	0	0	0	0	0	-	-	-	-	2	0
1988/89	1 (1)	0	1 (1)	0	0 (1)	0	-	-	1	0	3 (3)	0
1989/90	0	0	0	0	1	0	-	-	0	0	1	0
Total	3 (1)	0	1 (1)	0	1 (1)	0	0	0	1	0	6 (3)	0

Watson, Tom

NEWCASTLE-BORN Tom Watson started his managerial career at Newcastle's East End and West End clubs and helped to change football forever on Tyneside as he headed a deputation which resulted in the Newcastle Freemen and the Newcastle Corporation granting permission for football to be played on the site now known as St James' Park.

When Watson was appointed at Sunderland in 1889 he made an immediate impact. Not elected to the Football League until the year after he arrived, Sunderland won the First Division Championship in 1892, 1893 and 1895 as well as reaching the FA Cup semi-final three times. Watson weaved his magic at Sunderland, reflected upon by the *Echo's* Victor Hall. 'If there was one man who had the supreme gift of creating esprit de corps on a football team of eleven men, then that man was the same Tom who beat, and hammered, and forged to perfection the steel-tempered football machine that was in his day the "irresistible" Sunderland team. They were trained well, not molly-coddled, they were not overpaid, and they had Tom Watson as guide, philosopher and friend.'

WATSON also had one vital trick up his sleeve – he told his trainers to apply whisky to the sore limbs of his players at half-time and it often worked wonders! More trophies would probably have followed at Roker Park but in the summer of 1896 Liverpool made the most successful manager in the country an offer he couldn't refuse. Watson traded in his 'Team of the Talents' for the Second Division champions. His annual salary at Liverpool was £300, doubling what he had earned at Sunderland.

ONLY 37 years old at the time of this move, Watson was still a relatively young man, certainly for a football manager. This was a radical change to Liverpool's set-up, as the *Cricket and Football Field* reported. 'The team have never had a "boss" off the field, and there have been too many on, so that a central figure, and one that commands respect, should work wonders in this direction.' Watson implemented a strict diet and a new coaching regime. Breakfast at 8.30am consisted of weak tea, chops, eggs, dry toast or stale bread. A glass of beer or claret was recommended at dinner, but butter, sugar, milk, potatoes and tobacco were to be 'sparingly used'. Liverpool exercised two times a day, at 9.45am and 3.30pm, along with a half-hour stroll at 7.30am and a one-hour stroll at 7.30pm; when 'out walking the whole of the players must keep together and accompany the trainer'. Watson did not allow his players to even see a ball during training, a fact that, he confessed to the *Evening Express* in 1899, was considered injudicious by some people, but few could argue with the success his sides enjoyed. Watson orchestrated Liverpool's

rise to the top, a common sight for Reds, observing the game 'well muffled up with a ruby complexion and inevitable cigar just visible below the brim of his cap'.

LIVERPOOL'S game against The Wednesday on 1 September 1896 was Watson's debut as well as the first game the team wore red shirts and white 'knickers' instead of the blue and white outfit that the club's followers were so familiar with. Following the 2-1 win, Liverpool failed to score in two matches in a row and a club director was strongly of the opinion that 'the close passing game is almost played out, as it is so much overdone, and more goals will accrue, he thinks, if the swinging moves from wing to wing were indulged in.' Whether Liverpool did overpass the ball or not the goals soon arrived and Watson delivered fifth place, a big improvement on the previous top-flight campaign that had ended in relegation.

WATSON was not only an accomplished manager but he liked a song as well, as his players discovered on a day out at Roscommon Music Hall in November 1896. 'Tom Watson is a man of many parts, but his presence on the stage as a singer was never expected by those that know him,' the press noted. A favourite of his was 'Bricks and Mortar', the words were simple, the melody easy, and the sentiment irreproachable: 'Farewell to bricks and mortar, Farewell to dirty lime, Farewell to gangways and gangplanks, And to hell with overtime!' Watson went to Scotland to look for young talent as he had done many times before with great success, but the endeavour was not without risk, as he had many a venture down lonely lanes at dead of night in Scotland where he 'looked to them like the butcher who has come to take away the pride of the flock', as Watson described his harrowing experiences. 'And I had to flee, or rather, the horse had. How often have I regretted at such crises in my existence that I am not a cyclist.'

Progress was almost as quick at Liverpool as it had been at his previous club. Two FA Cup semi-finals were reached before the turn of the century and, 90 years before the crucial final league match with Arsenal in 1989, Liverpool were also involved in a 'winner takes all' end to the season. Liverpool travelled to Birmingham to face Aston Villa, a win necessary against their Midland rivals to secure the club's first major title – the Villans had won their previous game 7-1 and thus ensured a better goal average. By the interval the Reds, who had conceded only 28 goals in their previous 33 league matches that season, had inexplicably let in another five and the match was over as a contest, as was Liverpool's title dream.

Season	Division	P	W	D	L	GF	GA	Pts	Pos	Win %	FA Cup
1896/97	1st Division	30	12	9	9	46	38	33	5	40.00	Semi-Final
1897/98	1st Division	30	11	6	13	48	45	28	9	36.67	3rd Round
1898/99	1st Division	34	19	5	10	49	33	43	2	55.88	Semi-Final
1899/1900	1st Division	34	14	5	15	49	45	33	10	41.18	2nd Round
1900/01	1st Division	34	19	7	8	59	35	45	1	55.88	1st Round
1901/02	1st Division	34	10	12	12	42	38	32	11	29.41	2nd Round
1902/03	1st Division	34	17	4	13	68	49	38	5	50.00	1st Round
1903/04	1st Division	34	9	8	17	49	62	26	17	26.47	1st Round
1904/05	2nd Division	34	27	4	3	93	25	58	1	79.41	1st Round
1905/06	1st Division	38	23	5	10	79	46	51	1	60.53	Semi-Final
1906/07	1st Division	38	13	7	18	64	65	33	15	34.21	4th Round
1907/08	1st Division	38	16	6	16	68	61	38	8	42.11	3rd Round
1908/09	1st Division	38	15	6	17	57	65	36	16	39.47	2nd Round
1909/10	1st Division	38	21	6	11	78	57	48	2	55.26	1st Round
1910/11	1st Division	38	15	7	16	53	53	37	13	39.47	2nd Round
1911/12	1st Division	38	12	10	16	49	55	34	17	31.58	2nd Round
1912/13	1st Division	38	16	5	17	61	71	37	12	42.11	3rd Round
1913/14	1st Division	38	14	7	17	46	62	35	16	36.84	Runners-Up
1914/15	1st Division	38	14	9	15	65	75	37	13	36.84	2nd Round
Total	**-**	**678**	**297**	**128**	**253**	**1123**	**980**	**722**	**-**	**43.81**	**-**

LIVERPOOL slipped to 10th the following season but recovered to mount a serious challenge for the championship. The 1901 title was won by two points from, ironically enough, Watson's former employees Sunderland, and seemed to herald a new and exciting era. But, rather surprisingly, results took a turn for the worse and the club was relegated only three years later, only to bounce back at the first time of asking and follow that with their second league title just 12 months later, becoming the first club to achieve the 'double' feat of winning the Second and First Division Championships in successive seasons. In 1906 Watson suffered the disappointment for the sixth time of being the manager of a losing FA Cup semi-finalist, this time to Everton, who went on to lift the trophy by beating Newcastle. League results for the

next few years were rather erratic and only in 1910, when finishing runners-up to Aston Villa, did Liverpool come seriously close to taking another championship. In 1914 Watson at last overcame his cup semi-final jinx as Liverpool progressed to the final, but the big day at London's Crystal Palace ground ended in disappointment against Burnley.

As World War One broke out, Tom Watson was preparing for his 19th season in charge at Anfield. It was to be his last. He had visited his native Newcastle for his 56th birthday on 8 April. Three weeks later he was back at work when he was seized with a severe chill. A few days later it had developed into a fatal attack of pneumonia. Tom Watson died on 6 May 1915. He had been a popular and successful manager and that was reflected in the turnout for his funeral, where many of the players he signed acted as pall-bearers on his final journey. Alex Raisbeck, Ned Doig, Arthur Goddard, Charlie Wilson, Maurice Parry, George Fleming and Bobby Robinson as well as the club trainer William Connell carried his coffin. Watson is buried at Anfield Cemetery.

TOM WATSON was clearly one of the most beloved figures to have ever graced the football club. The day after his death he was remembered by the *Echo's* Bee. 'Bluff, hearty, jovial, fond of a joke and … always prepared to listen to one, Tom was a favourite all over the country. And how worthily Tom bore out the confidence then placed in him at the time and the proud records of the Liverpool Club have since shown. He brought fame and fortune to his players and to his club, and enjoyed here, as he often admitted to the writer, some of the warmest and most cherished friendships of his whole life.' Watson is the club's

longest-serving manager to date, a legendary man who is worthy to dine at the exclusive table of manager legends Bill Shankly and Bob Paisley.

FACTFILE

BORN
8 April 1859, Byker, Newcastle upon Tyne
DIED
6 May 1915
OTHER CLUBS
Newcastle West End, Newcastle East End, Sunderland (1889–96)
SIGNED FROM
Sunderland, 27 July 1896
DEBUT GAME
1 September 1896
CONTRACT EXPIRY
Until death
HONOURS
League Championship 1900/01, 1905/06; Second Division Championship 1904/05

Websites

ANFIELD Online was established in 1997 and has been at its current address *Anfield-Online. co.uk* since 1999. According to their editors, priorities for their website are 'coverage of the important Liverpool news stories, great match reports, the introduction of multimedia LFC content and forum discussion'.

Editor Michael Owen (no, not that one) provides match reports, news articles and comment pieces on *TheAnfieldOpinion.com*. He has a number of columnists such as Martin Kelly (no, not that one).

TheAnfieldWrap.com, established in 2011, is built around an award-winning podcast that can be heard on CityTalk 105.9FM or downloaded from its website. This high-quality show involves passionate fans as well as well-known journalists and has even welcomed Rafa Benítez to its panel. The podcast is expertly moderated by Neil Atkinson.

EmpireoftheKop.com is an independent social-blog. 'What

makes this blog different from any other blog is that there are no editors, we value the opinion of all true Reds out there and anyone can have their say about our great club,' says owner Antoine Zammit.

Est1892.co.uk is a forum that has accumulated over 5,000 members since 2006.

Kjellhanssen.com is a treasure trove for fans interested in the club's colourful past. It is the

history of Liverpool FC through newspaper articles and this impressive collection is growing fast every day.

Kopsource.com is a popular blog established in 2009 offering debates on the many sensitive issues related to the club.

LfcInEurope.com is a superb site by Kevin Nealon that is becoming the definitive guide to Liverpool's exploits in Europe. You can browse through the site and find a varied collection of scans of newspaper articles, programmes, tickets and all kinds of memorabilia.

Arnie Baldursson and Gudmundur Magnusson, who are the authors of the very book you are reading, are respectively editor and webmaster of *LFChistory.net*, which was launched in September 2003. It is an accessible website with stats, historical articles and exclusive interviews. The site is based on detailed information on

every game in the club's history. Arnie and Gudmundur are ably assisted by regular contributor Chris Wood.

Shankly.com, *Bobpaisley.com* and *Billyliddell.com* are a trio of websites also in the possession of *LFChistory.net's* owners. *Billyliddell.com* was launched in January 2009 and is based on unique photos and press cuttings from Billy's life and times, donated by his only sister, Rena. The Shankly and Paisley sites were originally created by Derek Dohren in 1997 and 2001 respectively. Borne out of a dearth of information on the web at that time relating to the pair, the sites have become the definitive internet resource of football's greatest. The sites were relaunched by Arnie and Gudmundur in February 2009 and subsequently a lot of quotes, photos, stories and articles have been added regularly. *LFCOnline.com* has been on the net since 1999 and is currently the unofficial Liverpool Footymad fans site.

The blog *The-Liver-Bird.co.uk* is unique in the sense that it is the only female-run Liverpool website that we know of. Kirsty has been blogging regularly since 2009.

Michael Yip's shirts museum is on *LiverpoolKits.com*, and is an extensive collection that is worth taking a look at.

Liverpool's official site, *Liverpoolfc.com*, is one of the world's most popular football websites dedicated to a single club. You can get your latest news fix, purchase a wide range of Liverpool goods or watch *LFC TV* with an e-season ticket. Its roots can be traced to the start of the internet revolution in the 1990s. Email lists and usenet groups were formed and local fans shared their knowledge. The first Liverpool FC website, Alex Brown's *The Mighty Reds*, was created through a Liverpool mailing list. Alex hosted the site and programmed it and the users of the list provided the information. It was a truly collaborative effort, typical of the internet at the time, a resource for fans by fans. The site became more popular and Alex moved from New Zealand to Liverpool to work on it in an official capacity. Eventually the club took control of it as the Official LFC website.

Andy Philip has been tireless in providing material for *Liverweb. org.uk* since 2001. A great deal of information on the club can be found there.

RedAndWhiteKop.com is the most popular unofficial Liverpool website. Quite a few columnists have cut their teeth on there and gone on to make a living writing about Liverpool FC. The founders were voluntary moderators of the IRC room on the Official LFC site that *The Mighty Reds* had been transformed into. When Granada bought a 9.9 per cent stake in Liverpool it eventually closed the chat room previously hosted by Merseynet, which was the catalyst for a group of users to create their own forum and chat room at free servers such as *lpoolfc.f2s.com*. As free servers with any stability became rarer and the community size increased, the site *RedAndWhiteKop.net*, was established, initially on a shared server, in 2001. 'Ben S' provided the technological knowledge and Bob Kurac and 'Rushian' had the editorial vision. RAWK is mainly based on a forum that since 2001 has seen over 10 million posts on 150,000-plus subjects and has around 40,000 members!

SixCrazyMinutes.com, whose name is based on Liverpool's

incredible revival in Istanbul, is a forum that was established in 2006.

ThisIsAnfield.com was created by the merger of Matt Ladson's LFC Kop and Max Munton's Anfield FC in 2001. The site has excellent regular columnists and a forum.

TomkinsTimes.com is Paul Tomkins' subscription-based website that he established in 2009. He has written a number of books on the club that offer detailed analysis. Tomkins has talked openly about his battle with chronic fatigue syndrome that forced him to retire from a regular work environment. He is widely considered the best columnist on all things Liverpool FC bar none.

YNWA.tv has regular historic features such as 'Down Memory Lane', 'Double Agents' and 'On This Day in History', which are very informative for Reds fans. It also boasts one of the most popular forums that has seen over 2 million posts since 2002.

Welfare, Harry

HENRY "Harry" Welfare made his debut for the club in a home fixture with Sheffield Wednesday on 15 February 1913 in Bill Lacey's absence and his performance was promising according to the *Liverpool Echo*:

> *He worked like a 'brick' all through the game, and his dash, tired as he was from the three-quarters stage, was ever to be feared. Welfare used his weight fairly and with good result, and it was delicious to see him bowl over one of the Wednesday defenders. I was sorry the Northern Nomad amateur didn't get a goal, for he deserved one. His inward pass and his care for the wings were judicious and timed to the right fraction of a minute. It was his pass that gave Metcalf a chance to equalise.*

Welfare scored his only goal when Derby County were the visitors two weeks later. He played in the next match at Tottenham, but only figured once more in the first team, as club legends Lacey and Arthur Goddard were not easily shifted from the wings.

The amateur moved to Rio de Janeiro in August 1913 to work as a geography and mathematics teacher at Ginasio Anglo-Brasileiro, a second branch of a school founded by Charles W. Armstrong in 1909 that followed 'the example of the best schools in England'. The school's PE teacher, J.A. Quincey-Taylor, happened to be the first-team coach at Fluminense Football Club and he used Welfare's talents to their fullest for his team. It would be 20 more years before a professional league was formed in Brazil and as Welfare was top

of the scoring charts Liga Metropolitana challenged his amateur status. A statement from George Patterson, Liverpool's secretary, appeased the Brazilian league authorities. 'Mr Harry Welfare always played for us as an amateur,' Patterson wrote. 'Prior to joining our club he played for several local teams but always as an amateur and to our knowledge

> 'MR HARRY WELFARE ALWAYS PLAYED FOR US AS AN AMATEUR'
>
> **GEORGE PATTERSON**

was never a professional. I can trust this will put the matter right.' As well as scoring a plethora of goals Welfare made a valuable coaching contribution for his team-mates. He had an immensely successful career at Fluminense from 1913 to 1924, winning the Campeonato Carioca, the football league of the state of Rio de Janeiro, three years running from 1917 to 1919 and scoring no fewer than 163 goals in 166 games! As an amateur Welfare wasn't committed to one team and he turned out for Flamengo

in a December 1915 to January 1916 tour of Bélem, the capital of Pará, where he scored seven goals in four games. Welfare became Vasco da Gama's coach in 1927 and led the club to victory in Brazil's first professional league in its second season in 1934. He was considered the best coach in the country during his 10-year spell at Vasco. Despite switching allegiances in Rio, Welfare is remembered as a giant in Fluminense's colourful history. He passed away in Angra dos Reis, Brazil, on 1 September 1966.

FACTFILE

BORN
Wavertree, Liverpool,
20 August 1888
DIED
1 September 1966
POSITION
Right/left-winger
OTHER CLUBS
St Helens Recreation,
Sandown, Hoylake,
Southport Central (1911),
Northern Nomads (1911–12),
Fluminense (1913–24),
Flamengo (guest 1915–16)
JOINED
May 1912
LFC DEBUT GAME/GOAL
15 February 1913 /
1 March 1913
CONTRACT EXPIRY
May 1913

Season	League		FA Cup		Total	
	App	Goals	App	Goals	App	Goals
1912/13	4	1	0	0	4	1
Total	4	1	0	0	4	1

Welsh, Don

IN MARCH 1951 Liverpool persuaded Don Welsh to move north from the south-coast town of Brighton to replace George Kay, who had retired for health reasons two months earlier.

Welsh already had links to Merseyside because he had been a popular guest player for Liverpool from 1943 to 1945 during World War Two, scoring 44 goals in 39 games, and had also been keen to join Liverpool as a coach at that time, a move his then employers Charlton Athletic refused to allow. Don Welsh enjoyed his most successful time as a player at Charlton in the mid-1930s. He was the inspiration behind a meteoric rise that saw the south London club top the Third Division South in 1935, promoted as runners-up to Second Division champions Manchester United in 1936, and then finish as runners-up to United's neighbours City in the top division just a year later. After

the war, Charlton's league form faltered but Welsh helped them reach the FA Cup final in 1946 and to a 1-0 extra-time victory over Burnley in 1947.

WITH HIS playing days over, Welsh started his managerial career at Brighton & Hove Albion in November 1947. The Seagulls finished bottom of the Third Division South at the end of his debut season but there was no automatic relegation in those days. Brighton recovered to finish sixth and eighth in the next two years before Liverpool came calling for Welsh's services. He was appointed Liverpool manager on 5 March 1951. A simple three-page letter on headed notepaper in copper-plate script doubled up as his contract. He was paid £1,500 per year for three years with an addition of £500 for expenses. Welsh hadn't even applied for the job and was thrilled to accept. 'Liverpool asked me to go for an interview. The next day I was told that they had agreed to appoint me. It's a wonderful opportunity to put my ideas into practice.' Welsh wanted

Don Welsh receives a warm welcome to Anfield from Liverpool Chairman George Richards

to make training less monotonous and aimed to cut out the ceaseless lapping of the track, instead the players would keep fit by playing recreational games like leap-frog and tunnel-ball.

Unfortunately, Welsh inherited a Liverpool team that had been stagnating in mid-table for a few seasons and a board of directors that didn't seem particularly ambitious. The team relied too much on the mercurial Billy Liddell, but even the Scotsman couldn't stop the team's slide down the table. Despite strengthening the team with five new players in December 1953, the club finished bottom of the pile with only nine victories and 28 points. Welsh was downhearted but optimistic. 'They were good signings, but they came in at a bad time. Things were bad and confidence was low. Now for a new start, with all the players pulling together. From the chairman right down to the youngest member of the ground staff, we are all resolved to win promotion in one season.' Welsh kept his job but the writing was on the wall when the club could only manage an 11th-place finish in 1955 during a season that included a terrible 9-1 humiliation at the hands of eventual champions Birmingham City. A lot of money had been spent on players who were either past their best or didn't show the form they had been deemed capable of. The directors believed that a change was needed and Welsh was dismissed at the end of the 1955/56 season. 'I may quit football,' Welsh said downheartedly.

After leaving Liverpool, Welsh became a publican for a while in the West Country before the lure of football brought him back into club management again, this time at Bournemouth in the newly formed and non-regional Third Division just before the start of the 1958/59 season. After two average seasons finishing 12th and 10th,

Liverpool manager Don Welsh gives his players a team talk during training at Melwood

he was dismissed in February 1961 following a string of poor results. He managed non-league Wycombe Wanderers before returning to the club where he had enjoyed such success as a player, Charlton Athletic, to become a member of their administrative staff. Don Welsh wasn't a success as Liverpool manager, however much he wanted, following his popularity as a war-time guest player. The 1950s wasn't a good decade for Liverpool Football Club, apart from reaching a cup final at the start and appointing Bill Shankly at the end. Maybe Welsh was the wrong man at the wrong time? Unfortunately, the club was in a worse state when he departed than when he arrived.

FACTFILE

BORN
25 February 1911, Manchester
DIED
2 February 1990
OTHER CLUBS
Brighton & Hove Albion (1947–51), Bournemouth (1958–61), Wycombe Wanderers (1962–64)
SIGNED FROM
Brighton & Hove Albion, 5 March 1951
DEBUT GAME
23 March 1951
CONTRACT EXPIRY
4 May 1956

Season	Division	P	W	D	L	GF	GA	Pts	Pos	Win %	FA Cup
1950/51*	1st Division	8	3	2	3	7	10	8	9	37.50	-
1951/52	1st Division	42	12	19	11	57	61	43	11	28.57	5th Round
1952/53	1st Division	42	14	8	20	61	82	36	17	33.33	3rd Round
1953/54	1st Division	42	9	10	23	68	97	28	22	21.43	3rd Round
1954/55	2nd Division	42	16	10	16	92	96	42	11	38.10	5th Round
1955/56	2nd Division	42	21	6	15	85	63	48	3	50.00	5th Round
Total	-	**218**	**75**	**55**	**88**	**370**	**409**	**205**	-	**34.40**	-

* Welsh appointed on 5 March 1951 with Liverpool in 8th position

Welsh, John

A FORMER captain of England at various levels as well as Liverpool reserves, John Welsh is a small powerhouse of a central-midfielder. Welsh may be quiet off the field, but it's a different story on the pitch. In the 2004/05 season Welsh started in two Premier League games as well as featuring as a substitute in the 3-1 Champions League win over Bayer Leverkusen in the last 16.

Despite these highlights it was obvious Welsh would have to leave his beloved Liverpool for regular football. He swapped places with Hull's Paul Anderson in January 2006 and made 50 appearances in the Championship before he was released in June 2009. A month later Welsh became one of the first signings made by new Tranmere Rovers manager and former Liverpool player John Barnes. Welsh survived the cull that saw the management duo of Barnes and Jason McAteer leave the club in October. The captain at Prenton Park rejected a new deal at Tranmere and joined fellow

League One side Preston North End in May 2012. Welsh was voted Player of the Year by Preston supporters and his teammates in the 2012/13 season.

FACTFILE

BORN
Edge Hill, Liverpool, 10 January 1984
POSITION
Midfielder
OTHER CLUBS
Hull City (loan, 2005; permanent, 2006–09), Chester City (loan, 2008), Carlisle United (loan, 2008), Bury (loan, 2009), Tranmere Rovers (2009–12), Preston North End (2012–)
JOINED
1994; signed professional 29 January 2001
INTERNATIONAL CAPS
8 England U-21 caps (1 goal)
LFC DEBUT
4 December 2002
CONTRACT EXPIRY
1 January 2006

Season	League		FA Cup		League Cup		Europe		Other		Total	
	App	Goals	App	Goals	App	Goals	App	Goals	App	Goals	App	Goals
2002/03	0	0	0	0	0 (1)	0	0	0	0	0	0 (1)	0
2003/04	0 (1)	0	0	0	0	0	0 (1)	0	-	-	0 (2)	0
2004/05	2 (1)	0	1	0	0 (2)	0	0 (1)	0	-	-	3 (4)	0
Total	**2 (2)**	**0**	**1**	**0**	**0 (3)**	**0**	**0 (2)**	**0**	**0**	**0**	**3 (7)**	**0**

West, Alf

ALF WEST had the makings of the finest full-back in England but his career suffered from a few serious setbacks. He was described in the club programme as 'perhaps the best and classiest back that had been seen at Anfield and his style was perfect. His methods are such as commend themselves to all who desire to see football played with a maximum of skill and a minimum of physical force. West does not rely upon the latter quality; he calmly awaits the oncoming forward and judges the precise moment for intervention with admirable facility.'

West was signed in the autumn of 1903 having starred at Second Division Barnsley for two years since arriving from Ilkeston. Several big clubs were chasing his signature and Small Heath (later to become Birmingham City) had already had a bid turned down. West played in the remaining 24 First Division games of the 1903/04 season

as relegation was confirmed. He was absent until Christmas 1904 as Liverpool tried to make their way out of the Second Division due to an unfortunate shooting accident, as reported by the club programme:

West had been training for a 120 yards handicap and finished his preparation with a week at Lytham. Everything was complete, and he, accompanied by his trainer, went to take the final spin before leaving for Keswick where he was due to run the following day. Not having had much practice at starting with the pistol it was decided to adopt this method. Whilst the trainer was handling the weapon, it accidentally went off and West received a bullet under his right shoulder. He walked away some 200 yards, and then, staggering, fell into his trainer's arms. Fortunately the bullet did not penetrate the lungs, but spent itself by travelling along the outside of the ribs to the front part of the chest.

West was in a critical condition as he had been actually been shot with two bullets just above the heart by trainer William Norman 'who was naturally much upset'.

West missed just a single game as the club won its second First Division Championship in 1906. He could never easily forget the match against Leicester Fosse in the first round of the FA Cup on 13 January 1906 when he missed two penalties, one in each half! Thankfully for him Billy Bannister missed a penalty as well and Liverpool beat the Foxes 2-1, but were conquered by Everton in the semi-finals. West was injured against Middlesbrough after only four games had passed of the 1906/07 season and then, once he had recovered, 'the most severe family tragedy trouble

that could befall a man happened' [was not explained any further but most likely a loss of a child] and he missed the rest of the season. West was a regular the following season, but only played 15 games in his last two years at the club. After a brief stint with Reading at the end of the decade, he returned to Anfield in 1910 but only made five more appearances for Liverpool before being transferred to Notts County.

Season	League		FA Cup		Other		Total	
	App	Goals	App	Goals	App	Goals	App	Goals
1903/04	24	1	1	0	-	-	25	1
1904/05	16	1	2	0	-	-	18	1
1905/06	37	3	5	1	1	0	43	4
1906/07	4	0	0	0	-	-	4	0
1907/08	33	0	3	0	-	-	36	0
1908/09	10	0	0	0	-	-	10	0
1910/11	4	0	1	0	-	-	5	0
Total	**128**	**5**	**12**	**1**	**1**	**0**	**141**	**6**

Westerveld, Sander

SANDER WESTERVELD had gained quite a reputation after three seasons at Twente in the Eredivisie and had made his international debut, against Brazil, a week prior to him becoming the most expensive goalkeeper in England.

Westerveld was especially known for his drop-kick known as 'The Bomb'. He entertained team-mates at training and fans in pre-match warm-ups by launching the ball from his penalty area into the stands behind the opposite goal. Westerveld's monster efforts were never officially measured but

he was widely acknowledged to have the longest kick in Europe. He quickly won over the Anfield crowd, who had grown weary of the inconsistency of David James and Brad Friedel. Westerveld was a great shot stopper, but lacked dominance of the penalty area. He had an excellent first season behind the new central pairing

of Sami Hyypia and Stephane Henchoz as Gérard Houllier's team took shape.

THE TREBLE of the League Cup, FA Cup and UEFA Cup was won in Westerveld's second season but he had been way less impressive than in his first year. He punched the ball into his own net in the Chelsea game on 1 October 2000 as well as making other glaring errors. In January 2001 Liverpool were linked with Coventry's number one. 'I've been assured by Gérard Houllier that Liverpool haven't made a bid for Chris

Kirkland,' Westerveld said confidently. 'As long as we don't buy Edwin van der Sar or Peter Schmeichel I won't be worried because I don't mind who sits on the bench.' Westerveld had a disastrous UEFA Cup final, which almost cost the Reds the treble. Houllier had been looking for a replacement for quite a few months and only three games into the 2001/02 season he was given the perfect excuse to axe Westerveld for good after a speculative long-range shot from Bolton's Dean Holdsworth squirmed under his body.

Houllier signed not one but two keepers four days later! Westerveld was obviously not best pleased with the arrival of Jerzy Dudek and the aforementioned Chris Kirkland. 'When I returned from international duty last week Houllier told me that I was the number 3 keeper at the club. He said I was still allowed to train with the first team but I would be sitting in the stands on Saturday. I'm absolutely disgusted with that. There's no use staying at Liverpool as long as Gérard Houllier is there.'

WESTERVELD revived his career with a successful spell in Spain with Real Sociedad and helped the Basque club to the runners-up place in La Liga and Champions League qualification. In July 2005

Westerveld returned to English football with Portsmouth and was also signed on loan to Everton, who had suffered a mid-season injury crisis with Richard Wright and Nigel Martyn out injured. Westerveld only played twice for the Blues before returning to Portsmouth, who released him

in May 2006. Following spells in Spain, the Netherlands and Italy Westerveld, in his 37th year, moved to South Africa with Ajax Cape Town where he stayed two years.

When Westerveld was playing at Liverpool he admitted that he didn't appreciate Scouse humour but, more importantly, revealed his confidence was easily dented. 'Some people think it's funny to make jokes about goalkeepers when they come up to me but I've just about had enough. If someone two metres away from me drops their glass of beer on the floor you can bet that a wise guy has asked if it was me. Even my postman gets in on the act when he gives me my letters. "Watch you don't drop them,"

he says. I don't like these comments and they don't exactly help your confidence either.'

FACTFILE

BORN
Enschede, Netherlands,
23 October 1974
POSITION
Goalkeeper
OTHER CLUBS
Twente Enschede (1988–96),
Vitesse (1996–99),
Real Sociedad (2001–05),
Real Mallorca (loan, 2004),
Portsmouth (2005–06),
Everton (loan, 2006),
Almeria (2006–07),
Sparta Rotterdam (2007–08),
Monza (2009–11),
Ajax Cape Town (2011–13)
SIGNED FROM
Vitesse, £4million,
15 June 1999
INTERNATIONAL CAPS
6 Netherlands caps (5 at LFC),
1999–2001
LFC DEBUT
7 August 1999
CONTRACT EXPIRY
17 December 2001
HONOURS
FA Cup 2001;
League Cup 2001;
UEFA Cup 2001

Season	League App	League Goals	FA Cup App	FA Cup Goals	League Cup App	League Cup Goals	Europe App	Europe Goals	Other App	Other Goals	Total App	Total Goals
1999/2000	36	0	2	0	1	0	-	-	-	-	39	0
2000/01	38	0	6	0	4	0	13	0	-	-	61	0
2001/02	1	0	0	0	0	0	1	0	1	0	3	0
Total	**75**	**0**	**8**	**0**	**5**	**0**	**14**	**0**	**1**	**0**	**103**	**0**

Wheeler,
Johnny

JOHNNY WHEELER was strong in tackle, had a good engine and was dangerous in attack.

The 28-year-old was already an experienced player before arriving at Anfield, having played 101 league games for Tranmere in the

Third Division North and just over 200 games for First Division Bolton. Wheeler played in the famous 'Matthews final' which Bolton lost 4-3 after leading Blackpool 3-1, due to Stanley Matthews' brilliance on the day. Manager Phil Taylor put Wheeler's wealth of experience to good use as Liverpool tried to get promoted from the Second Division and made him club captain in the 1958/59 season. Wheeler was a versatile player who normally played at right-half, but many of his early appearances for Liverpool came as an inside-right forward. Wheeler was the star of the show against Port Vale early in November 1956 when, after Billy Liddell had equalised Vale's first-half goal, he scored one of the fastest hat-tricks ever recorded, his goals coming in the 81st, 82nd and 85th minute.

DURING 1960/61 Wheeler had to share the number 4 shirt with the young Gordon Milne and in the following season he was only selected once, covering for left-half Tommy Leishman when Plymouth Argyle visited

Anfield on 9 December 1961. Wheeler was appointed player-manager of New Brighton in May 1963, but didn't take up the post, becoming assistant trainer at Bury instead where he stayed until 1969.

FACTFILE

BORN
Crosby, Liverpool,
26 July 1928
POSITION
Right-half /
Inside-right forward
OTHER CLUBS
Tranmere Rovers (1944–51),
Bolton Wanderers (1951–56)
SIGNED FROM
Bolton Wanderers, £9,000,
7 September 1956
INTERNATIONAL CAPS
1 England cap, 1954
LFC DEBUT GAME/GOAL
15 September 1956 /
13 October 1956
CONTRACT EXPIRY
May 1963

Season	League App	League Goals	FA Cup App	FA Cup Goals	Other App	Other Goals	Total App	Total Goals
1956/57	28	10	1	1	-	-	29	11
1957/58	38	5	5	0	-	-	43	5
1958/59	41	1	1	0	-	-	42	1
1959/60	29	2	2	1	-	-	31	3
1960/61	27	3	1	0	3	0	31	3
1961/62	1	0	0	0	-	-	1	0
Total	**164**	**21**	**10**	**2**	**3**	**0**	**177**	**23**

Whelan,
Ronnie

A LONG-SERVING RED who scored in 14 consecutive seasons for Liverpool, Ronnie Whelan's background always made it likely that he would be successful in the sport as his father was an Irish international and his younger brother Paul also played in the League of Ireland for many years.

The Dubliner impressed as a youth with Home Farm in the city of his birth and a number of English clubs showed interest, including Manchester United where he was a trainee. Whelan went to Liverpool in the summer of 1979 for a two-week trial. 'I was pretty nervous about going there but my dad told me I might as well start at the top!' Shortly before the youngster's 18th birthday Liverpool 'compensated' him for giving up his amateur status with a £20,000 signing-on fee, as sought by his father. Whelan had to be patient but finally got his chance two days

after Liverpool had won the League Cup for the first time, on April Fools' Day 1981. Whelan slotted easily into Ray Kennedy's position on the left side of midfield and even surged forward just before the half-hour mark to calmly slip a shot past Stoke keeper Peter Fox. When Kennedy was sold to Swansea in January 1982 Whelan was preferred to Kevin Sheedy and it was soon clear that the Irishman would be a very capable successor. After sitting uncomfortably halfway down the table at New Year, an astonishing run of 11 successive First Division victories between 9 March and 1 May 1982 helped propel the team to a most unlikely championship success. Whelan scored four in this amazing run, including the goal that effectively wrapped up the title in the final home game against Tottenham. The White Hart Lane outfit had already suffered the 'Whelan factor' when he scored twice against them in the League Cup final at Wembley in March. Many expected Whelan to become one of the game's greats with the fantastic start he made to his career. He may have developed into a less spectacular player but he was still a damn good one.

During the next eight seasons Whelan played nearly 400 matches, scored 54 goals and regularly added medals and Irish caps to his collection. He was capable of the extraordinary when the team needed it most. Who can forget his curler against Manchester United in the Wembley League Cup final in 1983 and the belter against United as well in the FA Cup semi-final at Goodison Park in 1985? Whelan clearly had an eye for the spectacular when playing Manchester United, as his chipped back-pass from 30 yards sailed over Bruce Grobbelaar and into his own net on 18 March 1990. To date, it is considered one of the most bizarre own goals in top-flight history. Whelan moved into a more central midfield role after John Barnes arrived in 1987, controlling the tempo of the game. He was made captain in 1988/89 and his proudest moment came when he went up the Wembley steps to receive the FA Cup after Liverpool's thrilling 3-2 extra-time victory over Everton in May 1989.

'A lot of people said I would be on my way when John Barnes came but Kenny moved me back into the centre,' Whelan noted. 'That was my best years. I loved playing in the centre. I loved being involved all the time, although I didn't score as many goals because I was more defensive and Macca did the runs

FACTFILE

BORN
Dublin, Ireland,
25 September 1961
POSITION
Midfielder
OTHER CLUBS
Home Farm (1976–79),
Southend United (1994–95)
SIGNED FROM
Home Farm,
19 September 1979
INTERNATIONAL CAPS
53 Ireland caps (3 goals)
(51 (3) at LFC), 1981–95
LFC DEBUT GAME/GOAL
3 April 1981 / 3 April 1981
CONTRACT EXPIRY
1 June 1994
HONOURS
League Championship
1981/82, 1982/83, 1983/84,
1985/86, 1987/88, 1989/90;
FA Cup 1986, 1989;
League Cup 1982, 1983, 1984;
European Cup 1984

Season	League App	League Goals	FA Cup App	FA Cup Goals	League Cup App	League Cup Goals	Europe App	Europe Goals	Other App	Other Goals	Total App	Total Goals
1980/81	1	1	0	0	0	0	0	0	0	0	1	1
1981/82	31 (1)	10	3	0	8	3	3 (1)	1	0	0	45 (2)	14
1982/83	26 (2)	2	1	0	3 (3)	2	5	3	1	0	36 (5)	7
1983/84	20 (3)	4	0 (1)	0	4 (1)	3	5	2	0	0	29 (5)	9
1984/85	35 (2)	7	7	4	3	1	10	0	1 (1)	0	56 (3)	12
1985/86	39	10	7	1	7	3	-	-	4	0	57	14
1986/87	39	3	3	0	8	2	-	-	3	0	53	5
1987/88	26 (2)	1	2	0	3	0	-	-	-	-	31 (2)	1
1988/89	37	4	5	0	6	0	-	-	3	0	51	4
1989/90	34	1	8	1	3	0	-	-	1	0	46	2
1990/91	14	1	1	0	1	0	-	-	1	0	17	1
1991/92	9 (1)	0	3	1	0	0	0	0	-	-	12 (1)	1
1992/93	17	1	0	0	0	0	0	0	1	0	18	1
1993/94	23	1	0	0	0	0	-	-	-	-	23	1
Total	**351 (11)**	**46**	**40 (1)**	**7**	**46 (4)**	**14**	**23 (1)**	**6**	**15 (1)**	**0**	**475 (18)**	**73**

forward. I knew I was there to win the ball back and give it to the likes of Beardsley and Barnes. I didn't try to do anything spectacular. I couldn't dribble. I was a good passer of the ball. I could read the game well. The managers and the players appreciated the job more than some of the supporters.'

The 29-year-old Whelan was out with a fractured shin when Graeme Souness succeeded Kenny Dalglish as manager in April 1991 and was sidelined for seven months with a knee injury in the 1991/92 season. He returned to score a dramatic late equaliser at Highbury to earn a replay with Portsmouth in the FA Cup semi-final. Although he played in the Villa Park replay, which Liverpool won on penalties, Whelan missed the final against Sunderland because of injury. The 1992/93 and 1993/94 seasons

had a similar pattern. Whelan was a regular from the start of the season until he got injured come September or October and didn't return until February/March. Souness had an uneasy tenure as manager which finally came to an end and Roy Evans' reign began. 'Every time I got fit I'd get another injury. It was just non-stop for four years,' Whelan said. 'I was a bit disappointed with Souey when he took the club captaincy off me and gave it to Mark Wright. I'd worn the number 5 shirt for so many years and when the names and squad numbers were introduced I got number 12. It doesn't make you think you're wanted that much in the team.'

If his final four seasons at Anfield were not successful in terms of injuries received, games played and medals gained, nobody can be in any doubt that between 1981 and 1990 Ronnie Whelan was a hugely influential part of a very successful squad of players that brought him no fewer than six League Championship medals as well as two winners' medals in the FA Cup, three in the League Cup and one on the European stage when

Liverpool went into the lions' den in Rome to take the giant trophy away from the Roman hordes who mistakenly believed they only had to turn up to witness victory. Whelan's contract expired in the summer of 1994 and a few months later he became Southend United's player-manager. Whelan wanted to test pastures new and coached Panionios in Greece and Apollon Limassol and Olympiakos Nicosia in Cyprus.

WHELAN was a fantastic servant for Liverpool, greatly appreciated by the likes of Bob Paisley who, at the height of the club's dominance, said: 'And when those special matches come round and there are medals to be won and the pundits are asking whether the match winner will be Rushie or Kenny or Brucie, then I look past them all towards Ronnie Whelan and think to myself: "There's our man for the big occasion".'

Whitbread, Zak

CENTRE-HALF Zak Whitbread is a USA youth international, as he was born in Houston, Texas, where his dad Barry was running a 'soccer' coaching school.

His family moved back to England when he was only two years old. Zak was invited to join Liverpool's Academy at the tender age of eight, but his stint was cut short two years later when his family moved to Singapore when Barry became the assistant technical director for the Singapore national

team, later promoted to team manager. Zak progressed through the youth ranks of Singapore's Geylang United, a club that his future Liverpool team-mates were well aware of, as he explains. 'I did an interview with *FourFourTwo* magazine, which misprinted Geylang as 'Gayland'. The lads thought that was hilarious, asking me what we all got up to in the "gay-land" dressing room.' Barry moved the family back to England as he wanted Zak to pursue his dream of becoming a professional footballer. At 15 Zak rejoined the Reds and the Whitbread family's ties were further strengthened when Barry was appointed head

of recruitment at the Academy, where he served until 2007.

ZAK MADE six starts in his Liverpool career; in the local cups, where Liverpool admittedly featured an under-strength side and in the qualifying rounds of the Champions League. He couldn't remove either Sami Hyypia or Jamie Carragher from the first team, but was still compared with the great Finn because of his ability go forward. 'I'm aware that some people have been comparing me to Sami and I take that as a massive compliment. I'd like to think I'm better-looking than him though.' Whitbread returned to the Premiership with Norwich in the 2011/12 season, playing a few games alongside former Red Danny Ayala. But

FACTFILE

BORN
Houston, USA,
10 January 1984
POSITION
Centre-half
OTHER CLUBS
Millwall (loan, 2005;
permanent, 2006–10),
Norwich City (2010–12),
Leicester City (2012–)
JOINED
1992 (joined the Academy);
1999
LFC DEBUT
26 October 2004
CONTRACT EXPIRY
1994 (left the Academy);
13 June 2006

Whitbread's season was disrupted by injury and following his release by the Canaries he signed for Championship Leicester City in the summer of 2012.

Season	League		FA Cup		League Cup		Europe		Other		Total	
	App	Goals	App	Goals	App	Goals	App	Goals	App	Goals	App	Goals
2004/05	0	0	1	0	3	0	0	0	-	-	4	0
2005/06	0	0	0	0	1	0	1 (1)	0	0	0	2 (1)	0
Total	**0**	**0**	**1**	**0**	**4**	**0**	**1 (1)**	**0**	**0**	**0**	**6 (1)**	**0**

White, Bill

THE REFEREE SEEMED TO AMUSE WHITE.

BILL WHITE couldn't have started his Liverpool career better when he scored in the second minute of his debut against Everton in the first home game of the season.

According to the *Liverpool Courier* Raisbeck passed the ball to Bowen who 'dashed along the wing. He finished with a beautiful centre. The ball flashed past McGuigan and Raybould, but White received it, and slammed the leather into the net – a beautiful goal.' White played six games during the 1901/02 season, which Liverpool finished disappointingly in 11th place after winning their first Football League Championship the previous year. White ended his playing career at his first club, eventually working down the mine in Broxburn.

	League		FA Cup		Total	
Season	**App**	**Goals**	**App**	**Goals**	**App**	**Goals**
1901/02	6	1	0	0	6	1
Total	**6**	**1**	**0**	**0**	**6**	**1**

White, Dick

SCUNTHORPE-BORN Dick White arrived at Anfield in November 1955 after he had played 133 league matches for his home-town club. Liverpool manager Don Welsh and two club directors arrived in Scunthorpe on 10 November 1955, took manager Bill Corkhill away from a snooker game, and offered him £8,000 for White on the spot, the largest fee ever received by the club for a player.

White replaced regular centre-half Laurie Hughes at Barnsley on 10 March 1956 and made a further seven appearances for Liverpool before the end of that season. But Hughes missed only one league match in 1956/57 so it wasn't until the following season that White became a regular in the side. He only missed two matches over the next four league seasons. Ron Yeats took over as centre-half from White at the start of the 1961/62 season, but Shankly still

DICK WHITE
LIVERPOOL

found a spot for him at right-back. White and Jamie Carragher are the only players in Liverpool's history to score two own goals in a single game for the club. When Liverpool faced Middlesbrough on 7 October 1961 Yeats was out with a shoulder injury so White returned to his old position. In the 49th minute White was determined to prevent the lurking forward Alan Peacock from reaching the ball and mistimed his header so it went past his keeper, Bert Slater. Fifteen minutes later Gordon Milne's attempted clearance thumped against White's shoulder for his second own goal. These turned out to be the only goals in the match. 'What is the use of worrying? It was just one of those things – twice,' White told *Liverpool Echo's* reporter right after the game. White lost his spot in the team as well as the captaincy to Ron Yeats on Boxing Day 1961. White, had only been leading Liverpool out since the 1959/60 season. In January 1962 White added two appearances to amass a total of 25 for the campaign, leaving the club in May with a Second Division winner's medal.

	League		FA Cup		League Cup		Total	
Season	**App**	**Goals**	**App**	**Goals**	**App**	**Goals**	**App**	**Goals**
1955/56	8	0	0	0	-	-	8	0
1956/57	5	0	0	0	-	-	5	0
1957/58	41	0	5	1	-	-	46	1
1958/59	42	0	1	0	-	-	43	0
1959/60	41	0	2	0	-	-	43	0
1960/61	42	0	2	0	3	0	47	0
1961/62	24	0	1	0	-	-	25	0
Total	**203**	**0**	**11**	**1**	**3**	**0**	**217**	**1**

Whitehead, John

JOHN Whitehead was picked for the Test match against Bury at the end of the 1894/95 season in which William McCann and Matt McQueen had shared goalkeeping duties. Unfortunately, Liverpool lost this vital match played at neutral Blackburn and dropped into the Second Division.

Whitehead figured twice in 1895/96 with completely contrasting fortunes, a 5-1 home thrashing of Newcastle being followed by a 5-2 defeat at Newton Heath (later to become Manchester United).

Season	League		FA Cup		Other		Total	
	App	Goals	App	Goals	App	Goals	App	Goals
1894/95	0	0	0	0	1	0	1	0
1895/96	2	0	0	0	0	0	2	0
Total	2	0	0	0	1	0	3	0

FACTFILE

BORN
Liverpool, 1871
POSITION
Goalkeeper
OTHER CLUBS
Bootle (1890–92),
Everton (1892–94)
SIGNED FROM
Everton, 28 March 1894
LFC DEBUT
27 April 1895
CONTRACT EXPIRY
April 1896

Whitehurst, Albert

ALBERT WHITEHURST was transferred to Liverpool after scoring 116 goals in 168 games in the Third Division North for Rochdale. He was selected on the opening day of the 1928/29 season and responded with the second of Liverpool's three goals in their home win over Bury.

He played in seven of the first nine First Division fixtures but wasn't recalled until early in February 1929. That appearance at Leeds proved to be the last time he would wear a Liverpool shirt,

but he did sign off with a goal two minutes from time to save a point in a 2-2 draw. Whitehurst had only been a short while at Bradford when he scored seven goals in an 8-0 triumph over Tranmere Rovers on 6 March 1929. His 24 goals in 15 games helped his team win the Third Division North in his debut

season. Two years later Whitehurst moved to Tranmere, where he played at centre-half in the last stages of his career.

Season	League		FA Cup		Total	
	App	Goals	App	Goals	App	Goals
1928/29	8	2	0	0	8	2
Total	8	2	0	0	8	2

FACTFILE

BORN
Fenton, Stoke-on-Trent,
22 June 1898
DIED
1976
POSITION
Centre-forward
OTHER CLUBS
New Haden Colliery,
Stoke (1920–23),
Rochdale (1923–28),
Bradford City (1929–31),
Tranmere Rovers (1931–34)
SIGNED FROM
Rochdale, May 1928
LFC DEBUT GAME/GOAL
25 August 1928 /
25 August 1928
CONTRACT EXPIRY
February 1929

Whitham, Jack

JACK WHITHAM made a name for himself at Sheffield Wednesday where he scored 31 goals in 72 games in a struggling First Division team.

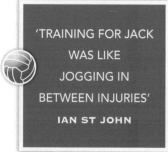

'TRAINING FOR JACK WAS LIKE JOGGING IN BETWEEN INJURIES'

IAN ST JOHN

Wednesday eventually got relegated in the 1969/70 season, but Whitham stayed in the top flight by moving to Liverpool, six months after Roger Hunt's departure. Sadly Whitham's injury problems that had halted his progress in Sheffield continued at Liverpool. John Toshack's arrival in November 1970 meant that Whitham's first-team opportunities became even more limited. He enjoyed some success towards the end of 1971, scoring two late goals in a win at Coventry and a hat-trick against Derby County at Anfield three weeks

later. One of Ian St John's favourite stories involves Whitham. 'Training for Jack was like jogging in between injuries,' the Saint told *LFChistory.net*. 'He was driving Shanks mad because he hated people who

FACTFILE

BORN
Burnley, 8 December 1946
POSITION
Forward
OTHER CLUBS
Holy Trinity,
Sheffield Wednesday
(1964–70),
Cardiff City (1974–75),
Reading (1975–76),
Worksop Town (1977–79),
Hallam (1979–82),
Oughtibridge (1982–83)
SIGNED FROM
Sheffield Wednesday,
£57,000, April 1970
LFC DEBUT GAME/GOAL
8 September 1970 /
12 December 1970
CONTRACT EXPIRY
1974

were like that. Finally he said one day to Jack in training, "You, go up to the corner, where the pigsty was [at Melwood], and train up there. I don't want you to contaminate the rest of the team." Poor Jack was jogging up there in the pigsty with the smell of the pigs.' But after making only one appearance in two seasons Whitham's contract was terminated. He joined Second Division Cardiff after being invited to a trial by manager Frank O'Farrell. He scored three goals

in 15 appearances before moving down the league ladder to Reading. He featured in 19 games as the Elm Park outfit was promoted from Fourth Division, his three goals that season all came in the same match against

Hartlepool United. Whitham moved into non-league football playing for Worksop Town, Hallam and finally Oughtibridge in the local Sheffield League. Whitham has been involved in football since 1993 as a scout for

Sunderland, Luton Town, Sheffield United and Wolves. He lives in Sheffield and away from football he is a well-known singer/songwriter around the acoustic music clubs in the South Yorkshire area.

Season	League		FA Cup		League Cup		Europe		Other		Total	
	App	Goals	App	Goals	App	Goals	App	Goals	App	Goals	App	Goals
1970/71	6	1	0	0	1 (1)	0	0	0	-	-	7 (1)	1
1971/72	9	6	0	0	0	0	0	0	0	0	9	6
1972/73	0	0	0	0	0	0	0 (1)	0	-	-	0 (1)	0
Total	**15**	**7**	**0**	**0**	**1 (1)**	**0**	**0 (1)**	**0**	**0**	**0**	**16 (2)**	**7**

Whitworth, George

GEORGE WHITWORTH signed for Liverpool in February 1950 but didn't make his first-team debut until two years later, away to Fulham.

There were 11 matches remaining of the season and he played in nine of them in Phil Taylor's absence at right-half. Liverpool

lost only one of those nine, which turned out to be Whitworth's final game for the club; a 4-0 defeat at Preston on 26 April 1952.

Season	League		FA Cup		Total	
	App	Goals	App	Goals	App	Goals
1951/52	9	0	0	0	9	0
Total	**9**	**0**	**0**	**0**	**9**	**0**

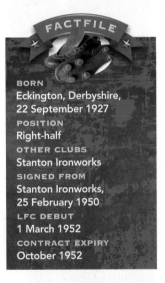

FACTFILE

BORN
Eckington, Derbyshire,
22 September 1927
POSITION
Right-half
OTHER CLUBS
Stanton Ironworks
SIGNED FROM
Stanton Ironworks,
25 February 1950
LFC DEBUT
1 March 1952
CONTRACT EXPIRY
October 1952

Wilkie, Tom

TOM WILKIE was a towering Scotsman at 5ft 11in (191cm), unusually tall for a left-back.

He was an integral part of the team that won the Second Division and made 25 consecutive First Division appearances before he was replaced by Billy Dunlop for the last seven matches of the 1896/97 season. Wilkie only played 13 games over the next two

campaigns before heading south to join Portsmouth Football Club, formed to replace the defunct Royal Artillery. He was also joined by fellow Liverpool teammates; Tom Cleghorn and Bobby Marshall as well as Dan Cunliffe, who played for Liverpool in the 1897/98 season. Wilkie became one of Pompey's most successful pioneers and played 178 matches for the club into the new century.

Season	League		FA Cup		Other		Total	
	App	Goals	App	Goals	App	Goals	App	Goals
1895/96	20	1	2	0	1	0	23	1
1896/97	25	0	3	0	-	-	28	0
1897/98	10	0	1	0	-	-	11	0
1898/99	2	0	0	0	-	-	2	0
Total	**57**	**1**	**6**	**0**	**1**	**0**	**64**	**1**

FACTFILE

BORN
Edinburgh, Scotland,
1876
DIED
8 January 1932
POSITION
Left-back
OTHER CLUBS
Hearts (1893–95),
Portsmouth (1899–1904)
SIGNED FROM
Hearts,
18 January 1895
LFC DEBUT GAME/GOAL
7 September 1895 /
9 November 1895
CONTRACT EXPIRY
1899
HONOURS
Second Division
Championship 1895/96

Wilkinson, Barry

BARRY WILKINSON joined Liverpool from famed amateur side Bishop Auckland.

He played 18 games in the First Division in the 1953/54 season while still in the RAF, so he had to get special permission to play for the club. Liverpool were relagated at the end of his debut season and once in the Second Division Roy Saunders was preferred to Wilkinson as the team's number four. Wilkinson returned to the first-team fold in April 1959 and started the 1959/60 season as a regular but in December a certain Bill Shankly arrived, who cut him from the team and sold him to Bangor City in the summer.

Season	League		FA Cup		Total	
	App	Goals	App	Goals	App	Goals
1953/54	18	0	1	0	19	0
1954/55	15	0	0	0	15	0
1955/56	1	0	0	0	1	0
1956/57	8	0	0	0	8	0
1957/58	10	0	0	0	10	0
1958/59	12	0	0	0	12	0
1959/60	14	0	0	0	14	0
Total	**78**	**0**	**1**	**0**	**79**	**0**

FACTFILE

BORN
Bishop Auckland,
16 June 1935
DIED
2004
POSITION
Right/left-half
OTHER CLUBS
West Auckland (1951–52),
Bishop Auckland (1952–53),
Bangor City (1960–63),
Tranmere Rovers (1963–64),
Holyhead Town (1964–66)
SIGNED FROM
Bishop Auckland,
October 1953;
signed professional
1 June 1954
LFC DEBUT
5 December 1953
CONTRACT EXPIRY
August 1960

Williams, Bryan

LOCAL LAD Bryan Williams had waited five years for his first-team debut when he replaced Phil Taylor in a 1-0 win over Birmingham on 12 March 1949.

He continued at right-half for five out of the next six games before his place was taken by Laurie Hughes. Williams did not feature at all in 1949/50 but deputised for right-back Ray Lambert for three consecutive games at the end of the 1950/51 season. Williams got a new lease of life as an inside-left in his final two seasons at the club, showing his versatility. Williams was a regular for Third Division North Crewe Alexandra for a number of seasons, playing nearly five times as many league matches for the Cheshire club as he had for Liverpool. Williams had a rocket-launch of a throw which he became known for, and was an excellent swimmer and sprinter.

Season	League		FA Cup		Total	
	App	Goals	App	Goals	App	Goals
1948/49	6	0	0	0	6	0
1950/51	3	0	0	0	3	0
1951/52	11	1	2	0	13	1
1952/53	11	4	1	0	12	4
Total	**31**	**5**	**3**	**0**	**34**	**5**

FACTFILE

BORN
Liverpool, 4 October 1927
POSITION
Inside-left forward /
Right-half
OTHER CLUBS
South Liverpool (1943–44),
South Liverpool (1953–54),
Crewe Alexandra (1954–58),
Rhyl (1958–61)
SIGNED FROM
South Liverpool,
March 1944; signed
professional August 1945
LFC DEBUT GAME/GOAL
12 March 1949 /
29 September 1951
CONTRACT EXPIRY
July 1953

Wilson, Charlie

UTILITY DEFENDER Charlie Wilson established himself in the 1899/1900 season when he played in 22 of the 34 First Division fixtures.

The highlight of his career was no doubt winning the First Division title in 1901 where he featured in 25 league games. His playing style was so described by the club programme: 'A sturdy, vigorous, and well-built youth, he plays football with all the energy he possesses, and his very exuberance of vitality is often mistaken for roughness by biased individuals.' The night before Liverpool were due to play Middlesbrough on 28 February 1903 Wilson told his room-mate, captain Alex Raisbeck, that he'd had a nightmare, as the Scotsman remembered in the *Daily News* in 1915:

> *We slept in the same room at night and we didn't sleep very well. As a matter of fact when we rose in the morning the question which each of us addressed to the other was how we had passed the night. 'A terrible dream I had,' said Wilson. 'I dreamt that my leg was broken.' I think I see the two of us smiling yet at the mere suggestion of such a calamity, but the game had not been half a minute in progress when he went in to meet Jones, who had visions doubtless, and certainly seemed to have every prospect of scoring, when there was a clash. You actually heard the snap of the broken limb.*

Wilson shattered his leg and did not return until eight months later, but only added nine appearances for Liverpool in two seasons. The club programme issued 15 December 1906 reflected on what might have been. 'Before he broke his leg Wilson was a sound centre-half, who studied the game, and played it accordingly. Indeed, there are many who think that he would have disputed pre-eminence with the great Raisbeck himself but for the unfortunate accident which practically stopped his First League career. He can score goals, and his offensive work was always splendid. Especially dangerous was he when corner kicks were taken. The juniors can learn much from Wilson if they will. He is bulky now, and must be one of the weightiest

men playing in Combination football.' Wilson's final appearance for Liverpool's first team came against Bolton Wanderers on 1 April 1905, but he stayed on at the club working as a scout and from 1928 onwards as a first-team trainer until 1938.

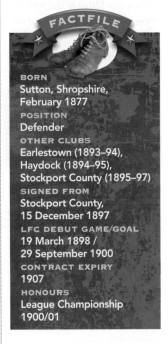

FACTFILE

BORN
Sutton, Shropshire, February 1877
POSITION
Defender
OTHER CLUBS
Earlestown (1893–94), Haydock (1894–95), Stockport County (1895–97)
SIGNED FROM
Stockport County, 15 December 1897
LFC DEBUT GAME/GOAL
19 March 1898 / 29 September 1900
CONTRACT EXPIRY
1907
HONOURS
League Championship 1900/01

Season	League		FA Cup		Total	
	App	Goals	App	Goals	App	Goals
1897/98	1	0	0	0	1	0
1898/99	7	0	0	0	7	0
1899/1900	22	0	2	0	24	0
1900/01	26	1	2	0	28	1
1901/02	8	0	3	0	11	0
1902/03	12	2	0	0	12	2
1903/04	4	0	0	0	4	0
1904/05	5	0	0	0	5	0
Total	**85**	**3**	**7**	**0**	**92**	**3**

Wilson, Danny

FACTFILE

BORN
Livingston, Scotland, 27 December 1991
POSITION
Centre-half / Left-back
OTHER CLUBS
Rangers (2007–10), Blackpool (loan, 2012), Bristol City (loan, 2012), Hearts (loan, 2012; permanent, 2013-)
SIGNED FROM
Rangers, £2million, 21 July 2010
INTERNATIONAL CAPS
5 Scotland caps (1 goal), 2010–11
LFC DEBUT
22 September 2010
CONTRACT EXPIRY
27 May 2013

DANNY WILSON made 24 first-team appearances for Rangers in his debut season in 2009/10 and not only won the Young Player of the Year award voted for by club supporters but was also crowned Young Player of the Year by both the Scottish FWA and PFA.

The *Daily Record* sports journalist Gordon Parks reckoned when Wilson moved to Liverpool that he had 'the potential to become the outstanding young Scottish defender of his generation'. Wilson was said to be a very mature player but it quickly became evident that he had a lot to learn before he was ready for a regular place in Liverpool's first team.

THE MAJORITY of the games he featured in at the club were in

the unfamiliar role of left-back. Wilson was loaned to Hearts in January 2013 where he made such a good impression that he signed a three-year contract for the Tynecastle club in May. Wilson impressed on loan at Hearts and signed a three-year contract to remain at the Edinburgh club. The Scottish Premier League initially refused to ratify this contract as Hearts was in administration, but the decision was later rescinded.

Season	League		FA Cup		League Cup		Europe		Total	
	App	Goals	App	Goals	App	Goals	App	Goals	App	Goals
2010/11	1 (1)	0	0	0	1	0	5	0	7 (1)	0
2011/12	0	0	0	0	1	0	-	-	1	0
Total	**1 (1)**	**0**	**0**	**0**	**2**	**0**	**5**	**0**	**8 (1)**	**0**

Wilson, Dave

ONE OF THE brave men at Second Division Preston who lost 3-2 to an injury-time winner against West Ham in the 1964 FA Cup Final, Dave Wilson made his only Liverpool appearance as a substitute for Gordon Milne in the 80th minute in the very last match of the 1966/67 season, a 3-1 home defeat to Blackpool.

He was transferred back to Preston, where he played in excess of 320 games in two spells and won the Third Division title in the 1970/71 season.

DAVE WILSON
LIVERPOOL

Season	League		FA Cup		League Cup		Europe		Other		Total	
	App	Goals	App	Goals	App	Goals	App	Goals	App	Goals	App	Goals
1966/67	0 (1)	0	0	0	-	-	0	0	0	0	0 (1)	0
Total	0 (1)	0	0	0	0	0	0	0	0	0	0 (1)	0

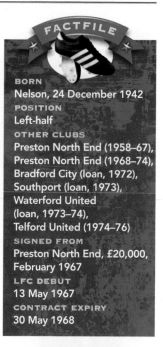

FACTFILE

BORN
Nelson, 24 December 1942
POSITION
Left-half
OTHER CLUBS
Preston North End (1958–67),
Preston North End (1968–74),
Bradford City (loan, 1972),
Southport (loan, 1973),
Waterford United
(loan, 1973–74),
Telford United (1974–76)
SIGNED FROM
Preston North End, £20,000,
February 1967
LFC DEBUT
13 May 1967
CONTRACT EXPIRY
30 May 1968

Wilson, David

DAVID WILSON (some sources claim his first name is Daniel) was a number of players tried in the absence of right-winger Jack Cox in the middle of the 1899/1900 season.

Wilson made just two first-team appearances, in consecutive First Division matches against Burnley (a 2-1 defeat) and Preston North End (a 1-0 win) early in December 1899.

Season	League		FA Cup		Total	
	App	Goals	App	Goals	App	Goals
1899/1900	2	0	0	0	2	0
Total	2	0	0	0	2	0

FACTFILE

BORN
1875
POSITION
Right-winger
OTHER CLUBS
East Bontas (1895–99),
Airdrieonians, Hamilton
Academical, Albion Rovers
SIGNED FROM
East Bontas, 7 May 1899
LFC DEBUT
2 December 1899
CONTRACT EXPIRY
20 July 1900

Wins

Biggest win

	Opponent	Competition	Date
11-0	Strømsgodset	ECWC	17 September 1974
10-0	Dundalk	European Fairs Cup	16 September 1969
10-0	Fulham	League Cup	23 September 1986
10-1	Rotherham Town	2nd Division	18 February 1896
10-1	Oulu Palloseura	European Cup	1 October 1980
9-0	Newtown	FA Cup Qualifier	29 October 1892
9-0	Crystal Palace	1st Division	12 September 1989
8-0	Higher Walton	Lancashire League	3 September 1892
8-0	Burnley	1st Division	26 December 1928
8-0	TSV Munich	European Fairs Cup	7 November 1967
8-0	Swansea City	FA Cup	9 January 1990
8-0	Stoke City*	League Cup	29 November 2000
8-0	Besiktas	Champions League	6 November 2007

Biggest away win

	Opponent	Competition	Date
8-0	Stoke City	League Cup	29 November 2000
7-0	Burton Swifts	2nd Division	29 February 1896
7-0	Crewe Alexandra	2nd Division	28 March 1896
7-0	Birmingham City	FA Cup	21 March 2006

All at home except the win over Stoke was at the Britannia Stadium

Biggest win in the 1st Division

	Opponent	Date
9-0	Crystal Palace	12 September 1989
8-0	Burnley	26 December 1928
9-2	Grimsby Town	6 December 1902
7-0	Stoke	4 January 1902
7-0	Tottenham	2 September 1978

All wins at home

Biggest away win in the 1st Division

	Opponent	Date
7-1	Derby County	23 March 1991
6-0	Wolverhampton Wanderers	28 September 1968
6-1	Grimsby Town	5 October 1946
6-1	Coventry City	5 May 1990
5-0	Manchester City	10 April 1982
5-0	Everton	6 November 1982
5-0	West Bromwich Albion	23 March 1985

Biggest win in the Premier League

	Opponent	Venue	Date
7-1	Southampton	Anfield	16 January 1999
6-0	Manchester City	Anfield	28 October 1995
6-0	Ipswich Town	Portman Road	9 February 2002
6-0	West Bromwich Albion	The Hawthorns	26 April 2003
6-0	Derby County	Anfield	1 September 2007
6-0	Newcastle United	St James' Park	27 April 2013

Biggest win in Europe, FA Cup and League Cup

(see "Biggest win" list)

Biggest win in the Champions League

	Opponent	Round	Date
8-0	Besiktas	1st Group Phase (H)	6 November 2007
5-0	Haka	3rd Qualifying round 1st leg (A)	8 August 2001
5-0	Spartak Moscow	1st Group Phase (H)	2 October 2002

Biggest aggregate win

	Home	Away	Opponent	Competition	Dates
14	10-0	4-0	Dundalk	European Fairs Cup 1st round	16-30 September 1969
12	11-0	1-0	Strømsgodset	European Cup Winners' Cup 1st round	17 September - 1 October 1974
11	10-0	3-2	Fulham	League Cup 2nd round	23 September - 7 October 1986
11	5-0	6-0	Exeter City	League Cup 2nd round	7-28 October 1981
10	6-1	5-0	KR Reykjavík	European Cup Preliminary round	17 August - 14 September 1964
9	10-1	1-1	Oulu Palloseura	European Cup 1st round	17 September - 1 October 1980
8	6-0	3-1	Real Sociedad	UEFA Cup 2nd round	22 October - 4 November 1975
8	4-1	5-0	Haka	Champions League Qualifier	8-21 August 2001
8	7-0	1-0	Oulu Palloseura	European Cup 1st round	16-30 September 1981
8	5-0	3-0	Kosice	UEFA Cup 1st round	15-29 September 1998

Most wins in a league season

		League	Games	Position
1978/79	30	1st Division	42	1
1904/05	27	2nd Division	34	1
1961/62	27	2nd Division	42	1
1987/88	26	1st Division	40	1
1922/23	26	1st Division	42	1
1963/64	26	1st Division	42	1
1965/66	26	1st Division	42	1
1981/82	26	1st Division	42	1
1985/86	26	1st Division	42	1

Fewest wins in a league season

		League	Games	Position
1894/95	7	1st Division	30	16
1903/04	9	1st Division	34	17
1953/54	9	1st Division	42	22
1901/02	10	1st Division	34	11
1897/98	11	1st Division	30	9

Most wins at Anfield in a league season

		League	Games	Position
1978/79	19	1st Division	21	1
1976/77	18	1st Division	21	1
1973/74	18	1st Division	21	2
1961/62	18	2nd Division	21	1

Most away wins in a league season

		League	Games	Position
1904/05	13	2nd Division	17	1
2008/09	13	Premier League	19	2
2001/02	12	Premier League	19	2
1981/82	12	1st Division	21	1
1946/47	12	1st Division	21	1

Fewest wins at Anfield in a league season

		League	Games	Position
1948/49	5	1st Division	21	12
1894/95	6	1st Division	15	16
2011/12	6	Premier League	19	8
1951/52	6	1st Division	21	11

Fewest away wins in a league season

		League	Games	Position
1894/95	1	1st Division	15	16
1953/54	2	1st Division	21	22
1938/39	2	1st Division	21	11
1935/36	2	1st Division	21	19
1903/04	2	1st Division	17	17
1901/02	2	1st Division	17	11

Wisdom,
Andre

IT HAS been a meteoric rise for Andre Wisdom, who had been at Bradford City less than six months when Liverpool made their move when he was still only 14 years old.

FACTFILE

BORN
Leeds, 9 May 1993
POSITION
Right-back
SIGNED FROM
Bradford City (youth),
24 January 2008
INTERNATIONAL CAPS
7 England U-21 caps
LFC DEBUT GAME/GOAL
20 September 2012 /
20 September 2012

Although officially an Under-16 player, Wisdom became a regular for the Under-18s and was an important part of the team that reached the FA Youth Cup Final in 2009, only to lose to Arsenal, led by Jack Wilshere, over two legs. Wisdom was also being closely watched by the England staff. He took part in the Under-17 European Championships in Liechtenstein in 2010. Midway through the first half of the final against Spain a shot deflected into the England net off young Wisdom, but he recovered his composure immediately, so much so that eight minutes later he strode upfield to head the equalising goal from a corner. A couple of minutes before half-time Conor Wickham guaranteed England's first age-group title since 1993.

Martin Kelly's injury early on in the 2012/13 season opened the first-team door for Wisdom under new boss Brendan Rodgers and he has had few problems adapting from the centre-half role to the right-back slot. He is strong and quick, has good heading ability and is a massive physical presence. Wisdom signed a new long-term contract for the club in January 2013. He recalled that Jamie Carragher made sure he kept his feet on the ground. 'Carra had a message for me. He said I'll be back at the Academy as soon as Martin Kelly is fit!'

Season	League		FA Cup		League Cup		Europe		Total	
	App	Goals	App	Goals	App	Goals	App	Goals	App	Goals
2012/13	12	0	2	0	1	0	4	1	19	1
Total	**12**	**0**	**2**	**0**	**1**	**0**	**4**	**1**	**19**	**1**

Woan,
Don

DON WOAN'S two league appearances for the Reds were in consecutive matches against Derby County and Everton in January 1951 as a stand-in for Jimmy Payne.

Liverpool beat Derby 2-1 at Baseball Ground but lost 2-0 to Everton at Anfield. Liverpool-born Woan was mainly a reserve at the club, featuring in 33 Central League games and scoring three goals. He became part of an exchange deal with Leyton Orient when Liverpool transferred Woan and paid £6,500 extra for 18-year-old Brian Jackson.

Season	League		FA Cup		Total	
	App	Goals	App	Goals	App	Goals
1950/51	2	0	0	0	2	0
Total	**2**	**0**	**0**	**0**	**2**	**0**

FACTFILE

BORN
Liverpool, 7 November 1927
POSITION
Right-winger
OTHER CLUBS
Bootle Athletic (1945–50),
Leyton Orient (1951–52),
Bradford City (1952–54),
Tranmere Rovers (1954–55),
Yeovil Town (1955–57)
SIGNED FROM
Bootle Athletic, £1,000,
October 1950
LFC DEBUT
13 January 1951
CONTRACT EXPIRY
5 November 1951

Worgan,
Arthur

ARTHUR WORGAN was in Liverpool's reserves in the club's first ever season, 1892/93.

He could play for any club as long as he remained an amateur and featured for Aigburth Vale in the early parts of the 1893/94 season before signing Football League forms and scoring two goals on his Liverpool debut at home to Burton Swifts on 3 March 1894. Worgan only made one additional first-team appearance for Liverpool in a home First Division clash with Sheffield United on 6 October 1894, after which the *Liverpool Mercury* said that he was 'much too light; but beyond that when he gets over his nervousness and becomes more used to the speed of First League matches he will prove a fairly good emergency man'. Arthur's brother Albert, who was a goalkeeper at Liverpool Casuals when Arthur played there, later became a director at Liverpool.

Season	League		FA Cup		Other		Total	
	App	Goals	App	Goals	App	Goals	App	Goals
1893/94	1	2	0	0	0	0	1	2
1894/95	1	0	0	0	0	0	1	0
Total	**2**	**2**	**0**	**0**	**0**	**0**	**2**	**2**

FACTFILE

BORN
Aigburth Vale, Liverpool,
1871
POSITION
Forward
OTHER CLUBS
Aigburth Vale (1893–94),
Chester City,
Liverpool Casuals
JOINED
Unaffiliated,
16 August 1893
LFC DEBUT GAME/GOAL
3 March 1894 /
3 March 1894
CONTRACT EXPIRY
1895

Wright,
Dave

DAVE WRIGHT'S breakthrough was when he scored six goals in 15 league appearances in the second part of the 1930/31 season. He made a terrific start to the 1931/32 season by netting five in the first four games, even overshadowing the great Liverpool inside-right Gordon Hodgson.

WRIGHT scored 27 goals in 70 matches in his two campaigns as a regular. Sam English took over the central role in Liverpool's attack at the start of the 1933/34 season and Wright was moved to inside-left. His 100th first-team appearance for Liverpool, at home to Derby County on the last day of March 1934, unfortunately turned out to be his last match for the club.

Season	League		FA Cup		Total	
	App	Goals	App	Goals	App	Goals
1929/30	1	0	0	0	1	0
1930/31	15	6	0	0	15	6
1931/32	35	13	4	0	39	13
1932/33	30	14	1	0	31	14
1933/34	12	2	2	0	14	2
Total	**93**	**35**	**7**	**0**	**100**	**35**

FACTFILE

BORN
Kirkcaldy, Scotland,
5 October 1905
DIED
August 1953
POSITION
Centre-forward,
Inside-left forward
OTHER CLUBS
Raith Rovers (1923–24),
East Fife (1924–26),
Cowdenbeath (1926–27),
Sunderland (1927–30),
Hull City (1934–35), Bradford
Park Avenue (1935–36)
SIGNED FROM
Sunderland, 12 March 1930
LFC DEBUT GAME/GOAL
12 April 1930 / 7 February 1931
CONTRACT EXPIRY
July 1934

Wright, Mark

FACTFILE

BORN
Dorchester,
1 August 1963
POSITION
Centre-half
OTHER CLUBS
Oxford United (1979–82),
Southampton (1982–87),
Derby County (1987–91)
SIGNED FROM
Derby County, £2.2million,
15 July 1991
INTERNATIONAL CAPS
45 England caps (1 goal)
(5 (0) at LFC), 1984–96
LFC DEBUT GAME/GOAL
17 August 1991 /
1 September 1992
CONTRACT EXPIRY
1 August 1998
HONOURS
FA Cup 1992

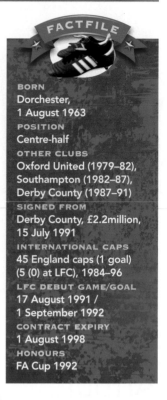

THE 19-year-old Mark Wright quickly established himself in the Southampton team under Lawrie McMenemy, who in 1984 guided the club to second place in the First Division, their highest ever finish to date in the top flight.

'Only' Liverpool stood in their way of capturing the league title. Newly promoted Derby County had big plans under owner Robert Maxwell and shattered their transfer record to bring in Wright along with his veteran team-mate Peter Shilton. After two successive promotions Derby finished 15th in the First Division in 1988 and climbed up to fifth a year later as new signing Dean Saunders was providing the necessary goals. Derby's decline was rapid, however, and the Baseball Ground outfit was relegated in 1991. Wright had been one of England's best performers during the World Cup in 1990 and Graeme Souness made the Derby captain the most expensive defender in Britain, hoping he would become Liverpool's defensive lynchpin. Kenny Dalglish had made a bid for Wright a year earlier, prior to the start of his last season as manager but the defender agreed to stay at Derby for at least 12 months. Wright didn't have particularly happy memories of Liverpool, as he had suffered a horrific leg break after a clash with Bruce Grobbelaar in the 1986 FA Cup semi-final.

WRIGHT was a master of bringing the ball out of defence and dominant in the air, with a smooth playing style reminiscent of Alan Hansen. Souness named Wright captain in the absence of the injured Ronnie Whelan, but his Liverpool career did not get off to the best of starts as he was injured only two games into the season and sidelined for three months. The season did end on a happy note when Wright lifted the FA Cup after a win over Sunderland. Following a run of bad results in September 1993, Wright lost his place temporarily to Torben Piechnik, along with the captaincy. The 1993/94 season was the last of Souness's reign and almost became Wright's last campaign as well. He had been absent through injury since March 1994 and in the 1994/95 pre-season Roy Evans criticised his poor form and attitude publicly. The double purchase of centre-halves Phil Babb and John Scales hardly increased Wright's chances. Wright returned to the first-team fold in March 1995, however, after an absence of 12 months, and had clearly learned his lesson. He seemed rejuvenated in the 1995/96 season in Roy Evans' 3-5-2 formation and his performances were of such high calibre that he made an unexpected return to the England national team at the age of 33, but an injury ruled him out of Euro 96 at the last minute. 'I loved bossing the defence,' Wright told *LFC Magazine*. 'I'm very vocal and I enjoyed doing all that. I played in a back four as well but I liked to read the game and in the centre of three I could do that.' Wright was voted the club's Player of the Year in the 1996/97 campaign, the highlight of which was a tremendous response from Liverpool against Paris St Germain at Anfield after a 3-0 defeat in Paris in the first leg of the semi-finals of the European Cup Winners Cup. 'That was some atmosphere and some noise. It still gives me goosebumps when I think about it today. I scored at the Kop end to make it 2-0, and I can still see the corner coming in and I got up and it was in.' Unfortunately, Liverpool couldn't add to the score. Injuries caught up with Wright in 1998 and he had to retire from the game, after enjoying the best spell of his Liverpool career. Wright has had a tumultuous managerial career during which he has been in charge of Chester City in three different spells and in 2012 he was briefly manager of Malta's Floriana, the Southern European country's oldest club.

Season	League App	League Goals	FA Cup App	FA Cup Goals	League Cup App	League Cup Goals	Europe App	Europe Goals	Other App	Other Goals	Total App	Total Goals
1991/92	21	0	9	0	1	0	4	0	-	-	35	0
1992/93	32 (1)	2	0	0	2 (2)	1	3	1	1	0	38 (3)	4
1993/94	31	1	0	0	5	0	-	-	-	-	36	1
1994/95	5 (1)	0	0	0	0	0	-	-	-	-	5 (1)	0
1995/96	28	2	7	0	3	0	4	0	-	-	42	2
1996/97	33	0	2	0	3	1	5	1	-	-	43	2
1997/98	6	0	0	0	0	0	1	0	-	-	7	0
Total	**156 (2)**	**5**	**18**	**0**	**14 (2)**	**2**	**17**	**2**	**1**	**0**	**206 (4)**	**9**

Wright,
Stephen

STEPHEN RRIGHT trained with his beloved Everton, but in the end chose Liverpool in July 1996. The right-back made his first-team bow for Liverpool as a substitute for Markus Babbel in the 8-0 League Cup humiliation of Stoke on 29 November 2000.

The historic 2000/01 cup-treble season largely passed him by, but he did enjoy a rare highlight in his short first-team career on 30 October 2001 when he scored with a header in front of the Kop in a 2-0 victory over Borussia Dortmund that secured top spot in Group B of the Champions League. Abel Xavier's arrival at Anfield meant that Wright's first-team chances were going to be limited and Gérard Houllier accepted a handsome offer of £3million from Sunderland. A lot of fans were unhappy that a player like Xavier should be able to push a local lad like Wright out of Anfield but his departure was inevitable. Xavier soon followed suit anyway.

THE BOOTLE BOY had a rocky six-year spell on Wearside, bouncing up and down between the Premier League and the Championship, and had dreadful luck with injuries. In the summer of 2009 Wright was appointed Coventry's club captain, but holding that position did not prevent him from being let go at the end of the 2009/10 season. Short-term deals at Brentford and Hartlepool United followed, but his main wish was to stay in the north west and he signed for Conference club Wrexham in 2012.

Season	League App	League Goals	FA Cup App	FA Cup Goals	League Cup App	League Cup Goals	Europe App	Europe Goals	Other App	Other Goals	Total App	Total Goals
2000/01	0 (2)	0	1	0	0 (1)	0	0	0	-	-	1 (3)	0
2001/02	10 (2)	0	1	0	1	0	2 (1)	1	0	0	14 (3)	1
Total	**10 (4)**	**0**	**2**	**0**	**1 (1)**	**0**	**2 (1)**	**1**	**0**	**0**	**15 (6)**	**1**

Wright,
Vic

AFTER AN excellent start to the 1930/31 season with Rotherham United in the Third Division North when he scored eight goals in seven matches, Vic Wright was sold to First Division Sheffield Wednesday. Wright struggled to get a game for Wednesday and returned the following season to Rotherham.

LIVERPOOL saw something worthwhile in him and he played in seven of the last nine league matches of that 1933/34 season, scoring twice. Wright was the epitome of the crowd-pleasing centre-forward: he was strong and brave, good in the air and difficult to knock off the ball once it came into his possession. In 1934/35 Wright and Gordon Hodgson scored 46 league goals between them. Wright could justifiably be proud of his contribution of 19 goals from 36 games and had well and truly proved that he could score goals at the highest level. However, he only managed six from 25 appearances in 1935/36 and by 1936/37 he featured more often for the reserves, but still scored four goals in the 13 first-team matches he was selected for in his final season.

Season	League App	League Goals	FA Cup App	FA Cup Goals	Total App	Total Goals
1933/34	7	2	0	0	7	2
1934/35	36	19	2	1	38	20
1935/36	25	6	2	1	27	7
1936/37	13	4	0	0	13	4
Total	**81**	**31**	**4**	**2**	**85**	**33**

Wyllie,
Tom

TOM WYLLIE was the first player to sign a professional contract for Liverpool Football Club. Wyllie scored in almost every other game in the Lancashire League and netted a total of five in three FA Cup games in the 1892/93 season.

> TOM WYLLIE WAS THE FIRST PLAYER TO SIGN A PROFESSIONAL CONTRACT FOR LIVERPOOL FOOTBALL CLUB

When the first derby between First Division Everton and Second Division Liverpool took place on 22 April 1893 in the Liverpool Senior Cup final, former Everton player Wyllie scored the game's only goal. The Merseyside teams were still at odds after John Houlding had quit Everton and formed Liverpool a year earlier.

In 1893 Wyllie stayed in the local league with third-placed Bury while Liverpool took the Second Division title. A year later Bury were elected to the Second Division, which the Greater Manchester club won at its first attempt. To be promoted, though, the Second Division champions would first have to defeat the

bottom club of the First Division to gain access to the top flight. Fate would have it that Bury's opponents were Wyllie's old club, Liverpool. Bury won 1-0 and Wyllie played two seasons in First Division before moving to Bristol City in the Southern League in the close season of 1897. He retired in 1898 and became a newsagent in Bedminster.

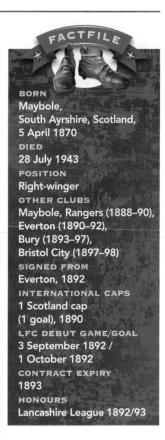

FACTFILE

BORN
Maybole,
South Ayrshire, Scotland,
5 April 1870
DIED
28 July 1943
POSITION
Right-winger
OTHER CLUBS
Maybole, Rangers (1888–90),
Everton (1890–92),
Bury (1893–97),
Bristol City (1897–98)
SIGNED FROM
Everton, 1892
INTERNATIONAL CAPS
1 Scotland cap
(1 goal), 1890
LFC DEBUT GAME/GOAL
3 September 1892 /
1 October 1892
CONTRACT EXPIRY
1893
HONOURS
Lancashire League 1892/93

Season	League		FA Cup		Other		Total	
	App	Goals	App	Goals	App	Goals	App	Goals
1892/93	-	-	3	5	22	10	25	15
Total	0	0	3	5	22	10	25	15

Liverpool players line up in front of the Kop in the 1920s

Xavier,
Abel

ABEL XAVIER has had as colourful a career as his hair suggests. He has played in seven countries: Portugal, the Netherlands, Italy, Spain, England, Turkey and the USA.

His international career has been unusual as well. Portugal had reached the semi-finals of the 2000 European Championships when deep into extra time against France Xavier handled the ball in the penalty area and Zidane scored the deciding penalty. Xavier went ballistic and his remonstrations to the referee earned him a six-month suspension from international football.

Nick Barmby crossed Stanley Park in summer 2001 and the following January Xavier became the second player in recent history to join Liverpool from Everton. Xavier didn't score in 49 games for

the Blues but it took him only 16 minutes to score on his debut for Liverpool at Ipswich, the first defender to accomplish that feat since Alec Lindsay in 1969. Xavier enjoyed a good run in the side managed by Phil Thompson while Gérard Houllier was recuperating from his heart operation and kept his place once the Frenchman returned. Xavier lost his spot in the team a few games into the 2002/03 season and he was loaned out to Galatasaray in January. His loan deal was set to last 12 months but he left the Turkish club in August after a dispute reportedly over unpaid wages. Houllier stated emphatically that Xavier was not to return to Liverpool as he was no longer part of his plans.

XAVIER returned to English football with Middlesbrough in August 2005. After failing a drugs test after the UEFA Cup tie against Greek club Xanthi on 29 September 2005 he was out of the game for 14 months. He had tested positive for an

anabolic steroid. Xavier was still under contract at Boro and made 20 appearances in the 2006/07 season. His next stop was the USA where he played one year alongside David Beckham at Los Angeles Galaxy.

On 22 December 2009 Xavier announced his retirement from professional football. He subsequently converted to Islam and changed his name to Faisal Xavier. 'It's an emotional

goodbye and I hope to participate in something very satisfying in a new stage of my life,' he said. 'In moments of grief, I have found comfort in Islam. Slowly, I learned a religion that professes peace, equality, freedom and hope. These are foundations with which I identify.'

FACTFILE

BORN
Nampula, Mozambique,
30 November 1972
POSITION
Left-back
OTHER CLUBS
Estrela Amadora (1987–93),
Benfica (1993–95),
Bari (1995–96),
Real Oviedo (1996–98),
PSV Eindhoven (1998–99),
Everton (1999–2002),
Galatasaray (loan, 2003),
Hannover 96 (2004),
AS Roma (2005),
Middlesbrough (2005–07),
LA Galaxy (2007–08)
SIGNED FROM
Everton, £750,000,
30 January 2002
INTERNATIONAL CAPS
20 Portugal caps (2 goals),
1993–2002
LFC DEBUT GAME/GOAL
9 February 2002 /
9 February 2002
CONTRACT EXPIRY
2 February 2004

Season	League App	League Goals	FA Cup App	FA Cup Goals	League Cup App	League Cup Goals	Europe App	Europe Goals	Other App	Other Goals	Total App	Total Goals
2001/02	9 (1)	1	0	0	0	0	5	1	0	0	14 (1)	2
2002/03	4	0	0	0	1	0	0	0	1	0	6	0
Total	**13 (1)**	**1**	**0**	**0**	**1**	**0**	**5**	**1**	**1**	**0**	**20 (1)**	**2**

Yeats,
Ron

RON 'ROWDY' YEATS served his role as captain of Liverpool with distinction from seasons 1961/62 to 1969/70. His father was a butcher and it was fitting the boy would grow up strong as an ox.

YEATS WAS an apprentice slaughterman at 15 years old in Aberdeen. He started work at three o'clock in the morning and finished about seven hours later. He captained Dundee United at a young age and also the British Army side during his National Service. Bill Shankly wanted to buy Yeats when he was manager of Huddersfield, but the board couldn't finance the deal.

In 1961 Shankly managed to convince Liverpool to finally get his man. He met Yeats and the board of Dundee United at a hotel in Edinburgh in July 1961.

Shankly took one look at Yeats and uttered words that have become legendary: 'Jesus, you must be seven feet tall, son?' Yeats replied: 'No, I am only six feet tall.' 'Well, that's near enough seven feet for me.' Yeats wasn't sure where Liverpool was on the map and asked Shankly a simple geographical question. 'Liverpool is in the First Division,' Shankly quipped. Yeats replied hesitantly that he thought Liverpool was still in the Second Division. 'With you in the side we will soon be in the First Division,' Shankly responded. If Yeats harboured any doubts about moving south they

evaporated during this meeting. Once his contract had been signed and Yeats headed south to Anfield, Shankly famously invited the press to walk around the giant centre-half.

'WE HAVE THE
GREATEST SKIPPER
ANY MANAGER
COULD EMPLOY
LET'S DRINK
SIX CRATES
TO BIG RON YEATS
BILL SHANKLY'S
PRIDE AND JOY'

Ian St John, who had arrived two months earlier, and Yeats were the last pieces in the puzzle of Shankly's Liverpool renaissance. Shanks later reminisced: 'They were the greatest signings and they were the beginning of Liverpool.' After only half a season in the side, Shankly gave the 24-year-old the captain's armband on Boxing Day; Yeats became the manager's eyes and ears on the field. Shankly's prediction soon came true as with Yeats in the side Liverpool clinched their place in the First Division on 21 April 1962. Two goals from Kevin Lewis gave Liverpool a 2-0 win against Southampton at a rainy Anfield. 'Just after the final whistle, everyone was going berserk and amid the celebrations I got thrown into the boys' pen!' Yeats remembers fondly. The Liverpool fans didn't want to let go of Yeats and it took him about 15 minutes to return to the dressing room. Shankly was very relieved to see his captain. 'Jesus Christ, son,

I thought we'd lost you forever!' Yeats always led by example and after heading in the winner against Manchester United at Old Trafford on 23 November 1963, which was his first goal for Liverpool, Shankly announced in his typically understated manner that 'Yeats is the greatest centre-half in the world today!'

YEATS' most glorious moment came in 1965 when he had the honour of lifting the FA Cup trophy that Liverpool had won for the first time in their 73-year

history. 'It was an emotional time getting the cup from the Queen. In fact I just wanted to throw it into the crowd, to the Liverpool supporters,' Yeats said. 'We won it now. Let's share it between us.' Liverpool repeated their 1964 League Championship success in 1966 and reached a European final for the first time, playing Borussia Dortmund in Glasgow with the European Cup Winners' Cup at stake. The game went into extra time after both sides had scored one goal after 90 minutes. In the 107th minute disaster

struck. Reinhard Libuda tried his luck from 30 yards and as the ball was heading straight for Liverpool's goal Yeats chased back, but unfortunately the ball hit the post and went in off his thigh. Dortmund celebrated victory.

At the heart of Liverpool's defence for so many years Yeats had a perfect partner in Tommy Smith, a formidable pairing if there ever was one! 'We let the ball go past us, but never the ball and the man. Tommy was hard as nails, but a great player as well. He had a bit of Sami [Hyypia] in him, he used the ball very well, a lot better than I did,' Yeats told *LFChistory.net*. 'I was a tackler, a header of the ball and read the game well. I got the ball and gave it to someone who could pass it. I knew my limitations. I was very left-footed. I would be lying if I said I would be comfortable on my right side.

Yeats with Liverpool's first European opponents, KR Reykjavík, in 2007

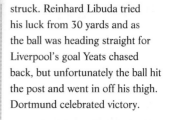

'IT WAS AN EMOTIONAL TIME GETTING THE CUP FROM THE QUEEN. IN FACT I JUST WANTED TO THROW IT INTO THE CROWD, TO THE LIVERPOOL SUPPORTERS, WE WON IT NOW LET'S SHARE IT BETWEEN US'

He was my right foot and I was his left. That's how we worked.'

Come the 1970/71 season Yeats had constant back aches and Shankly had found a replacement in Larry Lloyd. Yeats did play 16 games as left-back that campaign and scored with a bullet header in front of the Kop in a 2-0 victory over Burnley in October 1970. His last game in a Liverpool shirt was at Maine Road on 26 April 1971. Yeats was close to making the side that faced Arsenal in the FA Cup final but Lloyd was declared fit to play only two days prior to the game. Yeats moved to neighbours Tranmere Rovers, played around 100 matches and managed the team for three years. He certainly didn't enjoy his spell as manager. 'That was the worst decision I had ever made in my life. Nice people except one guy who was the chairman at the time. Three of our youngsters were playing in the first team and he sold every one of them within 18 months for a pittance of money,' Yeats said. 'He sold Steve Coppell to [Manchester] United for £40,000. He was worth over £100,000.' Yeats also had an unhappy stint as player-manager in California. He returned home when it became apparent that the owner couldn't pay his players any wages.

In 1986 Yeats asked Graeme Souness, then manager at Glasgow Rangers, about a job, as he wanted to get back into football. In the meantime Kenny Dalglish offered Yeats the role of chief scout at his beloved Anfield. Yeats went on to serve in the same role for Souness after Dalglish left, then Roy Evans, Gérard Houllier and Rafa Benítez. Yeats was awarded the Bill Shankly Memorial Award in 2002 for his fantastic service to the club. He retired in 2006 following Liverpool's FA Cup victory at the Millennium Stadium, a competition so close to his heart since 41 years earlier.

'Big Ronny is the best centre-half I have ever seen,' goalscoring legend Roger Hunt said in 1974. 'In the air he was great. Some people used to think he was weak on the ground, but I never saw

> 'BIG RONNY IS THE BEST CENTRE-HALF I HAVE EVER SEEN, IN THE AIR HE WAS GREAT. SOME PEOPLE USED TO THINK HE WAS WEAK ON THE GROUND, BUT I NEVER SAW ANYBODY GIVE HIM A CHASING. HE WAS THE RIGHT MAN FOR CAPTAIN. WITH HIM IN THE TEAM AND AT HIS BEST, WE USED TO THINK WE WERE UNBEATABLE'
>
> **ROGER HUNT**

anybody give him a chasing. He was the right man for captain. With him in the team and at his best, we used to think we were unbeatable.'

FACTFILE

BORN
Aberdeen, Scotland,
15 November 1937
POSITION
Centre-half / Left-back
OTHER CLUBS
Dundee United (1957–61),
Tranmere Rovers (1971–74),
Stalybridge Celtic (1975–76),
Los Angeles Skyhawks (1976),
Barrow (1976),
Santa Barbara Condors (1977),
Formby (1977–78)
SIGNED FROM
Dundee United, £22,000,
22 July 1961
INTERNATIONAL CAPS
2 Scotland caps, 1964–65
LFC DEBUT GAME/GOAL
19 August 1961 /
23 November 1963
CONTRACT EXPIRY
30 December 1971
HONOURS
League Championship
1963/64, 1965/66;
Second Division
Championship 1961/62;
FA Cup 1965

Season	League App	League Goals	FA Cup App	FA Cup Goals	League Cup App	League Cup Goals	Europe App	Europe Goals	Other App	Other Goals	Total App	Total Goals
1961/62	41	0	5	0	-	-	-	-	-	-	46	0
1962/63	38	0	6	0	-	-	-	-	-	-	44	0
1963/64	36	1	5	0	-	-	-	-	-	-	41	1
1964/65	35	0	8	0	-	-	9	1	1	0	53	1
1965/66	42	2	1	0	-	-	9	0	1	1	53	3
1966/67	40	2	4	0	-	-	5	0	1	0	50	2
1967/68	38	2	9	0	2	0	6	1	-	-	55	3
1968/69	39	2	4	0	3	0	2	0	-	-	48	2
1969/70	37	3	6	0	2	0	3	0	-	-	48	3
1970/71	11 (1)	1	2	0	0	0	2	0	-	-	15 (1)	1
Total	**357 (1)**	**13**	**50**	**0**	**7**	**0**	**36**	**2**	**3**	**1**	**453 (1)**	**16**

Yesil, Samed

SAMED YESIL has an impressive scoring record at youth international level: 25 goals in 29 appearances for Germany.

Yesil was second-top scorer in the 2011 Under-17 World Cup with six goals in seven matches as Germany finished third in Mexico. The youngster scored 57 goals in

71 matches for Bayer Leverkusen's youth teams in two years and had made one appearance for Sami Hyypia's club before joining Liverpool. He has already made two appearances for Liverpool in the League Cup, but it will be a while before he is fully ready for the first team.

FACTFILE

BORN
Düsseldorf, Germany,
25 May 1994
POSITION
Centre-forward
OTHER CLUBS
Bayer Leverkusen (2012)
SIGNED FROM
Bayer Leverkusen, £1million,
30 August 2012
LFC DEBUT
26 September 2012

Season	League		FA Cup		League Cup		Europe		Total	
	App	Goals	App	Goals	App	Goals	App	Goals	App	Goals
2012/13	0	0	0	0	2	0	0	0	2	0
Total	0	0	0	0	2	0	0	0	2	0

You'll Never Walk Alone

THIS Rodgers and Hammerstein show tune from the 1945 musical Carousel has become synonymous with Liverpool Football Club. In the second act of the musical, Nettie Fowler, the cousin of the female protagonist Julie Jordan, sings 'You'll Never Walk Alone' to comfort and encourage Julie after her husband had killed himself to avoid capture during a failed robbery.

LOCAL BAND Gerry and the Pacemakers introduced the song to Liverpudlians in the early 1960s, as singer Gerry Marsden explained to *LFC Magazine*: 'We were performing it around the clubs in Liverpool for more than a year before we recorded it

because we loved the song so much. The audience would just stop, stand there and listen. I just loved the words and melody.'

The band changed the lyrics ever so slightly from 'keep your chin up high' to 'hold your head up high'

and infused a bit more energy into the tempo of the song. Gerry wanted to release the song as the next single from their album, but legendary music producer George Martin (often referred to as the 'Fifth Beatle') and Brian Epstein (the Beatles' and the Pacemakers'

manager) were not as convinced as they felt it was too slow to catch on. 'Okay, but if it doesn't get to number one, on your head be it,' was their message to Gerry. In October 1963 the song became the third consecutive number one single for Gerry and the Pacemakers. Anfield DJ Stuart Bateman always played a rundown of the top-ten singles to entertain the crowd and as 'You'll Never Walk Alone' was number one it was played closest to kick-off. Liverpool fans took immediately to the song and have embraced it ever since, a unifying anthem in times of joy and times of sorrow.

> LIVERPOOL FANS TOOK IMMEDIATELY TO THE SONG AND HAVE EMBRACED IT EVER SINCE, A UNIFYING ANTHEM IN TIMES OF JOY AND TIMES OF SORROW

Liverpool players relaxing in the 50s

Younger,
Tommy

THE SCOTTISH international Tommy Younger won the Scottish League two years running in 1951 and 1952 with Hibernian. He did his National Service in West Germany where he was a PE instructor and had to fly back every weekend to play for Hibs. Due to his frequent trips home he was nicknamed 'Herr Tommy Offenback' and British European Airways presented him with a plaque for being the 'Best Customer of the Year'.

YOUNGER went straight into Liverpool's first team in 1956 and missed only a handful of games in the next three years. He added 16 internationals caps to his collection while at Liverpool and captained Scotland's 1958 World Cup squad. Younger was very courageous, some said foolhardy, and was an immense presence in goal. According to his younger brother Jim, his mother only saw him play once, when he was in goal for Hutchison Vale. He knocked himself out twice by hitting his head on the goalpost while diving and she vowed never to watch him again.

Younger once played up front for Liverpool against Derby on 19 October 1957. He got injured in the match and Ronnie Moran, in the days before substitutes, went in goal. When the keeper returned to the field of play after treatment, Liddell was switched to left-back and Younger went up front!

Younger lost his place to Bert Slater prior to the 1959/60 season and moved to Falkirk as player-manager. He made a return to England with Stoke in 1960 before a year later moving to Canada to play for Toronto City over the summer. Grocery magnate Steve Stavro had put together an all-star team to compete in the newly formed four-team Eastern Canada Professional Soccer League. Younger was paid a king's ransom to feature alongside luminaries such as Northern Ireland skipper Danny Blanchflower, who

captained Spurs' 1961 double-winning side, 46-year-old Sir Stanley Matthews, who was about to start his second spell with Stoke, and England captain Johnny Haynes, who wore the captain's armband at Fulham. While Toronto City relied on the cream of the crop from Britain, rivals Toronto Italia were represented by a number of players from Serie A in Italy. City won the league and Younger played so well that Matthews recommended him to Don Revie at Second Division Leeds, where he made his debut in September 1961. Younger played 36 games in his debut season and was allowed to coach his former club, Toronto City, during the off-season. Younger made his final appearance as a player against Bury at Elland Road on 5 September 1962 after adding six games to his Leeds total in 1962/63.

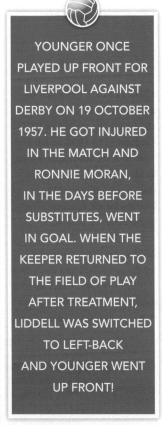

HE RETURNED to Hibernian in October 1969 and became a prominent board member at the club. Having served previously as vice-president he was voted president of the Scottish Football Association in May 1983. Younger died on 13 January 1984, at only 53 years of age.

FACTFILE

BORN
Edinburgh, Scotland,
10 April 1930
DIED
13 January 1984
POSITION
Goalkeeper
OTHER CLUBS
Hibernian (1946–56),
Falkirk (1959–60),
Stoke City (1960),
Toronto City (1961),
Leeds United (1961–62)
SIGNED FROM
Hibernian, £9,000, July 1956
INTERNATIONAL CAPS
24 Scotland caps (16 at LFC),
1955–58
LFC DEBUT
18 August 1956
CONTRACT EXPIRY
12 June 1959

Season	League		FA Cup		Total	
	App	Goals	App	Goals	App	Goals
1956/57	40	0	1	0	41	0
1957/58	39	0	5	0	44	0
1958/59	41	0	1	0	42	0
Total	**120**	**0**	**7**	**0**	**127**	**0**

Zenden,
Bolo

BOLO ZENDEN was voted the the Dutch Talent of the Year in 1997 while he starred at PSV Eindhoven. In 1998 he left his homeland for Barcelona where he played 89 games in three years before being sold to Chelsea for £7.5million prior to the 2001/02 season.

Zenden struggled to become a regular at Chelsea and was loaned to Middlesbrough, where he scored the club's winner against Bolton in the 2004 League Cup final. Zenden only signed a one-year contract at Boro but was voted the supporters' Player of the Year in the 2004/05 season. Liverpool came calling but his career at the Reds never really took off. Rafa Benítez put his faith in his experience in the 2006/07 Champions League season when Liverpool progressed to the Athens final. The Dutchman then joined Marseille on a two-year deal in July 2007 after his contract had expired at Liverpool. A quirk of fate brought Zenden quickly back to Merseyside when Marseille and Liverpool were paired in the same group in the Champions League. Marseille won 1-0 at Anfield in September

but two months later Liverpool beat them 4-0 in France. Zenden was reunited with Benítez in November 2012 when he was appointed assistant to Chelsea's interim manager.

Season	League App	League Goals	FA Cup App	FA Cup Goals	League Cup App	League Cup Goals	Europe App	Europe Goals	Other App	Other Goals	Total App	Total Goals
2005/06	5 (2)	2	0	0	0	0	6 (4)	0	0	0	11 (6)	2
2006/07	9 (7)	0	0	0	2	0	7 (4)	0	1	0	19 (11)	0
Total	**14 (9)**	**2**	**0**	**0**	**2**	**0**	**13 (8)**	**0**	**1**	**0**	**30 (17)**	**2**

Ziege,
Christian

A VETERAN German international and league title winner with Bayern Munich and Milan, Christian Ziege was certainly expected to strengthen Liverpool's left-back position considerably when he arrived in August 2000. He arrived in a blaze of controversy from Middlesbrough, who claimed Liverpool had made an illegal approach for the player, for which they were later fined £20,000 by the Football Association.

Ziege never fitted in at Anfield. Liverpool were victorious in his sole season at the club, winning a treble, but Ziege was rooted to the bench in four out of the last five games he was in the squad. Ziege was transferred to Tottenham Hotspur in July 2001, hardly worth the trouble it took to get

him to Liverpool. He played in 47 Premier League matches for Spurs during a three-year stay, scoring seven times. He suffered a horror injury against Charlton on Boxing Day 2002 that restricted him to 90 minutes of action in 13 months. Having been sent off on 23 December, he also received his marching orders in this match, after which he was rushed into hospital after his thigh muscle had blown to twice its normal size. He underwent emergency surgery that saved his right leg from amputation.

In 2004 the left wing-back returned to his homeland, joining Borussia Mönchengladbach, but he only played for a season before announcing his retirement at the age of 33. Ziege coached Gladbach's Under-17 team and served as the club's director of football from 2007 to 2008. He later had an unsuccessful spell as head coach of Armenia Bielefeld and works now for the German FA, coaching the Under-18 international side.

Season	League App	League Goals	FA Cup App	FA Cup Goals	League Cup App	League Cup Goals	Europe App	Europe Goals	Total App	Total Goals
2000/01	11 (5)	1	2 (1)	0	1 (3)	1	6 (3)	0	20 (12)	2
Total	**11 (5)**	**1**	**2 (1)**	**0**	**1 (3)**	**1**	**6 (3)**	**0**	**20 (12)**	**2**

Bibliography

Alan A'Court,
My Life in Football,
The Bluecoat Press, 2003.

Gary Ablett,
The Game of My Life,
Sport Media, 2012.

**Jeff Anderson
and Stephen Done,**
The Official Illustrated History,
Carlton Books, 2002.

**Arnie Baldursson and
Guðmundur Magnússon,**
Liverpool: A Complete Record,
deCoubertin Books, 2011.

John Barnes,
John Barnes: The Autobiography,
Headline, 1999.

Peter Beardsley,
My Life Story,
HarperCollins, 1996.

Jamie Carragher,
Carra: My Autobiography,
Transworld Publishers, 2009.

Kenny Dalglish,
My Liverpool Home,
Hodder & Stoughton, 2010.

Dixie Dean,
Dixie Uncut - The Lost Interview,
Trinity Mirror Sport Media, 2005.

Derek Dohren,
Ghost on the Wall,
Mainstream, 2004.

**Stephen Done
and David Walmsley,**
The Treasures of Liverpool FC,
Carlton Books, 2004.

Robbie Fowler,
Fowler: My Autobiography,
Pan, 2006.

**Steven Gerrard
and Henry Winter,**
Gerrard: My Autobiography,
Bantam Press, 2006.

Karen Gill,
The Real Shankly,
Trinity Mirror Sport Media, 2007.

Bruce Grobbelaar,
More Than Somewhat,
HarperCollins, 1986.

Didi Hamann,
*The Didi Man:
My Love Affair with Liverpool,*
Headline, 2012.

Alan Hansen,
A Matter of Opinion,
Partridge Press, 1999.

Emlyn Hughes,
Crazy Horse,
Arthur Barker, 1980.

Craig Johnston with Neil Jameson,
Walk Alone,
HarperCollins, 1990.

Kevin Keegan with John Roberts,
Arthur Barker, 1977

Stephen F. Kelly,
Dalglish,
Headline, 1997.

Stephen F. Kelly,
The Boot Room Boys,
Willow, 1999.

Stephen F. Kelly,
The Kop: Liverpool's Twelfth Man,
Mandarin Paperbacks, 1993.

Alan Kennedy,
Kennedy's Way,
Mainstream Publishing, 2005.

Ray Kennedy with Dr. Andrew Lees,
Ray of Hope,
Penguin Book, 1993.

Paul Lake,
I'm Not Really Here,
Arrow, 2012.

Doug Lamming,
Who's Who of Liverpool 1892-1989,
Breedon Books, 1989.

Billy Liddell,
My Soccer Story,
Stanley Paul, 1960.

Jan Mølby,
*Jan the Man:
From Anfield to Vetch Field,*
Orion, 2007.

Bob Paisley and Peter Oakes,
Bob Paisley - My 50 Golden Reds,
Front Page Books, 1990.

**Bob Paisley
as told to Clive Tyldesley,**
*Bob Paisley's Personal View of
the First Team Squad of 1986-87,*
Cablestar, 1987.

Bob Paisley,
My Autobiography,
Littlehampton Book Services,
1983.

Mark Platt and Gary Shaw,
At the End of the Storm,
Gary Shaw, 2009.

Mark Platt with Andrew Fagan,
Joe Fagan: Reluctant Champion,
Aurum Press, 2011.

Ken Rogers,
The Real Bob Paisley,
Trinity Mirror Sport Media, 2007.

John Rowlands,
*"John Houlding, the founder of
Liverpool Football Club,"*
History Magazine, Ian Nannestad,
Issue 12.

Bill Shankly and John Roberts,
Shankly, Arthur Barker, 1976.

Graham Sharpe,
*Free the Manchester United One:
The Inside Story of Football's
Greatest Scam,*
Robson Books, 2003.

Tommy Smith;
I Did It the Hard Way,
Littlehampton Book Services,
1980.

Graeme Souness,
No Half Measures with Bob Harris,
HarperCollins, 1985.

Ian St John,
Boom at the Kop,
Pelham Books, 1966.

Phil Thompson,
Stand Up Pinocchio,
Trinity Mirror Sport Media, 2005.

John Wark,
Wark On,
Know the Score! 2009.

John Williams,
*Red Men
- Liverpool Football Club:
The Biography,*
Mainstream, 2010.

Newspapers
and magazines

90 Minutes,
Athletic News,
Blackburn Standard,
Cambridge Independent Press,
Cricket and Football Field,
Daily Express,
Daily Mirror,
Daily News,
Derby Daily Telegraph,
Dundee Courier,
Edinburgh Evening News,
Evening Express,
Evening Telegraph,
Evening Times,
Field Sports,
FourFourTwo,
Glasgow Evening Times,
The Guardian,
The Independent,
*Joint Everton
& Liverpool Programme,*
Lancashire Daily Post,
Liverpool Courier,
Liverpool Daily Post,
Liverpool Echo,
Liverpool Evening Express,
Liverpool FC Official Magazine,
Liverpool Mercury,
Lloyds Weekly Newspaper,
Manchester Courier,
Morgunblaðið,
The People,
Scottish Sunday Express,
Sunday Chronicle,
The Times,
Toronto Star,
Yorkshire Herald.

ROLL OF

HONOUR

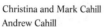

Arnie Baldursson
Guðmundur Þór Magnússon
Ásta Sól Kristjánsdóttir
Ólöf Haflína Ingólfsdóttir
Elena Arngrímsdóttir
Leon Bjartur Sólar Arngrímsson
Elísabet Ósk Guðmundsdóttir
Ólöf Arngrímsdóttir
James Corbett
William Corbett
Stefan Nygren
James Bueck
Steven Holliday
Brian Seery
Brian Drever
Andrew DC Dawson
David Locke
Jørgen Ringestad
Eric Lee
Jack Swainston
Mikael Remling
Todd Proper
Joseph Wright
David Hughes
Christine Andrade
Cathy and Vivek Ayer
Ole Damstuen
Chris and Alli Cummings
Peter Dojcsan
Daragh Kennedy
Chris Wood
Adrian Day
Jose D. Lima
Christopher M. Lima
Graeme Riley
David Hammarbro
Adrian Killen
Tore Hansen
David A. Madeiros
Mark Anthony
Ludwig Siemsen
Gerard Scully
Stuart Basson
Los Moutchatchos
Owen Serjeant
Ian Beardsley
Anthony Barnes & Katie Ditch
Kevin Neil Jenkins
Bob Blenkinsop
Matthew Shearer
Flosi Sigurðsson
Martin Brodetsky
Gavin Clarke
Rob Gowers
Jim Donnelly
Seamus Whelan
Ivan Potapov
Torbjørn Flatin
Bardhyl Bob Kallamata
Irene and Igor Nekrashevich
Gavin Foster
Christian von Simson
Andrew Coluton
Angela McKenna

Christina and Mark Cahill
Andrew Cahill
David France
Kim-André Odden Kjønigsen
John Corrigan
Jeff Gaydish
Oleg Gribin
Chris Goodwin
Hans Magne Opsahl
Lee Gray
Ray Roberts
Skapti Hallgrímsson
Simon Deninson
Elizabeth Hargreaves
Andy "Wally" Walterson
Patrick Brickley
Alan Hindley
Joe McCormick
Steven Horton
John Lewis
Hyder Jawad
Daníel Sveinsson
Gerald Jensen
Matthew Coles
John Jones
Sigurður Einar Einarsson
Hilmar Thors
Bob McCluskey
Baldur S. Sigurðsson
Kevin Nealon
Jóhann Ásgeirsson #11
Joe Neary
Malcolm Berry
Ron Parrott
Chasen McClanahan
Mark Platt
Guðmundur Þór Ámundason
Paul Plowman
Benedikt Jón Sigmundsson
Katharine Reidel
John Sowerby
Darren Riley
For 96 Brothers and Sisters RIP
Pete Sampara
Keith Coker
George Sephton
Westlee Wallace
Jacqueline Wadsworth
Reginald Riley
Dan Williams
Phil Brough

Frank Crowley
Paul Crowley
Vegard Heggem
Rena Liddell
Graeme Helen and Olivia Riley
Tim Pomfret
Alan Dunn
Jim Gardiner
Dave Usher
Allan Mather
Gyða Björk Jónsdóttir
Andreas Leth Bockhoff
Hörður Magnússon
Steinar Bjerkmann
Rósmundur Magnússon
Jussi Uotila
Jósep Svanur Jóhannesson
Ossi Nummelin
Hallgrímur Indriðason
Pasi Teini
Gestur Steinþórsson
Johan Wren
Karl Daníel Magnússon
Johann Petur Fleckenstein
Grétar Magnússon
Svavar Halldórsson
Hrólfur Þór Valdemarsson
Paul Burton
Árni Þór Freysteinsson
Guðmundur Ó Heiðarsson
Sveinn Waage
Ottar Hauge
Sigurður Hjaltested
Per-Inge Ölveborn
Helgi Tómasson
Pål Winther
Kristján Guðmundsson
Joseph Daniel Heyes
Guðni Ölversson
Geir Olav Kittelsrud
Gunnar Ómarsson
Jón Pétur Guðjónsson
Kristjan S. Thorsteinsson
Markús Einarsson
Lars Déman
Bergvin Gíslason
Madrid Reds LFC
Supporters Club

Stephen Jackie and Lilly
Joanne James Macy-Jo and JJ
Danny and Marianne
Andy and Tom Priestley
Sandra Barry and Alex Bibby
Ron Smith
John David Boyham
Danny Muirhead
Joanna Mallon
John Mallon
Steve Murray
Rolv Kristian Moldestad
Bergþór og Sigríður
Oliver Helgi S. Jensson
Haraldur Emilsson
Ged Rea
Ólafur Arnar Pálsson
Jóhannes R. Jóhannesson
Sigmar Helgason
Guðjón Engilbertsson
Anders Olsson
Unnar Hermannsson
Aðalheiður og Pétur
Daniel Hills
Jónína og Hjördís
Hayley A. Roberts
Miles T. Roberts
Bjørn Petter Røkenes
John Russell
Ian Watt Scott
Wayne Griffin
Sami Heinula
Jan Holten
Lionel J. Roper (1910-2003)
Lars Nilsson
Mark Chatterton
Keith Blower
Torbjörn Welam
Fredrik Runnström
Sigfús Guttormsson
Craig Stenhouse
Torkild Steinholt
David Duguid
John Teesdale
Paul Woods
Mark Howard
Alan Boynton
Kari Salla
Roald
Jack P. Walker
Owen J. Walker

Doreen and Leslie Priestley
Margaret and Lawrence Price
James and Joseph Price
Martha and Daniel Garrigan
Andrew 'Flatzie' Fitzgerald
The Ong Family
The Hunters
Anders Morén
Dan Cronin
J. Bratch
Martin Lang
Billy Lysaght
Issy Wong
Buster Wong
Dominic Wong
Eyþór Ólafsson
Anders Berglind
Michael Makison
Ben Wells
Desmond Ong and Family
Stirling Jarrad
Christopher Carver
Paul Connolly
Sheila Ruse
Kev Lynch
Adrian Day
William Doran
James Joseph Cotton
Christopher M. Williams
David Dinwoodie
Dennis Niittykoski
Darren William Creed
Emmet Murphy
Marcus Francis Howarth
Paul 'Dunner' Dunne
Kevin Neil Jenkins
Gunnlaugur Guðjónsson
Magnús Freyr Smárason
Gary Hims
Christopher V. Tench
Alex Twells
Peter Koinberg
Joachim Olovsson
Einar Jón Pálsson
Maureen Gallagher
Árni Brynjúlfsson
Asle Natås Lægreid
Jón Helgi Sveinbjörnsson
Ørjan Eriksen
Colin E Spiers - Happy 60th
Ali Sharif
Anthony Parsons
Sue Parsons
Norman Brereton
Alan Hurst
Lynne Kinsella
Terry Kinsella
Liam Gibbs
Michael Whitehead
Wayne Tymms
Paul Neilson
Gunnlaugur Helgason
Ólafur Haukur Guðmundsson
Phil Martin

"WE ARE LIVERPOOL"

THE COMPLETE HISTORY

LFCHISTORY.NET

The ultimate online reference for
LIVERPOOL FOOTBALL CLUB

LFChistory.net was launched in September 2003 by Arnie Baldursson and Gudmundur Magnusson.

Their mission was to create an accessible website for stats and historical articles on Liverpool FC. The site has grown from strength to strength and its stats are now considered the official stats for Liverpool Football Club. LFChistory.net has exclusive interviews, all the results from official games, every single LFC and opposition line-up and other match details since the 1892/93 season. The Icelanders' labour of love has become a significant resource for the study of Liverpool´s tremendous history.

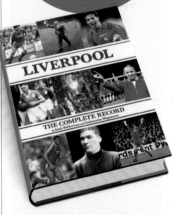

YOU'LL NEVER WALK ALONE

In the memory

of the

Liverpool fans

who so sadly

lost their lives

at Hillsborough

15 APRIL 1989